AMERICAN STUDIES

AN ANNOTATED BIBLIOGRAPHY

VOLUME II

AMERICAN STUDIES

AN ANNOTATED BIBLIOGRAPHY

VOLUME II

Edited by

JACK SALZMAN
Director, Columbia Center for American Culture Studies

on behalf of

THE AMERICAN STUDIES ASSOCIATION

The right of the
University of Cambridge
to print and sell
all manner of books
was granted by
Henry VIII in 1534.
The University has printed
and published continuously
since 1584.

CAMBRIDGE UNIVERSITY PRESS

CAMBRIDGE

LONDON NEW YORK NEW ROCHELLE

MELBOURNE SYDNEY

Published by the Press Syndicate of the University of Cambridge
The Pitt Building, Trumpington Street, Cambridge CB2 1RP
32 East 57th Street, New York, NY 10022, USA
10 Stamford Road, Oakleigh, Melbourne 3166, Australia

First published 1986

Printed in the United States of America

ISBN 0-521-26687-4 Vol. II
ISBN 0-521-32555-2 Set of three volumes

CONTENTS

MUSIC

PREFACE

A number of institutions provide important resources for American Studies in music. Most of the collections mentioned here are open to researchers, and most provide listening facilities for recordings and tapes. The most important institutional collection is the Music Division of the Library of Congress. As the major repository for scores and books on all varieties of American music, the Library houses more than four million items. Established in 1897 and expanded early in the 20th century under the directorship of Oscar Sonneck, the Music Division also contains a number of special collections and rare materials. In addition, the Music Division houses a National Library Service for the Blind and Physically Handicapped, which includes 30,000 braille scores, large print scores, and audio materials. Researchers interested in American folk music should be familiar with the Library's Archive of Folk Culture.

A number of institutions throughout the country offer collections that focus on particular aspects of music in America and American music. The Division of Musical Instruments of the Smithsonian Institution includes more than 2,000 instruments as well as books and other materials on instrument manufacture and use. This collection contains no scores or recordings. The Music Division of the New York Public Library at Lincoln Center comprises both circulating and reference libraries, and the American Collection includes a broad range of materials relevant to American Studies scholars. The Oscar Hammerstein Archive of Recorded Sound, also located at the Music Division, contains recordings from all countries and historical periods, including a large American music collection.

The focus at Chicago's Newberry Library is on American music from its beginnings to the early 20th century. The collection also includes a large number of 19th-century music periodicals. The music collections of the American Antiquarian Society in Worcester, Massachusetts emphasize early American music and musical activity. Researchers will find sheet

music printed prior to 1880, songsters, hymnals, and recordings of 18th-
and 19th-century American music. The Stephen Collins Foster Memorial
at the University of Pittsburgh contains early editions of Foster's songs,
arrangements, artifacts, recordings, and materials relating to Foster's
music and 19th-century American popular songs. Music of the American
Yiddish Theater can be studied at the American Jewish Historical Society
in Waltham, Massachusetts. This collection includes sheet music and the
papers of Abraham Ellstein, Walter Hart Blumenthal, Molly Picon, and others.

The American Music Center in New York City specializes in collecting
scores and other materials related to contemporary composers, specifically
those who are still active and those who have died within the past twenty-
five years. The Music Library at Yale University has a Twentieth Century
Music Archive that includes manuscripts and papers of Charles Ives, Carl
Ruggles, Kurt Weill, and other American composers. The Edwin A. Fleisher
Collection at the Free Library of Philadelphia includes 13,000 orchestral
scores and files on 1,400 American composers. Archival materials on Louis
Gruenberg and other composers are also housed in the Fleisher Collection.

The Institute of Jazz Studies at Rutgers University in Newark, New
Jersey includes more than 60,000 jazz and popular music recordings. The
collection also contains piano rolls, sheet music, books, periodicals,
and transcripts of more than 100 interviews compiled by the Jazz Oral
History Project under the auspices of the National Endowment for the Arts.
The materials at Bowling Green State University in Bowling Green, Ohio
include more than 200,000 recordings, most of popular music. This collection also contains monographs and periodicals relating to American
popular culture. The University of California at Los Angeles houses both
the Archive of Popular American Sheet Music and the Film and Television
Music Archive.

Researchers on musical topics in American Studies will want to begin
with The New Grove Dictionary of Music and Musicians (New York: Macmillan,
1980). Entries cover a broad range of relevant musical topics, from com-

posers, styles, and instruments to ethnomusicology. Space limitations
in The New Grove highlighted the need for a separate comprehensive dictionary of American music. The New Grove Dictionary of American Music
(New York: Grove's Dictionaries of American Music, 1986) devotes four
volumes to American composers, performers and performing organizations,
musical styles, and uses of music in American society. Other general
sources that incorporate more than one American musical genre include
JoAnn Skowronski, Black Music in America: A Bibliography (Metuchen, N.J.:
Scarecrow Press, 1981), which covers performers, musical history, and
general reference works, and Rita H. Mead, Doctoral Dissertations in American Music: A Classified Bibliography (Brooklyn, N.Y.: Institute for
Studies in American Music, 1974), which lists dissertations on composers,
performers and performing groups, education, theater, music theory, ethnomusicology, and related topics. The journal American Music, published
quarterly by the Sonneck Society and University of Illinois Press, includes
scholarly articles on all types of American music. The Musical Quarterly
also often publishes articles on American music. Popular Music: A Year-
book, published since 1981 by Cambridge University Press, presents multi-
disciplinary articles, book reviews, bibliographies, and discographies.
The Music Industry Directory, 7th ed. (Chicago: Marquis Professional
Publications, 1983) surveys musical organizations, competitions, awards
and prizes, education, resources, and various business aspects of American
music.

Country and folk music research can begin with Kenn Kingsbury, ed.,
Kingsbury's Who's Who in Country and Western Music (Culver City, Calif.:
Black Stallion Country Press, 1981). This volume includes entries on
artists, songwriters and publishers, country music radio, managers and
agents, and top-ten songs. Irwin Stambler and Grelun Landon have compiled
The Encyclopedia of Folk, Country and Western Music (New York: St.
Martin's Press, 1983) as a biographical survey of the contemporary folk
and country music industry. An older source is Linell Entry's A History

and Encyclopedia of Country, Western, and Gospel Music (Nashville, Tenn.: Clairmont, 1969). Traditional folk music receives extensive but no longer current treatment in Charles Haywood, A Bibliography of North American Folklore and Folksong (New York: Dover, 1961). The Academy of Country Music in Hollywood, California publishes a monthly newsletter that focuses on contemporary developments in the industry, and the Journal of Country Music in Nashville, Tennessee publishes primary source material and articles on traditional country music three times each year.

Publications about jazz abound. Macmillan publishes a Jazz Masters series of books about specific periods in the history of this characteristically American music. Leonard Feather and Ira Gitler, eds., Encyclopedia of Jazz in the Seventies (New York: Horizon Books, 1976) includes biographical articles, a guide to jazz films, a survey of colleges and universities where courses in jazz are offered, and a bibliography. In addition, Transaction Books in New Brunswick, New Jersey publishes an overview of scholarly research on jazz in its Annual Review of Jazz Studies.

Irwin Stambler's Encyclopedia of Pop, Rock, and Soul (New York: St. Martin's Press, 1974) provides an introduction to popular music through biographies of major artists and a brief bibliography. The American Society of Composers, Artists, and Publishers has revised its ASCAP Biographical Dictionary, 4th ed. (New York: Jacques Cattell Press, 1980), which includes entries on 8,000 ASCAP members.

E. Ruth Anderson's Contemporary American Composers: A Biographical Dictionary (Boston: G. K. Hall, 1982) provides information on composers born after 1870 who are U.S. citizens or residents. This volume does not contain information on jazz, folk, rock, or popular music composers. Neil Butterworth's A Dictionary of American Composers (New York: Garland, 1984) is similar in its focus on composers of concert music, although it includes popular music composers who have also written works for the concert hall or opera house. Two comprehensive bibliographies of early American music are A Bibliography of Early American Secular Music written by Oscar Sonneck and revised by William Treat Upton (Washington, D.C.: Library of Congress, 1945) and Richard J. Wolfe, Secular Music in America, 1801-1825 (New York: New York Public Library, 1964). The latter includes biographical entries and a discussion of music publishing in early 19th-century America. The Institute for Studies in American Music Newsletter, published twice a year at Brooklyn College, includes essays, reviews, and research reports on work in progress in American music, and the College Music Symposium, also published semiannually, focuses on current music research, including research on American music. Researchers in the history of American music in the concert hall can consult such historically significant periodicals as Dwight's Journal of Music, Musical America, The Musical Courier, The Musical Observer, and Modern Music, in addition to articles and criticism in the daily press.

Barbara L. Tischler
Barnard College

I.   GENERAL MUSIC

M 1.   AMMER, CHRISTINE. Unsung: A History of Women in American Music.
       Westport, Conn.: Greenwood Press, 1980. 317 pp.
This volume provides a comprehensive survey of the contributions of women
to a number of areas in American music. Ammer considers singers and instrumentalists as well as composers in a work that is intended to transcend
the contributions to the historiography of women in American music of
Sophie Drinker's Music and Women (1948), David Ewen's American Composers
Today (1949), and Music Annals: A Thousand Years of Patronage (1976).
Ammer analyzes the music of her subjects thematically, examining singers
and players in concert and popular music, composers whose music reflects
principally European influences and those who looked to local or regional
vernacular idioms for musical sources.

M 2.   AYARS, CHRISTINE MERRICK. Contributions to the Art of Music in
       America by the Music Industries of Boston, 1640-1936. New York:
       Wilson, 1937. 326 pp.
Ayars bases her research on the premise that musical performance depends
on the printing and instrument-making industries. She surveys the activities, first of individuals and later of large and small companies, in
these important areas. Focusing only on Boston, she discusses publishing,
educational publishing, music engraving and printing, pianoforte and organ
manufacturers, and other instrument makers. She also includes a chapter
on the bells and bell chimes cast by Paul Revere and later bell makers
in Boston.

M 3.   CARNEY, GEORGE O., ed. The Sounds of People and Places: Readings
       in the Geography of Music. Washington, D.C.: University Press
       of America, 1979. 336 pp.
This collection of fourteen articles by eleven academic geographers examines classical, country, gospel, folk, rock and roll, and popular music
and the historical, cultural, social, and geographical importance of these
various styles. Citing the folklorist Alan Lomax's statement, "The map
sings," the editors claim that "the music played, sung, written, and listened to by Americans is one of the best indicators of the cultural milieu
of our country . . . as diverse as the people who are found in the various
. . . areas of the country." Topics include "Music and Environment:
An Investigation of Some of the Spatial Aspects of Production, Diffusion,
and Consumption of Music," "From Down Home to Uptown: The Diffusion of
Country-Music Radio Stations in the United States," "The Development and
Spatial Diffusion of Gospel Quartet Music in the United States," "Woody
Guthrie and the Dust Bowl," "Geographic Factors in the Origin, Evolution,
and Diffusion of Rock and Roll Music," and "The Image of Place in American
Popular Music." The article, "The Roots of American Music," offers some
general conclusions about music and place in America.

M 4.   CHASE, GILBERT. America's Music from the Pilgrims to the Present.
       1955; Rev. ed. New York: McGraw-Hill, 1966. 759 pp.
Chase presents a synoptic history of American music from the Colonial
period to the mid-20th century. He focuses on folk music, popular song
genres, ragtime, spirituals, jazz, music from various ethnic traditions,
American Indian contributions to the development of culture in this country,
theater music, opera, and music for the concert hall. Chase argues for
the emergence of an early American folk music in the psalm singing of
early Puritan settlers, and he also devotes attention to the fasola movement of the early 19th century which was an indigenous attempt to establish
a system of notation. His chapters on the 20th century analyze folklore
in concert music, twelve-tone currents in American music, modern American
opera, and the various styles that have emerged since W.W. II.

M 5. DAVIS, RONALD L. A History of Music in American Life. Vol.
      I, The Formative Years, 1620-1865. Malabar, Fla.: Krieger, 1982.
      301 pp. Vol. II, The Gilded Years, 1865-1920. Huntington, N.Y.:
      Krieger, 1980. 268 pp. Vol. III, The Modern Era, 1920-Present.
      Malabar, Fla.: Krieger, 1981. 444 pp.
Davis's three-volume history, written from the viewpoint of a historian
rather than a musicologist, examines the function of music, both American
and European, within the changing social contexts in America from 1620
to the present. The first volume begins with a discussion of the limited
musical life of the New England Puritans and the first settlers of the
Middle and Southern Colonies, peoples who discouraged music and emphasized
reserve, control, and piety. He examines the careers of Colonial composers
Hopkinson and Billings and discusses the "Search for a National Identity"
in American cultural and musical life. He devotes two chapters to the
emergence of a concert life and interest in European opera, much of which
was fostered by the women of the upper classes, with the growth of urban
centers in the East. Other chapters discuss the sentimental songs of Stephen
Foster, the career and music of Louis Moreau Gottschalk, the age of minstrelsy, and the varied regional and ethnic folk musics of the U.S. Volume
II, which discusses the "Gilded Years" of American music, outlines the
rise of the symphony orchestra, the patronage of Grand Opera by the nou-
veau riche, the "growth of serious composition," and the careers of
MacDowell and Ives. He also charts the growth of various popular musical
forms, including musical theater, Tin Pan Alley, blues, ragtime, and early
jazz. The final volume discusses the maturation of concert life and opera
in this country; the careers of Copland and Gershwin; the music of the
Traditionalist, Modernist, and Experimentalist movements; and the evolution
of jazz. Final chapters examine American popular music, a field, Davis
claims, dominated by Afro-Americans and Jews; the rise of country music;
and contemporary rock and soul music. Throughout his survey, Davis asserts
that, although concert and "serious" music has gained ground and authority
in this country, the notable growth and innovations in American musical
life have occurred in popular and "vernacular" musical styles.

M 6. DeLERMA, DOMINIQUE RENE, ed. Black Music in Our Culture: Cur-
      ricular Ideas on the Subjects, Materials, and Problems. Kent,
      Ohio: Kent State University Press, 1970. 263 pp.
Some of the papers in this collection address curricular and philosophical
challenges of black music; black music in church and school; jazz history;
black composers and the avant garde; and black dance and its influence on
black music. It also includes a discussion of problems relating to publishing and recording music, and problems in administering such curricula.
Appendices include selective lists of scores, recordings, films, books,
articles, and sample curricular syllabi.

M 7. EDWARDS, ARTHUR C. and W. THOMAS MARROCCO. Music in the United
      States. Dubuque, Iowa: Brown, 1968. 179 pp.
In their brief survey of American music and musical activity from the
earliest sacred music to the music of the 1960s, Edwards and Marrocco
attempt to remedy the lack of scholarship on pre-20th century musical
achievement in this country. They discuss and define various styles such
as psalmody, fasola, and patriotic music, always noting the specific contributions of various immigrating sects and ethnic groups. They chart the
"rise of American music" in the 18th century, the growth of "musical sophistication" in the 19th century, and the simultaneous development of traditional styles and exploration of new styles, such as twelve-tone technique,
in the 20th century. Throughout their history Edwards and Marrocco are
concerned with examining American musical education and the various nationalistic elements of American music. A discography is included.

M 8. GELATT, ROLAND. The Fabulous Phonograph: 1877-1977. 1954; Rev.
ed. New York: Macmillan, 1977. 349 pp.
Gelatt's history of the phonograph encompasses the aesthetic, scientific,
and commercial aspects of its development. Beginning with the appearance
of Thomas A. Edison's primitive "tin-foil" apparatus in 1877, Alexander
Graham Bell's "graphophone" in 1887, and Emile Berliner's "gramophone"
in 1888, the early chapters detail such commercial events as entrepreneur
Jesse H. Lippincott's decision to launch the American Graphophone and
North American Phonograph Companies in 1888. The extensive discussion
of commercial recording gives prominence to the role played by such musicians as Enrico Caruso and Emilio de Gogorza, as well as to the impact
of the first jazz recordings in 1914. Later chapters deal with what Gelatt
calls the decisive moment in phonographic history: the appearance of
rock music in the 1950s and the subsequent transformation of musical recording into a mass market industry.

M 9. HAMM, CHARLES. Music in the New World. New York: Norton, 1983.
722 pp.
Inspired by the historical and musicological material brought to public
and scholarly attention by the American Bicentennial celebration, Hamm
continues in the recent tradition of scholars who shed light on the development of both music in America and American music. He begins with a chapter
on "Music of the Native American," an anthropological and cultural study
of the type not generally found in music surveys. His chronological survey
of American musical activities includes chapters on Colonial psalms and
hymns, concert and operatic music in Colonial and Federal America, the
music of the African slaves, the "Dawning of Classical Music in America
(1825-65)," "Stephen Foster and Indigenous American Song," "Shape-Note,
Camp Meeting, and Gospel Hymnody," the music of Tin Pan Alley, the roots
and rise of jazz, "The Search for a National Identity," country music,
the music of the American avant-garde, and rock music. Hamm includes
a discography and "A Note on New World Records, Recorded Anthology of
American Music."

M 10. HAMM, CHARLES, BRUNO NETTL, and RONALD BYRNESIDE. Contemporary
Music and Music Cultures. Englewood Cliffs, N.J.: Prentice-
Hall, 1975. 270 pp.
Using an "approach that focuses on music in the contemporary world, and
particularly on the way in which it interacts with those social, political,
and cultural processes that distinguish the twentieth century," the authors
have written a collection of essays which deal with a broad range of musical styles from American rural, urban, and elite societies. The first
essay is a general discussion of musical concepts and terminology, enabling
the reader "to consider music as the craft of the composer." The following
essays include "Changing Patterns in Society and Music: The U.S. Since
World War II," "The Western Impact on World Music: Africa and the American
Indians," "The Acculturation of Musical Styles: Popular Music, U.S.A.,"
"Words and Music: English Folksong in the United States," "The Performer
as Creator: Jazz Improvisation," and "Technology and Music: The Effect
of the Phonograph."

M 11. HARE, MAUDE CUNEY. Negro Musicians and Their Music. Washington,
D.C.: Associated Publishing, 1936. 439 pp.
The author includes discussions of both folk and "art" music and musicians.
Among the topics discussed are African music and its influences in America;
characteristics of black folk song, both secular and religious; origins
of black American folk songs; various kinds of black American music, such
as blues, ragtime, and jazz; black rhythm; use of black themes in art
music; Creole musicians in New Orleans; and such black musicians as William
Grant Still, Marian Anderson, and Paul Robeson. Appendices are included
on African musical instruments and black folk songs.

M 12. HITCHCOCK, H. WILEY. Music in the United States: A Historical
      Introduction. 1969; Rev. ed. Englewood Cliffs, N.J.: Prentice-
      Hall, 1974. 286 pp.
Hitchcock transcends a historical survey of American music to introduce
the concepts of cultivated and vernacular musical language in this country.
These categories allow him to consider folk and popular music, along with
operas and tone poems composed for the concert hall in his study which
is divided chronologically into several major periods of American music
development. This analytical framework allows him particular flexibility
in the last chapters, in which he considers the interaction of the cultivated and vernacular traditions. Hitchcock also stresses the importance
of America's continued musical relation with Europe, especially during
W.W. I. Rather than argue for American musical independence in this period,
he notes that American composers were involved in the critical debates
of the decade along with their European counterparts.

M 13. HITCHCOCK, H. WILEY, ed. The Phonograph and Our Musical Life:
      Proceedings of a Centennial Conference, 7-10 December 1977.
      Brooklyn, N.Y.: Institute for Studies in American Music, 1980.
      91 pp.
This monograph contains the proceedings of a symposium on the phonograph's
role in American musical life, marking the hundredth anniversary of
Edison's first phonograph. The conference opened with a "response" by
several prominent music critics and scholars to the performance of a new
work by John Cage entitled Address. In the session, "The Phonograph and
the Audience," the papers delivered included William Ivey's "Recordings
and the Audience for the Regional and Ethnic Musics of the United States,"
and Jane Jarvis's "Notes for Muzak." During the second session, "The
Phonograph and the Composer," William Bolcom gave a talk, "Composer, Performance, and Recordings," and Eric Salzman discussed "Technology and
Recent Dialectical Processes in Music." Focusing on "The Phonograph and
the Performer," Martin Williams examined the interrelationship between
the role of "Jazz, the Phonograph, and Scholarship," and Charlie Gillett
looked at the role of "The Producer as Artist." The fourth session, "The
Phonograph and the Scholar and the Critic," included John Rockwell's "The
Phonograph and the Music of Today," and Charles Hamm's "The Phonograph
as Time Machine." During the final session, devoted to "The Phonograph
and Other Media," Claire Brook examined "The Book Publisher and Recordings," and Allan Miller focused on "The Use of Recorded Sound and Its
Manipulation in Films."

M 14. HOWARD, JOHN TASKER. Our American Music. 1936; Rev. ed. New
      York: Crowell, 1942. 944 pp.
In this broad survey of American music Howard chronicles the institutional
history of this country's cultural development. Beginning with New England
psalmody and ending with the composers of the 1930s, Howard provides portraits of individual creative personalities and their major works. He
also devotes considerable attention to the performance of music, including,
for example, a discussion of Patrick S. Gilmore's Peace Jubilees of the
1970s. The bibliography provides an extensive list of sources on early
American music, with brief lists of works on folk and popular music and
modern musical currents. The broad sweep of Howard's analysis has served
as a model for later music historians who have attempted generalizations
about American culture based on its musical experience.

M 15. HOWARD, JOHN TASKER and GEORGE KENT BELLOWS. A Short History
      of Music in America. New York: Crowell, 1957. 496 pp.
Howard and Bellows observe that American musical culture was not sufficiently developed to produce a composer of genius until the latter part
of the 19th century. They assert that the absence of an early American
role model is partly responsible for the persistence of a diversity of

styles and traditions in this country's music. They include some analysis of jazz, Broadway music, and folk sources, and they consider the importance of institutions and performance organizations and of new musical technology to the development of the American composer's craft.

M 16. HUBBARD, W. L., ed. History of American Music. Toledo, Ohio:
    Irving Squire, 1908. 356 pp.
Hubbard's history is part of The American History and Encyclopedia of Music. It includes a chapter on "Music Education" by Frank Damrosch and other chapters on "Negro Minstrelsy," "Patriotic and National Music," "Opera in America," and "The Music Trades." These chapters provide less a chronological, narrative history of events and personalities than a series of case studies in the American musical experience.

M 17. KAUFMANN, HELEN L. From Jehovah to Jazz: Music in America from
    Psalmody to the Present Day. New York: Dodd, Mead, 1937.
    303 pp.
Kaufmann's history of American music proceeds from the "pious infancy of song inspired by Jehovah to a lusty but uncertain adolescence conditioned to jazz and dissonance." She discusses the early sacred music of the period before 1720; the growth of a native American music and music publishing industry between 1720 and 1800; the emergence of a tension between native and imported music after 1800, particularly in the opera houses; the resurgence of European musical traditions with the immigration of German and other musicians and music teachers after the European revolutions of 1848; and the emergence of jazz as a distinctive "manifestation of native musical personality." She includes chapters on the spiritual and folk songs of black Americans, various other folk strains, "Rah-Rah Songs of College and Country," the sentimental ballad, the growth of symphony orchestras, wandering minstrelsy, blues and ragtime music.

M 18. KEBEDE, ASHENAFI. Roots of Black Music: The Vocal, Instrumental,
    and Dance Heritage of Africa and Black America. Englewood Cliffs,
    N.J.: Prentice-Hall, 1982. 162 pp.
Kebede studies the lifestyle of Africa through its music and, by extension, certain aspects of both lifestyle and music among blacks in America. The book includes discussion of African regions often neglected by those who consider that black Africa only begins south of the Sahara—"oriental" Africa (the Islamic cultures of the North), the Nile cultures of the Northeast, surviving traces of the pre-Islamic elements of North Africa, and Madagascar with its influences from Southeast Asia. Kebede studies vocal music in all these regions of Africa; musical instruments; legend, magic, myth, and symbolism, including symbolism of musical instruments; dance and music; and Euro-American elements in today's African music. A final chapter surveys the music of black Americans—blues, jazz, and African-derived instruments, such as the banjo.

M 19. KINGMAN, DANIEL. American Music, A Panorama. New York: Schirmer
    Books, 1979. 577 pp.
Kingman invokes the 19th-century panorama, "an exhibition of the painter's art done on a mammoth scale," in this thematically organized text, which describes the route from folk art to fine art, "via a detour to popular art." He charts the parallel progress of seven "intermingling and mutually influential streams": folk, sacred music, country, blues, rock, jazz, and classical. In the first of the book's six sections, he discusses various folk music traditions: Anglo-American, Afro-American, Native American, Spanish and French strains, and modern American folk music. He then discusses the influence of the folk tradition on American sacred music in "Sacred Music in the Possession of the Folk." "Three Prodigious Offspring of the Rural South" is an examination of country music, rock, and blues. In "Broadway Galaxy" he discusses the music of Tin Pan Alley, Broadway,

and Hollywood. "Jazz: The Unique Tradition of the Performer's Art" analyzes American jazz and its origins in minstrelsy and ragtime. A final
chapter, "Fine Art Music: The Comprehensive Tradition of the Composer's
Craft," discusses classical and concert music, both in the context of
its use with other media and its use of technology.

M 20. **KMEN, HENRY A.** Music in New Orleans, the Formative Years 1791-
1841. Baton Rouge: Louisiana State University Press, 1966.
314 pp.
Kmen places his sketch of the music of the city of New Orleans against
the backdrop of the city's demography and population growth, climate,
politics, and artistic patronage. He devotes the first two chapters of
this work to a discussion of music for fancy dress balls, an important
activity in the early history of New Orleans. Seven chapters on opera in
the city are followed by chapters on band music (including the famous
marching funeral processions), concerts, and Negro music. An appendix
lists the pieces played in formal concerts in New Orleans between 1806
and 1841. Kmen provides extensive footnotes and a bibliography.

M 21. **LOCKE, ALAIN.** The Negro and His Music. Washington, D.C.: Associates in Negro Folk Education, 1936. 142 pp.
Claiming that "America is a great music consumer, but not as yet a great
music producer," Locke writes that "Negro music is the closest approach
America has to a folk music, and so Negro music is almost as important
for the musical culture of America as it is for the spiritual life of
the Negro." Negro folk music, he writes, has laid "the foundation for
native American music," along with the Irish and English folk strains
preserved in the mountains of the East. He charts the gradual acceptance
and absorption of black folk music traditions into popular music. His
discussion of black American musical tradition is broken down according
to seven periods: "Before 1830: The Age of Plantation Shout and 'Breakdown'" (African reminiscences and survivals), "1830-1850: The Age of
the Sorrow-Songs: The Classic Folk Period" (spirituals and folk ballads),
"1850-1875: The First Age of Minstrelsy" (Stephen Foster and the sentimental ballad), "1875-1895: The Second Age of Minstrelsy" (farce and
buffoonery, the "buck and wing," the "coon song," and the "folk blues"),
"1895-1918: The Age of Ragtime" (vaudeville and musical comedy), "1918-
1926: The Jazz Age" (the Stomp, the artificial blues, and dance comedy),
and "1926 to Date: The Age of Classical Jazz" (the dawn of classical
Negro music).

M 22. **McCUE, GEORGE,** ed. Music in American Society 1776-1976, From
Puritan Hymn to Synthesizer. New Brunswick, N.J.: Transaction
Books, 1977. 207 pp.
McCue presents twelve essays on diverse topics in American music. These
essays are connected by their attempt to analyze music in terms of the
broad social currents that existed around it. Charlotte J. Frisbie writes
about "The Music of the American Indian" and William Schuman contributes
an essay on "Americanism in Music: A Composer's View." The volume also
includes Edward Jablonski's "Music with an American Accent," Dan
Morgenstern's "Jazz as an Urban Music," and Frank Peters's "Musical Corporation in America."

M 23. **McDONALD, WILLIAM F.** Federal Relief Administration and the Arts.
Columbus: Ohio State University Press, 1969. 869 pp.
While McDonald provides an overview of the structure and operations of
Federal One, he devotes considerable attention to the specific programs
which emerged regionally and then in individual states under the auspices
of the Federal Music Project and later the Federal Music Program. Using
information from the American Federation of Musicians, he documents the
seriousness of the unemployment problem in music as a result of sound

pictures, recorded music, and the general impact of the Depression, and he offers many examples of specific programs that provided concerts, classes, and recreational music at the local level. McDonald also cites permanent examples of Music Project initiative and support, including the Buffalo and Utah Orchestras.

M 24. **MELLERS, WILFRED H.** Music in a New Found Land. New York: Knopf, 1965. 543 pp.
Mellers analyzes American music in terms of American cultural development. According to Mellers, "America is a polyglot culture, different from any other in that it is non-indigenous." With respect to this country's relationship to Europe, he contends that "America is an extreme evolution from the European consciousness; we see in America what happened to the 'mind of Europe' when, separated from the traditions of a civilized past, it was faced with 'nothing but land--not a country at all, but the material out of which countries are made.'" Mellers divides his analysis into two parts. In "The Pioneer and the Wilderness," he discusses "primitive" American music as well as the work of such pioneering composers as Charles Ives, Carl Ruggles, Elliott Carter, and Harry Partch. "The World of Art and the World of Commerce: The Folk Song of the Asphalt Jungle" considers 19th-century popular music, jazz, theater music, and modern popular music. He also includes appendices, a list of recommended books, a discography, and indexes of musical examples and literary quotations.

M 25. **ROACH, HILDRED.** Black American Music: Past and Present. 1973; Rev. ed. Boston: Crescendo, 1976. 199 pp.
Roach's account of Afro-American music provides a survey of the work of black composers from 1619 to the 1970s. In the first section, she discusses the emergence of Afro-American music during the years of slavery in the U.S. This section covers the African heritage, early folk music, and spirituals. The second section concentrates on the years between the 1870s and the 1950s. During this period, as Roach demonstrates, there was a major increase in the number of professional black musicians, especially those involved with the development of jazz. She then discusses the contemporary period of the black revolution in music and the continued development of jazz and the evolution of New Music. The volume concludes with appendices listing readings and recordings, musical terms, composers and publishers, and repositories.

M 26. **ROBERTS, JOHN STORM.** Black Music of Two Worlds. New York: Praeger, 1972. 286 pp.
Roberts argues that Afro-American music, formed from a meeting of African, Arabic, and European musical styles, exists in three areas of the New World--the U.S., the Caribbean, and Central and South America. African musical elements found in varying degree in each of the regions include complex cross-rhythms, a close relationship to the rise and fall of speech, a use of instruments as an extension of the voice, the call-and-response pattern in performance, and the frequent use of "blues notes," six-note scales with a flatted seventh. In his discussion of the music of each region, Roberts attempts to identify both African and European traits and to describe the effects of one upon the other. For instance, in his discussion of music in South America, he focuses on Brazil as having the most impressive black music and finds that many of its elements, such as a fondness for percussion and complex rhythms, were reinforced by similar musical elements from Spain and Portugal. A final chapter discusses the modern urban music of post-Colonial Africa. The volume includes photographs and a discography.

M 27. **ROCKWELL, JOHN.** All American Music, Composition in the Late Twentieth Century. New York: Knopf, 1983. 286 pp.
These essays focus on composers and their music since the late 1930s in
the U.S. Arguing that there is often a fusion of the cultivated and vernacular traditions, Rockwell notes that "music in the late twentieth century exists on a myriad of levels of technical complexity, historical
tradition, technological discovery and hybrid interaction, and no culture
in the world has a richer confluence of these cross-currents than the
United States." Rockwell writes about music in social and historical
terms in twenty separate but not unrelated pieces that include "The Rise
of American Art Music and the Impact of the Immigrant Wave of the Late
1930s," "The Return of Tonality, the Orchestral Audience and the Danger
of Success," and "Art-Rock, Black vs White and Vanguard Cross-Pollination."

M 28. **ROSENFELD, PAUL.** An Hour with American Music. Philadelphia:
Lippincott, 1920. 179 pp.
Rosenfeld offers his reflections on modern America and its music in eight
essays thematically organized. He discusses jazz, spiritual, and mountain
music in the context of their social environments. He analyzes the impact
that this music has had on composers of concert music, pointing out, for
example, that modern European composers have utilized the techniques and
sounds of jazz in many recent works. Immigrant American composers, modernists, nationalists, and composers with strong interests in popular music
are considered, and he devotes single chapters to Carlos Chavez and Edgard
Varese.

M 29. **RUBLOWSKY, JOHN.** Black Music in America. New York: Basic Books,
1971. 150 pp.
Noting that American popular music is a synthesis of many styles and traditions, the author nevertheless contends that black music has been the
dominant influence in the 20th century. Black musical characteristics
that now pervade American popular music are complex rhythms, the use of
instruments as an extension of the voice, the use of ostinato and other
black performance styles, and the close association of music with dance.
The author follows the history of black American music from its origins
in slave worksongs to the rise, after emancipation, of such song forms
as spirituals. Also in the 19th century, black musicians began to take
part in minstrelsy, a theatrical form that had previously been dominated
by whites imitating blacks. Finally, he traces the rise of ragtime and,
in the 20th century, the triumph of jazz which "represents the heart of
American music" and the eventual appearance of black musical influence
in rock and roll.

M 30. **SCHAUFFLER, ROBERT HAVEN** and **SIGMUND SPAETH.** Music as a Social
Force in America and the Science of Practice. New York: Caxton
Institute, 1927. 118 pp.
The first two essays in this volume, Schauffler's "Music Comes to Main
Street" and Spaeth's "Social Aspects of Music in America," describe com-
munity music; music in schools, churches, and other institutions; the
problem of Americanization and the role of music in this process; and
problems in establishing community music. The third essay, Schauffler's
"The Science of Practice," is a practice guide for players and singers.

M 31. **SIDRAN, BEN.** Black Talk. New York: Holt, Rinehart & Winston,
1971. 201 pp.
Sidran examines "how the music of Black America created a radical alternative to the values of Western literary tradition." He discusses the
social function of black music as well as its meaning as a language within
Afro-American culture. Sidran asserts that there is no separation between
art and life in Afro-American culture and that Afro-American music is
"not only a reflection of the values of black culture but, to some extent,

the basis upon which it is built." He claims that "the elements of black
music make a particularly strong 'mood synthesizer': the music can galvanize a group of individuals on an emotional, nonverbal level of experience." He also contends that it has "not only provided the basis for
a viable social structure during times of crisis for the black community,
but was at the heart of the ensuing black revolution as well." After
a general discussion of the relationship between music and the "orality"
of Afro-American culture, Sidran divides his study into four historical
periods: the early history before W.W. I, the Jazz Age of the 1920s,
the evolution of the "Black Underground" between 1930-47, and the period
of "Black Visibility" between 1949-69. He finally argues that black culture has failed to develop a "literate" tradition, opting rather for a
more fluid and fluent "oral" modality.

M 32. SOUTHERN, EILEEN. The Music of Black Americans: A History. 1971;
      Rev. ed. New York: Norton, 1983. 602 pp.
In the revised and expanded edition of her history of the popular and
concert music of Afro-Americans, Southern focuses on the New World experience. She examines African musical traditions, such as Ethiopian minstrelsy, to help explain the evolution and forms of Afro-American music.
The volume is arranged chronologically into four sections: in "Song in
a Strange Land, 1619-1775" she covers African musical legacies and Colonial
songs and hymns; in "Let My People Go, 1776-1866" she discusses the music
of the slave experience, including the black military music of the Revolutionary and Civil Wars, the music of the black churches, and the music
which grew out of the urban and rural lives of American blacks; in "Blow
Ye the Trumpet, 1867-1919" she traces the evolution of spiritual, gospel,
minstrel and ragtime music in post-Civil War and turn-of-the-century
America; in "Lift Every Voice, 1920-" she examines the music of the Jazz
Age, the "Black Renaissance" of the 1920s and 1930s, and offers an up-
to-date history of Afro-American music from the post-W.W. II period to
the present, including gospel music, new jazz music, urban blues, popular music, concert music, opera, black Broadway musicals, music education,
and the music of the "Black Revolution." A bibliography and a discography
are appended. A companion volume, Readings in Black American Music (1971;
Rev. ed. New York: Norton, 1983), reprints contemporary documents in
black music history from the 17th century to the present.

M 33. SPELL, LOTA M. Music in Texas, a Survey of One Aspect of Cultural
      Progress. Austin, Tex.: n.p., 1936. 157 pp.
Spell's history of music in Texas focuses on the influences of various
cultures that created their own music and often cross-fertilized the music
of other groups. Early chapters discuss the music of Indians, Texas missions, Spanish-American folk music, and Anglo-American folk music. She
then analyzes the relationship of Texas to the rest of the South. Later
chapters consider music education, opera, orchestras, other agencies that
support music, and music composed by Texans or in Texas. An appendix
offers a Texas concert calendar from 1920-21.

M 34. STEVENSON, ROBERT. Protestant Church Music in America: A Short
      Survey of Men and Movements from 1564 to the Present. New York:
      Norton, 1966. 168 pp.
Stevenson begins his history of Protestant church music in America with
a discussion of the Huguenot settlers in Florida teaching hymns to the
Indians in 1564 and concludes mentioning the 20th-century composers of
"elevated" church music: D. S. Smith, Roger Sessions, Randall Thompson,
and Leo Sowerby. He examines the various repertoires and psalters used
by the New England Puritans between 1620 and 1720, and the "Regular Singing" movement of the mid-18th century. He focuses on the contributions
of the Pennsylvania German musicians from Johannes Kelpius to Johann
Friedrich Peter, of American composers of the Middle Atlantic Colonies

such as Francis Hopkinson and James Lyon, and of Southern composers such as C. T. Pachelbell. He also discusses the singing-school masters, the "scientific" composers, shape notation, and fasola folk, and devotes a chapter to Negro spirituals. His final chapter, covering the period from 1850 to the present, discusses gospel hymnody and modern church music.

M 35. **TAWA, NICHOLAS.** A Sound of Strangers: Musical Culture, Accultura-tion, and the Post-Civil War Ethnic American. Metuchen, N.J.: Scarecrow Press, 1982. 304 pp.
This volume offers "a study of musical acculturation in those American ethnic communities that were first formed toward the end of the 19th cen-tury." The ethnic musical traditions discussed include those of the East-European Jews and the immigrants from Southern Italy, the Mideast, China, and Japan. Among the topics Tawa considers are "The Transplanting of Musical Culture," "The Role of Isolation in Perpetuating Ethnic Culture," "Music Education in an Ethnic Community," and "Musical Acculturation and the Crisis in Identity." A final chapter on "The Cultural Commonwealth" includes examinations of "The Decline of Ethnocentrism," "The Ethnic Com-poser's Contribution to American Popular Music," and "Music in the Ethnic Society of the late 20th Century." He appends a section of "Musical Exam-ples" of various ethnic musics, complete with original texts, translations, and music.

M 36. **WALTON, ORTIZ.** Music: Black, White, and Blue: A Sociological Survey of the Use and Misuse of Afro-American Music. New York: Morrow, 1972. 180 pp.
This is primarily a sociological account of Afro-American music, its development, and its meaning within Afro-American culture. Walton presents the components of musical practice--improvisation, antiphony, and syncopation--and examines them in terms of their social and aesthetic functions. While acknowledging the unity of black music, he uses such categories as religious music, slave music, blues, jazz, and ragtime to further delineate the various performance and text practices in terms of their particular social settings. Walton also includes a cross-cultural comparison (Western versus African and Afro-American) of the fundamental issues of world view, rationality, and technology and illustrates their impact on the black music tradition. He includes a discussion of Bebop as a musical reaction to the atrophy and content dissolution of the dance band era as well as an assessment of the impact of the music industry as both a catalyst to and inhibitor of the evolution of black music. Chapters are devoted as well to the careers of Edward Kennedy Ellington, Arthur Davis, and "The Need for Afro-American Musical Training Programs."

II.   CLASSICAL AND CONCERT

M 37. **ALDRICH, RICHARD.** Concert Life in New York, 1902-1923. 1934; Rev. ed. New York: Putnam, 1941. 795 pp.
Aldrich, the music critic for The New York Times from 1902-23, approaches the art and science of criticism from the perspective of a teacher. Noting that "there is still a majority in the higher walks of life who consider themselves educated in other things, to whom the thought of being led to an understanding of a higher aesthetic purport in music is assumed to be an affectation and to rest on a foundation of boredom, if the truth were confessed," he analyzes musical personalities, performances, musical organizations, and new music with the idea of educating as well as enter-taining the reading and listening public.

M 38. BARZUN, JACQUES. Music in American Life. Bloomington: Indiana
       University Press, 1955. 126 pp.
Barzun describes what he calls a "cultural revolution" in the status of
music in American society since the 1920s, which, he notes, "should give
the contemporary reader a somewhat more explicit account than he gives
himself about what he daily undergoes." He is particularly concerned
with the spread of music through technology and argues that music is a
pervasive, but not an active, part of our lives. This "passive avocation"
for Americans is also described in chapters on "The Musician and the Economy," "Paradoxes of Democratic Patronage," "Music in the Schools," "Modernism and Self-Consciousness," and "Music and the Literary Fallacy."

M 39. BORETZ, BENJAMIN and EDWARD T. CONE, eds. Perspectives on Ameri-
       can Composers. New York: Norton, 1971. 268 pp.
The articles in this volume represent a collection of composers' writings
about their own art and that of their colleagues. Patterned after Henry
Cowell's American Composers on American Music (see M 51), this volume
provides a variety of points of view on the state of modern American music.
Chapters include "Edgard Varese: A Few Observations on His Music" by
Milton Babbitt, "Ives' Quarter-Tone Impressions" by Howard Boatwright,
"Copland on the Serial Road: An Analysis of 'Connotations'" by Peter
Evans, "Open Rather than Bounded" by Chou Wen-chung, and "A Composer's
Influences" by Ernest Krenek.

M 40. BROOKS, HENRY. Olden-Time Music: A Compilation from Newspapers
       and Books. Boston: Ticknor, 1888. 283 pp.
Brooks presents a documentary history of early musical activity in the
U.S. He argues that church music was in a continual decline because of
the opposition of the clergy to musical development prior to the emergence
of the movement for "Regular Singing" in the 1720s. This movement gained
the support of many ministers who wanted to improve the quality of psalm
singing in church. Brooks sees in this movement the emergence of a unique
American culture, and he predicts a continued independent flowering of
music in this country.

M 41. BROWN, ROLLO WALTER. Lonely Americans. New York: Coward-McCann,
       1929. 319 pp.
Brown offers seven portraits of American thinkers and creators who charted
their own courses. One of these portraits is of the American Romantic
composer, Edward MacDowell. Brown notes that "it is extremely fashionable
[in 1929] to refer to MacDowell as a very docile German romantic. Yet
in those days of his impetuous youth, he was hailed as a revolutionary."
Comparing the composer to Walt Whitman in his spirit and faith in democracy,
Brown discusses MacDowell's activities as a composer and as the first
chairman of the music department at Columbia University at the turn of
the 20th century, a time when music was not highly regarded as an academic
subject.

M 42. BROWNE, C. A. The Story of Our National Ballads. 1919; Rev. ed.
       New York: Crowell, 1931. 315 pp.
Beginning with the premise that "singularly enough, not one of the great
National Hymns has been written by a great poet, and but rarely has a
trained musician created the music to a National Song," Browne presents
sixteen chapters, each devoted to an American "national" song. These
range from "Yankee Doodle" and "America the Beautiful" to "Home, Sweet
Home," "Dixie," and "John Brown's Body." His last chapters consider songs
of the Spanish-American War and W.W. I.

M 43. **CAMUS, RAOUL F.** Military Music of the American Revolution. Chapel
      Hill: University of North Carolina Press, 1976. 218 pp.
In this study, Camus attempts to refute the assumption of music historians
that "bands and band music were nonexistent in the Revolutionary period
and that bands were not authorized in the regular army of the United States
until 1835." Citing Victor Herbert's statement that "the important part
that military bands have taken in the development of musical knowledge
in America cannot be overstated," Camus notes that "at a time when symphony
orchestras were not generally available as in Europe, military and militia
bands were serving the musical needs of the new nation . . . , more Americans heard orchestral music in band transcriptions than in their original
form." He begins with a discussion of the traditions of British and European military music and the subsequent development of Colonial American
military bands. After an examination of the historical background from
the battle of Lexington to Valley Forge, he provides an analysis of the
different beats and signals of the drum. Finally the role and development
of military music in the battles of the North and the South and of the
last campaign at Yorktown are examined. His appendices include a list
of the "Bands of Music in British Regiments of Foot, 1775-1783."

M 44. **CARDEN, JOY.** Music in Lexington Before 1840. Lexington, Ky.:
      Lexington-Fayette County Historic Commission, 1980. 148 pp.
Carden documents the musical history of Lexington, Kentucky, during the
years when that community was on the route of the Westward migration.
She surveys all varieties of music, from popular entertainments at barbecue
outings to early concert life, and she considers such important musical
personalities in the life of the city as Anthony Philip Heinrich and
William Iucho.

M 45. **CASE, ROBERT O.** and **VICTORIA CASE.** We Called It Culture--The Story
      of Chautauqua. Garden City, N.Y.: Doubleday, 1948. 272 pp.
The Cases describe how the traveling Chautauqua movement "brought culture
to Main Street" in this history of the instrumentalists and singers who
entertained as many as thirty million Americans with the "right" music
in hundreds of small towns across the country in a single season. They
cite the popularity of "standard" European compositions, as concert performers around the turn of the 20th century found that "audiences would
take all the music they could get." In 1921, the works most often
requested were composed by Beethoven, Massenet, Mendelssohn, Dvorak, and
Wagner. The authors stress the original intention of the Chautauqua movement to bring high culture to the hinterlands and note that "when the
music began to feature saxophone solos, bird whistles, musical saws, and
other hokey attempts at entertainment, the movement began to fail."

M 46. **CHASE, GILBERT**, ed. The American Composer Speaks. Baton Rouge:
      Louisiana State University Press, 1966. 318 pp.
In this volume, Chase presents a collection of American composers' writings
from William Billings to Earle Brown. He notes that these excerpts reveal
"the rather awkward and sometimes painful emergence of 'the American composer,' both as a type and as an individual, through the vicissitudes
of his social, economic, artistic, and intellectual situation." Chase
stresses the inhospitable nature of the American environment with respect
to music and says that the history of the composer in this country reveals
the attempts of individuals to navigate "between the Scylla of academicism
and the Charybdis of commercialism."

M 47. Comment and Criticism on the Work of Henry F. Gilbert, Composer.
      Boston: n.p., 1926. 16 pp.
This pamphlet reprints newspaper reviews and excerpts from journal articles
which analyze the career and music of Henry F. Gilbert, a turn-of-the-
20th-century American musical nationalist. It also includes commentary

by Gilbert on his music and his intention to create a national expression from folk and popular music sources. Gilbert is called a nationalist, "not from patriotic or jingoistic motives, but from philosophic conviction. He early perceived that the greatest, the most significant, and the most characteristic art of the world is always the flower of a particular national consciousness."

M 48. COPLAND, AARON. Copland on Music. Garden City, N.Y.: Doubleday, 1960. 280 pp.
This volume is a collection of pieces from a variety of sources, most notably Modern Music, The Saturday Review, and The New Republic. Copland analyzes a range of musical experiences and offers profiles of personalities as diverse as conductor Serge Koussevitzky, composer and teacher Nadia Boulanger, and writer and critic Paul Rosenfeld. He includes reviews of new music from the late 1940s and early 1950s and reprints here four important articles on the state of American composition: "America's Young Men of Promise" (1926), "America's Young Men Ten Years Later" (1936), "The New 'School' of American Composition" (1949), and "Postscript for the Generation of the Fifties" (1959).

M 49. COPLAND, AARON. Music and Imagination. Cambridge, Mass.: Harvard University Press, 1952. 116 pp.
The six pieces in this volume comprise Copland's Charles Eliot Norton Lectures at Harvard University during the 1951-2 academic year. In "The Gifted Listener," "The Sonorous Image," "The Creative Mind and the Interpretative Mind," "Tradition and Innovation in Recent European Music," "Musical Imagination in the Americas," and "The Composer in Industrial America," Copland asks if the artistic creativity in the U.S. is fundamentally different from that of Europe. While suggesting that it has been only natural for American composers to emulate European models, he says that "there is a deep psychological need to look for present signs" of unique American musical creation, and American composers have been very original in their use of folk materials.

M 50. COPLAND, AARON. The New Music, 1900-1960. 1941; Rev. ed. New York: Norton, 1968. 194 pp.
This volume, a revised and enlarged version of the 1941 Our New Music, offers Copland's reflections on the progress of music in American life and the state of professional health of the American composer and his music. In his analysis of the quality of music produced by American composers, Copland notes: "Geniuses don't grow on little bushes. The great young American composer will not appear suddenly out of the West with an immortal masterpiece under his arm. He will come out of a long line of lesser men--half geniuses perhaps, each one of whom, in his own way and with his own qualities, will prepare the way for our mature music." Copland offers the suggestion that this time of musical maturity has arrived in the U.S.

M 51. COWELL, HENRY, ed. American Composers on American Music, A Symposium. Palo Alto, Calif.: Stanford University Press, 1933. 226 pp.
This collection contains thirty-one articles by American composers, most of which are about another composer and his or her music. The volume also contains some general reflections on American music, such as Cowell's "Trends in American Music" and Amadeo Roldan's "The Artistic Position of the American Composer." Cowell writes that this work is "an experiment unprecedented in musical history, that of obtaining critical estimates from composers who may not always have a polished literary style but who know their subject, instead of from reviewers who are clever with words but do not know the principles of composition." The introduction contains a brief bibliographic essay on works that focus on American concert music.

M 52. CRAWFORD, RICHARD. American Studies and American Musicology, A
    Point of View and a Case in Point. Brooklyn, N.Y.: Institute
    for Studies in American Music, 1975. 33 pp.
In "American Studies and American Musicology," the first of the two essays
in this monograph, Crawford outlines some of the particular problems inherent in the study of American music. He stresses the need for scholars
to see music created and performed in this country "on its own terms,"
and he argues for greater consideration of the vernacular tradition in
academic studies of American music. "A Hardening of the Categories:
'Vernacular,' 'Cultivated,' and 'Reactionary' in American Psalmody" provides a case study in American musicology. Crawford notes that the idea
of an American composer has been slow to gain credence and that compilers
of psalm tunes in the 18th century, such as Andrew Law, expressed doubt
about the quality of music produced here.

M 53. DAVID, HANS T. Musical Life in the Pennsylvania Settlements of
    the Unitas Fratrum. Winston-Salem, N.C.: Moravian Music Foundation,
    1959. 44 pp.
David argues that the Moravians in 18th-century America, at a time when
"Puritan circles objected even to organs in their churches," were creating
a rich musical tradition. They were unique among East coast religious
settlements in their talent for and love of music. David discusses the
political and religious background of the Moravians, as well as their
musical heritage. The Moravian Brethren cultivated the musical talent
of the Bohemians of both Czech and German extraction, to which they were
closely related. David mentions, in particular, Count Zinzendorf, a
talented poet who found expression for his religious thoughts and feelings
in the improvised hymn. Also mentioned is the composer Johann Friedrich
Peter, the most gifted of Moravian composers, who brought over to the
New World not only the earliest preserved chamber music in the form of
his own compositions but also a first-hand knowledge of Haydn.

M 54. DAVISON, ARCHIBALD T. Protestant Church Music in America. Boston:
    Schirmer Books, 1933. 182 pp.
Davison writes that his book aims "to point out attitudes and conditions
which now govern our church music; to make clear certain powers and limitations of music in general which specifically apply to the present problem;
to define, through technical analysis, the main features of sacred as
opposed to secular style; to propose an ideal of Protestant church music;
and finally, to state what means and material are suitable for the realization of the ideal." In Part I, he examines the historical and social
backgrounds of several of these "attitudes and conditions," including
"indifference," "isolation," "deficient music education," "individualism,"
"tradition," and "prejudice." Part II, "The Theory and Substance of Church
Music," examines "The Uses of Music in Worship," "The Material of Sacred
Music," "Music to Fit the Ideal," and "Choirs and Instruments." He appends
"Four Brief Lists of Hymns, Anthems, Organ Selections, and Junior Choir
Selections."

M 55. DRUMMOND, ROBERT R. Early German Music in Philadelphia. New York:
    Appleton, 1910. 88 pp.
Originally a dissertation, this short book surveys the German contribution
to the musical scene in Philadelphia from the earliest settlements through
the early 19th century. Stressing the cooperation of German and English
musical practitioners in the "growth of musical taste in Philadelphia,"
Drummond includes chapters on church and secular music, teachers, music
dealers, and concert music. He also devotes chapters to the contributions
of Alexander Reinagle, Philip Roth, and Philip Phile. The appendix is
a list of Reinagle's compositions.

M 56. EDWARDS, GEORGE THORNTON. Music and Musicians of Maine: A History
of the Progress of Music in the territory which has come to be
known as the State of Maine from 1604 to 1928. Portland, Me.:
Southworth Press, 1928. 542 pp.
Edwards's work provides a compendium of detailed information about music
in Maine in a chronological framework. Some representative sections and
the periods to which they apply are "First Musicians of Maine" (1497-1639),
"Music Sinks to a Low Plane" (1640-1775), "Native Music Applauded" (1776-
1819), "How Music Was Used to Avoid the Blue Laws" (1820-1835), "Forming
of the Penobscot Musical Association" (1836-1856), "The Haydn Association
of Portland" (1857-1896), and "Maine Composers" (1897-1926). The last
chapter discusses "more than eighteen hundred living Maine musicians."

M 57. ELSON, LOUIS C. The History of American Music. 1904; Rev. ed.
New York: Macmillan, 1925. 423 pp.
Elson sketches the history of American music from the early New England
settlers to the composers of his own day. He finds the beginnings of
an American music in hymn and psalm singing and considers William Billings
the "first of the native composers." But in general, Elson sees little
real American creativity prior to the 1870s, arguing that during the previous decades "there was more of ambition than of true achievement and
the performances were generally slipshod and far below any classical standard." He focuses his attention on late 19th-century composers and includes
a chapter on "American Women in Music." The revised edition contains
a supplement on many early 20th-century composers, and the bibliography
provides sources on early music in America.

M 58. ELSON, LOUIS C. The National Music of America and Its Sources.
1899; Rev. ed. New York: Page, 1924. 367 pp.
Elson includes a wide variety of musical genres, creative personalities,
and cultural themes in his analysis of "national" music. He discusses
Pilgrim and Puritan music, the Regular Singing movement in 18th-century
New England, William Billings, "Yankee Doodle," "The Star Spangled Banner,"
sea songs, folk songs, and Civil War songs. After the first ten chapters,
he departs from his original theme somewhat to consider concert music,
Boston's Handel and Haydn Society, music in New York, the Boston Symphony
Orchestra, and the progress of music since 1900. His appendix offers
"More About Yankee Doodle."

M 59. EPSTEIN, DENA J. Music Publishing in Chicago Before 1871: The
Firm of Root & Cady, 1858-1871. Detroit, Mich.: Information Coordinators, 1969. 243 pp.
For her "study approaching mid-nineteenth century music in the United
States from the viewpoint of the publishers," Epstein uses a collection
in the University of Illinois library of over 800 sheets of music published
in Chicago before 1871, when the city's "thriving music trade" was drastically crippled by the great fire. She focuses on the career and publications of one of the "most interesting houses" in pre-fire Chicago,
the firm of Root & Cady. Epstein devotes separate chapters to "Chicago
Music Publishers Other Than Root & Cady," the partners of the firm, the
history and publications of the firm from its founding in 1858 to the
Civil War, the firm's support of the Union war effort through the publication of war songs during the Civil War, its expansion in the prosperous
post-War years, and the final years of the firm's existence from 1868-
71. Her appendices include a list of the publications of Root & Cady
and a directory of the music trade in Chicago before 1871.

M 60. EWEN, DAVID. Music Comes to America. New York: Crowell, 1942.
　　　295 pp.
Ewen analyzes the interaction between the European musical tradition and
the American environment. He discusses composers and their works, musical
organizations, and the audience. Once music made inroads into American
society and culture, Ewen argues, Americans could free themselves of European influences to create a musical culture of their own. Commenting
on the period after W.W. I during which the modern movement asserted its
influence on American composers, Ewen noted that, even in music, "the
American became more sure of himself, less inclined to look across the
ocean for models, more confident than ever before in American potentialities and resources. This reorientation, a postwar phenomenon, was a most
significant trend. Once the American no longer felt himself inferior
to Europe, he could cultivate his own music in his own way and achieve
unrestricted fertility."

M 61. FFRENCH, FLORENCE, ed. Music and Musicians in Chicago: The City's
　　　Leading Artists, Organizations and Art Buildings. Chicago: pri-
　　　vately printed, 1899. 236 pp.
Ffrench's collection of newspaper pieces on various musical activities
spans the period from the first official concert in the city in 1836 to
the end of the 19th century and was inspired by a special edition on music
in Chicago in The Musical Courier in 1897. She is interested in "the
story of the musical advancement made by this great Western metropolis,
its failures, disappointments, difficulties, and varying vicissitudes,
culminating in the vast triumph that has made Chicago, musically, as well
as in other directions, second to no city on this continent, with the
possible exception of New York."

M 62. FISHER, WILLIAM ARMS. Notes on Music in Old Boston. Boston: Ditson,
　　　1918. 100 pp.
Fisher's perspective in this volume is that of the observer from historic
Boston Common, the site of a new building that houses "the oldest publishing concern in the United States," Oliver Ditson Co. He discusses the
history of music shops, theaters, performance sites, and publishing establishments between 1630 and 1918. His numerous illustrations include various views of the Boston Common during different periods, concert halls,
portraits of composers and important musical personalities, and musical
examples. The volume also includes a chronology of the Oliver Ditson
Co.

M 63. FOOTE, HENRY WILDER. Three Centuries of American Hymnody. Cam-
　　　bridge, Mass.: Harvard University Press, 1940. 418 pp.
Foote provides chapters on the English heritage in American church music,
the Bay Psalm Book, the revival of singing in 18th-century New England,
the early hymn singing of the German settlers in America, the transition
from psalmody to hymnody, and 19th- and 20th-century American hymns.
Two appendices discuss in detail the controversies in the 1720s over the
practice of "lining out" psalms versus "Regular Singing." Foote includes
an index of psalm and hymn books and first lines of hymns.

M 64. GAGNE, COLE and TRACY CARAS. Soundpieces: Interviews with Ameri-
　　　can Composers. Metuchen, N.J.: Scarecrow Press, 1982. 418 pp.
Gagne and Caras present interviews with twenty-four American composers
whose works have not been often discussed in print, including Charles Dodge,
Henry Brant, Conlon Nancarrow, and Ralph Shapey. The work attempts to
provide "a forum for the composers' ideas," and these edited interviews
allow for a substantive discussion of compositional philosophy, technique,
and concepts of musical style. Each composer also has the opportunity
to comment on ancillary but important issues, such as public reception
of new works, government support for the arts, and the problems of economic
survival.

M 65. **GERSON, ROBERT A.** <u>Music in Philadelphia</u>. Philadelphia: Presser,
1940. 422 pp.
This volume is a chronological history of organized and community-supported
music in Philadelphia. Gerson considers the influence of early settlers,
especially Germans and Swedes, on the musical life of the city, and he
chronicles the impact of talented and trained immigrant composers, such
as Raynor Taylor and Benjamin Carr, on concert life. He also pays considerable attention to church music and popular entertainment music.
He includes sections on the Philadelphia Orchestra, chamber music, opera,
singing societies, music in schools and colleges, conservatories, music
publishers, and other musical organizations, such as the Manuscript Music
Society and the Musical Art Club. Part II is an index-dictionary of music
in Philadelphia.

M 66. **GOLDIN, MILTON.** <u>The Music Merchants</u>. New York: Macmillan, 1969.
242 pp.
Goldin provides an account of the progress of musical institutions, artists and their impressarios, and patrons. Noting that a consciousness
of "culture" can emerge where it is least expected, he says of P. T.
Barnum's promotion of Jenny Lind's famous tour in 1850 which, although
it was "conceived by a promoter with no previous interest in serious music,
supported by a public with no interest in serious music, . . . shook the
nation into an enjoyment of serious music." His chapters are divided
under the headings "Impressarios," "Patrons," and "Organizers." On support
for musical activity in his own day, Goldin argues that "when more Henry
Higginsons (founder and patron of the Boston Symphony Orchestra) and Morton
Baums (activist leader of the City Center in New York) decide what they
like and take leadership, the arts in America are going to be well-
nourished, whether with corporate, with foundation or with government funds."

M 67. **HART, PHILIP.** <u>Orpheus in the New World, The Symphony Orchestra
as an American Cultural Institution--Its Past, Present and Future</u>.
New York: Norton, 1973. 562 pp.
Hart's analysis of symphony orchestras in America and of the orchestra
as an American institution is divided into three parts. In the first,
he surveys the careers of five personalities: conductor Theodore Thomas,
Boston Symphony Orchestra Patron Major Henry Lee Higginson, union leader
James Petrillo, concert master Arthur Judson, and Helen Thompson of the
American Symphony Orchestra League. In the second section, he offers
case studies of six orchestras (Philadelphia, Utah, Cincinnati, Louisville,
Buffalo, and Albuquerque) to illustrate current problems. Part three
considers the economics of orchestra survival, concert repertory, the
concert audience, and education efforts. Fourteen appendices offer additional information on issues raised in the main body of the text.

M 68. **HARWELL, RICHARD B.** <u>Confederate Music</u>. Chapel Hill: University
of North Carolina Press, 1950. 184 pp.
Harwell states that the South has a long musical history that both precedes
and continues after the brief existence of the Confederate States of
America between 1861 and 1865. But he has chosen this brief period for
his study because of the unusual intensity of music publishing and distributing in the South during this time. The first section of his volume
is historical, with discussions of singing soldiers, the publication of
popular sheet music, sentimental and patriotic songs, and John Hewitt
Hill, the "bard of the Stars and Bars." The second section is an alphabetical listing of all sheet music published in the Confederate States.
Harwell also lists Confederate publishers and music dealers who were active
between 1861 and 1865.

M 69. HIPSHER, EDWARD ELLSWORTH. American Opera and Its Composers. Phila-
        delphia: Presser, 1927. 478 pp.
Hipsher devotes little attention to early American opera, concentrating
his attention on the late 19th and early 20th centuries. He discusses
the problem of presenting opera in English and concludes that opera in
the vernacular is vital to the development of what he calls "native opera"
in this country. Chapters 9-55 are brief portraits of composers, mainly
of the early 20th century, who have turned their talents to opera. He
celebrates the progress made in the U.S. in opera composition and performance, declaring that the "day of Native American Opera is at hand!"

M 70. HOWARD, JOHN TASKER. The Music of George Washington's Time. Washing-
        ton, D.C.: United States George Washington Bicentennial Commission,
        1931. 96 pp.
This pamphlet discusses the music of the Revolutionary and early Federal
periods in the context of the upheavals and Constitutional innovations
of the time. Howard cites, for instance, the resolution passed by the
Continental Congress in 1774 to "discourage every species of extravagence
and dissipation," which, of course included all forms of entertainment,
including musical performances. He also discusses the composition of
the "Federal March" in honor of the ratification of the U.S. Constitution,
by Alexander Reinagle. Howard concludes with an analysis of the musical
outpourings of emotion on Washington's death.

M 71. HOWE, MARK ANTONY DeWOLFE and JOHN N. BURK. The Boston Symphony
        Orchestra, 1881-1931. Boston: Houghton Mifflin, 1931. 272 pp.
Howe and Burk trace the history of the Boston Symphony Orchestra from
its founding in 1881 by Major Henry Lee Higginson through its first fifty
years. They trace the development of the orchestra's style under a number
of German conductors, the last of whom was Dr. Karl Muck who was deported
as a dangerous alien shortly after W.W. I, through the tenures of Henri
Rabaud, Pierre Monteux, and Serge Koussevitzky. Using contemporary press
editorials and news stories, they narrate the details of the Karl Muck
affair, analyzing the implications of this example of "musical 100% Americanism" for other conductors and orchestras.

M 72. HUGHES, RUPERT. Contemporary American Composers. Boston: Page,
        1900. 456 pp.
The composers described in this book are those whose styles and reputations
were formed at the end of the 19th century. Hughes surveys the backgrounds,
important stylistic characteristics, and major works of more than thirty
composers. He cites an improving situation for the American composers
at the beginning of the 20th century, as more orchestras were beginning
to program American pieces. "Now that Americanism is rife in the land,"
he notes, "some of the glowing interest in things national might well
be turned toward an art that has been too long neglected among us. The
time has come to take American music seriously. The day for boasting
is not yet here--if indeed it ever comes; but the day of penitent humility
is surely past."

M 73. JOHNSON, H. EARLE. Hallelujah, Amen! The Story of the Handel and
        Haydn Society of Boston. Boston: Humphries, 1965. 256 pp.
This volume first appeared on the occasion of the Handel and Haydn Society's 150th anniversary. It chronicles the history of the Society, first
founded for the purpose of performing Handel's "Messiah" and Haydn's "Creation," through its performances of other music and its community activities
in Boston. Johnson describes the repertoire of the Society under each
of its conductors and the reception it received over the years from
Boston's musical press, and he devotes particular attention to early 20th-
century critics H. T. Parker and Philip Hale who felt that the emphasis
on "standard" choral music should be modified to include newer pieces

in the Society's concerts. Johnson also includes a number of photographs and illustrations.

M 74. **JOHNSON, H. EARLE.** Musical Interludes in Boston, 1795-1830. New York: Columbia University Press, 1943. 366 pp.
Inspired in part by the questions raised in Oscar Sonneck's Early Concert Life in America (see M 113), Johnson "surveys the territory" of music in the 18th and 19th centuries. He focuses on the limited terrain of music in Boston, which he nevertheless finds to be fertile ground because of the activities of the Von Hagen family in publishing, Gottlieb Graupner in performance, composition, and publishing, and Dr. George K. Jackson as a conductor and organist. Johnson also studies other publishers, music dealers and manufacturers, performers, and teachers. Appendices provide lists of publications by the Von Hagen family, Graupner, and other firms, as well as a partial list of copyrighted music composed in Boston during this period.

M 75. **KAUFMAN, CHARLES H.** Music in New Jersey, 1665-1860. Rutherford, N.J.: Fairleigh Dickinson University Press, 1981. 297 pp.
This chronological history of music in New Jersey from early settlement to the beginning of the Civil War considers all musical genres and varieties of performance under the rubrics of sacred and secular music. Kaufman's analysis of sacred music concentrates on the music of particular churches in two categories: Lutheran (German Lutheran, Moravian, and Swedish Evangelical) and Calvinist (Reformed Dutch, Presbyterian, Protestant Episcopal, and Baptist). His discussion of secular music examines education, music publication, concert life, and various published "views on music," including early criticism. The volume includes appendices and a bibliography.

M 76. **KEEFER, LUBOV.** Baltimore's Music: The Haven of the American Composer. Baltimore, Md.: n.p., 1962. 343 pp.
Keefer justifies calling Baltimore "The Haven of the American Composer" by noting that, even though the city has not produced a major American composer, "nowhere in early America did music form a closer and more integral part of the whole man." In this survey of the cultivation of taste and the integration of music into daily life in Baltimore from the founding of the Maryland colony in 1649 to the post-W.W. I period, Keefer discusses life in the early town of Baltimore, Fort McHenry, George Peabody, music festivals, Americana, the "gay nineties," and the founding of an orchestra in the city. Keefer includes a bibliography.

M 77. **KOLODIN, IRVING.** The Metropolitan Opera 1883-1966, A Candid History. 1936; Rev. ed. New York: Knopf, 1966. 809 pp.
Kolodin writes: "Opera was given continuously at the Metropolitan Opera House, 1423 Broadway, New York City, for nearly eighty-three years-- from its first season of 1883. During that time no work by a native American--indeed, no work created on the North American continent--had any lasting success in its repertory. In this as well as in other ways, the Metropolitan took on a coloration peculiarly American." He argues that the lack of government support and the presentation of operas in their original languages rather than in the vernacular also set the "Old Met" apart from other world famous houses. Kolodin discusses patrons, management, the early seasons of opera in German, other New York City opera companies at the end of the 19th century, the influence of W.W. I and the Depression upon opera production, and the building of Lincoln Center. He also provides a compilation of works, which indicates the total number of performances for each opera.

M 78. **KREHBIEL, HENRY EDWARD.** Chapters of Opera, Being Historical and Critical Observations and Records Concerning the Lyric Drama from Its Earliest Days Down to the Present Time. New York: Holt, 1908. 435 pp.

Krehbiel, a music editor for the New York Tribune, surveys the early history of the Metropolitan Opera House on the occasion of its twenty-fifth anniversary. In Chapters I-VII, he offers a background to the present history, examining the introduction of opera in New York, the rise and popularity of Italian opera, and the growth of smaller New York opera houses. In Chapters VIII-XXIV, Krehbiel gives a detailed history of the Metropolitan Opera itself from 1883 to 1908. He discusses the rise of German opera in New York, the enthusiasm for Wagner, the brief return of Italian opera in 1891 and 1892, the careers of various performers, and the managerial terms and strategies of Maurice Grau, Heinrich Conried, and Oscar Hammerstein.

M 79. **KREHBIEL, HENRY EDWARD.** More Chapters of Opera, Being Historical and Critical Observations and Records Concerning the Lyric Drama in New York from 1908 to 1918. New York: Holt, 1919. 474 pp.

This book continues the history of the Metropolitan Opera House which Krehbiel began in Chapters of Opera (see M 78), covering the events of the decade from 1908 to 1918. He discusses the effect of W.W. I on the opera, the popular dislike of German opera (the Met's specialty), and the new era of operatic management. His chapters concern managerial controversies, the first season of dual administration (1908-09), rivalries between the Manhattan and the Metropolitan Opera Houses (and the demise of the former), popular opera at the Century Theater, the administration of Giullo Gatti-Casazza, experiments with English and Russian operatic works, and the coming to America of Giacomo Puccini, Engelbert Humperdinck, Amelita Galli-Curci, and Arturo Toscanini. The volume includes forty-three photographs, cast lists, repertoires for the decade at the Metropolitan and for the last seasons of the Manhattan Opera House.

M 80. **KRUEGER, KARL.** The Musical Heritage of the United States: The Unknown Portion. New York: American Society for the Preservation of the American Musical Heritage, 1973. 237 pp.

The "unknown portion" of America's musical heritage that Krueger describes is the support, or lack thereof, for American music in this society's cultural institutions. He analyzes publishing, the founding of major symphony orchestras, and the emergence of conservatories and college music departments in this country to preserve, perform, and provide training for American composers. His focus is on the period between 1825 and 1925 when, he argues, American composers became important in their own country. Krueger's history includes a listing of American Society for the Preservation of the American Musical Heritage's Archive of Recorded Performances, Music-in-America Series.

M 81. **KUPFERBERG, HERBERT.** Those Fabulous Philadelphians, The Life and Times of a Great Orchestra. New York: Scribner, 1969. 257 pp.

This volume is a history of the Philadelphia orchestra from its founding in 1900 to the late 1960s. Kupferberg provides chapters on "The City and the Orchestra," "The Early Years," "The Stokowski Era," "The Ormandy Era," and "The Life of the Orchestra." Appendices present a listing of the Philadelphia Orchestra's first performances, an alphabetical listing of all orchestra members from 1900 to 1969, and a discography.

M 82. LAHEE, HENRY CHARLES. Annals of Music in America, A Chronological
Record of Significant Musical Events, from 1640 to the Present
Day, with Comments on the Various Periods into Which the Work Is
Divided. Freeport, N.Y.: Books for Libraries Press, 1922.
298 pp.
Lahee presents a chronicle of performances, book publications, and appear-
ances of noted musicians in the U.S. between the publication of the Bay
Psalm Book in 1640 to the presentation of Sergei Prokofiev's "Love for
Three Oranges" by the Chicago Opera Association on December 30, 1921.
He also includes an index of compositions and listing of "Miscellaneous
Items."

M 83. LANG, PAUL HENRY, ed. One Hundred Years of Music in America. New
York: Schirmer Books, 1961. 322 pp.
Lang offers a collection of essays to celebrate the centenary of the pub-
lishing house founded in New York by Gustav Schirmer. The essays are
divided into four categories: "Musical Life," "The Business of Music,"
"Music as a Field of Knowledge," and "Music, Government, and the Law."
Contributions include "The Evolution of the American Composer" by Nathan
Broder, "Band Music in America" by Richard Franko Goldman, "Music on
Records 1877-1961" by Roland Gelatt, "Copyright and the Creative Arts"
by Robert J. Burton, and "The Taste-Makers: Critics and Criticism" by
Edward Downes.

M 84. LEVY, ALAN HOWARD. Musical Nationalism, American Composers' Search
for Identity. Westport, Conn.: Greenwood Press, 1983. 168 pp.
Levy analyzes "the shifting of international ties in American art music
from 1865 to 1930." He argues that this was an important period during
which the influence of German composers and German Romantic music declined
in this country with a concomitant rise in the influence of French music
and musicians. In his survey, which synthesizes chronological narrative
and thematic analysis, he considers "The German Orthodoxy," "Americanism
and French Impressionism," "Paris and Neoclassicism," "Expatriates, Frivo-
lous and Serious," "Ray Harris and Strident Americanism," and "Aaron
Copland." His study offers the conclusion that it was foreign, specifically
French, influence that briefly helped American composers find an identity
of their own in the period after W.W. I.

M 85. LOWENS, IRVING. Music and Musicians in Early America. New York:
Norton, 1964. 328 pp.
This volume of eighteen essays asserts the existence of a viable musical
culture in 17th- and 18th-century America. Arguing that the early New
England colonists demonstrated "extraordinary intellectual vitality and
thrust," Lowens asks, "is there any reason why music should have been
excluded from the range of their endeavors?" His descriptions of the
interaction of European traditions with the New World environment provide
evidence of a vital, if previously unrecognized, musical culture. Lowens
also analyzes the influence of politics on musical development after the
Revolution and the rejection of America's own music in urban cultural
centers by the second decade of the 19th century. He discusses attempts
to create American "national" music in the 19th century and speculates
about the validity of concepts of a unique and representative American
music in the 20th century.

M 86. LOWENS, IRVING. Music in America and American Music. Brooklyn,
N.Y.: Institute for Studies in American Music, 1978. 61 pp.
In "Music in America," the first of the two essays in this monograph,
Lowens discusses the problem of the popular perception of American music
and the reaction against music created here, especially as relations with
Europe improved after the Revolutionary War. Lowens notes the presence
of interesting and original music inland, away from the major centers

of commerce, trade, and interaction with Europe as well as other parts
of the rapidly developing U.S. In "American Music," he considers the
theme of musical nationalism and notes that the concept of an American
music was anachronistic by the 1970s.

M 87. MASON, DANIEL GREGORY. The Dilemma of American Music. New York:
      Macmillan, 1928. 306 pp.
Mason's volume contains eight articles on present-day American music,
along with four papers on more general musical subjects. The title piece,
which first appeared in the January 1926 issue of The American Mercury,
argues that modern American composers have many styles that tend to
"dilute, confuse, and cancel each other out." Mason denigrates musical
folklorism and finds little of positive value in the various strands of
the modern movement emanating from Europe. Noting that "the music of
the whole world has battered our ears" since W.W. I, he characterizes
the music of the period between 1914 and 1928 as "Music of Indigestion."

M 88. MASON, DANIEL GREGORY. Tune In, America: A Study of Our Coming
      Musical Independence. New York: Knopf, 1931. 206 pp.
Mason's study includes essays previously printed in The American Magazine
of Art, The American Mercury, Harper's, The Virginian Quarterly Review,
and other popular and scholarly journals. Mason stresses the future promise rather than the past achievements of American concert music, noting
that "in recent years it has been growing increasingly evident that America
is drawing toward the end of her long, necessary period of musical childhood and timid dependence on Europe, that she is even now in the somewhat
awkward self-conscious stage of adolescence, and that before long she
will be musically adult." He examines American music between 1925 and
1930 and includes an appendix of American pieces performed by six major
orchestras outside of New York during that period. Other chapters discuss
conductors and concert programs and the activities on behalf of American
music at the Eastman School of Music in Rochester, New York.

M 89. MATHEWS, W. S. B. A Hundred Years of Music in America: An Account
      of Musical Effort in America. Chicago: Howe, 1889. 715 pp.
This volume begins its chronological narrative with Colonial New England
psalmody but focuses most of its attention on musical institutions and
personalities in the 19th century. Mathews discusses the personal history
and contributions of artists, composers, music educators, inventors, and
journalists, including chapters on teaching music as a profession and
literary factors affecting musical progress in the U.S., specifically
the attitudes of critics toward music created and performed here. The
volume ends with historical and biographical sketches of important musical
personalities.

M 90. McCORKLE, DONALD M. The Moravian Contribution to American Music.
      Winston-Salem, N.C.: Moravian Music Foundation, 1956. 10 pp.
McCorkle discusses the music of the Pennsylvania and North Carolina model
communities of German settlers who came to be known as "Moravians." His
focus is on the period of active creativity and performance in these communities, from about 1740 to 1840. He argues that Moravian musicians'
contribution to the musical heritage of the U.S. includes the trombone
choir (derived from the German Stadtpfeiffer, or town piper, tradition),
the Collegium Musicum as a performing organization, and European instruments in the performance of sacred and secular music, as well as a body
of music by Moravian composers.

M 91. MERTENS, WIM. American Minimal Music. Translated by J. Kautekeit.
New York: Broude, 1983. 124 pp.
Mertens presents an analysis of the musical styles of contemporary minimalist composers LaMonte Young, Terry Riley, Steve Reich, and Philip Glass.
In the second portion of this volume, he provides some historical background to the current minimalist movement with a discussion of the music
of Anton Webern, Karlheinz Stockhausen, and John Cage. Part three, "Ideology," discusses Theodor Adorno's "Libidinal Philosophy," "a critical analysis of the negative dialectic," and the relationship of this approach
to minimalist composition.

M 92. MUELLER, JOHN H. The American Symphony Orchestra, A Social History
of Musical Taste. Bloomington: Indiana University Press, 1951.
437 pp.
This volume analyzes musical taste in 20th-century America by surveying
the activities of major symphony orchestras. Mueller provides a brief
historical sketch of the growth of the symphony orchestra as an American
institution, and he discusses some of the forerunners of the modern orchestra, such as the music festivals of the late 19th century and the orchestras led by Louis Antoine Julien and Theodore Thomas. He offers profiles
of seventeen major American orchestras, discusses the composers whose
works are most often performed, from Beethoven to Roy Harris, and includes
sections on orchestra audiences, unions and management, and the formation
of musical taste.

M 93. Music in Colonial Massachusetts 1630-1820, Vol. I Music in Public
Places. Boston: Colonial Society of Massachusetts, 1980.
404 pp.
This volume contains papers drawn mostly from a conference in May 1973
on "Music in Colonial Massachusetts." The essays all focus on secular
music and include "Selected American Country Dances and Their English
Sources" by Joy Van Cleef and Kate Van Winkle Keller, "Military Music
of Colonial Boston" by Raoul Francois Camus, "Songs to Cultivate the Sensations of Freedom" by Arthur F. Schrader, and "Broadsides and Their Music
in Colonial America" by Carleton Sprague Smith. Each essay includes its
own bibliography.

M 94. MUSSULMAN, JOSEPH A. Music in the Cultured Generation: A Social
History of Music in America, 1870-1900. Evanston, Ill.: Northwestern University Press, 1971. 298 pp.
In his contribution to the "history of music as a social act," Mussulman
discards the view that the musical life of 19th-century America was conventional, trite, artificial, sentimental, and governed solely by economic
considerations. To gain a "clearer understanding of a significant but
long-neglected episode in American musical life," he refers to the "tremendous body of critical and reportorial writing about music" in such
magazines as the Atlantic Monthly, Harper's New Monthly Magazine, Scribner's Magazine, and Century Illustrated Monthly Magazine between 1870
and 1900. He begins by discussing the histories, editors, and writers
of the four magazines and depicting the readers as members of a self-
consciously "cultured class." Mussulman examines the public conception
of the role of music as a "civilizing agency," music education, the "search
for a national musical costume," the American folk tradition, the "essence
of musical Americanism," the predicament of opera in America, the
"Mendlessohnism" and "Wagnerism" of the late 19th century, and the musical
lives of the parlor and the church. He includes four appendices which
list the articles pertaining to music in the four monthly magazines which
he has used as sources.

M 95. OLSON, KENNETH E. Music and Musket: Bands and Bandsmen of the
       American Civil War. Westport, Conn.: Greenwood Press, 1981.
       299 pp.
Olson discusses the era of the brass band in the 19th century, the social
and political functions the bands served, and their musical repertoire.
He analyzes a collection of primary source materials to illustrate the
impact of the brass bands during and after the Civil War, both in terms
of the music the bands played and their visual impressions. He presents
the bands in the context of a variety of military ceremonies, citing examples from music used in those ceremonies.

M 96. OWEN, BARBARA. The Organ in New England: An Account of Its Use
       and Manufacture to the End of the Nineteenth Century. Raleigh,
       N.C.: Sunbury Press, 1979. 629 pp.
This regional study is part of a growing literature on the manufacture
and use of musical instruments in the U.S. The narrative begins with
the installation of the first organ in a church in Boston in 1713. The
Brattle Square Church refused Thomas Brattle's gift of a small instrument,
but King's Chapel accepted the organ. Owen devotes several chapters to
organ builders and organists and to the increasingly important role of
the instrument in New England churches in the 18th and 19th centuries.

M 97. PICHIERRI, LOUIS. Music in New Hampshire, 1623-1800. New York:
       Columbia University Press, 1960. 297 pp.
Pichierri provides a study of musical life in New Hampshire which developed
out of his initial interest in music education. He discusses the importance of musical instruments, religious and secular music, music for public
occasions, opera before and after the American Revolution, concert life,
music theory, and music teachers. He also places the careers of composer
Samuel Holyoke and critic John Hubbard in historical perspective and discusses The Village Harmony, a singing book used for teaching the rudiments
of music which had gone through seventeen editions between 1795 and 1821.

M 98. PRATT, WALDO SELDEN. The Music of the Pilgrims, A Description of
       the Psalm-book Brought to Plymouth in 1620. Boston: Ditson, 1921.
       80 pp.
Pratt analyzes the contents and uses of the Ainsworth Psalter, a psalm
book printed in Amsterdam in 1612 and used in Plymouth Colony from its
founding at least until the merger with the Massachusetts Bay in 1692,
by which time it had generally been replaced by the Bay Psalm Book. He
provides technical descriptions of the versification in the Ainsworth
Psalter, musical examples, and analyses of the structure of the psalm
settings. He also reprints many harmonized psalm tunes. This book derives
its inspiration from the tercentenary of the settlement of the Plymouth
Colony.

M 99. REESE, GUSTAVE, ed. A Birthday Offering to Carl Engel. New York:
       Schirmer Books, 1943. 233 pp.
This collection of essays was compiled in honor of composer and musicologist Carl Engel, president of G. Schirmer music publishers. Several of
the essays are about Engel and his varied activities and accomplishments.
"Henry F. Gilbert: Nonconformist" by Olin Downes describes the career
and music of this turn-of-the-century American musical nationalist. In
his article "The Wa-Wan Press: An Adventure in Musical Idealism," Edward
N. Waters discusses Arthur Farwell's attempts to further American music,
specifically by publishing pieces which expressed a nationalist consciousness with his own publishing enterprise.

M 100. REIS, CLAIRE RAPHAEL. Composers, Conductors, and Critics. New
York: Oxford University Press, 1955. 264 pp.
Reis, an active supporter of the League of Composers and proponent of
modern music and modern composers in the 1920s and 1930s, writes about
the "crusading atmosphere" of the 1920s, in which composition in the U.S.
was influenced by the most current trends of the European avant-garde.
She offers insights into the operation of the League, with its various
publication, commission, and concert activities, arguing that the League
"upheld the most forward attitude, the most productive principles, of any
of the established musical institutions here [in New York]." Reis also
notes the unique quality of the period of experimentation in modern American music, stating that "somehow in 1949 the mood could not be recaptured."

M 101. RITTER, FREDERIC LOUIS. Music in America. New York: Scribner,
1883. 423 pp.
Ritter sees two distinct forces at work in the development of American
music. For him, the traditions of psalm singing and art music are not
complementary, and he attributes the absence of an American music to Puritan influence. "The American landscape," he writes, "is silent and monoto-
nous and imparts a melancholy impression, though Nature has fashioned
it beautifully." His interests lie outside the realm of indigenous American music, and he concentrates on opera, orchestras and other musical
institutions, and immigrants and their impact on American musical life.

M 102. SABLOSKY, IRVING L. American Music. Chicago: University of Chicago Press, 1969. 228 pp.
Sablosky provides a survey of American music, with a focus on the democratization of concert music, the development of a broader audience, and a
concomitant broadening of the base of financial support for music, all
of which were 20th-century developments. In his chapters on the early
20th century, he devotes particular attention to the founding of musical
institutions and to the interaction between what he calls an "Anglo-
European" tradition which stressed cultural "uplift" and a musical tradition
based on the Afro-American experience. He also writes about the growth
of the audience and of the number of prizes and fellowships available
to American composers after W.W. I.

M 103. SCHICKEL, RICHARD. The World of Carnegie Hall. New York: Messner,
1960. 438 pp.
Schickel offers a history of Carnegie Hall from its opening in 1891 to
the end of the 1950s. He focuses on the history of the music performed
and the musicians who made the hall famous, but he also considers the
social context in which these cultural developments occurred. On the
construction of Carnegie Hall, for example, he notes that in the early
1890s, "the new rich stood at the zenith of their untrammeled power, at
the height of their prestige. And it is one of the ironies of Carnegie
Hall's history that it achieved landmark status during the half-century
in which the thrust of American history was toward reform of the excesses
committed by the very class that had erected it." Schickel's history
attempts to expand its focus to present a general picture of New York's
cultural history.

M 104. SCHOLES, PERCY A. The Puritans and Music in England and New England:
A Contribution to the Cultural History of Two Nations. London:
Oxford University Press, 1934. 428 pp.
Scholes seeks to refute the notion that there was no musical activity
or appreciation among Puritans and to affirm the essential role of music,
both sacred and secular, in this community. By way of introduction, he
offers "a brief preliminary sketch of the history of protestantism and
puritanism and the founding of the Puritan colonies." Although the greater
part of his study examines the musical life of the English Puritans, he

devotes chapters to the "Charge Against the English Puritans" that they
were an unmusical people, "The 'Blue Laws' of Connecticut," "Instrumental
Music and the New England Community," "Puritanism and the Dance on Both
Sides of the Atlantic," "Puritan Church Song in England and New England,"
and "A Glimpse at Musical Life in a Non-Puritan Colony," about music in
Virginia. He offers eleven appendices on various specific issues, including a "Description of the Genuine 'Blue Laws' of Connecticut," "Some Early
Cases in Court in Massachusetts" and "The Quakers and Music," and a glos-
sary of musical terms.

M 105. SESSIONS, ROGER. The Musical Experience of Composer, Performer,
        Listener. Princeton, N.J.: Princeton University Press, 1950.
        127 pp.
Sessions presents a series of reflections on music as an experience and
the place of that experience in society and proposes that music, "of all
the arts, seems to be the most remote from the ordinary concerns and preoccupations of people, of all things created by man, its utility, as that
word is generally understood, is least easy to demonstrate. Nevertheless,
the effort to explain at least a part of the composer's craft, the ways
in which that art is transmitted, and how it is received by listeners
seems to be a worthwhile undertaking." He celebrates the presence of
composers in academic communities, for instance, because teaching allows
a composer to earn a living and train the next generation of composers.
Writing of his own generation of composers, he notes that, while his predecessors Schoenberg, Bartok, and Stravinsky, "have left music decisively
changed from what it was before them," his own generation in the 1920s
and 1930s "was not at all a revolutionary one."

M 106. SESSIONS, ROGER. Reflections on the Musical Life of the United
        States. New York: Merlin Press, 1956. 184 pp.
In this volume of observations on music and the American scene Sessions
stresses the fluidity of American culture and the ambivalence manifest
in our society toward the validity of musical composition as a worthwhile
activity. He points to two phenomena in our culture that influence trends
in music. The first, "colonialism," implies a reliance on Europe for
cultural direction, and the second, "frontierism," is a revolt against
European culture and, sometimes, even against high culture itself.
Sessions sees the university as a liberalizing force which can help to mitigate both tendencies, and he celebrates the fact that, in 1956, "one finds
more or less distinguished names [of composers] on university faculties
all over the country, and of the young native composers a characteristically great number are university graduates."

M 107. SESSIONS, ROGER. Roger Sessions on Music: Collected Essays.
        Edited by Edward T. Cone. Princeton, N.J.: Princeton University
        Press, 1979. 388 pp.
Sessions wrote the essays collected here between 1927 and 1975. Many
of them concern music and musical life in America, although most of them
address developments in European music. The essays are organized according
to various subjects, including "The Composer's Craft," "The Composer and
His Audience," "Education and Training," "The Limits of Theory," and "Music
and the World Conflict." Sessions deals with the composer's message,
issues confronting the composer, the relation between art and freedom
of expression, the American avant-garde, "Music in a Business Economy,"
the composer as teacher, American music and the coming of political crisis
(written at the beginning of W.W. II), the influx of European musicians
at the beginning of W.W. II, and the future of American music.

M 108. **SHANET, HOWARD.** Philharmonic--A History of New York's Orchestra.
Garden City, N.Y.: Doubleday, 1975. 788 pp.
Shanet provides a comprehensive history of the New York Philharmonic Orchestra. Building on previous histories by Henry Krehbiel, James Gibbons
Huneker, and John Erskine (see M 109), he expands the scope of his history
beyond the orchestra itself to encompass musical life in New York and
in the U.S. as a whole. He notes, for instance, that "the German domination of symphonic music in New York, and indeed everywhere in the United
States, has too long been underestimated. It is a domination that has
largely determined the aesthetics and the sociology of orchestral concert-
going in this country." He provides details of music performed by the
orchestra in its history since 1842 and includes commentary by contemporary
critics on the orchestra's progress.

M 109. **SHANET, HOWARD,** ed. Early Histories of the New York Philharmonic.
New York: Da Capo Press, 1979. 481 pp.
This compilation provides a single sourcebook for histories of the New
York Philharmonic Orchestra published previously to Shanet's own work
(see M 108). It includes Henry Edward Krehbiel's The Philharmonic Society
of New York: A Memorial; Published on the Occasion of the Fiftieth
Anniversary of the Founding of the Philharmonic Society (New York and
London: Novello, Ever, 1892), James Gibbons Huneker's The Philharmonic
Society of New York and Its Seventy-Fifth Anniversary: A Retrospect (no
imprint, no date, presumably published for the Society, 1917), and John
Erskine's The Philharmonic-Society of New York: Its First Hundred Years
(New York: Macmillan, 1943). Shanet's introduction summarizes each work
and provides critical commentary, biographical sketches, and a list of
corrections.

M 110. **SHEAD, RICHARD.** Music in the 1920s. New York: St. Martin's Press,
1977. 148 pp.
Shead analyzes the impact of American music, particularly American popular
music, on modern European music in the 1920s. He emphasizes ballet, opera,
and other types of stage pieces in which music, text, and scene interact
to form an artistic whole. He notes that the 1920s was a decade of experimentation which was influenced by a variety of styles, including jazz,
neoclassic music, and popular music. This music was centrally concerned
with expressing varied images of America. The works of Erik Satie, Darius
Milhaud, Igor Stravinsky, Kurt Weill, and Ernst Krenek are discussed.

M 111. **SMITH, CECIL.** Worlds of Music. Philadelphia: Lippincott, 1952.
328 pp.
Smith attempts to explain the pervasiveness of music in modern American
society by analyzing the dynamics of the music business. The "worlds"
of music that he explores include those of Columbia Artists Management,
the audience, the performer, the New York music scene, music outside New
York, opera, orchestras, composers, dancers, music education, and electronic music.

M 112. **SOKOL, MARTIN L.** The New York City Opera: An American Adventure.
New York: Macmillan, 1981. 562 pp.
Sokol uses the minutes of the New York City Opera's Board of Directors,
public materials, and private papers to provide an account of the company's
history from its founding in 1943 to the assumption of directorial duties
by Beverly Sills. He examines the NYCO's perennial lack of funds and
the efforts of individuals to keep it solvent. In addition to a general
chapter on opera's origins, and the emergence of opera as entertainment
and art in New York City, Sokol discusses opera on radio and television,
and the influence of long-playing recordings and tape recordings. He
also considers the ways in which jet travel has facilitated the engagement
of artists whose schedules require precise coordination. The annals list

and describe each of the NYCO's performances from February 21, 1944, through April 26, 1981.

M 113. SONNECK, OSCAR GEORGE THEODORE. Early Concert Life in America (1731-1800). Leipzig: Breitkopf & Hartel, 1907. 338 pp.
Sonneck's early study of institutional-sponsored concerts in the U.S. covers material not previously considered in monographs on the history of music in America. His analysis implies an interest in secular music, which, he argues, has a lively history of its own. He offers this conclusion as a corrective to earlier emphases on religious music in the history of American musical development. Written as a source book, this volume is organized by locality, and he includes chapters on early concerts in Charleston and the South, Philadelphia, New York, and Boston and New England. Sonneck also offers the conclusion that, prior to 1800, England was the primary cultural model for Americans and instrumental music prevailed over choral music. With the influence of German immigrants and the choral forms of opera and oratorio in the 19th century, both of these patterns would soon change.

M 114. SONNECK, OSCAR GEORGE THEODORE. Early Opera in America. New York: Blom, 1915. 230 pp.
This volume appeared originally as a series of articles in New Music Review (June-August 1907). The historical scope of the book is the time of the early settlements to about 1800, a period when, according to Sonneck, "opera played a secondary part in the theatrical affairs of our country." Ballad operas, "light English operas in which the plot is carried on in spoken dialogue instead of by recitative," receive attention here. The section on opera from 1793-1800 is organized by city, treating New York, Philadelphia, Boston and New England, and Charleston and the South separately. The epilogue considers the impact of French opera on American performance and composition around the turn of the 19th century.

M 115. SPALDING, WALTER RAYMOND. Music at Harvard, A Historical Review of Men and Events. New York: Coward-McCann, 1935. 310 pp.
Spalding offers a portrait of musical organizations and personalities. He states that musical activity in the U.S. began at Harvard in 1808, with the founding of the Pierian Sodality Orchestra. He discusses the establishment of a music department under the leadership of John Knowles Paine in the 1870s, various university clubs related to music, and includes a chapter on Memorabilia Musicalia. Spalding provides a list of holders of degrees in music from Harvard and also includes a chapter on prizes, bequests, and benefactions.

M 116. STOUTAMIRE, ALBERT. Music of the Old South: Colony to Confederacy. Rutherford, N.J.: Fairleigh Dickinson University Press, 1972. 349 pp.
This volume focuses almost exclusively on Virginia. Stoutamire concentrates on music in churches, in theaters, and in concert halls, as well as what he calls "music merchantry." He also considers the various European influences on antebellum Southern music and the importance of musical events to Richmond's elite social life. Two appendices provide discussions of public buildings used for musical performances and of selected programs in Richmond from the period 1797 to 1865.

M 117. SWAN, JOHN C., ed. Music in Boston--Readings from the First Three Centuries. Boston: Public Library of the City of Boston, 1977. 99 pp.
This book is a compilation of writings about music in Boston, ranging from The Whole Booke of Psalmes Faithfully Translated Into English Metre (1640) to the 20th-century writings of Henry Taylor Parker in the Boston Evening Transcript. Cotton Mather takes up the question of "Whether Instru-

mental Musick may lawfully be introduced into the Worship of God, in the Churches of the New Testament?" in his Magnalia Christi Americana (1702), and John Sullivan Dwight argues for "good" European music as a tool with which Americans can become better citizens in Dwight's Journal of Music in the 19th century. Swan does not provide editorial commentary but allows the sources to speak for themselves.

M 118. SWOBODA, HENRY, ed. The American Symphony Orchestra. Washington, D.C.: Voice of America, 1967. 218 pp.
This volume is a collection of seventeen interviews and lectures by various composers, conductors, teachers, broadcasters, and writers, which were originally broadcast as Forum lectures by the Voice of America. The pieces represent a "selective overview of achievements, shortcomings, and trends, as well as cultural and financial aspects of our symphonic life." Among other topics, the participants discuss nationalism in American symphonic music, the role of the composer as conductor, the career of the orchestral musician, the university symphony orchestra, the dissemination of symphony music by radio and television, and the financial situation of the American orchestra.

M 119. THOMPSON, OSCAR. Practical Musical Criticism. New York: Whitmark, 1934. 178 pp.
Thompson, an associate editor of Musical America, professor of criticism at the Curtis Institute of Music, and music critic of the New York Evening Post from 1928-34, presents his views on the importance of objectivity in criticism and articulates the problems faced by American critics at a time when the music of American composers was beginning to gain attention. His image of the critic is of a person who possesses "a liberal education, good breeding, [and] the ordinary attributes of a gentleman." He argues that the American critic must choose to become either a propagandist or a staunch upholder of his own musical standards. "Any sort of vacillation between the two positions," he writes, "is likely to be fatal to respect."

M 120. THOMSON, VIRGIL. American Music Since 1910. New York: Holt, Rinehart & Winston, 1970. 204 pp.
In the introduction to this survey of 20th-century currents in American concert and stage music, Nicholas Nabokov delineates some of the important features of our century's music: a "quickening pace of change," experimentation, the breakdown of academic rules and traditions, the proliferation of a variety of styles and approaches to composition, an increased support of musical institutions by cities, and greater participation by the mass media in making music available to a broader public. In the body of the volume, Thomson describes the trends that Nabokov lists, providing evidence and examples of the phenomena. Thomson concludes that, in the "Tower of Babel" of modern music, "the American voice becomes more and more distinct as the volume of our work augments."

M 121. UPTON, WILLIAM TREAT. Art-Song in America, A Study in the Development of American Music. Boston: Ditson, 1930. 279 pp.
Upton analyzes the progress of art song in America founded "upon the solid rock of German study and tradition," for which, he says, "we cannot be too thankful." But his study, which ranges from 18th-century composers in the English tradition such as Francis Hopkinson to composers such as Charles Tomlinson Griffes who eschewed the German tradition for French Impressionism, also celebrates the liberation of American song from its German influence. He argues: "The advent of such men as Charles M. Loeffler and Ernest Bloch in our midst exerted tremendous pressure toward a modifying of our hitherto strongly entrenched Teutonic ideals. And justly so, for we had developed these ideas and ideals to such an extent that it was time for the introduction of some new ingredient to lighten and brighten what was in danger of becoming a bit stale."

M 122. VAN VECHTEN, CARL. Music and Bad Manners. New York: Knopf, 1916.
243 pp.
Van Vechten cites what he sees as a "misunderstanding, lack of sympathy,
and enmity" toward new music in the U.S. "There is many a man who weeps,"
he writes, "because he may grow up to like music without melody! Music
has changed, of that there can be no doubt. Don't go to a concert and
expect to hear what you might have heard fifty years ago." Van Vechten
analyzes the music and ideology of the Futurist composers, including the
American, Leo Ornstein. He calls Ornstein's music "a modern expression,
untraditional, and full of a strange soothing emotion."

M 123. WELLS, KATHERINE GLADNEY. Symphony and Song: The Saint Louis
Symphony, The First Hundred Years. Woodstock, Vt.: Countryman
Press, 1980. 227 pp.
Wells traces the history of the U.S.'s second oldest civic orchestra (New
York's Philharmonic Society was the first) from its origins as an amateur
ensemble to its present status as a major American orchestra under the
direction of Leonard Slatkin. She focuses on the contributions in the
orchestra's early years of German immigrant performers and audiences that
provided the financial base for the ensemble's success, and she traces
the activities of each of the conductors of the Saint Louis Symphony.
Wells also covers the orchestra's tours, children's and popular music
concerts, and entry into the realm of radio broadcasting. The Symphony
Women's Association and its supportive efforts also receive consideration.

M 124. WELLS, L. JEANETTE. A History of the Music Festival at Chautauqua
Institution from 1874 to 1957. Washington, D.C.: Catholic University Press, 1958. 310 pp.
Wells traces the course of American music through the history of the Chautauqua Institution, a summer gathering designed to promote education for
Sunday School teachers, and to provide a cultural forum for general audiences. She stresses the "correct" quality of the hymns, choral and orchestral works, and stage pieces presented at the summer festival, a forerunner
of future summer music festivals throughout the U.S. Wells argues that
the cultivation of good musical taste in aesthetically untrained audiences
was a significant goal of the concert organizers. She lists concert programs, visiting artists, orchestras and their conductors, and newspaper
reviews to support her argument that culture emerged under the influence
of the Chautauqua movement and took hold in its American audiences.

M 125. WETZEL, RICHARD D. Frontier Musicians on the Connoquenessing,
Wabash and Ohio. Oberlin: Ohio University Press, 1976.
294 pp.
Wetzel presents a history of the music and musicians of George Rapp's
Harmony Society and their descendants between 1809 and 1906. The Harmon-
ists, a millennialist community led by Rapp, settled in the Ohio Valley
in the 19th century, bringing with it a strong tradition of religious
and community music from Germany. Wetzel traces the history of the Harmony
Society under Rapp and later leaders Jacob Henrici and John S. Duss, analyzes Harmonist music, and chronicles a shift from music created in Europe
to pieces composed in the American settlements. Appendices reproduce
examples of vocal and instrumental music from the Harmony Society and
a Catalog of the Music Collection of Economy Village in Ambridge, Pennsylvania.

M 126. WILSON, RUTH MACK and KATE VAN WINKLE KELLER. Connecticut's Music
in the Revolutionary Era. Hartford: American Revolution Bicentennial Commission of Connecticut, 1980. 142 pp.
In this volume Wilson and Keller offer a portrait of music in Connecticut
during the 18th century. Using contemporary diaries, sermons, and speeches,
they discuss the controversy over Regular Singing that erupted in the

region in the 1720s. They also consider the influence of European, specifically English, dance music and ballad operas, and the influx of immigrant musicians to New England, particularly after the Revolutionary War. The War itself provided the inspiration for an increase in musical activity and the creation of patriotic pieces to further the American cause.

M 127. WISTER, FRANCES ANNE. Twenty-Five Years of the Philadelphia Orchestra. Philadelphia: Women's Committees for the Philadelphia Orchestra, 1925. 253 pp.
Wister presents an institutional history of the Philadelphia Orchestra's first twenty-five years. Her concern with public support for the orchestra throughout Pennsylvania and surrounding states, in the form of various Women's Committees, equals her interest in musical accomplishment. She provides accounts of Philadelphia's early musical history, the formation of the Philadelphia Orchestra with its attendant financial problems, the leadership of Leopold Stokowski, music during W.W. I, the audience, and the press. Appendices list various officers and directors of the Philadelphia Orchestra Association, members of the Women's Committees, and summaries of concerts.

M 128. WOLFE, RICHARD J. Early American Music Engraving and Printing: A History of Music Publishing in America from 1787 to 1825 with Commentary on Earlier and Later Practices. Urbana: University of Illinois Press, 1980. 321 pp.
Wolfe's study of "early American music engraving and printing" is intended to serve as a companion piece to Oscar Sonneck's A Bibliography of Early Secular American Music (18th Century) (1945) and his own Secular Music in America, 1801-1825; A Bibliography (1964). He discusses the "engraving, printing, publishing, and selling of music in America during the colonial and federal periods . . . when professional musicians and music publishers came to America in increasing numbers and began to form a music-publishing industry." Prefacing his history with three chapters on the "Anglo-European background," "Music-Publishing in the American Colonies," and "Printing Music from Type before 1825," he then discusses the arrival of German and English musician-publishers and the introduction of the "punching and stamping" technique which led to the growth of a permanent music-publishing industry in the post-Revolutionary era. He includes four chapters on the technical innovations, tools, and materials of the trade. The last two chapters examine the "customs and conditions of the trade" and the crucial question of dating early American music by the identification of printing techniques. Three appendices, "Account Book of Simeon Wood, 1818-21," "Inventory of George E. Blake, 1871," and "Watermarks in American Music Sheets, 1787-1830," are included.

M 129. ZANZIG, AUGUSTUS DELAFIELD. Music in American Life, Present and Future. New York: Oxford University Press, 1932. 560 pp.
In the foreword to this volume, Daniel Gregory Mason emphasizes a growing passivity in American musical consumption, citing statistics on decreased piano purchases and increased radio listening to support his point. Zanzig's study, prepared for the National Recreation Association, explores the relationship of music to American society and seeks explanations for the trends Mason notes. Zanzig studies school and community music, adult education, government aid to music, churches, playgrounds, settlement houses, art museums, and summer camps as loci of musical activity.

M 130. ZUCK, BARBARA ANN. A History of Musical Americanism. Ann Arbor, Mich.: UMI Research Press, 1980. 383 pp.
This book provides a history of the various attempts to create music for the concert hall and stage that would reflect American nationality. Zuck contends that the 1930s and 1940s marked the last efforts by a group of American composers to create a "specifically 'American' music." She pays

special attention to the Composers' Collective of the early 1930s and
the Composers' Forum Laboratory Concerts under the auspices of the Federal
Music Project as examples of a national spirit, a spirit that, during
the Depression in particular, "turned leftward." Using the categories
of "cultivated" and "vernacular" music, drawn from the work of H. Wiley
Hitchcock (see M 12), Zuck is concerned with her own subject of nationalism
as well as with a narrative history of musical events and compositions.
She includes both art music and popular music in this analysis of the
national theme in American music.

III.   FOLK AND COUNTRY

M 131. **AMERICAN FOLKLIFE CENTER.** Ethnic Recordings in America: A
        Neglected Heritage. Washington, D.C.: Library of Congress, 1982.
        269 pp.
Collected here are eight scholarly essays by participants in a conference
held at the American Folklife Center in January 1977. The contributors
explore the interactions between the various ethnic musical traditions,
the recording industry, the technology of sound recording, and the relation
of folk music to the world of popular music. Included are in-depth discussions of Irish-American recordings, the Mexican-American folk singer
Lydia Mendoza, and the Polish-American music publisher Wladyslaw Sajewski.
The final chapter is a biblio-discographic essay by Norm Cohen and Paul
F. Wells, "Recorded Ethnic Music: A Guide to Resources."

M 132. **AMES, RUSSELL.** The Story of American Folk Song. New York: Grosset
        & Dunlap, 1955. 276 pp.
Ames's history of American folk song from the Colonial period to the mid-
20th century focuses on the influence of British folk music. He orients
his history within the relevant historical and cultural contexts. Ames
divides his study into ten chapters, including examinations of the songs
of particular moments in history such as the Revolutionary War, the War
of 1812, and the Gold Rush; different types of song such as the broadside
ballad; the songs of various ethnic and occupational groups, such as Negro
spirituals and cowboy and miners' songs; and the relationship between
blues and prison music.

M 133. **ARTIS, BOB.** Bluegrass: From the Lonesome Wail of a Mountain Love
        Song to the Hammering Drive of the Scruggs-Style Banjo: The Story
        of an American Musical Tradition. New York: Hawthorn Books,
        1975. 182 pp.
In this volume Artis offers a history of "country music's other world"
from 1940 to the present. He describes bluegrass as the "modern heir"
of the folk music tradition brought from the British Isles, distinctive
for its use of the fiddle, and later, the banjo. After a background history of the rise of country music, Artis devotes separate chapters to
the careers and music of several key figures in bluegrass, including Bill
Monroe, the Stanley Brothers, Lester Flatt and Earl Scruggs, and the
Osborne Brothers. He focuses on the financial dilemma of bluegrass musicians, their turn to religious music and sponsorship, and the recent emergence of "newgrass," despite the traditionalist pressure. His appendices
include lists of bluegrass recordings, radio stations, and organizations.

M 134. BOYER, WALTER E., ALBERT F. BUFFINGTON, and DON YODER, eds. Songs
        Along the Mahantongo: Pennsylvania Dutch Folksongs. Lancaster:
        Pennsylvania Dutch Folklore Center, 1951. 231 pp.
The first complete volume on the subject of Pennsylvania Dutch folk songs,
this is a collection of songs with music and lyrics in both Dutch and
English. Some songs are of German origin, in which case the lyrics are
in both German and English. These songs reflect the habits, beliefs,
and life-styles of the Pennsylvania Dutch, and though there is a variety
of themes, the essential ones are: childhood, courtship and marriage,
and farming. Full of historical notes and anecdotes, the book is as revealing of the people of the Mahantongo Valley as it is of their music.

M 135. BRAND, OSCAR. The Ballad Mongers: Rise of the Modern Folk Song.
        New York: Funk & Wagnalls, 1962. 240 pp.
Brand presents an admittedly subjective history of the modern folk movement.
He begins by transcending the International Folk Music Council's definition
of folk song as "music that has been submitted to the process of oral
transmission" to include "a kind of 'simple noise' . . . , the result
of an artless, unself-conscious quality in the music and lyrics." Sources
of American songs, the folk song's enduring popularity, and the pioneering
work of the Lomaxes and other collectors and archivists are discussed.
Brand chronicles the spread of folk music through the music business.
He focuses on the Weavers as an illustration of the effects of modern
recording techniques, marketing ploys, and of the damage caused by the
blacklisting efforts against political singers in the 1950s. He also
touches on the folk movement of the early 1960s, the difficult questions
of censorship in civilian and military musical life, and the "legal tangle"
over the ownership of songs. Finally, Brand makes some predictions about
the future of folk music and proposes a solution to the "Purist vs. Popularizer" controversy.

M 136. BRONSON, BERTRAND HARRIS. The Ballad as Song. Berkeley: Uni-
        versity of California Press, 1969. 324 pp.
Most of the eighteen essays in Bronson's collection center on the Child
ballads and questions of methodology. All of these chronologically
arranged essays, written between 1940 and 1967, are firmly rooted in a traditional, historical approach. The articles which focus on American folk
music are the four book reviews of George Pullen Jackson's Down-East
Spirituals and Others (1943) and Frank Clyde Brown's four-volume collection
of North Carolina folklore (1952, 1957); the historical articles, "Folk-
Song in the United States, 1910-1960" and "Cecil Sharp and Folk Song";
the study of a specific American ballad, "Samuel Hall's Family Tree";
and the articles on methodology, "The Morphology of the Ballad Tunes,"
"Toward the Comparative Analysis of British-American Folk-Tunes," and
"Folk-Song and Live Recordings."

M 137. CAMPA, ARTHUR LEON. Spanish Folk-Poetry in New Mexico. Albuquer-
        que: University of New Mexico Press, 1946. 224 pp.
Campa begins his survey of New Mexican folk music with a historical sketch
of the region since the Narvaez expedition in 1527. He then discusses
the troubadours, legendary and modern, and credits them with saving a
significant number of songs from obscurity. The body of the book consists
of the lyrics of more than 120 songs and their variants, accompanied by
notes on origins and historical context. Campa divides these lyrics into
four categories. The oldest genres, the "Romance" and the "Decima" are
of Spanish origin and are rarely sung by modern troubadours. The "Cor-
rido," a narrative song of eight-syllable verse derived from the Romance,
and the "Cancion," a broad category lacking any formal regularity, are
the two other genres represented in this collection.

M 138. CARR, PATRICK, ed. The Illustrated History of Country Music.
        Garden City, N.Y.: Doubleday, 1979. 359 pp.
This collection of essays by eight editors of Country Music magazine examines the roots and evolution of country music in America. Taken together
the essays trace the development of the musical genre from its origins
in the British-American ballad. The authors note the particular journalistic purpose and moralistic tone of the American ballads and folk songs.
These songs were characteristically handed down through oral transmission,
often within the family, and through sheet music publication. The rise
of country music in the 1930s and its commercialization at the hands of
producer Ralph Peer are discussed. The years of the Great Depression,
the time of the emergence of radio barn dances, are seen as years of great
experimentation and creativity. Other chapters discuss the music of Texas,
the career of Hank Williams, the emergence of Nashville as the center
for country music in the 1940s, the emergence of rockabilly and modern
country music, and the influence of studio technology.

M 139. COHEN, NORM. Long Steel Rail: The Railroad in American Folksong.
        Urbana: University of Illinois Press, 1981. 710 pp.
This book chronicles the impact of the railroad upon American music utilizing commercial recordings as sources, especially those blues and hillbilly
records produced between 1920 and 1950. Non-commercial field recordings
from the Library of Congress Archive of Folk Song are also used. The
author has interpreted the "phrase 'railroad song' liberally, including
pieces about trains . . . railroaders . . . railroad construction . . .
and railroad travelers." Songs which use railroad imagery metaphorically
are also discussed. The three introductory chapters offer a history of
the railroad in America, a history of American folk and popular music,
and an overview of American railroad songs from 1830 to 1970. In the
remaining nine chapters, the songs are divided according to type and subject. Each chapter opens with a general introduction which refers to
the historical and social contexts outlined in the introductory chapters;
each song within the chapter is followed by a discussion of its history
and background and a biblio-discography. Appendix I is a biblio-discography of two genres of song excluded from the study: work songs and
instrumentals. Appendix II lists recommended recordings of railroad songs.

M 140. COOK, HAROLD E. Shaker Music: A Manifestation of American Folk
        Culture. Lewisburg, Pa.: Bucknell University Press, 1973.
        312 pp.
Cook opens his discussion of Shaker music with a discussion of the social
and historical background of the religious group. He then examines "The
Development of Shaker Hymnody," "Shaker Notation," the relation between
"Shaker Theory and American Tune-Book Theory," the "Technical Aspects
of Shaker Musical Practice," and the "Performance of the Music," and analyzes various song types. Cook focuses his discussion on the influence
of British music on Shaker song, the revitalization of the sect and its
music with the Great Revival of the early 19th century, the relation of
Shaker singing schools to the non-Shaker shaped-note schools, the effect
of printing upon the original modal state of the songs, and the drastic
change of Shaker music into a "colorless, methodic sort of expression,"
with "the coming of harmony, printed hymnals, musical instruments, professional singing teachers, and constant contact with a non-Shaker business
world" after the Civil War. Appendices include a "Collation of the Manuscript Hymnals" and a list of printed Shaker hymnals.

M 141. CORNFIELD, ROBERT and MARSHALL FALLWELL, Jr. Just Country: Coun-
        try People, Stories, Music. New York: McGraw-Hill, 1976.
        176 pp.
This book describes the history, musical forms, and major performers of
the American country music tradition. The authors take the "family" rather
than the scholarly approach to their subject, with Mother Maybelle Carter
playing the "Queen Mother" role, Jimmy Rodgers playing the "Father of
the Country," and the Grand Ole Opry as its first home. The focus is
on such famous personalities as Roy Acuff, Bob Wills, Ernest Tubbs, Jerry
Lee Lewis, Merle Haggard, Bill Monroe, Hank Williams, and Tom Hall. The
chapters are divided according to musical type, including barn dances,
Western swing, honky tonk, Appalachian bluegrass, the music of the Memphis
rebellion, and the rise of Nashville. The final chapter examines potential
Nashville stars of tomorrow.

M 142. COURLANDER, HAROLD. Negro Folk Music U.S.A. New York: Columbia
        University Press, 1963. 124 pp.
Courlander's work is an attempt to see the various genres of black folk
music against the cultural continuity of other existing traditions. He
examines the evidence of a large and significant oral tradition running
through the music. His various topics are: anthems and spirituals; cries,
calls, whooping, and hollers; work songs; blues, ring games, and playparty
songs; Louisiana Creole songs; ballads and minstrelsy; dances such as
calindas, buzzard lopes, and reels; and such instruments as drums, gut-
buckets, and horns. The volume includes both words and music of forty-
three songs, along with notes, discography, and sources of notated songs.

M 143. DENISOFF, R. SERGE. Great Day Coming: Folk Music and the American
        Left. Urbana: University of Illinois Press, 1971. 219 pp.
A sociological study of the use of folk music as a weapon to achieve political ends, Denisoff's work focuses on the protest songs used by the American
Left during the 1930s and 1940s and by the New Left during the 1960s.
Denisoff traces the emergence and development of a "folk consciousness"
and raises the question, "Why folk music as a propaganda tool in an industrial urban setting?" He describes the formation of such groups as The
Almanac Singers, People's Songs Inc., and People's Artists Inc. and follows
the "political-intellectual fad of the sectarian left into the mass media,
where it emerged as a commodity to be sold in the market place of popular
music." A selected discography of American protest songs is included.

M 144. DENISOFF, R. SERGE. Sing a Song of Social Significance. Bowling
        Green, Ohio: Bowling Green University Popular Press, 1983.
        255 pp.
Using a functional approach to protest music which stresses "the content
and usage of the musical and lyrical tradition" rather than "the motivation
or intent of the composer," the sociologist Denisoff discusses the singers
and audiences of protest songs, the effectiveness of "songs of persuasion"
as forces of communication and propaganda, and their place in the modern
popular music tradition. "Having outlined the properties of political
propaganda songs," Denisoff writes, "we will be concerned with their use
by religious movements, segments of the new and old Left, especially emphasizing the American Communist movement." Denisoff also examines the political statements made in top-forty music, "stressing the impact of these
songs on their listeners" and what Karl Mannheim has called "'the confusion
of tongues' in popular music." Primarily concerned with the "social milieu
of musical statements of dissent," Denisoff includes chapters on the
counterculture, the musical tastes of teen-agers, "Kent State, Muskogee,
and the Ghetto," "Christianity, Communism, and Commercialism," and the
"Sociology of Popular Music."

M 145. DENSMORE, FRANCES. Cheyenne and Arapaho Music. Los Angeles, Calif.:
Southwest Museum, 1936. 111 pp.; Chippewa Music. 2 vols. Washington, D.C.: United States Government Printing Office, 1910, 1913.
557 pp.; Choctaw Music. Washington, D.C.: United States Government Printing Office, 1943. 188 pp.; Mandan and Hidatsa Music.
Washington, D.C.: United States Government Printing Office, 1923.
192 pp.; Menominee Music. Washington, D.C.: United States Government Printing Office, 1932. 230 pp.; Music of Acoma, Isleta,
Cochiti, and Zuni Pueblos. Washington, D.C.: United States Government Printing Office, 1957. 117 pp.; Music of Santo Domingo Pueblo,
New Mexico. Los Angeles, Calif.: Southwest Museum, 1938. 186 pp;
Nootka and Quileute Music. Washington, D.C.: United States Govern-
ment Printing Office, 1939. 358 pp.; Northern Ute Music. Washing-
ton, D.C.: United States Government Printing Office, 1922. 213
pp.; Papago Music. Washington, D.C.: United States Government
Printing Office, 1929. 229 pp.; Pawnee Music. Washington, D.C.:
United States Government Printing Office, 1929. 129 pp.; Seminole
Music. Washington, D.C.: United States Government Printing Office,
1956. 223 pp.; Teton Sioux Music. Washington, D.C.: United
States Government Printing Office, 1918. 561 pp.; Yuman and Yaqui
Music. Washington, D.C.: United States Government Printing Office,
1932. 216 pp.

Densmore's monographs constitute one of the pioneering studies of American
Indian music. Based on her extensive fieldwork, stretching from 1901
until her death in 1957, the monographs follow a consistent pattern.
In each volume, Densmore describes the social life of the tribe, the
general character of its music and instruments, and the particular roles
different types of songs occupy in the tribe's social and religious life.
Tunes are transcribed from recordings and accompanied by musical analyses
and explanations of their content. Many volumes also include comparative
analyses between the tribe under consideration and ones previously studied.

M 146. DeTURK, DAVID A. and A. POULIN, Jr. The American Folk Scene:
Dimensions of the Folksong Revival. New York: Dell, 1967.
334 pp.

Divided into four sections, this collection of thirty-two essays, many
reprinted from journals, touches on a number of the social, commercial,
and artistic issues of the folk movement of the 1960s. Musicians, music
and social critics, academics, musicologists, and one ex-senator contribute
essays, ranging from Peter Tamony's etymological search of the word "hoote-
nanny" to a symposium featuring Phil Ochs, Chad Mitchell, and Moses Asch
on topical songs. The first section deals with the history of folk music
and its phenomenal rise in stature in the early 1960s, focuses on issues
of definition and interpretation, and outlines the traditional-modern
controversy. The second section examines various topical-protest songs.
The third section is devoted to the careers and music of the singers Woody
Guthrie, Pete Seeger, Joan Baez, and Bob Dylan. The last section discusses
the commercialization of folk music and the relation of folk music to
folkrock in such essays as "Folk, Rock, Cash, and the Future."

M 147. DJE DJE, JACQUELINE COGDELL. American Black Spiritual and Gospel
Songs from Southeast Georgia: A Comparative Study. Los Angeles:
Center for Afro-American Studies, University of California, Los
Angeles, 1976. 105 pp.

This case study, based upon the author's fieldwork in her hometown of
Jessup, Georgia, and its environs, addresses some larger issues regarding
the meaning and functions of spirituals and gospel in black religious
communities. Spirituals are divided into three groups: call-and-response
chant, long melody, and the syncopated melody. American black gospels
(called "Jubilee" or "new spirituals") began in the 1930s. The author
ties patterns of musical expression to denominations, religious patterns,

and social class membership of churches. She combines musicological and
ethnographic analysis to discover the differences between the two types.
Sample transcriptions of gospel and spiritual songs and a glossary are
included.

M 148. DUNSON, JOSH. Freedom in the Air: Song Movements of the Sixties.
        New York: International, 1965. 127 pp.
Dunson discusses the history and development of two parallel movements
which emerged in the climate of social and political unrest of the 1960s:
"the Broadside-type of songs in the North and the songs of the freedom
movement in the South." The Northern topical song is grounded in the
traditions of the Anglo-American ballad and the union movement and its
songs, and was revived through the efforts of the singers Woody Guthrie
and Pete Seeger, the singer-songwriters Bob Dylan, Phil Ochs, and Tom
Paxton, and by the foundation of Broadside magazine. Dunson further examines the Southern folk tradition and the rise of the freedom song in the
Civil Rights Movement, noting in particular the role of Guy Carawan in
focusing the leaders' and demonstrators' attention on song as an instrument
of protest, the emergence of the Albany Movement, and the Freedom Singers.
He also discusses the 1964 "Sing for Freedom" meeting in Atlanta, where
the Northern and Southern song movements converged.

M 149. EPSTEIN, DENA J. Sinful Tunes and Spirituals: Black Folk Music
        to the Civil War. Urbana: University of Illinois Press, 1977.
        433 pp.
This study of the roots and growth of the early Afro-American musical
tradition is based on extensive research in obscure contemporary accounts
of slave music and dance. Topics range from early accounts of black music
in French and British America to the emergence of recognizable black folk
music by the time of the Civil War. Two final chapters discuss the first
published collection of black songs—Allen's Slave Songs of the United
States published in 1867 (see M 202). Three appendices include musical
excerpts from Allen's manuscript diary, a table of sources documenting
the development of the banjo, and the earliest published versions of "Go
Down Moses." The volume includes extensive notes, musical facsimiles,
photographs, bibliography, and index.

M 150. FERRIS, WILLIAM and MARY L. HART, eds. Folk Music and Modern Sound.
        Jackson: University Press of Mississippi, 1982. 215 pp.
The essays collected here were originally presented as lectures at a conference held in April 1980 at the University of Mississippi on American
folk music by such scholars as William Ivey, A. L. Lloyd, Bill C. Malone,
Robert Palmer, and Charles K. Wolfe. As Ferris explains in the introduction, these essays describe "the process through which traditional folk
music assumes new forms," which is mainly through "urbanization, industrialization, migration, new technology, and . . . the invigorating mix
of cultures from many lands." The text is divided into six sections which
deal with British and various ethnic folk strains, religious influences
on folk music, folk's relation to country music, "Myths and Heroes," and
"Blacks and Blues." Biographical sketches of the contributors are included.

M 151. FISHER, MILES MARK. Negro Slave Songs in the United States. Ithaca,
        N.Y.: Cornell University Press, 1953. 223 pp.
One of the first attempts to refute the "white-to-black" theory of the
development of spirituals put forth by George Pullen Jackson (see M 164
and M 223), this work uses song texts as historical documents. Fisher
believes that spirituals revealed much that the slave felt about slavery,
religion, relations with his or her master, and other problems of slave
life. Taking his chapter titles from the lyrics of the spirituals, he
organizes his discussion according to themes such as escape, African cult
meetings, exhortations to be dutiful and obedient, return to Africa, and

life after death. Fisher argues that the evolution of the spiritual was
influenced by various elements, including African musical traditions,
European religious and secular musical traditions, conversion to Christianity, and recorded events of early American history.

M 152. FONER, PHILIP S. American Labor Songs of the Nineteenth Century.
        Urbana: University of Illinois Press, 1975. 356 pp.
A history of American labor as reflected in songs, Foner's work spans
the years from the beginnings of the Republic to the rise of an indigenous
socialism at the end of the 19th century. Foner chose the more than 550
songs which he discusses for the subjects or issues they address rather
than for their inherent literary or musical merit. These songs, originally
published in the various papers of the labor press (which Foner calls
the "advocate and symbol of hope" for its audience), may not all have
entered the oral tradition, but all are valuable "social documents" which
provide insight into many causes and events of the labor movement. The
discussions of the songs are grouped in chapters according to period and
subject; each chapter contains an introductory section and explanatory
notes. The chapters examine the songs of the Revolutionary War period;
the songs of the era of Jacksonian democracy; the songs of the pre-Civil
War period; the songs of foreign-born and black workers; the songs of
the Civil War and post-Civil War eras; the songs of the 1873-9 depression;
the songs of the Knights of Labor, the AFL, miners, populists, and early
socialists; and songs about the eight-hour day movements, the Haymarket
Riot, and the labor unrest of 1880-1900.

M 153. GAILLARD, FRYE. Watermelon Wine: The Spirit of Country Music.
        New York: St. Martin's Press, 1978. 236 pp.
Gaillard argues that the tension between tradition and change, between
old ways and new, provides a source of creativity and innovation in modern
country music. He further states that a second dialectic between musical
and poetical creativity and the commercialization of American popular
music threatens the future of this most characteristically American musical
tradition. Gaillard conceives of country music as a form of popular poetry
expressing in its lyrics the common experiences, values, and aspirations
of its audience. He focuses on the songwriters, singers, music, and
audiences of country music, and on the struggle to resist commercialization. He also provides detailed analyses of representative songs and
discussions of the relationships between the contents of the songs and
the autobiographies of the composers.

M 154. GRAME, THEODORE C. America's Ethnic Music. Tarpon Springs, Fla.:
        Cultural Maintenance Associates, 1976. 323 pp.
The twelve chapters of this study are keyed to the fifteen broadcasts
in the "One Land, Many Voices" series prepared for National Public Radio.
Concerned with the music of "the non-dominant class," Grame organizes
the chapters around settings or occasions such as the industrial city,
rites of passage, and the festival, or themes such as "derision and conflict," American religion, or "the melting pot," rather than by ethnic
group. Grame avoids the simpler "melting pot" model and gathers evidence
for the sustained importance of ethnic music in modern, urban folk communities. He includes a bibliography of the music of thirty-six ethnic groups.

M 155. GREEN, ARCHIE. Only a Miner: Studies in Recorded Coal-Mining
        Songs. Urbana: University of Illinois Press, 1972. 504 pp.
Making considerable use of commercial phonograph recordings, "this work
is intended as a statement on sound recordings as cultural documents and
communicative devices, and is restricted to a handful of songs which
appeared on discs between 1925 and 1970." After two general introductory
chapters on folk music in its social setting and on "race" and hillbilly
records, Green studies the recorded versions of seven well-known mining

songs, offering insights into the interrelationship between labor history, popular culture, and folk tradition. Each chapter includes a checklist of recordings of the subject song and an appendix documenting the work of individuals important in early recordings of folk music. Chapter Ten is a case study of three Southern blues songs as "compelling human documents which reveal aspects of American coal miners' working and conditions and value systems." Chapter Eleven deals with the evolution of the 7-inch 45 rpm disc and the 12-inch 33 rpm disc in the context of the "folksong revival." Chapter Twelve, "Slack from the Gob Pile," is a final discussion of his "avocational-centered, cross-disciplinary, and horizontal" methodological approach.

M 156. GREEN, DOUGLAS B. Country Roots: The Origins of Country Music. New York: Hawthorn Books, 1978. 238 pp.
Green discusses both the historical and generic divisions of country music. He mentions the minor figures who helped to shape the evolution of country music as well as the major contributors. Chronologically ordered, the book includes chapters on "Old-Time Music" (Grand Ole Opry and National Barn Dance), blues, radio comedy, "singing cowboys," Cajun music, bluegrass, western swing, gospel, rockabilly, and honky tonk music. Green includes a chronology of major events and a discography.

M 157. GREENWAY, JOHN. American Folksongs of Protest. New York: Octagon Books, 1970. 348 pp.
Attempting to "open a previously unexploited vein of American folk culture," Greenway calls his study "an introduction rather than a scientific analysis, an impressionistic panorama rather than a blueprint." He includes an introduction which describes the position of protest songs in folk literature and the genesis and structure of the protest song, and a historical survey which traces protest music from the Dorr Rebellion and the New York Anti-Rent War through the Populist movement of the late 19th century. Individual chapters examine the protest music of Afro-Americans, textile workers, miners, migratory farm workers, farmers, and unionized laborers. The "song-makers" Aunt Molly Jackson, Ella May Wiggins, Woody Guthrie, and Joe Glazer are the subjects of his final chapter. Appendices include a list of "songs of social and economic protest on records," a list of composers, and a list of songs and ballads.

M 158. HEAPS, WILLARD A. and W. PORTER. The Singing Sixties: The Spirit of Civil War Days Drawn from the Music of the Times. Norman: University of Oklahoma Press, 1960. 423 pp.
Heaps and Porter examine the Civil War songs of both the North and the South and stress their "historical quality and purpose." The authors' aim is to "illustrate the human as well as the historical and contemporary elements involved in the Civil War through its music." They begin with a history of music-making during wartime and a general introduction to the music of the Civil War. They divide their discussion of the songs themselves, which are taken from sheet music produced between 1860 and 1865, into chapters according to their content. All of them are historically interesting for their expression of the ideals and temperaments of either side and in their narration of the specific events of the war. The various sections examine the expression of patriotism in the songs, their use in the appeal for volunteers, their description of the organization of the armies, their narrations of specific battles, their examination of the situation of Southern blacks, their expression of civilian support, and their vision of the final victory of the North and defeat of the South.

M 159. HEMPHILL, PAUL. The Nashville Sound: Bright Lights and Country
Music. New York: Simon & Schuster, 1970. 289 pp.
Hemphill's book is an informal study of the contemporary country music
scene in Nashville, with particular emphasis on the dynamics of change
and the conflicts between the older generation of traditional country
musicians and the younger writers and performers who have homogenized
and nationalized country music. The first section is structured around
a series of interviews and describes the city of Nashville and the economics of the Nashville music business. A second section follows the
evolution of country music from the Anglo-American ballads to Appalachian
mountain music to modern country music. The third section describes the
nationalization of country music in the 1960s.

M 160. HERNDON, MARCIA. Native American Music. Norwood, Pa.: Norwood,
1980. 233 pp.
Herndon's study is a response to the need to approach Native American
music from a topical, historical, and above all, Native American point
of view. She claims that the definitions used in Euro-American scholarship
do not pertain to Native American music; Native American music is neither
"primitive" nor "folk" music. It is inextricably tied to rituals, ceremonies, and performances. Herndon briefly discusses the string, wind,
and percussion instruments used in Native American music. She traces
the history of the Euro-American study of Native American music from the
mid-19th century on, and identifies the problem of approaching this point
of view. The Native American aesthetic is defined in opposition to the
Euro-American aesthetic: Native American art is "intuitive-experiential,"
an art of "utility," "participation," and "efficacy through action."
After a chapter outlining the various "culture area systems" used by
scholars, Herndon discusses the relationship between music and mana (power);
the role of music in Nativistic movements, taking the Ghost Dance (1888-
96) as an example; the role of music in the Native American Church, often
called the "Peyote cult"; and the idea of music as a "transformational
agent" in ceremonials and initiation rites. In conclusion, she defines
six "musical areas" according to the outlines of Bruno Nettl's North American Indian Musical Styles (see M 175).

M 161. HERRERA-SOBEK, MARIA. The Bracero Experience: Elitelore Versus
Folklore. Los Angeles: UCLA Latin American Center, 1979.
142 pp.
Herrera-Sobek discusses the culture of the Mexican bracero--the migrant
or temporary worker in the U.S.--as it is recorded in such "elitelore"
as fiction and such "folklore" as oral histories and folk songs. Whereas
the "elitelore" version of the bracero experience is dark and pessimistic,
the "folklore" version offers a more positive and optimistic testimony.
Herrera-Sobek closely analyzes the lyrics of several songs, finding in
them a portrait of the bracero as a picaresque figure who uses intelligence
and wit to survive the terrible social conditions in which he lives.

M 162. HUDSON, ARTHUR PALMER. Folklore Keeps the Past Alive. Athens:
University of Georgia Press, 1962. 63 pp.
This book is a collection of three lectures given by Hudson at Mercer
University Center. As a folklorist familiar with British and American
literature and folk music, Hudson informs his lectures on folk music with
allusions to these fields. In the first lecture, he examines two old
folk songs, "The Holy Bluff" and "Perry Merry Dectum Domini." The second
lecture is a concise overview of the history of the South as it has been
inscribed in folk songs. The final lecture illustrates the role of folk
songs in American poetry and fiction, focusing on many 19th-and 20th-
century writers, including Henry Wadsworth Longfellow, John Greenleaf
Whittier, Carl Sandburg, Wallace Stevens, Robert Frost, Elizabeth Madox
Roberts, Sherwood Anderson, Dorothy Scarborough, and Thomas Wolfe.

M 163. JACKSON, BRUCE, ed. Wake Up Dead Men: Afro-American Worksongs
from Texas Prisons. Cambridge, Mass.: Harvard University Press,
1972. 326 pp.
This volume describes the words and tunes of sixty-five work songs sung
by black prisoners in various Texas prisons. The songs were collected
by Jackson between 1964 and 1966. In his introduction he insists upon
the importance of understanding the context in which these songs are used
as survival tools. The context--the work, the conditions, the prisoners--
is described by the prisoner-singers themselves in the series of taped
interviews printed in the following chapter. Jackson analyzes the content
and functions of the songs and the song-leading system and arranges the
songs according to the type of work they accompany. Notes describe the
work and locations, give variant titles, and provide general commentary.
A glossary and a discography are appended.

M 164. JACKSON, GEORGE PULLEN. White Spirituals in the Southern Uplands:
The Story of the Fasola Folk, Their Songs, Singings, and "Buck-
wheat Notes." Chapel Hill: University of North Carolina Press,
1933. 444 pp.
In the first part of his study of Anglo-American spiritual music, "The
Old Fasola Folk," Jackson discusses the origins of group singing in New
England, the movement of these early shape-note singing schools to the
West and to the South, the various groups and major figures which emerged
there, dance tunes, the growth of the ballad, the camp meeting, and the
abandonment of the indigenous Southern traditions by urban churches.
Two of the more controversial chapters in the first part of his study
examine white fasola songs as the sources of Negro spirituals and compare
various texts of the two traditions. In Part II, "Fasola Offspring, the
Dorayme Folk," Jackson describes the introduction of the Do-re-mi system,
various notational innovations in the South and the West, the normal music
schools, music in the rural churches, and shape-note and Dorayme songs
among the Indians.

M 165. KANAHELE, GEORGE S., ed. Hawaiian Music and Musicians: An Illustrated History. Honolulu: University Press of Hawaii, 1979.
543 pp.
Arranged alphabetically by topic, like an encyclopedia, this volume contains a great deal of original research by scholars at the Hawaiian Music
Foundation. The history of Hawaiian music is divided into seven distinct
periods. During the first period, between the arrival of the missionaries
and the establishment of the Royal Hawaiian Band by Henry Berger in 1872,
there were two major musical genres, hymns, and secular chants. The second
period, 1872-1900, saw the heyday of the Royal Hawaiian Band and the royal
music clubs. The third period, extending to about 1915, marks the beginning of the influence of such American musical forms as ragtime. During
the fourth period, 1915-1930, "jazzed-up" Tin Pan Alley versions of hapa
haole songs spread to mainland America. The fifth period, 1930-60, was
characterized by the commercialization and internationalization of hapa
haole music. The sixth period, 1960-70, saw a lack of interest in Hawaiian
music. The seventh period--the present--fraught with new social problems,
has "led to an avid search for ethnic identity in accelerating urban
environments . . . reflected in Hawaii by an energetic revival of old
Hawaiian music." At issue are the defining characteristics of Hawaiian
music, the importance of the music to the islands' tourist economies,
the cultural dynamism of ethnic influences, the development and impact
of the himeni, and the internationalization of Hawaiian music. Three
main genres of music, chant, hapa haole, and Hawaiian song, are examined.
An extensive discography is appended.

M 166. **KREHBIEL, HENRY EDWARD.** Afro–American Folksongs: A Study in Racial
and National Music. New York: Schirmer Books, 1914. 176 pp.
Krehbiel's stated purpose is to bring "a species of folksong into the
field of scientific observation" and present it as "fit material for artistic treatment." His study of the characteristics and sources of Afro-
American folk music grows out of a series of articles he wrote as the
music reviewer for the New York Tribune on "folksongs and their relation
to national schools of composition." He first determines the nature of
the folk songs "in respect of their origin, their melodic and rhythmical
characteristics and their psychology." Krehbiel addresses the question,
"Are they American?" and discusses the extent to which this folk music
is influenced by African and/or Anglo–American music traditions. He also
refutes "the theory which has been frequently advanced that the songs
are not original creations of the slaves, but only the fruit of the negro's
innate faculty for imitation." Noting the primarily religious character
of the songs, he describes camp-meetings, spirituals, "shouts," work songs,
and voodoo ceremonies. Examining 527 songs from six collections, Krehbiel
outlines their distinctive musical characteristics and structural features.
He looks at Afro–American dances from Louisiana and the songs of the black
Creoles as two examples of the particular "hybrid art" to emerge from
the Afro–American experience.

M 167. **KURATH, GERTRUDE PROKOSCH,** with **ANTONIO GARCIA.** Music and Dance
of the Tewa Pueblos. Santa Fe: Museum of New Mexico Press, 1970.
309 pp.
Based upon eight years (1957-65) of fieldwork, this monograph describes
the music, dance, movement, and ceremonies of the Tewa Pueblo near the
Rio Grande in New Mexico. Kurath grounds these ceremonial arts in the
religious, social, and aesthetic symbolic systems of the group. She
focuses on three features of Tewa ceremonialism: directional symbolism,
gesture codes, and sacred clowns. She also examines the effects of contact
with other cultures, both Indian and white, upon the Tewa ceremonies.

M 168. **LAWS, G[EORGE] MALCOLM,** Jr. Native American Balladry: A Descriptive Study and a Bibliographical Syllabus. 1950; Rev. ed. Philadelphia: American Folklore Society, 1964. 298 pp.
Laws substantially revised his original text for the 1964 edition, adding
a new chapter and much new material to Appendixes I and II. He devotes
the first chapter to defining native American balladry. Laws notes that
his study is confined to North American ballads which have been "recovered
from tradition" and printed by collectors. English contributions are
considered only if "sufficiently reworked in [the U.S.] to acquire separate
identity as American pieces." In Chapter II, Laws classifies various
types of American ballads, including songs about war, sea, murder, tragedy,
and disasters,as well as those about lumberjacks, sailors, criminals,
and outlaws. In later chapters he discusses American ballads as dramatic
and historical narratives, their origin and distribution, forms and variants, the British and Afro–American influences, and the "spirit of American
balladry." Four appendices are attached. The first appendix classifies
about 250 ballads into nine groups. The other three list American–Canadian
ballads, those of "Doubtful Currency in Tradition," "Ballad-like pieces,"
and imported ballads.

M 169. **LOMAX, JOHN A.** Adventures of a Ballad Hunter. New York: Macmillan,
1947. 302 pp.
Generally regarded as the father of native American folk song collectors,
Lomax, the founder of the Archive of American Folksong in the Library
of Congress, recounts his personal experiences collecting folk songs and
ballads in the prisons, cow camps, fields, bars, streets, and isolated
communities of the Southern and Western U.S. The narrative concentrates
largely on the people who made and sang the songs and only incidently
on Lomax and the members of his family who travelled with him.

M 170. **MALONE, BILL C.** Country Music U.S.A.: A Fifty-Year History.
Austin: University of Texas Press, 1968. 422 pp.
Malone offers a history of the development of country music in the U.S.
from its commercial founding in the 1920s to its present big-business
status, emphasizing its social and economic milieu. Although country
music "has absorbed the styles, songs, instruments, and influences from
a multitude of nonwhite and noncountry sources," Malone focuses upon the
white Protestant Anglo-Celtic tradition. Beginning with a discussion
of the folk background and early period of commercial hillbilly music,
he then recounts the emergence of the first country singing star, Jimmie
Rodgers. He next discusses the growth of country music with the development of radio and advanced recording technology during the Depression
and its national expansion with the movement of populations to defense
jobs and army camps during W.W. II. The 1950s are portrayed as the "boom
period" of country music, the traditions of which began to give way to
country pop and the Nashville sound. In the 1960s, Malone concludes,
traditional country music was reinvigorated and restored by the honky-
tonk and saga song, by bluegrass and by the urban folk revival.

M 171. **MALONE, BILL C.** Southern Music, American Music. Lexington: University Press of Kentucky, 1979. 203 pp.
According to Charles Proland, the editor of the series New Perspectives
on the South, of which this book is a part, the South's most distinctive
form of artistic expression is music. Malone surveys the folk origins
of Southern music, examining the various influences of British, African,
Irish, German, Cajun, and Mexican cultures. He focuses on "the folk music
of the South and upon the popular forms that emerged from it," and emphasizes those political, economic, and social factors which have shaped
this music: poverty, slavery, religious fundamentalism, cultural isolationism, and the musical traditions of the minstrels and mountaineers.
The late 19th and early 20th centuries saw the rise of ragtime, blues,
and jazz. In the 1920s and 1930s, hillbilly, Cajun, and gospel music
also came to the forefront of the musical scene. Malone notes the advances
in musical technology in the 1930s and the subsequent nationalization
of Southern music in the 1940s. He ends his study with examinations of
the rock, gospel, and soul music of the 1960s and 1970s and the recent
resurgence of country music under the auspices of the Country Music Association.

M 172. **MALONE, BILL C.** and **JUDITH McCULLOH**, eds. Stars of Country Music:
Uncle Dave Macon to Johnny Rodriguez. Urbana: University of
Illinois Press, 1975. 476 pp.
Seeking to remedy the "lack of recognition of country music as a significant part of American culture . . . by the academy and the entertainment
industry alike," the editors provide a series of biographical essays by
musicologists, journalists, and fans about such early pioneers of country
music as Uncle Dave Macon, the Carter Family, Jimmie Rodgers, Gene Autry,
Ernest Tubb, and Hank Williams, as well as such contemporary figures as
Johnny Cash, Loretta Lynn, Charley Pride, and Johnny Rodriguez. Also
included are more general articles about "Early Pioneers" by Norm Cohen
and "A Shower of Stars: Country Music Since World War II" by Bill C.
Malone. Other contributors include Charles Wolfe, D. K. Wilgus, Douglas
B. Green, Charles R. Townsend, and Paul Hemphill. Each chapter is followed
by a discography of the performer's work.

M 173. **NETTL, BRUNO.** Folk and Traditional Music of the Western Continents.
1965; Rev. ed. Englewood Cliffs, N.J.: Prentice-Hall, 1973.
258 pp.
This revised version of Nettl's general history of Western folk music
includes new chapters on Latin American music by Gerard Behague. Although
only three chapters of this work are devoted specifically to North American
folk and traditional music, Nettl's study provides background, definitions,
and formal descriptions. Following a discussion of folk music both as
a part of the oral tradition and a form of national expression, Nettl
devotes a chapter to the structure and style of folk music. Chapters
3-7 examine the musical traditions of Europe and Africa. Chapter 8 examines the major American Indian traditions of folk music, including discussions of "Music in Indian Thought" and "Indian Music in Modern America."
Chapter 10 includes discussions of Afro-American instruments and black
folk music in the U.S. Chapter 11, fully revised, deals with "Ethnic
Minorities in Rural America," "The Role of Folk Music in Urban American
Culture," and "The Rural Anglo-American Tradition."

M 174. **NETTL, BRUNO.** Folk Music in the United States: An Introduction.
1960; Revised by Helen Myers. Detroit, Mich.: Wayne State University Press, 1976. 187 pp.
The third edition of Nettl's introductory history includes new material
on Afro-American, urban, and Hispanic-American folk musics. Nettl examines
how the "interlocking, interacting ethnic networks" of folk music are
superimposed upon an Anglo-American musical tradition, and how the dissemination of folk music through the mass media leads to the popularization
and hybridization of various ethnic musical traditions. The author outlines the problems of defining folk music and its distinctive uses and
styles, and offers case studies of various folk music traditions, including
Native American, British, Afro-American, and Hispanic-American. He also
discusses the movement of folk music from rural to urban areas, and devotes
the last three chapters to "Studying Folk Music," "Folk Music and the
Professional Singer," and "Folk Music and the Composer."

M 175. **NETTL, BRUNO.** North American Indian Musical Styles. Philadelphia:
American Folklore Society, 1954. 51 pp.
Nettl claims that the study of North American Indian music is central
to the history of comparative musicology in general. The study of this
music, he contends, provided the initial inspiration and techniques for
the science. Noting that the great variety of tribes in North America
provide an abundance of material for the musicologist, Nettl focuses on
six areas in which these tribes have identifiable musical styles: Eskimo-
Northwest Coast, Plains-Pueblo, California-Yuman, Great Basin, Athabascan,
and Eastern. The essays explore and attempt to answer the following questions: are there stylistic traits common to all Indian music north of
Mexico; if not, how do stylistic traits differ; and how do language and
culture effect musical style? Included is an appendix of musical examples.

M 176. **ODUM, HOWARD W.** and **GUY B. JOHNSON.** The Negro and His Songs:
A Study of Typical Negro Songs in the South. Chapel Hill: University of North Carolina Press, 1925. 306 pp.
Odum and Johnson offer an analysis of some 200 songs collected in northern
Mississippi and northern Georgia, with a few songs included from North
Carolina and Tennessee for comparison. Their study includes both formal
and functional analyses of three broad classes of Afro-American folk song:
religious songs and spirituals on such subjects as Heaven, Hell, and scriptural characters; social songs on such topics as love, jealousy, and sexual
relationships; and work songs, which were sung in unison to facilitate
labor and expressed a range of attitudes, including veiled criticism of
"the boss." A final chapter on "Imagery, Style, and Poetic Effect"--unique

for studies of this period--attends to the "descrip tive art" of the songs and includes discussion of their imagery, their expressions of personality and the "dominant self," and their use of conditional sentences, exclamations and variations, onomatopoetic words, rhyme, rhythm, and vowel rhymes.

M 177. ODUM, HOWARD W. and GUY B. JOHNSON. Negro Workaday Songs. Chapel
     Hill: University of North Carolina Press, 1926. 278 pp.
Approaching their work "primarily as sociologists," Odum and Johnson consider the "Negro workaday song" to be one of the best examples of that "self-portraiture" noted by Alain Locke, which illustrates the attitudes, values, and lifestyles of the American black. They focus on the group of songs current in certain areas in North Carolina, South Carolina, Tennessee, and Georgia, during the years 1924-25, and employ a new technique--the study of phonophotographic records and musical notations. The analysis of the songs is divided according to topic: songs of work and sorrow, travelling songs, "bad man ballads," songs of jail, chain gangs and policemen, songs of construction camps, "man's song of woman," "woman's song of man," and religious songs. They also discuss the folk song portraits of the hobo Left Wing Gordon and the workingman-hero John Henry. The last two chapters offer examples of typical Negro tunes and phonophotographic records of Negro singers.

M 178. PAIGE, HARRY W. Songs of the Teton Sioux. Los Angeles, Calif.:
     Westernlore Press, 1970. 201 pp.
Paige's study of the poetry and music of the Teton (or Western) Sioux investigates "the origins and methods of Indian poetry as well as the human needs which inspired its development." Paige analyzes the poetry of the Sioux song to discover its method, construction, and purpose, and discusses the various types of song such as "individual and ceremonial, spiritual and secular, pure, and those showing evidence of cultural contact with outside influence." Introducing his study with a chapter on "The People," Paige continues with chapters on "The Primitive Imagination and the Purpose of Song," and "The Nature of Primitive Song." He devotes chapters to "individual songs," which put forth an individual interpretation of experiences and styles, and to ceremonial songs, which are traditional, collaborative, ritualized songs, designed to "seek the aid of the supernatural." In the last chapter, Paige examines the value of Sioux songs as indicators of the course and problems of acculturation.

M 179. PAREDES, AMERICO. A Texas-Mexican "Cancionero": Folksongs of
     the Lower Border. Urbana: University of Illinois Press, 1976.
     194 pp.
This representative collection spans two centuries of folk songs indigenous to the Lower Rio Grande Border area, beginning with the 1750s, when Mexicans first settled in the region, and closing with the 1960s. In his general introduction Paredes describes the border singers and the kinds of situations in which they sing the songs. He then details the historical information relevant to each song in the prefatory notes to the book's five sections: "Old Songs from Colonial Days," "Songs of Border Conflict," "Songs for Special Occasions," "Romantic and Comic songs," and "The 'Pocho' Appears." Paredes's persistent concern is with the Mexican cultural identity and with their struggle to preserve that identity within the U.S.

M 180. PATTERSON, DANIEL W. The Shaker Spiritual. Princeton, N.J.:
     Princeton University Press, 1979. 562 pp.
In his study of the 8,000 to 10,000 songs preserved in Shaker manuscripts between the 1780s and the 20th century, Patterson focuses on the "interplay between the songs and the beliefs and practices of the Shakers." The songs, he claims, provide a unique and "exciting opportunity . . . to study the complete life history of a well-documented folk-song repertory

created by one distinctly bonded group." In four introductory chapters, he discusses "Early Forms of British and American Religious Folk Songs," "The Institutional Background of Shaker Song," and "The Relation of the Shaker Spiritual to Traditional Song," and offers "A Note on Shaker Notation and My Tune Transcriptions." Patterson divides his discussion of the songs themselves into thirteen parts, ordering them according to such types as ballads, hymns, occasionals, and work songs. He provides a general introduction for each section and notes on each song. He also describes the dances and rituals that often accompanied the songs, and includes checklists of Shaker song manuscripts and additional cited manuscripts.

M 181. PIETROFORTE, ALFRED. Songs of the Yokutes and Paiutes. Healdsburg, Calif.: Naturegraph, 1965. 64 pp.
Transcriptions of twenty-five songs of these two California Native American tribes comprise the bulk of this volume. Pietroforte provides English paraphrases for each song, descriptions of the Yokut "singing stick," and brief biographical sketches of the Native American singers recorded as part of this study. As an introduction, Pietroforte gathers several first-hand accounts by 18th- and 19th-century missionaries about the musical practices of Native Americans in California.

M 182. PRICE, STEVEN D. Old as the Hills: The Story of Bluegrass Music. New York: Viking Press, 1975. 110 pp.
Price describes bluegrass as a "direct descendant of the bagpipe and fiddle tunes" brought from Britain. The distinctive sound of bluegrass has been created by the inclusion of the banjo from Africa. He devotes chapters to the definition and origins of bluegrass, and its nationalization after the arrival of recording agents and radio in the Appalachians. Focusing attention on the major and minor figures of this musical tradition, Price discusses Bill Monroe and the Bluegrass Boys; Lester Flatt, Earl Scruggs, and The Foggy Mountain Boys; and "parking lot pickers" and bluegrass festivals. A discography is appended.

M 183. PRICE, STEVEN D. Take Me Home: The Rise of Country and Western Music. New York: Praeger, 1974. 184 pp.
Price considers country and western music to be an important part of America's musical heritage which expresses the nation's "growing concern with honesty and living in harmony with nature." He describes the development of this music from its European and African antecedents. Price defines country as "rural-oriented" music characterized by simple lyrics, "visceral" rather than "cerebral" imagery, "straightforward" melodies, and "relaxed" performances. He divides his study into separate chapters on love songs, work songs, and adventure songs, illustrates his points with song stanzas, and prefaces each chapter with a fictional narrative to characterize the people who play and listen to country music. The chapter on love songs emphasizes the influence of the British ballads; the chapter on work songs emphasizes the contributions of Afro-American music; and the chapter on adventure songs explores the fusion of the two traditions. A fourth chapter centers on the appeal of country music and its influence on other musical styles and forms. A short biographical section on country's key performers and a selected discography are appended.

M 184. RICKS, GEORGE ROBINSON. Some Aspects of the Religious Music of the United States Negro: An Ethnomusicological Study with Special Emphasis on the Gospel Tradition. New York: Arno Press, 1977. 419 pp.
Fundamental to this inquiry is the recognition of two traditions in black religious music: one in which folk elements originating in the experience of slavery are dominant, and which has historically been claimed by blacks of low social status, limited education, and relative isolation; and one

which embraces the Euro-American hymn style, originating with the Fisk
Jubilee Singers during the 1860s, and which has historically been claimed
by educated upper and middle class blacks. Ricks asserts that Gospel
music, which developed during the early 1900s among urban black communities, retains the basic musical values of its antecedent folk forms:
the Spiritual (pre-Civil War) and the Jubilee (post-Civil War). To support
this claim Ricks subjects the three styles to quantitative musicological
analysis for comparison. This statistical approach is complemented by
socio-historical portraits of the black populace during those periods
when each of the styles were dominant.

M 185. RIDDLE, RONALD. Flying Dragons, Flowing Streams: Music in the
Life of San Francisco Chinese. Westport, Conn.: Greenwood Press,
1983. 249 pp.
Riddle seeks to understand the musical culture of the Chinese in America
from 1852 to the present by examining the case of San Francisco's Chinese
community. He recounts five stages of the development, decline, and
regrowth of Chinese theater, but he also describes the functions of music
in other settings: in gambling houses, in restaurants, at banquets, at
dances, in brothels, in ceremonies (especially funerals), and in several
sorts of music clubs (Cantonese-Opera clubs, Peking-Opera clubs, instrumental music clubs, etc.).

M 186. ROBB, JOHN DONALD. Hispanic Folk Music of New Mexico and the Southwest. Norman: University of Oklahoma Press, 1980. 891 pp.
A supplement to and expansion of Robb's earlier book, Hispanic Folk Songs
of New Mexico (1954), this work is a collection of music and lyrics, accompanied by an in-depth study of the evolution of this particular folk music.
Robb's book is both a large assembly of music and lyrics and a musical
history of a people. Through the music, photos and numerous notes, Robb
portrays a unique culture in the American Southwest, one which has its
own idiosyncratic sense of such timeless themes such as birth, love, and
death. Though the greatest influences on Southwestern folk music are
Spanish and Mexican, the music has been affected by the American Indian
and Anglo cultures as well. Robb emphasizes the living nature of folk
music, pointing out that it varies and changes (though often through fixed
forms) to better express the attitudes of the folk culture. A certain
kind of natural selection is at work in the transmission of folk music.
As a part of an oral tradition, song must both improve as it changes and
remain appropriate to the people who have adopted it in order to survive.
The songs are in Spanish with English translations. Included are: instrumental melodies, piano-vocal arrangements, a glossary of definitions,
a bibliography, and a discography.

M 187. RODNITZKY, JEROME L. Minstrels of the Dawn: The Folk-Protest
Singer as a Cultural Hero. Chicago: Nelson-Hall, 1976.
192 pp.
The author examines "the history of American folk-protest with particular
stress on the evolution of the protest song, the protest singer and the
social forces that shaped the protest tradition during the twentieth century, with special emphasis on the 1960s." Rodnitzky contends that folk
music, by reason of its idealistic content, simple form, and easy appeal
to young people, was a "logical cultural weapon" in the counter cultural
movement of this period. The folk singers themselves become "cultural
heroes for many American young people who could no longer find heroes
in the traditional fields of politics, business, and sports." In Part
One Rodnitzky examines the "folk-protest mystique," focusing on the history
of the American protest song and the function of protest music as both
"religious experience" and "radical influence." Part Two contains "social
and cultural portraits of four key writer-performers who became cultural
heroes during the 1960s": Woody Guthrie, Joan Baez, Phil Ochs, and Bob

Dylan. A final chapter, "The Day the Music Died," discusses the absorption of protest music into popular music during the late 1960s. Rodnitzky includes a selected discography of protest music.

M 188. ROHRER, GERTRUDE MARTIN, ed. Music and Musicians of Pennsylvania.
Philadelphia: Presser, 1940. 121 pp.
This account of the beginning and development of music in Pennsylvania is introduced by a discussion of a memorial built for Pittsburgh composer Stephen Collins Foster. Brief essays then treat such topics as the music of Pennsylvania Indians; the relation between folklore and folk music; music in the public schools; the history of the Pennsylvania Federation of Music Clubs; the Presser Foundation of Philadelphia, a philanthropic organization founded in 1916 to further musical education; and Pennsylvania musicians of note. The most lengthy essay in this volume, "Three Hundred Years of Music in Pennsylvania," focuses on the major events, composers, teachers, performers, orchestras, choral groups, operas, and music halls of the state, with attention paid to indigenous and ethnic forms.

M 189. ROSEN, DAVID M. Protest Songs in America. Westlake Village, Calif.:
Aware Press, 1972. 159 pp.
In his case study of the social functions of popular music--which he considers to be a "social barometer"--Rosen describes the history and evolution of American protest songs from 1765 to 1970. He divides his work into three parts, topically and chronologically. The protest songs of the first period, 1765-1915, voice anti-British protest, anti-Civil War protest, anti-slavery protest, anti-upper class protest, and the protests of the labor and agrarian movements. They are characterized by "individualism," "moralism," and "naivete." Those of the second period, 1915-60, address the concerns of radical labor and agrarian factions and express the unrest resulting from the Depression, racism, and U.S. war involvements. According to Rosen, they manifest an increasing "class-consciousness," "urbanism," and "sophistication." The songs of the last period, the 1960s, center on the issues of civil rights, war, personal freedom, love, campus and urban problems, and religion, and express a social consciousness that transcends class lines.

M 190. SCARBOROUGH, DOROTHY. On the Trail of Negro Folk-Song. Cambridge,
Mass.: Harvard University Press, 1925. 289 pp.
Scarborough here recounts her adventures in collecting black folksongs--"shy elusive things"--and includes 140 songs with music. One of her discoveries was that black Southerners had for generations preserved and transmitted orally many white English and Scotch ballads and songs, and often had their own versions of them. In a chapter on ballads, she reports finding that, although the original version of a ballad may have used the third person voice, blacks quite freely used the first person. Chapters on dance songs or "reels," children's game songs and lullabies, songs about animals, work songs, railroad songs, and blues are included in the volume.

M 191. SEEGER, PETE. The Incompleat Folksinger. Edited by Jo Metcalf
Schwartz. New York: Simon & Schuster, 1972. 596 pp.
This book is a collection of Seeger's writings on a wide variety of subjects, drawing on his career as a folksinger and activist. He considers the possibility of a folk rivival; the "Folk Process," by which various cultural traditions of America, Britain, and South Africa are synthesized to form the folk identity; racism and the folk singer; the commercial music industry and its relationship to folk music; and the expression of patriotism through music. Seeger includes profiles of Huddie Ledbetter ("Leadbelly") and Woody Guthrie. Describing the fusion of old melodies and traditions with new lyrics and issues, he narrates the stories of such union, civil rights, and protest figures as Mother Jones, Joe Hill, Aunt

Molly Jackson, Uncle Dave Macon, and John Chapman ("Johnny Appleseed").
Seeger includes the music and lyrics of the songs he discusses and a
discography.

M 192. TOSCHES, NICK. Country: The Biggest Music in America. New York:
　　　　Stein & Day, 1977. 258 pp.
In this volume, Tosches offers a colloquial and informal history of country
music. He examines the social and cultural milieux which gave rise to
the country music of the 1940s and 1950s, focusing on the careers and
music of such performers as Emmett Miller, Jerry Lee Lewis, Roy Rogers,
and Spade Cooley. Tosches examines various black musical traditions,
from minstrelsy to blues, and their relation to the development of country
music. He also discusses the role of record companies and radio stations
in promoting this music.

M 193. UNDERHILL, RUTH MURRAY. Singing for Power: The Song Magic of
　　　　the Papago Indian of Southern Arizona. Berkeley: University
　　　　of California Press, 1938. 158 pp.
This study of the "song magic" of the Papago Indians is based on
Underhill's fourteen months of fieldwork. She examines the relation of
the mass of song tradition, what she calls the "Papago Bible," to various
aspects of Papago culture, including rituals, ceremonies, life cycles,
relations with animals, events of Papago history, the making of war, and
healing practices. Throughout the volume, the texts of numerous songs
are reproduced.

M 194. VASSAL, JACQUES. Electric Children: Roots and Branches of American
　　　　Folkrock. Translated and adapted by Paul Barnett. New York:
　　　　Taplinger, 1976. 270 pp.
This work, originally written in French, traces the history of U.S. folk
music from its roots up to the folk rock of 1976. The first section discusses the origins of folk music, showing the interrelation of black,
white, and American Indian traditions. The second section discusses four
representative musical figures and movements: Woody Guthrie, the urban
folk revival, Bob Dylan, and the new generation. The last section, written
largely by Paul Barnett, discusses more recent varieties of American and
British folk rock. Also covered are the musical origins and careers of
many performers. The final chapter speculates about the future status
of American folk music.

M 195. WALKER, WYATT TEE. "Somebody's Calling My Name": Black Sacred
　　　　Music and Social Change. Valley Forge, Pa.: Judson Press, 1979.
　　　　208 pp.
Walker places the tradition of black sacred music in its social and historical contexts. He claims that all music in the U.S. has its roots
in this music, and that the music, religion, and culture of black Americans
are essentially African. African oral traditions combine with Western influences to produce a hybrid culture. He treats, in turn, the Afro-American
spiritual, black music adapted from white hymns, and what he calls
"hymns of improvisation" (i.e., "gospelized hymns," Euro-American in origin). The author acknowledges that he omits two important phenomena:
spirit possession and the role of the Pentecostal movement among black
Americans.

M 196. WHITE, JOHN I. Git Along, Little Dogies: Songs and Songmakers
　　　　of the American West. Urbana: University of Illinois Press,
　　　　1975. 221 pp.
White has collected several of his essays as well as original pieces for
this review of the songs and songwriters of the American West. He includes
the texts of many Western songs and analyzes their relevance to the life
of the cowboy. White devotes separate chapters to the careers and songs

of the novelist Owen Wister, D. S. "Kid" O'Malley, Gail Gardner, Badger Clark, and Carl T. Sprague. The volume concludes with a chapter on N. Howard "Jack" Thorp and John Avery Lomax, two pioneer Western song collectors.

M 197. WHITE, NEWMAN IVEY. American Negro Folk-Songs. Cambridge, Mass.: Harvard University Press, 1928. 501 pp.
Discussing the origins of the Afro-American folk song, White writes: "The American Negro song was not at first original with the Negro. It originated in an imitation frustrated by imperfect comprehension and memory, and by a fundamentally different idea of music." White insists, however, that "the songs of the Negro to-day are beyond question the Negro's songs, not the white man's," and he explores the interrelationship between these songs, the tradition of minstrelsy, and white commercial music. White organizes his discussion of the more than 800 songs he has collected into thirteen groups according to function, setting, and theme, including social songs, work songs, songs about animals, songs about women, and songs about current events.

M 198. WOLFE, CHARLES K. Kentucky Country: Folk and Country Music of Kentucky. Lexington: University Press of Kentucky, 1982. 199 pp.
Wolfe explains why early Anglo-American ballads were so popular in Kentucky, using the song "Pearl Bryan" as an illustration of the process a folk song goes through to achieve legitimacy. Chapter II deals with early 20th-century Kentucky folk singers such as Dick Burnett, who wandered through the South, teaching and singing folk songs. According to Wolfe, a Richmond farmer named Dennis W. Taylor was Kentucky's first booking and recording agent, cutting the state's first record in October 1925. Wolfe also describes the influence of radio on Kentucky music, the origins of the American Folk Song Festival held in 1932 near Ashland, and such figures as John Jacob Niles and John Lair, who served as conduits between Kentucky's music and the greater American public. Wolfe feels that Kentucky offers a unique musical style because of its geographic location as "a melting ground for northern and southern cultures," its strong sense of heritage, and its accessibility.

M 199. WOLFE, CHARLES K. Tennessee Strings: The Story of Country Music in Tennessee. Knoxville: University of Tennessee Press, 1977. 118 pp.
Wolfe views country music as a "unique American art form that began as regional folk art." He puts this music into a social context, looking at both the folk or traditional aspect of country and the pop element found in the Nashville scene. The author believes that "because Tennessee has been able to maintain both of these cultures," it offers the "best environment" for country music. Wolfe introduces his study with a discussion of Cecil Sharp's 1916 transcriptions of folk songs. He covers the role of the fiddle in early country music, showing how Bob Taylor, twice the governor of Tennessee and later a U.S. Congressman, helped to popularize this instrument. He analyzes the changes brought about by records and radio in the 1920s and describes each particular region's contribution to Tennessee country music. Wolfe discusses George Hay and the Grand Ole Opry and many of the major figures of the 1940s and 1950s, including Roy Acuff, Ernest Tubb, Hank Williams, Eddy Arnold, Ernie Ford, and the Blue Grass Boys. He also examines Nashville's role in the recording business and Sam Philips's association with the stars of rockabilly, including Carl Perkins, Elvis Presley, Johnny Cash, and Jerry Lee Lewis.

M 200. WORK, JOHN WESLEY. Folk Song of the American Negro. Nashville,
Tenn.: Fiske University Press, 1915. 131 pp.
Work begins his study of Afro-American folk music with a brief analysis
of the content and style of African song. He then details "the transmi-
gration and transition" of these songs to the American continent and the
"favorable" conditions for the production and growth of a Negro folk music
found amidst the pain and sorrow of plantation life. Work examines "the
idiomatic peculiarity of Negro Folk Song," including its use of scripture,
its syncopated rhythms, and its use of "ejaculation at the dictates of
feeling." He attempts to enumerate and classify these folk songs in such
categories as "joy songs," "sorrow songs," "songs of faith," and "songs
of love." He also charts the "birth and growth of certain songs," notes
the efforts of such universities as Fiske, Hampton, Tuskegee, and Calhoun
to preserve and document Negro folk song, describes the tour of the original Jubilee Singers, and concludes with chapters on the psychological
significance of Negro folk song.

M 201. YODER, DON. Pennsylvania Spirituals. Lancaster: Pennsylvania
Folklife Society, 1961. 528 pp.
In this study, Yoder focuses on the "Bush-Meeting Dutch," a group of early
American Methodists who developed their own version of revivalism during
the Second Awakening and spawned such new native sects as the United
Brethren, the Evangelicals, and the Church of God. Chapters I-V are
general introductions to the spiritual tradition in America and, more
locally, in Pennsylvania, and to the sociological importance of bush-meeting
(or camp-meeting) religion. Chapter VI presents 150 song-texts, with
notes on each. Chapters VII and VIII discuss the sources of the spirituals
and their publication in early hymnal and broadside literature. Chapter
IX traces the diffusion of the tradition among other groups, including
discussion of its use by the Russian-Germans of the Plains states, in
the American gospel song, in the Pennsylvania local color novel, and in
the parodies by the "Church" groups. Chapter X analyzes the themes of
the songs.

IV. BLUES

M 202. ALLEN, WILLIAM FRANCIS, CHARLES RICHARD WARE, and LUCY McKEM
GARRISON, eds. Slave Songs of the United States. New York:
Simpson, 1867. 115 pp.
A thirty-eight page introduction, written primarily by Allen, notes that
no systematic effort to collect and preserve black melodies had ever been
made and that this collection was an effort to do so before the songs
"inspired by slavery" disappeared. In addition, the introduction, written
before the invention of the field recorder and phonograph, includes an
early discussion of a problem that would plague students of black music
for years--the near impossibility of reproducing black performance style
on paper. Finally, Allen, who as an official of the Freedmen's Bureau,
had his major contact with blacks on South Carolina's Sea Islands, discusses the "phonetic decay" of their dialect, now called Gullah, which
Allen likened to a foreign language. Extensive notes accompany the text
and music of 136 spirituals.

M 203. BASTIN, BRUCE. Crying for the Carolines. London: Studio Vista,
1971. 112 pp.
The Piedmont style of blues heard in Virginia, North and South Carolina,
and Georgia is characterized by a gentle and rollicking dance rag style.
Heavily influenced by country and mountain music, including the mountain
fiddle, it lacks the melancholy of Delta blues or the pulsating electric

drive of Chicago blues. Although an insular style, it reflects stylistic variations within the region. Some of the sub-regions and musicians Bastin discusses are Durham, North Carolina (Sonny Terry and Brownie McGhee); Greenville, South Carolina (Josh White and the Reverend Gary Davis); Spartanberg (Pink Anderson); and North Georgia (Buddy Moss and the Hicks Brothers). It is in Atlanta, the author notes, that blues styles begin to show a stronger influence from Alabama and the Deep South. Bastin also contends that one of the most distinctive features of the Piedmont style was its emergence from W.W. II with little stylistic change. The style still appears on commercial releases, performed by musicians who journeyed north, taking the logical eastern route to Washington, D.C., Baltimore, New York, and New Jersey. The volume includes a discography.

M 204. **BROVEN, JOHN.** South to Louisiana: The Music of the Cajun Bayous.
        Gretna, La.: Pelican, 1983. 368 pp.
Broven documents the history of the Cajun, zydeco, and swamp-pop styles in South Louisiana and attempts to define the unifying elements of these styles, tracing their influence upon blues and rock and roll. He discusses Bayou music up through the current Cajun Revival and includes personal interviews with performers and record men, photos and nine appendices covering biographical data; lists of albums, singles, bands and Cajun clubs; oral histories of Cajun music; and a time chart. Broven discusses the lives and work of Johnnie Allan, Joe Barry, Vin Bruce, Stanley "Buck-wheat" Dural, Clifton Chenier, Huey "Cookie" Thierry, Fernest Arceneaux, Jimmy "C" Newman, Alphonse "Bois Sec" Ardoin, Michael Doncet, Lazy Lester, Rockin' Dopsie, Slim Harpo, and Lonesome Sundown, among many others.

M 205. **BROVEN, JOHN.** Walking to New Orleans: The Story of New Orleans
        Rhythm & Blues. Bexhill-on-Sea, England: Blues Unlimited, 1974.
        250 pp.
According to Broven, New Orleans, primarily associated with the development of jazz, also made a significant contribution to the development of rhythm and blues and rock and roll. In the 1950s, the city was a center of record-ing activity for small but influential labels. These included not only the local labels Ace and Minit but such important outside labels as Spe-cialty, Savoy, Chess, and Atlantic. While Broven's chief focus is on recordings as having the widest and most permanent influence, he also documents other elements in the New Orleans musical world, including radio stations, distributors, and the jukebox trade. Finally, he discusses musicians whose frequent live performances in the city had an impact on the music far beyond New Orleans--Fats Domino, Huey "Piano" Smith, Ray Charles, Professor Longhair, and Little Richard. The volume includes a chart showing musical influences on New Orleans rhythm and blues and a discography.

M 206. **CHARTERS, SAMUEL BARCLAY.** The Bluesmen: The Story and the Music
        of the Men Who Made the Blues. New York: Oak, 1967. 223 pp.
When the blues revival began, many of the musicians were not only unknown but elderly. Charters describes the extensive efforts by researchers in the early 1960s to discover, record, and document the lives and music of these men before it was too late. In this volume, Charters also uses some of the fruits of his own field research to discuss pre-W.W. II blues styles from Alabama, Mississippi, and Texas. Among the musicians discussed are Charley Patton, Robert Johnson, Son House, Skip James, Bukka White, Blind Lemon Jefferson, and Texas Alexander. He also seeks through study of the music to identify any still-traceable African elements in blues. Among those characteristics that he feels may be African-derived is the use of the call-and-response pattern and the unique use of instruments as an extension of the voice. A discography is included.

M 207. CHARTERS, SAMUEL BARCLAY. The Country Blues. New York: Rinehart,
        1959. 288 pp.
Charters's study is one of the first attempts to study blues as a distinctly American art form. Although essentially a historical study of
the blues styles, it focuses on the recording history of the genre.
Charters discusses the careers and music of several blues performers, including Lonnie Johnson, Blind Lemon Jefferson, Big Bill Broonzy, Brownie McGhee,
Robert Johnson, Muddy Waters, and Lightnin' Hopkins. He further analyzes
the marketing and sales of "race records," the category in which blues
recordings were then listed, including the Bluebird and Paramount labels
and the Columbia 1400 series. In his introduction to the 1975 Da Capo
Press reprint, Charters places the 1959 publication (and, by extension,
much of the writing on black music of this period) in historical and political perspective. Writing in the aftermath of the McCarthy era and against
the background of the accelerating Civil Rights Movement, Charters was
indicating his concern over American racism and his belief that black
culture is a necessary element in American society which can "effect a
change in the American consciousness." A discography is included.

M 208. CHARTERS, SAMUEL BARCLAY. Poetry of the Blues. New York: Oak,
        1963. 111 pp.
Calling blues lyrics "a great body of folk poetry," Charters writes that
"the poetic achievement of the blues is in many ways unique, and if it
is still little known this is another aspect of the same social discrimina-
tions which have forced it into being." For Charters, the blues are a
form of social expression that has arisen from the "almost intolerable
emotional position" of the black American faced daily with the manifestations of American racism. The themes of its lyrics are "the torment of
love . . . and sudden consciousness of sexuality . . . , the insecurity
and difficulty of much of Negro life, the discomfort and the loneliness
of the enforced wandering of many of the singers . . . and veiled protest
at the social situation" into which black Americans are forced. Focusing
on the love, work, and protest songs of the blues, Charters writes that
although this music makes use of traditional poetic devices, it "finds
its images in the cabins and the tenements, in the fields, the empty roads,
and the crowded streets of American Negro life," and is characterized
by its reflection of the "immediacy of experience," terse and unadorned
idiom, "free use of near rhyme," and development of the "three-line verse."

M 209. CHARTERS, SAMUEL BARCLAY. Sweet as the Showers of Rain: The Blues-
        men. New York: Oak, 1977. 178 pp.
In the second volume of his The Bluesmen (see M 206), Charters argues
that W.W. II was a time of transition for blues, which had long been moving
from a pure song form to a dance form. The strongest effect of the war
years, however, was a change in the blues audience from a rural to an
urban one as black migration from the South to Northern cities reached
large numbers. In addition, the electric guitar, introduced to urban
blues during the period, had a profound impact on blues style. However,
despite the style evolving in the cities, a characteristic of pre-war blues
was the strength of regional styles. Those on which Charters focuses
are the styles of Memphis and other Tennessee singers, including the Memphis Jug Bands, Memphis Minnie, Furry Lewis, and Sleepy John Estes; Atlanta
singers Peg Leg Howell, the Hicks Brothers, and Willie McTell; and Atlantic
Coast and Carolina singers Blind Blake, Blind Boy Fuller, and the Reverend
Gary Davis.

M 210. CONE, JAMES H. The Spirituals and the Blues: An Interpretation.
        New York: Seabury Press, 1972. 152 pp.
Blues has long been considered "the Devil's music" by members of the black
church. Cone, however, finds that blues is actually a "secular spiritual"
and that the two musical forms serve a common purpose as cultural expres-

sions of the black struggle for survival. Limiting his discussion to spirituals influenced by slavery and to early blues, he delineates both their differences and similarities. Spirituals, created and sung by a group, dealt with black life and historical realities present before the Civil War. In contrast, blues, created and sung by lone musicians, deals with daily matters and reflects black experience issuing from emancipation and segregation. In addition, spirituals focus on a heavenly future, while blues focuses on the present. Yet from both historical and theological viewpoints, the two musical forms express black unity, aspirations of self-determination, and a rejection of white cultural values.

M 211. COOK, BRUCE. Listen to the Blues. New York: Scribner, 1973. 263 pp.
Cook holds that blues is the fundamental American music and that through its characteristic use of "blue notes," its use of instruments as an extension of the voice, and through its performance style, it has given shape to all of today's American popular music. In chapters on the blues and blues musicians in the Mississippi Delta, in Texas and Tennessee, in New Orleans, and in Chicago, he traces a direct line from blues to black rhythm and blues, the forerunner of white rock and roll. In other chapters, Cook studies the impact of blues on other forms of American music—country, jazz, gospel, and soul. Also included are discussions on the commercial exploitation of bluesmen by the recording industry and promoters, and on the popularity of blues in Europe.

M 212. EVANS, DAVID. Big Road Blues: Tradition and Creativity in the Folk Blues. Berkeley: University of California Press, 1982. 379 pp.
This study focuses on the processes whereby folk blues is transmitted, learned, composed, recomposed, and finally entered into the repertoires of blues singers. Based on taped interviews with bluesmen in Drew, Mississippi, a small Delta town that has long been a center of blues activity, the volume focuses primarily on two blues performers and their approach to Tommy Johnson's "Big Road Blues." Evans also discusses the folk blues tradition in relation to the Anglo-American folk song tradition, and the place of blues tradition in the study of oral traditions in general.

M 213. FERRIS, WILLIAM. Blues from the Delta. Garden City, N.Y.: Anchor Press, 1978. 226 pp.
Based on extensive fieldwork, Ferris documents the roots and traditions of blues as they exist in the Mississippi Delta. He includes discussions of the composition of verses, the part that recordings play in recycling blues, the relationship between the "bluesmen and preachers," the relationship between black musicians and white audiences, and the cultural meaning of the blues in the lives of its performers. A unique feature of this volume is the inclusion of a transcription of a "blues talk" session, in which the performer and audience interact in the true blues tradition. The volume includes a discography and a filmography.

M 214. GARLAND, PHYL. The Sound of Soul. Chicago: Regnery, 1969. 246 pp.
Soul music, popular in the late 1960s, is usually defined as a fusion of blues, jazz, and gospel. Garland seeks the "soul" or distinctively black sound of these musical forms and the characteristics of each found in soul. Noting that the indispensable element in all black music is the beat, the author concludes that soul took its structure and flavor from gospel, the earthiness of its lyrics from blues, and its more complex instrumentation and call-and-response patterns from jazz. Besides Ray Charles, whom the author credits with introducing soul in 1954, Garland profiles bluesmen B. B. King and Albert King, soul singers Nina Simone and Aretha Franklin, and jazzmen Billy Taylor and John Coltrane. Included

is a chapter on the important recordings made in the Stax studio of Memphis during the period. The book also includes a discography.

M 215. **GARON, PAUL.** Blues and the Poetic Spirit. London: Eddison Press, 1975. 178 pp.

Noting that nothing has been written on the relationship between blues and creative thought processes, Garon draws on both poetic and psychological perspectives of blues to study the nature of human creativity in a repressive society. His specific viewpoint is that of Surrealism, which he believes throws light over all problems relating to human expression and is, above all, revolutionary. The Surrealist's interest in blues centers on the revolutionary and utopian messages coded in the black community's poetic response to repression. For instance, Garon states that "not in singing about or against white culture, but by refusing to accept it, does the blues singer become a revolutionary." Such perspectives turn the blues into a "poetic weapon." Garon gives some attention to what he sees as the tendency of blues lyrics to demean women, as well as to his belief that the black middle class has failed to recognize the vision expressed by an older generation of blues singers.

M 216. **GROIA, PHILIP.** They All Sang on the Corner: New York City's Rhythm and Blues Vocal Groups of the 1950s. Setauket, N.Y.: Edmund, 1973. 147 pp.

In the 1950s, black rhythm and blues quartets and quintets, primarily male, could be heard singing a capella on the streets in many of New York's black neighborhoods. Later, commercially recorded with accompaniments, many of the groups and some individuals became well-known performers. For instance, the groups of Morningside Drive and Convent Avenue included the Dominoes, which contributed both Clyde McPhatter and Jackie Wilson to the world of pop singers. More than an avocation for these groups, street singing became a life style in which it was often possible to discern the dynamics of relationships in an urban neighborhood from the kinship ties and friendships within the group. And, according to Groia, the groups had a major influence on American popular music through such innovations as the use of sweet, very high natural and falsetto lead voices on ballads, the use of bass voices on leads, and the performance of white swing music in a black style.

M 217. **GROOM, BOB.** The Blues Revival. London: Studio Vista, 1971. 112 pp.

The blues revival began in England in the 1950s as part of the British interest in folk music. It was, says Groom, essentially the "discovery of blues by a large and appreciative white audience." The author discusses many of the effects of this renewed interest. Researchers, primarily British and French, began to make field trips into the American South and many bluesmen--such as Sleepy John Estes and Son House--were discovered or rediscovered. Blues recordings were reissued on such labels as Folkways and Flyright. In addition, books by such early blues researchers as Samuel Charters and Paul Oliver began to appear and Blues Unlimited, the first blues magazine, began publication in Britain. Throughout the book, Groom makes some effort to link blues influence to its "progeny"-- rhythm and blues, rock and roll, and skiffle--and to its relatives--jazz and urban folk music. In the final chapter "White Blues," he traces the influence of blues on the contemporary popular music of, among others, the Beatles, Bob Dylan, and the rock group Canned Heat.

M 218. **GUIDA, LOUIS, LORENZO THOMAS,** and **CHERYL COHEN.** Blues Music in Arkansas. Philadelphia: Portfolio Association, 1982. 26 pp.

Guida gives a brief history, with contemporary photographs, of blues in Arkansas's Mississippi Delta. He focuses in particular on the legendary blues harmonica player Sonny Boy Williamson, and on the influential radio station KFFA. The station, which went on the air in Helena in 1941, was the first in the nation to broadcast blues music and is considered a major influence in popularizing and transmitting blues in the South.

M 219. HANDY, W. C., ed. Blues: An Anthology. New York: Boni, 1926. 180 pp.
In his twenty-four page introduction, Abee Niles, the noted jazz journalist, concentrates on the "written" blues--composed and published blues based on orally transmitted blues--and especially those written by W. C. Handy. The blues form, peculiar in its sixteen-bar structure, arose among lower-class black Southerners early in this century, and served as a means of expressing their moods of the moment. Handy, a trained musician in Memphis, recognized the potential of the form, wrote down many of the songs, and composed others based on the form. Among these were his first--"Memphis Blues" written in 1909--and the well-known "St. Louis Blues." These published blues, along with the phonograph record, were among the means by which "blue notes" and other blues characteristics were incorporated into American popular music. Niles discusses the characteristics of blues verse, structure, harmony, and performance style, and notes some of the pioneer performers and white composers who used blues elements. Among these are performers Ma Rainey, Alberta Hunter, Bessie Smith, and String Beans, and composers Jerome Kern, Irving Berlin, and George Gershwin. Extensive notes accompany the fifty songs, printed with music, included in the anthology.

M 220. HARALAMBOS, MICHAEL. Right On: From Blues to Soul in Black America. London: Eddison Press, 1974. 187 pp.
Arguing that changes in music can only be understood in the context of changes in society, Haralambos contends that a musical style ends when it no longer meets the need of its audience. In the 1960s, he perceived a decline in the popularity of blues and believed it was because the music was associated in the minds of younger blacks with slavery and segregation. Haralambos argues that instead, evolving against the background of the Civil Rights and Black Power movements, soul music had become established by the mid-1960s as the most popular musical style among blacks. A synthesis of gospel and blues, soul answered the demand of a black audience for a music that was undeniably black but not too close to blues with its overtones of suffering and submission. A discography is provided.

M 221. HEILBUT, TONY. The Gospel Sound: Good News and Bad Times. New York: Simon & Schuster, 1971. 350 pp.
The modern black gospel sound was barely forty years old when this study appeared. Deliberately created by gospel composer Tommy Dorsey, a former bluesman, the style combines Baptist hymns, including those of Isaac Watts, and the musical beat heard in black Sanctified and Holiness churches. It continues, however, a long tradition of singing, shouting, and preaching familiar to generations of black churchgoers. Noting that the influence of the gospel church had been seen clearly throughout the freedom marches and sit-ins of the Civil Rights Movement, Heilbut contends that, because of its widespread hold over its followers, black gospel is central to any study of ghetto culture. Among those performers through whose careers he traces the rise of the style are Tommy Dorsey, Sallie and Roberta Martin, Mahalia Jackson, the Soul Stirrers, Ira Tucker and the Dixie Hummingbirds, the Reverend W. Herbert Brewster, the Ward Singers, Sister Rosetta Tharpe, and Marion Williams. The volume includes a discography.

M 222. HOARE, IAN, CLIVE ANDERSON, TONY CUMMINGS, and SIMON FRITH. The Soul Book. London: Methuen, 1975. 257 pp.
In his introduction, Hoare discusses the origin of the term "soul" and its application to an evolving gospel-based black music. The book contains five chapters which constitute a history of the music and its place in

black American musical history. The chapters cover the early beginnings; the Motown story; Memphis and the South; black lyrics and soul's interaction with white culture; and soul in the 1970s. A discography is included.

M 223. JACKSON, GEORGE PULLEN. White and Negro Spirituals, Their Life Span and Kinship: Tracing 200 Years of Untrammeled Song Making and Singing among Our Country Folk, with 116 Songs as Sung by Both Races. New York: Augustin, 1943. 349 pp.
Jackson's thesis is that the black spiritual, rather than being a purely black form of expression with roots in Africa, actually owed its principal origin to white pioneer hymnody, thus launching the "white-to-black" controversy that still appears occasionally. Jackson first traces the development of congregational singing practices among Baptists, Methodists, Shakers, and other religious sects of frontier America. He then analyzes black religious folksong in comparison to the white tradition, noting many differences in text, melody, and rhythm of black variants of white hymns. Most of his argument is based on the data brought together in "The Tune Comparative List," which presents 116 melodies Jackson considers white compared with their black variants.

M 224. JOHNSON, JAMES WELDON, ed. The Book of American Negro Spirituals. New York: Viking Press, 1925. 187 pp.
In his preface, Johnson maintains that black American spirituals are "purely and solely" the creation of American blacks. He bases his belief on the African characteristics he identifies in the form, including the music's rhythm form and intervallic structure; its use of incremental leading lines and choral iteration; and its use of the African call-and-response pattern. On the other hand, it was from the Christianity of the New World that black singers took their more melodic tunes and complex harmonies. This was also true of the lyrics of the spirituals, many of which were based on Biblical subjects. Johnson notes the efforts of early collectors to preserve the songs, as well as the introduction of the songs to the American public by the Fisk Jubilee Singers and other black university choral groups. The words and music of sixty-one spirituals are included in the volume, with musical arrangements by J. Rosamond Johnson and additional numbers by Laurence Brown.

M 225. KEIL, CHARLES. Urban Blues. Chicago: University of Chicago Press, 1966. 231 pp.
When this study was published, the blues revival had begun, but its focus was on rural blues as folk music; Keil claims that its advocates exhibited the mistaken belief that an authentic bluesman had to be old, obscure, and have spent most of his life as a sharecropper. Keil sets out to prove that there is a thriving blues tradition that has been transposed to the cities. At the same time, he is "primarily concerned with an expressive male role within urban lower-class Negro culture—that of the contemporary bluesman." He argues that the matrifocality in black families leads to a confused and misdirected male role model. Keil sees the role of "bluesman" as one of the few desirable role models available for black men. He discusses Afro-American music in general and the importance of particular regional blues styles, including those of Chicago, Kansas City, and Memphis.

M 226. LIEB, SANDRA R. Mother of the Blues: A Study of Ma Rainey. Amherst: Univeresity of Massachusetts Press, 1981. 226 pp.
Gertrude Pridgett Rainey, known as "Ma Rainey," was one of the earliest singers of the "classic blues" and one of the first major women blues singers. The classic blues, a style popular in the 1920s, was sung almost exclusively by women and was marked by a combination of blues and other material from black minstrel shows and vaudeville. The author contends

that Rainey, whose style never became as sophisticated as that of Bessie
Smith and other classic blues singers, represents the strongest link
between folk blues and black show business. In support of this the author
shows that, although Rainey's ninety-two extant recordings cover a wide
variety of material, her vocal style and three-quarters of her recordings
were directly influenced by twelve-bar blues. In two other chapters,
Lieb also provides a thematic analysis of Rainey's recorded blues songs.
Here she demonstrates that the lyrics had a clear message for women about
how to handle reversals in love and how to interpret and deal with other
areas of life such as alcoholism and poverty. Included in the volume
are appendices classifying Ma Rainey's recordings by types of song, and
a discography.

M 227. LOVELL, JOHN, Jr. The Black Song, the Forge and the Flame: The
Story of How the Afro-American Spiritual Was Hammered Out. New
York: Macmillan, 1972. 686 pp.
In Part One of this volume, Lovell seeks to refute the theory that white
pioneer hymnody was the chief source of the black spiritual. He contends
that the Afro-American spiritual was an independent folk song born of the
union of African tradition and American slavery. Among the differences
he delineates are not only musical structure and rhythm but differences
in religious thought, lyrics, and harmony. In Part Two, using many of
the lyrics included here, Lovell studies the slave community that created
them. His particular focus is on themes found in the songs, among them
goals of freedom and deliverance, Biblical characters and places, and
themes of nature. Part Three outlines the development of the spiritual
as a world phenomenon, discussing the scholarship on the music conducted
in this country and in twenty-five foreign countries.

M 228. LYDON, MICHAEL. Boogie Lightning: How Music Became Electric.
New York: Dial Press, 1974. 229 pp.
Lydon focuses on the historical significance of the wedding of music and
electricity which reached a symbolic peak in the instrumentation of rock
and roll. While he gives some attention to the role of radio and the
phonograph in spreading popular music, his chief discussion concerns the
electrical amplification of instruments, particularly the guitar. Amplified as early as the 1930s, the electric guitar was first used by slide
guitarists in Hawaiian and country music. However, it was in the 1940s
and 1950s that the electric guitar was introduced in virtuoso performances
by such bluesmen as T-Bone Walker and Muddy Waters and was adopted by
rock and roll musicians. Lydon gives interview-profile chapters on Ralph
Bass, John Lee Hooker, Aretha Franklin, Bo Diddley, The Chiffons, and
Ray Charles.

M 229. MIDDLETON, RICHARD. Pop Music and Blues: A Study of the Relationship and Its Significance. London: Gollancz, 1972. 271 pp.
The author sees the blues as the single most important influence on popular
music. The basic blues characteristics that he finds recurring in popular
music are tonal harmony, melody (often pentatonic), and ambiguity of rhythm.
In addition, popular music uses harmonic progressions within a basic framework of variation and repetition; harmonic formulae are also found. Vocal
technique is strongly related to speech patterns, and instruments are
used as an extension of the voice. Call-and-response techniques are common,
as is the use of ostinato. Middleton studies four styles of popular music
discussing representative performers of each style. These are rock and
roll (Fats Domino, Chuck Berry, Elvis Presley, Little Richard, Jerry Lee
Lewis); the Merseyside Beat (the Beatles, Bob Dylan); rhythm and blues
(the Rolling Stones, the Animals, the Yardbirds, the Who); and soul (James
Brown, Jimi Hendrix, the Supremes, Martha and the Vandellas, and the Four
Tops).

M 230. **OLIVER, PAUL.** <u>Blues Fell This Morning</u>: <u>The Meaning of the Blues</u>.
London: Cassell, 1960. 355 pp.
Oliver believes that blues became popular among American blacks in the
early 20th century--an age of repression and segregation--not only for
its musical qualities but because its verses had meaning for every black
American. In an analysis of the subject matter of 350 recorded blues
texts, he identifies themes that largely pervade the blues, including
crime, homicide, bootlegging, jail, vicious sheriffs, and unjust judges.
Other themes concern the singer's problems with work and "The Man," his
difficulties with tenant farming and with the ubiquitous boll weevil that
destroys meager cotton crops, and his often frustrating familial and sexual
relationships. The volume includes a discography.

M 231. **OLIVER, PAUL.** <u>Conversations with the Blues</u>. London: Cassell,
1965. 217 pp.
Oliver questions whether blues, a long musical tradition that had survived
in relative obscurity, will any longer survive as folk music now that
it has become visible, popular, and imitated. At such a vital juncture
in the history of the music, Oliver attempts to place on record what blues
have meant in the lives of mostly unknown singers of folk blues. The
reminiscences of some blues musicians are included. Much sociological
information may be found in the backgrounds of informants who as migrant
bluesmen had played in sawmill and levee camps, up and down the river
and the railroad, and in juke joints and barrelhouses. Other musicians
who were interviewed had played exclusively for a circle of friends and
relatives in one locality.

M 232. **OLIVER, PAUL.** <u>Savannah Syncopators</u>: <u>African Retentions in the
Blues</u>. London: Studio Vista, 1970. 112 pp.
Jazz historians usually link the origins of jazz, a largely instrumental
music, with the drum-dominated percussion music of rain forest coastal
West Africa. Oliver contends that, while this may be true for jazz, it
may be largely untrue for blues. As Oliver notes, blues is largely a
vocal music performed, especially in its formative years, by lone musicians
accompanying themselves on stringed instruments. He argues that music
found among the tribes of such present-day countries as Senegal, Gambia,
and Mali in the sub-Saharan savannah area of Africa, may have been more
influential in the development of blues. Among the possible links that
he finds are the importance of vocal music, the popularity of such stringed
instruments as the lute-harp, and <u>halam</u>, the more prevalent practice of
embellishment of the sung line. The latter characteristic, Oliver believes,
may be a result of the influence of the Muslim Sudan to the North. The
book includes a glossary of instruments, an index of tribes and people,
and a discography.

M 233. **OLIVER, PAUL.** <u>Screening the Blues</u>: <u>Aspects of the Blues Tradition</u>.
London: Cassell, 1968. 294 pp.
Oliver contends that, as blues evolved during the age of segregation,
it became an important medium through which black opinion and attitudes
were shaped. In his study of recorded blues, he finds that blues verses
may have had "coded" meanings for a black audience which may have remained
obscure to a non-black audience. For example, a large number of verses
in the song "Policy Blues" refer to the numbers racket. Other types of
verses discussed are those in which the singer voiced his comments on
religion; <u>The Forty-Fours</u>, a basic traditional composition in which,
through recordings, a complex family tree of blues recycling can be followed;
and the extensive body of blues carrying sexual connotations. He also
discusses the metaphors of travel and flight often found in blues verses.

M 234. **OLIVER, PAUL.** The Story of the Blues. Randor, Pa.: Chilton Book, 1960. 176 pp.

Based on a photographic exhibition that Oliver mounted for the American Embassy in London, this book attempts to place the blues singers in the context of the times and places in which the blues evolved. It also seeks not only to show the music's history but also to demonstrate some of its rich variety. The volume ranges from the post–Civil War period when freed slaves could travel, spreading a musical form which would produce not only blues but gospel, ragtime, and jazz. In chapters on Memphis jug bands, Beale Street, and the rise of urban blues in Chicago, New York, and Detroit, Oliver discusses vaudeville, minstrel and tent shows, blues on radio, and finally the rise of 1960s-style rhythm and blues.

M 235. **OSTER, HARRY.** Living Country Blues. Detroit, Mich.: Folklore Associates, 1963. 464 pp.

Much of the recording of the 230 examples included here was done in the Louisiana State Penitentiary at Angola between 1955 and 1961. However, the songs are typical of a much wider area. Oster gives a brief history of the blues and a definition of the form; he then discusses the themes and functions of the music. He also discusses certain conventions of imagery, style, and structure. The book includes annotated texts of songs and a discography.

M 236. **PALMER, ROBERT.** Deep Blues. New York: Viking Press, 1981. 310 pp.

Palmer contends that Delta blues is the cornerstone of American popular music, especially of rock and roll. In tracing the influence of the style through its migration to Chicago and eventual transmutation into urban blues, he focuses on the career of Muddy Waters. Born McKinley Morganfield in Rolling Fork, Mississippi, Muddy Waters moved to Chicago in the 1940s and formed his own blues band. Seeking a way to cut through the noise of Chicago's juke joints, he was among the first to use an electrified guitar, one of the innovations that was to transform urban blues into one of the seminal sources of rock and roll. In addition to Muddy Waters, Palmer discusses the contributions to urban blues of many other Delta bluesmen who made the trek to Chicago. The book includes a discography.

M 237. **RAMSEY, FREDERIC.** Been Here and Gone. New Brunswick, N.J.: Rutgers University Press, 1960. 177 pp.

This volume is a photographic essay based on fieldwork done in Alabama, Mississippi, and New Orleans between 1951 and 1957. As a member of the first generation of researchers on black music in the South, Ramsey had as his goal the documentation of the lives and social backgrounds of some of the South's little-known black musicians. At the time he saw such documentation as imperative, citing the rapid changes then occurring as mechanized agriculture and urbanization spread across the region. Among the musical forms discussed by Ramsey's subjects are gospel songs, work-songs, blues, dance music, and brass bands.

M 238. **REDD, LAWRENCE N.** Rock Is Rhythm and Blues: The Impact of the Mass Media. East Lansing: Michigan State University Press, 1974. 167 pp.

Redd argues that rhythm and blues (later soul music) and rock and roll "are the same musical idiom," although the mass media have tried to separate them into two different styles along racial lines. He addresses two questions: where did the music actually come from, and why has a distinction in terms been made in the course of its emergence as widely popular rock? Redd traces the connection between rhythm and blues, African work songs, blues, and jazz, and discusses the contributions of pioneers of the rhythm and blues style. Exploring the adoption of rhythm and blues by white-controlled media, he addresses the role of radio, movies, and television, in such chapters as "Development of African-American Radio," "Discovery of Rhythm Films," "Blackboard Jungle and Rock Around the Clock," "African-Americans and Early Television," and "Billy Ward and the Arthur Godfrey Show." Citing Brownie McGhee's statement, "For commercial purposes . . . people have changed the blues title, but they haven't changed the blues," Redd concludes "that rock and roll was initially rhythm and blues and that mass communications media really created the dichotomy between the synonymous musical terms." The second part of the book consists of interviews with B. B. King, Brownie McGhee, Dave Clark, Arthur "Big Boy" Crudup, Jerry Butler, and Jessie Whitaker.

M 239. RUSSELL, TONY. Blacks, Whites, and Blues: Negro and White Folk
        Traditions. New York: Stein & Day, 1970. 112 pp.
Russell attempts to draw together the parallel yet almost completely separate lines of discussion of Afro-American folk music and of white American folk music. Describing the two musics and their interactions, Russell argues that neither the music nor the ethos of the blues has ever belonged entirely to blacks, but rather that there has been cross-influence from earliest times. Black singers in post-plantation Southern society borrowed from white hillbilly and country music and church themes, and both poor blacks and poor whites shared a depressed condition that produced similar themes in their musical expressions. Russell appends a discography of blues recordings.

M 240. SHAW, ARNOLD. Honkers and Shouters: The Golden Years of Rhythm
        and Blues. New York: Macmillan, 1978. 555 pp.
Shaw studies rhythm and blues as a black art form and style, focusing on the period from 1945-60 when that style became an identifiable sound. In a text organized by region, he emphasizes the artists, writers, singing groups, record producers, and record companies who created and sustained the music. Among these are performers James Brown, Leroy Carr, B. B. King, Johnny Otis, and Muddy Waters. Important record companies were Atlantic, Chess, and Bihari Brothers. A unique feature of the book is a discussion of the many dances that evolved along with the music, among them the "Funky Chicken," the "Watusi," and "Walkin' the Dog." A discography is included.

M 241. SHAW, ARNOLD. The World of Soul. New York: Cowles Book, 1970.
        306 pp.
Shaw contends that soul music, which became a musical force in the mid-1950s, was the product of a new feeling of dignity, self-respect, and militancy among blacks. He writes that "Soul is black nationalism in Pop." However, it was only after the collapse of the Civil Rights Movement that it gained its stridency and tension. Crediting Ray Charles and James Brown with introducing the style, Shaw believes that, while soul had roots in blues, it was derived most directly from gospel and other black church music. Through a survey of blues and its evolution into urban rhythm and blues, the author shows that blues has a certain degree of control, reserve, and detachment which helps the singer face whatever he must face. Soul, on the other hand, is precisely the opposite, displaying deep personal involvement in fighting the adversities of the world. Among the many soul singers discussed in the volume are Nina Simone, James Brown, Jimi Hendrix, Otis Redding, Aretha Franklin, and Ray Charles. The volume includes a discography.

M 242. STEWART-BAXTER, DERRICK. Ma Rainey and the Classic Blues Singers.
        New York: Stein & Day, 1970. 112 pp.
Deploring the overclassification of blues styles by researchers, the author contends that the styles of the "classic blues" singers, women singers of the 1920s and 1930s, were hybrid styles. In every case, the singers

had two things in common, a wide range of material, including many songs other than blues, and a past history of appearing in tent shows and on the vaudeville stage. Indeed, the author believes that it was because they were professional entertainers and not itinerant male bluesmen that they had been ignored up until this study. Yet, as he shows, these singers were important because, beginning in 1920, they were the first blues singers to be recorded. Thus was launched the "race record" industry, so important for the later spread and popularity of blues music. Some of the singers studied in this volume are Mamie Smith, Ma Rainey, Bessie Smith, Victoria Spivey, Lucille Hegamin, and Alberta Hunter. The book contains a discography.

M 243. TITON, JEFF TODD. Early Downhome Blues: A Musical and Cultural Analysis. Urbana: University of Illinois Press, 1977. 296 pp. Titon analyzes the blues style known as "downhome blues," using that music's earliest reliable documents: commercial phonograph records from the 1930s. Describing the society of the so-called "Black Belt" region as a fluid one, he contends that the black church and the blues were both functional and structural counterparts. The preacher and the blues singer shared similar roles as community spokesmen. He also finds that black oral sermons and downhome blues share certain characteristics: formulaic composition and improvisation; repetition; ideas that cohere associatively; and the use of tone of voice to express emotion. Forty-four representative examples of early downhome blues are included in the volume and are subjected to musical analysis. The lyrics are also analyzed for formulaic structure and meaning. The final section of the book discusses cutting of the records and the cultural significance of the advertising used to sell downhome blues or "race records." The recording industry, Titon shows, was faced with advertising a music it did not understand to a consumer group it did not understand. In its advertisements the industry treated downhome blues as a folk music thus attempting to put the black in his place--far away in time and place, or newly arrived as country bumpkin and in awe of the city. His appendices include a discussion of "Patterns of Record Purchase and Listening," and a transcript of a "Sermon by the Reverend Emmett Dickinson: 'Is There Harm in Singing the Blues?'"

M 244. ZUR HEIDE, KARL GERT. Deep South Piano: The Story of Little Brother Montgomery. London: Studio Vista, 1970. 112 pp. The guitar has always been the favorite blues instrument, but the piano has followed as a close second. Despite this, the blues piano tradition in the South is less documented than that of the guitar. Zur Heide's study of Eurreal Wilford "Little Brother" Montgomery helps to illuminate the tradition since his story is similar to that of many other self-taught blues pianists of the period. Born in a sawmill camp in Louisiana in 1906, Little Brother, one of ten children in a musical family, began teaching himself to play piano at age five. He learned from many of the musicians who played the lumber camps, including Jelly Roll Morton, and by age eleven was playing piano for a living. By the time he moved to Chicago at the beginning of W.W. II, he had traveled many miles with his band, the Southland Troubadours, through Alabama, Mississippi, and Louisiana to play juke joints, dances and barrelhouses. The book includes a "Who's Who" of 120 musicians mentioned by Little Brother who played with him or were known by him through 1942. It also includes transcriptions of lyrics of Little Brother's songs, and a discography.

V.   JAZZ

M 245. **ALLSOP, KENNETH.** The Bootleggers: The Story of Chicago's Prohibition Era. New Rochelle, N.Y.: Arlington House, 1961. 379 pp.
Although the text deals primarily with gangsters in Chicago during the
Prohibition era, Allsop provides insights into the role, musical developments, and images of the early jazz musicians and their music in that
city. Chapter 17, entitled "The Jazz Baby," describes jazz's transplantation from New Orleans to Chicago and considers the multi-faceted relationship between jazz and prohibition Chicago. The author considers both
the positive and negative aspects of this relationship, using the recollections of Mezz Mezzrow, Pee Wee Russell, and others. Allsop is primarily
concerned with the historical and sociological aspects of his topic; consequently, no attempt is made to discuss early jazz in any musical detail.

M 246. **BACKUS, ROB.** Fire Music: A Political History of Jazz. 1964;
Rev. ed. Chicago: Vanguard Books, 1976. 104 pp.
To portray the evolution of jazz music as a reflection of the protest
of the oppressed Afro-American people, Backus uses the words of the musicians themselves. His study centers on "the historical conditions and
the politics of the Negro musicians' movement of the 1960s and 1970s."
To understand this movement, he briefly examines the cultural history
of the Afro-American, focusing on the function of music in the black
slave's life, the Civil War, the emergence of the blues, the Reconstruction
period, the Ku Klux Klan, and the tradition of minstrelsy. Describing
the birth of jazz, Backus concentrates on New Orleans and its enforced
social stratification. He relates the Northern migration of blacks to
the development of classic blues and jazz, and discusses musical life
during the Depression, W.W. II, and the post-War years, the emergence
of the bebop and "cool" styles, and the role of record companies. The
chapter, "Life in the Be-Bop Business," details the continuing aesthetic,
political, and personal struggles of the musicians. Chapter IX, "The
Musicians Fight Back," examines the guilds, festivals, associations, and
unions formed by black musicians as support networks. The final chapters
consider the function of jazz music as a political statement.

M 247. **BALLIETT, WHITNEY.** Dinosaurs in the Morning: 41 Pieces on Jazz.
Philadelphia: Lippincott, 1962. 224 pp.
This is a collection of forty-one of Balliett's essays on jazz and its
creators which originally appeared in the New Yorker between 1957 and
1962 and have been revised for this publication. The title is derived
from the eleventh essay in which the author recalls hearing a Vanguard
album entitled "Spirituals to Swing." Balliett notes that hearing the
memorable selections, recorded by John Hammond at Carnegie Hall in 1938
and 1939, is like "getting up one morning . . . and seeing a dinosaur
walk by." The essays, all of which are quite brief, often chronicle a
recent concert, acquaintance, or passing thought of the author. These
writings provide the reader with the perspective of an influential critic
at a turning point in the evolution of jazz: the emergence of the "avant-
garde" and "third-stream" styles. Balliett focuses on the contributions
of past artists to the present state of jazz music.

M 248. **BALLIETT, WHITNEY.** Ecstasy at the Onion: Thirty-one Pieces on
Jazz. Indianapolis, Ind.: Bobbs-Merrill, 1971. 284 pp.
Each of these thirty-one essays on jazz originally appeared as articles
in the New Yorker Magazine. This collection serves as a continuation
of Balliett's chronicles found in Sound of Surprise, Dinosaurs in the Morning (see M 247), Such Sweet Thunder, and Super-Drummer: A Profile of
Buddy Rich, covering the development of jazz between 1966-71. The first
section is primarily a diary from the Monterey and Newport Jazz Festivals.

The second section represents the author's ongoing interest in the works of Duke Ellington. The third section contains a collection of short reviews of such artists as Bobby Hackett, John Coltrane, Benny Morton, and Art Tatum. The fourth section is a discussion of noted jazz practitioners and promoters. The retrospective character of these essays conveys the author's pessimism about the current state of jazz. At this writing, Balliett considers jazz to be a dwindling, though not dying, medium.

M 249. BALLIETT, WHITNEY. Improvising: Sixteen Jazz Musicians and Their Art. New York: Oxford University Press, 1977. 263 pp.
This book contains thirteen essays and interviews in which Balliett focuses on sixteen leading jazz improvisors. The artists under consideration are Henry Red Allen, Joe King Oliver, Earl "Fatha" Hines, Mary Lou Williams, Pee Wee Russell, Jess Stacy, Red Norvo, Sidney Catlett, Buddy Rich, The Modern Jazz Quartet, Stephane Grappelli, Jim Hall, and Bob Culber. Several of the essays appeared previously in other collections, and of those some are out of print. The remainder of the essays have never appeared in book form. As the title suggests, this volume is primarily concerned with the nature and art of improvisation. Balliett examines the ocncepts, methods, and approaches of each of the musicians to illustrate the many processes involved in creating a jazz improvisation. many of the essays also provide information about the early musical background of the artists.

M 250. BALLIETT, WHITNEY. New York Notes: A Journal of Jazz, 1972-1975. Boston: Houghton Mifflin, 1976. 250 pp.
Most of the entries in Balliett's jazz diary originally appeared in somewhat different form in The New Yorker between 1972 and 1975. Balliett offers a selective record of the most significant jazz events and activities. Included here are recollections about jazz masters of the past as well as descriptions of the more recent activities of the Jazz Composer's Orchestra Association (JCOA) and other "new music" ensembles and players. The author presents tributes to recently deceased artists, which focus on their contributions to the development of jazz. Balliett is more optimistic about the future and quality of contemporary jazz music in this work than he is in such other collections as Ecstasy at the Onion (see M 248).

M 251. BALLIETT, WHITNEY. Night Creatures: A Journal of Jazz, 1975-1980. New York: Oxford University Press, 1981. 285 pp.
This book is a collection of the author's critical essays and profiles of musicians written between 1975 and 1980. All of these pieces originally appeared in The New Yorker magazine, and each has been revised for this publication. The essays focus on jazz in New York City, and deal with jazz on stage, records, television, and radio, as well as in books. Balliett continues to view the innovations of the present as direct extensions of the musical past, despite the dramatic changes brought about by the "new music" and "creative music" movements of the 1970s.

M 252. BARAKA, IMAMU AMIRI [Leroi Jones]. Black Music. New York: Morrow, 1967. 221 pp.
This work, a collection of Baraka's reviews and essays from 1959 to 1967, represents the author's distinct evolution as jazz enthusiast and culture critic. Discussions of "Jazz and the White Critic" and "The Changing Same (R&B and New Black Music)" are of particular interest. In both instances, Baraka places his discussion within the context of a racist and class-minded society, a society in which even black people participate in their own oppression. Noting the "oppositions" within black music as artificial, the author asserts that the "New Black Music" and rhythm and blues are merely particular aspects of a larger whole. Among the artists discussed by Baraka are John Coltrane, Wayne Shorter, Cecil Taylor, Thelonious Monk, and Archie Shepp.

M 253. **BARAKA, IMAMU AMIRI** [Leroi Jones]. Blues People: The Negro Experience in White America and the Music that Developed from It. New York: Morrow, 1963. 244 pp.
This is primarily a social and cultural critique of black Americans through their music. Baraka's thesis is that an analysis of black music which employs a musicological and socio-anthropological framework will yield information about the essential nature of the Negro's existence in this country. He notes, for example, that there are specific "stages" in the Negro's conversion from African to American and that those "stages" are most graphically represented in his music. Baraka discusses the slave experience, Christian religion, and the Negro's attempt to enter mainstream American life. In so doing, he illustrates how the various forms of black music reflect the conflicting sentiments of defiance, unity, powerlessness, and self-hatred among the Afro-American people.

M 254. **BARKER, DANNY AND JACK V. BUERKLE.** Bourbon Street Black: The New Orleans Black Jazzman. New York: Oxford University Press, 1973. 244 pp.
This is a sociological and cultural study of the black jazzmen in New Orleans. It is not a study of the music but rather a study of the musicians themselves. Buerkle and Barker determine the distinctive individual and group characteristics of these musicians and the particular historical circumstances which surrounded them. The tradition of the "second line," the importance of Creole culture, and the particular African synthesis which took place in New Orleans are considered in detail. The authors illustrate the relationship of Louisiana's 18th- and 19th-century legal history to the development of the black community in Louisiana. Based on interviews with fifty-one members of the black musicians' union, Buerkle and Barker uncover the human aspects of the Bourbon Street black community from the perspective of the musician and his family.

M 255. **BERENDT, JOACHIM ERNST.** The Jazz Book: From New Orleans to Rock and Free Jazz. Translated by Dan Morgenstern, Helmut Bredigkeit and Barbara Bredigkeit. New York: Laurence Hill, 1975. 459 pp.
The aim of this work is to present a comprehensive survey of the various jazz styles and movements. Berendt divides his study into eight broad categories: musical styles, elements, musicians, vocalists, instruments, big bands, combos, and contemporary European jazz. An abundance of musical detail is provided to demonstrate the logic and continuity of jazz's evolution. Berendt discusses many of the lesser known innovators and their specific contributions to the art of improvisation. He analyzes the jazz combo, using the term "integration." The term "integration," originally coined by John Lewis and the Modern Jazz Quartet, refers to the ways in which solo jazz expression is integrated into the musical collective or combo. Berendt asserts that jazz is "at once music of the individual and music of the collective."

M 256. **BERLIN, EDWARD A.** Ragtime: A Musical and Cultural History. Berkeley: University of California Press, 1980. 248 pp.
Dismissing much of the existing literature on ragtime as superficial, Berlin employs a rigorous critical method in his examination of ragtime. He makes substantial use of original source materials, analyzing over 1,000 piano rags and consulting numerous newspapers, books, and magazines of the period. In addition to presenting a detailed stylistic study of ragtime music, Berlin re-examines many of the social and aesthetic issues which emerged with the music, including ragtime's origins, racial content, potential for artistic development, and its effect on cultural and moral concerns. The author asserts, for example, that the original conceptions of ragtime differ sharply from the present-day notion of ragtime as a primarily piano-oriented music. In fact, Berlin contends, ragtime was more often considered to be a highly syncopated popular vocal music form.

M 257. **BLESH, RUDI.** Eight Lives in Jazz: Combo U.S.A. New York: Hayden
        Book, 1971. 240 pp.
Blesh organizes this essay, which focuses on various styles of early jazz,
as if it were a performance of a jazz suite. Chapter I, "Tuning Up,"
defines a combo as "a combination of musical instruments put together
to play an American music, jazz," and discusses how a combo functions
as a unit. This is followed by portraits of eight seminal figures in
jazz: Louis Armstrong, Sidney Bechet, Jack Teagarden, Lester Young, Billie
Holliday, Gene Krupa, Charlie Christian, and Eubie Blake. The final chapter, "Tag" (a jazz term for the final motive or recapitulation), is a
brief summary of the study of the combo. The author utilizes the artist's
own words as the basic material for each portrait and supplements them
with additional historical and discographical information.

M 258. **BLESH, RUDI.** Shining Trumpets: A History of Jazz. New York:
        Knopf, 1946. 410 pp.
This volume represents one of the first attempts at a comprehensive study
of the history of jazz. Blesh is concerned with the nature and development
of jazz as well as with establishing the artistic quality of the Afro-
American form. His chronological study begins with an examination of
the foundations of African culture and music; he ends with a discussion
of the emergence of "real" jazz forms in the 1930s. Blesh defines as
"real" the authentic styles of Dixieland and New Orleans jazz. For Blesh,
the music of the commercial swing band of the early 1930s represents an
artistic and aesthetic regression. In this work he also includes discussions of the Afro-American folk song, blues, classical jazz, and the boogie-
woogie piano style. Blesh contends that once the true artistic quality
of jazz is recognized, jazz music will be an important factor in alleviating racial tensions between blacks and whites in America.

M 259. **BLESH, RUDI and HARRIET JANIS.** They All Played Ragtime. New York:
        Knopf, 1950. 345 pp.
Blesh and Janis attempt to reconstruct the genesis and development of
ragtime by interviewing and corresponding with the surviving creators
and producers of the music. Although they claim that Sedalia, Missouri,
is the cradle of ragtime, they also explore the ragtime story in New
Orleans and the Midwest. They regard the development of ragtime in the
East as a separate phenomenon and include discussions about its relationship to Tin Pan Alley. In addition to surveying ragtime's origins in
the folk music of Afro-Americans, this work considers the creative, commercial, and social impact of ragtime at the turn of the century. The
authors attempt to differentiate ragtime in its "classic" sense from the
more commercially viable versions. They also include a discussion of
the many early pedagogical methods to facilitate the learning and performance of ragtime.

M 260. **BRUNN, HARRY O.** The Story of the Original Dixieland Jazz Band.
        Baton Rouge: Louisiana State University Press, 1960. 268 pp.
This book traces the origins, development, and decline of ODJB (Original
Dixieland Jazz Band). Brunn claims that the ODJB was the first band to
popularize jazz in the major cities of the world, and therefore holds
an important place in the creation of jazz. This essay is based on interviews with the surviving members of the band, including Nick LaRocca,
the leader of the ODJB, and on previously unknown primary materials and
documents now in the LaRocca Collection of the Archive of New Orleans
Jazz at Tulane University. Brunn considers the musical development of
the band, the relationship between jazz and the underworld, the moral
and social environments with which the band had to contend, and the role
of the phonograph in the musical and cultural revolutions of the beginning
of the 20th century. He includes information about the early recording
industry, the recording activity of the ODJB, and the musicians and ragtime
bands prominent in New Orleans before the "Chicago Exodus."

M 261. BUDDS, MICHAEL J. <u>Jazz in the Sixties</u>. Iowa City: University
        of Iowa Press, 1978. 124 pp.
Budds examines the radical expansion of musical resources and techniques
employed by jazz performers since 1960. After summarizing the various
jazz styles before 1960, he considers the new trends toward direct borrowing from African music and musicians and the growing interest in the
traditional musics of India, Asia, and Latin America. Budds relates the
black nationalist sound explorations of Ornette Coleman, John Coltrane,
and Sonny Rollins to the extension of expressive devices employed by avant-
garde European composers. In addition, he considers the reasons for and
the impact of using other European orchestral and electronic instruments
not previously associated with jazz. This work analyzes the changing
aesthetic of jazz which led to the new approaches to melody, texture,
instrumentation, color, and form.

M 262. CERULLI, DOM, BURT KORALL, and MORT NASATIR. <u>The Jazz Word</u>. New
        York: Ballantine Books, 1960. 192 pp.
This volume is a collection of jazz documents, recording the thoughts,
reflections, and reminiscences of Dom Cerulli, Bill Simon, Mercer Ellington,
Miles Davis, Lil Armstrong, Jack Kerouac, William Morris, Studs Terkel,
Burt Korall, Billy Taylor, Dari Brubeck, Bill Coss, Gery Kramer, and Nat
Hentoff, among others. The book includes poetry, personal accounts,
descriptions of the jazz experience, and thoughts on the developments and
future of jazz.

M 263. CHARTERS, SAMUEL BARCLAY and LEONARD KUNSTADT. <u>Jazz: A History
        of the New York Scene</u>. Garden City, N.Y.: Doubleday, 1962.
        382 pp.
Charters and Kunstadt outline the history of the jazz scene in New York
from the turn of the century to the late 1950s. Making a case for the
centrality of New York in the development of jazz music, they focus on
early ragtime music, the influence of such New Orleans bands as the Original Dixieland Jazz Band, the role of W.W. I Negro military bands, the
first blues recording by Mamie Smith, the importance of female artists
in the initial popularity of the blues, the growth of jazz from the obscurity of vaudeville shows to the respectability of the main stage with the
music of Paul Whiteman, the development of a distinctive New York style
by such musicians as Fletcher Henderson and Don Redman, the emergence
of the jazz ensemble, the evolution of the swing era, and the rise of
the bebop style of Dizzy Gillespie, Charlie Parker, and Thelonious Monk.
The authors also discuss the social and entertainment practices of both
black and white New Yorkers, the musical organizations which maintained
the various performing ensembles of the period, and the more obscure black
concert and classical scene.

M 264. COLLIER, JAMES LINCOLN. <u>Inside Jazz</u>. New York: Four Winds Press,
        1973. 176 pp.
Collier examines the basic characteristics and features of jazz. Noting
that jazz is not a type of music but rather a way of playing music, he
identifies the two most important features of jazz: its improvised nature
and the feeling (he terms it "jazz rhythm") required to perform it. Collier
discusses the origins of jazz, its various schools and styles, the jazz
life, and contemporary trends in jazz. The closing quarter of the text
is devoted to a consideration of specific jazz recordings representative
of the various styles.

M 265. COLLIER, JAMES LINCOLN. <u>The Making of Jazz: A Comprehensive His-
        tory</u>. New York: Dell, 1978. 534 pp.
Collier surveys the history of jazz, emphasizing the contributions of
such performers as Jelly Roll Morton, Bix Beiderbecke, Earl Hines, Coleman
Hawkins, and John Coltrane. He contends that many jazz practices, though

they may bear a strong resemblance to European musical elements, are governed by radically different conceptions. Consequently, he maintains that jazz must be viewed and evaluated on its own terms. Collier seeks to demythologize both jazz music and musicians through extensive use of recent research in musicology, history, and related disciplines. The issue of race is shown to be a significant component of jazz's evolution, and in a discussion entitled "The Atlantic Crossing," Collier deals with the advent of a black jazz presence in Europe and the emergence of such European practitioners as Django Reinhardt, John Dankworth, and Martial Solal.

M 266. CONDON, EDDIE and RICHARD GEHMAN, eds. Eddie Condon's Treasury of Jazz. New York: Dial Press, 1956. 488 pp.
This book is a collection of reprinted short stories and articles about jazz of all types. Most of the entries appear here in their original form although a few contain additional comments or rebuttals from the editors. The authors represented in this collection include the editors, Ernest Borneman, Nat Hentoff, Gilbert Millstein, Whitney Balliett, John Crosby, George Avakian, Otis Ferguson, Al Silverman, George Frazier, Carlton Brown, Leonard Feather, Marshall Stearns, and John Hammond. The pieces are mostly profiles of such musicians as Bix Beiderbecke, Fats Waller, Lee Wiley, Bill Davison, Dave Rough, Dizzy Gillespie, Pee Wee Russell, Duke Ellington, Count Basie, Glenn Miller, and the Dorsey Brothers. Included are discussions of bop and bebop.

M 267. DANCE, STANLEY. The World of Swing. New York: Scribner, 1974. 436 pp.
In this in-depth examination of the swing era, its music, and its musicians, the author provides a series of profiles of forty performers, principally drawn from their own words. Dance maintains that although the concept of swing originated within Afro-American culture in general, the swing era was particularly influenced by the innovations of Louis Armstrong. The author attributes the language and grammar of the swing era to the phraseology of Armstrong, claiming that virtually no instrumentalist was left unchanged after hearing Armstrong's improvisational technique. Dance also considers the role of arrangers, the interchange of ideas between the black and white bands, and the development of dance bands into show bands. He focuses on black musicians of the swing period, noting that the white jazz musicians have been "generally written about more extensively—even disproportionately—in the past." The musicians considered include Claude Hopkins, Elmer Snowden, Willie Smith, Jonah Jones, Roy Eldridge, Coleman Hawkins, Chick Webb, Mildred Bailey, Billie Holiday, Tiny Grimes, and Cozy Cole.

M 268. DAVIS, NATHAN. Writings in Jazz. Scottsdale, Ariz.: Gorsuch Scarisbrick, 1978. 172 pp.
Davis's thesis is that "any serious study of jazz must pay careful attention to its origins . . . both musical and extra-musical." He presents the social and cultural history of the Afro-American as a backdrop to the development of the various jazz styles. Davis considers the impact of African and Afro-American religious traditions upon jazz music. He discusses the role of voodoo, secret societies, and religion within this musical tradition. In addition, this work contains discussions of "Free Jazz and the Avant Garde" (about the music of the 1960s), "Jazz Rock" (about the music of the 1970s), and "The Role of Women in Jazz."

M 269. DE TOLEDANO, RALPH, ed. Frontiers of Jazz. New York: Ungar, 1962. 178 pp.
This book is a collection of critical essays on jazz and biographical profiles of its practitioners. The editor has selected articles which either generated widespread comment at the time of their publication,

or articles which are still pertinent to the serious exploration of jazz
and its creators. The book's first section, entitled "The Anatomy of
Jazz," deals with general critical issues of the definition, styles, and
performance practices of jazz. Included are Jean-Paul Sartre's essay,
"Jazz in America," and Roger Pryor Dodge's "Harpsichords and Jazz Trumpets." The latter essay considers the parallels between jazz improvisation
and the improvisational traditions of Haydn, Mozart, and Beethoven. The
second section, "The Men Who Made Jazz," contains biographical sketches
of King Oliver, The New Orleans Rhythm Kings, Bunk Johnson, Jelly Roll
Morton, Sidney Bechet, Bix Beiderbecke, Duke Ellington, Benny Goodman,
and James P. Johnson. Other contributors to the collection are Abbe Niles,
William Russell, Preston Jackson, George Beall, Morroe Berger, Hugues
Panassie, Ernst Anserment, George Johnson, Wilder Hobson, Frank Norris,
Otis Ferguson, and Ross Russell.

M 270. DEXTER, DAVE. Jazz Cavalcade. New York: Criterion Music, 1946.
        258 pp.
This survey of the history of jazz seeks to clarify what music and which
musicians may be appropriately defined by the term. Dexter maintains
that the early jazz activity in New Orleans and Chicago fits squarely
within the jazz tradition. He notes, however, that the emergence of the
Paul Whiteman orchestra and similar ensembles in New York City created
a great deal of confusion about the notion of "true jazz." In addition
to presenting general discussions about the various styles of jazz through
the 1940s, Dexter discusses the many films about jazz produced during
the 1940s and considers the state of jazz in Europe during the 1930s and
1940s, including a discussion of the prohibition of jazz in Germany by
the Nazi party.

M 271. DEXTER, DAVE. The Jazz Story from the '90s to the '60s. Englewood
        Cliffs, N.J.: Prentice-Hall, 1964. 176 pp.
This history of jazz covers developments from "the primitive New Orleans
bands right on up to 'the new thing'" of Ornette Colman and Charlie Mingus.
In his first chapter, "The Scene Today," Dexter claims that, despite the
changes in American musical life which have moved the musician out of
the nightclubs into "hotel orchestras" and "combos," the jazz musician
can still make a career from concerts, recordings, festivals, and even
college courses. In "How It Started," he writes: "With the growth of
the Louisiana Territory . . . African harmony, rhythm, and melody were
synthesized with the folk music of the booming Southern states" to create
jazz music. Dexter focuses on the early jazz bands and jazzmen of New
Orleans, the exodus of jazzmen to Chicago after the closing of Storyville
during the Prohibition, the "Golden Age of Jazz" in the gangster world
of Chicago, the devastating impact of the 1929 stock market crash upon
jazz musicians, and the late blooming of New York as a jazz center. Other
topics include the growth of jazz in the West, the careers of jazz singers,
the 1930s swing era, the musical "revolution" of rebop, the death of the
big bands, the advent of the "cool" school, and the international jazz
scene. Dexter includes a selected discography.

M 272. ERLICH, LILLIAN. What Jazz Is All About. 1962; Rev. ed. New
        York: Messner, 1975. 255 pp.
Erlich presents a general history of jazz, highlighting the contributions
of such famous performers as Duke Ellington, Count Basie, Charlie Parker,
and Ella Fitzgerald. Erlich suggests that the origins of jazz lie in
the traditional African music of the slaves and the European folk music
of the early white settlers. Historical in approach, this work examines
the various impacts of the slave experience, the early Afro-Christian church,
and the minstrel tradition on the modern jazz tradition. The final chapter makes some preliminary observations about the "jazz-rock" movement
of the 1960s and 1970s. An extensive collection of photographs of jazz
performers is included as a preface to the first chapter.

M 273. **FEATHER, LEONARD.** Inside Bebop. New York: Robbins, 1949.
103 pp.
Reprinted as Inside Jazz by DaCapo Press in 1977, this volume provides
a general survey of the bebop tradition and its many adherents. Feather
maintains that bebop represented a synthesis of the musical ideas of many
musicians—past and present. He cites Lester Young's improvisations as
prototypical of the qualities and nuances that later developed into bebop.
Substantial use of musical examples enables the author to illustrate many
of the performance innovations associated with the bebop style. In addition to discussing bop phrasing and the common harmonic practice of using
altered 9th, 11th, and 13th chords, Feather examines the changing sensibilities toward rhythm and rhythmic accent. He also notes the common
bop tradition of superimposing new melodies upon chord progressions of
existing tunes. The final section of this work contains ninety-two brief
biographies of musicians who were involved in the development and maintenance of the new musical style.

M 274. **FERNETT, GENE.** Swing Out: Great Negro Dance Bands. Midland,
Mich.: Pendell, 1970. 176 pp.
Fernett's book briefly discusses a large number of black jazz innovators
and their bands. He includes biographical sketches of such artists as
Jim Europe, Fletcher Henderson, Charlie Cook, Alphonso Trent, Noble Sissle,
Chick Webb, Don Redman, Cab Calloway, Earth "Fatha" Hines, and Claude
Hopkins, and of such better-known figures as Duke Ellington, Count Basie,
Louis Armstrong, Ella Fitzgerald, Billie Holiday, and Dizzy Gillespie.
Fernett also has collected in this volume 145 photographs, many of them
rare, and from the early jazz periods of the first half of the century.

M 275. **FERNETT, GENE.** A Thousand Golden Horns. Midland, Mich.: Pendell,
1966. 171 pp.
This book is a collection of classic photographs accompanied by brief
biographical passages on each of the performers featured. These include
Benny Goodman, Chick Webb, Hal Kamp, Glenn Miller, Jon Savitt, Count Basie,
Duke Ellington, the Dorsey Brothers, Artie Shaw, Harry James, Bunny Berigan,
Jack Teagarden, Bob Crosby, Jimmie Lunceford, Andy Kirk, and Erskine
Hawkins. Fernett includes a partial list of theme songs and a list of
band members for each.

M 276. **FINKELSTEIN, SIDNEY.** Jazz: A People's Music. New York: Citadel
Press, 1948. 274 pp.
Contending that distinctions between "classical" and "popular," "high
brow" and "low brow" are artificial and obsolete, Finkelstein aims his
essay at understanding jazz as part of world music. He considers the
aforementioned distinctions to be artificial because they have been imposed
on the music for financial, rather than artistic, reasons. He also seeks
to destroy the divisions between improvised and written composition.
Finkelstein examines such topics as "The African Myth," "What Jazz Teaches
About the Classics," "The Blues as a Language," and "The Future of Jazz."
He also discusses stylistic advances and emerging forms of jazz in the
context of various societal needs.

M 277. **FRANCIS, ANDRE.** Jazz. Translated and revised by Martin Williams.
New York: Grove Press, 1960. 189 pp.
The author provides an overview of jazz in which the music is considered
from aesthetic, historical, and technical points of view. In addition
to presenting the various styles of jazz and jazz performance from the
New Orleans style to the style of the "cool school," Francis considers
many practitioners of the period who have received little attention in
print. Discographical information is provided throughout the text to
supplement the issues of style and individual performance.

M 278. **GAMMOND, PETER.** Scott Joplin and the Ragtime Era. New York:
 St. Martin's Press, 1975. 223 pp.
Gammond presents a general survey of the ragtime era, focusing primarily
on the life and works of Scott Joplin, and secondarily on such other ragtime composers as Tom Turpin, James Scott, Joseph Lamb, and Louis Chauvin.
Gammond defines ragtime, in the strictest sense, as the highly syncopated,
written piano music published between 1897 and 1915, and, in the broadest
sense, as the ragtime-influenced Tin Pan Alley tunes and early jazz bands.
In addition to an extended discussion about proper ragtime performance
practices, Gammond attempts to reconstruct Joplin's early musical life
to illustrate the environment and social causes of the new style. He
contends that Joplin was strongly influenced by the march tradition of
John Philip Sousa, the songs of Stephen Foster, and popular piano music
of Brahms, Chopin, and Gottschalk.

M 279. **GIDDINS, GARY.** Riding on a Blue Note: Jazz and American Pop.
 New York: Oxford University Press, 1981. 313 pp.
This volume is a collection of Giddins's writings about jazz and the jazz-
influenced popular music of the 1970s. All of these essays, with the
exception of two, originally appeared as articles in the Village Voice.
Giddins has revised each of the essays for this publication. Giddins
considers the proverbial "blue note" to be the common ground shared by
the diverse artists and stylistic traditions represented here. Artists
discussed include Elvis Presley, Bobby Bland, Betty Carter, Frank Sinatra,
Jack Teagarden, Joe Venuti, Count Basie, and Professor Longhair. Also
included are extended discussions about composers Scott Joplin, Duke
Ellington, Charles Mingus, and Ornette Coleman. Giddins provides information about the musical collective movement of the 1960s, and notes how
the transplantation of Chicago's Association for the Advancement of Creative Music (AACM) to New York played a major role in revitalizing the
jazz scene there. Throughout, he makes strong connections between disparate styles to illustrate the unity and shared musical value system
of American popular music as a whole.

M 280. **GITLER, IRA.** Jazz Masters of the Forties. New York: Macmillan,
 1966. 290 pp.
This work centers on the development and impact of the bebop tradition
along with considerations of its many practitioners. Gitler, focusing
on the lives and works of Charlie Parker and Dizzy Gillespie, recounts
the musical and extra-musical circumstances which led to this radical
musical style. Biographical and interview materials provide insight into
the perspective and sentiments of the musicians themselves. Stories about
Charlie Parker and Dizzy Gillespie, for example, illustrate the often
disparate relationships between the artist's personal life and his creative
output. The remainder of the study of bebop is divided into discussions
according to musical instrument. Oscar Pettiford, for example, is presented within the context of bebop bassists in general. Other musicians
highlighted in this study include Bud Powell, Thelonius Monk, Fats Navarro,
J. J. Johnson, Charlie Christian, Kenny Clarke, Max Roach, Dexter Gordon,
Lennie Tristano, and Lee Konitz.

M 281. **GLEASON, RALPH J.**, ed. Jam Session: An Anthology of Jazz. New
 York: Putnam, 1958. 319 pp.
This volume is a collection of thirty-five short writings and reminiscences
from the 1940s and 1950s by such prominent jazz musicians and cultural
critics as Huddie Ledbetter ("Leadbelly"), Jelly Roll Morton, Bunk Johnson,
Iola and Dave Brubeck, Baby Dodds, Arna Bontemps, Anatole Broyard, Jack
Conroy, Henry Pleasants, and the editor. The essays are divided into
six sections, focusing on the musical roots of jazz in blues and spirituals;
the growth of "jazz culture"; the jazz revival; various jazz personalities,
including Earl "Fatha" Hines, Fats Waller, Dizzy Gillespie, Eddie Condon,

and Bix Beiderbecke; the emergence of "modern" jazz; and miscellaneous topics. An annotated selective discography is included.

M 282. **GODDARD, CHRIS.** Jazz Away from Home. New York: Paddington Press, 1979. 319 pp.
Goddard examines the period after the arrival in 1917 of American jazz musicians in Europe, focusing on the difficulties Europe encountered in assimilating the new musical movement. He also focuses on the activity in Paris and London, and reconsiders the claim that Europeans appreciate jazz more than Americans do. This work includes discussions of jazz-influenced music in the theater of the 1920s, the social attitudes of European high society, and the adaptation of jazz elements by European composers. Goddard notes that the first black American musicians moved to Europe to escape from the racial prejudice prevalent in the U.S., but adds that their hope was only partially fulfilled. This and other social factors in America at that time are juxtaposed with the social climate in Europe to produce some conclusions about the rejection of jazz by the European intellectual establishments, and about the simultaneous acceptance of jazz by a minority community of artists.

M 283. **GOFFIN, ROBERT.** Jazz from the Congo to the Metropolitan. New York: Doubleday, Doran, 1944. 254 pp.
Goffin starts his history of jazz with a discussion of tom-tom in New Orleans, moves to ragtime, and then to jazz itself. He focuses on Louis Armstrong, Benny Goodman, and Duke Ellington, but discusses many other bands, black and white. Goffin devotes one chapter to rating the best musicians and records. He concludes with his thoughts about the future of jazz, recalling its African origins. He describes jazz as "a democratic creation," and a "rich and tragic folklore." "Jazz," he contends, "is on its way to conquering the world."

M 284. **GOLDBERG, JOE.** Jazz Masters of the Fifties. New York: Macmillan, 1965. 246 pp.
This is a collection of twelve essays on several noted jazz performers who have come to prominence since the bebop era. The artists considered are the members of the Modern Jazz Quartet, Gerry Mulligan, Thelonious Monk, Art Blakey, Miles Davis, Sonny Rollins, Charles Mingus, Paul Desmond, Ray Charles, Cecil Taylor, John Coltrane, and Ornette Coleman. Although each of these artists is a performer of the bebop style, this essay focuses on the diverse stylistic paths chosen by each of them during the 1950s. These individual profiles also provide information about the major post-bop developments such as "funky bop," "hard bop," and "the third stream." The author's method is to combine the comments of the musicians, record producers, and music critics and then comparing their remarks with the musical product.

M 285. **GREEN, BENNY.** Drums in My Ears, Jazz in Our Time. New York: Horizon Press, 1973. 188 pp.
This volume is a collection of the author's own writings on jazz between the late 1950s and the early 1970s. The assortment of music reviews, book reviews, biographical sketches, and satires on jazz culture and popular music constitutes a body of jazz criticism from a distinctly British perspective. Green considers a wide range of jazz personalities and topics. The penultimate chapter, entitled "Avant Garde," describes the careers and musics of Miles Davis, Sonny Rollins, Ornette Coleman, and Horace Silver.

M 286. GRIDLEY, MARK C. Jazz Styles. Englewood Cliffs, N.J.: Prentice-
        Hall, 1978. 421 pp.
This is a general examination of the many styles and performance practices
associated with the history of jazz. Designed for the lay reader, the
work provides a guide for appreciating jazz and maintains that a knowledge
of jazz history is not essential to such an aim. Emphasis is put on the
melodic and harmonious components of the various styles. Gridley notes
the cross-fertilization of jazz with other musics of the world and emphasizes the relationship of jazz to the rock and roll innovations of the
1960s and 1970s. Focusing his attention on the saxophone, trumpet, and
piano, the author asserts that although a particular style may not change,
its practitioners often do.

M 287. GRIFFIN, NARD. To Be or not to Bop. New York: Workman, 1948.
        24 pp.
Griffin begins his short work by explaining the term "Bebop" as a popular
and convenient term for the "new and unusual element in modern music."
He notes the popularization of the term in a recording called "Bebop"
by Dizzy Gillespie. Pointing out that "bebop" is really a movement or
"advancement of modern jazz" rather than a type of music, Griffin discusses
the roles of the musicians Gillespie, Charlie Parker, Thelonious Monk,
the disc jockeys Fred Robbins and Symphony Sid, and the critic Leonard
Feather in this movement. Other figures discussed include Tadd Dameron,
Lester Young, Coleman Hawkins, Trummie Young, and Ross Russell.

M 288. GROSSMAN, WILLIAM L. and JACK T. FARRELL. The Heart of Jazz.
        New York: New York University Press, 1956. 315 pp.
In their study of jazz, Grossman and Farrell are concerned with "the exposition and critical evaluation of jazz content," an endeavor they consider
to be too often neglected in the study of jazz. They claim that "the
current renaissance of New Orleans jazz and of other traditional jazz
represents . . . the most important development in American popular music
. . . , one that derives . . . from a reversion to early models and
ideals." For Grossman and Farrell, the "heart of jazz" lies in the particular synthesis of Christian and secular content and musical style that
characterizes the traditional jazz of New Orleans. In developing their
argument, they consider such questions and topics as "Can jazz be defined?";
the Christian and secular elements of New Orleans jazz; jazz as a synthesis
of Christian, secular, Anglo-American, and Afro-American musical traditions; and "Mass-man's taste in jazz." The authors illustrate their discussions with examinations of the careers and music of prominent jazz
performers, and with analyses of the development of various jazz styles
and schools.

M 289. HADLOCK, RICHARD. Jazz Masters of the Twenties. New York:
        Macmillan, 1965. 255 pp.
Primarily concerned with the music of a select group of musicians of
the 1920s, Hadlock acknowledges the impact of economic and sociological
factors upon the music but does not discuss them in any detail. The main
subjects of this book are examined not only because of their individual
musical contributions but also because of their overall influence on the
development of early jazz. The volume is divided into eight chapters,
focusing on the lives and work of Louis Armstrong, Earl Hines, Bix
Beiderbecke, Fletcher Henderson, James P. Johnson, Jack Teagarden, Bessie
Smith, Eddie Lang, Dan Redman, and Fats Waller. A ninth chapter, entitled
"The Chicagoans," focuses on eight practitioners who had a collective
effect on jazz: Benny Goodman, Jess Stacy, Joe Sullivan, Frank
Teschemacher, Gene Krupa, Dave Tough, Bud Freeman, and Pee Wee Russell.
In providing an overview of the state of jazz during the 1920s, the author
hopes to dismantle the many myths and misunderstandings which continue
to obscure the jazz tradition. Throughout, Hadlock maintains that the

mass confusion about jazz and its creators created a spirit of camaraderie among the musicians which transcended the racial, ethnic, economic, and musical barriers of the time.

M 290. HARRISON, MAX. A Jazz Retrospect. Boston: Crescendo, 1976. 223 pp.

This is a collection of the author's reviews of jazz concerts and albums, biographical profiles of jazz musicians, and essays on a variety of jazz topics. Many of the essays appeared originally in Jazz Monthly and have been revised for the publication of this text. Harrison often elects to discuss topics which are either under-represented in the literature or which he feels have been completely overlooked. For example, he considers Ornette Coleman's violin-playing rather than his contributions on the alto saxophone. Throughout this text, the author wrestles with the aesthetic definition of jazz as a creative form. Like many British and continental critics, Harrison approaches jazz criticism by comparing it with the evolution of European classical forms. He also challenges many of the generally held presuppositions about jazz's African roots and includes a discussion of contemporary cross influences and their possible impact on the future of jazz.

M 291. HASKINS, JIM. The Cotton Club. New York: Random House, 1977. 169 pp.

This book explores the history of the famed Cotton Club in New York City. The author details both musical and extra-musical history to illustrate the complex social scene of which the Cotton Club was a part. Haskins examines the changed lifestyles of American blacks after W.W. I, and describes the transformation of Harlem from an affluent white suburb to a prosperous black community soon to be faced with the urban difficulties of prostitution, illegal drug sales, and overcrowding. He depicts the black Harlem of the 1920s as a new center of interest for the white, intellectual socialite. For whites, Harlem became a "primitive, yet thrilling" place to be entertained. Haskins also discusses the association of Duke Ellington with the Cotton Club, the impact of prohibition and the Depression, organized crime, and the Cotton Club revues on Broadway.

M 292. HENTOFF, NAT. Jazz Is. New York: Random House, 1976. 288 pp.
In this volume, Hentoff examines the jazz life, its practitioners, and its music. He attempts to uncover the nature of the music via an exploration of the varied lives, life styles, and perspectives of the jazz musicians. Several chapters focus on the lives and works of distinguished jazz artists, including Duke Ellington, Billie Holliday, Louis Armstrong, Teddy Wilson, Gerry Mulligan, Miles Davis, Charlie Mingus, Charlie Parker, John Coltrane, Cecil Taylor, and Gato Barbieri. A chapter entitled "The Political Economy of Jazz" examines the changing attitudes of musicians toward a more self-deterministic and militant stance. This chapter includes a discussion of the continued neglect and ignorance of black music among academics. The final chapter, entitled "Last (open-ended) Chorus," deals with the particular innovations presently taking root in the avant-garde or "new music" movement in the U.S.

M 293. HENTOFF, NAT. The Jazz Life. New York: Deal Press, 1961. 255 pp.

This is an explanation of the social, economic, and psychological contexts of modern jazz. Several of the chapters appeared previously as articles in various jazz periodicals and contemporary American magazines. Hentoff suggests that the basic attraction of jazz for those who perform it is that it affords them more freedom to express themselves than any other form of Western music. This freedom allows, and ultimately requires, the jazz person to be both imaginative and individualistic. The Jazz Life delves into the lives and lifestyles of the musician. "Paying dues," apprenticeship, and the pay scale on which jazz musicians are forced to live are all discussed. In addition, Hentoff discusses the racial tensions and "reversal of prejudice" in the jazz world along with what he describes as "the sizeable problem of narcotics addiction among jazz musicians of all shades during the past twenty years." Much of this work is based on the author's close professional association with jazz music and musicians.

M 294. HENTOFF, NAT and ALBERT J. McCARTHY, eds. Jazz: New Perspectives on the History of Jazz by Twelve of the World's Foremost Jazz Critics and Scholars. New York: Rinehart, 1959. 387 pp.
This volume is a collection of essays on jazz, jazz history, and jazz performers. Ernest Borneman addresses the issue of "The Roots of Jazz," Charles Edward Smith discusses the central role of New Orleans in the jazz tradition, and John Steiner analyzes "Chicago-style" jazz. The relationships of other musical traditions to jazz are examined in Guy Waterman's "Ragtime," Paul Oliver's "Blues to Drive the Blues Away," Max Harrison's "Boogie Woogie," and Hsio Wen Shih's "The Spread of Jazz and the Big Bands." The careers and musical styles of various performers are the subjects of Martin Williams's "Jelly Roll Morton," Gunther Schuller's "The Ellington Style," and Max Harrison's "Charlie Parker." Franklin S. Driggs deals with the early history of jazz in the Midwest and the Southwest in his essay. Finally, various aspects of contemporary jazz are outlined in Martin Williams's "Bebop and After," Alfred J. McCarthy's "The Re-emergence of Traditional Jazz," and Nat Hentoff's "Whose Art Form? Jazz at Mid-century." A discography is appended.

M 295. HOBSON, WILDER. American Jazz Music. New York: Norton, 1939. 230 pp.
Hobson defines "genuine jazz" as "an intricate, invigorating, spirited music," derived from the "principle of continuously suspended rhythm" of ragtime music. He devotes individual chapters to jazz's origins in Afro-American folk music; to the definition of "jazz language" and its expressive elements of tone color, rhythm, swing, melody, and harmony; and to the discussion of commercial and concert jazz. Tracing the musical evolution of jazz, Hobson devotes further chapters to New Orleans jazz, Chicago jazz, New York jazz, the swing era, and "hot" jazz. In the final chapter, he provides a selected list of thirty records, chosen and annotated to trace the development of jazz from folk music sources.

M 296. HODEIR, ANDRE. Jazz: Its Evolution and Essence. Translated by David Noakes. New York: Grove Press, 1956. 295 pp.
This essay deals with the principal characteristics and problems of American jazz from the perspective of the European critic. Hodeir asserts that jazz is to be understood as a complement to European culture rather than as an "antidote to the poisons of intellectualism." He evaluates jazz's influence on European music through the work of Ravel, Milhaud, and Stravinsky. Although he notes the reciprocity of influences between American jazz and European music, he suggests that only jazz is able to fully utilize and assimilate its European borrowings.

M 297. JACKSON, ARTHUR. The World of Big Bands: The Sweet and Swinging Years. New York: Arco, 1977. 130 pp.
In his brief history of big band music from pre-W.W. I Chicago to the present day, Jackson writes that "dance music, or swing . . . has, as an offshoot of jazz . . . always been an essentially American idiom which the British and continental bands have necessarily followed." His chronological survey begins in 1912 with the bands of Wilbur Sweatman, Paul Whiteman, and Rudy Vallee, and moves to the Golden Age of Lew Stone and Ray Noble in the 1930s, through the swing era of Duke Ellington and Glenn Miller, to the post-W.W. II sounds of Ted Heath and Sauter-Finegan and the current revival of the big band sound. Jackson focuses on the popu-

larization of big band music through the Hollywood productions of such movies as The King of Jazz (1930), the vital function of radio in the growth of big band music, the service bands of Glenn Miller and Sam Donohue during W.W. II, and the European adoption of the big band sound.

M 298. JASEN, DAVID A. and TREBOR JAY TICHENOR. Rags and Ragtime: A Musical History. New York: Seabury Press, 1978. 310 pp.
Although the bulk of the text is a chronologically arranged compositional history of ragtime music from 1897 to 1978, which gives short biographical notes on each composer/performer and an annotated list of his "rags," the introductory chapter places the music in a larger cultural context. After defining ragtime as a composition for the piano with a particular rhythm, Jason and Tichenor admit that "ragtime is a paradoxical art form with a perplexing history": "In an age of rigid racial divisions, ragtime appeared as a racially ambiguous commodity whose earliest composers had no common racial identity." Because it was primarily a "performance medium," ragtime can only be studied through the sheet music which began to appear from New York to San Francisco after 1898. The authors claim that the "pre-sheet music origins" of the music, as well as the origin of its name, have been "lost in an undocumented lower-class tradition of saloon and whorehouse piano-playing." They note the popularity of the music between 1906 and W.W. I, the homogenizing influence of Tin Pan Alley publishing business, the foreshadowing of ragtime in the "coon songs" of the 1890s, and the cake walk craze of the 1920s, the key roles of Scott Joplin and Jelly Roll Morton in the development of ragtime, and the recent ragtime revival.

M 299. JONES, R. P. Jazz. New York: Roy, 1963. 96 pp.
Jones examines the origins of jazz in Africa and Europe, and the roles of religion, slavery, emancipation, secret societies, and minstrelsy in the evolution of folk and work songs. The New Orleans-Storyville era is discussed in the context of the birth of the Dixieland and New Orleans styles. Jones treats the mass migration to the North, particularly to Chicago, which marked the beginning of what he calls "The Jazz Age." Focusing on the growth of the big band and the role of the Harlem community in the development of jazz, Jones discusses the musical careers of Paul Whiteman, Bix Beiderbecke, Bessie Smith, King Oliver, Jelly Roll Morton, Louis Armstrong, Fletcher Henderson, and Duke Ellington. He continues his history with examinations of the Depression, the role of Kansas City, the advent of swing, the "revival" of jazz, and the careers of Bennie Moten and Count Basie. He concludes with discussions of the coming of bop, the relation between jazz expression and social unrest, the growth of "cool jazz," the increased influence of white audiences and performers, and the beginning of rock and roll.

M 300. KAUFMAN, FREDRICK and JOHN P. GUCKIN. The African Roots of Jazz. New York: Alfred, 1979. 148 pp.
This study dissects the various musical elements of jazz and examines them in light of the cultural and musical practices found in traditional West Africa. It traces the prehistory of jazz up to the slave experience of the 16th and 17th centuries and views jazz as a product of the trans-plantation of West African culture to the New World. Noting that black African culture is not monolithic, the authors provide specific cultural detail about several of the most influential African societies situated in what is known today as Dahomey (Benin), Togo, Nigeria, and Ghana. Discussions of witchcraft, musical instrumentation, the riff, the falsetto break, and the blues are considered in terms of their place in both African and Afro-American cultures. This volume includes chapters on the present state of African music and jazz's relationship to dance, visual art, classical music, and language.

948

M 301. **KOFSKY, FRANK.** Black Nationalism and the Revolution in Music. New York: Pathfinder Press, 1970. 280 pp.
Kofsky is concerned with the social, political, and aesthetic parameters which frame black music and its continuing evolution. He maintains that jazz, like revolutionary black nationalist ideology, is born out of the oppressive experience of the black working class. Kofsky claims that black intellectuals and artists in other areas are forced to appropriate the "canons of European culture" as there are no established canons of black culture for the black musicians to draw from. In addition, this work deals with the problems of the jazz critic and the economics of the music industry. John Coltrane and Malcolm X, viewed by Kofsky as pivotal figures in the revolution, are dealt with in great detail.

M 302. **LANG, IAIN.** Jazz in Perspective: The Background of the Blues. London: Hutchinson, 1947. 148 pp.
Lang states: "Jazz is a music that expresses the life of common people, white and coloured." He traces the music back to New Orleans around 1900, describing the social conditions of the "common people" at that time. Lang insists that jazz is neither a solely black nor a solely white musical form; in fact, he finds that "it is the result of a Negro trying to sing a white tune." He seeks out native African influences on jazz, and traces the influence of American culture upon the content and development of jazz music, as in songs about the railroads and the Mississippi River. Lang stresses the significance of the exodus of Southerners from New Orleans to Chicago throughout the early 1900s, when and where Louis Armstrong figures prominently. Lang also discusses boogie-woogie, the Harlem scene, and the blues. A short discography is also included.

M 303. **LEE, EDWARD.** Jazz, an Introduction. London: Kahn & Averill, 1972. 188 pp.
Lee's approach to jazz is both historical and critical. He analyzes the various musical components of jazz, both in terms of their historical origins and their specific musical functions. His work is a comparative study, comparing jazz to both traditional African music and European classical music. Of particular note is his interpretation of the ways in which jazz resolves the various musical conflicts inherent in a music parented by the cultures of both Africa and Europe.

M 304. **LEONARD, NEIL.** Jazz and the White Americans: The Acceptance of a New Art Form. Chicago: University of Chicago Press, 1962. 215 pp.
This study examines the American reaction to jazz from 1917 to 1940 in the context of the longstanding controversies between traditionalist and modernist schools of artistic thought. Leonard notes that the controversies over jazz began in the 1890s and that the most heated controversy occurred between the two World Wars when intellectuals, clergymen, educators, artists, and patrons began to take sides. In addition to examining the rapid change in the taste for jazz in America, this essay seeks to answer several of the questions posed in Morroe Berger's article, "Jazz: Resistance to the Diffusion of a Culture-Pattern" (Journal of Negro History, XXII, January 1947). Leonard describes the gradual acceptance of jazz according to a Hegelian dialectical pattern in which a thesis (traditional music and values) and an antithesis (jazz and its related value system) were resolved in an aesthetical and ethical synthesis of the two opposing systems. In addition, Leonard discusses the role of jazz in American life and the world of art, its effect on the sensibilities of the young, and the impact of the gulf between the sensibilities of jazz artists and their potential audience.

M 305. LEVEY, JOSEPH. The Jazz Experience. Englewood Cliffs, N.J.:
Prentice-Hall, 1983. 158 pp.
Levey discusses jazz within the broader context of American popular music.
Noting that jazz has always made use of popular American musical idioms,
he presents the parameters of the reciprocal relationship between the
two forms, examining how they have influenced each other. He provides
working definitions of the two traditions, cites both their common ground
and dissimilarities, and discusses a wide range of jazz-related topics
including improvisations, jazz singing, and jazz dance.

M 306. LONGSTREET, STEPHEN. Sportin' House: A History of the New Orleans
Sinners and the Birth of Jazz. Los Angeles, Calif.: Sherbourne
Press, 1965. 293 pp.
Writing from years of personal observation, Longstreet describes the atmosphere in New Orleans' tenderloin district, Storyville, which was the spiritual birthplace of "stone age jazz." He describes life in the sporting
houses, the social phenomena revolving around sex and pleasure, street
"spasm" bands, the practice of voodoo, the nightclubs, and Tom Anderson's
Blue Book, the directory of Storyville whorehouses.

M 307. LYTTLETON, HUMPHREY. The Best of Jazz: Basin Street to Harlem,
1917-1930. London: Robson Books, 1978. 214 pp.
This book is the first volume of Lyttleton's "Best of Jazz" series. He
explores the styles and development of early jazz's most influential
figures. Each of the fourteen chapters is devoted to a particular artist
or group. These include The Original Dixieland Jazz Band, James P. Johnson,
King Oliver, Sidney Becket, Bessie Smith, Jelly Roll Morton, Fletcher
Henderson, Louis Armstrong, Bix Beiderbecke, Duke Ellington, Jimmy Noone,
Earl Hines, and Luis Russell. Lyttleton's study is based upon the recorded
works of the various artists. He analyzes the recordings, the artists'
stylistic innovations, the evolving functions of various instruments within
the early jazz band, and the varied approaches to improvisation and syn-
theses of existing trends.

M 308. LYTTLETON, HUMPHREY. The Best of Jazz 2: Enter the Giants, 1931-
1944. London: Robson Books, 1981. 239 pp.
This is the second volume of Lyttleton's "Best of Jazz" series (see M
307). The author provides a study of the styles of eleven jazz performers
who exerted a strong influence in their own and subsequent jazz eras.
The artists considered are Louis Armstrong, Fats Waller, Johnny Hodges,
Benny Carter, Dicky Wells, Lester Young, Billie Holiday, and Roy Eldridge.
This study is primarily based on the recorded works of these artists.
Lyttleton provides detailed discussions of the songs and performance prac-
tices which best exemplify the distinctive qualities of each player.

M 309. McCARTHY, ALBERT. Big Band Jazz. New York: Putnam, 1974.
368 pp.
McCarthy sets out to provide an overview of the big band jazz tradition.
Citing the on-going controversy over whether or not the commercially successful swing bands actually represent jazz big bands, the author acknowledges the great difficulty he had in determining which bands to include
in this study. He includes the jazz-oriented dance bands of Will Hudson
and Bob Zurke and excludes the Glenn Miller band. McCarthy claims that
the big bands were a national American phenomenon, not limited to the
major cities, but found in almost every region of the country. Accordingly,
McCarthy discusses many of the lesser known regional bands as well as
the even more obscure nightclub "housebands." In addition to profiling
the various bands, he details the personnel and circumstances that contributed to their success and failures. This examination includes discussions of the early syncopated orchestras, the pre-swing pioneers of
Chicago and New York, and the white bands of the period. McCarthy empha-

sizes the role of Fletcher Henderson and Don Redman in the development of the big band. He suggests further that it was arranger Redman who essentially laid the foundation for the big band jazz, and concludes with a consideration of the many factors which led to the decline of the big band era.

M 310. McCARTHY, ALBERT. The Dance Band Era: The Dancing Decades from Ragtime to Swing, 1910-1950. London: November Books, 1971. 176 pp.
This is primarily a study of pre-1950 white dance bands in the U.S. and abroad. Although the author does not provide specific criteria for differentiating between the early jazz bands and the early dance bands, he clearly perceives the black ensembles of Fletcher Henderson, Duke Ellington, Luis Russell, and Bennie Moten to be outside the scope of this book. He does, however, mention the seminal roles of James Reese Europe and Wilbur Sweatman. McCarthy recounts the musical and extra-musical factors which contributed to the idiom, citing the roles of the phonograph record, the advent of the radio broadcast, and heavy volume of sheet music sales. In addition, the author traces the development of the dance bands in Europe and the impact of W.W. II. McCarthy also discusses the business aspects of the dance band era. He provides information on the incomes of the various bands, the 1941 dispute between ASCAP (American Society of Composers, Authors and Publishers) and the radio networks, the birth of BMI (Broadcast Music, Inc.), and the AFM (American Federation of Musicians) strike of 1942.

M 311. McRAE, BARRY. The Jazz Cataclysm. New York: Barnes, 1967. 184 pp.
McRae chronicles the gradual transition in the 1950s from bop and "cool" jazz to "free form" jazz. He diagnoses the ailing "quintet formula"-- a "string of solos sandwiched between unison passages"--as having sunk into banality. He begins by discussing "cool" jazz as a reaction to bop and "a vital stage in the revolutionary and counter-revolutionary process," a process common to the development of all art forms. McRae praises Lee Konitz, Gerry Mulligan, and Stan Getz as the major "cool" innovators, and calls Dave Brubeck and his quartet "inconsequential." Things began to change with the work of Max Roach, Clifford Brown, Art Blakey, Horace Silver, and Cannonball Adderley. He recalls the English critic Benny Green's observation that "because jazz is becoming more complex, there are fewer players who can be classed as brilliant on the current scene." McRae claims that Sonny Rollins, John Coltrane, Charlie Mingus, and Ornette Coleman are four who can. He considers Miles Davis briefly. McRae notes that jazz creates its own rules and sets its own standards. He claims that the freedom inherent in the "free form" jazz could make it "more the property of the people."

M 312. MORGAN, ALAN and RAYMOND HORRICKS. Modern Jazz: A Survey of Developments Since 1939. London: Gollancz, 1956. 240 pp.
The authors describe their book as "a survey of the modern movement and of the contemporary jazz scene [and] a collation of our opinions and . . . our feelings with regard to the various major events in the evolution and development of modernism." They discuss swing as "the exertion of an organized state upon the authentic Negro style which emerged as jazz from New Orleans." Morgan and Horricks focus on the progressive movement revolving about Henry Minton's club in Harlem, led by guitarist Charlie Christian. Charlie Parker and Dizzy Gillespie figure prominently in the "post Minton development," along with Thelonious Monk, Kenny Clarke, Max Roach, and Lester Young. The authors also examine the early "white school," focusing on Woody Herman and activity of the West Coast. A chapter is devoted to Miles Davis. The last chapters concern the orchestras of Stan Kenton, Duke Ellington, Count Basie, and the "Modern Jazz Scene in Europe." The book also includes an extensive discography.

M 313. MORGENSTERN, DAN. Jazz People. New York: Abrams, 1976.
        300 pp.
In his introduction to Morgenstern's study of jazz musicians and their
music, the jazz trumpeter Dizzy Gillespie claims that jazz music is "a
truly universal language." Morgenstern examines elements in Part I, "Where
Jazz Came From, Where It's Been, and Where It's Going," seconding
Gillespie's claim: "Jazz has become the first truly global art alongside
the other form intrinsic to the 20th century, the motion picture." He
focuses on the beginnings of jazz in New Orleans, the roles of the marching
band and the red light district in the evolution of jazz, the relationship
of jazz to ragtime and blues, the legitimization of jazz by such white
groups as the Original Dixieland Jazz Band, the migration of jazz musicians
and music to Paris, the emergence of swing, the movement and the growth
of bebop. In Part II, Morgenstern examines the careers and music of jazz
performers, composers, and singers from Louis Armstrong to Ornette Coleman.
A selected discography is included and the volume is illustrated with
photos by Ole Brask.

M 314. MORRIS, RONALD L. Wait Until Dark: Jazz and the Underworld 1880-
        1940. Bowling Green, Ohio: Bowling Green University Popular
        Press, 1980. 231 pp.
Morris contends that jazz, without the long-standing sponsorship of mob-
sters and racketeers, could not have survived. He further claims that
most leading jazz entertainers between 1880 and 1940 were closely associated with racketeers for purposes of both encouragement and marketing.
Morris seeks to determine the nature of this relationship, the extent
of contact, and the implications of the cultural interaction. The author
suggests that the musician-mobster relationship also greatly influenced
the stylistic and artistic development of jazz as a whole. He examines
the simultaneous development of early jazz and the emergence of organized
crime organizations in the nation's urban centers. Re-examining the social
stigma attached to blacks, as well as to Jews and Italians, the author
seeks to show how the jazz nightclub became a meeting ground for musical
radicals and various social outcasts.

M 315. NANRY, CHARLES, ed. American Music: From Storyville to Woodstock.
        New Brunswick, N.J.: Transaction Books, 1972. 290 pp.
Based on the papers presented at a jazz and sociology conference at The
Rutgers Institute of Jazz Studies, the essays in this collection discuss
jazz in its social context from the 1920s to the 1950s, focusing mainly
on the social, cultural, and economic conditions that contribute to the
complexion of American music and the roles that jazz and rock play as
barometers of American life. Part I, "Bix Lives to Bird Lives: The Jazz
Phenomena," includes Neil Leonard's "The Impact of Mechanization," Howard
S. Becker's "The Culture and Career of the Dance Musician," Robert A.
Stebbins's "A Theory of the Jazz Community," and Richard A. Peterson's
"A Process Model of the Folk Pop and Fine Art Phases of Jazz." The shorter
Part II, "The Beat Goes On: Rock Comes of Age," includes Robert R.
Faulkner's "Hollywood Studio Musicians: Making It in the Los Angeles Film
and Recording Industry," and Irving Horowitz's "Rock, Recordings, and
Rebellion."

M 316. NANRY, CHARLES and EDWARD BERGER. The Jazz Text. New York: Van
        Nostrand Reinhold, 1979. 276 pp.
Nanry presents a sociological study of the history of jazz and considers
the cultural and sociological dimensions of jazz. He discusses the impact
of the race issue in America in general and within the black community
in particular, focusing on the schism between the creole and black musicians in New Orleans and Chicago. The text is divided into three parts.
The first part deals with the prehistory and origins of early jazz and
defines the basic musical components of the genre. The second part con-

siders the development of jazz, its various styles, and some selected practitioners. The third part presents a guide to jazz research and an extended survey of the various sociological approaches to the study of jazz, including applications of "reference group theory" and Max Weber's "theory of bureaucracy." The authors maintain throughout that, contrary to popular opinion, jazz is not a catalyst for social change but rather lags behind and reflects the environment in which it finds itself.

M 317. OSGOOD, HENRY O. So This Is Jazz. Boston: Little, Brown, 1926.
258 pp.
This text is one of the earliest attempts in the U.S. to explore the origin, history, and development of jazz. Osgood considers the nature of discussions about jazz in the 1920s. He dislikes the "hot jazz" associated with black jazz performers, preferring instead the more "refined" approach of Paul Whiteman and his contemporaries. The musical aspects of jazz, as well as the numerous social concerns of the jazz era, are discussed. Osgood presents an apology for the "sweet jazz" forms of Whiteman and Gershwin, and compares the intense criticism of jazz to the early reactions of the European music establishment to Arnold Schoenberg, an acquaintance of the author.

M 318. OSTRANSKY, LEROY. The Anatomy of Jazz. Seattle: University of
Washington Press, 1960. 362 pp.
Ostransky sets out to place jazz in its proper place for those whose primary interest is in "serious" or classical music. At the same time, he attempts to introduce the jazz-oriented listener to the problems of non-jazz composers and performers by relating jazz to the history of music in general. He further attempts to relate jazz theory to traditional music theory and to discuss the present position of jazz within the broader world of music. Intended as an introduction to the semantic, philosophic, and analytic difficulties associated with jazz, this book seeks to establish the common ground between jazz and classical enthusiasts in order to facilitate a mutually beneficial dialogue. In addition to detailing the various jazz styles, Ostransky discusses the musical elements of jazz and the nature of jazz improvisation. The final chapter entitled "Towards the Future" contains the author's speculations about future evolutions in jazz. He suggests that the 20th-century, 12-tone row technique, as conceived by Arnold Schoenberg, holds great promise for jazz.

M 319. OSTRANSKY, LEROY. Jazz City: The Impact of Our Cities on the
Development of Jazz. Englewood Cliffs, N.J.: Prentice-Hall,
1978. 274 pp.
Ostransky maintains that the story of jazz is intricately bound to the history of America in general, and to the history of America's urban centers in particular. He explores the complex of relationships that have bound jazz to certain major U.S. cities at specific points in our social history. Under particular scrutiny are New Orleans, Chicago, Kansas City, and New York City. The book seeks to discover why these cities were so conducive to the development of jazz while others were not. To this end, the author details the early histories and distinguishing characteristics of the cities. By considering the nature of the "jazz district" in each of these municipalities, Ostransky seeks to illustrate the causal relationship between the development of jazz and the "special conditions" in each city. These "special conditions" include the political, social, economic, and military developments which appear to be necessary to a vital jazz scene.

M 320. **OSTRANSKY, LEROY.** Understanding Jazz. Englewood Cliffs, N.J.:
        Prentice-Hall, 1977. 367 pp.
Ostransky offers a general introduction to the history of jazz, exploring
both the social and musical aspects of the tradition. To clarify his
method he presents the numerous difficulties involved in a critical examination of this type and compares the divergent perspectives of several leading jazz writers. Ostransky discusses the role of improvisation, the
importance of style, and the analytical means by which one artist may
be differentiated from another. This chronological investigation begins
with the military bands of the late 19th century and ends with an overview
of the musical developments of the 1970s.

M 321. **PANASSIE, HUGUES.** Hot Jazz: The Guide to Swing Music. Translated
        by Lyle Dowling and Eleanor Dowling. New York: Witmark, 1936.
        363 pp.
In this study of jazz (first published in French in 1934), Panassie notes
that his goal is "to give a precise idea of jazz in its definitive form,
to put an end to the deplorable misunderstandings about jazz." He devotes
his first chapter to defining the jazz style in opposition to the classical
music tradition. He distinguishes jazz from other musical forms by its
emphasis on the performer (whether a single musician or an entire orchestra) rather than the composer; in jazz, the performer, not the composer,
is "the creator." Panassie describes the two most important musical elements of jazz as "binary rhythm," the "gift" of "Negro swing," and jazz
"dissonance." In "The Hot Style," he records the evolution of the style,
differentiating it from "straight" jazz on the basis of intonation, melodic
style, and use of improvisation. Further chapters discuss Louis Armstrong
as soloist, other jazz improvisors, the Chicago style, Duke Ellington,
and principal arrangers and orchestras. An extensive discography is
included in an appendix.

M 322. **PANASSIE, HUGUES.** The Real Jazz. Translated by Anne Sorelle
        Williams. 1942; Rev. ed. New York: Barnes, 1960. 284 pp.
Panassie asserts that "real jazz," as opposed to "fake" or commercial
jazz, must be true to the spirit of its Southern Afro-American origin.
He defines Southern Afro-American music as music in which "creation" cannot
be separated from interpretation and where collective creation dominates
the individual effort. Panassie revises his emphasis on white musicians
in his earlier study, Hot Jazz (see M 321), and presents discussions of
various early jazz styles and stylists and the role of a black aesthetic.
His comparison of jazz to classical music further develops his notions
about jazz as a primitive music, in which the musician creates primarily
out of the need to express himself. For Panassie the intent of an artist
is as important as his execution in creating an authentic jazz creation.

M 323. **PLACKSIN, SALLY.** American Women in Jazz. New York: Seaview Books,
        1982. 332 pp.
Placksin examines the contributions of women to the history of jazz.
Her study is based on extant materials as well as on a series of interviews
with surviving artists in the various styles. She discusses female jazz
musicians from 19th-century black all-woman brass bands to female performers of the "New Music" of the 1970s. Placksin also explores the reasons
for the lack of recorded and written materials and discusses the role
of women in society in general, and in jazz in particular. By relating
the background, aspirations, and achievements of the female jazz performer,
the author raises questions about the influence of little known female
jazz instrumentalists and the professional and personal associations
between male and female jazz performers.

M 324. PLEASANTS, HENRY. Death of a Music? The Decline of the European
        Tradition and the Rise of Jazz. London: Gollancz, 1961.
        191 pp.
Pleasants's discussion of contemporary music is divided into two parts:
"The Crises of Evolution in European Music" and "The Crises of Evolution
in American Music." In the former, he discusses the problems confronted
by the "modern" classical composers of Europe whose work is not accorded
the attention that traditional classical works ordinarily receive. In
the second part, the American jazz scene and its music are defined and
discussed. Pleasants despairs about the serious music community's refusal
to accept jazz, examines the use of jazz elements in musical theater,
and compares the relation of musical theater and opera to that of jazz
and classical music. Pleasants argues that jazz must be more widely appreciated and recognized as a new form of art music rather than as a continuation of pop music traditions.

M 325. PLEASANTS, HENRY. Serious Music--And All That Jazz! An Adventure
        in Music Criticism. New York: Simon & Schuster, 1969. 256 pp.
Pleasants's purpose is to explore the dual function of contemporary music
as art and entertainment. He argues that classical European music--
"serious music"--is an exhausted tradition, and turns to Afro-American
music for a new and vital style. Examining the current state of jazz
music, Pleasants seeks to define it and to analyze the nature of its crisis,
which he sees as similar to the transition between the Renaissance and
the Baroque in Europe. Reviewing both the bop and "free jazz" styles
and perceiving states of aesthetic crisis, Pleasants turns to Afro-American
blues, gospel, and rock vocal styles as sources of new and needed musical
vigor. He also discusses the possibilities for the future latent in musical theater and the music of the cinema.

M 326. RAMSEY, FREDERIC. Been Here and Gone. New Brunswick, N.J.: Rut-
        gers University Press, 1960. 177 pp.
This photo-essay chronicles Ramsey's five trips to the rural South between
1951 and 1957 to uncover traces of the musical past and present of black
American folk culture. Numerous interviews, reviews of musical performances, and photographs serve as the resource materials for this essay.
Ramsey's investigations surveyed parts of rural Alabama and Mississippi
as well as the black sections of New Orleans. The author describes in
words and pictures many of the factors which served as the foundation
for the blues, jazz, and gospel forms of today. He includes discussions
of various sacred and secular folk texts, descriptions of various instruments and playing methods, and some general considerations of the themes,
images, and metaphors which run throughout both folk and contemporary
black culture.

M 327. RAMSEY, FREDERIC and CHARLES EDWARD SMITH, eds. Jazzmen. New
        York: Harcourt Brace Jovanovich, 1939. 360 pp.
This volume is an anthology of essays written by editors Ramsey and Smith,
William Russell, Wilder Hobson, and others. Although the essays cover
a wide range of early jazz topics and trends, the volume maintains the
primacy of the New Orleans jazz tradition. Much of the work is based on
interviews with the musicians under consideration. The volume is divided
into four sections which focus on the jazz traditions of New Orleans,
Chicago, and New York, and on the evolution of the "hot jazz" substyle.
The articles include Smith's "White New Orleans," E. Simms Campbell's
discussion of the relation of the blues to jazz in Chicago, Wilder Hobson's
"New York Turns on the Heat," and Richard Pryor Dodge's "Consider the
Critics."

M 328. REISNER, ROBERT G. The Jazz Titans, Including "The Parlance of
Hip." Garden City, N.Y.: Doubleday, 1960. 168 pp.
In the first part of this study, Reisner presents thirty-three brief profiles of noted jazz performers. The author notes that all of these "jazz
titans" are composers and have had a great influence on the development
of jazz. The second section, entitled "The Parlance of Hip," deals with
jazz slang. The author provides a short glossary of jazz or "hip" terms.

M 329. RIVELLI, PAULINE and ROBERT LEVIN, eds. Black Giants. New York:
World, 1970. 126 pp.
For Rivelli and Levin, the black giants are the Afro-American innovators
associated with the "New Music" movement of the 1960s and 1970s. This
volume is a collection of interviews with and essays about a selected
group of improvisors in the "New Music" tradition. The artists interviewed
or discussed include Oliver Nelson, John Coltrane, Alice Coltrane, Archie
Shepp, Leon Thomas, Ornette Coleman, Gary Bartz, Horace Tapscott, Sunny
Murray, Elvin Jones, John Carter, Bobby Bradford, and the Association
for the Advancement of Creative Musicians (AACM). The authors include
Frank Kofsky, David C. Hunt, John Szwed, Will Smith, and Nat Hentoff.
Taken as a whole, the volume suggests that the "New Music" practitioner
uses many different musical elements and styles in his or her assertive,
self-definitive effort to create a new black aesthetic.

M 330. ROSE, AL and EDMOND SOUCHON. New Orleans Jazz: A Family Album.
Baton Rouge: Louisiana State University Press, 1967. 338 pp.
Primarily a photo album of hundreds of musicians and musical sites in
New Orleans, this volume offers a wealth of visual detail to the contemporary jazz researcher. The evolution of musical instruments over the
past eighty years, for example, can be quickly assessed through one good
photograph. Examining the musical instruments and instrumentation of
the early New Orleans bands, this volume illustrates the multiracial character of the New Orleans tradition. Many of the early bands and musicians
noted here are not documented on recordings. The authors supply brief
biographical sketches of the musicians as well as street addresses for
many of the significant music and dance halls of New Orleans.

M 331. RUSSELL, ROSS. Jazz Style in Kansas City and the Southwest.
Berkeley: University of California Press, 1971. 292 pp.
In this volume, Russell offers a consideration of jazz in Kansas City
and explores both the musical traditions and social history which produced
such major figures as Charlie Parker, Lester Young, Charlie Christian,
and Count Basie. Russell views jazz as a folk art which persists within
the framework of the commercial music industry. He suggests further that
Kansas City jazz, unlike its Chicago counterpart, is not based upon the
music of New Orleans but rather developed in cultural and commercial isolation, away also from the publishing houses and recording companies of
New York. Thus the distinct Kansas City style was possible precisely
because of its isolation from the mainstream of popular American culture.
After detailed examinations of the political and social environments which
spawned the style, Russell considers the impact of the folk song and country
blues tradition upon jazz. Also included are discussions of noted territorial bands, the Kansas City origins of bebop, and the specific characteristics of the Kansas City style.

M 332. SARGEANT, WINTHROP. Jazz; Hot and Hybrid. 1946; Rev. ed. New
York: Da Capo Press, 1975. 302 pp.
Sargeant discusses the origins and basic grammar of "Hot Jazz" and raises
questions of exactly what is attributable to Afro-American, African, and
European cultures. He makes strong distinctions between the "purely
Negroid" improvisations of "Hot Jazz" and the more stylized and arranged
compositions of the "Sweet Jazz" dance ensemble. Although he asserts

that jazz is a hybrid art form uniquely rooted in both the rural and urban American experiences, Sargeant also discusses the particular means by which other world cultures have influenced the development of the music. Tin Pan Alley, for example, was not only a wellspring of popular tunes but also the conduit of many Anglo-Celtic, Central European, Russian, and Balkan Jewish religious and folk music practices. The author analyzes jazz models of syncopation, polyrhythms, and cross rhythms, then compares them to their European counterparts. Although Sargeant suggests that jazz is a fine art form which maintains its own aesthetic, he dismisses the notion that it can be linked to any particular moral or social ideology.

M 333. SCHAFER, WILLIAM J. Brass Bands & New Orleans Jazz. Baton Rouge: Louisiana State University Press, 1977. 134 pp.
This study is based, in large part, on the oral biography and interview materials at Tulane University's William Ransom Hogan Jazz Archive. The author complements this research with interviews with several surviving musicians and observers of the brass band tradition in New Orleans. Schafer traces the development and dissemination of the brass band in America as well as the particular parallel development of the brass band in New Orleans. He also summarizes the social and cultural history of New Orleans. He asserts that the story of the black brass band in New Orleans in the 20th century describes a symbiotic relationship of "two musics co-existing and mingling but never quite merging." Schafer also discusses the many roles of the brass band in the development of jazz, the transformation of the strict 19th-century military band style into the ragtime style, improvising street bands of New Orleans, and several of the often overlooked musicians and early bands associated with this music. Included are chapters on cultural traditions such as the "Second Line" and the "musical funeral."

M 334. SCHAFER, WILLIAM J. and JOHANNES RIEDEL. The Art of Ragtime. Baton Rouge: Louisiana State University Press, 1973. 249 pp.
Schafer and Riedel present an in-depth study of the ragtime style and consider its impact upon subsequent musical developments in the U.S. and abroad. The authors note the influence of ragtime upon American popular music, several 20th-century European composers, and the musical theater. They maintain that ragtime is the first Afro-American music to achieve wide commercial success. In addition, the authors suggest that ragtime is the bridge between the Afro-American oral traditions and the subsequent scored versions of jazz and popular dance musics, communicating both the black folk styles and black conceptions of Western art music. This volume is intended to provide a critical examination of ragtime's form, structure, and performance techniques. Four appendices, which constitute almost a third of the text, deal with such matters as the history of the cover illustrations for ragtime sheet music and Scott Joplin's Treemonisha.

M 335. SCHULLER, GUNTHER. Early Jazz. New York: Oxford University Press, 1968. 401 pp.
Schuller presents a systematic and comprehensive history which deals with the specifics of jazz music. The volume is designed to bridge the gulf between the more general histories of Goffin, Hobson, and Panassie (see M 283, M 295, and M322) and the more analytical writings of Sargeant and Hodeir (see M 296 and M 332). Schuller discusses the jazz tradition up to the era of the Depression and considers the early 1930s as a transitional period which set the stage for the swing era. Topics included in this work are the history of jazz and its musical antecedents, Louis Armstrong ("The First Great Soloist") and Jelly Roll Morton ("The First Great Composer"). Schuller also evaluates the various regional big band traditions, the virtuoso instrumentalists of the 1920s, and Duke Ellington.

M 336. SHAPIRO, NAT and NAT HENTOFF. Hear Me Talkin' to Ya: The Story
        of Jazz by the Men Who Made It. New York: Rinehart, 1955.
        414 pp.
This volume is an overview of the musical and extra-musical aspects of
the jazz life. The authors seek to present a composite portrait of the
jazzmen based on the recollections and perspectives of the musicians themselves. They cover the beginnings of jazz in New Orleans through to the
"Cool School" and Dixieland revivals of the 1950s. Also included are
discussions of jazz activity in various regions of the country, and the
many Afro-American and pre-jazz forms which created the foundations for
jazz. Shapiro and Hentoff combine discussions of significant social
factors and jazz events with a presentation of the musicians' viewpoints,
including Louis Armstrong's recollections of the closing of Storyville
in 1917, and Charlie Parker's response to the issue of narcotics usage.

M 337. SHAPIRO, NAT and NAT HENTOFF, eds. The Jazz Makers. New York:
        Rinehart, 1957. 368 pp.
This book is a collection of original essays devoted to the lives and
works of twenty-one significant contributors to the development of jazz.
The artists considered are Jelly Roll Morton, Warren "Baby" Dodds, Louis
Armstrong, Jack Teagarden, Earl "Fatha" Hines, Bix Beiderbecke, Pee Wee
Russell, Bessie Smith, Fats Waller, Art Tatum, Coleman Hawkins, Benny
Goodman, Duke Ellington, Charlie Parker, Fletcher Henderson, Count Basie,
Lester Young, Billie Holiday, Roy Eldridge, Charlie Christian, and Dizzy
Gillespie. The contributors represent a cross-section of noted jazz
critics and essayists, including Charles Edward Smith, John Wilson, George
Hoefer, Bill Simon, Orrin Keepnews, Leonard Feather, and George Avakian.
Some authors concentrate on biographical information, while others focus
on musical achievements.

M 338. SHAW, ARNOLD. The Street that Never Slept. New York: Coward,
        McCann & Geoghegan, 1971. 378 pp.
Shaw presents a social history and commentary on Manhattan's 52nd Street,
a center of jazz activity from the mid-1930s to 1950. Based on a collection of twenty-six taped interviews with noted jazz performers, producers,
and writers, this study reconstructs the many musical and extra-musical
factors which helped to create the 52nd Street musical boom. Shaw examines
52nd Street's relationship to three major style periods: the small "hot
jazz" ensembles of the 1920s, the swing era of the 1930s and 1940s, and
the post-W.W. II era of "bop and cool." In addition, Shaw illustrates
how "the Street" served as the middleground and meeting place for the
black artists of Harlem and mainstream white society. Jazz traditions
such as the "jam session" and "sitting in" are considered as well as the
external social realities of Prohibition and segregation.

M 339. SIMON, GEORGE T. Simon Says: The Sights and Sounds of the Swing
        Era, 1935-1955. New Rochelle, N.Y.: Arlington House, 1971.
        492 pp.
Simon has here put together a collection of his essays, interviews, and
music reviews which originally appeared in Metronome magazine. These
unrevised essays cover a wide range of jazz-related topics and are presented here with their original bylines. Although Simon acknowledges
that many of his musical opinions have changed over the years, he maintains
that there is some value in representing the writings exactly as they
appeared previously. He notes with some regret, for example, his earlier
perspective and remarks about the black bands and musicians of the period.
Topics considered in this volume include band reviews and histories, interviews with jazzmen and popular singers, and interviews with a wide range
of composers and arrangers. The volume provides both a sense of the times
and the critical perspective which influenced many listeners' reception
or rejection of the jazz and popular music movements between 1935 and
1955.

M 340. SINCLAIR, JOHN and ROBERT LEVIN. Music and Politics. New York:
        World, 1971. 133 pp.
This volume consists of a collection of articles, reviews, and interviews
which originally appeared in Jazz & Pop magazine. Each essay is representative of a generation of political writings on music which sought to
unify a diverse collection of revolutionary ideologies under the umbrella
of the "New Music" movement. Both authors assert that the avant-garde
tradition of the 1960s and 1970s is a sign and symbol of a cultural revolution in which the "masses" of the world will be united. Of particular
interest is Sinclair's discussion of "self-determination music." This
type, characterized by the recorded works of Sun Ra, Stanley Crouch, Sonny
Sharrock, and Roy Ayers, "liberates" the musician as he plays it; the
music, in turn, liberates the listener as he listens. Sinclair examines
the relationship of the self-deterministic new black music to the Black
Panther Party, the National Liberation Front of South Vietnam, the People's
Republic of China, and the Cuban Living Revolution. Levin's contributions
include an interview with Sonny Murray which recalls the early rejection
of new music even within the jazz community and an essay entitled "The
New Jazz and the Nature of Its Enemy." The latter discusses the critical
hostility toward the new form and the causal relationship between it and
the rise of black nationalism.

M 341. SMITH, LEO. Notes (8 Pieces) Source a New World Music: Creative
        Music. New Haven, Conn.: Leo Smith, 1971. 37 pp.
Composer/trumpeter Smith asserts that every black artist must self-
consciously document for himself the nature of his creative output. To
this end, the author seeks to define his music in the context of the
nascent "creative" music movement in the U.S. Smith maintains that creative
music represents the synthesis of two disciplines--improvisation and composition. He further asserts that musical art is in its purest form when
the musician (improvisor) creates without any prior guideline (music)
or external director (conductor). Smith sets forth the basic tenets of
the creative music movement. He includes discussions of the Association
for the Advancement of Creative Musicians or AACM (of which he is a member),
the role of the music critic, and the impact of the record industry on
this improvised form.

M 342. SPELLMAN, A. B. Four Lives in the Bebop Business. New York:
        Pantheon Books, 1966. 241 pp.
This work, based on interviews with Cecil Taylor, Ornette Coleman, Herbie
Nichols, and Jackie McLean, describes and analyzes the state of modern
black jazz at the height of the avant-garde movement of the 1960s.
Spellman uses the lives, struggles, and triumphs of these four disparate
artists to illustrate the peculiar status of the "serious" black jazz
musician in America. In so doing, he provides a commentary on the emerging
characteristics of serious black jazz and America's response to it.
Spellman asserts that America is indifferent to those aspects of Afro-
American culture which reflect the black artist's conscientious move away
from the "entertaining" folk and popular art forms. He notes the relationship between the avant-gardist's interest in "high" art and the audience's
steadily declining interest in jazz as it moves away from the barroom
and dance floor.

M 343. STEARNS, MARSHALL. The Story of Jazz. New York: Oxford University
        Press, 1956. 367 pp.
Stearns presents a general survey of the history of jazz. By offering
a documented outline of the music's development, Stearns seeks to discuss
jazz as a separate and distinct art form complete with its own aesthetic.
He begins by assessing the relationship of jazz to West African music
both in terms of the past and the present. He includes discussions of
the role of the West Indies and New Orleans, the various styles and inno-

vators, and speculations about the future of jazz. Stearns also offers psycho-sociological analyses of the "appeal of jazz" and "the role of the Negro in jazz."

M 344. STEARNS, MARSHALL and JEAN STEARNS. Jazz Dance: The Story of
American Vernacular Dance. New York: Macmillan, 1964. 464 pp.
This volume examines the history of the American vernacular dance traditions associated with jazz and jazz rhythms. Such popular dances as the
cakewalk, the lindy hop, the slop, and the twist are a few of the many
steps considered. The Stearns distinguish vernacular jazz from the modern
jazz dance techniques taught in the nation's dance studios; they note
that the latter is a blend of European and American styles that owes little
to jazz or jazz rhythms. Analyzing the parallel development of jazz dance
and jazz music, the authors begin their investigation with the African
and West Indian antecedents of jazz dance and end with a discussion of
the demise of jazz dance in the 1960s. Included is a selected list of
films and kinescopes on the subject as well as an extensive analysis section in labanotation.

M 345. STEWART, REX. Jazz Masters of the Thirties. New York: Macmillan,
1972. 223 pp.
The twenty articles by jazz trumpeter Stewart that comprise this volume
originally appeared in Down Beat and Melody Maker magazines between 1965
and 1967. Seventeen of the twenty chapters focus on the careers and music
of prominent jazz musicians and bands. The figures and groups highlighted
include the Jean Goldkette Band, Fletcher Henderson, Louis Armstrong,
Jimmy Harrison, Coleman Hawkins, Red Norvo, Duke Ellington, Sidney Catlett,
Benny Carter, and Art Tatum. In the other three chapters, Stewart takes
on three central issues in jazz history: the emergence, functions, and
impact of the recording business; the 1939 Duke Ellington tour of Europe
and the relation of the European audience and culture to American jazz
and jazz musicians; and the "cutting session" as a rite of passage or
a "test of strength" for the jazz performer.

M 346. TANNER, PAUL O. W. and MAURICE GEROW. A Study of Jazz. 1964;
Rev. ed. Dubuque, Iowa: Brown, 1981. 226 pp.
The authors discuss the evolution of jazz by examining the various performance styles of each jazz era. Based on their findings, Tanner and
Gerow attempt to present a precise definition of jazz and illustrate the
continuity that binds the many styles together into a discrete whole.
After presenting such musical elements as improvisation, rhythm, form,
and jazz interpretation, the authors provide a discussion of listening
techniques, noting what to listen for and why. They then proceed with
a survey of the history of jazz--from its African and European antecedents
to the jazz/rock innovations of the 1970s--emphasizing general style patterns rather than particular jazz practitioners. In addition, the volume
contains discussions of jazz and the film media, possible future directions,
and the impact of recent advances in electronic technology upon present
jazz practice.

M 347. TAYLOR, ARTHUR. Notes and Tones: Musician-to-Musician Interviews.
New York: Putnam, 1982. 296 pp.
This volume is a collection of "musician-to-musician" interviews, taped
between 1968 and 1972. Taylor, a drummer, seeks to provide an "insider's
view" of the jazz musician's thoughts on music, travel, religion, critics,
drugs, racism, the Black Power movement and other political strategies,
Bud Powell and Charlie Parker, the word "jazz," and a variety of other
topics. The older musicians interviewed also voice their reactions to
the "new music" and "free jazz" movements. The roster of musicians interviewed includes such artists as Miles Davis, Ornette Coleman, Philly Joe
Jones, Ron Carter, Charles Tolliver, Eddie "Lockjaw" Davis, Max Roach,

Dizzy Gillespie, Carmen McRae, Nina Simone, Tony Williams, Sonny Rollins, Don Cherry, Hampton Hawes, Kenny Clarke, Art Blakey, Hazel Scott, and Betty Carter.

M 348. TAYLOR, BILLY. Jazz Piano: A Jazz History. Dubuque, Iowa: Brown, 1982. 264 pp.
In this survey of the various styles and genres of jazz music, Taylor focuses on piano playing to illustrate the particular characteristics of each style. He begins with a discussion of the history and development of the jazz piano and the basic elements of jazz improvisation. He then considers the musical aspects of several prominent jazz styles. These include: blues-boogie, ragtime-stride, urban blues, swing and pre-bop, bebop, cool, hard bop, progressive jazz, funky jazz, third stream, post-bop, neo-gospel, abstract jazz, modal jazz, electronic jazz, and fusion.

M 349. TERKEL, STUDS. Giants of Jazz. 1957; Rev. ed. New York: Crowell, 1975. 210 pp.
Terkel has put together a collection of musical and biographical profiles of thirteen significant jazz personalities. The artists considered are Joe Oliver, Louis Armstrong, Bessie Smith, Bix Beiderbecke, Fats Waller, Duke Ellington, Count Basie, Billie Holiday, Woody Herman, Dizzy Gillespie, Charlie Parker, and John Coltrane. Each of the brief sketches begins with an examination of the artist's early years, and then isolates and discusses some particular aspect of his or her career. The profiles are based on interviews with various musicians and on existing writings of noted critics, musicians, and jazz scholars. The final chapter, entitled "Jazz Is the Music of Many," discusses the nature of jazz, including its constant propensity for change. This chapter also mentions some of the emerging leaders of the contemporary jazz scene.

M 350. TIRRO, FRANK. Jazz: A History. New York: Norton, 1977. 457 pp.
Tirro provides a general survey of the history of jazz. He incorporates recent research in cultural anthropology and American history as well as the traditional methods of musicology and music theory into his study. Almost a third of the text is devoted to jazz's pre-history. Tirro's topics are "The State of Music in the U.S. in the Late Nineteenth Century," "African Music," "Jazz Before the Name 'Jazz' Emerged," "Ragtime," and "The Blues." He devotes later chapters to "The Early Years of Jazz, 1900 to 1917"; the Jazz Age of the 1920s; the emergence of great figures in the swing era; the evolution of the substyle of bebop; the proliferation of jazz styles in the 1950s; the relation of jazz to such groups as classical musicians, the Beat poets, musical educators, and the churches; and the modern movement of "free jazz." The volume is designed to complement Martin Williams's anthology of jazz recordings, The Smithsonian Collection of Classic Jazz.

M 351. TRAVIS, DEMPSEY. An Autobiography of Black Jazz. Chicago: Urban Research Institute, 1983. 543 pp.
This book presents a survey of the history of black jazz, as related by musicians, promoters, and supporters intimately associated with the music. The discussion emphasizes the jazz activity in Chicago. An oral history, this book offers a semi-autobiographical history of jazz, which recalls lynching, segregated housing for black musicians on tour, and verbal abuse by white patrons. The "color issue" as it existed within the black community is also discussed. The interviews with white jazzmen Bud Freeman and Barret Deems provide additional information and perspective on the black jazz scene. The author examines the nightlife of the noted Chicago jazz clubs, the many vocalists, dancers, and comedians who played there, and the impact of the Jim Crow seating policy on the jazz practitioners and patrons alike.

M 352. TURNER, FREDERICK. Remembering Song: Encounters with the New
        Orleans Jazz Tradition. New York: Viking Press, 1982. 123 pp.
This book, the author warns, is not "a jazz book" in that it does not
assume "a deep familiarity with the history of jazz and thus an interest
in such details," nor is it "a complete history of New Orleans traditional
jazz." Rather it "is a book about a particular aspect of American cultural
history, the folk origins and subsequent development of a musical tradition." Turner interviews Sidney Bechet on the "hot" dances of Congo Square,
discussing the role of Buddy Bolden, whom he calls the "first folk hero"
of jazz. He traces the career of Bunk Johnson, from the "diaspora" of
New Orleans jazz performers into the North between 1910 and 1920 to the
New Orleans revival of the 1940s. In one chapter, Bill Russell, Willie
Humphrey, and Louis Keppard "remember vanished songs." The book ends
with a reflection on the life and career of Jim Robinson.

M 353. ULANOV, BARRY. A Handbook of Jazz. New York: Viking Press, 1957.
        248 pp.
Ulanov proposes to supply a basic introduction to jazz for the "old and
new" generations of jazz enthusiasts and practitioners who know very little
about each other. His study is directed toward a lay audience and the
generalized jazz-related topics include musically oriented presentations
on jazz instrumentation and the elements of jazz. In addition, there
are discussions of the "morality of jazz," the "professions of jazz,"
and the "musicians of jazz." Of special interest is a short glossary of
the jazzman's vocabulary which is included in a chapter titled "The Language of Jazz." Ulanov maintains that the influence of African music
on jazz is much less significant than it is commonly held to be. He suggests that careful listening will reveal a close association between jazz
and the folk songs of Western Europe.

M 354. ULANOV, BARRY. A History of Jazz in America. New York: Viking
        Press, 1952. 382 pp.
This history of jazz is directed toward a lay audience. Ulanov considers
a variety of topics ranging from jazz's origins to a discussion of the
"cool jazz" period of the 1950s. Much of this volume is devoted to a
series of anecdotes about the musicians and the circumstances which led
to their musical contributions. For example, much detail is provided
about the early New Orleans and Chicago bands, including information about
personnel and performance sites. A secondary goal of this text is to
establish a critical standard of evaluation for jazz. Ulanov couples
this new "standard" with a discussion of the value of criticism in the
arts.

M 355. UNTERBRINK, MARY. Jazz Women at the Keyboard. Jefferson, N.C.:
        McFarland, 1983. 184 pp.
Unterbrink discusses the often neglected lives and works of female jazz
composers and pianists. She considers prominent artists such as Marian
McPartland, Mary Lou Williams, and Joanne Brackeen, as well as such lesser
known figures as Joyce Collins, Valerie Capers, and Jane Jarvis. The
careers of these performers are presented in the context of a general
history of jazz. The author provides a biographical profile and selected
quotations from each of the artists. The final chapter, entitled "Present
Progress, Future Expectations," provides information on the current state
of women in jazz. This chapter includes details about women's jazz festivals and other institutions which support performances by women in jazz.

M 356. VULLIAMY, GRAHAM. Jazz and Blues. Boston: Routledge & Kegan
        Paul, 1982. 158 pp.
This work traces the nature and development of jazz and blues as well
as their relationship to more recent developments in rock and roll and
rhythm and blues. The author is primarily concerned with outlining the

962

overall characteristics of these musical genres and illustrating the continuity of the black music tradition within them. In addition, Vulliamy considers the transplantation of rhythm and blues to England. He notes the significant impact that American blues had on such British rock groups as The Rolling Stones, The Beatles, The Animals, and The Who. American blues, Vulliamy asserts, served as the foundation of British popular music after 1960.

M 357. **WALDO, TERRY.** This Is Ragtime. New York: Hawthorn Books, 1976. 244 pp.
Waldo examines the history of ragtime music from its origins in the Afro-American folk song to its present forms in ragtime revival movements across the country. He notes various definitions of the genre. After examining the Afro-American and European antecedents of ragtime, Waldo considers the roots of ragtime in 19th-century marches and minstrel shows. The book includes discussions of the ragtime era, the classic rag, commercial ragtime, and the state of black music in the East. In this regard, the author views the 1940s ragtime revival as a response to the swing band and the "unimaginative solo-after-solo small group" of the 1930s. In the 1950s revival, on the other hand, ragtime developed a distinctly piano-based and honky-tonk style. The final chapter presents a variety of opinions and perspectives on the role of and proper place for ragtime, the proper performance practices, and the present state of the genre.

M 358. **WHITEMAN, PAUL.** Jazz. New York: Sears, 1926. 298 pp.
Although much of this volume is autobiographical in character, it contains a wealth of information about early black jazz from a white jazzman's perspective. Whiteman claims to be the one who put jazz on a "real musical footing." The essay recounts his activity as band leader, orchestrator, and popular music impressario. In addition, this work contains Whiteman's response to his many detractors and his perspective on the strengths (rhythmic vitality) and weaknesses (raucous and crude nature) of the early black jazz idiom.

M 359. **WILLIAMS, MARTIN T.** Jazz Masters of New Orleans. New York: Macmillan, 1967. 287 pp.
This text focuses on the lives and works of several seminal figures of the New Orleans jazz tradition. Williams discusses the many careers and extra-musical factors which helped to shape early New Orleans jazz. The featured artists in this volume include Buddy Bolden, the Original Dixieland Jass Band (O.D.J.B.), Jelly Roll Morton, Joe Oliver, the New Orleans Rhythm Kings (N.O.R.K.), Sidney Bechet, Louis Armstrong, Zutty Singleton, Edward "Kid" Ory, Bunk Johnson, and Henry "Red" Allen. Williams limits the coverage of each musician either to his activity in the nascence of the New Orleans jazz tradition or to his later musical contributions in the same style. He explores many of the questions and controversies about the "true" originators of jazz and includes pertinent background information about the unique social history of New Orleans. In addition, Williams provides many details about the jazz clubs, recordings and recording sessions, and the early recording industry.

M 360. **WILLIAMS, MARTIN T.** Jazz Masters in Transition, 1957-69. New York: Macmillan, 1970. 288 pp.
This volume is a collection of reviews, interviews, album liner notes, and profiles of musicians which focuses on the jazz scene between 1957 and 1969. Williams discusses newly emerging artists as well as the activity of several more established practitioners during the period. He considers the various stylistic innovations which emerged during the decade, and offers assessments of rock and roll, "third stream," and the avant garde.

M 361. WILLIAMS, MARTIN T. The Jazz Tradition. New York: Oxford University Press, 1970. 232 pp.
The essays collected here appeared in somewhat different forms in Evergreen Review, Saturday Review, and Down Beat during the 1960s. Williams attributes the theoretical aspect of his work to the influence of Andre Hodeir. In the first essay, "A Question of Meaning," he asserts that jazz did not exist before the 20th century. He discusses such motifs as the blues scales and the twelve-bar blues, and notes the Afro-American aspects of jazz. He then describes the particular innovations and styles of Jelly Roll Morton, Louis Armstrong, Bix Beiderbecke, Coleman Hawkins, Billie Holiday, Duke Ellington, Count Basie, Lester Young, Charlie Parker, Thelonious Monk, The Modern Jazz Quartet, Sonny Rollins, Horace Silver, Miles Davis, John Coltrane, and Ornette Coleman. Williams provides discographical notes on each of the artists.

M 362. WILLIAMS, MARTIN T., ed. The Art of Jazz: Essays in the Nature and Development of Jazz. New York: Oxford University Press, 1959. 237 pp.
The twenty-one essays collected in this volume span a forty-year period (1919-59), and reflect a wide variety of approaches, methods, and perspectives in jazz circles. The authors include Williams, Ernest Ansermet, Marshall Stearns, Ross Russell, Paul Oliver, Andre Hodeir, and George Avakian. Each essay is preceded by a short preface which explains the context in which the material originally appeared. These general writings are historically significant because they recall the immediate reactions to a style or musical movement at its very onset. An example would be Ernest Ansermet's first impressions (1919) of the "new Negro music" via his contact with Sidney Bechet and Will Marion Cook's Southern Syncopated Orchestra.

M 363. WILLIAMS, MARTIN T., ed. Jazz Panorama. London: Crowell-Collier Press, 1965. 318 pp.
This book is a collection of reviews of various albums and performers which appeared in The Jazz Review between 1958 and 1962. Most prominently discussed are Jelly Roll Morton, King Oliver, Fats Waller, Art Tatum, Louis Armstrong, Bix Beiderbecke, Lester Young, Andy Kirk, Miles Davis, Jimmie Lunceford, Billie Holiday, Gil Evans, Charlie Parker, Stan Getz, Thelonious Monk, Sonny Rollins, Tony Scott, Ornette Coleman, Ray Charles, and Lightnin' Hopkins. Four pieces "introduce" Steve Lacy, Wilbur Ware, Scott La Faro, and Eric Dolphy. Reviewers include the editor, Nat Hentoff, Mait Edey, Glenn Coulter, Hsio Wen Shih, Julian "Cannonball" Adderley, Larry Gushee.

M 364. WILMER, VALERIE. As Serious as Your Life: The Story of the New Jazz. Westport, Conn.: Hill, 1980. 296 pp.
Wilmer focuses on the "new jazz," the broad creative music movement which has flourished since the 1960s. She considers the more well known innovators such as John Coltrane, Ornette Coleman, Cecil Taylor, and Sun Ra, as well as pivotal, though more obscure, figures and institutions such as Albert Ayler, Bill Dixon, Leo Smith, and the Association for the Advancement of Creative Musicians (AACM). Wilmer provides a framework for the understanding and appreciation of the more radical approaches to jazz utilized over the last two decades. She implies that the black artists' passion for musical freedom is a direct response to the social realities which delimit their personal freedom. Wilmer bases much of her work on the sentiments and statements of musicians themselves--voices rarely heard in this context. She notes the evolving interests in sound rather than melodic structure, rhythm without metric construct, and the changing attitudes toward repetition and harmony. Wilmer also includes discussions of the role of women, politics, new music collectives, and the impact of the music industry on the new movement. This work contains a biographical

section which includes many musicians not listed elsewhere. The author, a photo-journalist, also provides an extensive photographic supplement.

M 365. WILSON, JOHN STEUART. Jazz: The Transition Years, 1940-1960. New York: Appleton-Century-Crofts, 1966. 185 pp.
Wilson proposes that the post-W.W. II period of jazz history has not been sufficiently or thoroughly studied and sets out to fill in the gap between the study of the swing and bop styles and the study of the more recent experimental forms. He discusses the roles, careers, and music of many musicians, dividing his study into five chronological stages which mark radical changes in these musicians' attitudes toward and practice of jazz. The first stage of "revolution" saw the emergence of the bop music of Roy Eldridge, Dizzy Gillespie, and Charlie Parker. The second stage involved a "reaction," which took the form of the "cool" jazz of Stan Getz, Miles Davis, and others. The third stage of "reevaluation" saw a return to older and more traditional forms of jazz in the music of Lightnin' Hopkins, Ray Charles, and John Coltrane. The "intellectualization" of jazz, evident in the music of Dave Brubeck and The Modern Jazz Quartet, marked the fourth stage of development in these "two explosive decades." The fifth and final stage involved a "reacceptance" of previous jazz forms by the "revivalists." Wilson also discusses the careers and music of non-American artists in "Jazz Around the World" and the emergence of jazz into mainstream culture through television, radio, and music festivals in "Jazz and the Mass Audience."

VI. POPULAR AND ROCK

M 366. ANTHONY, GENE. The Summer of Love: Haight-Ashbury at Its Highest. Milbrae, Calif.: Celestial Arts, 1980. 184 pp.
Anthony discusses the major events, bands, musicians, poster artists, poets, spiritualists, community organizers, and street people who contributed to the 1966 "Summer of Love" in the Haight-Ashbury district of San Francisco. In particular he considers the roles of The Jefferson Airplane and The Grateful Dead in this community. The values of friendship, togetherness, sharing, and love, he says, were the basis not only of what was happening there, but of many of the cultural sentiments that swept the nation throughout the rest of the decade.

M 367. BELSITO, PETER, BOB DAVIS, and MARIAN KESTER. Street Art: The Punk Poster in San Francisco, 1977-1981. San Francisco: Last Gasp, 1981. 128 pp.
This is a collection of posters distributed on the streets of San Francisco to advertise performances by local bands. Each reproduction is accompanied by a title, the name of the artist, and the year. The text comments on the bands, their musical and social philosophies, and the nature of youth rebellion. The authors see the posters as symbols of the self-consciously transient nature of the punk movement, whose members tend to portray themselves as losers constantly seeking fun because it is forbidden by society.

M 368. BELZ, CARL. The Story of Rock. 1969; Rev. ed. New York: Oxford University Press, 1972. 286 pp.
In this general history of rock music, Belz places rock in the long tradition of folk art in America. Centrally concerned with the aesthetic distinctions between folk art, fine art, and popular art, Belz divides his history into four chronological periods. Examining the beginning of rock (1954-56), he describes the sources of rock in rhythm and blues and country and western, the careers of Bill Haley and Elvis Presley,

the roles of radio and disc jockeys, and the record industry. The years of "expansion" (1957-63) saw the emergence of Chuck Berry as the "Folk Poet of the Fifties," the spread of rockabilly, the fad of the twist, the surfing scene, and the Payola Hearings of 1959-60. The period of the "maturity" of rock (1964-68) witnessed the influx and predominance of British rock, the heyday of Bob Dylan, the revival of rhythm and blues, and the emergence of the "San Francisco scene." Belz describes the period from 1969 to 1971 as "troubled." He includes a selected discography for the years 1953-71.

M 369. BRAUN, D. DUANE. Toward a Theory of Popular Culture: The Sociology and History of American Music and Dance, 1920-1968. Ann Arbor, Mich.: Ann Arbor Publishers, 1969. 165 pp.
Braun's essay treats the social dynamics of the history of musical tastes and fads, and argues for the significance of contributions from individuals as opposed to a theory drawing on "societal reflection." Two chapters focus on the formation, legitimization, and fragmentation of the rock culture. These chapters relate changes in music and dance to such cultural developments as the white singers' imitation of black musical style and such political developments as the Civil Rights Movement and the Vietnam War. Braun finds three common elements, or stages, for all innovations in music and dance: humble origins, legitimization by white middle and upper classes, and institutionalization in the culture.

M 370. BROWN, CHARLES T. The Art of Rock and Roll. Englewood Cliffs, N.J.: Prentice-Hall, 1983. 205 pp.
Brown begins by stating that rock music is a legitimate art form whose roots are in American folk, jazz, and popular music. He traces the history of rock from the arrival of African slaves through the Afro-American music of the 19th century, the relation of rock to jazz, and rock's formal appearance in the early 1950s. Such major musicians as Elvis Presley, Bill Haley, and The Beatles are discussed as representative of specific movements. Brown develops a model for intelligently listening to music and making legitimate statements about it, following each chapter with a recommended listening list. He also analyzes the relationship between music and society, contending that music is a reflection of society's values and concerns.

M 371. BUSNAR, GENE. It's Rock 'n' Roll. New York: Wanderer Books, 1979. 247 pp.
Busnar takes the phenomenon of the 1970s nostalgia for the 1950s as his point of departure for discussing the real 1950s era and its various rock and roll styles: Northern band music (Bill Haley and the Comets), New Orleans (Lloyd Price, Shirley and Lee, Professor Longhair, Fats Domino, Little Richard, and Cajun and Creole influences on this style), rockabilly (Carl Perkins, Elvis Presley, Jerry Lee Lewis, and Buddy Holly), Chicago-style (Chuck Berry, Bo Diddley, and the influences of Muddy Waters and Howlin' Wolf), vocal group music (The Platters, The Shirelles, and The Orioles), and soul (The Isley Brothers, Ray Charles). The period of 1954-63 he calls the "Rock 'n' Roll Years," and he proceeds year by year to discuss the trends, politics, and fads of that period, including the phenomenon of "teen idols" and Dick Clark's "American Bandstand."

M 372. CHAPPLE, STEVE and REEBEE GAROFALO. Rock 'n' Roll Is Here to Pay. Chicago: Nelson-Hall, 1977. 354 pp.
The authors claim that "this book is meant to be a reasonably comprehensive listing of the pop music industry in America and at the same time a muckraking analysis of the way popular culture is manhandled in corporate society." Included among the seven chapters are "Black Roots, White Fruits: Racism in the Music Industry," "Long Hard Climb: Women in Rock," and discussions of the financial aspects of the Monterey Pop and Woodstock

Festivals. The authors provide a comprehensive chart of pop music styles and trends.

M 373. CHRISTGAU, ROBERT. Any Old Way You Choose It: Rock and Other Pop Music, 1967-1973. Baltimore, Md.: Penguin Books, 1973. 330 pp.
This volume is a compilation of essays, most of which were first published in The Village Voice and Newsday. The essays present Christgau's commentary on the figures, events, issues, and trends of rock music in the late 1960s and early 1970s. Christgau also includes his "Consumer Guide" feature from both papers, a series of brief and often strongly opinionated reviews, with letter grades, of various albums.

M 374. COHN, NIK. Rock from the Beginning. Briarcliff Manor, N.Y.: Stein & Day, 1969. 256 pp.
Cohn's volume, one of the first histories of rock music, chronicles musical developments in England and America from the early 1950s to the late 1960s. The author devotes a chapter each to major artists, eras, locations, and styles. Among the artists discussed are Bill Haley, Elvis Presley, Eddie Cochran, P. J. Proby, The Beatles, The Rolling Stones, Bob Dylan, and The Who. Cohn discusses separate "eras" that include "the beginning," and music in America after 1960, and in London in 1964-65. The locations he focuses on are Britain and California. Styles treated are Spectorsound, soul, British rhythm and blues, folk rock, and superpop.

M 375. DALLAS, KARL. Singers of an Empty Day: Last Sacraments for the Superstars. Birkenhead, England: Kahn & Averill, 1971. 208 pp.
Dallas examines the phenomenon of superstardom by which rock stars are created and often destroyed. The book focuses on the problems rock stars face in a culture that makes them into mythical heroes. Dallas uses the lives and careers of such entertainers as Janis Joplin, Jimi Hendrix, Bob Dylan, and John Lennon to illustrate the superstar's dilemma, the impossible expectations of fans, the star's need for a personal relationship with the audience, and the often necessary sacrifice of a meaningful personal life. Dallas gives particular attention to the careers of Joplin and Hendrix, for whom the dilemma proved fatal. Mick Jagger's career is highlighted as an example of a rock star's survival.

M 376. DENISOFF, SERGE. Solid Gold: The Popular Record Industry. New Brunswick, N.J.: Transaction Books, 1975. 504 pp.
Denisoff examines the combination of social trends, promotional strategies, and musical and performance styles that contribute to the making of a hit record or a star performer. The popularity of Elton John in the early 1970s is used as a case study. Denisoff traces the development of a musical product from its dissemination by the recording industry to its final reception by the public. He demonstrates how various audiences are defined by age, race, and class, and how a performer's popularity is based on a new system of the music industry's recruiting audiences rather than on direct audience response.

M 377. DENISOFF, SERGE and RICHARD A. PETERSON, eds. The Sounds of Social Change: Studies in Popular Culture. Skokie, Ill.: Rand McNally, 1972. 332 pp.
This anthology collects twenty-five scholarly and journalistic essays on the social context and use of popular music, which is broadly defined to include jazz, country, soul, Tin Pan Alley, and rock. The emphasis is on the song as protest, propaganda, and social influence. Selections range from articles from the American Journal of Sociology to polemics by Spiro Agnew and the John Birch Society; most were written in the late 1960s or early 1970s. The editors provide introductions to the six sections which examine music as protest, music in social movements, rock, changing musical tastes, musicians, and the music industry.

M 378. **DENNISON, SAM.** Scandalize My Name: Black Imagery in American Popular Music. New York: Garland, 1982. 594 pp.
This is a study of the predominantly racist images of blacks presented in American popular music. It begins with very early, pre-minstrel songs and continues to the present day, although over half of the book deals with pre-1900 songs. The social, political, psychological, economic, and musical causes and consequences of these images are studied. Appendices include a discussion of Charles Mathews and American minstrelsy and an explanation of the methods used in the study. Dennison quotes extensively from the song lyrics which comprise about half of the text.

M 379. **DRANOV, PAULA.** Inside the Music Publishing Industry. White Plains, N.Y.: Knowledge Industry, 1980. 185 pp.
Dranov's study provides a contemporary account of the size, scope, structure, and function of the music publishing industry. Currently overshadowed by recording companies, the publishing industry now chiefly serves as the monitor of performance royalties. Dranov also covers marketing and demographic factors that presently shape the industry. These factors are presented in tabular form as well as incorporated into the author's discussions. Dranov includes a list of the leading music publishers.

M 380. **EISEN, JONATHAN,** ed. The Age of Rock: Sounds of the American Cultural Revolution. New York: Vintage Books, 1969. 388 pp.
This collection of essays about the rock music and culture of the late 1960s reprints pieces that originally appeared between 1966 and 1969. The first essays posit a sociology of rock that is tied to the theories of Marshall McLuhan: Nat Hentoff, H. F. Mooney, Burton Wolfe, Stanley Booth, and Ralph Gleason trace significant shifts in the social structure which have affected rock music. Most of the rest of the essays discuss such performers and groups as The Rolling Stones, The Beatles, Joan Baez, Bob Dylan, Frank Zappa, James Brown, Joni Mitchell, and Jim Morrison. The essayists include Richard Farina, Jon Landau, Robert Christgau, Murray Kempton, Ned Rorem, Richard Poirier, Tom Wolfe, Joan Didion, and Harry Shearer. The volume also includes an interview with Frank Zappa, who discusses his politics, message, and methods.

M 381. **EISEN, JONATHAN,** ed. The Age of Rock, 2: Sights and Sounds in the American Cultural Revolution. New York: Vintage Books, 1970. 339 pp.
Similar to Eisen's first compilation of essays (see M 380), this volume gathers together forty-two pieces by a wide range of writers including Andy Warhol, George Paul Csicsery, T. Proctor Lippincott, Ian Whitcomb, Nick Browne, Geoffrey Canon, A. Martynova, J. Oliphant, Walter Breen, Peter Stampfel, Lenny Kaye, and Richard Meltzer. The stated object is "to get a handle on the culture generally, the rock culture more specifically." Eisen warns that "there is no central point," to this collage of generally interrelated viewpoints. Breen writes about types of experience in music, religion, and drug use; Csicsery about the Altamont concert; Canon about Bob Dylan; Meltzer about Pythagorus and Jimi Hendrix; Warhol interviews Meltzer. Also included are a New York Times article about rock in the schools, and a New York Daily News article about the tragedy of Altamont.

M 382. **EISEN, JONATHAN,** ed. Altamont: Death of Innocence in the Woodstock Nation. New York: Avon Books, 1970. 272 pp.
This anthology presents a number of views about the disastrous free Rolling Stones concert at the Altamont Speedway in Livermore, California, in 1969. At this concert, four people died, one of whom was beaten to death by The Hell's Angels. Eisen presents the Altamont case as the focal point for a discussion of identity and social crisis among American youth. The essays deal with the social and political situations as contexts for

what happened at the concert. The book draws together a range of views and a wealth of anecdotes, including an interview with Sonny Barger, the Hell's Angels's leader at the time.

M 383. ESCOTT, COLIN and MARTIN HAWKINS. Sun Records: The Brief History of the Legendary Record Label. 1975; Rev. ed. New York: Quick Fox, 1980. 184 pp.
Originally published under the title, Catalyst: The Sun Records Story, this book examines the social environment that gave rise to modern popular music, and traces the history of Sun Records, one of the most important of the independent companies. The history centers on Elvis Presley's early years. Presley was discovered in Sam Phillips's search for a new sound, blending country with rhythm and blues. The nature of performances, the relationships between Phillips and the artists, and the reasons for the decline of the company are explored. The authors examine the attitudes of performers as they were shaped by their environment and background, considering, among other questions, race relations and the ambivalence of Jerry Lee Lewis toward religion. Artists discussed are Carl Perkins, Carl Mann, Johnny Cash, Billy Riley, Malcom Yelvington, Booker T, Sleepy La Beef, Charlie Feathers, Onie Wheeler, Jerry Lee Lewis, and Ray Smith. Appendices include a list of all records released on the Sun, Flip, and Phillips International labels; a list of current Sun Albums; a list of other Memphis record labels; and a discography.

M 384. EWEN, DAVID. All the Years of Popular Music. Englewood Cliffs, N.J.: Prentice-Hall, 1977. 850 pp.
Ewen attempts to capture "the entire world of popular music in all of its varied facets within a single volume." The numerous styles and fields discussed include: ballads and war songs, instrumental and novelty songs, songs of Tin Pan Alley, folk songs, songs of the labor movement, ragtime, hillbilly music, country-western, symphonic jazz, vaudeville operettas, and rock musicals. Topics peripheral to music are also covered, from the history of the Roseland Ballroom to case studies in musical plagiarism to the histories of various musical awards. In his comprehensive history, covering the years 1620 to the present, Ewen also discusses the careers of popular musicians and composers, as well as the places where they congregated.

M 385. EWEN, DAVID. Great Men of American Popular Song: The History of the American Popular Song Told Through the Lives, Careers, Achievements, and Personalities of Its Foremost Composers and Lyricists--From William Billings of the Revolutionary War Through Bob Dylan, Johnny Cash, and Burt Bacharach. 1970; Rev. ed. Englewood Cliffs, N.J.: Prentice-Hall, 1972. 404 pp.
Ewen presents a broad spectrum of American popular songwriters in an effort "to portray a complete picture of the American popular song as seen through the careers of its creators." He briefly analyzes their lives and careers, claiming that "woven into the texture of these biographies are the social and political milieus that often inspired the songwriting activities." Each of the approximately thirty periods presented is seen through one to three representative artists: for example, Dan Emmett represents "Songs of the Blackface Minstrel"; George M. Cohan represents "Songs from Musical Comedy"; Gershwin, Rodgers and Hart, and Cole Porter represent "Songs of the 1920s and 1930s"; and Bob Dylan represents "Songs of Protest."

M 386. EWEN, DAVID. Men of Popular Music. Chicago: Ziff-Davis, 1944. 212 pp.
This study traces the evolution of American popular music by focusing on the careers and achievements of fifteen significant composers and artists. Ewen contends that the rise of a uniquely American popular music corresponds with the growth of a national consciousness dating from the

turn of the century, and the complexity of this music reflects the economic, social, and political growth of the period. The fifteen representative composers are King Oliver, Irving Berlin, Louis Armstrong, W. C. Handy, Meade Lux Lewis, Duke Ellington, Paul Whiteman, Ferde Grofe, George Gershwin, Jerome Kern, Richard Rodgers, Lorenz Hart, Cole Porter, Benny Goodman, and Raymond Scott.

M 387. EWING, GEORGE W. The Well-Tempered Lyre: Song and Verse of the Temperance Movement. Dallas, Tex.: Southern Methodist University Press, 1977. 298 pp.
Ewing's book, a history of the temperance movement in song and verse, is "an attempt to rescue from oblivion an interesting utterance of an age now irrevocably past." The last chapter devotes itself to songs depicting the "evils" of alcohol abuse.

M 388. FAULKNER, ROBERT R. Hollywood Studio Musicians: Their Work and Careers in the Recording Industry. Chicago: Atherton, 1971. 218 pp.
This is a sociological study of the small group of free-lance musicians working in the film industry. The work describes the ways in which these musicians are used in film production and the division of labor within the studio. The author discusses the conflict faced by young studio musicians between artistic aspirations and commercial career choices. Through interviews, musicians present their responses to their profession, focusing on their personal dignity in the face of exploitation and their financial concerns.

M 389. FAULKNER, ROBERT R. Music on Demand: Composers and Careers in the Hollywood Film Industry. New Brunswick, N.J.: Transaction Books, 1983. 281 pp.
Faulkner's purpose in this volume is threefold: to provide an ethnographic profile of the musicians in the film industry; to analyze the film industry's social structure, with a particular focus on transactions between free lancers and filmmakers; and to "articulate a perspective on commercial work as a subjective experience." The author's interest lies in the processes and structures of film music. The volume is arranged chronologically. The early chapters are devoted to the struggles of newcomers to the field. Subsequent chapters demonstrate the neophyte's adaptation to the requirements of the industry. Faulkner's emphasis is on an overall pattern of social and professional organization rather than on the lives and careers of particular composers. The final chapter, "Big Hollywood, Little Hollywood," demonstrates the interaction between the industry's "inner circles" and its "periphery" through an analysis of the distribution of industry credits, connections, and rewards, all of which tend to exclude all but certain groups within that "periphery."

M 390. FAWCETT, ANTHONY. California Rock, California Sound: The Music of Los Angeles and Southern California. Los Angeles, Calif.: Reed Books, 1978. 160 pp.
This book discusses the experiences and musical growth of some of the major performers and groups who emerged from the Southern California region in the 1960s and 1970s. Those included are Crosby, Stills, and Nash, Neil Young, Joni Mitchell, Jackson Browne, America, Linda Ronstadt, The Eagles, J. D. Souther, Karla Bonoff, and Warren Zevon. Fawcett emphasizes the influence of the Los Angeles area on the music of these artists. The text is based on extensive interviews, and seeks insights into the artists' personalities and lifestyles.

M 391. **FRITH, SIMON.** Sound Effects: Youth, Leisure and the Politics
of Rock'n'Roll. New York: Pantheon Books, 1981. 294 pp.
Frith presents a sociological analysis of rock music as a mass medium
aimed at a youth market. He explores the "relationship between music
as a means of popular expression and music as a means of making money."
In Part One, "Rock Meanings," Frith examines the roots of rock and its
relation to mass culture. In Part Two, "Rock Production," Frith analyzes
the recording industry's relationship to its market and artists, and other
commercial aspects of record production. In Part Three, "Youth," he examines what music means to the young. Frith concludes that rock is "capitalist music," which "draws its meanings from the relationships of capitalist production."

M 392. **GILBERT, DOUGLAS.** Lost Chords: The Diverting Story of American
Popular Songs. Garden City, N.Y.: Doubleday, Doran, 1942.
377 pp.
Gilbert focuses on the popular song from the Civil War to W.W. I. He
provides a survey of the subjects and musical styles of approximately
500 songs, prints the lyrics of about 100 of these, and places them in
the context of an anecdotal social history. Brief discussions of American
popular songs between the World Wars are included. Gilbert laments the
passing of America as a "melodic nation," expressing contempt for the
modern "rhythmic nation" of swing and its passive audience.

M 393. **GILLETT, CHARLIE.** Making Tracks: Atlantic Records and the Growth
of a Multi-Billion-Dollar Industry. New York: Dutton, 1975.
305 pp.
Gillett traces the development of Atlantic Records from its beginnings
as a jazz label in the late 1940s to its growth into a major record company.
The story is told through interviews with such key personnel as producer
and vice-president Jerry Wexler and songwriters Jerry Leiber and Mike
Stoller. Although he is sometimes critical of Atlantic's business tactics,
Gillett attributes the success of the company primarily to its enlightened
management.

M 394. **GILLETT, CHARLIE.** The Sound of the City: The Rise of Rock and
Roll. 1970; Rev. ed. New York: Pantheon Books, 1983. 515 pp.
Gillett sets out to analyze rock in the context of urban society, claiming
that rock is inherently an urban musical expression which celebrates and
reproduces the characteristics of city life. The author maintains and
demonstrates that "audiences or creators can determine the content of
a popular art communicated through mass media [because the] businessmen
who mediate between the audience and the creator can be forced by either
to accept a new style." Accordingly, he continues by showing how regional
musical dialects were integrated as potent influences into the national
medium of rock and roll. Using the social theory of Talcott Parsons,
Gillett explains that minority groups such as blacks were at first
"excluded" from the mainstream of society, and thus from its media. Later,
favored minority elements were "assimilated" into white culture by a few
black singers who sang like whites and a few white singers who sang black
songs. Finally, as the mainstream audience took interest in black culture,
the white media were forced to "include" black music with all its "distinctive characteristics." At the same time, audiences required more
honest, "real" representations of life and love, and these changes together
made rock and roll different from previous pop music forms. Gillett also
examines the roles and fortunes of the major and independent record labels
and their struggle to cope with changing tastes and values in their audiences.

M 395. **GOLDBERG, ISAAC.** <u>Tin Pan Alley</u>: A <u>Chronicle of American Popu-
    lar Music</u>. 1930; Rev. ed. New York: Ungar, 1961. 371 pp.
Goldberg begins his account with a discussion of American popular music's
roots in Puritan New England. The volume continues with chapters devoted
to minstrelsy, the transformation of minstrelsy to vaudeville, and the
roots of Tin Pan Alley music in sentimental ballads and ragtime. Goldberg
also traces the rise of musical comedy during the 1890s in a discussion
of the works of John Philip Sousa, Reginald de Koven, and Victor Herbert.
The chronicle continues with examinations of "ballyhoo," or how popular
songs were marketed; the period between the Spanish-American War and W.W.
I which saw the rise of jazz as an influence on popular music; the dominance of jazz following W.W. I; and the influence of the music associated
with motion pictures. The volume concludes with a supplement, "From Sweet
and Swing to Rock 'n' Roll," which discusses rock's roots in American
popular music.

M 396. **GOLDMAN, ALBERT.** <u>Freakshow</u>: <u>The Rocksoulbluesjazzsickjewblack-
    humorsexpoppsych Gig and Other Scenes from the Counter-Culture</u>.
    New York: Atheneum, 1971. 387 pp.
This volume is a collection of Goldman's 1960s essays from various papers
and magazines, including <u>The New Republic</u>, <u>Life</u>, and <u>The New York Times</u>.
In his section on rock, Goldman covers some of the major social, musical,
stylistic, financial, and psychological aspects of the music. He includes
pieces on the emergence of rock, rock theater, soul, the blues, "nostalgia"
in the rock revival, various portraits of individual performers, and the
death of rock in the 1970s with the separation of The Beatles, the "orgies"
of Mick Jagger, and the deaths of Janis Joplin and Jimi Hendrix. Other
sections of the book address "Sick Jew Black Humor," "Jazz: The Art that
Came in From the Cold," and what Goldman calls "Sexpoppsych."

M 397. **GROSSMAN, LOYD.** <u>A Social History of Rock Music</u>: <u>From the Greasers
    to Glitter Rock</u>. New York: McKay, 1976. 150 pp.
Grossman's analytic survey examines rock's impact on fashion, language,
art, sexual and political attitudes, and the social situation in America
between 1954 and the mid-1970s. He discusses hundreds of individuals
and groups briefly, but details only those whom he feels were significant
in the evolution of rock in this period (such as Elvis Presley, Chuck
Berry, The Beatles, The Rolling Stones, The Who, The Yardbirds, Cream,
Bob Dylan, The Jefferson Airplane, Janis Joplin, Led Zeppelin, Jimi Hendrix,
and Traffic). Grossman's topics include "Teen Culture in the Eisenhower
Era," "Pop Style and Fashion Renaissance," "Woodstock Nation Sells Out,"
"The New Transatlantic Style," "Women in Rock," and "Rock and Roll Technol-
ogy."

M 398. **GURALNICK, PETER.** <u>Feel Like Going Home</u>: <u>Portraits in Blues and
    Rock and Roll</u>. New York: Dutton, 1971. 222 pp.
This series of profiles portrays a progression of musical styles from
country blues to rock and roll. The early period of blues is presented
through profiles of Blind Lemon Jefferson, Charley Patton, Son House,
Robert Johnson, and Tommy Johnson. The later period of blues is seen
through portraits of Muddy Waters, Johnny Shines, Skip James, Robert Pete
Williams, and Howlin' Wolf, while rock and roll is shown through portraits
of Jerry Lee Lewis and Charlie Rich. Guralnick emphasizes the conflicts
between commercial success and authentic feelings, and he includes a commentary on the importance of the record industry in a section on Sam
Phillips and the Chess family.

M 399. GURALNICK, PETER. Lost Highways: Journeys and Arrivals of American
        Musicians. Boston: Godine, 1979. 362 pp.
This volume is a biographical history of the blues, country, and rock.
In a series of essays about such individual performers as Ernest Tubb,
Hank Snow, Deford Bailey, Bobby Bland, Charlie Rich, Waylon Jennings,
Merle Haggard, Howlin' Wolf, Otis Spann, and Big Joe Turner, Guralnick
develops definitions of the three genres. This collection of twenty essays
is centered on his idea of "the road" as a controlling metaphor in the
lives and music of these performers: "For each . . . the road has become
journey, arrival, process, definition." He also notes the effects of
the music business on the artists' lives and careers. A selective discography is included.

M 400. HAMM, CHARLES. Yesterdays: Popular Song in America. New York:
        Norton, 1979. 533 pp.
Hamm charts the history of the American popular song from the 18th century
to the mid-1970s. In his discussion of these songs, which focuses on
sheet music rather than on live or recorded examples, Hamm stresses the
primacy of old world influences, as in his considerations of "British
Concert and Stage Music in Early America," and the importation of Irish
and Scottish melodies, Italian operatic songs, and German song in the
19th century. Hamm expands on minstrelsy as the genesis of native American songwriting: one chapter deals entirely with Stephen Foster, followed
by sections on the Civil War and post-war songs. His study of the 20th
century focuses on Tin Pan Alley. Hamm deals briefly with rock as a fusion
of traditional musical forms and the expression of social turmoil. Seven
appendices provide "Most Popular Song" lists for several periods between
1800 to "Your Hit Parade" (1935-1958).

M 401. HENDLER, HERB. Year by Year in the Rock Era: Events and Conditions
        Shaping the Rock Generations That Reshaped America. Westport,
        Conn.: Greenwood Press, 1983. 350 pp.
Hendler examines the years 1955 to 1981 in a year-by-year analysis of
rock music and the various forces influencing artistic creation. Each
year's presentation covers the main popular artists, the top hits, and
the news that influenced songwriting. Details about the lifestyles current
in each year are presented with the intention of placing the year's music
in its sociological context.

M 402. HIRSCH, PAUL MORRIS. The Structure of the Popular Music Indus-
        try: The Filtering Process by Which Records Are Pre-Selected
        for Consumption. Ann Arbor: University of Michigan, Institute
        for Social Research, 1969. 72 pp.
Hirsch discusses the disc-jockey-and-hit-records formula for the promotion
of music that has influenced the development of the American system of
record production and distribution. This investigation of the preselection
system in the record industry breaks down the organization of the industry
into six stages of creation, filtration, and consumption.

M 403. HOPKINS, JERRY. Festival! The Book of American Music Celebrations.
        New York: Macmillan, 1970. 191 pp.
Hopkins sees the period 1965-69 as the era of the great rock festivals,
and he analyzes its principal events: the Newport Folk Festival, Woodstock,
the Monterey Jazz Festival, the Ann Arbor Blues Festival, and the Big
Sur Folk Festival, among others. Hopkins sees the Altamont concert, which
occurred during the writing of this book, as the end of the Festival tradition. Historical background information and sociological commentary
accompany the recollections of various observers and descriptions of organizational strategies.

M 404. HOPKINS, JERRY. The Rock Story. New York: Signet, 1970.
222 pp.
Hopkins's popular history of rock music ranges from 1954 to 1968 and is
divided into two sections. The first section is a general history of
rock which ranges from the emergence of the blues to the popularity of
The Doors. Hopkins emphasizes the "pop" aspect of rock, offering, for
example, an anecdotal history of Dick Clark's "American Bandstand" in
the chapter titled "The Other Philadelphia Story." The second section
is a collection of essays which focuses on various aspects of the rock
and roll world through detailed portraits of individual careers. "The
Story of a Hit" describes Aretha Franklin's "I Never Loved a Man." "Radio:
This Is Where It's Happening" analyzes the role of radio through the
description of the career of an underground disc-jockey. "My God, The
Rock Star" focuses on the social world of the groupie. The dynamics of
rock group membership are detailed in a case history of Buffalo Springfield.

M 405. KANTER, KENNETH AARON. The Jews on Tin Pan Alley: The Jewish
Contribution to American Popular Music, 1830-1940. New York:
KTAV, 1982. 226 pp.
Kanter claims that "both as a business and as an expression of talent
and creative artistry, American popular music was in large part shaped
and formed by Jews." The Jewish domination of the music business is evi-
denced by the careers of the songwriters Richard Rodgers and Oscar
Hammerstein, Irving Berlin, Lorenz Hart, Jerome Kern, George and Ira
Gershwin, Irving Caesar, Charles K. Harris, Henry Russell, and Monroe
Rosenfeld. Kanter also focuses on the careers of the Jews involved in
the music publishing industry centered in what came to be known as Tin
Pan Alley, including M. Witmark, Joseph Stern, Shapiro and Bernstein,
Harry Von Tilzer, and Leo Feist.

M 406. LAING, DAVE. The Sound of Our Time. Chicago: Quadrangle Books,
1970. 198 pp.
This volume is a historical survey of rock music from its roots in blues
and folk music through its development in the 1960s. The first part emphasizes the effects of the mass media upon the structure of popular music
in the 20th century. The rise of rock in the late 1950s is discussed
in the second part. The third part discusses the careers and musical
development of such major artists and groups as The Beatles, The Who,
and Bob Dylan. In the last section, "Towards a Theoretical Framework,"
Laing uses semiological theory to examine the cultural significance of
rock music and the contradiction evident in the dual status of pop music
as art form and industrial product.

M 407. LANDAU, JON. It's Too Late to Stop Now: A Rock and Roll Journal.
San Francisco: Straight Arrow Books, 1972. 227 pp.
Landau's volume is a collection of his journalistic and critical writings,
many originally published in Rolling Stone between 1966 and 1971. Landau
agrees with other contemporary writers that rock is properly a folk music,
performed and listened to by the same group of people. At the end of
the five years represented by these essays, Landau states that he sees
the business of creating rock stars as having become too routine and formu-
laic. The book is divided into two sections: "White Rock" and "Black
Rock." In the former, he writes about Bob Dylan, Creedence Clearwater
Revival, Van Morrison, Joni Mitchell, Paul Simon, The Grateful Dead, and
The Band. In the latter, the articles cover Otis Redding, B. B. King,
Muddy Waters, Aretha Franklin, Ray Charles, King Curtis, Valerie Simpson,
Sly and the Family Stone, Wilson Pickett, and the Motown record label.
Landau also discusses "Rock and Art," music engineering, and the death
of Janis Joplin.

M 408. LEVY, LESTER S. Flashes of Merriment: A Century of Humorous Songs
        in America, 1805-1905. Norman: University of Oklahoma Press,
        1971. 370 pp.
Levy examines the humorous songs that flourished during the 19th century
for their content and musical composition. He locates the roots of these
American songs in English popular music as well as in European classical
music. The volume is arranged by chapters devoted to the humorous tale
set to music, the comic situation of awkward "boy and girl" relationships,
the comic use of unassimilated foreign accents, and the nonsense song
with silly or unintelligible punch lines. Throughout, Levy demonstrates
the links between particular songs and various social and political events
and movements of their time. He also includes the lyrics and music for
many of the songs discussed.

M 409. LEVY, LESTER S. Give Me Yesterday: American History in Song,
        1890-1920. Norman: University of Oklahoma Press, 1975.
        420 pp.
In this volume, Levy examines the record of historical and cultural events
in American popular music. There are ten sections in the book, each
devoted to a particular type of song. Among the topics treated in these
essays are show business figures, modes of transportation, Presidents,
other political figures, women and femininity, entertainment events, progress, and general political and social trends. The volume includes the
lyrics and music for many of the songs discussed.

M 410. LEVY, LESTER S. Grace Notes in American History: Popular Sheet
        Music from 1820 to 1900. Norman: University of Oklahoma Press,
        1967. 410 pp.
Levy devotes his book to what he calls the "grace notes" of American
history—that is, the commentary of the "crowds," especially as evidenced
in popular sheet music. He stresses the importance of the popular song
as a medium of expression and communication, which reflects the mass opinion of contemporary issues and events. The songs are divided into two
groups: those concerning mores, and those concerning history. From these
he summarizes lyrical commentaries on such social phenomena and topics
as popular heroes, figures of ridicule, movements, female dress, drinking
and temperance, Presidents and candidates, transport, Indians, disasters,
and the Civil War. The music itself is not discussed. The book is illustrated with ninety-four plates of sheet music covers, and many lyrics
and melodies are reprinted.

M 411. MABEY, RICHARD. The Pop Process. London: Hutchinson Educational,
        1969. 190 pp.
Mabey's analysis of the social significance of the pop scene, its roots,
its music, its fashions, its heroes, and its subcultures deals primarily
with the London scene, but it does attend to the U.S. in a comparative
framework. After a brief consideration of the roots of pop culture, Mabey
examines the manner in which fashions and trends in the pop music scene
are propagated and spread by both the "audiences" and the "operators."
He includes a case history of Bob Dylan as a popular protest musician
who fuses moral allegory with the fundamental personal sense and "catch-
phrase" structure of the popular song. Mabey concludes that the cumulative
effect of the pop scene is "the consolidation of a sort of pop geist,
that exaggerates the importance of social change, activity, and exposure,
and persistently sabotages any growth toward thoughtfulness."

M 412. MARCUS, GREIL. Mystery Train: Images of America in Rock 'n' Roll
        Music. New York: Dutton, 1975. 275 pp.
This study of rock music focuses on six artists and bands: the "ancestors"
of rock, Robert Johnson and Harmonica Frank; and the "inheritors" of rock,
The Band, Sly and the Family Stone, Randy Newman, and Elvis Presley.

Marcus writes that his study "is not a history, nor a purely musical analysis, nor a set of personality profiles," but rather "an attempt to broaden
the context in which the music is heard; to deal with rock and roll not
as youth culture, or counter-culture, but simply as American culture."
He defines rock and roll as a democratic art in which the best performers
both draw on and change the shared experience of popular culture. The
originators of rock and roll were a handful of people who broke through
musical and social restrictions to become part of a radical, almost transcendental, movement. An extensive discography is appended.

M 413. MARCUS, GREIL, ed. Rock and Roll Will Stand. Boston: Beacon
        Press, 1969. 182 pp.
This volume is a collection of essays by various writers from the Berkeley
area during the 1960s. Longer essays explore, among other topics, the
conscious use of metaphor in rock music, the "New Mythology," the politics
of The Rolling Stones, early rhythm and blues music, and the history of
the foundation of Country Joe and The Fish. Shorter pieces offer various
impressions of concerts and other rock-related experiences in The Bay
area. Five of the twenty essays are written by Marcus; other authors
include Mike Daly, Stewart Kessler, Steve Strauss, and Sandy Darlington.

M 414. MARCUS, GREIL, ed. Stranded: Rock and Roll for a Desert Island.
        New York: Knopf, 1979. 303 pp.
This book collects essays by twenty journalists and critics on their favorite records. The authors argue for the merit of importance of such
diverse performers as The Ronettes, The Ramones, Captain Beefheart, Little
Willie John, and The New York Dolls. They emphasize neglected early figures and later experimenters. Marcus concludes with fifty pages annotating
several hundred of his own favorite albums. In addition to Marcus, the
writers include Nick Tosches, Simon Frith, Ellen Willis, Robert Christgau,
and John Rockwell. Among the artists discussed are The Kinks, Bruce
Springsteen, The Velvet Underground, Jackson Browne, Huey "Piano" Smith,
Neil Young, Van Morrison, Linda Ronstadt, and the "5" Royales.

M 415. McCUTCHEON, LYNN ELLIS. Rhythm and Blues: An Experience and Adven-
        ture in Its Origin and Development. Arlington, Va.: Beatty,
        1971. 306 pp.
McCutcheon examines the development of the rhythm and blues strain of
black popular music, describing three eras: the "Pioneer" era from 1946
to 1956, the "Rock and Roll" era from 1955 to 1963, and the "Soul" era
from 1964 to 1971. The first section traces the origins of rhythm and
blues and distinguishes the types of the music. The second presents a
chronological account of record companies, artists, records, and events.
The final part presents major artists, and the conclusion looks at rhythm
and blues music in the 1970s.

M 416. MILLER, JIM, ed. The Rolling Stone Illustrated History of Rock
        & Roll. New York: Rolling Stone, 1980. 474 pp.
This history of rock and roll is a collection of articles by the Rolling
Stone rock critics, including Robert Palmer, Peter Guralnick, Nik Cohn,
Griel Marcus, Jon Landau, Dave Marsh, Jim Miller, John Rockwell, and Robert
Christgau. Chronicling the growth of rock and roll from a scandal to
an important movement to a multi-billion dollar industry, the forty-two
short articles focus on individual performers from Elvis Presley to Aretha
Franklin to Elvis Costello, and on groups from the Everly Brothers to
The Doors to Steely Dan. Included also are such trends and movements
as rockabilly, the "rise of Top 40 AM," "girl groups," the blues revival,
"proto-punk" rock, rock festivals, art rock, jazz rock, disco, New Wave,
and reggae. Each article includes a discography.

M 417. MORSE, DAVID. Motown and the Arrival of Black Music. New York:
        Macmillan, 1971. 143 pp.
Morse describes the "Motown Sound," as engineered by Berry Gordy's independent Detroit record company, as the prototype of black soul music geared
to the tastes and demands of the national, predominately white audience.
He defines Motown music as "essentially a bridge between gospel and popular
music which by-passed traditional rhythm-and-blues." Beginning with an
overview of Motown music and a chapter on the critical response to Motown,
Morse focuses specifically on Martha Reeves, Smokey Robinson, The Supremes,
The Temptations, and The Four Tops. He argues that the music benefited
from three main factors: the changes in popular taste after the emergence
of rock and roll, the improvements in technology, and the recording of
several Motown songs by The Beatles.

M 418. NOEBEL, DAVID A. The Marxist Minstrels: A Handbook on Communist
        Subversion of Music. Tulsa, Okla: American Christian Press,
        1974. 346 pp.
Noebel attempts to tie together Pavlovian psychological theory and the
histories of rock music, drug use, folk music, record companies, and youth
culture to support his theory that music is being used to wage a Communist
takeover of America. He states his belief that this cultural offensive
is under way, and that Communists in fact dominate the world of popular
music. He notes two strategies in the "subverter's use of music": "removing the barrier between classical music and certain types of popular music
by substituting perverted form (e.g., jungle noises) for standardized
classical form," and "the communist use of music directed at destroying
the mental and emotional stability of America's youth through a scheme
capable of producing mass neurosis." Part One addresses the "Communist
Use of Mind Warfare." Part Two describes the "Nature of Red Record Companies." Part Three focuses on the degenerating and immoral effects of
rock music. Part Four indicts such folk musicians as Pete Seeger and
Woody Guthrie, and describes the role of folk music in the "Negro Revolution" and the "College Revolution." Parts Five and Six explore the
evidence of this subversive plot in six appendices.

M 419. ORLOFF, KATHERINE. Rock 'n' Roll Lady. Freeport, N.Y.: Nash,
        1974. 109 pp.
Orloff presents a series of interviews with major women figures in rock
music, including Rita Coolidge, Terry Garthwaite, Maria Muldauer, Bonnie
Raitt, Carly Simon, Linda Ronstadt, Grace Slick, and Wendy Waldman. Orloff
attends to the definition of a "women's music" and the emergence of Feminist themes in music. The personal and career challenges each faces, the
relationships of the artists to the women's movement, and the mutually
supportive attitudes among the performers are discussed.

M 420. PALMER, ROBERT. A Tale of Two Cities: Memphis Rock and New Orleans
        Roll. Brooklyn, N.Y.: Institute for Studies in American Music,
        1979. 38 pp.
Palmer focuses on "the contributions of Memphis and New Orleans, the most
important Southern recording centers in the transition from rhythm and
blues and country and western music—two popular idioms identified with
particular racial and socioeconomic groups—to rock and roll, a phenomenon
that cut across existing racial and musical barriers." He compares the
musical histories of the two cities, tracing the development of rhythm
and blues in New Orleans and the growth of rock and roll in Memphis.
The importance of white audiences for black performers is emphasized,
and larger questions about the nature of rock and roll and how it differs
from rhythm and blues and white country music are raised.

M 421. PALMER, TONY. All You Need Is Love: The Story of Popular Music.
        New York: Grossman, 1976. 323 pp.
Originating in a BBC-TV documentary series entitled "All My Loving,"
Palmer's history is highly visual, illustrated with many archival photographs and posters. Palmer sees the beginnings of American popular music
in African drum music and Afro-American blues, claiming that "popular
music--in the sense of jazz, rock and roll, blues, swing, soul, and their
related progeny--began soon after and probably as a result of The Day
of Jubilee, the freeing of the slaves, September 22, 1862." He devotes
subsequent chapters to the various forms of popular music: ragtime, jazz,
blues, vaudeville, Tin Pan Alley, the musical, swing, rhythm and blues,
country music, songs of war and protest, and rock and roll. Palmer argues
throughout that the music industry curbs musical individuality in its
desire to create a predictable and marketable product--a dynamic that
has been particularly damaging to black performers.

M 422. PICHASKE, DAVID. A Generation in Motion: Popular Culture and
        Music in the Sixties. New York: Schirmer Books, 1979. 248 pp.
Pichaske examines the role of rock music in the creation, flourishing,
and dissolution of the counter-culture of the 1960s. First, he discovers
the roots of 1960s thought and behavior in the counter-culture of the
late 1950s, discussing the Beat Generation, the social critics/comedians,
anti-nuclear sentiment, and such "subversive" rock and rollers as Elvis
Presley, Chuck Berry, and Little Richard. He determines four types of
"the angry no" as expressed by the counter-culture: the "nonviolent"
protest of Martin Luther King and the singers of the folk revival, the
"violent" protest of the Black Panthers and The Jefferson Airplane, the
"holy goof" of Abbie Hoffman and Frank Zappa and The Mothers of Invention,
and the artistic expression of social criticism by Phil Ochs, The Who,
Simon and Garfunkel, and Bob Dylan. Pichaske examines the "transcendent
yes" evident in the self-exploration of the 1960s counter-culture and
the search for alternative lifestyles from drug use to flower power to
black power to independent music companies. In conclusion, he examines
the tactics used by the power structure to deal with the threat of the
counter-culture and its music, and presents Elvis Presley as a paradigm
of co-option. In the 1970s, Pichaske argues, rock turned either to arti-
ness or excess, and rock musicians retired into privacy.

M 423. PLEASANTS, HENRY. The Great American Popular Singers. New York:
        Simon & Schuster, 1974. 384 pp.
Pleasants surveys the vocal performance techniques of some of the principal
stars of the various styles of popular music. He develops a general
description of the vocal art of American popular song, relating it to the
Italian "bel canto" tradition, which also used song as "a lyrical extension
of speech." He emphasizes the significance of the microphone in the
development of vocal style, analyzes the distinctions between popular and
classical performance, and notes the predominant influence of Afro-American
musical idioms. The performers focused upon include Al Jolson, Bessie
Smith, Louis Armstrong, Bing Crosby, Billie Holiday, Ella Fitzgerald,
Frank Sinatra, Hank Williams, Elvis Presley, Judy Garland, Johnny Cash,
Aretha Franklin, and Barbara Streisand.

M 424. POLLOCK, BRUCE. When the Music Mattered: Rock in the 1960s.
        New York: Holt, Rinehart, & Winston, 1983. 243 pp.
Pollock sees the 1960s as a decade of conflict and change, in which middle-
class life was totally disrupted; rock played a central role in this disruption. Defining rock music as a vehicle through which young people
could confront themselves, Pollock argues for a revival of this type and
function of music. He draws on the testimony of survivors of the period.
Dave Van Ronk describes the early 1960s folk scene in Greenwich Village.
Jiggs Meister of the Angels and John Kuse of the Excellents recall the

fun and innocence of teen music in the years before the Kennedy assassination, and the difficulty of recapturing that feeling afterwards. Paul Simon and Roger McGuinn discuss their careers, the lack of real change in the 1960s, and bringing intelligent music to Top 40 radio. Tracy Nelson and Marty Balin describe the blending of folk, blues, and acid rock, in the Bay Area. Peter Tork talks about the struggle to make the Monkees a viable act in the midst of the optimistic Beatles productions and Jimi Hendrix's flamboyant performance style. Tuli Kupferberg of the Fugs and Essra Mohawk reminisce about their efforts to create an alternative musical style, addressing important social issues, and John Sebastian relates the ups and downs of his career and the deaths of all his friends who lived too wildly.

M 425. PRENDERGAST, ROY M. A Neglected Art: A Critical Study of Music in Films. New York: New York University Press, 1977. 268 pp. Prendergast claims that the use of music to accompany film is a relatively new phenomenon, so new that it has gone practically unnoticed. He attempts to fill that void by focusing on three areas: history, aesthetics, and technique. Part I, the historical section, includes chapters on "Music in the Cartoon and Experimental Animated Film," and "Music in the Silent Film." Part II deals with "The Aesthetics of Film Music" and "Film Music with Form." Part III is a general discussion of the technical parameters within which the film music composer must work. The text includes musical examples.

M 426. ROBERTS, JOHN STORM. The Latin Tinge: The Impact of Latin American Music on the United States. New York: Oxford University Press, 1979. 246 pp. Roberts undertakes to show that "Latin music has been the greatest outside influence on the popular music styles of the United States" in the past century. Tin Pan Alley, stage and film music, jazz, rhythm and blues, country, and rock have all been influenced throughout their development by the musical idioms of Brazil, Argentina, Cuba, or Mexico. Some borrowings have been overt--like tango, rhumba, conga, samba, salsa, and various dance band styles--while other influences, starting in the middle of the last century, have been more subtle. Roberts devotes a chapter to each decade in the 20th century to emphasize the continual reintroduction of Latin influence into American music throughout the century. There is a glossary with extensive explanations of styles, instruments, and other Latin musical terms, as well as a discography.

M 427. ROGERS, DAVE. Rock 'n' Roll. Boston: Routledge & Kegan Paul, 1982. 148 pp. Rogers discusses youth styles and popular music in the 1950s in both England and the U.S. Important "behind-the-scenes" artists such as Alan Freed--the disc jockey involved in what came to be The Payola Scandal-- and recent producer Sam Phillips are discussed. The various styles of 1950s music this book mentions are skiffle, rhythm and blues, rockabilly, doo-wop, rock and roll, and popular music. Recording artists discussed are Bill Haley and The Comets, Hank Williams, Carl Perkins, Jerry Lee Lewis, Gene Vincent, Fats Domino, Chuck Berry, Little Richard, Lonnie Donegan, Tommy Steele, Terry Dene, Buddy Holly and The Crickets, Eddie Cochran, Ricky Nelson, the Everly Brothers, Marty Wilde, Cliff Richard, Billy Fury, and Johnny Kid and The Pirates. Rogers argues that popular music and culture in the 1950s were bland until the arrival of rock and roll and the counter-culture.

M 428. **SANDER, ELLEN.** <u>Trips: Rock Life in the Sixties</u>. New York:
Scribner, 1973. 272 pp.
Sander writes of the growth of the counter-culture of the 1960s as it
emerged from the teen culture of the late 1950s. Discussing The Beatles's
concerts, life at Haight-Ashbury, the music festivals at Monterey and
Big Sur, and the life of the yippies, Sander reports her personal feelings
and observations. These are supplemented by retrospective interviews
with members of The Byrds, as well as with such individual performers
as Cass Elliot, Paul Krassner, Eric Burdon, Stephen Stills, Grace Slick,
and Paul Kantner. She ends with what she calls a "Rock Taxonomy": a
list of the most important albums in various genres within rock and roll.

M 429. **SAVAGE, WILLIAM W., Jr.** <u>Singing Cowboys and All That Jazz: A
Short History of Popular Music in Oklahoma</u>. Norman: University
of Oklahoma Press, 1983. 185 pp.
Savage discusses the history of popular music in Oklahoma, contending
that it is richer and more complex than its reputation would indicate.
In the 19th century, Oklahoma became a major musical crossroads due to
the influence of the cowboys, the Plains Indians, slaves, and other musicians. Savage traces traditions in jazz, country and western, folk, and
rock and roll music, including brief descriptions and drawings of such
major figures to emerge from Oklahoma as Woody Guthrie, Bob Wills, Lester
Young, Gene Autry, and Leon Russell. Savage ends with an analysis of
the state's cultural crisis during the Depression, which he compares to
a "cultural firebreak," in that nothing major has been produced since
then.

M 430. **SAVARY, LOUIS M., ed.** <u>Popular Songs and Youth Today</u>. New York:
Association Press, 1971. 160 pp.
This collection of essays analyzes the themes of the music of the 1970s,
which addressed such concerns as personal values, human injustice, problems
in human relations, and societal reform. Part I presents a history of
the meaning of rock music through comments of various critics and performers. Part II analyzes the themes of popular songs, including "Images
of Man and Woman," "Images of Alienation," and "Images of the World."

M 431. **SCHAFER, WILLIAM J.** <u>Rock Music: Where It's Been, What It Means,
Where It's Going</u>. Minneapolis, Minn.: Augsburg, 1972. 128 pp.
Schafer writes as a concerned but not unsympathetic outsider, intending
to describe the rock culture to an audience with religious interests.
Briefly outlining the history of rock, he shows how rock music has been
a shaping force for young people, an alternative to mainstream culture,
and an expressive channel for the black culture in America. He judges
that the influence of rock can be uplifting, but sees reasons for concern
in its strongly hedonistic tendencies. Schafer gives particular attention
to The Beatles, The Who, Randy Newman, and Van Dyke Parks.

M 432. **SCHWARTZ, H. W.** <u>Bands of America</u>. Garden City, N.Y.: Doubleday,
1957. 320 pp.
Schwartz provides a history of big bands in America from the mid-19th
century through W.W. I. He focuses on the careers of band leaders, Patrick
S. Gilmore and John Philip Sousa. He also devotes chapters to the careers
and bands of Antoine Julien, Alessandro Liberati, Frederick N. Innes,
Thomas Preston Brooke, Giuseppe Creatore, Bohumir Kryl, Arthur Pryor,
Patrick Conway, and Albert Sweet.

M 433. **SHAW, ARNOLD.** <u>The Rockin' 50s: The Decade that Transformed the
Pop Music Scene</u>. New York: Hawthorn Books, 1974. 296 pp.
Shaw divides this study into three sections: the demise of Tin Pan Alley
and the crooners, 1950-53; the upheaval in pop, 1954-55; and the rock
and roll years, 1956-60. At the center of the early story is Elvis Presley.

As a music-business insider, Shaw takes special interest in Presley's relationship with the businessmen who guided him, Sam Phillips and Tom Parker. The rest of the history Shaw constructs out of short studies of many individuals and a sequence of landmark events, including the Payola scandals, youth fads, and fashions. His prime concern is with the conflict of generations in the making of a new music. Shaw provides discographies for each section.

M 434. SHEPHERD, JOHN. Tin Pan Alley. Boston: Routledge & Kegan Paul, 1982. 154 pp.
This book describes the major personalities and events in the history of Tin Pan Alley from about 1895 to 1955. Shepherd explores the beginnings of the pop world and describes how the music industry started to adopt the outlook and methods of big business. His account deals with the way in which this change occurred, the ways in which songwriters organized themselves to get their choice of subject matter, and the many stars who came to fame by taking a walk down the Alley. A glossary of musical terms and suggestions for further reading and listening are included.

M 435. SIMON, GEORGE T. The Big Bands. New York: Macmillan, 1967. 614 pp.
This book is both an encyclopedic reference work and a compendium of critical opinion. An opening section sets the scene of big band entertainment, describing the leaders, musicians, media, business figures, and public from the mid-1930s to the mid-1940s, during which time Simon followed and reviewed the bands for Metronome magazine. The rest of the book consists of short, critically evaluative chapters on seventy-two major bands and bandleaders from Count Basie and the Dorsey Brothers to Guy Lombardo and Lawrence Welk. Simon includes discussions of the horn-playing, reed-playing, piano-playing, violin-playing, and singing band leaders. He concludes with a discussion of the present state of the big bands and appends a selective discography of big band music and a list of big band theme songs.

M 436. SLOBIN, MARK. Tenement Songs: The Popular Music of the Jewish Immigrants. Urbana: University of Illinois Press, 1982. 213 pp.
Slobin argues that "popular culture, especially the music that lay at the heart of public and private entertainment, played a significant role in giving the immigrants a sense of identity" and in helping them to "keep their footing on these slippery shores." Noting the "survival value" of the Jewish immigrants' music as a "cultural adhesive," he examines the use of music in such Yiddish theaters as the one established by Abraham Goldfadn and the historical connection between artistic self-expression and the idea of upward mobility in Jewish culture. Slobin discusses the Jewish beliefs about music and musicians, the traditions of music and music-making brought from Europe, and the character of ethnic music in America. His survey, which begins at the time of Edison's invention of the phonograph and ends with the birth of radio, focuses on the heyday of sheet music between 1897 and 1920. He analyzes the content of Jewish-American sheet music as a "primary source material for understanding immigrant adaptation and maintenance of internal values."

M 437. SPAETH, SIGMUND. The Facts of Life in Popular Song. New York: Whittlesey House, 1934. 148 pp.
Spaeth looks at some of the humorous and revealing aspects of the popular songs of his day, contending: "The popular song has become a most revealing index to American life in general. It sums up the ethics, the habits, the slang, the intimate character of every generation." The first chapter, for example, analyzes suggestive and graphic details about "the facts of life"; the third sees popular music as stabilizing grammatical errors

in society's lexicon. Other chapters treat the use of rhyme errors, self-pity, nostalgia, baby talk, love, nature imagery, and nonsense words in popular songs.

M 438. SPAETH, SIGMUND. A History of Popular Music in America. New York: Random House, 1948. 729 pp.
In the introduction to his history of American popular music, Spaeth writes: "Popular music is an index to the life and history of a nation. . . . The manners, customs, and current events of every generation have been given expression in popular music." Spaeth's account of popular music in America focuses on the late 18th and 19th centuries, discussing the conception of such songs as "Yankee Doodle," the careers of such composers as William Billings and Stephen Foster, the tradition of minstrelsy, the boom of popular music during the Civil War Era, the growth of sentimental ballads and Negro spirituals in the 1870s and 1880s, and the prolific though mediocre song production of the 1890s. He chronicles the emergence of Tin Pan Alley, ragtime, and jazz in the 1920s, and concludes with a discussion of "the perplexing present." A list of further popular song titles from the Colonial times to the present is appended.

M 439. SPITZ, ROBERT STEPHEN. Barefoot in Babylon: The Creation of the Woodstock Music Festival, 1969. New York: Viking Press, 1979. 515 pp.
Spitz examines the business negotiations and deals leading up to the Woodstock festival as examples of the contradictions contained in, and not always faced by, the "Woodstock generation." He tells the story of the day-by-day running of the festival, and then surveys the festival's major figures ten years later. He reveals bigotry, pettiness, and greed, but he retains admiration for the people he presents and for the unprecedented event they achieved.

M 440. STOKES, GEOFFREY. Star-Making Machinery: Inside the Business of Rock and Roll. New York: Vintage Books, 1977. 234 pp.
Stokes calls his volume the record of "the Odyssey of an Album," reflecting his strategy of analyzing the rock recording business by means of the case history of a single album. He traces the recording, production, and promotion of a 1974 album by Commander Cody, entitled Commander Cody and His Lost Planet Airmen, to illustrate the processes, strains, and successes of marketing music in the early 1970s.

M 441. TAWA, NICHOLAS E. Sweet Songs for Gentle Americans: The Parlor Song in America, 1790-1860. Bowling Green, Ohio: Bowling Green University Popular Press, 1980. 273 pp.
This book examines the early evolution of American popular sheet music, based on the surviving collections of various families who accumulated, bound, and ultimately passed them on to public and university libraries. Tawa found more than 500 volumes in Boston, Cambridge, Mass., and Providence, R.I., and analyzes them in historical contexts. Chapters are devoted to the public, the economics, the subjects, and the music of such songs. Tawa also investigates the connections of parlor songs to music education and to the generally less genteel songs deriving from minstrel stage shows of the same era. The volume concludes with several appendices listing the most popular songs, their composers, and years of publication. Tawa also includes a selective bibliography and a musical supplement of the music and lyrics to sixteen parlor songs.

M 442. WEISSMAN, DICK. Music Making in America. New York: Ungar, 1982. 147 pp.
The premise of this book is that while music plays an integral part in the lives of many Americans, the professional musician has a difficult time earning a living in our society. Music making is considered a luxury

vocation compared to such "real" work as plumbing, mail delivery, law, and medicine. Weissman discusses the lives of professional musicians, focusing on their training, work habits, and relationship to American culture. A special chapter, written by songwriter, record producer, and performer Artie Traum, deals with what he calls "the infantry" of music. Other topics include "The Contemporary Music Education," "Muzak and the Listener," and "The Musician's Union in the 1980s."

M 443. WHITCOMB, IAN. After the Ball: Pop Music from Rag to Rock. New York: Simon & Schuster, 1972. 312 pp.
This volume is a wide-ranging history of popular music which concerns itself partly with the author's memoirs of his career as a musician, partly with anecdotes from the music scene in the U.S. and Britain, and centrally with the development of popular music in this century. About a quarter of the volume is devoted to British pop, but the rest focuses on the dominant American scene as Whitcomb reconstructs the evolution of rock and roll from its birth in ragtime and Tin Pan Alley to jazz and swing. His analysis is directed at explaining the "road" to the rock music of the 1960s.

M 444. WILDER, ALEC. American Popular Song: The Great Innovators, 1900-1950. Edited by James T. Mober. New York: Oxford University Press, 1972. 536 pp.
This volume is an analytical history of a half-century of the sophisticated New York popular music of Broadway and Tin Pan Alley. Wilder writes as a colleague as well as a scholar of the figures whose work he studies. He focuses on the music and careers of such major composers as Jerome Kern, Irving Berlin, George Gershwin, Richard Rodgers, Cole Porter, Harold Arlen, and Arthur Schwartz as well as such lesser-known figures as Hoagy Carmichael, Harry Warren, Jimmy McHugh, Ray Noble, Burton Lane, Hugh Martin, and Vernon Duke. Attending more to the music than to the lyrics, Wilder devotes a final chapter to "Outstanding Individual Songs: 1920-1950."

M 445. WILLIAMS, PAUL. Outlaw Blues: A Book of Rock Music. New York: Dutton, 1968. 191 pp.
Williams, a songwriter/critic/entrepreneur, collects his writings from his own magazine, Crawdaddy. He discusses many of the contemporary performers and performance styles with the greatest emphasis on The Beach Boys, The Byrds, Buffalo Springfield, Bob Dylan, and The Doors. Seeing rock not as a phenomenon but "as a means of expression, an opportunity for beauty, an art," he calls his book "an attempt to convey what I feel from the music." He devotes one chapter, "Outlaw Blues," to a discussion of rock as protest music and explores the question of "how rock communicates" in a final chapter. A discography is appended.

POLITICAL SCIENCE

The compilation of this bibliography was undertaken for the purpose
of providing the researcher with a survey of the literature defining the
present discipline of Political Science. The entries chosen for this
bibliography attempt to bring together the significant literature in the
field. This includes not only what is considered to be the "classic"
literature in Political Science, but also the literature that is directing
the present development of the discipline. Given the enormous amount
of material being published in the field, and the limited space available,
a bibliography such as this can never hope to be definitive, or all-
inclusive. At best, a representative sampling of materials can be expected.

No reference works, textbooks, or biographies have been included
within this bibliography. Political Science textbooks are constantly
revised to remain as current as possible. These textbooks also suffer from
the problem of generality, often failing to provide in-depth information.
Biographies are excluded because they are generally more concerned with
personalities than politics. Biographies of Presidents, Congressmen,
or Supreme Court Justices are more likely to illustrate an individual's
own practice within a political institution than to clarify the nature
of such an institution.

Anyone interested in pursuing the study of Political Science has
at her/his disposal a variety of reference materials. Frederick Holler,
Information Sources of Political Science, 3rd ed. (Santa Barbara, Calif.:
ABC-Clio, 1981); Clifton Brock, The Literature of Political Science:
A Guide for Students, Librarians, and Teachers (New York: Bowker, 1969);
Lubomyr R. Wynar, Guide to Reference Materials in Political Science (Denver:
Colorado Bibliographic Institute, 1966-68); and Raymond McInnis and James
Scott, Social Science Research Handbook (New York: Barnes & Noble, 1974),
all provide inventories of information and reference sources. Robert
B. Harmon, Political Science: A Bibliographic Guide to the Literature

(New York: Scarecrow Press, 1965), provides a record of other published bibliographies in Political Science.

General information about the discipline and history of Political Science can be acquired by consulting the International Encyclopedia of Social Science, David L. Sills, ed. (New York: Macmillan, 1972), and The Handbook of Political Science, Fred Greenstein and Nelson Polsby, eds. (Reading, Mass.: Addison-Wesley, 1975). For those who need a key to the language of Political Science, the Political Science Thesaurus (Washington, D.C.: American Political Science Association, 1975) provides a useful guide. It is suggested that anyone interested in locating government documents and information refer to one of the guides to resource materials mentioned above.

Since much of the work being done in the field is published in journals and periodicals, there are sourcebooks available to aid the researcher in locating such materials. B. F. Hoselitz, A Reader's Guide to the Social Sciences (New York: Free Press, 1970), and Carl White, Sources of Information in the Social Sciences (Chicago: American Library Association, 1973), both include lists of important recent publications in Political Science. The best sources for locating journal articles are the Social Sciences Index (Bronx, N.Y.: H. W. Wilson), a quarterly publication which provides author and subject indices to recent articles in the field, and the Social Sciences Citation Index (Philadelphia, Pa.: Institute of Scientific Information), which lists works that have been cited in the footnotes of bibliographies of journal articles. Other guides to journal articles include ABCPOLISCI: Advance Bibliography of Contents: Political Science and Governments (Santa Barbara, Calif.: ABC-Clio), which publishes the tables of contents of U.S. and foreign-based periodicals in Political Science and related fields; the International Bibliography of Political Science (Paris: UNESCO), which prints selective lists of books, as well as articles; the International Political Science Abstracts (Paris: UNESCO); and the United States Political Science Documents (Pittsburgh, Pa.: University Center for International Studies), which contains detailed indices, and abstracts from materials published in approximately 120 Political Science journals.

Certain journals published by Political Science associations may be examined to discern the current state and interest of the discipline. These journals include The American Political Science Review, Political Science Quarterly, Western Political Quarterly, American Journal of Political Science, Journal of Politics, and Polity. Anyone interested in alternatives to the mainstream approach to the discipline should look at Politics and Society and New Political Science, both of which challenge the conventional methods and ideological bases of Political Science.

A bibliography of the literature in Political Science may demonstrate nothing more than the compiler's own notion of the field. However, the bibliography presented here should demonstrate, if nothing else, that there does exist a common ground upon which to initiate the discourse about the nature of American politics.

Florindo Volpacchio
Columbia University

I.   NORMATIVE POLITICAL THEORY

PS 1.   ACKERMAN, BRUCE A. Social Justice in the Liberal State. New Haven,
        Conn.: Yale University Press, 1980. 392 pp.
Ackerman argues that neither the myth of a social contract nor the search
for social utility can do justice to the liberal ideal. He argues instead
for a theory of liberal political dialogue that is based on a principle
of neutrality between persons. To demonstrate the power of neutral dialogue in resolving social issues, Ackerman follows the conversational
path pursued by liberal society as it determines who will be born, how
children will be educated, how much each adult will receive, how adults
will exchange their labor and capital with one another, and how much they
must leave for succeeding generations. Within this context, he discusses
various social issues such as abortion, genetic engineering, education,
the distribution of wealth, and the role of the Supreme Court. He then
develops the minimum requirements that must be fulfilled by any democratic
society aspiring to the liberal ideal.

PS 2.   ALT, JAMES E. and K. ALEC CHRYSTAL. Political Economics. Berkeley:
        University of California Press, 1983. 276 pp.
Alt and Chrystal argue that the fundamental question of political economics
involves governmental responsibility for economic policy. Most of the
book focuses on the role of elected governments in the mixed economies
of Western industrial democracies. The authors begin by elaborating the
basic issues involved in analyzing state activity in the market economy
from the point of view of political economic theory. They then outline
the constraints on policy imposed by political institutions, economic
ideas, and the international environment. This is followed by a discussion
of methods for analyzing the public sector and the growth of government.

PS 3.   BACHRACH, PETER. The Theory of Democratic Elitism: A Critique.
        Washington, D.C.: University Press of America, 1980. 109 pp.
Bachrach claims that democratic elitism as an empirical theory is generally
unsound. Democratic elitism argues that within a democratic system there
is a natural division of labor between elite rule and non-elite interest.
As long as it can provide procedural democracy and properly serve the
people, it functions in the public interest. Democratic elitism calls
for a minimal amount of citizen participation. Bachrach argues that this
is a paradox. The true democrat cannot justify imposing his decisions
and hierarchical ordering on others. Democratic theory traditionally
favors the opportunity for individual development which arises from participation in meaningful political decision; the benefit is not merely
in the end result, but also in the process of participation. Democracy
explicitly refers to self-determination. Democratic elitism resists self-
determinism and mass participation. Bachrach argues that a theory of
democracy should allow fuller participation, not only in decision-making
but also within the community and private sector.

PS 4.   BARBER, BENJAMIN R. Superman and Common Man: Freedom, Anarchy,
        and the Revolution. New York: Praeger, 1971. 125 pp.
Barber's essays on political concepts and issues assail certain basic
liberal beliefs. He begins with a critique of anarchism, then turns to
the liberal notion that men can be forced to be free. This is followed
by an essay in which he argues that tolerance ought not always to be tolerated. Here he examines the relations between individualism and the common
good. Barber concludes with an essay which argues that revolution or
social change can be made only by the common actions of persons who speak
for the majority.

PS 5. BAY, CHRISTIAN. Strategies of Political Emancipation. Notre Dame, Ind.: University of Notre Dame Press, 1981. 240 pp.
Bay tries to develop rationalist-humanist priorities for the understanding and advancement of freedom, basing his theory on a human rights approach to politics. He begins with a critical examination of the liberal understanding of liberty. Bay tries to establish a connection between freedom and need: if people are to be free, then basic human needs must be fulfilled. The author analyzes the principal modes of oppression—domination, coercive oppression, and alienation—for the purpose of developing alternative approaches to the study of freedom. He looks at each of these categories of oppression conceptually and empirically to develop appropriate strategies for emancipation. Bay then examines the international aspects of the problem of human emancipation. He concludes with a call for the solidarity of human communities in the fulfillment of basic needs.

PS 6. BOOKCHIN, MURRAY. The Ecology of Freedom: The Emergence and Dissolution of Hierarchy. Palo Alto, Calif.: Cheshire Books, 1982. 385 pp.
Bookchin argues for a radical social ecology, attributable to the existence of social hierarchy within the community. In its place, he argues for a free society based on ecological principles which recognize the importance of nature for the human community, and for an acknowledgment that such recognition must coincide with the abolition of repressive authority. Bookchin supports a technology which can make use of local natural resources and can be operated by decentralized communities. This argument is followed by a call for direct democracy—urban decentralization with a high measure of self-sufficiency based on communal social life. The author develops these ideas by analyzing social institutions, technologies, and political structures with regard to the relations between person and person, and humankind and nature.

PC 7. BOORSTIN, DANIEL. The Genius of American Politics. Chicago: University of Chicago Press, 1948. 201 pp.
Boorstin raises the question of why the U.S. has not had a political theorist of world stature; the outstanding American thinkers, by and large, have been statesmen who addressed practical questions—for example, Jefferson, Madison, and Lincoln. Boorstin finds the answer to his question in what he calls the "givenness" of American institutions. He says that Americans have found their principles in their institutions—the Constitution and the Declaration of Independence—and thus they have never been tempted to go beyond them to formulate their values. In this sense, the American political theory is "given" in these institutions.

PS 8. BRZEZINSKI, ZBIGNIEW, et al., eds. The Relevance of Liberalism. Boulder, Colo.: Westview Press, 1978. 233 pp.
This volume examines the relevance of liberalism in light of the sudden expansion of popular political consciousness which is transforming the character of political values and actions. The overall theme of the essays is the continuing viability of liberalism; the question of whether it is universally applicable or limited to the Western world at a specific moment of social and economic development; the interaction between liberalism and democracy; the relationship of liberalism to Socialism; and the question of whether its influence should extend beyond the borders of the U.S. The volume concludes with a look at the future prospects of liberalism.

PS 9. BURNS, JAMES MacGREGOR. Leadership. New York: Harper & Row, 1978. 530 pp.
Burns examines the crisis of leadership in contemporary politics. He discusses the essence of leadership and the standards by which to measure, recruit, and reject it. In so doing, he brings together the literature

992

on leadership and the literature on audiences, masses, and voters—the people who follow leaders. In his description, leadership is based on a structure of action that engages persons to varying degrees, at all the levels of society. Leadership is distinguished from mere powerholding. Burns identifies two basic types of leadership: transactional and transforming. Transactional leadership approaches followers with a view toward exchanging one thing for another, for example, jobs for votes. Transforming leadership recognizes and exploits a potential follower's existing needs or demands. The primary aim of the book is to search for the moral foundations of leadership, those acts of leadership that serve to help release human potentials now locked in ungratified needs and thwarted expectations.

PS 10. BURNS, JAMES MacGREGOR. The Vineyard of Liberty. New York: Knopf, 1982. 741 pp.
This volume is the first in Burns's massive history of the U.S., and focuses on American political history beginning with the Constitutional Convention. Burns examines the development of the party system, the ideological basis of the Constitution, and the events which led to the Civil War. Much of the volume is concerned with the moral and political issues surrounding the institution of slavery, especially in light of the American ideal of equality. Burns concludes his study with a discussion of the Emancipation Proclamation.

PS 11. COCHRAN, CLARKE E. Character, Community, and Politics. University: University of Alabama Press, 1982. 195 pp.
Cochran tries to move away from the paradigm of autonomous individualism usually associated with American political thought by elaborating a communal theory of political order. His chief concerns are with the ideas of commitment, responsibility, and character, concepts which deal with the recognition of the rights of others rather than the assertion of one's own rights. These ideas are developed through a discussion of authority, freedom, pluralism, and the common good. The author then attempts to redirect political theory toward an understanding of human nature, which he feels is essential to comprehending the relation between the individual and the community. He analyzes the role that the community plays in individual self-determination, and the relationships between restraint and self-determination, individual rights and political order, individual development and communal stability. Cochran concludes with a discussion of the way in which public policy may attain justice and the common good by promoting specific qualities of community and character.

PS 12. COFFEY, JON W. Political Realism in American Thought. Lewisburg, Pa.: Bucknell University Press, 1977. 217 pp.
In this book Coffey assesses the meaning of American Realism as a political philosophy. He focuses on three of the principal advocates of this dominant American political philosophy: Reinhold Niebuhr, George Kennan, and Hans Morgenthau. Coffey is not so much concerned with the formal thought of these individuals as he is with reviewing domestic political issues that concern these thinkers and specific foreign policy positions related to their Cold War stands. Throughout, Coffey's purpose is to see what Realism means to these intellectuals as a way of looking at political problems.

PS 13. CONNOLLY, WILLIAM. Appearance and Reality in Politics. New York: Cambridge University Press, 1981. 218 pp.
Connolly examines the connections between the quest for personal identity, the construction of the welfare state, and the legitimacy of that state in the eyes of the citizens to whom it is formally accountable through elections. His analysis reveals the ways in which the collective effort to save appearances in public life contributes to a process of social

dissolution, while concealing the dynamics of this process from public discourse.

PS 14. CONNOLLY, WILLIAM, ed. The Bias of Pluralism. New York: Atherton Press, 1969. 261 pp.

The essays in this volume undertake a reevaluation of pluralist theory, contending that conventional formulations of the pluralist interpretation of politics are defective. The volume begins with a critique of pluralist theory in American politics. It then turns to a diagnosis of the notion of power within pluralism and interest-group liberalism, and looks at the role the military-industrial complex plays in a pluralist society. The book then presents standards and strategies of change, reexamining the notions of public interest and participatory democracy, and discusses relevant political approaches to social change.

PS 15. DAHL, ROBERT A. Dilemmas of Pluralist Democracy: Autonomy vs. Control. New Haven, Conn.: Yale University Press, 1982. 229 pp.

Dahl argues that the independent organizations which are an outcome of democracy are necessary to the functioning of the democratic process. But independence also creates an opportunity to do harm. This is the dilemma of pluralist democracy which threatens to undermine democracy itself: organizations ought to possess some autonomy, but at the same time they should be controlled. Dahl explores the nature of this dilemma and the function of control and autonomy within a pluralistic democracy.

PS 16. DAHL, ROBERT A. Polyarchy: Participation and Opposition. New Haven, Conn.: Yale University Press, 1971. 257 pp.

Dahl examines the ways in which political opposition develops. Specifically, he discusses the conditions which shape all opposition, rivalry, or competition between a government and its opponents. He argues that in a democracy, public opposition is an important means by which a government learns what its citizens demand. Dahl discusses the conditions which may increase or decrease the chances of public contestation in open societies, and concludes with an examination of the implications of his theory for political action and foreign policy.

PS 17. DAHL, ROBERT A. A Preface to Democratic Theory. Chicago: University of Chicago Press, 1956. 155 pp.

Dahl seeks to distill and formalize what he sees as the two main threads in American political thought: Madisonian democracy and populistic democracy. In addition, he tries to develop from observation a formal description of American democracy as it now exists, which he calls "polyarchal" democracy. The central problem of all three threads involves the conflict between the majority, who wish to rule, and the minority, who resist tyranny. Dahl believes that "polyarchal" democracy, as practiced in the U.S., strikes a reasonable balance between these opposing claims.

PS 18. DEVINE, DONALD J. Does Freedom Work? Liberty and Justice in America. Ottawa, Ill.: Green Hill, 1978. 192 pp.

The author argues that the liberty and justice inherent in free Capitalism make it morally legitimate as well as a superior economic system. He explains what American capitalist institutions are, and how they can justly solve the problems of modern society, including the problems of civil rights and welfare: he presents data showing that private means, not government planning and regulation, have been most successful in dealing with these problems in the U.S. Moreover, he argues, Capitalism is consistent with traditional religious and family values, which are still maintained in capitalist America.

994

PS 19. DIGGINS, JOHN P. and MARK E. KANN, eds. The Problem of Authority in America. Philadelphia: Temple University Press, 1982. 255 pp.

This anthology draws upon the disciplines of history, political theory, literature, and psychology to examine the nature of authority in America. The first part of the volume deals with the various expressions of authority as reflected in the writings of early theologians and political thinkers. It also deals with the recent issue of authority as it pertains to the idea of the state and to the politics of social control, arguing that the American government lacks the authority to lead. The second part explores the meaning of authority in the works of William Faulkner, Ezra Pound, and T. S. Eliot, concluding that American culture lacks a consensus of values that would give coherence to the social rules. The third part addresses itself to the alleged decline of the family and to the treatment of questions of authority in psychology, anthropology, and classical literature.

PS 20. DWORKIN, RONALD. Taking Rights Seriously. 1977; Rev. ed. Cambridge, Mass.: Harvard University Press, 1978. 371 pp.

This book is a collection of essays that tries to define and defend a liberal theory of law. Within these essays Dworkin also undertakes a critique of legal positivism and utilitarianism, showing how they are interdependent. Dworkin distinguishes two forms of rights: background rights, which an individual may always assert to protect himself against community decisions; and institutional rights, which hold against a decision made by a specific institution. Dworkin discusses such issues as judicial activism and judicial restraint, legislative rights, and compliance with the law; he also tries to reconcile the ideas of equality and individualism.

PS 21. EISENSTEIN, ZILLAH R. The Radical Future of Liberal Feminism. New York: Longman, 1981. 260 pp.

Eisenstein examines classical 19th-century feminist writing and compares them with contemporary feminist writings. She points to the contradictory character of liberal Feminism--contradictory because liberalism is patriarchal and individualistic, while Feminism is based on sexual egalitarian and collectivist notions. The author views liberalism as a specific ideology which protects and reinforces patriarchal and capitalist society and is antithetical to the true goals of Feminism. The intent of the author is to identify the radical feminist tendencies that exist theoretically within liberalism and practically within significant sectors of liberal feminist politics in order to clarify the basis for building a revolutionary feminist politics.

PS 22. FEINBERG, JOEL. Rights, Justice, and the Bounds of Liberty. Princeton, N.J.: Princeton University Press, 1980. 318 pp.

This book, a collection of essays, begins with a look at freedom; this is followed by a discussion of whether death is a "harm." The author then discusses whether offensive actions should face coercive restraints, and undertakes a criticism of legal paternalism. He next looks at the nature and value of rights as they pertain to humans, animals, and unborn generations. Feinberg then considers abortion, and follows this with a discussion of euthanasia. He concludes with an examination of the unfairness of false judgments against individuals.

PS 23. FISHKIN, JAMES. Justice, Equal Opportunity, and the Family. New Haven, Conn.: Yale University Press, 1983. 200 pp.

Fishkin argues that equal opportunity is the central doctrine in modern liberalism for legitimizing the distribution of goods in society. But if the theory of fair and equal opportunity were taken to its radical extreme, it would mean intrusion into the family--the original and crucial source of social inequality. Thus, the liberal's concern with maintaining procedural fairness by promoting the principle of merit and the equality of life contradicts his concern with maintaining the autonomy of the family. Fishkin's point is that the procedural equalities of modern liberalism can be maintained only at a substantial cost to liberty: one must either ignore background inequalities or intrude into the family and remove them. The author argues for a limited liberalism, one committed only to the resolution of conflicting principles in particular cases.

PS 24. FISHKIN, JAMES. Tyranny and Legitimacy: A Critique of Political Theories. Baltimore, Md.: Johns Hopkins University Press, 1979. 138 pp.
Fishkin argues that all of the principles currently prominent in political theory have the capacity of justifying a legitimate government tyranny. He undertakes a critique of procedural principles, such as majority rule; structural principles, such as utilitarianism; and absolute rights principles, such as natural rights. The author desires to expose the limitations of these principles. Rather than rejecting them uniformly, Fishkin argues that these principles must be qualified or limited in certain specific ways depending on the problems to which they have to adapt.

PS 25. FLATHMAN, RICHARD E. The Practice of Political Authority: Authority and the Authoritative. Chicago: University of Chicago Press, 1980. 274 pp.
Flathman's primary purpose is to identify the constellation of concepts, rules, institutions, and arrangements through which political obligations are assigned, understood, and acted upon. He assesses the practice of political obligation in light of practical questions regarding political behavior. His thesis is that the practice of political obligation operates only if men choose certain actions because they believe there are good reasons for accepting and obeying those actions. Flathman argues that political obligation, if it is to reflect human intentions and choice, must be understood in terms of action.

PS 26. FLATHMAN, RICHARD E. The Practice of Rights. New York: Cambridge University Press, 1976. 250 pp.
Flathman attempts to identify, analyze, and assess the patterns of thought and action that make up the practice of rights. He argues that a right provides the agent with a warrant for taking or refusing to take action that he conceives to be in his interest or to his advantage. Flathman identifies his conception of the practice of rights as civic individualism, which he sees as a form of individualism that is consistent with liberal principles. It locates the individual and individual actions in the socio-political context, and gives suitable emphasis to the aspects of the practice of rights that bear directly on the role of the citizen and his civic life. Flathman's goal is to restore to a theory of rights a primary concern for their political value and significance.

PS 27. FRIEDMAN, KATHI V. Legitimation of the Social Rights and the Western Welfare State: A Weberian Perspective. Chapel Hill: University of North Carolina Press, 1981. 269 pp.
Friedman seeks to discover the underlying values that make various methods and degrees of wealth redistribution acceptable to populaces in the Western democratic welfare states. Her theoretical rationale for the legitimacy of the Western welfare state is that it arose out of the 19th-century laissez-faire, liberal state. The author looks at the problems which arise in administering the welfare state and trying to decide how social goods are to be distributed. She shows how the attempt to redistribute societal surplus according to a set of principles is often frustrated by a bureaucracy based on contradictory principles. Friedman argues that Western governments gain legitimacy when they make redistribution of surplus goods into a formal social right.

PS 28. FRIEDMAN, MILTON. Capitalism and Freedom. 1962; Rev. ed. Chicago:
        University of Chicago Press, 1982. 202 pp.
The topic of this book is the role of competitive Capitalism--the organization of economic activity through private enterprise in a free market--
as a necessary condition for political freedom. It also examines the
role government should play in a society dedicated to freedom and relying
primarily on the market to organize economic activity. Friedman begins
with an elaboration of traditional liberalism and its roots in free market
theory. He then applies his principles to a variety of problems such
as the control of money, international financial trade agreements, fiscal
policy, education, discrimination, and other social issues.

PS 29. FRYER, RUSSELL G. Recent Conservative Political Thought: American
        Perspectives. Washington, D.C.: University Press of America,
        1979. 429 pp.
The main purpose of this volume is to evaluate recent conservative political thought. Fryer begins with an examination of the unique relationship between conservative and liberal thought in America. He identifies
those authors who have been most concerned with the tie between policy
and politics in American political life, and offers an examination of
both ideological and nonideological conservatism. Fryer concludes his
study with a consideration of conservatism's relation to contemporary
aspects of liberal and radical thought.

PS 30. GUTMANN, AMY. Liberal Equality. New York: Cambridge University
        Press, 1980. 318 pp.
Gutmann undertakes a discussion of liberal equality in order to justify
a more equal distribution of goods within contemporary liberal democratic
societies. The book begins with a consideration of both the foundation
and the limits of a liberal theory of equality. The foundation of liberal
equality is discovered in two strands of classical liberal theory: the
first describes people as equal beings, the second justifies a more equal
distribution of income. Gutmann then explores the modern development
of liberal egalitarian theory. This is followed by an examination of
the limits of liberal equality and the arguments against it. Gutmann
tries to reconcile the fundamental value of redistributive and participatory justice and explores several of the possible implications of her
theory for recent problems in American society.

PS 31. HARRINGTON, MICHAEL. Decade of Decision: The Crisis of the Ameri-
        can System. New York: Simon & Schuster, 1980. 354 pp.
Harrington tries to provide an explanation for the simultaneous existence
of inflation and high unemployment that was the cause of economic problems
in the U.S. in the 1970s. The author goes beyond economic explanations
and examines cultural and social reasons for these problems. This leads
him to present the roots of the current crisis as structural, and to argue
that the U.S. is entering a period dominated by "scrapping and rearranging"
the existing structure. Harrington then presents his own theory regarding
how this readjustment should take place. This theory defines the meaning
of a "structural" crisis and locates the causes in a system where corporate
priorities pervade government policy.

PS 32. HARRINGTON, MICHAEL. The Politics at God's Funeral: The Spiritual
        Crisis of Western Civilizations. New York: Holt, Rinehart &
        Winston, 1983. 308 pp.
Harrington argues that the Judeo-Christian tradition no longer determines
the norms that govern and provide understanding for our daily life. The
loss of religious motivation and divine inspiration in public life has
created a moral vacuum. Capitalism has transformed Western society into
one characterized by hedonism and selfishness. It no longer allows the
translation of private individual belief into public life. To meet this

moral crisis, Harrington appeals for a set of overarching principles which
would avoid the mystifications of the old beliefs and build a moral and
political structure that meets the needs of people in public life.

PS 33. HARTSOCK, NANCY. Money, Sex, and Power: An Essay on Domination
        and Community. Boston: Northeastern University Press, 1983.
        310 pp.
Hartsock is concerned with examining how relations of domination along
gender lines are constructed and maintained. The book undertakes a critique of power relations, especially of the ways sexist power is constructed, legitimated, and reproduced. She seeks to develop a theory that
can provide a more complete understanding both of power and dominance
relations and of the transformations necessary to create a more egalitarian
society. This study focuses on how male dominance is constructed and
maintained, rather than on women's oppression.

PS 34. HARTZ, LOUIS. The Liberal Tradition in America: An Interpretation
        of American Political Thought Since the Revolution. New York:
        Harcourt, Brace, 1955. 329 pp.
Hartz argues that American political culture is unique in the degree to
which it is dominated by liberal concepts of natural rights and natural
equality. Since Americans lacked the feudal institutions that restrained
liberalism in Europe, liberalism developed unimpeded. As a consequence,
American liberalism and the institutions that it generated never confronted
the kinds of class ideologies that arose in Europe. Thus, liberal individualism has been able to maintain a monolithic position in the American
political structure. The danger in this, according to Hartz, is that
the universal acceptance of liberal assumptions has led many Americans
to regard those who accept rival ideologies (e.g., Communism) as traitors
and as "un-American." He urges Americans in the modern era to understand
the uniqueness of their experience, and to accept the inevitable process
by which other nations adopt other kinds of political institutions.

PS 35. HUNTINGTON, SAMUEL. American Politics: The Promise of Disharmony.
        Cambridge, Mass.: Harvard University Press, 1981. 303 pp.
In this book, Huntington challenges the theories of the progressives
(Charles Beard and C. Wright Mills), the consensualists (Louis Hartz),
and the pluralists (Arthur Bentley). He argues that these theories cannot
explain four key reform movements: the American Revolution, the Jacksonian
era, the Progressive movement, and the Civil Rights and anti-Vietnam movements. Huntington argues that these theories fail to understand that
the importance of individualism in American society creates a tension
between the citizen and the government. Government cannot promote, and
is often in conflict with, what American idealism understands to be the
pursuit of individual happiness. This is a source of political motivation
which the dominant theories of American politics often fail to take into
account.

PS 36. KADARKAY, ARPAD. Human Rights in American and Russian Political
        Thought. Washington, D.C.: University Press of America, 1982.
        242 pp.
Kadarkay traces the intellectual origins of the American and Russian views
of human rights. He then brings the history of both these traditions
to bear on the contemporary Soviet-American confrontation over human rights,
arguing that the U.S.-Soviet confrontation arises from the nature of American and Russian political thought on human rights. The confrontation,
in short, is an outcome of the different moral attitudes of each society.

PS 37. KAPLAN, MORTON. Justice, Human Nature, and Political Obligation.
New York: Free Press, 1976. 283 pp.
Kaplan argues that conceptions of the good and the just are the products
of a continual interaction between human beings, society, and environment.
On this basis, he seeks to recapture the naturalistic tradition of political theory. He argues that justice has an objective ground--that conceptions of justice which present it as a transitive and closed system mis-
represent its character. Rather, different rules, goods, conditions,
and consequences coexist in equilibrium and jointly govern decisions.
The author uses the methods of systems analysis to build his model.

PS 38. KELSO, WILLIAM A. American Democratic Theories: Pluralism and
Its Critics. Westport, Conn.: Greenwood Press, 1978. 288 pp.
Kelso defends the pluralistic theory of democracy. He identifies and
compares four types of pluralist democratic theory: (a) polyarchy, which
sees the essence of democracy as competition among elites, (b) pluralism,
which conceives of democratic government as a twofold process involving
competition among elites and bargaining among interest groups, (c) populism,
which equates democracy with maximizing the power of the majority to decide
substantive political issues, and (d) participatory democracy, which views
democratic government as a form of community decision-making in which
all citizens can actively participate on a daily basis. Kelso then turns
to recent findings in voter behavior, participation, decision-making,
and public administration and analyzes the ramifications of these studies
for pluralism and democratic theory.

PS 39. KRISTOL, IRVING. Two Cheers for Capitalism. New York: Basic
Books, 1978. 274 pp.
Kristol analyzes the arguments against liberal Capitalism. In response
to this criticism, the author argues that Capitalism is the only economic
system conducive to individualism and a free society. Furthermore, Capitalism works: people who subscribe to a capitalist order improve their
social conditions. However, the author also considers some of the problems
that arise from the capitalist economy, such as the growth and domination
of bureaucratic forms of organizations, the generation of a spiritual
malaise and cultural crisis, and the rise of the welfare state and its
pursuit of social justice.

PS 40. KRISTOL, IRVING and PAUL WEAVER, eds. The Americans, 1976: An
Inquiry into the Fundamental Concepts of Man Underlying Various
U.S. Institutions. Lexington, Mass.: Heath, 1976. 370 pp.
This study examines the political ideas about human nature underlying
the American system of government, and how such ideas shape government
policy. The volume begins with an essay that examines the American idea
of man held by the Founding Fathers. This is followed by essays on social
policy, the family, crime and punishment, the military, education, mental
health, urban planning, economics, law, foreign policy, and American political ideology. The implicit intention of these essays is to challenge
the dominant approaches to American study which consider human nature
irrelevant. The essays, therefore, criticize the "scientific" study of
American politics and the tendency to sacrifice questions of statesmanship
to methods of technical control of the polity.

PS 41. LASLETT, PETER and JAMES S. FISHKIN, eds. Philosophy, Politics
and Society. New Haven, Conn.: Yale University Press, 1979.
312 pp.
The essays in this volume deal with democratic theory and its relation
to Rawlsian conceptions of justice. After presenting an essay by John
Rawls on the well-ordered society, and responses to his theory, the volume
takes up several other issues: first, how the growth of human populations
and its environmental impact will affect the growth of Western democratic

societies; second, what should be the size of any human community so that a proper political society may appear; and third, what are the obligations owed to their polity by the subjects of contemporary authoritarian states.

PS 42. LEVINE, ANDREW. Liberal Democracy: A Critique of Its Theory. New York: Columbia University Press, 1981. 216 pp.
Levine attempts to differentiate liberal and democratic theory through a critical examination of liberal democracy. He argues that conceptual difficulties arise when one attempts to combine liberalism and democracy into a coherent political philosophy. Levine believes that democratic liberalism is theoretically defective because it lacks distributional principles. It has become operationally feasible only because of peculiar historical conditions. He then examines some conceptual aspects of the historical link between liberal democracy and Capitalism and speculates on the prospects for going "beyond" liberal democracy, while retaining continuity with liberal democracy's core theory of rights.

PS 43. MANSBRIDGE, JANE J. Beyond Democracy. New York: Basic Books, 1980. 398 pp.
Mansbridge argues that American democracy is based on the notion that the interests of citizens are in constant conflict. She calls this notion "adversary democracy." Such democracy, she believes, violates the principles of reasoned discourse and consensus-building which have been essential to traditional democracy. Mansbridge calls democracy based on common interest "unitary democracy." Although she believes these two forms of democracy to be contradictory, Mansbridge argues that both the unitary and the adversary forms of democracy embody worthy democratic ideals, depending on the political context. The author bases this argument on case studies of a New England town meeting and a small democratic workplace. From these experiences, the author tries to knit two fundamentally different democratic practices into a single institutional system that advances common interests and resolves conflicts.

PS 44. MANSFIELD, HARVEY C., Jr. The Spirit of Liberalism. Cambridge, Mass.: Harvard University Press, 1978. 130 pp.
This book is a collection of essays defending liberalism against the criticism of the New Left. It begins with a look at liberal democracy and its principles. Mansfield discusses Lowi's The End of Liberalism (see PS 488) and the issues that Lowi addresses. In the context of considering Charles Reich's The Greening of America and Robert Dahl's After the Revolution, he also discusses the necessity of reconstructing the relation between consciousness and politics. Mansfield argues that modern liberalism has lost the capability of revolution, which was one of its original precepts. He concludes the book with a discussion of John Rawls and Robert Nozick and their relation to the classical liberalism represented by John Locke.

PS 45. MARCUSE, HERBERT. Counter-Revolution and Revolt. Boston: Beacon Press, 1972. 138 pp.
Marcuse argues that maintaining the capitalist system requires the organization of counter-revolution. He examines how it is possible for Capitalism to expand its repressive base without creating a revolutionary situation. Fearing revolution, Western capitalist countries undertake the organized inhibition of protest. Marcuse examines the Radicalism of the 1960s American counter-culture, arguing that the student movement, by drawing into the political struggle a discussion of non-material, subjective needs, was the forefront of the critical movement against Capitalism.

PS 46. MARCUSE, HERBERT. <u>An Essay on Liberation</u>. Boston: Beacon Press, 1969. 91 pp.

Marcuse challenges the avoidance of utopian speculation in contemporary social theory. He argues that what is frequently labeled utopian is not the historically impossible or the ideal. Rather, what is identified as utopian is the attempt to realize repressive interests and overturn contemporary social relations of domination. Utopian speculation, he argues, should be reemphasized; it provides the motivation to seek out needs different from the repressive ones which now define society. He describes how the reliance on technology for the satisfaction of needs has made the individual dependent on the development of organizational and technological rationality, and how moral development is surrendered to promote this.

PS 47. MARGOLIS, MICHAEL. <u>Viable Democracy</u>. New York: St. Martin's Press, 1979. 211 pp.

Margolis looks at the problems of providing viable democratic government in the last decades of the 20th century. His contention is that the contemporary citizen has lost control of his government. This is due to the fact that 18th-century institutions, which are the basis of American government, cannot deal with 20th-century problems. The author provides an outline of how political institutions and processes can be rearranged to cope with modern methods of popular participation and control. He begins with a criticism of community-based views on democratic government. He then turns to a criticism of empirical democratic theories. Margolis concludes with his own theory of modern democracy.

PS 48. NORDLINGER, ERIC A. <u>On the Autonomy of the Democratic State</u>. Cambridge, Mass.: Harvard University Press, 1981. 239 pp.

Nordlinger examines the extent to which the democratic state is an autonomous entity capable of pursuing its own authoritative actions. The author attacks the prevailing belief that the policy preferences of societal groups control the resources and the authoritative actions of the democratic state. He intends to demonstrate how the preferences of the state itself are as important as those of the pluralistic forces of civil society in determining the political direction of the state. According to Nordlinger, the state has autonomy and its own definitive preferences, and is capable of acting upon them even when they diverge from the demands of the most powerful groups in civil society. Public officials have their own agendas and means of pursuing them. They are not constantly pandering to the demands of special-interest groups. Nordlinger believes a distinction should be made between state and society in order to assess the impact of the interests of the state upon public policy independent of the constraints and supports of societal actors.

PS 49. NOZICK, ROBERT. <u>Anarchy, State, and Utopia</u>. New York: Basic Books, 1974. 367 pp.

Nozick argues for a political theory recognizing absolute rights that are so far-reaching that no person or group can violate them. He raises the question of how the state is to behave toward an individual with regard to these rights. Nozick identifies the minimal state, limited to the narrow functions of protection against force, theft, fraud, enforcement of contracts, etc., as the only justifiable one. A more extensive state would violate persons' rights not to be forced to do certain things. Nozick develops his entitlement theory to criticize theories of distributive justice which argue for a more extensive state.

PS 50. O'BRIEN, MARY. The Politics of Reproduction. Boston: Routledge
& Kegan Paul, 1981. 250 pp.
O'Brien develops a feminist political theory concerned with the process
of reproduction and the political significance of that process. The study
begins with a critical examination of the more influential feminist works.
O'Brien argues that the reliance of these works on existing social theories
perpetuates elements of a male stream of thought which weaken feminist
theory. She then turns to an examination of how the notion of work has
been separated from the experience of procreation in traditional theory;
this has separated the public realm and politics from the private realm
and the family, relegating women to the latter. O'Brien concludes that
the ideology of male supremacy in traditional political theory is manifested in how it ignores the crucial role that reproduction plays as a
dynamic of political theory.

PS 51. PITKIN, HANNA F. The Concept of Representation. Berkeley: University of California Press, 1967. 323 pp.
Pitkin explores the various meanings of the concept of "representation":
representation as a symbol, as "standing for" someone, and as "acting
for" someone. She concludes with a plea for addressing representation
as a rich blend of varied roles, rather than singling out one particular
role.

PS 52. RAWLS, JOHN. A Theory of Justice. Cambridge, Mass.: Harvard
University Press, 1971. 607 pp.
Rawls develops a modern social contract based on a theory of justice.
For Rawls, the central issue in justice is fairness. The compact of society is located in certain original procedural constraints which are
designed to lead to an agreement on principles of justice. The principles
of justice set forth are those that free and rational persons in a position
of relative equality would accept. Rawls also undertakes a critique of
utilitarianism. He then applies his theory to the philosophical basis
of constitutional liberties, the problems of distributive justice, and
the definition of the grounds and limits of political obligation.

PS 53. SANDEL, MICHAEL. Liberalism and the Limits of Justice. New York:
Cambridge University Press, 1982. 191 pp.
Sandel challenges the ideas behind the form of contemporary liberalism
which argues that society is comprised of a plurality of persons, each
with his own aims, interests, and conceptions of the good, and thus best
arranged when governed by principles that do not presuppose any particular
conception of the good. By leaving citizens as free as possible to choose
their own values and ends, liberal society tries to avoid imposing a single
way of life. But in being concerned only with individual notions of rights,
liberalism provides no social ethos toward which individuals may orient
themselves morally. Contemporary liberalism's emphasis on the person
leaves people without an adequate concept of community.

PS 54. SCHAUER, FREDERICK. Free Speech: A Philosophical Inquiry. New
York: Cambridge University Press, 1982. 237 pp.
Schauer discusses freedom of speech as a question of legality. He begins
by trying to find the philosophical foundation for free speech as an independent principle. As his argument develops, however, he shows that free
speech is in fact founded on a collection of interrelated principles.
The principle which applies is often dependent upon the context within
which free speech is asserted. Recognizing the great impact speech has
on others, the author wishes to define proper boundaries and avoid absolute
generalizations about free speech. Finally, Schauer links a theory of
free speech to a theory of rights.

PS 55. SCHRAM, GLENN N. Toward a Response to the American Crises. Washington, D.C.: University Press of America, 1981. 134 pp.
This volume is a collection of essays about the American crises of confidence in itself and in the general moral and material progress of society. The author begins with an essay vindicating democracy. Next, he offers an essay which argues that the moral reconstruction of society may be pursued through an interpretation of the Constitution which would allow a greater place for religion and for restraint in the society. The third essay argues for the alleviation of the crisis through public support of private education and shows how state aid to private education could be made constitutional. This is followed by an essay arguing for a restoration of traditional constitutional government as a means of overcoming contemporary political problems. The concluding essays deal with educational reforms, especially within the field of political science.

PS 56. SEN, AMARTYA and BERNARD WILLIAMS, eds. Utilitarianism and Beyond. New York: Cambridge University Press, 1982. 290 pp.
These essays examine utilitarianism and its possible alternatives. The issues raised range from moral and political philosophy to economics and social choice theory. Utilitarianism is specifically discussed in two ways: as a theory of personal morality and as a theory of public choice. The editors argue that this discussion allows utilitarianism to recover its lost psychological and political dimensions.

PS 57. SIMMONS, A. JOHN. Moral Principles and Political Obligations. Princeton, N.J.: Princeton University Press, 1980. 236 pp.
Simmons argues that political obligation is grounded in a moral bond between the citizen and his government. He examines the motive and character of political obligation by identifying principles which define duty and obligation. Specifically, he looks at how tacit consent, fair play, and gratitude are moral principles which yield political obligations. The moral principle in political obligation, argues the author, is demonstrated in everyday practices of the citizen in a normal political environment.

PS 58. SIMONI, ARNOLD. Crisis and Opportunity. New York: Schocken Books, 1983. 235 pp.
Simoni deals with many current problems, such as pollution, the economy, war, and the loss of natural resources. He argues that present institutions are incapable of dealing with these crises and that it is up to ordinary men and women to rescue the world. The aim of the book is to heighten public awareness about the seriousness of the problems facing society. Simoni attributes the absence of public sensitivity to the belief in progress. He discusses how the present responses to crises fail because they still adhere to a commitment to progress, and fail to address certain essential human needs. Simoni then turns to a close examination of the dangers of a growth-oriented economy which promotes military expansion and encourages war.

PS 59. SPRAGENS, THOMAS A. The Irony of Liberal Reason. Chicago: University of Chicago Press, 1981. 443 pp.
Spragens argues that the same liberal tradition that descends from and protects Western humanism has developed within itself tendencies that threaten human values. He explores this development by identifying first the key features of the "ideal type" conception of politics within liberal rationalism. He then explains some of the intellectual dynamics that produced the key features of liberalism, illuminates and criticizes their internal weakness, their empirical flaws, and their normative inadequacies, and finally suggests the main features of a neo-liberal humanism based on an adequate and up-to-date assessment of human reason.

PS 60. STERBA, JAMES. The Demands of Justice. Notre Dame, Ind.: University of Notre Dame Press, 1980. 164 pp.
Sterba theorizes about the demands of justice and the reasons for accepting them. He begins with an examination of how a justification for the demands of justice and morality can be provided by showing that ethical egotism is inconsistent, irrational, and involves the denial of the will of other persons. This leads to the articulation of the principle of fairness as a foundation for justice. Sterba then proceeds to derive principles of distributive and retributive justice based on fairness, showing how a fairness requirement can be used to support the welfare rights of distant people and future generations. He also considers the implications of his welfare rights theory for the liberals' defense of abortion on demand. Sterba concludes with a look at the conditions under which the demands of justice may be overridden by other values.

PS 61. THOM, GARY. Bringing the Left Back Home: A Critique of American Social Criticism. New Haven, Conn.: Yale University Press, 1979. 303 pp.
Thom undertakes a critical examination of leftist and left-liberal critiques of American society with the purpose of reorienting democratic theory. He begins with a discussion of pluralism, political science, and the proposed democratic theory arising from the American left. He then turns to more radical critiques of American society which discuss alienation and attempt to give social theory a psychological basis. Using Durkheim's concept of anomie, Thom suggests that social criticism should concern itself with what is satisfying to the individual.

PS 62. THOMAS, JOHN L. Alternative America: Henry George, Edward Bellamy, and Henry Demarest Lloyd, and the Adversary Tradition. Cambridge, Mass.: Harvard University Press, 1983. 399 pp.
This book is a study of George's Progress and Poverty, Lloyd's Wealth Against Commonwealth, and Bellamy's Looking Backward. Thomas shows how these books reassured an American public which was apprehensive about the costs of rapid modernization and the reality of progress, while at the same time trying to establish alternative social arrangements based on diversity and cooperation, small economic units, and simplicity in government. Each book proposed a new course of national policy for America. They sought a social reform that owed allegiance neither to the large-scale capitalist model then emerging, nor to the bureaucratic Socialism on the left. In this context, Thomas explores the political criticism of these authors and how they anticipated the Progressive Movement, the New Deal, and the counterculture of the 1960s.

PS 63. WALZER, MICHAEL. Radical Principles. New York: Basic Books, 1980. 310 pp.
Walzer's political essays, written over a fifteen-year period, respond to a variety of circumstances and times. The essays cover four main topics: the retreat of liberalism in the 1970s, the New Left of the 1960s, social change, and democratic Socialism. All of them, however, center primarily on elucidating democratic principles for a leftist politics. The essays are essentially concerned with the development of ideas of procedural justice for democratic Socialism and the distribution of decision-making power. Walzer believes that such readjustment of procedural justice and decision-making power is important because it challenges established powers and well-worn patterns of control and obedience.

PS 64. WALZER, MICHAEL. Spheres of Justice: A Defense of Pluralism and Equality. New York: Basic Books, 1983. 345 pp.
Walzer states that there is no single criterion, or single set of interconnected criteria, for all forms of distributive justice. He argues that to search for a unitary principle of distributive justice misunder-

1004

stands its pluralist character. Rather, he contends, the principles of
justice are themselves pluralistic; different social goods ought to be
distributed for different reasons, in accordance with different procedures,
by different agents; and all these differences derive from different under-
standings of the social goods themselves.

PS 65. WASSERSTROM, RICHARD A. Philosophy and Social Issues: Five Studies.
          Notre Dame, Ind.: University of Notre Dame Press, 1980. 187 pp.
Wasserstrom discusses five important social issues in contemporary American
life: racism and sexism, preferential treatment, the obligation to obey
the law, punishment, and conduct and responsibility in war. The essays
have a normative focus. They try to discern what is morally defensible
and justifiable in respect to these issues. The essays were written over
a fifteen-year period in response to the Civil Rights movement, crime,
and American conduct in the Vietnam War. All of the essays are philosophical inquiries into the justifiability of distinct social practices, laws,
and institutions. They present the events which inspired the essays,
as well as substantive moral arguments for specific positions on the issues.

PS 66. WOLFE, ALAN. The Limits of Legitimacy: Political Contradictions
          of Contemporary Capitalism. New York: Free Press, 1977. 432 pp.
Wolfe seeks to establish the effect of Capitalism on democracy. He examines this in the context of developing a theory of the state for American
politics. Arguing that the history of politics in capitalist society
is the history of the tensions between liberal and democratic conceptions
of the state, he examines how Capitalism has tried to solve this tension
without success. The author then turns to a discussion of the political
stagnation which has set in under the advanced capitalist state; it cannot
develop goals for public policy. Furthermore, politics becomes the pursuit
of power for its own sake, while citizens are frustrated by the absence
of any real political life. This leads to a questioning of state authority.
Wolfe believes that with no political or governmental answers to the failure of liberal democracy, the ruling class begins to consider authoritarian
alternatives.

PS 67. WRONG, DENNIS. Power: Its Forms, Bases, and Uses. New York:
          Harper & Row, 1979. 236 pp.
This book attempts to define the nature of power. Wrong begins by drawing
on debates that took place among social scientists in the 1960s, in addition to classical political theory, to elucidate his own notion of power.
After establishing his definition of power as the capacity of some persons
to produce intended and foreseen effects on others, Wrong turns to a discussion of forms of power—force, manipulation, persuasion, and authority—
and the legitimation of power. This is followed by a look at the bases
of power in individual and collective choices, as well as in political
democracy.

II.   METHODOLOGY AND EMPIRICAL THEORY

PS 68. ABRAMS, ROBERT. Foundations of Political Analysis: An Introduction
          to the Theory of Collective Choice. New York: Columbia University
          Press, 1980. 357 pp.
Collective choice theory is concerned with the problems of voting and how
social choice is made. Abrams begins by summarizing certain normative
democratic principles which collective choice theory must presume. He
presents the many different parts of the theory as well as different theories of voting methods. He then analyzes the rules for making collective

decisions, how such rules were decided upon, and how different voting methods compare with each other.

PS 69. BUCHANAN, JAMES M. Freedom in Constitutional Contract: Perspectives of a Political Economist. College Station: Texas A&M University Press, 1977. 311 pp.
Buchanan argues that constitutional contract is the only way individuals can secure and retain freedom. Making the liberal market economy the basis of his social order, he begins with a look at alternative political paradigms that seem inconsistent with a desirable constitutional order of society. This is followed with an articulation of a constitutionalist-contractarian attitude, along with a treatment of the limits of the contractarian position. Buchanan then takes up the problem of insuring that groups and persons will act in accordance with the agreed-upon rules. Here he also discusses economic implications of his position. Buchanan concludes with a diagnosis of the current condition of "constitutional anarchy" and prescribes reforms for it.

PS 70. BUCHANAN, JAMES M. The Limits of Liberty: Between Anarchy and Leviathan. Chicago: University of Chicago Press, 1975. 210 pp.
Buchanan argues that the idea of the social contract should serve as the legitimate basis of society. He establishes his own notion of constitutional contract, in which rights are delineated, and the post-constitutional contract, where rights are exchanged. The author argues for distinguishing two stages of social interaction, one which involves the selection of rules and one which involves actions within these rules. Buchanan begins with a critique of the anarchist position on society, and then turns to a discussion of the constitutional contract and the post-constitutional contract, which are founded on the free market. He then looks at the role of government and law in providing constraints and protecting freedom. Buchanan concludes with a discussion of what he perceives to be the disarray of the American constitutional structure, and his proposals for constitutional change.

PS 71. BUCHANAN, JAMES M. and GORDON TULLOCK. The Calculus of Consent: Logical Foundations of Constitutional Democracy. Ann Arbor: University of Michigan Press, 1962. 361 pp.
Buchanan and Tullock attempt to formalize the process by which organizations composed of rational beings undertake the writing of a constitution. Their major contribution lies in the analysis of the adoption of voting rules which state the number of votes required for the passage of a bill or resolution. They break the costs of decision-making into two parts: externalities placed on the minority when the adopted action takes place; and communication costs incurred in forming a majority. The authors demonstrate a theoretical voting rule which minimizes costs for a group.

PS 72. CORTES, FERNANDO, ADAM PRZEWORSKI, and JOHN D. SPRAGUE. Systems Analysis for Social Scientists. New York: Wiley, 1974. 336 pp.
This technically and mathematically oriented book adapts systems analysis as it is applied by engineers to the social sciences. The authors argue that social scientists should not look at isolated causal relationships, even those which might use numerous independent variables, to operate on a single dependent variable (that is, multiple regression). Rather, they should analyze the causal flow among a set of variables. Techniques are presented for how this may be done.

PS 73. CRICK, BERNARD. The American Science of Politics: Its Origins
        and Conditions. Boston: Routledge & Kegan Paul, 1959. 252 pp.
Crick traces the ideas, the institutions, and the individuals who have
had an impact on American political science. The book undertakes this
exploration within the framework of a critical examination of the idea
of politics as science in American political thought. Crick identifies
the unique methodological concerns of American political scientists as
outcomes of the liberal tradition. He argues that the American science
of politics is based on the notion of science found in ordinary American
social thought, the idea of common citizenship training, the generalization
of the habits of American democracy, and the common belief in inevitable
progress or manifest destiny for American society.

PS 74. DAHL, ROBERT A. Modern Political Analysis. 1963; Rev. ed. Engle-
        wood Cliffs, N.J.: Prentice-Hall, 1976. 118 pp.
Dahl deals with the nature of political analysis, the meaning of political
influence, types of political systems and regions, and types of political
behavior, in an attempt to provide a theoretical framework for understanding the politics behind policy decisions. He develops a strategy of
inquiry to improve the quality of political decision-making by providing
methods for researching empirical knowledge, arriving at a standard of
evaluation, and clarifying the meaning of terms and concepts.

PS 75. DAHL, ROBERT A. and CHARLES LINDBLOM. Politics, Economics, and
        Welfare: Planning and Politico-Economic Systems Resolved into
        Basic Processes. New York: Harper, 1953. 557 pp.
Dahl and Lindblom develop their theory of political economy by utilizing
a systems theory approach to socioeconomic organizations. They try to
uncover the conditions under which individuals can maximize the attainment
of their goals through the use of social mechanisms. They show how a
theory of rational social action, through large-scale processes of hierarchy, polyarchy, bargaining, and price system, can provide a framework
for the attainment of collective goals.

PS 76. DEUTSCH, KARL W. The Nerves of Government. New York: Free Press,
        1963. 316 pp.
Deutsch develops a theory of politics that is based on the philosophy
of science and cybernetic theories of communication and control. This
theory intends to elaborate the channels of communication and decision-
making within the body politic. The book suggests that governmental behavior should be examined less as a problem of power and more as a problem
of steering. Steering is presented as a matter of communication. Deutsch
examines the implications of this viewpoint for the analysis of governmental institutions, political behavior, and political ideas.

PS 77. DOMHOFF, G. WILLIAM. Who Really Rules? New Haven and Community
        Power Reexamined. New Brunswick, N.J.: Transaction Books, 1978.
        189 pp.
Domhoff provides a detailed study of the power structure and the policy-
making process in New Haven, Connecticut. The book itself is a methodological statement on how power structures should be studied. It provides
a theoretical framework for understanding local power structures in general
by showing how they function within the overall context of the power structures of the national corporate community and the national ruling class.
The study is a response to Robert Dahl's Who Governs? (see PS 193). The
author wants to reestablish the significance of elite theory, as opposed
to Dahl's pluralism, in understanding American politics.

PS 78. DOWNS, ANTHONY. An Economic Theory of Democracy. New York: Harper
    & Row, 1957. 310 pp.
Downs develops a simple formal model of elections and political parties
that reflects economic models of rational choice. He assumes that voters,
party leaders, and the government are rational actors, that party leaders
desire to control the government, and that they compete with each other
for votes. As a result voters give their votes to party leaders who promote the interests of the voters. Downs's main contribution is his discussion of the importance of uncertainty in the various exchanges which
take place between voters and leaders.

PS 79. EALY, STEVEN D. Communication, Speech and Politics: Habermas
    and Political Analysis. Washington, D.C.: University Press of
    America, 1981. 245 pp.
The author utilizes the work of Jurgen Habermas to provide a comprehensive
theoretical framework for understanding and investigating the connection
between language and politics. He applies this to a case study in administrative politics, the Georgia classification survey conducted by the State
Merit System from 1975-78. The study provides an example of the type
of communication problems which arise in political and administrative
organizations. From this, the author seeks to assess the utility of
Habermas's communication theory for the study of American state politics.
The author discovers that Habermas's theory explained many of the communication problems encountered in the case study of the Georgia classification
survey, although it was not adequate for the analysis of all types of
political speech.

PS 80. EASTON, DAVID. A Framework for Political Analysis. Chicago:
    University of Chicago Press, 1979. 142 pp.
Easton tries to establish systems analysis as a theory for the examination
of political systems. The book develops a logically integrated set of
categories with strong empirical relevance that will make possible the
analysis of political life as a system of behavior. The intent is to
unveil the basic processes through which a political system, regardless
of its generic or specific type, is able to persist as a system of behavior
in a stable or changing world. The attention, then, is mainly focused
on the processes of political systems, not on their ideological structures.

PS 81. EASTON, DAVID. The Political System: An Inquiry into the State
    of Political Science. New York: Knopf, 1953. 320 pp.
Easton deals with the condition of political science in the U.S., especially the relation between its causal theories and general political
research. He is critical of the separation of theory from research that
has occurred in political science. Political science, he argues, has
become desensitized to the problems that stand in the way of the development of a comprehensive or general theory of political activity. Furthermore, the neglect of theory has imperiled its attempt to understand the
major problems of political life. If American political science is to
pursue proper scientific inquiry, it requires the development of a scientific method which will provide the theoretical framework for research.
Finally, the American political scientist's flight from scientific reasoning in the area of political life is characteristic of the movement away
from the rational attitude toward life and toward a greater dependence
on emotion, faith, and opinion.

PS 82. EASTON, DAVID. A Systems Analysis of Political Life. New York:
    Wiley, 1965. 507 pp.
Easton examines the life processes of a political system: how it performs
its characteristic work, how it functions under stress, and how it persists
even under the pressures of frequent or constant crisis. In so doing,
he examines what stress and crises threaten the political system and how

they arise, as well as how the system deals with them. Generally, Easton conceives of politics as a system in which demands on the political system and support for it enter the system as "inputs" and are transformed into "outputs" (policies), which in turn feed back to influence further inputs. The political system is presented as a self-regulating mechanism.

PS 83. EDELMAN, MURRAY. Political Language: Words that Succeed and Policies that Fail. New York: Academic Press, 1977. 164 pp.
Edelman analyzes American politics through an examination of the ways in which leaders use language as a strategic tool. He concentrates on the use of language by American leaders to encourage mass acquiescence to their rule, despite widespread waste, injustice, and inequality.

PS 84. EULAU, HEINZ. Micro-Macro Political Analysis: Accents of Inquiry. Chicago: Aldine, 1969. 400 pp.
The book is a collection of essays dealing with the relationship between individual and collective political behavior. The author argues that an individual's "relatedness" to the political process is largely a function of the degree to which he has internalized his role as citizen, and the degree to which he evaluates this role as being an efficacious one, in the sense that performance of the role will make a difference in political affairs. This is followed by an examination of the meaning of social class for individual political behavior. Eulau also studies intergenerational occupational mobility as a political variable, and the effect of early socialization on adult political behavior. Finally, he discusses the relation between the behavioral sciences and liberalism.

PS 85. EULAU, HEINZ. Technology and Civility: The Skill Revolution in Politics. Stanford, Calif.: Hoover Institution Press, 1977. 111 pp.
This volume is a collection of lectures which defend the behavioral approach to political science. Eulau is critical of those people within the profession who advocate technological solutions as a means of solving social problems, as well as those who advocate an expansion of participatory democracy through a return to communal living. Both the technological and anti-technological futurists distrust the democratic and civil politics that fail to reinforce their utopian aspiration, despite their democratic protestations.

PS 86. FALCO, MARIA J., ed. Through the Looking Glass: Epistemology and the Conduct of Inquiry: An Anthology. Washington, D.C.: University Press of America, 1979. 409 pp.
This anthology is devoted to finding a basis for the establishment and validation of truth claims in political inquiry. The contributors address the problem of establishing an authoritative base with which to explain the nature of reality, examining which methodologies emerge as ideologies for bureaucratic or political control, and what the relation is between methodology and political theory. Part of the volume considers the role of methodology in the decision-making process of empirical political research, and the relations between methodology and public policy.

PS 87. FIELD, G. LOWELL and JOHN HIGLEY. Elitism. Boston: Routledge & Kegan Paul, 1980. 135 pp.
Lowell and Higley present a new form of elite theory for the study of the social sciences. Arguing for a more serious consideration of elitist hypotheses as a way of advancing social knowledge and professional social sciences, they show that a much more explicitly elitist viewpoint among persons in influential positions generally is necessary to meet the current problems of developed and developing societies realistically and practically. The authors trace the historical, intellectual development of elite theory before presenting their own paradigm. Then they discuss

the relationship between elitism and liberalism, the obligation of elitism, and the relation between elites and world problems.

PS 88. FROHLICH, NORMA, JOE A. OPPENHEIMER, and ORAN R. YOUNG. <u>Political Leadership</u> <u>and</u> <u>Collective</u> <u>Goods</u>. Princeton, N.J.: Princeton University Press, 1971. 161 pp.
The authors apply a classic rational choice theory of entrepreneurship to problems of political leadership. They argue that the entrepreneur's decision to provide a public good (such as clean air or highways) is contingent upon repayment and competition among suppliers, in addition to the entrepreneur's charismatic personality. The authors go on to develop a model of collective goods provision.

PS 89. GOODIN, ROBERT E. <u>Manipulatory</u> <u>Politics</u>. New Haven, Conn.: Yale University Press, 1980. 250 pp.
Goodin catalogues various modes of political manipulation and assesses them from a moral point of view. The book begins by explaining what is meant by the manipulation of politics and power. Essentially, the author argues that the concept of manipulation itself refers to the evil aspect of power. Goodin begins to identify the more well-known ways in which political manipulation takes place. He looks at the politics of lying, the use of linguistic traps, rhetorical treachery, the use of political rituals as forms of manipulation, and how the obviousness of political solutions can be manipulated through political processes. Goodin concludes with suggestions on how to avoid political manipulation.

PS 90. GOODIN, ROBERT E. <u>Political</u> <u>Theory</u> <u>and</u> <u>Public</u> <u>Policy</u>. Chicago: University of Chicago Press, 1982. 286 pp.
Goodin looks at the failure of the policy sciences to blend theory and practice in order to bring values back into the positivistic sciences. He attributes the antitheoretical cast of policy studies to the influence of incrementalism, a doctrine which maintains that theoretical understanding of the social system is unnecessary and undesirable for policy-making. Goodin believes that empirical relationships and moral values are best discovered by trial and error. He tries to show how incrementalism is an unwise strategy for ascertaining empirical truths and a restrictive method of obtaining social guidance. Goodin specifically examines energy and defense to demonstrate how theoretically informed analysis can illuminate particular policy studies.

PS 91. GOODIN, ROBERT E. <u>The</u> <u>Politics</u> <u>of</u> <u>Rational</u> <u>Man</u>. New York: Wiley, 1976. 210 pp.
Goodin develops a rational choice model of politics for a theory of integration. This general model of social cooperation among rational, self-interested individuals also draws on contemporary social contract theory. The author begins with an explication of the notion of rationality. He then develops the position that although rational actors will strive to coordinate their behavior, under certain conditions government is required for coordination to be effective. Goodin next turns to a discussion of principles by which rational actors would guide their collective activities and shape their social and political institutions. He concludes with an illustration of how his theory can apply to the politics of environmental protection.

PS 92. GREENSTEIN, FRED I. and NELSON W. POLSBY, eds. <u>Handbook</u> <u>of</u> <u>Political</u> <u>Science</u>. 9 vols. Reading, Mass.: Addison-Wesley, 1975. 3688 pp.
This handbook is comprised of nine volumes, each addressing a distinct general topic; within each volume, there are chapters written by various authors discussing different aspects of the central topic. For example, the volume <u>Political</u> <u>Science</u>: <u>Scope</u> <u>and</u> <u>Theory</u> contains a chapter entitled

"Political Science: Tradition, Discipline, Profession, Science, Enterprise"; and Policy and Policy Making includes the chapter "Making Economic
Policy: The Role of the Economist." Scattered throughout subsequent
volumes are chapters on revolutions, polimetrics, Federalism, and world
politics. These subsequent volumes include: Micropolitical Theory, Macro-
political Theory, Nongovernment Politics, Governmental Institutions and
Processes, Strategies of Inquiry, and International Politics; the final
volume in the set is a cumulative index.

PS 93. LASSWELL, HAROLD D. The Future of Political Science. New York:
        Atherton Press, 1963. 256 pp.
Lasswell looks at the future of political science from the viewpoints
of scope, method, and impact. Political science, argues Lasswell, is
inextricable from human society. Looking at the professional roles that
political scientists play, he argues that they must be independent intermediaries between the public and government. Lasswell discusses and evaluates the present research methods and theories advocated by the discipline
for developing public policies. He also discusses how political scientists
must cultivate creativity and collaborate with allied professors in other
disciplines. Lasswell concludes with a call for a better organizational
form for the discipline.

PS 94. LASSWELL, HAROLD D. Politics: Who Gets What, When, How. 1936;
        Rev. ed. New York: World, 1958. 222 pp.
Lasswell argues that the study of politics is the study of influences
and the influential. He defines the influential as those who get the
most of what there is to get, specifically deference, safety, and income.
Those who get the most are the elite. Lasswell examines such characteristics of the elite as skill, class, personality, and attitude. The fate
of an elite is profoundly affected by the ways it manipulates the environment by the use of violence, goods, symbols, and practices. The book
examines the methods used by the elite to remain influential and the consequences of their methods for themselves and society.

PS 95. LASSWELL, HAROLD D. A Pre-View of Policy Sciences. New York:
        Elsevier, 1971. 173 pp.
Lasswell clarifies and plots the future development of policy sciences.
He argues that the policy sciences offer a contextual, problem-oriented,
multi-method viewpoint which can overcome the fragmentation which exists
in the social sciences. He wants to develop a policy science approach
which links normative and legal theory with the instruments of policy
analysis. Lasswell looks at the intellectual tasks awaiting policy sciences and the synthesis of methods to be pursued. This is followed by
a discussion of how the policy process itself works and how the policy
scientist should be trained.

PS 96. LASSWELL, HAROLD D., NATHAN LEITES, and Associates. Language of
        Politics. New York: George W. Stewart, 1949. 398 pp.
The central theme of this book is that political power can be better understood to the degree that language is better understood, and that the language of politics can be usefully studied by quantitative methods. The
book provides a general theory of language as a factor in power and in
political response. It pursues the search for a quantitative method
because of the scientific and policy gains that can come of it. The authors
deal with the technical problems surrounding the quantification of language.
They then take up the application of this method, especially to the language of Communism.

PS 97. LINDBLOM, CHARLES E. The Intelligence of Democracy. New York:
Free Press, 1965. 352 pp.
Lindblom makes the case for partisan mutual adjustment as a rational
decision-making process for political leaders. By "partisan mutual adjustment," Lindblom means bargaining and negotiation between two decision-
makers, as well as unilateral decisions taken in anticipation of another
decision-maker. Lindblom argues that such decisions do result in a kind
of coordination which is a byproduct of the decision process. This coordination, in turn, connects decisions rationally. This unplanned coordination is contrasted with central coordination, which Lindblom criticizes.
Lindblom organizes this study around the thesis that leaders fail to behave
rationally because they are engaged in disjointed incrementalism rather
than synoptic problem-solving.

PS 98. LINDBLOM, CHARLES E. and DAVID K. COHEN. Usable Knowledge: Social
Science and Social Problem Solving. New Haven, Conn.: Yale University Press, 1979. 129 pp.
This book is a study in social problem-solving, policy-making, and political analysis. It considers social science and social research not only
in their governmental uses but in their uses by people in business enterprises and other private groups. The authors also raise questions about
the nature of social science research itself. They claim that social
science and social research are poorly understood by their own practitioners. This study's basic aim is to apply social science research to
the trade itself.

PS 99. LIPSET, SEYMOUR M., ed. Politics and the Social Sciences. New
York: Oxford University Press, 1969. 320 pp.
The essays in this volume consider the relationship of political science
to its neighboring disciplines in the social sciences. The authors look
at the degree to which political science is an autonomous discipline rather
than a hybrid of other social sciences, and whether it should join other
social sciences to form one comprehensive science of man. Also discussed
within these contexts are the values and liabilities of interdisciplinary
collaboration for political scientists.

PS 100. MEADOW, ROBERT G. Politics as Communication. Norwood, N.J.:
Ablex, 1980. 269 pp.
Meadow proposes that communication be viewed according to the role it
plays in political institutions and processes, and according to the role
politics play in shaping communication processes. He begins with a review
of the literature on political communication and is critical of the traditional approach. Meadow then argues that concepts such as power, conflict, political participation, political development, political integration, and political socialization can be based on communication and should
be considered by political communication researchers. He next looks at
aspects of political institutions and processes in the U.S. in which communication phenomena play crucial roles, and concludes with an examination
of how the centrality of communication has made communication itself an
important issue in political systems.

PS 101. POLSBY, NELSON W. Community Power and Political Theory: A Further
Look at Problems of Evidence and Inference. New Haven, Conn.:
Yale University Press, 1980. 245 pp.
Polsby is concerned with uncovering the sources of local community power:
how large groups in communities make demands on one another and how they
collectively determine policy. However, another major concern of this
book has to do with the proper theory and methods for such studies. The
author's studies of various American communities serve as vehicles for
demonstrating Polsby's own methodology and theory, which argues that power
is a subsidiary aspect of the community's social structure. The political

theory guiding current research on community power is the primary object
of attention.

PS 102. RAE, DOUGLAS, et al. Equalities. Cambridge, Mass.: Harvard
University Press, 1981. 210 pp.
This book examines the many ways the notion of equality is used in American
politics. The authors begin by developing their own abstract notion of
equality in a model society. The book then turns to an elaboration of
the authors' notions of equality and how it applies to societal structures,
social issues, and differences in individuals. In the process, the authors
sketch the difference between absolute and relative equalities. They
show how the criteria of relative equality depend upon circumstances.
Finally, they note that equality itself does not necessarily imply human
prosperity.

PS 103. RIKER, WILLIAM H. Liberalism Against Populism: A Confrontation
Between the Theory of Democracy and the Theory of Social Choice.
San Francisco: Freeman, 1982. 311 pp.
Riker uses social choice theory to explicate the theory of democracy.
Social choice theory tries to explain how individual persons' choices
are amalgamated and summarized into the choices of a collective group
of society. The book examines the feasibility of the political ideal
of democracy in terms of the practical constraints that the social choice
analysis reveals. The author hopes to demonstrate the relevance of social
choice analysis to normative concerns. The book's social choice analysis
is also aimed at providing an analytic theory for interpreting the behavior
of political institutions. It argues that social choice analysis can
explain the rise and decline of issues, the ways in which certain political
issues are chosen over others, and the patterns of voter behavior.

PS 104. RIKER, WILLIAM H. The Theory of Political Coalitions. New Haven,
Conn.: Yale University Press, 1962. 300 pp.
Riker here presents his theory of "size principle." According to this
principle, the ideal size of a coalition is a size large enough to win,
but no larger. If it is too small to win, none of its members will benefit;
but if it is larger than necessary, the spoils of victory must be divided
among too many members and each single member gains less than could have
been the case with a smaller coalition. The book develops this point,
detailing various conditions which must be met if a "minimal winning coalition" (one of the optimal size) is to be formed.

PS 105. RIKER, WILLIAM H. and PETER C. ORDESHOOK. An Introduction to
Positive Political Theory. Englewood Cliffs, N.J.: Prentice-
Hall, 1973. 387 pp.
This book introduces an important school of political theory in America--
the so-called "positive theoretic" school. Members of this school start
from the assumption that political actors are rational, and seek individually to maximize their utility. From this, there follows a varied set
of theories regarding elections and voters' behavior, formation of coalitions, power in legislatures, committee bargaining, regulation and public
policy, and so on. The method used is generally that of micro-economics,
emphasizing logical argument rather than empirical investigation.

III.   PRESIDENCY AND CONGRESS

PS 106.   ABSHIRE, DAVID and RALPH D. NURNBERGER. The Growing Power of
Congress. Beverly Hills, Calif.: Sage, 1981. 328 pp.
Abshire takes up four issues: (1) the motivation for increased Congressional involvement in the 1970s and the implications of such involvement
for the future course of U.S. foreign policy; (2) Congressional leadership
and its impact upon effective participation in foreign policy; (3) the
apparent trend in Congress toward policy extremes in foreign policy-making;
and (4) the legitimate parameters of Congressional participation in a
decision to go to war. These issues are approached through accounts of
how Presidential administrations and Congress have interacted to forge
foreign policy in the past. Abshire concludes that Presidential resistance
to Congressional efforts to gain more control over foreign policy is likely
to lead to more conflict between these two branches of the government
in the future.

PS 107.   BAKER, ROSS K. Friend and Foe in the U.S. Senate. New York:
Free Press, 1980. 301 pp.
Baker investigates the friendships and hostilities which develop among
working senators, and the effect which intimate personal relations have
on the legislative process. The author uses the term "institutional kinship" to describe those senatorial friendships which are based on trust,
integrity, hard work, and a tolerance for the opinions of one's adversary.
Baker explores the conditions which give rise to institutional kinship,
evaluates them, and distinguishes among different forms of friendship.
He focuses especially on the loner, the senator who has no close ties
with his colleagues. Also considered are the ways in which personal relations, as sources of conflict or cooperation, influence politics. Most
of the information was gathered through interviews with U.S. senators.

PS 108.   BARBER, JAMES D. Power in Committees: An Experiment in the Governmental Process. Chicago: Rand McNally, 1966. 189 pp.
Barber's study provides a close observation of twelve local government
committees working out a set of standardized problems. Included are examinations of the criteria selected by the committees to develop decisions;
how a committee perceives and evaluates its power relations; and how the
committee system functions internally. Essentially, Barber tries to
uncover the presence and use of political power in committees, thus illuminating interactions between individual members and the committee chair.
Finally the book outlines various types of action which can be initiated
by a committee member to enhance his power, and considers the resources
and personal characteristics associated with each variety of power.

PS 109.   BARBER, JAMES D. The Presidential Character. 1972; Rev. ed.
Englewood Cliffs, N.J.: Prentice-Hall, 1977. 479 pp.
Barber presents a two-fold typology which he asserts is useful in understanding the performance of 20th-century American Presidents. He examines
the degree to which each President has been active or passive in his role
as President, and the extent to which each President is positive or negative, that is, likes or dislikes his work. Barber distinguishes four
types of Presidents: active-negatives, whose basic motive is to obtain
and maintain power and who engage in compulsive activity because of low
self-esteem; passive-negatives, who are motivated by a sense of civic
duty and citizen virtue, who do not work very hard at being President
but agree to do it because they must somehow serve the people; passive-
positives, who are motivated by a need for love and affection and meet
this need by obtaining the approval of others through their political
activities; and active-positives, who are problem solvers, are flexible
and productive, with high self-esteem.

PS 110. BRAUER, CARL M. John F. Kennedy and the Second Reconstruction.
         New York: Columbia University Press, 1977. 396 pp.
Brauer argues that Kennedy did respond to the efforts of blacks to improve
their status in American life, and played a significant role in leading
the U.S. through a "Second Reconstruction." The political necessity of
appeasing the Southern wing of the Democratic party, which was especially
powerful in Congress, explains the apparent caution of Kennedy and his
administration. The author explains how, in the context of the period,
alterations in practice and policy which appear minor were of real importance to blacks and civil rights partisans. The pressure of events, especially those in Birmingham, heightened the administration's commitment
and led Kennedy to propose far-reaching civil rights legislation.

PS 111. BRECKENRIDGE, ADAM C. The Executive Privilege: Presidential
         Control over Information. Lincoln: University of Nebraska Press,
         1974. 188 pp.
Breckenridge presents a study of the conflicts that have arisen between
Congress and the President over the power of executive privilege. He
examines only those cases in which the President has participated directly
in invoking the privilege. Also considered are some related issues involving information that should be public, as distinguished from what the
Congress or its committees claim should be given to the public. The author
argues that the privilege is essential if there is to be any real constitutional and political independence of the executive. Breckenridge also
demonstrates how the exercise of executive privilege has not led to a
stalemate in government, showing the variety of ways in which it has been
successfully policed.

PS 112. CALIFANO, JOSEPH A. Governing America: An Insider's Report from
         the White House and the Cabinet. New York: Simon & Schuster,
         1981. 474 pp.
This is an account of Califano's thirty months as Secretary of Health,
Education, and Welfare during the Carter years. He begins by discussing
his years under Lyndon Johnson and his role in forming the Great Society
programs. He then relates how this experience influenced his work at
HEW (in the process, he recounts personal experiences with Washington's
political leaders, who are portrayed as dedicated public servants). The
book's main focus, however, is an account of how the author managed HEW.
Califano discusses how interest groups maneuver, how political deals are
made and broken, how Presidents make decisions, and what it is like for
a Cabinet officer to deal with the White House, the Congress and the media.
He also discusses various issues examined by HEW during his administration,
such as abortion, a national health plan, health costs, preventative health
care, civil rights, welfare reform, and social security.

PS 113. CLARKE, JAMES W. American Assassins: The Darker Side of Politics.
         Princeton, N.J.: Princeton University Press, 1982. 321 pp.
Clarke's study treats sixteen assassination attempts from 1835 to
Hinckley's attempt on President Reagan in 1981. Clarke's sources include
court testimonies, medical documents, government transcripts, and personal
diaries. Offering an alternative to the political or psychiatric
approaches, Clarke assesses each assailant in terms of personality and within
a social, situational, and cultural context. He sees four main assassin
"types" and organizes his study within this framework. In a final chapter
he summarizes his study and comments on media exposure, security procedures,
and handgun regulation.

PS 114. COOPER, JOSEPH and CALVIN G. MACKENZIE, eds. The House at Work.
         Austin: University of Texas Press, 1981. 369 pp.
Most of the contributors to this volume, which examines the workings of
the House of Representatives in the 1970s, were members of the U.S. House
Commission on Administrative Review. The essays cover topics concerning

1015

the non-policy-making functions of House members. The public's perception of Congress and its members is discussed in conjunction with the way in which legislators define their roles as representatives and as policy-makers. Also examined are the time-management problems of overburdened members, the problems of running a staff, and the acquisition of information about legislation by members of Congress and Congressional research agencies.

PS 115. CRONIN, THOMAS E. The State of the Presidency. Boston: Little,
        Brown, 1975. 355 pp.
Cronin analyzes the contemporary Presidency after Watergate. He finds that Americans have come to expect too much of the President, imagining him to be much more powerful than he really is, and that they are too ready to blame the President when things go wrong. At the same time, though, Cronin finds that the swelling of staff and the "imperial" trap-pings of power tend to isolate the President from people and from real problems, and encourage an excessive concern with image. Cronin looks at the problems inside the executive branch (for example, Cabinet relations, use of staff) most closely, with some attention to outside relations (for example, Congress, the public). He considers a variety of reform proposals, rejecting many (for example, a single, six-year term), and advocating mostly standard ones (for example, stronger parties, more openness).

PS 116. CRONIN, THOMAS E. and SANFORD D. GREENBERG, eds. The Presidential
        Advisory System. New York: Harper & Row, 1969. 375 pp.
This collection of twenty-nine essays attempts to report and analyze the sources of advice and advocacy available to the modern American President. Most of the contributors are social scientists, and the majority have had practical experience working in or advising the Executive branch. Much space is devoted to recounting events and reflecting upon experiences. There is considerable criticism, but mostly from a "mainstream" perspective. The book treats "inside" advisers, such as the Council of Economic Advisers; "outside" advisers, such as commissions and intellectuals; the politics of advising; and reform proposals.

PS 117. DAVIS, VINCENT, ed. The Post-Imperial Presidency. New York:
        Praeger, 1980. 190 pp.
Davis has compiled a collection of essays which examines the history of and expectations for the American Presidency in the 1980s. The preliminary essays discuss the Presidential selection process and citizen participation in that process. The President's role in national unity and his relation to Congress and the Defense Department is subsequently considered. One essay addresses whether or not the President might be better served by an executive cabinet. Also examined is the President's role in providing an economic stabilization policy. The book concludes with an examination of the Presidencies of Richard Nixon and Jimmy Carter.

PS 118. DODD, LAWRENCE C. and BRUCE I. OPPENHEIMER, eds. Congress Recon-
        sidered. 1977; Rev. ed. Washington, D.C.: Congressional
        Quarterly Press, 1981. 442 pp.
The essays in this book reassess the role of Congress and its internal structure in light of recent changes. Contributors look at the Congres-sional reforms by which the power of senior members of both houses has been lessened, the reassertion of Congressional authority in light of the Watergate scandals and the Vietnam War, and the apparently increasing insulation of Congressmen from electoral defeat. The revised edition includes essays that trace the effects of electoral, organizational, and membership changes on the behavior of Congressional members. It also provides a broad environmental, historical, and theoretical perspective on Congress, and on those factors that will influence Congress in the 1980s.

PS 119. DUGGER, RONNIE. On Reagan: The Man and His Presidency. New
York: McGraw-Hill, 1983. 616 pp.
Dugger has collected a comprehensive range of remarks made by Ronald Reagan
from the 1960s to his rise to the Presidency. Describing Reagan as a
right-wing ideologue, Dugger divides his book into chapters dealing with
distinct political issues (taxes, the environment, foreign policy, etc.).
This allows a view of the historical and biographical development of
Reagan's more controversial remarks. The author uses unpublished transcripts of more than 500 five-minute radio commentaries which Reagan broadcast from 1975-79. He draws from this recently available material in
order to throw more light on Reagan's activities as a propagandist and
on his uncompromised thinking prior to becoming a Presidential candidate.

PS 120. EDWARDS, GEORGE C. Presidential Influence in Congress. New York:
Freeman, 1980. 216 pp.
Edwards begins with an examination of the varying degrees of success that
Presidents have had with getting proposals passed. This is followed by
a comparison between the President's influence on Congress in domestic
and foreign policy-making. The author then looks at several sources of
conflict between the President and Congress, including their different
constituencies. He next examines the effectiveness of potential sources
of influence such as political party affiliations. The author's empirical
research discloses that there is a lack of Presidential coattails, and
that Presidential legislative skills are relatively unimportant. Furthermore, there are limitations to bargaining and only House members of the
President's own party are responsive to Presidential popularity.

PS 121. EDWARDS, GEORGE C. and STEPHEN WAYNE, eds. Studying the Presidency.
Knoxville: University of Tennessee Press, 1983. 312 pp.
Edwards and Wayne offer a collection of essays dealing with the scope
and methodology of research on the Presidency. The book begins with a
look at approaches, cases, concepts, methods of quantitative analysis,
and a comprehensive overview of the major perspectives that have been
employed: legal, institutional, political, and psychological. The book
then turns to an examination of data sources and techniques for collecting
data. Chapters here contain discussions of legal research, interviewing,
and primary and secondary documentary material, including that in Presidential libraries.

PS 122. FENNO, RICHARD F. Congressmen in Committees. Boston: Little,
Brown, 1973. 302 pp.
Fenno's thesis is that the decisions made by the House committees can
be explained in terms of two independent variables: individual members'
goals and environmental constraints on the committee. Fenno's categorization of committee members (based on personal interviews) distinguishes
among those who desire to join committees that have significant influence
within the House (e.g., Appropriations, Ways and Means) from those who
want to make good public policy (Foreign Affairs, Education, and Labor)
or to help constituents and thereby insure re-election (Interior and Post
Office). Environmental constraints, which vary in their significance
from committee to committee, include party leaders. In comparing the
two Houses, Fenno observes that Senate committees are less important as
a source of chamber influence, less preoccupied with success on the floor,
less autonomous within the chamber, less personally expert, less strongly
led, and more individualistic in decision-making than House committees.

PS 123. FENNO, RICHARD F. Home Style: House Members in Their Districts.
Boston: Little, Brown, 1978. 306 pp.
In preparation for this book, Fenno traveled with eighteen members of
the House of Representatives for several years as they visited and worked
with their constituents. Fenno describes how the members perceived and

presented themselves to their constituents. He analyzes the ways in which their relationship to their constituents affect, and are affected by, their activities in Washington. In addition to this analysis, Fenno includes an appendix describing his method of research.

PS 124. FENNO, RICHARD F. The President's Cabinet: An Analysis in the
Period from Wilson to Eisenhower. Cambridge, Mass.: Harvard
University Press, 1959. 327 pp.
Fenno provides a political analysis of the President's Cabinet, arguing that the Cabinet is a distinct institution. He examines the Cabinet's origins, its growth, its personnel, and its meetings, to better comprehend it as a decision-making and coordinating body. He also examines the close President-Cabinet relationship. This is done to illuminate how the Cabinet influences the President, how members are selected by the President, and how Cabinets limit the control of the President. Finally, Fenno examines the influence which the President and his Cabinet have on the larger political system; the political factions which influence Cabinet appointments; and the impact which partisan groups, the legislature, and the departmental bureaucracy have on the President-Cabinet relationship.

PS 125. FIORINA, MORRIS P. Representatives and Their Constituencies.
Lexington, Mass.: Lexington Books, 1974. 143 pp.
Fiorina develops an abstract model for the relationship between a representative and his or her constituents. A key assumption of this model is that constituents are generally "ungrateful," that is, the anger of those with whom the representative has not sided will be greater than the pleasure of those with whom he or she has sided. Fiorina argues that the critical condition, if Congressmen are to please their constituents and survive, is that members of their constituency be more or less agreed on policy issues. If this is not true, that is, if the constituency is heterogeneous, then he concludes that there is no way for a Congressman to build up a dependable base of support over time. Fiorina's point is that heterogeneity, rather than electoral marginality, is the source of electoral insecurity for Congressmen. A side benefit of the study is Fiorina's conceptual clarification of such terms as "marginality" of districts and "moderation" of Congressmen's votes.

PS 126. FISHER, LOUIS. The Constitution Between Friends: Congress, the
President, and the Law. New York: St. Martin's Press, 1978.
274 pp.
Fisher looks at the extent to which the Constitution is circumvented for political goals and how personal judgments often override institutional judgments in the struggle between the legislative and executive branches of government. He tries to clarify the central legal and institutional conflicts between the President and Congress. The book begins with a discussion of the Constitution and its doctrines of separated and implied powers. It then looks at specific Federal powers and presents cases which illuminate the conflicts which arise between the executive and the legislative branches. Specifically examined are the conflicts over the removal of power, the Presidential and legislative veto, control over the administration, Congressional investigation, impeachment, executive privilege, the power of the purse, and the treaty and war powers.

PS 127. FISHER, LOUIS. Presidential Spending Power. Princeton, N.J.:
Princeton University Press, 1975. 345 pp.
Fisher examines how the President executes the Federal budget after Congress appropriates funds for Federal agencies. Specifically, he looks at how the President impounds, transfers, reprograms, or shifts these funds. He also examines the President's authority to use these funds in confidential and covert ways, then shows how the decisive commitment to spend funds is not made by Congress but by executive officials. The

discussion begins with a description of the evolution of various forces
that led to the delegation over time of greater spending power to the
President. Then Fisher studies specific instruments of discretionary
actions, such as spending authority, appropriation accounts, and the
impoundment of funds, especially in light of how they were used to finance
the Cambodian War from 1970 to 1973. The author calls for greater Congressional understanding of the budget process to assure that Congress
will not have its power of the purse usurped.

PS 128. **FOLEY, MICHAEL.** The New Senate: Liberal Influence on a Conservative Institution, 1959-1972. New Haven, Conn.: Yale University
Press, 1980. 342 pp.
Foley examines the evolution of the Senate from a conservative institution
in which liberals were frustrated and ostracized in the 1950s to the
liberal majority of the 1960s. He assesses this change by looking at the
activities, behaviors, and policy successes of Senate liberals. The transformation of the Senate by liberals, the author asserts, also led to the
transformation of liberal Senators by the institutionalization of their
own policy processes. Foley defines what he means by "liberal" during
the period from 1959 to 1972 by articulating criteria drawn from the public
record. These criteria are then used to identify and rate liberal Senators.

PS 129. **FRANCK, THOMAS M.** The Tethered Presidency: Congressional
Restraints on Executive Power. New York: New York University Press,
1981. 299 pp.
Franck describes the weakening of Presidential authority in foreign policy-
making, and the historical origins of foreign relations conflicts between
the branches of government. He then examines the costs and benefits of
Congressional resurgence and its frustrations in light of Presidential
prerogatives. His essays deal with such subjects as Congressional concern
with international human rights and Congressional attempts to investigate
intelligence agencies and the Defense Department. These issues are discussed in view of how Congress now freely asserts its authority in foreign
policy, and has taken away the President's authority to speak for the
national interest and provide leadership in foreign policy.

PS 130. **GLAD, BETTY.** Jimmy Carter: In Search of the Great White House.
New York: Norton, 1980. 546 pp.
Glad provides a personal and psychological portrait of Carter which suggests that his great drive for political office was not motivated by any
overarching purpose. In a discussion of Carter's earlier career in Georgia
politics, she concludes that his administrative mentality and centralist
positions were characteristic of his whole political career. The 1976
campaign and Carter's Presidency demonstrate, Glad believes, that he was
more interested in procedure than in politics, and was both practical
and uncreative. Glad argues that Carter's attempts to manipulate images
of himself did not hide the administration's lack of purpose, and that
this strategy led to the electorate to believe that he was not in command
of events and precipitated his eventual defeat.

PS 131. **GOLDSTEIN, JOEL K.** The Modern American Vice-Presidency. Princeton,
N.J.: Princeton University Press, 1982. 409 pp.
Goldstein assesses the contemporary office of the Vice-Presidency by focusing on the activities of its occupants from 1953 to 1981. He relates
the growth of the office to larger developments in the American political
system since the New Deal. The importance of the Vice-Presidency, argues
Goldstein, lies in the maintenance of continuity of executive authority
in case of Presidential incapacity; furthermore, those who occupy the
office are then considered for the Presidency. The author notes that
the Vice-President also participates in decision-making processes and
is observed as a public figure and spokesman of the governing administration.

PS 132. GRABER, DORIS, ed. The President and the Public. Philadelphia: Institute for the Study of Human Issues, 1982. 310 pp.
Graber provides an account of how the President utilizes his public image. She describes the expectations of the public about what kind of person the President should be, and she examines how people get to know and like previously unknown Presidential candidates. The process through which the news media analyze Presidential activities is considered, thus eluci-dating trends in White House media coverage. Graber's study includes an examination of communication strategies used by incumbent Presidents in their bids for reelection; an evaluation of how well Presidents do in relating to the public; and an assessment of Presidential popularity polls.

PS 133. GREEN, MARK. Who Runs Congress? 1972; Rev. ed. New York: Viking Press, 1979. 343 pp.
Green looks at how the demands of special interest groups affect Congres-sional behavior and divert public interest. He then suggests that the public's general interest can reclaim control of Congress from special interest groups. Green begins with a look at the influence of big money on government. This is followed by an examination of the power of the most influential special interest groups and lobbyists, especially within the committee system. The author also examines corruption, and looks at the decline of Congressional powers in its relation to the Presidency. He concludes with suggestions for citizen action.

PS 134. HALPERIN, MORTON H. and DANIEL HOFFMAN. National Security and the Right to Know. Washington, D.C.: New Republic Books, 1977. 158 pp.
The authors relate how the system of secrecy regarding national security worked under the Nixon administration. They examine three episodes that illustrate how it functioned: the Pentagon Papers, the bombing of Cambodia, and the secret intervention in Angola. They show how secrecy in these cases undermined the constitutional prerogatives of Congress and the elec-torate, and led to the infringement of civil liberties. The authors con-clude with a case for a more open system and detail the kind of legislation that would lessen abuse of secrecy in national security matters.

PS 135. HARDIN, CHARLES M. Presidential Power and Accountability. Chicago: University of Chicago Press, 1974. 257 pp.
Hardin argues that Presidential abuse of power had been occurring seriously and getting worse for decades prior to the Watergate scandal of Nixon's administration. His position is that Congress has proven incapable of handling this growing abuse of Presidential power and of providing an alternative to Presidential government. The problem of Presidential abuse of power is a product of inherent structural faults, and is not attribut-able to one administration or one series of events. The author argues that only a new constitution can solve these longstanding problems. He then presents his own diagnosis and prescription for a new constitution, which centers on the establishment of a strong President, but one whose authority is limited by an opposition party government in the legislative branch.

PS 136. HEINEMAN, BEN W. and CURTIS A. HESSLER. Memorandum for the Presi-dent: A Strategic Approach to Domestic Affairs in the 1980s. New York: Random House, 1980. 404 pp.
Heineman and Hessler argue that in the 1980s a President's resources will be limited by the constraints placed on his or her powers. To guard against failure, the President must develop and follow a "strategic approach" to the domestic Presidency. The authors draw suggestions for this approach from examining the fundamental mistakes of the Carter adminis-tration. They propose that the President should know the constraints

placed on his office by other groups or institutions in order to establish realistic expectations; furthermore, the President should be able to differentiate among priorities and concern himself with Presidential issues, while dealing with sub-Presidential issues through the delegation of authority.

PS 137. HINCKLEY, BARBARA. Stability and Change in Congress. New York: Harper & Row, 1971. 216 pp.
Hinckley argues that both change and stability in Congress must be explained in dynamic terms. Her attention centers on three points: the stability of membership, the structure of the norms and values through which influence is distributed, and the leadership. In the final chapter, she identifies nine interrelationships among those phenomena. However, primary emphasis is given to membership because dynamic change is possible principally through changing membership. Her thesis is supported by the large number of Congressional changes and higher than normal membership turnover since 1972.

PS 138. INGRAM, HELEN, NANCY K. LANEY, and JOHN R. McLAIN. A Policy Approach to Political Representation: Lessons from the Four Corner States. 1968; Rev. ed. Baltimore, Md.: Johns Hopkins University Press, 1980. 370 pp.
This is an empirical study of the problems of representation, which argues that there is considerable agreement about policy preferences between legislators and voters. Using questionnaires sent to voters and interviews with legislators in Arizona, New Mexico, Colorado, and Utah, the authors sought links between the actions of state legislators and the opinions of their constituents. They found a marked consistency of viewpoint between voters and legislators in these states.

PS 139. IPPOLITO, DENNIS S. Congressional Spending: A Twentieth Century Fund Report. Ithaca, N.Y.: Cornell University Press, 1981. 286 pp.
The author looks at the efficacy of the Congressional budget reforms of 1974. He concludes that they failed to reduce Congressional spending and to produce fiscal responsibility. Part one shows how the budget reforms were a response to growing Presidential budgetary power and heightened criticism of Congress as fiscally irresponsible. Part two examines the implementation and operation of the reforms. Here Ippolito argues that the existence of two Congressional budget committees producing different budgets, and the growth of the Congressional Budget Office, made all attempts to place constraints on spending ineffective. Part three contains the author's own suggestions for controlling Congressional spending. He argues that only a balanced budget amendment would force Congress to make funding decisions based on program priorities.

PS 140. JOHNSON, HAYNES. In the Absence of Power: Governing America. New York: Viking Press, 1980. 339 pp.
Johnson argues that the U.S. has become a nation in danger of being unable or unwilling to govern itself. He claims that although this malaise set in during the administration of Jimmy Carter, it originated in the events of the 1960s and 1970s. Generally, this book provides a journalistic account of the problems faced by Carter during his administration, especially the failure to mobilize the people and the political system behind him. The author concludes that despite Carter's qualities, he presided at a time when many Americans lost faith in government.

PS 141. JONES, ROCHELLE and PETER WOLL. The Private World of Congress. New York: Free Press, 1979. 264 pp.
The authors look at staff conferences, the inner offices of Senators and Congressmen, the private meetings of Congressional groups, and the workings of the committee system in order to understand where legislative strategy and public policy are made. They analyze how the members of Congress scramble for the positions and signs of power--committee chairmanships, assignments to prestigious committees, having large and expert staffs, and gaining legislative victories. The authors also look at how Congressional aides use their positions, their bosses, and their expertise to advance their own power. They conclude with a consideration of how this competition for power affects public policy.

PS 142. KESSEL, JOHN H. The Domestic Presidency: Decision-Making in the White House. North Scituate, Mass.: Duxbury Press, 1975. 147 pp.
Kessel reveals how domestic policy was formulated in the White House of Richard Nixon. He specifically examines the impact that the President's aides had on the decision-making process. The author studies the group dynamics operating among the Presidential aides. He is concerned with uncovering how Presidential aides generally are organized to serve the interests of the President; how a consensus is reached if disagreements arise; how staff support is arranged; and how communications networks are established. Kessel also examines how authority is delegated and how accountability is maintained.

PS 143. KINGDON, JOHN W. Congressmen's Voting Decisions. New York: Harper & Row, 1973. 313 pp.
Kingdon examines how Congressmen make their decisions when voting in the House of Representatives. Rather than focusing on decision-making in general, Kingdon asks individual Congressmen to give a life history of one specific decision, describing the political actors to whom he paid attention and the considerations he weighed to reach a decision. He discovers that fellow Congressmen supply the most useful type of information: "digested," explicitly evaluative information which takes account of the political as well as policy implications of legislative issues. Kingdon reports that the next most important factor is the perceived position of the Congressman's constituency. The Executive office--though always on the minds of those members belonging to the President's party--and the party leadership appear to be relatively weak influences.

PS 144. LIGHT, PAUL C. The President's Agenda: Domestic Policy Choice from Kennedy to Carter (with Notes on Ronald Reagan). Baltimore, Md.: Johns Hopkins University Press, 1982. 246 pp.
Light's book covers the Presidencies from that of John Kennedy to that of Ronald Reagan to examine how domestic social policies are selected. Specifically, the author examines the development of what he calls the "No Win" Presidency in which the President faces cross pressures, with no room to compromise, between short-term political influence and long-term policy effectiveness. Light discovers that policy choices are based primarily on the benefits the President expects from them. He also looks at how agenda decision-making processes are characterized by internal conflict, staff coalition-building, standard operating procedures, and organizational learning.

PS 145. LYNN, LAURENCE E. Managing the Public's Business: The Job of the Government Executive. New York: Basic Books, 1981. 211 pp.
Lynn presents a proposal for effective management of government organizations, drawing from his experience on the National Security Council and in the Departments of the Interior, Defense, and Health, Education,

and Welfare. Lynn provides insights into the nature of the responsibilities of appointed executives, and the forces that diminish the capacities of these officials to perform with distinction and competence in government. He reviews those features of the American political system that jeopardize and diminish the political executive's effectiveness.

PS 146. MACKENZIE, CALVIN. The Politics of Presidential Appointments. New York: Free Press, 1981. 298 pp.
MacKenzie analyzes the procedures recent Presidents have used for selecting appointments which require Senate approval. This is followed by an examination of how the Senate renders its advice and consent when examining Presidential appointments. The author suggests that the appointment process reflects the nature of the Presidency, the Senate, and the relationships between them. The book provides a history of White House personnel operations to show how the selection of appointees is linked to the requirements of a particular President. Mackenzie concludes that the selection of appointees is part of policy-making in general, and not simply a system of political patronage or a process of personnel management.

PS 147. MALBIN, MICHAEL J. Unelected Representatives: Congressional Staff and the Future of Representative Government. New York: Basic Books, 1980. 279 pp.
Malbin examines the role that Congressional staff play in the formation of government policy. He examines the staff's considerable indirect influence and the tenuous controls Congressmen have over their staff, especially as Congress fails to cope with its increasing workload. He also presents case studies of committee staffs to illustrate various stages of the legislative process, discussing how staff members persuade their bosses to adopt their ideas, how staffs negotiate and act on behalf of their members in other stages of the legislative process, and how staffs direct the flow of information within Congressional committees. The author concludes with suggestions for the role of Congressional staffs in a representative democracy.

PS 148. MANLEY, JOHN F. The Politics of Finance: The House Committee on Ways and Means. Boston: Little, Brown, 1970. 395 pp.
Manley describes and analyzes the House Ways and Means Committee's recruitment, the internal relations of the Committee, the crucial role played by its chairman, and relations of the Committee to the House, the Senate, and the Executive branch. He emphasizes several findings. First, part of the success of the Committee in the 1960s depended on the skillful leadership and flexibility of the chairman, Wilbur Mills. Second, the Ways and Means Committee has been highly successful in the House largely because it has faithfully reflected the general policy preferences of a majority of the members of the House (which at the time was relatively conservative). Third, the results of elections have profound implications for the internal relations and policy decisions of the Ways and Means Committee. Fourth, Ways and Means has not yielded control over tax policy to the Executive branch (specifically the Treasury Department), for the Committee seems better able than the Executive branch to assimilate tax demands from various groups.

PS 149. MANSFIELD, HARVEY, Sr., ed. Congress Against the Presidency. New York: Praeger, 1975. 199 pp.
This book deals with the redistribution of influence within the national legislature after Richard Nixon's resignation, and how this affected Congress's capacity to confront the Executive. The first essay describes the growth, operations, and spread of power in Congress. Next, the media's current role in the political system is considered. Subsequent essays deal with how the present political system has had to adapt to a permanent large-scale military establishment and to global diplomacy. These essays include a discussion of foreign policy and the security agencies.

PS 150. MATTHEWS, DONALD R. U.S. Senators and Their World. Chapel Hill:
         University of North Carolina Press, 1960. 303 pp.
Based partly on biographical research and partly on personal interviews
conducted in 1957, this book describes the socio-economic backgrounds,
religious affiliations, education, and career histories of U.S. Senators.
Matthews assesses their relationships with the press and the unwritten
codes of behavior that prevail among them--their "folkways." He then
measures the impact of these factors on the Senators' influence.

PS 151. MATTHEWS, DONALD R. and JAMES A. STIMSON. Yeas and Nays: Normal
         Decision-Making in the U.S. House of Representatives. New York:
         Wiley, 1975. 190 pp.
This study examines why members of the House of Representatives vote as
they do. Matthews and Stimson note that preceding studies have assumed
that individuals freely choose how to vote on each issue as it arises.
However, with over 150 roll-call votes each year, a member of the House
would have to work very hard to build a personal basis for deciding how
to vote on each issue. The authors argue that Congressmen pick some significant member--the chair of a relevant subcommittee, the Speaker of
the House, or a party leader, for example--and simply vote in the same
way as that person. This assumption enabled Matthews and Stimson to predict the votes of House members with impressive accuracy.

PS 152. MAYHEW, DAVID R. Congress: The Electoral Connection. New Haven,
         Conn.: Yale University Press, 1974. 194 pp.
Operating on the assumption that Congressmen act with the sole motivation
of being reelected, Mayhew examines what activities are considered useful
by the Congressman, and what happens when a group of people so motivated
tries to legislate. He argues that the most important activities pertaining to reelection are advertising one's name, claiming credit to create
an image of power and influence, and devising methods of expressing opinions to please a wide variety of constituencies. Mayhew contends that
as an organization, Congress is able to operate effectively because its
structure of offices, committees, parties, and even functions serve the
ends of reelecting members and maintaining the institution.

PS 153. McADAMS, ALAN K. Power and Politics in Labor Legislation. New
         York: Columbia University Press, 1964. 346 pp.
McAdams uses the Landrum-Griffin Act, a labor law, to demonstrate the
impact of government on the economy. He examines the passage of this
legislative bill to show how the public decided the outcome of the 1959
battle over labor reform, thus elucidating the role of the voters in passing a bill into law. McAdams then discusses the labor movement in the
U.S. in order to provide background information. He concludes that passage of the bill reflected the strength of the labor movement and the influence of public opinion on Congress.

PS 154. MELTSNER, ARNOLD, ed. Politics and the Oval Office: Toward Presi-
         dential Governance. San Francisco: Institute for Contemporary
         Studies, 1981. 332 pp.
Meltsner offers prescriptions for meeting challenges to Presidential governance. He first examines the political environment in which the President
must operate, analyzing public opinion and popular moods, changing electoral behavior, declining political parties, the "imperial media,"
Presidential-Congressional relations, the President's problems with the
bureaucracy, and the Federal courts. Then he deals with the Presidential
office, the obstacles it presents to leadership, and how these might be
overcome. In the final part the author explores the current policy agenda
regarding the economy, energy, and national security, and evaluates alternatives in the context of the constraints imposed by the domestic political
environment and the Presidential office.

PS 155. MUELLER, JOHN E. War, Presidents, and Public Opinion. New York: Wiley, 1973. 300 pp.
Mueller examines public support for U.S. involvement in Korea and in Vietnam, and finds that support and opposition to involvement was similar for the two Wars. Beyond this, he charts the popularity of U.S. Presidents as indicated in Gallup polls, relating changes in popularity to the length of time the President had been in office, to various international crises, to the condition of the economy, and to the experiences in Korea and Vietnam. One of the author's most noteworthy conclusions is that a President's popularity steadily declines during his term in office.

PS 156. NATHAN, RICHARD. The Administrative Presidency. New York: Wiley, 1983. 180 pp.
Focusing on the relationship between bureaucrats and politicians, Nathan argues that it is appropriate for political executives to seek greater managerial influence over the bureaucracy. He defends his argument by examining the managerial objectives and accomplishments of Richard Nixon and Ronald Reagan. Nathan pays special attention to Reagan's successful administrative actions as demonstrations of the correct path for an American President to follow in managing a bureaucracy.

PS 157. NEUSTADT, RICHARD E. Presidential Power: The Politics of Leadership, with Reflections on Johnson and Nixon. New York: Wiley, 1976. 224 pp.
Basing his analysis partly on logic, partly on historical evidence, and partly on personal interviews with those who have worked with Presidents, Neustadt concludes that a President's real power is much less than his formal power. He states that in order to maintain real power, a President must build political "capital" by cultivating both public prestige and prestige among Washington "insiders." Neustadt further argues that a President must not squander this power by tolerating minor insubordination and by relying more on the ability to persuade than on the power to command.

PS 158. ORMAN, JOHN. Presidential Secrecy and Deception: Beyond the Power to Persuade. Westport, Conn.: Greenwood Press, 1980. 239 pp.
Orman presents a theoretical analysis of the problems involved in the covert use of power by an American President. He discusses several factors which influence Presidential use of covert activity, including the President's personality, the exigencies of the office, and the situational factors. He then explains recent covert operations in view of these factors. Orman considers the role of Presidential advisers, such as Henry Kissinger, in determining foreign policy. He concludes that illegal, unconstitutional, or unethical acts are never proper, though sometimes necessary, and that means and ends must be compatible.

PS 159. PEABODY, ROBERT L. Leadership in Congress: Stability, Succession, and Change. Boston: Little, Brown, 1976. 522 pp.
Peabody looks at formal party leadership in both the House and the Senate, using case studies of leadership contests for historical comparisons. He explores how and why particular leaders were chosen by the majority and minority parties and what factors condition their success—or lack of it—in the office. Four influences on leadership are presented: individual power, position, institutional arrangements, and such external forces as the mass media, intervention by the President, or interest group views. The personality and skill of the contestants also appear to be important. The study indicates that successful candidates usually come from the "safe districts" and from the ideological mainstream of their respective parties, especially those who party colleagues describe as having "leadership potential." Though the predominant pattern of leadership selection Peabody delineates is retention of incumbents, Republicans (the minority party) are more likely to contest leadership change.

PS 160. PFIFFNER, JAMES P. The President, the Budget, and Congress:
         Impoundment and the 1974 Budget Act. Boulder, Colo: Westview
         Press, 1979. 165 pp.
Pfiffner looks at the clash between Richard Nixon and the Congress over
fiscal power, policy priorities, and constitutional prerogatives. He
examines how, by means of the Congressional Budget and Impoundment Control
Act of 1974, Congress reasserted its constitutional prerogatives. Within
the discussion of this constitutional crisis, the author also examines
the partisan politics which were involved. He argues that Congress's
response to Nixon's practice of impoundment was motivated by a fear that
its Congressional spending power was being impaired by the growth of the
"imperial Presidency."

PS 161. PIERCE, NEAL R. and LAWRENCE D. LONGLEY. The People's President:
         The Electoral College in American History and the Direct Vote
         alternative. 1968; Rev. ed. New Haven, Conn.: Yale University
         Press, 1981. 342 pp.
The authors examine the history and current status of the Electoral College.
They regard it as ineffective, pointing out that it has overruled the
popular vote in the past, and that it threatened to do so again in 1976.
They consider the Electoral College a danger to democracy—one which may
cause a modern Constitutional crisis by throwing responsibility for deciding an election into the House of Representatives. After analyzing past
and present proposals for the reform of the Electoral College, they conclude that the only sure solution is to abolish it and establish a direct
popular vote for selecting the President.

PS 162. POLSBY, NELSON W. Political Promises: Essays and Commentary
         on American Politics. New York: Oxford Universeity Press, 1974.
         279 pp.
Polsby's seven essays examine a variety of features of the political scene
of the early 1970s. Rather than advocating profound revision of America's
political institutions, he claims that the institutions are here to stay.
Polsby favors nurturing dilapidated institutions rather than attacking
them. Subjects he addresses include Watergate and the Administration's
accountability; the 1972 election; the legislation, operation, and composition of Congress; social stratification; press coverage of political
events; and the political extremism of Joseph McCarthy and campus radicals.

PS 163. RANNEY, AUSTIN, ed. The Past and Future of Presidential Debates.
         Washington, D.C.: American Enterprise Institute, 1979. 226 pp.
The essays in this book address the issues surrounding the televised Presidential debates. The topics discussed include the origins, conduct, and
impact of the debates; their changing Constitutional and legal status;
and their impact on voter interest, knowledge, and choices of candidate.
Information is provided on how the candidates make the decision to participate in debates and their perceived strategic needs. The formats of the
debates are also examined: how these were ad hoc compromises among sponsors and candidate representatives, with each participant seeking to maximize his advantages and minimize his handicaps.

PS 164. RIESELBACH, LEROY N. The Roots of Isolationism: Congressional
         Voting and Presidential Party Leadership in Foreign Policy.
         Indianapolis, Ind.: Bobbs-Merrill, 1966. 240 pp.
Rieselbach examines the substantial opposition to American participation
in foreign affairs that persists among both politicians and votes. He
argues that Congress and the people are reluctant to provide the government
with the tools for the exercise of world leadership. He looks at how
the President tries to secure Congressional acceptance of, and support
for, his foreign policy. In the process, he tries to uncover specific
attributes of the isolationist Congressman and what factors determine

Congressional voting choices. This examination provides an understanding of the voting process in Congress and illuminates the ways the President can intervene in the legislative process to mobilize support for his programs.

PS 165. ROSEBOOM, EUGENE H. and ALFRED E. ECKES. A History of Presidential Elections from George Washington to Jimmy Carter. 1957; Rev. ed. New York: Macmillan, 1979. 355 pp.
Roseboom and Eckes provide a brief overview of all Presidential elections up to Jimmy Carter's, as well as an analysis of party alignments, regional voting blocks, and the ideological orientation of the various candidates. Intra-party rivalries, the emergence of third-party movements, and the activities of prominent politicians all receive attention. The authors also assess Vice-Presidential nominees, party platforms, electioneering tactics, the crucial issues that dominated each campaign, and the influence of the campaign on the relationships between politicians and the electorate.

PS 166. SCHLESINGER, ARTHUR M., Jr. The Imperial Presidency. Boston: Houghton Mifflin, 1973. 505 pp.
Schlesinger argues that the experiences of Vietnam and of Watergate demonstrate how the constitutional Presidency could become the "imperial Presidency." The book essentially deals with the appropriation by the President of powers which the Constitution and long historical practice have reserved for Congress. Schlesinger argues that the expansion of Presidential power was the result of the increased importance of foreign policy matters, and the President's appropriation of the decision to go to war. He examines the history of the war-making powers, and concludes that Constitutional restraints on the Presidency must be restored.

PS 167. SCHLESINGER, ARTHUR M., Jr. and ROGER BRUNS, eds. Congress Investigates, 1792-1974. New York: Chelsea House, 1975. 507 pp.
These essays examine the political controversies and constitutional questions surrounding selected investigating committees throughout the history of the U.S. Congress. The essays emphasize the legal and constitutional problems of Congressional investigation, rather than their historical significance. The study looks at the struggles of Congressional committees to exercise what the editors call "inquisitorial power." The authors examine the degree to which Congressional investigations infringe upon the powers of the judiciary; the extent of the power of Congress to subpoena; the potential for violation of the personal liberties of witnesses interrogated by Congress; and the political and partisan motivations behind certain committee investigations.

PS 168. SCHNEIDER, JERROLD E. Ideological Coalitions in Congress. Westport, Conn.: Greenwood Press, 1979. 270 pp.
Schneider argues that there exists a high ideological consistency across issues among members of Congress, and criticizes the pluralist view of politics. Pluralism argues that Congressional coalitions are flexible and vary widely according to the substance of issues, interests, and policies. The author tests the pluralist and ideological theories by examining and comparing the consistency of Congressional behavior in foreign policy, coalition formation, voting patterns, and economic policy. Schneider concludes that his results show very high ideological consistency along all policy dimensions.

PS 169. SCHWARZ, JOHN E. and L. EARL SHAW. The United States Congress in Comparative Perspective. Hillsdale, Ill.: Dryden, 1976. 421 pp.
The authors examine the operation of the U.S. Congress by comparing it to three national representative legislatures—the British House of Commons, the French National Assembly, and the West German Bundestag. They provide

a brief descriptive overview of each legislature's institutional characteristics (and its relationship to other aspects of the polity) as well as
narrative case studies on the law-making process in each system. Their
thesis is that a legislator's behavior is a joint result of motivational
characteristics (political career ambition, affective and normative dis-
positions) and the environment, including the relevant actors with their
various values to the legislator, as well as the more stable aspects of
the political setting.

PS 170. SEYMOUR-URE, COLIN. The American President: Power and Communi-
         cation. New York: St. Martin's Press, 1982. 190 pp.
Seymour-Ure investigates the President's approach to public communication,
and what role communication plays in the achievement of Presidential goals.
He begins with an analysis of the relationship between communication processes and various types of power, as well as the factors influencing the
President's public communication. He then turns to a short critique of
the literature on Presidential power and evaluates the use of public communication as an instrument of power by Presidents since 1945.

PS 171. SHELLEY, MACK C. The Permanent Majority: The Conservative Coali-
         tion in the United States Congress. University: University
         of Alabama Press, 1983. 201 pp.
Shelley provides an analysis of Congressional conservatism since the 1930s.
He argues that enduring policy alliances of conservative politicians have
formed a coalition that is one of the most important factors determining
policy decisions in Congress. (This coalition consists mainly of Republicans and Southern Democrats.) Focusing on the way in which party lines
are crossed to form bipartisan conservative groups, Shelley demonstrates
how the concept of a cross-party coalition provides a more flexible framework for comprehending why public policy assumes specific forms, as well
as for predicting the outcome of policy-making activity in Congress.

PS 172. SHICK, ALLEN. Congress and Money: Budgeting, Spending and Taxing.
         Washington, D.C.: Urban Institute, 1980. 604 pp.
Shick provides an insider's perspective on the budget process. His objective is to compare current behavior to Congressional budget practices
prior to the reforms of the 1970s. The author examines the budget wars
of the late 1960s and early 1970s that convinced Congress that budget
reform was necessary. He records the process and negotiations that brought
about the reform: the Congressional committees, the politics of resolution-
writing in the House and the Senate, and the attempts to build coalitions
for the passage of budget resolutions. He then considers the impact of
the budget reform on other Congressional taxing and spending committees,
and concludes that the institutionalized budget provides a useful mechanism
for the management of budgetary conflict.

PS 173. SHULL, STEVEN A. Domestic Policy Formation: Presidential-
         Congressional Partnership? Westport, Conn.: Greenwood Press,
         1983. 218 pp.
Shull argues that the process of policy-making depends upon the strategies
and interactions of political actors as they confront the particular functional and substantive content of public policy issues. He examines processes, actors, and content in policy-making within the context of agenda-
setting, initiation, modification, and adoption. Shull focuses on Congress
and the President as the ultimate deciders (primary actors) in national
policy formation. He concludes with recommendations for greater cooperation and accountability in the policy-making process, since policy output
is, in his study, seen to be influenced increasingly by actors not subject
to Presidential control.

PS 174. SIFF, TED and ALAN WEIL. Ruling Congress: A Study of How the
House and Senate Rules Govern the Legislative Process. New York:
Grossman, 1975. 299 pp.
The authors present an analysis of how Congress concentrates power and
determines the legislative process. The authors begin with an examination
of the legislative circuit and how it works in Congress. They then turns
to a discussion of the important role of the parliamentarians in Congress.
The authors look at the power of committees and their chairmen, especially
in the rules and administration committees of both chambers, and they
analyze the role floor debates and conference committees play in the legislative process.

PS 175. SINCLAIR, BARBARA. Congressional Realignment, 1925-1978. Austin:
University of Texas Press, 1982. 201 pp.
Sinclair investigates the impact of realignment upon Congress, showing
how, between 1925 and 1978, policy transformation occurred only when there
was critical realignment in the electorate. Since major policy change
requires Congressional action, the author considers the process by which
a legislature ordinarily capable of making only incremental policy changes
is transformed into a body which can propose a transformation of the Congressional political agenda. The author also examines the role of Congress
in transforming the major issues, or the new political agenda during times
of critical realignment, into public policy.

PS 176. SMITH, PAUL A. Electing a President: Information and Control.
New York: Praeger, 1982. 239 pp.
Smith examines the flow of information between the candidates of a Presidential campaign and their constituencies. He looks at the importance
of true competition among candidates as a means of bringing out the issues
and uncovering underlying dissatisfaction among the electorate. Smith
argues that insofar as campaigns do not reveal much about the candidate,
or do not reach substantial portions of the electorate, their essential
functions are not being performed. After discussing the rules and theories
of American campaign politics, the author turns to the primary campaigns,
the national conventions, and the general election of 1980 to show how
campaigning is a political process of communicating with voters.

PS 177. SORENSEN, THEODORE C. Decision-Making in the White House: The
Olive Branch or the Arrow. New York: Columbia University Press,
1963. 93 pp.
Sorensen argues that every President develops a certain pattern for making
decisions; the same basic forces and factors will repeatedly shape those
decisions regardless of how the institution and apparatus of government
may be organized. Sorensen discusses the role of advisers in the White
House and how decisions were reached on some of the events which occurred
during the Kennedy administration. This leads to a presentation of how
the President tries to build a consensus on a decision. Sorensen also
discusses the role of public opinion. He concludes that a good President
knows the limitations of his office.

PS 178. SORENSEN, THEODORE C. Watchman in the Night: Presidential Accountability After Watergate. Cambridge, Mass.: MIT Press, 1975.
177 pp.
Sorensen discusses what effect Watergate might have on the future of the
American Presidency. He argues for changes in the Presidency which take
into account the lessons of Watergate and hold the President accountable.
Sorensen discusses the illusion of unlimited Presidential power and points
to the institutional and personal limitations on the President. He then
presents specific analyses of how the President can be made more accountable to the Congress, the courts, and the people.

PS 179.   SPRAGENS, WILLIAM C. and CAROLE ANN TERWOOD. From Spokesman to
          Press Secretary: White House Media Operations. Lanham, Md.:
          University Press of America, 1980. 243 pp.
Spragens and Terwood provide a close-up look at the role of recent White
House Press Secretaries, using biographical materials, interviews, and
discussions. Specifically, they look at the White House Secretaries from
the Kennedy to the Carter administrations. The authors begin with a consideration of White House operations and the rise in importance of Press
Secretaries with the growth of the power of the modern media. They then
present background information on specific Secretaries, gauging how they
are viewed by their White House colleagues. Finally, they present a cor-
respondent's perception of the Press Secretaries, and assess the importance
of the office.

PS 180.   THOMPSON, KENNETH W. The President and the Public Philosophy.
          Baton Rouge: Louisiana State University Press, 1981. 219 pp.
Thompson examines the responsibility an American President has to define
and promote a public philosophy—the goals and beliefs toward which the
society should strive. He argues that it is the President who sets the
tone, shapes moods and expectations, and provides or fails to provide
a framework for public understanding. This has become more important,
he asserts, because of the growth of special interest groups which generate
a divisive factionalism, the diminishing participation of citizens, and
the prevalent loss of public trust in institutions and ideals.

PS 181.   WEATHERFORD, J. McIVER. Tribes on the Hill. New York: Rawson,
          Wade, 1981. 300 pp.
Weatherford provides an account of the U.S. Congress, and the rituals,
ceremonies, and behavior that characterize its daily activities. He uses
theories of tribal life as articulated by anthropologists to examine Congressional activity. The purpose of this approach is to explain the political behavior of Congress as a cultural phenomenon which can be compared
to other social institutions. Weatherford concludes that Congress has
become an "endangered tribe" which appears to have become weaker with
the increasing power of the Presidency, and that it is stagnating as the
legislative process becomes increasingly drawn out.

IV.   FEDERALISM, STATE GOVERNMENT, AND
       URBAN POLITICS

PS 182.   ARKES, HADLEY. The Philosopher in the City: The Moral Dimensions
          of Urban Politics. Princeton, N.J.: Princeton University Press,
          1981. 465 pp.
Arkes develops a political theory for the study of urban politics by applying moral principles to the problems of cities. He uses legal cases and
arguments as well as public disputes and arguments over urban policy as
examples of incidents that reflect and test our understanding of the principles of moral judgment. Arkes's purpose is to offer a moral perspective
on the city and to draw out the implications of this perspective for the
politics of the city.

PS 183.   BACHRACH, PETER and MORTON S. BARATZ. Power and Poverty. New
          York: Oxford University Press, 1970. 220 pp.
Bachrach and Baratz undertake a critical examination of elitist and pluralist approaches to the nature of power in American society. Finding contemporary approaches inadequate, they offer their own conceptions of power,
authority, and influence, as well as the novel concept of the "non-
decision" of political events. The authors defend the empirical worth of

their theories by analyzing the relationship of the 1960s anti-poverty campaign to the political process in Baltimore, Maryland. The study shows how political attitudes affected issues which were decided as well as those which were neglected. It thus analyzes participation in the decision-making process as a means of determining who exercises power and how, and of obtaining clues to the nature and extent of non-decision-making.

PS 184. BANFIELD, EDWARD. The Unheavenly City Revisited. 1970; Rev. ed. Boston: Little, Brown, 1974. 358 pp.
In this revised version of his 1970 The Unheavenly City, Banfield makes use of census data which were not available at the time of the work's original publication. This is particularly important in his analysis of metropolitan development and in his discussion of the "lower classes." Banfield asserts that urban problems are not confined to cities, and do not automatically lead to "the urban crisis." He discusses the contribution of economic, demographic, and technological developments to metropolitan growth, and outlines the cultural perspectives of various social classes and their impact on urban issues. The author discusses the importance of race in city life, arguing that "the most conspicuous fact of life in the city is racial division." In the latter two-thirds of the book he turns his attention to issues of public policy, suggesting that many existing efforts to solve problems are misguided at best and are often destructive. This section focuses on unemployment, poverty, education, and crime, and culminates in a chapter entitled "Rioting for Fun and Profit." Banfield concludes that the problems of the city are largely the result of disproportionately large numbers of lower class residents, and he suggests specific policy measures to reduce crime, unrest, and disorder.

PS 185. BANFIELD, EDWARD and JAMES Q. WILSON. City Politics. Cambridge, Mass.: Harvard University Press, 1963. 362 pp.
This book emphasizes the political and informal rather than the formal structural and administrative dimensions of city decision-making. It stresses that social cleavages and political organizations are the setting in which city government occurs. There is a section on the role of cities in the American Federal system which stresses the interactive political nature of that system. This is followed by a discussion tracing the political development of large cities, beginning with a description of urban machines, the role of reform, and the implications of reform (e.g., non-partisanship), and concluding with a discussion of the increasing importance of professional city managers and master planning. The final section analyzes the roles of several of the major political actors in city politics—city employees, businessmen, civic leaders, labor, minorities, and the press.

PS 186. BARBER, JAMES D. The Lawmakers: Recruitment and Adaptation to Legislative Life. New Haven, Conn.: Yale University Press, 1965. 314 pp.
Barber's study of the state legislature of Connecticut is based on personal interviews with 100 legislators conducted in 1959. Emphasizing the importance of the mode of recruitment in members' careers in the legislature, Barber distinguishes four types of legislator: (1) "advertisers," who are in the legislature in order to make a public name for themselves and do not plan to remain for long; (2) "reluctants," who serve as a matter of duty; (3) spectators," and (4) "lawmakers," who take an active role. Barber claims that only about one-third of the Connecticut legislature fell into the latter category.

PS 187. BARFIELD, CLAUDE E. Rethinking Federalism: Block Grants and Federal, State and Local Responsibilities. Washington, D.C.: American Enterprise Institute for Public Policy Research, 1981. 99 pp.

Barfield analyzes the workings of block grants. He explores the administrative and political results of the Reagan administration's proposal to consolidate almost a hundred existing categorical grant-in-aid programs into six large grants to states in light of the questions it raises regarding the nature and function of American Federalism. This exploration leads to a suggested framework for reordering Federal, state, and local responsibilities. The author proposes that the national government move to complete the national social agenda by assuming policy and financial responsibility for welfare reform and national health insurance. In turn it would hand over to state and local governments a number of functions and programs in such areas as education, transportation, community and economic development, social services, law enforcement, health, and environment.

PS 188. BEST, MICHAEL and WILLIAM CONNOLLY. The Politicized Economy. Lexington, Mass.: Heath, 1982. 241 pp.

The authors explore the relationship between democracy and an economy of growth. They argue that the reciprocal relationship expected between democratic politics and a free-enterprise economy has proved to be inconsistent and volatile. They grant that the affinity between democracy and Capitalism has been close; nevertheless, they assert, the relationship is becoming more tenuous and problematic in the U.S. A large proportion of the American population is employed by institutions which exist primarily to control and regulate others or are themselves the object of these regulations. To continue productively, the economy requires social control and regulation. The state, furthermore, now assumes more subsidization, enforcement, and discipline in the economy. The authors discuss the tension between the need for this control and the maintenance of democratic institutions.

PS 189. BISH, ROBERT L. The Public Economy of Metropolitan Areas. Chicago: Markham, 1971. 176 pp.

This work offers a discussion of the public choice and political economic approaches to understanding decision-making processes in American metropolitan regions. Explanations are developed from assumptions used in economic analysis, which are primarily the assumptions of individual self-interest and of rationality in the presence of scarce resources. Bish uses these concepts to describe the variety and mix of American political units. Early in the book, he summarizes the background concepts, including public goods, externalities, and collective action, and their relationship to the political process commonly operating at the local level. He then analyzes in some detail two metropolitan regions (Los Angeles County, California, and Dade County, Florida) as well as two urban public functions (education and the control of air pollution). Finally, Bish compares the public choice approach to more traditional approaches to the discussion of metropolitan governmental reform.

PS 190. BRADBURY, KATHERINE, ANTHONY DOWNS, and KENNETH A. SMALL. Urban Decline and the Future of American Cities. Washington, D.C.: Brookings Institution, 1982. 309 pp.

The authors define urban decline in two ways: (1) the decrease in population or employment; and (2) the loss of major services and social opportunities that make urban life desirable. The book's key finding is that jobs follow people: firms are attracted to areas where the population is growing, for such areas provide an expanding local market. Employment responds to population growth. Considering the demographic, economic, and social evidence, the authors conclude that present urban trends are irreversible; Federal and state intervention are called for if the present decline is to be slowed or halted. Rather than attracting new industries or groups, policy-makers should deal directly with urban problems. The authors make policy recommendations that try to circumvent the Federal biases against big cities, using Cleveland to simulate a test for their recommendations.

PS 191. BREAK, GEORGE F. Financing Government in a Federal System. Washington, D.C.: Brookings Institution, 1980. 276 pp.
Break deals with the problem faced by the national government in providing Federal financing to state and local governments. He deals with the question of how spending responsibilities should be assigned among levels of government. He also asks how taxing sources and powers should be coordinated; what the uses and misuses of intergovernmental grants-in-aid are; and what the best means of confronting the special financial difficulties of large urban areas might be. The study provides an examination of fiscal relations in the Federal system and urban fiscal system, and the tax coordination between the two. It also looks at the economics of intergovernmental grants and the functioning of the U.S. grant system. In short, Break examines the problem of intergovernmental relations in light of the difficulties presented by the economic problems of the 1980s.

PS 192. CLARK, TERRY N., ed. Urban Policy Analysis: Direction for Future Research. Beverly Hills, Calif.: Sage, 1981. 296 pp.
This volume, a collection of papers from a conference on urban policy research, is divided into four areas. The first considers urban politics and policy outputs. The second section examines the degree to which the availability and delivery of public services depend on political manipulation of the bureaucratic process, and the economic effects this has on the community. The third section looks at urban political cultures and the responsiveness of urban governments in developing policy proposals that meet citizens' preferences. The fourth section looks at economic development and decline within the central city and the effect on demographic shifts. The volume as a whole examines recent trends in urban policy analysis and suggests areas for further study.

PS 193. DAHL, ROBERT A. Who Governs? Democracy and Power in an American City. New Haven, Conn.: Yale University Press, 1961. 355 pp.
Dahl examines the city of New Haven, Connecticut, to understand how the American values of democracy and equality are practiced in an urban community. Generally, he provides a pluralist theory of politics to explain the distribution of power. Dahl begins by studying the nature of inequality in resources and political influence to show how elites, influential leaders, and public officials are susceptible to the politics of democratic institutions. Dahl argues that the emergence of pluralist politics created "a profound alteration in the way political resources are distributed among the citizens of New Haven." This has not necessarily brought about perfect equality. But it has brought about a shift from cumulative inequalities to noncumulative or dispersed inequalities, sparing any one group from carrying the entire burden of inequality and spreading around the inequalities which must be carried.

PS 194. DOWNS, ANTHONY. Neighborhoods and Urban Development. Washington, D.C.: Brookings Institution, 1981. 189 pp.
Downs describes the problems facing metropolitan areas as a result of their deterioration, and offers suggestions for dealing with the present urban problems. He begins the book by describing the context in which urban development unfolds from neighborhood to neighborhood, and from core to periphery. He then explores the interaction of all regions and functional services in a metropolitan area to understand urban development. Downs expounds on this under the presupposition, however, that both deteri-

oration and poverty are conditions of urban life. Urban problems are a result of tensions inherent in the metropolitan system. He thus challenges the theory that neighborhood revitalization stabilizes a section of a town and prepares the way for development in adjacent neighborhoods. The author's recommendations for holding off urban decline include redistributing incomes within metropolitan areas, limiting suburban growth, distributing social costs and mortgages more fairly, coping with housing deterioration, and transferring the delivery of some services and government authority to the neighborhood level.

PS 195. EULAU, HEINZ and KENNETH PREWITT. Labyrinths of Democracy: Adaptations, Linkages, Representation, and Policies in Urban Politics. Indianapolis, Ind.: Bobbs-Merrill, 1973. 713 pp.
This book is an attempt to begin a careful analysis of representation and governmental policy-making. Originating as a report on city councils in the San Francisco bay region, it has expanded well beyond this. No single finding or theory characterizes the book; rather, it attempts to bring together in a consistent way all aspects of urban government. To this end, the authors often develop a specialized vocabulary and deal extensively with taxonomy and theory.

PS 196. FOSTER, R. SCOTT and RENEE A. BERGER, eds. Public-Private Partnership in American Cities: Seven Case Studies. Lexington, Mass.: Heath, 1982. 363 pp.
Foster and Berger provide a series of case studies undertaken by the Committee for Economic Development examining the changing relationships between the public and private sectors in seven cities. The essays show how the public sector has reached a limit in its commitment of major new resources to America's urban areas, while the Federal government has become less able and less willing to address the diversity of local conditions. Communities must therefore organize private and public sector cooperation to fill the gap. Each study focuses on projects developed in cities to mobilize public and private sectors to improve the economy and the community.

PS 197. GANS, HERBERT J. People and Plans: Essays on Urban Problems and Solutions. New York: Basic Books, 1968. 395 pp.
This book is a collection of essays that critically examine city planning and city problems. Gans argues that decisions should be based on the goals people are seeking and on the most effective programs to achieve them. But city planning has not paid much attention to people's goals or to the urgent problems of the cities. Planning has become a profession dedicated to a set of narrowly articulated architectural goals, to land-use, and to designing programs for realizing these goals. Furthermore, Gans contends, the outcome of urban planning often has little impact on people's behavior patterns and values. Planning that aims to improve living conditions often fails to address the economic, social, and political conditions which are the real forces that shape a community's environment. Planners often plan communities according to their own values rather than those of the community they wish to change.

PS 198. GARNETT, JAMES. Reorganizing State Government: The Executive Branch. Boulder, Colo.: Westview Press, 1980. 245 pp.
Garnett discusses the reorganization of state governments on a cross-state basis. He offers strategies for and points out obstacles to reorganization: when it should be attempted, how comprehensive it should be, how to deal with bureaucratic resistance to administrative reforms, and the resistance of clientele groups affected by reorganization. The major part of the book, however, is devoted to an in-depth quantification of the effects of reorganization across the country. Garnett also undertakes a comprehensive review of all reorganization efforts in all states between 1914 and 1975.

PS 199. GOVE, SAMUEL and LOUIS H. MASOTTI, eds. After Daley: Chicago
         Politics in Transition. Urbana: University of Illinois Press,
         1982. 244 pp.
This group of essays studies Chicago politics after the era of Mayor
Richard Daley. However, the problems they examine can be generalized to
all the major urban centers in the Great Lakes Region. The volume explores
electoral processes, the city's infrastructure, and external pressures.
It examines the emergence of new political forces: blacks as a dominant
group; the importance of geographic-residential patterns over traditional
ethnic white interests; the increasingly powerful public-employer unions;
and the professional administrative class in the city's bureaucracy.

PS 200. GREENSTONE, J. DAVID and PAUL E. PETERSON. Race and Authority
         in Urban Politics: Community Participation and the War on Poverty.
         New York: Russell Sage, 1973. 364 pp.
Greenstone and Peterson analyze the impact of the Federal requirement
for citizen participation through Community Action Agencies on the politics
of the five largest U.S. cities (New York, Chicago, Los Angeles, Philadelphia, and Detroit). They suggest that the Community Action Program
was in many ways the most radical part of the War on Poverty (developed
during the Johnson administration) because it had the effect of shifting
the major basis for conflict in large cities from social and economic
class to race. The book analyzes the agency's evolution in the context
of the elitist-pluralist debate over the character of urban political
power. The authors conclude that the changes wrought by the urban turmoil
of the late 1960s and their aftermath require substantial modification
of the pluralist perspective.

PS 201. HALE, GEORGE E. and MARIAN LIEF PALLEY. The Politics of Federal
         Grants. Washington, D.C.: Congressional Quarterly Press, 1981.
         178 pp.
Hale and Palley examine the function and governance of the politics of
the intergovernmental grant process. They begin by relating the modern
grants system to traditional concepts of Federalism, tracing the evolution
of grants programs through the stages of the policy-making process—agenda
setting, policy adoption, and Federal implementation. The authors then
look at the effects of Federal grants on local jurisdictions, specifically
in urban and rural areas. They conclude with an assessment of the implications of the grant system for policy-making and the Federal system.

PS 202. HOUSE, PETER W. and ROBERT G. RYAN. The Future Indefinite:
         Decision-Making in a Transition Economy. Lexington, Mass.: Heath,
         1979. 175 pp.
House and Ryan argue that the reason for scientific-technological confusion
about America's future is that American society is in the process of a
massive cultural transition. They choose the urban environment and the
energy issue as examples of problems that will not respond to past policies
because of this confusion. Beginning with an analysis of how the American
economy is undergoing a transition period, they then turn to urban blight
and the battle that is emerging between the Sunbelt and the Frostbelt
over scarce economic resources. The authors conclude with suggestions
on how to develop tools and techniques for coping with this transition.

PS 203. KARNIG, ALBERT K. and SUSAN WELCH. Black Representation and Urban
         Policy. Chicago: University of Chicago Press, 1981. 179 pp.
The authors look at the conditions affecting the election of black mayors
and city council members, and what influence black elected officials have
on city budgets. Their study shows that blacks are underrepresented in
mayoral and council seats in cities where there is a substantial black
population. The level of representation is found to be dependent on the
level of black resources in that city, i.e., the size, education, and

income of the black population. The authors conclude that if blacks can get nominated in partisan cities, they benefit from the partisan system. Furthermore, the presence of black mayors is found to bring about more consistent increases in expenditures than black council representation, but the increases are neither powerful nor significant.

PS 204. KATZNELSON, IRA. City Trenches: Urban Politics and the Patterning of Class in the United States. New York: Pantheon Books, 1981. 267 pp.

Katznelson analyzes the urban crisis of the 1960s as a problem of class relations. He argues that what has been special about class relations in the U.S. is traceable to the ways in which workers understood the separation of work and home (or community) in early industrial cities. What emerged was a dichotomy between the politics of the worker in the work place and his politics in the community. Katznelson uses a case study of urban revolt in the 1960s in a community of northern Manhattan to explain how the traditional urban system worked, how it was challenged, and how it was ultimately reconstructed. The author concludes with a look at what his theory means as a political theory of urban community.

PS 205. LADD, BRUCE. Crisis in Credibility. New York: New American Library, 1968. 247 pp.

Ladd traces the government's loss of credibility to its unwarranted and unjustified concern with secrecy; its refusal to reveal information which is properly in the public domain; lying by government officials; and the government's adeptness at devising new ways to mislead the public and the press through manipulation of information and news management. The book is a journalistic account of the government's information policy. Ladd defends the role of the press to be a watchdog over government. He argues that denying the public proper information is a threat to the democratic system because it leaves the people uninformed and affects the credibility of government.

PS 206. LEAVITT, JUDITH W. The Healthiest City: Milwaukee and the Politics of Health Reform. Princeton, N.J.: Princeton University Press, 1982. 294 pp.

Leavitt examines Milwaukee's municipal efforts to deal with the health problems resulting from sudden urban expansion and industrial growth in the period from 1867 to 1930. She focuses on case studies from each of the three major areas of public health activity—infectious diseases, sanitation, and food control—to identify and analyze the major components of health reform in urban America. She also studies the effects that medical or technical knowledge, economic interests, interurban competition, political ideologies, ethnic diversity, corruption, and inefficiency had on public health. The author concludes that the city was capable of consequential action which led to the improvement of health conditions.

PS 207. LEVINE, CHARLES, IRENE S. RUBIN, and GEORGE G. WOLOHOJIAN. The Politics of Retrenchment: How Local Governments Manage Fiscal Stress. Beverly Hills, Calif.: Sage, 1981. 223 pp.

This study looks at the ways in which American cities are dealing with fiscal crises. The authors examine how fiscal crisis affects the capacity of policy-makers to govern, and the effect it will have on the physical conditions of cities and the ability of city government to deliver services at the necessary levels. This information is drawn from four case studies of major American cities. The authors develop a model of organizational retrenchment drawn from the experiences of New York City and apply this model to their case studies. They conclude with recommendations on how a city should respond to a fiscal crisis.

PS 208. **LIPSKY, MICHAEL.** Protest in City Politics: Rent Strikes, Housing, and the Power of the Poor. Chicago: Rand McNally, 1970. 214 pp.
Lipsky began his study of the rent strike movement in the fall of 1964, when it appeared to him that aspects of the civil rights movement were emerging in Northern cities. His concern was with the ability of the American political system to respond to the needs of relatively powerless groups. Out of these case materials, Lipsky develops a theory of protest in American city politics particularly applicable to groups that are usually excluded from participation in the political system. Lipsky's perception is that political pressure applied by the powerless is indirect rather than direct, and must rely on reaching the communications media and the reference groups of those who are the targets of the protest. Lipsky concludes that it is possible, in some instances, for relatively powerless groups to raise issues and make successful demands on the political system. However, the lack of organizational resources makes it virtually impossible for such groups to sustain this effort and become a regular part of a responsive, pluralistic system of government.

PS 209. **LIPSKY, MICHAEL** and **DAVID J. OLSON.** Commission Politics: The Processing of Racial Crisis in America. New Brunswick, N.J.: Transaction Books, 1977. 476 pp.
In this study, Lipsky and Olson provide an overview and developmental analysis of the process by which the American political system managed the racial crisis of the late 1960s. Specifically, Lipsky and Olson concentrate on the creation of riot commissions as the response to civil disorder. They study the commissions, their decision processes and their recommendations, as well as the extent to which the recommendations were implemented. The authors includes a historical survey of race riots in the U.S., and in a concluding chapter discuss the problem of maintaining political stability in the presence of persisting social inequality and discontent. The authors suggest that riots have not significantly changed attitudes about racial matters.

PS 210. **NATHAN, RICHARD P.**, **FRED C. DOOLITTLE**, and Associates. The Consequences of Cuts: The Effects of the Reagan Domestic Program on State and Local Government. Princeton, N.J.: Princeton Urban and Regional Research Center, 1983. 221 pp.
This book examines the changes in the domestic policies of the U.S. government under the Reagan administration's "new Federalism." The most important of these were put into effect by the Omnibus Budget Reconciliation Act of 1981. The authors examine how this act significantly cut domestic spending and reduced the Federal government's role in domestic program areas, and how these changes affected state and local governments. The focus is on grants-in-aid to state and local governments and non-profit organizations, and the ways in which states replaced lost funds.

PS 211. **PATTERSON, SAMUEL C.**, **RONALD G. HEDLUND**, and **G. ROBERT BOYNTON.** Representatives and Represented: Bases of Public Support for the American Legislatures. New York: Wiley, 1975. 212 pp.
The authors present a data-intensive study of attitudes toward the Iowa State Legislature. They examine the attitudes of five groups occupying different positions in the political strata: legislators, lobbyists, county political party chairmen, attentive constituents, and the general public. The study focuses on a broader concept of representation ("diffuse support" or legitimacy of the legislature as an institution) rather than on the instrumental version which emphasizes specific supports and demands. A hierarchy of support emerged, from the mass public through the sub-elites (lobbyists, party leaders, etc.) to legislators.

PS 212. RANSONE, COLEMAN B., Jr. The American Governorship. Westport,
          Conn.: Greenwood Press, 1982. 197 pp.
This study presents a description of the functions of the modern day office
of governor. Ransone begins with a look at the impact of the party concept
on the governorship, the governor's role in intergovernmental relations,
and the formal powers of the office. This is followed by an examination
of the problems involved in being elected. Ransone compares the governor's
functions in the 1950s and the 1970s and describes the changes that have
taken place. He then turns to the governor's role in policy formation.
Ransone concludes with predictions of what may be expected of the
governor's role in the future.

PS 213. RATNER, SIDNEY. Taxation and Democracy in America. 1942; Rev.
          ed. New York: Wiley, 1967. 600 pp.
"Taxes," comments Ratner (quoting Justice Holmes), "are the price we pay
for civilization." With this in mind, Ratner focuses less upon the economics of taxation than he does on the potential offered by taxes as instruments of social and economic reform. His concern in this survey is primarily with the politics of taxation and the clash of economic interests
in policy-making. He examines the Congressional debates and Supreme Court
decisions involved in the formulation and passage of tax legislation since
the late 18th century and the effects of taxation on the distribution
of wealth. Ratner pays relatively little attention to state and local
taxes, concentrating instead on Federal taxes on income, profits, and
inheritances. He criticizes the inequities of indirect taxation and is
favorably inclined to "progressive" direct taxation as a viable instrument
of social and economic engineering.

PS 214. RICH, WILBUR C. The Politics of Urban Personnel Policy: Reformers,
          Politicians, and Bureaucrats. Port Washington, N.Y.: Kennikat
          Press, 1982. 178 pp.
Rich examines the politics of urban personnel management in New York City
during the fiscal crisis of 1973. The book begins with an outline of
the political context of the city's personnel policies. Rich stresses
the significance of personnel policies regarding the allocation of jobs
and the regulation of income, as well as the values governing these policies. He then turns to an analysis of the perspectives, values, and
actions of several crucial interest groups and how they influence municipal
administrative policies. This is followed by an assessment of the impact
of reform politics on mayoral control of the personnel system, and the
central role played by public-employee unions in the politics of employee
relations.

PS 215. RIKER, WILLIAM H. Federalism. Boston: Little, Brown, 1964.
          169 pp.
Riker defines a Federal constitution and states that two conditions—a
willingness to compromise and a recognized need for military unity—are
necessary for the creation of Federalism. He examines the conditions
necessary for the survival of a Federal system and proposes that the system
of political parties (not the administrative system, as is commonly supposed) maintains the Federal arrangement. Lastly, Riker considers whether
Federalism is worth maintaining.

PS 216. ROURKE, FRANCIS E. Secrecy and Publicity: Dilemmas of Democracy.
          Baltimore, Md.: Johns Hopkins University Press, 1961. 236 pp.
American democracy, Rourke warns, is in grave danger of falling victim
to the suppression of information and manipulation of public opinion,
particularly in the areas of foreign affairs and defense policy. The
government's desire to control the public voice threatens to give it too
much control over "the electorate to which it is in theory subordinate."
Rourke traces the history of the manipulation of opinion in the U.S. and

the range of issues it has affected. He delineates the means by which such control is achieved by the President, Congress, and the courts. Although he insists that no democracy can exist where such manipulation of opinion occurs, he is aware that an open government can operate only at the expense of a certain measure of national security.

PS 217. RUBIN, IRENE S. Running in the Red: The Political Dynamics of Urban Fiscal Stress. Albany: State University of New York Press, 1982. 167 pp.
Rubin examines what causes urban fiscal crises and how cities respond to these crises. The author deals with such questions as the migration of the poor, tax-base erosion, and political structure and leadership. She then examines the social, political, and economic causes of urban fiscal crises. Rubin applies the major contemporary theories of urban fiscal stress to her case study. The conclusion summarizes the study in terms of the strengths and weaknesses of these explanatory propositions. She makes her own theoretical contributions, and suggests how cities facing fiscal crises may resolve them.

PS 218. SABATO, LARRY. Goodbye to Good Time Charlie: The American Governor Transformed, 1950-1975. Lexington, Mass.: Heath, 1978. 283 pp.
Sabato presents an overview study of the recent transformation in the quality and character of American governors. He argues that there is a trend toward a higher quality governor. Sabato begins by scrutinizing the characters and careers of 321 governors. This is followed by an examination of recent structural alterations in state governments, and the changes in the personal powers of the governor's office. Sabato then examines the relationship between the states and the other layers of the Federal system. Finally, he comments on the recent resurrection of the governorship as a route to the Presidency.

PS 219. SHARKANSKY, IRA. The Maligned States. New York: McGraw-Hill, 1972. 169 pp.
The author argues that state governments are unjustly maligned. In marshalling his defense, Sharkansky first describes the regional diversity which he believes justifies strong state government. Next he describes the impressive record of states in gathering revenues and in providing services. In particular, he admires the states' ability to provide higher education and urban aid. Sharkansky believes that Federal dominance in policy is largely a myth, and he argues that states have made contributions even in areas heavily funded by the Federal government.

PS 220. SMITH, MICHAEL P. The City and Social Theory. New York: St. Martin's Press, 1979. 315 pp.
Smith argues that what are often labeled "urban problems" are in fact society-wide ills produced by economic and social inequalities. He analyzes the writings of five social theorists—Louis Wirth, Sigmund Freud, Georg Simmel, Theodore Roszak, and Richard Sennett—who depict the modern city as a repressive social institution which is the source of alienation. In a critique of their theories, the author shows that many social pathologies thought to be rooted in ecological, biological, or technological necessity are in fact attributable to the social structure and economic organization of particular societies. He concludes with a description of the contemporary American urban milieu as a by-product of the development of corporate Capitalism and criticizes the role that urban planners have played in legitimizing the unequal distribution of the social costs and benefits of that development.

PS 221. SUNDQUIST, JAMES L. Making Federalism Work. Washington, D.C.: Brookings Institution, 1969. 293 pp.
Sundquist's book is a study of inter-governmental relations in the U.S. The author is concerned with the problem of coordination in a Federal system. Using interviews with 700 people, he examines coordinating devices at the community level. He gives a historical account and a description of the workings of three coordinating structures: community action and model cities in metropolitan areas, and economic development programs in rural areas. Sundquist proposes his own models for coordination. He advocates a differential approach to Federal-state relations whereby the Federal government grants broad discretion to administratively competent states and retains its power over less competent ones.

PS 222. WALKER, DAVID B. Toward a Functioning Federalism. Cambridge, Mass.: Winthrop, 1981. 267 pp.
To study the recent growth of government, Walker begins by looking at the intent of the founding fathers. He then examines three eras of American inter-governmental history (1620-1789, 1790-1960, 1960-1980) to illuminate how today's pattern of inter-governmental relations is a break with previous ones. The author argues that the present system is a departure from the minimal inter-governmental interaction intended by the Founding Fathers and previously practiced. The recent trend which Walker examines is the tendency to thrust nearly every facet of domestic American policy into the inter-governmental arena. This has created major problems in the areas of finance, administration, and official accountability.

PS 223. WILLIAMS, OLIVER P. Metropolitan Political Analysis: A Social Access Approach. New York: Free Press, 1971. 118 pp.
Williams describes the process by which individuals develop strategies to improve their access—in geographical and social terms—to the things they want. He applies this framework to several major aspects of the contemporary urban scene, including the way in which the distribution of households depends on the desire of individuals to locate in more or less homogeneous neighborhoods. He also applies his framework to the interaction between entrepreneurs and local political units throughout the metropolitan region. Finally, he considers the implications of his approach for both centralization and decentralization of metropolitan policies, and the prospects for future reorganization of metropolitan governmental structures.

PS 224. WILSON, JAMES Q. The Amateur Democrat: Club Politics in Three Cities. Chicago: University of Chicago Press, 1962. 378 pp.
Wilson examines the activities of "amateur" (liberal, issue-oriented, idealistic) political activists in Democratic party clubs in America's three largest cities: Chicago, where the "regular" (patronage and victory-oriented, more conservative) party organization has been very strong; Los Angeles, where party organization is almost non-existent; and New York, where a once-strong party "machine" is failing. The reasons that amateurs join and remain in political clubs are examined, as are their attitudes toward patronage and party organization. Wilson concludes that the amateurs' approach tends to destroy party organization and its capacity for consensus-building; thus, the amateurs' activities are self-defeating and undesirable for the club.

PS 225. WILSON, JAMES Q. Thinking About Crime. New York: Random House, 1975. 231 pp.
Wilson has revised and collected a number of his essays on crime. He takes issue with conventional explanations of criminality and prefers an economic approach; that is, that people commit crimes because the benefits of crime exceed its costs by a wider margin than the benefits of working exceed the costs of working. In the first section Wilson describes

crime in the U.S. and its impact on the community. In the second section
he provides the views of statesmen and criminologists on crime. In the
third section he discusses some ways of dealing with crime--better police,
drug control, sentencing, corrections, and the death penalty.

PS 226. WRIGHT, DEIL S. Understanding Intergovernmental Relations. North
        Scituate, Mass.: Duxbury Press, 1978. 409 pp.
Wright explores the nature and changing character of inter-governmental
relations in American politics. The author compares the American form
with alternative models of inter-governmental relations in order to clarify
the concept of Federalism. He then explores the character of relations
between local, state, and national governments with respect to fiscal
issues of public policy. Wright also examines the attitudes of officials
at all levels toward inter-governmental relations. The book concludes
with an assessment of the issues which shape such relations and the course
they are likely to take what lies in the future.

PS 227. YIN, ROBERT K. and DOUGLAS YATES. Street-Level Governments.
        Lexington, Mass.: Heath, 1975. 276 pp.
Yin and Yates examine the movement toward decentralization in urban administration, especially the desire to bring government which controls urban
services closer to those who receive them. They support the position
that urban decentralization is chiefly influenced by, and at the same time
involves a structuring of, the relationship between those who govern and
those who are governed. They maintain that residents should participate
in discussions of public policy which affect their neighborhoods. The
authors draw from numerous case studies to evaluate the effects of decentralization.

V.   LAW AND THE COURTS

PS 228. ABRAHAM, HENRY J. Freedom and the Court: Civil Rights and Liber-
        ties in the United States. New York: Oxford University Press,
        1977. 335 pp.
Abraham's work deals with Supreme Court decisions, principally in the
areas of civil liberties litigation, freedom of expression (speech, press,
assembly), religion, and race. Abraham also undertakes theoretical discussions of the meaning of due process. He presents arguments for and
against "the double standard" of deferential treatment accorded the protection of property as opposed to civil rights, and the incorporation
doctrine issue--that is, whether the due process clause in the Fourteenth
Amendment makes the Bill of Rights applicable to state governments. There
is also an analysis of the distinction between substantive and procedural
due process.

PS 229. ABRAHAM, HENRY J. The Judicial Process: An Introductory Analysis
        of the Courts of the United States, England, and France. 1962;
        Rev. ed. New York: Oxford University Press, 1975. 381 pp.
In this comparative study of judicial process, Abraham draws primarily
on the American system for a judicial model. The introduction contains
definitions of the concept of law. In his discussion of the typologies
of law, Abraham discusses his "bias" toward comparative analysis on the
common ground of Anglo-American law: his main concerns are with equity,
common law, and statutory law. Institutional description (what different
courts are and how they are staffed) and process orientation (how courts
determine dockets and decide cases, external and internal influences on
judges) are the principal topics. Abraham includes an extensive discussion

of judicial review. To conclude his assessment of judicial power, Abraham offers "sixteen great maxims of judicial restraint." An appendix contains bibliographies on American and comparative Constitutional law.

PS 230.   ABRAHAM, HENRY J.   Justices and Presidents: A Political History of Appointments to the Supreme Court. New York: Oxford University Press, 1974. 310 pp.
Abraham's central thesis is that there "is indeed a considerable element of unpredictability in the judicial appointing process." Moving through Court periods—Federalist, Jacksonian, late 19th century, pre-Roosevelt New Deal, and the "almost immediate past"—Abraham provides limited generalizations about factors important in selection, such as judicial experience, party affiliation, geography, religion, and personal friendship. Abraham assesses judicial performance by linking it to Presidential expectations. In an appendix he rates all Supreme Court Justices on a five-point scale from "greats" to "failures."

PS 231.   ALTESON, JAMES.   Values and Assumptions in American Labor Law. Amherst: University of Massachusetts Press, 1982. 240 pp.
Alteson argues that decisions in American labor law are not incoherent, as is presently believed. Alteson intends to show that underlying American labor law is a set of rarely expressed values that, although illegitimate under contemporary modes of legal thought, help to explain the judicial and administrative decisions reached. These values and assumptions predate the statutes and can be found in 19th-century judicial opinions. Legal decisions, argues Alteson, are explained by such factors as notions of inherent property rights, the need for capital mobility, and the interest in continuing productivity.

PS 232.   BECKER, THEODORE L. and MALCOLM M. FEELEY, eds.   The Impact of Supreme Court Decisions: Empirical Studies. New York: Oxford University Press, 1969. 247 pp.
This anthology presents a sampling of the most sophisticated research using impact and compliance concepts. Becker and Feeley broaden the scope of "impact" to include the effect of decisions upon the President and Congress. Other sections include impact studies upon other courts, state and local governments (examining such diverse areas as school desegregation, Bible reading, obscenity regulation, police interrogation, reappointment, and juvenile justice), and public opinion. There is also a section on theory building. Among other things, the editors argue for more work which will help to adequately assess reasons for the "tragically wide gulf between the ideals of Constitutional doctrine and the reality of political life."

PS 233.   BELKNAP, MICHAL, ed.   American Political Trials. Westport, Conn.: Greenwood Press, 1981. 316 pp.
This book is a collection of articles discussing some of the more famous political trials in U.S. history. The essays all try to show the role political trials have played in the development of the U.S. The cases are discussed with regard more to their historical milieu than to the court procedures. The articles look at a pre-Revolutionary War trial on press censorship, and the prosecution of British Loyalists after the Revolutionary War; the attempt to impeach Samuel Chase; the treason trials of Fugitive Slave Law opponent Castner Hanway and Indiana agrarian Lambden Milligan; the Pullman strike case; and the trials of accused Communist Benjamin Gitlow, black activist Angelo Herndon, Nazi Joseph E. McWilliams, the Rosenbergs, and the Chicago Seven.

PS 234. BERGER, RAOUL. Death Penalties: The Supreme Court's Obstacle
Course. Cambridge, Mass.: Harvard University Press, 1982.
242 pp.
Berger argues that the Court's position on the death penalty is based
primarily on moral feelings and is not founded on constitutional analysis.
The author wants to examine constitutional arguments which favor the death
penalty in order to show that there does exist a constitutional basis
for capital punishment. He argues that the Supreme Court is legislating
and making policy choices, which goes beyond its constitutional role when
it tries to revise the "cruel and unusual punishment" clause to outlaw
capital punishment. As a result, death penalty and sentencing legislation
were left by the Constitution to the discretion of individual states.

PS 235. BERGER, RAOUL. Government by the Judiciary: The Transformation
of the Fourteenth Amendment. Cambridge, Mass.: Harvard University Press, 1977. 483 pp.
Berger argues that free-wheeling judicial activism in the name of "libertarian" interpretations of the Constitution (particularly of the Bill
of Rights and Fourteenth Amendment) violates the conception of the judicial function intended by the founders of the American Republic. The
purpose of this book is to demonstrate that the Supreme Court was not
designed to act as a "continuing constitutional convention." The role
assigned to it was to police the boundaries drawn in the Constitution.
Berger categorically rejects the notion of a "double standard": there
is no justification for increased judicial intervention in the name of
protecting civil rights and liberties, just as there was no justification
for a similar mission before 1937 to protect the rights of private property.

PS 236. BICKEL, ALEXANDER M. The Least Dangerous Branch: The Supreme
Court at the Bar of Politics. Indianapolis, Ind.: Bobbs-Merrill,
1962. 303 pp.
Bickel argues that the U.S. Supreme Court is the "most extraordinarily
powerful court of law the world has ever known." Much of his book is
concerned with the origins and evolution of the doctrine of judicial review.
One of Bickel's principal theses is that the court exercises a tribunal
function. Its decisions ought to be based on fundamental presuppositions
rooted in the fabric of society. As part of the "evolving morality of
our tradition," the justices should transcend the limits of their own
attitudes or will. Bickel is critical of the excesses of judicial power
generally equated with "activism."

PS 237. BICKEL, ALEXANDER M. The Morality of Consent. New Haven, Conn.:
Yale University Press, 1975. 156 pp.
Bickel describes two traditions in Western politics: liberal-contractarian
(rooted in John Locke) and conservative-Whig (rooted in Edmund Burke).
He favors the latter model, arguing that the U.S. would correspond more
closely today to the contractarian model if its constitutional development
had relied more on the privileges and immunities clause of the Fourteenth
Amendment, rather than upon the due process and equal protection clauses.
As it is, constitutional development has deviated from the contractarian
model because of the inclination of the Supreme Court to be timely, incremental, pragmatic, and (he argues with respect to the Warren Court) "result
oriented." Courts must play a limited role in policy-making because they
are removed by several orders of magnitude from a pragmatic political
world that succeeds in making tentative, non-principled decisions. Judicial legitimacy rests ultimately on craftsmanship, on a process in which
appeal to fundamental moral principles is the rule, not the exception.

PS 238. BICKEL, ALEXANDER M. The Supreme Court and the Idea of Progress.
         New York: Random House, 1970. 210 pp.
Bickel argues that comparisons between the Warren Court and earlier courts
(particularly since the Civil War) with respect to the qualities of judicial statesmanship are futile: standards of comparison are either nonexistent or imprecise. Moreover, such comparison "really does not matter
one way or the other, for intellectual incoherence is not excusable and
is no more tolerable because it has occurred before." Bickel is critical
of the modern Court for allowing the vagaries of subjective individual
judgments to serve in place of Constitutional law, for misreading history
(with respect to the intent of the Fourteenth Amendment), and for attempting to exceed the limited judicial function in the interest of social
progress. "The Court is the place for principled judgment, disciplined
by the method of reason familiar to the discourse of moral philosophy,"
Bickel says.

PS 239. BLASI, VINCENT, ed. The Burger Court: The Counter-Revolution
         that Wasn't. New Haven, Conn.: Yale University Press, 1983.
         326 pp.
These essays argue that despite the appointments of Chief Justice Warren
Burger and five other Justices by Republican Presidents, the Court has
not taken a turn to the right. It has not, as was feared, forced a roll-
back of the liberal doctrines of the Warren Court. In fact, the essays
show not only how the Burger Court has confronted the precedents set down
by its predecessor, but also how it has consolidated and extended some
of the doctrines established by the Warren Court. The essays provide
a narrative survey of a number of important decisions and identify and
evaluate the themes, trends, and problems of the Burger Court. But the
examinations demonstrate how the Court cannot be characterized categorically. In certain areas it has shown a retrenchment from the Warren years,
but it has not produced a conservative counter-revolution. If anything,
the Court appears to be drifting, still trying to discover its identity.

PS 240. BOLES, JANET K. The Politics of the Equal Rights Amendment:
         Conflict and the Decision Process. New York: Longman, 1979.
         214 pp.
Boles traces the ERA from its original appearance on the political agenda
to the resolution of the issue through authoritative decision-making.
She also examines the role interest groups and community conflict played
in American state politics in the attempt to get the ERA ratified. The
study is based primarily on the political events surrounding the ERA
between January and May 1974 in the states of Texas, Georgia, and Illinois.
It also includes interviews with those active at the national level in
ERA ratification. The study shows the difficulty that the ERA faced when
opponents represented the amendment as a threat to traditional beliefs
and values. The backers of the ERA were able to get state ratification
only when opposition was minimal or nonexistent; in the face of opposition,
these backers retreated to a display of the amendment as a moral imperative
rather than a legal necessity. In retrospect, the author thinks that
the ERA may have been introduced prematurely.

PS 241. BUELL, EMMETT H. and RICHARD BINBIN, Jr. School Desegregation
         and Defended Neighborhoods: The Boston Controversy. Lexington,
         Mass.: Heath, 1982. 203 pp.
The authors consider why white opposition to busing in Boston was so hostile, as well as the conditions that frustrated the implementation of
Federal court orders and prevented the local political system from resolving community conflict over desegregation. In trying to understand the
violence and the difficulty in implementing and complying with court decisions, Buell and Binbin set forth an historical account of Boston's ethnic
areas to show how residents developed a communal identity and dependence

1044

on their neighborhood. They also analyze the legal precedents which created political conflicts that made implementation of busing difficult, which in turn led to an erosion of the legitimacy of judicial authority. The authors, critical of the decisions of the local judge, draw conclusions that seek to avoid this problem in the future.

PS 242. CARDOZO, BENJAMIN. The Nature of the Judicial Process. New Haven, Conn.: Yale University Press, 1921. 180 pp.
In this collection of lectures, Cardozo recounts how he decided cases while on the New York Court of Appeals. Cardozo argues that judges make laws, and that they have several methods at their disposal in the task of interpretation. The method of philosophy favors reasoning by analogy to prior cases; it provides logical consistency in the growth of law. The method of history casts law in terms of its evolution and development. If philosophy and history fail to fix the direction of a legal principle, then judges may appeal to the methods of tradition and sociology. The former suggests that law is a reflection of dominant norms and customs in the society; the latter argues for the welfare of society and the power of social justice. By proposing that judges might appeal to methods outside the traditional factors of logic and history, Cardozo lays the foundation for sociological jurisprudence.

PS 243. CASPAER, JONATHAN D. American Criminal Justice: The Defendant's Perspective. Englewood Cliffs, N.J.: Prentice-Hall, 1972. 178 pp.
Caspaer's book is mainly descriptive, putting forth defendants' views on arrests and police, plea bargaining, counsel (retained and appointed), prosecutors, judges, and crime. Seventy-one individuals were interviewed, all charged with felonies in Connecticut. By Caspaer's own admission, the sample size is limited and consists predominantly of people who were ultimately convicted. However, the compilation of statements of defendants--in their own words with minimal editing--challenges common wisdom and provides evidence of th eproblems and failures of American criminal justice.

PS 244. CHASE, HAROLD W. Federal Judges: The Appointing Process. Minneapolis: University of Minnesota Press, 1972. 240 pp.
Chase provides a thorough study of judicial recruitment and selection of Federal judges in Constitutional or Article III courts. Such judges serve lifetime tenures on the U.S. Court of Appeals, District Courts, Court of Claims, and Court of Customs and Patent Appeals. In addition to archival material and historical records, Chase has relied on interviews and conversations in the Justice Department, on Capitol Hill, and with forty Federal judges and thirty lawyers who practice before Federal courts. Chase concludes "that our present appointment system nets a good but not outstanding array of Federal judges." As a possible alternative which would require Constitutional amendment but which might improve quality, Chase proposes that selection be made the responsibility of the U.S. Supreme Court.

PS 245. CORWIN, EDWARD S. The "Higher Law" Background of American Constitutional Law. Ithaca, N.Y.: Cornell University Press, 1955. 89 pp.
Corwin discusses the legal philosophers who posited the notion of a law superior to the jus civili, providing the philosophic basis for elevating Constitutional law to a loftier position during the American Revolution. Just as natural law constrained the highest early powers, so Constitutional law (infused with the principles of the jus naturale) provided the basis for limitations on governmental power. From such a hierarchy and from the limitations imposed by the "higher law," the American doctrine of judicial review evolves. Corwin argues that the principal job of the

doctrine in the 19th century was to protect the natural right of private property—hence a concern with the doctrine of vested rights—and that in the last fifty years the focus has been on civil rights.

PS 246. COX, ARCHIBALD. The Warren Court: Constitutional Decision as an Instrument. Cambridge, Mass.: Harvard University Press, 1968. 144 pp.
This work presents some of the major decisions of the Warren Court in the areas of civil rights, free speech and association, voting rights, and the reform of criminal procedure. Cox argues that the Court was presented with the problem of achieving society's goals without impairing its own usefulness. The Court was pushed into this position of activism by the failure of other branches of the government and the states to respond to the problems of the era. He maintains that the Court's decisions were a response to fundamental forces in American society, including the commitment to egalitarianism, the belief in the sanctity of personal liberty and privacy against governmental intrusion, the demand for racial justice, and the findings of modern psychology. Cox's work places the Warren Court squarely in the mainstream of American history.

PS 247. CROSSKEY, WINSLOW and WILLIAM JEFFREY, Jr. Politics and the Constitution in the Political History of the United States. 3 vols. Chicago: University of Chicago Press, 1953-1980. 2002 pp.
The first two volumes of this series, written by Crosskey, examine the legislative intent of early American Congressional legislators by using diaries, correspondence, and press accounts from the period. These sources, for Crosskey, provide information regarding the ways early American legislators formed the Federal Constitution and the reasoning behind their actions. The author examines contemporary political and economic theories as a background for a discussion of the issue of Federal control over commerce and the function of the developing Supreme Court. Volume Three, cowritten by Crosskey and Jeffrey, focuses on the movement to abandon the Articles of Confederation of 1777 and the political and legal issues dealt with at the Constitutional Convention of 1787.

PS 248. FELLMAN, DAVID. The Defendant's Rights Today. Madison: University of Wisconsin Press, 1976. 446 pp.
Fellman examines how notions of procedural due process evolved through Court interpretations of the Fourth through the Eighth Amendments. He stresses the positions the Supreme Court has taken, since these decisions tend to establish minimal national standards for all other courts. Fellman begins with a discussion of procedure, using the two models of the criminal process (due process; crime control) created by Herbert L. Packer. The remaining chapters provide extensive information on the course of a defendant's rights, and on the multiplicity of judicial tests and standards which the Court has developed since the early due process cases of the 1930s.

PS 249. FRIEDMAN, LEON and FRED L. ISRAEL, eds. The Justices of the United States Supreme Court, 1789-1978: Their Lives and Major Opinions. 5 vols. New York: Chelsea House, 1980. 3900 pp.
The initial four volumes of this work contain original essays on ninety-seven Supreme Court justices who served through 1978. The essays, written by thirty-eight scholars (e.g., Robert McCloskey, Alpheus T. Mason, Stanley Kutler, John P. Frank, Gerald Dunne), are supplemented by excerpted representative Court opinions and a selected bibliography. A fifth volume provides information on "Burger Court" Justices of the 1970s, as well as "hold-over" Justices from the Warren Court and retirees of the last decade. The Appendix contains valuable charts and tables, including one listing all acts of Congress deemed unconstitutional by the Supreme Court, and another showing all Supreme Court decisions which have been overruled.

PS 250. FUNSTON, RICHARD Y. Constitutional Counterrevolution? The Warren and the Burger Courts: Judicial Policy Making in Modern America. New York: Schenkman, 1977. 399 pp.

Funston has written a detailed comparison of the U.S. Supreme Court under Chief Justices Earl Warren and Warren Burger using both descriptive and critical approaches. In his initial chapter on the nature of the Supreme Court, he argues against "result-oriented jurisprudence" in favor of sound judicial reasoning. His central thesis is that "opinions based upon reasoned principle are necessary to the very self-preservation of the Supreme Court." Treating the principal topics of contemporary constitutional interpretation (race relations, reapportionment, the rights of accused persons, search and seizure, religion, and obscenity), Funston assesses the areas of continuity and discontinuity in these two courts.

PS 251. GLICK, HENRY R. Courts, Politics and Justice. New York: McGraw-Hill, 1983. 355 pp.

Glick looks at the judicial process in all types and levels of U.S. courts in order to present a broader perspective of the judicial system and a better understanding of how the judicial system functions from the initial considerations of a court case to the system as a whole. The author utilizes recent social science research to explain what courts do. Social science research, Glick feels, provides a more complete and realistic account of judicial behavior than formal law. Finally, Glick links courts to politics. He explains judicial behavior by considering the broader social and political context within which the courts operate. They are treated as major and integral parts of state and national politics, not independent of institutions affected by a political world outside of themselves.

PS 252. GLICK, HENRY R. and KENNETH N. VINCES. State Court Systems. Englewood Cliffs, N.J.: Prentice-Hall, 1973. 111 pp.

Glick and Vinces provide a general description of state courts, especially the litigation within them and their organization. A chapter on selection and recruitment presents five different selection systems used by the states, systems which range from partisan election to "meritocracies" based primarily upon professional influence. Glick and Vinces define judicial role types within state supreme courts, the typology of which includes law-interpreters, lawmakers, and pragmatists. Using personal interviews of justices in four states, and generalizing from a sample of twenty-four individuals, the authors provide some empirical evidence regarding the distribution of role types.

PS 253. GOLDMAN, SHELDON and THOMAS P. JAHNIGE. The Federal Courts as a Political System. New York: Harper & Row, 1976. 292 pp.

The authors analyze the workings of the Federal courts as a subsystem of the larger American political system. The introduction presents an adaptation of David Eastonian's systems model to describe Federal judicial institutions and environments. The organization of the book follows the Eastonian typology; chapter subjects include regime rules (organization, procedure, norms), the authorities (recruitment and backgrounds), input (litigation, including a useful explanation of gatekeeping functions which limit litigation), conversation (decision-making, particularly in collegial appellate courts), output (adjudication as policy-making), impact, and feedback.

PS 254. GOLDWIN, ROBERT A. and WILLIAM A. SCHAMBRA, eds. How Democratic Is the Constitution? Washington, D.C.: American Enterprise Institute, 1980. 150 pp.

This collection of essays contains a wide range of perspectives--from the neo-conservative to the radical--on the democratic nature of the U.S. Constitution. The essays argue, respectively, that the Founders intended to create a wholly democratic constitution; that the representative structure of the Constitution is undemocratic but responsive to public needs; that the central fact of the Constitution is not that the Constitution is or is not democratic, but that it secures natural rights by protecting the private realm. The essays argue that the Constitution was intended to counter a variety of governmental abuses in the states, and that the development of an extended republic was an accommodation by conservative elites of radical democratic elements.

PS 255. HALPERIN, MORTON H. and DANIEL HOFFMAN. Freedom vs. National Security. New York: Chelsea, 1977. 594 pp.
The authors examine how the courts have attempted to balance the requirements of national security against the constitutional rights of Americans. The book begins with an analysis of the ways in which the courts have addressed the claim that the President has a prerogative in foreign affairs to take whatever action he deems necessary, and he is not subject to Congressional limitations. The authors then deal with the government's power to control access to information relating to national security matters. Halperin and Hoffman also look at the issues of government surveillance and government infringement on civil liberties. They conclude with a discussion of whether people whose rights have been violated in the name of national security can be vindicated in court.

PS 256. HALPERN, STEPHEN C. and CHARLES M. LAMB, eds. Supreme Court Activism and Restraint. Lexington, Mass.: Heath, 1982. 436 pp.
These essays categorize Supreme Court Justices as judicial activists or exercisers of judicial self-restraint. The essays, however, illustrate that few Justices can be strictly placed in one category or the other. All Supreme Court decisions have political ramifications and, insofar as they assert one position over another, have an element of activism. In general, the essays conclude that the categories as they are now understood are not very useful for identifying consistent positions over time. However, they may be helpful in making distinctions within specific time periods and within the context of specific issues.

PS 257. HOROWITZ, DONALD L. The Courts and Social Policy. Washington, D.C.: Brookings Institution, 1977. 309 pp.
Horowitz's thesis is that in the 20th century judicial power in the U.S. has grown so extensively that courts have seized the initiative in lawmaking; the American tendency to adjudicate social problems has accelerated the trend. Horowitz argues that the range of social and political issues brought before judges casts them in a role for which they have neither the capacity nor the legitimate authority. To support his thesis, he examines four cases: citizen participation in the 1966 Model Cities Program, the definition of equality in school resources, the creation of a procedural Bill of Rights for minors, and application of the "exclusionary rule" for admissibility in state courts of unconstitutionally seized evidence.

PS 258. JACOB, HERBERT. Crime and Justice in Urban America. Englewood Cliffs, N.J.: Prentice-Hall, 1980. 198 pp.
Jacob presents an overview of criminal justice in American cities. He is particularly interested in the way in which the intricate political life of a city "complicates the pursuit of justice." After sections on victims, criminals, and the police, this study focuses on urban court systems. Jacob offers case studies of New York, Chicago, Los Angeles, and Prairie City, as well as discussions of such topics as the urban bar, provision of legal services, and dispute processing. The volume concludes with more general thoughts about crime, justice, and city politics.

PS 259. **JACOB, HERBERT.** Justice in America: Courts, Lawyers and the
         Judicial Process. Boston: Little, Brown, 1978. 237 pp.
This is a descriptive work on the politics of justice as it is administered
by American courts. Jacob argues that "the distribution of justice does
not simply result from partisan politics, social cleavages, interest group
activity, or election outcomes," and that justice is not simply the outcome
of the adversary process, or of neutral principles in the interpretation
of the law, or of lawyers' expertise. Many factors contribute to giving
justice its special part in the policy process. Jacob assesses the functions of courts, of participants in the judicial process, and of the structure and rules of adjudication.

PS 260. **KLUGER, RICHARD.** Simple Justice: The History of Brown v. Board
         of Education and Black America's Struggle for Equality. New
         York: Knopf, 1976. 823 pp.
Kluger's Simple Justice is a study of the school desegregation decision
of 1954. The purpose of the book is to suggest "how law and men interact, how social forces of the past collide with those of the present,
and how the men selected as America's ultimate arbiters of justice have
chosen to define that quality with widely varying regard for the emotional
quality of life itself." Kluger analyzes the inner workings of the Warren
Court shortly after Earl Warren was appointed Chief Justice of the U.S.
in 1963. That Warren was able to effect a unanimous decision in Brown
attests to the leadership abilities that he brought to the office.

PS 261. **KRISLOV, SAMUEL.** The Supreme Court and Political Freedom. New
         York: Free Press, 1968. 239 pp.
Krislov explores the evolution of First Amendment protections designed
to maximize both representative government and protection of individual
conscience. The primary purpose of the First Amendment "is basically
motivated by the political needs of the society." In a series of analytic
chapters, Krislov explores the history and development of First Amendment
interpretation. He discusses such issues as the incorporation doctrine,
the preferred freedoms doctrine, absolutism versus balancing, state action,
and the nature of judicial review.

PS 262. **MALBIN, MICHAEL.** Religion and Politics: The Intention of the
         Authors of the First Amendment. Washington, D.C.: American
         Enterprise Institute, 1978. 40 pp.
Malbin argues that the debates in the First Congress suggest that Congress
did not mean the establishment of religion clause to require strict neutrality between religion and irreligion. Aid to religion was to be permitted as long as it furthered a purpose and as long as it did not dis-
criminate among sects. Malbin argues that a fully enforced nondiscrimina-
tion requirement perhaps would not change many of the Supreme Court's
recent decisions on the issue of separation of church and state, but that
a return to the original conception might have an effect on future legislation and court cases.

PS 263. **MASON, ALPHEUS T.** The Supreme Court from Taft to Burger. Baton
         Rouge: Lousiana State University Press, 1978. 250 pp.
Mason's treatise blends political and case narrative with an analysis
of the nature of judicial power in the American system of government.
Beginning with the Taft Court (1921-30), Mason argues that the Supreme
Court reached a zenith of judicial activism in the name of protecting
private property and capital from government regulation and intervention.
Mason goes on to explore the judicial crisis of 1935-6, a period of
unabated abnegation of New Deal policies; the "Constitutional Revolution
of 1937"; and the Supreme Court's search for a role in the 1940s. In
his examination of the Warren and Burger Courts, Mason assesses the nature
of judicial review as it applies to civil rights and liberties.

PS 264. McCLOSKEY, HERBERT and ALIDA BRILL. Dimensions of Tolerance:
What Americans Believe About Civil Liberties. New York: Russell
Sage, 1983. 512 pp.
McCloskey and Brill examine what makes individuals advocates of civil
liberties rather than blind conformers to political duty and obligation.
The authors survey civil libertarian attitudes among opinion leaders,
the public, lawyers and judges, police officials, and academics. They
analyze levels of tolerance on a range of civil liberties issues and discover that social learning is the most productive method for breeding
civil libertarian norms.

PS 265. McCLOSKEY, ROBERT G. The American Supreme Court. Chicago: University of Chicago Press, 1960. 260 pp.
McCloskey attempts to understand the role of the Supreme Court, particularly its responsibilities as a constitutional tribunal exercising the
power of judicial review. Beginning with a discussion of the genesis
of judicial power (and the philosophic origins of judicial review as these
relate to natural law precepts), the author moves era by era from the
early Marshall Court (to 1810) to the modern court of the post-New Deal
period (1937-60). McCloskey characterizes the principal constitutional
and political issues of each period: he integrates doctrinal developments
with the individual contributions of major Supreme Court Justices to produce a succinct institutional history.

PS 266. McCLOSKEY, ROBERT G. The Modern Supreme Court. Cambridge, Mass.:
Harvard University Press, 1972. 376 pp.
In this work, McCloskey focuses on the history of the Supreme Court after
1937. Since he tends to see the Court as a political force rather than
as a source of legal doctrine, one of his major concerns is the Court's
increasing role in American society and the way it has seized initiative
from less enterprising branches of government. McCloskey argues that
the Court's dominant concern since 1937 has been the protection of individual rights against government and society; therefore, much of this
volume is a history of the Court's activities in the area of civil rights.

PS 267. MILLER, ARTHUR S. Democratic Dictatorship: The Emergent Constitution of Control. Westport, Conn.: Greenwood Press, 1981.
268 pp.
Miller argues that, as the powers of government increase with new demands
made upon it, conflicts may arise between expanding demands and unsatisfied
needs. He looks at crisis (emergency) government as a response to such
conflicts and how it may lead to an authoritarian government. He also
examines the means employed by the U.S. in the past to confront revolutionary changes and natural disasters. Miller then turns to the inadequate
present-day government reaction to similar changes and struggles, and
projects possible political and constitutional consequences. He next
considers how a crisis government may exercise its authority without becoming authoritarian, and concludes by speculating about the probable repressive nature of future American Constitutionalism.

PS 268. MILLER, ARTHUR S. Social Change and Fundamental Law: America's
Evolving Constitution. Westport, Conn.: Greenwood Press, 1979.
395 pp.
Miller proposes that the fundamentals of law must be adaptable to changing
circumstances if we are to have a "living" Constitution. The author provides outlines for a modernized study of Constitutional law. He argues
that the Constitution involves affirmative duties as well as negative
limitations, and these affirmative duties should be exercised in light
of social change. This leads to a discussion of the problems of policy-
making by judicial decision and how it may conflict with the principle
of the separation of powers. Miller also discusses the constitutional
questions surrounding Watergate and the Congressional veto.

PS 269. MILLER, ARTHUR S. The Supreme Court: Myth and Reality. Westport,
    Conn.: Greenwood Press, 1978. 388 pp.
Miller argues that the decisions of the Supreme Court are shaped by the
issues of contemporary American politics, not the strict interpretation
of the law. He believes that the Supreme Court should be studied as one
of the policy-making agencies of the Federal government and as a target
of pressure groups. The principal functions of the Supreme Court have
been to validate constitutional change and to make it fit the exigencies
of succeeding generations. Miller intends to correct the myth that the
Supreme Court epitomizes the idea of government under law. The essays
look at the justices' reasoning behind cases; the power of the Court to
alter behavior patterns and attitudes of Americans; the question of public
confidence in the judiciary; and the Court's treatment of personal privacy
issues.

PS 270. MILLER, ARTHUR S. The Supreme Court and American Capitalism.
    New York: Free Press, 1968. 259 pp.
Miller examines how developments in constitutional theory have affected
American business since the early 19th century. He argues that the decisions made before the Civil War by the Marshall and Taney Courts, which
altered the legal status of corporations, made it possible for the corporation to emerge as the dominant form of business organization. Through
his discussions of the Marshall and Taney decisions, the proliferation
of corporations between the Civil War and the 1930s, and the eventual
decline of the Court's influence on economic policy after the 1930s, Miller
hopes to describe the relationship between legal and political institutions
and the distribution of resources in the U.S.

PS 271. MOORE, W. S. and RUDOLPH G. PINNER, eds. The Constitution and
    the Budget: Are Constitutional Limits on Tax, Spending, and
    Budget Powers Desirable at the Federal Level? Washington, D.C.:
    American Enterprise Institute, 1980. 155 pp.
The authors debate the proposal for a constitutional amendment requiring
a balanced Federal budget. The book begins with a look at ways in which
an amendment may be established, including the possibility of amending
the Constitution by convention. The articles discuss such matters as
the amending powers established in Article Five of the U.S. Constitution,
the effects of constitutional restraints on economic policy-making, and
how constitutional restrictions on the budget affect fiscal authority.
The book concludes with a discussion of the policy issues raised by proposals for constitutional limits on the Federal budget.

PS 272. MURPHY, WALTER F. Elements of Judicial Strategy. Chicago: Uni-
    versity of Chicago Press, 1964. 249 pp.
Murphy applies concepts of social psychology to the analysis of the U.S.
Supreme Court. He begins with the premise that "in settling disputes,
judges inevitably play a part in the shaping of public policy." He is
also concerned with intra-court power issues among justices. His analysis
includes a discussion of external political checks and influences upon
the Court. In a chapter entitled "Marshalling the Court," Murphy outlines
the tactics available to a Justice carrying out efforts to influence policy
choice: persuasion based on merits, increasing personal power, sanctions,
and bargaining.

PS 273. MURPHY, WALTER F. and JOSEPH TANENHAUS. The Study of Public Law.
    New York: Random House, 1972. 242 pp.
Murphy and Tanenhaus assess the state of public law in the early 1970s.
They concentrate on the work of American scholars, but not exclusively
on American courts. In an attempt to build hypotheses and middle-range
theories about judicial policy-making and behavior, Murphy and Tanenhaus
compare the courts of Australia, Canada, India, Ireland, Japan, and West

Germany. The central reference point remains the U.S. judicial system and, more directly, the U.S. Supreme Court.

PS 274. NEELY, RICHARD. How Courts Govern America. New Haven, Conn.: Yale University Press, 1981. 233 pp.
Neely argues that American courts, both state and Federal, are the central institutions which make American democracy work. He denies the assertion that such courts are undemocratic because judges are not elected and cannot be held politically accountable for their actions. Instead, Neely argues that the courts serve a democratic role by alleviating the dangerous structural deficiencies of the other institutions of government. He contends that it is the job of the courts to protect society from the potential dangers that exist in American political institutions; by keeping a check on the other areas of American politics, the courts preserve participatory democracy.

PS 275. NICHOLAS, SUSAN C., ALAN PRICE, AND RACHEL RUBIN. Rights and Wrongs in Women's Struggle for Legal Equality. New York: McGraw-Hill, 1979. 89 pp.
The authors examine women's legal battle to gain the right to participate and contribute to society as full and equal citizens. The book begins with a look at how women have struggled to gain equal protection under law and full recognition of their rights under the Constitution. It also looks at how the law has regarded the family, marriage, and property in ways which have repressed women. The book then turns to an examination of women in the marketplace and the struggle against sex discrimination. This is followed by a discussion of rape and abortion, and the right of women to control their bodies. The book concludes with a summation of the breakthroughs women have made and how much more remains to be accomplished.

PS 276. O'BRIEN, DAVID M. Privacy, Law, and Public Policy. New York: Praeger, 1979. 262 pp.
O'Brien examines the constitutional and public boundaries of the political ideal of privacy. He begins with a look at privacy as a political value, then turns to a consideration of the way privacy is defined within the Constitution and how the legal principle of privacy is integrated into the U.S. judicial system. O'Brien also discusses personal privacy as an issue of contemporary public policy, especially in light of information-gathering technology. In addition he assesses public policies designed to safeguard privacy.

PS 277. O'BRIEN, DAVID M. The Public's Right to Know: The Supreme Court and the First Amendment. New York: Praeger, 1981. 205 pp.
O'Brien tries to reconcile the First Amendment with the need for government secrecy. He examines "the public's right to know" in terms of constitutional politics as interpreted and enforced by the Supreme Court, and considers the basis for asserting a constitutionally enforceable right to know. O'Brien then turns to the historical origins of this right. He concludes that the public's right to know has been enhanced by the Supreme Court's broad interpretation of the First Amendment, but that even this interpretation has at times been balanced by the need to protect governmental secrecy and judicial review.

PS 278. PELTASON, JACK W. Federal Courts in the Political Process. New York: Random House, 1955. 81 pp.
Judges, Peltason argues, are engaged in the same political struggles as legislators and administrators. His study focuses on the relation of judicial activity to the rest of the American political process. Judicial activity involves the support of political groups and legislative bodies, and the organization and constitution of the judiciary reflects this inter-

action. Peltason examines judicial organization, environment, recruitment, decision-making, and interest-conflict in terms of their relation to the political process. Competing groups struggle over the selection of judges, the power of individual courts, the implications of decisions, and their influence over those decisions. Peltason characterizes such constitutional issues as desegregation in terms of the interplay and conflict among interested groups.

PS 279. PERRY, MICHAEL J. The Constitution, the Courts, and Human Rights: An Inquiry into the Legitimacy of Constitutional Policy-making by the Judiciary. New Haven, Conn.: Yale University Press, 1982. 241 pp.
Perry addresses the courts' decisions in areas concerning freedom of expression, equal protection, and substantive due process. He begins with a distinction between constitutional policy-making and constitutional interpretation. He then examines the courts' constitutional policy-making in cases regarding the separation of powers. Perry next turns to constitutional policy-making on issues concerning the proper relationship between the individual and the government. Here the author makes his case for the necessity of constitutional policy-making for the protection of human rights.

PS 280. PRITCHETT, CHARLES HERMAN. The American Constitution. 1959; Rev. ed. New York: McGraw-Hill, 1977. 719 pp.
Pritchett provides an interpretation of the evolution and development of American Constitutional law relating to judicial review, interstate relations, jurisdiction, taxation, commerce, executive powers, equal protection, and due process. He explains the various approaches to constitutional interpretation which the Supreme Court has adopted, and relates them to the almost innumerable tests and standards the justices have used to bring both rationality and continuity to the task of judicial interpretation. Even though Pritchett is principally concerned with doctrinal analysis of the Court output, he also emphasizes the "impact of individual judicial minds upon Constitutional development."

PS 281. ROHDE, DAVID W. and HAROLD J. SPAETH. Supreme Court Decision Making. New York: Freeman, 1976. 229 pp.
Rohde and Spaeth develop models for predicting voting behavior of justices. They base their models upon prior decisions of individual justices in a variety of categorized cases. Early chapters examine jurisdiction, norms, precedent, reasoning, and the status and role definition of Justices. In presenting their theory of Supreme Court decision-making, the authors argue that Court decisions are the consequence of three factors: goals, rules, and situations. To identify the Justices' personal policy preferences, Rohde and Spaeth analyze the psychological components of personal preference: beliefs, attitudes, and values.

PS 282. ROSSITER, CLINTON. The Supreme Court and the Commander in Chief. 1951; Rev. ed. Ithaca, N.Y.: Cornell University Press, 1976. 231 pp.
Rossiter attempts to show how the Supreme Court interprets the President's status and authority as commander-in-chief. His major theme is that in times of stress and under the cloud of war a President can reasonably assume that he can act without systematic institutional restraint from other sectors of American government. The first part of the study examines the Court's construction of the President's war power. Rossiter then turns to five specific problems regarding war powers which the Court has addressed, and the varied implications for Presidential authority. The expanded edition, prepared by R. P. Longaker, provides a look at developments after 1950. Longaker argues that during the Korean and Vietnam Wars, Presidents claimed unprecedented power with regard to internal and external security.

PS 283.   RUBIN, EVA R.   Abortion, Politics, and the Court: Roe v. Wade
          and Its Aftermath. Westport, Conn.: Greenwood Press, 1982.
          211 pp.
Rubin provides an account of the litigation campaign, the historical antecedents, and some of the political and legislative consequences of the
Roe v. Wade decision. She traces the origin of the social movement which
pressed to legalize abortion, and examines the effect this pressure had
on the Supreme Court decision. She also considers the growth of opposition
in the 1960s to state anti-abortion policy, the attempts to change these
policies by legislation and litigation, and how these attempts influenced
the Supreme Court. Rubin concludes with a look at the debates and political activity that followed the decision in Roe v. Wade.

PL 284.   SCHMIDHAUSER, JOHN R.   The Supreme Court: Its Politics, Personali-
          ties and Procedures. New York: Holt, Rinehart & Winston, 1960.
          163 pp.
Schmidhauser depicts the Supreme Court in terms of its internal dynamics
and, specifically, the process of appellate adjudication. In three sections, the book presents descriptive information on judicial selection,
external political and legal forces operating on the Court, and internal
procedures and customs. Schmidhauser provides information on operating
procedures to assess the Court in its collegial (or small group) capacities.
Moving across historical periods, he discusses such factors as majority
opinions, leadership, dissent, role definition, gatekeeping, and opinion
writing. The author also attempts to draw some correlations between the
social backgrounds of Justices and their voting patterns.

PS 285.   SCHUBERT, GLENDON.   The Judicial Mind: The Attitudes and Ideolo-
          gies of Supreme Court Justices, 1946-1963. Evanston, Ill.:
          Northwestern University Press, 1965. 295 pp.
Schubert's Judicial Mind tries to construct a psychometric model of U.S.
Supreme Court Justices' attitudes. The assumptions which underlie such
models are that ideologies form the basis for judicial decisions, and
that the more sophisticated understanding of attitudes, the more likely
the success in predicting outcomes in appellate court cases. Schubert
uses factor analysis (applied to voting data from the Supreme Court, 1946-
63) to rank Justices along liberal and conservative dimensions. These
dimensions are broken down further into pragmatic and dogmatic components.
The model itself has both descriptive and analytic uses.

PS 286.   SCHUBERT, GLENDON.   Judicial Policy Making: The Political Role
          of the Courts. Glenview, Ill.: Scott, Foresman, 1974.
          212 pp.
Schubert argues that judges share with other governmental officials the
political power and responsibility to make policy decisions. Much of
this volume is descriptive, relying on systems analysis for the discussion
of judicial structures and institutions. In later chapters Schubert
devotes attention to decision-making procedures and policy-making analysis,
employing theories of social psychology regarding leadership, sociometric
relationships, social norms, and attitude configurations for Justices
on the Burger Court. One of the final chapters seeks to draw relationships
between judicial role definitions (activism, restraint) and ideology.

PS 287.   SCHWARTZ, BERNARD.   The Great Rights of Mankind: A History of
          the American Bill of Rights. New York: Oxford University Press,
          1977. 279 pp.
Schwartz's study is a history of the creation of the American Bill of
Rights--government restrictions which James Madison deemed the "great
rights of mankind." Schwartz's approach is chronological, starting with
the great charters of English liberty, continuing through Colonial and
Revolutionary texts, then into the political and social movement that
led to the drafting and passage of the Bill of Rights.

PS 288. SCHWARTZ, BERNARD and STEPHEN LESHNER. Inside the Warren Court.
Garden City, N.Y.: Doubleday, 1983. 279 pp.
This book is based on information from conference notes, personal testimony,
correspondence, diaries, memoranda, and draft opinions of several Supreme
Court Justices who served under Earl Warren. It also draws on information
from the Warren Archives. The result is a biographical account of Earl
Warren and of those with whom he worked during his tenure as Supreme Court
Justice. It contains anecdotal and behind-the-scenes accounts of the
nature of the Supreme Court, suggesting that, in determining Court decisions, personal, nonjudicial opinions and feelings came into play but
were always tempered by respect for the law.

PS 289. SHAPIRO, MARTIN. Law and Politics in the Supreme Court: New
Approaches to Political Jurisprudence. New York: Free Press,
1964. 364 pp.
Shapiro argues for regarding the U.S. Supreme Court as an integral part
of the political process. In a conscious attempt to break away from the
view of judging as "discovery of the law" by objective, nonpolitical judges,
Shapiro emphasizes the similarities between the Supreme Court and such
other political agencies as regulatory commissions and Congressional committees. Shapiro argues for a "political jurisprudence." He attempts
to treat the Supreme Court as one government agency among many in the
American policy-making process. His analysis embraces fully the "behavioral approach," in which judges are to be viewed as political actors.
"It is behavior that is being examined, not law," Shapiro states.

PS 290. SIEGAN, BERNARD H. Economic Liberties and the Constitution.
Chicago: University of Chicago Press, 1980. 383 pp.
Siegan contends that it is up to the Supreme Court to loosen economic
restraints so that all segments of society may benefit from the free play
of market forces. The legislative and administrative processes which
promote economic liberties are seriously flawed because they are forced
into compromise by different interest groups, political factions, and
voter ignorance. Siegan calls on the Court to control government regulation of business. The Court, he asserts, also must assume responsibility
and control government spending on social problems, all of which have
proved harmful to the market and economic liberties. Siegan claims that
the protection of traditional property rights and commerce is guaranteed
by the Constitution, and it is the responsibility of the Court to make
sure such guarantees are carried out.

PS 291. SORAUF, FRANK J. The Wall of Separation: The Constitutional
Politics of Church and State. Princeton, N.J.: Princeton University Press, 1976. 394 pp.
Sorauf analyzes the judicial interpretation of the First Amendment prohibition of laws "respecting an establishment of religion" through an investigation of sixty-seven cases decided by state supreme courts, U.S. Courts
of Appeal, and the U.S. Supreme Court from 1951 to 1971. Sorauf's analysis
presents the litigation of church-state relations in terms of the "group
basis of politics," portraying the plaintiffs, attorneys, and the groups
seeking judicial decision in terms of their strategies and goals as well
as their successes and failures. Dividing the group into "separatists"
and "accommodationists," he assesses the impact of their respective cases
on the political and ideological content of church-state litigation during
the two decades covered.

PS 292. SUMMERS, ROBERT S. Instrumentalism and American Legal Theory.
Ithaca, N.Y.: Cornell University Press, 1982. 295 pp.
Summers develops a general theory of what he calls pragmatic instrumentalism in American legal theory. Pragmatic instrumentalism as a legal
theory emerged around the beginning of the 20th century in the U.S. It

considers the primary task of legal theory to be the establishment of
ideas which will make law publicly useful. Instrumentalism also considers
the various goals laws may serve, and how laws are implemented. Summers
traces the development of instrumentalism in American legal theory.

PS 293. WESTIN, ALAN. Privacy and Freedom. New York: Atheneum, 1967.
          487 pp.
Westin looks at the problem of the invasion of privacy in light of developments in surveillance techniques. He first defines what is meant by privacy. This is followed by an inquiry into the ways in which American
society has reacted to the new surveillance techniques. Westin provides
information regarding recent developments in the evolution of our norms
of privacy and whether there are trends in interest-group and general
public opinion that may help to guide Americna policy-makers. Finally,
he undertakes a discussion of how American law has dealt with the issue
of privacy and surveillance, as the backdrop for an analysis of specific
measures that public and private authorities might take to ensure the
preservation of privacy.

PS 294. WHITE, G. EDWARD. The American Judicial Tradition: Profiles
          of Leading American Judges. New York: Oxford University Press,
          1976. 441 pp.
White maintains that there is a tradition of American appellate judging,
and examines this tradition through a series of individual and group portraits. Eight chapters describe the judicial traditions developed in
the 19th century, a period when judging was not regarded as an exercise
in making law. White calls this the "oracular theory," for judges were
regarded as oracles who discovered and interpreted the law. In the 20th
century, judges, in response to social and economic developments and the
growth of sociologic jurisprudence, have been acknowledged to be lawmakers
rather than law-finders. White's concluding seven chapters are devoted
to the traditions of judicial liberalism and process jurisprudence.

PS 295. WILKINSON, J. HARVIE, III. From Brown to Bakke: The Supreme
          Court and School Integration, 1954-1978. New York: Oxford Uni-
          versity Press, 1979. 368 pp.
Wilkerson's study is primarily a history of the Supreme Court's role in
public school integration in the years 1954-78. He begins with Brown
v. Board of Education, evaluating the Court's decision both in terms of
its historical precedents and antecedents, and the perspectives on education and race which were revealed in the case. He then examines the
Court's attempts over the next fifteen eyars to implement Brown in the
South. He contends that as the rural South began to integrate its schools,
the focus of the Court shifted away from that area, and concentrated more
and more on the nation as a whole, and particularly on the nation's urban
centers. The third section of the book examines court-ordered busing,
most prevalent in the urban centers, and desegregation in the late 1960s
and learly 1970s. Wilkinson concludes with a discussion of the Bakke
case, a case which he points to as signaling a return to the Court's pre-
Brown v. Board of Education focus--integrating colleges and graduate schools.
Wilkerson's approach is contemporary, social, and at times journalistic.
He draws on the work of lawyers, journalists, historians, and social scientists.

VI. BUREAUCRACY AND PUBLIC ADMINISTRATION

PS 296. AARON, HENRY J. and JOSEPH A. PECHMAN, eds. How Taxes Arrect Economic Behavior. Washington, D.C.: Brookings Institution, 1981. 466 pp.
Aaron and Pechman have collected essays on policy proposals for income tax reduction. The articles are based on empirical research on the effect of taxes on labor and supply, equipment investment, corporate finance, stock prices, capital gains, housing, savings, and charitable contributions. The research also explores the economic effects of tax policies on public finance and budgetary policy. In trying to uncover the best quantitative estimate for alternative tax policies, these essays provide a report on the state of economic research. The emphasis throughout the book is on the effect of taxes on economic behavior within society.

PS 297. ACKERMAN, BRUCE A. and WILLIAM T. HASSLER. Clean Coal/Dirty Air: Or How the Clean Air Act Became a Multibillion Dollar Bail Out for High Sulphur Coal Producers and What Should Be Done About It. New Haven, Conn.: Yale University Press, 1981. 193 pp.
The authors examine the application of the Clean Air Act of 1970 as an example of administrative lawmaking. They seek to understand how decision-makers perceived, defined, and solved problems within the evolving framework of environmental regulation in order to determine which experiments in administrative design succeeded. The study begins with the ways in which Congress set about to control the environment in the 1970s and how it tried to come up with a new way for administering the Clean Air Act. This is followed by an examination of how coal burners became the concern of Congressional deliberation when they were being seriously threatened by the Clean Air Act. The study then considers how Congress balanced the relationship between economic costs and ecological benefits presented by alternative regulatory policies.

PS 298. ALFORD, ROBERT. Health Care Policies. Chicago: University of Chicago Press, 1974. 294 pp.
Alford presents a critique of pluralism and proposes a new interest group theory of politics—the structural interest theory. He applies his theory to health care crises in New York City in order to explain why reform efforts do not succeed. Alford believes health care institutions are understood theoretically as a continuing struggle among the professional monopolists (doctors who dominate the system), the corporate rationalizers (for example, hospital administrators) who challenge the monopolists, and the poor. The monopolists and rationalizers are major structural interests; the poor are a repressed structural interest. The major structural interests respond to crises by initiating symbolically reassuring investigations by committees whose reports call for coordination and integration of the health delivery system.

PS 299. ALFORD, ROBERT and HARRY M. SCOBLE. Bureaucracy and Participation: Political Cultures in Four Wisconsin Cities. Chicago: Rand McNally, 1969. 244 pp.
Alford and Scoble study four Wisconsin cities and classify their political systems according to the degree of bureaucratization and professionalization of their governments and the level of participation and interest group activity that characterizes their political life. The authors propose that the key independent variable for understanding particular local political systems is the character of a community's economic base. They classify the cities as trading, manufacturing, or professional centers to demonstrate the relationship between the economic character of the city and its level of bureaucratization and citizen participation. The

main body of the book reports on each of the four cities in turn, and
then analyzes their bureaucratic and participatory characteristics. The
authors conclude that the modern city is highly bureaucratized; formal
and public mechanisms are used over informal and private ones for the
resolution of conflicts.

PS 300. ART, ROBERT J. The TFX Decision: McNamara and the Military.
        Boston: Little, Brown, 1968. 202 pp.
Art analyzes the establishment and success of civilian control of military
leadership in a series of decisions to purchase the ill-fated TFX fighter
plane. The time span of the case is 1959-62, most of which is the early
era of Robert McNamara's tenure as Secretary of Defense. The book
describes the TFX episode and the application of various management techniques to procure military weapons. It is also a case study of civilian
control of the military.

PS 301. BALL, HOWARD, DALE KRANE, and THOMAS P. LAUTH. Compromised Com-
        pliance: Implementation of the 1965 Voting Rights Act. Westport,
        Conn.: Greenwood Press, 1982. 301 pp.
The principal focus of this book is the section of the Voting Rights Act
(VRA) which froze all voting patterns in the covered jurisdictions as
of November 1964, in order to prevent them from passing new legislation
that could abridge or dilute the voting strength of blacks. The authors
also look at the way in which the government tried to enforce the Act
through its implementation, examining the evolution of the bureaucratic
structures that tried to administrate the Act, as well as the impact of
court decisions on the implementation of the Act. They conclude that
there exist substantial inconsistencies and discrepancies between the
intent of the legislation and its enforcement by the Justice Department.
Despite the guarded achievements of the VRA, its policy implementation
was frustrated by the fact that its enforcement had to be pursued not
through the threat of withholding Federal funds, but through bargaining
between the Justice Department and local officials that led to compromises
and trade-offs.

PS 302. BARTLETT, ROBERT. The Reserve Mining Controversy: Science, Tech-
        nology and Environmental Quality. Bloomington, Ind.: Indiana
        University Press, 1980. 293 pp.
Bartlett examines the effect of public opinion on the environmental policy
processes surrounding the Reserve Mining Company's pollution of Lake Superior. His examination centers on the question of whether the advancement
of industrial science and technology necessarily conflicts with ecological
concerns. Bartlett shows that the policy process is torn between industrial technological advances and environmental protection, and finds it
difficult to reconcile the two. The case illustrates how policy-makers
succumb to public pressure for industrial restrictions despite the absence
of sufficient scientific evidence to prove that the Reserve Mining Company's pollution was endangering the public. Bartlett believes that decisions involving environmental policy are determined by political and subjective motives rather than by scientific proof.

PS 303. BAUER, RAYMOND A., ITHIEL de SOLA POOL, and LEWIS A. DEXTER.
        American Business and Public Policy: The Politics of Foreign
        Trade. Chicago: Atherton, 1972. 499 pp.
This is a study of interest group involvement in the decision to initiate
the "Kennedy round" of negotiations for a mutual lowering of tariffs
between the European Common Market and the U.S. in the early 1960s. The
major conclusion of the study is that interest group involvement was not
nearly so intense nor so effective as had previously been thought. Expressions of opinion by individual businessmen were few and were dominated
by people from large firms. Formal lobbying groups in Washington did

little but talk to those who were already convinced. In the Congress, general procedure, members' views of their roles, the activities of the President, and the pressure of time had more to do with the final outcome than the pressure of interest groups.

PS 304. BERGER, PETER and RICHARD NEUHAU. To Empower People: The Role of Mediating Structures in Public Policy. Washington, D.C.: American Enterprise Institute, 1977. 45 pp.
The authors argue that alternative mechanisms are capable of replacing the services often demanded of the welfare state. They call these mechanisms mediating structures. The structures stand between the individual in his private life and the large institutions of public life. Those dealt with specifically in this book are the family, the church, the neighborhood, and voluntary associations. These mediating structures can provide many necessary services often demanded from government, and may also satisfy the general anti-government attitude that exists among most Americans. Without an institutionally reliable process of mediation, the political order becomes detached from the values and realities of individual life. Public policy should protect and foster mediating structures; and public policy should use mediating structures for the realization of social purposes. The authors believe this program will return power to the community.

PS 305. BERGERSON, FREDERICK. The Army Gets an Air Force: Tactics of Insurgent Bureaucratic Politics. Baltimore, Md.: Johns Hopkins University Press, 1980. 216 pp.
Bergerson examines the importance that bureaucratic politics played in the revival of the Army Air Force. The case is used to demonstrate how bureaucratic insurgency is its own form of social movement within a large scale organization. The concept of bureaucratic insurgency here refers to some form of open protest by the bureaucrat against organizational policy, which remains a loyal form of protest oriented toward reform for the good of the organization. The bureaucratic insurgency in this story involves a loose fraternity of middle-ranking officers and technicians who were motivated by a common conviction that the Army placed too low a priority on close air support for land operations. Bergerson shows how bureaucratic insurgents can make use of the system to hasten what is usually perceived as a stolid, ponderous, and plodding institution.

PS 306. BREYER, STEPHEN. Regulation and Its Reform. Cambridge, Mass.: Harvard University Press, 1982. 472 pp.
Breyer provides a summary of how regulation works, when it needs to be changed, and how it can be changed. His book is directed toward the regulator or legislator who must make policy judgments regarding the effects of regulation. Breyer pragmatically argues for policy decisions based primarily on factual information. He emphasizes suggestions for helping bureaucratic and organizational structures to facilitate the processing of regulatory policy.

PS 307. BROWN, PETER G., CONRAD JOHNSON, and PAUL VERNIER. Income Support: Conceptual and Policy Issues. Totowa, N.J.: Rowman & Littlefield, 1981. 378 pp.
This book is a collection of essays which explore the theoretical, economic, social, and moral issues underlying recent welfare reform efforts. It provides suggestions for future policy decisions regarding welfare reform. The philosophical essays in the first section analyze the moral authority and proper goals of income support policy. The second section looks at how normative concerns are actually applied to policy objectives. The final section tries to provide future alternatives for the welfare reform debate by looking at recent welfare reform and policy changes.

PS 308. CAMPBELL, BALLARD. Representative Democracy: Public Policy and
Midwestern Legislatures in the Late Nineteenth Century. Cambridge,
Mass.: Harvard University Press, 1980. 260 pp.
This book examines the daily businesses of three state legislatures for
the period 1886-95. Campbell discovers what effects the socio-economic
change and the political ferment of that time had on political party alignments and major areas of public policy. Individual legislators, he shows,
were primarily elected on the basis of ethnic and religious considerations.
The constituencies of the parties were divided along such lines, and no
other consideration, except for occasional party loyalties, played a major
role in explaining voting patterns. Ethnic and religious concerns, furthermore, made moral issues the source of the strongest partisan divisions.
Social issues proved more divisive than economic issues. Campbell demonstrates how the historical study of state legislatures provides an important mirror for the understanding of political development.

PS 309. CARNOY, MARTIN, DEREK SHEARER, and RUSSELL RUMBERGER. A New Social
Contract: The Economy and the Government After Reagan. New
York: Harper & Row, 1983. 243 pp.
The authors undertake a critical study of Reaganomics and present alternatives regarding the role the U.S. government should play in the economy
and society. They outline a new liberal economic policy which would redistribute resources to create more jobs, reduce unemployment levels, and
meet public needs without increasing the tax burden. The authors propose
the creation of public corporations and labor-intensive service industries
to compete with private enterprise. Public needs would dictate investment
policy. The authors also stress regional and local planning. The book
chronicles the failure of conservative economic policies, as exemplified
by the Reagan administration, in light of the crisis of liberal economics
in the 1960s and 1970s. It then goes on to analyze the role the government
has played as an employer, provider of human services, and contractor
of military hardware.

PS 310. COLLINS, ROBERT M. The Business Response to Keynes, 1929-1964.
New York: Columbia University Press, 1981. 293 pp.
Collins traces the developing response of certain major segments of the
business community to the Federal government's adoption of a Keynesian
fiscal policy in 1938, from initial rejection to ultimate acceptance.
The Chamber of Commerce, the National Association of Manufacturers, and
the Committee for Economic Development are the business groups primarily
under study. Collins discovers that each group responded differently
to the government's new economic policy. Historically, the book is divided
into three periods: the New Deal, W.W. II, and the postwar years. Special
attention is paid to a specific piece of Keynesian economic legislation
for each period: the Industrial Recovery Act of 1933, the Employment
Act of 1946, and the Kennedy-Johnson tax cut of 1964.

PS 311. CRENSON, MATTHEW A. The Un-Politics of Air Pollution. Baltimore,
Md.: Johns Hopkins University Press, 1971. 227 pp.
Crenson's study is an exploration of Peter Bachrach and Morton Baratz's
concept of "non-decision-making" (see PS 183). Using survey data from
urban political leaders to judge the political prominence of the air pollution issue, Crenson seeks to explain why some cities have failed to
cope with dirty air. After taking into account the actual level of local
air pollution, he looks for statistical relationships between neglect
of the air pollution issue and political characteristics of local leaders
and institutions. In addition to the aggregate statistical analysis,
he conducts case studies in Gary, Indiana, and East Chicago, two heavily
polluted industrial cities.

PS 312. DAVID, PAUL T. and ROSS POLLOCK. Executives for Government:
Issues of Federal Personnel Administration. Washington, D.C.:
Brookings Institution, 1957. 186 pp.
This study examines the problems the Federal government has in obtaining,
developing, and holding a sufficient supply of qualified executives.
It begins with the problem of the size of government. Government is so
big that it appears impossible to manage, and frightens off many potential
executives. The government executive also has special burdens and responsibilities, such as maintaining peace, promoting growth, and advancing
general welfare. Other deterrents include the complexities that result
from trying to reconcile political and administrative factors in staffing
the upper echelons of the executive branch. Furthermore, the authors
contend, there is inadequate compensation, limited prestige, and special
harassments arising out of executive-legislative relations. David and
Pollock offer suggestions for acquiring competent executives and establishing a more effective career service system.

PS 313. DOWNS, ANTHONY. Inside Bureaucracy. Boston: Little, Brown,
1967. 292 pp.
Downs seeks to develop a theory of bureaucratic decision-making and bureau
behavior from three premises: bureaucracies are rational; they have complex goals; and their environment influences their internal processes.
From these, Downs elaborates a definition of "bureau," and develops theories regarding how one functions. He treats such subjects as internal
structure, communication and control in bureaus, the aging and rigidifi-
cation of bureaus, decision processes, bureaucratic ideologies, and relationships among bureaus, while developing a typology of officials and
advancing a justification for the existence of bureaus.

PS 314. DUNN, WILLIAM M., ed. Values, Ethics, and the Practice of Policy
Analysis. Lexington, Mass.: Heath, 1983. 241 pp.
This book argues that the practice of policy analysis involves much more
than simply the production of information about the causes and consequences
of public policies. Policy analysis is also normative; it produces information about the value of public policy. The essays in this volume investigate the impact of values and ethics on the practice of academic and
government policy analysis. Thus they run counter to the present trend
wherein methods that resist ethical reasoning are used in the analysis
of public policy. The contributors to this book are critical of the belief
that scientific policy analysis can be value neutral, ethically detached,
and confined to predicting the consequence of alternative policy actions.
They argue that the traditional separation between fact and value sought
by public policy analysis is neither possible nor desirable. Personal
and professional social ethics and values always come into play in the
determination of public policy.

PS 315. DYE, THOMAS R. Who's Running America? The Reagan Years. Englewood Cliffs, N.J.: Prentice-Hall, 1983. 285 pp.
Assessing national leadership and elite government during the Reagan
administration, Dye defines the terms, concepts, and methods of identifying
the nation's institutional elite. He provides a description of the centers
of power in the U.S., such as industry, the government, and the news media.
He also describes the type of persons who occupy top institutional leadership positions in the various power sectors of society, identifying and
providing biographical sketches of some of the more powerful individuals.
Dye then undertakes a systematic investigation of interlocking and specialization among elites, overlapping elite membership, recruitment paths,
socioeconomic backgrounds, previous experience, racial and sexual bias,
competition and consensus, and patterns of interaction in policy-making.

PS 316. DYE, THOMAS R. and VIRGINIA GRAY. The Determinants of Public
         Policy. Lexington, Mass.: Lexington Books, 1980. 227 pp.
The essays in this volume develop specific theories and models of policy
determination. They introduce a wide array of social, economic, cultural,
and political variables which are considered to be influential in determining policy. The authors deal with a variety of substantive policy
areas and treat different political systems from the local to the national
level. They also describe public policy, determine its causes, and assess
its consequences, in order to find out what governments do, why they do
it, and what difference it makes.

PS 317. EDWARDS, GEORGE C. and IRA SHARKANSKY. The Policy Predicament:
         Making and Implementing Public Policy. San Francisco: Freeman,
         1978. 336 pp.
Edwards and Sharkansky concentrate on the problems that hinder the smooth
translation of public needs into benefits through policy. They are skeptical of the influence of public opinion on policy-making and the capacity
of officials to make policy on the basis of a rational selection of the
best options. They also look at the economic and political constraints
on policy makers, describing decision-making under existing conditions.
The authors conclude that the complexities of the problems faced by policy
makers and the procedural complications faced by policy-making hinder
any simple and successful attack on most of the world's problems.

PS 318. ENGLER, ROBERT. The Politics of Oil: A Study of Private Power
         and Democratic Directions. Chicago: University of Chicago Press,
         1961. 565 pp.
Engler's book is a study of the power and behavior of the American oil
industry functioning as an interest group in the American political process.
Detail is provided on the industry's growth, its national, international,
economic, and political activities, and its internal structure. Engler
portrays the industry as a highly organized monopoly whose power, employed
for private interests, undermines the public interest. The oil industry
represents a private government with substantial independent control over
energy matters affecting the public. Accordingly, Engler calls into question the validity of American pluralist theory as a description and justification of interest group activity and roles in the political process.

PS 319. FEDER, JUDITH, JACK HADLEY, and JOHN HOLAHAN. Insuring the
         Nation's Health: Market Competition: Catastrophic and Compre-
         hensive Approaches. Washington, D.C.: Urban Institute, 1981.
         227 pp.
This book analyzes the health programs of Congressman James Martin, Senators Edward Kennedy and Henry Waxman, and President Jimmy Carter. The
various plans emphasize either comprehensive or catastrophic coverage
as a basis for a national health insurance. The book analyzes the impact
any of the plans would have on coverage, income distribution, cost control,
urban health services, and market competition. The authors then compare
the feasibility of Martin's plan, which aims at a national health insurance
policy by enhancing competition, with the Kennedy-Waxman and Carter plans,
which utilize regulatory approaches. They also look at the impact a
national health insurance policy would have on employment in the cities,
contending that any of the plans would be more beneficial to urban areas
than the present government insurance programs. The authors prefer the
Kennedy-Waxman proposal for its overall promise of large-scale policy
change, though they acknowledge that it is the least practically feasible.

PS 320. FEDER, JUDITH, JOHN HOLAHAN, and THEODORE MARMOR, eds. National Health Insurance: Conflicting Goals and Policy Choices. Washington, D.C.: Urban Institute, 1980. 721 pp.
The contributors to this volume look at the issue of national health insurance with regard to the administrative concerns of its implementation. Considering what can be accomplished under various managements and administrations given the existing corporate, governmental, and professional systems, they argue that the implementation of policy is the key to the success of any national health care system. The authors show how state and local government can be involved in the administration of a national health care system; they also examine several different national health care proposals as well as the kind of policy choices they will require under the present arrangements. The book concludes with its own proposals for broader access to health care.

PS 321. FISCHER, FRANK. Politics, Values, and Public Policy: The Problem of Methodology. Boulder, Colo.: Westview Press, 1980. 230 pp.
Fischer addresses the growing concerns about norms and values in policy assessment. He tries to develop a methodology for the political evaluation of public policy which is designed to move policy evaluation beyond its current emphasis on efficient achievement of goals by focusing on the acceptability of the goals themselves. Fischer raises problems associated with the fact-value distinction. He points to the methodological integrations of empirical and normative data as a major barrier to a relevant social science contributing to policy questions, and offers an alternative avenue for avoiding the epistemological impasse. He then demonstrates the effectiveness of his methodology by applying it to an urban decentralization argument.

PS 322. GILBERT, NEIL. Capitalism and the Welfare State: Dilemmas of Social Benevolence. New Haven, Conn.: Yale University Press, 1983. 196 pp.
Gilbert studies the American welfare state as it went from an era of public approval and expansion under the Great Society programs of the 1960s to a period of disfavor and retrenchment in the early 1980s. He begins with a series of analyses on the merging of economic and social markets--such as the influx of profitmaking organizations to stimulate competition among providers of social services--to illustrate the trend toward the commercialization of the social market. He then turns to an analysis of the expansion in scope and purpose of social services that occurred with the growth of the welfare state, and the impact this had on markets. This is followed by a study of the growing emphasis on the provision of aid through the voluntary sector. Gilbert concludes with suggestions for creating a workable balance between the welfare state and the market.

PS 323. GOODWIN, CRAUFURD D. Energy Policy in Perspective: Today's Problems, Yesterday's Solutions. Washington, D.C.: Brookings Institution, 1981. 728 pp.
Goodwin's book is a study of the largely abortive efforts to develop national energy policies in the U.S. since the end of W.W. II. Each chapter analyzes the energy policies of a Presidential administration, from Truman through Carter. The study shows that, for most of the time covered by this book, the U.S. did not have a national energy policy which coordinated the supply and use of the major energy sources, but only individual fuel policies. In part, this was due to the fact that there was no central office dealing specifically with energy until the 1970s. In addition, energy policy had become confused because of national security issues. Finally, Goodwin argues that some of the problems regarding energy stem from the fact that there is little competition in the energy business.

PS 324. GRAY, VIRGINIA and ELIHU BERGMAN, eds. Political Issues in United
         States Population Policy. Lexington, Mass.: Heath, 1974.
         212 pp.
Gray and Bergman have collected research on politics and population policy
in the U.S. Population policy is conceived of as government action that
influences population characteristics (the size, distribution, composition,
and rate of growth of population). The volume includes several empirical
studies of the impact of population on public policies. Another section
considers the political implications of population policies, particularly
for relatively disempowered groups such as women and blacks, as well as
the ethical implications of various policies. The methodological articles
include an application of cohort analysis and a critical analysis of science as a social movement.

PS 325. GREENBERG, EDWARD S. Serving the Few: Corporate Capitalism and
         the Bias of Government Policy. New York: Wiley, 1974. 275 pp.
Greenberg explains the rise and ongoing operation of the modern welfare
state in the U.S. He demonstrates that modern government is not a set
of neutral institutions responsive to the public will. Instead, it is
the instrument by which corporate Capitalism attempts to fashion for itself
a stable environment conducive to steady expansion and health profitability.
Greenberg begins with a look at the modern state and the dominance of
corporate Capitalism within it. This is followed by an assessment of
the distribution of wealth, income, and legal justice. He then discusses
government spending and how it benefits specific classes. The study concludes with a look at the function of the welfare state.

PS 326. HADWIGER, DON. The Policies of Agricultural Research. Lincoln:
         University of Nebraska Press, 1982. 230 pp.
Hadwiger examines the political decisions behind the agricultural research
institutions that have caused a revolution in agricultural technology
and food production. This revolution in farm production, which was responsible for raising the American standard of living, brought with it human
and environmental costs. American agricultural research is now having
its traditional goals challenged. The goals of food abundance and leisure
for the farmer are being questioned. Hadwiger criticizes American agricultural research and its supporters for ignoring such consequences of agricultural technology policy as environmental contamination, health risks to
consumers, and the wasting of natural resources.

PS 327. HAEFELE, EDWIN T. Representative Government and Environmental
         Management. Baltimore, Md.: Johns Hopkins University Press,
         1973. 188 pp.
Haefele argues that most policy decisions are mandated by executive decision rather than legislative action. In order to return to the true spirit
of representative government he feels we must reassess legislative and
senatorial representation among the states, redress the balance between
executive and legislative power in government, alter the two-party system,
and eradicate seniority and committee rule in legislatures, among other
changes in legislative policies. Most of his essays concern legislative
management of "common-property resources" such as air and water, which,
being the property of no one in particular, have received the least attention. Haefele proposes ways of achieving greater citizen participation
in environmental quality management, and advocates a return to technical
efficiency as the primary goal of resource policy development.

PS 328. HALPERIN, MORTON, et al. The Lawless State: The Crime of U.S. Intelligence Agencies. Baltimore, Md.: Penguin Books, 1976. 328 pp.
This volume documents the efforts of the Central Intelligence Agency, Federal Bureau of Investigation, and the Internal Revenue Service to intrude into the private lives of U.S. citizens--often using illegal tactics and motivated by political ends. The dubious activities of these agencies range from character assassination at home to plotting political murders abroad, from illegal electronic eavesdropping to burglary. The authors conclude by suggesting a number of reforms which range from limiting the powers of intelligence agencies to enforcing criminal statutes.

PS 329. HANRAHAN, JOHN. Government by Contract. New York: Norton, 1983. 354 pp.
Hanrahan argues that Federal contractors constitute a bureaucracy that parallels the official civil service bureaucracy. The activites of Federal contractors, however, are largely hidden from public view. The increase in big government in recent decades has not been due to the expansion of the civil service bureaucracy, but to the ascendancy of the contractors' bureaucracy. Hanrahan demonstrates that while discussion and criticism of big government focuses on social programs, military spending, or the civil service bureaucracy, little attention has been devoted to the largely hidden contractors' bureaucracy which received one-fourth of the annual Federal budget each year. Much of the study concentrates on the Defense and Energy departments.

PS 330. HASKELL, ELIZABETH. The Politics of Clean Air: EPA Standards for Coal-Burning Power Plants. New York: Praeger, 1982. 206 pp.
Haskell provides a case study of the Environmental Protection Agency's (EPA) successful attempt in the late 1970s to set a pollution control standard for future coal-fixed power plants to be built by the electric utility industry. She documents the fight between the EPA, Congress, the White House, and utility interests to establish a national environmental air pollution policy for the emission of sulfur dioxide. She also chronicles the way in which the agency tried to establish a policy which would consider all the interests involved and balance economic interests with air quality needs and energy constraints. Recommendations for the improvement of environmental decision-making are offered by the author.

PS 331. HAVEMAN, ROBERT H., ed. A Decade of Federal Antipoverty Programs. New York: Academic Press, 1977. 381 pp.
Haveman presents seven papers evaluating the success of the "war on poverty" (the expansion of social services from 1964 to 1974). Several different areas of policy are evaluated--education, health, income maintenance, community action, legal services, and antidiscrimination. The authors conclude that the war on poverty improved access to medical care, legal services, and political participation. The education and training programs, on the other hand, failed to increase incomes. The success of antidiscrimination policy and income maintenance progams was mixed.

PS 332. HOOLE, FRANCIS W., ROBERT L. FRIEDHEIM, and TIMOTHY M. HENNESSEY, eds. Making Ocean Policy: The Politics of Government Organization Management. Boulder, Colo.: Westview Press, 1981. 291 pp.
Most of the essays in this volume argue that social sciences can provide important insights into the problems of U.S. ocean policy. The volume is divided into four major parts: "History," "Advocacy," "Analysis," and "Studying Ocean Policy." The essays propose various policies, such as recommending that the governance of Federal ocean policy not be centralized. Federal ocean authority should be distributed among the existing

agencies and left to state and local coastal zone management. Overall, the essays deal with the ways in which the social sciences can improve management and administrative techniques for ocean policy decision-making.

PS 333. HOROWITZ, IRVING L. and JAMES E. KATZ. Social Science and Public Policy in the United States. New York: Praeger, 1975. 187 pp.
The authors examine social science and public policy under a neo-capitalist, post-industrial system. They approach the U.S. as a social system largely directed by a bureaucratic sector responsive but not always responsible to other social classes. The mass society does not have a level of political power beyond the voting process. The authors try to show how social science links up with policy efforts to satisfy the bureaucratic needs of managing a post-industrial economy and the competing claims of entrenched social classes. They argue that the role of social science should involve advocacy as well as analysis--that is, giving voice or representation to the mass general interest over special interests.

PS 334. HOUSE, PETER. The Quest for Completeness: Comprehensive Analysis in Environmental Management and Planning. Lexington, Mass.: Heath, 1976. 245 pp.
The purpose of House's book is to present the arguments concerning the uses and limitations of comprehensive analysis in answering environmental questions. House provides case studies and draws on his experiences with the Environmental Protection Agency to examine strategies of comprehensive analysis. He concludes that the slow response of government agencies to environmental problems will only change if there is a major environmental crisis in the future.

PS 335. HOUSE, PETER. The Urban Environment System: Modeling for Research, Policy-Making and Education. Beverly Hills, Calif.: Sage, 1973. 316 pp.
House discusses the building of an environmental model for education, training, research, and policy-making. The first part of the book divides the concept of such a model into five categories: data base, executive routing, input, operating programs, and output. The author presents a paradigm for describing any model which is designed for computerization. He then takes the general theoretical structure of his model and subjects it to the rigor of a working model. The General Environmental Model developed is shown to be a computer-assisted, decision-making model that can be used to represent economic, social and governmental decision-making entities within regional, metropolitan, or urban areas.

PS 336. HUMMEL, RALPH P. The Bureaucratic Experience. 1977; Rev. ed. New York: St. Martin's Press, 1982. 282 pp.
Hummel treats bureaucracy as an organized social life--a new environment with its own work life, society, culture, psychology, language, and politics. Also, it is a new way of exercising power. Hummel analyzes this new form of social organization and elucidates its psychological processes. The revised edition contains writings by leading scholars, analyzing organizational problems of advanced modern societies. Hummel provides a final chapter offering alternative approaches to diagnosing and curing unproductive and stressful aspects of modern organization.

PS 337. JONES, CHARLES O. Clean Air: The Policies and Politics of Pollution Control. Pittsburgh, Pa.: University of Pittsburgh Press, 1975. 373 pp.
In this book, Jones develops a "policy process model"--a type of research involving the following sequence of action: problem identification, policy formation, legitimization, implementation, and evaluation. Jones examines this sequence with regard to U.S. air pollution policy, as administered by local, state, and national agencies. He concludes that without public

support, the regulators come to depend on the organizations being regulated. Jones examines the state of Pennsylvania and Allegheny County as case studies of pollution control policies.

PS 338. KAMIENIECKI, SHELDON. Public Representation in Environmental Policy-Making: The Case of Water Quality Management. Boulder, Colo.: Westview Press, 1980. 131 pp.
Kamieniecki's environmental study conducted among citizens of the Niagara Falls Frontier examines citizens' beliefs and the leaders' beliefs (as well as their perceptions of public beliefs) about water quality issues. The author's concern is the need for greater citizen participation in the development and implementation of Federal water pollution legislation. Kamieniecki discovers that there is misunderstanding in the leaders' perceptions of public opinion, despite the fact that the actual beliefs of citizens and leaders are similar on many issues. The discrepancy highlights the lack of communication between the citizenry and leaders. The author concludes by discussing mechanisms through which officials can get more accurate information on public opinion.

PS 339. KAUFMAN, HERBERT. The Forest Ranger: A Study in Administrative Behavior. Baltimore, Md.: Johns Hopkins University Press, 1960. 259 pp.
Kaufman focuses on the problem of controlling a large, decentralized bureaucracy. Relying upon documents, interviews, and especially upon intensive field investigation in five Forest Service districts across the country, Kaufman attributes the Forest Service's success to its effective use of three management techniques. First, the Service attempts to "preform" as many decisions as possible by writing detailed guidelines for field officers (rangers) to follow in dealing with varied situations. Second, rangers are regulated by requirements for exhaustive reporting of activities, coupled with systematic field inspections and frequent transfers. Third, the Service carefully selects and indoctrinates its recruits.

PS 340. KINNARD, DOUGLAS. The Secretary of Defense. Lexington: University Press of Kentucky, 1980. 252 pp.
Kinnard examines the careers of seven men who have served as Secretary of Defense since the Truman Adminsitration, giving the most attention to relations between the Secretary, the President, and Congress. He also looks at the evolution of the Secretary's staff in order to delineate the constellation of bureaucratic power of which the Secretary has often attempted to be (though he seldom has been) the center. The volume concludes with an essay which draws together these various themes and attempts to arrive at a number of theories concerning the role of the Secretary in the formulation of domesticated foreign policy.

PS 341. KLOMAN, ERASMUS H., ed. Cases in Accountability: The Work of the GAO. Boulder, Colo.: Westview Press, 1979. 254 pp.
Kloman presents twenty-eight case studies--most prepared by staff members of the General Accounting Office (GAO)--exemplifying the various types of work the office performs. Sub-sections address how the GAO evaluates whether legislative desires and objectives are achieved; whether resources are managed effectively; and whether financial matters are conducted properly and legally, and fairly represented in reports. There are also studies addressing how the GAO handles special cases, mostly coming from Congressional constituent inquiries, and various other minor problems. The book is intended to supplement Frederick Mosher's 1979 study of the GAO (see PS 361).

PS 342. KOLKO, GABRIEL. Wealth and Power in America: An Analysis of
Social Class and Income Distribution. New York: Praeger, 1962.
178 pp.
Kolko examines economic inequality in America and concludes that inequality
in the 1960s was about the same as inequality at the turn of the century,
whether this be measured in income, wealth, or economic power. Furthermore,
these inequalities have been unaffected by such government policies as
aid for unemployment and progressive taxation of incomes.

PS 343. KRISLOV, SAMUEL. Representative Bureaucracy. Englewood Cliffs,
N.J.: Prentice-Hall, 1974. 149 pp.
Noting the pervasiveness and importance of bureaucracy in modern states,
Krislov urges the development of an adequate political theory of administration. Thus, he focuses upon the question of bureaucratic "representativeness," arguing that bureaucracies, requiring specialized skills
and talents, can never be accurately representative of the population.
However, Krislov asserts that bureaucracies can, and often do, represent
the population in the sense of incorporated elements of the major social
groupings, and thus social divisions and tensions, in a country. He concludes that bureaucracies can be effective in dealing with such social
tension to the degree that they mirror it.

PS 344. KRISLOV, SAMUEL and DAVID H. ROSENBLOOM. Representative Bureaucracy and the American Political System. New York: Praeger,
1981. 209 pp.
In response to the anti-bureaucratic mood of the 1970s, Krislov and
Rosenbloom try theoretically to combine the existence of independent bureaucratic authority with representative Republican government. Arguing that
attempts to fight the bureaucracy are best served by augmenting the effort
to maximize the political representativeness of public bureaucracy, they
move from a consideration of the relationship between bureaucratic organization and democratic government to an assessment of public bureaucracy's
representative potential in terms of personnel, structure, responsiveness
to political authorities, and interaction with the public. The authors
conclude that, although there are inherent limitations on representative
bureaucracy, there is also great potential that must be fulfilled if public
bureaucracy and American democracy are to be integrated more successfully.

PS 345. LARSON, GARY O. The Reluctant Patron: The United States Government and the Arts, 1943-1965. Philadelphia: University of Pennsylvania Press, 1983. 314 pp.
Larson studies the attempt to establish a program of Federal arts patronage
in the years between the Works Project Administration and the National
Endowment for the Arts. He begins with a look at the failure to establish
Federal arts patronage through the WPA, then turns to the subsequent social
and cultural concerns which influenced Federal arts patronage: the post-
war conservatism and the origins of the cold war, the anti-Communist fears
of the 1950s, and the mixed national pride and self-consciousness of the
1960s. Larson shows how, during this period, legislative schemes interacted with private plans both for and against a new Federal arts community
in America. Finally, he demonstrates how the increasing desire for cultural legislation led to the formation of the National Endowment for the
Arts in 1965.

PS 346. LEVI, MARGARET. Bureaucratic Insurgency: The Case of Police
Unions. Lexington, Mass.: Heath, 1977. 165 pp.
Levi studies the development of labor unions among public workers by examining the cases of police unions in three American cities--New York, Detroit,
and Atlanta. In New York, she notes the rise of the Patrolman's Benevolent
Association in the face of strong opposition; and in the case of Detroit,
she discovers successful rank-and-file militancy. In Atlanta, by contrast,

the story is one of the difficult, early stages of unionizing. Levi notes
that successful unionization has tended to escalate union demands. She
raises questions concerning the considerable power to disrupt both economy
and society implicit in the right of public employees to strike.

PS 347. LEVINE, CHARLES H. and IRENE RUBIN, eds. Fiscal Stress and Public
Policy. Beverly Hills, Calif.: Sage, 1980. 314 pp.
These essays explore the links between policy, economics, and management,
and provide an examination of the effects of austerity on the public sector.
The first group of essays defines and examines the sources and extent
of fiscal stress at the societal level. The volume then turns to an
examination of the immediate impact of fiscal stress on budgetary and financial management. The essays which follow discuss emerging policy choices
and limits on the range of governmental responses to fiscal stress.

PS 348. LIPSET, SEYMOUR M. and WILLIAM SCHNEIDER. The Confidence Gap:
Business, Labor, and Government in the Public Mind. New York:
Free Press, 1983. 434 pp.
The authors examine the changing public perceptions of American institutions and leaders in light of the crisis of authority which occurred in
the 1960s. They trace the trends in public confidence over the past fifty
years by examining public opinion. Specifically, Lipset and Schneider
try to ascertain what Americans like or dislike about government, business,
labor, and the causes and consequences of such opinions. They argue that
the public has lost faith in the leadership of major U.S. institutions,
primarily as a result of the racial and social conflict of the 1960s,
the experiences of Watergate and the Vietnam War, and the economic troubles
of the 1970s. But the distrust is aimed mostly at those who run the institutions. It is a crisis of confidence in leadership. There remains an
underlying faith among the public in the institutions themselves.

PS 349. LOWI, THEODORE and ALAN STONE, eds. Nationalizing Government.
Beverly Hills, Calif.: Sage, 1978. 454 pp.
The contributors look at the way government handles problems that are
considered to require governmental rather than individual or private action.
They document the disenfranchisement of state and local agencies regarding
attempts at national direction--attempts which only occasionally succeed.
A second theme is bureaucratization, the increasing delegation of problem-
solving activities to administrative agencies because such agencies
generally have greater expertise, time, and flexibility to cope with the
problems. The contributors also consider the need for legal and political
restraints on the government and the relationship between private ownership
and government involvement in the economy.

PS 350. LYNN, LAURENCE E. The State and Human Services: Organizational
Change in a Political Context. Cambridge, Mass.: MIT Press,
1980. 217 pp.
Lynn presents an analysis of public policy and bureaucratic administration
in human service programs and agencies in Arizona, Florida, Georgia, Minnesota, Pennsylvania, and Washington. He examines the problems that bureaucratic and political institutions create whenever public policy is directed
at institutional reorganization. His case studies draw the conclusion
that organizational change is successful when it comes from top state
officials, but that such officials have a greater desire for efficiency
and economy than for providing effective human services.

PS 351. MARCUS, ALFRED. Promise and Performance: Choosing and Implementing an Environmental Policy. Westport, Conn.: Greenwood Press, 1980. 204 pp.

This book analyzes the problems of the EPA through case studies of policy implementation. Marcus argues that the administrative difficulties encountered by the EPA since its inception result from its being pulled in many directions by the different constituencies to which it must answer (the White House, Congress, and environmentalists). Further confusion was created when its research, policies, and programs operated at cross purposes from one another.

PS 352. MARMOR, THEODORE R. The Politics of Medicare. Chicago: Aldine, 1973. 150 pp.

Marmor provides a study of the passage of Medicare (free medical care for the aged). He relates how Medicare was placed on the policy agenda and the type of response it drew from the public and from interest groups. The Medicare proposal was more successful than previous efforts at formulating the problem because governmental elites decided to confine their efforts to partial hospitalization coverage for the aged, rather than full coverage for the general population. Marmor describes the enactment of Medicare in great detail. In the final chapter he turns his attention to fitting this case study into more general theoretical frameworks.

PS 353. MELMAN, SEYMOUR. From Military to Civilian Economy: Issues and Options. Los Angeles, Calif.: Center for the Study of Armament and Disarmament, 1981. 50 pp.

Melman argues that the military economy of the U.S. is not a source of income and jobs, but the cause of inflation and unemployment. The U.S., he claims, is primarily based on a war economy: military production is a continuing and important activity that utilizes a major portion of the nation's productive resources. Melman considers how a war economy generates unemployment because of the non-competitive nature of the industry, and because production is transferred to cheaper, foreign markets. The war economy also produces inflation through huge governmental military expenditures. Melman suggests that the U.S. convert from a military to a civilian economy, and considers how civilian industries may be reconstructed.

PS 354. MELMAN, SEYMOUR. Pentagon Capitalism: The Political Economy of War. New York: McGraw-Hill, 1970. 290 pp.

Melman argues that an industrial management has been installed in the Federal government under the Secretary of Defense to control the nation's largest network of industrial enterprises. By transforming itself into a new state management, the government has combined and concentrated within itself economic, political, and military decision-making. The new institution of state management control has been undertaken for the declared purposes of adding to military power and economic efficiency and reinforcing civilian, rather than professional, military rule. The state management has replaced the military-industrial complex, and has become the largest industrial administrative office in the U.S. and the most powerful decision-making unit of government.

PS 355. MELMAN, SEYMOUR. Profits Without Production. New York: Knopf, 1983. 344 pp.

Melman traces the fundamental sickness of American industry to the pursuit of huge profits despite the collapse of productivity. He is concerned with showing that the military economy is an integral part of and a major contributor to the transformations in American management, technology, and productivity. The author identifies the main features of managerialism and how they have been changing. He then discusses the impact of managerial development and technological change, and the roles played by private and state managers. Melman concludes that if the present developments in management, technology, and productivity continue, the deterioration in production competence will become irreversible.

PS 356. MELMAN, SEYMOUR, ed. The War Economy of the United States. New York: St. Martin's Press, 1971. 247 pp.
This volume is organized in sections that portray the characteristics of the military-industrial firm, the nature of its impact on the economy as a whole, and the problem of conversion from military to civilian economy. The essays demonstrate how the military-industrial firm and the effects of its operation have changed the internal economics of the firm and have altered key features of industrial Capitalism as a whole. The autonomy of private firms used to exist in the power of their own management. In the military-industrial firm, the traditional entrepreneurial autonomy has been supplanted by the Department of Defense, which behaves like a monopolistic buyer—intervening in the internal affairs of the supplying firm to suit the convenience of the monopoly buyer.

PS 357. MESSER, ROBERT. The End of an Alliance: James Byrnes, Roosevelt, Truman and the Origins of the Cold War. Chapel Hill: University of North Carolina Press, 1982. 292 pp.
Messer examines the career of James Byrnes as Secretary of State in the context of his relationship with Presidents Roosevelt and Truman. Messer begins with a short biographical essay on Byrnes, and then discusses Byrnes's quest for the Vice-Presidency under Roosevelt. The main focus of the work is Byrnes's performance both as diplomat abroad and as Administration spokesperson in the Congress. The conferences at Yalta, Potsdam, and Moscow are all analyzed in this light, as is Byrnes's work on the Interim Committee. Messer concludes with Byrnes's fall after the Moscow Conference, and his subsequent attacks on the Truman Administration.

PS 358. MEYER, MARSHALL W. Change in Public Bureaucracies. New York: Cambridge University Press, 1979. 251 pp.
Meyer argues that the behavior and structure of public bureaus are largely shaped by environmental forces. Social and political forces have more influence on bureaucratic change than internal processes. Bureaucracies are not rigid, closed systems, but are responsive to external pressures, including the effect leadership and territorial battles have on bureaucratic change. Meyer discovers that despite these forces, bureaucracies do not change fast enough. They reach a point where the social and political forces they serve become extremely dissatisfied with them and push for reorganization.

PS 359. MILLER, S. M. and DONALD TOMASKOVIC-DEVERY. Recapitalizing America. Boston: Routledge & Kegan Paul, 1983. 215 pp.
The authors try to discredit the belief that increasing the power and profitability of private capital will solve the cyclical and structural problems of the U.S. economy in the 1980s. Reactionary recapitalization is the term used to describe the organized campaign by business leaders to convince citizens and politicians that business needed relief from regulation, access to capital funds, and lower taxes. The authors view Reaganism as one political variant of reactionary recapitalization. Another industrial policy which they oppose is the reduction of political and economic questions to technical questions. The pursuit of technological development masks the political question of who bears the burdens of economic and social policy changes. Miller and Tomaskovic-Devery conclude by trying to connect the criticism of current economic programs with the realistic politics of coalitions and movements.

PS 360. MORGAN, RICHARD E. Domestic Intelligence: Monitoring Dissent in America. Austin: University of Texas Press, 1980. 194 pp.
Morgan traces the way in which governmental agencies become involved with domestic intelligence gathering. He reviews the record of intelligence abuses revealed in the mid-1970s and examines the intelligence reforms adopted thus far in order to suggest what additional reforms are necessary. He also looks at the role of the FBI in domestic intelligence, covert techniques, and the constitutional questions surrounding domestic intelligence. Morgan argues that limited domestic intelligence operations are justifiable only when undertaken on the basis of some reasoned expectation that criminal activity is contemplated by a particular group or individual.

PS 361. MOSHER, FREDERICK C. The GAO: The Quest for Accountability in American Government. Boulder, Colo.: Westview Press, 1979. 387 pp.
Mosher describes the evolution of the General Accounting Office (GAO), and provides an intensive analysis of its roles in American government and society today. He describes the independent authority which the GAO has acquired, and its responsibility with regard to holding other branches of government accountable. The GAO's relations with Congress are examined in this light. Mosher also considers its relations with the executive branch and other political institutions. He discusses the internal practices, problems, and trends in the organization, and concludes with a survey of the issues surrounding the role of the GAO.

PS 362. MOYNIHAN, DANIEL P. Maximum Feasible Misunderstanding: Community Action in the War on Poverty. New York: Free Press, 1969. 218 pp.
Moynihan provides an account of the major effort in the early-1960s to develop a national policy that would end hard-core poverty in the U.S. His analysis is particularly concerned with the role of community action organizations in the war on poverty, especially the requirement that such organizations involve "maximum feasible participation" (of the residents of the areas). Moynihan traces the intellectual and political history of the anti-poverty program, particularly the radical requirement that their development and implementation at the local level include residents and others directly affected by the programs, even though this would diminish their control by city officials.

PS 363. MURPHY, THOMAS, DONALD E. NUECHTERLEIN, and RONALD J. STUPAK. Inside the Bureaucracy: The View from the Assistant Secretary's Desk. Boulder, Colo.: Westview Press, 1978. 221 pp.
The authors focus on real actors in the policy process by presenting the comments and opinions of those who have served in the position of assistant secretary. Assistant secretaries are seen as the key linchpin for effective government. They allow the President to gain control over the bureaucracy, mediating between the political and bureaucratic elements of government. Furthermore, they face the greatest pressure from interest groups and electoral demands. By focusing on the assistant secretary's position, the authors attempt to highlight the conflicts and problems within democratic processes.

PS 364. NAGEL, STUART S., ed. Environmental Politics. New York: Praeger, 1974. 376 pp.
Nagel combines a survey of the literature on environmental politics with an analysis of the issues which the literature addresses. The essays are organized by fields within the political science. The underlying theme of most of the essays is that the adoption of antipollution technology by industrial or commercial concerns is not likely to occur without governmental incentives. They emphasize the importance of the role of

governmental activity in minimizing pollution, regulating environmental
quality, and planning land-use effectively.

PS 365. NELSON, RICHARD R. and DOUGLAS YATES, eds. Innovation and Implementation in Public Organizations. Lexington, Mass.: Heath,
1978. 186 pp.
The essays collected here investigate in detail a particular institution
or program with a view toward uncovering the life history and evolution
of some deliberate attempt to innovate and implement. Drawing from their
own personal experiences in public organizations, the authors reveal how
organizational innovation may be the product of conflict over issues,
ambition, professionalism, or politics. The essays cover such fields
as health, education, the penal system, and urban resources.

PS 366. NETZER, DICK. The Subsidized Muse: Public Support for the Arts
in the United States. New York: Cambridge University Press,
1978. 289 pp.
Netzer argues that a greater commitment should exist on the part of the
government in its public policy support of the arts. The study explores
the various means and policy instruments the government may choose for
its support of the arts, drawing on the experiences of other nations to
evaluate which policies would be best for the U.S. Netzer evaluates the
effects of public support in light of public expectations; he also examines
the rationales for public subsidies that economic theory provides, concluding with his own policy suggestions.

PS 367. NEUSTADT, RICHARD and HARVEY FINEBERG. The Epidemic that Never
Was: Policy-Making and the Swine Flu Scare. 1978; Rev. ed.
New York: Vintage Books, 1982. 293 pp.
This study, originally published as The Swine Flu Affair, is a revised
edition of the official report prepared by the Department of Health, Education and Welfare on Federal decision-making in regard to the swine flu
program. It is a case study of public policy-making. The authors argue
that the administrative machinery for implementing the program was badly
handled. Problems resulted from the over-confidence of specialists in
theories spun from meager evidence; zeal by health professionals; insufficient questioning of scientific logic; and insensitivity to media relations. The authors also sketch the open issues in the swine flu's wake:
a national commission, liability legislation, and a new immunization initiative.

PS 368. O'BRIEN, DAVID M. and DONALD A. MARCHAND, eds. The Politics of
Technology Assessment: Institutions, Processes and Policy Disputes. Lexington, Mass.: Heath, 1982. 307 pp.
The essays in this volume explicate the role of different political institutions and policy-making processes while considering specific technology-
policy disputes. The book begins with an examination of the respective
roles of the private sector, the Congress, and the Executive branch, as
well as the Judiciary, in assessing and advancing technologies. It then
turns to several case studies, illuminating the complex and dynamic processes of assessing or resolving technology-policy disputes and illustrating the uses and potential contributions of technology assessment.

PS 369. O'CONNOR, JAMES. The Fiscal Crisis of the State. New York:
St. Martin's Press, 1973. 276 pp.
O'Connor sets forth a theory of government budget-making based on an investigation of the sociological foundations of government and state finances.
He elucidates the relationship between private and state sectors and
between private and state spending in the U.S. since W.W. II to interpret
the period's economic development and crisis tendencies. O'Connor argues
that the capitalistic state must try to fulfill two basic and often mutu-

ally contradictory functions—accumulation and legitimization. The state
must try to maintain—or create through fiscal budget—conditions in which
profitable capital accumulation is possible, while it must also try to
maintain or create conditions for social harmony.

PS 370. OLSON, LAURA KATZ. The Political Economy of Aging: The State,
         Private Power and Social Welfare. New York: Columbia University
         Press, 1982. 272 pp.
Olson uncovers some of the structural issues of the current crisis in
old age policies and programs. She explores the reasons why a large percentage of the elderly continue to suffer from inadequate retirement income,
housing, medical care, and other services, despite vast resources ostensibly committed to their welfare. Her analysis is set in the context
of changes in the political, social, and economic order in the U.S., and
the deleterious effects of these changes on the elderly population. Olson
argues that social disadvantages among the elderly population stem from
market and class relationships, along with racist and sexist institutions,
that negatively affect workers and their families throughout their life
cycles.

PS 371. OSTROM, VINCENT. The Intellectual Crisis in American Public
         Administration. University: University of Alabama Press, 1973.
         165 pp.
Ostrom observes that the study of public administration in America has
failed both to yield a theoretical understanding of the nature and significance of public bureaucracy and to give useful advice to policy-makers.
He suggests a new paradigm developed from a synthesis of ideas current
in political economy and the philosophy of Madison and Hamilton. Ostrom's
key point is that administration is best when it functions through decentralized, multiple structures, not when it is organized strictly hierarchically.

PS 372. PALMER, JOHN L. and ISABEL V. SAWHILL, eds. The Reagan Experiment:
         An Examination of Economic and Social Policies Under the Reagan
         Administration. Washington, D.C.: Urban Institute, 1982.
         530 pp.
This book examines Ronald Reagan's programs for economic recovery with
regard to his economic, budget, tax, and regulatory policies. It then
turns to a discussion of Reagan's attempt to redesign the relations between
the Federal government, and state and local government. This is followed
by essays which discuss Reagan's social policy shifts in employment training, health, social services, education, income security, housing, and
transportation. The volume concludes with a look at the regional impact
of Reagan's program and how it has affected the well-being of families.

PS 373. PALUMBO, DENNIS J., STEPHEN B. FAWCETT, and PAUL WRIGHT, eds.
         Evaluating and Optimizing Public Policy. Lexington, Mass.:
         Heath, 1981. 271 pp.
These essays argue that implementing and evaluating are strongly interrelated and that it is necessary to understand the linkages among them
in order to optimize public policy. This contradicts the traditional
approach which views evaluating and optimizing as two separate activities.
The writings show that public policies invariably change while they are
being implemented and that this has important consequences for both optimizing and evaluating public policy.

PS 374. PALUMBO, DENNIS J. and MARVIN A. HARDER, eds. Implementing Public
         Policy. Lexington, Mass.: Heath, 1981. 169 pp.
These essays examine how policies are invariably changed during implementation. The authors look at the changes that are likely to occur during
implementation, the changes that lead to these changes, and how implemen-

tation can be improved through evaluation. They show what happens when a policy and its form of implementation are communicated by the policy-makers; how a policy undergoes incremental change through implementation until it is substantially altered; the problem of relating goals to implementation; the importance of staff performance; the effects of new technology; and the absence of an adequate means for evaluating the success of an implemented policy proposal.

PS 375. PATTERSON, JAMES T. America's Struggle Against Poverty: 1900-1980. Cambridge, Mass.: Harvard University Press, 1981. 261 pp.
Patterson explores the changing attitudes, especially of reformers, toward poverty and welfare. Focusing specifically on the increasing government involvement in social welfare from 1930-80, he attempts to see what effect changing attitudes toward poverty had on public policy, and how the popular view of poverty, prescriptions of reformers, and governmental programs affected the poor. Patterson identifies demographic changes, the nationalization of politics, the growing power of pressure groups, and the bureaucratic expansion as forces affecting public policy toward the poor.

PS 376. PEIRCE, WILLIAM SPANGAR. Bureaucratic Failure and Public Expenditure. New York: Academic Press, 1981. 318 pp.
Peirce looks at the conditions under which a bureaucracy will fail to respond to political leaders and their policies. He begins with a look at the hierarchy of bureaucratic control, locating some of the reasons for bureaucratic failure in the political control of bureaucracy and in the internal management of bureaucracies. Peirce then turns to case studies based primarily on General Accounting Office audits, which compare legislated goals with bureaucratic performance. He utilizes his findings to analyze the standard economic theory of the role of government in a market society. Peirce demonstrates how structural features make it possible to predict success or failure at the moment when legislation is before Congress, and how individual participants pursue their own interests.

PS 377. PERTSCHUK, MICHAEL. Revolt Against Regulation: The Rise and Pause of the Consumer Movement. Berkeley: University of California Press, 1982. 165 pp.
Pertschuk draws from his experience as chairman of the Federal Trade Commission and in the Senate Commerce Committee to examine the growth of the consumer movement and the setbacks it encountered under the Reagan administration. Pertschuk examines the FTC's battles with Congress in the late-1970s to characterize the revolt against government regulation. He begins, however, with a brief chronicle of social regulatory legislation enacted by Congress during the mid-1960s through the early-1970s. Pertschuk then looks at the role business PACs have had in consumer strategies during the first years of the 1980s.

PS 378. PIVEN, FRANCES F. and RICHARD A. CLOWARD. Regulating the Poor: The Functions of Public Relief. New York: Random House, 1971. 389 pp.
Piven and Cloward present a radical critique and analysis of the role of public welfare (relief giving) in the U.S. They argue that welfare programs, far from being the benevolent institutions they claim to be, actually serve as engines of social and political control, forcing the poor into the labor market. Relief arrangements are expanded when mass unemployment threatens to produce civil disorder. When political stability is restored the relief system contracts. The authors relate their theory to the relief explosion of the Great Depression of the 1930s and the affluent years of the 1960s.

PS 379. PORTER, ROGER B. Presidential Decision-Making: The Economic
        Policy Board. New York: Cambridge University Press, 1980.
        265 pp.
Porter presents a case study focusing on the structures and operations
of the Economic Policy Board during the Ford administration. He details
the functions of the Board during some of the more controversial policy-
making moments, such as the U.S.-U.S.S.R. grain agreement. Porter's objective is to examine the process of decision-making--especially in light
of the fragmentation of the decision-making processes of the Executive
branch--and to assess the interrelationship of policy issues. The book
emphasizes the bureaucratic workings of the Board rather than the politics
of the decisions reached.

PS 380. RANNEY, AUSTIN, ed. Political Science and Public Policy. Chicago:
        Markham, 1968. 287 pp.
The essays in this book aim to redirect the attention of professional
political scientists toward examining the content of public policies,
not the processes by which policy is made. The volume seeks to discover
what the skills and obligations of a political scientist are when it comes
to examining the contents of public policy. It attempts to discover what
problems of conceptualization, data collection, and analysis must be solved
if studies of policy are to be of value. It also asks how policy-makers
will be served if political science emphasizes the study of policy contents,
and how this approach will be useful to the policy-makers.

PS 381. REAGAN, MICHAEL D. Science and the Federal Patron. New York:
        Oxford University Press, 1969. 346 pp.
Reagan argues that the present inaccessibility of scientific knowledge
to the non-scientifically trained public is creating a danger for the
status of science in public life. While science is demanding ever greater
support for research, the public and government demand the practical justification of all money spent on scientific research. The consequence of
this is that research is now justified on the grounds that it will develop
technological applications for the society and will serve the public interest. Reagan shows how science, the government, and the public can communicate and cooperate regarding the Federal support of science.

PS 382. SELZNICK, PHILIP. TVA and the Grass Roots: A Study in the Sociol-
        ogy of Formal Organization. Berkeley: University of California
        Press, 1949. 274 pp.
Selznick traces the development of the Tennessee Valley Authority (TVA)
as an early American experiment in public management. He studies the
interaction between an organization and its environment, developing the
concept of "cooptation," which refers either to the control of a clientele
group by a bureaucracy or the reverse. The latter occurred within the
TVA, as a faction of valley farmers became influential in Authority policy-
making, significantly affecting the goals and operations of TVA. The
manner in which such "informal" transfers of power, viewed as adaptation
by the organization to its environment, can interact with the ideology
and priorities of the organization comprises the main focus of Selznick's
theoretical analysis.

PS 383. SHARKANSKY, IRA. The Politics of Taxing and Spending. Indianapo-
        lis, Ind.: Bobbs-Merrill, 1969. 210 pp.
Sharkansky examines the raising and spending of revenues by all levels
of government in the U.S. He integrates local, state, and national policies toward taxation and expenditure, describing the norms and expectations
which guide decisions about the role of the government in the economy.
Next, Sharkansky details institutional, structural, and economic constraints on taxing and spending. He pays special attention to historical
influences on spending, such as depressions and wars. Sharkansky questions

the relationship between spending and performance, concluding that high spending is unrelated to high measures of service.

PS 384. SIMON, HERBERT A. _Administrative Behavior_. 1947; Rev. ed. New York: Macmillan, 1976. 259 pp.
Simon seeks to demolish prior claims to a "scientific" understanding of administration, substituting a theory based on the ideas of rational choice. He first develops his rational-choice model, then examines factors in the organizational environment that influence behavior (e.g., authority, communication, loyalties), and finally shows how the fact/value distinction on which his model is based can shed light on the problem of organizational design. Simon denounces current theory and accepts positivism as the basis for scientific theory. In the revised edition Simon focuses more upon the limitations organizational environments place on rationality, qualifying his assumption that humans choose rationally.

PS 385. SPANIER, JOHN, ed. _Congress, the Presidency, and American Foreign Policy_. New York: Praeger, 1981. 211 pp.
This collection of essays by American political scientists examines the evolution of the relationship between the Executive and the Legislature in the formulation of American foreign policy. Changes in the influence of the Congress from the Cold War to the post-Vietnam period are considered in terms of institutional rivalry with the President, political partisanship, and a shared mandate from the Constitution. A variety of specific cases are then discussed, including ratification of SALT, economic sanctions against Rhodesia, and energy policy.

PS 386. STOVER, DONALD W., Jr. _Seabrook and the Nuclear Regulatory Commission: The Licensing of a Nuclear Power Plant_. Hanover, N.H.: University of New England Press, 1980. 248 pp.
Stover examines the questions about the powers and procedures of the NRC raised during the opposition to the building of the Seabrook Nuclear Power Plant. He begins by presenting the administrative procedures utilized by the NRC to authorize the building of the nuclear power plant, finding that the NRC's decision-making process was devoid of public input and allowed the utility to invest heavily in the project before the NRC held public hearings on the matter. Furthermore, the study shows the NRC to have been inefficient, unable to evaluate nuclear policy properly, and dependent on information provided by the utility to render its decisions. The NRC, Stover argues, does not concern itself with public opinion, and openly compromises its objectivity during the processing of license applicants.

PS 387. STRAIGHT, MICHAEL. _Twigs for an Eagle's Nest: Government and the Arts, 1963-1978_. Berkeley, Calif.: Devon Press, 1979. 181 pp.
This book contains personal reminiscences from the author's tenure as deputy chairman of the National Endowment for the Arts from 1969-78. It provides insights into the policy-making process during the NEA's formative years. Straight describes how the agency tried to establish itself on principles of "cultural egalitarianism" and the commitment to government "non-intervention" while always being fearful of possible adverse public or Congressional reaction to government funded cultural projects.

PS 388. STRUYK, RAYMOND J. _A New System for Public Housing: Salvaging a National Resource_. Washington, D.C.: Urban Institute, 1980. 263 pp.
Struyk offers a new strategy aimed at alleviating the problems associated with housing projects administered by twenty-nine of the nation's largest public housing authorities, established by the Housing Act of 1937 and overseen by the U.S. Department of Housing and Urban Development (HUD).

Many public housing projects, Struyk notes, have become the slums they were supposed to replace. To improve the management of local public housing authorities he proposes that local government, rather than HUD, administer public housing, and that public housing authorities be turned into marketplace competitors. This, he claims, would avoid the inevitable mismanagement of public housing by centralized agencies such as HUD.

PS 389. THAYER, FREDERICK. An End to Hierarchy and Competition: Administration in the Post-Affluent World. 1973; Rev. ed. New York: Franklin Watts, 1981. 242 pp.
Thayer argues that American society is undergoing an organizational revolution which is causing the old hierarchical walls of formal organizations to fall. This revolution is being impeded by outmoded theories of policies and economics which are especially problematic for democratic societies because they are based on hierarchical authority. The problem is worsened when competition is offered as an answer to this problem. Competition only leads to chaos. Thayer's purpose is to explore a non-hierarchical meaning for democracy, one which emphasizes cooperation rather than competition.

PS 390. THOMPSON, FRANK J. Health Policy and the Bureaucracy: Politics and Implementation. Cambridge, Mass.: MIT Press, 1981. 334 pp.
Thompson explores the politics of health and the role of the bureaucracy in deciding who gets what from Federal health programs. The author demonstrates that the efforts to improve the public's health heavily depend on the politics pervading implementation processes. He studies particular health care institutions, such as the National Health Service Corps, Medicaid, Medicare, the Veteran Administrations Medical Program, and OSHA. Thompson shows how these institutions are concerned primarily with economy and efficiency.

PS 391. TOLCHIN, SUSAN and MARTIN TOLCHIN. Dismantling America: The Rush to Deregulate. Boston: Houghton Mifflin, 1983. 323 pp.
The Tolchins examine the present government movement toward deregulation and what is happening to the regulatory agencies. They examine closely the role of Congress and the efforts of the Carter and Reagan administrations to gain control of regulatory mechanisms. The authors are especially critical of the Reagan administration's attempt to dismantle regulatory legislation. They claim the Reagan administration lacks a public mandate to do so and is proceeding without due political process. Regulation has too easily become a national whipping boy for all of America's problems. The Tolchins argue for the necessity of regulation to avoid the industrial excesses of the past.

PS 392. TRATTNER, WALTER I., ed. Social Welfare or Social Control: Some Historical Reflections on "Regulating the Poor." Knoxville: University of Tennessee Press, 1983. 161 pp.
This book is a collection of essays by historians of social welfare responding to Frances Piven and Richard Cloward's Regulating the Poor (see PS 378). Piven and Cloward argue that the public welfare programs and institutions have not been, and are not, philanthropic or benevolent in nature; rather, they are intended to maintain social and political control and to force the poor into the labor market. The authors of the essays in this volume examine various periods in American history in order to test Piven and Cloward's thesis. All the contributors express doubts and criticisms about the work of Piven and Cloward. The book concludes with a response to the critics by Piven and Cloward.

PS 393. VAN HORN, CARL E. Policy Implementation in the Federal System: National Goals and Local Implementors. Lexington, Mass.: Lexington Books, 1979. 178 pp.
Van Horn deals with the implementation of inter-governmental programs, emphasizing the tension between the goals of programs provided with Federal dollars and the realities these programs face when they are implemented by state and local elected officials. Van Horn specifically examines three laws that emerged from the reform movement known as the New Federalism as examples of policy formation and implementation. These laws deal with revenue sharing, job training through CETA, and community block grants. Van Horn traces their development under successive Presidential administrations and Congresses in order to learn lessons about the problems of policy implementation. The study concludes with an analysis of who truly governs--Federal authorities or local implementors--in the implementation of public policy.

PS 394. VICTOR, RICHARD H. K. Environmental Politics and the Coal Coalitions. College Station: Texas A&M University Press, 1980. 285 pp.
Victor examines the evolution of Federal environmental policies relevant to coal energy and the political processes that guided that evolution. In response to growing environmental interests, coal interests have formed a united coalition which presses for coal development by lobbying and public relations campaigns. Through its extensive resources, the coal coalition exercises almost total control over technical information during the formulation and implementation of coal-related legislation. The coal coalition thus has blunted the impact of the environmental movement by becoming the source for the technical information that shapes the compliance standards of environmental legislation.

PS 395. VITERITTI, JOSEPH P. Bureaucracy and Social Justice: The Allocation of Jobs and Services to Minority Groups. Port Washington, N.Y.: Kennikat Press, 1979. 199 pp.
Viteritti argues that in decentralizing our local bureaucracies, reformers may be dismantling the very institutions which respond to the needs of the poor. Furthermore, by advocating citizen and group participation in the administrative process, these reformers are politicizing bureaucratic decision-making to such a degree that it is no longer responsive to the poor. Viteritti begins by discussing norms of representation and social equality in order to clarify the concept of justice within a bureaucratic framework. He then applies his normative and theoretical position to research on the bureaucracy of New York in order to see how an American city pursues the goal of social justice.

PS 396. WALDO, DWIGHT. The Administrative State. New York: Ronald Press, 1948. 227 pp.
Waldo studies the literature on public administration from a theoretical standpoint, regarding the writings of public administrators as "a chapter in the history of American political thought." He reviews the ideological background of this literature and identifies the network of ethical values--individualism, materialism, peace, liberty, urbanization, and equality--which the architects of the "Good Society" held sacred. Waldo notes the misuses of the term "science" common in many works. Claims of "scientific" status were made both for normative assertions and for common-sense suppositions. Waldo observes that the authors of public administration literature frequently failed to distinguish between facts and values.

PS 397. WEIMER, DAVID L. Improving Prosecution? The Inducement and Implementation of Innovations for Prosecution Management. Westport, Conn.: Greenwood Press, 1980. 237 pp.
Weimer's research deals with the development, diffusion, and implementation of Case Management Information Systems (CMIS) by prosecutors' offices. In theory, a CMIS enhances a prosecutor's management capabilities by providing data bases to detect deviations from stated policy, to identify assistants and branch offices straying from office norms, and to provide feedback to assistants on case outcomes. The author concludes, however, that the benefits promised by this system had not been realized three years after it was launched, and that the system was launched solely because of bureaucratic incentives, without an initial evaluation of what benefits it could provide.

PS 398. WILDAVSKY, AARON. How to Limit Government Spending. Berkeley: University of California Press, 1980. 197 pp.
Wildavsky argues that the growth of government, particularly at the expense of the private sector, is not desirable. Controlling the expansion of Federal spending will reduce inflation, lower taxes, and improve efficiency. An absolute limit on spending or a balanced budget is inferior to keeping the percentage growth of Federal outlays to the percentage of the growth of the GNP. Implementation of this goal cannot be achieved by administrative regulation or statute. Instead, only a constitutional amendment is sufficiently powerful to compel all governmental or quasi-governmental actors to submit to the same discipline. Resource addition will be replaced by real resource allocation if a Constitutional outlay limit is established.

PS 399. WILDAVSKY, AARON. The Politics of the Budgetary Process. 1964; Rev. ed. Boston: Little, Brown, 1974. 271 pp.
This is a treatment of the national budgetary process in the U.S. based on interviews and transcripts of appropriations hearings of twenty-five agencies over a fifteen year period. The revised edition adds chapters on program budgeting and Congressional control. Wildavsky describes the calculations the participants make in deciding how much to ask for or how much to spend. He then describes the strategies adopted by each set of actors. Finally, he reviews several proposals to reform the budgetary process, devoting most of his criticism to program budgeting.

PS 400. WILSON, JAMES Q. The Investigators: Managing FBI and Narcotics Agents. New York: Basic Books, 1978. 228 pp.
Wilson compares the performance and management of two American law enforcement agencies, the Federal Bureau of Investigation (FBI) and the Drug Enforcement Agency (DEA). Wilson argues that the management techniques employed by both agencies have often been irrelevant to their tasks and incapable of altering or affecting their effectiveness. Rather, management has been primarily responsive to outside pressures, especially Congress. Until recently, the FBI enjoyed virtual autonomy within the government. The DEA has had to endure secondary status and a certain amount of criticism. Wilson explores the consequences of their status in government for management, especially in regard to attempts to change priorities.

PS 401. WILSON, JAMES Q., ed. The Politics of Regulation. New York: Basic Books, 1980. 468 pp.
This is a collection of empirical studies on regulatory enterprises. Wilson's theory is that there is a politics of regulation, and it is based on how goals are determined, conflicts resolved or managed, standards set, and policy enforced. The contributors are critical of most political theories of regulation, specifically those which emphasize the economics of policy-making. The essays specifically look at the politics behind the policy developments of such Federal regulatory agencies as the Civil

Aeronautics Board and the Food and Drug Administration. They attempt
to explain the origins of regulation agency behavior, as well as the
dynamic of the regulatory system.

PS 402. WIRT, FREDERICK M. and MICHAEL W. KIRST. The Political Web of
           American Schools. Boston: Little, Brown, 1972. 285 pp.
In an effort to bring educational policy under the scrutiny of political
scientists, Wirt and Kirst argue that school policy-making is political.
They explode the myth that educators and educational policy-makers act
in a political vacuum. Instead, they argue, in each subsequent political
era new demands arise and the government's needs of the populace change.
The authors examine the process by which these demands are converted into
new educational policies. They concentrate on policy implementation in
three major areas—special aid for impoverished children, desegregation,
and curriculum change.

PS 403. WISE, ARTHUR. Legislated Learning: The Bureaucratization of
           the American Classroom. Berkeley: University of California
           Press, 1979. 219 pp.
Wise looks at the problems in education that have come about as a result
of the interference of the state and Federal governments, and the courts.
Education is being taken out of the hands of the schools and colleges
by government bureaucracies. This is leading to a new hierarchy of control
within the education system, with the Federal government at the top.
The true motive behind this, argues the author, is the desire to make
educational institutions more efficient and more effective, rather than
to improve academic achievement. For evidence, Wise points to the ways
in which new educational policies draw upon the tradition of scientific
management.

PS 404. WISE, DAVID. The Politics of Lying: Government Deception, Secrecy,
           and Power. New York: Random House, 1973. 415 pp.
Wise looks at the erosion of confidence between people and government.
He deals with the issue of governmental deception and the resultant loss
of public trust. The book begins with a look at government deception,
the system of secrecy, and the spread of misinformation. It then turns
to an examination of the role of the press, and how it unintentionally
mediates government deception to the public. Wise concludes with a discussion of how a deceptive government providing the public with misinformation threatens democracy.

PS 405. YARMOLINSKY, ADAM. The Military Establishment. New York: Harper
           & Row, 1971. 433 pp.
Yarmolinsky looks at how the American military establishment affects the
lives of individuals; how it affects the nature of society; how it makes
alternatives known and possible to political decision-makers; and how
it affects the decision-making process. Yarmolinsky begins with an examination of the rise of the U.S. military and the weakness of the countervailing powers which try to control it. He then examines the use of military
power and its influence in U.S. society as well as the impact of the military establishment.

VII.   ELECTORAL POLITICS AND POLITICAL PARTIES

PS 406.   ABRAMSON, PAUL R.   Generational Change in American Politics.
Lexington, Mass.: Lexington Books, 1975. 140 pp.
Abramson follows voting trends from 1945 to 1974 with regard to the relationship between voter class and party vote as well as the extent to which
the people feel bound to one political party. He demonstrates that the
decline in class voting and in voter attachment to one party has occurred
mainly through generational replacement (that is, by older, class-oriented
partisans dying and being replaced by young voters), rather than by individuals changing their behavior. The book attributes the decline of voter
participation to the "problem of generations."

PS 407.   ABRAMSON, PAUL R., JOHN H. ALDRICH, and DAVID W. RHODE. Change
and Continuity in the 1980 Elections. Washington, D.C.: Congressional Quarterly Press, 1982. 257 pp.
The authors explore the 1980 Presidential election and the contest between
the candidates seeking their party's nomination. They offer a study of
voting behavior in the 1980 elections, exploring the motivations of and
major influences on the voters. In addition, they provide evidence to
substantiate the assertion that the 1980 Presidential election was more
a rejection of President Carter than it was a statement of support for
President Reagan. The authors also provide a description of the 1980
Congressional elections and analyze the causes of the recent decline in
voter turnout.

PS 408.   ALDRICH, JOHN. Before the Convention: Strategies and Choices
in Presidential Nominations. Chicago: University of Chicago
Press, 1980. 257 pp.
Aldrich utilizes rational choice theory to analyze the 1976 Presidential
campaign. He relies on quantitative methods to examine the backgrounds
and motivations of Presidential candidates, the institutional context
of the campaign, and the degree of citizen participation. Aldrich analyzes
the strategic problems of the allocation of resources during an evolving
campaign, the choice for primary candidates of which states to compete
in, and the debate over which issues candidates should be identified with.
He also examines the willingness of political candidates to take risks
and the political tradeoffs made by the voting public between preferred
candidates and those who are electable. All this leads to the development
of a mathematically logical methodology for predicting the outcome of
Presidential nomination campaigns.

PS 409.   BARBER, JAMES D. Citizen Politics: An Introduction to Political
Behavior. Chicago: Markham, 1979. 199 pp.
Barber studies the present movement of citizen participation in policy
decisions. He begins by looking into the present patterns of actual citizen participation, including the ways motives, opportunities, and resources
work together. The study examines the extent of the citizenry's political
knowledge by looking at individuals and groups to see how the typical
citizen thinks about politics. Barber explores the positive and negative
impact of political debate in aiding citizens to make rational choices.
He also takes up the question of when citizens should resist government
actions. The book then turns to the effect professional public relations
campaigns and political propaganda have in mobilizing citizen participation,
taking into account the political cultures of communities. Barber argues
that governments which fail to adapt quickly to rapid, fundamental social
changes may become illegitimate in the eyes of their citizens.

PS 410. BARBER, JAMES D., ed. Choosing the President. Englewood Cliffs, N.J.: Prentice-Hall, 1974. 207 pp.
This book contains seven essays which raise questions concerning the relationship of the American people to their President. Erwin Hargrove asks, "what kind of President do we want?" and concludes that the President should be "democratic" in character and style. Donald Matthews considers how candidates are chosen, focusing on the importance of early campaigning to a candidate. Austin Ranney reviews changes in party nominating procedures, while John Kessel analyzes campaigns, with emphasis on building and maintaining coalitions. Fred Greenstein examines public attitudes toward the President; Murray Edelman is concerned with Presidential manipulation of the public. Finally, Richard Boyd projects future trends, seeing an electorate characterized by cynicism and disaffection.

PS 411. BERELSON, BERNARD, PAUL F. LAZARSFELD, and WILLIAM N. McPHEE. Voting: A Study of Opinion Formation in a Presidential Campaign. Chicago: University of Chicago Press, 1954. 395 pp.
This study emphasizes the social processes by which a community, and social groups in the community, make a collective choice through an election. It utilizes voting studies of the town of Elmira, New York, during the 1948 election. Particular emphasis is placed on the ways in which various groups—trade unions, religious groups, groups of friends or of fellow workers—helped to mold the choices of their members, and the effect of this interaction on the election campaign.

PS 412. BICKEL, ALEXANDER M. Reform and Continuity: The Electoral College, the Convention, and the Party System. New York: Harper & Row, 1971. 121 pp.
Bickel presents essays on three aspects of the American electoral system and prospects for their reform. In examining the Electoral College, Bickel defends the status quo. He feels that the Electoral College, by giving an advantage to large, industrial states, balances Congress's bias toward small states; moreover, he finds reform proposals seriously flawed. Considering party conventions, however, he generally endorses reforms, particularly those proposed following the tumultuous 1968 Democratic Convention. Finally, Bickel examines the legal status of third parties, especially their ability to qualify candidates for the ballot in the various states. Again, he tends to endorse reform, arguing that laws handicapping third parties should be invalidated.

PS 413. BONOMI, PATRICIA, JAMES M. BURNS, and AUSTIN RANNEY, eds. The American Constitutional System Under Strong and Weak Parties. New York: Praeger, 1981. 142 pp.
This volume examines the sweeping changes affecting U.S. political parties since 1968. The editors do so by presenting a collection of essays which deal with the historical experience and current status of U.S. political parties. The book begins with an examination of Presidential leadership and the Congressional Caucus in political parties during the ante-bellum period. This is followed by a look at the progressive reforms undertaken from 1880-1920. Two different tendencies of reform are identified in this period which are carried down to this day: one toward democracy and another toward bureaucracy. The reforms since 1968, the book argues, actually further incapacitated political parties. The enfeeblement of parties is traced not to political interests, but to intellectual insensitivity to the institutional requirements of representative democracy. The volume concludes with a discussion of whether the party system can be saved.

PS 414. BOYTE, HARRY C. The Backyard Revolution: Understanding the New
    Citizen Movement. Philadelphia: Temple University Press, 1980.
    257 pp.
Boyte seeks to identify, describe, and analyze emerging social movements
in American politics. He describes contemporary forms of citizen organizing, and the formation of grass roots organizations. Many of the social
movements the author identifies--such as neighborhood groups, farmers'
protests, consumer activism, new forms of workplace organizing--are historically linked to what Boyte calls the citizen advocacy tradition.
Contemporary social movements have been enriched with ideas that grew
out of the movements of the 1960s, but draw on the citizen advocacy tradition. In part, Boyte argues that the citizen movement is a necessary
adaptation to the growing inflation, urban fiscal crises, and corporate
reaction of the 1970s. The networks and organizations which these movements establish are found to have a firm democratic base. The new citizens
movement is presented as an alternative popular democratic thread of insurgency in modern society.

PS 415. BRAMS, STEVEN J. The Presidential Election Game. New Haven,
    Conn.: Yale University Press, 1978. 242 pp.
Brams presents models for the three major phases of the Presidential election game: state primaries, national party conventions, and the general
election. He also develops models of coalition politics, drawing on examples from early and recent Presidential campaigns to demonstrate how coalitions form and break up. Brams examines Richard Nixon's confrontation
with the Supreme Court and his subsequent resignation as a case study
in how an election mandate can be overturned. He concludes with a proposal
for a new form of voting. Its theoretical properties are analyzed along
with its likely empirical effects.

PS 416. BRECKENRIDGE, ADAM. Electing the President. Washington, D.C.:
    University Press of America, 1982. 157 pp.
Breckenridge provides a review of the literature proposing reform of the
Electoral College system. He reviews not only professional literature,
but Senate hearings, public debates, and published reports on the subject.
He also looks at the various alternatives which have been advanced to
replace the Electoral College. However, Breckenridge's primary focus
in on the direct national popular vote plan and its advantages and disadvantages. He concludes with a defense of the Electoral College system,
and minor suggestions for reform.

PS 417. BURNHAM, WALTER DEAN. Critical Elections and the Mainsprings
    of American Politics. New York: Norton, 1970. 210 pp.
Burnham develops V. O. Key's notion of "critical elections" (see PS 443).
He produces evidence suggesting a periodicity to critical realignments,
noting that they recur about every forty years. Furthermore, he claims
to show a general decline in the importance of parties as sources of influence in electoral results over the last seventy years. Burnham attempts
to identify the underlying cleavage patterns in several elections of the
1960s which brought about the realignment of the 1970s. He sees the emergence of a new liberal coalition composed of minorities and upper-income
white intellectuals, with blue-collar whites excluded.

PS 418. BURNHAM, WALTER DEAN. The Current Crisis in American Politics.
    New York: Oxford University Press, 1982. 330 pp.
Burnham provides a collection of his essays--written between 1964 and
1981--which focus on the degeneration of the contemporary American electoral market and its institutions. Burnham's main concern is with the
causes, characteristics, and implications of the periodically recurring
critical realignment of the electorate. The author pursues his thesis
that abnormal and general crises in American politics express themselves

1084

by critical realignments of parties and political elites. Critical realignments are an expression of ideological polarization. They are abrupt but enduring shifts in the nature and social location of party coalitions in the electorate, and result in major changes in the shape and direction of public policy. Critical realignment, argues Burnham, has become America's substitute for revolution. The essays focus primarily on the changing nature of the American electorate over the course of history. Burnham tries to explain the causes of the declining involvement of the American electorate in recent elections.

PS 419. BURNS, JAMES MacGREGOR. Deadlock of Democracy: Four-Party Politics in America. Englewood Cliffs, N.J.: Prentice-Hall, 1963. 388 pp.

Burns argues that in reality the U.S. has four parties—the Democrats and Republicans, each with a "presidential" wing (aware of nationwide concerns, internationalist, and progressive on social issues) and a "congressional" wing (parochial, narrow, and cautious). Thus the distribution of power goes beyond institutional divisions to pit against each other a President and a Congress who respond to different portions of the electorate. Presidential candidates must devote special attention to marginal "swing" areas, while Congress is dominated by the representatives of safe one-party areas. Because of the confusion ensuing from the existence of four parties, Burns argues that the formation of working alliances is difficult and that policy is made by fits and starts, with long delays in needed programs.

PS 420. CAMPBELL, ANGUS, PHILIP E. CONVERSE, WARREN E. MILLER, and DONALD E. STOKES. The American Voter. New York: Wiley, 1960. 573 pp.

This is a study of the social-psychological character of the American voter, stressing the elements that contribute to an individual's choice of which party to support. Particular emphasis is given to the concept of "party identification," an emotional attachment which the authors see as central to an individual's political development. Much of the book consists of an elaboration of this concept. The authors argue that this identification, rather than ideology or policy questions, is what drives electoral development. Though their emphasis is on individuals, they interpret larger issues such as their theory of individuals' choice, the nature of elections, the nature of Congressional representation, and the political role of various social groups such as farmers or the working class.

PS 421. CAMPBELL, ANGUS, PHILIP E. CONVERSE, WARREN E. MILLER, and DONALD STOKES. Elections and Political Order. New York: Wiley, 1966. 385 pp.

This study examines the aggregate properties of the electorate and the party system in the U.S. by looking at Presidential and Congressional elections. Drawing information from national surveys conducted in the period between 1946 and 1960, the authors attempt to reveal the character of the collective vote. This information is then applied to an analysis of how elections function in the political system. The authors also examine the competition between parties in the American political system, the nature of the party controversy, and the relation of ideological positions to the vote.

PS 422. CEASER, JAMES W. Reforming the Reforms: A Critical Analysis of the Presidential Selection Process. Cambridge, Mass.: Ballinger, 1982. 201 pp.

Ceaser examines the way in which the desire to reform the Presidential selection process spread to every American institution during the 1960s and 1970s. By the end of the 1970s, the author argues, the American political climate began to change; the reform movement subsided, and the efficacy of previous reforms came to be questioned. Ceaser examines the impulse to reform the Presidential selection process by examining the evolution of the Presidential nominating process from 1789 to 1968. The book concludes with a discussion of the state of American political parties in the 1980s.

PS 423. CHAMBER, WILLIAM N. and WALTER DEAN BURNHAM, eds. The American
         Party System: Stages of Political Development. 1962; Rev. ed.
         New York: Oxford University Press, 1975. 379 pp.
The essays in this book analyze a party's development through an examination of its history and activity. The book also examines the impact and behavior of parties. The volume begins with an historical essay on party development in mainstream American politics. Half of the essays are historical in nature, examining the role of the political party during significant periods such as the post-Revolutionary War and the Civil War eras. The rest of the essays examine the present state of political parties in America. The volume concludes with an essay examining the future of American parties in light of the critical realignment of the electorate.

PS 424. CONVERSE, PHILIP E. The Dynamics of Party Support: Cohort-
         Analyzing Party Identification. Beverly Hills, Calif.: Sage,
         1976. 175 pp.
In responding to Paul Abramson's rejection of the long-accepted idea that Americans become more partisan as they age (see PS 406), Converse presents a close empirical examination of the decline in attachments to parties in the late 1960s. He concludes that the decline was due not to differences in the generations, but to the tensions of the civil rights movement and the Vietnam War. In refuting Abramson, Converse presents an example of the method of "cohort analysis," a technique by which an investigator attempts to distinguish the effects of aging from changes effected by the replacement of older generations by newer ones.

PS 425. COTTER, CORNELIUS and BERNARD C. HENNESSY. Politics Without Power:
         The National Party Committee. New York: Atherton, 1964. 246 pp.
This study examines the national organization and operations of the two major American political parties. The authors' primary theme contrasts the apparent formal power of the National Committees and their chairmen with their actual lack of resources, stable organization, and, often, political power. Cotter and Hennessy review all aspects of their subject: committee organization, members and their backgrounds, chairmen and their backgrounds, performance of party functions (e.g., publicity and research), finance, policy roles, and relationships with other political actors (e.g., Presidents and special interest groups). Their findings suggest, among other things, that the "out" party's organization is more important than the "in's," that the Republicans tend to be better organized than the Democrats, and that strong chairmen can have real impact. They conclude by recommending stronger parties, and they offer suggestions to that end.

PS 426. CROTTY, WILLIAM J. Decision for the Democrats. Baltimore, Md.:
         Johns Hopkins University Press, 1978. 318 pp.
Crotty examines some of the reforms undertaken by the Democratic Party from 1968 to 1972. His focus is primarily on the serious attempts at major institutional change put forward by the Democratic reform committees. Specifically, Crotty looks at how the committees introduced due process guarantees, and attempted to force an equitable representation of minority groups in party affairs. He also examines the committees' attempts to modernize the national nominating convention, showing the extent to which these reform bodies succeeded and the difficulties they encountered.

PS 427. CROTTY, WILLIAM J., ed. Paths to Political Reform. Lexington,
Mass.: Lexington Books, 1980. 366 pp.
Crotty's essays analyze the continuing controversy over political reforms
in the 1960s and 1970s. The book begins by looking at changes in the
American electorate. It tries to redefine the American electorate in
light of the issues which concern voter decision-making. It then considers
the public mood and the declining public confidence in American institutions. (The decline of political parties is traced to the erosion in
popular support.) The book also looks at the controversies surrounding
reform in voter registration and the electoral parties. It then turns
to the Presidential nominating process; public office campaigns and the
way they are financed; and the way in which Congress responds to the public
will.

PS 428. DAVID, PAUL T. and JAMES W. CEASER. Proportional Representation
in Presidential Nominating Politics. Charlottesville: University
Press of Virginia, 1980. 298 pp.
David and Ceaser provide a comprehensive study of the Democratic Presidential nominating process of 1976 and of delegate behavior at that year's
convention. The book begins with an analysis of the selection process.
It describes the various selection systems used and traces the origin,
growth, and potential future consequences of the new system of proportional
representation. This is followed by case studies of the nomination process
in six states. This part also shows how party rules affected the division
of delegates, and demonstrates the uniqueness of each state nomination
race.

PS 429. DAVID, PAUL T., RALPH GOLDMAN, and RICHARD BAIN. The Politics
of National Party Conventions. Washington, D.C.: Brookings
Institution, 1960. 592 pp.
The authors analyze the convention system as a means of selecting nominees
for the Presidency and Vice-Presidency. Their analysis is based on a
review of the history and evolution of the major national parties as evidenced in and affected by their national conventions. The authors draw
on historical materials to appraise the nominating process. They examine
the problems particular to the party out of power and the party holding
office. The leadership centers of the out-party and in-party are described,
with particular attention to the way various leadership elements have
functioned in the nominating process since 1876.

PS 430. DAVIS, JAMES W. National Conventions in an Age of Party Reform.
Westport, Conn.: Greenwood Press, 1983.
Davis examines the basic purpose of national conventions in light of the
recent efforts at making parties, especially the Democratic party, more
representative. The importance of national conventions as decision-making
bodies has significantly declined, but the national convention remains
an important political event that continues to serve an indispensable
brokering function, especially when a close race develops in the party
primaries. Furthermore, the conventions place a stamp of legitimacy on
the nominee, telling party members and the nation that the party stands
behind the nominee. Davis also examines various alternatives that have
been recommended as replacements for the national convention.

PS 431. ELDERSVELD, SAMUEL. Political Parties: A Behavioral Analysis.
Chicago: Rand McNally, 1964. 613 pp.
Eldersveld attempts to disprove Robert Michels's assertions that political
parties will always be controlled by an oligarchic elite. Through an
intensive study of party organization in Detroit, Michigan, at the time
of the 1956 election, he shows that there is little central control or
coordination within the parties. The book provides an informative examination of local party structure.

PS 432. **EVERSON, DAVID H.** American Political Parties. New York: New
Viewpoint, 1980. 244 pp.
Everson argues that the recent changes in American political parties
reflect an evolution in the direction of greater responsibility. He examines parties from the perspective of democratic theory, beginning with
an elaboration of the central concepts of responsible parties, followed
by a presentation of the characteristics of the traditional two-party
system, and he then describes the major changes that have taken place.
Everson examines electoral realignment and the possibility of developing
a more responsible electorate. He also assesses recent changes in the
Presidential nomination process.

PS 433. **FERGUSON, THOMAS** and **JOEL ROGERS**, eds. The Hidden Election:
Politics and Economics in the 1980 Presidential Campaign. New
York: Pantheon Books, 1981. 342 pp.
The Hidden Election is a collection of essays that analyze the effect
of domestic and international economic issues on the 1980 Presidential
campaign. It looks at the election as a moment of realignment among the
electorate. It also tries to show the impact of elitist politics on the
campaign. In general, the essays provide a Leftist critique of the 1980
elections.

PS 434. **GREENSTEIN, FRED.** The American Party System and the American
People. Englewood Cliffs, N.J.: Prentice-Hall, 1963. 115 pp.
Greenstein presents research on electoral psychology as applied to the
relationship between American political parties and the American people.
The book concentrates on the degree to which political parties contribute
to enhancing a democratic political system. Greenstein inquires into
the way in which the institution affects the adequacy of governmental
policy-making. He analyzes the citizen base of the American political
party system and considers the role of parties in the electorate and their
impact on public opinion and voting. He also seeks to find the extent
to which citizens control party leaders, paying special attention to the
urban political machine.

PS 435. **HACKER, ANDREW.** Congressional Districting: The Issues of Equal
Representation. Washington, D.C.: Brookings Institution, 1963.
132 pp.
Hacker examines the consequences of the Supreme Court's decision in the
Baker v. Carr Congressional redistricting case. (The case opened the
way for the reform of antiquated and inequitable patterns of representation
in state legislatures.) He looks at the Congressional districts at the
time of the decision in order to discuss what problems were anticipated
from the reapportionment. In the process, Hacker discusses the constitutional and historical background of Congressional districting; state
and judicial action; reasons for the disproportion between votes and seats
won; and the extent and consequences of inequalities in representation
in the House of Representatives.

PS 436. **HILL, DAVID B.** and **NORMAN R. LUTTBERG.** Trends in American Electoral Behavior. 1980; Rev. ed. Itasca, Ill.: Peacock, 1983.
200 pp.
Hill and Luttberg review the extent of actual change in American electoral
behavior, as evidenced by Presidential and Congressional elections from
1952 to 1982. They begin with a description of voter behavior drawn from
pre-1960s electoral research. This description provides a review of previous findings and theories regarding electoral behavior. They then turn
to questions of party decline, declining political participation, and
declining political trust.

PS 437. HINCKLEY, BARBARA. Congressional Elections. Washington, D.C.:
          Congressional Quarterly Press, 1981. 173 pp.
Hinckley provides a comprehensive examination of the influences at work
in Congressional elections. She surveys the literature while examining
the major topics involved in Congressional elections. She also provides
a framework for analyzing the decline in interest in Congressional races
and examines how voters receive and process information about candidates
and issues. This is followed by a discussion of the powerful impact of
incumbency and party influence, and the effect of issues. Hinckley then
compares midterm Congressional races with Presidential election year races.

PS 438. JACOBSON, GARY C. Money in Congressional Elections. New Haven,
          Conn.: Yale University Press, 1980. 251 pp.
Jacobson argues that what incumbents spend in election campaigns makes
relatively little difference whereas for non-incumbents, spending is important: whether or not campaigns are seriously contested depends on the
resources mobilized by non-incumbents. The author looks at the people
and groups that supply campaign funds and how they determine which races
are competitive and which are not. This is followed by an examination
of how changes in the law regulating campaign finance can alter the competitive environment decisively. Jacobson provides an examination of
the context of Congressional elections, emphasizing the decline in competition and voter participation. He looks at the problem of fundraising
itself, especially for a non-incumbent, and concludes with an interpretation of the politics of campaign finance reform.

PS 439. JACOBSON, GARY C. The Politics of Congressional Elections. Boston:
          Little, Brown, 1983. 216 pp.
Jacobson provides a systematic account of Congressional elections in order
to show how electoral politics reflect and shape other components of the
political system. The author's central argument is that the political,
economic, and social problems of the 1960s and 1970s led to public discontent and mistrust of political leaders and institutions; however, the
political incapacity of Congress, and public discontent, are both outcomes
of the Congressional election process. Electoral politics, Jacobson argues,
have produced a Congress that combines high individual responsiveness
with high collective irresponsibility. This suggests that the way in
which Congress is elected has contributed strongly to the incapacity of
government to deal effectively with pressing national problems, and to
the consequent loss of faith in political leaders and institutions.

PS 440. JACOBSON, GARY C. and SAMUEL KERNELL. Strategy and Choice in
          Congressional Elections. New Haven, Conn.: Yale University
          Press, 1981. 111 pp.
Jacobson and Kernell try to reconcile apparently contradictory phenomena:
national political events obviously influence the outcomes of subsequent
Congressional elections, but voters polled seldom claim to have been
affected by such events in their voting choices. In order to reconcile
these phenomena--and to repudiate theorists who attend only to macro-level
political analysis and ignore voter input--they emphasize the role of
candidates and campaign coordinators as strategic intermediaries between
the electorate and those events which apparently shape elections. Political events such as Watergate or the hostage crisis in Iran do influence
election results, but only indirectly. Politicians shape campaigns according to the current political climate and present candidates in such a
way as to make them appear suitable and capable. Thus, the authors argue,
although most voters claim to be voting for the best candidate regardless
of national issues and current events, their vision of the best candidate
and of the candidates themselves, has indeed been shaped by these issues
and events.

PS 441. KEECH, WILLIAM R. and DONALD R. MATTHEWS. The Party's Choice.
         Washington, D.C.: Brookings Institution, 1976. 258 pp.
The authors examine the manner in which the two major American political
parties nominated their candidates for President in ten elections between
1936 and 1972. They seek common patterns and develop a modest typology
of situations. Their main contribution, however, lies in their identification of the two or three years before the "formal" start of the campaign
as more critical than either the primary elections or party conventions.
The main problem Keech and Matthews see in the nomination system is that
too few candidates, and perhaps not the best ones, begin their campaigns
strongly enough to have a reasonable chance.

PS 442. KESSEL, JOHN. Presidential Campaign Politics: Coalition Strate-
         gies and Citizen Responses. Homewood, Ill.: Dorsey, 1982.
         298 pp.
Kessel argues that coalition strategies and citizen choice are equally
important parts of the same political process. These are explored within
the context of Presidential campaigns. Kessel notes how the purpose of
coalitions is to recruit delegates in order to win the nomination and
persuade voters in order to win an election. He thus analyzes the linkages
that exist between parties and voters. He begins with a look at nomination
politics and then turns to electoral politics. This is followed by a
discussion of the Presidential campaign strategies of the 1960s and 1970s.
Kessel then turns to an examination of how an individual becomes informed
about Presidential politics, establishes a party identification, and makes
a Presidential choice.

PS 443. KEY, V. O., Jr. The Responsible Electorate: Rationality in Presi-
         dential Voting, 1936-1960. Cambridge, Mass.: Harvard University
         Press, 1966. 158 pp.
This book is a response to Angus Campbell's The American Voter (see PS
420) and Bernard Berelson's Voting (see PS 411). Key contends that those
studies under-emphasized the role of individual free will among voters
in determining election results. Through the use of survey data, he shows
that over a series of elections most of those who changed their vote did
so because of some policy issue.

PS 444. KEY, V. O., Jr. Southern Politics in State and Nation. New York:
         Knopf, 1949. 675 pp.
Key presents a study of political party structure and the conduct of elections in the American South as of 1948, a time when the South was virtually
a one-party system. In an effort to paint a picture of mass politics
in the South for the rest of the nation, he offers state-by-state analysis
of the South's political elites and economic alignments. He then assesses
the political implications of the South's one-party system, extreme factionalism, and racial segregation, the latter particularly in view of limits
on imposed suffrage, such as the literacy test and the poll tax. Key
views the region's intricate system of racial discrimination as the primary
obstacle to political rejuvenation.

PS 445. KLEPPER, PAUL. Who Voted? The Dynamics of Electoral Turnout:
         1870-1980. New York: Praeger, 1982. 238 pp.
Using statistical analysis of ninety years of county-level election returns,
Klepper links changes in the level of composition of turnout to the ethnicity, income, education, and religion of constituencies. He finds the
period from 1840 to 1900 to be a "mobilization era" in which tight party
competition and conflict between "pietist" Republicans and "liturgical"
Democrats made for a comparatively high level of electoral participation.
He analyzes the "demobilization" of 1896-1928, the "remobilization" of
the electorate under Roosevelt in the years 1930-60, and the "demobilization and disillusionment" of the years 1964-80, in which a loss of faith

in parties and elections among low income and poorly educated potential voters led to an increase in upper-class bias in government.

PS 446. LADD, EVERETT C. Where Have All the Voters Gone: The Fracturing of American Political Parties. 1978; Rev. ed. New York: Norton, 1982. 138 pp.
Ladd assesses the parties and election system that emerged from the collapse of the New Deal program. The book begins with a discussion of the conditions of American political parties, with emphasis on the weakness of the present parties as political organizations. Ladd criticizes some of the reforms instituted by these parties, then turns to what he calls the continuing march among American voters toward realignment: rather than a turn toward another party, he asserts that there is a continuing decline of all forms of party allegiance. He then examines Republican and Democratic leaders' assessments of the 1980 voting and of the divisions between the parties following the election. Ladd concludes with a look at the prospects of the two major parties in view of post-election developments, including the Reagan administration's performance.

PS 447. LADD, EVERETT C. and CHARLES D. HADLEY. Transformations of the American Party System: Political Coalitions from the New Deal to the 1970s. New York: Norton, 1975. 371 pp.
Ladd and Hadley chart the evolution of voting coalitions in Presidential and Congressional elections from 1924 to 1972, with an emphasis on the breakdown of the New Deal coalition of labor, Catholics, and white Southerners, and the evolution of the new coalitions that replaced it. They also chart the changing directions of the polity within the larger context of a changing social order. Changes in party coalitions are observed as reflections of social change. The book proceeds from this to determine what coalitions will emerge as dominant and what conflicts the new coalitions will generate.

PS 448. LIPSET, SEYMOUR MARTIN, ed. Party Coalitions in the 1980s. San Francisco: Institute for Contemporary Studies, 1981. 480 pp.
The essays Lipset has collected here discuss the future prospects of the party system. The discussions are based to a large extent on interpretations of the politics of the 1970s and the 1980 elections. The book begins with background information about the political party system and an analysis of the issues surrounding the 1980 election. This is followed by essays on the nature of party coalitions and their transformations throughout the history of the U.S. The book then looks at contemporary politics, issues of party coalitions, and the strategies of the two parties in the 1980 election. The final essay addresses the question of whether there was a realignment among voters in the 1980 election and what it means for the future of American politics.

PS 449. MAISEL, LOUIS S. From Obscurity to Oblivion: Running in the Congressional Primary. Knoxville: University of Tennessee Press, 1982. 173 pp.
Maisel provides a personal account of his own campaign in order to study the problems faced by Congressional primary candidates and to answer questions about the nature of Congressional primaries in general. The author tries to discover why people run for Congress; how decisions are made; and how campaigns are organized and financed. He also deals with the way in which issues and political agenda are formulated and the tactics used during a campaign. Maisel concludes with a discussion of the important public policy questions raised by Congressional primary elections.

PS 450. MAZMANIAN, DANIEL A. Third Parties in Presidential Elections.
Washington, D.C.: Brookings Institution, 1974. 140 pp.
Mazmanian assesses the origins of third parties, their impact on public
policy and the party system, and the episodic nature of their appearance.
The author discusses the leading third parties that have contended for
the Presidency over the past 140 years. His analysis reveals the conditions necessary for significant third party voting and the effects of
third parties on Presidential elections, the party system, and public
policy. Mazmanian argues that the promotion of nearly permanent minor
parties is a way of enriching the Presidential contest. He also recommends
a national election code which would ensure the survival of strong minor
parties. Mazmanian concludes by anticipating change in the traditional
two-party system from pressures placed on it by significant third party
movements.

PS 451. McCORMICK, RICHARD. The Presidential Game: The Origin of American
Presidential Politics. New York: Oxford University Press, 1982.
279 pp.
McCormick offers an explanation of the development of the Presidential
selection process between the Constitutional Convention and 1844. He
identifies four major successive attempts made during this period to devise
alternatives to the Constitutional Convention's proposed election method.
McCormick claims that the party system of Presidential selection was at
odds with the republican ideology, but argues that once the party system
of Presidential selection became entrenched, it maintained its basic character until the post-1868 rule changes.

PS 452. MILLER, WARREN and TERESA A. LEVITAN. Leadership and Change:
The New Politics and the American Electorate. Cambridge, Mass.:
Winthrop, 1976. 267 pp.
This is a study of the "new politics" in the U.S. and its influence from
1970 to 1974. The term "new politics" is shorthand for a constellation
of social issues that threatened to replace the traditional lines of economic cleavage in American politics. Advocates of the "new politics"
were those sympathetic to political protest and the "counterculture,"
and hostile to agents of social control and the doctrines of law and order.
Opposed to this movement were those labelled by the authors as the "silent
majority," who held more conservative views on the issues of political
protest and law and order. They suggest that the "new force" in American
politics could generate a realignment in partisan loyalties.

PS 453. NIE, NORMAN H., SIDNEY VERBA, and JOHN R. PETROCIK. The Changing
American Voter. Cambridge, Mass.: Harvard University Press,
1976. 399 pp.
The authors present this study as an examination of the changes in the
American electorate which have taken place since the publication of Angus
Campbell's The American Voter (see PS 420). Their thesis is that Americans
have, over the intervening years, become less partisan and much more prone
to choose leaders on the basis of issues and ideology. They buttress
this claim with many sets of survey results.

PS 454 NIEMI, RICHARD G. and HERBERT F. WEISBERG, eds. Controversies
in American Voting Behavior. San Francisco: Freeman, 1976.
543 pp.
Niemi and Weisberg present thirty articles which address the following
questions about voting behavior: (1) Is it rational to take the trouble
of voting in an election, when it is almost certain that one's single
vote will not determine the result? (2) How ideological is the American
electorate? (3) Are elections primarily determined by partisan preferences,
by the attractiveness of candidates, or by particular political issues?
(4) Are Congressional elections inherently more partisan than Presidential

elections? (5) Is the party balance in the U.S. currently changing?
(6) Are parties becoming irrelevant to elections? (7) Was the electorate
of the 19th century a more active, informed electorate than that of the
20th century?

PS 455. O'ROURKE, TIMOTHY G. The Impact of Reapportionment. New Brunswick,
N.J.: Transaction Books, 1980. 213 pp.
O'Rourke provides a comparative study of the impact of reapportionment
on six state legislatures during the period 1962-72. He examines the
effect of reapportionment on legislative turnover, legislator characteristics, constituency relations, party competition for legislative seats,
urban-rural and partisan conflict in the legislature, legislative procedure
and organization, and legislative policy-making. The author concludes
that reapportionment had its strongest impact in those states in which
malapportionment had created an artificial rural majority in the legislature.

PS 456. PAGE, BENJAMIN I. Choices and Echoes in Presidential Elections:
Rational Man and Electoral Democracy. Chicago: University of
Chicago Press, 1978. 336 pp.
Page examines the behavior of political parties and candidates during
elections, drawing on information from a number of elections from 1932
onward. He gauges the extent to which choices and differences exist
between candidates; the effect of public opinion on candidates; the extent
to which candidates stand firm on issues; and how candidates shape their
images. Page is concerned with uncovering how the politician's behavior
influences and is influenced by the voters, and how these processes affect
electoral democracy. This leads to his discussion of how candidates influence voters during elections. His theoretical presumption is that electoral behavior is rational and that individual behavior may be explained
and predicted once assumptions about people's goals and beliefs are elabo-
rated. Statistical information is utilized toward the determination of
electoral behavior.

PS 457. PIERCE, JOHN C. and JOHN L. SULLIVAN, eds. The Electorate Reconsidered. Beverly Hills, Calif.: Sage, 1980. 293 pp.
This is a collection of papers on voter behavior. The book includes material on voter attitudes toward the President during the Watergate affair.
It analyzes the instability of the opinions of survey respondents, arguing
that many "unstable" patterns of response indicate real attitude change.
There is also a reevaluation of the classic findings on political tolerance,
which measures intolerance, not merely toward left-wing groups, but toward
right-wing groups as well. Another study uses rational choice theory
to explain that when voters are uncertain of the political position of
a candidate, they are likely to vote for the one who will offer the fewest
surprises when elected.

PS 458. POLSBY, NELSON W. Consequences of Party Reform. New York: Oxford
University Press, 1983. 267 pp.
Polsby examines the reforms of the Presidential nomination process that
have taken place since 1968. He argues that many of the most significant
problems of American government and politics today are rooted in the way
we nominate our Presidents and prepare them for office. Polsby specifically examines the reforms undertaken by the Democratic Party to show
how these reforms failed to broaden democratic participation and take
Presidential nominations away from political bosses. (They made elections
less rather than more responsive to majority rule, and more susceptible
to pressure group influence.) Though Polsby defends the role of American
political parties, the reform movements they have undertaken have greatly
diminished their influence in Presidential nomination processes.

PS 459. POLSBY, NELSON W., ed. Reapportionment in the 1970s. Berkeley:
         University of California Press, 1971. 296 pp.
Polsby has assembled a collection of essays on reapportionment--the regular
redrawing of legislative boundaries to take population changes into account
or to reflect changing standards for proper representation. Essays address
the relation of reapportionment to Constitutional law, state legislatures,
Congress, and the philosophical basis of representative government, and
they assess the practical political effects of reapportionment policy.

PS 460. RAINE, ALDEN. Change in the Political Agenda. Beverly Hills,
         Calif.: Sage, 1977. 60 pp.
Raine presents arguments against the supposition that the Presidential
elections of the late 1960s and the early 1970s represented new party
realignment among the American people. To support his position, the author
points toward the events that followed Richard Nixon's reelection: his
resignation, the economic adversity of the early 1970s, and the Democratic
election victories in 1974 and 1976. Raine claims that even if a realignment based on the social issues of the 1960s was well underway in 1972,
it would have to survive the economic issues of the 1970s. Furthermore,
the research documenting realignment has failed to demonstrate conclusively
that voting choices reflected an enduring realignment.

PS 461. RANNEY, AUSTIN. Curing the Mischiefs of Faction: Party Reform
         in America. Berkeley: University of California Press, 1975.
         218 pp.
Ranney reviews the development of the American political parties as institutions. His particular concern is reform, from the abolition of Congressional caucuses as Presidential nominators in 1824 to the radically democratized rules introduced by the Democrats in 1972. In general, such reforms
have sought to eliminate the evils of parties by empowering "the people"
to control them. While not unsympathetic to this goal, Ranney views it
critically, asking not only whether reforms always attain their desired
ends, but whether they have some significant costs. In particular, Ranney
worries that recent reforms might weaken the parties' ability to nominate
candidates who can win.

PS 462. RANNEY, AUSTIN. The Federalization of Presidential Primaries.
         Washington, D.C.: American Enterprise Institute, 1978. 40 pp.
Ranney summarizes the main proposals for federalizing Presidential primaries. These proposals are shown to pose two important constitutional
questions: (1) does Congress have the power to regulate the manner in
which Presidential elections are held; and (2) does whatever power Congress
has to regulate Presidential elections include the power to regulate Presidential primaries? Ranney examines the legality of federalized Presidential primaries; the issues of participation, campaigns and candidates;
and the impact federalization would have on parties. Ranney concludes
with a discussion of the costs and benefits of federalizing Presidential
primaries.

PS 463. RUBIN, RICHARD. Party Dynamics: The Democratic Coalition and
         the Politics of Change. New York: Oxford University Press,
         1976. 203 pp.
Rubin focuses on the growing instability of the Democratic Presidential
coalition. Seeking to explain the decline in the power and consistency
of the majority coalition, he focuses on the developments within the Democratic party since W.W. II, and he analyzes the voting behavior of the
urban groups which once were the source of Democratic power in order to
assess the future of the party. The study shows how major migrations
and demographic changes have weakened the traditional base of support.
Rubin also discusses the internal battles between key factions of the
Democratic party. He then turns to the problems of reconciling the desires

of the electorate and the demands of the party in selecting a Presidential
nominee.

PS 464.   SABATO, LARRY J.   The Rise of Political Consultants: New Ways
          of Winning Elections.   New York: Basic Books, 1981.   376 pp.
Sabato looks at the use of consultants and the growth of new campaign
technology, and doubts that either has been significantly useful to politicians.   He questions the extent to which consultants are committed to
their clients, implying the absence of any political or ideological commitment.   Besides pursuing their own ambitions, the author argues, consultants
have trivialized American politics, emphasizing personality over issues
and exploiting negative themes.   Sabato asserts that consultants have
replaced party leaders in key campaign roles.   He calls for a revitalization of the political party as a check on the unethical activities of
consultants.

PS 465.   SANDOZ, ELLIS and CECIL V. CRABB, Jr., eds.   A Tide of Discontent:
          The 1980 Elections and Their Meaning.   Washington, D.C.: Con-
          gressional Quarterly Press, 1981.   254 pp.
Sandoz and Crabb present articles that consider whether the 1980 elections
were a moment of critical realignment among the electorate.   They begin
with a profile of the 1980 election and a historical overview which places
the election in perspective.   This is followed by a discussion of the
Presidency, the struggle for the House of Representatives, and the capture
of the Senate by the New Right Republicans.   Other articles look at the
changed roles of the parties, the media, and the pressure groups which
influenced the outcome of the election, and discuss the economic and foreign affairs issues which affected the elections.

PS 466.   SCAMMON, RICHARD M. and BEN J. WATTENBERG.   The Real Majority.
          New York: Coward, McCann & Geoghegan, 1970.   347 pp.
Scammon and Wattenberg argue that many candidates in the 1968 election,
particularly, though not exclusively leftist Democrats, ignored the concerns of the "real majority" of Americans: "racial problems, crime . . .
student disruption, pot, pornography, morals, school integration, and
raucous dissent."   Terming this constellation of subjects "the social
issue," they document how it was regarded by the majority of the electorate
(the "unyoung, unpoor, and unblack"), how it was treated by political
candidates in 1968 and 1969, and how it should be exploited by future
seekers of public office.   The authors are more concerned with how politicians can best appeal to the electorate than with how to solve "the
social issue," but they favor a hard-line, law-and-order approach in
general, and claim that most Americans do also.

PS 467.   SHAFFER, WILLIAM R.   Party and Ideology in the United States.
          Washington, D.C.: University Press of America, 1980.   362 pp.
Shaffer makes the case that American political parties offer the electorate
a choice and are different, that Democrats and Republicans are divided
considerably over major issues.   The author evaluates the liberal-
conservative dimension in and between the parties.   He also provides profiles
of ideologically typical Congressmen and Senators to demonstrate the partisanship and ideological differences between Democrats and Republicans.
Schaffer examines party ideology in terms of regional breakdown and state
delegation.   He concludes that as a whole the Democrats tend to be ideologically liberal and the Republicans ideologically conservative.   Shaffer
argues that the absence of successful third party candidates is due, in
part, to the fact that existing parties do offer a choice to the electorate.

PS 468. SILBEY, JOEL, ALLAN C. BOGUE, and WILLIAM H. FLANIGAN, eds. The
History of American Electoral Behavior. Princeton, N.J.: Princeton University Press, 1978. 384 pp.
This volume is a collection of essays that try to show how quantitative
mathematical methods are used to address specific historical problems
of electoral behavior. The contributors address such problems as improving
the conceptualization and classification of electoral patterns, accounting
for electoral outcomes, examining the nature and impact of constraints
on participation, and the relation of electoral behavior to subsequent
public policy. The essays have a broad chronological focus, covering
most of the history of electoral behavior in America.

PS 469. SIMPSON, DICK and GEORGE BEAM. Strategies for Change: How to
Make the American Political Dream Work. Chicago: Swallow Press,
1976. 258 pp.
This book provides suggestions for political action that will lead to
reform. Simpson and Beam argue that governmental and political outcomes
are the result of policy decisions made within structural limits. The
goal of reform-oriented political action should be to gain control of
policy-making positions and to force existing policy-makers or enforcement
officials to make decisions favorable to democratic goals. The book primarily focuses on strategies for affecting electoral politics, administrative politics, and interest-group politics. The authors provide case
studies of successful strategies that have produced reform, and the cases
are analyzed for decisive strategies which might be adopted by others.

PS 470. SORAUF, FRANK. Political Parties in the American System. Boston:
Little, Brown, 1964. 194 pp.
Sorauf asks how the structures and roles of the parties are determined
and how the functioning party relates to the entire political process.
He explores these questions by analyzing and interpreting the nature and
operations of the American political party system. Beginning with an
examination of the functioning roles and structures that define a political
party, he then proceeds to analyze a party system, with special emphasis
on the American two-party system. This is followed by a discussion of
party organizations, issues, incentives, and uses of power. Sorauf concludes with suggestions toward the development of a theory of the political
party.

PS 471. SUNDQUIST, JAMES L. Dynamics of the Party System: Alignment
and Realignment of Political Parties in the United States. Washington, D.C.: Brookings Institution, 1973. 388 pp.
Sundquist's topic is the composition of American parties and the process
of realignment, wherein the coalitions that comprise the parties change.
To that end he traces the history of the American party system, concentrating upon periods of major realignment. He concludes that realignments
are precipitated by the rise of a dominant, polarizing issue or issue
cluster that cuts across existing party lines, rendering the existing
party system incapable of dealing with it.

PS 472. VERBA, SIDNEY and NORMAN NIE. Participation in America: Political
Democracy and Social Equality. New York: Harper & Row, 1972.
428 pp.
This study of political participation examines in great detail the varying
forms of participation available--voting, writing letters to leaders,
forming local political groups, informal persuasion, holding office--as
well as the ways in which different social groups participate. Most importantly, it seeks to assess whether a high level of mass participation
increases the agreement between political leaders and the mass electorate.
The authors produce strong evidence that it does. Leaders are more in
agreement with the general population in communities in which participation

is high, and in those communities they are in closest agreement with citizens who participate the most.

PS 473. WAYNE, STEPHEN. Road to the White House: The Politics of Presidential Elections. New York: St. Martin's Press, 1980. 269 pp.
Wayne offers a discussion of the way in which the political campaign system works. He summarizes the nature of Presidential electoral politics, beginning with examinations of the Electoral College, campaign finance, and the political environment, then moving on to the distinct stages of the Presidential campaign: delegate selections, nominating conventions, and the general election. Wayne also looks at reforms within the nominating process and the purpose of the nominating convention. He addresses the role of the media and the creation of candidate images, and concludes with a look at the Presidency itself.

PS 474. WOLFINGER, RAYMOND E. and STEVEN J. ROSENSTONE. Who Votes? New Haven, Conn.: Yale University Press, 1980. 158 pp.
This book draws on an analysis of survey samples to study individual political behavior. Wolfinger and Rosenstone argue that the motivation of individuals to vote may best be understood in terms of the benefits and costs to the individual. They utilize statistical information and demographic characteristics to measure how individuals voted. They also measure the effects of socio-economic status, age, sex, registration laws, and political issues and political culture on voter turnout. The authors summarize their findings and conclude that education turns out to be the most important variable in raising the probability of voting.

VIII. INTEREST GROUPS AND THE MEDIA

PS 475. BERRY, JEFFREY M. Lobbying for the People. Princeton, N.J.: Princeton University Press, 1977. 329 pp.
Berry addresses the question of how public opinion is aggregated and preferences expressed in the day-to-day political world. Public-interest groups are seen as a means of participating collectively in politics and of influencing public policy outcomes. The study compares public and private interest groups, and argues that public groups are distinguished by the motivational basis of their membership and the internal structure of their organizations. Berry illustrates his thesis by a survey of lobbyists of national public-interest groups in Washington. He examines the development and maintenance of public-interest groups: their resources, the recruitment and background of lobbyists, decision-making structures, and the strategies and tactics of lobbying. He also explains how interest groups communicate with the government.

PS 476. CULHANE, PAUL. Public Lands Politics: Interest Group Influence on the Forest Service and the Bureau of Land Management. Baltimore, Md.: Johns Hopkins University Press, 1981. 398 pp.
Culhane analyzes how local Federal land administrators and groups interested in the management of public lands try to influence national policy decisions. He focuses on the Forest Service and Bureau of Land Management's responsiveness to interest groups. Culhane utilizes a pluralist analysis to measure the effects of interest group pressure. He uses mathematical representation to measure the power, value preferences, and access of the groups involved in the policy process. His research reveals that the demands of interest groups and their anticipated reaction to policy are in fact considered when public policy on land-use is drafted, and that administrators seek to avoid conflict and achieve a more moderate position on conflicting demands.

PS 477. ENLOE, CYNTHIA H. Ethnic Conflict and Political Development.
         Boston: Little, Brown, 1973. 282 pp.
Enloe looks at ethnicity in this comparative study as one of the most
significant planes of political cleavage, and disputes the idea that,
as the nation-state develops, ethnicity attenuates. She suggests that
one explanation for the persistence of ethnic identity is that it meets
primary and communitarian needs. She also shows how ethnic groups function
as political interest groups.

PS 478. FUCHS, LAWRENCE, ed. American Ethnic Politics. New York: Harper
         & Row, 1968. 304 pp.
The essays in this volume discuss the interrelationships between ethnicity
and politics in the U.S. The book begins with an examination of how important ethnicity has become in American politics, and why American politics
has been so important to ethnic groups. It then presents a series of
articles on various ethnic groups and their confrontations with the American polity. Other essays discuss the kinds of issues faced by scholars
and the different methods they employ in their attempt to understand the
interrelationships that exist between ethnicity and politics.

PS 479. GERSON, LOUIS L. The Hyphenate in Recent American Politics and
         Diplomacy. Lawrence: University of Kansas Press, 1964.
         325 pp.
Gerson studies the effect of hyphenates--Americans of foreign origin--
on American foreign policy and on the political system as a whole, suggesting that politicians have cultivated a sort of artificial ethnicity
in their attempt to win votes. The politicians are not alone in their
efforts, however. Gerson also looks at the ethnic representative--the
professional ethnic--who claims to speak for a distinct voting bloc.
His concern lies in what he sees to be the danger of the special affections
of ethnic groups to prudent national decision-making.

PS 480. GLAZER, NATHAN and DANIEL PATRICK MOYNIHAN. Beyond the Melting
         Pot. 1963; Rev. ed. Cambridge, Mass.: Harvard University Press,
         1970. 363 pp.
Glazer and Moynihan study the role of ethnicity in New York City, focusing
on blacks, Puerto Ricans, Jews, Italians, and Irish Americans. They offer
a history of each ethnic community, and argue that understanding ethnicity
is the key to understanding the social, economic, and political life of
the city. They contend that social and economic problems, as well as
political issues, appointments, and strategies are substantially related
to ethnicity. Ethnic groups act and are regarded as distinct interest
groups in New York City politics; the interplay of ethnic, political,
and economic structures sustains the viability of ethnic political cohesion.
Thus, in the view of the authors, the idea of a "melting pot," where groups
are assimilated into American life, is called into question by groups
which retain their identity through generations.

PS 481. GREENSTONE, J. DAVID. Labor in American Politics. 1969; Rev.
         ed. Chicago: University of Chicago Press, 1977. 408 pp.
Greenstone provides a case study of American labor, focusing on the origins
and electoral activities of the leadership of the AFL-CIO. Labor is portrayed as a major force in American electoral politics, particularly within
the Democratic party. Employing original interview data from leaders
in Detroit, Chicago, and Los Angeles, Greenstone arrives at a description
and explanation of labor's electoral politics. He argues that labor is
divided among many groups (outsiders) competing for access to the decision-
makers within the different parties (insiders) but has nonetheless become
an integral part of the Democratic party.

PS 482. HANDLER, EDWARD and JOHN R. MULKERN. Business in Politics: Campaign Strategies of Corporate Political Action Committees. Lexington, Mass.: Heath, 1982. 128 pp.
Handler and Mulkern focus on such activities of corporate PACs as fund-
raising and fund-disbursing. They examine the internal organizational
life of several PACs which were active in the elections of 1978 and 1980.
They also question the degree of influence that PACs exert and the degree
of political cohesion within the business community. The authors discover
that two broad streams of corporate PAC donation emerged in the 1978 and
1980 elections: money was spent either to cultivate access to incumbents,
or it was spent to help bring about change in the political composition
of Congress. However, the authors discover that an internal pluralism
exists also within the business community (demonstrated by variations
in corporate-PAC contributions), and claim that this pluralism limits
corporate political influence.

PS 483 HANNA, MARY T. Catholics and American Politics. Cambridge, Mass.:
Harvard University Press, 1979. 262 pp.
Hanna examines how the churches have become political interest groups
and how religion has become the basis for interest-group activity. She
specifically examines American Catholics as an ethnic interest group.
Hanna examines Catholics both because they comprise one fourth of the
population and because they have provided much of the intellectual and
organizational leadership for the ethnic consciousness and ethnic group
associations in America. The author examines the Catholic political interest group at three levels: the Catholic people as a whole, their institutional Church leaders, and their political leaders.

PS 484. HAYES, MICHAEL T. Lobbyists and Legislators: A Theory of Political Markets. New Brunswick, N.J.: Rutgers University Press,
1981. 200 pp.
This is a study of the role of organized interest groups in the legislative
process. It specifies those legislative circumstances in which interest
groups are important. Hayes advances a typology of policy-making processes
in an effort to identify those areas in which groups play a major role.
Furthermore, he argues for the recognition of the interdependence of legislators and lobbyists which does not underestimate the significance of
either group in the policy process. Hayes shows that the relationship
between legislators and lobbyists is a symbiotic one.

PS 485. HOLTZMAN, ABRAHAM. Interest Groups and Lobbying. New York:
Macmillan, 1966. 154 pp.
Holtzman provides an overview of the structure of American interest groups,
the political environment within which they operate, and their style of
behavior. Interest groups are seen as bringing to the political arena
a diverse set of resources (e.g., lobbying skills, finances, sizeable
membership), which they employ to their advantage in competition with
other interest groups seeking access to decision-makers in the legislative,
judicial, and executive branches of government. Once access is attained,
group representatives attempt to persuade decision-makers to implement
policy favorable to particular group interests. Holtzman explains interest
group strategy and success in terms of group skill in accommodating the
American political structure.

PS 486. LIPSET, SEYMOUR MARTIN, MARTIN A. TROW, and JAMES S. COLEMAN.
Union Democracy: The Internal Politics of the International
Typographical Union. New York: Free Press, 1956. 455 pp.
The authors attempt to test Robert Michels's thesis that voluntary organi-
zations come to be run by oligarchies. They examine the International
Typographical Union, one of the few American labor unions that has a well-
organized set of competing factions which contest all union elections,

and they conclude that the ITU is a result of unusual historical and situational factors. While the ITU demonstrates that it is possible for an interest group to be internally democratic, the analysis of the union does not suggest reforms which would enhance internal democracy in other groups. In this sense, the authors' conclusion is almost as pessimistic as Michels's.

PS 487. LOWE, CARL, ed. New Alignments in American Politics. New York: Wilson, 1980. 216 pp.
These essays examine how special interest groups have come to replace the major parties, traditional coalitions, and well-established voting blocks in American politics. The success of special interest groups is attributed to the erosion of the traditional parties. In turn, the growth of the mass media has filled the vacuum left by the decline of parties, and has become the voters' chief source of political information. The essays examine the political realignments and special interests that emerged in the late 1970s, beginning with an overview which traces the roots of political programs that seek to appeal to these new interest groups.

PS 488. LOWI, THEODORE J. The End of Liberalism: Ideology, Policy, and the Crisis of Public Authority. New York: Norton, 1969. 322 pp.
Lowi undertakes a wide-ranging attack on pluralism, which he characterizes as "interest-group liberalism." This system, Lowi claims, encourages the competitive application of pressures on government by interest groups and assumes that out of the resulting pressure and bargaining, proper policy will result. Lowi examines several areas of policy in the U.S. and charges that pluralism (1) leads to unrealistic expectations about participation; (2) renders government impotent and prevents planning; (3) makes it impossible for government to achieve justice; and (4) undermines formal democracy. Lowi concludes by recommending an alternative called "juridical democracy," a form of government founded on law rather than equilibrium.

PS 489. MALBIN, MARTIN, ed. Parties, Interest Groups, and Campaign Finance Laws. Washington, D.C.: American Enterprise Institute, 1980. 384 pp.
The essays in this collection probe the impact of campaign finance reform on interest groups, political parties, and campaign strategies. The book begins with a look at the efficacy of the campaign finance laws in curbing the power of the "special interests." It also shows how the growth of political action committees is a response to such laws. The book then assesses the effect of the campaign finance laws on political parties, including an analysis of the centralizing and bureaucratizing effects of the 1974 and 1976 laws on national party organizations. The book also provides an historical outline of campaign finance regulations in the U.S.

PS 490. McCONNELL, GRANT. Private Power and American Democracy. New York: Knopf, 1966. 397 pp.
McConnell presents a major critique of American pluralist theory. He argues that a decentralized American society breeds a multitude of small groups maintaining monopolistic control over their respective areas of interest rather than fostering a competitive interaction of interest groups resulting in a stable and nationally representative public policy. Interest groups exercise control over their constituencies and over the public sector by penetrating and manipulating the agencies designed to regulate them. McConnell suggests ways to serve the public and national interests "by correcting for small constituencies, autonomy, self-determination, self-regulation, and decentralization."

PS 491. McQUAID, KIM. Big Business and Presidential Power: From FDR
to Reagan. New York: Morrow, 1982. 383 pp.
McQuaid looks at the patterns of interaction between big business and
the government. He examines foreign and domestic economic policy to draw
out these patterns, arguing that big business is indebted to the institutional alliances it has made with government for its successes in the
20th century. McQuaid concludes with a discussion of the coalition of
economic policy-makers that backed Ronald Reagan—supply-siders, monetar-
ists, and Republican traditionalists. He looks at how these three groups
are battling to influence Reagan, and how they have been responsible for
framing the relationship between Reaganomics and the corporate elite.

PS 492. MILBRATH, LESTER W. The Washington Lobbyists. Chicago: Rand
McNally, 1963. 431 pp.
Milbrath provides an overview of lobbyists and their activities in Washington, D.C. According to Milbrath, lobbying relates only to governmental
decision-making, is motivated by a desire to influence governmental decisions, and implies the presence of an intermediary—the lobbyist—between
citizens and their representatives. Lobbying therefore constitutes a
representative act between private groups and governmental decision-makers.
Employing a communication model, Milbrath outlines Washington lobbyists'
recruitment processes, backgrounds, roles, relationships to groups, and
styles of action. Lobbying is evaluated normatively and in terms of effectiveness.

PS 493. MOE, TERRY M. The Organization of Interests: Incentives and
the Internal Dynamics of Political Interest Groups. Chicago:
University of Chicago Press, 1980. 282 pp.
Moe analyzes the organization of interest groups. He begins by classifying
individual and organizational behavior. He looks at the individual's
decision to join an organization, and assesses organizational formation,
maintenance, and internal politics. He then demonstrates that group goals
in most cases are not the key to group membership, and that economic interest groups appear to rest primarily upon non-political foundations.

PS 494. NOVAK, MICHAEL. Further Reflections on Ethnicity. Middletown,
Penn.: Jednota Press, 1977. 85 pp.
Novak explores the new ethnicity: the movement of self-knowledge among
third and fourth generation Americans. Dealing specifically with how
this phenomenon has arisen among descendants of Southern and Eastern Europeans, Novak presents the new ethnicity as a coming to consciousness of
a new spirit of self-assertion. It is a matter of politics insofar as
it involves an awakening from passivity, and the expression of new responsibilities. The value of this new ethnicity for American society, argues
Novak, lies in how it creates a new cultural pluralism, producing a more
culturally differentiated social policy.

PS 495. NOVAK, MICHAEL. The Rise of the Unmeltable Ethnics: Politics
and Culture in the Seventies. New York: Macmillan, 1972.
321 pp.
This book deals with the new awakening of ethnic consciousness among descendants of Southern and Eastern European immigrants. The desire to reestablish traditional ethnic identities is traced to a desire for a new form
of political assertion. Novak begins with an overview of new ways in
which ethnic identity has been asserted, and of the issues faced by white
ethnic Americans. He then examines the relationships of intellectuals
to this new movement. Novak concludes with a discussion of the political
attitudes and movements that have come about as a result of the new ethnic
identity.

PS 496. ROSE-ACKERMAN, SUSAN. Corruption: A Study in Political Economy.
New York: Academic Press, 1978. 258 pp.
Rose-Ackerman addresses the problem of corruption in the political economy.
She first devotes her attention to legislative corruption, and discusses
such topics as corruption among politicians, and interest group activity.
The second half of the volume deals with the various forms and levels
of bureaucratic corruption. In conclusion, the author argues for a more
synthetic approach to the problem of corruption, and attempts to relate
the different concerns of economics, politics, and morality.

PS 497. ROUCEK, JOSEPH S. and BERNARD EISENBERG, eds. America's Ethnic
Politics. Westport, Conn.: Greenwood Press, 1982. 403 pp.
The essays in this collection synthesize the available information on
the background and trends of the new ethnic awareness in American society
and the political demands made by selected American minorities. The essays
deal with the foreign roots of ethnic minorities, the difficulties faced
in the "melting pot," and the specific conditions leading to ethnic politics. They also deal with ethnic influences in America's local, state,
national, and international affairs. The central concern of the book
is the irony that ethnic politics has assumed increasing importance at
a time when the foreign-born population has declined in numbers.

PS 498. SCHATTSCHNEIDER, E. E. The Semisovereign People: A Realist's
View of American Democracy. New York: Holt, Rinehart & Winston,
1960. 147 pp.
This book is primarily a theoretical analysis about political organization
and the scope of political conflict. The assumption is made throughout
that the nature of political organization depends on the conflicts
exploited in the political system. Schattschneider argues that the key question in a political conflict is whether or not its scope is to be expanded
or contracted. The main strategic considerations of the contestants
involve gauging the scope of conflict advantageous to them, with the weaker
side constantly trying to expand the scope and the stronger side trying
to maintain the scope as it is. From this basic insight, Schattschneider
derives interpretations of how democracy in America has developed, how
political realignments take place, and why non-voting occurs.

PS 499. THUROW, LESTER C. The Zero-Sum Society: Distribution and the
Possibilities of Economic Change. New York: Basic Books, 1980.
230 pp.
Thurow argues that American society has been paralyzed by the responsiveness of government to sectarian interests. There no longer exists any
cumulative consensus by which to forge policy in the public interest
because the political system is unable to confront conflicts with vested
interests. The author proposes that the market system has to be restructured within the framework of international trade and international competition. Government should compensate individuals dislocated by economic
progress, and not firms that go under. Thurow calls for more economic
justice and equality through a restructured economy, one that contains
a "socialized sector" which generates job opportunities for all and has
fewer discrepancies between the highest and lowest-paid workers.

PS 500. TRUMAN, DAVID B. The Governmental Process: Political Interests
and Public Opinion. New York: Knopf, 1951. 544 pp.
Truman presents a theory of politics as a fluid competition among groups—
organized and unorganized—for access to governmental decision-makers.
The book is a contribution to the development of "pluralist" theory, which
sees politics as properly consisting of free competition among a multiplicity of groups—a model of politics which parallels in many ways a
"free market" model of the economy.

PS 501. WEYL, NATHANIEL. The Jew in American Politics. New Rochelle, N.Y.: Arlington House, 1968. 375 pp.
Weyl presents a general survey of the unique role played by Jews in the American political system. He claims this role cannot be explained by using the standard terms of public opinion and voting behavior. For although American Jews tend to be in the middle class and upper-middle class, they also tend to be liberal-to-radical in terms of ideology and voting behavior. The devotion of American Jews to the liberal tradition does not correlate to their economic or educational status. This paradox has deep roots in the religious, economic, and political history of the Jewish people, Weyl maintains, and is the result of their centuries-long fight for equality of opportunity and against persecution.

PS 502. WILSON, GRAHAM K. Interest Groups in the United States. New York: Oxford University Press, 1981. 161 pp.
Wilson argues that interest groups in the U.S., though poorly developed, remain a conspicuous part of the policy-making process, especially with the decline of political parties. He recognizes that there is a trend for interest groups to become more efficient and certainly more effective; they are undergoing a change which is increasing their importance, and which Wilson says reflects a new policy of pluralism. Within the study, the author specifically looks at the agricultural, union, and business interest groups.

PS 503. WILSON, JAMES Q. Political Organizations. New York: Basic Books, 1973. 359 pp.
Wilson calls into question the pluralist assumptions that individuals will act collectively in groups to advance their interests and that groups have greater influence on political decisions than do individuals acting alone. Instead, he asserts that the dynamics of groups is closely linked to the activity of group leaders seeking to maintain and enhance the organization and their position in it. Employing a theoretical perspective based on organization incentives, Wilson studies political parties, labor unions, business associations, and civil rights groups. He treats internal organization processes, the interaction of groups with their environments, and political initiatives.

PS 504. ZEIGLER, L. HARMON and MICHAEL BAER. Lobbying: Interaction and Influence in American State Legislatures. Belmont, Calif.: Wadsworth, 1969. 210 pp.
Zeigler and Baer assess the impact of lobbying in the state legislatures of Oregon, North Carolina, Massachusetts, and Utah. They focus on both legislators and lobbyists, portraying role perceptions, recruitment, and lobbying techniques. They also provide a partial description and explanation of the effectiveness of lobbying.

PS 505. ZEIGLER, L. HARMON and G. WAYNE PEAK. Interest Groups in American Society. Englewood Cliffs, N.J.: Prentice-Hall, 1972. 309 pp.
This study is a survey of interest groups in American society detailing the myriad economic and non-economic groups in society and their role in the electoral, legislative, judicial, and administrative arenas. A brief summary of American pluralist theory is followed by an elaboration of the relationship between American society and its interest groups within the framework of the pluralist tradition.

IX. POLITICAL SOCIALIZATION AND PSYCHOLOGY

PS 506. ADORNO, THEODOR W., BETTY ARON, MARIA HERTZ LEVINSON, and
WILLIAM MORROW. The Authoritarian Personality. New York: Norton,
1950. 990 pp.
This study is an attempt to reveal the authoritarian personality traits
possible within American individuals. Its concern is with the potentially
fascistic individual, one who has a personality structure that makes him
or her particularly susceptible to antidemocratic tendencies. The author
focuses on personality, he argues, because of the necessity for mass cooperation in any fascist movement. After determining that individuals differ
in their susceptibility to antidemocratic tendencies, Adorno tries to
find what potentially fascistic individuals have in common and in what
ways they are susceptible to fascist propaganda. He tries to discover
what part of the population would be immediately ready to accept fascism
in the U.S., and seeks correlations between what a person thinks and the
sociological factors operating in an individual's background.

PS 507. APPLE, MICHAEL, ed. Cultural and Economic Reproduction in Education: Essays on Class, Ideology and the State. Boston:
Routledge & Kegan Paul, 1982. 350 pp.
Apple has collected studies representing radical approaches to educational
analysis. The essays explore the structural roots of domination and exploitation, and demonstrate the role education plays in reproducing not only
these structures but a labor force stratified by gender, class, and race.
In an attempt to address the core problems facing advanced industrial
societies, they examine the role education plays as a state apparatus.
Other essays focus on the cultural reproduction of class relationships
by examining the ideologies found in schools, and the way class and gender
actors respond to and contest the ideological messages those institutions
are presenting.

PS 508. ARONOWITZ, STANLEY. Working Class Hero: A New Strategy for Labor.
New York: Pilgrim Press, 1983. 229 pp.
Aronowitz traces the change in character of the modern American labor
movement, beginning with Samuel Gompers and the founding of the AFL,
through John Lewis and labor's relationship with post-New Deal America.
He discusses the increasing distance between trade union leadership and
rank-and-file membership, and shows how this is a direct result of our
corporate economy, with its technological and professional demands.
Aronowitz argues that as workers have changed so have their grievances;
labor's strategy must change its New Deal orientation and address the
problems that the working class is still facing within the changed technology and skill operations. Aronowitz offers suggestions on how to reorganize labor to fit into the framework of our current political and economic program.

PS 509. BARAN, PAUL and PAUL SWEEZY. Monopoly Capital: An Essay on the
American Economic and Social Order. New York: Monthly Review
Press, 1966. 401 pp.
Baran and Sweezy attempt to analyze systematically the U.S. as a monopoly
capitalist society. They examine the generation and absorption of the
economic surplus--the difference between what a society produces and the
costs of producing it--under the conditions of monopoly Capitalism. The
amount of surplus generated represents the wealth of a nation. Baran
and Sweezy show how business, government, and the military absorb this
surplus and contribute to the concentration and centralization of capital.
Furthermore, they argue, the utilization of this surplus links the economic
foundation of society to its ideological, cultural, and political forms.

They demonstrate that the typical capitalist economic unit is the large-scale enterprise which produces a significant share of the output of an industry and is thus able to control its prices, the volume of its production, and the type and amount of its investments.

PS 510. BELL, DANIEL. The Cultural Contradictions of Capitalism. 1976; Rev. ed. New York: Basic Books, 1978. 301 pp.
Bell argues that capitalist society has made accumulation an end in itself, divorced from the moral values and principles from which the free pursuit of economic activity arose. The contradictions of Capitalism are expressed in antagonistic principles that underlie the technical-economic, political, and cultural structure of society. The economy is concerned with efficiency, policy with equality, and culture with self-realization. Contradictions arise, he argues, as the organizations and norms of the economic realm conflict with the norms of self-realization central to culture. Bell concludes that Capitalism has generated an unrestrained economic impulse and undermined the work ethic, that hedonism has been justified by the culture, and that Western society lacks both a spontaneous willingness to make sacrifices for the public good, and a political philosophy to justify rules governing priorities and allocations.

PS 511. BELL, DANIEL. The End of Ideology: On the Exhaustion of Political Ideas in the Fifties. Glencoe, Ill.: Free Press, 1960. 416 pp.
Bell argues that as industrial societies mature in the post-war period, political conflict between rival ideological systems will be replaced by instrumental arguments which revolve around means instead of ends. The wreckage of the 20th century has provided an object lesson in the dangers of ideological politics. At the same time, the problems that confront modern capitalist societies are increasingly technical ones, and this condition encourages pragmatic politics. Moreover, he concludes that the productive powers of modern economies will generate the technology and the wealth to address these issues successfully.

PS 512. BELL, DANIEL, ed. The Radical Right: The New American Right. Garden City, N.Y.: Doubleday, 1963. 468 pp.
Bell has assembled fourteen articles written between 1955 and 1962 by himself, Richard Hofstadter, David Riesman, Nathan Glazer, Peter Viereck, Talcott Parsons, Alan Westin, Herbert Human, and Seymour Lipset. Stimulated by the phenomenon of McCarthyism, he uses the insights of his colleagues to explain the role of the radical right in American politics. According to Bell, the radical right represents a small minority trying to protect its social and political position in a society that its members perceive to be increasingly hostile toward them. Throughout the volume, a variety of rightist groups are examined in terms of their origins, their diverse activities, and their effect on American society.

PS 513. BENELLO, C. GEORGE and DIMITRIOS ROUSSOPOULOS, eds. The Case for Participatory Democracy: Some Prospects for a Radical Society. New York: Grossman, 1971. 385 pp.
These essays are critical of the pervasive depersonalization of advanced industrial society. They argue that the development of neo-Capitalism has produced institutions exercising a highly centralized social control, and that the self-appointed elites who manage technology make decisions which are political in nature because of their far-reaching influence. The book argues for the introduction of democratic processes into the major organizations of society which are now considered private. It seeks to overturn the elitist and hierarchical nature of the capitalist corporate structure by introducing citizen participation into the workplace and the community.

PS 514. BLUESTONE, BARRY and BENNETT HARRISON. The Deindustrialization
of America: Plant Closings, Community Abandonment and the Dismantling of Basic Industry. New York: Basic Books, 1982.
323 pp.
Bluestone and Harrison argue that the high rate of unemployment, the slug-
gish growth in the domestic economy, and the U.S.'s failure to compete
successfully in the international market can all be traced to the deindustrialization of America. Deindustrialization in this case means a widespread, systematic disinvestment in the nation's basic productive capacity;
capital has been divested from our basic national industries into nonpro-
ductive speculation. The authors assert that the conflict between capital
and community is at the root of deindustrialization, since it destroys
communities and leaves them without space or work. Bluestone and Harrison
conclude with suggestions on how to build a stable community and still
have economic growth, arguing that the exigencies of global competition
and capital mobility foreclose any strategies that rely on individual
corporations to act in the public interest.

PS 515. BOTSCH, ROBERT E. We Shall Not Overcome. Chapel Hill: University
of North Carolina Press, 1981. 237 pp.
Botsch provides an in-depth study of populist sentiment in the American
South. The author interviews fifteen white and black males in the hope
of discovering populist feelings. He discovers, to the contrary, that
there are no stirrings of a populist movement in the South despite the
recognition of class distinctions, the continued economic misery of the
working class, and the passing of race issues. Fatalistic and resigned
individualism, religion, the belief in the attainment of status through
merit, and the continued existence of racial prejudice all stand in the
way of a populist victory. Few of the study's respondents were involved
politically, and these not beyond voting. Those interviewed did not view
politics as a mechanism to right the wrongs of society. The study concludes that an organized, class-based politics is not likely in the South.

PS 516. BOWLES, DAVID GORDON and TOM WEISSKOPF. Beyond the Wasteland:
A Democratic Alternative to Economic Decline. Garden City, N.Y.:
Doubleday, 1983. 465 pp.
The authors reject the argument that American economic difficulties in
the 1970s and 1980s stem from capital shortage, stating that the U.S.
economy is a "slack economy," with huge stocks of available resources
which are being allowed to go to waste rather than being used for investment and growth. The problems facing the U.S. economy are traced to the
costs of maintaining a faltering system of private corporate power, not
to a failure of technique or a dearth of productive machinery. The proposed key to economic recovery is to stop the waste that causes the economy
to fall far short of its productive potential. The authors argue that
the system of private corporate waste cannot be stopped by the intrusion
of government. What they propose is a practical program for a democratic
economy which can sustain a popular mobilization against private corporate
waste.

PS 517. BRAVERMAN, HARRY. Labor and Monopoly Capital: The Degradation
of Work in the Twentieth Century. New York: Monthly Review
Press, 1974. 465 pp.
Braverman examines the development of the processes of production and
labor in capitalist society. He systematically examines the consequences
that particular kinds of technological change characteristic of the monopoly capitalist period have had on the nature of work. Braverman traces
these changes first through the developing relations between labor and
management, focusing especially on the effects that scientific management
have had on the workplace. Then he turns to the scientific-technical
revolution, and its effects on machinery, work, and management. Braverman

next looks at the current status of monopoly capital, and analyzes contemporary occupations and transformation of skills. He argues that, despite the changes in the nature of work, the working class still faces many of the same problems.

PS 518. BRETTON, HENRY L. The Power of Money: A Political-Economic Analysis with Special Emphasis on the American Political System.
         Albany: State University of New York Press, 1980. 418 pp.
Bretton discusses the importance of money as a political force and the dangers it poses to a democracy. He argues that money is not a neutral instrument of exchange, but a means of controlling resources, exercising power, and shaping social relations. His thesis is that monetarized society reveals the incompatibility between Capitalism and substantive democracy. It produces ever-greater wealth and power for the few and more scarcity and hardship for the many, despite democratic trappings. In the first half of the book, Bretton criticizes the economists, political theorists, and social thinkers who, over the centuries, have failed to see the link between money and political power; in the second half he shows how money is used to buy political influence. Political analysis at all stages and in all areas, the author concludes, is inadequate without reference to the centrality of money.

PS 519. BROWN, BERNARD E. Intellectuals and Other Traitors. New York:
         Ark House, 1980. 196 pp.
Brown argues that a sizeable minority of the intellectual class has withdrawn from the democratic consensus, and that they are traitorous because they weaken the democratic politics that offer them autonomy and independence. The intellectuals he refers to are the Marxists and New Leftists of the 1960s who were united by their opposition to the Vietnam war and the feeling of social alienation. (Although these intellectuals lack a highly unified organization, they have established a power base within the universities.) Brown claims that American intellectuals blame social problems such as poverty on the evils of Capitalism. He argues that this is a poverty of perception, that the deprivation of the poor is a result of an abysmal lack of discipline. In Brown's analysis, they lack the motivation to seek work and to acquire the skills that would enable them to function in a modern society. Traditional institutions such as the church, the family, and the schools, he argues, no longer provide such discipline.

PS 520. BURNHAM, DAVID. The Rise of the Computer State. New York: Random
         House, 1983. 273 pp.
Burnham looks at the possible dangers of the growing computer and telecommunications industries and their growing influence over daily life. He examines how the widely acknowledged and heavily advertised ability of the computer to collect, organize, and distribute information enhances the power of information-gathering organizations. He also looks at how the computer, as utilized by the institutions of our society, is affecting our values. Burnham reviews how large organizations are using such systems and how these systems influence what we think, how we behave, and how we make choices.

PS 521. BUTTERFIELD, HERBERT. The Politicization of Society: Essays
         by Herbert Butterfield. Indianapolis, Ind.: Liberty Press,
         1979. 541 pp.
Butterfield's essays deal with the growth of the modern state, its intrusion into civil society, and the significance of this for the individual. In the context of specific subjects such as politics, law, economy, history, ideology, and individual liberty, the essays look at the rapid extension of the authority of the state and its increasing capacity to control, discipline, and subordinate the individual and all types of social insti-

tutions. The fundamental purpose of these essays is to show how the state intrudes on the autonomy of the marketplace, the privacy of the family, and the values of society. Butterfield claims that the state has replaced the church in determining how we should behave.

PS 522. CARSON, CLAYBORNE. In Struggle: SNCC and the Black Awakening.
Cambridge, Mass.: Harvard University Press, 1981. 359 pp.
Carson shows how the Student Nonviolent Coordinating Committee (SNCC) represented a mixture of idealism, spontaneity, and sacrifice, but was also consumed by a burning sense of frustration and a radical disillusion-ment with black and white allies and with American society. He looks at the SNCC's organizational evolution and ideological development through the tactics and strategies used to fight social discrimination in the South. The group originally believed in the use of non-violence and Chris-tian radicalism to fight segregation, spur voter registration, and advance the cause of civil rights. They attempted to educate local leaders and build community-based organizations. Carson shows how, in the North, the Committee met with frustration and failure: the methods successful in the South could not be transplanted to the North. He also details how the development of black nationalism led to a more revolutionary and violent rhetoric, and how this corroded the original aims of the SNCC, and alienated and excluded whites. All this eventually led to violent police suppression and FBI infiltration that destroyed the SNCC.

PS 523. CASTELLS, MANUEL. The Economic Crisis and American Society.
Princeton, N.J.: Princeton University Press, 1980. 285 pp.
Castells attempts to explain the contemporary crisis of advanced Capitalism on a theoretical level that draws on several contemporary neo-Marxist approaches (such as Structuralism and dependency theory), and he then tries to elaborate his theory by applying it to the crisis in the structure of the American political-economic system. He emphasizes the importance of considering the political and ideological dimensions of the problem along with the economic dimension. The theory itself emphasizes factors that affect the profit rate, especially factors that dampen it, such as the increase in the organic composition of capital. In the case of the U.S., Castells argues that attempts by the state and corporations to stimu-late demand have tended to lower productivity in the long run, stimulate inflation, and reduce profits. Castell's examination of corporate and state structures demonstrates the applicability of neo-Marxist theories to advanced industrial society.

PS 524. COCKBURN, ALEXANDER and JAMES RIDGEWAY, eds. Political Ecology.
New York: Times Books, 1979. 421 pp.
The essays in this volume provide information for a general program of political ecology. The book begins with a look at the problems of energy. Essays provide criticism of the oil and nuclear power industries, and recommend alternative energy sources and technologies. The book then examines housing, land, and transport. It discusses the erosion of cities and the rise of the Sunbelt in light of ecological developments. This is followed by discussions on agriculture, health, and technology. The editors set the topics in their historical context, and explore the funda-mental political nature of the topics.

PS 525. CONNELL, R. W. The Child's Construction of Politics. Melbourne,
Australia: Melbourne University Press, 1971. 251 pp.
Connell traces the development of a child's political consciousness from infancy through adolescence. In Part One, he examines the beginning of political consciousness at ages five and six, characterizing this level of thought as "intuitive." Around the age of six or seven, he notes, there develops what he calls a "task pool"; children have a pool of ideas about what public figures do, and when questioned about any one particular

public figure, the children draw their answers more or less randomly from this pool. Around the age of ten or eleven, children begin to develop a more coherent knowledge of hierarchy and of the organization of the political world. They begin to construct the political order, to understand the idea of political power, and to form some realistic notion of formal law. In Part Two of the book, Connell presents transcripts from his interviews with five of his subjects, ranging in age from seven to fifteen. Connell's effort is an attempt to relate Piaget's concepts of cognitive development to the process of political socialization.

PS 526. DeBENEDETTI, CHARLES. The Peace Reform in American History. Bloomington: Indiana University Press, 1980. 245 pp.
DeBenedetti examines organized citizen activism for peace from the Colonial period to the modern day. Peace activism is examined within the context of national and international events, and as it relates to other movements. The author shows how these movements have denounced war and worked for alternative means of resolving conflicts; over the years, the movements have tried to form ideal communities that would serve as working models for the larger society. DeBenedetti illustrates how the peace movements have been an essential part of the American reform tradition.

PS 527. DENNIS, JACK, ed. Socialization to Politics: A Reader. New York: Wiley, 1973. 527 pp.
This reader contains twenty articles on such topics as the development of preadult political learning, the political learning process, the agencies of political socialization, subcultural and cross-national variations in political learning, elite socialization, and problems of methodology in socialization research. Other essays demonstrate that the usually benign imagery of government is less benign among black youngsters than among middle-class whites, and that the high school civics curriculum has little if any impact upon the development of attitudes toward the political system and government, except among black children, upon whom it has some modest impact.

PS 528. DRUCKER, PETER F. Men, Ideas and Politics. New York: Harper & Row, 1971. 278 pp.
Drucker's book is a collection of essays dealing with "political ecology," or the environment of society. The essays range in subject matter from the structural change in the economy in the 1960s, to essays on Henry Ford and Thomas Jefferson, to the counter-culture movement. The author defines political ecology as the understanding that society, polity, and economy, all man's creations, are "natural" to man. Man cannot be understood apart and outside of them. The essays in this volume are concerned with the early diagnosis of fundamental social and economic change; the relationship between thought (economic, political, or social) and actions; the ideas that work in the American tradition; and conditions for effective leadership in the complex structures of industrial society and giant government.

PS 529. DRUCKER, PETER F. Technology, Management and Society. New York: Harper & Row, 1967. 209 pp.
Drucker's intent is to show how technological development revolves around human institutions and organizations. The author criticizes the 19th-century notion that divided man's society into "culture," and "civilization" (which deals with artifacts and things). Instead, he argues that man's personality is tied into the technology he develops for his civilization. Technology also relates to the expression of ideas, aspirations, and values. Drucker's essays deal with technology and its history, management and managers, and the role of the computer in modern culture.

PS 530. FREEDMAN, ANNE and P. E. FREEDMAN. The Psychology of Political
        Control. New York: St. Martin's Press, 1975. 269 pp.
The Freedmans are fervent Skinnerians, and assume that all behavior is
controlled, that man is an animal subject to the laws that govern the
behavior of all other animals, and that behavior is thus environmentally
determined. The text covers in detail the use of positive "aversive"
conditioning (the use of fear to control behavior), how to socialize "good
citizens," what to do in the event of a breakdown in political control,
and how to effect attitude change and resocialization. The Freedmans
draw on cross-national as well as American research and examples, and
espouse the use of operant conditioning to control the behavior of citizens.

PS 531. GREENSTEIN, FRED I. Children and Politics. 1965; Rev. ed. New
        Haven, Conn.: Yale University Press, 1969. 199 pp.
Most adult political attitudes, claims Greenstein, originate between the
ages of nine and thirteen, when children move from near ignorance of political figures and operations to a semblance of political awareness. Most
of the knowledge gained in these years comes through the "civic instruction
which goes on incidental to the normal activities in the family." The
media play a less significant role and formal education almost none at
all. Children of lower socio-economic status tend to be less politically
sophisticated than children from the upper classes, and girls less so
than boys. Greenstein attributes these differences less to educational
factors than to children's perceptions of their respective, appropriate
social roles. He concludes with some proposals for improving the political
socialization of children.

PS 532. GREENSTEIN, FRED I. and MICHAEL LERNER, eds. A Source Book for
        the Study of Personality and Politics. Chicago: Markham, 1971.
        572 pp.
This book is a collection of essays on the literature dealing with personality and politics. All the essays focus on the connections between
personal psychology and political life. The book begins with a look at
general theoretical and methodological statements about personality-and-
politics research. This is followed by sections dealing respectively
with: (1) analysis of individual political actors; (2) typological analysis of classes of political actors; and (3) analysis of how individual
and type aggregates form the complex social processes that comprise politics.

PS 533. GROSS, BERTRAM. Friendly Fascism: The New Face of Power in
        America. New York: Evans, 1980. 410 pp.
Gross examines the tendencies in American democracy that can lead to despo-
tism. He begins with a look at classical Fascism. This is followed by
an examination of rising authoritarianism in corporation-dominated societies, and the possibility of Fascism arising from democratic elections.
Gross argues that the source of this potential fascism is trans-national
growth and the faltering responses to mounting world crises. He looks
at political alternatives that counter the potential for fascism and lead
to stronger democracies. Gross sees true democracy as the decentralization and counter-balancing of power.

PS 534. HIRSCHMAN, ALBERT O. Exit, Voice and Loyalty: Responses to
        Decline in Firms, Organizations, and States. Cambridge, Mass.:
        Harvard University Press, 1970. 162 pp.
Hirschman develops a general theory of how people react to policies and
problems in an association. "Association" here is broadly conceived as
any formal group of people--a family, a political party, a state, and
so on. Members of the association may respond to a problem by "voice"
(working to solve it) or by "exit" (leaving and joining another association
in which the problem does not exist). Their choice will depend on relative
costs, and on the resources available to them to meet these costs.

PS 535. HOROWITZ, IRVING L. Ideology and Utopia in the United States, 1956-1976. New York: Oxford University Press, 1977. 464 pp. Horowitz discusses the movement of American politics into a phase of illegality, mass apathy, and social conflict among ethnic, racial, and interest groups. The essays range from a discussion of the Pentagon Papers to the FBI's domestic activities. Horowitz also discusses the status of various political ideologies, the failure of the working class to look after its political interests, the ideological framework of American social sciences, and the role of government and the state in protecting class interests.

PS 536. HOROWITZ, IRVING L. and SEYMOUR M. LIPSET. Dialogues on American Politics. New York: Oxford University Press, 1978. 194 pp. This book is a discussion between Lipset and Horowitz on American politics. Each represents a different wing and professional force in political sociology. The debate covers issues surrounding the polity, equality, the presidency, and the U.S. role in Third World development. In the process, the authors converse on the nature of ideology in American politics and the American two-party system; the question of affluence and poverty; and the electoral process as a structural entity in American society, over and against the political processes involved in the nominating procedures.

PS 537. JENNINGS, M. KENT and RICHARD NIEMI. The Political Character of Adolescence. Princeton, N.J.: Princeton University Press, 1974. 357 pp. Jennings and Niemi analyze a national survey of high school seniors and their parents. They present a detailed analysis of adolescents' ideas and evaluations of political parties, public policy issues, and citizenship roles. The authors find that the civics curriculum provides mostly redundant information; that high school teachers have little influence on the political opinions of their students, except as they reinforce the values and opinions of the nuclear family; and that parents have the most influence on matters of political party preference and candidate preference, while peers have somewhat more influence on specific issues and matters of political efficacy.

PS 538. KANN, MARK E. The American Left: Failures and Fortunes. New York: Praeger, 1982. 238 pp. Kann examines the present state of the American Left. He begins with a look at its past failures and argues that its lack of political influence lies in the Left's failure to develop strong democratic credentials. He then looks at some contemporary trends that suggest that the American Left is verging on becoming a radical democracy. Kann examines the potential of the democratic Left to reveal the elite's vulnerability to legitimate opposition, and to counter the present dominance of antidemocratic conservative thought. He concludes with his own theory of radical democracy.

PS 539. KANN, MARK E., ed. The Future of American Democracy: Views from the Left. Philadelphia: Temple University Press, 1983. 305 pp. Kann offers a collection of essays which looks first at the challenge to the Left presented by the Reagan administration and the conservative climate of contemporary American society. This section presents essays which discuss how the government is feeding the military-industrial complex at the expense of economic prosperity. Other essays examine the use of science in contemporary American politics, the struggle for democracy within the present conservative environment, and what the future holds for American politics. The last section of the book examines U.S. foreign policy and what the proper democratic response to it should be.

PS 540. KLEHR, HARVEY. Communist Cadre: The Social Background of the
American Party Elite. Stanford, Calif.: Hoover Institution Press,
1978. 141 pp.
Klehr provides a biographical profile of the U.S. Communist Party leadership, especially of those who served on the Central Committee. He examines
the kinds of people that rose to leadership positions in the organization,
then tries to discover what kinds of people were joining the Communist
Party in different periods, and why they left. The author utilizes this
information to argue that a distinction must be made between party members
and the party cadre, and he highlights the differences between the two.
In the course of the discussion, Klehr details the internal dynamics of
the American Communist movement.

PS 541. KNUTSON, JEANNE. The Human Basis of the Polity. Chicago: Aldine,
1972. 360 pp.
Knutson writes from the perspective of humanistic psychology, emphasizing
the need hierarchy proposed by Abraham Maslow, who asserts that all humans
have the same hierarchically arranged needs, and that when lower level
needs are met the higher order needs will become activated. These needs
progress from basic physiological needs to the needs for safety and security, affiliation and love, esteem, and self-actualization or self-
fulfillment. Knutson uses this theory to organize a review of the voluminous literature on the authoritarian personality, dogmatism, manifest anxiety, intolerance of ambiguity, security-insecurity, alienation, and political efficacy. The second half of her book is an attempt to test the political implications of Maslow's need hierarchy.

PS. 542. KOHLBERG, LAWRENCE. Essays on Moral Development: The Philosophy
of Moral Development. New York: Harper & Row, 1981. 441 pp.
This volume applies the idea of justice to moral development and education.
Kohlberg argues that justice, interpreted in a democratic way as equity
or equal respect for all people, is the goal of moral development.
Kohlberg utilizes the cognitive developmental theory of moral psychology
to present a framework for his theory of virtue as justice. He argues
that there are stages of moral reasoning and judgment, that the core of
each stage is an underlying conception of justice, and that at each successive stage people are better at resolving problems of justice. He
applies his theories to problems in humanities, political philosophy and
the philosophy of law, focusing specifically on Supreme Court decisions
dealing with capital punishment and religious observance in school.

PS 543. LANE, ROBERT E. and DAVID O. SEARS. Public Opinion. Englewood
Cliffs, N.J.: Prentice-Hall, 1964. 120 pp.
This book is a survey of the interplay between political science and social
psychology in the study of public opinion. Topics include cognitive balance; the role of family, secondary groups, and political leaders in forming people's opinions; and the problems of rationality, conformity, and
intensity in public opinion.

PS 544. LASSWELL, HAROLD. Power and Personality. New York: Norton,
1948. 262 pp.
Lasswell attempts to delineate the relationship between power—defined
as "relations in which severe deprivations are expected to follow the
breach of a pattern of conduct"—and personality. More specifically,
he addresses the question of whether there are political types—that is,
personalities who seek power, whose inner motivation toward the exercise
of power leads them to careers in politics rather than in business, education, or some other profession. He concludes that there is such a type,
and that the political type, the power seeker, is motivated by a basic
insecurity rooted in a lack of self-esteem.

PS 545. LASSWELL, HAROLD. Psychopathology and Politics. 1930; Rev.
ed. New York: Viking Press, 1960. 319 pp.
The author utilizes psychoanalytic methods to uncover psychopathological
characteristics of major public and historical characters for the purpose
of expanding our knowledge of human nature in politics. Lasswell presents
psychological developmental profiles of different types of public characters in order to find relations between the personal experiences of
people in influential or powerful positions and their specific political
traits and interests. By applying psychoanalysis to politics, the author
provides an examination of personality types and the psychopathologies
of public figures.

PS 546. LIPSET, SEYMOUR MARTIN, ed. Political Man: The Social Basis
of Politics. 1959; Rev. ed. Baltimore, Md.: Johns Hopkins
University Press, 1981. 586 pp.
This book is a collection of essays which deal with democracy as a characteristic of social systems. It begins with a restatement of classic
theories of the sociology of politics. The principal topics discussed
are the conditions necessary for democracy in societies and organizations;
the factors which affect participation in politics, particularly voting
behavior; and the sources of support for values and movements which sustain
or threaten democratic institutions. The revised edition contains two
additional parts by Lipset in which he discusses his concept of ideology
in light of political and social events since the original publication
of the book.

PS 547. LIPSET, SEYMOUR MARTIN, ed. The Third Century: America as a
Post-Industrial Society, Stanford, Calif.: Hoover Institution
Press, 1980. 471 pp.
These essays examine what has happened to different institutions and groups
in post-industrial society, beginning with an essay by the editor on the
future of this society. This is followed by an examination of the demographic changes that are occurring in America. Other essays discuss the
status of religion in America; the present condition of Constitutionalism, Federalism, the judiciary, the Presidency, and the American party
system; the present conditions of the labor movement, Catholics, Jews,
blacks, and women; and the future of the American university and intellectuals. The volume concludes with a look at continuity and change in
the American national character.

PS 548. MARABLE, MANNING. How Capitalism Underdeveloped Black America:
Problems in Race, Political Economy and Society. Boston: South
End Press, 1983. 343 pp.
Marable presents a critique of black American labor. His basic argument
is that the structures of racism and Capitalism have led to the economic
underdevelopment of black Americans. Marable traces the emergence of
the black working class, black poor, and black prisoners to demonstrate
his theory. He then turns to the black elite to explain the contradictory
role of black entrepreneurs, politicians, and educators within this system
of underdevelopment. He concludes with proposals for overcoming patterns
of underdevelopment by arguing for a socialist society.

PS 549. MILLS, C. WRIGHT. The Power Elite. New York: Oxford University
Press, 1956. 423 pp.
Mills develops the thesis that the major political decisions in the U.S.
are dictated by an interlocking elite of corporate managers, political
officials, and military leaders. The power of this elite has been aug-
mented in the modern era by the concentration of the communications media,
which allows the elite to dictate the political agenda to the fragmented
and powerless public. The "major decisions," in Mills's view, concern
questions of war and peace, which are decided without reference to the

interests of the people. Thus, the Cold War is fueled by the interests
of the large corporations and political and military elites. Unlike elites
in other societies, however, Mills argues that the American elite proceeds
without the slightest regard for the welfare of society at large. Thus,
it is both undemocratic and irresponsible. Mills suggests the creation
of a truly professional civil service to counteract this problem.

PS 550. MULLER, EDWARD N. Aggressive Political Participation. Princeton,
      N.J.: Princeton University Press, 1979. 305 pp.
Muller tries to formulate and test a general multivariate theory of individual participation in acts of political aggression, with the intention
of developing an understanding of aggressive political participation that
is applicable to all advanced industrialized democracies. The author
examines aggressive political participation as a form of "strong" collective participation. Fundamentally, Muller's point is to demonstrate the
systematic political character of what is usually considered uncivil behavior.

PS 551. NIMMO, DAN and JAMES E. COMBS. Subliminal Politics: Myths and
      Mythmakers in America. Englewood Cliffs, N.J.: Prentice-Hall,
      1980. 256 pp.
This book explores the assumptions, conceptions, and "myths" people have
about politics and history. It shows the necessity of myth for social
organization and how the accretion of it over time has given Americans
a "usable past" by which to identify and feel proud about themselves and
their country, despite the fact that much myth is contrived. The book
also examines the media, politicians, pop culture, and political scientists
as mythmakers and purveyors of myths. Nimmo and Combs conclude that though
human society cannot live without myths, the commitment to scientific
thought and a less neurotic reliance on myths can assuage certain cultural
problems.

PS 552. NISBET, ROBERT. The Twilight of Authority. New York: Oxford
      University Press, 1975. 287 pp.
Nisbet argues that American institutions are experiencing a process of
decline and erosion, and that there is a vacuum in the moral order—a
degradation of values and a corruption of culture. At the same time,
there is a promotion of military power, and this, Nisbet notes, creates
the spectre of war, since such a society will turn to war when its own
internal problems become too difficult. This thesis is examined as symptomatic of the waning of the historic political community and the twilight
of authority. In his conclusion, Nisbet identifies the essential social
elements for an alternative to the twilight age, arguing for a political
society committed to the concept of citizenship and a government structured
around pluralism.

PS 553. NOVAK, MICHAEL, ed. The Denigration of Capitalism: Six Points
      of View. Washington, D.C.: American Enterprise Institute, 1979.
      64 pp.
The authors of the essays in this collection deal with anti-capitalist
attitudes within the intellectual disciplines. They assert the virtues
of democratic Capitalism, and criticize the theories and practices of
Socialism. The book begins with a discussion of how the moral values
of Capitalism are being subverted by current educational, intellectual,
and especially religious institutions. The authors reassert the morality
of Capitalism as an expression of choice and individual freedom. The
essays also deal with the relation of Christianity to Capitalism and public
policy in the U.S.

PS 554. NOVAK, MICHAEL, et al. The Family: America's Hope. Rockford,
Ill.: Rockford College Institute, 1979. 127 pp.
The essays in this book are based on the belief that the weakening of
family ties, traditions, and rules of conduct poses the greatest single
threat to America's capacity to sustain responsible liberty. The book
begins with an essay on the American family as an embattled institution.
Other essays discuss the significance of the family for childhood and
adult life, and the relation between religion and the family. The book
concludes with an analysis of the status of the family in modern culture
and a discussion of ways to uphold principles of family solidarity.

PS 555. POWERS, THOMAS. The War at Home. New York: Grossman, 1973.
348 pp.
This book is about events during the four-year period from the Tonkin
Gulf incident of 1964 to early 1968. Powers views the events of early
1968 as a turning point, when U.S. policy moved from escalation to disengagement. His thesis is that Johnson was forced into policy changes
by political protests, the rebellion within his own administration, and
the challenges raised by Eugene McCarthy and Robert Kennedy as the result
of a broad-based popular opposition to the war. The opposition brought
the U.S. to a point of profound political crisis in late 1967 and early
1968. Powers examines the public reactions to the war and how the government was forced to reorganize its military policies.

PS 556. PRESTHUS, ROBERT. The Organizational Society. 1962; Rev. ed.
New York: St. Martin's Press, 1978. 323 pp.
In this volume, Presthus addresses the effects that complex organizations
have upon the lives of the people who must work within them. He charts
the growth of bureaucracy and describes its consequences: the development
of a hierarchy, differentiation of tasks, specialized careers within the
organizations, and the rationalization of authority. Presthus maintains
that bureaucratic organization has invaded all spheres of modern life,
so that nearly everyone must adapt to its logic. Whatever ways people
adapt, he suggests that there is an inevitable cost in frustration, anxiety,
or alienation. The logic of large-scale enterprise leads to bureaucratic
organization, but this replaces social bonds with rules and subordinates
the individual's need for autonomy to the requirements of organizational
life.

PS 557. RENSHON, STANLEY. Psychological Needs and Political Behavior.
New York: Free Press, 1974. 300 pp.
The focus of Renshon's study is the origins and political consequences
of the need for personal control. People differ in their need for personal
control, he argues, because they differ in the way their physiological
needs are met in early childhood: if childhood needs are met consistently,
children begin to experience a sense of personal control, whereas if they
are not met, they begin to experience an exaggerated need for personal
control. The factors which influence need for personal control are consistency of rule enforcement by parents and the amount of autonomy allowed
by parents. An exaggerated need for control, Renshon contends, leads
to a lack of faith in government, increased alienation, and a tendency
to blame individuals rather than broader forces for the problems of society.

PS 558. ROELOFS, H. MARK. Ideology and Myth in American Politics: A
Critique of a National Mind. Boston: Little, Brown, 1976.
262 pp.
Roelofs argues that even though it is broadly evident that the American
political system is corrupt and inefficient, Americans never cease to
be shocked by this corruption and always maintain a residual faith in
the system. He attempts to deal with the paradoxes of Americans' governmental behavior by locating in the American "political mind" three dis-

parate sources of myth and ideology in American politics: (1) the bourgeois ideology, (2) the Protestant myth, and (3) rational/professional
mentality. In Roelofs's critique, myth gives meaning to national existence
and endeavor, and ideology gives patterns for political action. He argues
that the discrepancy between myth and ideology is crippling American politics, and that the claims on myth and ideology are not being satisfied.

PS 559. RULE, JAMES and DOUGLAS McADAM. The Politics of Privacy: Planning
         for Personal Data Systems as Powerful Technologies. New York:
         Elsevier, 1980. 212 pp.
Rule and McAdam show how privacy emerged as a political issue with the
development of an advanced industrial society in which complex organizations place a premium on gathering personal information about their clients.
They then offer a critique of the incremental development of Federal privacy protection practices. The authors conclude that further legislation
and procedural reforms are inadequate to safeguard privacy interests in
computerized record systems; they find legal safeguards generally insufficient and dismiss them as concessions toward social convention. The
authors recommend that organizations be less discriminating in their treatment of individuals. This in itself would decrease the demands for personal information and enhance the prospects for personal privacy.

PS 560. SCHLESINGER, ARTHUR M., Jr. The Crisis of Confidence. Boston:
         Houghton Mifflin, 1969. 313 pp.
These essays are a response to the political and social turmoil of the
1960s. Schlesinger argues that these events have created a crisis of
confidence, that Americans are doubtful about the country's capacity to
solve its problems. This crisis of confidence, in Schlesinger's view,
is creating a loss of faith in American values, leaders, and institutions.
The book assesses the problem of violence in American life and in foreign
affairs, including a discussion of the Cold War and Vietnam. The author
concludes by looking at how political institutions have responded to the
crisis of confidence.

PS 561. SCHWARTZ, DAVID and SANDRA SCHWARTZ, eds. New Directions in Politi-
         cal Socialization. New York: Free Press, 1975. 340 pp.
This work is an attempt to develop a political socialization theory which
focuses more on the individual and on different age groups and subcultures
than traditional studies. Groups of essays address the influence of individual characteristics on political socialization, explain the processes
of political socialization (rather than merely describing it as previous
studies have done), and investigate the socialization of such diverse
groups as preschoolers and Vietnam veterans, as well as such socializing
agents as popular music and popular culture.

PS 562. SOWELL, THOMAS. Race and Economics. New York: McKay, 1975.
         276 pp.
Sowell argues that the basic principles of economics can deepen our understanding of race-related social problems. He looks at the effect of racial
discrimination on the market for goods and services and on the factors
of production; how the experiences and reactions of ethnic minorities
worsen or improve their economic situation; and what sorts of markets
are more likely to disregard race. Sowell discusses the historical experiences of ethnic groups, then turns to the economics of race in the market
and in government-directed economic activities. He concludes with a look
at the future of the economics of race.

PS 563. USHER, DAN. The Economic Prerequisite to Democracy. New York:
    Columbia University Press, 1981. 160 pp.
Usher studies how society protects democratic government by entrusting
the economy with the task of assigning income and other advantages. He
argues that it is the normal procedure in economic analysis to rank social
options on the basis of economic efficiency, but that this system does
not consider whether democratic government is made more or less secure
by these rankings. In its place, the author proposes that choices about
the form of economic organization and the analysis of policy issues be
based not on efficiency, but on whether the system of equity is streng-
thened or attenuated. The book examines the role and limitations of welfare government, as well as the formation of economic policy in light
of efficiency, equality, and equity.

PS 564. WILLIAMSON, EDWARD C. American Political Writers, 1801-1973.
    Boston: Twayne, 1981. 190 pp.
This volume examines some of the major American political writers from
Thomas Jefferson to Richard Nixon. The writers range from utopian ideal-
ists to practical realists. Topics emphasized include Jacksonian democracy,
slavery, and the rise of the Republican party. The book also includes
sections on Reconstruction, and on the relationship between political
thought and the rise of industrialism, Populism, and imperialism. Special
emphasis is given to Populist writers because of the effect they had on
the Progressive movement. The modern period deals with the debates between
conservatives and liberals, the civil rights revolt, and the Vietnam war.

PS 565. WILLS, GARRY. Lead Time: A Journalist's Education. Garden City,
    N.Y.: Doubleday, 1983. 389 pp.
Wills presents a collection of magazine articles and essays written during
the 1960s and 1970s that deal with important political events and figures
of those decades, including the Civil Rights movement, Martin Luther King,
Jr., Richard Nixon's role in the Alger Hiss case and his actions during
Watergate, recent Presidential nominating conventions, and most of the
Presidents from Truman to Reagan. Wills also examines the careers of
other prominent politicians of the 1960s and 1970s, and devotes a section
to religion in America.

PS 566. WILSON, WILLIAM J. The Declining Significance of Race: Blacks
    and Changing American Institutions. 1978; Rev. ed. Chicago:
    University of Chicago Press, 1980. 243 pp.
Wilson studies the significance of class in understanding issues of race.
The American preoccupation with race and racial conflict has obscured
fundamental problems that derive from the respective influence of class
and race. He traces the development of black class structure and relates
it to what he perceives to be the declining influence of race in the economic sector from pre-industrial America to the present time. He also
pays particular attention to how the modern welfare state and structural
changes in the economy have displaced racial antagonisms from the economic
to the socio-political realm. Wilson then examines the connection between
social class and different types of protest movements, and the relevance
of black urban power in declining central cities.

PS 567. WOLFE, ALAN. America's Impasse: The Rise and Fall of the Politics
    of Growth. New York: Pantheon Books, 1981. 293 pp.
Wolfe argues that America's impasse is caused by the fact that political
traditions--especially liberalism capable of organizing power in a coherent
way--were sidetracked after W.W. II to ensure that growth could take place
in an unhampered fashion. There was, he claims, a contradiction between
the liberal ideals of the post-W.W. II political system and the promotion
of free business. Wolfe concludes that when the economy stopped growing
the liberal vision was sacrificed, leaving an absence of political structure, and leading ultimately to Reagan's victory.

X. FOREIGN POLICY

PS 568. ABELLERA, JAMES, ROGER P. LaGRIE, and ALBERT C. PIERCE. The FY
1982-86 Defense Program: Issues and Trends. Washington, D.C.:
American Enterprise Institute, 1981. 70 pp.
This book focuses on the five defense spending plans presented by the
Reagan administration in March 1981. It looks at the underlying logic,
assumptions and impacts of defense spending, planning, and procedures.
The analysis has two purposes: (1) to provide a basis for evaluating
Congressional changes in the plan; (2) to provide insights not suggested
in the mainstream analysis of the chronic debate over defense spending.

PS 569. ABSHIRE, DAVID M. and RICHARD V. ALLEN, eds. National Security:
Political, Military, and Economic Strategy in the Decade Ahead.
New York: Praeger, 1963. 1039 pp.
These essays, first presented at a conference sponsored by Georgetown
University's Center for Strategic Studies, bridge the gap between research
in strategic and economic problems. Part one focuses on U.S. foreign
policy toward China and the Soviet Union, as well as Sino-Soviet relations.
This includes an examination of trade policy as well as military policy,
with a special emphasis on how growth affects Sino-Soviet relations.
The following section examines the political requirements for U.S. foreign
policy in Europe and parts of the Third World. Turning to a consideration
of U.S. military and economic strategy around the world, the essays then
pay attention to how the build up of nuclear arms and the arms race affect
this strategy, and how U.S. foreign policy can be linked to U.S. military
policy. The final section contains essays examining the difficulty of
meeting national security needs in the face of rising costs, the problem
of meeting Federal budget requirements, and the growth requirements of
a free economy.

PS 570. ACHESON, DEAN. Present at the Creation: My Years in the State
Department. New York: Norton, 1969. 798 pp.
Acheson gives an account of his professional experiences with the State
Department from 1941-53. These years cover his experiences from Under-
Secretary to Secretary of State under Truman. Acheson provides insight
into the important events of U.S. foreign affairs during his service.
He also discusses the impact which domestic events and foreign policy
had on each other, as in the case of McCarthyism and the Chinese revolution.
Acheson concludes with a retrospective summation.

PS 571. ADLER, SELIG. The Uncertain Giant, 1921-1941; American Foreign
Policy Between the Wars. New York: Macmillan, 1965. 340 pp.
In this survey intended for the nonspecialist, Adler describes American
attitudes toward the rest of the world during the period between the two
World Wars. He focuses on the prevailing isolationist attitude which
developed from the disillusionment with the results of W.W. I and from
American preoccupation with the enjoyment of material comfort. This
resulted in the dilemma as to whether America should ignore the turmoil
which was to become W.W. II or to make an effort to arrest it, causing
Adler to name the U.S. "The Uncertain Giant."

PS 572. ALLISON, GRAHAM T. Essence of Decision: Explaining the Cuban
Missile Crisis. Boston: Little, Brown, 1971. 338 pp.
Allison argues that the literature relevant to foreign policy formulation
can be organized into three categories that correspond to models of policy
formulation. One model is entitled "rational actor" and is based upon
the assumption of many nuclear strategists that nations act as rational
units. A second model, "organizational process," incorporates organiza-

1118

tional theory and asserts that foreign policy actions are largely the result of standard operating procedures. A third model, "bureaucratic politics," views decisions as the result of intra-bureaucracy politics; this model is based upon studies of the U.S. Presidency by Neustadt, Hilsman, and others. Each of these models is applied to evidence from the 1964 Cuban missile crisis.

PS 573. ALLISON, GRAHAM T. and PETER SZANTON. Remaking Foreign Policy: The Organizational Connection. New York: Basic Books, 1976. 238 pp.

This book is a proposal for changing the structures of the U.S. foreign policy apparatus. Clarified by six brief case studies, the argument of the book is that structure matters, that inadequacies of the current structure include a bias toward policy formulation rather than implementation, and that the current structure is more suited to problems of the 1940s than to those of the 1970s. Recommendations include the abolition of the National Security Council, initiation of an "advocacy role" for the State Department, establishment of an "Ex-Cab" for high level review of issues that have domestic and foreign policy significance, creation of Congressional committees of interdependence, and a division of the CIA into a Foreign Assessment Agency and a Special Services operations organization.

PS 574. AMBROSE, STEPHEN E. The Rise to Globalism: American Foreign Policy Since 1938. Baltimore, Md.: Penguin Books, 1971. 352 pp.

Ambrose traces American foreign policy from American reactions to Hitler to the beginnings of the arms race and the Vietnam War, arguing that there has been nothing less than "a revolution in means and methods" in American foreign policy since 1938. The military, whose role was primarily defensive, was transformed in such a way as to become a protector of American hegemony worldwide. Ambrose argues that American attitudes have shifted as well, from a distrust of war to a belief in the necessity of aggressive containment overseas.

PS 575. BALL, DESMOND. Politics and Force Levels: The Strategic Missile Program of the Kennedy Administration. Berkeley: University of California Press, 1980. 322 pp.

Ball's book is a political and strategic analysis of the missile programs undertaken by the Kennedy administration. It covers the period from the "missile gap" to the imposition of a quantitative ceiling on U.S. strategic forces, roughly 1958-65. The focus of the analysis, though, is on the Kennedy-McNamara years. Ball believes the Kennedy missile build-up of this period has not been adequately explained. This study addresses both the theoretical and policy implications of the build-up of strategic forces.

PS 576. BALL, GEORGE W. The Past Has Another Pattern: Memoirs. New York: Norton, 1982. 527 pp.

Ball narrates the events of his life from childhood to the period of the Carter Administration. The author describes his different government projects during W.W. II, including his work on lend-lease. He recounts his research in Germany at the war's end on the effects of Allied bombing, his association with Adlai Stevenson, and his involvement in the politics of the 1950s. He provides accounts of his work on foreign policy in the Kennedy and Johnson administrations, including such matters as the Cuban missile crisis, the Congo War, and policy toward the Third World. Ball discusses the Johnson years with a specific focus on Vietnam, speaking as one of the War's few original highly placed critics.

PS 577. BARNET, RICHARD J. The Alliance: America, Europe, Japan: Makers of the Postwar World. New York: Simon & Schuster, 1983. 511 pp.
Barnet presents an account of the "small circle of politicians, diplomats, industrialists, bankers and generals on three continents who created and shaped the postwar world by building an alliance of North America, Europe and Japan." The book describes the complex and "ingenious" political, military, economic, and cultural relations created under American leadership, and the effects of these relations both on the international system and on the domestic politics of the countries involved. The analysis culminates with the author's interpretations of recent events, which he believes manifest the unraveling of the familiar postwar world and the twilight of the Western alliance.

PS 578. BARNET, RICHARD J. Real Security. New York: Simon & Schuster, 1981. 127 pp.
This book examines U.S. efforts to remain secure from a Soviet nuclear attack from the 1950s to the present. The U.S.'s perceptions of Soviet strength and political will are assessed, and then compared with the current force structure and size of the U.S. arsenal. Trends in U.S. military doctrine since W.W. II are discussed, with emphasis on the adoption of "flexible response," and on the impact of the Vietnam War on the U.S. military. Barnet concludes with an essay concerning the usefulness of arms control, and the sources of American national security.

PS 579. BARNETT, A. DOAK. U.S. Arms Sales: The China-Taiwan Triangle. Washington, D.C.: Brookings Institution, 1982. 70 pp.
Barnett examines U.S. arms sales to Taiwan and to the People's Republic of China (PRC), which have confounded U.S. relations with both countries since 1981. The historical evolution of the present impasse is briefly discussed, followed by an assessment both of the basic points of contention and of policy options available to Washington. The author believes that relations with the PRC will not progress without concessions on arms sales to Taiwan. Barnett argues that U.S. political relations with the PRC should have priority over military agreements, and that the U.S. should place less emphasis on military relations with both Taiwan and the PRC.

PS 580. BARTON, JOHN H. and RYUKICHI IMAI, eds. Arms Control II: A New Approach to International Security. Cambridge, Mass.: Oelgeschlager, Gunn & Hain, 1981. 328 pp.
This collection of essays by American and Japanese scholars examines arms control efforts during the post-W.W. II period in the broader context of U.S.-Asian relations. The authors consider the current ensemble of arms control instruments, including institutions and treaties, in terms of the interests of various geopolitical groups. The study also discusses the obstacles to arms control such as continual technological advances, transfer of armaments technology, and the economics of arms control. Half of the book is devoted to case studies on the implications of arms control for Korea, Southeast Asia, China, and Japan.

PS 581. BERES, LOUIS RENE. Mimicking Sisyphus: America's Countervailing Nuclear Strategy. Lexington, Mass.: Heath, 1983. 142 pp.
Beres undertakes a critical examination of how the U.S. pursues national security by tying it to what he considers the futile acquisition of nuclear weapons. The author provides an assessment of the development of current U.S. nuclear politics, and urges that the U.S. should move immediately from a counterforce strategy to one of minimum deterrence. He also offers suggestions on how to achieve nuclear arms reduction, a comprehensive test ban treaty, a no first-use pledge, and a bilateral nuclear freeze.

PS 582. BERGSTEN, C. FRED. The United States in the World Economy: Selected Papers of C. Fred Bergsten, 1981-82. Lexington, Mass.: Lexington Books, 1983. 245 pp.
Bergsten's essays discuss the many problems and policy conflicts confronting the U.S. since it became heavily dependent on the world economy. The book is an analysis of the U.S. international economic situation in the 1980s. It surveys themes ranging from the relationships of currency, merchandise, and investment of flows, to issues in North-South economic relations. All of the essays conclude with general or specific prescriptions.

PS 583. BERMAN, EDWARD H. The Influence of the Carnegie, Ford, and Rockefeller Foundations on American Foreign Policy: Ideology of Philanthropy. Albany: State University of New York Press, 1983. 227 pp.
As its title indicates, this book describes the considerable impact of three major American philanthropic foundations on decisions affecting American foreign policy. The author contends that the work of the foundations at home and abroad is not exclusively humanitarian; rather foundation programs are designed "to further the foreign policy interests of the United States." Moreover, they serve as "vital cogs in the ideological support system of state capitalism," although these two closely linked functions are seldom overt. The primary thrust of the foundations' contribution to American foreign policy has been in the cultural sphere (particularly in their support for selected universities), where they have "perfected methods whereby their educational and cultural programs would complement the cruder and more overt forms of economic and military imperialism. . . ." Basing his study on extensive research in the foundations' archives, Berman contends that one of the major features of foundation activities abroad has been their "public adherence to democratic principles and their support of a carefully selected and nurtured elite to implement their programs at home and abroad."

PS 584. BERMAN, LARRY. Planning a Tragedy: The Americanization of the War in Vietnam. New York: Norton, 1982. 203 pp.
Berman gives an account of the policy-making process which led to President Johnson's July 1965 decision to fully commit the U.S. military to the conflict in Vietnam. Working from recently declassified documents from the Johnson Library, he depicts the human element in the President's and advisers' vain search for a way of avoiding war. The documents are used to demonstrate how the events of the day shaped and constrained policy choices and flexibility; how individual world-views influence the definition of a situation; how institutional rank can place advisers in unequal advocacy positions; how adviser role definitions can influence advocacy strategy; and how no one decision can be studied in isolation from decisions that preceded it.

PS 585. BERTRAM, CHRISTOPH, ed. The Future of Strategic Deterrence. Hamden, Conn.: Archon Books, 1981. 108 pp.
This collection of essays by American scholars and former government officials assesses the ability of the U.S. to deter a Soviet nuclear attack. Targeting doctrine and force structure are both considered, as are arms control and efforts to prevent horizontal proliferation of nuclear weapons. Various policy options are reviewed, including the counterforce mission against the Soviet Union. The book also investigates the implications of nuclear capabilities in China and the Third World for the U.S.'s strategic doctrine.

PS 586. BETTS, RICHARD K. Soldiers, Statesmen, and Cold War Crises.
         Cambridge, Mass.: Harvard University Press, 1977. 292 pp.
Betts analyzes the influence of the U.S. military on Cold War decision-
making policy. He considers how and why the proportion of military to
civilian influence has varied since 1945; and how that influence has varied
between military departments, commands, and responsibilities. In the
context of numerous case studies, Betts discusses the structure and role
of the Joint Chiefs, organizational doctrine, careerism, professionalism,
and the interaction of policy, strategy, capabilities, and choices.

PS 587. BETTS, RICHARD K., ed. Cruise Missiles and U.S. Policy. Washing-
         ton, D.C.: Brookings Institution, 1982. 61 pp.
In this book, Betts presents a technical discussion of the cruise missile.
He also looks at its cost-effectiveness and its role in the U.S. nuclear
theater and in conventional strategy. Betts also examines the missile's
effect on the politics of defense planning, acquisition, and arms control.

PS 588. BISSELL, RICHARD E. South Africa and the United States: The
         Erosion of an Influence Relationship. New York: Praeger, 1982.
         147 pp.
This book deals with the apparently intractable dilemma South Africa presents for U.S. policy: it is an important ally against the spread of
Communism in southern Africa, yet its racial policies are offensive to
U.S. ideals. The study deals with the strategic, political, economic,
cultural, and moral questions of U.S. policy; it focuses particularly
on the failure of U.S. policy to influence South Africa to take steps
toward the removal of apartheid. Bissell also examines the personalities
and leaders who have been involved in shaping relations between the U.S.
and South Africa.

PS 589. BLACK, LLOYD D. The Strategy of Foreign Aid. Princeton, N.J.:
         Van Nostrand Reinhold, 1968. 176 pp.
Black's study of U.S. foreign aid emphasizes the pragmatic basis of the
policy: that it cannot be separated from foreign policy and national
interests. The major questions Black examines concern what constitutes
foreign aid, what purposes it serves, who receives it, what benefits the
U.S. receives from it, and what the attitudes are of the developing countries toward external assistance. Black also discusses the foreign aid
programs of Western Europe and the "Sino-Soviet Bloc."

PS 590. BLECHMAN, BARRY M. and STEPHEN S. KAPLAN. Force Without War:
         U.S. Armed Forces as a Political Instrument. Washington, D.C.:
         Brookings Institution, 1978. 584 pp.
This study provides a historical record of the U.S.'s use of military
operations to support its diplomacy in the postwar era. The authors focus
on the political incidents in which the military has been used to carry
out foreign policy. Thirty-three incidents are analyzed in order to evaluate the effectiveness of military force as a political instrument. The
authors discover that military operations have been generally successful in stabilizing situations for short-term benefits in long-range diplomatic policies.

PS 591. BRODIE, BERNARD, ed. The Absolute Weapon: Atomic Power and World
         Order. New Haven, Conn.: Yale Institute of International Studies,
         1946. 212 pp.
Brodie presents his prescient analysis of the historic impact of atomic
weapons upon warfare and security. Brodie predicts that the unprecedented
destructive power of these weapons, the relative abundance of the means
for their production, and the fundamental inadequacy of defense against
them will encourage the rapid development of delivery systems and undermine
world security. Arnold Wolfers and Percy E. Corbett discuss the impact

of atomic weapons on U.S.-Soviet relations and international organization. William T. R. Fox examines the prospects for the international control of atomic weapons, and Frederick S. Dunn discusses some human dimensions of life in the nuclear age.

PS 592. **BROWN, HAROLD.** Thinking About National Security: Defense and Foreign Policy in a Dangerous World. Boulder, Colo.: Westview Press, 1983. 288 pp.

Brown presents a broad approach to national security issues, looking at not only military factors, but diplomatic, political, economic, and social factors as well. He undertakes a policy-oriented analysis along functional and geographical lines, assuming an interdependent and tenuous international system. Brown defines the scope of U.S. national security interests in general terms, in relation to the Soviet Union, and in each world region. He discusses the economic, energy, and resource questions surrounding defense spending and various security issues. Brown also addresses defense management, reform, and arms control.

PS 593. **BROWN, HAROLD** and **LYNN E. DAVIS.** Nuclear Arms Control Choices. Boulder, Colo.: Westview Press, 1984. 55 pp.

This essay examines three general approaches to U.S.-Soviet arms control negotiations. It analyzes their impact on the strategic balance, their political viability, and their contributions to U.S. and Soviet objectives. The first option, to extend or modify the SALT II treaty, encompasses the present Soviet-START proposal. A second option entails the significant restructuring of nuclear forces, including as possible components the U.S. START proposal, a missile build-down through the nuclear freeze, and the adoption of single warhead missiles. A third approach argues for an "overall equivalence" of U.S. and Soviet forces at lower levels. The authors discuss the inclusion of British and French forces in the U.S.-Soviet arms talks and the combination of START and theater nuclear force negotiations.

PS 594. **BROWN, SEYOM.** The Faces of Power: Constancy and Change in United States Foreign Policy from Truman to Reagan. New York: Columbia University Press, 1983. 397 pp.

This book focuses on the premises policy-makers have about national interests and purposes, and the ability of the U.S. to realize these interests and purposes. The concept of power as a multifaceted, often elusive entity is central to this study, which asks: What means have leaders considered most appropriate to realize basic national purposes in the international arena? Brown's thesis is that major changes in foreign policy are due more to changes in the premises of power than to changes in the foreign policy goals of nations.

PS 595. **BRZEZINSKI, ZBIGNIEW** and **SAMUEL P. HUNTINGTON.** Political Power: USA/USSR. 1963; Rev. ed. New York: Viking Press, 1964. 461 pp.

This study in comparative Soviet and American politics attempts to integrate recent developments in two normally independent fields. The authors are interested in the similarities and differences, and the strengths and weaknesses of the two systems particularly with regard to the nature and role of political power in each. Among the other topics discussed are the role of ideology for the individual, and the process of leadership recruitment, circulation, and succession in each system. Topics are examined by comparing case studies in both systems: for example, the power struggles of Kennedy and Khrushchev; the crises of civilian authority in the challenges of MacArthur and Zhukov; and the attempt to control the internal affairs of territorial neighbors in the cases of Cuba and Hungary.

PS 596. BULL, HEDLEY. The Control of the Arms Race: Disarmament and
Arms Control in the Missile Age. 1961; Rev. ed. New York:
Praeger, 1965. 235 pp.
Bull discusses the arms race and the means by which it may be controlled.
The author distinguishes between disarmament and arms control. The former
is the reduction of arms, unilateral or multilateral, controlled or uncontrolled; the latter is the international restraint of the arms race.
He then discusses the objectives and conditions of arms control and disarmament, and the prospects for arms control without disarmament. Bull argues
that the core problem of the arms race is not nuclear weapons in themselves,
but the continuous innovation of weapons systems.

PS 597. BUNDY, WILLIAM P., ed. Two Hundred Years of American Foreign
Policy. New York: New York University Press, 1977. 251 pp.
This collection of articles written for the American bicentennial addresses
broad historical themes in U.S. foreign policy. Alistar Buchon writes
on America's role in the European balance of power, John Paton Davies
on America and East Asia. George Kennan discusses U.S.-Soviet relations
since 1917, and Abraham Lowenthal U.S. hegemony in Latin America. Charles
Kindleberger analyzes U.S. foreign economic policy. Felix Gilbert discusses America's ideological roots.

PS 598. BURT, RICHARD, ed. Arms Control and Defense Postures in the 1980s.
Boulder, Colo.: Westview Press, 1982. 230 pp.
These articles stress the need for a complete reassessment of U.S. security
interests and for an arms negotiations strategy that is connected to
defense policy. The authors argue that future arms limitation talks must
allow for an effective unilateral response to new classes of military
problems and technologies. Each contributor addresses a specific area
of arms negotiations, identifies options, outlines potential outcomes,
and discusses whether arms talks actually focus on the right military
issues. An overview of previous U.S. arms limitation strategies is provided. The Soviet approach to integrating national security and arms
control policies is also described.

PS 599. CALLEO, DAVID P. The Imperious Economy. Cambridge, Mass.:
Harvard University Press, 1982. 265 pp.
Calleo presents an economic interpretation of U.S. foreign policy during
the 1960s and 1970s. The author explains the failure of five administrations to achieve the international objectives of U.S. foreign policy.
Calleo argues that U.S. foreign policy during that period was based on
economic interest, and that its failure can be traced to shortcomings
in the economic theory behind that interest. Calleo's analysis tries
to correlate domestic economic issues with foreign policy in order to
challenge the perspective of policy-makers.

PS 600. CALLEO, DAVID P. and BENJAMIN M. ROWLAND. America and the World
Political Economy: Atlantic Dreams and National Realities.
Bloomington: Indiana University Press, 1973. 317 pp.
The authors state that it is difficult for Americans to conceive of international cooperation without also assuming American hegemony. They discuss
the establishment and subsequent decline of U.S. hegemony in the Atlantic,
which was based on liberal trading and monetary systems. Early parts
of the book focus on the political and intellectual roots of U.S. advocacy
of liberal economic ideas, espoused in particular by Cordell Hull, who
saw free trade as a way of promoting international integration. The
authors see the rise and fall of U.S. control in the Atlantic as a result
of U.S. government abuse of the very economic systems it had established.
The inapplicability of "Atlanticist" policies for Japan and the Third
World is discussed. The book argues that regional groupings are appropriate, that our world is unavoidably mercantile, and that hegemonic

efforts to establish a single world economic system ignore political realities.

PS 601. CATUDAL, HONORE. Kennedy and the Berlin Wall Crisis: A Case Study in U.S. Decision-Making. Berlin: Berlin-Verlag, 1980. 358 pp.
This volume recounts the actions of the U.S. and other governments during the events leading to the first blockades of West Berlin. The study shows the State Department was caught by surprise and unprepared when it first learned of the Berlin Wall, even though some sort of East German action to stop the mass exodus from East Berlin had been expected. Furthermore, there was bickering within the U.S. government and between Washington and its allies in the months prior to the construction of the Berlin Wall, resulting in the West's relative paralysis. The crisis was successfully handled only because President Kennedy rose above bureaucratic inertia to take personal command of foreign policy.

PS 602. CHOMSKY, NOAM. Towards a New Cold War: Essays on the Current Crisis and How We Got There. New York: Pantheon Books, 1982. 498 pp.
In this collection of essays on America's role in the international system, Chomsky criticizes the conventional Western approach to international relations in terms of superpower conflict. For Chomsky, loss of hegemony and economic decline confront the Soviet Union as well as the U.S.; what is significant is the decline of the Cold War system which both superpowers have manipulated to control their respective alliance systems. Chomsky addresses a wide range of topics within this highly critical approach, including the role of intellectuals in the state, Indochina, Kissinger's White House Years (PS 703), and Israel and Palestine.

PS 603. CLARKE, DUNCAN L. Politics of Arms Control: The Role and Effectiveness of the U.S. Arms Control and Disarmament Agency. New York: Free Press, 1979. 277 pp.
Clarke discusses the American arms control policy process and the role of the U.S. Arms Control and Disarmament Agency (ACDA). Specifically, he claims that the ACDA, which has legal responsibility for arms control policy under the President, was left out of decision-making on several crucial issues. This circumstance diluted the impact of arms control considerations within the executive branch. The study suggests ways to enhance ACDA's position and to integrate arms control policy more fully with overall U.S. national security policy.

PS 604. CLINE, RAY. World Power Trends and United States Foreign Policy in the 80s. Boulder, Colo.: Westview Press, 1980. 173 pp.
The theme of this book is the relative strength of the world's nations measured in quantitative terms. Cline sets forth this assessment as a guide for military planning in the 1980s. He uses several criteria—including population, territory, economic and military strength, national will—as elements of an equation to compute the "perceived power" of a given nation. Cline provides a number of charts which explain the numerical value he assigns to each state for each attribute.

PS 605. COFFEY, KENNETH J. Strategic Implications of the All-Volunteer Force: The Conventional Defense of Central Europe. Chapel Hill: University of North Carolina Press, 1980. 210 pp.
This book focuses on the evolution and mission of the All-Volunteer Military Force (AVF) in the U.S. and its implications for the defense of Central Europe. The formation of the AVF and its evolution into an army drawn largely from disadvantaged racial minorities are the central concerns of Coffey. However, the book is prefaced with a chapter concerning resistance to the draft during the 1970s and the responses made by the government

in the draft reform measures of the 1970s. Coffey offers some detailed
explanations on the performance of the American military in the absence
of the draft and some possible changes of the defense system. However,
he proposes debate and not criticisms or solutions in this book.

PS 606. COHEN, BERNARD C. The Public's Impact on Foreign Policy. Boston:
         Little, Brown, 1973. 222 pp.
This book focuses on the impact of public opinion on the decision-making
approach to foreign policy analysis in the U.S. While orthodox scholars
have argued that American public opinion imposes constraints on policy-
makers, radical critics believe that public opinion has been manipulated
in support of predetermined policies. Cohen argues that these scholars'
analysis of the relationship of public opinion and foreign policy-making
lacks consideration for the linkage between what the public believes and
how policy-makers behave. Cohen proposes that the best way to discover
the degree of the impact of public opinion on decision-makers is through
interviews. Based on two series of informal interviews with officials
of the State Department, Cohen reports that officials rarely perceive
mass opinion as a constraint. While they welcome favorable public opinion,
they discount unfavorable public reaction. On the other hand, elite
opinion is held as more salient and respected by these officials. In
general, officials regarded opinion digests as a waste of time and money.

PS 607. COHEN, WARREN I. Dean Rusk. Totowa, N.J.: Cooper Square, 1980.
         375 pp.
Cohen offers a study of Dean Rusk's impact on foreign policy, exploring
Rusk's service from his early career to his tenure under Johnson and
Kennedy. He explains Rusk's method of formulating foreign policy and providing advice to these Presidents. Rusk experienced stormy years under
Kennedy--their conflict is presented as one between the mature, reasonable
foreign policy expert and the young, impetuous politician--but had more
positive relations with Johnson. He is depicted as a cautious, thoughtful
adviser who believed that the U.S. needed to honor its international commitments, especially in light of the Communist threat. Unlike his peers,
Rusk felt that attention should be paid equally to developing countries.
Cohen presents Rusk as a professional whose foremost concern was the best
interests of the U.S. at a time (in Rusk's view) of deteriorating U.S.
foreign policy.

PS 608. COLLINS, JOHN M. U.S. Defense Planning: A Critique. Boulder,
         Colo.: Westview Press, 1982. 337 pp.
Collins appraises U.S. national defense planning with five objectives
in mind: to set assessment standards; to study the principles of U.S.
planning; to evaluate the practices of U.S. planning; to identify U.S.
planning problems; and to present optional courses of corrective action.
The author shows how domestic and foreign policy inputs from the White
House, the National Security Council and the State Department affect
defense planning. The detailed discussion, however, focuses on the attempts
of the Office of the Secretary of Defense and the Joint Chiefs of Staff
to produce sound military strategies.

PS 609. CRABB, CECIL V., Jr. and PAT M. HOLT. Invitation to Struggle:
         Congress, the President and Foreign Policy. Washington, D.C.:
         Congressional Quarterly Press, 1980. 234 pp.
This book discusses the role of Congress in foreign policy in the period
following the Vietnam War. It presents a particularly stormy chapter
in the historic rivalry between Congress and the Executive for the control
of foreign policy. Crabb and Holt discuss three issues concerning the
process of policy-making. First, the President's role and the problem
of achieving a coherent, unified policy with Congressional oversight are
discussed. Second, the authors examine Congress and the effect that cer-

tain legislative changes have had on its foreign policy domain. Third,
the role of public opinion and interest groups is examined. The concluding
chapter is a more theoretical discussion of the consequences of these
developments for America's international position.

PS 610. CUMINGS, BRUCE. Child of Conflict: The Korean-American Relation-
           ship, 1943-1953. Seattle: University of Washington Press, 1983.
           335 pp.
This collection of articles studies the historical origins of U.S. involvement in Korea after W.W. II; it relies on recently declassified American
documents from the late 1940s and early 1950s. The essays include an
examination of Korean resistance to the American presence and a study
of the guerrilla war waged prior to 1950. Other articles discuss the
little-known dispute between the State and War Departments over the U.S.
commitment to Korea, and analyze the diplomatic and military history of
this period. The book also includes a bibliographical essay on the
archival literature.

PS 611. CUMINGS, BRUCE. The Origins of the Korean War: Liberation and
           the Emergence of Separate Regimes, 1945-1947. Princeton, N.J.:
           Princeton University Press, 1981. 606 pp.
In this first of a projected two-volume study of the Korean War, Cumings
shows that the roots of the Korean conflict are to be found in the years
1944-47 rather than 1949-50. Indigenous Korean revolutionary nationalism,
not North Korean-inspired or Stalin-inspired Communism, was at work in
producing what was essentially a genuine civil war and a war of national
revolution. Containment of Communism was the guiding force behind U.S.
policy from the start; the U.S. Command in Korea opposed any "deals" with
Stalin, and American assistance in the restoration of native rules, some
of them collaborators with the Japanese, resulted in the 1946 uprising;
this uprising was in turn perceived by American officials as Communist.
The ultimate outcome was the imposition of the South Korean regime and
the final division of the Korean peninsula. Cumings provides examples
of his thesis in close analyses of important Korean provinces.

PS 612. DALLEK, ROBERT. The American Style of Foreign Policy: Cultural
           Politics and Foreign Affairs. New York: Knopf, 1983. 313 pp.
This is a survey of the subjective influences historically affecting U.S.
diplomatic policy. It singles out the moods, climates, symbols, impressions, impulses, and internal tensions within American society that affect
foreign policy. Dallek is struck by how the domestic mood shapes foreign
policy. He does not reject the importance of politics, strategy, or economics, but suggests that a relationship exists between style and substance:
subjective and objective factors must be considered together. Dallek
begins in the 1890s with a narrative of the relation between U.S. social
history and foreign policy and concludes with the Nixon-Kissinger years.

PS 613. DALLEK, ROBERT. Franklin D. Roosevelt and American Foreign Policy
           1932-1945. New York: Oxford University Press, 1979. 657 pp.
This study of Franklin D. Roosevelt's foreign policy begins by describing
the President's cosmopolitan internationalism. Dallek narrates the progress of Roosevelt's Presidency through the stages of nationalism (1933-
34), isolationism (1935-38), and the final evolution from neutrality to
war and broader international foreign policy. Among the topics Dallek
examines are the London Economic Conference of 1933; the Spanish Civil
War; the Quarantine Address; Munich; the Welles Mission; the 1941 Atlantic
Conference; wartime policy with China and Russia; participation of the
U.S. in the War; the Unconditional Surrender Doctrine; the Morgenthau
Plan; and the atomic bomb. The author is particularly intrigued by
Roosevelt's enigmatic, self-contained leadership style. Roosevelt's politi-
cal success is attributed to his ability to integrate realist ends with
idealist means.

PS 614. DALY, JOHN CHARLES, et al. How Should the U.S. Meet Its Military Manpower Needs? Washington, D.C.: American Enterprise Institute for Public Policy Research, 1980. 36 pp.
This is the text of a debate between three members of Congress and a Secretary of Defense on the merits of military conscription. Issues discussed include the strategic needs of the U.S., and Congressional and popular support for a return to the military draft. The relative effectiveness of the All-Volunteer Force and the difficulties of training and retaining draftees are also assessed.

PS 615. DE SANTIS, HUGH. The Diplomacy of Silence: The American Foreign Service, the Soviet Union and the Cold War, 1933-1947. Chicago: University of Chicago Press, 1979. 270 pp.
De Santis presents an alternative theory on the origins of the Cold War, based upon a survey of U.S. career diplomats serving in Eastern Europe and the Soviet Union from 1944 to 1946. It is intended as a response to the ideological, political or economic explanations based on deterministic ideas. The author offers a humanistic and contingent thesis, which focuses on the culturally determined professional views of foreign service officials. He looks beyond the views of Kennan and Bohlen to discover neither monolithic conciliation nor hostility, but considerable vacillation toward the U.S.S.R. within the distinct schools of thought.

PS 616. DESTLER, I. M. Making Foreign Economic Policy. Washington, D.C.: Brookings Institution, 1980. 244 pp.
This study focuses on two primary objectives related to policy-making processes in the U.S.: (1) it attempts to analyze the role of government, private organizations, and individuals in formulating the processes of U.S. foreign policy-making toward trade and food; and (2) it tries to determine whether organizational changes are necessary for the improvement of U.S. foreign economic policy-making. Destler concludes that in considering domestic and international economic affairs, more attention should be given to overseas economic policy-making.

PS 617. DESTLER, I. M. Presidents, Bureaucrats and Foreign Policy: The Politics of Organizational Reform. Princeton, N.J.: Princeton University Press, 1972. 329 pp.
In this book Destler considers the irrationality of government policy-making and possible ways to treat the problem. His interest is primarily in the coordination of government action in foreign policy. He is less concerned with particular policies than with the process of policy development. Destler discusses the implications of bureaucratic organization by looking at different strategies of foreign policy decision-making under Kennedy, Johnson, and Nixon; the continuing difficulties between the Department of State and the President; and the changing nature and use of bureaucratic staffs. He offers organizational strategies and approaches to facilitate coherent policy-making.

PS 618. DINERSTEIN, HERBERT S. The Making of the Missile Crisis: October 1962. Baltimore, Md.: Johns Hopkins University Press, 1976. 302 pp.
Through the use of commentary from the Soviet state-controlled press, Dinerstein presents the story of the Cuban Missile Crisis from the Soviet perspective. The 1954 CIA-sponsored coup in Guatemala taught the Soviets that the U.S. would not permit independent, anti-American governments to be established in the Western hemisphere. Khrushchev nevertheless supported Castro, in part due to his desire to retain revolutionary leadership in the world, a claim being rivalled by the bellicose Chinese Communist regime. The failure of the Bay of Pigs invasion in April 1961 led Khrushchev to conclude that the introduction of Russian missiles into Cuba would be tolerated and could advance the Soviet position. The Kennedy Administration's reaction was therefore a surprise to the Soviets.

PS 619. DISKIN, MARTIN, ed. Trouble in Our Backyard: Central America
         and the United States in the Eighties. New York: Pantheon Books,
         1983. 269 pp.
This collection of critical essays deals with U.S. foreign policy reaction
to the contemporary political and social upheavals in Central America.
It begins by establishing the historical background of U.S. involvement
in the region, emphasizing U.S. military support of right-wing governments.
All the essays examine U.S. foreign policy in light of its failure to
address the specific causes of social upheaval. The authors criticize
the tendency of U.S. foreign policy to blame the Soviet Union as the source
of troubles in the region. Besides considering U.S. relations under Reagan
with Nicaragua, El Salvador, Guatemala, and Honduras, the book has essays
on the role of the Roman Catholic Church in the region.

PS 620. DIVINE, ROBERT A. Blowing in the Wind: The Nuclear Test-Ban
         Debate 1954-1960. New York: Oxford University Press, 1978.
         393 pp.
This book examines the development of a public consensus for a ban on
nuclear weapons testing in the U.S. from 1954-60. Early tests, including
the Bravo and Castle detonations, are examined in order to demonstrate
the attitude of the U.S. government toward testing. Divine then examines
Atomic Energy Commission hearings, the U.S. Congress, and the 1956 presidential election to show how the danger of nuclear fallout became a political issue. The impact of SANE (Safe Alternatives to Nuclear Energy),
Linus Pauling, and relations with the NATO allies are also considered.

PS 621. DIVINE, ROBERT A. Eisenhower and the Cold War. New York: Oxford
         University Press, 1981. 181 pp.
Divine presents a sympathetic view of Eisenhower which differs from the
traditional evaluation of his administration by scholars. He sees
Eisenhower as an exception to the normal pattern of U.S. presidents who bring
to office domestic political expertise and little foreign policy experience.
Eisenhower succeeded in ending the Korean War and in maneuvering through
Cold War crises with both a sense of national legitimacy and an astute
appreciation of power. Divine does not attempt a systematic account,
but an anecdotal narrative of prominent events from Korea through the
U-2 incident in order to demonstrate Eisenhower's skill and purposive-
ness.

PS 622. DIVINE, ROBERT A. The Illusion of Neutrality. Chicago: Univer-
         sity of Chicago Press, 1962. 370 pp.
Divine provides a historical narrative of the isolationist movement which
became a dominant political force in the second half of the 1930s. Prior
to the Depression, the U.S. had maintained an international role, as the
Washington Conference and the Kellogg-Briand Pact suggest. The Depression,
however, catalyzed isolationism while Japanese conquests of China and
Hitler's rise intensified it. Divine focuses on neutrality legislation
of the 1930s, from its origins in events of the 1920s to its decisive
revision in 1939. The author also studies the debates between isolation-
ists and their opponents over how best to prevent American involvement
in a future conflict.

PS 623. DIVINE, ROBERT A., ed. Exploring the Johnson Years. Austin:
         University of Texas Press, 1981. 280 pp.
This is the first investigation of the presidency of Lyndon B. Johnson
based on the materials available at the Lyndon B. Johnson Library. A
collection of essays on the conduct of both foreign and domestic policies
during the Johnson Administration, this report contains reviews and analysis of issues such as foreign policy--specifically toward Vietnam and
Latin America--domestic reform movements--Civil Rights, the War on Poverty,
education--and Johnson's relationship with the media. The book is prefaced

with a survey of available resource material, both published and unpublished, in the holdings of the Johnson Library.

PS 624. DONOVAN, ROBERT J. Conflict and Crisis: The Presidency of Harry S. Truman, 1945-1948. New York: Norton, 1977. 473 pp.
Donovan's biographical study of Truman's first three years in the White House begins by detailing the immediate problems faced by the new administration: the smooth transition of power, the decision to drop the atomic bomb, and the Potsdam Conference. Donovan then discusses the postwar years, chronicling such events as the Hurley Affair, Harold Ickes's resignation, and the firing of Henry Wallace. Part III details the beginning of the Cold War, and Part IV takes the reader up to the 1948 campaign and Truman's re-election.

PS 625. DONOVAN, ROBERT J. The Tumultuous Years: The Presidency of Harry S. Truman, 1949-1953. New York: Norton, 1982. 444 pp.
This book is the second of Donovan's two-part study of the embattled Truman Presidency. It starts with Truman's startling 1948 election victory and recounts the political events of his second administration: the North Atlantic Treaty, the "loss of China," the H-Bomb decision, NSC-68, McCarthyism, and the MacArthur problem. Particular emphasis is placed on Truman's conduct of the Korean War. The book concludes by considering the meaning of the end of twenty years of Democratic presidential leadership with the election of Eisenhower.

PS 626. DRAPER, THEODORE. Present History. New York: Random House, 1983. 458 pp.
Draper presents a collection of articles and essays written over a ten-year period. He analyzes present-day events in an historical context and offers political commentary. The book begins with an article and an exchange with Caspar Weinberger over nuclear war. These are followed by articles reviewing the Western European alliance and the U.S. role in Europe's security system. The author then looks at Vietnam, the diplomacy of Henry Kissinger, and the Arab-Israeli War. The last part of the book deals with theories of the neo-conservatives and the role of intellectuals in politics.

PS 627. DULLES, FOSTER RHEA. America's Rise to World Power, 1898-1954. New York: Harper & Row, 1955. 314 pp.
Dulles provides a narrative synthesis of U.S. foreign policy from the Spanish-American War to the Eisenhower Administration that includes analyses of the effects of diplomacy itself, public opinion, political and economic factors, and U.S. policy decision-making. The fundamental conflict over policy in these years, Dulles argues, was between those attempting to retain an isolationist stance and those who felt that the growth of the U.S. demanded that it assume new responsibilities abroad.

PS 628. ELLIOTT, MARK. Pawns of Yalta: Soviet Refugees and America's Role in Their Repatriation. Urbana: University of Illinois Press, 1982. 287 pp.
Elliott discusses the reluctance of Russian prisoners to return to the Soviet Union at the end of W.W. II. The Soviets, motivated by a desire to punish Nazi collaborators, to corroborate propaganda regarding Party solidarity, and to replenish depleted populations, demanded the immediate return of all displaced persons and POWs. Americans, ignorant of the reasons for the prisoners' reluctance to return (some committed suicide to avoid repatriation) and eager to please the Soviet Union, initially tried to return expatriates as quickly as possible. Too late, deteriorating U.S.-Soviet relations caused the U.S. to reverse its policy on forced repatriation. Elliott compares American treatment of Soviet expatriates to the hostility and filth encountered by American POWs at the hands of

the liberating Red Army. He criticizes American diplomats at Yalta for
making inadequate provision for reciprocal cooperation in the returning
of POWs. The later chapters examine the reception of repatriated Russians
by the Soviet Union, the subsequent history of Soviet attitudes toward
their repatriates (a gradual repudiation of Stalin), and the relation
of the repatriation episode to the emerging Cold War.

PS 629. ELLIS, LEWIS ETHAN. Republican Foreign Policy, 1921-1933. New
        Brunswick, N.J.: Rutgers University Press, 1968. 404 pp.
Ellis studies the impact of public opinion on the formulation of policy
toward Europe, Latin America, and Asia. He believes that U.S. leaders
involved in foreign affairs were uneasy and finally unwilling to make
strong commitments to overseas action; the Kellogg-Briand peace pact is,
for Ellis, a perfect example of the divided mind of U.S. policy-makers.
Ellis also examines how Hoover and Stimson established the groundwork
for the 1930s "good neighbor" policy toward Latin America.

PS 630. ENTHOVEN, ALAIN C. and K. WAYNE SMITH. How Much Is Enough? Shap-
        ing the Defense Program, 1961-1969. New York: Harper & Row,
        1971. 364 pp.
In the atmosphere of virulent debate over defense spending which began
to emerge in the waning years of the Vietnam War, Enthoven and Smith review
the 1960s defense programs of Secretary of Defense Robert McNamara in
an effort to determine what the powers of the Defense Secretary should
be and to develop a means of analyzing national security requirements.
Their concern is with "the process of planning military strategy, forces,
and budgets," rather than with military operations during the period.
Through a detailed statistical analysis of various fields of U.S., NATO,
and Soviet military capabilities, they highlight some of the fortuitous
decisions and major debacles of 1960s military planning. Enthoven and
Smith, former Defense Department officials, favor a balance between civilian and military personnel in military development, with the Defense Secretary holding the most authority.

PS 631. ETHERIDGE, LLOYD. A World of Men. Cambridge, Mass.: MIT Press,
        1978. 178 pp.
Etheridge investigates the impact of the individual on the making of U.S.
foreign policy, taking a psychological approach to his subject. He
describes the role of personality, emotional syndromes, and the need for
self-expression in the behavior of upper- and middle-level bureaucrats.
The book quantifies the statistics which represent this behavior in an
attempt to ascribe a coherent pattern to the causes of misperceptions
and mistakes which plague the conduct of foreign affairs in the U.S.

PS 632. ETZIONI, MINERVA. The Majority of One: Towards a Theory of
        Regional Compatibility. Beverly Hills, Calif.: Sage, 1970.
        238 pp.
This book examines the Organization of American States (OAS) in the wider
context of world order, with specific reference to the U.N. Etzioni
approaches the U.N.-OAS relationship as a matter of constitutional, organizational, and diplomatic history. She demonstrates the extent to which
U.S. diplomacy, by using OAS to endorse its own policies in the region,
has undermined the expectations of the organization's charter. The author
uses this study to illustrate what she calls "incompatible regionalism"
in the U.N.-OAS relationship.

PS 633. FALLOWS, JAMES. National Defense. New York: Random House, 1981.
        204 pp.
This book deals with the long-range issues confronting national defense,
specifically with such factors as the size, purpose, and composition of
military forces. Fallows discusses the restoration of the military draft,

the role of high technology, methods of evaluating and promoting officers, methods of weapons acquisition, and defense contracting. Three themes run throughout the author's discussion: the danger of theory obscuring practical considerations in defense-related discussion; the qualitative difference between war, the planning of war, and other forms of human activity; and a belief that the fundamental problems in this field cannot be solved simply through increased military spending.

PS 634. FEINBERG, RICHARD E. The Intemperate Zone: The Third World Challenge to U.S. Foreign Policy. New York: Norton, 1983. 287 pp.
Feinberg outlines the problems posed by the Third World for U.S. foreign policy in the 1980s. He then tries to construct appropriate policy guidelines for dealing with these problems. He adopts "Neorealism" as a philosophical approach which directs foreign policy toward defending American vital interests. Neorealism seeks to take into account the increasing difficulty governments have in controlling the range of private and organizational actors, especially in the Third World. The author, a member of the State Department Policy Planning Staff under Carter, applies his thesis of Neorealism to economic issues and to Soviet competition with the U.S. in the Third World.

PS 635. FEIS, HERBERT. The Atomic Bomb and the End of World War II.
Princeton, N.J.: Princeton University Press, 1966. 213 pp.
Originally published in 1961 as Japan Subdued: The Atomic Bomb and the End of the War in the Pacific, Feis's book explores the role of the atomic bomb in ending W.W. II. Feis argues that the bomb was necessary to obtain a prompt end to the war. In the process, he recounts the discussion within the U.S. government over the use of the bomb, considers whether an earlier opportunity to end the war had been missed, and discusses those who wanted Russia to enter the war.

PS 636. FEIS, HERBERT. Between War and Peace: The Potsdam Conference.
Princeton, N.J.: Princeton University Press, 1960. 367 pp.
In this study of the Potsdam Conference, Feis examines the complex issues between Russia and the Western powers that came with victory over Germany, including the Polish question; the multiple Germany question; the position of France, Italy, the Near East, Iran, and Spain; the transfer of German satellites to similar status in the Soviet Union; and the creation of a new alliance of nations. For the West, the fear of Soviet Communist domination of Europe overshadowed the fear of defeated Germany during the conference.

PS 637. FEIS, HERBERT. The China Tangle: The American Effort in China from Pearl Harbor to the Marshall Mission. New York: Atheneum, 1966. 445 pp.
Feis evaluates the American government's response to China during W.W. II and during the critical period of peace-making. Part one focuses on the American effort to sustain Chinese resistance and gives way to a fuller analysis of the factors that determined China's future in the Pacific. In particular, Feis considers internal forces—including the interaction between the Chinese government and the Chinese Communists—and external forces embodied in the diplomatic discussions concerning the role of the United Nations in the Pacific. As the author explains, the Chinese were basically involved in a civil war in which "American diplomacy and military planning got entangled, stumbled; and we failed in our attempt to shape the vast country of China into the image of our desires."

PS 638. FEIS, HERBERT. The Road to Pearl Harbor: The Coming of the War Between the United States and Japan. Princeton, N.J.: Princeton University Press, 1950. 356 pp.
Beginning his account in 1937, Feis sifts through the origins of the conflict between the U.S. and Japan, examining the diplomatic maneuverings that steered the two nations into war. He studies the actions of such figures as Cordell Hull, Kichisaburo Nomura, Yosuke Matsuoka, Funimar Konoye, and Roosevelt and Churchill. He discusses the complex negotiations and failed attempts to maintain peace during the years before the bombing of Pearl Harbor.

PS 639. FERRELL, ROBERT H. American Diplomacy in the Great Depression: Hoover-Stimson Foreign Policy, 1929-1933. New Haven, Conn.: Yale University Press, 1957. 319 pp.
Ferrell discusses U.S. foreign policy from the Wall Street Crash to the advent of the New Deal. He focuses on Herbert Hoover and Secretary of State Stimson, and examines the Kellogg-Briand pact, the problem of war debts, and the emergence of the "Stimson Doctrine" in response to the Japanese invasion of Manchuria. Changes in Latin American policy and the conflict between isolationism and Wilsonian internationalism are also discussed in depth. Ferrell concludes his study with an investigation of the interaction between the economic chaos of the Depression years and the role of force in foreign policy.

PS 640. FITZGERALD, FRANCES. Fire in the Lake: The Vietnamese and the Americans in Viet Nam. Boston: Little, Brown, 1972. 491 pp.
Fitzgerald surveys the impact of Americans and the war on the people of Vietnam. The primary focus of the work is the role of the U.S. government in Southeast Asia since 1954; Fitzgerald's major theme is that practically everything America did in Vietnam was wrong in both theory and execution. She provides an account of Vietnamese society and culture, using both psychological and anthropological methods, to argue for the primacy of the Vietnamese village over a national state and of social unanimity over pluralism.

PS 641. FRANCK, THOMAS M. and EDWARD WEISBAND. Foreign Policy and Congress. New York: Oxford University Press, 1979. 357 pp.
The authors argue that the Vietnam War led to a revolutionary redistribution of power within the U.S. government, with Congress gaining new controls over foreign policy. They consider how Congress has reasserted control over war powers and established its right to oversee military aid, human rights conduct, nuclear export policy and the intelligence community. In addition, the authors look at the ability of Congress to distinguish national interests from special interests; Congressional methods of leadership and expertise; and the prospects for establishing a foreign policy consensus through Congressional leadership.

PS 642. FREEDMAN, LAWRENCE. U.S. Intelligence and the Soviet Strategic Threat. Boulder, Colo.: Westview Press, 1977. 235 pp.
Freedman studies the development of the ways in which the U.S. intelligence services estimate Soviet strategic forces. He observes that the content and quality of estimates often depend on political arrangements within the intelligence community and between the intelligence services and the defense establishment. The book studies the major intelligence debates of the 1940s and 1950s, particularly the "missile gap" scare of the late 1950s. These are then compared to the debates of the 1960s and 1970s, which were based on improved methods of intelligence gathering and centered on the issue of ICBM's vulnerability. The relationship between the U.S. assessment of Soviet forces and U.S. strategic force policy is also discussed.

PS 643. FREEDMAN, LAWRENCE, ed. The Troubled Alliance: Atlantic Relations
in the 1980s. New York: St. Martin's Press, 1983. 170 pp.
Freedman has collected essays that debate the nature of the alliance
between the U.S. and Western Europe. The essays cover a range of public
issues, including security, trade, and monetary policy. In the process,
they also emphasize the history of the problems this alliance has faced
and the different national perspectives brought to it. Freedman focuses
on the fundamental questions implicit in the discussions, which include
the future of the alliance, its competence in dealing with policy problems,
and alternative patterns of relationship between the U.S. and the European
nations.

PS 644. FREELAND, RICHARD M. The Truman Doctrine and the Origins of
McCarthyism: Foreign Policy, Domestic Politics, and Internal
Security, 1946-1948. New York: Knopf, 1972. 419 pp.
Freeland advances a broad thesis on the origins of McCarthyism which seeks
to explain the intensity of anti-Communist emotions in America. He discusses the events which preceded McCarthy and led to the growth of anti-
Communism: the Soviet Union's explosion of an atomic weapon, Mao's successful conquest of China in 1949, the Alger Hiss case, and the invasion of
South Korea in 1950. However, Freeland argues that the essential force
behind McCarthyism and the Cold War consensus was the Truman administration's effort to mobilize support for the Marshall Plan in 1947-48.

PS 645. GADDIS, JOHN L. Strategies of Containment: A Critical Appraisal
of Post-War National Security Policy. New York: Oxford University Press, 1982. 432 pp.
Gaddis analyzes U.S. policy toward the Soviet Union since W.W. II. Policy
failures are attributed to the inability to devise strategies which effectively coordinated political means and ends. Gaddis divides the strategic
approaches which have characterized U.S. diplomatic history into five
periods: 1947-49, which saw Kennan's original formulation pursued prior
to NSC-68; 1950-53, which was dominated by the Korean War; 1953-61, the
period of Eisenhower's "New Look"; 1961-69, when "Flexible Response" became
the policy; and the detente era of 1969-79, which was terminated by the
Soviet invasion of Afghanistan.

PS 646. GADDIS, JOHN L. The United States and the Origins of the Cold
War, 1941-1947. New York: Columbia University Press, 1972.
396 pp.
Gaddis presents an analysis of the evolution of U.S. policy toward the
Soviet Union from 1941-47. He conceives of foreign policy as a product
of both internal and external influences and seeks to address a wide range
of factors affecting policy. But his central theme is the narrow range
of realistic alternatives available to American policy-makers. He discusses America's vision of a post-War world and the American belief that
the purpose of war was to secure a particular type of peace, not merely
to defeat an enemy. Gaddis concludes with a look at the changes that
took place in foreign policy under Truman.

PS 647. GANSLER, JACQUES. The Defense Industry. Cambridge, Mass.: MIT
Press, 1980. 346 pp.
This book investigates the U.S. defense industry, especially during the
post-Vietnam era. It explores this major sector of the American economy
from both an economic and a strategic perspective. The study concludes
that the industrial base of the defense industry is becoming economically
inefficient and unresponsive to a potential strategic emergency. The
specific factors that Gansler believes will result in a weakening of U.S.
security are identified and quantified. The book then offers explicit
policy proposals aimed at improving U.S. security.

PS 648. GATI, CHARLES, ed. Caging the Bear: Containment and the Cold
         War. New York: Bobbs-Merrill, 1974. 228 pp.
Gati has collected a number of documents and articles on the history of
the Cold War. In the introduction, he provides an overview of the concept
of containment in the Cold War era. The volume includes the 1947 "Truman
Doctrine" address (in which Truman promulgated containment while requesting
military aid for Greece and Turkey); and George Kennan's "X" and "Mr.
X" articles, along with Kennan's more recent views on containment. Also
included are articles by J. William Fulbright, William Zimmerman, Donald
Zagoria, John Spanier, Zbigniew Brzezinski, Marshall Shulman, and a bibliographical essay by Toby Trister.

PS 649. GATZKE, HANS W. Germany and the United States: A "Special Rela-
         tionship?" Cambridge, Mass.: Harvard University Press, 1980.
         314 pp.
Gatzke's treatment of 200 years of U.S.-German relations focuses on the
post-W.W. II era. His premise is that three components must be present
for a "special relationship" to exist between two nations: common political and economic interests; identity of basic goals and values; and empathy
between peoples. Gatzke argues that historians have overstated the friendliness of U.S.-German relations prior to W.W. I; even German immigration
failed to build a significant "bridge" between the two countries. W.W. I
changed the relationship fundamentally by fostering both the "bad German"
image and an American sense of duty to reform Germany; U.S. aid to Germany
in the 1920s was substantial but not sufficient to restore the country.
Nazism resulted, understandably, in revulsion and "Germanophobia," bringing
relations to "point zero." Postwar anticommunism forged a new alliance,
encouraged by economic ties and favorable public opinion born of travel
and cultural exchange. Gatzke concludes that detente resulted in "fluidity" and "uncertainty" in U.S.-German relations; and that to apply the
term "special relationship" would be both too restrictive and too complac-
ent.

PS 650. GELB, LESLIE H. with RICHARD K. BETTS. The Irony of Vietnam:
         The System Worked. Washington, D.C.: Brookings Institution,
         1979. 387 pp.
By exploring the history of the decision-making process that increased
U.S. involvement in Vietnam, the authors seek to show that the process
worked, and that it was the policy itself that failed. The U.S. system
can be said to have worked according to three general criteria: (1) the
main consensual goal of postwar foreign policy (containment of communism)
was pursued consistently; (2) differences of both elite and mass opinion
were accommodated by compromise, and policy never strayed very far from
the center of opinion either within or outside of the government; (3)
virtually all views and recommendations were considered and virtually
all important decisions were made without illusions about the odds of
success.

PS 651. GELLMAN, IRWIN F. Good Neighbor Diplomacy: United States Policies
         in Latin America, 1933-1945. Baltimore, Md.: Johns Hopkins
         University Press, 1979. 296 pp.
Gellman credits Roosevelt's administration, not Hoover's, with the real
origin of the "good neighbor" policy toward Latin America. U.S. interests
remained paramount, and continued influence and possible intervention
were assumed. Gellman emphasizes the individuals involved in formulating
policy, including Roosevelt, Secretary of State Cordell Hull, Henry Wallace,
and Sumner Wells. With the coming of the Cold War rivalry with the Soviet
Union and the passing of these individuals from the policy-making scene,
the "good neighbor" policy no longer dominated, and was replaced by relative indifference and inattention.

PS 652. GEORGE, ALEXANDER L. Presidential Decision-Making in Foreign
         Policy: The Effective Use of Information and Advice. Boulder,
         Colo.: Westview Press, 1980. 267 pp.
This study examines the various ways in which the judgments of foreign
policy decision-makers are distorted by the misuse of information and
analysis. In particular, the book looks at how individual executives
or small policy-making groups try to cope with the stress of making difficult decisions. George then discusses methods of organizing and managing
in order to reduce the likelihood of such distortions. He notes the impact
of presidential styles and personalities on policy-making and discusses
how collegial relationships with a policy-making group can improve analysis
and decision.

PS 653. GEORGE, ALEXANDER L. and RICHARD SMOKE. Deterrence in American
         Foreign Policy: Theory and Practice. New York: Columbia Uni-
         versity Press, 1974. 666 pp.
This book presents a critical examination of deterrence theory and strategy
as they have been applied in American foreign policy since the end of
W.W. II. Rather than focusing on strategic deterrence (the deterrence
of general war between the U.S. and the Soviet Union), the study is concerned with the effort to deter limited conflicts that might start through
encroachment by other countries on U.S. allies or neutral states. The
authors attempt to conceptualize deterrence processes more clearly and
to organize them in a general theory for policy applications. They also
provide a historical analysis, a theoretical essay, and fifteen case
studies.

PS 654. GIMBEL, JOHN. The Origins of the Marshall Plan. Stanford, Calif.:
         Stanford University Press, 1976. 344 pp.
Gimbel analyzes the Marshall Plan in the context of the long-standing
academic dispute over the origins of the Cold War. His central thesis
is that the intent of the Marshall Plan had little to do with the concerns
of the Cold War, as traditional and revisionist historians tend to argue.
Rather, it was an ad hoc "crash program," which grew out of squabbles
over the cost of German occupation and which was conceived by rival State
Department and Army bureaucrats to coordinate German recovery with that
of the rest of Europe. These bureaucrats, with little disposition or
opportunity for long-range planning, worked toward disparate and often
contradictory objectives.

PS 655. GRABER, DORIS A. Public Opinion, the President and Foreign Policy:
         Four Case Studies from the Formative Years. New York: Holt,
         Rinehart & Winston, 1968. 379 pp.
The book looks at four case studies from early American history of the
role of public opinion in the formation of foreign policy. The case
studies treat John Adams's mission to France, the Louisiana Purchase, the
War of 1812, and the Monroe Doctrine. The author tries to learn why the
nation's founders deemed it so essential to consider public opinion in
making policy decisions. She also looks at the scope of the influence
of public opinion and at the mechanisms by which public officials ascer-
tained what the public wanted. The study is based both on the theories
contained in the founders' writings and on their practical application.
Graber concludes by comparing the original role of public opinion in foreign policy with its modern role.

PS 656. GRAEBNER, NORMAN A. Cold War Diplomacy, 1945-1960. Princeton,
         N.J.: Van Nostrand Reinhold, 1962. 191 pp.
Graebner analyzes American foreign policy from 1945 to 1960. The first
portion of the work is a narrative account of the era while the second
part is given over to documents relating to American foreign policy, such
as speeches by Cordell Hull, Truman, Marshall, Acheson, and Dulles.

Graebner argues that America wished to return to an isolationist stance immediately following W.W. II but was thwarted in this by the expansionist policies of the Soviet Union. He further contends that the major failing in America's response to the post-War world was its tendency to pursue abstractions rather than concrete interests; this led to a lack of clearly defined objectives for American foreign policy.

PS 657.   GRAY, COLIN S.   Strategic Studies and Public Policy: The American Experience.   Lexington: University Press of Kentucky, 1982.   230 pp.
Gray presents a history of American foreign policy in the nuclear age. After W.W. II, the U.S. was compelled to consider a peacetime military strategy, which it never before had needed to do.   Strategy is defined as the relationship between military power and political purpose, and encompasses a broad conceptual range that includes nuclear strategy, deterrence, limited war, the role of arms control, and new strategies.   The study also deals with strategic concepts such as flexible response, crisis management, counter-insurgency, and nation-building.

PS 658.   GRAY, COLIN S.   Strategy and the MX.   Washington, D.C.:   Heritage Foundation, 1980.   66 pp.
Gray believes that the current debate surrounding the MX missile overlooks the central issues.   He defends the MX by arguing that the missile plays an important role in operational aspects of strategy; it provides the U.S. with the capability to strike more Soviet targets, more effectively, and within a wider range of possible threats.   In this way, the MX contributes to the deterrence of both a major war and Soviet aggression.   In the process, Gray also discusses the U.S. Nuclear Weapons Employment Policy (NUWEP), the "MX Firebreak," and the effect of the MX on the arms race.

PS 659.   GREENWOOD, TED, HAROLD A. FEIVESON, and THEODORE B. TAYLOR.   Nuclear Proliferation: Motivations, Capabilities, and Strategies for Control.   New York: McGraw-Hill, 1977.   210 pp.
These essays, products of the "1980s Project" of the Council on Foreign Relations, propose strategies to manage several aspects of the nuclear proliferation problem.   Ted Greenwood discusses the task of reducing the incentives and increasing the disincentives for the acquisition of nuclear weapons.   He includes suggestions on the management of the international nuclear industry and on the control of independent groups seeking nuclear arms.   Harold A. Feiveson and Theodore B. Taylor also discuss strategies for the international control of nuclear power.

PS 660.   GRISWOLD, A. WHITNEY.   The Far Eastern Policy of the United States.   1938; Rev. ed.   New Haven, Conn.:   Yale University Press, 1962.   530 pp.
Griswold begins his study in 1898, a time when U.S. aims in the Far East were commercial rather than political.   This policy began to change with Theodore Roosevelt's annexation of the Philippines, which sparked the development of American political interest in the area.   Griswold argues that financial interest in China and Japan frequently masked political interest.   He traces European influence in the Far East, suggesting that the U.S.   seriously misjudged British interest in the area.   Japanese immigration to the U.S. further complicated Far Eastern policy.   Griswold concludes his study in 1938, with FDR's announcement of a "24-hour policy" and its implication of an uncertain future for American involvement in the Far East.

PS 661. GROSE, PETER. Israel in the Mind of America. New York: Knopf,
         1983. 361 pp.
From the Puritan roots of the New World to the current dilemmas of American-
Israeli relations, Grose examines the ideological ties between Americans
and Jews. He focuses primarily on the events surrounding the U.S. recognition of Israel. His study is based in part on American, British, and
Israeli archival sources which provide fresh perspectives on older sources.
The author analyzes American attitudes and policies toward Zionism in
order to show what he claims is the unique spiritual bond between two
sovereign peoples. He sees a mutual "grafting" of two heritages: Judaic
tradition influenced America's early settlers and shaped the American
Republic; in turn, "the American dream" had its effect on the formation
of Israel.

PS 662. GROSSER, ALFRED. The Western Alliance: European-American Rela-
         tions Since 1945. Translated by Michael Shaw. New York: Con-
         tinuum, 1980. 375 pp.
This account of the U.S.'s relations with Western Europe synthesizes much
existing literature, and looks at the relations between political strategy,
international economics, diplomatic and inter-governmental relations.
It examines the effect of commercial, corporate, and banking interactions
on U.S.-European relations, as well as the role of unions, churches, the
media, intellectuals, and cultural relations in the Western alliance.
Grosser's themes are those of continuity and change, specifically in the
attitudes of France and West Germany toward each other and toward the
U.S. He sees the Western alliance as intrinsically disharmonious, yet
the relationship has paradoxically endured because it rests on the three
"pillars" of defense, economics, and political-cultural ties.

PS 663. HALLE, LOUIS J. and KENNETH W. THOMPSON, eds. Foreign Policy
         and the Democratic Process: The Geneva Papers. Washington,
         D.C.: University Press of America, 1978. 90 pp.
Halle and Thompson consider the difficulty of formulating and sustaining
effective foreign policy in a democracy. The volume looks at a number
of related issues: the quality of political leadership and its effect
on the resolution of problems; the function and limits of American leadership in world politics; the challenge of reconciling professional diplomacy
with democratic decision-making; the influence of mass media and public
opinion on foreign policy; and the relationship between democratic societies and authoritarian regimes. The book concludes with a review of
the relationship between U.S. democracy and the Third World.

PS 664. HALPERIN, MORTON H. Defense Strategies for the Seventies. Boston:
         Little, Brown, 1971. 149 pp.
Halperin discusses various aspects of the impact of modern weapons on
defense. The early chapters consider force and warfare in the nuclear
age, including different kinds of wars, alternative strategies for deterrence, and limits on the use of quantitative techniques for analyzing
strategic questions. One chapter each is devoted to Soviet, Chinese,
and U.S. military strategy. Other chapters discuss the Nixon administration's criterion of "sufficiency" of U.S. strategic forces, deterrence
in the context of Europe and Asia, and efforts to obtain partial arms
control.

PS 665. HALPERIN, MORTON H., PRISCILLA CLAPP, and ARNOLD KANTER. Bureau-
         cratic Politics and Foreign Policy. Washington, D.C.: Brookings
         Institution, 1974. 340 pp.
This book analyzes American foreign policy based on the memoirs of 100
American policy-makers since 1945. In three parts, the authors introduce
the participants in the foreign affairs bureaucracy, the ways in which
these participants maneuver and promote their policy positions, the influ-

ential factors resulting in a presidential decision, and the processes
of implementing policy decisions. The book concludes with observations
about the implications of the bureaucratic politics approach for understanding international events.

PS 666. HANSEN, ROGER D. Beyond the North-South Stalemate. New York:
McGraw-Hill, 1979. 329 pp.
This book focuses on the complex issues of the North-South nexus of relations. It examines the evolution of Third World relations with developed
countries, gives an academic as well as protagonistic analysis of the international system—specifically North-South relations—and focuses on how
this challenge should be met in the 1980s.

PS 667. HANSEN, ROGER D. United States Foreign Policy and the Third World.
New York: Praeger, 1982. 321 pp.
This book focuses on U.S. commitments to assist Latin American development
in the areas of economics, food, and national security. This collection
of essays by five political scientists examines the various institutions
created by the U.S. as a part of the aid program to Latin America. A
statistical abstract describing economic conditions in Latin America comprises half the work.

PS 668. HARRISON, SELIG S. China, Oil, and Asia: Conflict Ahead? New
York: Columbia University Press, 1977. 317 pp.
Based on interviews with 300 oil and energy specialists, this book deals
with the energy policy in East and Southeast Asia with special emphasis
on Chinese viewpoints and interests. Harrison argues that the Chinese
approach to energy policy-making could increase tensions in Asia and
endanger Chinese claims to off-short petroleum rights. The book focuses
on a detailed description of the national interests of ten states that
have claims of varying magnitude to the resources in the East China Sea,
the Yellow Sea, the Taiwan Strait and the South China Sea.

PS 669. HART, ROBERT A. The Eccentric Tradition: American Diplomacy
in the Far East. New York: Scribner, 1976. 277 pp.
Hart explores the complexities of American policies in the Far East.
The volume presents an overview of American relations with the Orient
from 1783 to the present. Hart argues that American interests were often
lost due to emotional reactions which caused Americans to fall back from
policies of flexibility, realism, and balance. He contends that such
American characteristics as impulsiveness and over-simplification were
destructive in a region known for its complexity and subtlety.

PS 670. HECKELMAN, A. JOSEPH. American Volunteers and Israel's War of
Independence. New York: KTAV, 1974. 304 pp.
After reviewing the major events and battles of Israel's War of Independence, Heckelman considers how much credit should be given to Americans
when evaluating Israel's victory. The role of Americans in procuring
equipment is analyzed, and a tally of the Americans and Canadians killed
in the war is also provided. Americans contributed most in the Israeli
Air Force, so four chapters are devoted to this subject. Heckelman concludes that American volunteers were "indispensable" to the war effort.

PS 671. HERO, ALFRED O. Jr., and JOHN BARRATT, eds. The American People
and South Africa. Lexington, Mass.: Lexington Books, 1981.
229 pp.
This collection of essays considers the impact of American public opinion
and corporate ventures upon the formulation of U.S. policy toward South
Africa. The essays also look at the export of American culture to South
Africa through religious and educational institutions. Finally, the book
discusses the Reagan Administration policies which call for the easing

1139

of apartheid in order to stabilize the Botha government and to secure
U.S. political and economic interests in South Africa.

PS 672. HERRING, GEORGE C. America's Longest War: The United States
    and Vietnam 1950-1975. New York: Wiley, 1979. 298 pp.
Herring presents an overview of American involvement in Vietnam. The
Vietnamese "problem" is examined in the context of the demise of French
colonialism; the interaction between the U.S., the French, and the Vietnamese is seen in terms of the larger development of the Cold War policy
of containment. The partnership between Kennedy and Diem and Johnson's
decision to escalate U.S. involvement in the war are also detailed.
Herring's analysis focuses on the Tet Offensive of 1968 and Nixon's "Viet-
namization" policy. Herring concludes with an analysis of the way Nixon
and Kissinger handled the final disengagement.

PS 673. HERSH, SEYMOUR M. The Price of Power: Kissinger in the Nixon
    White House. New York: Summit Books, 1983. 698 pp.
Hersh presents an account of Henry Kissinger's control over U.S. foreign
policy during Nixon's first term in the White House. He examines the
relationship between the diplomatic strategies the administration pursued
and the personal ambitions and personalities of those involved. Hersh
is critical of Kissinger and the Nixon White House and sees their performance as marred by political self-interest, mistakes, unethical conduct,
and internal corruption. He tries to show that despite the apparent foreign policy successes of Kissinger and Nixon, their conduct of foreign
policy was in many respects reprehensible.

PS 674. HILSMAN, ROGER. To Move a Nation: The Politics of Foreign Policy
    in the Administration of John F. Kennedy. Garden City, N.Y.:
    Doubleday, 1967. 602 pp.
In this book Hilsman focuses on foreign policy debates during the Kennedy
years. He draws from his experience as a participant in foreign policy
decisions during the Kennedy administration in order to provide insights
into the nature of the policy-making process. The book applies a theory
of the politics of policy-making to the development of foreign policy
toward Laos, Cuba and Vietnam. Hilsman concludes that the Vietnam tragedy
might have been avoided by reorganizing the political nature of that country in a way consistent with more unilateral American action in Asia.

PS 675. HOFFMAN, STANLEY. Primacy or World Order: American Foreign Policy
    Since the Cold War. New York: McGraw-Hill, 1978. 333 pp.
This essay confronts the issues of the post-Cold War, post-containment
international system. Hoffman addresses the following questions: What
have we learned? What kind of world are we facing? What policies make
sense? What are our assets and handicaps? He discusses the legacy of
Vietnam, Kissinger's statecraft, classical models of international relations, interdependence, the nature of conflict, the conduct of foreign
policy by executive and Congressional bodies, human rights, and nuclear
proliferation.

PS 676. HOLLICK, ANN. U.S. Foreign Policy and the Law of the Sea. Prince-
    ton, N.J.: Princeton University Press, 1981. 496 pp.
This book focuses on American decision-making processes, with special
emphasis on the evolution of American policy in response to commercial,
environmental, strategic, technological developments, and to a changing
international political system. History of the UNCLOS and the effect
of domestic politics and international incidents in this area are also
discussed by Hollick. As a chronological study of the forty-year period
from W.W. II through the ninth session of the Third United Nations Conference on the Law of the Sea (UNCLOS) in 1980, this book draws on interviews, correspondence, published documents of the United Nations, unpublished State Department records, and some secondary sources.

PS 677. HOPKINS, RAYMOND F. and DONALD J. PUCHALA. Global Food Interdependence: Challenge to American Foreign Policy. New York: Columbia University Press, 1980. 214 pp.
The authors examine the U.S.'s role as the world's chief supplier of foodstuffs in the context of present, uneven patterns of production, distribution, and consumption. Factors affecting supply and demand are considered, including growth in consumption, malnutrition, and worldwide shortages of food. The authors then look at the political economy of food trade, and at the U.S.'s efforts to alleviate the current crisis through Public Law 480 and through a variety of organizations established by the Executive branch of government.

PS 678. HUNT, MICHAEL H. The Making of a Special Relationship: The United States and China to 1914. New York: Columbia University Press, 1983. 416 pp.
Hunt gives a portrayal of China from both the American and Chinese points of view. The issue of Chinese immigration to the U.S. continually strained relations between the two countries, producing divisions within each country's policy-making circle. While the U.S. called for the "open-door," it was reluctant to act to bring it about. Hunt's epilogue traces U.S.-Chinese relations since these early years, and argues that the American notion of a "special" relationship with China made U.S. understanding of the Communist revolution far more difficult.

PS 679. HUNTINGTON, SAMUEL P. The Common Defense: Strategic Programs in National Politics. New York: Columbia University Press, 1961. 500 pp.
Huntington studies U.S. national security policy-making from 1945-1960, a period of profound political change for the U.S. military. He focuses more on the process of decision-making than on the substantive policies pursued. He examines the conflict between those who desired an aggressive military policy and those who sought to transform the guiding strategy from constant mobilization to deterrence. Huntington also studies the process by which the executive branch formulates legislative bills concerning military programs and tries to balance military with economic strength.

PS 680. IMMERMAN, RICHARD H. The C.I.A. in Guatemala: The Foreign Policy of Intervention. Austin: University of Texas Press, 1982. 291 pp.
Immerman studies C.I.A. involvement in the overthrow of the Guatemalan government of Jacobo Arbenz Guzman in 1954; the C.I.A. was intent on removing the Communist regime and protecting the United Fruit Company. The author sees the fall of Arbenz as an important chapter in Cold War history, since it set a precedent for U.S. intervention. Immerman concludes that C.I.A. activities paved the way for a return to authoritarian government in Guatemala and led to the Bay of Pigs fiasco and to present U.S. dilemmas in Central America.

PS 681. IRIYE, AKIRA. Across the Pacific: An Inner History of American-East Asian Relations. New York: Harcourt, Brace & World, 1967. 361 pp.
Iriye's book is a history of foreign policy between the U.S. and China and Japan from 1780 to the present. The author emphasizes the general cultural perceptions that Americans and Far Eastern peoples have had of one another and the patterns of accommodation that these perceptions have undergone. Iriye is concerned with the impact of westernization on China and Japan and how these factors are related to the U.S. "open door" policy. The importance of the Far East to the U.S. between the two World Wars is discussed, and the reaction of U.S. politicians to the Chinese Civil War is put in the context of the U.S.'s overall posture toward Communism in the post-W.W. II era.

PS 682. IRIYE, AKIRA. Power and Culture: The Japanese-American War 1941-
         1945. Cambridge, Mass.: Harvard University Press, 1981. 304 pp.
Iriye portrays the Pacific War as an interpower and intercultural conflict.
He asserts that this war was between two nations who had more in common
than they realized. The book starts with the events of 1939-40, and the
U.S. attempts to support China in order to prevent an alliance between
a German-dominated Europe and a Japanese-dominated Asia. However, China
was not willing to side with Western powers against Japan. With the invasion of Russia by Germany, the Japanese moved into Vietnam. In retaliation,
the U.S. stopped the flow of oil to Japan. Iriye views the Pacific War
in the context of U.S.-Japan and China-Japan conflicts and of Russia's
relationship with the U.S., China and Japan. Special emphasis is given
to the role of generals in power during this period. He concludes that
international relations may be studied on three levels: power, culture,
and the interaction of these two sets of relations. Iriye presents a
narrative of the political events and social circumstances of the war
in the broader cultural manifestations of national self-image and destiny.
The war is seen as a catalytic event that profoundly shaped the progress
of international relations, as well as subsequent Japanese social history.

PS 683. ISRAEL, JERRY. Progressivism and the Open Door: America and
         China, 1905-1921. Pittsburgh, Pa.: University of Pittsburgh
         Press, 1971. 222 pp.
Israel's theme in this study is Americans' ambivalence in intervening
in Chinese affairs in the early 20th century, as they were torn between
competitive and cooperative urges. He discusses the struggles of those
Americans favoring independent U.S. action and those who were for cooperative action by all the foreign powers. Israel shows that the "open door"
in 1905 did not mean "equal opportunity" for all to trade with China,
but rather an opening of China's markets to American ideas, products,
and investment.

PS 684. JANIS, IRVING. Groupthink: Psychological Studies of Policy Deci-
         sions and Fiascoes. Boston: Houghton Mifflin, 1982. 349 pp.
Janis advances the theory that leaders and policy-makers tend toward social
conformity in group situations when faced with pressures to retain group
approval. Janis develops this thesis by examining several case studies
in which he believes "groupthink" contributed to policy failures: the
Bay of Pigs, the Korea stalemate, Pearl Harbor, Vietnam, and the Watergate
cover-up. He also discusses cases wherein "groupthink" has had successful
results.

PS 685. JERVIS, ROBERT. The Logic of Images in International Relations.
         Princeton, N.J.: Princeton University Press, 1970. 281 pp.
Jervis discusses "the ways states can affect the images others have of
them and thereby exercise influence without paying the high costs of altering their own major policies." He studies the signals states send out
to create an image for themselves and to manipulate other states within
the international system. He evaluates strategies of sending out ambiguous
signals and lying, and then examines the significance of image making
in the nuclear era.

PS 686. JONAS, MANFRED. Isolationism in America, 1935-1941. Ithaca,
         N.Y.: Cornell University Press, 1966. 315 pp.
According to Jonas, pre-W.W. II isolationism should not be dismissed as
an ignorant mainstream American response to foreign and domestic development. By examining isolationism in the rhetoric and literature of its
proponents, Jonas seeks to explain the strength of isolationism in this
period. He also discusses the causes of its eradication after the Pearl
Harbor attack.

PS 687. KAHAN, JEROME H. Security in the Nuclear Age: Developing U.S.
Strategic Arms Policy. Washington, D.C.: Brookings Institution,
1975. 361 pp.
Kahan surveys nuclear weapons problems that have arisen in the U.S. since
the Eisenhower administration, concentrating on "doctrinal and diplomatic
issues related to strategic arms" rather than on specific details of weapons systems or the connection between nuclear policy and U.S. foreign
policy in general. He details the history of Soviet nuclear policy and
the SALT talks in Part One of this book; in Part Two he discusses future
strategic policy issues, concluding with guidelines for a policy of "stable
deterrence."

PS 688. KAHN, HERMAN. On Thermonuclear War. 1960; Rev. ed. New York:
Free Press, 1969. 668 pp.
Kahn "examines the military side of what may be the major problem that
faces civilization, comparing some of the alternatives that seem available
and some of the implications of these choices." This book consists of
three lectures delivered at Princeton University in 1959, "The Nature
and Feasibility of Thermonuclear War," "The Formulation and Testing of
Objectives and Plans," and "World War I through World War VIII." Kahn
concludes that in a nuclear world a nuclear deterrent cannot work unless
a nation's leaders make potential enemies aware that they are willing
and able to use it; he argues for first-strike capability. In the revised
edition Kahn responds to some of his critics and reassesses his findings
in light of 1969 conditions, when the world climate had come to seem more
safe--a misleading impression, argues Kahn.

PS 689. KAISER, KARL and HANS-PETER SCHWARZ, eds. America and Western
Europe: Problems and Prospects. Lexington, Mass.: Lexington
Books, 1977. 447 pp.
The articles in this volume assess the importance, utility, and viability
of the Atlantic Alliance in the face of the significant world political
changes of the 1970s. These changes include the collapse of the Bretton
Woods system, the oil crisis of 1973-74, the aggravation of North-South
tensions, and global recession. The articles are organized around the
following analytic categories: public opinion, culture, and relations
between elites; the Western economy system; dimensions of security; and
structural problems in the West. In their conclusion, the editors examine
a few of the tasks which they consider to be particularly important to
an agenda of political action.

PS 690. KALB, MADELEINE G. The Congo Cables: The Cold War in Africa
from Eisenhower to Kennedy. New York: Macmillan, 1982.
466 pp.
This book recounts the U.S.-Soviet Union clash over the Congo from 1960
to 1968. It is based upon State Department documents and cables of that
period between Leopoldville and Washington. The cables provide a record
of the struggle between the two superpowers as well as of the battles
between the Congolese national factions. Kalb also discusses the policy
conflicts concerning the Congo that occurred within the Eisenhower and
Kennedy administrations, especially those between the State Department,
the Pentagon, the U.S. Mission to the U.N., and the embassy at Leopoldville.

PS 691. KATTENBURG, PAUL M. The Vietnam Trauma in American Foreign Policy,
1945-1975. New Brunswick, N.J.: Transaction Books, 1980.
354 pp.
Kattenburg, the State Department's Vietnam Desk Officer from 1952 to 1956
and the Director of Vietnam Affairs in 1963-64, was opposed to the Vietnam
war from the outset. He argues that American involvement was an outcome
of: (1) the victorious war against Japan which left the U.S. the dominant
power in Asia after 1945; (2) U.S. military power which created the temp-

tation to armed intervention; (3) American anti-Communism which overrode anti-Colonial traditions and made the Vietnamese struggle against the French into a component of the U.S.'s containment policy; and (4) U.S. fear of being perceived as weak-willed which meant a predisposition to the use of force. The tragedy of Vietnam, concludes Kattenburg, was that the U.S. had little specific interest in Vietnam and its national problems, but was motivated by a broad intent to oppose Communism.

PS 692. KAUFMANN, WILLIAM W. The McNamara Strategy. New York: Harper
& Row, 1964. 339 pp.
The author explains the national security changes McNamara pursued as Secretary of Defense. McNamara's management techniques are believed to have revolutionized the system of program planning at the Pentagon. Furthermore, his leadership and the work of his "whiz kids" signalled the growing influence of civilian managers on U.S. defense policy. Instead of a discussion of McNamara's quantitative evaluation methods, the book is a narrative of his general approach to major policy issues.

PS 693. KAUFMANN, WILLIAM W., ed. Military Policy and National Security.
Princeton, N.J.: Princeton University Press, 1956. 274 pp.
The articles in this volume discuss the reformation of U.S. military policy. Among the conclusions reached are that Soviet-American parity will not by itself remove the possibility of aggression and warfare. Furthermore, if the U.S. is to maintain a dominant position, it must acquire an ample force of both conventional and nuclear power. William W. Kaufmann writes on deterrence in foreign policy and on limited war; Roger Hilsman discusses nuclear strategy and alliances; Klaus Knorr examines passive air defenses and military potentials; and Gordon Craig discusses relations between NATO and Germany.

PS 694. KENNAN, GEORGE F. American Diplomacy, 1900-1950. Chicago: University of Chicago Press, 1951. 146 pp.
In this series of lectures, Kennan discusses the theoretical basis of America's foreign relations. He looks at the assumptions and concepts which have guided statesmen attempting to adjust to and define America's changing international role. The study considers in particular several turning points in U.S. diplomatic history, such as the advent of the U.S. as a world power around the turn of the century. Despite its gains in power, Kennan argues, the nation's security has declined since 1900. The volume also includes "Sources of Soviet Conduct" (the "X" article), originally published in 1949.

PS 695. KENNAN, GEORGE F. Memoirs: 1925-1950. Boston: Little, Brown,
1967. 583 pp.
Kennan recounts his professional experience in the foreign service from his training as a Soviet specialist through his long tenure in Moscow in the 1930s and during W.W. II. He also discusses his interludes in other Eastern European capitals, and his central role in influencing U.S. policy immediately after the war. The account concludes with his departure from public service in 1950. It also provides Kennan's views of the prospects for Europe and his recommendations for U.S. diplomatic conduct with the Soviet Union.

PS 696. KENNAN, GEORGE F. The Nuclear Delusion: Soviet-American Relations
in the Atomic Age. New York: Pantheon Books, 1982. 207 pp.
This collection of essays focuses on the argument that the nuclear arms race has never been based on a fully realistic assessment of the Soviet Union. In fact, the acceleration of and reliance on nuclear deterrence constitute a disastrous policy which should be immediately discontinued. Kennan provides explanations of Soviet policies and objectives since 1917. He discusses detente, the crises in Afghanistan and Poland, and American failure to construe correctly Soviet strategic objectives.

PS 697. KENNAN, GEORGE F. Soviet-American Relations, 1917-1920: Russia
Leaves the War. Princeton, N.J.: Princeton University Press,
1956. 544 pp.
In this volume, Kennan traces Russo-American relations, beginning with
the overthrow of the Tsar during the first Revolution of 1917, and covering
both the Bolshevik Revolution of 1917 and the withdrawal of Soviet Russia
from W.W. I in 1918. The collapse of the Russian front and the final
capitulation of Russia to the German military eliminated the eastern front
from the War. This altered both the Germans' and the Allies' estimation
of the duration and outcome of the War. Kennan argues that this withdrawal
was the basis for allied and American distrust of the Bolshevik regime.

PS 698. KENNAN, GEORGE F. Soviet-American Relations, 1917-1920: The
Decision to Intervene. Princeton, N.J.: Princeton University
Press, 1958. 513 pp.
In the second volume of his study of Soviet-American relations, Kennan
discusses the intervention of U.S., Allied, and German forces into the
Soviet Union between 1918 and 1923. The invasion began in order to force
Russia to return to the War effort and to forestall Germany from gaining
spheres of influence promised by the Treaty of Brest-Litovsk. In addition,
the threat that Germany might march beyond treaty boundaries, as well
as a desire to reapply pressure on Germany from the East, were the primary
reasons for intervention. These motivations, according to Kennan, were
soon replaced by Allied attempts to maneuver for postwar position in newly
organized Eastern Europe, and by the desire to overthrow or quarantine
the Bolshevik regime.

PS 699. KENNEDY, ROBERT F. Thirteen Days: A Memoir of the Cuban Missile
Crisis. New York: Norton, 1969. 224 pp.
Kennedy describes how work within the White House during the Cuban missile
crisis was organized. He discusses the debates that took place among
the President's advisers on whether to use military attack or maritime
quarantine to stop the placement of missiles in Cuba. He presents the
behind-the-scene dialogues that went on between the Kremlin and the White
House. The book also offers a character profile of President Kennedy,
displaying his determination and flexibility in the crisis.

PS 700. KING, ANTHONY, ed. The New American Political System. Washington,
D.C.: American Enterprise Institute, 1978. 407 pp.
This book contains contributions of nine political scientists and deals
with significant changes in all aspects of American politics since the
presidency of John F. Kennedy. Special emphasis is given to the evolution
of the roles and functions of different branches of the Federal government
and their impact on policy-making and party politics. King concludes
that "American politics has become, to a high degree, atomized."

PS 701. KISSINGER, HENRY A. The Necessity for Choice: Prospects of American Foreign Policy. New York: Harper, 1961. 370 pp.
Kissinger discusses what he believes are the fundamental failures and
omissions in American foreign policy, arguing that the U.S. lacks criteria
by which to determine policy choices and suffers from a tendency toward
passivity in international conduct. Furthermore, U.S. national security
policy needs a strategic doctrine and a coherent military policy. The
author examines the dilemmas of deterrence and limited war, U.S.-Western
Europe security relations, difficulties in arms control and negotiations
with the Soviet Union, the prospects for a liberal transformation of the
Soviet system, and the relationship between policy-makers and intellectuals.

PS 702. KISSINGER, HENRY A. The Troubled Partnership: A Re-appraisal
         of the Atlantic Alliance. New York: McGraw-Hill, 1965.
         259 pp.
In this study of U.S.-European relations, Kissinger analyzes the structural,
political, and strategic problems that have hindered collaboration and
integration within Europe and across the Atlantic. The structural problems
result from the European economic recovery, the recession of the Soviet
threat, and the release of Colonial burdens, encouraging Europe's political revitalization and desire for self-assertion. Political friction
results from competing French and American images of European unity.
The strategic issues arise from Europe's enormous dependence on U.S. forces
as a deterrent threat. The author discusses future prospects for U.S.-
European relations, emphasizing Germany's central role.

PS 703. KISSINGER, HENRY A. The White House Years. Boston: Little,
         Brown, 1979; Years of Upheaval. New York: Little, Brown, 1982.
         1283 pp.
These volumes comprise Henry Kissinger's memoirs of Richard Nixon's first
and second administrations. The White House Years deals with Nixon's
first term and Kissinger's tenure as Assistant to the President for
National Security Affairs. This book also makes it clear that Kissinger
could have run the domestic operations of the Nixon Administration if
he would have so wished. Years of Upheaval begins with Kissinger's appointment as Secretary of State. It discusses all aspects of his foreign policy
with particular attention to the Middle East negotiations.

PS 704. KITCHEN, HELEN, ed. Options for U.S. Policy Toward Africa. Wash-
         ington, D.C.: American Enterprise Institute, 1979. 76 pp.
Kitchen presents six distinct policy options for the U.S. in Africa.
These policies range from the "geo-strategic option," which focuses on
the Soviet threat in the Third World, to the "Afro-centric perspective,"
which aims at helping Africa to transform itself. The latter would entail
a progressive role for the U.S. in Africa. Each option is summarized;
its assumptions and objectives are identified along with its risks.
Experts contribute brief articles in support of each option.

PS 705. KOLKO, JOYCE and GABRIEL KOLKO. The Limits of Power: The World
         and United States Foreign Policy, 1945-1954. New York: Harper
         & Row, 1972. 820 pp.
The authors argue that violence and conflict were the inevitable consequences of a U.S. foreign policy that sought to create a world order hos-
pitable to U.S. commercial interests. The pursuit of such an order
required the U.S. to promote conservative, dependent regimes in the Third
World. The traditional Cold War approach to U.S. foreign policy is criticized for focusing on U.S.-Soviet relations to the exclusion of the global
context and goals of U.S. policy.

PS 706. KRASNER, STEPHEN D. Defending the National Interest: Raw Mate-
         rials Investments and U.S. Foreign Policy. Princeton, N.J.:
         Princeton University Press, 1978. 404 pp.
The principal purpose of this book is to present and defend a "statist"
approach to the analysis of foreign policy. This approach treats the
state as an autonomous actor rather than a passive reactor to political
pressures. As evidence in support of this approach, Krasner examines
U.S. foreign policy in raw materials between 1950 and 1955: specifically,
in Liberian rubber and in Middle Eastern and Iranian oil. Krasner also
shows how U.S. foreign policy was oriented toward the protection of foreign
investment, giving special attention to cases involving the use of military
force.

PS 707. KUNIHOLM, BRUCE R. The Origins of the Cold War in the Near East: Great Power Conflict and Diplomacy in Iran, Turkey and Greece. Princeton, N.J.: Princeton University Press, 1980. 439 pp.
This book focuses on the origins of the Cold War in the Near East, with special emphasis on the role of the "Great Power" rivalry in Greece, Turkey and Iran. Kuniholm asserts that the historical struggle for power in this region was an important factor in the development of the Cold War. He explores the domestic struggles of these three countries to define their national destiny during and immediately after W.W. II. He also focuses on the Soviet Union's patterns of behavior in its pursuit of interests in the region. Kuniholm views the U.S.'s policy formulation as a response to Soviet pressure.

PS 708. LaFEBER, WALTER. America, Russia, and the Cold War, 1945-1966. New York: Wiley, 1967. 295 pp.
LaFeber views the Cold War as the result of years of suspicion that began after W.W. II when America's hope for an open world ran up against Russia's desire to protect its security through the establishment of satellites in Eastern Europe. He argues that U.S. Cold War policy was set when the Truman administration tried to break down Russian hegemony through economic power and the atomic monopoly in 1945 and 1946. After trying to combat Communism through foreign aid and military alliances, American policy solidified into rigid anti-Communism because of the Korean War and McCarthyism. During the 1950s the Cold War shifted from Europe to the Third World and emerging nations; the Vietnam War was a direct result of this shift. LaFeber argues against the U.S. anti-Communist preoccupation and calls for a new appraisal of American foreign policy.

PS 709. LaFEBER, WALTER. Inevitable Revolutions: The United States in Central America. New York: Norton, 1983. 357 pp.
In this book LaFeber focuses on the U.S. response to Central American revolutions. He asserts that the U.S. tends to see the development of indigenous politics in Central America as the result of foreign interference in the region. Surveying the history of U.S. involvement in Costa Rica, Guatemala, Honduras, El Salvador and Nicaragua, LaFeber argues that the region is tightly integrated into the U.S. economic and security systems. However, the U.S. has been ignoring Central America as an economic problem since W.W. II. He asserts that this dependency together with strong economic inequalities existing in the region have given rise to guerrilla movements and revolutions. LaFeber concludes that the revolutionary movements will persist in this region as long as U.S. policy follows its traditional trends. However, as long as the guerrilla movements continue their activities, there is no hope that U.S. policy in the region will change.

PS 710. LANGLEY, LESTER D. The United States and the Caribbean, 1900-1970. Athens: University of Georgia Press, 1980. 324 pp.
Langley's study of U.S. policies toward Caribbean nations (including Central America) is chronological and uses the case study method for both countries and specific problems; he discusses both substantive U.S. policies and the developmental thinking behind them. Before 1945, America was generally successful in controlling Caribbean nations which were deemed of strategic importance; since then, however, the trend has been in the other direction, owing to increased Caribbean nationalism, the rise of Castroism in Cuba, economic difficulties in the region, and American preoccupation elsewhere. Langley includes a bibliographical essay.

PS 711. LAQUEUR, WALTER. The Political Psychology of Appeasement: Fin-
         landization and Other Unpopular Essays. New Brunswick, N.J.:
         Transaction Books, 1980. 283 pp.
These essays deal with European issues such as "Finlandization," Euro-
Communism, and Russia after Brezhnev, and with the topic of "futurism."
Laqueur also includes a number of articles on terrorism and the possibilities for peace in the Middle East. Finally, he addresses U.S. foreign
policy, dealing with such issues as human rights, the psychology of appeasement, the Third World, and President Carter's foreign policy.

PS 712. LASH, JOSEPH P. Roosevelt and Churchill, 1939-1941: The Partner-
         ship that Saved the West. New York: Norton, 1976. 528 pp.
Lash chronicles the Churchill-Roosevelt exchanges in American foreign
policy from the invasion of Poland to Pearl Harbor. Lash argues that
Roosevelt justifiably led the nation toward intervention in W.W. II.
He presents both Churchill and Roosevelt as the great leaders demanded
by the times; although they occasionally mistrusted each other, by 1941
they had developed a deep sense of openness and honesty in their relations.

PS 713. LASSWELL, HAROLD D. National Security and Individual Freedom.
         New York: McGraw-Hill, 1950. 259 pp.
Lasswell deals with the question of how to maintain a proper balance
between national security and individual freedom in a continuing crisis
of national defense. The book begins with an examination of the reason
and the need for national defense in a threatening international order.
Lasswell then reviews the basic principles and values of American foreign
policy, which is dominated by the belief that the danger of war is always
present. The author warns, however, that a comprehensive national defense
does not rely solely on armaments; it requires a civilian commitment to
the society, which in turn requires the protection of civil liberties.

PS 714. LEDEEN, MICHAEL and WILLIAM LEWIS. Debacle: The American Failure
         in Iran. New York: Knopf, 1981. 256 pp.
Combining journalistic methods with scholarly analysis, this book presents
both a historic overview of dynastic rule in Persia and an account of
more recent history: the Washington-Tehran link since the 1940s, the
significance of the Massadegh affair, and Iran's place in U.S. policy
since the Shah's installation. The majority of this work is an analysis
of events under Jimmy Carter: the crises preceding the Shah's fall, the
revolution, and the consequences of the Ayatollah's rule for future U.S.-
Iranian relations.

PS 715. LENS, SIDNEY. The Maginot Line Syndrome: America's Hopeless
         Foreign Policy. Cambridge, Mass.: Ballinger, 1982. 194 pp.
Lens offers a critical examination of the U.S. policy of "containment"
toward the Soviet Union. He argues that this policy has led to an escalation of the arms race and to misperceptions of the true causes of international conflict, national revolution and social upheaval. Lens argues
that the Cold War foreign policy strategies that were to have guaranteed
American predominance have instead worked to undermine social institutions
and to create spiritual malaise in American society. He concludes with
a plea for the establishment of an international agency to oversee disarmament and the destruction of nuclear weapons on both sides.

PS 716. LEVERING, RALPH B. The Public and American Foreign Policy, 1918-
         1978. New York: Morrow, 1978. 192 pp.
Using data drawn from public opinion polls, Levering investigates the
interaction of public opinion and foreign policy between the end of W.W.
I and 1978. He analyzes the American electorate's views of foreign policy
in terms of ethnicity, education, and political affiliation; he also traces
the increasing importance of the media in influencing foreign policy.

Levering argues that prior to 1936 domestic concerns were of primary importance to Americans, and that this was a key factor in the isolationism
of the period. After W.W. II the public view of foreign policy was closely
related to a general anti-Communist sentiment and that this was followed
by a "new realism" in the post-Vietnam era.

PS 717. LEVIN, N. GORDON. Woodrow Wilson and World Politics: America's
Response to War and Revolution. New York: Oxford University
Press, 1968. 340 pp.
Levin undertakes an integrated analysis of the theory and practice of
Wilsonian foreign policy from 1917 to 1919. Levin argues that Wilson's
main international objective was the attainment of a peaceful liberal-
capitalist order based on international law and safe from both revolutionary Socialism and traditional Imperialism, with which a missionary America
could assume moral and economic preeminence. This basic vision, Levin
argues, persists today.

PS 718. LEWY, GUENTER. America in Vietnam. New York: Oxford University
Press, 1978. 540 pp.
Lewy analyzes U.S. involvement in Vietnam, beginning with a detailed empirical record of U.S. actions. He relies heavily on previously classified
military records, after-action reports, staff studies, and classified
intelligence. Lewy concludes that the war might have been won by the
U.S. and attributes the failure to a basic misunderstanding of the political and social dynamics of the conflict. He defends the American conduct
of the war, though, denying charges of large-scale, officially condoned
illegal and immoral activities.

PS 719. LIFTON, ROBERT J. and RICHARD FALK. Indefensible Weapons: The
Psychological Case Against Nuclearism. New York: Basic Books,
1982. 301 pp.
Lifton and Falk discuss what they call the problem of "nuclearism"--the
psychological, political, and military dependence on nuclear weapons as
an apparent solution to the problem of national security. The early part
of the book addresses individual and collective psychological responses
to "the bomb." Given its tremendous destructive capacity, nuclear technology dictates to the mind-set of American citizens rather than the mind-
set controlling the technology. The results are various "absurd" or at
least undesirable mental attitudes toward the nuclear threat, including
passivity or "numbness," resignation, the illusion of "security," a sense
of "futurelessness," etc. "Nuclearism" also has a corrosive effect on
the legitimacy of the nation's political institutions. Rather than capitu-
late to the illusions or the negative premises of "nuclearism" (the authors
argue), a broad-based movement for positive change should be mounted:
organized labor, physicians, and religious and educational institutions
should work toward increasing public awareness and encouraging candid
public discourse on the nuclear issue.

PS 720. LIPPMAN, WALTER. U.S. Foreign Policy: Shield of the Republic.
Boston: Little, Brown, 1943. 177 pp.
This book argues that failure to readjust America's foreign policy to
the changing international system, especially since the advent of American
prominence around 1900, has left the country in a dangerous situation.
America is ill-prepared for war or for peace, and its people are divided
on how to proceed on many foreign issues. Despite the building of a powerful navy and the extension of the U.S. sphere of influence to Asia and
the Pacific, America's foreign policy has remained essentially unchanged.
Lippman discusses the expanding international American commitment from
1898-1941, the "bankruptcy of American foreign relations" in this period,
and relations with the Atlantic community, Russia, and China.

PS 721. LISKA, GEORGE. Imperial America: The International Politics
of Primacy. Baltimore, Md.: Johns Hopkins University Press,
1967. 115 pp.
In an effort to determine the character of America's status as the "manifestly preponderant world power," Liska examines ancient and recent historical examples of states which attempted to establish order on a global
level, arguing that world order is inevitably structured around the actions
of major imperial powers. He believes that equilibrium in the "multipolar"
world political situation can be achieved only under the leadership of
the U.S. To achieve such equilibrium the U.S. must consolidate diplomatic
strength in Europe and promote allegiance among Afro-Asian states.
Although the contemporary war in Vietnam is mentioned only intermittently,
Liska's essay is a tacit defense and analysis of that action.

PS 722. MADDOX, ROBERT JAMES. The New Left and the Origins of the Cold
War. Princeton, N.J.: Princeton University Press, 1976.
169 pp.
This book is a critique of seven "New Left" histories of the Cold War;
Maddox's method is to compare the original sources which these authors
used with their resulting interpretations. Among the authors investigated
are William Appleman Williams, Gar Alperovitz, and Gabriel Kolko. Maddox
concludes that their carelessness with the sources led them to grievous
errors of interpretation, and that the "revisionists" are guilty of using
gross double standards when comparing the actions of U.S. and Soviet policy-
makers. Maddox makes no interpretation of or comment on U.S. foreign
policy in these years; the book is strictly a critical examination of
the work of the seven revisionists.

PS 723. MAHONEY, RICHARD D. JFK: Ordeal in Africa. New York: Oxford
University Press, 1983. 338 pp.
This account of the conduct of U.S. policy toward Africa in the early
1960s focuses primarily on the Congo, Ghana, and Portuguese Angola. The
book is an examination both of Kennedy's foreign policy style and method
and of African politics and superpower rivalry for control of the continent.
Mahoney concludes that Kennedy's approach was an exception to the antina-
tionalist tendency in American foreign policy; Kennedy believed that
nationalism was a robust force capable of sweeping away Communism as it
had colonialism.

PS 724. MAY, ERNEST R. Imperial Democracy: The Emergence of America
as a World Power. New York: Harcourt, Brace, 1961. 318 pp.
During the period of the Spanish-American War, the U.S. ascended rapidly
to international power. Examining American foreign policy during the
important decade of the 1890s, May discusses the changing image of the
U.S. as the European attitude shifted over a period of only a few years
from condescension to recognition of America as a world power. The policies of the McKinley administration and public opinion leading up to
involvement in the war with Spain are interpreted in this volume.

PS 725. MAY, ERNEST R. "Lessons" of the Past: The Use and Misuse of
History in American Foreign Policy. New York: Oxford University
Press, 1973. 220 pp.
May presents three theses on U.S. foreign policy: first, that policy-
makers base present decisions on past lessons. He provides examples from
W.W. II, the Cold War, Korea, and Vietnam. Second, May argues that policy-
makers frequently misuse and misinterpret history, and are guilty of narrow
thinking, relying often on simplistic reasoning and selective observation.
Third, he claims that American policy-makers can learn to use historical
lessons with greater discrimination and effectiveness, citing several
cases in support of this thesis.

PS 726. McCLENNAN, ROBERT. The Heathen Chinee: A Study of American Attitudes Toward China, 1890-1905. Columbus: Ohio State University Press, 1971. 272 pp.

The various attitudes of Americans toward China since the mid-19th century are the focus of this study. Prior to 1894, McClellan shows, Chinese immigrants were welcomed by Americans as potential railroad laborers. Eventually, however, resentment built up against the Chinese workers and legislation was enacted to ban Chinese labor. McClellan then details the second major American encounter with the Chinese which took place through American missionary and trade work in China. Their description of the Chinese and of American interests in China led to political interest in the Far East and made Americans aware of its growing role in world affairs. Throughout these encounters, McClennan asserts, a single American attitude dominated: an interpretation of the Chinese derived almost entirely from individual and immediate concerns of Americans and not from consideration of the Chinese. Consequently, U.S. policy in China has been the protection of American lives and property. A selected bibliography is included.

PS 727. McCORMICK, THOMAS J. China Market: America's Quest for Informal Empire, 1893-1901. Chicago: Quadrangle Books, 1967. 241 pp.

McCormick presents a study of U.S. economic Imperialism during the administrations of Grover Cleveland and William McKinley. He examines the debate between anti-Imperialists and expansionists, which culminated in 1898 with the triumph of anti-Imperialism, when the U.S. definitively turned to economic rather than political or military expansionism. McCormick's thesis is that Americans who desired commercial expansion into China "analyzed the causes of social instability as economic," and thus sought an economic solution to social instability through "overseas mercantile expansion." Thus the U.S. sought an "informal empire" through controlling markets.

PS 728. McGEEHAN, ROBERT. The German Rearmament Question: American Diplomacy and European Defense After World War II. Urbana: University of Illinois Press, 1971. 280 pp.

This study of the American effort to rearm Germany in the 1950s looks specifically at the impact of the Korean War, which prompted the American decision to seek a German military contribution to Western security. McGeehan looks at the diplomatic contest between France, which resisted American efforts to rearm Germany, and the Federal Republic of Germany, which bargained for national sovereignty. The conclusion considers the degree to which American diplomacy was successful, and how German rearmament served or damaged U.S. interests.

PS 729. MENDEL, DOUGLAS. American Foreign Policy in a Polycentric World. Belmont, Calif.: Dickenson, 1968. 132 pp.

Mendel examines the inability of American foreign policy to be prepared for the international political crises that arose in the post-W.W. II period. He traces this problem to the development of what he calls "polycentrism": in the modern age, each nation is more capable of an independent foreign policy based on a unique national interest. Foreign policy can no longer be dictated simply by the relations between the U.S. and the U.S.S.R., but must understand the multiple balance of power involving other nations. The book begins by examining how the U.S. government, in its domestic politics responds to international crises. This is followed by an examination of American foreign policy problems in Europe, the Middle East, and other key spheres of American influence. Finally the book identifies problem areas where, in the future, American foreign policy may confront international crises, and it offers contingency plans to meet them.

PS 730. MILLER, STUART CREIGHTON. "Benevolent Assimilation": The American
Conquest of the Philippines, 1899-1903. New Haven, Conn.: Yale
University Press, 1982. 340 pp.
Miller recounts the American response to the Philippine insurrection which
followed U.S. conquest of Spain in the 1898 war. The focus is on the
military in the Philippines, rather than on decision-makers in far-off
Washington. Miller blames the U.S. military for causing the Filipino
uprising through its total misunderstanding of the situation. He shows
the ineffectiveness of the efforts of the anti-Imperialists in the U.S.
to arouse opposition to the war, which the general public strongly supported. Miller closes his study with a comparison of the Philippine Insurrection and the Vietnam War.

PS 731. MYERS, RAMON H., ed. A U.S. Foreign Policy for Asia: The 1980's
and Beyond. Stanford, Calif.: Hoover Institution Press, 1982.
144 pp.
The articles in this volume advance an alternative foreign policy program
for Asia. The authors collectively recommend that Asia's strategic importance to the U.S. be considered as equivalent to that of Europe. The
book provides a new framework for examining the Afghan and Cambodian conflicts. The strategic importance of India is presented as comparable
to that of China. The authors stress the need for the U.S. to strengthen
and improve its relations with the Asian-Pacific Basin countries. A strong
naval and air force presence in the Indian and Pacific Oceans is recommended. Furthermore, American allies in the region should be encouraged
to cooperate with the American military.

PS 732. MYRDAL, ALVA. The Game of Disarmament: How the United States
and Russia Run the Arms Race. 1976; Rev. ed. New York: Pantheon
Books, 1982. 433 pp.
Myrdal provides a study of disarmament from an international point of
view, stating reasons for disarmament and for holding the military capacities of superpowers to a sensibly low level by mutual agreement. The
book begins by suggesting that the arms race may have its origins in the
general malaise of our era. Myrdal recounts the political failures that
mark the history of disarmament talks between the U.S. and the U.S.S.R.
The book also contains constructive proposals for resolving these problems
and sketches an international strategy for reaching agreement on disarmament.

PS 733. NATHAN, JAMES A. and JAMES K. OLIVER. Foreign Policymaking and
the American Political System. Boston: Little, Brown, 1983.
273 pp.
The authors argue that, since W.W. II, the U.S. has pursued an activist
foreign policy based on the belief that American security is closely tied
to the dynamics of world order. In the first years after W.W. II, America
attained strategic and economic superiority among nations, and the Soviet
Union appeared to be the only obstacle to U.S. foreign policy objectives.
In the 1960s and 1970s, international conditions began to constrain U.S.
foreign policy, specifically the diffusion of military capability to other
nations and the Soviet Union's achievement of military parity with the
U.S. The authors analyze three aspects of the American political system
which shaped postwar U.S. foreign policy: first, the constitutional framework within which American government deals with foreign and national
security policy; second, the foreign policy bureaucracy; and third, the
role of public opinion and interest groups in the formation of national
security policy.

PS 734. NEFF, DONALD. Warriors at Suez: Eisenhower Takes the U.S. into the Middle East. New York: Simon & Schuster, 1981. 479 pp.
The Suez crisis of 1956 is analyzed from the perspectives of the nations and the leaders involved. Neff begins with a historical essay tracing the history of European involvement in the region from the 19th century. The development of the crisis is then examined in the context of Egyptian-Israeli relations, British and French Colonial interests in Egypt, and the Cold War between the U.S. and the U.S.S.R. Neff analyzes the personal interests of the various heads of state, military leaders, and diplomats who participated in the Suez crisis.

PS 735. NEWHOUSE, JOHN. Cold Dawn: The Story of SALT. New York: Holt, Rinehart & Winston, 1973. 302 pp.
This book focuses on the complicated political and technical problems of the Strategic Arms Limitation Talks (SALT), particularly the implications of SALT I negotiations of 1972. Newhouse analyzes the problems of survival, nuclear limitation, the contrast between U.S. and Soviet strategic concepts, and diplomatic bureaucracies. Newhouse provides background information on the political and strategic circumstances which led to the convening of the negotiations. He also tries to analyze the relationship of SALT to the Nixon-Kissinger policy-making system.

PS 736. NEWHOUSE, JOHN, with MELVIN CROAN, EDWARD R. FRIED, and TIMOTHY W. STANLEY. U.S. Troops in Europe: Issues, Costs, and Choices. Washington, D.C.: Brookings Institution, 1971. 177 pp.
This book focuses on the American commitment to the defense of Western Europe, and explores the American concerns about this commitment. Based on public documents, secondary sources and media releases, the study looks at American policy and its possible alternatives in Western Europe. The book concerns itself with questions such as: Does the changing east-west political environment in Europe mean the military-political threat to Western Europe is diminishing? Is there a military balance between NATO and Warsaw pact forces in Central Europe, and how important are U.S. forces to that balance? Can Western Europe assume a greater share in NATO defense? The financial cost of alliance with Europe, and American concerns over U.S. deficits in international trade balance are also discussed.

PS 737. ODELL, JOHN S. U.S. International Monetary Policy: Markets, Power and Ideas as Sources of Change. Princeton, N.J.: Princeton University Press, 1982. 385 pp.
This study focuses on America's role in the operation, collapse, and reformation of the international monetary system during the 1960s and 1970s. It suggests a new conceptual framework for analyzing how economic policy is made and changed. According to Odell, explanations that rely on the properties of international systems, or on bureaucratic and domestic politics, are inadequate. Instead, he emphasizes how ideas in monetary theory affect policy.

PS 738. OSGOOD, ROBERT E. Ideals and Self-Interest in America's Foreign Relations: The Great Transformation of the Twentieth Century. Chicago: University of Chicago Press, 1953. 491 pp.
This interpretation of American attitudes toward world politics since 1900 takes for its central theme the tension between national self-interest and the universal ideal of a community of nations. Osgood studies the underlying motives of American international conduct and seeks to apply his analytical concepts to specific historical situations. He argues that "realism" based upon self-interest and devoid of ideals is self-defeating, and that America's moral leadership is indispensable to its survival as a nation.

PS 739.   OSGOOD, ROBERT E.   Limited War: The Challenge to American Strategy.
          Chicago: University of Chicago Press, 1957. 315 pp.
Osgood focuses on the necessity of America's preparation for limited as
well as large-scale war. The book is divided into three parts: (1) "War
and Policy," in which Osgood examines the differences of U.S. and Soviet
approaches to war; (2) "The Lessons of History," in which the decline
of limited war and the increasing possibility of total war in the 20th
century are discussed; (3) "American Strategy," which focuses on American
war policy since W.W. II, including containment policy. Osgood deals
with the question: "How can the U.S. employ military power as a rational
instrument of foreign policy when the destructive potentialities of war
exceed any rational purpose?" This issue is complicated by the unprecedented destructive power of modern weapons. Osgood's approach is a fundamental rethinking of traditional American attitudes concerning the nature
of war and its relationship to policy. It supports adoption of an overall
national strategy.

PS 740.   OSGOOD, ROBERT E.   Limited War Revisited. Boulder, Colo.: West-
          view Press, 1979. 124 pp.
This book focuses on the development of limited-war strategies since W.W.
II and analyzes the impact of the Vietnam war on these strategies. Osgood
calls for taking the Vietnam case as a lesson for U.S. policy-making toward
the Third World. Osgood asserts that limited war "will be an essential
part of U.S. military strategy." He concludes that U.S. commitments should
not be based solely on preventing the expansion of Communism in the Third
World.

PS 741.   OSGOOD, ROBERT E.   NATO: The Entangling Alliance. Chicago:
          University of Chicago Press, 1961. 416 pp.
This study of post-W.W. II American foreign policy examines the military
and strategic issues that challenged the North Atlantic alliance, the
pre-eminent instrument of security in the Cold War period. Osgood looks
at the role of military power in the nuclear age; the influence of military
strategies and capabilities upon international politics; and the political
and psychological ramifications of peacetime military collaboration within
NATO.

PS 742.   OSGOOD, ROBERT E., ROBERT W. TUCKER, HERBERT S. DINERSTEIN,
          FRANCIS E. ROURKE, ISAIAH FRANK, LAURENCE W. MARTIN, and
          GEORGE LISKA. America and the World: From The Truman Doctrine
          to Vietnam. Vol. I. Baltimore, Md.: Johns Hopkins University
          Press, 1970. 434 pp.
This volume is the first in a projected series of volumes that were to
appear in the year following each Presidential election. Robert Osgood
provides an introductory essay reappraising the U.S. response to the Cold
War; Robert W. Tucker discusses U.S. foreign policy and Herbert S.
Dinerstein Soviet policy; Francis E. Rourke, Osgood and Isaiah Frank then
address domestic issues in the formulation of policy, military issues,
and economic restraints, respectively. Finally, Laurence W. Martin discusses the European arena, and George Liska the Third World.

PS 743.   OSGOOD, ROBERT E., ROBERT W. TUCKER, HERBERT S. DINERSTEIN,
          FRANCIS E. ROURKE, LAURENCE W. MARTIN, DAVID P. CALLEO,
          BENJAMIN M. ROWLAND, and GEORGE LISKA. America and the World:
          Retreat from Empire: The First Nixon Administration. Vol. II.
          Baltimore, Md.: Johns Hopkins University Press, 1973. 350 pp.
The authors provide individually written essays on foreign policy topics
under the Nixon Administration. Robert E. Osgood and Robert W. Tucker
provide introductory essays; Herbert S. Dinerstein surveys the Soviet
outlook in regard to the U.S., Europe, and China; Benjamin M. Rowland
discusses U.S. policy toward Latin America; and the other authors provide

essays on such topics as strategic parity, the Third World, and the political economy of allied relations.

PS 744. OYE, KENNETH, ROBERT LIEBER, and DONALD ROTHCHILD. Eagle Defiant: United States Foreign Policy in the 1980s. Boston: Little, Brown, 1983. 404 pp.
This collection of articles addresses the foreign policy opportunities available to the Reagan administration and to policy-makers in general in the 1980s. The first section discusses the Reagan approach in the context of international and domestic politics, with articles by Oye and Schneider. Section II deals with functional problems, and contains articles by Posen and Van Evera on defense policy, Cohen on economic relations, Feinberg on Reaganomics and the Third World, and Lieber on energy policy and national security. Section III discusses U.S. policy in specific regions, containing articles by Dallin and Lapiders on the Soviet Union and Eastern Europe, Lowenthal on Latin America, Rothchild and Ravenhill on Africa, and Rubin on the Middle East.

PS 745. PACKENHAM, ROBERT A. Liberal America and the Third World: Political Development Ideas in Foreign Aid and Social Science. Princeton, N.J.: Princeton University Press, 1973. 395 pp.
This work is about notions of political development in the postwar era. Packenham believes the theories of policy-makers and scholars were profoundly affected by implicit premises of liberal ideology. This book studies and ultimately supports the "exceptionalist" hypothesis on the confrontation of liberal ideology with an obdurate reality. Packenham discusses the evolution of these doctrines and theories separately, demonstrating their common ideological roots. He discusses their utility and failures, and offers prescriptions in his conclusion.

PS 746. PATERSON, THOMAS. On Every Front: The Making of the Cold War. New York: Norton, 1979. 279 pp.
Paterson examines the evolution of U.S.-Soviet relations from 1945 to 1949. Domestic politics, economic stability at home and in Europe, and security against Soviet attack are given as the primary factors influencing U.S. policy during this period. The development of NATO, the Marshall Plan, and the conferences at Potsdam and Yalta are all considered. Paterson discusses Soviet internal political struggles and aggression in Eastern Europe, as well as the Soviet attempt to establish economic relations with Western Europe. The book also contains a chapter which deals with the impact of Congress and public opinion on U.S. foreign policy formulation.

PS 747. PERKINS, BRADFORD. The Great Rapprochement: England and the United States, 1895-1914. New York: Atheneum, 1968. 341 pp.
Using political and library materials, Perkins recounts the numerous ways in which closer ties between England and the U.S. were formed. He argues that as England found its power declining in this era it welcomed the increase of American power and sought closer ties as a barrier against the expansion of Russian and German influence. In essence the British accepted the Roosevelt Corollary to the Monroe Doctrine; the U.S. would keep political and commercial order in its hemisphere. Roosevelt, a key figure in this book, was representative of the American elite which sought closer ties with England; he is portrayed as a strong supporter of the doctrine of Anglo-Saxon racial and cultural superiority.

PS 748. PERKINS, DEXTER. A History of the Monroe Doctrine. Boston: Little, Brown, 1963. 463 pp.
Perkins believes that the Monroe Doctrine lies at the heart of America's foreign policy creed. He argues that there are few principles of U.S. diplomatic history as important, as consensual, and yet as misunderstood

as this doctrine. Perkins treats some of these misconceptions: for example, that the Monroe Doctrine prevented a re-conquest of South America
by a combination of European powers, that Theodore Roosevelt staved off
a German occupation of Venezuela and that the Monroe Doctrine proscribes
American involvement in European affairs.

PS 749. PFALTZGRAFF, ROBERT L., Jr., ed. Contrasting Approaches to Stra-
         tegic Arms Control. Lexington, Mass.: Lexington Books, 1974.
         350 pp.
These articles address the important arms control issues that grew out
of the SALT I treaty and would constitute the agenda for SALT II. Among
these issues are the negotiating differences between the U.S. and the
Soviet Union, bureaucratic decision-making regarding weapons systems in
the U.S. and the Soviet Union, and the implications of SALT for the U.S.-
Soviet military balance. The study also looks at the effect of alternative
types of arms agreements on U.S. alliances, in particular those with NATO
and Japan. Finally, the volume considers the perspectives of smaller
powers on the SALT agreement, the prospects for smaller nations becoming
nuclear powers, and the implications of SALT for the development of new
technologies.

PS 750. PIERRE, ANDREW J., ed. Nuclear Weapons in Europe. New York:
         Council on Foreign Relations, 1984. 118 pp.
This volume consists of essays by two European and two American experts
concerning the deployment of new American nuclear missiles in Europe.
The essays provide contrasting views on such questions as: Should Western
Europe continue to rely on the U.S. for its security? What role should
nuclear weapons play in the defense against a conventional or full force
attack? Should NATO adopt a "no first use" declaratory policy? Should
the INF (intermediate-range nuclear forces) and START (strategic arms
reduction talks) negotiations be merged? In his introduction, Andrew
J. Pierre provides the historical background, notes the basic issues,
and traces the official rationales for NATO's policies.

PS 751. PLATT, ALAN and LAWRENCE WEILER, eds. Congress and Arms Control.
         Boulder, Colo.: Westview Press, 1978. 277 pp.
This volume focuses on how the changing role of Congress in foreign policy
has affected various arms control issues such as SALT, nonproliferation,
arms sales, and weapons procurement. It also discusses the role of secrecy
in arms negotiations, the involvement of the Senate Foreign Relations
Committee in the formulation of arms control policy, and the European
perspective on Congressional involvement in defense issues. The contributors are Alton Frye, Les Aspin, Thomas Dine, Dick Clarke, Philip J. Farley,
Warren H. Donnelly, Kurt Lauk, Alan Cranston, and the editors.

PS 752. PLISCHKE, ELMER, ed. Modern Diplomacy: The Art and the Artisans.
         Washington, D.C.: American Enterprise Institute, 1979.
         456 pp.
This collection of essays by such statesmen, diplomats, and academicians
as Thomas A. Bailey, Charles W. Thayer, and Dean Rusk discusses modern
diplomacy and its practitioners. The editor claims that the volume's
perspective differs from conventional treatments of diplomacy, which study
such issues as power politics and comparative policy analysis; these essays
are concerned, rather, with the "concept, nature, scope, and development
of diplomacy." Essays by George F. Kennan and Clare Boothe Luce, among
others, discuss the question of professional and non-professional diplomats;
Harry S. Truman, Hugh S. Gibson, and William M. Franklin address democratic
and "open" diplomacy; and Fred Charles Ikle and Henry Kissinger discuss
the functions of diplomats, from negotiation to observance of protocol.

PS 753. **PRANGE, GORDON W., with DONALD M. GOLDSTEIN and KATHERINE V. DILLON.** At Dawn We Slept: The Untold Story of Pearl Harbor. New York: McGraw-Hill, 1981. 873 pp.
Prange presents an account of the attack on Pearl Harbor, including both the Japanese and American points of view. This study is divided into three parts: a discussion of the plans of the Japanese Naval General Staff in 1941, including Admiral Yamamoto's Pearl Harbor project; the putting of the Pearl Harbor attack plan into action; and the aftermath of the attack. Military and political leaders in Hawaii and Washington are judged to be guilty of enormous errors, but Japanese skill and determination are stressed, too. Many Japanese who planned the attack were interviewed for this study.

PS 754. **PRANGE, GORDON W. with DONALD M. GOLDSTEIN and KATHERINE V. DILLON.** Miracle at Midway. New York: McGraw-Hill, 1982. 469 pp.
Prange's book is an account of the June 1942 American naval victory over Japan at Midway island. The focus is on the exercise of military command. Prange used archives and conducted interviews on both sides of the Pacific. The implications of Midway for the future conduct of naval warfare are considered. The Midway triumph meant that the U.S. had seized and would sustain the offensive in the Pacific theater.

PS 755. **PRUITT, DEAN G. and RICHARD C. SNYDER.** Theory and Research on the Causes of War. Englewood Cliffs, N.J.: Prentice-Hall, 1969. 314 pp.
This collection of articles summarizes recent scholarship in the U.S. on the causes of war. It discusses the motives that impel states into war; the political perceptions which precede entry into war and how these perceptions change as war progresses; military and non-military conditions that restrain nations from entering war; and the statistical correlates of war. The book also discusses various research methods under development and the prospects for an integrated theory.

PS 756. **QUANDT, WILLIAM B.** Decade of Decisions: American Policy Toward the Arab-Israeli Conflict, 1967-1976. Berkeley: University of California Press, 1977. 313 pp.
Quandt presents an analysis of U.S. foreign policy in the Middle East during the Arab-Israeli conflict of 1967-76, a decade of intense and repeated clashes. His chronological narrative takes four complementary perspectives on the conflict, which seek to provide an understanding of U.S. conduct. The "national interests perspective" encompasses traditional explanations offered by participants. The "domestic politics perspective" emphasizes the influence of interest groups and public opinion on policy. The "bureaucratic politics perspective" and the "Presidential leadership perspective" focus, respectively, on the actions and interests of the executive branch organizations, and of the President and his close advisers.

PS 757. **RADOSH, RONALD.** American Labor and United States Foreign Policy. New York: Random House, 1969. 463 pp.
Radosh examines the cooperation between organized labor and the Federal government in foreign policy matters since the turn of the century. His analysis is based on the theory that labor unions perceive themselves as junior partners to large corporations, and that union leaders seek only those gains that are acceptable to the corporate community. These leaders do not challenge corporate foreign policy with its continuing Cold War premises for fear that such challenges will threaten both corporate profits and union gains. To end this situation, the author calls for an independent union movement controlled by the rank-and-file and not tied to the machinery of the state.

PS 758. RAMAZANI, RUHOLLAH K. The United States and Iran: The Patterns
         of Influence. New York: Praeger, 1982. 179 pp.
This book focuses on the contemporary relationship between the U.S. and
Iran, with special attention to U.S. interference with Iran's domestic
and foreign policies during the Shah's reign from 1941 to 1979. Ramazani
attempts to analyze the nature of U.S. influence in Iran by examining
the historical development of U.S. policy toward that country. He concludes that Iranian domestic policies were directly linked with Iran's
foreign policy toward the U.S., and that this linkage contributed to the
Iranian revolution.

PS 759. RAVENAL, EARL C. Never Again: Learning from America's Foreign
         Policy Failures. Philadelphia, Pa.: Temple University Press,
         1978. 153 pp.
Ravenal examines what Americans believe they have learned from recent
foreign policy experiences, specifically from Vietnam. He describes five
types of lessons drawn from Vietnam, all of which conclude, though for
different reasons, that the U.S. must never again involve itself in such
a situation. The author favors the "strategic" critique, which implies
a foreign policy aimed at reconciling U.S. interests with the changed
character of the international system. He sees two possible directions
for the U.S. policy: either U.S. involvement in managed internationalism
or a less institutionalized system with U.S. disengagement.

PS 760. RECORD, JEFFREY. The Rapid Deployment Force and U.S. Military
         Intervention in the Persian Gulf. Cambridge, Mass.: Institute
         for Foreign Policy Analysis, 1981. 84 pp.
Record analyzes the existing deficiencies in the Rapid Deployment Force
(RDF), especially in its capacity to intervene in the Persian Gulf and
keep the oil lanes open in periods of crisis. Despite RDF's origins as
a force designed to respond principally to Middle East emergencies, the
author finds that it lacks even this capacity. The main problems are
inadequate strategic and tactical mobility, an insufficient forcible-entry
capacity, a confused and divided command apparatus, and the absence of
assured access to Middle East territory in a crisis. After developing
his criticism, Record proposes certain reforms which would improve the
capacities of the RDF.

PS 761. REVELEY, W. TAYLOR III. War Powers of the President and Congress:
         Who Holds the Arrows and Olive Branch? Charlottesville: Univer-
         sity Press of Virginia, 1981. 394 pp.
Reveley begins with two basic questions: What are "war powers"? How
has control of war powers evolved since 1789? He establishes a conceptual
framework by focusing on the historical struggle for authority between
Congress and the Executive branches of government, and on the Constitution's war powers provisions which tend to support Congressional dominance,
although with ambiguities. Reveley also discusses the original intentions
of the Constitution's authors. The remainder of the text discusses the
evolution of war powers from 1789 to date, specifically tracing the erratic
growth in executive war power. Recommendations are offered which integrate
the original intentions of the Constitution with current circumstances.

PS 762. ROBBINS, CARLA ANNE. The Cuban Threat. New York: McGraw-Hill,
         1983. 351 pp.
Robbins examines many of the assumptions and myths that have guided U.S.
policy toward Cuba, and attempts to examine how real the Cuban threat
is and how the U.S. must respond. She begins with a presentation of Cuba's
early efforts to export revolution in South America, and the origins of
U.S.-Cuban hostilities. This is followed by a look at Cuba's other foreign
relations, especially with the Soviet Union and Angola. The author concludes with an argument which tries to debunk the Cuban threat as myth,
and proposes steps toward a new American policy.

PS 763. ROSE, LISLIE. The Roots of Tragedy: The U.S. and the Struggle
         for Asia, 1945-53. Westport, Conn.: Greenwood Press, 1976.
         262 pp.
This book is a study of the American failure to respond to anti-Colonial
nationalism in Vietnam, Indonesia, Korea, and China during the years following W.W. II. Rose tries to determine why the American response to
that revolt was "so tragically inappropriate." While the book provides
an historical account of U.S. involvement in the region, it is more an
interpretive essay than a comprehensive historical analysis. The author
concludes with a consideration of the Korean War which views it as an
inevitable prelude to the Vietnam War.

PS 764. ROSENAU, JAMES N., ed. Domestic Sources of Foreign Policy. New
         York: Free Press, 1967. 340 pp.
This collection of articles contrasts domestic political processes and
behavior in the framework of foreign policy. Rosenau argues in his introduction that institutional analyses and case studies are insufficient
tools for studying nongovernmental variables and their impact on foreign
policy. This volume contains essays by political scientists and sociologists; among them are Milton Rosenberg's "Attitude Change and Foreign
Policy in the Cold War Era," Warren Miller's "Voting and Foreign Policy,"
Scott Greer's "Urbanization, Parochialism and Foreign Policy Crisis,"
and Theodore Lowi's "Making Democracy Safe for the World: National Politics and Foreign Policy." Rosenau argues that the essays reveal two themes:
first, that foreign policy grows out of tensions between groups with differing interests; and, second, that leaders are variously conceived as
"perpetuators and reconcilers" of these clashes.

PS 765. ROSTOW, WALT W. The Diffusion of Power: An Essay in Recent His-
         tory. New York: Macmillan, 1972. 739 pp.
Rostow offers first-hand accounts of American foreign policy from 1957-
72. He emphasizes that presidential problems are inherited to some degree
and that history and foreign policy are part of a developing process which
does not abruptly change to reflect a change in leadership. The primary
thesis of the book is that the diffusion of world power may be a stabilizing rather than a disruptive force. Rostow applies this thesis to the
presidencies and foreign policy of Eisenhower, Kennedy, Johnson, and Nixon.
The work is also the author's attempt to define his role in the Johnson
administration, where he was an early and persistent advocate of strong
American involvement in Vietnam.

PS 766. ROSTOW, WALT W. The United States in the World Arena: An Essay
         in Recent History. New York: Harper, 1960. 568 pp.
Rostow sketches patterns of relationships between American society and
world politics. He starts with the panorama of world history from the
19th century, and elaborates on details of 20th-century history with the
U.S. always as focal point. Rostow's central concern is with the prospective alternatives of U.S. relationsips to world affairs, giving special
attention to American ways of problem-solving in domestic and international
affairs. The questions he addresses include: (1) How has the nature
and evolution of American life at home affected the nation's foreign and
military policy performance? (2) What foreseeable problems on the world
scene must the U.S. solve in order to protect its interests? (3) How
may these be solved while maintaining the quality of domestic society?
Rostow closes with a discussion of possible future developments.

PS 767. ROTHSTEIN, ROBERT. The Third World and United States Foreign
         Policy. Boulder, Colo.: Westview Press, 1981. 271 pp.
This book examines U.S. policy toward Latin America, South Asia, and sub-
Saharan Africa in the context of the "North-South" dialogue. Rothstein
delineates the specific national interests of this group of states, and

the relevance of these interests to U.S. foreign policy imperatives. The focus of the book is the responsibility of the U.S. toward these nations in matters of food policy, economic trade, and the management of world debt. The book concludes with a discussion of the relationship between U.S. policy toward the Third World and East-West relations. The threat of social and political disintegration in the Third World is also considered.

PS 768. **ROURKE, FRANCES.** Bureaucracy and Foreign Policy. Baltimore, Md.: Johns Hopkins University Press, 1972. 80 pp.
The author argues that foreign policy is the product of a system of collective decision-making in which the President and his political appointees play a leading role and career bureaucrats are often relegated to minor parts. Rourke discusses the process by which bureaucratic decision-making in foreign policy occurs to show that bureaucrats do not wield an exclusive or monopolistic kind of authority. Reform of the foreign policy process should not be sought in administrative reorganization, but through a reordering of the basic political structure. Rourke argues for the establishment of limits on the Presidential monopoly over the conduct of foreign affairs.

PS 769. **RUBIN, BARRY.** Paved with Good Intentions: The American Experience and Iran. New York: Oxford University Press, 1980. 426 pp.
Rubin presents a survey and analysis of U.S.-Persian relations since the beginning of the 20th century. The author is concerned with explaining how the U.S. was "transformed in Iranian eyes from their nation's savior to the world-devouring satan of the Khomeini era." Rubin provides a brief account of Persian history before beginning a detailed account of more recent events. He notes the persistent mutual ignorance that has characterized U.S.-Iranian relations, particularly the U.S. tendency to ignore the currents of Mideast politics in formulating otherwise rational policy.

PS 770. **RUSSETT, BRUCE M.**, ed. Peace, War, and Numbers. Beverly Hills, Calif.: Sage, 1972. 352 pp.
These articles are quantitative "macroscopic" studies of war. J. David Singer, Stuart Bremer and John Stuckey explore the impact of capability distribution and uncertainty on major wars. Michael D. Wallace focuses on status inconsistency and armament levels. Nazli Choveri and Robert C. North look at the long-term dynamics of population and technology in four countries. National differences are linked to foreign conflict behavior by Jonathan Wilkenfeld, while R. J. Rummell uses attribute and behavior distances to explain U.S. conflict involvement. Steven Rosen finds that wealth and "capability to suffer" are useful predictors of victory in war. Escalation sequences are studied by Jeffrey Milstein in the context of Arab-Israeli violence, and John D. Sullivan examines the connection between U.S. symbolic commitments and escalation in Vietnam. Bruce Russett examines U.S. public opinion changes regarding defense spending.

PS 771. **RUSSETT, BRUCE M.**, ed. What Price Vigilance? The Burdens of National Defense. New Haven, Conn.: Yale University Press, 1970. 261 pp.
This book is an empirical investigation into the reasons for and the consequences of high levels of expenditure on U.S. defense. It presents correlations between Congressional voting on defense and on other national spending issues; analyzes both the effect of treaty alliance commitments on major military power and the opportunity cost of U.S. defense; and compares the U.S. defense burden with defense spending in other nations. The appendix is a discussion of mathematical models of arms races.

PS 772. SAFRAN, NADAV. Israel: The Embattled Ally. Cambridge, Mass.:
          Harvard University Press, 1978. 633 pp.
Safran describes U.S.-Israeli relations from the Balfour Declaration to
1978. He argues that the 1969 and 1973 wars, as well as the "war of attri-
tion" in 1969-70, resulted in the evolution of the American-Israeli relationship "from a connection of qualified friendship to a bond of alliance
between friends." He traces this relationship through four stages: in
the first, from 1948-57, the U.S. concern was to bring Israel into their
anti-Soviet plan. In the second, from 1957-67, the U.S. ceased trying
to enlist the Arab countries as allies and began to see Israel, politically
stable and militarily strong, as a possible asset; in the 1967 crisis
the U.S. stood firmly by Israel. In the third stage, 1967-73, the decision
to support Israel on the territorial issue "brought the real American
interest in complete harmony with the moral interest in Israel." In the
years from 1973 to 1975 the U.S. intervened dramatically in the Middle
East with arms and financial assistance. Safran argues that in the next
stage "a formal American-Israeli mutual security pact" must replace the
"present tacit alliance."

PS 773. SAUNDERS, HAROLD H. The Middle East Problem in the 1980s. Washing-
          ton, D.C.: American Enterprise Institute, 1981. 83 pp.
Saunders's essay begins by asserting that, for a variety of reasons, U.S.
effectiveness in the global politics of the 1990s will be substantially
determined by its handling of the Middle East problems of the 1980s.
He examines how forces at work in the Middle East will challenge the ability of the U.S. to pursue its interests in this critical region and will
weaken the U.S. position in the world. The politics of the Middle East
are analyzed in the context of a systematic examination of U.S. interests
in the area, including oil, Arab-Israeli peace, and the global strategic
balance. In conclusion, the author devises a national policy to meet
these challenges.

PS 774. SCHECHTMAN, JOSEPH. The United States and the Jewish State Move-
          ment: The Crucial Decade, 1939-1949. New York: Thomas Yoseloff,
          1966. 474 pp.
Schechtman studies the American government's policy toward Zionism and
Palestine during, and immediately after, W.W. II. It was in these years
that the U.S. emerged as a major actor in the Middle East. The author
attends not only to the foreign policy aspects of the Palestine question,
especially as regards Anglo-American and Soviet relations, but also to
Zionism as a factor in the American political scene. He bases his work
on federal government records, documents and official publications of
Zionist organizations, writings of American statesmen, and contemporary
reportage.

PS 775. SCHELLING, THOMAS C. and MORTON H. HALPERIN. Strategy and Arms
          Control. New York: Twentieth Century Fund, 1961. 148 pp.
The authors explore the significance of arms control in the era of inter-
continental weapons, attempting to integrate arms control with foreign
and national security policy. While recognizing that the arms race is
more a result than a cause of antagonism between nations, the authors
note that the superpowers also have a common interest in arms control.
Arms control is discussed in relation to the incentive for premeditated
attack, limited war, crises, technological progress, the tempo of decision-
making, political-military interrelations, the strategic balance, and
bargaining.

PS 776. **SELZER, MICHAEL.** Israel as a Factor in Jewish-Gentile Relations in America: Observations in the Aftermath of the June, 1967 War. New York: American Council for Judaism, 1968. 27 pp.
Selzer considers the impact of Israel's Six Day War on American social and political life, emphasizing the divergent responses of American Jewish, Protestant, and black organizations and what these responses reveal about the capacities of these groups to work cooperatively. The pamphlet stresses the role of Jewish tradition in shaping the ideal and reality of the modern Jewish state, and examines how that tradition influenced discussions of Zionism in the late 1960s, both among American Jews and Americans concerned with ecumenical dialogue and among a larger group of civil rights advocates concerned with the moral problems of a democracy. Selzer is ultimately critical of narrow self-interests and urges American Jews to assist the black struggle for equal rights.

PS 777. **SHEEHAN, NEIL,** et al. The Pentagon Papers. New York: Quadrangle Books, 1971. 810 pp.
This narrative history of U.S. government involvement in Indochina from W.W. II to May 1968 is condensed from the original 3000-page study which Secretary of Defense McNamara commissioned in 1967. It was intended as a top secret, candid inquiry into the origins of America's dilemma in Vietnam. The Pentagon Papers became part of Vietnam era history when they were leaked to the New York Times and published in 1971, despite government attempts to suppress their release. The Papers describe, often in the words of the decision-makers themselves, how and why the key decisions were made which drew the U.S. ever deeper into the Vietnam War.

PS 778. **SHERWIN, MARTIN.** A World Destroyed: The Atomic Bomb and the Grand Alliance. New York: Knopf, 1975. 315 pp.
Sherwin focuses on the impact of the atomic bomb on international diplomacy during the period after W.W. II. His book centers on four questions: (1) Did the development of the atomic bomb affect American policies toward the Soviet Union? (2) Was diplomatic consideration toward the Soviet Union a factor influencing the use of the bomb against Japan? (3) Did diplomatic considerations regarding postwar relations with the Soviet Union influence the formulation of Roosevelt's atomic energy policies? (4) How did these policies affect the development of atomic energy and the diplomatic policies of successive administrations? Sherwin argues that the decision to drop the atomic bomb on Hiroshima was as much a means to justify the massive public expenditure as it was an act of strategy or diplomacy.

PS 779. **SILK, LEONARD** and **MARK SILK.** The American Establishment. New York: Basic Books, 1980. 351 pp.
This book examines the private sources that have influenced policy-making in the U.S. from the Kennedy administration to the present. Silk examines in particular the influence of Harvard University and the Protestant Church on various policy-makers. Short histories of research institutions, such as the Council on Foreign Relations, the Brookings Institution, and the Ford Foundation, are included to indicate the relations between government and the private sector, and their impact on the formulation of both domestic and foreign policy. Silk concludes with a chapter assessing the function of private forces in American political culture, and describing the populist challenge to these forces.

PS 780. **SMITH, GERARD.** Doubletalk: The Story of the First Strategic Arms Limitation Talks. Garden City, N.Y.: Doubleday, 1980. 555 pp.
This is an analysis of the first SALT talks by the U.S. Chief Delegate. Smith presents a picture of the international negotiations that took place within the departments of the U.S. government as well as the negotiations

with the Soviet delegation. The book considers the internal politics
of the SALT talks, pointing out the two central weaknesses of these talks:
the lack of adequate attention to ICBM protection and the failure to deal
with MIRVs. Smith is seriously critical of Nixon-Kissinger "back-channel"
negotiations which often undermined the work of the U.S. delegation.

PS 781. SNETSINGER, JOHN. Truman, the Jewish Vote, and the Creation of
Israel. Stanford, Calif.: Hoover Institution Press, 1974.
208 pp.
Snetsinger offers a case study of the ways in which U.S. foreign policy
can be decisively influenced by domestic political pressures. The Truman
Administration's support for the new Jewish state did not, Snetsinger
contends, emerge out of a commitment to the Zionist program or a disinterested consideration of the national interest. Instead, it was a felt
need to cultivate the Jewish vote in anticipation of the 1948 elections
that was most crucial in moving the President away from previous vacil-
lating policies. Snetsinger works from official documents, personal interviews, published sources, and manuscript collections, most importantly
the Harry S. Truman and Clark Clifford papers.

PS 782. SOFAER, ABRAHAM D. War, Foreign Affairs and Constitutional Power:
The Origins. Cambridge, Mass.: Ballinger, 1976. 533 pp.
This book is a product of the social and political protests and the large
and various legal debates precipitated by the war in Vietnam. The essential question the work addresses is what right "the executive had to commit
armed force to hostilities without congressional authorization." Sofaer
turns to American history for precedents for the Vietnam War. In doing
so he examines the Constitution and its background; other presidents,
such as John Adams and Thomas Jefferson, and their policies; and the changing nature of executive power. Sofaer examines how the controversy between
Congress and the President during the Vietnam War was not really new;
it was perhaps a symptom of similar unresolved controversies that had
plagued other administrations in the past. From a legal point of view,
the author considers the meaning of the Constitution and the "vexing question of the separation of powers."

PS 783. SORENSEN, THOMAS C. The Word War: The Story of American Propaganda. New York: Harper & Row, 1968. 337 pp.
Sorensen discusses the American government's efforts to influence foreign
public opinion, tracing the history of U.S. propaganda from W.W. I to
the 1960s. He analyzes and evaluates American foreign information programs,
particularly the strengthening of the U.S. Information Agency that took
place under the directorship of Edward R. Murrow. Sorensen concludes
with a look at the strengths and weaknesses of the present U.S.I.A. He
suggests that schools of international affairs concentrate more on providing education that prepares graduates to communicate effectively with
foreign public opinion.

PS 784. SPANIER, JOHN. American Foreign Policy Since World War II. New
York: Praeger, 1977. 354 pp.
Using an approach that emphasizes conflict between states, this work begins
by describing the formation of the international state system based on
"balance-of-power," and the origins of the distinct style of U.S. diplomacy.
Spanier then examines the evolution of American foreign policy, including
the implementation of the Marshall Plan and the creation of NATO under
Truman, U.S. efforts to contain Communist expansion in Asia and Communist
infiltration at home, the increasing importance of the Third World in
U.S. policy considerations, and the transformation of the state system
into a bipolar arrangement.

PS 785. SPANIER, JOHN. Congress, the Presidency, and American Foreign
         Policy. New York: Praeger, 1974. 180 pp.
This book discusses the connection between the decision-making process
and the formulation of foreign policy in the U.S. since W.W. II. Spanier
focuses on the conflict between bureaucratic interests and Executive prerogative in the making of foreign policy. He describes the configuration
of agency interests which spring up around various issues of foreign policy,
including as case studies the anti-ballistic missile decision, the mining
of Haiphong harbor, and the passage of the War Powers Act. These events
are examined in the context of the conflicting Constitutional authorities
enjoyed by the President and the Congress.

PS 786. SPANIER, JOHN and ERIC M. USLANDER. Foreign Policy and the Demo-
         cratic Dilemmas. New York: Praeger, 1978. 264 pp.
This is a study of how America's foreign policy is made, with special
attention to the difference between the process of foreign policy-making
and that of domestic policy-making. The rational actor and bureaucratic
modes of decision-making are employed in the discussion of five case
studies: the Cuban missile crisis, the Iranian hostage crisis (1979-1981),
the enactment of ABM legislation by the Johnson and Nixon administrations,
the SALT II debates in the Senate, and energy legislation in the Congress.
The study addresses these specific dilemmas: governmental checks and
balances versus Presidential concentration of power, democratic process
versus policy output, and broad democratic participation versus foreign
policy-making by a small elite.

PS 787. SPYKMAN, NICHOLAS. America's Strategy in World Politics. New
         York: Harcourt Brace, 1942. 500 pp.
Spykman undertakes a study of what he feels is the most basic issue of
American foreign policy, the choice between isolation and intervention.
He applies the special circumstances of American security to the general
experiences of states and the nature of international relations. From
this he offers an analysis of America's future strategic options in terms
of geography and power. Writing at the outbreak of W.W. II, which effectively sealed the dispute between isolationism and integration for a time,
Spykman argues that isolation, with its deep roots in the American political psyche, will reemerge.

PS 788. STEINBRUNER, JOHN D. and LEON V. SIGAL, eds. Alliance Security:
         NATO and the No-First Use Question. Washington, D.C.: Brookings
         Institution, 1983. 222 pp.
The debate over the use of nuclear weapons in defense of Europe was intensified in the 1980s by two events: the 1979 NATO decision to deploy U.S.
nuclear missiles in response to Soviet deployments, and the public advocacy
by four prominent Americans for the formal renunciation of a "first use"
of nuclear weapons. This latter position was immediately contested by
prominent West Germans insisting on the maintenance of a U.S. deterrent
force against conventional attack. In this volume, American and European
scholars examine the underlying security issues involved.

PS 789. STOBAUGH, ROBERT and DANIEL YERGIN, eds. Energy Future: Report
         of the Project at the Harvard Business School. 1979; Rev. ed.
         New York: Random House, 1983. 459 pp.
The articles in this collection analyze the world energy supply and the
energy market in order to clarify the policy issues which confront the
U.S. The study looks at the potential and problems of alternative energy
sources for the U.S. economy. Individual studies look at the prospects
of oil, natural gas, coal, nuclear energy, solar energy, and better conservation. The authors advance moderate, "balanced" energy programs,
combining traditional and alternative approaches to energy supply.

PS 790. SWANSON, ROGER. _Intergovernmental Perspectives on Canada-U.S. Relations_. New York: New York University Press, 1978. 278 pp.

This book traces U.S. relations with Canada from the 1940s to the present, with specific reference to economics, strategic interests, and cultural affairs. Swanson describes the differences between governmental institutions in the two countries--including the relative power of the executive and legislative branches--and discusses the significance of the diplomatic corps. A number of organizations which regulate trade and transnational relations are examined, including those dealing with fishery rights, mutual security, and commerce. A comparative study of relations between Federal and state or province governments in each nation is also included.

PS 791. THOMPSON, JAMES C. _Rolling Thunder_. Chapel Hill: University of North Carolina Press, 1980. 199 pp.

This book details the planning and the failure of a U.S. bombing campaign against Vietnam early in the Johnson Administration. Thompson attributes the failure to bureaucratic disputes which surrounded the formulation and implementation of the program. Bureaucratic and personal self-interest, organizational characteristics, and Presidential concerns are all considered as elements in the program's ineffectiveness. Thompson's analytic framework is explained through an overview of the "bureaucratic politics" literature in which the work of Richard Cyert, James March, John Steinbruner, and Morton Halperin is discussed.

PS 792. THOMPSON, JAMES C., PETER STANLEY, and JOHN CURTIS PERRY. _Sentimental Imperialists: The American Experience in East Asia_. New York: Harper & Row, 1981. 352 pp.

This volume examines the changes in U.S. foreign policy toward the Far East and its relation to American cultural conceptions of the area. The opening of Japan and the evolution of the "open door" policy in China are viewed as expressions of the U.S.'s desire to "civilize" the Far East at a profit. Imperialism and the acquisition of Pacific islands during the Spanish American War are seen by these authors as part of a process of expansionism that culminated in W.W. II. U.S. reactions to the Chinese Revolution and the gradual increase in U.S. involvement in Vietnam are also discussed.

PS 793. THOMPSON, KENNETH W. _Foreign Assistance: A View from the Private Sector_. Notre Dame, Ind.: University of Notre Dame Press, 1972. 160 pp.

Thompson presents a study of the nature and activities of the foreign assistance programs of private foundations. He especially focuses on the Rockefeller Foundation aid program and its activities toward cultural, educational, public health, and agricultural programs. Thompson argues that private programs usually have clear objectives, qualified personnel and participation of aid recipients. These aid programs are often more successful than government aid programs which are often short-term and have multi-purpose objectives. Thompson tries to underline the value of the private sector in foreign assistance and international cooperation, especially in light of the decline of foreign assistance from government sources.

PS 794. THOMPSON, KENNETH W. _Interpreters and Critics of the Cold War_. Washington, D.C.: University Press of America, 1978. 113 pp.

This book is a survey of American literature on the Cold War since the 1950s. Thompson discusses the impact that different perspectives on the Cold War have had on the method of discourse utilized by various writers. Thompson focuses on the opinions of four persons--diplomat George F. Kennan, journalist Walter Lippmann, theologian Reinhold Niebuhr, and political philosopher Hans J. Morgenthau. The positions these men have held toward

American foreign policy and toward the Soviet Union have deviated from the orthodoxy at the White House. All four have consistently advocated that "national interest and not a set of noble universalistic goals is the best overall guide to foreign policy."

PS 795. THOMPSON, KENNETH W. Morality and Foreign Policy. Baton Rouge: Louisiana State University Press, 1980. 197 pp.
Thompson focuses on the dilemma of morality and politics on the international scale. He reviews this issue from ancient Rome to President Carter's emphasis on human rights. Instead of presenting new alternatives, this book provides a comprehensive review of the literature in this area.

PS 796. TIEN, HUNG-MAO, ed. Mainland China, Taiwan, and U.S. Policy. Cambridge, Mass.: Oelgeschlager, Gunn & Hain, 1983. 270 pp.
These articles discuss the complex triangular politics between the Republic of China (Taiwan), the People's Republic of China (PRC), and the U.S.; the contributors, scholars of Chinese origin, present a wide range of views. U.S. arms sales to Taiwan are discussed in the context of their implications for U.S. relations with Communist China and Taiwan. The efforts of the PRC at peaceful reunification are examined from the perspectives of both Chinas, and of the native Taiwanese. Other articles address the political, social, and cultural developments which have taken place in China and Taiwan. The volume also looks into the future prospects for PRC-Taiwan relations.

PS 797. TILLMAN, SETH P. The United States in the Middle East: Interests and Obstacles. Bloomington: Indiana University Press, 1982. 333 pp.
Tillman examines U.S. politics and interests in the Middle East, and provides a brief review of the region's history. He then examines the main actors in the region: Saudi Arabia, Israel, the Palestinians, and the Soviet Union. The author concludes by considering ways in which peace might be achieved and U.S. interests secured in the region. He favors an agreement among the conflicting parties in accordance with U.N. Resolution 242, along with a firmer American resolve to enforce the resolution.

PS 798. TOW, WILLIAM T. and WILLIAM F. FEENEY, eds. U.S. Foreign Policy and Asian-Pacific Security: A Transregional Approach. Boulder, Colo.: Westview Press, 1982. 264 pp.
This book addresses the Reagan Administration's re-establishment of an American military presence in Asia and the Pacific, and examines the problems raised by this new commitment. Some of the problems discussed are the differences between U.S. and Japanese views on Japanese defense expenditures and force levels, and the ASEAN's (Association for Southeast Asian Nations) anxiety over U.S. military ties to China. Also considered are plans to expand ANZUS (the U.S.'s pact with Australia and New Zealand), and the problems confronting the U.S. basing of forces. The volume is sympathetic to the American role in the region and emphasizes the region's importance to the U.S.

PS 799. TUCHMAN, BARBARA. Stilwell and the American Experience in China, 1911-1945. New York: Macmillan, 1971. 621 pp.
The career of General Joseph Stilwell is the focus of this book. Stilwell was a military liaison officer during the 1940s and an influential figure in the relationship between China and the U.S. There are two themes running through this history: a biographical account of the life of the colorful Stilwell, and an analysis of foreign relations with China over a thirty-five year period. Tuchman examines the crucial events from the 1911 Chinese revolution to the end of W.W. II alongside the personality and career of a single individual.

PS 800. TUCKER, ROBERT W. The Purposes of American Power: An Essay on
National Security. New York: Praeger, 1981. 190 pp.
Tucker argues that American policy and America's role in the international
system are at a critical juncture in history. He seeks to analyze the
main features of U.S. policy in the 1970s, a period of American decline.
He examines the conceptual and practical flaws of detente, and the significance of Central America, the Third World, and the Persian Gulf for
U.S. security interests. Tucker comments on the role and significance
of U.S. allies, and discusses two variants of containment theory. Finally,
he offers alternative policy options for the future.

PS 801. TYSON, JAMES. U.S. International Broadcasting and National Security. New York: Ramapo Press, 1983. 153 pp.
In this book, Tyson focuses his attention on U.S. international broadcasting activities. He asserts that these activities, such as Radio Free
Europe, Radio Liberty and USIA Voice of America, work as elements of
national security.

PS 802. U.S. CONGRESS, COMMITTEE ON FOREIGN AFFAIRS, SUBCOMMITTEE ON
AFRICA. U.S. Interests in Africa. Washington, D.C.: U.S. Govern-
ment Printing Office, 1980. 540 pp.
The text reports the testimony of experts and committee members who
appeared before the House Subcommittee on Africa during the fall of 1979.
These hearings provided a general examination of U.S. interests in Africa,
encompassing military, diplomatic, humanitarian, and developmental concerns.
The witnesses were primarily academic and government authorities.

PS 803. U.S. CONGRESS, SENATE COMMITTEE ON FOREIGN RELATIONS. The SALT
II Treaty: (Report). Washington, D.C.: U.S. Government Printing
Office, 1979. 551 pp.
This report of the U.S. Senate committee on the flaws of the SALT II treaty
provides an analysis of the meaning and relative importance of each section
of this complex agreement. It also summarizes the debates and testimony
of witnesses covering all major issues raised by the treaty, including
verification, the vulnerability of ICBMs, the implications for strategic
balance and stability, and the issue of the Backfire bomber.

PS 804. VERNON, RAYMOND. Sovereignty at Bay: The Multinational Spread
of U.S. Enterprises. New York: Basic Books, 1971. 326 pp.
According to Vernon, multinational corporations are eroding the sovereignty
of states, which seem unable to devise ways of controlling or cooperating
with them. The author's analysis defines the multinational enterprise
and studies particular types; for example, manufacturing industries and
those that deal in raw materials. He studies their impact on national
economies and societies, and the problems created by their presence.
The general problem is summarized as a conflict between the state trying
to manage its resources in pursuit of legitimate goals, and the multinational enterprise with sufficient economic power not to be accountable
to other authority. Future patterns and policy choices are examined.

PS 805. VLAHOS, MICHAEL. America: Images of Empire. Washington, D.C.:
Johns Hopkins Foreign Policy Institute, 1982. 124 pp.
Vlahos contrasts characterizations of America as an imperialist power
with America's historic self-image as a physical and spiritual sanctuary
from empire. The author studies the validity of America's vision of uniqueness along five thematic lines: (1) the range of American images of empire;
(2) national patterns of behavior; (3) the "elasticity" of American geophysical vision; (4) America's inherent fear of subversion; and (5)
America's attempts to defend itself. Vlahos's central thesis is that
America's unstated mythologies of national experience continue to shape
the ways in which Americans view themselves and attempt to reshape the
world.

PS 806. WEIL, MARTIN. A Pretty Good Club: The Founding Fathers of the
U.S. Foreign Service. New York: Norton, 1978. 268 pp.
This is an account of a small group of men who founded the profession
of diplomacy in America. It discusses their experiences in the State
Department and in embassies abroad during the period that saw Communism
triumph in Russia, Hitler rise to power, and Franklin Roosevelt mobilize
America to fight a global war. These men--for example, Joseph Grew,
William Phillips, Loy Henderson, James Dunn, George Kennan, Charles Bohlen,
Jay Pierrepont Moffat, and Sumner Welles--all shared a common aristocratic
and religious heritage, held lengthy tenure, and achieved notable successes
as public servants.

PS 807. WEXLER, IMANUEL. The Marshall Plan Revisited: The European Perspective. Westport, Conn.: Greenwood Press, 1983. 327 pp.
In this book, Wexler argues that the Marshall Plan was an economic instrument in pursuit of specific economic ends, rather than an institutional
or foreign policy response to the European situation after W.W. II. The
study focuses on the four particular goals set by Congress: (1) strong
production; (2) the expansion of foreign trade; (3) the creation and maintenance of financial stability; and (4) the development of economic cooperation. The author devotes his study primarily to analyzing how these
objectives were pursued, and the extent to which they were achieved by
the time the program was terminated in 1951.

PS 808. WHALEN, CHARLES W., Jr. The House and Foreign Policy: The Irony
of Congressional Reform. Chapel Hill: University of North Carolina Press, 1982. 207 pp.
In this study, former Congressman Whalen questions many of the House of
Representatives' recent foreign policy actions. He believes that the
questionable performance of the House in foreign policy is partially the
consequence of Congressional rule changes that occurred in the 1970s.
To demonstrate this, he studies the evolving Constitutional roles and
prerogatives of the House, the Senate, and the Executive on foreign policy
issues. Whalen shows how the executive and legislative branches have
learned to cooperate, changing the substantive nature of U.S. foreign
policy in the 1970s.

PS 809. WHITAKER, JENNIFER SEYMOUR, ed. Africa and the United States:
Vital Interests. New York: New York University Press, 1978.
255 pp.
This study is a major re-examination of U.S. policy toward Africa conducted
by the Council on Foreign Relations. The articles discuss various aspects
of American interests in Africa. Gordon Bertolin and Guy F. Erb both
deal with economic issues. Geoffrey Kemp and Robert Legvold consider,
respectively, U.S. and Soviet military and foreign policy strategy in
Africa. I. William Zartman examines the possible political problems Black
Africa will face. Finally, Andrew Nagorski and Jennifer Whitaker discuss
U.S. policy and the options open to the U.S. in Africa.

PS 810. WHOLSTETTER, ROBERTA. Pearl Harbor: Warning and Decision. Stanford, Calif.: Stanford University Press, 1962. 426 pp.
Wholstetter's work is a case study of the interaction of military intelligence and policy-making by Americans prior to the attack on Pearl Harbor.
It examines the available intelligence warning of the attack, how it was
processed and transmitted--or not transmitted--to policy-makers and com-
manders, and how the signals were lost and mishandled. The Japanese
strategy of surprise attack succeeded, despite good U.S. intelligence,
in part because of excessive "noise" (competing signals or information)
in numerous intelligence channels.

PS 811. WILLRICH, MASON and JOHN B. RHINELANDER. SALT: The Moscow Agreements and Beyond. New York: Free Press, 1974. 361 pp.
This collection contains articles about the SALT I treaty, the process of negotiating, the treaty's strategic implications, its political significance to other nations (e.g., Japan, China, and Europe), and other related issues. Contributors are Chalmers M. Roberts, J. P. Ruina, Alton Frye, Marshall D. Shulman, John B. Rhinelander, Herbert Scoville, Jr., Ian Smart, Morton Halperin, George W. Rathjens, and Mason Willrich. The SALT I treaty and related documents are in the appendix, including the Jackson Amendment, the Revised Hot Line Agreement, and Basic Principles of Negotiations on the Further Limitation of Strategic Offensive Arms.

PS 812. WOLFE, ALAN. The Rise and Fall of the "Soviet Threat": Domestic Sources of the Cold War Consensus. Washington, D.C.: Institute for Policy Studies, 1979. 94 pp.
Wolfe argues that recent fears about Soviet military build-up have much more to do with U.S. domestic policies than with national security. Domestic problems which force the Cold War issues are: a disequilibrium in party politics; the existence of domestic threats to the hegemony of the Presidency; an outbreak of intra-governmental rivalry; conflict within the foreign policy establishment over the proper focal point of U.S. policy; and the coming to power of political coalitions seeking to spur economic growth. If the American political system succeeds in alarming the American public into belief in a Soviet threat, this will result in increased military spending. This result in turn impedes prosperity, creates inflation, erodes gains for minorities and women, and reduces popular respect for the rights of others around the world, while endangering civil liberties at home.

PS 813. WOLFE, THOMAS. The SALT Experience. Cambridge, Mass.: Ballinger, 1979. 405 pp.
This book focuses on the SALT negotiations of the decade before 1979, and gives special emphasis on the institutional setting of the negotiation process in the U.S. and the Soviet Union. Wolfe shows how the SALT II agreement was directly influenced by the Vladivostok accord of 1974 and how it affected the strategic nuclear forces in the U.S. Parts of this book were previously published as RAND papers.

PS 814. YAGER, JOSEPH A., ed. Nonproliferation and U.S. Foreign Policy. Washington, D.C.: Brookings Institution, 1980. 438 pp.
This study analyzes the nonproliferation programs of U.S. foreign policy. The principal focus is on coping with the incentives that foreign countries have to acquire nuclear weapons. Attention is also paid to civil nuclear policies and how they lead to the spread of facilities capable of producing weapons fuels. Joseph A. Yager studies Japan, Taiwan, and South Korea. Richard K. Betts studies India, Pakistan, Iran, and South Africa. Henry S. Rowen and Richard Brody discuss the Middle East, and William H. Courtney writes on Brazil and Argentina.

PS 815. YARMOLINSKY, ADAM and GEORGE FOSTER. Paradoxes of Power: The Military Establishment in the Eighties. Bloomington: Indiana University Press, 1973. 154 pp.
The authors identify four major paradoxes surrounding the U.S. military today: (1) the theory of deterrence which argues for a military buildup as a means of preventing war; (2) the theory of limited response which forces a great power to limit its military objectives to avoid escalation; (3) the problems of the military bureaucracy caused by its size and complexity; and (4) the problem of how peace can be preserved when the military establishment plays such a dominant role in national affairs. The study takes a look at the conflicting demands placed on the military by political and civilian authorities. The authors then turn to an examina-

tion of the military in the American economy and society. The book concludes with a look at the failure of the military and at arms control as a key determinant of that failure.

PS 816. YERGIN, DANIEL. Shattered Peace: The Origins of the Cold War
         and the National Security State. Boston: Houghton Mifflin,
         1977. 526 pp.
Yergin studies the events leading to the Cold War between the U.S. and
the Soviet Union. This study focuses on the American-Soviet alliance
during W.W. II and the beginning of the arms race of the Cold War. Yergin
analyzes the role of diplomacy and ideology in shaping the Cold War.
He addresses the difficulty of American policy-making in understanding
the relationships between Soviet foreign policy and totalitarian Marxist-
Leninism. He concludes that the diplomatic break between the U.S. and
the Soviet Union was mainly initiated by the U.S.

PS 817. ZASLOFF, JOSEPH. Communist Indochina and United States Foreign
         Policy: Postwar Realities. Boulder, Colo.: Westview Press,
         1978. 221 pp.
This book examines U.S. relations with and policy toward Laos, Vietnam,
and Cambodia. The work is prefaced with a chapter describing the impact
of the Vietnam War on the formulation and implementation of U.S. foreign
policy. Zasloff delineates those issues of importance to the U.S.
government--including admission of Vietnam to the United Nations, the recovery of MIAs (soldiers missing in action), and economic aid to Southeast
Asia--and then discusses the needs of the new governments in Southeast
Asia. Zasloff describes the structure and function of these individual
governments and the U.S.'s responsibility toward each.

POPULAR CULTURE

It is still _de rigueur_ in some circles to inveigh against popular
culture and to warn that it is eroding the quality of American art. But
as movies and television, comics and bestsellers have taken off, so too
has scholarly enthusiasm. Fortunately, bibliographic guides to that scholarship have proliferated apace.

Foremost in GENERAL overview is the three-volume _Handbook of American
Popular Culture_, edited by M. Thomas Inge (Westport, Conn.: Greenwood
Press, 1978-81), which divides the territory into some fifty related concerns. Each chapter, written by a recognized authority, includes a historic outline of the genre, its history and criticism, research centers
and archives, a bibliography, and periodicals to consult. Already, the
most useful of these essays have been revised and updated in the _Concise
Histories of American Popular Culture_, edited by M. Thomas Inge (Westport,
Conn.: Greenwood Press, 1982), a single volume which offers those new
to popular culture the best place to begin.

Brief but no less diverse is the ground-breaking work in Russel
B. Nye's _The Unembarrassed Muse: The Popular Arts in America_ (New York:
Dial Press, 1970), whose bibliography amounts to a series of bibliographic
essays, chronologically arranged. Nye covers all the familiar popular
genres and then some, and his command of earlier studies is still the
envy of scholars in the field. Similarly broad and more recent, Larry
Landrum's _American Popular Culture: A Guide to Information Sources_
(Detroit, Mich.: Gale Research, 1982) offers brief annotations for nearly
2,200 "unabashedly eclectic" items, most focusing on genres rather than
individual artists. More inclusive is the computer-assisted _American
Popular Culture: A Historical Bibliography_, edited by Arthur Frank
Wertheim (Santa Barbara, Calif.: ABC-Clio, 1984), which elicits titles
from 2,000 journals in forty-two languages between 1973 and 1980.

As these guides suggest, the field is now active enough to encourage
bibliographies of more specialized interests, even across the popular
culture spectrum. For example, Leslie J. Friedman's Sex Role Stereotyping
in the Mass Media: An Annotated Bibliography (New York: Garland Publishing, 1977) provides substantial descriptive annotations for 1,018 entries
in advertising, film, broadcast and print media, and such popular genres
as comic strips and books, and science fiction. Oriented toward the college students who have most often asked for help, this bibliography
includes studies, content analyses, published opinions, and U.S. government
documents. In another vein, Katherine Fishburn's Women in Popular Culture:
A Reference Guide (Westport, Conn.: Greenwood Press, 1982) offers seven
bibliographic essays on popular literature, sports, comics, and all aspects
of the media, as well as histories and theories.

Annual bibliographies of shorter studies are also on hand. Abstracts
of Popular Culture, published biannually by the Popular Press at Bowling
Green University, scans more than 300 journals, including many not
abstracted elsewhere. With thousands of entries in the "New Humanities"
each year, it remains the only source specifically oriented to popular
culture. Complementing it is the Alternative Press Index, published quarterly though irregularly, which indexes over 180 underground journals and
newsletters—Marxist, feminist, ethnic—that would otherwise be ignored.
Similarly, the New Periodicals Index, begun in 1977, surveys alternative
and new age magazines, journals, newspapers and newsletters: non-scholarly
publications that have much to say on subjects like the media and comics.
Finally, Robert M. Bottorff's Popular Periodical Index, published twice
a year since 1973, is worth consulting for individual authors or texts
rather than genres, except where very broad.

Altogether, the range and depth of the general bibliographic work
in popular culture is both cheering and daunting. Those new to the field
will find their way eased by Gordon Stevenson's "The Wayward Scholar:
Resources and Research in Popular Culture" (Library Trends, 25 [April

1174

1977], 779-818), an excellent survey of the rise and expansion of popular
culture study in America. Stevenson pays particular attention to what
general sources are commonly available, and he concludes with suggestions
on where research may fruitfully begin. Those whose research has already
commenced may call upon more specific bibliographic aid.

In FILM, bibliographic guides have long been available and continue
to proliferate. The most comprehensive work on books, from original paperbacks to doctoral dissertations, is George Rehrauer's The Macmillan Film
Bibliography: A Critical Guide to the Literature of the Motion Picture,
2 vols. (New York: Macmillan, 1982), which combines and updates his
three earlier volumes in the Cinema Booklist series. Vol. 1 provides
6,762 entries, most with descriptive and evaluative annotations; Vol.
2 is a 519-page Index, which makes the guide remarkably easy to use.

The standard source for pre-1940 articles has long been Harold
Leonard, ed., The Film Index: A Bibliography, originally published in
1941 by New York's Museum of Modern Art and enlarged and updated through
1985 (New York: H. W. Wilson, 1985). Sponsored by the WPA, it is a massive volume with more than 8,000 books, articles and reviews indexed.
Updating Leonard's guide is The New Film Index: A Bibliography of Magazine
Articles in English, 1930-1970, edited by Richard Dyer MacCann and Edward
S. Perry (New York: Dutton, 1975), which surveys about forty periodicals
plus additional general magazines, provides short descriptive annotations
for most entries, and concludes with a lengthy "Index to the Index" for
more efficient use. Extending that coverage is Jack C. Ellis, Charles
Derry, and Sharon Kern's hefty The Film Book Bibliography, 1940-1975
(Metuchen, N.J.: Scarecrow Press, 1979), a guide to over 5,400 film books
and monographs. For those in need of interpretive works, Robert A.
Armour's Film: A Reference Guide (Westport, Conn.: Greenwood Press, 1980)
offers selective bibliographic essays that identify basic books in genre
criticism, film and related arts, film and society, and the like, with
information on reference works, periodicals, and research collections.

Two annual indexes have already become standard sources for the year's scholarship in journals. The Film Literature Index, begun in 1973 and edited by Vincent J. Aceto, Jane Graves, and Fred Silva, scans a core of 125 film journals, plus 150 more general periodicals; it is intelligently indexed, easy to use, and extensive, though unannotated. In addition, the International Index to Film Periodicals, begun in 1972 and variously edited, surveys more than eighty film periodicals and (since 1979) forty television journals; it annually provides more than 7,000 entries, briefly annotated in English and well organized, with a detailed subject index. More limited and thus more accessible updates on book publication are the annual book round-up to which Film Quarterly devotes an entire issue, and the review essays and shorter book reviews in the Journal of Popular Film and Television.

Off the general track are several studies worth noting. I. C. Jarvie's Movies and Society (New York: Basic Books, 1970) concludes with a lengthy annotated bibliography, an impressive guide to out-of-the-way sources. Erik Barnouw's Documentary: A History of the Non-fiction Film (New York: Oxford University Press, 1974) likewise offers a particularly thorough bibliography; it is unannotated, but of great help in so specialized an area. As interest in film grows, its popular impact is also receiving attention: Bruce A. Austin's The Film Audience: An International Bibliography of Research (Metuchen, N.J.: Scarecrow Press, 1983) includes 1,233 entries, most descriptively annotated, and demonstrates how social science methods may further the study of film in a larger context.

Those just entering such developed critical territory can take heart: Larry N. Landrum's "Sources for the Study of Popular Film" (Journal of Popular Film and Television, 7 [1978], 108-119) assembles basic books and articles on all aspects of popular film, together with brief descriptive annotations. Since Landrum emphasizes film in its cultural dimension, his survey should encourage American Studies scholars to see what they might productively explore.

In the realm of the MEDIA at large, the principal guide is Eleanor Blum's Basic Books in the Mass Media: An Annotated Selected Booklist Covering General Communications, Book Publishing, Broadcasting, Editorial Journalism, Film, Magazines, and Advertising, 2nd ed. (Urbana: University of Illinois Press, 1980), which now includes 1,179 entries, descriptive annotations, and a detailed subject guide. Blum favors broad assessments of communications rather than specific studies or biographies; she includes popular culture, publishing, broadcasting, and film, along with an annotated list of indexes to periodicals, newspapers, and dissertations.

Of note in a canvass of important bibliographies are Erik Barnouw's lengthy checklists in his landmark, three-volume History of Broadcasting (New York: Oxford University Press, 1966-70); Barnouw condensed and updated these checklists in his Tube of Plenty: The Evolution of American Television (New York: Oxford University Press, 1975), whose extensive bibliographic notes offer a guide to principal sources and additional readings. More broadly, Warren C. Price and Calder M. Pickett provide 2,172 entries with brief descriptive annotations in An Annotated Journalism Bibliography, 1958-1968 (Minneapolis: University of Minnesota Press, 1970), which picks up where Price's once standard bibliography, Literature of Journalism, leaves off. More recently and more sociologically, Communications and Society: A Bibliography on Communications Technologies and Their Social Impact, compiled by Benjamin F. Shearer and Marilyn Huxford (Westport, Conn.: Greenwood Press, 1983) offers a selected bibliography of 2,732 unannotated entries, which consider the social effects of the mass media as creators and reflectors of public opinion.

Bibliographic guides have also appeared on the individual media themselves. Access to journalism studies, for instance, is promoted by Joseph Patrick McKerns in "The History of American Journalism: A Bibliographic Essay" (American Studies International, 15 [Autumn 1976], 17-34), a survey of newspapers and printing from the 16th and 17th centuries to the present, together with the major scholarship they have inspired.

1177

Alan R. Havig reviews radio historiography in "Beyond Nostalgia: American Radio as a Field of Study" (Journal of Popular Culture, 12 [1978], 218-227); he concludes by suggesting areas to investigate. William E. McCavitt extends the parameters of investigation in compiling Radio and Television: A Selected Annotated Bibliography (Metuchen, N.J.: Scarecrow Press, 1978), and Supplement One, 1977-1981 (1982), which together provide 1,666 listings with descriptive annotations on such subjects as Society, Audience, Video (Home and Corporate), and Satellites. Finally, Felix Chin's Cable Television: A Comprehensive Bibliography (New York: IFI/Plenum, 1978) surveys general reference works and periodicals of interest, notes texts in seven categories, and provides impressive appendices.

Keeping up with media research is a full-time business in Communication Booknotes: Recent Titles in Telecommunications, Information and Media, a newsletter that appeared as Mass Media Booknotes until 1982. Edited by Christopher Sterling, it offers two special issues a year—on recent U.S. government documents in August and on cinema books in December—as well as a series of three annotated and regularly revised bibliographies, on telecommunications policy, media, and international/ foreign communications. More inclusively, Journalism Quarterly provides a column on Research in Brief, a sizeable book review section, and a listing of articles in mass communications in American and foreign journals. Also useful are the Journal of Communication, which notes recent research and includes a substantial book review section, and Gazette: International Journal for Mass Communication Studies, which is published quarterly at the Hague and provides an international bibliography organized by topic in each issue.

Two recent bibliographic essays do much to simplify access to the criticism that the media have spawned. Joseph P. McKerns, Carole McNall, and Elizabeth M. Johnson provide a brief summary of the field in "Mass Media Criticism: An Annotated Bibliography" (Mass Comm Review, 3 [Winter 1975/76], 9-18). More specific in scope, Jennifer Tebbe's "Mass Media and American Culture, 1918-1941; A Bibliographic Essay" in Catherine L. Covert and John D. Stevens, eds., Mass Media Between the Wars: Perceptions of Cultural Tension, 1918-1941 (Syracuse, N.Y.: Syracuse University Press, 1984, pp. 221-43), provides an exemplary survey of the resources covering the 1920s and 1930s. Tebbe's bibliographic work on the media in a cultural context suggests that similarly specific cultural studies may well be in the offing.

In SPORTS, bibliographic guides have appeared more recently, as have the cultural analyses they index. Robert J. Higgs offers fourteen bibliographic essays with a humanistic approach in Sports: A Reference Guide (Westport, Conn.: Greenwood Press, 1982). Particularly useful is Chapter 4, "Sports and Popular Culture," probably the best place to begin. Much more extensive, though unannotated, is the Handbook of Social Science of Sport, edited by Gunther R. F. Luschen and George H. Sage (Champaign, Ill.: Stipes Publishing, 1981); classified by major subject areas, its 5,147 entries include an extensive international bibliography, in many languages. Dwarfing all other efforts in the field is the Sport Bibliography/Bibliographie du Sport, 8 vols. (Ottawa: Sport Information Resource Centre, 1981), with a two-volume update in 1983. Published by a computerized documentation center and listed in Sport data base, the bibliography indexes over 70,000 books, periodical articles, theses, microforms, and conference proceedings—primarily after 1974—on all subjects related to sports and physical activity. Vol. 7 on Humanities and Social Sciences is pertinent for cultural research, especially in Native American activities.

Continuing surveys of sports scholarship have already begun to appear. The computer-assisted Sociology of Leisure and Sports Abstracts, issued from Amsterdam three times a year, provides over 1,000 abstracts annually. Begun in 1980, it scans current journals, conference proceedings, unpublished papers, theses, monographs, and government documents. Plans have been announced to publish five-year specialized bibliographies from time to time, on subjects like "Sport and Social Mobility" and "Leisure and Cultural Development." Also useful is the Journal of Sport History, which abstracts articles in its "Journal Surveys" and includes such subjects as popular culture and social history in compiling its "Booknotes." Finally, Complete Research in Health, Physical Education and Recreation, appearing annually, includes theses and dissertations along with published research, plus an extensive index to cross references.

Popular ENTERTAINMENT studies of tent shows, vaudeville, striptease, and the like are also on the increase, as recent bibliographic work testifies. Of particular interest in Don B. Wilmeth's American and British Popular Entertainment: A Guide to Information Sources (Detroit, Mich.: Gale Research, 1980), which provides close to 2,500 entries with descriptive, sometimes evaluative, annotations. Emphasizing live entertainment, Wilmeth surveys general sources, popular entertainment forms, and popular theater. More selectively, Wilmeth offers twelve bibliographic essays on individual forms in Variety Entertainment and Outdoor Amusements: A Reference Guide (Westport, Conn.: Greenwood Press, 1982), an extension of his work in the Handbook of American Popular Culture. Each essay summarizes the history of the form, surveys the scholarship, and provides a checklist of major sources, including graduate theses and periodicals.

More specialized in its focus is Raymond Toole-Stott's majestic Circus and Allied Arts: A World Bibliography, 4 vols. (Derby, England: Harpur, 1958-71). International in scope, spanning centuries, Toole-Stott's more than 13,000 entries in thirteen languages make his work indispensible, especially since he generally annotates his sources and extends his compass to include melodrama, pantomime, architecture, and special effects. Closer to home is The American Stage to World War I: A Guide to Information Sources, again edited by Don B. Wilmeth (Detroit, Mich.: Gale Research, 1978), which surveys roughly 225 periodicals and serials and thus provides a useful supplement to his work on Popular Entertainment per se. Stressing detailed studies rather than overviews, Wilmeth here provides an annotated guide to 1,461 sources on all aspects of the American stage. A complementary bibliography, from W.W. I to the present, is in preparation.

Three journals customarily indicate recent work touching upon popular entertainment. The Educational Theatre Journal (re-titled Theatre Journal in 1979) indexes "Doctoral Projects in Progress in Theatre Arts" in its May issue, and always provides a substantial book review section that includes studies of popular entertainment in its various forms. Nineteenth Century Theatre Research has annually assessed current research in its Autumn or Winter issue. Lastly, the Drama Review provides brief annotations on new books to conclude each issue.

Two essays offer a handle on scholarship in popular entertainment and thus provide a place to begin. John H. Towsen's "Sources in Popular Entertainment" (Drama Review, 18 [March 1974], 118-22) includes a list of basic research tools, libraries and museums, related organizations, and a select unannotated bibliography of standard works. Happily, the article appears in an issue devoted entirely to Popular Entertainments and is worth reading. In addition, Don B. Wilmeth offers a scaled-down version of his later coverage in "American Popular Entertainment: A Historical Perspective" (Choice, 14 [October 1977], 987-1004). Assessing the major studies in the field, Wilmeth concludes this bibliographic essay with a checklist of 235 sources on the specific forms he expertly surveys.

POPULAR LITERATURE has become so popular among scholars that its study has already subdivided several times over. So distinct are its current territories that they are most often pulled together bibliographically by specialized interests as they arise. James J. Best, for example, ranges freely in American Popular Illustration: A Reference Guide (Westport, Conn.: Greenwood Press, 1984), a series of six bibliographic essays that promote an overview of the popular literature industry while concentrating on its significant visual artists. The Journal of Popular Culture has also run occasional review essays of less familiar periodicals in

1181

several genres: Robert E. Briney, for instance, considers pulps, fantasy, science fiction, and Westerns in "Popular Literature Periodicals" (Journal of Popular Culture, 3 [1969], 352-54). But sweeps of these various sub-genres are becoming less the rule as scholarly research becomes more focused.

Of all popular genres, BESTSELLERS are probably the most read and least studied, comparatively at any rate. James D. Hart's early assessment, The Popular Book: A History of American Literary Taste (New York: Oxford University Press, 1950), remains the best guide to articles, books, and monographs written since "bestsellers" first hit the charts; his extensive bibliography is still cited. Alice Payne Hackett and James Henry Burke's 80 Years of Best Sellers, 1895-1975 (New York: Bowker, 1977) also con-cludes with "Books and Articles about Best Sellers," briefly annotated. As to periodical updates, much of the energy goes into compiling primary bibliographies rather than surveys of the year's scholarship (Dime Novel Roundup is a case in point). For that reason, the most useful biblio-graphic introduction is Suzanne Ellery Greene's essay in the Handbook of American Popular Culture.

The study of CHILDREN'S LITERATURE likewise produces numerous primary bibliographies each year, but librarians have been particularly resourceful in gathering scholarship. Children's Literature: A Guide to Reference Sources, edited by Virginia Haviland (Washington, D.C.: Library of Con-gress, 1966) annotates international sources on history and criticism, guides to children's reading, and works on folklore and storytelling. With its First Supplement (1972) and Second Supplement (1977), Haviland's guide compiles well over 2,500 entries in an exhaustive survey of the litera-ture.

More recently, Suzanne Rahn's Children's Literature: An Annotated Bibliography of the History and Criticism (New York: Garland Publishing, 1981) offers a selective bibliography that favors historical and literary analysis, most usefully in her section on formula fiction. Also useful

historically is Elva Smith's The History of Children's Literature: A
Syllabus with Selected Bibliographies, recently updated by Margaret Hodges
and Susan Steinfirst (1937; Rev. & enl. Chicago: American Library Association, 1980), which is annotated and particularly good on books and
articles about the 19th century. More specialized is Folk Literature
and Children: An Annotated Bibliography of Secondary Materials, compiled
by George W. B. Shannon (Westport, Conn.: Greenwood Press, 1981), which
focuses on fairy tales and surveys the scholarship published through 1979,
including ERIC documents.

The most scholarly periodical in the field is Children's Literature:
An International Journal, which publishes an annual annotated listing
of Dissertations of Note, as well as longer book reviews. The Children's
Literature Association Quarterly (once Newsletter) provides an annotated
bibliography of recent books, essays, bibliographies and special journal
issues, plus news of current research. The journal's own plans include
a Summer 1987 issue on "Children's Literature and Popular Culture," to
be edited by Janice Alberghene. In addition, Phaedrus: A Journal of
Children's Literature Research focuses on research into media and children,
and lists periodical literature, selected dissertations, and recent bibliographies published in the United States and abroad.

In this welter of possibilities, Jacqueline Faustino provides a
place to begin with "Basic Reference Materials for Children's Literature:
An Annotated Bibliography" (North Carolina Libraries, 38 [Summer 1980],
30-36). She surveys reference, bibliographies, biographies, and storytelling, and she provides brief descriptive annotations for the sources she
identifies.

Amateur devotion to the genre has long made MYSTERY AND DETECTIVE
FICTION the subject of comment, and scholars have willingly joined the
throng. In fact, professionals are emerging from the closet along with

the skeletons, as Jacques Barzun and Wendell Hertig Taylor reveal in A Catalogue of Crime (New York: Harper & Row, 1971). Based on decades of reading, reacting, and corresponding, their guide to primary works includes a survey of over 150 secondary sources; their annotations are a delight, and their prefaces and introductory essays are useful.

Just as idiosyncratic is Jon L. Breen's What About Murder: A Guide to Books About Mystery and Detective Fiction (Metuchen, N.J.: Scarecrow Press, 1981), which provides full evaluative annotations for 239 general histories, technical manuals, coffee-table books and the like. More temperate is Crime Fiction Criticism: An Annotated Bibliography, edited by Timothy W. Johnson, et al. (New York: Garland Publishing, 1981), a comprehensive guide to over 2,000 general works and some 250 individual authors considered in books, dissertations, articles, and book sections. International in scope and interdisciplinary in emphasis is Crime, Detective, Espionage, Mystery, and Thriller Fiction and Film: A Comprehensive Bibliography of Critical Writing Through 1979, compiled by David Skene Melvin and Ann Skene Melvin (Westport, Conn.: Greenwood Press, 1980), an unannotated but soundly cross-referenced guide which includes over 1,600 items from twenty-five countries.

Two bibliographic essays can make this corpus more manageable. In "Sleuthography: Reference, Research and Reprint Publishing in Detective Fiction" (Choice, 14 [October 1977], 1004-13), Virginia Clark surveys secondary literature beginning with H. Douglas Thomson's Masters of Mystery (1931) and concluding with a checklist of useful titles, both primary and secondary. Robin W. Winks in "American Detective Fiction" (American Studies International, 19 [Autumn 1980], 3-16) offers a selected bibliography of general guides, histories, periodicals, listings for individual writers, and more; he includes brief evaluative annotations, and his titles are all fairly recent. In addition to these, The Armchair Detective, now published by New York's Mysterious Press, provides an annual bibliography of secondary sources.

Bibliographic guides often link FANTASY to science fiction, especially in updating their critical surveys. But two sources do provide a way into the field and places to go from there. Marshall B. Tymn's "Recent Critical Studies on Fantasy Literature: An Annotated Checklist," Exchange Bibliography #1522 (Monticello, Ill.: Council of Planning Librarians, 1978) indicates, in brief, what proportions scholarship has assumed. Extending that initial list and furthering its guidance is Fantasy Literature: A Core Collection and Reference Guide, assembled by Marshall B. Tymn, Kenneth J. Zahorski, and Robert H. Boyer (New York: Bowker, 1979), which briefly annotates both books and articles in fantasy scholarship and lists over 240 seminal works in high fantasy fiction.

Of related interest is the larger genre of GOTHIC AND ROMANCE FICTION, which may be wholly or partially a female precinct, depending upon who edits the bibliography. Horror Literature: A Core Collection and Reference Guide, edited by Marshall B. Tymn (New York: Bowker, 1981) offers six historical overviews of fiction and poetry, from gothic romances to pulps, plus an extended annotated section on reference sources, periodicals in the field, and organizations of interest. Dan J. McNutt incisively establishes the genre in The Eighteenth-Century Gothic Novel: An Annotated Bibliography of Criticism and Important Texts (New York: Garland Publishing, 1974), but his texts are largely British. For that reason, a more relevant survey is Frederick S. Frank's Guide to the Gothic: An Annotated Bibliography of Criticism (Metuchen, N.J.: Scarecrow Press, 1984), which divides the territory by nationality, offers over 550 entries on its American development, and emphasizes individual authors. Frank's introduction assesses the genre's growth, together with its scholarly study; it thus provides a good place to begin.

The broadest survey of the genre as a whole is Kay Mussell's Women's Gothic and Romantic Fiction: A Reference Guide (Westport, Conn.: Greenwood Press, 1981), which includes bibliographic essays on bibliographies and related genres, literary and social history approaches, popular commentary and the like. Mussell also provides a useful introduction to this disputed scholarly terrain, where the gothic and the romance are now uneasily joined.

To keep abreast of the field, the Gothic Press in Baton Rouge has published two journals, consecutively. _Gothic: The Review of Supernatural Horror Fiction_, which appeared in 1979 and 1980, initiated an annual compilation of secondary literature. That bibliographic enterprise has recently resurfaced in expanded form as the _Bibliography of Gothic Studies_, an annual survey first published in 1983 with a review of 1980 scholarship.

Scholarly interest in SCIENCE FICTION has intensified in recent years, especially since the first seminar in science fiction was held at the Modern Language Association in 1958 and the Science Fiction Research Association was founded in 1970. One of the first scholarly bibliographies to appear was Thomas D. Clareson's _Science Fiction Criticism: An Annotated Checklist_ (Kent, Ohio: Kent State University Press, 1972), a comprehensive guide to general studies, literary studies, book reviews, visual arts, futurology, utopia and dystopia, classroom and library, publishing, specialist bibliographies, checklists and indices, and the contemporary scene. It remains a good source for articles in scholarly journals and popular magazines, which have been excluded from the more recent _Research Guide to Science Fiction Studies: An Annotated Checklist of Primary and Secondary Sources for Fantasy and Science Fiction_, compiled and edited by Marshall B. Tymn, Roger C. Schlobin, and L. W. Currey (New York: Garland Publishing, 1977), which surveys over 400 of the best and most comprehensive studies, and includes an unannotated bibliography of doctoral dissertations, together with a guide to special journal issues. More compactly, Marshall B. Tymn offers neophytes a twelve-page introduction to the territory in "A Basic Reference Shelf for Science Fiction Teachers," Exchange Bibliography #1523 (Monticello, Ill.: Council of Planning Librarians, 1978), which includes biographical guides, bibliographies, indexes to anthologies and magazines, surveys and histories, author studies, and film guides, generously annotated.

As science fiction studies continue to multiply, so do the journals which keep track of them. Extrapolation: A Journal of Science Fiction and Fantasy is the oldest academic journal in the field. Each year its December issue assembled "The Year's Scholarship in Science Fiction and Fantasy," which annotates all American scholarship, some from Britain, and criticism from established fanzines. Two four-year cumulations, 1972–75 and 1976–79, have been published separately; from 1980, the bibliography has been expanded and published as a separate monograph, under the general editorship of Marshall B. Tymn.

Complementing that coverage is Foundation: The Review of Science Fiction; published by the British Science Fiction Foundation, it offers reliable scholarly reviews of recent titles. In addition, Science-Fiction Studies devotes part of each issue to numerous review articles and several briefer reviews, with a specialized bibliography upon occasion.

WESTERNS have also inspired both lore and scholarship, much of it as steady and dispassionate as Western heroes purport to be. Leading the field is Richard W. Etulain's A Bibliographic Guide to the Study of Western American Literature (Lincoln: University of Nebraska Press, 1982), which surveys bibliographies, anthologies, general works, special topics like the Western film or the Beats, and works on over 350 individual authors. A companion volume for scholars is Fifty Western Writers: A Bio-Bibliographical Sourcebook, edited by Fred Erisman and Richard W. Etulain (Westport, Conn.: Greenwood Press, 1982), which includes both Western (popular) and western (regional) writers. Each essay, written by an expert in the area, provides a brief biography, major themes, a survey of criticism, and a bibliography of primary and secondary works.

Carrying the genre a step further, John G. Nachbar's Western Films: An Annotated Critical Bibliography (New York: Garland Publishing, 1975) provides a selective survey of articles and books in ten related categories,

like Western Film Criticism, Theories of Western Film, and The Western
Audience. Michael D. Gibson concentrates on the female Western in "The
Western: A Selective Bibliography" (Journal of Popular Culture, 7 [1973],
743-48), which appears in an issue highlighting Western fiction. Keeping
up to date with such scholarship is Western American Literature, whose
annual bibliographies appear in its Winter issues.

The study of COMICS has fared less well in academic preserves, perhaps because its primary sources are more ephemeral than most. Correcting
that misfortune somewhat is The World Encyclopedia of Comics, edited by
Maurice Horn (New York: Chelsea House, 1976), a hefty A-Z volume on all
aspects of the comic industry, with appendices identifying comic book
publishers and newspaper syndicates. The notes on contributors also provide a useful index of who's at work in the field. Even more helpful
is The World Encyclopedia of Cartoons, edited by Maurice Horn (New York:
Chelsea House—Gale Research, 1980), an exhaustive survey that covers some
200 years and produces close to 1,200 entries in dictionary format. The
volume is well illustrated and concludes with a bibliography of references
on cartoons in print and animated. Plans have been made to update, revise,
and enlarge the survey at regular intervals.

Charting initial criticism in the genre is David Manning White's
The Comic Strip in America: A Bibliography (Boston: Boston University,
School of Public Relations and Communication, 1961), a checklist of 450
items, with a short list of theses and dissertations. Robert M.
Overstreet's annual The Comic Book Price Guide (New York: Harmony Books),
begun in 1970 for dealers and collectors, has since been expanded and
revised each year; it is now an extensively illustrated, comprehensive.
listing of comic book titles since 1933, and thus an important source
of information. More farflung is the International Bibliography of Comics
Literature, edited by Wolfgang Kempkes (New York: Bowker, 1971), which
tallies up 3,831 entries in all phases of comic literature since 1896,
including the structure of comics, their readership, and their effects.

Thomas W. Hoffer's assessment of related scholarship, _Animation:_
_A_ _Reference_ _Guide_ (Westport, Conn.: Greenwood Press, 1981) offers a series
of selective bibliographic essays, with an annotated guide to periodicals
and a briefly annotated survey of articles in the trade journals and the
popular press. The best introduction to these various aspects of a less
familiar genre is M. Thomas Inge's essay in the _Handbook_ _of_ _American_ _Popular_
Culture or his more succinct "American Comic Art: A Bibliographic Guide"
(_Choice_, 11 [January 1975], 1581-93), which is especially helpful on selected
periodicals and the best books with which to begin.

Since the primary sources in MATERIAL CULTURE are of mutual interest
to museum curators and university professors, scholarship in the field
has drawn from both faculties and profited from their differing perspectives. Writing from the National Museum of History and Technology at
the Smithsonian, Harold Skramstad examines decorative arts and architecture,
historical and industrial archeology, and the academic object-orientation
in "American Things: A Neglected Material Culture" (_American_ _Studies_
International, 10 [Spring 1972], 11-22), a bibliographic essay which he
concludes with a suggested reading checklist. More recently, _Material_
Culture _Studies_ _in_ _America_, compiled and edited by Thomas J. Schlereth
(Nashville, Tenn.: American Association for State and Local History,
1982), closes with Schlereth's "Selective Bibliographic Essay," a more
noticeably academic guide to available bibliographies, anthologies, journals and newsletters, dissertations and exhibition catalogues, together
with an unannotated checklist of representative studies.

With work advancing from both camps, the field has grown active
enough to have produced bibliographies on specialized interests. Bernard
Mergen's _Play_ _and_ _Playthings:_ _A_ _Reference_ _Guide_ (Westport, Conn.: Greenwood Press, 1982) offers a history of children's play in America over
three centuries, plus an extensive bibliographic guide to its study and
the study of toys. Alvar W. Carlson's "Bibliography on Barns in the United
States and Canada" (_Pioneer_ _America_, 10 [June 1978], 65-71) provides an

unannotated listing of 120 sources on barns, largely written after the 1940s. _Theatre_ _and_ _Cinema_ _Architecture_: _A_ _Guide_ _to_ _Information_ _Sources_, edited by Richard Stoddard (Detroit, Mich.: Gale Research, 1978) includes over 1,800 entries, many of them annotated, in a format that is easy to use. Tracking studies like these is _Material_ _Culture_ (whose title changed from _Pioneer_ _America_ in 1984), a journal which regularly reviews books, will eventually review films, and consistently provides commentary on relevant issues and scholarship in "The Research Notebook."

Material culture is a field both new enough to arouse scholarly curiosity and old enough to have invited two reasoned bibliographic introductions. Patrick H. Butler's "Material Culture as a Resource in Local History: A Bibliography" (_Newberry_ _Papers_ _in_ _Family_ _and_ _Community_ _History_, #79-1 [March 1979], 1-21) reviews methodological literature, surveys, specialized studies, and museological literature, with emphasis on an interdisciplinary approach to the study of artifacts. Thomas Schlereth's "American Studies and American Things" (_Pioneer_ _America_, 14 [1982], 47- 66) defines material culture as "all the things that people leave behind" and surveys its study by considering representative texts. He concludes by identifying "present trends" and "future opportunities" in the field.

The study of popular culture in its multiple genres can only benefit when more of the major bibliographies go on-line. At the very least, they will be more uniformly current. Scholarship will likewise benefit from the various popular culture archives across the country, which are harder to get to but easier to locate. They are crucial in genres whose primary sources do not ordinarily reappear: television, comics, or material culture. The Museum of Broadcasting in New York City, the San Francisco Academy of Comic Art, and the Margaret Woodbury Strong Museum in Rochester are all centers that provoke ideas and encourage their spread. Similar collections of all genres have been cited in the _Handbook_ _of_ _American_ _Popular_ _Culture_, as well as in the many general guides listed here.

Already it is possible to duplicate bibliographic work in popular culture.

That, in itself, is a fair sign that boom times are coming.

Kathleen Diffley
University of Iowa

I.   GENERAL

PC 1. BERTOLOTTI, DAVID S., Jr. Culture and Technology. Bowling Green,
         Ohio: Bowling Green State University Popular Press, 1984.
         153 pp.
Through an analysis of several historical episodes, Bertolotti provides
an examination of the reciprocal relationship between culture and technology by looking for examples of "culture-technology interface." The
examples chosen reflect different historical and philosophical perspectives.
The development and building of the Panama Canal show a view of the machine
as a means for attaining and furthering the concept of Manifest Destiny.
An analysis of W.W. II aviation and the atomic bombing of Hiroshima traces
the displacement of an essentially mechanical world by science in the
atomic age. A final topic examines the Salk Anti-Polio vaccine as a reflection of the "Better Living Through Chemistry" philosophy. The impact
of culture on technological advances is evaluated through an examination
of how these advances were treated in the print media.

PC 2. BIGSBY, C. W. E., ed. Approaches to Popular Culture. Bowling Green,
         Ohio: Bowling Green University Popular Press, 1976. 280 pp.
This collection is an assortment of essays defining approaches to popular
culture study and applying popular culture criticism to particular case
studies. The first section of the book includes seven essays detailing
perspectives on popular culture study, including linguistic, structuralist,
and Marxist approaches. This is followed by a photo essay, "As We See
Ourselves," which forms a bridge to the concluding section. The final
six pieces apply various analytical techniques, not necessarily those
described in the first unit, to particular cultural expressions, including
film, television, and music.

PC 3. BIGSBY, C. W. E., ed. Superculture: American Popular Culture and
         Europe. Bowling Green, Ohio: Bowling Green University Popular
         Press, 1945. 225 pp.
Bigsby brings together essays devoted to the study of the impact of American popular culture on Europe. Because Europe is not a homogeneous culture,
the particular studies are unified by a concept of an "Anglo-American
connection" and by the concept of America as a superculture which provides
the basic direction in modern popular culture in other countries. American
culture is traced in Europe by looking at its effects on language, vernacular architecture, food and food technology, advertising, religious groups,
detective and science fiction, comic forms, television series, and the
Hollywood film formulas.

PC 4. BOORSTIN, DANIEL J. The Image: A Guide to Pseudo-Events in America.
         New York: Atheneum, 1962. 315 pp.
Boorstin examines the substitution of image for reality in American life.
His book is about "our arts of self-deception, how we hide reality from
ourselves." Boorstin claims that Americans are ruled by "extravagant
expectations" of what the world holds, and of their power to shape the
world. He describes how what he terms "pseudo-events" form a "new kind
of synthetic novelty which has flooded our expectations." News coverage,
images of national heroes, tourism, art and literature, and the definition
of the American Dream are discussed as specific examples of the making
of cultural illusions.

PC 5. BROOKS, JOHN. Showing Off in America, From Conspicuous Consumption
to Parody Display. Boston: Little, Brown, 1979. 296 pp.
Brooks applies Thorstein Veblen's theory of conspicuous consumption and
the rise of the leisure class to modern American society. Examining the
ways in which Americans "show off," he argues that parody and display
have become an American way of boasting, of presenting the self as worthy
and successful. Brooks argues that personal qualities such as wit and
intelligence are displayed in the same manner that the symbols of wealth
and power are used to demonstrate the achievement of the individual.
He looks at American sports, games, fashion, eating and drinking, and
the styles of everyday life in contemporary society, finding a shift during
this century from "straightforward display of money to more complex and
sophisticated forms of showing off style, acquired sense of taste, and
playful irony."

PC 6. BROWNE, RAY B., ed. Forbidden Fruits: Taboos and Tabooism in Culture. Bowling Green, Ohio: Bowling Green University Popular Press,
1984. 192 pp.
Taboos, as examined in this collection, are a response to a basic dualism
in human nature, that of positive and negative social impulses. Society
responds to human inclination by establishing sanctioned and non-sanctioned
behavior. Taboos reflect time-honored efforts to control the "dark side"
of personality and disposition. Accordingly, there is a reluctance to
study taboos as social and cultural phenomena, yet such study--the contributors argue--is richly rewarding for the student of folk and popular
culture. Browne includes essays on such topics as taboos in architecture,
horror films, detective novels, fairy tales, sexual literature, and sports.

PC 7. BROWNE, RAY B., ed. Objects of Special Devotion: Fetishes in Popular Culture. Bowling Green, Ohio: Bowling Green University Popular
Press, 1982. 364 pp.
According to Browne, a fetish, like an icon, is an "object, person, concept,
theory, or philosophy believed to possess extraordinary magical, or supernatural power," but fetishes are viewed as "bastard icons." They are
sinister, primitive, and somewhat obscure parts of the culture. The fetish
is the dark side of the icon; but, like the icon, it serves a necessary
function in American society. This collection attempts to define and
label fetishes in order to understand them better. Some of the essays
look at old definitions of fetishes, fetishism, and fetishists to find
meaning in new fetishes (as in the linking of Jack the Ripper to contemporary sex crimes), while others update old concepts. The collection
includes analyses of the fetishes of sex crimes, love, 19th-century dolls,
mystery fiction, sports, graveyards, The National Enquirer, Jewish sons,
college fraternities, food, mail order cults, mechanical fetishes (such
as airplanes and computers), and various superstitions.

PC 8. BROWNE, RAY B., ed. Popular Culture and the Expanding Consciousness.
New York: Wiley, 1973. 200 pp.
This volume traces the growth of an expanding consciousness in the study
of popular culture from old elitist attitudes to an awareness of the importance of the popular in our culture. The old attitudes are characterized
by their elitist orientation, the belief being that the "popular" nature
of popular culture renders it unworthy of study. The first section of
this collection attempts to define popular culture, and to illuminate
the old attitudes. A second section on "changing concepts" illustrates
the shift to a more open-minded approach as the distinctions made between
high and low culture become less important, and new definitions of art
based on pleasure rather than on aesthetics alone emerge. The final section offers an analysis of the link between different expressions and
types of popular culture with the new expanding awareness, including the
Western, the detective story, comics, science fiction, music, and the
movies.

PC 9. BROWNE, RAY B. and MARSHALL W. FISHWICK, eds. The Hero in Transition. Bowling Green, Ohio: Bowling Green University Popular Press, 1983. 324 pp.
The editors begin with the assumption that "cultural relocations" coincide with "heroic transformations." The changes in the culture expressed in media, ideology, and lifestyles are reflected in our heroes. This collection of essays questions the influence and power of the media, and asks whether the influence of the media will eventually produce a new type of hero. In the first essay, Peter Rollins makes a distinction between celebrities and heroes, and looks at the process by which an entertainer becomes a hero. This is followed by individual essays on types of heroes: the accidental hero (Lenny Skutnik), the political hero (Ronald Reagan, John Glenn), and the historical hero (George Washington, Abraham Lincoln). The largest group of essays focuses on the popular hero, specifically the media-produced hero (Tarzan, Columbo, the soap opera hero, and the Western hero), the sports hero, and the cult hero (Marilyn Monroe).

PC 10. BROWNE, RAY B., MARSHALL FISHWICK, and MICHAEL T. MARSDEN, eds. Heroes of Popular Culture. Bowling Green, Ohio: Bowling Green University Popular Press, 1972. 190 pp.
This collection of essays examines the hero in American culture since 1953. In his introduction, Fishwick contends that the 1960s counterculture caused changes in the presentation of the heroic style from an oral and verbal tradition to the multisensory and electronic "pop goes the hero." The shift in emphasis marks the rise of the antihero in the 1960s, and the image remains strong in the 1970s. After an essay defining the heroic style, the volume offers an analysis of some of the heroes of our culture: the tenant farmer, the sports hero (Ty Cobb, Babe Ruth, Joe DiMaggio), the media-produced hero (Perry Mason, "Mr. Belvedere"), the music hero (Joan Baez, Burt Bacharach), and the dog as hero.

PC 11. CANTOR, NORMAN F. and MICHAEL S. WERTHEIM, eds. The History of Popular Culture. New York: Macmillan, 1968. 788 pp.
This anthology defines popular culture as "what people do when they are not working; it is man in pursuit of pleasure, excitement, beauty and fulfillment." The book surveys popular culture from ancient times to the present, dividing the vast range of material into seven chronological periods. The editors consider leisure activities and public rituals, as well as the popular arts.

PC 12. CHEEK, NEIL H., DONALD R. FIELD, and RABEL J. BURGE. Leisure and Recreation Places. Ann Arbor, Mich.: Ann Arbor Science, 1976. 172 pp.
The authors assimilate the current findings and research in the field of recreation and identify the central characteristics of leisure and recreation places in America, focusing on the relationship between society, the community, the individual, and the kinds of behavior that occur at a place of recreation. They also include a section on recreation, participation, and ethnicity, in which they identify differences in leisure behavior between whites and blacks. The authors suggest possible problems in leisure programs that are directed toward black and white low-income populations.

PC 13. CHENOWETH, LAWRENCE. The American Dream of Success: The Search for Self in the Twentieth Century. North Scituate, Mass.: Duxbury Press, 1974. 237 pp.
This text provides an interdisciplinary study of American society from the turn of the century through the 1960s in an attempt to show how the society's "traditional guides to living" have failed to keep up with social changes. The result has been tensions leading to "fantasy, helplessness, loneliness, and insignificance." Chenoweth emphasizes middle class

America's search for pleasure values. He utilizes popular culture as a way of examining the search which has emphasized finding answers over questioning beliefs. Reader's Digest (1926–69), The Saturday Evening Post (1917–67), self-help books (1917–69), and comic strips were chosen because of the extent of their popularity. Chenoweth's application of popular culture to the five major periods of stress (Industrialism, the Depression, W.W. II, the Cold War, and the 1960s) reveals that society has developed responses to the tensions which impede the questioning of dysfunctional beliefs.

PC 14. CIRINO, ROBERT. We're Being More than Entertained. Honolulu, Hawaii: Lighthouse Press, 1977. 224 pp.
Cirino explores the political messages in mass media, providing an analysis of ways in which to recognize and to counter the prevailing political biases he finds in media content. He outlines four basic political perspectives: socialist, liberal, conservative, and libertarian. The author examines television drama for its assumptions and biases, providing examples of possible alternative message-structures from one of the four political points of view. He also deals with newspaper reporting, mass-circulated magazines, game shows, media for the young, cartoons, and other sources for analysis. Cirino calls for the establishment of alternative systems of public communication which might serve the public with a range of viewpoints and perspectives.

PC 15. CORWIN, NORMAN. Trivializing America. Secaucus, N.J.: Lyle Stuart, 1983. 286 pp.
Corwin argues that mass culture trivializes American life and society. He cites the popular arts among "forces in our culture and society that tend to reduce us, to fragment our concentration, erode our standards, fritter away our native genius. . . ." He discusses various media manifestations which represent this process as well as the social forces responsible for it.

PC 16. DEER, IRVING and HARRIET DEER, eds. The Popular Arts: A Critical Reader. New York: Scribner, 1967. 336 pp.
This anthology deals with popular arts—Westerns, science fiction, detective stories—rather than with such mass media as television or newspapers. The editors are concerned with the relationship between the popular and the traditional arts, and the essayists included tend to approach the popular arts from the perspective of conventional literary criticism. Contributors to the volume include John A. Kouwenhoven, William Whyte, Jr., Norman Podhoretz, Jacques Barzun, Reuel Denny, Gilbert Highet, James Agee, and Abraham Kaplan.

PC 17. DeGRAZIA, SEBASTIAN. Of Time, Work, and Leisure. New York: Twentieth Century Fund, 1962. 559 pp.
DeGrazia examines concepts of leisure, work, and time in modern, industrial America. He notes that contemporary leisure is measured in units of time, and that work is the antonym of free time. Leisure and free time, however, are different, leisure referring to a state of being. From the perspectives of political philosophy, the author explores the origin of the ideal of leisure, the relationship between leisure and work, the commercialization of free time, how Americans use their leisure, how free time can be transformed into leisure, and the future of leisure in the U.S. He concludes that "leisure, given its proper political setting, benefits, gladdens, and beautifies the lives of all. It lifts up all heads from practical workday life to look at the whole high world with refreshed wonder."

PC 18. DORFMAN, ARIEL. The Empire's Old Clothes: What the Lone Ranger,
        Babar, and Other Innocent Heroes Do to Our Minds. New York:
        Pantheon Books, 1983. 225 pp.
In this book, Dorfman, a Chilean critic, provides a Marxist analysis of
how our popular culture, particularly in works oriented toward children,
supports status quo social and political ideals. His close explication
of Babar, Donald Duck, the Lone Ranger, Superman, Reader's Digest, and
other familiar artifacts reveals the story of capitalism, American cultural
imperialism, and the hegemony of the "power elite" in the Western world.

PC 19. DULLES, FOSTER RHEA. America Learns to Play: A History of Recrea-
        tion, 1607-1940. New York: Appleton-Century-Crofts, 1940.
        446 pp.
The author of this history of popular recreation in the U.S. regards
the ways in which Americans play as a means of evaluating American culture.
Dulles has limited his study to forms of organized public recreation which
have reached a wide range of people. In tracing the trends in recreation
over the last three centuries, he discusses the effects of the Puritan
work ethic on the recreation movement in America. He points as well to
the gradual transformation from an agrarian economy to the complexity
of the machine age, with its growth of leisure time, as a key factor in
determining popular recreation in the U.S. Dulles focuses on significant
individuals who have contributed to the growth of recreation in America,
and illustrates this work with black-and-white drawings and photos.

PC 20. EWEN, STUART and ELIZABETH EWEN. Channels of Desire: Mass Images
        and the Shaping of the American Consciousness. New York: McGraw-
        Hill, 1982. 312 pp.
Beginning with the rise of the machine and the emergence of consumerism
as a way of life, the authors discuss the ways in which mass production
transformed the U.S. from a handicraft and agrarian society into an industrial giant, while consumerism posed radically new ways of seeing the
world and altered concepts of value and integrity. The Ewens focus on
specific areas to demonstrate the power of images in American life: the
role of film in the Americanization of immigrants; how clothing and fashion
functioned to give shape to American ideas about democracy and sexuality;
the collaboration of media images in building a moral climate for war.

PC 21. FISHWICK, MARSHALL W. Common Culture and the Great Tradition:
        The Case for Renewal. Westport, Conn.: Greenwood Press, 1982.
        230 pp.
Fishwick examines the significance of popular culture for the modern world,
arguing that an examination of world-wide sources reveals that we have
much in common. He traces the evolution of modern Western societies,
noting processes of division and of reunification, the latter resulting
largely from electronic technologies of communication employed in the
production and dissemination of popular art forms. Among the topics on
which he focuses are myths and dreams, land and lore, heroes, sports culture, celebrities, counter-culture styles, and literary art. Fishwick
argues that the future demands a greater understanding of the global significance of modern popular culture and ways of dealing with common and
disparate images and experience.

PC 22. FISHWICK, MARSHALL W. and RAY B. BROWNE, eds. Icons of Popular
        Culture. Bowling Green, Ohio: Bowling Green University Popular
        Press, 1970. 128 pp.
Icons are described as "symbols and mindmarkers" that are tied closely
to "myth, legend, values, idols, aspirations." The editors compare and
contrast the traditional social role of icons as symbols of stability
with newer popular icons which reflect a culture of continual change.
Essays in the collection examine such icons as the Coke bottle, automobiles,
matchbox labels, media images, and various folk and popular artifacts.

PC 23. GANS, HERBERT J. Popular Culture and High Culture: An Analysis and Evaluation of Taste. New York: Basic Books, 1974. 179 pp.
Concluding that traditional mass culture critique serves high culture interest, Gans offers instead an "argument for cultural democracy." "Taste cultures" and "taste publics" form the conceptual foundation of this alternative. Gans describes five taste cultures and publics: high culture, upper-middle culture, lower-middle culture, low culture, and quasi-folk culture. Each of these subcultures reflects aggregates of different values, and people who make similar choices among these cultural offerings constitute taste publics. While Gans feels that higher cultures are better than lower because they are more comprehensive and informative, he considers taste publics to be equal to the degree that they serve their respective constituents. He laments cultural conditions that block people's opportunities to participate in higher cultures, and at the same time deny lower groups access to good programming within their taste cultures.

PC 24. GEIST, CHRISTOPHER D. and JACK NACHBAR, eds. The Popular Culture Reader. 1978; Rev. ed. Bowling Green, Ohio: Bowling Green University Popular Press, 1983. 347 pp.
This reader examines four major areas of popular culture: popular mythologies, popular objects, popular arts, and popular rituals. Popular culture is said to "impose structures upon experience that allow us to make sense of a world that often seems absurd and to find expression for ideas, beliefs, and values that often seem inexpressible." The sections of the book explore popular myths, popular icons, stereotypes, heroes, rituals, and formulas. Issues in popular culture criticism are summarized and discussed.

PC 25. GIRGUS, SAM B., ed. The American Self: Myth, Ideology, and Popular Culture. Albuquerque: University of New Mexico Press, 1981. 248 pp.
Girgus brings together essays which represent the development of American Studies scholarship—including popular culture inquiry—over the past several decades. The first set of essays shows how the traditional American Studies interest in myth and ideology remains under scrutiny; the second set reflects the growing concern for the diversity of cultural experience in America. Popular culture topics inform both approaches to the study of our culture and society, here reflected in essays dealing with the cowgirl figure, popular narrative, baseball, autobiography, movie heroes, and New Mexico folklore.

PC 26. GOWANS, ALAN. The Unchanging Arts: New Forms for the Traditional Functions of Art in Society. Philadelphia: Lippincott, 1971. 433 pp.
In this second of a three-part study of history and art, Gowans explores the changed character of what we call art. He traces what has happened to the "social functions painting abandoned, the history of those arts variously called 'popular,' 'mass,' or 'commercial' that picked them up, one after the other, and perform them still—these arts, in a word, whose function has been changeless." The book presents a discussion of the bases of distinction between the popular and fine arts, with a specific focus on photography, commercial design, decoration, such forms of illustration as narrative painting and prints, comics, movies, television, cartoons, architecture, and advertising. Gowans concludes with a discussion of the unchanging and the revolutionary aspects of art.

PC 27. HALL, JAMES B. and BARRY ULANOV, eds. Modern Culture and the Arts. 1967; Rev. ed. New York: McGraw-Hill, 1972. 574 pp.
Hall and Ulanov attempt to "raise issues central to the arts in our time" through an examination of the nature of art and the relationships to be found among the various arts. Essential to such a study is an evaluation

of the split between high culture and the popular arts. The editors have
divided this collection into sections dealing with various cultural expressions of modern society. Each section begins with an essay presenting
the traditional point of view, and the rest of the essays examine the
traditional point of view from a modern perspective. Included are essays
on music (Stravinsky, Copland, Ulanov), art (Gombrich, Kandinsky, Klee,
Picasso, Jaffe), the novel (James, Fiedler, Barthes), poetry (Valery,
Cummings, Auden, Thomas), theater and dance (Shaw, Brecht, Wigman), television (Panofsky, Sarris, Bergman, Callenbach, Commager), photography
(Szarkowski, Bazin, Abbott), and architecture (Gropius, Pei, Soleri).

PC 28. **HALL, STUART** and **PADDY WHANNEL**. The Popular Arts: A Critical
Guide to the Mass Media. Boston: Beacon Press, 1967. 480 pp.
According to the authors, "the struggle between what is good and worthwhile
and what is shoddy and debased is not a struggle against the modern forms
of communication, but a conflict within these media." The book provides
critical methods for evaluating mass media. Part I explores definitions
of media and society, minority art, folk art, popular art, and mass culture.
Part II deals with popular forms, popular artists, violence on the screen,
fantasy and romance, and the young audience. Part III deals with critical
approaches to mass culture and Part IV focuses on curriculum and projects
for teachers. An appendix presents materials on books, journals, records,
film, television, and organizations.

PC 29. **HAMMEL, WILLIAM**. The Popular Arts in America: A Critical Reader.
1972; Rev. ed. New York: Harcourt Brace Jovanovich, 1977.
501 pp.
This reader focuses on the mass media, arguing that "these new arts contain
some of the most exciting artistic developments of our time, and that
anyone who seriously hopes to understand American culture cannot possibly
ignore the popular arts." Essays include a general account of the popular
arts and specific studies of film, television, popular music, popular
books, and journalism. Writers such as Russel Nye, Leo Rosten, James
Baldwin, John Cawelti, Gilbert Highet, Stanley Kauffman, Robert Warshow,
James Agee, Ingmar Bergman, Margaret Mead, Spiro Agnew, Eric Sevareid,
Leroi Jones (Imamu Amiri Baraka), Charles Schulz, and Jules Feiffer reflect
the range of opinion, background, and interest devoted to discussing mass
media as social and cultural phenomena.

PC 30. **HUEBEL, HARRY RUSSELL**. Things in the Driver's Seat: Readings
in Popular Culture. Chicago: Rand McNally, 1974. 270 pp.
Huebel's readings are organized into two time periods: 1865-1945 and
1945-70. The first section deals with the impact of urban and commercial
forces on American culture, including the significance of technology and
new industrial products for production and distribution. Discussions
look at Currier and Ives lithographs, Uncle Remus, The Wizard of Oz, the
baseball umpire, the automobile, European borrowing of American popular
culture, adventure comics, and the gangster-image in American popular
art. The selections in the second section indicate the growing complexity
of American culture, including the emergence of a counter-culture "underground." Topics dealt with include jazz, colloquial language, Mickey
Spillane, James Dean, Elvis Presley, Halloween, Pueblo baseball, Western
movies, romance magazines, and Mormon jokes.

PC 31. **INGE, M. THOMAS**, ed. Concise Histories of American Popular Culture.
Westport, Conn.: Greenwood Press, 1982. 504 pp.
This collection includes fifty chapters, each providing a brief history
of a significant aspect of American popular culture and a checklist of
important books and references. The book combines various portions of
Inge's three-volume Handbook of American Popular Culture to form what
the editor terms "a combined history, bibliography, and textbook designed

to encourage and further our understanding of the cultural environment
in which we live." Chapters are devoted to such diverse subjects as animation, children's literature, fashions, foodways, jazz, romantic fiction,
sports, television, women, and Westerns. An essay by Michael Bell discusses approaches to the study of popular culture.

PC 32. JACOBS, NORMAN, ed. Culture for the Millions? Mass Media in Modern
        Society. Boston: Beacon Press, 1964. 200 pp.
These essays emerged from a seminar on mass culture, mass society, and
the mass media; the volume includes a transcript of the panel discussion
which followed the original presentations. Such social critics as Edward
Shils, Hannan Baldwin, Arthur Schlesinger, Jr., Gilbert Seldes, and Sidney
Hook comment on the impact that popular culture has on society. The volume
is characterized by the sense of urgency with which the influence of the
mass media and the nature of modern mass society were discussed in the
late 1950s and early 1960s.

PC 33. JEWETT, ROBERT and JOHN SHELTON LAWRENCE. The American Monomyth.
        New York: Anchor Press, 1977. 263 pp.
Jewett and Lawrence locate an American monomyth in the artifacts of popular
culture. According to this book, a very basic myth in which a paradise
of harmony and tranquility is threatened, the community disrupted, and
an heroic rescue is undertaken recurs continually in our popular arts.
The symbols in this story reveal the basic underpinnings of American society, including our fear that our social institutions are inadequate and
that we will have to be redeemed by a hero with special, supernatural
powers. To illustrate their contentions, Jewett and Lawrence analyze
such sources as "Star Trek," Playboy, "Death Wish," "Heidi," the work
of Walt Disney, and science fiction. The authors trace changes in the
myth over the years and evaluate its cultural and social significance,
seeing it as escapist, undemocratic, hostile to individualism, and supportive of passivity.

PC 34. KANDO, THOMAS M. Leisure and Popular Culture in Transition. St.
        Louis, Mo.: Mosby, 1975. 308 pp.
In this general sociological introduction to the field of leisure and
popular culture, Kando examines America's changing attitudes toward work
and leisure and the resulting changes in national consciousness and lifestyle. The first part of this study is chiefly theoretical in nature,
defining the concepts of game, recreation, and play; the second part
focuses on specific leisure forms and practices related to mass leisure
and mass culture. Kando investigates the dominant recreational behavior
in contemporary America, speculates about the future of leisure in America,
and attempts define the desirable forms of leisure, culture, and lifestyle.

PC 35. KETCHUM, ALTON. Uncle Sam: The Man and the Legend. New York:
        Hill & Wang, 1975. 90 pp.
The story of Uncle Sam, an actual historical figure, is chronicled in
this work. Drawing on period newspapers as well as local lore, Ketchum
traces the nation's search for a national symbol from Pocahontas, Columbia,
and Yankee Doodle to Brother Jonathan, and finally to "Sam." The text
is illustrated with period drawings dating from Sam Wilson's inaugural
depiction in 1832 up to the mid-1970s. Citing the potency of the cartoon
medium, Ketchum shows how "Sam" became the vehicle by which much of the
nation's internal and international struggles have been expressed. He
discusses "Sam" as he is depicted by Thomas Nast; Joseph Keppler (the
originator of the "I Want You" poster); James Montgomery Flagg; England's
John Leech; and by the Italian, Latin American, and Soviet presses.

PC 36. KLAPP, ORRIN E. Heroes, Villains, and Fools: The Changing American
        Character. Englewood Cliffs, N.J.: Prentice-Hall, 1962. 176 pp.
This book is a study of several social character-types in America--heroes,
villains, and fools--and of their role as models for belief and behavior.
Klapp presents the character-types as exemplars of positive and negative
social conduct and as images which guide public attitudes. He studies
popular language as a key element in the development of our attitudes
toward behavior, and examines such sources as literature, art, news coverage, biography, and mythology as vehicles for transmitting images. A
separate chapter is devoted to each character-type, and additional chapters
explore such issues as the deterioration of the hero, American anomic
types, and mockery of the idea of the hero.

PC 37. KLAPPER, JOSEPH. The Effects of Mass Communication. New York:
        Free Press, 1960. 302 pp.
Klapper evaluates the literature on the psychological and sociological
impact of mass culture, noting the limitations of certain studies and
questioning whether the media are as persuasive as some commentators maintain. His first section explores theoretical studies of mass communication,
including theories of reinforcement and conversion, and studies of the
processes of opinion and attitude formation. The second part examines
specific questions, such as those pertaining to crime and violence and
to the effects of media on children. Among other topics discussed are
escapist literature, adult TV shows, and audience passivity.

PC 38. LAFORSE, MARTIN W. and JAMES A. DRAKE. Popular Culture and American
        Life: Selected Topics in the Study of American Popular Culture.
        Chicago: Nelson-Hall, 1981. 257 pp.
The authors analyze several prominent of popular culture expressions of
20th-century American society. An introduction briefly discusses definitions of popular culture and common critical and theoretical viewpoints
on popular culture, contrasting the popular arts with high culture and
folk culture. Specific studies are devoted to popular music (particularly
jazz), the popular theater, the broadcast and film media, the development
of racial and ethnic stereotypes in popular culture, and the development
of sports in America. The authors stress the role of the entertainment
media in the formation of a popular culture in contemporary America.

PC 39. LARRABEE, ERIC and ROLF MEYERSOHN, eds. Mass Leisure. Glencoe,
        Ill.: Free Press, 1958. 429 pp.
This collection of essays focuses on leisure as a social phenomenon in
the modern world, especially in America. Leisure is described as "deeply
connected with the cultivation of the self." It is linked to mass culture
and has become increasingly more available to the modern industrial societies of the West. In these work-oriented societies, leisure vies with
work, and poses problems and choices in the allocation of time. The essays
approach the subject from a variety of disciplinary perspectives, including
those of history, sociology, anthropology, philosophy, and economics.
General analysis seeks to define leisure, to relate it to work, to discuss
the "leisure class," and to discover the meaning of play; and more specific
inquiries examine hobbies, holidays, sports, fads, and other issues.
The volume includes a bibliography devoted to studies of leisure.

PC 40. LEWIS, GEORGE, ed. Side-Saddle on the Golden California Pacific
        Palisades. Pacific Palisades, Calif.: Goodyear, 1972. 388 pp.
Lewis employs the structure of the Hegelian dialectic of thesis, antithesis,
and synthesis as a theoretical framework for the analysis of the relationship of social structure to expressions of popular culture. This collection of essays examines cultural "artifacts" to illustrate changes occurring in the society. After a working definition of popular culture is
provided through the writings of Russel Nye and Ray Browne, the thesis,

emphasizing the expressions of cultural artifacts in the "larger social system," is outlined in essays on the significance of Marlboro cigarettes, the demolition derby, radio evangelists, and hamburgers. The volume also considers subcultural artifacts, such as those of black and youth culture, which offer antithetical alternatives to the established social structure. A concluding section questions whether a synthesis of mainstream culture and subcultures is possible.

PC 41. **LOWENTHAL, LEO.** Literature, Popular Culture and Society. Palo Alto, Calif.: Pacific Books, 1961. 169 pp.
Lowenthal begins by making a clear distinction between literature as an art form and literature as a "popular commodity": the former is described as a complex probing of human nature and society, and the latter as a more shallow reflection of mass interests without significant truth or insight. Great writers, he contends, achieve an expression of truth in "the realization of the ideal"; popular art expresses more ephemeral pre-occupations.

PC 42. **LYNES, RUSSELL.** The Tastemakers. New York: Harper, 1949. 362 pp.
According to Lynes, "taste is our personal delight, our private dilemma, and our public facade." He explains that the shaping of American taste is an essential activity of American capitalism. Lynes provides the personal histories of men and women who reflect changing tastes, and includes inquiries into such topics as art missionaries, packaged taste, stately homes, suburbia, highbrow-lowbrow-middlebrow taste distinctions, and the relationship between public, private, and corporate tastes.

PC 43. **MANNING, FRANK E.** The Celebration of Society: Perspectives on Contemporary Cultural Performance. Bowling Green, Ohio: Bowling Green University Popular Press, 1983. 208 pp.
This collection of essays explores the "relationship between celebration and the social realities of those who experience it." In these ethnological, cross-cultural studies, celebration is presented as performance and entertainment, as public spectacle and participatory event. Topics examined include professional wrestling, gambling, Carnaval in Rio, cowboy celebrations in Canada, and Indian powwow festivals. Celebration is analyzed as responding to deep-seated social, psychological, and cultural needs and beliefs. It is related to processes of change and of supporting social stability, to modernity, and to hierarchical structure.

PC 44. **MATLAW, MYRON,** ed. American Popular Entertainment. Westport, Conn.: Greenwood Press, 1977. 338 pp.
The contributors to this volume represent both the scholarly world and that of the producers, distributors, and performers of popular entertainment. In addition to an overview of popular entertainment and its study, papers dealing with such topics as the minstrel theater, vaudeville, burlesque, tent shows, circus, medicine shows, dance, and environmental entertainment (for example, amusement parks, street theater) provide a history of American popular culture. The volume concludes with a bibliography.

PC 45. **McLUHAN, MARSHALL.** Understanding Media: The Extension of Man. New York: McGraw-Hill, 1964. 359 pp.
For McLuhan media are "extensions of man" that have progressively altered the human environment. What was once done with the body and the senses is now done by machine. Furthermore, every medium has as its content another medium. McLuhan follows media evolution from "hot" high-information print through "cool" low-definition television, with its "tactile" appeal and total involvement. He explores such varied media as numbers, roads, wheels, clocks, money, automobiles, games, radios, and telephones. McLuhan sees "understanding media" as a way to mitigate the confusion they cause in our sensory perceptions.

PC 46. MENDELSOHN, HAROLD. Mass Entertainment. New Haven, Conn.: College
    & University Press, 1966. 203 pp.
Mendelsohn focuses on the role of mass media in the gratification of human
needs for pleasure. He looks at television, film, radio, novels, newspapers, and magazines from a sociological perspective, and notes that
discussion of the effects of mass media is linked with the consideration
of values and with the attempts to define "the good life" in contemporary
culture. Mendelsohn calls for a multi-disciplinary inquiry into the
motives and functions of the media, to be financed by the entertainment
industries.

PC 47. MONACO, JAMES. Celebrity: The Media as Image Makers. New York:
    Dell, 1978. 258 pp.
According to Monaco, we are surrounded by mass media-produced fictional
images that emerge out of our "collective fantasies," and we live through
the roles that they project. This collection of essays attempts to rein-
state "the balance between life and fiction" by looking at the basic characteristics of celebrity status. Three categories of celebrities are
studied: "heroes, stars, and quasars: heroes for the things they do,
stars for who they are, and quasars which are totally media created and
transmitted entities fulfilling the expectations we have for them." After
commenting on the nature of celebrity, Monaco describes the role of the
media promoting the celebrity's image in the society. He follows this
with a discussion of the casualties of celebrity (Patty Hearst, Mary Ann
Vecchio, and Katherine Blum). Celebrities considered include Farrah
Fawcett, Douglas Fairbanks, Jr., Greta Garbo, and Ingrid Bergman.

PC 48. MONACO, JAMES, ed. Media Culture: Television, Radio, Books, Maga-
    zines, Newspapers, Movies. New York: Dell, 1978. 335 pp.
In this volume, Monaco examines the mass media in the late 1970s, and
provides an analysis of the producers, the product, and the effect of
the media on our culture. The history of the media is defined through
the history of technology as it was shaped by the forces of distribution,
capital, and profit-motive. The non-print media are basically oligopolistic in nature, and the print media have lost much of their diversity.
This collection of essays looks at who controls the media, what is produced,
and how the effect of the media culture is measured.

PC 49. MYERS, ROBERT J. and THE EDITORS OF HALLMARK CARDS. Celebrations:
    The Complete Book of American Holidays. Garden City, N.Y.: Double-
    day, 1972. 386 pp.
A broad social history of forty-five major American holidays, with summary
information on fourteen more, this volume includes discussion of all
nationally observed holidays and of many local and ethnic events that
receive national attention. Myers provides a history of important secular
and religious observances, with information on how and why they started,
and the customs associated with them. Also included is a list of purely
local observances. Religious holidays include Christmas, Easter, Passover,
Yom Kippur and Hanukkah. Secular holidays include New Year's, Washington's
Birthday, Mother's Day, Father's Day, Independence Day, Labor Day, and
Thanksgiving. Ethnic and local celebrations include the Mardi Gras, American Indian Day, St. Patrick's Day, Pan American Day, and the Chinese New
Year. Other holidays include Martin Luther King's Birthday, Inauguration
Day, April Fool's Day, Reformation Day, and National Aviation Day. Myers
examines each day for its place in American culture, providing summaries
of public attitudes and of the historical significance of the day at various periods.

PC 50. NYE, RUSSEL. The Unembarrassed Muse: The Popular Arts in America. New York: Dial Press, 1970. 497 pp.

Nye explores the history of American popular arts, "the arts of commercial entertainment." Dependent on mass media technology and a complex of social, political, and economic factors, these popular arts emerged in the 19th century along with mass society. Accordingly, consensus defines popular art as speaking for the majority and confirming their experience. Nye looks at six aspects of the popular arts: popular fiction and poetry; popular theater, dime novels and comics; detective and science fiction; Western stories; popular music; and movies, radio, and television. He concludes with a statement on popular arts and the critics, seeing the removal of boundaries between elite and popular cultures as beneficial.

PC 51. PETERSON, RICHARD A., ed. The Production of Culture. Beverly Hills, Calif.: Sage, 1976. 144 pp.

The eight essays in this volume take a sociology of art perspective, discussing the production and distribution of popular culture, including the roles of government, educational institutions, religion, and patronage; the economics of popular art production; and the conditions under which the popular arts are created and made available. This approach to understanding popular culture is advanced as central to any cultural examination of art and entertainment.

PC 52. POWERS, RICHARD GID. G-Men: Hoover's FBI in Popular Culture. Carbondale: Southern Illinois University Press, 1983. 356 pp.

This study traces the rise and fall of the FBI's public image from the 1930s to the present. It is an account of how the FBI and the mass entertainment industry cooperated to transform the FBI's biggest cases into popular mythology by tailoring them to fit public preconceptions about crime, criminals, and detectives. The book attributes Hoover's success to his early ability to satisfy important needs in popular America culture, and his decline to his failure to perceive and adapt to changing cultural conditions.

PC 53. REAL, MICHAEL R. Mass-Mediated Culture. Englewood Cliffs, N.J.: Prentice-Hall, 1977. 289 pp.

Real applies different methods of popular culture analysis, such as ethnography, exegesis, and propaganda theory, to case studies of mass media phenomena. He offers this work as an example of cultural studies—a bridge between the approaches of social science and the humanities. With a McLuhanesque view of media as human extensions, he analyzes Disneyland, the Super Bowl, television medical programs, Nixon's Committee to Re-Elect the President, Billy Graham's evangelism, and, as a cross-cultural example, the Aymaras tribe in Peru. Operating from a structuralist-Marxist perspective, Real sees capitalist, Western, white males controlling the mass media. He condemns the use of the media to perpetuate injustice and calls for a reorientation of the media to serve the people's needs. The book offers a survey of modern media criticism as well as Real's own solutions to the problem of the influence of mass media.

PC 54. ROSENBERG, BERNARD and DAVID MANNING WHITE, eds. Mass Culture: The Popular Arts in America. New York: Free Press, 1957. 561 pp.

Rosenberg and White outline the critical debate concerning the social impact of mass culture, with Rosenberg summarizing the various anti-popular culture positions and White explaining several possible defenses. The volume contains forty-nine essays. Some of the essays are purely theoretical considerations of the likely functions of popular art in a mass society; others look more specifically at particular popular genres and their audience.

PC 55. ROSENBERG, BERNARD and DAVID MANNING WHITE, eds. Mass Culture Revisited. New York: Van Nostrand & Reinhold, 1971. 473 pp. In this update of their Mass Culture (see PC 54), the editors continue to present a theoretical discussion of popular culture's effects on society, with Rosenberg again stating the case against popular culture and White writing as an advocate. Several of the contributors to the volume take sides in this debate, while others take closer views of particular genres such as television, film, magazines, spy fiction, and advertising. The editors provide various disciplinary perspectives, including those of psychology, philosophy, sociology, and journalism.

PC 56. ROSZAK, THEODORE. The Making of a Counter Culture. Garden City, N.Y.: Doubleday, 1969. 303 pp. Roszak defines the technocratic society as a "social form in which an industrial society reaches the peak of its organizational integration." It is against this structure that the youthful counter-culture emerges to rebel against the passivity of an adult population which accepts the power structure. Because of the "repressive desublimation" of the tech- nocracy, which absorbs the discontents and rebels, a theoretical framework must be built around the issues. Roszak looks at the psychological insights of Herbert Marcuse and Norman O. Brown, and at mysticism, drugs and utopianism, and concludes that a complete transformation of the way people view reality is needed, together with experimentation with forms that subvert the traditional structure. People need to examine the culture with a critical eye and live their lives outside of the dominant character- istics of consumption that define technological progress.

PC 57. SANN, PAUL. Fads, Follies and Delusions of the American People. New York: Crown, 1967. 570 pp. In this pictorial study, Sann traces 20th-century popular tastes--or, as he refers to them, fads, follies, and delusions. The book explores America's heroes, social follies, money schemes, mind-and-body fads, game rages, messianic leaders, popular entertainers, campus fads, and crowd gatherings. Specifically, Sann studies why children are attracted to Batman, Hula Hoops, Davy Crockett's coonskin cap, skateboards, Zorro, and bubblegum. Adult tastes include Billy Graham, Ouija boards, and Bing Crosby. Popular to both teenagers and adults are fads like marathons, mini-skirts, rock-n-roll, and Frank Sinatra. Sann also looks at changing campus activities from goldfish swallowing to anti-war marches. He con- cludes that these happenings often derive from the bewildering variety of promises held out to the "panting masses." These promises include: something-for-nothing, easy money, mental contentment, physical health, boundless vigor in the boudoir, and delightful excursions into fantasy land.

PC 58. SELDES, GILBERT. The Public Arts. New York: Simon & Schuster, 1956. 303 pp. Seldes writes positively about the popular arts, but he is also aware of the possible negative effects of popular culture on the mass audience. He is concerned with the potential of the electronic media to replace communication on an individual basis with larger, more unified, "sacred" images. He looks specifically at radio programs, quiz shows, television personalities, and other mass media issues, noting the links between the producers, the texts, and the audiences for whom they are intended. Accord- ing to Seldes, the popular arts belong to the people, but, in the modern media configuration, exercising control over the arts becomes more prob- lematic.

PC 59. SELDES, GILBERT. The Seven Lively Arts. 1924; Rev. ed. New York: Sagamore Press, 1957. 306 pp.

Seldes examines both the aesthetic nature and the sociological significance of the popular arts. The revised version of the book updates the analysis with more contemporary examples, but his earlier interest in popular culture is unchanged. The author recognizes that popular culture contains "bogus art"--productions which are either pretentious or oriented to mass commercial appeal rather than to sincere expression; but he also outlines areas of artistic endeavor--comic strips, motion pictures, musical comedy, vaudeville, radio programs, popular music, and dance--in which the popular arts are indeed "lively." Among the specific examples studied are the productions of Florenz Ziegfeld, the Negro cabaret theater, Al Jolson, Charlie Chaplin, Fanny Brice, Keystone comedy, "Krazy Kat," the circus, and burlesque theater.

PC 60. STEIN, BENJAMIN. The View from Sunset Boulevard. New York: Basic Books, 1979. 156 pp.

Stein considers the content of American television by examining its relationship to the political opinions, backgrounds, and lifestyles of the people who write, direct, and produce the programs. His thesis is that the small, homogeneous (white, male, over thirty-five, Jewish) group of people who control the making of television has a distinct ideological perspective: it is pro-labor, anti-business, anti-military, and critical of small-town society. He notes that the world of television is a very particular slice of American life, edited to conform to the tastes, beliefs, needs, and concerns of the artists, and to what they think their audience wants or needs. The author uses ethnographic examination of the television industry as well as various critical approaches to its product.

PC 61. TRUZZI, MARCELLO, ed. Sociology and Everyday Life. Englewood Cliffs, N.J.: Prentice-Hall, 1968. 371 pp.

Truzzi takes a sociological approach to the "mundane," the "salient," and the "hip" manifestations of culture in everyday life. The volume contains twenty-nine essays organized in sections labeled "Sociology and Everyday Life," "Social Differentiation," "Everyday Interactions," "Occupations," "Youth," "Minority Groups," "Religion," "Deviance and Crime," "Social Change," and "Terminating Processes." Topics covered include card playing, comic strips, the Beatles, MAD Magazine, nudist camps, religious cults, Santa Claus, and the circus.

PC 62. ULANOV, BARRY. The Two Worlds of American Art: The Private and the Popular. New York: Macmillan, 1965. 528 pp.

Ulanov compares and contrasts two types of cultural production: popular and private. According to the author, popular art is based in the mass media; it panders to the largest possible audience and is dominated by concerns for commercial viability. The private artist, on the other hand, seeks to elevate himself above mass taste and to cultivate a special, sophisticated audience which is capable of appreciating his or her unique gifts. Ulanov develops his comparison with specific references to various musical forms, graphic arts, literary endeavors, theatrical performance, and mass media expression.

PC 63. WAGNER, GEOFFREY. Parade of Pleasure: A Study of Popular Iconography in the USA. New York: Library Publishers, 1955. 192 pp.

Wagner evaluates American popular art from a social perspective, looking at movies, comics, and pin-ups, as well as TV, radio, jazz, and murder mysteries. In all such "drivel," Wagner discovers a lustful and sadistic violence, a celebration of primitive appetites which poses a particular threat to the minds of the young. While he does not argue for censorship, he encourages prompt official investigation of questionable popular offerings.

PC 64.   WHETMORE, EDWARD J.   Mediamerica: Form, Content, and Consequence
         of Mass Communications.   Belmont, Calif.: Wadsworth, 1982.   365
         pp.
Whetmore provides an introduction to mass media in America, emphasizing
both a historical perspective and current trends and issues.   The book
is divided into three sections: print media, electronic media, and media-
related topics.   The print media section includes examination of books,
newspapers, New Journalism, comics, magazines, and the relationship between
government and the press.   Electronic media discussed include radio, television, music, and film; and topics in the final section are advertising,
news, public relations, popular culture, and international communication.

PC 65.   WHITE, DAVID MANNING, ed.   Pop Culture in America.   Chicago: Quad-
         rangle, 1970.   279 pp.
White has selected articles dealing with popular culture from the New
York Times in order to provide a closer focus on popular art criticism
as well as on the various genres themselves.   In this book, the editor
reflects his view that it is time to go beyond purely theoretical discussion of the pros and cons of popular culture to a more sophisticated analysis of the arts themselves, their themes, and their popular reception.
Contributors to the collection include Bruce Boiven, Marya Mannes, Richard
Schickel, and Benjamin DeMott.

PC 66.   WHITE, DAVID MANNING and JOHN PENDLETON, eds.   Popular Culture:
         Mirror of American Life.   Del Mar, Calif.: Publisher's Inc.,
         1977.   360 pp.
The unifying theme of this anthology is that popular culture provides
a "mirror" in which our society can be viewed and explored.   Essays examine
popular culture's institutions, the question of popular culture and social
change, and the future of popular culture.   Contributors include Russel
B. Nye, Reuel Denney, Oscar Handlin, John Cawelti, Daniel Boorstin, Michael
Real, and Betty Friedan.

PC 67.   WHITE, EDWARD M., ed.   The Pop Culture Tradition: Readings with
         Analysis for Writing.   New York: Norton, 1972.   196 pp.
These essays seek to explicate the popular art text with the same critical
tools used in the criticism of the fine arts.   Popular song lyrics, comics,
movies, and magazines, among other sources, are analyzed and evaluated
in three sections: "Understanding Assumptions: Art and Society"; "Understanding Implications: Art and Behavior"; and "The Uses of Evidence:
Art and Popular Art."   Readings include works by George Orwell, John Updike,
Franz Kafka, David Reisman, Marshall McLuhan, Randall Jarrell, and William
Shakespeare.

II.   LITERATURE

GENERAL WORKS

PC 68.   AUSTIN, JAMES C. and DONALD A. KOCH, eds.   Popular Literature in
         America: A Symposium in Honor of Lyon N. Richardson.   Bowling
         Green, Ohio: Bowling Green University Popular Press, 1972.
         205 pp.
The essays collected in this volume elucidate the major themes in American
popular literature, with a focus on the 19th century.   The volume is
divided into three sections, each of which addresses a specific approach

to popular literature. The first section, "Romancers," includes essays
on popular taste in Cleveland, Ohio (which is taken as a microcosm of
the nation), detective fiction, the role of the feud in Southern mountain
literature, and the cowboy in popular literature. in Section II,
"Jesters," the essays examine the role of satire, the use of dialect,
and the Americanization of burlesque in mid-19th-century America. The
final section, "Homilists and Heretics," is comprised of essays on the
roots of reform literature in the 19th century, women militants, the uncer-
tainties of authorship in the post-Civil War South, and a final essay on
the function of television in the American way of life.

PC 69. BEER, THOMAS. The Mauve Decade: American Life at the End of the
        Nineteenth Century. Garden City, N.Y.: Garden City Publishing,
        1926. 268 pp.
Beer's analysis of American life at the end of the 19th century focuses
on the lives and works of literary and social figures. He draws on published and unpublished letters and journals as well as on personal reminiscences to portray an era which he feels is characterized by the superficial-
ity of American civilization and culture. In particular, he identifies
the problems as American materialism, ignorance, and the predominance
of mob rule. Beer incorporates the rise of literary Realism and the rapid
growth of American railroads and industry into his discussions, which
also include special chapters devoted to American religious sentiment
and to American magazines.

PC 70. BROWN, HERBERT ROSS. The Sentimental Novel in America, 1789-1860.
        Durham, N.C.: Duke University Press, 1940. 407 pp.
Brown focuses on "social trends, forces, creeds, movements, and literary
fashions" to account for the rise of the "sentimental" novel. These forces
emerged in 18th-century England, where the novels of Samuel Richardson
and Laurence Sterne made sentiment and sensibility fashionable for popular
fiction, and in Germany, with Goethe's The Sorrows of Young Werther.
In America, writers (mostly women) applied these values to a variety of
subjects: scientism, intemperance, domestic entanglements, slavery, and
religion. Brown emphasizes the flawed morality of a literature that created victims, especially when their "natural goodness" depended upon compromise and repression.

PC 71. BURNS, REX. Success in America: The Yeoman Dream and the Indus-
        trial Revolution. Amherst: University of Massachusetts Press,
        1976. 212 pp.
Focusing on the period 1825-60, Burns investigates "both the existence
of the yeoman idea and its varying mutations." He begins his discussion
by examining Puritan and Enlightenment views of "traditional" success
that emphasized the three elements of competence, independence, and morality. Interpreting popular literature, children's literature, labor periodicals, and the novels of Hawthorne, he analyzes the equating of success
with wealth in the mid-19th century. The yeoman dream, Burns remarks,
persisted in the late 19th century, but the dominant notion of success
became one of material well-being competitively achieved; in the new industrial age, the yeoman idea began to assume a defensive posture responding
to radical social change.

PC 72. CAWELTI, JOHN G. Adventure, Mystery, and Romance: Formula Stories
        as Art and Popular Culture. Chicago: University of Chicago Press,
        1976. 336 pp.
This book examines the narrative structure and general audience appeal
of popular story formulas. Cawelti contends that because they express
collectively held beliefs, such fictional formulas reveal and are shaped
by cultural patterns. In general, he considers the problems and possibilities of analyzing formulaic literature. Further, he describes the "art-

fulness" of writers and genres typically considered simple and aesthetically uninteresting. After an extended discussion in which Cawelti relates
formulaic analysis to other literary and cultural approaches (genre study
and myth-symbol analysis, for example), he focuses on several major formulas in particular: crime literature (the classical detective story and
hardboiled fiction); the Western; and the popular social melodrama.

PC 73. **CAWELTI, JOHN G.** Apostles of the Self-Made Man: Changing Concepts
of Success in America. Chicago: University of Chicago Press,
1965. 279 pp.
This volume focuses on the differing American definitions of the idea
of success, and the way in which interpretations of the self-made man
have changed. Cawelti examines three main sources for the self-improvement
theme: individual figures such as Benjamin Franklin, Thomas Jefferson,
Ralph Waldo Emerson, Horatio Alger, and John Dewey, who either played
a major role in shaping the success ideal or were associated with it in
the public mind; success manuals and guides from the late 18th century
to 1900; and the self-made man as the central character in fictional narratives. Cawelti analyzes "the characteristic complex of ideas about
the self-made man" that reveal connections between social conditions and
the divergent notions of success.

PC 74. **DETTELBACH, CYNTHIA GOLOMB.** In the Driver's Seat: The Automobile
in American Literature and Popular Culture. Westport, Conn.:
Greenwood Press, 1976. 139 pp.
This volume considers the depiction of the car in American letters and
popular culture in order to explore the significance of the automobile
as an artistic device and as a major phenomenon in 20th-century society.
Dettelbach introduces films, music, popular poems, and novels, as well
as the literary endeavors of William Faulkner, F. Scott Fitzgerald, John
Steinbeck and Flannery O'Connor, to analyze the car as "a metaphor or
microcosm of our ambivalent dream/nightmare experiences." She divides
the chapters into categories of wish-fulfillment and anxiety: Youth,
Freedom, Success, Possession. Dettelbach concludes that the "original
American Dream is as dependent upon a car as the ensuing nightmare. . . .
In America, the automobile shapes—and haunts—the imagination."

PC 75. **FIEDLER, LESLIE.** The Inadvertent Epic: From Uncle Tom's Cabin
to Roots. New York: Simon & Schuster, 1979. 85 pp.
Fiedler reconstructs an American epic of domesticity and race by exploring
Uncle Tom's Cabin, spin-offs of Harriet Beecher Stowe's book, Gone with
the Wind, and Roots. Rejecting charges of sentimentality and structural
weakness, Fiedler admires these works for their myth-making power, and
their ability to express both the seamy and the sunny characteristics
of the popular consciousness. This collective mythology is feminine and
pro-family, but it is also troubled by racial tension. Stereotypical
blacks and whites may not work well as fictional constructs, argues Fiedler,
but they should be studied for the insights they provide into our night-
mares and hopes concerning racial relationships.

PC 76. **FIEDLER, LESLIE.** What Was Literature?: Class Culture and Mass
Society. New York: Simon & Schuster, 1982. 258 pp.
Fiedler addresses the issue of an "anti-hierarchical" criticism—one that
would account for "low" literature as well as "high"—by appealing to
the mythopoeic power of texts from Moby Dick to Gone with the Wind, and
their ability to cross class and racial barriers and communicate to a
mass audience. He devotes considerable attention to traditional responses
to popular art, and to the relation of elite culture to mass culture.
Fiedler suggests that neither elite nor mass culture is intrinsically
better, nor should one be celebrated to the exclusion of the other. After
debunking as myth the solitary American artist who despises commercial

success, Fiedler reviews the systematic subversion of critical standards by popular culture, and discusses the degree to which that subversion has opened up the literary canon.

PC 77. FILLER, LOUIS, ed. A Question of Quality: Popularity and Value
         in Modern Creative Writing. Bowling Green, Ohio: Bowling Green
         University Popular Press, 1976. 264 pp.
Citing the significance of "democratic esthetics," Filler describes his collection of essays as an endeavor "to give the immediatist some reasonable relationship to past enthusiasms." Rather than dismissing popular writers for their financial success, the volume focuses on "essences of style or treatment which help explain the author as a changing human being," and makes "the transitions from old popularity to new popularity more understandable." Some of the essayists comment on the phenomenon of a specific bestseller within a writer's career--Erich Segal's Love Story, James Gould Cozzens's By Love Possessed, Ross Lockridge's Raintree County, Meyer Levin's Compulsion--while others explain the general popularity of a prolific author (Irving Wallace) or analyze a major contributor to a given genre (Ring Lardner, Dashiell Hammett). Many of the essays re-evaluate writers who have received attention as "serious" artists, such as the poets Vachel Lindsay, Stephen Vincent Benet, and Edna St. Vincent Millay, and the novelists James T. Farrell, John Dos Passos and John Steinbeck.

PC 78. GOULART, RON. Cheap Thrills: An Informal History of the Pulp
         Magazines. New Rochelle, N.Y.: Arlington House, 1972. 192 pp.
Goulart offers a general history of the pulp magazines from the turn of the century to the present time, with an in-depth focus on the "heyday" of the pulps--1920-40. He begins with an account of Frank Munsey, who developed the format of pulpwood fiction, and of Street and Smith Publishing Company, which initiated the printing of Popular Magazine in 1903. Goulart perceives the pulps as "major packages of fiction heroes" and devotes chapters to the most popular characters: the Lone Ranger, Doc Savage, Tarzan, the cowboy, the detective, the FBI agent. A final chapter provides nostalgic remembrances of the influence of these heroic figures on the lives of individual readers.

PC 79. GREENE, SUZANNE ELLERY. Books for Pleasure: Popular Fiction,
         1914-1945. Bowling Green: Bowling Green University Popular Press,
         1974. 200 pp.
On the premise that popular novels reflect the "attitudes and values" of their readers, Greene compiles a list of 145 long-time bestsellers and identifies characteristics of their audience: generally young, well-educated, evenly male and female, middle to upper class, and predominantly Northeastern or Far Western. By rating changes in fictional characters and themes, Greene pinpoints equivalent changes in popular thought and feeling, at least for "this select but very powerful group." Greene organizes the group's attitudes into four periods: 1914-16, 1918-27, 1928-37, 1938-45. By 1945, shifts from individual to social concerns, from a fragmented to an interrelated world, and from domestic to international affairs reveal that the popular audience has "matured."

PC 80. HART, JAMES D. The Popular Book: A History of America's Literary
         Taste. New York: Oxford University Press, 1950. 351 pp.
Hart examines the sale and distribution of books, relative costs, population figures, and literacy rates to discover what books were read and why. His study opens with The Mayflower and considers a range of literary tastes, including piety, reason and common sense, sentiment and the home, social crusades, Western allure, genteel culture, medieval romance, local color, Jazz Age cynicism, and Americana. Since book sales reflect the "popular psyche," Hart argues, literary tastes can be tied to major shifts

in the reading public's concept of destiny. Bearing in mind class and regional distinctions in the reading public, Hart seeks to chart the "lasting impressions" of "invisible but unyielding forces" on the American mind.

PC 81. **JOHANNSEN, ALBERT.** The House of Beadle and Adams and Its Dime and Nickel Novels: The Story of a Vanished Literature. 2 vols. Norman: University of Oklahoma Press, 1950. 919 pp.
This book "by collectors for other collectors" relates the history of the first dime novel publishing house and provides a complete bibliography of its titles. There are sections on "pre-Beadle" novels and the history of the Beadle and Adams firm, a numerical list of the various series of Beadle novels, and biographies of dime novel authors. The House of Beadle and Adams published thousands of novels in the second half of the 19th century. These novels were the "literary outcropping of a pioneer people," owing more to Cooper than to Walter Scott, and had an enormous audience— from idle Union Army troops to urban schoolboys. Although the novels came under harsh criticism from the pulpit and from educators later in the century, they remained popular. The firm closed down with the deaths of Beadle and Adams in the mid-1890s.

PC 82. **LEE, CHARLES.** The Hidden Public: The Story of the Book-of-the-Month Club. Garden City, N.Y.: Doubleday, 1958. 236 pp.
Lee discusses the rise and development of the Book-of-the-Month Club, the influence of its merchandising success and revolutionary distribution practices on readers, the book industry, and American culture. In Part I, he chronicles the Club's origins, including the controversies which its methods of operation generated within the book community. Focusing on procedures and membership, Part II examines such topics as judges and selection, promotion and mail delivery, advertising, and the role played by the Club's magazine. Part III provides a list of selections, dividends, and alternates, from 1926 to 1957. Lee's appendices offer reactions from reviews and publishers, and introduce statistics regarding selections which have appeared on bestseller lists.

PC 83. **MEYER, DONALD.** The Positive Thinkers: Religion as Pop Psychology from Mary Baker Eddy to Oral Roberts. 1965; Rev. ed. New York: Pantheon Books, 1980. 396 pp.
Meyer examines the development of popular beliefs concerning the close relationship of wealth, health, and peace of mind. Beginning with Mary Baker Eddy, Meyer offers evidence which links the popular psychologies under scrutiny with "pervasive disturbance in the capacity of established ideas and institutions to satisfy." Part I, "Peace in God: Theology as Psychology," discusses "mind cure" teachings which provided an ideological foundation for a distinctive way of life. Part II, "Peace in the System: Sociology as Psychology," presents beliefs about industry and businessmen that influenced the way in which individuals perceived themselves after 1900. Part III, "Peace in Peace: Psychology as Psychology," explores the post-W.W. II growth of a therapeutic orientation which often sought to replicate, especially in the writings of Norman Vincent Peale, the inspirational dimensions of theology.

PC 84. **MITCHELL, SALLY.** The Fallen Angel: Chastity, Class, and Women's Reading, 1835-1880. Bowling Green, Ohio: Bowling Green University Popular Press, 1981. 223 pp.
Investigating the motif of feminine purity in English publications during the 19th century, Mitchell pursues two objectives: (1) to trace the changes in the popular image of women's nature and role in this era of the birth of feminism; and (2) to analyze variations in theme, moral intent, and literary style in fiction directed at different reading audiences. She traces the portrait of the unchaste woman in a variety of publications:

penny weekly family magazines; sensation and problem novels; middle-class novels about love, morals, and sexual relations outside of marriage; and magazines featuring new heroines possessed of a sense of economic self-sufficiency. Mitchell remarks that feminists in 1835 responded to the literature of chastity by beginning a struggle "to become human beings instead of angels"; she believes, however, that writers continued to stress the innocence and victimization of the woman rather than emphasizing the opportunities derived from a freedom of choice.

PC 85. MOTT, FRANK LUTHER. Golden Multitudes: The Story of Best Sellers in the United States. New York: Macmillan, 1947. 357 pp.
Mott defines a bestseller as a book with sales figures representing 1% of the total U.S. population during the decade of the volume's publication. Excluding bibles, dictionaries, pamphlets, and series books, he finds 324 titles. These range from the first bestseller, the poem "The Day of Doom" (1662) by Michael Wigglesworth, to the sentimental novel Charlotte, A Tale of Truth (1791) by Susanna Rowson, works by Shakespeare from the 1790s onward, The Scarlet Letter (1850) by Nathaniel Hawthorne, Erich Maria Remarque's war novel All Quiet on the Western Front (1929), and Margaret Mitchell's Gone with the Wind (1936). Mott's study disputes two prevalent misconceptions: that there is only one bestseller public at any given time, and that a "typical" bestseller exists.

PC 86. MOTT, FRANK LUTHER. A History of American Magazines, 5 vols. I. 1741-1850, New York: Appleton, 1930; II. 1850-1865, III. 1865-1885, IV. 1885-1905, V. Sketches of 21 Magazines, 1905-1930. Cambridge, Mass.: Harvard University Press, 1938-68. 3558 pp.
Mott's work outlines the development of magazine history in America from the pre- and post-Independence years (Volume I) to the Civil War period (Volume II), the Reconstruction period (Volume III), and the period of advertising development (Volume IV). Volumes I to IV are structured as a "running history" of the period's leading events and characteristics, followed by separate sketches of the most important periodicals. Volume V provides sketches of twenty-one magazines from 1905 to 1930.

PC 87. NOEL, MARY. Villains Galore . . . The Heyday of the Popular Story Weekly. New York: Macmillan, 1954. 320 pp.
In the field of popular literature, the literary weeklies arose in the 1830s as predecessors to the standard family story papers, which maintained themselves as a literary format from 1845 to 1885. Noel concentrates on economic factors influencing in the production methods of these periodicals, such as The Philadelphia Courier, The Flag of Our Union, and The New York Ledger. She traces the rise and fall of various contributions to the form, with the eventual success of Beadle & Co. in the 1860s. Later chapters examine character, plot, setting, and authors. Noel discusses standard components of the story paper: editorials, serials, and correspondence columns. Concluding with an analysis of the reading audience, she also evaluates the role of women, the role of labor, and the use of propaganda in the way this literature was presented.

PC 88. PAPASHVILY, HELEN WAITE. All the Happy Endings: A Study of the Domestic Novel in America, the Women Who Wrote It, the Women Who Read It, in the Nineteenth Century. New York: Harper & Row, 1956. 231 pp.
Papashvily investigates the domestic novel, that "peculiar literary form of the 19th century," to discover the dream world of women: the fears, hopes, and frustrations that heroines and readers shared. She discusses women's fiction against the backdrop of the Industrial Revolution, which centralized production, reduced the prestige of women, spawned a new breed of readers, and encouraged subscription libraries, public schooling, and

technological advances in home life. What resulted, Papashvily contends, were "handbooks of another kind of feminine revolt": sentimental novels that celebrated the home, ordinary women, and daily routines, while disparaging the world of the male.

PC 89. **PATTEE, FRED LEWIS.** The Feminine Fifties. New York: Appleton-Century, 1940. 339 pp.
Pattee explores the decade which saw the publication of Susan B. Warner's Wide, Wide World, the movement for women's rights, and the "high tide of feminine fiction." As "daughters" of Boston Brahmins, who had no literary sons, the writers of the 1850s responded to an era of political tension with a literature that Pattee calls "hysterical." The Civil War foreclosed on what Southern literature might have been, but not before the welcome advent of the Atlantic Monthly and the folksongs of Stephen Foster.

PC 90. **PEARSON, EDMUND LESTER.** Dime Novels; or, Following an Old Trail in Popular Literature. Boston: Little, Brown, 1929. 280 pp.
Pearson offers a historical survey from the publication of the first Beadle dime novel in 1860 to the end of the 19th century, when this popular medium was replaced by the boys' weeklies. According to Pearson, the early contributors "reverently" followed the framework established by Walter Scott and James Fenimore Cooper; by 1881 the dime novel had reached the peak of its popularity and became more formulaic in content and form. Characters such as "Broadway Billy," "Cap Collier," and "Deadwood Dick" captured the imagination of youngsters by offering "tales of adventure and combat." To determine the attraction of this literary medium, Pearson concludes with nostalgic reminiscences by former readers of the dime novel.

PC 91. **RAINWATER, CLARENCE E.** The Play Movement in the United States: A Study of Community Recreation. Washington, D.C.: McGrath Publishing Company and National Recreation and Park Association, 1922. 371 pp.
This study surveys the history of the play movement in the U.S. from the early 17th century to 1920. Rainwater analyzes the structure and function of the play movement, asserting that the early 20th century has seen the regeneration of the play movement, which in the late 19th century had been undermined by massive immigration to the cities and the commercialization of leisure activities. In the 20th century, the play movement has become institutionalized in the form of directed play activities and specialized structure.

PC 92. **REEP, DIANA C.** The Rescue and Romance: Popular Novels Before World War I. Bowling Green, Ohio: Bowling Green University Popular Press, 1982. 144 pp.
Noting that popular formulas and conventions "synthesize" diverse American values and beliefs, Reep focuses on the convention of the rescue: a "voluntary act" which "controls the progress and development of the romance." She examines fifty popular novels, some of them from the crucial development period before James Fenimore Cooper's Precaution. In these books she discovers four major variations: child rescued, woman rescued from physical danger by a man (most popular), woman rescued from a dilemma by a man, and man rescued by a woman (least consistent and most interesting). Throughout, these novels emphasized that good actions would be rewarded and class differences would be maintained, together with the "solid social value of male dominance and female submission."

PC 93. **REYNOLDS, QUENTIN JAMES.** The Fiction Factory; or From Pulp Row
to Quality Street. New York: Random House, 1955. 283 pp.
Reynolds provides a history of the first hundred years of Street and Smith
Publishing Company of New York. His work introduces an analysis of the
magazines published from the 1850s to the 1950s--including the New York
Weekly, Log Cabin Library, Nick Carter Weekly, New York Five Cent Library,
Ainslee's, Sea Stories Magazine, Western Story Magazine, Mademoiselle,
and Astounding Science Fiction. Reynolds attributes Street and Smith's
longevity to its practice of ceasing publication of magazines showing
"signs of age," thereby enabling the company to keep up to date with contemporary issues, interests, and concerns. The volume concludes with
a list of Street and Smith publications, and the dates of their initial
appearance.

PC 94. **SCHICK, FRANK.** The Paperbound Book in America: The History of
Paperbacks and Their European Background. New York: Bowker,
1958. 262 pp.
Schick describes the growth of the American paperbound book trade from
Colonial times to 1957. Discussing the history of paperbounds in Europe
and America from 1639 to 1939, Part I indicates how technological advances
in printing and new methods of distribution stimulated a proliferation
in newspaper extras and cheap libraries. Focusing on the period 1939
to 1957, Part II introduces an account of the publishing scene, in both
the commercial and government sectors, and provides a chronology of important developments in the trades. Part III offers case histories of individual publishing firms, which handled pocket books, magazine and pulp
publications, and religious paperbacks. Schick writes that the history
of paperbounds in America embodies "the evolutionary unfolding of a format
. . . rather than the story of a 'revolution.'"

PC 95. **SCHNEIDER, LOUIS and SANFORD M. DORNBUSCH.** Popular Religion:
Inspirational Books in America. Chicago: University of Chicago
Press, 1958. 174 pp.
Examining popular "inspirational religious literature," the authors employ
content analysis in documenting the themes and trends found in forty-six
bestsellers published between 1875 and 1955. They consider the changing
definitions of man, faith, God, and nature, as well as the varied concepts
of selfhood related to health, material well-being, and other "manifestations" of personal salvation. Schneider and Dornbusch observe that such
literature was "produced for everyday people with the avowed aim of helping
them to meet their everyday problems." Finally, they trace the changes
in American values--such as the appearance of psychological and psychiatric
orientations in the 1930s and the growing support for institutional religion after the 1940s--which may occur within the context of the Judeo-
Christian tradition.

PC 96. **SIEGEL, ADRIENNE.** The Image of the American City in Popular Literature, 1820-1870. Port Washington, N.Y.: Kennikat Press, 1981.
211 pp.
Investigating the emergence of a popular urban literature during the period
1820-70, Siegel contends that publications written for a mass audience
serve as a "window through which we can view the cultural mentality of
a generation shaken by accelerated and disruptive urbanization." She
indicates how popularizers, often differing in their depiction of city
life from the writers of traditional belles-lettres, "whetted the appetite"
of the common person for the urban experience. Seeking to reconstruct
the image of a changing America "from the bottom up," Siegel discovers
a variety of topics in this literature: the urban aristocracy, the working
class, ethnics, folk heroes and villains, the hazards of city life, places
of forbidden pleasure, the lure of corruption, the pageantry of urban
culture, and moral opportunities and the American Dream.

PC 97. **SMITH, HERBERT F.** The Popular American Novel, 1865-1920. Boston: Twayne, 1980. 192 pp.
Against the backdrop of the traditional canon, Smith highlights minor writers whose work embodied the enthusiasms and national ideals of a mass audience. Smith surveys post-Civil War social fiction, the sentimental novel, the decline of New England's authority, the rise of historical fiction in the South, the emergence of exotics, fanatics, and cowboys, the shift to the political novel, and the stylistic experiments of modernists. Popular writers of the 19th century, he discovers, approved the Protestant ethic of success, reform, and piety, as well as the sentimental triumph of virtue; in the 20th century, new forms and genres replaced Christian piety with class conflict. Consistently, major writers acknowledged prevailing popular themes, but in their formal strategies they sought to subvert these thematic limitations and to reshape popular taste.

PC 98. **SMITH, ROGER,** ed. The American Reading Public: What It Reads, Why It Reads. New York: Bowker, 1964. 268 pp.
This compilation of essays reprinted from Daedalus addresses issues related to the "faithful reader"--students, teachers, executives--for whom "reading is an act of engagement, whether for professional reasons or recreation or both." In considering the role of the publishing industry in shaping public taste, the volume treats American textbooks and education; university presses; commercial publishers; the "mass media of print"; the status of literary criticism and book reviewing. Smith observes that these essays represent a "definitive portrait" of a most important segment of communications in America during the 1960s.

PC 99. **STERN, MADELEINE B.,** ed. Publishers for Mass Entertainment in Nineteenth Century America. Boston: G. K. Hall, 1980. 358 pp.
This collection of essays on forty-five American publishers includes biographical sketches of the chief officers of the companies, lists of major works published, a history of the firms, and lists of references used for each article. In her preface, Stern says of these figures: "Many nineteenth-century American publishers built their houses upon the thesis that millions had the right to affordable literature, and in so doing they not only launched a literary revolution but produced books that still reflect the reading tastes of their age."

PC 100. **STONE, GREGORY P.,** ed. Games, Sport and Power. New Brunswick, N.J.: Transaction Books, 1972. 228 pp.
The general orientation of these essays is sociological; games and sports are seen variously as amusements of the leisure classes, commodities for mass consumption, and social symbols of power struggles. The introduction develops a sociological structure for the interpretation of games and sports in differing times and contexts. Part I, on games, includes essays on pool playing and poolrooms, poker, and making and playing card games. Part II, on sports, discusses athletes as students, baseball players and salaries, professional baseball rituals and taboos, and Brazilian soccer. Part III, on control of play versus play as control, discusses classical music as a status symbol, jazz audiences, dance studios and instruction, museums as mass media, and authority in the comics. Also included in the book are discussions of American popular culture and its effects on Europe, and of some contrasts between European and American treatments of similar recreational activities.

PC 101. **STUCKEY, W. J.** The Pulitzer Prize Novels: A Critical Backward Look. 1968; Rev. ed. Norman: University of Oklahoma Press, 1981. 277 pp.
Joseph Pulitzer, who acquired a fortune through his newspapers, established the Pulitzer Prize in 1903 to honor the American novel "which shall best present the wholesome atmosphere of American life and the highest standard

1215

of American manners and manhood." Although Columbia University (the trustee of the funds) and the Advisory Board have modified these standards several times since Pulitzer's death in 1911, few major critics--according to Stuckey--value the awards. Stuckey argues, however, that the prize-winning novels (e.g., Gone with the Wind, The Magnificent Ambersons, The Caine Mutiny) reveal popular taste in fiction and embody traditional American values.

PC 102. **SUTHERLAND, JOHN.** Bestsellers: Popular Fiction of the 1970's. London: Routledge & Kegan Paul, 1981. 268 pp.
Sutherland examines hundreds of bestsellers from the 1970s which he considers "corporate ventures" involving author, agent, editor, and salesman. Concentrating on blockbusters over genre paperbacks, Sutherland reviews works by Arthur Hailey, women's fiction from The Thorn Birds to Erica Jong, Star Wars and Jaws, the "new Western," fashionable crime, and disaster epics. These he sees as inextricably bound to the "host culture" by a "productive apparatus" which guarantees their common economic function even while their ideological messages vary in instructive ways. Artistically unendangered by such "Trivialiteratur," the "serious" novel is nonetheless produced with much of the same machinery.

PC 103. **WALKER, ROBERT H.** The Poet and the Gilded Age: Social Themes in Late 19th Century American Verse. Philadelphia: University of Pennsylvania Press, 1963. 387 pp.
This volume considers the social role of the poet and the function of poetry both generally and with specific reference to the last quarter of the 19th century. Walker argues that the poet is uniquely suited to express the main concerns of his culture. He stresses the social relevance of Gilded Age poetry rather than applying biographical or aesthetic approaches to the study of verse. Walker applies content analysis to the concerns of the Gilded Age's "post-citizens" by establishing categories of public interest (attitudes toward explorers, the economy, politicians, immigration, among others) and tabulating how frequently Gilded Age poets refer to these categories.

PC 104. **WASSERSTROM, WILLIAM.** Heiress of All the Ages: Sex and Sentiment in the Genteel Tradition. Minneapolis: University of Minnesota Press, 1959. 157 pp.
Insisting that commonplaces about Victorian culture have proved inadequate, Wasserstrom reconsiders the historical underpinnings of the genteel code, its ideals, and the contemporary awareness that those ideals would not be met. The results were the competing paradigms that Wasserstrom studies: such varying combinations of sex, love and freedom as Steel-Engraving Ladies and Gibson Girls, Lily and Prairie Flower, Nymph and Nun. To replace "the twin principles of manliness and womanliness," Wasserstrom proposes the American girl, whose various roles symbolized "a living victory of the spirit over the flesh." The English sentimental novel was thus reshaped in America by the "shared American dream of justice and freedom for all," a project that eventually fell apart when genteel "idealism" was lost.

PC 105. **WEISS, RICHARD.** The American Myth of Success: From Horatio Alger to Norman Vincent Peale. New York: Basic Books, 1979. 276 pp.
Weiss examines the myth of success, "one of the most enduring expressions of American popular ideals," in the nation's "massive" literature. The volume explores the attitudes and values embodied in a success myth which has shaped men's world view and experiences in a broad social context. Weiss presents a chronological study of the long tradition of American guides to living. The self-help literature of the Puritans, Ben Franklin, Horatio Alger, Christian novels, conduct-of-life literature, "New Thought" idealism, and Norman Vincent Peale's "mind-power" writings convey how

the American promise of material rewards became merged with the faith
in a divine order.

PC 106. WERTHAM, FREDERIC. The World of Fanzines: A Special Form of
Communication. Carbondale: Southern Illinois University Press,
1973. 144 pp.
Wertham perceives "fanzines" to be noncommercial, amateur-produced magazines that have suffered from critical neglect because of their lack of
a literary orientation. He focuses on the historical development of science fiction and fantasy fanzines by analyzing them as a system of communication bringing together individuals of similar interests. The fanzines facilitate relationships between fans by helping to define and organize a "paraculture" through which clubs, conventions and associations
emerge. Wertham considers fanzines to be a unique medium, distinguished
from other publications by their independent nature, their amateur orientation, and their lack of profit motive. He explores the style, content,
and production of the fanzine in order to determine its importance and
function within American society.

PC 107. WYLLIE, IRVIN G. The Self-Made Man in America: The Myth of Rags
to Riches. New York: Free Press, 1954. 210 pp.
Wyllie explores the application of the "rags-to-riches" motif to America's
business civilization. He focuses upon 19th-century success manuals as
a resource for intellectual history, "the realm of ideas about self-help
under American conditions of opportunity." The leading proponents of
the national cult of the self-made man emphasized that the secret to success rested upon individual capabilities, not upon the influences of society. To prove persuasive, the advocates of this doctrine synthesized
religion, business, and the techniques of journalism. Wyllie finds that,
although opinions concerning the gospel of success change, the myth of
the self-made man persisted to the end of the 19th century.

CHILDREN'S LITERATURE

PC 108. BADER, BARBARA. American Picturebooks from Noah's Ark to the
Beast Within. New York: Macmillan, 1976. 615 pp.
Bader calls the picturebook "a social, cultural, historical document;
and, foremost, an experience for a child." She presents an overview of
what types of picturebooks 20th-century children have been offered, keeping
in mind the influence of art, commerce, technology, and social change.
Genre studies of French imports, holiday stories, and the presentation
of black characters are interspersed with analyses of authors, beginning
with E. Boyd Smith, through Roger Duvoisin, Dr. Seuss and Maurice Sendak,
and concluding with the modern fabulists.

PC 109. BETTELHEIM, BRUNO. The Uses of Enchantment: The Meaning and
Importance of Fairy Tales. New York: Knopf, 1976. 328 pp.
This psychoanalytic consideration of folk fairy tales delineates how such
stories, representing "in imaginative form what the process of healthy
human development consists of," contribute to children's positive growth
and maturation. In Part I Bettelheim examines fairy tale imagery and
speculates on its use in civilizing the chaotic pressures and drives of
the unconscious--an orientation touching upon such themes as vicarious
satisfaction, externalization, separation anxiety, and eventual integration.
In Part II he interprets nine popular favorites, among them "Cinderella"
and "Jack and the Beanstalk." Throughout, emphasis is on the fairy tale
as both an art form and a powerful psychological tool in confronting existential anxieties.

PC 110. BRATTON, J. S. The Impact of Victorian Children's Fiction. Totowa, N.J.: Barnes & Noble, 1981. 230 pp.
Although an analysis of British fiction, this text provides methodological insights for Americanist scholars. A context of Victorian conventions in writing is provided--incorporating assumptions about children--to examine the didacticism of the moral tale. Writers' intentions are deemed of vital importance in such a transmission of cultural values and are considered in a framework shaped by Northrop Frye's notion of romance and James Britton's "spectator role" theory of reader response. Analysis includes the development of juvenile publishing, evangelical writing, distinctive themes created for both boys and girls, and fin-de-siecle transitions in expressed values.

PC 111. BRODERICK, DOROTHY M. Image of the Black in Children's Fiction. New York: Bowker, 1973. 219 pp.
This study represents a historical, literary, and critical analysis of the portrait of the black that emerges from the children's books published between 1827 and 1967. Broderick offers a close examination of what white children have been told in their reading about significant events of black history and about blackness itself. Chapters on slavery, segregation, and stereotypes criticize white liberal attitudes toward blacks. The volume indicates that racism is as much a socioeconomic problem as it is one between individuals, and concludes that "landmark titles" which break through the barrier of mere "tolerance" (or that of blacks' accommodation to whiteness) should be encouraged.

PC 112. DARLING, RICHARD L. The Rise of Children's Book Reviewing in America, 1865-1881. New York: Bowker, 1968. 452 pp.
Darling provides an examination of the criticism of children's literture in thirty-six periodicals during the seventeen years following the Civil War. He includes the most important literary and children's magazines, with a sampling of religious, educational, and book-trade journals. The period is seen as a time of expansion in both quality and quantity, as entertainment and aesthetic values replaced didacticism, with consequential trends in children's publishing encouraging this shift. Darling claims the emphasis placed on critical reviewing of children's books by gifted and noteworthy authors of this period remains unparalleled.

PC 113. EGOFF, SHEILA A. Thursday's Child: Trends and Patterns in Contemporary Children's Literature. Chicago: American Library Association, 1981. 323 pp.
Evaluating trends in children's literature between 1957 and 1982, and Egoff maintains that the best modern writers examine the psychological transition from childhood to adulthood and create young protagonists who "bear their own burdens of self-awareness and responsibility." After examining historical changes in emphasis in children's "classics," she considers the genres of realistic fiction, the problem novel, fantasy, science fiction, folklore and myth, poetry, and the picture book. The study is limited to imaginative writings, primarily those originally written in English, although the final chapter traces universal themes in translated European children's novels.

PC 114. EGOFF, SHEILA A., G. T. STUBBS, and L. F. ASHLEY, eds. Only Connect: Readings on Children's Literature. New York: Oxford University Press, 1969. 471 pp.
These writings on children's literature discuss and judge the genre according to the professional standards applied to other branches of literature. The collection is divided into the following categories: didacticism, fantasy, historical fiction, great writers, illustrations, and the modern scene. Addressing librarians, parents, teachers, and students, the editors emphasize a rejection of "nostalgic or sentimental analyses" in favor of more informed consideration.

PC 115. FRASER, JAMES H., ed. Society and Children's Literature. Boston: Godine, 1978. 209 pp.
The Simmons College Symposium on research, social history, and children's literature--held in Boston in May 1976--was the first American attempt at a European-style interdisciplinary children's literature conclave, bringing together "researchers from various disciplines outside the field of education as well as librarians and individuals engaged in service to children." These twelve essays were presented at that symposium and explore a variety of topics in children's literature. Those contributions most specifically related to cultural study include analyses by Anne Scott MacLeod on antebellum didacticism, R. Gordon Kelly on late 19th-century children's periodicals, Fred Erisman on American regionalism, and James H. Fraser on foreign language publishing in the U.S.

PC 116. HAVILAND, VIRGINIA, ed. Children and Literature: Views and Reviews. Glenview, Ill.: Scott, Foresman, 1973. 461 pp.
This collection of essays and criticism emphasizes theories and judgments on the creation, distribution, and reading of American children's litera-ture, and is aimed at library science and teacher education students. It provides historical background in children's literature and addresses what makes a classic, what children should or should not read, how one writes for children, and how one illustrates for children. Genre studies analyze folk literature, fantasy and science fiction, poetry, and histori-cal fiction, while closing chapters scrutinize the "international scene," criticism and awards. Haviland introduces each topic with a brief sum-marizing essay.

PC 117. JORDAN, ALICE M. From Rollo to Tom Sawyer, and Other Papers. Boston: Horn Book, 1948. 160 pp.
Jordan investigates the available books for and reading habits of American children in the 19th century. Consideration is also given to such impor-tant figures as Susan Warner and Peter Parley, who are examined for their shaping of a sentimental and didactic ethos. Jordan places the rise of the publication of children's books between the proliferation of magazine publications on the one hand and the influence of the more elite New England writers on the other to explain that rise and its eventual influence.

PC 118. KELLY, R. GORDON. Mother Was a Lady: Self and Society in Selected American Children's Periodicals, 1865-1890. Westport, Conn.: Greenwood Press, 1974. 233 pp.
This study examines cultural transmission of values in fiction over a twenty-five year span, in St. Nicholas, Our Young Folks, and The Youth's Companion. Kelly views the magazine as a medium for the dramatization of the ideals of a "gentry elite," who attempted to pass on their concepts of the proper roles of a gentleman and a lady. The importance of education, moral vision, and self-reliance are stressed in these periodicals, as are a strong sense of a rural setting's nurturing characteristics and a disdain for "fashionable society." The introduction discusses theoreti-cal implications; the bibliographic essay surveys work done in the socio-historical analysis of children's literature.

PC 119. KIEFER, MONICA. American Children Through Their Books, 1700-1835. Philadelphia: University of Pennsylvania Press, 1948. 248 pp.
This work traces the changing status of American children and the general shifts in their cultural and social roles through an analysis of children's literature. Kiefer's historical overview of the "emancipation" of the child differentiates between the theological age, in which a child was considered to be in a state of total depravity (1700-1775), and the utili-tarian age, in which industry and wisdom were stressed (1775-1835). The study demonstrates how spiritual standards shifted from theological foun-dations to a secular moral basis, and the American Revolution is cited as the beginning of the modern concept of childhood.

PC 120. KINGSTON, CAROLYN T. The Tragic Mode in Children's Literature.
New York: Teachers College Press, 1974. 177 pp.
Focusing on tragedy in "highly regarded" children's realistic fiction
for eight-to-twelve-year-olds, Kingston maintains that selections of this
subgenre follow great literary patterns, consider the audience, grapple
with real problems, and end in affirmation and heightened compassion.
Emphasizing the fiction of the 1950s and 1960s, she defines "tragic
moments" as a "series of tragic essences that build toward a climax, which
results in a new understanding of the problem"; she considers the themes
of rejection, entrapment, sensitivity, war, and loss.

PC 121. LANES, SELMA G. Down the Rabbit Hole: Adventures and Misadven-
tures in the Realm of Children's Literature. New York: Atheneum,
1971. 239 pp.
This is a compendium of what the author considers the best works of "artistic inspiration and literary merit" for listeners and readers up to the
age of eight. St. Nicholas, Kate Greenway, Maurice Sendak, and Dr. Seuss
are included in the study, as are fairy tales, Golden Books, the role
of black characters, publishing procedures, and the idea of "first favorites." The appendix contains a briefly annotated bibliography of suggested
readings for a variety of early childhood age ranges.

PC 122. LYSTAD, MARY. From Dr. Mather to Dr. Seuss: 200 Years of American
Books for Children. Boston: G. K. Hall, 1980. 264 pp.
This volume focuses on changes in the content of American children's literature between 1698-1977 by using a random sampling of 1000 titles from
the Rare Books Division of the Library of Congress. Lystad's statistical
results plot historical trends in content, purpose, authors' backgrounds,
and publishing history. She is particularly concerned with "changes in
beliefs about the nature of children and the nature of society, of perceptions of proper ways of socializing children, and of definitions of
social values." Colonial didacticism is seen to give way by 1850 to an
increasing interest in the family; by 1920 the trend is toward a concern
for the child's individual needs and desires.

PC 123. MacCANN, DONNARAE and OLGA RICHARD. The Child's First Books:
A Critical Study of Pictures and Texts. New York: Wilson, 1973.
135 pp.
Accepting the premise that environment has the greatest effect on both
the growth of general intelligence and the school achievement of young
children, these authors argue that critical care should be taken in the
creation of aesthetically pleasing and stimulating picture books. Picture
books are defined as works in which the written narrative is brief and
the story line is presented through illustrations, but "profusely illustrated short stories" are also included in this study's scope. Literary
and graphic elements receive the greatest emphasis and are discussed separately in critiques of exemplary works, while historical perspective,
typography, binding, and a need to review Caldecott Award standards are
also considered.

PC 124. MacCANN, DONNARAE and GLORIA WOODWARD, eds. The Black American
in Books for Children: Readings in Racism. Metuchen, N.J.:
Scarecrow Press, 1972. 223 pp.
This volume stresses the need for a black perspective in children's books,
a concept referred to as "thinking black," "wearing the shoe of the black
American," writing from "inside rather than outside." MacCann and Woodward
advocate the creation of aesthetically effective and socially and psychologically authentic stories about blacks; the publishing of better children's books requires a reconsideration of the relative absence of black
characters. Some attention is given to the question of censorship vis-
a-vis racism.

PC 125. MacCANN, DONNARAE and GLORIA WOODWARD, eds. Cultural Conformity in Books for Children: Further Readings in Racism. Metuchen, N.J.: Scarecrow Press, 1977. 205 pp.
This collection of essays urges those involved in book selection for children to insure that a positive identification be made with the children's specific ethnic or racial groups. Part I calls for cultural pluralism and equal intellectual opportunities. Part II considers the application of the cultural perspective in children's literature for Native Americans, Chicanos, Puerto Ricans, Asian Americans, and black Americans. Part III provides strategies to combat racism to be used by librarians, teachers, and those interested in multicultural education.

PC 126. MacLEOD, ANNE SCOTT. A Moral Tale: Children's Fiction and American Culture, 1820-1860. Hamden, Conn.: Shoe String Press, 1975. 196 pp.
Analyzing the cultural values presented in highly didactic antebellum stories written for children under the age of twelve, MacLeod notes an uneasiness with rapid social change on the part of the authors, and their consequent attempt to instill a strong inner character in their readers. Realism was subordinated to didacticism in these moral tales, which, broadly speaking, presented the social attitudes of "a democratic middle-class society." As change accelerated and the U.S. moved toward civil war, these stories stressed, through sentimentality and drama, a moral order to the universe, though a "sense of apprehensiveness" pervaded the literature.

PC 127. MASON, BOBBIE ANN. The Girl Sleuths: A Feminist Guide. Old Westbury, N.Y.: Feminist Press, 1975. 144 pp.
The author proposes to give critical attention to the form and substance of some of the series books popular with young girls, to consider the possible impact on their imagination, and to examine the stereotypes which have been popularized by those works. Chapters such as "Bobbsey Bourgeois" and "Nancy Drew: The Once and Future Prom Queen" capture both the appeal and the racism and snobbery of books which depict independent heroines, from Louisa May Alcott's Jo to more recent girl sleuths. The girl sleuth is paradoxical: on the one hand, a thrilling model of independence and courage; on the other, a cool and dainty "lady," eternally feminine and devoted to the preservation of middle-class values.

PC 128. MEIGS, CORNELIA, ANNE THAXTER EATON, ELIZABETH NESBITT, and RUTH HILL VIGUERA. A Critical History of Children's Literature. 1953; Rev. ed. New York: Macmillan, 1969. 708 pp.
This chronological survey of children's books in England and America is divided into four sections: the distant past to 1840; 1840 to 1890; 1890 to 1920; and 1920 to 1967. Each section has chapters focusing on genres, specific authors, or popular subjects. Historical context is considered (Henry Steele Commager wrote the introduction), but the emphasis is on critical evaluation. The volume indicates what the contributing librarians and academicians consider to be good in children's literature, both aesthetically and didactically.

PC 129. PIERPONT MORGAN LIBRARY. Early Children's Books and Their Illustration. New York: Pierpont Morgan Library, 1975. 263 pp.
This collection of 225 "milestones" from the past two thousand years of children's literture, from Aesop's Fables to The Little Prince, is based largely on the Pierpont Morgan Library holdings. Especially intended for the student or collector of illustrated children's books, the work emphasizes Anglo-American publications and traces the gradual shift in focus from didacticism to entertainment. An introductory essay by historian J. H. Plumb discusses the socio-historical interrelationships of children, schools, and book publishing in 18th-century England.

PC 130. PRAGER, ARTHUR. Rascals at Large, or, The Clue in the Old Nostalgia. Garden City, N.Y.: Doubleday, 1971. 334 pp.
A member of the generation "that fell between the sharp pincers of the Depression on one side and World War II on the other," Prager reflects upon some of his favorite serial readings as an adolescent in this combined literary history and memoir. He considers Tarzan of the Apes, Fu Manchu, Nancy Drew, the Hardy Boys, Tom Swift, the Moving Picture Boys, the Rover Boys, Frank Merriwell, and Don Sturdy. The formulas, conventions, and style of Edward Stratemeyer, who wrote many of these serials under sixty-five pseudonyms, are discussed at length.

PC 131. ROBINSON, EVELYN ROSE. Readings About Children's Literature. New York: McKay, 1966. 431 pp.
This collection of sixty-three reprinted articles is intended for parents, teachers, librarians, and students of children's literature. Three goals inherent in all these selections are an understanding of the child as reader, a knowledge of accepted criteria for book selection, and identification of a broad range of literature that meets those criteria.

PC 132. SALE, ROGER. Fairy Tales and After: From Snow White to E. B. White. Cambridge, Mass.: Harvard University Press, 1978. 280 pp.
Applying textual analysis to "classic" children's stories, this work makes a plea for a more clearly defined literary history of this genre. A discussion of fairy tale origins emphasizes the need for historically grounded cultural awareness, and is followed by a look at the transcription of oral traditions. After animal stories are considered as a subgenre, Sale turns his attention to the works of Lewis Carroll, Beatrix Potter, Kenneth Grahame, Rudyard Kipling, L. Frank Baum, Walter R. Brooks, and E. B. White.

PC 133. SLOANE, WILLIAM. Children's Books in England and America in the Seventeenth Century: A History and a Checklist, Together with the Young Christian's Library, the First Printed Catalogue of Books for Children. New York: King's Crown Press, 1955. 251 pp.
Seeking to redress what he sees as the scholarly neglect of 17th-century children's literature, Sloane divides his study into two sections: (1) a history of English and American children's books in the 1600s; (2) a "chronological checklist" of these volumes. The first part identifies children's reading habits, the kinds of works written for them, the most popular volumes, and the form in which these books were published. Sloane's second section provides a definition of children's books (works written exclusively for that audience), the full title of each book, an account of how the checklist was designed, the location of libraries where copies of each volume may be found, and other comments concerning items cited on the checklist.

PC 134. TOWNSEND, JOHN ROWE. A Sense of Story: Essays on Contemporary Writers for Children. Philadelphia: Lippincott, 1971. 215 pp.
Convinced that children's literature should be appraised "as a stimulus and discipline for author and publisher," and thereby improved as a genre, Townsend has selected nineteen English-speaking authors for critical review. Claiming personal preference as his criterion for selection, he includes Australian and British writers as well as the following Americans: Meindert DeJong, Eleanor Estes, Paula Fox, Madeleine L'Engle, Andre Norton, and Scott O'Dell. Each author is assessed for literary contributions; autobiographical notes and bibliographical data are also included.

PC 135. TUCKER, NICHOLAS. The Child and the Book: A Psychological and
        Literary Exploration. New York: Cambridge University Press,
        1981. 259 pp.
In this work an educational psychologist draws on psychoanalytic theory
and Piaget's cognitive psychology to describe the changing nature of the
relationship between children and literature from infancy through adolescence. Children are divided into four consecutive age groups for analysis.
While Tucker draws upon British children's literature to document his
general observations, international applications of his study are also
suggested. Closing chapters consider how it is determined which books
will reach the juvenile audience and how contemporary social and media
factors affect current reading habits.

PC 136. WHALLEY, JOYCE IRENE. Cobwebs to Catch Flies: Illustrated Books
        for the Nursery and Schoolroom, 1700-1900. Berkeley: University
        of California Press, 1975. 163 pp.
Mainly an overview of instructional works of the Anglo-American tradition,
this study is intended as an introduction to children's literature as
a cultural artifact, with general observations of interest to beginning
students. Emphasis is on British publications, yet some comparisons are
made to French and German contemporary equivalents in the genre. After
commenting on illustrations, the author considers in turn the following
categories: alphabet books, reading books, counting books, religious
instruction, moral improvement, history, geography, occupations, science,
grammar, music, and languages.

PC 137. WOMEN ON WORDS AND IMAGES. Dick and Jane as Victims: Sex Stereo-
        types in Children's Readers. Princeton, N.J.: Women on Words
        and Images, 1972. 58 pp.
Establishing the point that primary school readers are an important tool
in the transmission of social and cultural values, this study proceeds
to examine the way girls are portrayed in such literature, and to call
for a departure from sexist stereotyping. One hundred thirty-four elementary readers from fourteen different publishers are included in the
analysis, and the emphasis in activity mastery, adult role models, and
biographies is found to be overwhelmingly on positive male role models,
while women's roles tend to emphasize housekeeping or motherhood.

DETECTIVE, MYSTERY, AND SUSPENSE FICTION

PC 138. AISENBERG, NADYA. A Common Spring: Crime Novel and Classic.
        Bowling Green, Ohio: Bowling Green University Popular Press,
        1980. 271 pp.
Aisenberg contends that through allegory and archetypal characterization
the crime novel not only provides an accurate social history but also
helps readers to cope with their deepest fears and anxieties. Drawing
mainly on C. G. Jung, Claude Levi-Strauss, Vladimir Propp, and Northrop
Frye, Aisenberg demonstrates that basic motifs from myth and fairy tale
are rehearsed in the British and American detective novel; among these
are the thematic situations of pursuit, quest, identity, the scapegoat,
and poetic justice. She also explores how crime novel themes and structures were employed by Charles Dickens, Joseph Conrad, and Graham Greene.
A Common Spring includes a brief historical overview of the evolution
of the crime novel.

PC 139. BALL, JOHN, ed. The Mystery Story. San Diego: University Extension, University of California, 1976. 390 pp.
These seventeen essays, many by mystery writers themselves, concern the
conventions and characterizations of mystery fiction. Hillary Waugh discusses the structure of policy procedurals, and Donald Yates describes
the locked room story. Several essays focus on the detectives: Otto
Penzler describes the appeal of "The Amateur Detective"; James Sandoe
analyzes the "Private Eye"; and Michelle Slung examines "Women in Detective
Fiction." The Mystery Story also includes a checklist of hardboiled fiction, an annotated bibliography of criticism, and—by the editor—a historical overview of the mystery story.

PC 140. CHAMPIGNY, ROBERT. What Will Have Happened: A Philosophical
and Technical Essay on Mystery Stories. Bloomington: Indiana
University Press, 1977. 183 pp.
In this theoretical study of the mystery story, Champigny distinguishes
between "ludic interest" in the mystery, which he describes as a reader's
enjoyment in reading a text for the first time, and aesthetic appreciation
which is based on the rereading experience; his chief concern is with
the latter, a "kind of sport" serving as "embroidery" which provides a
narrative's character "with an appropriately tailored setting." Further,
the author argues that a stress on content of the stories distracts from
"basic semantic and esthetic questions." Champigny analyzes the stylistic
and structural patterns of the mystery, and he considers how characters
in a story communicate a "fictional viewpoint" to the reader. He draws
from English, French, and American sources, paying significant attention
to Poe, Chandler, Christie, Joel Townsley Rogers, and Simenon.

PC 141. CHARNEY, HANNA. The Detective Novel of Manners: Hedonism, Morality, and the Life of Reason. Rutherford, N.J.: Fairleigh Dickinson University Press, 1981. 125 pp.
In her close structural reading of the conventions and language of the
detective novel, Charney contends that it has adopted "the format of the
novel of manners." She regards detective fiction as "minor literature,"
which at once mimics the forms of the novel of manners and also establishes
its own standards. Charney also considers the popularity of the detective
novel and suggests that it presents a reality in which crime is extirpated
so that society may again function. She examines, and quotes from, a
wide range of English and American writers, including Agatha Christie,
P. D. James, Dorothy Sayers, Georges Simenon, and Rex Stout.

PC 142. COOPER-CLARK, DIANA. Designs of Darkness: Interviews with Detective Novelists. Bowling Green, Ohio: Bowling Green University
Popular Press, 1983. 239 pp.
In the introduction to these thirteen interviews, Cooper-Clark discusses
the origins of the critical prejudice against detective fiction. Throughout these interviews, she asks authors—among them Ross Macdonald, Julian
Symons, and Dick Francis—to respond to what she sees as an unfortunate
division of "serious" and "formula" writing. These novelists comment
on changes in the genre, especially the trend toward more complex and
ambivalent characterizations. As Cooper-Clark notes in her introduction,
several themes emerge from the interviews: the similarities between criminals and detectives; the increasing use of women as characters; and speculations about future directions.

PC 143. CRAIG, PATRICIA and MARY CADOGAN. The Lady Investigates: Women
Detectives and Spies in Fiction. New York: St. Martin's Press,
1981. 252 pp.
Craig and Cadogan provide a history of the fictional female detective
in England and America from 1861 to the present. The authors discern
two essential character types: the woman who succeeds through special

"feminine" knowledge; and the woman who competes on equal terms with men.
They cite the stereotype of feminine "nosiness" and the opportunity to
present the female detective "fancifully" or "comically" as significant
reasons for the proliferation of female sleuths. The categories of female
detectives receiving particular attention include women spies of W.W.
II, hardboiled "she-dicks," the teenage girl detective, and the "elderly
busybody" grandmother.

PC 144. DOVE, GEORGE N. The Police Procedural. Bowling Green, Ohio:
Bowling Green University Popular Press, 1982. 274 pp.
Dove examines the police procedural novel, a form of fiction in which
police detectives solve the mystery by following ordinary police practices.
He points out that the heroes of this genre are drawn from real life, and
chronicles the real police experience of the twenty-five writers he dis-
cusses. Dove considers both the European and American police procedural,
and he pursues how these novels evoke the image of police subcultures.
He focuses on several police detective types--the woman, the black, the
Jew, the Hispanic--and devotes separate chapters to nine authors, including
Hillary Waugh, Ed McBain, and Collin Wilcox.

PC 145. ECO, UMBERTO and THOMAS A. SEBEOK, eds. The Sign of Three: Dupin,
Holmes, Peirce. Bloomington: Indiana University Press, 1983.
236 pp.
These ten essays draw on C. S. Peirce's theories of reasoning and knowledge
to explain the logic of fictional detectives, in particular the creations
of Edgar Allan Poe and Arthur Conan Doyle. Sebeok considers Peirce's
division of induction, deduction, and abduction, the last depending on
the reader's our hope to determine the likelihood of a given phenomenon,
and describes Sherlock Holmes as a "consulting semiotician." Other contributors analyze the logical structure of Doyle's abductions and Poe's
ratiocination by employing Peirce's theory as a point of reference. By
way of conclusion, Eco categorizes varieties of abductions illustrating
the reasoning processes identified with detection. The editors provide
an international bibliography of references to detective fiction and to
theories of logic and knowledge.

PC 146. FREEMAN, LUCY, ed. The Murder Mystique: Crime Writers on Their
Art. New York: Ungar, 1982. 140 pp.
These eleven essays by members of the Mystery Writers of America concern
various types of mystery fiction. Essays in Section I discuss the rise
of the mystery in England and America, with Thomas Chastain focusing on
the American private eye; Freeman charts the development of what she terms
the "whydunit." Section II concerns strategies and objectives for writing
and marketing mystery fiction. Edward D. Hoch discusses film and television adaptations; Eleanor Sullivan comments upon the motives for writing
mysteries; and Franklin Bandy explains why mysteries are published in
paperback. Ken Follett contributes an essay on the spy as hero and villain.

PC 147. GARDINER, DOROTHY and KATHERINE SORLEY WALKER, eds. Raymond
Chandler Speaking. Boston: Houghton Mifflin, 1962. 271 pp.
This volume of excerpts from Raymond Chandler's letters concerns his own
career in particular and mystery fiction in general. The letters--mainly
from the 1940s and 1950s--contain numerous brief critiques of mystery
writers and also reveal Chandler's impatience with critics and agents;
blaming both foolish marketing and occasional bad writing, he decries
the poor critical reputation of mystery fiction. Chandler's views on
several issues are compiled in individual chapters: the craft of writing
and revising; television and film treatment of detective fiction; publishing; and his own stories and hero, Philip Marlowe. The editors include
Chandler's "Casual Notes on the Mystery Novel" and "Notes on Famous
Crimes."

PC 148. **GEHERIN, DAVID.** Sons of Sam Spade: The Private-Eye Novel in
the '70's: Robert B. Parker, Roger L. Simon, Andrew Bergman.
New York: Ungar, 1980. 168 pp.
This study examines ten novels by three authors who have inherited and
revitalized the hardboiled detective fiction associated with Dashiell
Hammett, Raymond Chandler, and Ross Macdonald. Geherin provides brief
biographies of the authors and offers plot summaries and critical analyses
of their novels. He considers how these novelists imitate traditional
conventions and characterizations of the genre while establishing their
own particular approaches. Simon's hero, Moses Wine, for example, combines
the cynicism of Philip Marlowe with a Marxist political philosophy; and
Bergman parodies the hardboiled genre as he sets his mysteries in the
1940s. Geherin contends that the contemporary detective has become "more
complex, more humanized, more vulnerable."

PC 149. **GILBERT, MICHAEL FRANCIS,** ed. Crime in Good Company: Essays
on Criminals and Crime Writing. London: Constable, 1959.
242 pp.
Derived from the "table talk" of a group of authors--among them Raymond
Chandler and Eric Ambler--this compilation presents the writers' analysis
of their craftsmanship as armchair detectives. Gilbert defines the three
basic methods of approaching crime writing as: an "intellectual exercise"
which describes the interaction--the parrying back and forth--between
the detective and the criminal; a close exploration of the violent acts
of the criminal; and an examination of the motives, rather than the "who"
or "how," of the crime. All three approaches are deemed acceptable, as
long as the writer remains true to the conventions of the genre and does
not intentionally mislead the reader. The volume introduces a variety
of topics, including the image of the criminal (from the perspectives
of the doctor, lawyer, and policeman), the rules of writing detective
fiction, and the general intentions and specialized techniques of its
practitioners.

PC 150. **HARPER, RALPH.** The World of the Thriller. Cleveland, Ohio:
Press of Case Western Reserve University, 1969. 139 pp.
In describing the world of the thriller, Harper identifies thirteen separate thematic categories of thrillers; he notes, for instance, the emphasis
on situation, crisis, terror, danger, chaos, and violence. His main concern is with the "inner world" of the reader and the subjective experience
of reading. Offering a "phenomenology" of reading, Harper considers
several questions: how does a thriller provide the reader with a sense
of escape; how does a reader appreciate the "thrill" even as he recognizes
aesthetic shortcomings; how does the reader come to identify with characters in the novel; and how does the reader construct a personal dream
world based on this form of fiction?

PC 151. **HAYCRAFT, HOWARD.** Murder for Pleasure: The Life and Times of
the Detective Story. 1941; Rev. ed. New York: Biblo & Tannen,
1968. 409 pp.
In this history of detective fiction, Haycraft writes affectionately of
a genre which he regards as occupying a "vital position . . . in modern
civilized existence." He begins his survey of the development of the
detective story with Edgar Allan Poe, and emphasizes individual authors--
Arthur Conan Doyle, Agatha Christie, Dorothy Sayers, "S. S. Van Dine,"
Dashiell Hammett--because of the popularity of their technical contributions, and not because of their enduring literary merit. He looks at
the evolution of the genre in England and America during "The Romantic
Era" (1890-1914), "The Golden Age" (1918-30), and the age of "The Moderns."
Haycraft also examines techniques of writing and the state of the detective
fiction market. Murder for Pleasure includes a bibliography of criticism,
a list of "cornerstones" in the genre's history, and a list of detective
fiction characters.

PC 152. HAYCRAFT, HOWARD, ed. The Art of the Mystery Story: A Collection
         of Critical Essays. New York: Simon & Schuster, 1946. 565 pp.
Haycraft calls this compilation of fifty-three critical essays the "first
and definitive anthology" devoted solely to detective fiction. Apart
from chapters on Edgar Allan Poe and Arthur Conan Doyle, these essays
address the characteristics of the genre as a whole in England and America,
rather than offering detailed observations of individual authors. The
opening section, "The Higher Criticism," introduces essays by Dorothy
Sayers, R. Austin Freeman, Williard Huntington Wright (S. S. Van Dine),
and Howard Haycraft. In "Care and Feeding of the Whodunit," writers and
editors (Raymond Chandler and John Dickson Carr, among others) discuss
the craft of detective fiction. Professional reviewers contribute remarks
in "Critic's Corner," and four writers (including Dashiell Hammett) consider "Detective Fiction vs. Real Life." The volume also provides sections
on "The Lighter Side of Crime" and the future of the genre, and three
bibliographical essays.

PC 153. KNIGHT, STEPHEN. Form and Ideology in Crime Fiction. Bloomington:
         Indiana University Press, 1980. 202 pp.
Knight discusses Edgar Allan Poe as the first author to introduce the
figure of the isolated and intelligent detective into fiction; Raymond
Chandler as not a realist but an idealist, whose detective figures (modern
knights errant) challenged a deterministic, nationalist world-view; and
Ed McBain as the writer responsible for the introduction into crime fiction
of an objective, bureaucratic approach to crime investigation, supplemented
by technology and systematic procedures.

PC 154. LANDRUM, LARRY N., PAT BROWNE, and RAY B. BROWNE, eds. Dimensions
         of Detective Fiction. Bowling Green, Ohio: Bowling Green Uni-
         versity Popular Press, 1976. 290 pp.
The editors introduce this collection of twenty-three essays with a survey
of the origins and evolution of detective fiction in England and America.
The first of three sections concerns the forms and conventions of the
genre. Section II focuses mainly on individual authors and their works;
included are essays on Eric Ambler, Mickey Spillane, John D. MacDonald,
and an interview with Ross Macdonald. In Section III, "The Genre
Extended," the contributors speculate on the future direction of detective
fiction.

PC 155. MADDEN, DAVID, ed. Tough Guy Writers of the Thirties. Carbondale:
         Southern Illinois University Press, 1968. 247 pp.
The seventeen essays in this volume focus on the hardboiled detective
novel of the 1930s. These essays depict the tough detective as reacting
to the "indifferent, violent, deceptive world that made him." The volume
includes a survey of "The 'Black Mask' School" in general and Dashiell
Hammett in particular ("The Poetics of the Private Eye" and "Focus on
The Maltese Falcon"). Herbert Ruhm discusses Raymond Chandler, and Joyce
Carol Oates writes about the novels of James M. Cain. Other contributors
comment on "The Gangster Novel," "The Hollywood Novel," and "Horace McCoy's
Objective Lyricism." The three concluding essays consider later manifestations of tough-guy writing: the carnival novel; Jim Thompson's 1950s
fiction; and the works of John D. MacDonald.

PC 156. MARGOLIES, EDWARD. Which Way Did He Go?: The Private Eye in
         Dashiell Hammett, Raymond Chandler, Chester Himes, and Ross
         Macdonald. New York: Holmes & Meier, 1982. 97 pp.
Margolies begins by tracing the evolution of the hardboiled detective
and finds in his ancestry not only Edgar Allan Poe's detective but also
the rugged hero of the Western adventure tale. He emphasizes Hammett's
merging of the "Poe-like puzzle element" with suspenseful--often violent--
episodic adventure. In addition to providing biographies of these four

authors, Margolies considers the nature of their fictional detectives by pointing out how they represent both popular notions of the sanctity of the individual and a mistrust of official authority. These detective heroes reaffirm commonly held beliefs, he observes, because no popular author can diverge from what his readers take for granted. Margolies prefaces his work with a bibliographic essay on crime and detective fiction.

PC 157. **MERRY, BRUCE**. Anatomy of the Spy Thriller. Montreal: McGill-
Queen's University Press, 1977. 253 pp.
This study of the 20th-century spy thriller describes the "ground rules" and "standard recurrent situations" of the genre. Merry emphasizes the structure of the spy thriller by indicating how individual authors mold the standard situations—setting of traps, double agents, recognition scenes, and agent meetings. He also explains the adversarial relationship between author and reader as a significant dimension of the spy thriller's appeal; the writer challenges the comprehension of the reader as time runs out within the novel. The emphasis is on British authors, most notably John Le Carre, and, as an example of early espionage fiction, Joseph Conrad. A final chapter explains the popularity of the genre by drawing upon the theories of Erving Goffman and Vladimir Propp.

PC 158. **MOST, GLENN W.** and **WILLIAM W. STOWE**, eds. The Poetics of Murder:
Detective Fiction and Literary Theory. New York: Harcourt Brace
Jovanovich, 1983. 394 pp.
This collection of twenty essays—primarily by literary critics and academics—offers diversified explanations for the persistent popularity of the genre. Certain scholars point to the narrative structure of detective fiction: Umberto Eco considers reader response to plot manipulation; and Dennis Porter, drawing on Roland Barthes (also reprinted in the anthology), argues that popularity is derived from suspense created by standard narrative techniques. Offering a sociological perspective, several authors relate the popularity of detective fiction to the political and social structures of Western society, while other contributors account for the genre's appeal by drawing on psychoanalytic theory.

PC 159. **MURCH, ALMA ELIZABETH**. The Development of the Detective Novel.
New York: Philosophical Library, 1958. 272 pp.
Murch explores the origins of detective fiction, the emergence of its techniques, and the evolution of its narrative structure. Finding the earliest roots of the genre in France and England, Murch discerns national differences in a field she generally regards as international. Throughout, Murch ties the development of detective fiction to the particulars of social history; for example, she comments upon the rise of middle-class demand for fiction. She also observes how technological advances are reflected in the fiction. Murch gives special attention to: Edgar Allan Poe, women writers, Sherlock Holmes, and the post-W.W. I "Golden Age." She confines her focus to the detective story, to be distinguished from crime fiction and mystery fiction in general.

PC 160. **NEVINS, FRANCIS M., Jr.**, ed. The Mystery Writer's Art. Bowling
Green, Ohio: Bowling Green University Popular Press, 1971.
338 pp.
This collection of essays on mystery fiction introduces contributions by mystery writers—among them Ellery Queen, John Dickson Carr, and Ross Macdonald—academics, and film scholars. Part I provides a bibliography of criticism and "appreciations" of Edgar Allan Poe, Sax Rohmer, R. Austin Freeman, Henry Wade, Dashiell Hammett, Erle Stanley Gardner, and Alfred Hitchcock's Psycho. Part II, "Taxonomy," considers the genre's important attributes (discussed, for example, in Jacques Barzun's "Detection and the Literary Art") and subgenres such as the locked-room story and occult

fiction. Essays in Part III, "Speculation and Critique," include Macdonald's view of his own depiction of the detective hero, and comment upon future directions for detective fiction.

PC 161. PALMER, JERRY. Thrillers: Genesis and Structure of a Popular Genre. New York: St. Martin's Press, 1979. 232 pp.
In this exploration of the history and form of detective thrillers, Palmer examines the genre's portrayal of hero and villain and emphasizes its world view of "competitive individualism." Attributing the appeal of the thriller to narrative repetition rather than to artistic innovation, Palmer considers how authors such as Ian Fleming, Mickey Spillane, and Raymond Chandler rise above the genre. Palmer suggests a socio-historical explanation for the appearance of the thriller in the 19th century, as he remarks upon the "emergence of a specific class structure in a laissez-faire economy" and upon the era's new attitudes regarding crime. The volume includes a chapter on genre theory and its application to the thriller novel.

PC 162. PORTER, DENNIS. The Pursuit of Crime: Art and Ideology in Detective Fiction. New Haven, Conn.: Yale University Press, 1981. 267 pp.
Porter considers the popularity of detective fiction in this study of its forms and ideologies. He examines how writers achieve "readability" within the formula of the genre and borrows from psychoanalytic theory to describe the pleasure associated with suspense. In his discussion of ideology, Porter argues that the popular detective novel embodies a world view; he demonstrates, for instance, how Dashiell Hammett and Raymond Chandler "Americanized" the genre, expressing particular American values. Further, Porter examines the manner in which the style of detective fiction—language, character, the depiction of landscape—changes to communicate changing ideologies. Six authors are discussed extensively: Wilkie Collins, Arthur Conan Doyle, Agatha Christie, Hammett, Chandler, and Georges Simenon.

PC 163. RUEHLMANN, WILLIAM. Saint with a Gun: The Unlawful American Private Eye. New York: New York University Press, 1974. 155 pp.
Saint with a Gun is a study of both American detective fiction and the character of the American reading public. Arguing that popular fiction reflects fundamental cultural values, Ruehlmann asserts that popular culture presents "an exaggerated portrait of a nation's psychic nature." He further argues that the popularity of private eye fiction derives from reader identification with the detective; the hero expresses the American attitude that occasionally the rules must be broken in the name of justice. Ruehlmann proceeds chronologically, tracing the evolution of the detective's character. His most extensive chapter, "The Kid from Cyanide Gulch," is devoted to the hardboiled detective of the Black Mask writers.

PC 164. STEWART, R. F. . . . And Always A Detective: Chapters on the History of Detective Fiction. North Pomfret, Vt.: David & Charles, 1980. 351 pp.
Stewart considers the origin of the generic term "detective fiction" in the late 19th century, while noting that Edgar Allan Poe was writing what the Victorians regarded as "sensation fiction." Focusing on the evolution of the detective to demonstrate the continuity between sensation fiction and detective fiction, the author remarks in detail on how the latter emerges as a unique genre, more serious and intellectual in nature, after 1900. He emphasizes English (and, to a lesser extent, French and American) sources in examining what the modern detective owes to the Victorian sensation novel. Further, Stewart argues that such origins—not detective fiction from the 1920s and 1930s—provide the basis for comparative judgments of later examples of the genre.

PC 165. SYMONS, JULIAN. Mortal Consequences: A History from the Detective
        Story to the Crime Novel. New York: Harper & Row, 1972. 269 pp.
Symons, an English crime novelist and critic, offers a history of the
development of the detective story. He discusses American writers such
as Edgar Allan Poe, Raymond Chandler, and Dashiell Hammett extensively,
although he acknowledges his bias toward English detective fiction. Mortal
Consequences is both a literary and social history of the genre. Symons
closely traces the evolution of the detective hero and the establishment
of the "rules" of mystery fiction. Throughout, he indicates the significance of social, technological, and economic changes as they relate to
the writing and marketing of detective fiction.

PC 166. THOMSON, HENRY DOUGLAS. Masters of Mystery. London: Collins,
        1931. 288 pp.
In his introduction to the 1978 republication of Masters of Mystery, E.
F. Bleiler calls Thomson's study the first English-language work devoted
to serious criticism and history of the detective story. Thomson is especially concerned with establishing an aesthetic of detective fiction;
he regrets the diminution of such fiction as mere popular entertainment.
His critical criteria are indicative of the standards of his day; a
"fair"--and therefore worthwhile--story was one in which the reader could
logically puzzle out the solution. The fiction of Edgar Allan Poe receives
prominent treatment, while Thomson gives greatest attention to British
authors: Arthur Conan Doyle, Agatha Christie, and Dorothy Sayers, among
others.

PC 167. WINKS, ROBIN W. Modus Operandi: An Excursion into Detective
        Fiction. Boston: Godine, 1982. 131 pp.
In this "intensely personal essay," Winks considers the structure, appeal,
and reputation of detective fiction in England and America. He analyzes
the popularity of the mystery by comparing it to the appeal of baseball
and football; he recalls the tone of Edward Arlington Robinson's poetry
to reflect the mood of Ross Macdonald. Winks accounts for the poor critical reputation of detective fiction by suggesting that factors more complicated than "mere snobbery" are at work. He also examines how the mystery responds to the needs of the reader, who is allowed to "move up close
to sins" which one normally cannot contemplate.

PC 168. WINKS, ROBIN W., ed. Detective Fiction: A Collection of Critical
        Essays. Englewood Cliffs, N.J.: Prentice-Hall, 1980. 246 pp.
Winks's introduction considers the structure and unique appeal of detective
literature as "moral fiction" mirroring society. Providing an overview
of the genre, the first section includes Dorothy Sayers's "Aristotle on
Detective Fiction" and a critique by Edmund Wilson. Part II offers three
historical surveys of the genre, while the following section is devoted
to serious aesthetic analyses of detective fiction, among them essays
by John Cawelti on literary formulas and Julian Symons on the short story.
Specific authors--Ross Macdonald, Agatha Christie, Sayers--are discussed
in Part IV; Winks and George Dove contribute closing speculations on the
future of the genre. This volume also includes synopses of two Yale University courses on detective fiction and a bibliography of the critical
and historical literature.

FANTASY AND THE OCCULT

PC 169. **APTER, T. E.** Fantasy Literature: An Approach to Reality. Bloomington: Indiana University Press, 1982. 161 pp.
For Apter, fantasy literature does not represent an escape but "an investigation of human reality." Fantasy may be considered "therapeutic,"
for it enables the reader to draw upon the unconscious to cope with everyday problems; fantasy also aggravates "disintegration" by revealing "how
awful, how limiting and imprisoning the world is." Utilizing psychoanalytic theory, the volume includes discussions of Nathaniel Hawthorne,
Joseph Conrad, Franz Kafka, Nikolai Gogol, Fyodor Dostoevsky, and Vladimir
Nabokov.

PC 170. **ATTEBERY, BRIAN.** The Fantasy Tradition in American Literature:
From Irving to Le Guin. Bloomington: Indiana University Press,
1980. 212 pp.
This text begins with the author's definition of fantasy as a narrative
form treating "an impossibility as if it were true," and then traces the
history and development of the genre from its 18th- and 19th-century literary antecedents to the post-Tolkien writers of the 1970s. Attebery elucidates the "high fantasy" practiced by William Morris, C. S. Lewis and
J. R. R. Tolkien that has helped to define the American portrayal of a
"sense of wonder." He devotes an entire chapter to Frank Baum's Oz, which
he identifies as the first "coherent American fantasy world." He also
emphasizes the contributions of James B. Cabell, Robert Zelazny, and Ursula
Le Guin in carrying on fantasy's heritage and traits--its setting in the
Other World, its relationship to fairy tales, the conflict between limited
human heroes and superhuman and immortal protagonists, and the establishment
of a "sphere of significance" suggestive of a coherent and understandable
order of things.

PC 171. **CARTER, LIN.** Imaginary Worlds: The Art of Fantasy. New York:
Ballantine, 1973. 278 pp.
Defining fantasy literature as a genre set in an invented milieu that
includes magic as an integral part of the natural world, Carter provides
critical and technical analysis of the major American and British fantasy
writers of the 20th century. The study begins with a summary of the life
and work of such contributors as William Morris, Lord Dunsany, E. R.
Eddison, and James Branch Cabell, then chronicles the role of fantasy
in American pulp magazines and the impact of John W. Campbell's periodical,
Unknown. The writings of C. S. Lewis and J. R. R. Tolkien receive attention, preparatory to an in-depth study of the subgenre of sword and sorcery.
Carter concludes with a discussion of techniques for inventing fictional
worlds and for naming things within them appropriately.

PC 172. **de CAMP, L. SPRAGUE.** Literary Swordsmen and Sorcerers: The Makers
of Heroic Fantasy. Sauk City, Wis.: Arkham House, 1976. 313
pp.
An author of science fiction and tales of "sword and sorcery," de Camp
traces the development of "heroic fantasy" from its revival in the 1880s
to W.W. II. Discussing the evolution of the genre, he begins with William
Morris and interprets the lives and works of key British authors--Lord
Dunsany, Clark Ashton Smith, and J. R. R. Tolkien--as well as of the Americans H. P. Lovecraft, Robert G. Howard, and Fletcher Pratt. De Camp places
considerable emphasis on the genre's distinctive value as a form of psychological gratification: "Heroic fantasy is the purest escape fiction there
is; the reader escapes clean out of the real world."

PC 173. HOLTSMARK, ERLING B. Tarzan and Tradition: Classical Myth in
Popular Literature. Westport, Conn.: Greenwood Press, 1981.
196 pp.
Holtsmark challenges those "literal-minded critics" who fail to appreciate
Tarzan as more "than an unidimensional figure pandering to the lowest
common denominator of the vulgar masses." Considering Edgar Rice Burroughs
as a writer in the Homeric mode, Holtsmark places Tarzan within the context
of traditional myth and legend by interpreting the language and social
organization of the community of apes as allegorical reflections on the
"dual nature" of animal and man. The volume also explores Burroughs's
portrayal of parent-child relationships, the erotic hero, and the relevance
of Darwinian evolution.

PC 174. IRWIN, W. R. The Game of the Impossible: A Rhetoric of Fantasy.
Urbana: University of Illinois Press, 1976. 215 pp.
This critical study of fantasy in English and American literature from
1880 to the 1950s offers a theoretical rather than an historical approach
to the genre. For Irwin, conferring upon the impossible with the appearance of reality requires a transactional process in which the "writer
and reader knowingly enter upon a conspiracy of intellectual subversiveness,
that is, upon a game." He distinguishes the genre from other types of
prose fiction--fairy tales, gothic romances, ghost stories, science fiction,
pornographic stories. Fantasy, he asserts, "is governed by the requirement
and devices of rhetoric, much more than of art." He investigates a variety
of fantasy modes, including the supernatural, the utopian, parody, and
the tale of metamorphosis. The genre, Irwin finds, proves gratifying,
for it "invites the play of wit within a controlled situation."

PC 175. JACKSON, ROSEMARY. Fantasy: The Literature of Subversion. London:
Methuen, 1981. 211 pp.
Fantasy fiction, according to Jackson, is not a transcendent mode of creating a better world. Rather, "fantasy characteristically attempts to compensate for a lack resulting from cultural constraints: it is a literature
of desire, which seeks that which is experienced as absence and loss."
In the first half of the book, Jackson employs a structuralist approach
to identify varieties of narrative mode and examines how these varieties
reveal the workings of the psyche. In the second section, she discusses
certain historical and social forces which acted upon the development
of fantasy from The Castle of Otranto to The Crying of Lot 49.

PC 176. KING, STEPHEN. Danse Macabre. New York: Everest House, 1981.
400 pp.
King addresses the psychological appeal of the horror tale and contends
that its real meaning exists at a level close to the primitive: the horror
tale works on our "phobic pressure points." A variety of movies, books,
and radio shows are investigated for the way in which they achieve this
impact; while their ideological and allegorical aspects receive some attention, King stresses the theme that "the good horror tale will dance its
way to the center of your life and find the secret door to the room you
believed no one but you knew of."

PC 177. LOVECRAFT, HOWARD PHILLIPS. Supernatural Horror in Literature.
New York: Ben Abramson, 1945. 106 pp.
Lovecraft investigates the history and aesthetics of supernatural horror
literature from medieval times to the tales of the 20th-century masters.
Chapters on the Gothic emphasize the significance of Horace Walpole, "the
actual founder of the literary horror-story as a permanent form," Mrs.
Radcliffe, M. G. Lewis, C. R. Maturin, and the American Charles Brockden
Brown. Lovecraft includes a chapter on Edgar Allan Poe as the creator
of a new standard in literary horror, and traces the supernatural tradition
in America through Nathaniel Hawthorne, Ambrose Bierce, Henry James, and

F. Marion Crawford. Admitting that such literature may have a limited audience, Lovecraft nonetheless believes that the psychological dimensions of the genre deserve attention. "The one test of the really weird is this," he urges: "whether or not there be excited in the reader a profound sense of dread, and of contact with unknown spheres and powers."

PC 178. **MANLOVE, C. N.** The Impulse of Fantasy Literature. Kent, Ohio: Kent State University Press, 1983. 174 pp.
In this history of fantasy literature, Manlove cites the "insistence on and celebration of the separate identities of created things" as a recurrent theme of modern fantasy. After an introductory chapter on the origins of this genre in traditional fairy tales, he devotes chapters to individual authors of fantasy--Charles Williams, Ursula Le Guin, George MacDonald, T. H. White, and Mervyn Peake--and comments on the contributions of William Morris, Lord Dunsany, E. R. Eddison, and Peter Beagle. Fantasy literature in England and America, Manlove maintains, shares the assumption that the "relationship between the writer and his material towards which he continually strives is permanent: and this is the basic condition from which the overt concern with wonder in all its forms is generated."

PC 179. **MESSENT, PETER B.,** ed. Literature of the Occult: A Collection of Critical Essays. Englewood Cliffs, N.J.: Prentice-Hall, 1981. 188 pp.
This collection of critical pieces focuses on British and American literary works, beginning with the Gothic novel's "rationally unexplainable" use of the supernatural and including a consideration of important modern texts. Occult literature is appreciated for its many polarities: rational and irrational, dark and light, good and evil, the spirit world and the physical world. Categorization within the genre serves as the theme of some contributors, as in Tzvetan Todorov's delineations between the uncanny and the marvelous, and Jack Sullivan's examination of the archetypal ghost story. Two essays comment on the role of spiritualism. Some of the analyses focus on authors--such as Edgar Allan Poe, Bram Stoker, and H. P. Lovecraft--while others discuss the "numinous" (non-rational) factor of Victorian fiction, or more contemporary concerns, such as the anthropological insights of Carlos Castaneda.

PC 180. **PENZOLDT, PETER.** The Supernatural in Fiction. London: Nevill, 1952. 271 pp.
Penzoldt introduces psychoanalytic methods to interpret the authors of 19th- and 20th-century English short stories of the supernatural. He opens with a general survey of this genre--its origins, structure, uniqueness, and "the principal superstitions that seem to haunt the tellers of ghostly tales." He also considers the significance of certain supernatural figures--the ghost, the vampire, the werewolf--as well as the presence of supernatural motifs in science fiction. The remainder of Penzoldt's volume offers analyses (with occasional references to American writers) of the major authors of weird fiction: Joseph Sheridan Le Fanu, Robert Louis Stevenson, Rudyard Kipling, Water de la Mare, Algernon Blackwood, and the practitioners of the "pure tale of terror." Commenting on the psychology of both writers and readers, Penzoldt notes that the tale of the supernatural remains "one of the most effective devices for combating that secret and persistent faith in the unknown."

PC 181. **RABKIN, ERIC S.** The Fantastic in Literature. Princeton, N.J.: Princeton University Press, 1976. 234 pp.
Rabkin's historical and critical study explores "the nature and uses of the fantastic." He investigates fairy tales, science fiction, detective fiction, religious allegory, and the broader scope of human psychology. Illustrating his observations with examples from later Victorian England, he also includes works from earlier periods and from America. Rabkin's

chapters on genre criticism and literary history seek to complement conventional methods of interpretation by analyzing reader response and perspectives. Assuming that the fantastic represents a basic mode of human knowledge, he notes: "Unless one participates sympathetically in the ground rules of a narrative world, no occurrence in that world can make sense or even nonsense."

PC 182. TIMMERMAN, JOHN H. Other Worlds: The Fantasy Genre. Bowling Green, Ohio: Bowling Green University Popular Press, 1983. 124 pp.

This work begins with the assumption that fantasy serves as a "parallel reality" allowing the reader sufficient distance to gain insight into the problems of the ordinary world. Timmerman devotes individual chapters to the six characteristics necessary to a definition of the "unique qualities" of the genre: Story, Common Characters and Heroism, Another World, Magic and the Supernatural, Struggle between Good and Evil, The Quest. He considers the distinctiveness of fantasy not only in relationship to literary tradition but also in comparison to the popular genres of the Western and science fiction.

GOTHIC FICTION AND ROMANCE

PC 183. BEER, GILLIAN. The Romance. London: Methuen, 1970. 88 pp.

Beer provides an historical study of European romance, the forerunner of the modern Gothic, from the 12th century to the end of the 18th century. She discusses two critical points in the history of the romance: the publication of Don Quixote and the beginning of the romantic revival. The romances, Beer observes, "allowed their readers--who were mainly women--to immerse themselves without responsibility in a hectic world which made real life pale by comparison." The appearance of the Gothic revealed a particularly powerful psychological dimension, for "the floodgates of fancy were opened, and the commitment to imagination as the source of inspiration . . . had begun." Studied closely, the romance may be perceived as providing both escape and an illumination of our assumptions about the experience of life.

PC 184. BELL, MICHAEL DAVITT. Hawthorne and the Historical Romance of New England. Princeton, N.J.: Princeton University Press, 1971. 253 pp.

Bell explores the Puritan past in Nathaniel Hawthorne's fiction by comparing the author's depiction of history with the fictional past found in works by his literary contemporaries, including many women writers. He discusses the manner in which the conventional romantic marriage plot was introduced to convey the historical romancers' attitudes toward the nature and direction of New England history. As in many Gothic tales, Hawthorne's heroines overcome their rebelliousness to assume a position of femininity and domesticity. Hawthorne, however, rejected the assumptions behind the conventional New England historical romances--"subordination of all to the heart, to romantic love, to nature"--in seeking a "balance between head and heart, between civilization and nature."

PC 185. BIRKHEAD, EDITH. The Tale of Terror: A Study of the Gothic Romance. New York: Dutton, 1920. 241 pp.

This early work traces the origin and development of Gothic romance and the tale of terror in English literature. The volume examines the classic Gothic romances, beginning with Walpole's The Castle of Otranto (1764), and offers a consideration of Walter Scott's relationship to the novel

of terror, satiric treatments of this genre, and the short story of terror.
In the chapter "American Tales of Terror," Birkhead discusses Gothic works
by Charles Brockden Brown, Washington Irving, and, most significantly,
Nathaniel Hawthorne and Edgar Allan Poe. She briefly explores the persistence of the element of terror in science, detective, and supernatural
fiction. Birkhead observes that the Gothic romance, appealing mainly
to women readers, "satisfies the human desire to experience new emotion
and sensations without actual danger."

PC 186. CECIL, MIRABEL. Heroines in Love, 1750-1974. London: Michael
         Joseph, 1974. 236 pp.
In this survey of British and American romance fiction, Cecil catalogues
the different types of heroines that have appeared in women's magazines
from 1750 to 1974. The chapters are arranged chronologically by character
types, and are followed by a reprint of a magazine story representative
of each period. Cecil stresses that magazine heroines have always conformed to conventional ideas about women, and notes the influence of novel-
istic heroines on magazine fiction. Eighteenth-century romance fiction,
modeled on Richardson's Clarissa, was preoccupied with how its heroines
avoided sex. Victorian women's magazines, such as America's Godey's Lady's
Book (1830-98), provided middle-class women with standards of propriety
and purity. In the 1950s, "the happy housewife heroine" appeared in
McCall's and other magazines. Cecil concludes her study with the new sexual
realism of Cosmopolitan, aimed at yet a different type of reader.

PC 187. FLEENOR, JULIANN E., ed. The Female Gothic. Montreal: Eden,
         1983. 311 pp.
This collection of essays explores the nature of women's literature as
illustrated in the female Gothic, a form of literature, Fleenor notes,
"shaped by the patriarchal paradigm." Such dichotomies as male and female,
good and evil, are addressed as they relate to the quest for autonomy
and the conflict with a powerful mother figure. The anthology's four
sections identify significant motifs: (1) "Mystique: The Popular Gothic";
(2) "Madness: Apocalypse and Transcendence"; (3) "Monsters: Sexuality
and Terror"; and (4) "Maternity: The Body as Metaphor." Fleenor's contributors present divergent opinions about the genre's relationship to
cultural assumptions. For some essayists, the Gothic represents the
"expression of rebellion and ambivalence toward the woman's sphere," while
for others it "affirms the popular role of women."

PC 188. GILBERT, SANDRA M. and SUSAN GUBAR. The Madwoman in the Attic:
         The Woman Writer and the Nineteenth-Century Literary Imagination.
         New Haven, Conn.: Yale University Press, 1979. 719 pp.
Gilbert and Gubar examine the distinctly female literary tradition begun
by English women writers in the 19th century. They argue that these
authors shared a "common female impulse to struggle free from social and
literary confinement through strategic redefinition of self, art, and
society." The discussion of Gothic and romance fiction appears in chapters
devoted to Jane Austen and Charlotte Bronte, as well as in the briefer
section on Mary Shelley. Other writers, including Emily Dickinson, are
also considered in order to trace the emergence of a recognizable female
imagination.

PC 189. HAZEN, HELEN. Endless Rapture: Rape, Romance, and the Female
         Imagination. New York: Scribner, 1983. 184 pp.
Hazen explores the relationship of feminist fiction to romances, pornog-
raphy, and Gothic literature. She considers classic Gothic novels--by
Walpole, Radcliffe and M. G. Lewis--as well as such modern works as Ira
Levin's Rosemary's Baby, Stephen King's The Shining, and Marge Piercy's
Small Changes. She criticizes the feminist Gothic novelist for stressing
the oppression of women's lives and for exhibiting a preference for unhappy

endings. Without "the use of rape as a metaphoric world view"--the emphasis upon the existence of evil male figures and sexual violence--feminist
fiction could not exist in its present form; the "error," Hazen contends,
"is that the reality that caused the recital of the misery, the reason
for the plot, remains unacknowledged."

PC 190. HENNESSY, BRENDAN. The Gothic Novel. New York: Longman, 1978.
        59 pp.
Hennessy presents a broad chronological view of the Gothic novel that
stresses the British literary traditions but also takes note of the genre's
presence in America (especially in the works of Edgar Allan Poe), France,
Germany, and Russia. His volume has two central objectives: (1) to trace
the importance of Gothic literature by discussing its medieval antecedents,
its influence on Romanticism, and its impact upon supernatural, detective
and speculative fiction; and (2) to demonstrate that a significant portion
of the Gothics written between 1765 and 1820 fail to receive serious attention "because a false distinction tends to be made nowadays between 'good'
and 'popular.'" Hennessy, in discussing the modern Gothic in several media,
indicates that both the horror film and Gothic fiction represent "collective dreams, expressions of and safety-valves for the unconscious of the
age, expressions of generally experienced desires and fears that tend
to be repressed by individuals."

PC 191. HOWELLS, CORAL ANN. Love, Mystery, and Misery: Feeling in Gothic
        Fiction. London: University of London, The Athlone Press, 1978.
        199 pp.
Howells approaches the Gothic novel, the most popular form of English
fiction between 1790 and 1820, as an experiment in the portrayal of feeling.
She analyzes distinctively Gothic moods--love, mystery, and misery--as
well as the techniques used to convey emotion, imagination, and sensibility.
Her chronological approach suggests changes in Gothic fiction during its
heyday. Through a detailed examination of novels by Mrs. Radcliffe,
M. G. Lewis, Regina Maria Roche, Jane Austen, C. R. Maturin, and Charlotte
Bronte, Howells reveals how the genre addresses the irrational element
in human beings by arousing suspense and fear.

PC 192. MacANDREW, ELIZABETH. The Gothic Tradition in Fiction. New York:
        Columbia University Press, 1979. 289 pp.
This volume investigates the appearance and continuity of Gothic literary
devices. MacAndrew contends that "authors writing in the Gothic tradition
employ the same structures, imagery, and methods of characterization
because their works have a common purpose--the exploration of human nature."
The shared features of Gothic characters, setting, and narrative structures
are analyzed. The study, which focuses on 19th-century British fiction,
also considers American authors (Edgar Allan Poe, Nathaniel Hawthorne,
Henry James) and continental European writing. MacAndrew provides a
broadly chronological approach to Gothic fiction, while introducing individual works to illustrate the stylistic devices of this "literature of
nightmare."

PC 193. MOERS, ELLEN. Literary Women. Garden City, N.Y.: Doubleday,
        1976. 336 pp.
Focusing on the contributions of major English and American writers since
the second half of the 18th century, Moers describes her work as "a celebration of the great women who have spoken for us all." The chapter
entitled "Female Gothic" explores the tradition established by such authors
as Ann Radcliffe, Mary Shelley, Emily Bronte, Christina Rossetti, and
Carson McCullers, writers of narratives "in which the central figure is
a young woman who is simultaneously persecuted as a victim and courageous
heroine." The chapter "Traveling Heroinism" stresses the tribulations
encountered by the central figures found in Mrs. Radcliffe's novels.

This form of the Gothic, Moers argues, "became a feminine substitute for the picaresque, where heroines could enjoy all the adventure and alarms that masculine heroes had long experienced far from home, in fiction."

PC 194. PUNTER, DAVID. The Literature of Terror: A History of Gothic Fictions from 1765 to the Present Day. New York: Longman, 1980. 449 pp.
Punter employs Marxist and sociological methods, as well as Freudian perspectives, in his critical study of the Gothic modes in fiction. In formulating a theory of the Gothic, his general assumption is "that an art-form of a genre derives its overall vitality . . . from its attempt to come to grips with and to probe matters of concern to the society in which that art-form or genre exists." Discussing British and American literary works, Punter explores the Gothic's concern with paranoia, barbarism, and the taboo. American authors treated include Charles Brockden Brown, Nathaniel Hawthorne, Edgar Allan Poe, Ambrose Bierce, Robert W. Chambers, and H. P. Lovecraft. In interpreting the impact on readers, Punter suggests that the central contradiction of the genre is that the "Gothic can at one and the same time be categorised as a middle-class and as an anti-middle-class literature."

PC 195. REDDEN, SISTER MARY MAURITA. The Gothic Fiction in the American Magazines (1765-1800). Washington, D.C.: Catholic University Press, 1939. 184 pp.
Redden presents a chronological study of Gothic fiction in American magazines to detail the basic elements of this genre. She compares characteristic devices of English and American fiction of the 18th century. Commenting on the genre's "stock-in-trade of horror and romanticism," Redden identifies six plot motifs: "The Castle Keep," Historical Background, Magic, Ghosts, "Tales Involving Clerical and Conventional Milieu," and Natural Phenomena. She briefly treats reader psychology, and observes that the Gothic satisfied a natural desire to experience violent emotions vicariously.

PC 196. RINGE, DONALD A. American Gothic: Imagination and Reason in Nineteenth Century Fiction. Lexington: University Press of Kentucky, 1982. 215 pp.
Ringe contends that a distinctively American mode of the Gothic developed from British and German roots, and that the genre, far from being "puerile," became an appropriate vehicle for the development of serious themes by American writers. He discusses the European Gothic imports which American authors drew on for their own tales and romances. Beginning with Charles Brockden Brown, Ringe emphasizes the growth of the American Gothic mode in Washington Irving, Edgar Allan Poe, and Nathaniel Hawthorne. He includes other writers--James Fenimore Cooper, James K. Paulding, William Cullen Bryant, Robert M. Bird, and William Gilmore Simms--to reveal the interrelationships of literary figures pursuing Gothic motifs. The decline of Gothic fiction after 1860 is also addressed.

PC 197. UTTER, ROBERT PALFREY and GWENDOLYN BRIDGES NEEDHAM. Pamela's Daughters. New York: Macmillan, 1936. 512 pp.
This literary history of British Gothics and romances--which includes occasional references to American literature--discusses the images of women in fiction since Samuel Richardson's Pamela. Two types of heroines, the submissive and the imperious, are identified. The characteristic plot, Utter and Needham indicate, uses "love for the starting-post and marriage for the finish line." An explanation of classic British romances and Gothics reveals a variety of themes concerning the nature of womanhood: the poor girl starving for domestic happiness, the importance of being a prude, the weeping heroine, fainting and the aristocracy, chastity, and changing social conventions.

PC 198. VARMA, DEVENDRA. The Gothic Flame. London: A. Barker, 1957.
264 pp.
Varma's history of the Gothic novel in England analyzes three main streams
of Gothic Romance derived from Horace Walpole's The Castle of Otranto:
The Gothic-Historical; The School of Terror of Mrs. Radcliffe; and the
works of Schauer-Romantik ("horror-romanticism"). The author traces the
"origins, efflorescence, disintegration, and residuary influences" of
the genre and suggests that the Gothic spirit restored mystery and innate
emotion to a literature permeated with rationalism. While the Gothic
has declined because of shifting popular tastes, "the same spirit is rein-
carnate in new forms." Varma's discussion of the impact of the Gothic
impulse on ghost stories, detective fiction, and romantic literature
applies to the study of both British and American literary figures.

SCIENCE FICTION

PC 199. ALDISS, BRIAN W. Billion Year Spree: The True History of Science
Fiction. Garden City, N.Y.: Doubleday, 1973. 339 pp.
Aldiss describes science fiction as "born in the heart and crucible of
the English Romantic movement," as a genre engaged in the "search for
a definition of man and his status in the universe which will stand in
our advanced but confused state of knowledge (science), and . . . characteristically cast in the Gothic or post-Gothic mould." Utilizing Mary
Shelley's Frankenstein as a model of excellence, he comments on the contributions of Edgar Allan Poe, Edward Bellamy, and H. G. Wells, discusses
the excesses of the American pulp tradition (reflected in the fantasies
of Edgar Rice Burroughs and the editorial policies of John Campbell),
and admits to a preference for authors (for example, Olaf Stapledon) who
transcended the boundaries of the magazine world. The final two chapters
emphasize the "liberalizing" preoccupation with environmental issues,
the role of women, and the theme of dehumanization articulated by writers
who rose to prominence in the 1950s and 1960s.

PC 200. ALDISS, BRIAN W. and HARRY HARRISON, eds. Hell's Cartographers:
Some Personal Histories of Science Fiction Writers. New York:
Harper & Row, 1975. 246 pp.
Aldiss's introduction places the diverse autobiographies of six contemporary science fiction authors--Robert Silverberg, Alfred Bester, Harry
Harrison, Damon Knight, Frederick Pohl, and Aldiss himself--within a generational context: these writers were heavily influenced by Hiroshima-
Nagasaki, had watched science fiction become "one of the bland flavour-
ings of the mass media," and yet remained confident that the genre "mirrors
the present in such a way as to dispense with inessentials and dramatize
new trends." Each reminiscence, accompanied by an account of personal
work habits, comments upon the author's childhood experiences and reading
tastes, initial encounters with the publishing world, the psychological
and financial reasons for occasionally undertaking other careers, and
the important stages of moving from obscurity to renown.

PC 201. AMIS, KINGSLEY. New Maps of Hell: A Survey of Science Fiction.
New York: Harcourt, Brace, 1960. 161 pp.
Based on Amis's 1959 lectures at Princeton University, this volume discusses both the institutional development of science fiction (its pulp
magazines and fan clubs) and the psychological implications of a literature
reflecting the "wishes, hopes, and fears" of a culture. He reserves his
greatest enthusiasm for dystopian literature, most successfully represented
in Frederick Pohl and Cyril Kornbluth's The Space Merchants, as "an instru-

ment" rendering "general and public what in the present context is only piecemeal and private." Amis suggests that science fiction will achieve the status of mainstream literature if its advocates reduce their sense of "hieratic self-importance," cease to pursue faddish beliefs, and develop a "growing concern for style."

PC 202. **ARMYTAGE, W. H. G.** Yesterday's Tomorrows: A Historical Survey of Future Societies. Toronto: University of Toronto Press, 1968. 288 pp.
Armytage observes that images of the future "reflect collective emotional tensions" played out in the form of "preparatory daydreams, imagined encounters, wish-fulfillments, and compensatory projections." Considering both optimistic and apocalyptic literature, he chronicles futuristic visions from ancient times to Herman Kahn and the RAND Corporation, and places these "heuristic" devices within the intellectual climate of the eras which produced them (for example, the faith in the "noble savage" and the "superman," the Darwinian concepts of evolution). The greatest emphasis upon American science fiction appears in the chapter "Virgils of the Dynamo," which discusses the significance of Hugo Gernsback, Ray Bradbury, and Frederick Pohl, as well as that of such magazines as Analog, Galaxy, and Fantasy and Science Fiction. Citing Marx, Freud, and Kierkegaard, Armytage concludes by speculating that fantasy in general may well prove to be "the inevitable antidote to the crushing logic of 1984."

PC 203. **ASIMOV, ISAAC.** Asimov on Science Fiction. Garden City, N.Y.: Doubleday, 1981. 334 pp.
Asimov reprints fifty-five editorials and essays which he produced on the topic of science fiction--many of them taken from Isaac Asimov's Science Fiction Magazine--and organizes them into eight categories. His first concern is to define the genre, his second to give tips on plot, language, and technique in writing. After discussing the power of prediction in science fiction, he traces the history of the field, giving some attention to Soviet contributions. Asimov devotes considerable space to the praise of specific writers, among them Jules Verne, Ray Bradbury, and Arthur Clarke. Final sections include a discussion of the important role of science fiction fans, some critical reviews by Asimov, and his personal reflections on the pursuit of a writing career.

PC 204. **BAILEY, JAMES O.** Pilgrims Through Space and Time: Trends and Patterns in Scientific and Utopian Fiction. New York: Argus, 1947. 341 pp.
Bailey's volume investigates the literary tradition of the "scientific romance"--works depicting the impact of an "imaginary invention or discovery in the natural sciences." In Part I, an account of scientific romances from 1800 to the 1940s, Bailey focuses on imaginary voyages and utopian societies, but also includes tales of the supernatural and of crime and detection. Part II, "And Space Anatomized," discusses formal attributes such as narrative methods, characterization, plot conventions and philosophical "creeds." Bailey emphasizes the importance of book-length fiction--for example, the work of Jules Verne and H. G. Wells-- and only occasionally comments on the contributions of the American pulp magazines. While placing science fiction within the traditions of the Middle Ages and the Renaissance, he also contends that by portraying the human response to technological change, the scientific romance may provide instruction to the world about the Atomic Age.

PC 205. BARR, MARLEEN S., ed. Future Females: A Critical Anthology.
         Bowling Green, Ohio: Bowling Green State University Popular
         Press, 1981. 191 pp.
Barr describes her anthology as a significant "communal" venture: feminists exchanging observations with male contributors; established scholars
collaborating with younger colleagues; literary critics joining with media
specialists and political scientists to recommend that science fiction
might form "a main current of feminist thought." Barr's volume seeks
to go "beyond science fiction's relationship to sexism." While some of
the essays document gender stereotyping (as found in the Star Trek series),
others comment on the genre's positive portrayals of women. A discussion
of the "conflicts of interest" encountered by such novelists as Suzy
Charnas and Marge Piercy illuminates the complex demands of contemporary
authorship, while two contrasting interpretations (by Barr and Norman
Holland) of Ursula Le Guin's fiction indicate the subtle, transactive
nature of reader response to a major science fiction writer. The volume
also includes a checklist of women writers and their works.

PC 206. BERGER, HAROLD. Science Fiction and the New Dark Age. Bowling
         Green, Ohio: Bowling Green University Popular Press, 1976.
         231 pp.
Berger contends that science fiction has not traditionally celebrated
progress, but rather illuminated a "syndrome . . . the tendency of scientific and social progress in this century to cause more problems than
it solves and even turn solutions into problems." Noting earlier studies
by Kingsley Amis and Mark Hillegas, Berger proposes a more detailed investigation of the thematic clusters of dystopian fiction: The Threat of
Science (man vs. machine, "ignoble utopias"), New Tyrannies ("mind invasion," "the revolt of youth"), and Catastrophe (nuclear war, population
explosion, race war). Berger discusses not only George Orwell, Kurt
Vonnegut, Jr., Frederick Pohl, Robert Silverberg, and Anthony Burgess,
but also Eric Fromm, Hannah Arendt, B. F. Skinner, and "mainstream" authors
such as Gore Vidal, in order to demonstrate a "crisis of confidence" concerning the future. He concludes that such an apparent malaise may prove
constructive, for dark visions offer warnings regarding "which paths must
not be taken."

PC 207. BLISH, JAMES (William Atheling, Jr.). The Issues at Hand: Studies
         in Contemporary Magazine Science Fiction. 1964; Rev. ed. Chicago:
         Advent, 1973. 158 pp.
This volume collects the critical pieces contributed by Blish to the fan
magazines of the early 1950s, an era when the genre began to emerge from
its "specialty classification" and attract "slick magazines" and book
publishers. As "William Atheling" (a pseudonym once employed by Ezra
Pound), Blish argues for an emphasis upon "technical competence" as the
"indispensible" criterion for judging literary endeavors. Adopting the
persona of "sour Bill," he critiques the major editors of science fiction:
John Campbell of Astounding, Horace Gold of Galaxy, and Anthony Boucher
of Fantasy and Science Fiction. This compilation also includes Blish's
updated observations regarding the emergence of religious motifs (for
example, A Canticle for Leibowitz) and the satiric methods of Kurt Vonnegut,
Jr. For Blish, rendering "sloppy work" obsolete performs a significant
function by fostering a "wider appreciation for writers who show reasonable
craftsmanship."

PC 208. BLISH, JAMES (William Atheling, Jr.). More Issues at Hand: Criti-
         cal Studies in Contemporary Science Fiction. Chicago: Advent,
         1970. 154 pp.
This second collection of Atheling's critical observations, primarily
from the mid- and late-1960s, reflects Blish's growing conviction that
science fiction had transcended its pulp origins and become a legitimate

1240

movement in the popular arts. Blish, who describes himself as a "technical critic" opposed to the excesses of impressionistic and ideological inter- pretations, proposes to diagnose the "universe of discourse" grounded in "the myths of twentieth century metaphysics." Defending Atheling's "waspish style," he focuses upon the genre's ambiguous institutional prog- ress: its participants have become preoccupied with awards and prizes at conventions; critics and historians, varying in their knowledge of literature and love of science fiction, are erratic in meeting the needs of an increasingly self-conscious audience; and a younger generation of writers, the "New Wave," has sought to revolutionize science fiction by confronting contemporary social issues and by imitating mainstream litera- ture.

PC 209. BRETNOR, REGINALD, ed. The Craft of Science Fiction. New York: Harper & Row, 1976. 321 pp.
This symposium by fifteen science fiction writers concentrates on how science fiction is written; the volume is intended not only for novice writers but also for teachers and scholars of this popular genre. The list of contributors includes Poul Anderson, Theodore Sturgeon, Frank Herbert, Harlan Ellison, and Frederick Pohl. The first of three sections overviews sources of inspiration: the writer's personal drive, the tra- dition of the saga, and changing applications of the physical and social sciences. Next, the symposium pursues some of the creative components of science fiction, among them extrapolation, aliens, and alternative social systems. In closing, contributors share trade secrets in charac- terization, word choice, and the use of a "video image," and offer advice on creating short stories and novels in order to become a "science fiction professional."

PC 210. BRETNOR, REGINALD, ed. Modern Science Fiction: Its Meaning and Its Future. New York: Coward-McCann, 1953. 294 pp.
This 1950s anthology contains diverse perspectives regarding the social role of science fiction. Editors (John Campbell, Anthony Boucher), critics (Boucher, Bretnor), and writers (L. Sprague de Camp, Isaac Asimov, Arthur Clarke) reflect on the field's relationship to "contemporary science, contemporary literature, contemporary human problems." The eleven essays discuss publishing, the function of the creative imagination, and sci- ence fiction's ability to respond to accelerated changes within Western society. The volume also considers science fiction in film, radio, and television, and compares the genre to mainstream literary endeavors.

PC 211. BRETNOR, REGINALD, ed. Science Fiction, Today and Tomorrow. New York: Harper & Row, 1974. 342 pp.
Contrasting the present collection of essays with his 1950s anthology Modern Science Fiction (PC 210), Bretnor maintains that the emergence of a "mandarin society" has deepened the need for non-conformity. Con- sisting of observations by the genre's authors and editors, the volume considers the practical dimensions of science fiction--the role of pub- lishers, the relationship to the literary mainstream, guidelines for craft- ing a successful narrative, and reading lists for prospective teachers. The compilation also addresses the centrality of science fiction in a rapidly changing world, as Frank Herbert applauds the confrontation with environmental issues, Theodore Sturgeon considers parallels with religious morality, and Ben Bova reflects on the human need for myth. Bretnor argues that science fiction, representing a "rational speculation regarding the human experience of science and its resultant technologies," should not abandon its scientific foundations for the academic "word games" and retro- gressive counter-culture encouraged by the mandarins of society.

PC 212. CARTER, PAUL. Creation of Tomorrow: Fifty Years of Magazine
        Science Fiction. New York: Columbia University Press, 1977.
        318 pp.
Carter provides an account of science fiction as an "imaginative extrapolation from the known into the unknown." Focusing on the 1930s and 1940s,
Carter uses editorials and letters to the editor as well as fictional
pieces in order to demonstrate the genre's preoccupation with the century's
political and technological issues: (1) the development of rocketry;
(2) the philosophical implications of "time machines" and of the concept
of the superman; (3) the rise of Hitler and of apocalpytic moods immediately prior to W.W. II; and (4) the depiction of ecological crises and
traditional sex roles. Carter comments briefly on the declining influence
of pulp magazines since 1950, and expresses the hope that science fiction
will cease to reflect contemporary "despair" and return to the balanced
critique of technological progress.

PC 213. CIOFFI, FRANK. Formula's Fiction?: An Anatomy of American Science
        Fiction, 1930-1940. Westport, Conn.: Greenwood Press, 1982.
        181 pp.
Cioffi examines the interaction of American society in the 1930s, the
"social-economic enterprise" of science fiction, and the "scientifically
explicable changes" found in the pulp magazines of the Depression. Focusing on the narrative structures of short stories and novellas in Astounding,
he identifies three formulaic patterns: "status quo" science fiction,
"subversive" science fiction, and "other world" tales. Cioffi traces
the increasing complexity of these formulas in the late 1930s and indicates
how each continued to be viable for "the media-bombarded, information-
saturated modern consciousness" of the 1970s; Cioffi's examples include
the film Alien, John Varley's "Persistence of Vision," and the short
stories of Thomas Disch. He concludes by recommending that future scholars
apply his observations to the evolution of science fiction between 1940
and 1975, to "premodern" science fiction, and to the other media of the
1930s.

PC 214. CLARESON, THOMAS D., ed. Many Futures, Many Worlds: Theme and
        Form in Science Fiction. Kent, Ohio: Kent State University
        Press, 1977. 303 pp.
Clareson's compilation of essays places science fiction within the literary
tradition of "unknown lands"--a form of writing which encompasses the
medieval travel book and the scientific romance--and argues that science
fiction is "not solely of this century." Philosophical essays comment
on the scientific basis of science fiction as well as on the genre as
"fictive history" and theological speculation. Several contributors analyze the literary and historical significance of character development
and specific settings, as in the portrayal of "lost lands and lost races,"
of oppressive governments, and of the role of women. Casey Fredericks
writes on the revival of ancient myths, Gary Wolfe on iconography, and
Patricia Warrick on man-machine relationships. The volume concludes with
writer Samuel Delany's recommendations concerning the critical methods
appropriate to an analysis of the genre.

PC 215. CLARESON, THOMAS D., ed. SF: The Other Side of Realism; Essays
        on Modern Fantasy and Science Fiction. Bowling Green, Ohio:
        Bowling Green University Popular Press, 1971. 356 pp.
Designed to "celebrate" the first decade of the MLA Seminar on Science
Fiction and of the Seminar's newsletter (Extrapolation), this anthology
establishes a dialogue between scholars--who cautiously recognize the
genre's "narrow critical and academic respectability because of its concerns with utopian and dystopian themes"--and "afficionados"--who traditionally share their experiences in the "subculture" of "fanzines," conventions, and specialist publishing houses. The compilation reprints essays

and notes from the 1960s to demonstrate the variety of approaches applicable to the genre: science fiction authors, including Samuel Delany and Norman Spinrad, reflect on the craft of their contemporaries; a number of academic contributors illuminate the philosophical or mythological dimensions of works by Edward Bellamy, Isaac Asimov, and Kurt Vonnegut, Jr.; other scholars--H. Bruce Franklin, Richard Mullen, and Mark Hillegas--apply historical and cultural perspectives.

PC 216. CLARESON, THOMAS D., ed. Voices for the Future: Essays on Major Science Fiction Writers, Volume One. Bowling Green, Ohio: Bowling Green University Popular Press, 1976. 283 pp.

Clareson describes this collection of essays as a selective analysis of specific authors "who have gained academic attention--at least in the classroom." Investigating major writers whose careers had begun by 1945, this compilation opens with Jack Williamson's reminiscences of H. G. Wells, Olaf Stapledon, and Arthur Clarke. Other pieces identify traditions shaping the artistry of American literary figures: the heritage of Hebraic and New England Calvinism is found in Isaac Asimov's Foundation series; Robert Heinlein's "adolescent dreams" of power and freedom are equated with our frontier past; Ray Bradbury's skepticism toward mechanization is placed within the national mainstream. Clareson's volume concludes with a discussion of the "Swiftian Satire" of Kurt Vonnegut, Jr., the writer benefitting most from the interest in science fiction on college campuses.

PC 217. CLARESON, THOMAS D., ed. Voices for the Future: Essays on Major Science Fiction Writers, Volume Two. Bowling Green, Ohio: Bowling Green University Popular Press, 1979. 208 pp.

This second volume of interpretive essays designed for students and teachers of science fiction emphasizes writers who began their careers in the 1950s and played an important role in the genre's emerging academic respectability. The opening essays stress the complex influences shaping an author's work: the allusions to comparative literature and literary criticism in the work of Robert Silverberg; Philip Jose Farmer's interest in Amerindian mythology; and the short stories of Walter Miller which show a concern for biological, technological and religious issues. The remaining essays focus on the prominent writers of the 1960s, an era often characterized as cultivating a pessimistic science fiction. J. G. Ballard's apocalyptic vision is considered a necessary prerequisite for social progress, while John Brunner is appreciated for his continued faith in rationality and science, Roger Zelazny for his "affection" and "wonder" toward his characters, and Ursula Le Guin for her ethical "celebration of life."

PC 218. DELANY, SAMUEL R. The Jewel-Hinged Jaw: Notes of the Language of Science Fiction. Elizabethtown, N.J.: Dragon Press, 1977. 326 pp.

"Science Fiction," Delany observes in these essays, "is a way of casting a language shadow over coherent areas of imaginative space that would otherwise be largely inaccessible." For Delany, science fiction forms a complex matrix as: (1) a "wanted commodity" subject to an "atrophied editorial image"; (2) a unique approach to language requiring close attention to stylistic needs (the "word-beast"); (3) an experiment--undertaken notably by Thomas Disch and Joanna Russ--in symbolism. Delany uses his personal journals to describe his experiences as a black youth in Harlem and his later preoccupation with linguistics, structural anthropology, the philosophy of science, and cybernetics. Analyzing the psychology of reading, Delany comments on Ursula Le Guin's The Dispossessed, a novel which only partially departs from "mundane" fiction.

PC 219. DEL REY, LESTER. The World of Science Fiction, 1929-1976: The
        History of a Subculture. New York: Ballantine, 1979. 416 pp.
Del Rey, citing his "years of participation and study" in the "extended
family" of science fiction, records the impact of the Depression and W.W.
II, the contributions of editors such as Hugo Gernsback and John Campbell,
and the role played by world conventions, book publishers and writing
workshops in the evolution of this popular art. Del Rey's definition
of science fiction--the "attempt to deal rationally with alternate possibilities in a manner which will be entertaining"--shapes his historical emphases; as he gives cursory attention to fantasy and utopian literature, expresses skepticism about science fiction motifs found in comic
strips and television, and censures both the controversial experimentation
of the 1960s New Wave and the contemporary emulation of mainstream literature. The volume concludes with optimistic observations about science
fiction's ability to prepare Americans for "future shock" and about the
cinematic quest for a revitalized mythology in films such as Star Wars.

PC 220. DUNN, THOMAS P. and RICHARD D. EHRLICH, eds. The Mechanical God:
        Machines in Science Fiction. Westport, Conn.: Greenwood Press,
        1982. 284 pp.
This volume investigates "the increasing mechanization of life itself,"
in particular science fiction's portrayal of "mechanical people"--computers,
robots, cyborgs. Brian Aldiss's introduction establishes a literary context for this theme, and is followed by: (1) critical essays devoted
to the image of the machine in individual authors such as Karel Capek,
C. S. Lewis, Isaac Asimov, Kurt Vonnegut, Jr., Frederick Pohl, and Roger
Zelazny; (2) a brief section devoted to the treatment of the robot in
children's literature; (3) essays analyzing human-machine relationships
as depicted by a wide range of authors; and (4) a section emphasizing
the philosophical and symbolic implications of the cyborg in literature.
The anthology concludes with a list of reference guides, anthologies,
fiction, films, music, criticism and background studies.

PC 221. ERLICH, RICHARD D. and THOMAS P. DUNN, eds. Clockwork Worlds:
        Mechanized Environments in SF. Westport, Conn.: Greenwood Press,
        1983. 369 pp.
A companion volume to Dunn and Erlich's The Mechanical God (PC 220), this
anthology emphasizes mechanization as a "metaphorical" phenomenon rather
than as a portrayal of "literal machines." Arthur Lewis's introduction
outlines the political and literary history of the theme of mechanization.
Part I, "Prototype and Archetype," provides interpretations of Dante,
Bellamy, and Wells as authors of "classic" dystopian literature. The
second part discusses major modern science fiction writers, such as Robert
Heinlein, Kurt Vonnegut, Jr., Philip K. Dick, and Harlan Ellison. Part
III introduces a "variety of viewpoints, methodological approaches, special
interests," among them images of the female computer, the dehumanization
of social welfare, science fiction films, and a structural analysis of
mythic portrayals of mechanization. The volume includes an annotated
listing of works--both critical and fictional--pertinent to the study
of automated futures.

PC 222. ESCHBACH, LLOYD ARTHUR, ed. Of Worlds Beyond: The Science of
        Science Writing. Reading, Pa.: Fantasy Press, 1947. 96 pp.
Eschbach describes his essays as a "handbook" for writing and selling
science fiction, which has evolved from its suspect status in the pulps
to become "the fiction of the Atomic Age." Providing brief biographies
of each contributor, the volume begins with Robert Heinlein's contention
that science fiction should not celebrate a "Glorious Technological Future"
nor indulge in "costume dramas" if it is to achieve the "bit pay" of
"general fiction magazines"; rather it must extrapolate "established facts"
to reveal how human beings cope with the dilemmas of new situations.

Other contributors include Jack Williamson, A. E. Van Vogt, L. Sprague de Camp, and "Doc" Smith. Finally, John Campbell, editor of Astounding, contends that science fiction represents "a prophetic application of the known," a maturing literature capable of becoming a "form of applied psychology" and "a science of sociology."

PC 223. FRANKLIN, H. BRUCE. Future Perfect: American Science Fiction of the Nineteenth Century. New York: Oxford University Press, 1966. 402 pp.
Primarily an anthology of 19th-century American short fiction, this volume includes introductory remarks encouraging the study of the "most important writers" and their relationship to science fiction. Describing science fiction as an offshoot of the 19th-century romance, Franklin analyzes the contributions of Edgar Allan Poe and Nathaniel Hawthorne in defining both the genre's role--to "present reality in terms of a credible hypothetical invention . . . extrapolated from that reality"--and its significance--to transcend the status quo more effectively than does literary Realism. Franklin organizes his anthology topically: Automata, Marvelous Inventions, "Into the Psyche," Space and Time Travel. While he includes some discussion of authors neglected by scholars (for example, Fitz-James O'Brien), the emphasis is on such major figures as Melville, Bellamy, Bierce, and Twain. For Franklin, the study of science fiction provides insight not only into 19th-century American society, but "into the predictions, expectations, and fantasies of the present."

PC 224. FRANKLIN, H. BRUCE. Robert A. Heinlein: America as Science Fiction. New York: Oxford University Press, 1980. 232 pp.
Though a Marxist literary critic, Franklin does not criticize Heinlein for his seemingly "right-wing" beliefs; rather, he attributes the writer's skepticism toward governmental authority to his growing up in a Midwest beset by aggressive corporate capitalism. Tracing the significant stages of Heinlein's career, Franklin discusses the tales contributed to John Campbell's Astounding, remarks on the implications of Heinlein's juvenile science fiction for its young reading audience, and explores Stranger in a Strange Land as a reflection both of Heinlein's psychology and of an American culture which embraced the novel as a cult phenomenon. Franklin concludes with an analysis of The Number of the Beast, a complex work representing Heinlein's return after a considerable hiatus.

PC 225. FREDERICKS, CASEY. The Future of Eternity: Mythologies of Science Fiction and Fantasy. Bloomington: Indiana University Press, 1982. 229 pp.
Fredericks describes his "comprehensive essay" as the work of a "professional classicist," responsive to "my own time and culture" and recommending "a comparative basis for the impact and importance of both SF and myth." Fredericks considers biblical and Greek myths--with an emphasis upon Prometheus and Odysseus--in order to dramatize the "rich ecology" of underrated works of science fiction and fantasy. Arguing that such scholars as David Ketterer have overemphasized the archaic nature of myth, Fredericks contends that a modern concern for cosmology, heroic fantasy, and the primitive--in the works of Fritz Leiber, Roger Zelazny, and Philip Jose Farmer--proves useful by "energizing and organizing our thoughts toward an as yet unrealized potential in man." Science fiction, by portraying encounters between man and superman, man and machine, man and alien, may serve to heal the split between the "two cultures" of scientific speculation and myth-inspired narration.

PC 226. GRIFFITHS, JOHN. Three Tomorrows: American, British and Soviet
Science Fiction. Totowa, N.J.: Barnes & Noble, 1980. 217 pp.
Griffiths contends that science fiction functions as a suggestive "litmus
test," communicating "certain things about social trends and about the
role of science in the development of different societies." Having worked
in England, the U.S., and the Soviet Union, he invokes the principles
of the sociology of knowledge to generalize about the differing portrayals
of disaster narratives, utopias and dystopias, cybernetics, and aliens
in the literature of the three cultures. Griffiths discovers that American
science fiction, with its faith in the superhero, celebrates an extreme
form of individualism and displays fascist tendencies; that British writers
propose a more modest hope for personal salvation through human group
behavior; and that Soviet authors perceive their works as an "instrument
of policy" for the collective state. Griffiths regrets the contemporary
willingness to deny the authority of scientific thought, and the attendant
loss of confidence in human autonomy.

PC 227. GUNN, JAMES. Alternate Worlds: The Illustrated History of Science
Fiction. Englewood Cliffs, N.J.: Prentice-Hall, 1975. 256 pp.
Gunn's emphasis is not on "isolated masterpieces," but on "basic" science
fiction works that have demonstrated the genre's impact upon the "public's
mind." Recapitulating his own experiences as a reader, he proposes to
"incorporate within an adult vision the ingenuous eyes of discovery."
He identifies science fiction as "mutated fantasy" shaped by the Industrial
Revolution, and perceives the genre to be responding significantly to
the "future shock" of the atomic era. Introducing each chapter with an
intellectual, economic, and technological context, Gunn pays considerable
attention to the premodern writings of Shelley, Verne, and others, and
addresses the role of pulp magazine editors, fan clubs, and world conventions in anticipating the expansion of science fiction into paperbacks,
films, and television. Gunn predicts that the shift from the "ghetto"
era to the diversified markets of contemporary fiction signals a new cycle
in the history of the genre.

PC 228. HASSLER, DONALD. Comic Tones in Science Fiction: The Art of
Compromise with Nature. Westport, Conn.: Greenwood Press, 1982.
143 pp.
A student of the Enlightenment, Hassler reflects upon the sensibility
shared by artists and intellectuals of the 18th century and science fiction
writers of more recent times. Individuals of both eras had to adjust
to changes in scientific principles, respond to the ambiguities fostered
by such changes, and seek the "survival effect of the comic." Hassler
credits Freud and the "anti-elitism" of structuralism and post-structural-
ism with enabling him to establish parallels between the 18th century's
preoccupation with the loss of a "Golden Age" and the contemporary author's
use of nostalgia and irony to confront "indeterminacy." After identifying
the assumptions of the late Enlightenment and the similarities between
Jane Austen and Ursula Le Guin, Hassler focuses on the pulp tradition
of science fiction: the self-conscious humanity of Theodore Sturgeon,
the emphasis on personal responsibility found in Isaac Asimov, and the
playfulness of writers such as Hal Clement and Frederick Pohl.

PC 229. HILLEGAS, MARK. The Future as Nightmare: H. G. Wells and the
Anti-Utopians. New York: Oxford University Press, 1967.
200 pp.
This study analyzes literary works devoted to "slave citizens," state
surveillance, and defeated individualism as "indexes to the anxieties
of our age." Stressing his commitment to "quality" science fiction,
Hillegas traces the origins of anti-utopian novels in the scientific
romances of the "angry young man," H. G. Wells, and the influence of
Wells's assault against Victorian complacency upon the generation of

writers--Forster, Zamyatin, Huxley, Lewis, and Orwell--who grew to maturity
in the first decades of the 20th century. Noting that social criticism
and satire eventually "filtered down" to the American pulp magazines,
Hillegas includes a chapter on the emergence of serious science fiction
in the U.S.--in particular Frederick Pohl and Cyril Kornbluth's The Space
Merchants, Ray Bradbury's Fahrenheit 451, and, most significantly, Kurt
Vonnegut, Jr.'s Player Piano.

PC 230. KETTERER, DAVID. New Worlds for Old: The Apocalyptic Imagination,
         Science Fiction, and American Literature. Garden City, N.Y.:
         Anchor Press, 1974. 347 pp.
Ketterer proposes to "open up" science fiction in an "explicatory manner
comparable in detail and rigor" to the investigation of classic authors,
and in the process to demonstrate that science fiction is as "endemically
American" as the Western novel. Comparing 20th-century science fiction
with such authors as Poe, Melville, Bellamy, Brown, and Twain, Ketterer
focuses upon three kinds of apocalyptic imagination: (1) the visionary
and mythic traditions found in Ursula Le Guin's The Left Hand of Darkness;
(2) the sociological, often satiric, emphases of utopian and dystopian
literature (for example, Walter Miller's Canticle for Leibowitz); and
(3) the philosophical dimensions offering new and radical perspectives,
as in Philip K. Dick's Man in the High Castle. Ketterer considers that
Kurt Vonnegut, Jr., embodies a successful blending of science fiction
and mainstream literature, an integration of the "satiric, philosophical
and visionary" strands of the apocalyptic tradition.

PC 231. KNIGHT, DAMON. The Futurians. New York: John Day, 1977.
         276 pp.
This history of the influential science fiction club of the late 1930s
and early 1940s examines the origins, growth, and disbandment of "a kind
of subculture," a "group of hungry young science fiction fans and would-
be writers" with "their own communal dwellings, their folklore, songs,
games, even their own mock religion." Knight traces the founding of the
Futurians to the family backgrounds of its initial members--including
Isaac Asimov, Frederick Pohl, Cyril Kornbluth, and Donald Wollheim--and
to the context of the Depression and the rise of European totalitarianism.
The volume also considers the origins and roles of later participants--
James Blish, Judith Merril, and Knight himself--and then pursues briefly
the successes and failures of individual members after 1945. Speculating
on the club's demise (and on the motives for its founding), Knight suggests
that the lonely childhood of many participants, the feeling of being "under-
dogs," and the sense of poverty and politics characterizing the Depression
ceased to be of major importance after W.W. II.

PC 232. KNIGHT, DAMON. In Search of Wonder: Essays on Modern Science
         Fiction. 1956; Rev. ed. Chicago: Advent, 1967. 306 pp.
Anthony Boucher's introductory remarks assert that Knight was science
fiction's pioneering professional critic, achieving a middle ground between
"scholarly distaste" and the undiscriminating enthusiasm of the "fanzines."
Knight argues that science fiction is "a field of literature worth taking
seriously," that "ordinary critical standards" of style, construction,
coherence and "sanity" may be applied meaningfully. Admitting that science
fiction frequently deserves its suspect reputation, Knight nonetheless
applauds writers such as Robert Heinlein, Isaac Asimov and Theodore
Sturgeon for conveying an "undiminished wonder at the mystery which surrounds us." Knight includes a number of post-1955 reviews and comments--
an investigation of "decadents" (for example, Philip Dick) and "amphibians"
(Kurt Vonnegut, Jr.), as well as an appraisal of contemporary British
writers and of H. Bruce Franklin's literary history, Future Perfect (PC
223)--in order to show the growing sophistication that followed the "boom"
period of the early 1950s.

PC 233. KNIGHT, DAMON, ed. Turning Points: Essays on the Art of Science Fiction. New York: Harper & Row, 1977. 303 pp.
This compilation emphasizes critical pieces from the 1950s, the decade immediately preceding academic attention to the genre, when criticism was "unencumbered by outside help (or, in most cases, by any formal training in literature)." Knight has selected "highly partisan" essays representing a "glorious collision of credos" by authors and editors who "joyfully invented SF criticism ab initio." The collection reprints definitions of the genre (by Isaac Asimov and Robert Heinlein), and discussions of its relationship to scientific practice (John Campbell) and religious revelation (C. S. Lewis and James Blish), as well as autobiographical reflections by Theodore Sturgeon and Arthur Clarke. In order to provide a comprehensive view of this "turbulent and perplexing field," Knight includes chapters from historical studies (by H. Bruce Franklin, Kingsley Amis, and Brian Aldiss), pieces found in the Bulletin of the Science Fiction Writers of America, and two original essays (by Knight himself) "to fill in the gaps."

PC 234. KREUZIGER, FREDERICK A. Apocalypse and Science Fiction: A Dialectic of Religious and Secular Sorteriologies. Chico, Calif.: Scholars Press, 1982. 247 pp.
Kreuziger views science fiction as "secular apocalyptic literature" illuminating the relationship between theology and contemporary writing. The text begins with a review of the critical literature based on the self-perceptions of science fiction's community of scholars. Looking at previous studies by James Bailey, Kingsley Amis, and David Ketterer, as well as at theories of structural fabulation, Kreuziger finds evidence that apocalyptic fiction is a literature of hope for and by individuals dissatisfied with the present and therefore longing for a new age. Applying a structural analysis to apocalyptic writing, he discovers an emphasis on salvation and deliverance that distinguishes this subgenre as the highest form of science fiction. The religious and secular "sorteriologies" pursued by Kreuziger include revelation, gnosticism, the myths of beginnings and endings, social and political alternatives, and the creation of future history.

PC 235. LE GUIN, URSULA K. The Language of the Night: Essays on Fantasy and Science Fiction. Edited by Susan Wood. New York: Putnam, 1979. 270 pp.
Le Guin's essays, speeches, introductions to her novels, and remarks at writing workshops provide the reflections of a practitioner of fantasy and "its modern offshoot," science fiction. Suggesting that science fiction abandon the formulaic habits of its pulp-magazine origins, Le Guin not only calls for a sensitive exploration of gender roles and human aggression, but, as a "petty bourgeois anarchist," recommends that any legitimate fiction should avoid an unthinking commitment to sociology and "the lure of the pulpit." She describes her own writing, which has been influenced by Jungian psychology, as a "translation" of nonverbal dream symbols into conscious language. Le Guin deplores the utilitarian excesses of America's Puritan heritage and identifies a subtler ethical function for fantasy and myth: to distance us from everyday routines, to depict "internal journeys" toward maturity, wisdom, and the responsibilities of freedom. The volume also includes a checklist of Le Guin's interpreters and published works.

PC 236. MALZBERG, BARRY N. The Engines of the Night: Science Fiction in the Eighties. Garden City, N.Y.: Doubleday, 1982. 199 pp.
Malzberg describes science fiction as a genre that emphasizes the encroachment of technology and its subsequent social repercussions. In this collection of essays, representing personal reflections and critical analysis, he evaluates some high points in the continuing evolution of science fic-

tion and describes its contemporary nature as necessarily conservative. Malzberg also discusses sex in science fiction, editorial decline, the role of ambivalence, the convention circuit, America's shifting political climate, tips for writers, archetypal plots, personal practices and preferences. He also pays tribute to certain authors (for example, John W. Campbell and Mark Clifton) and, in particular, to the generation of social satirists who made 1950s science fiction distinctively successful.

PC 237. MEYERS, WALTER EARL. Aliens and Linguists: Language Study and Science Fiction. Athens: University of Georgia Press, 1980. 257 pp.
Meyers responds to the relative linguistic "poverty" of works of science fiction by exploring the philosophical and technical challenges in the depiction of encounters with "aliens," monkeys, marine animals, machines, and representatives from other planets. Meyers argues that most American science fiction has circumvented these challenges by resorting to the convenient devices of automatic translators and telepathy. Surveying the erratic history of formal linguistics in science fiction, he discusses the unfortunate influence of Alfred Korzybski's "General Semantics" on authors such as Robert Heinlein. Meyers concludes his volume with a discussion of how writers of utopian and dystopian literature—George Orwell, B. F. Skinner, Ursula K. Le Guin—possess a unique opportunity in their "universe of discourse" to "say something about language, something liberating, and tolerant and entertaining."

PC 238. MOSKOWITZ, SAMUEL. Explorers of the Infinite: Shapers of Science Fiction. Cleveland, Ohio: Wald, 1963. 353 pp.
Moskowitz traces the emergence of science fiction by focusing on the important writers from the 17th century to 1940. The volume discusses the "major molders of the form" within the context of its "total impact" on television, film, radio, comic books, and paperbacks. Profiles on writers such as Edgar Allan Poe, Arthur Conan Doyle, H. G. Wells, Karel Capek, and Hugo Gernsback evaluate each author's contributions to science fiction and also serve to illustrate the relationship of the genre to mainstream literature.

PC 239. MOSKOWITZ, SAMUEL. The Immortal Storm. Atlanta, Ga.: Science Fiction Organization Press, 1954. 269 pp.
Originally published as a series of articles for fan magazines, this work provides details of the early history of science fiction. Moskowitz offers an anecdotal account of the feuds and affairs of science fiction "fandom" from the turn of the century to the first world convention in 1939. Emphasizing the role of Hugo Gernsback, who formulated the concept of fandom as a means for boosting circulation figures, Moskowitz not only introduces the rules of this subculture, but also chronicles the institutional development revealed in its clubs, associations, conventions, and magazines.

PC 240. MOSKOWITZ, SAMUEL. Seekers of Tomorrow: Masters of Modern Science Fiction. Cleveland, Ohio: World, 1966. 441 pp.
Moskowitz offers biographies of twenty-one science fiction writers in order to provide a "webwork" history of the genre from 1940 to 1965. He sees the "modern period" as characterized by a shift in emphasis from simple adventure stories to a more sophisticated and complex exploration of this literary form. Beginning with the influence of John Campbell in 1939, and concluding with the "taboo breaker" Philip Jose Farmer, Moskowitz discusses the major contributors to the genre during the modern era.

PC 241. MULLEN, R. D. and DARKO SUVIN, eds. Science-Fiction Studies:
         Selected Articles on Science Fiction 1973-1975. Boston: Gregg
         Press, 1976. 304 pp.
This sampling of contributions to Science-Fiction Studies during its first
two years of publication stresses structural, semiotic, and Brechtian
literary analyses illustrative of the editors' assumption that "consistently intelligent formalist criticism leads to consistently intelligent
sociological criticism." The journal often served as a forum for science
fiction writers (Stanislaw Lem, Joanna Russ, Ursula Le Guin, Brian Aldiss)
to reflect upon the theoretical implications of the genre, as well as
an opportunity for critics (H. Bruce Franklin, Frederic Jameson, Robert
Scholes) to exchange opinions on the merits of a Marxist approach to the
genre and its interpretation. Identifying the two poles of science fiction,
the volume reprints the special issues devoted to Philip K. Dick, the
"romantic" who envisions the "breakdown" of cultural taboos, and Le Guin,
the "classical" author who calls for a "collectivist system" and "integration."

PC 242. MYERS, ROBERT E., ed. The Intersection of Science Fiction and
         Philosophy: Critical Studies. Westport, Conn.: Greenwood Press,
         1983. 262 pp.
These seventeen essays explore connections between science fiction and
philosophy in the conceptual frameworks upon which literary narratives
are based. Part I establishes some useful working definitions of philosophy and science fiction, while Part II concentrates on the fundamental
concepts of time and space. Part III takes up the themes of nature and
human nature; Part IV pursues the implications of "being a person," and
includes a philosophical interpretation of Star Trek. According to the
contributors to Part V, perspectives of the alien can lead to insights
about the self; and Part VI emphasizes the complex role of language in
communication. The remaining two sections cover a variety of topics:
feminist science fiction, medical morals, heroes, the sublime, and theism.

PC 243. NICHOLLS, PETER, ed. Science Fiction at Large. New York: Harper
         & Row, 1976. 224 pp.
This compilation of lectures delivered at London's Institute of Contemporary Arts proposes to place its audience, "the silent majority," in
the "interface area . . . where science fiction meets real life." Along
with the reflections of science fiction writers--Ursula Le Guin, Thomas
Disch, Robert Sheckley, among others--the volume also includes the observations of the futurist Alvin Toffler and the psychologist Edward de Bono.
The lectures address the capabilities and practices of the genre in exploring the diversified issues of history, science, education, and the portrayal of human character and thought processes. While noting that science
fiction has "insinuated" itself by "osmosis, into the very style and air
of our lives," Nicholls remarks that the genre has reached a "stage of
discrimination," where its supporters may cease "missionary work" and
make it a great literature of metaphor articulating the hopes and fears
of modern society.

PC 244. NICOLSON, MARJORIE HOPE. Voyages to the Moon. New York:
         Macmillan, 1948. 297 pp.
Challenging the assumption that 19th- and 20th-century science fiction
writers initiated the depiction of space flight, Nicolson traces the long
literary heritage of this form of writing. She indicates that "Cosmic
Voyages" to the moon and to the stars have existed in literature from
Lucian to Cyrano de Bergerac to the present time. The volume covers a
substantial tradition which has influenced the works of Edgar Allan Poe,
Jules Verne, H. G. Wells, and C. S. Lewis.

PC 245. PARRINDER, PATRICK, ed. Science Fiction: A Critical Guide.
London: Longman, 1979. 238 pp.
Parrinder's collection of essays investigates the genre as "a small and
recently colonized planet" within "the solar system of literary fictions,
the galaxy of modern culture, the universe of human life as a whole."
Part I, "Early Landmarks," traces science fiction's literary evolution
up through the works of Jules Verne and H. G. Wells, while Part II analyzes
the "formative traditions" of utopian literature and of the scientific
world view. Four essays in Part III, "Science Fiction Today," clarify
trends of American science fiction since 1945: T. A. Shippey discusses
1950s magazine fiction as a serious "cover" for controversial social issues;
J. A. Sutherland relates the expanding consumption of science fiction
to political, sexual, academic and marketing changes of the 1960s; Scott
Sanders explains the genre's "disappearance of character" as a reflection
of modern society's regimentation; Tom Woodman addresses the emphasis
upon religion as an important response to the contemporary world.

PC 246. PIERCE, HAZEL BEASLEY. A Literary Symbiosis: Science Fiction/
Fantasy Mystery. Westport, Conn.: Greenwood Press, 1983.
255 pp.
Pierce explores how "idea-bound" science fiction and "situation-oriented"
mystery fiction may achieve a productive relationship because of their
compatible interests in logic and scientific methods as responses to the
disruption of the status quo. Part I analyzes Hal Clement's Needle, Alfred
Bester's The Demolished Man, and Isaac Asimov's Caves of Steel as "classical" case studies of a successful symbiosis and of a reading public "skeptical of easy solutions to any human problem." The remaining sections
discuss numerous novels, and the interaction of mystery fiction with the
"host" genre of science fiction and fantasy: the police procedural, the
"thriller," the Gothic mystery. Pierce also introduces literary motifs
(the "picaresque" hero), best-selling novelists (Ian Fleming and John
Le Carre) and theoretical observations (the supernatural modes of Gothic
fiction) to identify traditions that have contributed, or will contribute,
to a meaningful symbiosis.

PC 247. PLATT, CHARLES. Dream Makers: The Uncommon People Who Write
Science Fiction. New York: Berkley Books, 1980. 284 pp.
Platt's interviews with prominent American and British science fiction
writers support his contention that how a story is "conceived, written,
and published" cannot be divorced from "the commercial constraints, financial pressures, and other influences poisoning or fertilizing the creative
process." Introducing each author with "quick impressions" of "life-style
and environment," Platt encourages his subjects to reflect upon childhood
experiences, stylistic and narrative intentions, and the temptations of
the genre's current marketability. A reviewer-participant of the British
science fiction scene of the late 1960s and early 1970s, Platt visits
members of John Campbell's generation (Isaac Asimov, A. E. Van Vogt),
converses with those who achieved notoriety in the 1950s (Kurt Vonnegut,
Jr., Alfred Bester), describes the distinctive habits of the American
New Wave (Harlan Ellison), and exchanges reminiscences and expectations
with his peers--Michael Moorcock, John Brunner, Brian Aldiss--who shaped
the direction of contemporary British science fiction.

PC 248. PLATT, CHARLES. Dream Makers, Volume II: The Uncommon Men and
Women Who Write Science Fiction. New York: Berkley Books, 1983.
300 pp.
This volume not only accentuates science fiction's increasing marketability,
but also stresses the unfortunate consequences of the genre's commercial
success: while the right-wing Jerry Pournelle and his "high-tech" co-
author Larry Niven reach a large reading public, the literary ingenuity
of a John Sladek goes largely unnoticed. In Platt's second collection

of interviews (see PC 247), L. Ron Hubbard, Arthur C. Clarke, and Donald Wollheim represent voices of the older generation; remarks from William Burroughs and Alvin Toffler suggest an expansive definition of "science fiction"; and women authors--Joan Vinge, Joanna Russ, James Tiptree, Jr. (Alice Sheldon)--indicate the increasing staturs of female writers.

PC 249. RABKIN, ERIC S., MARTIN H. GREENBERG, and JOSEPH D. OLANDER, eds. The End of the World. Carbondale: Southern Illinois University Press, 1983. 204 pp.
Rabkin's introduction to this collection of essays interprets stories depicting the end of the world as individual wish-fulfillment on one level, and as a judgment of social values on another. Gary K. Wolfe considers cataclysm as a chance for a new beginning, while Robert Plank explores the image of the lone survivor and the psychological needs it answers. In "Ambiguous Apocalypse," Robert Galbreath investigates the question of transcendence in speculative fiction. The impact of a cyclical view of history on literary works of eschatology is the focus of W. Warren Wagar, who also reinforces Wolfe's emphasis on "the fresh start." The final two essays discuss the forces often identified as responsible for triggering a holocaust, with Brian Stableford stressing the role of "Man-Made Catastrophes" and Wagar "The Rebellion of Nature."

PC 250. RABKIN, ERIC S., MARTIN H. GREENBERG, and JOSEPH D. OLANDER, eds. No Place Else: Explorations in Utopian and Dystopian Fiction. Carbondale: Southern Illinois University Press, 1983. 278 pp.
These essays, by one Russian, seven British, and five American writers, explore literary interpretations of utopia and its antithesis, dystopia. Rabkin maintains that although themes of utopia might be seen as progressive planning for future development, they must also be understood as urges for the orderliness of childhood innocence, and as literary endeavors to console readers trapped in the present. Among the American works considered, B. F. Skinner's Walden Two is evaluated as a mixture of behaviorism and utopia, Kurt Vonnegut, Jr.'s Player Piano as an example of the threat of a technology directed by human nature, and Ray Bradbury's Fahrenheit 451 as an extrapolation from the socio-historical situation of the early 1950s. The concluding essays portray Robert Silverberg's The World Inside as a "cautionary dystopia" and Ursula Le Guin's The Dispossessed as an "ambiguous utopia."

PC 251. RILEY, DICK, ed. Critical Encounters: Writers and Themes in Science Fiction. New York: Ungar, 1978. 184 pp.
Intended for both the scholar and the fan, these nine essays are by academicians and free-lance authors. As the subtitle suggests, this collection focuses both on specific works--Frank Herbert's Dune, Arthur C. Clarke's Childhood's End, Robert Heinlein's Stranger in a Strange Land, Samuel Delany's The Einstein Intersection and Ursula Le Guin's The Left Hand of Darkness--and on specific themes: the use of robots in Isaac Asimov's works, Theodore Sturgeon's style, the role of invasion in Ray Bradbury's stories, and feminist science fiction.

PC 252. ROSE, MARK. Alien Encounters: Anatomy of Science Fiction. Cambridge, Mass.: Harvard University Press, 1981. 216 pp.
Rose identifies "the human in relation to the nonhuman" as the central narrative concern of science fiction. Tracing the genre's emergence to the romance of the early 19th century, he observes that science fiction, which once provided a middle ground between fantasy and reality, has increasingly explored the realm of metaphor. Rose addresses four chapters to important works in order to illustrate his heuristic categories: (1) "Space"--focusing on Journey to the Center of the Earth, War of the Worlds and Solaris; (2) "Time"--discussing the relationship of novels by H. G. Wells, Olaf Stapledon, Philip K. Dick, and J. G. Ballard to Darwinian

concepts of evolution; (3) "Machine"--comparing Stanley Kubrick's 2001, and the opinions of Ruskin, Carlyle, and Marx, and (4) "Monster"--which provides a general discussion of the ambiguous definition of selfhood manifested in the growing nostalgic and apocalyptic moods of science fiction.

PC 253. ROSE, MARK, ed. Science Fiction: A Collection of Critical Essays. Englewood Cliffs, N.J.: Prentice-Hall, 1976. 174 pp.
Rose's introduction applauds science fiction as a shift away from "meticulous psychological realism," and as the "characteristic romance form of the scientific age." His anthology brings together critical models that do not condemn such literature for its one-dimensional characters and its erratic record of prediction, but rather recognize its "quasi-religious mood of awe" and its allegorical dimensions. Part I ("Backgrounds") stresses the intellectual origins of science fiction and includes selections from Kingsley Amis's New Maps of Hell (PC 201) and Robert Scholes's Structural Fabulation (PC 255). Part II ("Theory") reprints Darko Suvin's discussion of "cognitive estrangement" and Eric Rabkin's distinctions between science fiction and fantasy. Part III ("Approaches") introduces a variety of specialized orientations (for example, Susan Sontag's analysis of science fiction movies, David Ketterer's exploration of American apocalyptic literature) and closes with John Huntington's observations regarding the conservative dimensions of visions of the future.

PC 254. SARGENT, PAMELA, ed. Women of Wonder: Science Fiction Stories by Women About Women. New York: Vintage Books, 1974. 363 pp.
Sargent's introduction to her anthology of twelve science fiction stories indicates the unique nature of a volume devoted to women writers whose female protagonists play an important function: "One can wonder why a literature that prides itself on exploring alternatives or assumptions counter to what we normally believe has not been more concerned with the roles of women in the future." Sargent offers a brief history of female science fiction writers and the past portrayal of female characters in a genre largely dominated by male authors. The writers selected by Sargent--among them Ursula Le Guin, Kate Wilhelm, Joanna Russ, Vonda McIntyre, and Ann McCaffrey--are included for their depiction of changing sex roles, thereby illustrating that science fiction "can provide women with possible scenarios for their own future development."

PC 255. SCHOLES, ROBERT. Structural Fabulation: An Essay on the Fiction of the Future. Notre Dame, Ind.: University of Notre Dame Press, 1975. 111 pp.
Describing these four revised Notre Dame lectures as "a kind of prolegomena to the serious reading of what we loosely call 'science fiction,'" Scholes urges his fellow teachers to introduce the genre into their classes, for to "live well in the present, to live decently and humanely, we must see into the future." The first two lectures are of a "polemical" and "speculative" nature, devoted to the contemporary "loss of faith" in both fantasy and realism and to the emergence of the "didactic romance" or "fabulation" as a literary form in which a radical discontinuity with the realm of experience ("sublimation") and an awakened perception of reality ("cognition") may become integrated. The remaining two lectures illustrate the application of Scholes's theories to specific cases of "cognitive estrangement": Daniel Keyes's Flowers for Algernon, Frank Herbert's Dune, Olaf Stapledon's The Star Maker, and, most significantly, Ursula Le Guin's Earthsea Trilogy and The Left Hand of Darkness.

PC 256. SCHOLES, ROBERT and ERIC RABKIN. Science Fiction: History--
Science--Vision. New York: Oxford University Press, 1977.
258 pp.
Introducing students to the history, scientific assumptions, and literary
significance of science fiction, this text illustrates the genre's growing
academic stature during the 1970s. The "brief literary history" contrasts
the adventure tales of a "pulpy America" with the innovations of a "political Europe"--Capek, Stapledon, Huxley--and the theological speculations
of C. S. Lewis; American writers of the 1960s and 1970s--Philip K. Dick,
Thomas Disch, Samuel Delany, Joanna Russ--are compared favorably with
mainstream literature. The text discusses the scientific principles and
mythic archetypes informing a variety of novels and short fiction, and
also considers the genre's relationship to fantasy and utopian literature
as well as its innovative treatment of sex and race. The final section
offers an analysis of ten "representative" novels--among them A Canticle
for Leibowitz and The Left Hand of Darkness--which are particularly suggestive of the "literary merits" and "the problems, issues and techniques
that have animated this form of literature."

PC 257. The Science Fiction Novel: Imagination and Social Criticism.
Chicago: Advent, 1959. 128 pp.
This publication of 1957 University of Chicago lectures by four writers--
Robert Heinlein, Cyril Kornbluth, Alfred Bester, and Robert Bloch--
represents an important stage in the evolution of science fiction's literary reputation. While Basil Davenport's introduction remarks upon the
lecturers' frequent disenchantment with existing science fiction, much
of the skepticism derives from their varied and high expectations:
Heinlein argues that the genre, the "only fictional medium capable of interpreting the changing head-long rush of modern life," proves far more challenging than mainstream literature; Kornbluth despairs that science fiction
has not matched the demonstrable impact of Uncle Tom's Cabin or The Jungle;
Bester, in a contrasting vein, calls for a literature addressed to the
"modern Renaissance Man . . . full of romantic curiosity and impractical
speculation"; Bloch suggests that science fiction may yet abandon its
devotion to suspect heroism or temporary reform for the cultivation of
"better citizens."

PC 258. SLUSSER, GEORGE E., GEORGE R. GUFFEY, and MARK ROSE, eds. Bridges
to Science Fiction. Carbondale: Southern Illinois University
Press, 1980. 168 pp.
Comprised of papers delivered at the first Eaton Conference on Science
Fiction and Fantasy Literature, this work constitutes the opening volume
of "Alternatives," a series designed "to serve the growing critical audience of science fiction, fantastic fiction, and speculative fiction."
The compilation consists primarily of contributions from literary scholars
who perceive science fiction as shaped by "the mainstream of our cultural
inheritance," rather than as a "wholly independent phenomenon." Opening
with Harry Levin's historical overview of the humanistic response to the
genre, the collection provides essays devoted to science fiction's relationships to medieval cosmology, to the philosophy of science, and to
the religious quest for revelation and transcendence. The volume then
pursues the genre's similarities to fairy tales, epic storytelling, and
the Gothic novel. George Slusser concludes with a structural analysis
of the universal human need to understand the past through speculations
about the future.

PC 259. SLUSSER, GEORGE E., ERIC S. RABKIN, and ROBERT SCHOLES, eds.
Coordinates: Placing Science Fiction and Fantasy. Carbondale:
Southern Illinois University Press, 1983. 209 pp.
These papers from the third annual Eaton Conference on Science Fiction
and Fantasy Literature seek to redress the "formlessness" of a growing
scholarly field and provide "well-defined analytical contexts" for achieving an "interactive resonance." Leslie Fiedler's observations, applauding science fiction for a "mythopoeic power" which transcends the conventional
standards of "linguistic subtlety," serve as a keynote for the volume.
The editors include papers of a general philosophical nature—the conflicting world views in novels by Jules Verne, Isaac Asimov, and Frank
Herbert—as well as essays addressing specific historical and ethical
contexts: the ideological implications of works by Robert Heinlein, Samuel
Delany and Ayn Rand; the publishing histories of Ray Bradbury's Fahrenheit
451 and the 1939 issues of Astounding; and the gender stereotypes of H.
Rider Haggard's She. The volume concludes with a discussion of the existential interaction of the self and the mythopoeic appeal of science fiction and fantasy.

PC 260. STAICAR, TOM, ed. The Feminine Eye: Science Fiction and the
Women Who Write It. New York: Ungar, 1982. 148 pp.
Aimed especially at scholars involved with the development of women's
studies, these nine essays examine the alternate realities created by
feminist science fiction writers, and their consideration of new possibilities for sex roles, child rearing, and matriarchal dominance. Contributors,
drawn from academe and from science fiction fandom, analyze the following
authors: Leigh Brackett, C. L. Moore, Andre Norton, C. J. Cherryh, James
Tiptree Jr. (Alice Sheldon), Suzy McKee Charnas, Marion Zimmer Bradley,
Suzette Haden Elgin, and Joan D. Vinge. Some of the themes considered
include role reversal, feminist handling of vampirism, the ethic of freedom
in Bradley's Darkover novels, and the work of Norton, Moore, and Brackett.

PC 261. SUVIN, DARKO. Metamorphoses of Science Fiction: On the Poetics
and History of a Literary Genre. New Haven: Yale University
Press, 1979. 317 pp.
Suvin's study is "an essay in definition, appreciation, and evaluation"
rather than a detailed literary history. Influenced by the theories of
Bertolt Brecht and Walter Benjamin, Suvin explores the "poetics" of a
"literature of cognitive estrangement." Remarking on the "mystifying
escapism" of most bourgeois "paraliterature," he uses science fiction
prior to H. G. Wells to illustrate his thesis that 20th-century fiction
often reflects the ideology of a mass culture and a "warfare-welfare
state." Suvin refers to science fiction as a small "fraction" existing
"above the silent surface of officially recorded culture," and analyzes
the "organized daydreams" of More, Swift, Shelley, Bellamy and Twain.
After investigating Jules Verne, the utopian speculations of Wells, and
the orientation of Russian science fiction, he concludes with the works
of Karel Capek, whose desire to "study the heroism of ideas as well as
inner simplicity" embodies Suvin's definition of meaningful science fiction.

PC 262. WAGAR, W. WARREN. Terminal Visions: The Literature of Last Things.
Bloomington: Indiana University Press, 1982. 241 pp.
Contending that we live in an "endtime," Wagar "explores the level of
intention, thought and meaning in the fiction of the end of the world."
Wagar, identifying the religious and secular origins of "terminal visions,"
explores how this perspective has permeated Western civilization since
the first decades of the 19th century. Beginning with Mary Shelley's
The Last Man (1826), he pursues the theme of a "dying culture" in a variety
of American and European authors, including Poe, Verne, London, Wells,
Capek, Stapledon, Lessing and Vonnegut.

PC 263. **WARRICK, PATRICIA S.** The Cybernetic Imagination in Science Fiction.
Cambridge, Mass.: MIT Press, 1980. 282 pp.
Warrick's introduction outlines the aims of her study: to write a history
of the sub-genre of "artificial or machine intelligence," to describe
"recurring images, patterns and meaning" in both fiction and the theoretical sciences, and to establish criteria so that scholars may arrive at
a "critical judgment of literary merit." Troubled by the "reactionary"
nature of post-W.W. II fiction devoted to computers and robots, Warrick
introduces a "systems approach" to identify three major kinds of writing:
(1) "isolated-system" fiction, investigating man-robot interaction in
a limited social environment; (2) "closed-system" fiction, offering a
dystopian view of how machines serve to enslave a society's citizenry;
and, most significantly, (3) "open-system" fiction (for example, Frank
Herbert's Destination Void), emphasizing how artificial intelligence may
enrich human existence. Warrick concludes with the work of Philip K.
Dick, which he sees as anticipating a new category, "futuristic fiction,"
which may "unite the prescientific consciousness of childhood with the
logic of scientific thought."

PC 264. **WARRICK, PATRICIA S., MARTIN H. GREENBERG,** and **JOSEPH OLANDER,**
eds. Science Fiction: Contemporary Mythology. New York: Harper
& Row, 1978. 476 pp.
This anthology, sponsored by the Science Fiction Writers of America and
the Science Fiction Research Association, represents a "cooperative undertaking of writer and critic." The volume reprints stories illustrative
of nine "mythic patterns" found within the genre, and each pattern is
introduced by authors and literary scholars identified with that specific
motif: Philip Jose Farmer co-authors the discussion of the "Remarkable
Adventure"; Isaac Asimov discusses the origins of robots in fiction;
Frederick Pohl traces the history of utopian and dystopian writing;
Patricia Warrick analyzes the ethical implications of cyborgs and androids;
and David Ketterer diagnoses the psychological appeal of apocalyptic literature. Warrick's introduction to the volume defines the relationship of
19th-century scientific models of the universe to the function of myth--
"a complex of stories which a culture regards as demonstrating the inner
meaning of the universe and of human life."

PC 265. **WILLIAMSON, JACK,** ed. Teaching Science Fiction: Education for
Tomorrow. Philadelphia: Owlswick Press, 1980. 261 pp.
This compendium of twenty-five essays indicates the growing pedagogical
interest in the genre during the 1970s. Part I considers synthesizing
studies of science and the humanities, science fiction as a component
of women's studies, and the genre's tie to literary tradition and intellectual history. Part II focuses on the role of the teacher, and on a
variety of classroom strategies in primary school and high school, and
in such diverse fields as English, the physical sciences, computer science,
psychology, religion, social and political science. Part III introduces
techniques for teaching science fiction film and concludes with a bibliography and summary of relevant library resources.

PC 266. **WILSON, ROBIN SCOTT,** ed. Those Who Can: A Science Fiction Reader.
New York: New American Library, 1973. 333 pp.
An anthology of science fiction short stories compiled by an organizer
of academic writing workshops, this volume accompanies each tale with
an account of its origin and evolution. Selecting authors on the basis
of their role as "teacher-writer," Wilson divides his collection into
six topical headings defining and exemplifying the narrative devices of
science fiction: Plot (illuminated by fictional pieces from Samuel Delany
and Jack Williamson), Character (with stories by Daniel Keyes and Harlan
Ellison), Setting (Joanna Russ, Robert Silverberg), Theme (Ursula Le Guin,
Damon Knight), Point of View (Kate Wilhelm, Robin Wilson), and Style (James

Gunn, Frederick Pohl). For Wilson, the volume's autobiographical reflections embody "an author's voyage into his own creative terra incognita."

PC 267. WOLFE, GARY K. The Known and the Unknown: The Iconography of Science Fiction. Kent, Ohio: Kent State University Press, 1979. 250 pp.
Wolfe focuses upon American and British science fiction of the late 1930s to the early 1960s, when a "somewhat inbred cadre of writers, fans and readers" gave an "unofficial seal of approval" to the major characteristics of the genre. Wolfe examines the process by which images become icons, achieve a "sense of wonder" apart from individual narratives, and prove "representative of fundamental beliefs and values" that "are embedded in our culture at large." Investigating the "ubiquitous image" of the "barrier" existing between the known and the unknown, he devotes chapters both to icons expressive of artificial or unnatural environments—the spaceship, the city, the wasteland—and to icons associated with a "distorted" humanity, such as the robot and the "monster." Wolfe suggests that scholars should now explore premodern and contemporary writers, the rituals of fandom, and such extraliterary forms as art, film, futurology and advertising for similar iconographic significance.

PC 268. WOLFE, GARY K., ed. Science Fiction Dialogues. Chicago: Academy Chicago, 1982. 227 pp.
This compilation, reflecting the objectives of the Science Fiction Research Association, illustrates the scholarly estimate of the history, present status, and future of the genre. For Wolfe, recent literature, film, and television demonstrates that science fiction has emerged from the "ghetto" to join the cultural mainstream; the genre has become legitimate, but in the process some "petrification" has taken place. Offering an historical perspective, essayists analyze the literary antecedents of H. G. Wells and Olaf Stapledon, the influence of publishing companies and of editors such as Horace Gold, and the relationship of individual authors (Hal Clement, Larry Niven) to science fiction's Golden Age. The anthology also explores feminist perspectives, the genre as a "literature of ideas," and the importance of the Pilgrim Award (granted to achievements in research). A final section provides information concerning resources, including scholarly works, international contributions, and science fiction conventions.

PC 269. WOLLHEIM, DONALD A. The Universe Makers: Science Fiction Today. New York: Harper & Row, 1971. 122 pp.
As a member of the "pioneering group, the fanatical fandom of the thirties," Wollheim admits that he is not writing conventional history, but rather a "flow of ideas" to edify "the legions of science fiction readers today." Commenting upon Verne and Wells as the founders of the genre's two major traditions, Wollheim prefers the thoughtfulness of the Wellsian heritage, and its critique of atomic warfare, pollution, and overpopulation. While he is also appreciative of the "galactic" scope of Isaac Asimov, he disapproves of Frederick Pohl and Cyril Kornbluth's cynicism as well as of John Campbell's uncritical "Vernian" acceptance of dianetics. Hopeful of finding an "overwhelming spirit" in the dark visions of younger writers such as Kurt Vonnegut, Jr. and Harlan Ellison, Wollheim concludes that "we have a capacity for survival—by our wits—that should not be underrated."

THE WESTERN

PC 270. **CAWELTI, JOHN G.** The Six-Gun Mystique. Bowling Green, Ohio: Bowling Green University Popular Press, 1971. 138 pp.
This essay defines the Western formula's basic structure--setting, characterization (in particular the portrayal of the hero), situation, plot-- and then uses divergent methods to interpret its significance in literature and, to some extent, in film. Cawelti explores the Western both as an art form, possessing its own laws, and as a cultural phenomenon. Formulaic fiction, he contends, should not be reduced to "simplistic cultural explanations" or dismissed as escapist entertainment, for the Western serves as a "social ritual," enabling individuals to play out aggressive impulses. Cawelti suggests that his analytical methods may be applied to other fictional forms which "follow a highly conventional pattern."

PC 271. **DURHAM, PHILIP** and **EVERETT JONES,** ed. The Western Story: Fact, Fiction and Myth. New York: Harcourt Brace Jovanovich, 1975. 369 pp.
Beginning with the premise that the figure of the cowboy "celebrates our past and establishes our national self-image," this compilation emphasizes the "historical fictions" of Western literature. The volume traces the evolution of the Westerner from his historical context (with Theodore Roosevelt serving as an example of the "cattleman's west of fact") to his emergence as a "mythic hero" in fictional works. Durham and Jones offer a sampling of Western writing--by Owen Wister, Jack London, Stephen Crane, Zane Grey, and Vardis Fisher, among others--in order to show how the literature contributed to the development of a mythology. In a final section, the editors offer interpretations of the West from the perspectives of literary scholarship, journalism, sociology, psychology, and history.

PC 272. **ETULAIN, RICHARD** and **MICHAEL T. MARSDEN,** eds. The Popular Western: Essays Toward a Definition. Bowling Green, Ohio: Bowling Green University Popular Press, 1974. 111 pp.
In this collection, Etulain and Marsden identify previous studies of the Western and introduce new approaches to analyzing its significance. Utilizing the methodologies of the literary critic, the historian, and the American Studies scholar, the anthology provides an overview of the development of the genre. The concept of the American West is traced through an analysis of selected authors, including Zane Grey, Vardis Fisher, Luke Short, and Jack Schaefer. Treating the Western as a viable literary form, the essayists "attempt to assess its value in understanding American culture."

PC 273. **FOLSOM, JAMES K.** The American Western Novel. New Haven, Conn.: College and University Press, 1966. 224 pp.
The meaning of the Western, Folsom contends, does not reside in anecdotal history but in the cultural myths conveying how Americans view themselves and their country; the Western is "a story about history, but not of it." Folsom discusses the influence of James Fenimore Cooper on the evolution of the genre, and stresses the aesthetic merits of works--by Owen Wister, Zane Grey, A. B. Guthrie, and others--which he considers to be the most impressive in the body of Western literature.

PC 274. **FOLSOM, JAMES K.,** ed. The Western: A Collection of Critical Essays. Englewood Cliffs, N.J.: Prentice-Hall, 1979. 177 pp.
Folsom's introduction observes that the American attitude toward the West has tended to oppose primitivism to the ambiguous merits of civilization, thereby leading to a "cultural dilemma . . . of a society that, though founded in perfection, aspired to progress." For Folsom, writers have

rarely achieved the synthesis of James Fenimore Cooper, who perceived progress fulfilling the incomplete state of the frontier. The first section of essays analyzes Western heroes and seeks to explain the popularity of this literature in terms of the "American cultural myth." The second part, "Fidelity to What?," addresses the literary West's relationship to the historical West and suggests that a mixture of fact and fiction is desirable. A third section provides a cross-cultural comparison of the American cowboy and the gaucho, illustrating that the same frontier environment does not necessarily lead to similar literary interpretations. The volume concludes with a consideration of the new historiography devoted to the Western genre.

PC 275. FRANTZ, JOE B. and JULIAN CHOATE, Jr. The American Cowboy: The Myth and the Reality. Norman: University of Oklahoma Press, 1955. 232 pp.
This study explores the three levels of the cowboy's contribution to American society: the historical, the fictional, and the folkloristic (or mythic). Frantz and Choate begin with the account of the historical cowboy, with an emphasis on the town of Abilene, Texas, the cattle drives, and the physical locales of the ranch and the range. The authors then trace the emergence of a composite figure created from the positive characteristics of many real Western heroes—their courage, code of honor, colorful dress, and superb horsemanship—as they confronted the lawlessness of society. The volume's second section investigates the evolution of the cowboy folk hero in literature, from his 19th-century image in dime novels to the elaboration of a heroic figure through Owen Wister's The Virginian and the works of Andy Adams, O. Henry, Hamlin Garland and Zane Grey. For Frantz and Choate, the cowboy remains an important aspect of the nation's culture, embodying "a living and present reality in the American folk mind."

PC 276. HARRIS, CHARLES W. and BUCK RAINEY, eds. The Cowboy: Six-Shooters, Songs and Sex. Norman: University of Oklahoma Press, 1976. 167 pp.
This compilation seeks to illuminate the "unique historical character" of the cowboy between 1860 and 1910, asserting that Western literature has tended toward "fictive accounts" that either romanticize the cowboy or are too "adventure oriented." The essays place an emphasis on the historical cowboy and differentiate between the "myth" and the "reality." In an attempt to dispel many of the romantic notions that have emerged in film, literature, and music, Harris and Rainey include topics such as the supposed shooting skills and sexual prowess of the cowboy, and trace the evolution of the "dude cowboy."

PC 277. HAZARD, LUCY LOCKWOOD. The Frontier in American Literature. New York: Crowell, 1927. 308 pp.
Hazard analyzes the importance of the frontier to the shift from visualizing literature as a solely European invention to producing a national literature which is distinctly American in its content and style. Hazard focuses on three different frontiers and the eras of their exploration, and associates each with representative writers: the regional frontier (Cooper, Irving); the industrial frontier (Twain, Dreiser); and the "spiritual" frontier (Anderson, Lindsay, Lewis). The emergence of this last frontier signifies not "the development of the continent but the development of the character," the formation of a new idealism reluctant to accept "the assertive redblooded heroes of regional or industrial pioneering."

PC 278. JONES, DARYL. The Dime Novel Western. Bowling Green, Ohio: Bowling Green University Popular Press, 1978. 186 pp.
Focusing on the years between 1860 and 1902, Jones examines the influence of the dime novel Western on the development of the Western formula. Jones analyzes the dime novel Western as a popular form of expression dependent on audience expectations and publishers' demands. The dime novels, he remarks, contained the characteristic elements which contributed significantly to the definition and history of the Western genre. As cultural artifacts, they also "responded to the anxieties and aspirations of the age."

PC 279. LEE, ROBERT EDSON. From West to East: Studies in the Literature of the American West. Urbana: University of Illinois Press, 1966. 172 pp.
Lee traces the image of the West portrayed by explorers (Lewis and Clark), Easterners traveling West (Irving, Parkman), the Westerner traveling East (Twain), the adopted Westerner (Cather), and the native Westerner (De Voto). He comments on the obstacles confronting those who sought to translate the frontier experience into a unique literature. Lee indicates that authors often filtered or altered their impressions to meet the Eastern reading audience's demands for romance and adventure, for a celebration of freedom and individuality as distinctly American traits. Lee argues that in seeking to cast off the "shadow of England" in order to develop a national literature, writers created a West of "metaphor," a symbolic place where actuality proved less important than the romantic image of the frontier.

PC 280. MILTON, JOHN R. The Novel of the American West. Lincoln: University of Nebraska Press, 1980. 341 pp.
The Western novels chosen by Milton are principally concerned with humankind's relationship to nature--more specifically, with the articulation of "an almost religious response to the land" (although much of the Western novelist's importance lies in his ability to transcend location and offer universal themes). Milton first discusses popular Westerns in order to contrast them with the superior but neglected literature of the West. He then focuses on six novelists--Vardis Fisher, Walter Van Tilburg Clark, Frederick Manfred, A. B. Guthrie, Harvey Fergusson, and Frank Waters--to illustrate their contribution to our "knowledge of the American Character."

PC 281. PETTIT, ARTHUR G. Images of the Mexican American in Fiction and Film. Edited by Dennis E. Showalter. College Station: Texas A & M University Press, 1980. 282 pp.
Proposing "general models of popular culture images," Pettit analyzes Anglo-American attitudes toward the Mexican people of the Southwest as expressed in literature and film. Pettit argues that the Southwest has been perceived by Anglo-Americans--in "conquest fiction," for example--as a foreign country and its inhabitants as aliens. He describes the ways in which the media have encouraged contradictory stereotypes--Mexicans have been applauded as "noble savages," and they have also been dismissed as "shiftless, unreliable and decadent."

PC 282. PILKINGTON, WILLIAM T., ed. Critical Essays on the Western American Novel. Boston: G. K. Hall, 1980. 275 pp.
Bringing together a "cross-section of critical approaches" to the study of the Western genre, the collection provides a general criticism of the Western novel as well as an analysis of individual Western writers. Pilkington places the novelists into three historical periods: the early 20th century (Emerson Hough, Owen Wister), the classical period (A. B. Guthrie, Louis L'Amour), and the contemporary Western (William Eastlake, Edward Abbey). A final section examines two minority writers (N. Scott

Momaday, Rudolfo Anaya). The emphasis throughout the text is on the Western novel as the basic literary form for expressing the themes inherent in the myth of the American West.

PC 283. ROSA, JOSEPH G. The Gunfighter: Man or Myth? Norman: University of Oklahoma Press, 1969. 229 pp.
Rosa discusses "the gunfighter of fact and fiction" by tracing "the myth of the hero without fear, fault or flaw" in literature, television, and film. From a historical perspective, Rosa indicates, the cowboy should not be considered the central participant in the settlement of the West, but should be placed in the context of the different social groups migrating to the frontier. Noting the actual experiences of numerous "shootists," he suggests that only Wild Bill Hickock and Bat Masterson led lives resembling the legends which have been associated with them.

PC 284. SAVAGE, WILLIAM W., Jr. The Cowboy Hero: His Image in American History and Culture. Norman: University of Oklahoma Press, 1979. 179 pp.
This volume explores the transmission of the image of the cowboy through the various media of film, television, literature, and music. Savage comments on the elusiveness of the "real" cowboy, noting that Americans do not possess a "clear historical idea" of his identity. Savage proposes that the image of the Westerner is an illuminating "cultural artifact," for the cowboy has become a "composite" serving a political and an economic function in America by reinforcing social values and selling merchandise.

PC 285. SONNICHSEN, C. L. From Hopalong to Hud: Thoughts on Western Fiction. College Station: Texas A & M University Press, 1978. 201 pp.
Sonnichsen emphasizes the Western genre's articulation of "cultural symbols"—the elucidation of America's past, present, and sense of destiny—rather than analyzing its literary merits. He begins with chapters identifying the prevalent mythology associated with the West. A second section seeks to dispel a number of cultural stereotypes and cliches through an investigation of such topics as the Indian and the Mexican in Western literature, the cowboy as heroic and unheroic figure (the "Wyatt Earp Syndrome"), and the role of the sharecropper in fiction. Sonnichsen's final section suggests areas requiring additional research.

PC 286. STAUFFER, HELEN WINTER and SUSAN J. ROSOWSKI, eds. Women and Western American Literature. Troy, N.Y.: Whitston, 1982. 331 pp.
On the premise that scholars have neglected the portrayal of women found in the literature of the American West, Stauffer and Roskowski have brought together a collection of essays which explore how "myth filters reality" by contrasting the actual condition of women on the frontier with the female characters imagined by writers of fiction. The volume also considers individuals—Constance Rourke, Mary Austin, Eudora Welty, among others—who have sought to create a new orientation by reinterpreting the "male-oriented model."

PC 287. STECKMESSER, KENT LADD. The Western Hero in History and Legend. Norman: University of Oklahoma Press, 1965. 281 pp.
This work focuses on four "heroes" of the 19th-century frontier—Kit Carson, Billy the Kid, Wild Bill Hickock, and George Custer—and demonstrates that they were created from a "fusion of history and legend." Steckmesser seeks to distinguish between the actual and the symbolic achievements of these important figures. Serving as personifications of a specific historical era, these heroes shared, in the public's view, "genteel qualities, clever traits, prowess, and epic significance." Celebrated by East-

ern writers who romanticized the frontier, the legendary stature of the Western hero often proved more important than his historical influence or his actual exploits.

PC 288. TATUM, STEPHEN. Inventing Billy the Kid: Visions of the Outlaw in America, 1881-1981. Albuquerque: University of New Mexico Press, 1982. 242 pp.
Tatum's study traces the evolution of the legend of Billy the Kid to determine how the Kid has been "invented" since his death in 1881, as well as to interpret images associated with the outlaw and what they reflect about the "cultural preoccupations" of individual writers. Tatum first sketches the historical Billy the Kid and then discusses the mythology that has emerged as a direct result of such major events as Prohibition, the Cold War, and Watergate. A final section provides an analysis of the differing motivations and visions of society of those who fostered the Billy the Kid legend.

OTHER GENRES: FICTION AND NON-FICTION

PC 289. AICHINGER, PETER. The American Soldier in Fiction, 1880-1963: A History of Attitudes Toward Warfare and the Military Establishment. Ames: Iowa State University Press, 1975. 143 pp.
Aichinger discusses the changing attitudes of U.S. citizens toward warfare and military establishments by examining a number of representative American war novels. Dividing the volume into four major epochs (1880-1917, 1917-39, 1939-52, and 1952-63) he considers the role of historical, economic and political events in reorienting public and literary opinion. For Aichinger, the genre of the war novel has possessed archetypal importance since 1880 and may be studied meaningfully by tracing its development as a literature of crusade and protest, as a depiction of the absurd, and as pop art. In this vein, he examines war novels by, among others, Wharton, Cather, Cummings, Dos Passos, Hemingway, Faulkner, Jones, Shaw, Mailer, Styron, Heller, and Michener.

PC 290. BERGER, ARTHUR ASA. Li'l Abner: A Study in American Satire. New York: Twayne, 1970. 191 pp.
Berger engages in a stylistic analysis of "Li'l Abner," the comic strip by Al Capp, and argues that it exemplifies the way in which humor reflects "value configurations" of American culture. In Part I, following a defense of studying popular culture, he compares Italian and American comics in order to defend his claim that the stylistic differences between the two result from cultural differences. He then traces the satirical antecedents of "Li'l Abner" to show how the comic strip draws on the tradition of American humor, in general, and American Southwestern humor, in particular. Part III presents a literary analysis of "Li'l Abner" that has an eye on Capp's use of language, narrative strategy, and graphics. Berger concludes in Part IV with a discussion of how the strip reflects specific American values.

PC 291. BERMAN, NEIL DAVID. Playful Fictions and Fictional Players: Game, Sport, and Survival in Contemporary American Fiction. Port Washington, N.Y.: Kennikat Press, 1981. 112 pp.
In discussing contemporary literature's depiction of sports, Berman follows Johan Huizinga and Erik Erikson in assuming that to define play in a culture is to define that culture, and that work and play, usefulness and gratuitousness, are really inseparable concepts. Berman distinguishes between the various purposes and degrees of healthfulness of play presented

by American writers, and draws parallels between their attitudes toward play and towad society. He devotes separate chapters to Leonard Gardner's Fat City, Peter Gent's North Dallas Forty, Don Delillo's End Zone, Lawrence Shainberg's One on One, and Robert Coover's The Universal Baseball Association. Berman believes that Coover portrays a complete subordination of work and achieves a fictional world convincingly structured by the rules of play.

PC 292. DIZER, JOHN T. Tom Swift & Company. Jefferson, N.C.: McFarland, 1982. 183 pp.
Dizer places the publications of the Stratemeyer Syndicate in the context of series books that emerged at the turn of the century. He emphasizes the significance of the Tom Swift series, which he considers symbols of national ingenuity, technological progress, and the American Dream. Dizer also traces the "blood lines of juvenile science fiction" in the Stratemeyer works devoted to science, invention, futurism and space travel. Commenting upon the portrayal of race in series publications, Dizer concludes that Stratemeyer "appears as unusually objective and liberal for the times in his literary treatment of the Blacks." A Stratemeyer bibliography is also included in this volume.

PC 293. HELLMAN, JOHN. Fables of Fact: The New Journalism as New Fiction. Urbana: University of Illinois Press, 1981. 164 pp.
Hellman proposes a "reconsideration" of the characteristics and significance of the New Journalism. Disputing what he sees as typical explanations of the form, Hellman regards New Journalism texts as "transforming literary experiments" combining the facts of journalism with the fable of fiction. He treats the development of New Journalism along with that of fabulist fiction, for he perceives both as reactions against the limitations of conventional newsgathering and realistic literature. Hellman notes, for example, how writers such as John Barth, Thomas Pynchon, and Donald Barthelme construct alternate, autonomous worlds to comment on the actual world. He devotes individual chapters to the major works of Norman Mailer, Hunter Thompson, Tom Wolfe, and Michael Herr, and suggests that each author combines "a journalistic subject with certain fabulist techniques."

PC 294. HOLLOWELL, JOHN. Fact and Fiction: The New Journalism and the Nonfiction Novel. Chapel Hill: University of North Carolina Press, 1977. 190 pp.
This volume analyzes the origins and styles of New Journalism—nonfiction writing that incorporates the narrative techniques of fiction to report contemporary events. Hollowell focuses on the changing climate in both literature and journalism in the 1960s. He asserts that the nonfiction novel exemplifies the increasing irrelevance of distinctions between elite and popular art. To support this view, Hollowell introduces the "speculations" of historians, social scientists, and journalists. Fact and Fiction includes separate chapters devoted to the work of Truman Capote, Norman Mailer, and Tom Wolfe; these three, the author contends, have contributed the best examples of the genre.

PC 295. JOHNSON, MICHAEL L. The New Journalism: The Underground Press, the Artists of Nonfiction, and Changes in the Established Media. Lawrence: University Press of Kansas, 1971. 177 pp.
In exploring the broad changes in journalism in the 1960s, Johnson not only considers the style and techniques of such New Journalists as Truman Capote, Norman Mailer, and Tom Wolfe, but also discusses rock journalism, underground radio, and what he calls "the New Muckrakers." He notes the limitations of established media, and contends that new forms of journalism have done a more thorough and honest job of responding to the profound political and social changes in the 1960s. The New Journalism emphasizes

three categories of written journalism: underground publications; New Journalistic books; and examples of how established media have borrowed New Journalistic approaches. Johnson provides a brief history of the underground press and concludes with a chapter speculating on the future of New Journalism.

PC 296. **LEISY, ERNEST E.** The American Historical Novel. Norman: University of Oklahoma Press, 1950. 280 pp.
"Historical fiction," says Leisy, "is concerned with historical truth" and is set "at an earlier time" from that of the author; it has been the most popular form of the novel in America, particularly in the years 1815-50, 1890-1910, and 1930-50. Although Leisy devotes a few pages to James Fenimore Cooper and William Gilmore Simms, he does not emphasize individual authors. Rather he chronologically arranges the subject matter of the historical novels so that readers may study the appeal of such historical events as the Revolution, the Westward Movement, the Civil War and Reconstruction, and National Expansion. A list of "Additional Historical Novels" is appended.

PC 297. **MILLER, WAYNE CHARLES.** An Armed America, Its Face in Fiction: A History of the American Military Novel. New York: New York University Press, 1970. 294 pp.
Miller observes that the study of war novels provides a "historical and cultural perspective from which the American military man and military machine may be better understood and controlled." Beginning with James Fenimore Cooper and the historical romance's portrayal of the American Revolution, Miller traces the influence of the Civil War, of literary realism (Crane, Bierce, Kirkland), of W.W. I, and of the novel of social protest (Hemingway, Dos Passos, Cummings, Dalton Trumbo) on the development of the American military novel. He then investigates the divergent views concerning W.W. II and the military elite in the works of Leon Uris, Herman Wouk, Norman Mailer, James Jones, John P. Marquand, and James Gould Cozzens. After devoting a chapter to Joseph Heller's Catch 22, Miller concludes with a discussion of the role of the war novel--especially the works of James Michener, Eugene Burdick and Harvey Wheeler, and Peter George--during the nuclear age.

PC 298. **ORIARD, MICHAEL.** Dreaming of Heroes: American Sports Fiction, 1868-1980. Chicago: Nelson-Hall, 1982. 382 pp.
Oriard focuses on novels devoted to baseball, football, boxing, and basketball. He argues that sports offer American writers "a vehicle for a distinct representation of reality," and that they provide "a metaphor of American life and an escape from . . . banality and complexity." After surveying the history of sports fiction, Oriard traces the treatment of sports themes in the works of such authors as Gilbert Patten (the creator of the Frank Merriwell series), Jack London, Robert Coover, Philip Roth, Dan Jenkins, and Peter Gent. He describes how shifting perceptions of myth and of such fundamental polarities as youth and age, country and city, and masculinity and femininity have remade the archetypal hero in ways distinct to each cultural era of the 20th century. He also includes a checklist of sports novels published in America through 1980.

PC 299. **WALDMEIR, JOSEPH J.** American Novels of the Second World War. The Hague: Mouton, 1969. 180 pp.
Waldmeir discusses W.W. II novels, focusing on the influence of combat on individual psychology and the role of ideology in a wartime society. Contrasting novelists of the two world wars, Waldmeir stresses the significance of fascism in shaping the direction of literature in the 1940s. In works such as Norman Mailer's The Naked and the Dead and John Horne Burns's The Gallery, fascism became the picture of evil in both Nazi Germany and American culture. For Waldmeir, Herman Wouk and James Gould

Cozzens offer a dissenting opinion, stressing the importance of winning the war and limiting their anti-fascism to depictions of the German enemy. While indicating that novelists of W.W. II revived the tradition of social criticism, Waldmeir also observes that their emphasis on individualism, responsibility, commitment, collectivism and the anxiety of choice led them to the "threshold of existentialism."

PC 300. **WALSH, JEFFREY.** American War Literature, 1914 to Vietnam. New York: St. Martin's, 1982. 218 pp.
According to Walsh, American novelists and poets of the 20th century have "often come to understand their own country, its social character, institutions and relations with the world, through metaphors of battle." Organized chronologically, Walsh's study traces such themes as: protest, alienation, redemption, and brotherhood in W.W. I poetry; the Lost Generation and radical literature; W.W. II fiction and poetry; and, lastly, the portrayal of Vietnam. Working from the premise "that modern American war literature shares the nature of debate, discourse and consciousness rather than static form," Walsh analyzes the use of language and the formal and generic problems represented in this literature.

PC 301. **WEBER, RONALD.** The Literature of Fact: Literary Nonfiction in American Writing. Athens: Ohio University Press, 1980. 181 pp.
Focusing on "nonfiction with a literary purpose," this book examines journalism of the 1960s and 1970s. In Part I, "The Background," Weber describes the critical context of literary nonfiction by noting, for example, controversies over the direction and purpose of both journalism and the novel. He sees literary nonfiction as a "complex counterpointing" of history and literature, and distinguishes between literary nonfiction and literary journalism. In Part II, Weber begins with an exploration of how James Agee and John Hersey contributed to a continuing tradition. He devotes extensive attention to Truman Capote, Tom Wolfe, Gay Talese, Jane Kramer, Norman Mailer, John McPhee, and C. D. B. Bryan as significant representatives of this narrative approach. A final chapter surveys the literary nonfiction scene at the close of the 1970s.

PC 302. **WEBER, RONALD,** ed. The Reporter as Artist: A Look at the New Journalism Controversy. New York: Hastings House, 1974. 312 pp.
This volume includes reprints of twenty-eight articles, reviews, book chapters, interviews, or critiques concerned with the New Journalism. In Part I, "Personal Journalism," several New Journalists, among them Tom Wolfe and Gay Talese, consider the techniques and objectives of the form. Also included are interviews with Talese and Gloria Steinem. Magazine editors evaluate "The Article as Art" in Part II. Part III investigates the possibility of regarding New Journalism as literature and features George Plimpton's interview with Truman Capote. Part IV reprints the work of critics and journalists who have emphasized the shortcomings of this form of news reporting.

PC 303. **WOLFE, TOM** and **E. W. JOHNSON,** eds. The New Journalism. New York: Harper & Row, 1973. 394 pp.
Wolfe's introduction to this anthology of examples of the New Journalism is part autobiography, part history, and part analysis. He defines the form as "journalism that would read like a novel," and discovers its origins among 1960s newspaper feature writers impatient with their lack of prestige and eager to write novels. Wolfe recalls his own excitement, for example, at the possibility of communicating not only the facts of the matter, but also the subjective "feel" of the scene. Wolfe traces the various experimental narrative devices employed in the New Journalism in order to render the "status life" (symbolic details of everyday experi-

ence) of its subjects. The twenty-three anthologized pieces illustrate the wide range of subjects and styles encompassed by the New Journalism; the editors include contributions by Gay Talese, Truman Capote, Hunter Thompson, Joan Didion, and Wolfe himself.

PC 304. YATES, NORRIS W. The American Humorist: Conscience of the Twentieth Century. Ames: Iowa State University Press, 1964. 310 pp.

This book examines the characteristic beliefs expressed in literary humor and satire from 1900-1950. Yates treats three recurring character types: the crackerbarrel sage; the public-spirited, middle-class citizen; and the harried Little Man. He notes the similarities among these types, stressing what he sees as the continuity of American literary humor. All three figures represent everyday common sense, stable family life, and monogamous marriage in the face of an often unstable society. After introductory chapters on 19th-century humor, the author considers five crackerbarrel philosophers, including Will Rogers. He then focuses on those "small-town" humorists who emerge as "defenders of Rational Man"-- H. L. Mencken, Ring Lardner, and Don Marquis. Finally, Yates investigates the depiction of the Little Man by writers such as Robert Benchley, Dorothy Parker, James Thurber, and E. B. White.

III.   COMICS

PC 305. BECKER, STEPHEN. Comic Art in America. New York: Simon & Schuster, 1959. 387 pp.

This is a social history of comic art which is based on the thesis that "All art says something about the society that produces it; and often-- cumulatively, over a period of years--the impress of an art alters the face of its society." In addition to five chapters surveying the development of the comic strip, the book also considers film animation, humorous and comic periodicals, comic books, sports cartoons, and editorial cartoons. A special essay of appreciation discusses the work of six "lyric clowns"-- George Herriman, Walt Kelly, Crockett Johnson (David Johnson Leisk), Charles Schulz, Milt Gross, and Rube Goldberg.

PC 306. BERGER, ARTHUR ASA. The Comic-Stripped American. New York: Walker, 1973. 225 pp.

Berger here offers a collection of impressionistic sociocultural analyses of selected comics which he believes reflect American values and elements of the national character. The volume includes essays on the Yellow Kid, the Katzenjammer Kids, Mutt and Jeff, Krazy Kat, Little Orphan Annie, Buck Rogers, Blondie, Dick Tracy, Flash Gordon, Superman, Batman, Pogo, Peanuts, Marvel comic books, and underground comic books.

PC 307. COUPERIE, PIERRE, MAURICE C. HORN, PROTO DISTEFANIS, EDOUARD FRANÇOIS, CLAUD MOLITERNI, and GERALD GASSIOT-TALABOT. A History of the Comic Strip. Translated by Eileen B. Hennessy. New York: Crown, 1973. 246 pp.

This study of comic strip art was prepared from an historical and ideological perspective in conjunction with the first international exhibition of comic art held in Paris in 1967. Throughout the book the authors emphasize that comic strip content is the product of an elaborate network of influences and traditions, both conscious and unconscious. The creators, the form, the style, and the audience of comics are all analyzed.

PC 308. DANIELS, LES. Comix: A History of Comic Books in America. New
    York: Outerbridge & Dienstfrey, 1971. 198 pp.
Comix consists of eight chapters devoted to the birth of comic books,
funny animal tales, the products of the E.C. firm, the comics code controversy, post-code adult titles, the Marvel comics phenomenon, and the
development of underground comic books. The text primarily offers summaries that are complemented by reprints of numerous comic book stories.

PC 309. DORFMAN, ARIEL and ARMAND MATTELART. How to Read Donald Duck:
    Imperialist Ideology in the Disney Comic. Translated by David
    Kunzle. New York: International General, 1975. 112 pp.
Dorfman and Mattelart's study of Donald Duck and his companion comic
figures is an examination of what the authors see as a latent capitalist-
imperialist ideology in the comic art of Walt Disney. Written during
the Chilean revolution of 1971, the book attempts to deflate the popular
impression that the characters of Disney's world are simple, pure, non-
partisan, spontaneous, respectful of parents, and loving to friends.

PC 310. ESTREN, MARK JAMES. A History of Underground Comics. San Fran-
    cisco: Straight Arrow, 1970. 320 pp.
Estren explores the art of underground comics in this historical and thematic study. Filled with black-white-and-red comic illustrations, the
chapters address definition, historical origins, content analysis, and
censorship. Estren explains that underground comics "are truly three-
dimensional, at least figuratively." The artists deal with all subjects—
religion, race relations, education, the supernatural, sex, violence,
and horror—in uncompromising visual and verbal terms and usually criticize
the censors severely. In his final chapter, Estren examines the extent
to which censorship has disrupted, but not completely impeded, the development of comic art. A listing of underground comics and publishing houses
by Clay Geerdes and an interview with Harvey Kurtzman, critic and one-
time writer and editor of Mad magazine, are appended.

PC 311. GOULART, RON. The Adventurous Decade. New Rochelle, N.Y.: Arling-
    ton House, 1975. 224 pp.
Goulart presents an impressionistic survey of the development of the adventure comic strip in the 1930s with chapters on the beginnings of the adventure genre and on the following varieties: science fiction, aviation,
detective, child adventurer, Western, and military. He incorporates interviews with such cartoonists as Roy Crane, Milton Caniff, and Alfred
Andriola, and with numerous writers of comics.

PC 312. HESS, STEPHEN. The Ungentlemanly Art. New York: Macmillan,
    1968. 252 pp.
This is an illustrated history of the political cartoon and caricature
in the U.S. The cartoons provide a record of public views on politics,
dress, speech, and tastes in humor at various periods. Hess studies such
prominent symbolic figures as Uncle Sam, the Gerrymander, the Democratic
donkey, and the Republican elephant. He traces the development of symbols
and conventions of political cartooning, and audience reaction to cartoons
and cartoonists. He also studies the careers and work of such famous
artists as Nast, Herblock, Mauldin, Feiffer, Oliphant, and Conrad and
discusses the cartoon as propaganda, particularly during W.W. II.

PC 313. HORN, MAURICE, ed. The World Encyclopedia of Cartoons. New York:
    Chelsea House, 1981. 787 pp.
Using the model of the World Encyclopedia of Comics (see PC 314), Horn
and twenty-two contributors have written almost 1,200 entries on cartoonists, animators, editors, producers, and the works they have created in
the fields of animation, gag cartoons, syndicated comic panels, editorial
cartoons, caricature, and sports cartoons. The entries are supplemented

with an overview of caricature and cartoons, a brief history of humor magazines, a world summary of animated cartoons, a chronology of important events in the history of cartooning, a glossary of cartooning terms, and a history of the humor periodicals Puck, Life, and Judge. There are more than 900 illustrations in black-and-white and color.

PC 314. HORN, MAURICE, ed. The World Encyclopedia of Comics. New York: Chelsea House, 1976. 790 pp.
Horn and numerous other contributors have put together an extensive survey of comics. Filled with over 800 illustrations, many in color, the book offers more than 1200 cross-referenced entries on comic features, artists, and writers from the U.S. and abroad. The biographical entries provide summaries of the lives and careers of artists, with emphasis on their thematic and stylistic contributions and their influence on other artists. The bibliographical entries offer a brief history of the comic features, the names of artists and writers who created and worked on them, a summary of themes, plots, and leading characters, a discussion of the place held by each feature in comic history, and their adaptations to other media. Supplementing the entries are a brief world history of comics, a world comics chronology, an analytical summary dealing with language, themes, and structure of comics, a history of news syndication and a glossary of comic terms.

PC 315. LUPOFF, DICK and DON THOMPSON, eds. All in Color for a Dime. New Rochelle, N.Y.: Arlington House, 1970. 263 pp.
In this volume, eleven contributors offer appreciations and analyses of such topics as Superman, Captain Marvel, Popeye, Captain America, the Justice Society of America, Planet Comics, Jingle Jangle Comics, Fawcett comic book titles, boys' gangs in comic books, and Saturday afternoon film serials based on comic strip and book characters.

PC 316. MURRELL, WILLIAM. A History of American Graphic Humor. Vol. 1, New York: Whitney Museum of American Art, 1933; Vol. 2, New York: Macmillan, 1938. 271 pp.
Murrell's two volumes constitute a pictorial history of graphic humor from 1750 to 1938, with a limited emphasis on satire. The first volume traces the development from the days of Benjamin Franklin and Paul Revere, when antique engravings were crowded with allegory and explanatory remarks. Murrell continues his survey by discussing such 19th-century artists as Edward W. Clay, who was known for his social caricatures, and Thomas Nast, America's first successful political cartoonist. Murrell's second volume looks at the years 1865-1938, when graphic humor represented the economic and social crises of the times. Exploring such social cartoonists as Art Young and Jacob Burch and such political cartoonists as J. N. Darling and Herbert Johnson, Murrell concludes that the future of graphic humor in America is in the hands of the newspaper and magazine publishers, not of the artists.

PC 317. REITBERGER, REINHOLD and WOLFGANG FUCHS. Comics: Anatomy of a Mass Medium. Translated by Nadia Fowler. Boston: Little, Brown, 1972. 264 pp.
Reitberger and Fuchs's historical, sociological, and contextual study of comic strips made in America from 1900 to 1971 serves as an introduction to the genre. The authors divide comic strip history into five periods, each characterized by a different type of strip: funnies (1900-30); adventures (1930-40); superheroes (1940-54); recession (1955-62); and the new boom (1962-70). In addition to offering a historical introduction, Reitberger and Fuchs analyze archetypal patterns in the strips and their psychological effects on readers. The analysis also looks at the effects of American-based comics upon readers in European countries. The authors conclude that the comic can no longer be regarded as a medium purely for

children--if it ever was. The subject matter of strips deals with social values and, therefore, appeals to all age groups at every level of society. A chronology of comic strip history and an index by comic strip title are appended to the study.

PC 318. **ROBINSON, JERRY.** The Comics: An Illustrated History of Comic Strip Art. New York: Putnam's, 1974. 256 pp.
Robinson's historical-sociological study is a broad overview of comic art. Illustrated with black-and-white and color prints, the chapters trace the comic strip's origins, explore its relationship to other media forms, and emphasize the importance of comic art in both reflecting and influencing our mores and illusions. Concentrating on the comic strip, the newspaper panel, and comics abroad, Robinson looks at the historical development of comic art from the Egyptian period through the Benjamin Franklin years and into the 20th century's Golden Age of comics. Like American culture, Robinson contends, the comic strip is in constant flux.

PC 319. **THOMPSON, DON** and **DICK LUPOFF**, eds. The Comic-Book Book. New Rochelle, N.Y.: Arlington House, 1973. 360 pp.
The editors of All in Color for a Dime (see PC 315) assemble another thirteen appreciations of comic book characters and genres, with essays on Plastic Man, Mickey Mouse in the comics, the Frankenstein monster in comic books, the Spirit, Donald Duck, Wonder Woman, Tarzan, the E.C. comic book series, magicians in the comics, aviation comic book titles, and radio adaptations. The contributors include Bill Blackbeard, Ron Goulart, Dick O'Donnell, and Maggie Thompson.

PC 320. **WALKER, MORT.** Backstage at the Strips. New York: Mason/Charter, 1975. 311 pp.
This work is a partly autobiographical account of contemporary comic strips, with some history of the genre. The book is based on Walker's own experience as a cartoonist and an officer in the National Cartoonists' Society. Walker describes how strips are created, drawn, and published, and gives examples from strips of all types, including those featuring adventure, romance, humor, and satire. He provides a full survey of his own Beetle Bailey from the first concept to the 1970s. Walker also discusses other strips created by him and his close colleagues: Hi and Lois, Hagar the Horrible, and Boner's Ark. He also provides a detailed discussion of audience response to different strips and plots, often with excerpts from letters. The book includes humorous anecdotes and is illustrated with photographs, sketches, rough drafts, and reproductions of entire panels and strips.

PC 321. **WAUGH, COULTON.** The Comics. New York: Macmillan, 1947. 360 pp.
Based on extensive research in newspaper files, as well as on Waugh's own experience as a cartoonist (he replaced Milton Caniff on the comic strip Dickie Dare in 1934), the book is both a detailed historic overview of the medium and a critique of the aesthetics of the more successful examples. Waugh finds comic books to be raw and ugly--"there is a soulless emptiness to them, an outrageous vulgarity"--and he does not approve of the movements toward realism and serious subject matter. It is in light-hearted humor and imaginative fantasy that "the medium is most itself and performs its most native function."

PC 322. **WHITE, DAVID MANNING** and **ROBERT H. ABEL**, eds. The Funnies: An American Idiom. New York: Free Press, 1963.
This volume is a collection of fourteen previously published and eight original articles on the comic strip and its social importance in America. Essays focus on the content of comic strips, their reflection of values and sexual roles, their influence on children and adults, their status

as art, and the reasons for their popularity, often based on statistical data and surveys. Two appreciative essays are devoted to George Herriman's Krazy Kat. A bibliography of social science and popular articles on comics is included.

IV.   ENTERTAINMENT

PC 323. ATKINSON, BROOKS. Broadway. New York: Macmillan, 1970.
         484 pp.
Atkinson defines Broadway as the theater district in midtown Manhattan and traces the history of its stars, producers, and critics from 1900 to 1950. This study is divided into three overlapping time periods: 1900-18, the "era of good feeling" in which unsophisticated but lively theater was being produced; 1918-39, which saw the recovery from the war and a great burst of energy in serious theater; and 1938-50, the last years of active Broadway theater. A postscript briefly views the years 1950-70.

PC 324. BANKS, ANN, ed. First Person America. New York: Knopf, 1980.
         287 pp.
The eighty life histories collected in this volume are drawn from interviews undertaken as part of the Federal Writers' Project between 1939 and 1942. Two sections ("Troupers and Pitchmen" and "The Jazz Language") deal with the life of small-time entertainers and Chicago jazz musicians. Many of the vaudeville comedians, troupers, and pitchmen interviewed were no longer practicing in the 1930s; their reminiscences, which hark back to the turn of the century, celebrate early freewheeling show business. The Chicago jazz musicians also speak of an earlier, richer time (1925-29), and frequently mention other jazzmen of the 1920s and 1930s (particularly Bix Beiderbecke).

PC 325. BARAL, ROBERT. Revue: The Great Broadway Period. New York:
         Fleet Press, 1962. 296 pp.
Writing in the style of Variety, Baral provides a documentary chronicle of revue with a focus on the 1920s and 1930s. He offers a brief history of the colorful and eccentric showmen who originated the shows and then covers, year by year, the accomplishments and developments of the shows. Those covered include: Flo Ziegfeld and the Ziegfeld Follies, the Shuberts's Passing Show, John Murray Anderson's Greenwich Village Follies, George White's Scandals, the Music Box Revue started by Irving Berlin, and the Earl Carroll Vanities. Baral also covers many lesser-known shows, performances of the 1940s and 1950s, and London and Paris shows.

PC 326. BAUMOL, WILLIAM J. and WILLIAM G. BOWEN. 1966; Rev. ed. Performing Arts--The Economic Dilemma; a Study of Problems Common to Theater, Opera, Music and Drama. New York: Twentieth Century Fund, 1967. 582 pp.
This book studies the financial problems of the performing arts and shows the implications of these problems for the future of American arts. The first part describes the economic situation of the performing arts in the U.S., including extensive data on certain organizations, the audience, and the performers. Part II investigates the technology of the performing arts (for example, ticket pricing policies) and examines its effects on the economic future. Part III identifies sources (for example, private individuals, the government) which might counter financial gaps which exist within the performing arts. The authors conclude that a "cultural boom" is occurring, but largely for a narrow, highly educated,

and financially well-off community. They see a healthy future for amateur activity but not for professional works.

PC 327. BORDMAN, GERALD. American Musical Comedy: From Adonis to Dream-girls. New York: Oxford University Press, 1982. 244 pp.
A companion volume to Bordman's study on American operetta (see PC 328), this book examines musical comedy as a second genre in American musical theater. The study concludes that, unlike the history of operetta, there is no clear development in the evolution of musical comedy. Bordman chrono-logically examines the changes that have occurred in musical comedy from the musical burlesque of the 19th century to the contributions of such directors as Michael Bennett and the success of the recent musical Dream-girls.

PC 328. BORDMAN, GERALD. American Operetta: From H.M.S. Pinafore to Sweeney Todd. New York: Oxford University Press, 1981. 206 pp.
Bordman maintains that the modern musical play is simply latter-day oper-etta and that modern musicals from Oklahoma! to Sweeney Todd represent a logical and inevitable step in operetta's evolution. He traces the history of operetta in America from The Bohemian Girl and Offenbach opera comique to A Little Night Music and Sweeney Todd, assessing trends in operettas and comparing different styles.

PC 329. BROWN, T. ALLSTON. History of the American Stage Containing Bio-graphical Sketches of Nearly Every Member of the Profession That Has Appeared on the American Stage, from 1733 to 1870. New York: Dick & Fitzgerald, 1870. 421 pp.
Brown, a former theater critic and agent, chronicles the history of the American stage from 1733 to 1870 through alphabetically arranged biographi-cal sketches. He provides a checklist of major and minor figures, from Mr. and Mrs. William Abbot to Marie Zoe, with special attention paid to actors, playwrights, managers, singers, and minstrels.

PC 330. CHINDAHL, GEORGE L. A History of the Circus in America. Caldwell, Idaho: Caxton, 1959. 279 pp.
Chindahl's history of the circus covers the U.S., Canada, and Mexico. Beginning with the period before 1800, this work is divided into seven chronological sections. The author's objective in recording the evolution of the circus is to "point out the factors that have determined its form and quality." The effects of the Civil War on the circus and the advent of the railroad are covered, as is the growth of motorized and indoor circuses. A final section deals with such topics as types of entertainment, the circus performer, horsemanship, clowning, circus acts, side shows, publicity, labor relations, and advertising. A list of circus menageries (1771 to 1956) is appended.

PC 331. CHRISTOPHER, MILBOURNE. The Illustrated History of Magic. New York: Crowell, 1973. 452 pp.
Written by a practicing magician and historian of magic, this work covers magic throughout the world, with extensive coverage of magic as a perform-ing art in the U.S. Among the major American magicians analyzed, Christopher gives special attention to Houdini, Thurston, Dante, Blackstone, and Dunninger. A separate chapter is devoted to the "Great Vaudeville Specialists."

PC 332. CHURCHILL, ALLEN. The Great White Way: A Re-creation of Broadway's Golden Era of Theatrical Entertainment. New York: Dutton, 1962. 310 pp.

In this work, Churchill recreates the Golden Era of Broadway from the opening of Florodora in 1900 and Actor's Equity Strike in 1919. During this period Americans were particularly theater-conscious, and the popularly known actors (William Gillette, John Drew), actresses (Sarah Bernhardt, Minnie Maddern Fisk, Laurette Taylor), playwrights (Ned Sheldon, Eugene Walter), and producers (David Belasco, George M. Cohan) are covered, as are such shows as Peter Pan. Churchill provides insight into the attitudes of people associated with the popular theater, and discusses their involvement with the Syndicate which was founded by (among others) producer Charles Frohman.

PC 333. CHURCHILL, ALLEN. The Theatrical Twenties. New York: McGraw-Hill, 1975. 326 pp.

This work traces, year by year, the entertainment productions and personalities of the 1920s. Each chapter focuses on several actors, actresses, and playwrights for that year and reviews the changes in entertainment production. In 1920, theater was "king" in the entertainment world, and Eugene O'Neill was the major playwright. Churchill discusses Al Jolson, Lynn Fontanne, and Alfred Lunt in 1921; John Barrymore and the Theatre Guild in 1922; the Ziegfeld Follies and humor in 1923; serious playwrights such as Laurence Stallings and Maxwell Anderson in 1924; Jean Engels and musical comedies (for example, the Marx Brothers) in 1925; the "play of the decade," Broadway, in 1926; talkies in 1927; Jed Harris in 1928; and the decline of Broadway entertainment in 1929. Each chapter provides a "roundup"--a list and description of the major productions of the year.

PC 334. CORIO, ANN, with JOE DiMONA. This Was Burlesque. New York: Grosset & Dunlap, 1968. 204 pp.

This book includes commentary on, as well as illustrations and photographs of, the great stars of burlesque during the 1930s. One of the practitioners of the form, Corio suggests several possible origins for the striptease. She places the phenomenon in a historical perspective and in the context of earlier burlesque forms, before the striptease.

PC 335. CSIDA, JOSEPH and JUNE BUNDY CSIDA. American Entertainment: A Unique History of Popular Show Business. New York: Watson-Guptill, 1978. 448 pp.

The Csidas trace the history of show business from 1700 to the 1970s through capsule histories and reproductions of articles, advertisements, and photographs from Billboard, the oldest show-business trade paper. The work is divided into five chronological time periods: 1700-1893, the beginning of show business; 1894-1904, the heyday of live shows; 1905-18, the rise of radio and motion pictures; 1919-46, the era of talking movies; and 1947-77, the period dominated by television. A sixth section discusses entertainment music. All forms of entertainment are covered, including burlesque, film, the circus, and rock concerts.

PC 336. DiMEGLIO, JOHN E. Vaudeville U.S.A. Bowling Green, Ohio: Bowling Green University Popular Press, 1973. 259 pp.

This study describes the challenges a vaudevillian faced while playing the various circuits of the U.S. and Canada, and examines the relationship between the artist and their audiences. DiMeglio discusses the managers and vaudeville magnates, the variety of acts found in vaudeville, the audiences that attended the shows, censorship, the entertainer and his life, the black vaudevillian, geographical areas played by vaudevillians, the importance of New York City, and small-time vaudeville.

PC 337. DRUXMAN, MICHAEL B. The Musical: From Broadway to Hollywood. South Brunswick, N.J.: Barnes, 1980. 202 pp.
The author describes the way in which a stage musical is transformed into a motion picture, and discusses the success or failure of past adaptations. He pays particular attention to production processes and directors' approaches. Many musicals are examined, including On the Town, Pal Joey, and Cabaret.

PC 338. ENGEL, LEHMAN. The American Musical Theater. 1967; Rev. ed. New York: Macmillan, 1975. 266 pp.
Engel begins this work with a brief history of the American musical theater. He then selects fifteen shows and discusses the libretto--the key to a successful musical--in relation to other elements of the show (music, dancing, acting and decor). According to Engel, all factors must work together to support the resolution of dramatic conflict between the characters. Furthermore, since musical theater is not a passive entertainment, the audience must feel compelled to see such a resolution take place. Engel also treats American opera, which he claims "descended from Broadway," and plotless rock musicals.

PC 339. EWEN, DAVID. The Life and Death of Tin Pan Alley: The Golden Age of American Popular Music. New York: Funk & Wagnalls, 1964. 380 pp.
Tin Pan Alley, a major source of American popular music, is here traced from 1880 to 1930. Tin Pan Alley is both a location--28th Street in Manhattan--and an epoch in American popular music. As a location, it was the center of music publishing houses and the place where many young composers (for example, Kern, Gershwin, Berlin) got their start. As an epoch, it saw the growth of a new way of writing, publishing, and promoting American popular music. Ewen links the demise of Tin Pan Alley to the advent of talking pictures and to depressed sales of sheet music. He discusses popular songs and their composers, and offers comments on American life as reflected in song.

PC 340. EWEN, DAVID. New Complete Book of the American Musical Theater. New York: Holt, Rinehart & Winston, 1970. 800 pp.
The purpose of this work is to bring together and order all aspects of American musical theater. Ewen divides his work into two sections: an alphabetically arranged overview of almost 500 musical productions from 1866 to the late 1960s; and over 160 biographies of leading composers, librettists, and lyricists. An appendix provides a chronology of the musical theater. Lesser known works by well-known masters such as Gershwin, Rodgers, Porter, and Berlin are included, as are rock musicians and their works.

PC 341. EWEN, DAVID. The Story of America's Musical Theater. 1961; Rev. ed. Randor, Pa.: Chilton, 1968. 278 pp.
Ewen examines the beginnings of musical theater in the 18th and 19th centuries and establishes November 20, 1894, the production date of Victor Herbert's Prince Ananias, as the "birth" date. Through the works and lives of significant composers, Ewen traces this unique American form from the fairy tale operettas of the late 1800s to the musical comedies and plays of the 1960s. Burlesque, extravaganza, and revue are examined for their contribution to musical comedy. The growth and change of the musical theater in the 1920s (the Golden Age) and the more sober 1930s are explored through the works of Richard Rodgers, Lorenz Hart, George Gershwin, Irving Berlin, Cole Porter, George M. Cohan, and Jerome Kern.

PC 342. FIEDLER, LESLIE. Freaks: Myths & Images of the Secret Self.
     New York: Simon & Schuster, 1978. 367 pp.
Fiedler investigates the role of the freak from classical times to the
present era of film and pop-culture "freaking out." The freak is variously
characterized as a holy figure, a living good-luck charm, a kind of household pet, a showpiece and a source of entertainment, an object of pity
and scorn, a symbol of the human condition, and a symbol for the future
possibilities of man. Fiedler analyzes the freak in all its forms, both
natural and unnatural, and looks at the subject in literature, film, art,
and mythology.

PC 343. GAGEY, EDMOND M. The San Francisco Stage: A History. New York:
     Columbia University Press, 1950. 271 pp.
Gagey traces the history of the San Francisco stage from 1850 to 1924.
Relying largely on newspaper accounts of theatrical activity in the city,
Gagey focuses on the stars of the stage, including the Booths, the Starks,
Adah Menken, and John McCullough; the rise and fall of such theaters as
the Metropolitan, the California, the Bella Union, the Tivoli, and the
Alcazar; and the San Francisco audience. Playwright-impresario David
Belasco, and Tom Maguire and his theatrical empire, are given particular
attention. Gagey indicates which shows and actors were native to San
Francisco and which were imported from the East or elsewhere. Though
much San Francisco theater was original, Gagey contends, the ties with
the East were such that the history of this city's theater is essentially
the history of Broadway during the same period.

PC 344. GILBERT, DOUGLAS. American Vaudeville: Its Life and Times.
     New York: McGraw-Hill, 1940. 428 pp.
Though the origins of vaudeville are uncertain, Gilbert begins his history
with Tony Pastor's variety show of 1881. The main ingredient of vaudeville,
humor (often topical), is viewed in its transformations from racial and
frequently vulgar humor to the refined "clean" humor of Tony Pastor and
the tramps and blackface acts of the Golden Days (1900). Female vaudevillians and the death of vaudeville are given attention in the last section. The death of vaudeville is attributed to many causes (for example,
mechanized entertainment), and Gilbert contends that when vaudeville moved
from low comedy to a more sophisticated entertainment it became devitalized
and brought about its own destruction. Throughout, Gilbert offers show
lyrics, short biographies of major figures in vaudeville, and analyses
of the economic aspects of this entertainment form.

PC 345. GOTTFRIED, MARTIN. Broadway Musicals. New York: Abrams, 1979.
     353 pp.
The Broadway musical is, according to Gottfried, America's most significant
contribution to world theater. The Broadway musical is a unique form
which emerged from the "past's rowdy stages," a "rhythmic spiel of New
York"; it is entertainment, not art. Gottfried begins by defining and
analyzing the elements of a Broadway musical: the music, lyrics, and
design. He looks at selected major directors--Abbott, Robbins, and Fosse--
and the "giants" among composers--Kern, Rodgers, Porter, Gershwin, and
Berlin. Through numerous photographs, Gottfried's intent is to capture
the spirit of the Broadway musical, not to explain how it works; the "why"
of a successful musical is the magic, the flamboyance, and energy of the
performance. It is this spirit which makes up for technological shortcomings which occur, according to Gottfried, because the Broadway musical
is still in the process of development.

PC 346. **GRAHAM, PHILIP.** Showboats: The History of an American Institution. Austin: University of Texas Press, 1951. 224 pp.
Graham provides a complete record of America's floating theaters from the first in 1831 to the last true showboat, tied up at a St. Louis dock in 1937. He includes coverage of the vehicles, stages, entertainments, entertainers, audiences, businessmen, and progress of its various forms.

PC 347. **GREEN, ABEL** and **JOE LAURIE,** Jr. Show Biz from Vaude to Video. New York: Holt, 1951. 613 pp.
Interspersed with biographical data on Sime Silverman, the founder, editor, and publisher of Variety, this volume traces the history of show business from 1905--the "hoopla years"--to the television shows of the 1950s. The authors adopt a journalistic perspective and use "Varietyese" (Variety slang) to describe the evolution of Show Biz from Vaude (Vaudeville) to Pix (motion pictures), sound film, radio, and finally video (television).

PC 348. **GREEN, STANLEY.** Ring Bells! Sing Songs! Broadway Musicals of the 1930s. New York: Galahad Books, 1971. 358 pp.
This is an illustrated history of musical theater from Strike Up the Band (January 1930) to DuBarry Was a Lady (December 1939). A year-by-year account focuses on 175 new productions during this decade: sixty-eight musical comedies, thirty-two operettas, fifty-six revues, seventeen all-black musical comedies or revues, and two operas. Casts and credits for each of these productions are included at the conclusion of the narrative, in addition to lists of London productions and film versions of Broadway musicals of the 1930s, a bibliography, and discography.

PC 349. **GREEN, STANLEY.** The World of Musical Comedy: The Story of the American Musical Stage as Told Through the Careers of Its Foremost Composers and Lyricists. 1960; Rev. ed. New York: Barnes, 1968. 541 pp.
Though musical comedy is a large and variously defined genre, including operetta, comic opera, musical play, revue, and extravaganza, Green locates one common factor: music. He therefore traces the history of musical comedy through the lives of the most prominent composers and lyricists. Green contends that the period of musical comedy from 1920 to 1960 was largely concerned with the improvement of song and the integration of song and story. He begins his history in the 20th century with Victor Herbert and George M. Cohan. He then discusses the major talents of the 1920s--George and Ira Gershwin, Cole Porter, and Oscar Hammerstein II-- and the innovations of Jerome Kern and Otto Harbach during the 1930s. Green argues that the mature librettos of Rodgers and Hammerstein high-lighted the 1940s, while the emergence of director-librettists, and director-choreographers George Abbott and Joshua Logan, distinguished the 1950s and 1960s.

PC 350. **HARRIS, NEIL.** Humbug: The Art of P. T. Barnum. Boston: Little, Brown, 1973. 337 pp.
In this work, Harris discusses Barnum's public role and his use of popular taste for private gain. He depicts Barnum as a symbol of the individual "New Man" of Jacksonian America, challenging and exploding established rituals. At the same time, Harris sees Barnum as more than a symbol; he was aware of public tastes, of the new democratic sensibility of the times, and of his own accomplishments. Understanding the success of Barnum's show world is therefore to understand the times. Throughout, Harris focuses on this relationship as well as on Barnum's mastery of showmanship and his ability to mix high art and vulgar entertainment.

PC 351. HODGE, FRANCIS. Yankee Theatre: The Image of America on the
Stage, 1825-1850. Austin: University of Texas Press, 1964.
320 pp.
This study focuses on the "stage Yankee" during its peak period, and illustrates how this native American-type character developed in early plays
of American authorship. Hodge examines the full range of Yankee theatrical
activity, including the actors and the playmakers, as he re-evaluates
the contribution of the Yankee to the growth of the American stage. In
two appendixes, Hodge includes "A Note on Yankee-Theatre Stage Speech"
and "David Humphreys's Glossary of Yankee Words."

PC 352. HOYT, HARLOWE R. Town Hall Tonight. Englewood Cliffs, N.J.:
Prentice-Hall, 1955. 292 pp.
Hoyt has written a history of the entertainment offered on the stages
of town halls in the 1880s and 1890s. Though he focuses on his home town
in Wisconsin, he contends that the story of this theater was typical
throughout the U.S., insofar as most theaters performed standardized plays and
experienced the same economic problems. Giving a personal account, Hoyt
reconstructs the town and theater setting, the often melodramatic performances, and changes in the stock companies such as the disappearance of
the "star system," which was replaced by local companies with weekly show
changes. He also treats the showboat, the last small-time entertainment
to disappear. The passing of local theater is attributed to technological
advances in entertainment, the rise of traveling shows, and a growing
sophistication in entertainment.

PC 353. ISAACS, EDITH J. R. The Negro in the American Theatre. New York:
Theatre Arts, 1947. 143 pp.
Isaacs identifies four significant moments in the history of blacks in
American theater: the heyday of minstrelsy in which Billy Kersands, James
Blend, and Sam Lucas became prominent; the turn of the century, which
featured comedians Bob Cole, Earnest Hogan, and Bert Williams; the year
1914, which saw the rise and success of Ridgely Torrence's Granny Maumee;
and the 1940s, with Paul Robeson, Duke Ellington's Beggar's Holiday, and
the revival of Porgy and Bess. Isaacs envisions a "brighter" period in
which black theater is no longer viewed as separate from American theater
as a whole.

PC 354. KAYE, MARVIN. The Story of Monopoly, Silly Putty, Bingo, Twister,
Frisbee, Scrabble, et Cetera. New York: Stein & Day, 1973.
196 pp.
This journalistic survey of the American toy industry and the place of
toys and games in contemporary American culture discusses the importance
of playthings for children and adults, and gives a general perspective
on how playthings are designed, marketed, and used. Individual chapters
consider dolls, models, educational games, adult games, advertising, and
government regulation of the toy industry. Kaye discusses such famous
toys and games as Monopoly, Scrabble, and Silly Putty in detail, including
their cultural impact.

PC 355. KISLAN, RICHARD. The Musical: A Look at the American Musical
Theater. Englewood Cliffs, N.J.: Prentice-Hall, 1980.
262 pp.
In this work, the author examines the history of the musical, its most
influential creative artists, and the major elements that make up a musical
theater production. Kislan traces the musical's evolution through the
eras of minstrelsy, vaudeville, burlesque, revue, and comic opera up to
the present day. He deals in some detail with Jerome Kern, Rodgers and
Hammerstein, and Stephen Sondheim.

PC 356. KYRIAZI, GARY. The Great American Amusement Park: A Pictorial
         History. Secaucus, N.J.: Citadel Press, 1976. 256 pp.
This is a pictorial history of the American amusement park from the early
19th-century picnic groves and beer gardens to its present form. The
most detailed section covers Coney Island from its early days as a seaside
resort for the rich to its great days with Luna Park, Dreamland, and
Steeplechase Park and finally to its decline in recent years. Included
are chapters on Disneyland and the theme parks, as well as a list of
America's top 100 parks.

PC 357. LA PRADE, ERNEST. Broadcasting Music. New York: Rinehart, 1947.
         236 pp.
La Prade discusses the entire process of broadcasting music from planning
to production, and underlines the technical aspects of this process.
The work also presents a historical outline of the early days of broadcasting and includes a discussion of arranging, composition, conducting,
and final productions.

PC 358. LAUFE, ABE. Broadway's Greatest Musicals. 1969; Rev. ed. New
         York: Funk & Wagnalls, 1977. 529 pp.
According to Laufe, the artistic success of Broadway is to be measured
by its commercial appeal and return on production costs. Laufe offers
a discussion of selected musicals, which not only marked epochs in musical
theater, but were box office markers as well: Oklahoma, Showboat, South
Pacific, My Fair Lady, and others. Productions discussed date from 1884
to the 1970s.

PC 359. LAURIE, JOE, Jr. Vaudeville: From the Honky-Tonks to the Palace.
         New York: Holt, 1953. 561 pp.
Laurie, who was a hoofer, singer, comedian, and monologist, as well as
show business historian, offers a history based on anecdotes and reminiscences. His own experience in small-time vaudeville is reflected in his
discussion of life in the old-time boardinghouses and theatrical hotels,
as well as of the small-time chiselers and big-time operators that characterized vaudeville. Laurie writes about all types of vaudeville acts:
shadowgraphists, animal acts, musicians, contortionists, minstrels, escape
artists, sharpshooters, mind readers, monologists, and many more. He
also includes examples of routines seen in vaudeville.

PC 360. LEWIS, PHILIP C. Trouping: How the Show Came to Town. New York:
         Harper & Row, 1973. 266 pp.
The object of this book is to reconstruct the theatrical milieu on the
road from 1850 to 1905, a period when, according to the author, the inter-
action between the theater and American society was at its most vigorous.
Lewis's story is peopled with some of the more interesting theatrical
personalities of this era, such as Joseph Jefferson, Junius Brutus Booth,
James O'Neill, Denman Thompson, Edwin Booth, Lotta Crabtree, Lillian
Russell, and Adah Isaacs Menken. Lewis also touches on the rise of the
musical, from the minstrel show to the operettas of Victor Herbert and
Gilbert and Sullivan.

PC 361. MacMINN, GEORGE R. The Theater of the Golden Era in California.
         Caldwell, Idaho: Caxton, 1941. 529 pp.
In this narrative history, the author describes a brief period in the
history of California theater: the first decade of the Gold Rush. Throughout, the focus is on San Francisco, Sacramento, and numerous mining camps.
MacMinn draws heavily on primary sources (production notices, actors'
memoirs, and critical appraisals) to document his study. There are chapters on such topics as early performers (Jenny Lind), the popularity of
Shakespeare, music, the circus, and minor forms of entertainment, and
mainstream theater.

PC 362. MANGELS, WILLIAM F. The Outdoor Amusement Industry: From Earliest
          Times to the Present. New York: Vantage Press, 1952. 206 pp.
Stating that the "public has always craved spectacles," Mangels describes
outdoor public amusements, first in their early European forms and then
as developed and perfected in America. He covers the early American amusement park, a development of the "picnic grove," and focuses on the most
famous park, Coney Island. Mangels notes that the need for greater and
more exciting amusement gave rise to numerous inventions, such as the
carousel, the roller coaster, and the ferris wheel.

PC 363. MARKER, LISE-LONE. David Belasco: Naturalism in the American
          Theatre. Princeton, N.J.: Princeton University Press, 1975.
          248 pp.
This study of the dramatist, director, and producer David Belasco attempts
to reassess his place in theatrical and dramatic history by means of
detailed production reconstructions. The four productions, representing
different styles and concepts, are Sweet Kitty Bellairs (1903), The Girl
of the Golden West (1905), The Easiest Way (1909), and The Merchant of
Venice (1922). Marker provides background on Belasco's life, career,
and production methods, and throughout emphasizes the playwright's sensitivity to changing styles and developments in the theater.

PC 364. MATES, JULIAN. The American Musical Stage Before 1800. New Bruns-
          wick, N.J.: Rutgers University Press, 1962. 340 pp.
Mates recounts the earliest history of musical theater in the U.S. from
the adaptations of European musical and theatrical conventions and the
first truly American innovations seen in the Colonies in the early 1700s
to the elaborate production of The Archers at the John Street Theatre
in 1796. This latter work by William Dunlap and Benjamin Carr is considered by Mates to be the first extant musical both performed in the U.S.
and written by Americans. The various elements of this production--the
stage, orchestra, company, librettists, composer, and critical reception--
are examined closely by the author. Mates also attempts to establish
a relationship between early works and modern musical comedy.

PC 365. MATLAW, MYRON, ed. American Popular Entertainment: Papers and
          Proceedings of the Conference on the History of American Popular
          Entertainment. Westport, Conn.: Greenwood Press, 1979.
          352 pp.
This is a collection of twenty-six papers which comprised a major conference on American popular entertainment held in the U.S. (at the Library
of the Performing Arts, Lincoln Center, New York) in November 1977. The
volume contains contributions in six major categories: an overview of
popular entertainment; minstrel shows, vaudeville, and burlesque; tent
repertoire shows; the circus, Wild West shows, and medicine shows; dance;
and environmental entertainment. Among the contributors are Robert C.
Toll, Ralph G. Allen, Laurence Senelick, Marcello Truzzi, William L. Slout,
and Ray B. Browne.

PC 366. MATTHEWS, BRANDER. A Book About the Theater. New York: Scribner,
          1916. 334 pp.
In this collection of essays, Matthews addresses a broad range of topics,
many outside the definition of theater in the strict sense. Although
the topics are not limited to the American scene, a majority of the essays
focus on American entertainment. Matthews includes chapters on top theaters, puppetry, dance, acrobatics, minstrelsy, variety, magic, American
women dramatists, the dramatization of novels, the novelization of plays,
the evolution of scene-painting, and the problems with contemporary
dramatic criticism in the U.S.

PC 367. MAY, EARL CHAPIN. The Circus from Rome to Ringling. New York:
Duffield & Green, 1932. 332 pp.
May's thesis is that "in spite of its ancient, foreign origin and its
popularity in every civilized country, the circus has reached its greatest
size and efficiency in America through what we may call 'Yankee genius'."
His history is composed of brief chapters on all aspects of the circus.
In addition to a chronological narrative, chapters are included on such
topics as advertising, horsemanship, famous women of the circus, the plan-
ning of a circus bill, and important circus pioneers (such as the Ringling
Brothers).

PC 368. McCARTHY, ALBERT. The Dance Band Era: The Dancing Decades from
Ragtime to Swing 1910-1950. Radnor, Pa.: Chilton Book, 1971.
176 pp.
McCarthy describes the development of the dance band, defining it in relation to instrumentation and rhythmic structures. From the acceptance
of syncopated music in popular circles to the post-War big bands, this
work describes the performers, composers, groups, and bandleaders who
created, maintained, and perfected the dance band scene.

PC 369. McKENNON, JOE. A Pictorial History of the American Carnival.
3 vols. 1972; Rev ed. Sarasota, Fla.: Carnival Publishers
of Sarasota, 1981. 640 pp.
These volumes cover many aspects of the carnival. McKennon begins by
looking at the European and American roots of the carnival, and at the
1893 World's Columbian Exposition. Volume II contains biographical
sketches of "carnies," a discussion of itineraries, a glossary of carnival
words and terms, carnival titles, and a chronological breakdown of the
carnival to the present. In Volume III, the carnivals of the 1970s are
covered.

PC 370. McLEAN, ALBERT F., Jr. American Vaudeville as Ritual. Lexington:
University of Kentucky Press, 1965. 250 pp.
McLean looks at vaudeville "as a manifestation of psychic and social forces
at work in American history." His major concern is to isolate this form's
social-historical significance. The central theme that emerges is that
vaudeville as an entirety was a "manifestation of the belief in progress,
the pursuit of happiness, and the hope for material success basic to the
American character." The work is both an analysis of the form and an
attempt to place the vaudeville ritual in its mythic and historical contexts.

PC 371. McNAMARA, BROOKS. Step Right Up: An Illustrated History of the
American Medicine Show. Garden City, N.Y.: Doubleday, 1976.
233 pp.
This book covers the evolution and decline of various forms of the American
medicine show, from the earliest European mountebank and charlatan to
the demise of the form in the mid-1960s. The medicine show proper, according to McNamara, is a fusion of the mountebank shows and 19th-century
American popular entertainment. This unique form, which flourished in
the U.S. between 1870 and 1930, was essentially a theatrical production,
interrupted by sales pitches. McNamara covers Pitchmen, Wizard Oil,
Kikapoo Shows, and Indian Shows. Included is a portfolio of colored reproductions of trade and advertising cards from the William Helfand Collection.

PC 372. MEISELAS, SUSAN. Carnival Strippers. New York: Farrar, Straus,
& Giroux, 1976. 148 pp.
This is a photo-journalistic examination of the girlie shows attached
to small carnivals that travel through rural New England and the South.
Over a three-year period photographer Meiselas followed several of these
shows in order to provide the seventy-three photographs and text (culled

from over 100 hours of interviews with the dancers, talkers, and managers) which form a documentary portrait of this American subculture.

PC 373. MESSICK, HANK and BURT GOLDBLATT. The Only Game in Town: An Illustrated History of Gambling. New York: Crowell, 1976. 214 pp.
This study chronicles the history of gambling in America. After a brief survey of gambling in ancient civilizations, Messick and Goldblatt provide anecdotes of prominent people to illustrate the pervasive nature of gambling in American culture. They examine the birth of the gambling casino and its association with organized crime; various forms of gambling in the U.S., including dream books, lotteries, sports, and gambling machines; the evolution of the bookie in the gambling world; and governmental efforts to reduce corruption in gambling.

PC 374. MEYER, ROBERT, Jr. Festivals: U.S.A. & Canada. New York: Ives Washburn, 1967. 280 pp.
The author provides a general survey of major festivals taking place annually in the U.S. and Canada. He notes in his introduction that North American festivals began to flourish in the 1930s, in part due to improved transportation and increased recreation time. Meyer contends that the various types of festivals reflect the cultural, economic, historical, religious, and social character of individual communities. The text describes representative festivals taking place in North America. The last section is a calendar of annual festivals in the U.S. and Canada.

PC 375. MICKEL, JERE C. Footlights on the Prairie: The Story of the Repertory Tent Players in the Midwest. St. Cloud, Minn.: North Star Press, 1974. 236 pp.
Mickel provides an examination of the tent-show theater groups that traveled Middle-Western small towns from the mid-1850s to W.W. II. He looks at the use of tents and indoor spaces and at the "silly kid" character Toby, who, he says, ultimately undermined the quality of material presented and the standards of production. Mickel provides a detailed analysis of the stars, the show operations, the tent-show vocabulary, and the touring practices of representative companies.

PC 376. MOODY, RICHARD. America Takes the Stage. Bloomington: Indiana University Press, 1955. 330 pp.
This study looks at romanticism in American drama and theater from 1750 to 1900. Moody shows how wars, the struggles of the frontiersman, and the natural wonders of the land were readily adapted to lavish stage productions. From these theatrical adaptations came familiar American stage stereotypes. Moody deals predominantly with the Yankee, the black-face minstrels, and romanticism in stage design. He includes a selected play list for the 150-year period under investigation.

PC 377. MORDDEN, ETHAN. Better Foot Forward: The History of American Musical Theater. New York: Grossman, 1976. 369 pp.
According to Mordden, the truly American musical comedy began with Showboat. The history of the American musical before 1920 is a gradual one, with music, dance, and lyrics variously asserting themselves. Mordden traces this evolution through comic opera, musical comedy, revue, and operetta, to Showboat, in which words and music worked together to tell a story. With this model, the American musical grew and undersent innovation. Mordden traces the development of this genre to the 1970s.

PC 378. MORDDEN, ETHAN. Broadway Babies: The People Who Made the American Musical. New York: Oxford University Press, 1983. 244 pp.
Mordden chronicles the development of musical comedy from 1900, primarily through biographical discussions of influential figures on Broadway. Foremost in this group are Florenz Ziegfeld, Harold Prince, Bert Lahr, Gwen Verdon, Angela Lansbury, Victor Herbert, Liza Minnelli, and Stephen Sondheim. To Mordden, as important as the authors and composers are, other key figures also deserve attention (actors, directors, choreographers, and producers). During the 1920s big stars dominated; Mordden demonstrates how this pattern was disrupted by various authors and how the genre was transformed.

PC 379. MORRISON, THEODORE. Chautauqua: A Center for Education, Religion, and the Arts in America. Chicago: University of Chicago Press, 1974. 315 pp.
In this history of Chautauqua, Morrison traces the 100-year development of the institution from its beginning with the establishment of a summer assembly in 1874. The founders, John Heyl Vincent and Lewis Miller, originally conceived of Chautauqua as a serious place of study. It has always been a music center, but in addition it has fostered virtually all of the arts, including theater. Morrison discusses the abundance of activities at Chautauqua, such as Sunday Schools, traveling tent shows, and lectures. Morrison contends that Chautauqua, today as in the past, reflects "the opinions and trends of intellectual and cultural leaders of the United States." A photographic section features a series on the arts.

PC 380. NATHAN, GEORGE JEAN. The Entertainment of a Nation or Three-Sheets in the Wind. New York: Knopf, 1942. 290 pp.
Nathan looks at various aspects of popular entertainment in an effort to identify what keeps audiences entertained. Beginning with a comment on the deterioration of "American Male Playwrights" (except Eugene O'Neill), Nathan writes about such trends in American theater as the death of sophistication and the rebirth of sentiment; the appeal of stage film musical shows; the end of Bonanzas; and the appeal of mystery plays. Using contemporary examples, Nathan critically discusses all aspects of theater from the producer to the actors and actresses, and examines genres from cabarets and striptease to the circus. Nathan offers advice to the aspiring actress, the new actress, novice playwrights, and producers. The need for novelty in popular entertainment is seen in Hellzapoppin and Hold On To Your Hats, and more recently in certain motion pictures. According to Nathan, it is only through such innovations that the audience will not "die of ennui."

PC 381. NATHAN, GEORGE JEAN. The Popular Theater. New York: Knopf, 1918. 236 pp.
Nathan examines the nature of popular theater to reveal what makes a work popular with "the mob." Success and fame in the popular theater do not stem from talent; according to Nathan, a popular play is generally a bad play. Popular theatergoers expect to see their own thoughts and emotions reflected on the stage; therefore the form is bound and limited by the spectator. Yet talent does exist. Nathan identifies good as well as bad plays, actors, and movies, as he attempts to provide a new critical approach in evaluating aspects of this entertainment form. Within this critical view, Nathan adopts a pragmatic notion about the role of theater: it is simply a diversion for the "well-educated, well-bred, well-fed man." Topics addressed include the audience, criticism, first nights, and a typical season.

PC 382. **NATHAN, HANS.** Dan Emmett and the Rise of Early Negro Minstrelsy.
Norman: University of Oklahoma Press, 1962. 496 pp.
Nathan chronicles the development of minstrelsy from black impersonations
in 18th-century England to the death of Dan Emmett in 1904. He focuses
on Emmett, whose works as a banjoist, fiddler, singer, and comedian are
not only important to the history of American popular theater, but are
of intrinsic significance for their humor, freshness, and native value.
Rooted in a living tradition, Emmett's work, according to Nathan, is a
folk art, a truly American art. Throughout, Nathan describes minstrelsy
with details of specific dance numbers, musical scores, and lyrics.

PC 383. **POWLEDGE, FRED.** Mud Show: A Circus Season. New York: Harcourt
Brace Jovanovich, 1975. 374 pp.
This book follows the Hoxie Brothers Circus, a medium-sized tented circus
that toured from town to town during the 1974 season. The author provides
an evocation of a dying American institution, as he looks at the people
who travel with the circus. Their frustrations, moments of glory, boredom,
excitement, and secrets are discussed in this work.

PC 384. **RAHILL, FRANK.** The World of Melodrama. University Park: Pennsylvania State University Press, 1967. 334 pp.
Rahill treats the theater as a social institution and contends that melodrama was a genre of significance during the 19th century. Although his
coverage is not limited to the U.S. (there is a great deal on England
and France), Part III deals exclusively with melodrama in America. Here
Rahill explores such areas as Wild West melodrama, the drama of "ten,
twent', thir'," music in melodrama, and the propaganda melodrama. He
concludes with a chapter on melodrama in the films, including the Western.

PC 385. **REVETT, MARION S.** A Minstrel Town. New York: Pageant Press,
1955. 335 pp.
The author examines the history of traveling entertainment in Toledo,
Ohio, from 1840 to the turn of the century. While a discussion of the
theater and circus is included, the work centers on minstrel shows and
local music. Revett also provides more general, biographical discussions
of the development of movable entertainment prior to the early days of
Broadway.

PC 386. **RICE, EDWARD LeROY.** Monarchs of Minstrelsy, from "Daddy" Rice
to Date. New York: Kenny, 1911. 366 pp.
Rice traces the history of minstrelsy in America through short biographical
sketches of the chief minstrels, beginning with the first "blackface"
comedian, Thomas Dartmouth "Daddy" Rice, who created the "Jim Crow" song
and dance routine in 1828. Newspaper accounts, letters, and personal
reminiscences document the careers of these "blackface" actors.

PC 387. **ROOT, DEANE L.** American Popular Stage Music 1860-1880. Ann Arbor,
Mich.: UMI Research, 1981. 284 pp.
This work defines popular music as music which develops distinctive char-
acteristics according to the tastes of the expanding middle class. The
author identifies prevailing forms and styles of musical theater in the
U.S. between 1860 and 1880. Since most primary music discussed in this
study is not extant, much evidence is gathered from secondary sources.
The author includes lists of composers, arrangers, and works.

PC 388. **ROURKE, CONSTANCE.** Troupers of the Gold Coast, or the Rise of
Lotta Crabtree. New York: Harcourt, Brace, 1928. 275 pp.
From the perspective of an American cultural historian, Rourke presents
a biographical study of the actress Lotta Crabtree--"the San Francisco
Favorite." Although Crabtree is the major focus of this study, Rourke
also provides an examination of mid-19th-century theater, from New York

and Boston to San Francisco, with the major focus on California. She
also gives the reader glimpses of many of Crabtree's most important theatrical contemporaries, including Adah Menken, Lola Montez, Caroline Chapman,
Minnie Maddern, and the young Edwin Booth.

PC 389. RUSSELL, DON. The Wild West: A History of the Wild West Shows.
Fort Worth, Tex.: Amon Carter Museum of Western Art, 1970.
155 pp.
This is a history of traveling Wild West shows of the late 19th and early
20th centuries. Russell examines these "exhibitions of skill and daring"
and documents their rise and decline, analyzing the form for its innovation,
longevity, and uniqueness. Russell shows that the image of the American
West in popular thought is largely due to the Wild West exhibition and
especially to the contributions made by Buffalo Bill Cody.

PC 390. SAMPSON, HENRY T. Blacks in Blackface: A Source Book on Early
Black Musical Shows. Metuchen, N.J.: Scarecrow Press, 1980.
562 pp.
Sampson provides information about the pioneer efforts of black musical
shows. Employing certain black newspapers as his major sources, he begins
with an overview of black musical theater and proceeds to a closer look
at the money-men, theater-builders, and show producers who made this form
a reality. Later chapters provide extensive information on productions
and performers.

PC 391. SAMUELS, CHARLES and LOUISE SAMUELS. Once Upon a Stage: The
Merry World of Vaudeville. New York: Dodd, Mead, 1974.
286 pp.
This history of vaudeville contains chapters on the beginnings of vaudeville, with special attention given to Tony Pastor and other vaudeville
pioneers; on the singing women of vaudeville (such as Anna Held, Mae West,
Nora Bayes, Elsie Janis); on vaudeville legends (Sophie Tucker, Mae West,
Emma Carus, Louise Dresser, Trixie Friganza, Fritzi Scheff); on comics
in vaudeville (Eddie Foy, Dolly Sisters, the Marx Brothers, among others);
on various specialty acts; and on the Palace Theatre, the mecca for vaudeville stars.

PC 392. SLOUT, WILLIAM LAWRENCE. Theatre in a Tent: The Development
of a Provincial Entertainment. Bowling Green, Ohio: Bowling
Green University Popular Press, 1972. 153 pp.
The repertoire tent show which flourished from the last half of the 19th
century and into the 20th century was a distinct form of theater. Slout
traces the development of a typical tent show by describing the small
town opera house from which the repertoire show grew, and the troupes
which performed there. Economic and other problems led the repertoire
to move from established theaters to canvas tents, which were originally
used by the circus. Slout provides an examination of the development
of repertoire shows, including the literature, out of which emerged Toby--
the "traditional rustic of low comedy."

PC 393. SMITH, BILL. The Vaudevillians. New York: Macmillan, 1976.
278 pp.
This look at vaudeville is presented through interviews with thirty-one
vaudevillians. Among the entertainers telling their "inside" stories
are George Jessel, Edgar Bergen, John Bubbles, Milton Berle, George Burns,
Jack Durant, Jack Haley, Benny Rubin, Ken Murray, Rudy Vallee, Joe Smith,
and Rose Marie.

PC 394. SMITH, CECIL and GLENN LITTON. Musical Comedy in America: From the Black Crook to Sweeney Todd. 1950; Rev. ed. New York: Theatre Arts Books, 1981. 368 pp.

The first three sections of this work contain Smith's original Musical Comedy in America, which is a historical survey of America's musical theater from 1866 to 1949. Litton has added three additional sections to cover the musicals of the 1950s, 1960s, and 1970s. The authors categorize musicals and describe the historical development of the form. Smith states that the musical comedy is not America's only contribution to theater, nor is it wholly American, having derived in part from European forms of musical theater. He concludes that musicals are for entertainment and are only incidentally art. Both authors take into account the effect of historical events (wars, the Depression, Watergate) on musical theater.

PC 395. SOBEL, BERNARD. Burleycue: An Underground History of Burlesque Days. New York: Farrar & Rinehart, 1931. 284 pp.

Sobel begins this history of burlesque in 1869 with Lydia Thompson and the British Blondes. The early reactions to the exposed legs and blond heads are recorded, as are later attitudes toward the "forbidden pleasures" and bawdy humor of the burlesque stage. The star comedians (Leon Errol, James Barton, Fannie Brice, and Sam Barnard) and the "goddesses" of the form (Annie Ashley, Rose Sydell, Mollie Williams, and Truly Shattuck) are covered in this attempt to characterize the "joie de vivre" of burlesque. Sobel also describes the origin, operation, and production methods of the shows.

PC 396. SPEAIGHT, GEORGE. The Book of Clowns. New York: Macmillan, 1980. 128 pp.

Speaight presents an overview of the circus clown with one chapter devoted exclusively to the American clown. His objective is to capture the spirit of the clown's art and craft in both words and pictures; the volume includes color photography by Malcolm Fielding, Ralph Gobits, and Homer Sykes. The American clowns discussed and analyzed include Dan Rice, the most famous of 19th-century clowns; Emmett Kelly, a prime example of the hobo or tramp clown; Felix Adler, a producing clown (who devises acts for others); and Lou Jacobs, the quintessential image of the circus clown.

PC 397. SPEAIGHT, GEORGE. A History of the Circus. New York: Barnes, 1980. 216 pp.

Speaight focuses on the circus in England and America. He demonstrates the special way in which the circus grew in the U.S., where three-ring circuses were transported over vast distances by railroad. Among the topics covered are: menageries and animal acts; competition and combinations; permanent circus buildings; railroad shows; "leapers" and other acrobatic specialists; three-ring circuses; truck shows; and American features (for example, multi-rings, midway, menagerie tents, seat divisions, pre-circus concerts, after-shows). An appendix lists permanent or semi-permanent buildings that have been used for circuses in London, New York, and Paris.

PC 398. TAYLOR, JOHN RUSSELL and ARTHUR JACKSON. The Hollywood Musical. New York: McGraw-Hill, 1971. 278 pp.

Taylor begins his history of the Hollywood musical by exploring the backgrounds of the stage musical and its relationship to the film musical. The Hollywood musicals of the 1940s and 1950s rewrote the story, altered the score, and revised the use of dance, retaining only the title of the original Broadway show. This trend ended in the 1960s with a reversion to the Broadway musical and with the emergence of large production musicals. Taylor dissects the Hollywood musical into its separate parts: the music, composers, singers, and dancers. An extensive filmography is provided by Jackson.

PC 399. TOLL, ROBERT C. Blacking Up: The Minstrel Show in Nineteenth-
Century America. New York: Oxford University Press, 1974.
310 pp.
Toll describes minstrelsy as the first American popular entertainment
form to become a national institution, setting precedents and trends that
would influence later fields, especially burlesque and vaudeville. The
social and entertainment milieu in which minstrelsy emerged is described,
and the form's evolution is chronicled. Toll addresses the popularity
and function of minstrelsy, arguing that it both reflected and shaped
American attitudes. The social role of this entertainment form is explored
in chapters which cover the image of blacks in antebellum minstrelsy;
the support minstrels gave the Union during the Civil War; and the social
commentary which dominated the content of 19th-century white minstrelsy.

PC 400. TOLL, ROBERT C. The Entertainment Machine: American Show Business
in the Twentieth Century. New York: Oxford University Press,
1982. 284 pp.
Toll discusses the entertainment revolution generated by the application
of modern electronic technology to traditional popular art forms. He
focuses on film, phonograph recordings, and broadcast media as distinct
forms for expressing familiar themes and for creating an opportunity for
familiar entertainment functions. He also examines popular culture artifacts as reflecting popular tastes, needs, and inclinations, looking
closely at Westerns, music, theater, and comedy, as well as at such themes
as crime and sexuality.

PC 401. TOLL, ROBERT C. On with the Show: The First Century of Show
Business in America. New York: Oxford University Press, 1976.
361 pp.
Toll traces the historical development of American show business, arguing
that it reflects the needs of average Americans. He maintains that "the
common people shaped show business in their own image," and that the study
of the reception of show business productions offers a better understanding
of the opinions and attitudes of average people. He devotes several chapters to the careers of important show business figures such as P. T. Barnum
and Florenz Ziegfeld as well as to prominent black entertainers, sexual
impersonators, and celebrities. Entertainment forms such as the minstrel
theater, musical comedies, burlesque and vaudeville shows, and the circus
also receive attention. Toll uses contemporary anecdotes and photographs
to recreate an impression of how show business was viewed in its own era.

PC 402. TOWSEN, JOHN H. Clowns. New York: Hawthorn Books, 1976.
413 pp.
This is a survey of the clown in all its various forms: fools and jesters,
medieval mimes, jongleurs and minstrels, Pueblo Indian delight makers,
Harlequins and Pierrots, circus clowns, and many others. Towsen focuses
on specific clowns representing various periods, approaches, or styles
of comedy. A large number of American clowns are included.

PC 403. WILMETH, DON B. The Language of American Popular Entertainment:
A Glossary of Argot, Slang, and Terminology. Westport, Conn.:
Greenwood Press, 1981. 326 pp.
This source attempts to collect in one book the special language of the
principal forms of American popular entertainment: circus, carnival,
vaudeville, burlesque, tent shows, popular theater, magic shows, medicine
shows, early optical entertainments, and fairs. Less prominent forms,
such as puppetry, pantomime, and the musical review, are given some attention. The approach is that of the theater historian attempting to record
words and phrases that have been (and in some cases still are) part of
a special vocabulary of substrata of American popular culture.

PC 404. WILMETH, DON B. Variety Entertainment and Outdoor Amusements:
A Reference Guide. Westport, Conn.: Greenwood Press, 1982.
255 pp.
The objectives of this guide are threefold. The first is to provide brief
historical overviews of major forms of American variety entertainment
and outdoor amusements, including in the final chapter showboats and tent
shows. The second objective is to evaluate the available literature,
including graduate theses, periodicals, collections, and organizations
relevant to each chapter topic. Last, a checklist of major sources for
each chapter is provided. There are ten chapters covering such topics
as outdoor amusements, the circus, the Wild West exhibition, the dime
museum and P. T. Barnum, the medicine show, the minstrel show, variety/
vaudeville, burlesque and the striptease, the musical revue and early
musical theater, and stage magic.

PC 405. WITTKE, CARL. Tambo and Bones: A History of the American Minstrel
Stage. Durham, N.C.: Duke University Press, 1930. 269 pp.
This is a history of black-face minstrelsy, its performers, its form and
structure, and its performance. Wittke's thesis is that the minstrel
show was "a unique development, a purely native form of entertainment,
and a distinctively American contribution to theatrical history." His
study is divided into five chapters. The first chapter examines the origins of minstrelsy; the second surveys early minstrel shows; the third
deals with the prosperity and decline of the minstrel show; and the fourth
analyzes the technique of the show. The final chapter, "Knights of the
Burnt Cork," presents biographical sketches of some of the more prominent
minstrels: Dan Emmett, Edwin P. Christy, George N. Christy, Luke West,
L. V. H. Crosby, John H. Carle, Charley Howard, John Washington Smith,
Dan Gardner, Joe Sweeney, "Eph" Horn, Charles White, William P. Spaulding,
Francis Leon, Dan Bryant, William W. Newcomb, E. Freeman Dixey, Ralph
Keeler, George H. Primrose, Lew Dockstader, Al G. Field, and several dozen
other performers.

PC 406. ZEIDMAN, IRVING. The American Burlesque Show. New York: Hawthorn
Books, 1967. 271 pp.
Burlesque, writes Zeidman, is primarily a "commercialized sex show" which
has always been seen as too dirty by the censors, or not dirty enough
by the audience. The history of burlesque, therefore, is a history of
producers' unsuccessful attempts to create a balance between these two
demands. Beginning in the 1880s, Zeidman traces the history of Broadway
burlesque from The Black Crook and its most bawdy times, to its more
refined periods. Often using anecdotes, Zeidman describes the shows, the
"queens" of the form, and the producers.

V.   FILM

PC 407. ADAIR, GILBERT. Vietnam on Film: From the Green Berets to Apocalypse Now. New York: Proteus Books, 1981. 190 pp.
This book explores Hollywood's portrayal of American involvement in the
Vietnam War, demonstrating how that portrayal reflected Americans' conflicting attitudes toward the war. Adair establishes a context for his
study by examining Hollywood's relationship to other wars and notes that
the Vietnam War was most frequently portrayed indirectly, either through
allegory by the appropriation of other genres (such as the Western), or
by portraying protesters and returning veterans. Protest films and films
portraying draft resisters--such as Zabriskie Point, Alice's Restaurant,
Medium Cool, and The Strawberry Statement--are viewed in light of the

proliferation of low-budget, youth-oriented films in Hollywood following
the box office success of Easy Rider. Adair examines the various depictions of returning veterans in motorcycle movies, the Billy Jack series,
Taxi Driver, and films concerned with Vietnam veterans' readjustment to
American society (such as Coming Home). Included are lengthy discussions
of the portrayal of Americans in Vietnam in The Green Berets, The Deer
Hunter, and Apocalypse Now.

PC 408. **AFFRON, CHARLES.** Cinema and Sentiment. Chicago: University
of Chicago Press, 1982. 202 pp.
This spectator-based film theory is predominantly concerned with melodramas
and sentimental films, but it is equally applicable to all types of fiction
film. Affron examines the role played by identification in the film
viewer's relationship to the film text, and discusses the simultaneous
presence in the cinema of fictional elements and realistic representation.
He also observes that films contain qualities of self-referentiality while
striving for an invisibility of technique. The book examines the roles
played by the film frame in positioning and defining the spectator and
by cinema's illusion of depth in sustaining audience attention. Mise-
en-scene, sound, performance, and shot scale are discussed in relation
to their impact on the spectator's relationship to a film.

PC 409. **AGEE, JAMES.** Agee on Film: Reviews and Comments by James Agee.
New York: McDowell, Obolensky, 1958. 432 pp.
This posthumous collection, consisting primarily of Agee's reviews for
the Nation and Time Magazine in the 1940s, contributed to the intellectual
community's growing sense that serious discourse about the "ephemeral"
art of the movies might be possible. Contending that the medium achieves
a unique "poetic vitality" by recording "unaltered reality," Agee seeks
out redeeming qualities of the cinema of 1940s America; and he considers
the moral implications of a wartime propaganda that poses as documentary
fact. Discontented with the "suffocating genteelism" of many Hollywood
productions, he confesses to an affection for Preston Sturges comedies
and Val Lewton horror movies; and disturbed by postwar anti-Communism,
he argues that Roberto Rossellini's Open City and Charlie Chaplin's
Monsieur Verdoux possess profound ethical messages for 20th-century society.
Two of his final pieces--on the tragic careers of D. W. Griffith and Sergei
Eisenstein--touch upon Agee's own unrealized talents and upon his eventual
mythic status as an eloquent advocate of the movies.

PC 410. **ALEXANDER, WILLIAM.** Film on the Left: American Documentary Film
from 1931 to 1942. Princeton, N.J.: Princeton University Press,
1981. 355 pp.
This chronological history discusses the accomplishments and present-day
relevance of radical left film organizations and filmmakers of the 1930s.
Alexander combines critical analyses of such films as Pie in the Sky,
The Wave, New Earth, The Plow That Broke the Plains, The City, and Power
and the Land with biographies of over fifteen major filmmakers (which
are based on extensive personal interviews). He discusses the importance
of cooperative film organizations such as The Workers' Film and Photo
League, Nykino, and Frontier Films. Throughout the book, Alexander compares and contrasts the work of these artists with that of left-liberal
filmmakers, concentrating especially on the influence of Joris Ivens.

PC 411. **ALLOWAY, LAWRENCE.** Violent America: The Movies 1946-1964. New
York: Museum of Modern Art, 1971. 95 pp.
This analysis of themes of violence in American films views the changing
depiction of violence as a realistic reflection of social and technological
change. Alloway considers film as an artistic complex of recurring images
and themes and identifies thematic trends during the period of his study:
the rise of new types of violent action films; the renewed popularity

of gangster and private eye films; and the establishment of the private
eye as a vernacular hero. Alloway sees the violence in films of this
period as arising directly from the social and political context of the
1940s, 1950s, and early 1960s, and he connects the cycles of recurring
themes and motifs with the ability of films to function as social myths.

PC 412. ALTMAN, RICK, ed. Genre: The Musical. Boston: Routledge &
Kegan Paul, 1981. 228 pp.
This anthology contains thirteen essays which reveal many of the theoretical and methodological conflicts of film theory and criticism in the 1970s.
Questions of authorship, the social function of films, the role of technology in film history, and the relationship of ideology and the movies
are among the issues raised throughout this volume. The problem of the
"auteur" approach in light of the realities of studio filmmaking is
addressed by several of the contributors. The roles played by both the
cinematic apparatus and the film text in positioning the spectator are
also explored. While all of the essays are concerned with the musical
film, and most look at individual films, these works represent a variety
of critical approaches and address issues that extend beyond the boundaries
of the musical film genre.

PC 413. ATKINS, THOMAS R. Sexuality in the Movies. Bloomington: Indiana
University Press, 1975. 244 pp.
Sexuality in the Movies contains a series of essays which depict the evolution of portrayals of sex in films. That evolution is viewed in relation
to the changing values of moviegoers. Atkins includes discussions of
the sensual nature of the medium and of the ways moviegoing became associated with sexual identity and behavior. One section of the book discusses the depiction of sexuality in certain important Hollywood films
of the 1950s and 1960s, concentrating on the sexual ingredients of classical horror films, movies depicting homosexuality, skinflicks, and hard
core pornography. The final section examines six films from the 1960s
and 1970s considered landmarks for their portrayal of sexuality: I Am
Curious Yellow, Deep Throat, Midnight Cowboy, Carnal Knowledge, Cries
and Whispers, and Last Tango in Paris.

PC 414. BAKER, M. JOYCE. Images of Women in Film: The War Years, 1941-
1945. Ann Arbor, Mich.: UMI Research Press, 1980. 176 pp.
Baker observes that the necessities of wartime mobilization required that
popular perceptions of women's capabilities coincide with the changes
in women's roles in society. Media forms, particularly the cinema, emphasized the changing status of women, but with little consideration of the
post-war implications. Through a detailed analysis of several representative films of the period, Baker reveals Hollywood's strong attachment
to traditional notions of a woman's role in society and to the portrayal
of women eager to return to their pre-war social positions. While the
influx of women into the workforce advanced the movement toward sexual
equality, Baker finds that without a popular dialogue addressing the
changes in women's social roles, Americans privately questioned such changes
and clung to old behavior models.

PC 415. BALIO, TINO. United Artists: The Company Built by the Stars.
Madison: University of Wisconsin Press, 1976. 323 pp.
This economic history of United Artists Corporation chronicles the evo-
lution of the business of American filmmaking. Originally founded by
Charles Chaplin, D. W. Griffith, Mary Pickford, and Douglas Fairbanks,
Sr., to allow them to retain financial and creative control of their films,
United Artists maintained throughout its history a film distribution enter-
prise geared to the independent producer despite the oligopolistic market
structure that characterized the American film industry. Balio begins
with the initial organization of United Artists and follows the corporation

through various reorganizations and internal squabbles. He provides a look at the ways in which such events as the acquisition of first run theaters, the adjustment to sound technology, the Depression, W.W. II, and the Paramount Consent Decree affected one major film distributor and the American film industry as a whole.

PC 416. BALIO, TINO, ed. The American Film Industry. Madison: University of Wisconsin Press, 1976. 499 pp.
This volume contains original essays and excerpts from other publications which examine how such factors as economics, technological advances, industry structure, and changing legal constraints influenced American motion picture form and content from 1894 to the mid-1970s. These essays trace the development of the motion picture industry from a structure characterized by hundreds of small businesses in healthy competition, follow its growth into a mature oligopoly composed of five vertically integrated companies, and expose the effects of the forced divestiture of exhibition interests from those of production and distribution. In addition to scholarly and historical studies, Balio includes a prospectus prepared by an investment house designed to attract investors to motion picture firms in the 1920s, an article on publicity by Carl Laemmle, founder of the Independent Motion Picture Company, and Fortune magazine's 1930s evaluations of MGM and Loew's Inc.

PC 417. BARNOUW, ERIK. Documentary: A History of the Non-Fiction Film. 1974; Rev. ed. New York: Oxford University Press, 1983. 360 pp.
Barnouw surveys the history of the documentary film from the crude documentaries of the Lumiere brothers at the turn of the century to the more sophisticated documentary films of the early 1980s. In defining the documentary, Barnouw declares that the documentarist must not invent what he sees but should select and arrange his images so that they express his personal point of view. This book traces different impulses of documentary filmmaking, linking them to the goals of filmmakers. Barnouw uses terms such as "explorers," "reporters," "advocates," "chroniclers," "poets," and "guerillas" to identify these impulses. The book examines certain trends that have occurred throughout the history of the documentary and highlights the work of individual filmmakers. An extensive bibliography of materials relating to nonfiction films is included.

PC 418. BARSAM, RICHARD MERAN. Nonfiction Film: A Critical History. New York: Dutton, 1973. 332 pp.
Barsam outlines the historical development of nonfiction filmmaking, identifying two kinds of nonfiction film practice: the documentary film (distinguished by its sociopolitical purpose) and the factual film (such as travel, training, and educational films). While concerned with nonfiction films of all national origins, this volume pays particular attention to important moments in American nonfiction filmmaking. In examining the political documentaries of the 1930s and 1940s, Barsam discusses filmmaker Pare Lorentz and the U.S. Film Service, the March of Time newsreel series, the films of independents such as the Frontier Film Group and Willard Van Dyke, as well as the nonfiction film's contribution to U.S. mobilization during W.W. II. From the beginnings of the direct cinema movement in the 1950s, Barsam follows the rise of cinema verite filmmaking and describes how certain technological developments allowed the conscious informality and the breaking down of barriers between filmmaker and subject which characterize cinema verite.

PC 419. BARSAM, RICHARD MERAN, ed. Nonfiction Film Theory and Criticism. New York: Dutton, 1976. 382 pp.
The essays in this volume--written from the 1930s to the mid-1970s--have been assembled in an attempt to present various theoretical, critical, and practical positions on the documentary film. The first section contains theoretical essays that define the documentary impulse. Other essays explore the social and historical contexts in which several important documentary films were produced. The films of such directors as Robert Flaherty, Frederick Wiseman, and Willard Van Dyke are described through several critical essays and interviews. The final section of the anthology contains essays by filmmakers describing their efforts to meet the technical challenges posed by the documentary form.

PC 420. BATAILE, GRETCHEN M. and CHARLES L. P. SILET, eds. The Pretend Indians: Images of Native Americans in the Movies. Ames: Iowa State University Press, 1980. 202 pp.
The Pretend Indians is a collection of essays concerned with the portrayal of Native Americans in film. The book contains essays on the relationship between myth and media stereotypes, a collection of early responses to Hollywood's depiction of American Indians (covering the period 1911-44), as well as recent essays on the stereotyping of Indians. Also included are a collection of contemporary reviews of American Indian films, a photographic essay on the Hollywood Indian, and an annotated checklist of articles and books on the image of Indians in American film. The volume reveals the ways in which the cinema's distorted view of American Indians has reflected national ideology, values, and trends.

PC 421. BATTCOCK, GREGORY, ed. The New American Cinema: A Critical Anthology. New York: Dutton, 1967. 256 pp.
Battcock documents the 1960s "underground" cinema movement by compiling a variety of primary sources that explicate the New York-based scene of experimental movies. Including statements from evangelists (Jonas Mekas), skeptics (Parker Tyler and Amos Vogel), and antagonists (Bosley Crowther and Dwight Macdonald), the volume defines the role of the avant-garde screen as an outspoken alternative to Hollywood, an Old American Cinema that can only claim to have achieved "the highest pitch of technical excellence." Battcock also includes the individual film artists--Stan Brakhage, Jack Smith, Andy Warhol, Stan Van Der Beek, among others--who exemplify a radical reevaluation of professional competence, social responsibility, and aesthetic intention. Such accounts not only contrast the underground with an impersonal film industry, but also measure the experimental cinema against all of the visual and dramatic arts of the 1960s revolution.

PC 422. BAXTER, JOHN. Hollywood in the Sixties. New York: Barnes, 1972. 172 pp.
This survey of the style and content of the films, as well as the careers of the stars and directors of the 1960s, describes a period of recession in the film industry. Baxter traces the decline of the studio system and the acquisition of studios by entertainment conglomerates, citing these as factors responsible for a decline in the quality of American films. A shift to lower production values, the use of minor actors instead of major stars, and an emphasis on size rather than content or quality characterized American film production during this period. "East coast tastes and ideas" influenced film style and techniques as never before, contributing to an imitative rather than creative period of filmmaking. Types of films surveyed include musicals, thrillers, detective stories, romances, comedies, Westerns, horror films, spectaculars, and two subgenres--the "fantastic effects film" and the "battle of the sexes film."

PC 423. BAXTER, JOHN. Hollywood in the Thirties. New York: Barnes, 1968. 160 pp.
This book is a broad survey of the themes, stars, and film developments of the 1930s, a decade of important growth and perfection in the cinema. Particular attention is given to the impact of sound, its popular reception, and the changes it produced in the film industry. The studio system is examined in light of its effect on film content. Baxter specifically disclaims the auteur theory, citing the collaborative nature of filmmaking and the large body of work produced by each major director. With an emphasis on feature films, he discusses each of the major studios, and many of the important directors, technicians, and actors. Baxter covers MGM, Paramount, Warner Brothers, Universal Studios, Howard Hawks, Lewis Milestone, Frank Capra, John Ford, King Vidor, David Selznick, Samuel Goldwyn, and other directors and producers. He also surveys the prominent film stars, and includes selected "forgotten names" in acting and production.

PC 424. BERGMAN, ANDREW. We're in the Money: Depression America and Its Films. New York: New York University Press, 1971. 200 pp.
Bergman sees the movies of the 1930s as a major cultural force expressing dissatisfaction with social and economic conditions and providing an acceptable channel for such feelings. Themes expressed in the films of this period include the wish to blame others or to escape; attempts to understand the Depression and its causes; the streamlining and reinforcing of traditional goals and assumptions about success; and attempts to sustain optimism. Bergman discusses major films in each of these categories, as well as the contributions of major actors and directors to films in the 1930s. For the years 1930-33, the book covers gangster films, corruption and the city, anarchic comedy, the Marx Brothers, W. C. Fields, female roles, movie musicals, and Busby Berkeley; for 1933-39, it considers King Kong, films of King Vidor, G-men and cowboys, and social consciousness in films; for 1933-37, the search for authority, Frank Capra, and screwball comedy; for 1931-41, juvenile delinquent films and the Dead End Kids.

PC 425. BISKIND, PETER. Seeing Is Believing: How Hollywood Taught Us to Stop Worrying and Love the Fifties. New York: Pantheon Books, 1983. 371 pp.
Biskind examines American films of the 1950s as cultural documents. His approach acknowledges that these films may be without explicit political content but have the potential to reveal the cultural attitudes and the political climate of the era in which they were produced. Biskind concentrates on individual films from a variety of genres and discusses both serious dramatic works and exploitation pictures. He reveals how films of the 1950s reflect the Cold War era through their depictions of domesticity, conformity, delinquency, sexuality, and dissent.

PC 426. BOGLE, DONALD. Toms, Coons, Mulattoes, Mammies, and Bucks: An Interpretative History of Blacks in American Films. New York: Viking Press, 1973. 260 pp.
This book provides a survey of black actors and racial stereotypes in Hollywood films from the early silents to the 1970s. The author emphasizes the importance of Birth of a Nation and Gone with the Wind in shaping the popular perception of blacks and their portrayal in motion pictures. Bogle surveys the evolution, transformation, and discarding of stereotypes, and the ways in which major actors were able to transcend stereotypical roles. Among the trends and the actors discussed are: blacks in 1920s comedies; black servants and the careers of Hattie McDaniel, Rochester, Stepin Fetchit, and Bojangles in the 1930s; black entertainers and the "new Negro" in the 1940s; the rise of such black stars as Sidney Poitier, Ethel Waters, and Dorothy Dandridge in the 1950s; and the greater militancy

shown by blacks in films of the 1960s. Included are interviews with actors
and detailed discussions of important films and roles.

PC 427. BRAUDY, LEO. The World in a Frame: What We See in Films. Garden
         City, N.Y.: Anchor Press, 1976. 274 pp.
Braudy distinguishes his theoretical consideration of film from others
by concentrating on the reception of films rather than on their creation.
Combining formal, sociological, thematic, and historical varieties of
criticism, he breaks his discussion of an audience's experience of a film
into three general concerns. He begins by discussing the form that film
takes, how objects appear in film, and in what ways they gain significance.
Placing the film experience in a context of social myth and reality, Braudy
discusses the influence of tradition and convention on films (giving particular attention to the Western and movie musical). He also examines
the psychological relationship between films and their audiences.

PC 428. BROSNAN, JOHN. Future Tense: The Cinema of Science Fiction.
         New York: St. Martin's Press, 1978. 320 pp.
Brosnan finds in science fiction films a tendency to endorse the prevailing
moral and political climate of their day, in contrast to the radical political and philosophical tones of most literary science fiction. The author
credits W.W. II with indirectly increasing the number and sophistication
of science fiction films through discoveries in rocketry and weaponry,
and traces the changes in iconography and themes of post-war science fiction films in order to identify connections between Cold War rivalries
and movies depicting alien invasion and possession. Brosnan describes
the adoption of the science fiction genre by exploitation film producers
in the mid-1950s and 1960s, and the domination of special effects to the
exclusion of social issues in recent science fiction films. He includes
detailed plot summaries and production notes of important films as well
as excerpts from interviews with science fiction authors and film production personnel.

PC 429. BROWNLOW, KEVIN. The Parade's Gone By . . . . New York: Knopf,
         1968. 580 pp.
Brownlow has assembled an extensive series of oral histories concerning
early silent era filmmaking in an attempt to counter the popular perception
that the period was characterized by crude or inept filmmaking. These
interviews with former actors, producers, directors, stuntmen, and technicians portray films and filmmaking both before and during the early
stages of the studio system. Individual films and filmmakers, as well
as such specific silent film techniques as tinting, titling, and acting
styles, are examined in detail.

PC 430. BROWNLOW, KEVIN. The War, the West, and the Wilderness. New
         York: Knopf, 1978. 602 pp.
Brownlow uses logbooks, diaries, personal correspondence, and interviews
to construct a documentary record of early filmmakers who worked outside
of film studios. He describes the conditions of production faced by newsreel filmmakers covering Pancho Villa, the Boxer Rebellion, and W.W. I,
as well as naturalists and explorers who made use of early film technology;
he discusses the production of such films as Wings and The Big Parade
as well as the works of filmmakers Robert Flaherty, King Vidor, and D.
W. Griffith. However, the majority of the book is devoted to the films
and experiences of lesser-known filmmakers.

PC 431. CALDER, JENNI. There Must Be a Lone Ranger: The American West
         in Film and in Reality. New York: Taplinger, 1975. 241 pp.
Calder's study of the imaginary American West describes the ingredients
of the Western movie and their contribution to the Western's appeal.
This appeal runs across normal demographic considerations, testifying

to the power of a myth that endures even when confronted with documented facts questioning its authenticity. Calder concentrates on film versions of the West made from the late 1940s into the mid-1970s, and examines the cultural and political implications as well as the current relevance of the Western myth.

PC 432. CAMERON, EVAN WILLIAM, ed. Sound and the Cinema: The Coming of Sound to the American Film. Pleasantville, N.Y.: Redgrave, 1980. 232 pp.
This anthology consists of the proceedings of a 1973 symposium on "The Coming of Sound to the American Film, 1925-1940." Essays in the first section of this volume establish the technological and economic context of the coming of sound. In the second section, members of the Hollywood filmmaking community (including cinematographer Hal Mohr, directors Frank Capra and Rouben Mamoulian, screenwriters Julius Epstein and Walter Reisch, and composer Bernard Herrmann) describe how the invention of sound filmmaking technologies affected their careers. Also included in this book are detailed studies of the impact of sound on the production techniques and final form of Applause (1929) and Citizen Kane (1941).

PC 433. CAMPBELL, EDWARD D. C., Jr. The Celluloid South: Hollywood and the Southern Myth. Knoxville: University of Tennessee Press, 1981. 212 pp.
Examining films from Birth of a Nation (1915) to Mandingo (1975), Campbell suggests that Hollywood's perpetuation of a mythical South is more revealing of contemporary society than of the society it attempts to portray. He looks at the silent film's glorification of plantation society, the importance of Gone with the Wind, revisionist portrayals of the South from 1941-80, and the needs in American culture that Hollywood's image of the South has addressed. The author traces the shift in the celluloid picture of the South from that of a proud, noble, but defeated nation to that of a decadent society characterized by sexual deviance, racism, and political corruption.

PC 434. CAMPBELL, RUSSELL. Cinema Strikes Back: Radical Filmmaking in the United States 1930-1942. Ann Arbor, Mich.: UMI Research Press, 1982. 387 pp.
Focusing on three American filmmaking collectives--The Workers' Film and Photo League, Nykino, and Frontier Films--Campbell discusses the radical cinema movement in American documentary filmmaking during the 1930s. According to the author, Leftist filmmakers were drawn to documentary forms because nonfiction filmmaking seemed to grow out of the doctrine of Socialist Realism. The resulting films provided a serious and systematic depiction of workers and the unemployed unavailable in Hollywood's commercial output. Campbell chronicles the financial problems and the sporadic lack of a working class organizational base which plagued many of the Leftist filmmakers' early efforts. He also examines how such problems were overcome through the efforts of the three collectives. Descriptions of such films as Heart of Spain, Return to Life, China Strikes Back, People of the Cumberland, and Native Land, as well as filmographies of the three collectives, are included.

PC 435. CARY, DIANA SERRA. Hollywood's Children: An Inside Account of the Child Star Era. Boston: Houghton Mifflin, 1979. 290 pp.
The author--a former child star who appeared in many popular silent comedies under the name "Baby Peggy"--surveys child stars of films and vaudeville, emphasizing Lotta Crabtree and her position as the prototype for all subsequent child stars. Cary includes biographies and career sketches of herself, Mary Pickford, Jackie Coogan, the "Our Gang" children, Shirley Temple, Mickey Rooney, Judy Garland, Jane Withers, Margaret O'Brien, Deanna Durbin, Jackie Cooper, and Freddie Bartholomew. In studying the operation

of the child star system, Cary analyzes the reasons for the popularity
and later decline of child films, financial arrangements with child stars,
and the psychological effects on children when their careers had ended.
Also included are discussions of several forgotten child stars and child
actors who never reached stardom.

PC 436. CAUGHIE, JOHN, ed. Theories of Authorship: A Reader. Boston:
         Routledge & Kegan Paul, 1981. 316 pp.
The three sections of Caughie's reader document the developmental stages
of theories about authorship in Hollywood: the "romantic" self-expression
imagined by pioneering auteurists; the analysis of directors as essentially
"bearers of structure"; and the deciphering of spectator-text relationships
in the course of a movie's "performance." Traditional auteur theory is
represented by a sampling of remarks from Andrew Sarris, Movie, and Cahiers
du Cinema as well as by a "dossier" on John Ford's career, while the structuralist methods inspired by Claude Levi-Strauss are taken from, among
others, Peter Wollen's writings and Cahiers du Cinema's appreciation of
Young Mr. Lincoln. For Caughie, the close reading of spectator-film discourse proves to be a commendable evolution: from a primitive "untidy
humanism" to a subtle, more "scientific" perspective, from an abundant
"idealism" to a sober objectivity compatible with the aims of semioticians,
feminists, and members of the avant garde.

PC 437. CAVELL, STANLEY. Pursuits of Happiness: The Hollywood Comedy
         of Remarriage. Cambridge, Mass.: Harvard University Press,
         1981. 283 pp.
Cavell offers a consideration of seven Hollywood films of the 1930s and
1940s: The Lady Eve, It Happened One Night, Adam's Rib, Bringing Up Baby,
The Philadelphia Story, His Girl Friday, and The Awful Truth. He finds
the precedent for the genre's structure, which he calls "comedies of remarriage," in Shakespearian romantic comedy. These films are as much about
self-realization, the "creation" of self, and the private/public nature
of marriage, as they are about the rejoining of a separated couple. In
particular, these films take as a heroine a married woman--a spirited
mature female protagonist--which was unusual for films of this era. Central to Cavell's thesis is the notion that the relationships of married
couples often provide a forum for the difficult struggle to achieve self-
knowledge. Paradoxically, self-knowledge in these films is usually
achieved through some kind of separation which the married couples undergo.
According to Cavell, authentic marriages must support the liberty and
dignity of both husband and wife.

PC 438. CEPLAIR, LARRY and STEVEN ENGLUND. The Inquisition in Hollywood:
         Politics in the Film Community 1930-1960. Garden City, N.Y.:
         Anchor Press, 1980. 536 pp.
Ceplair and Englund trace radical and liberal sentiment and the activities
of the Hollywood film community beginning with the founding of the Screen
Writers Guild in 1933. They also consider government and popular responses
to those activities. The authors discuss the Congressional hearings into
Communist activity in Hollywood that took place in October 1947 and again
from 1951-53. The case of the Hollywood Ten and the industry practice
of blacklisting are looked at in depth. The work includes a list of officers and board members of the Screen Writers Guild from 1933-45, a list
of political activists in Hollywood in the 1930s and 1940s who were classified as either radicals or liberals, a list of HUAC witnesses for the
October 1947 hearing, a list of informers, and a copy of the Waldorf Statement made by members of the Association of Motion Picture Producers deploring the actions of the Hollywood Ten.

PC 439. CLARENS, CARLOS. Crime Movies: From Griffith to The Godfather
         and Beyond. New York: Norton, 1980. 351 pp.
This genre study—which focuses on the American crime film from its inception in the early 1900s to the late 1970s—explores the genre's ability
to express changing American attitudes. According to Clarens, crime films
portray what is culturally, psychologically, and morally abnormal, thus
making individuals aware of behavior that society cannot, or will not,
tolerate. Beyond this function, Clarens examines such topics as: the
crime films of the silent era, the 1930s crime film, film noir, and the
more liberated and violent crime films of the late 1960s and early 1970s.
Clarens further explores ways in which audiences relate to the depiction
of historical and cultural realities in the genre film.

PC 440. COGLEY, JOHN. Report on Blacklisting: Volume I—The Movies.
         N.P.: Fund for the Republic, 1956. 312 pp.
Cogley's book outlines the institutionalization of the blacklist and
explores the nature and extent of Communist influence in Hollywood.
Included are interviews with motion picture industry executives, leaders
of theatrical unions and anti-Communist organizations, producers, writers,
directors, and actors which chronicle their experiences with blacklisting
and the "subversive" forces in Hollywood. Cogley discusses the 1947 HUAC
hearings, the case of the Hollywood Ten, and the House Committee's renewed
investigation in 1951. He describes attempts made to insure the loyalty
of Hollywood employees, including the establishment of the Motion Picture
Alliance for the Preservation of American Ideals; various "clearance"
systems set up to remove alleged Communists from employment; and Hollywood's cooperation with the American Legion; and the Legion's influence
on the practices of the motion picture industry. Also included are an
essay by Harold W. Horowitz on the legal aspects of the blacklist, and
Dorothy B. Jones's analysis of Communist influence on film content. Volume
II (see PC 742) discusses the blacklist in the radio and television industries.

PC 441. CONANT, MICHAEL. Antitrust in the Motion Picture Industry; Eco-
         nomic and Level Analysis. Berkeley: University of California
         Press, 1960. 240 pp.
Conant analyzes the impact of antitrust actions on the structure and behavior of the Hollywood motion picture industry, placing particular emphasis
on the case of U.S. vs. Paramount Pictures (1948). He makes extensive
use of exhibits from the Paramount case, Securities and Exchange Commission
reports, and trade journals, while describing the market structure and
trade practices of the American film industry at the time of prosecution
and the changes ordered by the divestiture decree. The book also includes
an historical summary of the American film industry with particular emphasis on the early antitrust cases, especially the many suits involving
the Motion Picture Patents Company.

PC 442. COOK, JIM and MIKE LEWINGTON, eds. Images of Alcoholism. London:
         British Film Institute, 1979. 82 pp.
This collection of essays discusses how films from the 1930s to the 1970s
portrayed the causes and medical treatments of alcoholism, identifying
an extremely consistent range of representations of alcoholism. The editors conclude that these dominant representations result from dramatic
and ideological restrictions rather than from a desire for realistic portrayals. Individual essays consider movie versions of the alcoholic hero,
women alcoholics, and alcoholic treatment agencies. The work also includes
a filmography of representative films that portray alcoholism.

PC 443. CRAFTON, DONALD. Before Mickey: The Animated Film 1898-1928. Cambridge, Mass.: MIT Press, 1982. 413 pp.
Crafton examines the origins and early development of the animated film by placing that development against a cultural and industrial background. Initially, a confusing array of characters, plots, and visual styles characterized the animated film. Crafton suggests an evolution in which the main influences on the early animated film (such as the commercial nature of film industry, technology, other popular arts, and the personalities of specific animators) determined the development of a relatively small number of codes, the primary function of which was the figuration of the animator. This book focuses on the popular arts which predated the animated film and shaped its development (the comic strip and lightening sketches), on important animators (Emile Cohl and John Randolph Bray), and on the development of mass production animation shops.

PC 444. CRIPPS, THOMAS. Black Film as Genre. Bloomington: Indiana University Press, 1978. 184 pp.
Cripps examines motion pictures aimed at black audiences and produced by black writers, directors, and actors, attempting to discover what these films reveal about the black experience in America. After a brief discussion of the evolution of the black film, Cripps analyzes six black genre films (The Scar of Shame, The St. Louis Blues, The Blood of Jesus, The Negro Soldier, Nothing But a Man, Sweet Sweetback's Baadasssss Song), placing them in social, cultural, and historical contexts and examining their impact upon black audiences. Cripps also includes a discussion of the criticism and scholarship of black films and a filmography of black genre films.

PC 445. CRIPPS, THOMAS. Slow Fade to Black: The Negro in American Film, 1900-1942. New York: Oxford University Press, 1977. 447 pp.
This social history of the role of blacks in American films ranges from 1900 to 1942 when the major studios met with the NAACP and agreed to begin integration of studio technicians and to abandon racial stereotypes. Cripps traces the slow emergence of Afro-American impact on the motion picture industry, connecting it with the larger struggle against racism in American society. He examines films made during the period of his study, discussing their ability to function as collective myths and reveal deep-seated American values and attitudes. Cripps also considers the survival of blacks within the motion picture industry, black protest against Hollywood abuses, and attempts to establish a black underground cinema.

PC 446. CURTIS, DAVID. Experimental Cinema. New York: Universe Books, 1971. 168 pp.
Curtis discusses the changing status of oppositional filmmaking in America. From the late 1920s to the early 1930s, experimentation within Hollywood studios yielded technological innovations which extended cinema's potential but were used only to reinforce dominant narrative practices. Later American experimental filmmakers were influenced by the European avant-garde. The post-W.W. I choice of the 16mm filmmaking format by the American avant-gardists cut them off from all but nontheatrical avenues of distribution, furthering their separation from the mainstream American film industry and requiring the development of alternative distribution systems. Curtis discusses the films and theoretical positions of such important avant-gardists as Maya Deren, Amos Vogel, Stan Brakhage, James Broughton, Kenneth Anger, Curtis Harrington, and Gregory Markopoulos, as well as the establishment of Cinema 16 and the founding of Film Culture magazine.

PC 447. DAVIES, PHILIP and BRIAN NEVE, eds. Cinema, Politics and Society
in America. New York: St. Martin's Press, 1981. 266 pp.
The editors stress the role of industrial economics in shaping motion
picture content. Certain essayists provide the continuity for Hollywood's
difficult transformation from the consensus-oriented studio system to
the present emphasis on independent productions aimed at a diversified
American public. Other contributors focus on individual decades (the
1930s, the 1940s), genres (the Western), and films (Elia Kazan's On the
Waterfront) to document how the movies, representing more than a casual
reflection of social climate, become filtered through a complex network
of economic and political interests. The concluding pieces, adopting
a topical approach--the distorted cinematic depiction of blacks, the working class, the police, and the automobile--reinforce a message pervading
much of the volume: that the American screen's penchant for evasion and
violence suggests an industrial hegemony, a subservience to middle-class
taste, which persists in spite of the departure of the traditional studio
bosses.

PC 448. DE LAURETIS, TERESA and STEPHEN HEATH, eds. The Cinematic Apparatus. New York: St. Martin's Press, 1980. 213 pp.
This compilation of papers from a 1978 conference at the University of
Wisconsin's Center for Twentieth Century Studies employs the concept of
the "cinematic apparatus" to synthesize a wide range of technological
and ideological matters related to the motion picture. In the first half
of this volume, the majority of the contributors--among them Peter Wollen,
Douglas Gomery, and Dudley Andrew--ground the debates over technical innovations for sound and color in a historical, largely American, context.
Many of the remaining essays, by such authors as Jean-Louis Comolli and
Bill Nichols, address issues of perception and spectator-text relationships:
the implications of deep-focus, the assumption-challenging role of the
avant-garde, the distinctive psychology of female viewers. De Lauretis's
concluding remarks summarize the conference's objectives: to appreciate
film as a "social technology" by uniting a "historical materialist theory"
with the decoding methods offered by structuralism, semiology, and psychoanalysis.

PC 449. DEMING, BARBARA. Running Away from Myself. New York: Grossman,
1969. 210 pp.
Deming declares that films offer "a portrait of ourselves" by facilitating
escape into a dream world that reflects the reality of audiences and the
culture in which a film was created. In this work she explores the potential for films to reflect cultural beliefs and morals, concentrating on
American films from the 1940s. Deming analyzes recurring character types
from the period such as the tough guy hero, the possessive heroine, and
the protagonists of success stories. She concludes that films reveal
not only the best aspects of the culture that produces them, but also
the worst, often presenting an uncompromising image of society.

PC 450. DE USABEL, GAIZKA S. The High Noon of American Films in Latin
America. Ann Arbor, Mich.: UMI Research Press, 1982. 317 pp.
This work examines the distribution of American films in Latin America
from 1919-51. Beginning with the conditions of film markets in the silent
era, de Usabel traces the activities of United Artists representatives
and the establishment of subsidiaries in Mexico, Brazil, Cuba, Argentina,
and Panama. In analyzing the growth of United Artists' interests in Latin
America the author reveals how the company's representatives overcame
such problems as language barriers, film piracy, and governmental or censorship restriction. De Usabel traces the increased interest in Latin American markets brought about by W.W. II, the effect of the "Good Neighbor
Policy" on United Artists, and the financial crisis which brought about
the dissolution of many Latin American branches in the post-war period.

PC 451. DOOLEY, ROGER. From Scarface to Scarlett: American Films in
the 1930s. New York: Harcourt Brace Jovanovich, 1979.
648 pp.
In this historical consideration of movies made during the 1930s, Dooley
examines the sociological significance of many of the Hollywood productions
of the Depression Era and groups these films into fifty distinct genres,
cycles, or trends, introducing each by suggesting the social, historical,
or psychological reasons for its development. He then traces these film
types through the decade, citing significant examples and discussing what
they reveal about American culture during the Depression. Among the film
categories discussed by Dooley are those based on intrigue, nostalgia,
escapism, and imperialism; as well as portrayals of the wealthy, criminals,
forces of law and order, and "everyday people."

PC 452. DOWDY, ANDREW. Movies Are Better Than Ever: Wide-Screen Memories
of the Fifties. New York: Morrow, 1973. 242 pp.
Dowdy sees the films of the 1950s as reflections of a general atmosphere
of fear, cynicism, and paranoia that arose from the Cold War and McCarthyism. He explores the dual function of movies in providing escape from
high culture and demythologizing previous idols. Chapters in this book
explore the impact of television on film, and the decline of several genres
and themes during the period (including "B" movies, the musical, movie
serials, and the image of the harmonious American family). New technological developments such as 3-D films, Cinemascope, and other wide screen
techniques are discussed, as are the proliferation of youth-oriented films.
Dowdy examines science fiction films, sexuality in movies, Western heroes,
and sexual symbols, placing them in the cultural context of the 1950s.
The volume was reprinted in 1975 under the title, Films of the Fifties:
The American State of Mind.

PC 453. DURGNAT, RAYMOND. The Crazy Mirror: Hollywood Comedy and the
American Image. New York: Horizon, 1970. 280 pp.
This analysis of the themes and images in Hollywood film comedy establishes
its theoretical context by defining comedy as a mixture of satire, slapstick, and sophisticated style, and by noting the capacity of the movies
to reflect society and social trends. Durgnat examines early cartoon
films and the silent comedies of Mack Sennett, Charles Chaplin, Buster
Keaton, and Harold Lloyd. He characterizes the early sound comedies of
the 1930s as sophisticated and possessing middle-class values. In his
discussion of 1940s film comedy, Durgnat describes the replacement of
the "comedy of manners" by "homely comedy." Noting a return to both sophistication and slapstick in 1950s film comedies, he chronicles the appearance
of sex as a comic subject and the abundance of optimistic themes. Durgnat
concludes his analysis with observations on the rejection of middle-class
assumptions in film comedies of the 1960s.

PC 454. DYER, RICHARD. Stars. London: British Film Institute, 1979.
204 pp.
Dyer merges two analytical methods--the sociological-industrial and the
semiotic--to understand the popular appeal of a select number of American
film stars: Greta Garbo, Marlene Dietrich, Bette Davis, Marilyn Monroe,
Marlon Brando, Jane Fonda, and Robert Redford. Assuming that all texts
may be deciphered as "social facts," he emphasizes three facets of celebrity status: the interaction of values, human needs, social structure
and the institutions of production and consumption; the star-image conveyed
through social types (the "independent woman," "the rebel," among others)
and the promotional tactics of fan magazines and publicity stills (as
in the case of Jane Fonda); and the function of performers in constructing
characters within specific film narratives (for example, Bette Davis in
The Little Foxes). For Dyer, the star phenomenon reflects a specific
ideology--Hollywood's ability to depoliticize America--which only apparently resolves society's deep-rooted conflicts of class and gender.

PC 455. EDGERTON, GARY R. American Film Exhibition and an Analysis of
the Motion Picture Industry's Market Structure, 1963-1980. New
York: Garland, 1983. 224 pp.
Beginning with the Paramount Decision of 1948 and its implications for
the American film industry, Edgerton undertakes a study of the changing
role of film exhibition and its relationship to film production and distribution. He also discusses the operation of American movie theaters
and the sociocultural implications of how theater design reflects American
society and embodies the business philosophy of movie exhibition. In
addition, he examines the developing symbiotic relationship between the
film industry and cable and video delivery systems, and the potential
consequences this relationship will have for the exhibition component of
the film industry.

PC 456. ERENS, PATRICIA, ed. Sexual Strategems: The World of Women in
Film. New York: Horizon Press, 1979. 336 pp.
This anthology consists of twenty-four essays that examine the roles women
play not only as characters in film but also as filmmakers. The text
is divided into two sections: "The Male Directed Cinema" and "The Women's
Cinema." The essays explore such issues as the complex and constantly
changing role of women in films and society, films which focus attention
on how men have come to perceive women, and the ways in which films have
aided or obstructed women's attempts to perceive themselves. Profiles
of Dorothy Arzner, Ingmar Bergman, Mai Zetterling, and Lina Wertmuller
are included.

PC 457. EVERSON, WILLIAM K. American Silent Film. New York: Oxford
University Press, 1978. 387 pp.
Everson surveys the cultural and historical significance of the silent
film from 1896 to the advent of sound in the late 1920s and early 1930s.
He describes the impact that motion pictures had on the American public
at the turn of the century, and how films grew from a novelty item at
amusement parks and vaudeville houses to a serious and profitable art
form by the time D. W. Griffith began making movies in the early 1900s.
Everson includes chapters on the evolution of such film genres as the
Western, the comedy, and the horror film, and describes Griffith's Birth
of a Nation, Intolerance, and his contributions to silent film during
the 1920s. Individual chapters examine the practice of subtitling and
the emergence and dominance of the female star. Everson concludes with
an appendix that discusses the state of film scholarship in America, a
bibliography that includes information on books, films, and archives of
interest to the student and historian of silent film, and a chronology
surveying the technical and artistic evolution of the silent film from
1893-1929.

PC 458. FARBER, MANNY. Negative Space: Manny Farber on the Movies.
New York: Praeger, 1971. 288 pp.
This collection of Farber's writings from the 1940s to the late 1960s
illustrates the reviewer's transformation from champion of the Hollywood
"B" picture to explicator of the European avant-garde. Explicitly set
apart from the critical traditions established by James Agee, who "shel-
lacked the reader with culture," Farber's pieces for the Nation and Commentary in the 1950s applaud the virtues of "termite art"--the male-action
dramas of Howard Hawks, Samuel Fuller, and Don Siegel--against "white
elephant art"--the "realm of celebrity and affluence" applauded by "long-
hairs" who embrace pretentious Hollywood and the "burnt-out sentimentality
and aesthetic cowardice" of European film-makers. Early Farber is consistently the advocate of a "seamless" naturalism and the opponent of
the Big Statement and the "disappearance of reality in the fog of interpretation." The late 1960s contributions to Artforum indicate that Farber,
preferring "formal excitements" over content, has exchanged the "tattoo

parlors" of 42nd Street for the New York Film Festival and the experimental ventures of a Jean-Luc Godard.

PC 459. FARBER, STEPHEN. The Movie Rating Game. Washington, D.C.: Public
      Affairs Press, 1972. 128 pp.
This volume arises out of Farber's 1969-70 fellowship appointment to the
Code and Rating Administration of the Motion Picture Association of America.
Farber describes the Administration's movie rating policies and procedures.
Designed as a guide to film content, the rating system's distinction
between classification and censorship has become blurred. Farber discusses
the rating system in light of the changing demographics of movie audiences
and the increasing demand made by filmmakers for the same freedoms as
other artists. The book contains a copy of the Motion Picture Association's original description of the rating system, a typical studio contract
ratings clause, a list of rating appeals through March 1972, and an extract
from the original Motion Picture Production Code's content restrictions.

PC 460. FELL, JOHN L. Film and the Narrative Tradition. Norman: Uni-
      versity of Oklahoma Press, 1974. 284 pp.
Fell views movies as the culmination of a long tradition of evolving narrative technique and discusses a number of impulses present in business,
art, and culture from 1886-1911 to reveal how they came together to shape
film storytelling of the nickelodeon era. Instead of identifying innovators or specific influences, he attempts to describe the development
of a "conventional narrative code," largely based upon the narrative tradition of representational painting. Fell begins by describing the setting
of the period, its population, technology, and merchandising techniques.
He then examines various amusements and leisure activities (19th-century
novel, comics, magazine illustrations, theater and popular entertainments),
discussing their depiction of space, time, movement, and consciousness,
and considering how these impulses culminated in the silent narrative
film.

PC 461. FELL, JOHN L., ed. Film Before Griffith. Berkeley: University
      of California Press, 1983. 395 pp.
The essays collected in Film Before Griffith offer a revision of some
of the more romantic histories of the early motion picture industry.
Fell has organized the essays into three sections. The first emphasizes
some of the early companies and filmmakers and includes essays which
address the connection between early filmmaking and ideology. Fell's second
section deals with early film exhibition and distribution practices.
Individual essays discuss the effects of copyright laws, describe the
role of the individual traveling exhibitor, and question the traditional
notions of early audience demographics. The final section addresses the
films themselves, viewing their form, content and social meanings, and
connecting some films to recent concerns such as Feminism and the avant-
garde.

PC 462. FENIN, GEORGE N. and WILLIAM K. EVERSON. The Western: From
      Silents to the Seventies. 1962; Rev. ed. New York: Grossman,
      1973. 396 pp.
This study of the Western film and its view of America provides a critical
analysis of the genre, its conventions, and its industrial and aesthetic
growth. The volume discusses both major films and "B" films, with a
detailed examination of specific classics of the genre. Topics include
Western history and the Hollywood version, the contents and moral influence
of Western films, early films, the Westerns of D. W. Griffith and Thomas
Ince, the 1920s, Western costume, the 1930s, the Western serial, the 1940s,
post-war trends (sex, neurosis, racial conscience), stuntmen and technicians, Western films for television, international audiences and the
international Western, the 1960s, Italian Westerns, Japanese Westerns,

and the future of the Western (anti-heroes, tolerance themes). The book also includes a discussion of major Western stars and their roles in shaping the genre. The authors see the Western's vision of America as one in which such qualities as courage, independence, individualism, idealism, and optimism are promoted.

PC 463. FERGUSON, OTIS. The Film Criticism of Otis Ferguson. Edited by Robert Wilson. Philadelphia: Temple University Press, 1971. 475 pp.
In his introduction, Wilson cites Ferguson, film reviewer for the New Republic from 1934 to 1941, as the pioneering influence on the tradition of journalistic film criticism that would later include James Agee and Pauline Kael. Andrew Sarris, in a foreword to the volume, sketches Ferguson's unique qualities--his "instinctive populism," "passion for music," "technocratic spirit," "American skepticism" regarding the highbrow, and faith in early sound-film realism--that would make him a lively advocate of stylized fluidity (screwball comedies, Alfred Hitchcock thrillers, and the personas of James Cagney and Fred Astaire), the outspoken enemy of pretension (MGM blockbusters, Soviet propaganda, Walt Disney's Snow White, and Orson Welles's Citizen Kane), and a much-welcomed voice of moderation (delineating the pros and cons of Warner Brothers' social realism). The collection includes Ferguson's detailed reports of early 1940s Hollywood as well as most of his New Republic reviews.

PC 464. FEUER, JANE. The Hollywood Musical. Bloomington: Indiana University Press, 1982. 131 pp.
Feuer describes the American musical's systematic appeal to audience emotions and its ability to deny change and affirm the cultural status quo. The genre's conservative themes and ability to give audiences intense pleasure lead Feuer to declare that the musical epitomized the Hollywood studio era. She identifies several techniques of the musical normally associated with modernist art. The films freely acknowledge their status as created artifice in their use of fragmented space, direct audience address, emphasis on the illusion of spontaneity, and multiple levels of reality. Thus, for Feuer, the American musical is both thematically conservative and formally innovative.

PC 465. FIELDING, RAYMOND. The American Newsreel, 1911-1967. Norman: University of Oklahoma Press, 1972. 392 pp.
This survey of the evolution and content of movie newsreels provides a critical look at an information medium that failed to fulfill its newsgathering or artistic potentials. Fielding discusses the function of the newsreel in American society, its role in the motion picture industry, and the conditions of its production. Topics covered by the author include silent newsreels, war coverage, the introduction of sound, style and operation of major producers in the 1920s, changes in content, film industry attitudes on production and distribution in the 1930s, and criticism of sound newsreels from 1926 to 1960. Finding the historical accuracy of newsreels to be suspect, Fielding describes how this form of nonfiction film became more of an entertainment and picture-showing medium than a disseminator of news.

PC 466. FIELDING, RAYMOND. The March of Time, 1935-1951. New York: Oxford University Press, 1978. 359 pp.
"The March of Time" was an interpretive newsreel, filling the place in film that Time magazine did in print. In this history, Fielding includes interviews with "March of Time" personnel, surveys of news coverage, a detailed study of coverage of Nazi Germany and W.W. II, and a discussion of editorial content and film scripting techniques. The author sees "The March of Time" as representative of the "new journalism" of the 1930s and 1940s and as an expression of the assumptions of America in that period.

PC 467. FORMAN, HENRY JAMES. Our Movie Made Children. New York:
         Macmillan, 1934. 288 pp.
Forman summarizes the conclusions reached by the Payne Fund studies, covering four years (1929 to 1933) and a dozen cities, in order to discuss
the moviegoing habits of children, the nature of the pictures they see,
and the subsequent influences on their physical and psychological well-
being as well as on their moral development. Forman contends that motion
pictures lacking moral and beneficial lessons in life possess no
"character-molding" attributes and prove harmful to children. Assuming that
the motion picture is "a potential boon to mankind," he cites the findings
from the volumes by Herbert Blumer, Edgar Dale, and other contributors
to the Payne Fund studies to provide "evidence of the influence of motion
pictures and their impersonation upon the character, conduct and behavior
of the vast numbers of our nation." Forman hopes that this study "will
bring us face to face with the facts" and, ultimately, to a solution.

PC 468. FRENCH, BRANDON. On the Verge of Revolt: Women in American Films
         of the Fifties. New York: Ungar, 1978. 165 pp.
French discusses certain films of the 1950s which on the surface promote
domestic roles for women but, more significantly, reflect the severe limitations of those roles. The author finds these films indicative of the
transition women underwent prior to the women's movement of the 1960s
and 1970s. French refers to some films of the early 1950s which depict
women asserting their equality without challenging their destiny as wives
and mothers. The portrayal of women's unhappiness as rooted in loneliness
and sexual deprivation is discussed in relation to films appearing in
1953-56. French identifies certain films from 1957-59 which reassert
women's equality and career options instead of marriage. The relationship
of 1950s attitudes, as reflected in films, to the women's movement is
discussed in analyses of Sunset Boulevard, Shane, Picnic, Some Like It
Hot, The Nun's Story, and other films.

PC 469. FRENCH, PHILIP. Westerns: Aspects of a Movie Genre. 1973; Rev.
         ed. New York: Oxford University Press, 1977. 208 pp.
French examines the proliferation of American movie Westerns from the
1930s to the 1970s, finding that the genre was sustained, in part, by
Hollywood's search for tame subject matter in the aftermath of the HUAC
investigation of Communist Party influence in Hollywood. The genre offered
a recognizable form through which controversial issues could be handled
at a distance. Westerns were also particularly suitable for the new wide-
screen processes. French finds that as the "B" movie Western was supplanted by television dramas, the feature-length Western underwent a
revitalization that resulted in more complex, self-conscious films. As
he discusses the depiction of heroes, villains, Indians, the landscape,
and violence, French connects the content of post-W.W. II Westerns with
the political climate of the time.

PC 470. FRENCH, WARREN, ed. The South and Film. Jackson: University
         Press of Mississippi, 1981. 258 pp.
In this anthology the contributors consider the role that the South has
played in Hollywood from D. W. Griffith's Birth of a Nation to Martin
Ritt's Sounder. Essays discuss individual films (Jezebel, Gone with the
Wind, The Southerner), the work of specific directors (Martin Ritt, John
Ford, Robert Altman), and the portrayals of women, the Civil War, hill-
billies, and New Orleans. Also included is a section on William Faulkner
and film. The South and Film reveals that despite an abundance of notable
films a regional genre has not developed around the American South and
the South has continued to be viewed in stereotypical terms. French
includes an extensive bibliography and an index to films which portray
the South.

PC 471. FRIAR, RALPH E. and FRIAR, NATASHA A. The Only Good Indian . . .: The Hollywood Gospel. New York: Drama Book Specialists, 1972. 332 pp.
The authors attribute the inaccuracies in Hollywood's portrayal of American Indians to a historical fallacy that views all Native Americans as part of one racial and ethnic group. This popular image of a single Indian culture is traced throughout film history. Dime novels, popular songs, the theater, and Wild West shows are viewed as the background upon which film portrayals of Native Americans were based. The development of Indian stereotypes in silent films (especially those of Cecil B. DeMille and William S. Hart) is discussed in light of later film portrayals of Indians as either noble savages or vicious killers. The Friars also attempt to reveal the hypocrisy of recent films such as A Man Called Horse, Tell Them Willie Boy Is Here, and Little Big Man, all of which were allegedly made on behalf of Native Americans. Included are descriptions of films, excerpts of dialogue and press books, and an extensive index to films concerned with Native American issues.

PC 472. FRIEDMAN, LESTER D. Hollywood's Image of the Jew. New York: Ungar, 1982. 390 pp.
Friedman attempts to connect film content to Jewish American cultural events and to the economic practices of a film industry dominated by Jewish-American ownership and management. Unlike films about other minorities, the production of films with Jewish American characters or themes was influenced by the minority they represent. From early films advocating a rejection of traditional Jewish values in favor of assimilation into American society, to a period of relative invisibility reflecting the success of that assimilation, culminating in a sense of ethnic conscious-ness in modern films, this book traces the changing portrayal of Jewish Americans in Hollywood films. Friedman includes a chronological list of films which deal with Jewish-American issues and sources for rental of these films.

PC 473. GEDULD, HARRY M. The Birth of the Talkies: From Edison to Jolson. Bloomington: Indiana University Press, 1975. 337 pp.
The desire to link recorded sound with the motion pictures predated the collaboration between Warner Brothers, Western Electric, and Bell Telephone that resulted in the Vitaphone system and The Jazz Singer. This volume begins with the invention of the phonograph and describes the early attempts to provide movies with sound accompaniment. Geduld describes the problems of poor sound quality, amplification, and synchronization and indicates how these problems were overcome. The effect of the introduction of sound on each of the major producers and distributors is analyzed. Geduld includes a section of responses to the introduction of sound tech-nologies by various actors, critics, and directors, and a list of Hollywood sound feature films produced in 1929.

PC 474. GOW, GORDON. Hollywood in the Fifties. New York: Barnes, 1971. 208 pp.
Gow surveys the changes in film technology, subject matter, and production methods that shaped Hollywood films in the 1950s. Characterized by a blending of genres, the films of this period defy simple categorization and are discussed in this book largely through thematic analyses. Gow finds a limited amount of social comment, few comedies, a number of films about show business, and an abundance of adaptations from other media in the films of the 1950s. Technological innovations (new color and wide screen processes), major authors (Arthur Miller, Tennessee Williams), directors (Alfred Hitchcock, John Huston, Elia Kazan), and stars (Marlon Brando, James Dean, and Marilyn Monroe), are examined to reveal the impact they had on films of the period. Characteristic films of the decade such as Sunset Boulevard, Suddenly Last Summer, The Gunfighter, The Defiant

Ones, and On the Waterfront, are singled out for closer consideration. Identifying television as the major cause of change in moviemaking, Gow suggests that the films of the 1950s were shaped by an attempt to provide something which television could not provide.

PC 475. GRANT, BARRY K., ed. Film Genre: Theory and Criticism. Metuchen, N.J.: Scarecrow Press, 1977. 249 pp.
This volume contains articles reprinted from books and journals on film or modern literature which explore aspects of film genre. Part I is concerned with genre theory, the definition of film genres, audience experience of genres, and genres in political contexts. Part II is an examination of particular genres: the screwball comedy, disaster films, epics, gangster films, horror films, musicals, science fiction films, and Westerns. The authors' theoretical concerns range through psychology, iconography, aesthetics, and poetics. Revealing the tension between genre and auteur approaches to film criticism, each article confronts the general problem of genre studies and the constraints imposed by the conventions of a genre as opposed to individual artistic expression.

PC 476. GREENBERG, HARVEY R. The Movies on Your Mind. New York: Dutton, 1975. 273 pp.
In this book Greenberg subjects films to a psychoanalyst's interpretation, justifying this practice by characterizing the cinema as a type of dream or fantasy catering to audience desires for omnipotence. Greenberg speculates on the cinema's vast appeal to the psyche and finds an inexpensive but potent catharsis in moviegoing. From this theoretical base, Greenberg applies his psychoanalytic techniques to nearly 100 films (most from America). Some are considered in detail, while others are referred to only as examples of a particular genre. Among the films analyzed in detail are The Wizard of Oz, The Treasure of the Sierra Madre, The Maltese Falcon, Casablanca, and Psycho. Greenberg also devotes several chapters to the horror and science fiction genres.

PC 477. GUBACK, THOMAS H. The International Film Industry: Western Europe and America Since 1945. Bloomington: Indiana University Press, 1969. 244 pp.
Guback observes that from 1940-69 the American motion picture industry evolved from a domestically oriented business, obtaining the majority of its revenues from national distribution, to an industry where international markets accounted for at least 50% of its income. After a discussion of film's status as a commodity, this book examines attempts made by both the European and American film industries to expand their markets. Included are economic data and studies of American film exhibition in Europe and foreign film distribution in America. Guback describes the cooperation between the American film industry and the federal government through a discussion of the changing role played by the American feature film as propaganda directed toward West Germany. The economic demand to distribute films abroad and its ability to shape American film content are viewed in relation to the importance of Western Europe as a market for American films.

PC 478. HAMPTON, BENJAMIN B. History of the American Film Industry from Its Beginnings to 1931. New York: Covici, Friede, 1931. 456 pp.
This book was previously released as A History of the Movies (New York: Covici, Friede, 1931). Hampton, writing from his background in business, attempts to construct a financial history of the movie industry through 1931. He describes Thomas Edison's attempts to control the industry through the formation of a patent pool and indicates how the Motion Picture Patents Company was outmaneuvered by independent companies producing films of greater length. Attempts to increase the quality of motion pictures

are discussed through analyses of the careers of D. W. Griffith and Mary Pickford, and through a look the early demands for censorship that resulted in the formation of the Motion Picture Producers and Distributors of America. Hampton also discusses the rise of the star system, battles for ownership of first-run theaters, foreign distribution of American films, and the standardization of production and distribution processes.

PC 479. HANDEL, LEO A. Hollywood Looks at Its Audience: A Report of Film Audience Research. Urbana: University of Illinois Press, 1950. 240 pp.
This book describes the methods used to measure the size and preferences of movie audiences as of 1950. Among the procedures examined are: sneak previews, analyses of box office returns, fan mail analyses, and the evaluation of exhibitor opinions. Handel also describes the extent to which the results of audience research affected the content of Hollywood films either in the selection of story types, actors, and actresses, or in the portrayal of certain kinds of behaviors. The book includes a detailed audience preference study for child actress Margaret O'Brien and a study of the relationship of film viewing to book or newspaper reading and radio listening.

PC 480. HARMON, JIM and DONALD F. GLUT. The Great Movie Serials: Their Sound and Fury. Garden City, N.Y.: Doubleday, 1972. 384 pp.
Harmon and Glut discuss the history of the Hollywood movie serial. Placing its origins in comic strips and radio serials, they trace its development through the film's transition to sound and into the television era. With the coming of sound, the plots of movie serials became progressively more simple but they always maintained a significant emphasis on action. While lacking in characterization and credibility, the movie serials were a cut above other "B" pictures in both special effects and musical scores. The book discusses several recurring features of the serial, including the role of women, jungle pictures, detectives, super heroes, serials set in outer space, and the portrayal of villains.

PC 481. HASKELL, MOLLY. From Reverence to Rape: The Treatment of Women in the Movies. New York: Holt, Rinehart, & Winston, 1973. 388 pp.
The capacity for films to function as cultural artifacts allows Haskell to uncover how women perceived themselves at various moments in recent American history. This book examines actresses, directors, trends in portrayal, and specific films from the 1920s to the early 1970s to demonstrate how American society's role definitions have been reflected in films. Particular emphasis is placed on the "women's film" of the 1930s and 1940s, melodramas of the 1940s and 1950s, the absence of women directors, and the pitting of love versus career in Hollywood narratives.

PC 482. HENDRICKS, GORDON. The Edison Motion Picture Myth. Berkeley: University of California Press, 1961. 216 pp.
In an attempt to address the romantic legend surrounding the beginnings of American film, Hendricks considers the commonly held assumption that Thomas Edison invented the motion picture apparatus. Examining work done at Edison's West Orange Laboratory from 1888 to 1892, this book credits Edison employee William Laurie Dickson with much of the creative effort that made motion photography possible. Through the use of Edison corporate records and Dickson's Kinetoscope notebook, Hendricks chronicles the conception, construction, refinement, and Patent Office actions involved in the development of the Edison Company's Kinetoscope. This book also reveals the efforts of Edison to obscure the actual events of the early development of motion pictures in an attempt to further the Edison myth. Also included in this volume are a biographical sketch of Dickson, original texts of the four motion picture caveats, and a list of motion picture inventions from other sources during the same period.

PC 483. HIGASHI, SUMIKO. Virgins, Vamps, and Flappers: The American
         Silent Film Heroine. St. Albans, Vt.: Eden Press Women's Publi-
         cations, 1978. 226 pp.
Higashi describes the changes in the popular image of women that reflect
larger cultural developments in this study of 165 American silent feature
films. The author discusses film archetypes of woman as virgin and vampire
that are similar to those of the Victorian era, focusing specifically
on the screen careers of Lillian Gish and Mary Pickford. The book also
discusses the portrayal of working girls, socialites, and flappers, and
the changes in their portrayals as reflected the popular image of women
during the Jazz Age.

PC 484. HIGHAM, CHARLES and JOEL GREENBERG. Hollywood in the Forties.
         New York: Barnes, 1968. 192 pp.
The authors of this broad survey of the themes, stars, and film developments of the 1940s find new techniques, more first-class scripts, and
great directors to be responsible for the resurgence in the film industry
and the numerous classic films produced in the decade. Their discussion
concentrates on selected major pictures, stars and directors, and on characteristic themes of the period. Casablanca is discussed at length as
the most characteristic film of the decade. Genres studied include melodrama, film noir, fantasy and horror, problem and sociological films,
war propaganda, prestige pictures, women's pictures, comedy, musicals,
biography and literary adaptation, action, and outdoor films. The historical context includes the impact of W.W. II and the Cold War on films,
the movie industry, blacklisting and "red scares," and the decline of
the large studios that had dominated American filmmaking.

PC 485. HOBERMAN, J. and JONATHAN ROSENBAUM. Midnight Movies. New York:
         Harper & Row, 1983. 338 pp.
Midnight Movies, a discussion of the evolution and cultural significance
of the cult movie, reflects the authors' belief that movies which acquire
a cult following accurately reflect certain moral, psychological, or sexual
trends deemed unfit or decadent by society. Hoberman and Rosenbaum profile
well-known cult movie directors such as Andy Warhol, David Lynch (Eraser-
head), Alexander Jodorowsky (El Topo), John Waters (Pink Flamingos), and
George A. Romero (Night of the Living Dead). They explain that the cult
movie reveals perceptive, and often tragic, insights into the individual's
attitudes toward society and self, whether the cult film addresses the
drug culture (Reefer Madness), the rock scene (Performance), or camp (Myra
Breckinridge).

PC 486. HUETTIG, MAE D. Economic Control of the Motion Picture Industry:
         A Study in Industrial Organization. Philadelphia: University
         of Pennsylvania Press, 1944. 163 pp.
Huettig's book is based on an economic study of Hollywood conducted from
1939 to 1941 and describes the organization of the American film industry
at a time when it was dominated by eight major companies with control
at the levels of production, distribution, and exhibition. Huettig
describes the origins of this vertical integration and its effects on the
industry as a whole. Included are various analyses of industry profitability as well as an examination of the marketing of films that includes
a description of block booking and the majors' ability to dominate exhibition through ownership of relatively few important theaters. Huettig
also discusses the initial attempts made by the Federal government to
break up the vertically integrated companies through antitrust proceedings.

PC 487. HUSS, ROY and T. J. ROSS, eds. Focus on the Horror Film. Engle-
         wood Cliffs, N.J.: Prentice-Hall, 1972. 186 pp.
This series of essays concerned with the history and criticism of the
horror film in America and abroad is divided into sections on general
and gothic horror, monster terror, and psychological thrillers. Articles
explore the popularity of these films and the relationship between
aesthetic play and shocks to perception. Essays in the first section trace
the historical development of the genre and present theoretical perspectives on its content and style. Gothic horror is examined through discussions of various productions of the Dracula story (in the novel, film,
and theater), a psychoanalytical reading of the vampire myth, and a discussion of some of the more provocative versions of the Jekyll and Hyde
story. Emphasizing the monster as the product of an age of moral and
ecological chaos, the third section explores films such as King Kong,
The Lost World, The Mummy, and The Beauty and the Beast. The final section
on the psychological thriller looks at movies such as Psycho, Repulsion,
and The Night Must Fall, concluding that these thrillers deal with disturbed protagonists but that the real nature of their disturbance is rarely
explained.

PC 488. ISENBERG, MICHAEL. War on Film: The American Cinema and World
         War I, 1914-1941. London: Associated University Press, 1981.
         273 pp.
Michael Isenberg's War on Film explores the ways in which Hollywood treats
historical incidents, discussing how historians can benefit from feature
films by viewing them as effective historical documentation. Restricting
his study of American film to the depiction of W.W. I, Isenberg shows
how American films shape a historical event so that its depiction will
function at the service of American ideas, attitudes, and values. Isenberg
finds this relationship between historical reconstruction and ideology
to be most vivid when culturally devastating events are portrayed.

PC 489. ISSARI, M. ALI and DORIS A. PAUL. What Is Cinema Verite? Metuchen,
         N.J.: Scarecrow Press, 1979. 208 pp.
The authors look to cinema verite's antecedents in the films of Dziga
Vertov and Robert Flaherty, and identify cinema verite as a style of filmmaking concerned with presenting "truth." This "truth" is informed by
both the filmmaker's culture and the culture of his or her subject. Three
decades of cinema verite filmmaking are traced from the points of view
of filmmakers, theorists, and critics from many countries, but this book
concentrates on two particular schools--French and American--as embodied
in the works of Jean Rouch and Richard Leacock. The authors acknowledge
that cumbersome production equipment had imposed limitations on filmmakers,
and analyze how the development of the 16 mm format, portable sound equipment, zoom lenses, and reflex viewing systems eliminated factors separating
the filmmaker from his subject and made cinema verite techniques possible.

PC 490. JACOBS, DIANE. Hollywood Renaissance. 1977; Rev. ed. New York:
         Dell, 1980. 276 pp.
This historical analysis of American feature filmmaking during the 1970s
focuses on the films and careers of Hal Ashby, Michael Ritchie, Robert
Altman, John Cassavetes, Francis Ford Coppola, Paul Mazursky, and Martin
Scorsese. Jacobs's thesis is that Hollywood films have been greatly
affected by the French New Wave movement of the late 1950s and early 1960s
and that the movement's influence is particularly noticeable in the work
of these seven directors. To support this claim, the author examines
the films of these directors, their major themes, and the origins of those
themes; Jacobs also makes note of the roles played by women in their films,
criticizing all but Mazursky for portraying women in a negative or a predictable light.

PC 491. JACOBS, LEWIS. The Documentary Tradition. 1971; Rev. ed. New
York: Norton, 1979. 594 pp.
This collection of essays and reviews, many by filmmakers, is predominantly
concerned with individual documentary films, and functions as a history
of important achievements in nonfiction and socially committed filmmaking.
Essays concern such subjects as similarities between literary naturalism
and the style of American documentary filmmaking in the 1920s, the use
of film for political persuasion in the 1930s, the appropriation of documentary film practice by the U.S. government in the 1950s, films of personal statements on the film medium, and a series of documentaries set
in urban areas during the 1950s. Lewis's anthology includes essays discussing the combination of forces that resulted in cinema verite filmmaking,
and several essays discussing various aspects of documentary film in the
1970s, including the connection between the Feminist movement and the
rise of women filmmakers in the U.S.

PC 492. JACOBS, LEWIS. The Rise of the American Film: A Critical History.
1939, Rev. ed.; New York: Teachers College, 1968. 631 pp.
This history of technical and cultural aspects of movies through the late
1940s provides a critical analysis of film's rise to the status of a mature
art form. Jacobs includes discussion of technical, artistic, and industrial aspects of filmmaking, critical interpretations of major films,
and analyses of the contributions of producers, actors, and technicians.
The historical survey covers early films (1896-1903), foundations of the
industry (1903-08), development of Hollywood and the star system (1908-
14), growth in sophistication (1914-18), film as big business (1919-29),
and maturity and consolidation during and after the Depression. Discussions of Birth of a Nation and Intolerance, and an essay on "Experimental
Cinema in America 1912-1947" are included. Martin S. Dworkin's foreword
discusses national images and international culture, and the impact film
has had on the world's perception of America.

PC 493. JARVIE, IAN C. Movies as Social Criticism: Aspects of Their
Psychology. Metuchen, N.J.: Scarecrow Press, 1978. 207 pp.
Jarvie devotes chapters to the social psychology of movies, their relation
to American civilization, the diversity of film audiences, movies and
reality, and the motion picture as social criticism. Disagreeing with
the notion that motion pictures represent mere "pap," he asserts that
studying audiences can be important in gauging the effects of "the unintended consequences of social phenomena," for films are meaningful sources
of information and misinformation concerning the fashions, social mores,
and many other aspects of American culture. Reflecting the response of
moviemakers to each era's preoccupations, the medium oscillates between
criticizing society and endorsing its status quo. Jarvie considers not
only the cinematic depiction of social issues (that is, marriage, racism,
adolescence, and family life), but also the impact that motion pictures
ultimately have on the psychology of the public.

PC 494. JENKINSON, PHILIP and ALAN WARNER. Celluloid Rock: Twenty Years
of Movie Rock. U.S.: Warner Brothers, 1976. 136 pp.
Jenkinson and Warner observe that the relationship between popular films
and American culture is so close that the rock-and-roll movie has been
consistently able to absorb emerging patterns and trends and then reintro-
duce them to the general public. They trace the roots of movie rock to
the mid-1940s collegiate musicals and follow its evolution from the early
1950s to 1973. Identifying trends in rock films as indicative of popular
attitudes of the period, the authors focus on significant performers and
films that have contributed to the growth of this movie genre.

PC 495. JEROME, V. J. The Negro in Hollywood Films. New York: Masses
& Mainstream, 1950. 64 pp.
Jerome's book is an expansion of a lecture delivered in New York in February 1950 under the auspices of the Marxist cultural magazine Masses &
Mainstream. The Negro in Hollywood Films critiques Hollywood's postwar
attempts to portray blacks and black issues realistically. Discussing
such films as Home of the Brave, Pinky, and Intruder in the Dust, Jerome
finds that Hollywood's postwar realism continued to perpetuate the negative stereotype that characterized earlier American filmmaking.

PC 496. JOHNSON, WILLIAM, ed. Focus on the Science Fiction Film. Englewood Cliffs, N.J.: Prentice-Hall, 1972. 182 pp.
This collection of essays, reviews, and excerpts from books and articles
on the science fiction film discusses themes and techniques of science
fiction filmmaking as well as important individual movies such as 2001:
A Space Odyssey, Destination Moon, Invasion of the Body Snatchers, and
Fahrenheit 451. While an essay on the cinema-like narrative of H. G.
Wells's Time Machine is included, the primary concentration of this anthology is on the 1950s, 1960s, and early 1970s. The volume includes brief
interviews with science fiction writers (Arthur C. Clarke, Robert Heinlein,
Isaac Asimov), and filmmakers (Roger Corman, Fritz Lang, Alain Resnais).
The essays describe the science fiction film as a special sub-genre, both
of film and of science fiction, which reflects popular perceptions of
the world and of science and deals with technological change and its
effects. Johnson attempts to define the nature of science fiction film,
its relationship to written science fiction, and its aesthetic value.

PC 497. JOWETT, GARTH. Film: The Democratic Art. Boston: Little, Brown,
1976. 518 pp.
In this social history of the motion picture and its place in American
culture, Jowett stresses the importance of the movies as a major socializing force in the first half of the 20th century. During this time film
developed from a disorganized collection of individual entrepreneurs into
a full industry characterized by a star system, feature length films,
an established distribution system, and studio film production. Jowett
surveys movie content, movies and education, censorship, moral and social
issues in movie content, and audience response. Included are the results
of early social science studies of movies as well as discussions of movies
and W.W. II, morale, propaganda, and politics. For the post-war period,
Jowett studies the decline of the industry, the proliferation of drive-
in theaters, and the impact of television. Jowett includes a survey of
film content from 1946-60, an analysis of the growth of the art film,
and a discussion of the American image abroad.

PC 498. JOWETT, GARTH and JAMES LINTON. Movies as Mass Communication.
Beverly Hills, Calif.: Sage, 1980. 149 pp.
Jowett and Linton seek to remedy the "piecemeal" aesthetic approach to
the motion picture by treating the movies as "non-art," as a segment of
the "economic and industrial complex" of "mass-mediated culture." The
authors investigate American film as a form of mass communication, responsive to an analysis of a sender (the movie industry) and its numerous
receivers (the American public). Hollywood is analyzed as a "business
enterprise," possessing "articles of faith" regarding formulas, cycles,
"tie-ins," industry awards, and exhibition. Three chapters consider the
complex question of audience behavior—attendance figures, the role of
movie stars, the applicability of psychoanalytic approaches, propaganda
and socialization, and the nation's general consumer habits. Jowett and
Linton, noting the rising prominence of video technology, speculate about
the future of theatrical movies, "one of the few tribal rituals left in
America."

PC 499. KAEL, PAULINE. I Lost It at the Movies. Boston: Little, Brown,
    1965. 323 pp.
In this first collection of her criticism, Kael assumes the persona of
a West Coast partisan, an advocate of "honest vulgarity," narrative coherence, and the pluralistic nature of human (cinematic) experience. Sus-
picious of New York trendsetters, she dissects Andrew Sarris's use of
the auteur theory; skeptical of the romantic myth of the alienated artist,
she castigates the apologists of the avant-garde screen. Kael devotes
much of her attention to the "fantasies of the art house audience" in
America--the acquiescence to the "Sick-Soul" of Europe (for example, the
work of Federico Fellini), the sentimental embrace of Soviet pacifism
(The Ballad of a Soldier), the preoccupation with British working class
malaise (Saturday Night and Sunday Morning) and the native liberal's distaste for criminal injustice (Twelve Angry Men).

PC 500. KAGAN, NORMAN. The War Film: An Illustrated History of the Movies.
    New York: Harcourt Brace Jovanovich, 1974. 106 pp.
This historical and thematic analysis of American war films from early
silent films to the 1970s examines the most popular and critically
acclaimed war films, seeking patterns and meanings common to films of certain
eras. For Kagan, these patterns reflect the beliefs and social attitudes
prevalent when the films were made and can be found in the depiction of
characters and historical events, as well as in what is suggested, left
out, or falsified. Kagan defines the special techniques and conventions
of the war film genre and the genre's relationship to other arts, particularly the war novel. He gives special attention to two film classics,
Birth of a Nation and Shoulder Arms. The book is separated into several
sections: early silent films, W.W. I, 1920s and 1930s, W.W. II, Korean
perspectives 1949-56, Vietnam perspectives 1957-73, the comedy of war,
and anti-war films.

PC 501. KAMINSKY, STUART M. American Film Genres: Approaches to a Criti-
    cal Theory of Popular Film. Dayton, Ohio: Pflaum, 1974. 232 pp.
Kaminsky's generic approach to the study of film places movies against
a background of mythology, psychology, religion, and anthropology. This
book focuses on American films from the 1920s through the mid-1970s, defining and examining in detail such film genres as the Western, the gangster
film, the musical, the horror movie, and the science fiction film. Also
included are analyses of the films and careers of John Ford and Don Siegel,
two directors who Kaminsky believes epitomize the genre director.

PC 502. KANE, KATHRYN. Visions of War: Hollywood Combat Films of World
    War II. Ann Arbor, Mich.: UMI Research Press, 1982. 174 pp.
Kane has examined the similarities among combat films made in America
from 1942-45 to determine if they can be considered a legitimate film
genre. She begins the book with a discussion of the nature of genres
and bases her study on previous efforts at genre criticism, particularly
studies of the Western. Ignoring auteurist and historical considerations,
Kane discusses films without reference to the creative or social forces
behind them. This book describes the setting, characters, and plots of
specific films and considers how those elements were used to justify U.S.
involvement in the war, to maintain moral superiority over the enemy,
and depict freedom, the home, and duty. Kane identifies a shift in concerns from 1943-45 from an emphasis on the moral purpose of involvement
to a growing sense of futility. She postulates that this revisionism
was due to the contradictions of earlier film presentations.

PC 503. KAPLAN, E. ANN. Women and Film: Both Sides of the Camera. New
York: Methuen, 1983. 259 pp.
Kaplan introduces structuralism and semiotics as means for deciphering
feminist issues conventionally "relegated to the outskirts of historical
discourse." Stressing psychoanalytic techniques in order to "unlock patriarchal culture," she focuses on the "controlling power" of the "male gaze"
found in three classic Hollywood films (Camille, Blonde Venus and The
Lady from Shanghai). Kaplan devotes the remaining portion of her study
to the alternatives provided by the Independent Women's Film in Great
Britain and the U.S.: the formalist or experimental avant-garde (for
instance, Yvonne Rainer); the political documentary tradition represented
in Harlan County U.S.A.; and the "avant-garde theory film" (Riddles of
the Sphinx), where feminists question the stylistic as well as the sociological conventions of a male-oriented Western culture. Kaplan closes
with an account of the problems--production, distribution and exhibition--
and the promise--a re-evaluation of mother-daughter relationships--facing
prospective feminist filmmakers.

PC 504. KAPLAN, E. ANN, ed. Women in Film Noir. London: British Film
Institute, 1980. 132 pp.
The majority of the authors contributing to this anthology view film noir
as a genre, looking to common thematic concerns, narrative structure,
and iconography as its identifying features. The essays examine the role
played by women in film noir and their conventional positioning under
the ideological control of a patriarchal culture. The film noir woman
is seen as essential to the central intrigue of the film, offering desirable and dangerous obstacles to the narrative's male quest, but is ultimately without a fixed role. Essays discuss Klute as a contemporary film
noir and as a feminist critique, the absence of the family in film noir,
film noir character types, and the portrayal of women in Mildred Pierce,
The Blue Gardenia, Gilda, and Double Indemnity.

PC 505. KARIMI, AMIR MASSOUD. Toward a Definition of the American Film
Noir, 1941-1949. New York: Arno Press, 1976. 255 pp.
Karimi identifies the film noir as a type of crime film that reached its
peak between 1941-49, and undertakes a thematic analysis of the origins,
influences, structure, and creators of the film noir. He outlines the
similarities in standard plot structures, atmosphere, and characters
between the film noir and the hard-boiled detective novel, finding film
noir's literary origins in mystery and detective fiction, and its film
origins in horror, mystery, and gangster films. Karimi traces the film
noir as it evolves from the standard crime film of the 1930s, examining
the shifts in style and content and the roles played by major contributors
to the genre. This book includes sections on the place of the film noir
in the American cinema, the depiction of violence, and the psychological
crime film.

PC 506. KARPF, STEPHEN LOUIS. The Gangster Film: Emergence, Variation,
and Decay of a Genre, 1930-1940. New York: Arno Press, 1973.
299 pp.
Karpf's study traces the development, proliferation, and progressive decay
of the American gangster film in the 1930s. Defining the genre based
on its continuity of actors and its archetypal characters and plot lines,
Karpf outlines the origins, conventions, development, and historical orientation of these films. This volume focuses on four movies that embody
the essential characteristics of the genre: Little Caesar (1930), Public
Enemy (1931), Scarface (1932), and The Petrified Forest (1936). It
includes a detailed examination of the four stars and their roles from these
films: Edward G. Robinson (Rico), James Cagney (Tom Powers), Paul Muni
(Tony Carmonte), and Humphrey Bogart (Duke Mantee). Attributing the wane
of the gangster film to the influx of uninspired genre films and the influ-

ence of censorship, the author identifies a socially conscious quality
of the genre that influenced a later group of historical documentary dramas.

PC 507. KAUFFMANN, STANLEY. A World on Film: Criticism and Comment.
New York: Harper & Row, 1966. 437 pp.
This first collection of Stanley Kauffmann's film reviews for the New
Republic (1958-65) offers a chronicle of the interaction between the journalist's "critical self" and a readership taking the movie medium with
increased seriousness. The opening section reprints Kauffmann's general
observations about certain facets of the Hollywood scene—the depiction
of war, biblical spectacles, and the relationship of film to drama and
literature. The longest section arranges Kauffmann's critical pieces
according to national cinemas, thereby providing an opportunity to measure
the contemporary American screen against the impressive backdrop of recent
contributions from the New Waves of Europe and Asia. Kauffmann closes
with an original essay expressing his ambivalence toward the new "Film
Generation," a phenomenon not only represented in the troubling "antihuman-
ism" and nihilistic stance of the American avant-garde, but also reflected
in the "appetite" for tradition and individual integrity found among an
educated middle class coping with the challenges of modern society.

PC 508. KAY, KARYN and GERALD PEARY, eds. Women and the Cinema: A Critical Anthology. New York: Dutton, 1977. 464 pp.
This anthology was assembled in an attempt to explore the history of feminist discourse on cinematic practice ranging from the avant-garde to Hollywood feature films. Kay and Peary combine historical articles, interviews,
autobiographical essays, and political and theoretical statements to reveal
the cinema's status as a medium where feminist culture has grown despite
the influence of patriarchal values. Though acknowledging occasional
enlightened "women's pictures" that came out of Hollywood, this volume
concentrates on how feminist issues were addressed outside of mainstream
filmmaking. The anthology is organized around such themes as: women
in studio era film production, avant-garde filmmakers and independents,
women and political films, and feminist film theory.

PC 509. KEYSER, LES. Hollywood in the Seventies. San Diego, Calif.:
Barnes, 1981. 264 pp.
Keyser's book discusses the changing business structure and content of
American filmmaking in the 1970s. The author describes the final rejection
of the studio system as Hollywood filmmaking became controlled by free-
lance, location-oriented, independent production companies. The major
studios were absorbed by conglomerates and consolidated their business
interests at the distribution level. Keyser cites the changing demographics of film audiences, a softening of censorship, the revival of old genres,
and the establishment of new genres (disaster movies, "blaxploitation"
films, etc.) as determining a 1970s film content characterized largely
by escapism. The content of American films of the 1970s is discussed
through descriptions of successful films and through consideration of
popular actors and actresses of the decade.

PC 510. KITSES, JIM. Horizons West, Anthony Mann, Budd Boeticher, Sam
Peckinpah: Studies of Authorship Within the Western. Bloomington:
Indiana University Press, 1969. 176 pp.
Kitses's book is an auteurist influenced discussion of the Western films
of three American directors: Anthony Mann, Budd Boeticher, and Sam
Peckinpah. After a brief survey of the elements of the Western form, Kitses
discusses how the structure of the Western genre can be manipulated and
thus reveal a director's personal vision. Through an examination of the
roles played by heroes and the landscape, Kitses describes the Westerns
of Anthony Mann as characterized by men stretching beyond their limits.
Kitses uses connections between Boeticher's personal life and his film

themes to describe an emphasis on individualism in Western films which take on qualities of morality plays and fables. Peckinpah's films are looked at for their contemporary relevance in the portrayal of emotionally and spiritually crippled characters searching for a personal identity.

PC 511. KNIGHT, ARTHUR. The Liveliest Art. 1957; Rev. ed. New York: Macmillan, 1978. 304 pp.
Knight traces the history of the American film--Edison's technical beginnings, D. W. Griffith's innovations, Marx Brothers's comedy, Orson Welles's ingenuity, the social messages of John Huston and Elia Kazan--while also giving due regard to the German and Russian silent screen, the 1930s French sound film and Italian neo-realism. Expanding his 1957 perspective, Knight includes "an international survey" up to the late 1970s. Independent production, he notes, has become "the way of life" for American moviemakers; Hollywood is no longer the center of world filmmaking, and scholars have had to pay increasing attention to the French New Wave, to modernist Italian directors, and to the Japanese screen and Third World cinema.

PC 512. KOLKER, ROBERT PHILLIP. A Cinema of Loneliness. New York: Oxford University Press, 1980. 395 pp.
A Cinema of Loneliness examines the careers of Arthur Penn, Stanley Kubrick, Robert Altman, Martin Scorsese, and Francis Ford Coppola. For Kolker, these filmmakers typify the shift in American filmmaking from studio structured and dominated films to more formally structured films which ask their audiences to perceive the cinema in different ways. Kolker's thesis is that all five filmmakers were (and, to a great extent, still are) influenced by the French New Wave movement of the late 1950s and early 1960s, and that this influence has greatly shaped their intellectual and emotional vision of the world. The author believes that one flaw all of the directors have in common is an inability to view American culture in ideologically new and challenging ways. He finds their films technically and cinematically innovative, but intellectually cold and emotionally vapid. The author appends filmographies of each director's work which include complete listings of cast and crew.

PC 513. KUHN, ANNETTE. Women's Pictures: Feminism and Cinema. London: Routledge & Kegan Paul, 1982. 225 pp.
This venture in "cultural politics" explores the interplay of sex roles, economics, history, and ideology within motion picture history. Influenced by the insights of Jacques Lacan and Christian Metz, Kuhn merges semiotics and psychoanalysis to dissect the subtle relationship of the spectator to film texts. Beginning with the representation of women in the "dominant cinema" of Hollywood, she not only considers the narrative organization of Mildred Pierce and The Big Sleep, but also diagnoses the gratification conventionally derived from the violent scenes of Psycho and from the "pornographic apparatus" of the movie industry. Kuhn then estimates the prospects for an alternative cinema, as she remarks on the compromises of modern Hollywood (for example, Alice Doesn't Live Here Anymore), the radical content of realistic documentaries (Union Maids), and the experimentation in form displayed by Daughter-Rite and Lives of Performers. The volume concludes by identifying the channels of production, distribution, and exhibition available to the aspiring feminist filmmaker.

PC 514. LAHUE, KALTON C. World of Laughter: The Motion Picture Comedy Short, 1910-1930. Norman: University of Oklahoma Press, 1966. 240 pp.
This analysis of the history and content of short silent comedy films focuses on themes and comedy techniques, not social history. Lahue claims that shorts were developed to supply an increasing demand for quality comedy in the early days of film. Major companies and directors of the early period discussed by Lahue include Universal Studios, the General Film Company, Mack Sennett, and Hal Roach. The author provides extensive

commentary on independent producers, early cartoons, and the change from one-reel to two-reel films, reviewing the plots and actors of many classic films. The genre, its conventions, and its themes were established in the decade 1910-19. Later films were characterized mainly by the personality of the comedian, including such figures as Charlie Chaplin, Harold Lloyd, and Buster Keaton.

PC 515. LEAB, DANIEL J. From Sambo to Superspade: The Black Experience in Motion Pictures. Boston: Houghton Mifflin, 1975. 301 pp.
Leab examines the extent to which the depiction of blacks both reflected American racial prejudices and contributed to the exclusion of blacks from American society. This history of the portrayal of blacks in films begins with silent motion pictures and examines the social effects of the repetition of negative stereotypes of blacks. Leab follows those stereotypes through the transition to sound, describing the efforts of the NAACP to convince Hollywood to produce films with more realistic black characters. Leab notes a divergence from racial stereotypes after W.W. II but finds in the films of the 1960s the sensationalist use of themes of miscegenation. Noting that today's movie industry is more aware of the financial power of black audiences, Leab describes the development of new stereotypes that are more pleasing to black audiences yet still lack humanity.

PC 516. LENIHAN, JOHN H. Showdown: Confronting Modern America in the Western Film. Urbana: University of Illinois Press, 1980. 214 pp.
Lenihan's examination of the Western and its relation to important political, social and intellectual issues and trends since W.W. II asserts that many of the concerns and attitudes of American society can be found in movie Westerns made after W.W. II. Looking at such films as The Gunfighter, High Noon, Broken Arrow, The Wild Bunch, and Lonely Are the Brave, Lenihan believes that an analysis of the postwar Western can reveal the nation's concerns about such controversial topics as racism, the Cold War, and the modern citizen's struggle to keep individuality and humanity intact.

PC 517. LEVIN, G. ROY. Documentary Explorations. Garden City, N.Y.: Anchor Press, 1971. 420 pp.
Levin attempts to develop a broad history of the documentary film as a genre by assembling fifteen interviews with documentary filmmakers from Britain, France, Belgium, and the U.S. He reveals a personal side to these filmmakers and evaluates the potential social implications of their films. Filmmakers appearing in this study were selected not as representatives of world documentary but for the influence they have had on current documentary practice in the U.S. and the West. Among the American filmmakers interviewed are Willard Van Dyke, Richard Leacock, D. A. Pennebaker, Albert and David Maysles, Frederick Wiseman, and Ed Pincus.

PC 518. LINDSAY, VACHEL. The Art of the Moving Picture. 1915; Rev. ed. New York: Macmillan, 1922. 324 pp.
Lindsay's volume, one of the first book-length discussions of film's cultural implications, introduces a variety of tactics to challenge the medium's sceptics. He formulates a typology (painting-in-motion, architecture-in-motion, sculpture-in-motion) to spotlight the photoplay's symbolic and patriotic superiority over the theater. In addition, he encourages architects to consider the motion picture as a crusading instrument and imagines film libraries to service future university extension courses. Finally, he envisions the photoplay as a benevolent machine which can pave the way for a more ecumenical society.

PC 519. LOUNSBURY, MYRON O. The Origins of American Film Criticism, 1909-1939. New York: Arno Press, 1973. 547 pp.

Lounsbury investigates the contention that America's literature about film has traditionally espoused a liberal philosophy which stresses the medium's social content at the expense of its formal virtues. Adopting a chronological approach, he places critics and their institutions (periodicals, book publishers, museums, film societies) within historical contexts. These include the role of sympathetic trade magazines, liberal journals, and artists during the Progressive Era; the 1920s intellectual community's response to an increasingly prominent film industry and its talking pictures; the transformation from aesthetic to political radicalism in the early years of the Depression; and the 1930s discovery of a native heritage of Realism in leftist and liberal magazines. Analyzing Lewis Jacobs's The Rise of the American Film (see PC 492) as a synthesis of the different theoretical stances, Lounsbury concludes that the critical tradition is a dialectical one between the devotees of formal value and the advocates of humane content.

PC 520. MacCANN, RICHARD DYER. Hollywood in Transition. Boston: Houghton Mifflin, 1962. 208 pp.

MacCann examines the many changes the American film industry underwent during the introduction and popularization of television. Chronicling the reduction in censorship, the shift away from studio-controlled film production, and the decreased importance of the domestic box office to financially successful films, MacCann explores the effects that these changes had on Hollywood and American film audiences. He profiles influential producers (David O. Selznick, Sam Spiegel, and Ross Hunter), directors (William Wyler, George Stevens, and Elia Kazan), writers (Dudley Nichols and Frank Gruber), and stars (William Holden, Marlon Brando, and Joanne Woodward) whose careers have been affected by the changes in film censorship, studio production, and box office economics.

PC 521. MacCANN, RICHARD DYER. The People's Films: A Political History of U.S. Government Motion Pictures. New York: Hastings House, 1973. 238 pp.

MacCann traces the U.S. government's use of documentary film from the Department of Agriculture's films of the early 1930s through the current use of television by the executive and legislative branches. MacCann discusses the films of Pare Lorentz (specifically The Plow That Broke the Plains and The River), the development of the U.S. Film Service, the war-time filmmaking activities of the Office of War Information, and armed forces documentaries (including the "Why We Fight" series). This volume also describes the filmmaking of the U.S. Information Agency (1962-67) and the relationship of film to foreign policy.

PC 522. MACDONALD, DWIGHT. Dwight Macdonald on Movies. Englewood Cliffs, N.J.: Prentice-Hall, 1969. 492 pp.

This compilation, consisting primarily of Macdonald's reviews for Esquire between 1960 and 1966, documents the changes of heart experienced by this critic of middlebrow America's fondness for kitsch. The few pieces reprinted from the 1920s and 1930s reveal Macdonald's admiration for the pioneers of the silent screen (D. W. Griffith and Sergei Eisenstein) and his distaste for their subsequent betrayal at the hands of Hollywood moguls and Soviet Stalinists. His acceptance of the reviewing post at Esquire indicates that New Waves from France, Italy, England and elsewhere had revived his faith in this 20th century art form, while the American screen--the "Doris Day syndrome," the psychoanalytic excesses of William Inge, and the humorless avant-garde--became the targets of his criticisms. Macdonald's closing column for Esquire summarizes the difficult role of an American critic.

PC 523. MADSEN, AXEL. The New Hollywood: American Movies in the Seventies. New York: Crowell, 1975. 183 pp.
Madsen describes the state of the American film industry in 1975. He discusses the roles of producers, directors (particularly Peter Bogdanovich and Francis Ford Coppola), writers, cinematographers (Haskel Wexler, Lazlo Kovacs, and Vilmos Zsigmond), and stars in modern filmmaking. He also considers pornography and violence in the movies and the shift in demographics of filmgoers to a better educated, more selective audience.

PC 524. MALTBY, RICHARD. Harmless Entertainment: Hollywood and the Ideology of Consensus. Metuchen, N.J.: Scarecrow Press, 1983. 417 pp.
In this volume, Maltby calls for a critical history of film based on the conviction that the American cinema is "primarily a commercial institution, engaged in manufacturing and selling a specific product in a capitalistic market place." After considering the economic and moral strictures placed on a business-like industry, Maltby focuses on the consensus achieved, through compromise, during the heyday of the studio system. He finds Frank Capra's "populist archetype" to be most representative of this consensus. However, as the author notes, compromise continued through the films of Elia Kazan and Stanley Kramer in the 1950s. Maltby's greatest criticisms are reserved for Martin Scorsese's Taxi Driver and Clint Eastwood's "Dirty Harry" series for their extreme departures from the "middle-of-the-road" productions discussed earlier in the volume.

PC 525. MALTIN, LEONARD. Of Mice and Magic: A History of American Animated Cartoons. New York: McGraw-Hill, 1980. 470 pp.
This historical work traces the evolution of the American cartoon at specific studios, chronicling the competition among the studios and the development of different characters and styles. Among the cartoonists and studios discussed are: Walt Disney, Max Fleischer, Paul Terry and Terrytoons, Walter Lantz, Ub Iwerks, the Van Beuren Studio, Columbia, Warner Brothers, MGM, Paramount, and UPA. Various animation techniques and technological innovations are examined to provide an insight into how they shaped the evolution of the American cartoon. Individual cartoonists are discussed, as are artists and inventors, in order to reveal the divisions of labor within the studio cartoon system.

PC 526. MAMBER, STEPHEN. Cinema Verite in America: Studies in Uncontrolled Documentary. Cambridge, Mass.: MIT Press, 1974. 288 pp.
Mamber traces the rise and proliferation of the alternative documentary filmmaking style in the 1960s. He describes the attempts made by cinema verite filmmakers to eliminate technical, procedural, and structural barriers between a film's subject and its audience. Mamber examines the films of the Maysles brothers, D. A. Pennebaker, Richard Leacock, Frederick Wiseman, and Drew Associates. The author includes a discussion of cinema verite's theoretical background, filmographies of cinema verite's major figures, an extensive bibliography, and a list of film rental sources.

PC 527. MANVELL, ROGER. The Film and the Public. Baltimore, Md.: Penguin Books, 1955. 352 pp.
Manvell documents the rise of American film from the early silent era to the mid-1950s, when television competed with film as a source of entertainment and communication. Major sections of this book include: "The Silent Film," "The Sound Film," "The Film and Industry," "The Cinema and Society," and "Television and Film." Manvell includes an extensive bibliography, as well as a detailed filmography that covers motion pictures from the silent era until 1954.

PC 528. MAPP, EDWARD. Blacks in American Films: Today and Yesterday.
Metuchen, N.J.: Scarecrow Press, 1972. 278 pp.
Mapp begins his study with a discussion of the American film's portrayal
of blacks during several periods of film history. He characterizes black
roles in the early silent period as limited to simple-minded characters,
while films from the 1930s contained occasional black roles which displayed
more sympathy and substance. Mapp observes that after W.W. II, American
films began to show concern for the problems of racial and religious minorities but these improvements continued to be overshadowed by one-dimensional,
stereotypical roles and the casting of white actors in black roles. Beginning with 1962 and continuing through 1970, Mapp devotes a chapter to
the depiction of blacks in films during each year. He notes a steady
increase in the number of black roles and a rise of black male stars.
Mapp illustrates his discussion with analyses of individual films and
includes an extensive bibliography and an evaluation of previous studies
of Hollywood's portrayal of blacks.

PC 529. MARCORELLES, LOUIS, in collaboration with Nicole Rouzet-Albagli.
Living Cinema: New Directions in Contemporary Filmmaking. Translated by Isabel Quigly. New York: Praeger, 1973. 155 pp.
This book considers two impulses present in early 1970s filmmaking that
reacted against naturalistic cinema. Both "direct cinema" and "concrete
cinema" reminded their audiences of the film's status as a created object
and acknowledged the work done during the cinematic process. The equipment,
techniques and aesthetic of "direct cinema" are viewed in relation to
the films of Richard Leacock and Jean Rouch and to these filmmakers' direct
participation in the material they were filming. The authors define "concrete cinema" as a synthetic mode of filmmaking entirely formed through
human craftmanship and cite animation and the American Underground Film
as examples. Throughout the book, these two alternative cinema strategies
are linked to the future potential of television. The political and theoretical implications and the problems involved with these new techniques
are stressed.

PC 530. MARSDEN, MICHAEL T., JOHN G. NACHBAR, and SAM L. GROGG, Jr. Movies
as Artifacts: Cultural Criticism of Popular Film. Chicago:
Nelson-Hall, 1982. 274 pp.
This volume is a collection of critical essays that reveal the variety
of ways in which films can reflect different aspects of American culture.
Among the major topics are the relationship between movies and their audiences, movie stars and American culture, the role of genres in American
film, and movies and their times. The authors include an annotated bibliography discussing historical, thematic, and generic film criticism,
film production, directing, screenwriting, and acting.

PC 531. MASON, JOHN L. The Identity Crisis Theme in American Feature
Films, 1960-1969. New York: Arno Press, 1977. 384 pp.
This book describes Hollywood's portrayal of the problem of constructing
a personal identity. Mason selects twenty-two dramatic fiction films
about young people made and set in the 1960s, placing particular emphasis
on five motorcycle films. Included in the book are interviews with seven
writers, directors and producers (including Roger Corman, Stanley Kramer
and Tom Mankiewicz) whose personal vision of the identity crisis shaped
its presentation in their films. In addition, Mason outlines a methodology
for film content analysis developed specifically for his study, but applicable to any study of dramatic films.

PC 532. MAST, GERALD. The Comic Mind: Comedy and the Movies. 1973;
       Rev. ed. Chicago: University of Chicago Press, 1979. 369 pp.
Mast examines film comedies in an attempt to reveal the presence of serious
thought in the comic film form. He begins by developing a theory of comedy
and explores the style as well as the content of film comedies to identify
social values and authorial insights transmitted by humorous films. Mast
surveys the historical and cultural importance of screen comedy from the
Lumiere brothers' L'Arroseur arrossee to Woody Allen's Annie Hall and
includes discussions of Mack Sennett, Charlie Chaplin, and Buster Keaton
and their contributions to the American silent film. Mast concludes with
a discussion of sound film comedy and the films and careers of Frank Capra,
Preston Sturges, Jacques Tati, Jerry Lewis, and Mel Brooks.

PC 533. MAST, GERALD. A Short History of the Movies. Indianapolis, Ind.:
       Bobbs-Merrill, 1976. 575 pp.
Mast surveys the history of the American motion picture from the early
experiments conducted during the mid-19th century that resulted in the
Zoetrope and the Stroboscope to the 1970s and the generation of young
American "auteurs" such as Peter Bogdanovich, Robert Altman, Stanley
Kubrick, and Francis Ford Coppola. Acknowledging significant trends in
international filmmaking such as Soviet experimentation with montage during
the 1920s, post-war Italian neorealism, and the French New Wave of the
late 1950s and early 1960s, Mast attempts to determine what effect these
innovative film practices had on American cinema. Profiles of D. W.
Griffith, Mack Sennett, and Charlie Chaplin illustrate the important role
played by these filmmakers in paving the way for the American film industry's rapid growth and maturation during the 1920s. Mast chronicles the
dominance of the Hollywood studio system until its deterioration in the
late 1950s and 1960s as the industry structure shifted to the current
arrangement of independent filmmakers whose work is distributed by large
entertainment conglomerates.

PC 534. MAST, GERALD, ed. The Movies in Our Midst: Documents in the
       Cultural History of Film in America. Chicago: University of
       Chicago Press, 1982. 766 pp.
Mast reprints over 100 original documents to record the cultural and historical evolution of the American motion picture from 1882-1977. Taken
from such diverse sources as filmmakers, audiences, church groups, economists, critics, and sociologists, these documents reveal cultural, moral,
and psychological insights into film and its relationship with society.
The book is divided into seven sections dealing with: the invention of
the motion picture apparatus, the daily growth of the American film industry, issues of film content and the rise of the Hollywood studio system,
the technological and economic aspects surrounding the inception of sound,
the American film industry during the 1930s and the 1940s, the post-war
investigations of the House Committee on Un-American Activities (including
sixty pages of testimony from the 1947 and 1951-52 hearings), and the
stormy relationship between film and television.

PC 535. MATTHEWS, J. H. Surrealism and American Feature Films. Boston:
       Twayne, 1979. 213 pp.
Matthews traces the influence of Surrealism on Hollywood feature films
from such 1930s films as Duck Soup and King Kong through the late 1970s
and Marty Feldman's The Last Remake of Beau Geste. He claims that Sur-
realists are extremely concerned with accurately portraying reality, though
their portrayal of it is highly stylized and individualistic. Citing
such Hollywood directors and films as Delmer Daves (Dark Passage), Henry
Hathaway (Peter Ibbetson), and Leo McCarey (Duck Soup), Matthews explores
the relationship between the Surrealist movement and Hollywood film practice. The book includes a filmography of American movies influenced by
Surrealist strategies and techniques, and a chronology that traces that
influence from the early 1920s to the late 1970s.

PC 536. MAY, JOHN R. and MICHAEL BIRD, eds. Religion in Film. Knoxville:
         University of Tennessee Press, 1982. 257 pp.
This volume explores the potentials for religious interpretation of film.
Essays apply such an interpretation to a diverse group of genres and films
including science fiction (Close Encounters of the Third Kind), horror
(The Exorcist), prison drama (Cool Hand Luke), and the rock musical (Tommy).
The anthology is divided into three parts which examine the use of religion
and the presence of religious meanings in films. Essays in Part I
address various theoretical positions surrounding religious interpretations
of film. Those in Part II consider particular film genres and cultural
trends which lend films a religious significance. Part III contains essays
examining thirteen directors (among them Alfred Hitchcock, Sam Peckinpah,
and Robert Altman) whose films are often associated with religious concerns
or lend themselves to religious interpretation.

PC 537. MAYNARD, RICHARD A. The American West on Film: Myth and Reality.
         Rochelle Park, N.J.: Hayden Book, 1974. 130 pp.
Maynard compares the historical realities of American westward expansion
with the mythic American West of movies. Juxtaposing letters and diaries
of Western homesteaders and cattle drovers with screenplay excerpts, movie
stills, and movie promotional material, he finds the reality of American
Western history drab and unromantic compared to the myth which overwhelms
that reality. That myth, characterized by the presence of militant individualism, violence, white supremacy, and a rigid sense of right and wrong,
is analyzed with excerpts of film scholarship by George Fenin, William
Everson, and Robert Warshow and an essay on the Western dime novel by
Henry Nash Smith.

PC 538. MAYNARD, RICHARD A. The Black Man on Film: Racial Stereotyping.
         Rochelle Park, N.J.: Hayden Book, 1974. 134 pp.
Maynard, viewing motion pictures as a mirror of society's attitudes,
attempts to understand why unrealistic stereotypes of blacks persisted
and how film images became expectations of black behavior and were thus
used to justify white racism. This volume includes a description of black
stereotypes in film, excerpts from essays written between 1922-55 discussing the portrayal of blacks, lengthy analyses of both Birth of a Nation
and the career of Sidney Poitier, as well as short, parallel studies of
American Indians and Jews in the Hollywood film.

PC 539. McARTHUR, COLIN. Underworld U.S.A. New York: Viking Press,
         1972. 176 pp.
In this auteurist-influenced study, Colin McArthur looks at the gangster
and thriller film genre as it appears in the films of Fritz Lang, John
Huston, Jules Dassin, Robert Siodmak, Elia Kazan, Nicholas Ray, Samuel
Fuller, Don Siegel and Jean-Pierre Melville. Like the Western, the gangster and thriller film developed a readily identifiable, recurrent iconography. McArthur believes that an examination of how these generic elements
were manipulated can reveal the personal vision of certain film artists.
Beginning with the film Little Caesar (1930), McArthur traces the development of the genre, its continuity of visual imagery, and its relationship
to America's urban technological society.

PC 540. McCARTHY, TODD and CHARLES FLYNN, eds. Kings of the Bs Working
         Within the Hollywood System: An Anthology of Film History and
         Criticism. New York: Dutton, 1975. 561 pp.
This comprehensive anthology of critical and historical essays on the
American "B" film contends that all films are of potential historical
value because of our constantly changing cultural perspectives. In the
first section of this volume, the editors have collected essays which
define the "B" film by budget, intention, and formula, and discuss the
relationship of audiences to such films at the time of their release.

                                 1319

A section describing the history of the "B" film from the 1930s through the 1950s follows. Brief biographical sketches of "B" directors and producers such as Roger Corman, Sam Katzman, and Val Lewton and analyses of specific "B" films (including Nightmare Alley and They Live by Night) comprise the next two sections. This volume concludes with a directorial filmography of 325 American directors compiled by McCarthy.

PC 541. McCLELLAND, DOUG. The Golden Age of "B" Movies. Nashville, Tenn.: Charter House, 1978. 216 pp.
McClelland examines the American "B" movie during its prime in the 1940s. Quickly and inexpensively produced, usually without stars, these relatively short films proliferated by the mid-1930s as distributors used double bills to boost Depression era movie attendance. These films functioned as apprentice programs for young actors, writers, and directors trying to break into Hollywood's studio system. Because of the low budgets and lack of expectations for success, the "B" movie allowed for some degree of experimentation. The bulk of McClelland's book describes fifty typical "B" movies from the 1940s.

PC 542. McCONNELL, FRANK D. The Spoken Seen: Film and the Romantic Imagination. Baltimore, Md.: Johns Hopkins University Press, 1975. 195 pp.
This literary study of film and its use of the themes, aesthetic, and traditions of Romance discusses film in terms of its creation of a dream reality, and bases its analysis on the audience's emotional response to the illusion created by the cinema. McConnell discusses trends in literary criticism, paying particular attention to structuralism and its applicability to film; film as language, communication mode, and political expression; film genre and the question of film authorship; and the overly rigid use of the auteur theory, which McConnell attacks on the grounds that actors and writers make major contributions to the finished film. The purpose of film, according to McConnell, is to promote a re-examination of the nature of reality, and thus to provide insight into the non-film world. McConnell attempts to demonstrate that it is possible to use film as a guide to the social realities of its audience and their culture.

PC 543. McGEE, MARK THOMAS and R. J. ROBERTSON. The J.D. Films: Juvenile Delinquency in the Movies. Jefferson, N.C.: McFarland, 1982. 197 pp.
McGee and Robertson examine the portrayal of juvenile delinquency in films, tracing its evolution from the early 1950s to the 1970s. They explore the reasons for the popularity of J.D. films in the 1950s, discuss how this type of film has tackled serious and controversial themes dealing with juvenile delinquency, and question why these films have rarely been taken seriously by either film critics or scholars. Among the films discussed are: The Wild One, The Blackboard Jungle, Rebel Without a Cause, Saturday Night Fever, Rock and Roll High School, and The Wanderers.

PC 544. MELLEN, JOAN. Big Bad Wolves: Masculinity in the American Film. New York: Pantheon Books, 1977. 365 pp.
Mellen traces the changes in Hollywood's portrayal of American men through each decade from the silent film era to the 1970s. By considering the relationships of screen males to violence, women, and other men, the author describes the creation of a violent and dominating male image, superior both to the Hollywood image of women and to film audiences. She concludes that Hollywood's male images leave their audience with a sense of inadequacy by presenting a male image which the audience could never hope to emulate. Mellen considers individual films and actors in each decade and their contribution to Hollywood's stylized portrayal of the American man.

PC 545. MELLEN, JOAN. Women and Their Sexuality in the New Film. New
        York: Horizon Press, 1973. 255 pp.
Mellen raises several concerns about the portrayal of women in the cinema
and its relationship to the psychological complexities of female sexuality.
She concludes that the international women's movement did not result in
a significant change in the cinema's patronizing portrayal of women and
finds that even the occasional depiction of a self-sufficient woman is
used to reinforce the repressions of the past. This book includes discussions on the portrayals of female sexuality and lesbianism in the movies,
essays on the films of individual directors such as Ingmar Bergman, Eric
Rohmer, Dusan Makavejev, Luis Bunuel, and Luchino Visconti, an examination
of the sexual politics in Last Tango in Paris, and a revisionist look
at the career of Mae West.

PC 546. MILLER, RANDALL M., ed. The Kaleidoscopic Lens: How Hollywood
        Views Ethnic Groups. Englewood, N.J.: Jerome S. Ozer, 1980.
        222 pp.
The essays in this anthology trace the origins, evolution, and significance
of representations of ethnic groups in American films. Nine ethnic groups
are discussed: American Indians, Asians, blacks, Germans, Hispanics,
Irish, Italians, Jews, and Slavs. The authors reveal that movie stereotypes were rarely created by Hollywood; rather they were derived from
other media. Inaccurate film stereotypes served only to reconfirm well-
established attitudes toward minority groups. These essays chronicle
how ethnic images in American film evolved due to such factors as war,
international diplomacy, changing racial attitudes, and the rise and fall
of the American studio system of filmmaking.

PC 547. MONACO, JAMES. American Film Now. New York: Oxford University
        Press, 1979. 540 pp.
Monaco considers the motion picture not just as an art form, but also
as a commodity produced and marketed by an industry. By concentrating
on the structure of the contemporary movie business, he is able to reveal
how economic considerations, to a large extent, determine the kinds of
films made available to American audiences. The author surveys the American film industry from the 1950s to the late 1970s and includes brief
commentaries on the work of specific actors, directors, cinematographers,
and producers. Monaco observes that, despite the concern for profits,
the film industry has become increasingly honest in its portrayal of sensitive subjects such as political corruption, racism, feminism, and sexual
deviance. He includes a chapter devoted to black directors as well as
speculations as to which filmmakers of the 1970s will serve as the models
for the filmmakers of the 1980s.

PC 548. MORDDEN, ETHAN. The Hollywood Musical. New York: St. Martin's
        Press, 1981. 261 pp.
This chronological history of the American musical film begins with the
first sound motion pictures in the 1920s and traces the genre through
the mid-1970s. Mordden details the development of the musical film through
discussions of various subgenres including backstage musicals, musicals
with the radio industry as a setting, college musicals, operettas, and
musical biographies. Specific films are highlighted to reveal the role
they played in the growth of the genre. Chapter-long examinations of
the dance musical, the musical comedy, and the fantasy and story musical
describe the genre at the height of its popularity and artistic achievement,
but Mordden also considers the wane of the musical during the 1950s.
Hollywood's adaptation of Broadway plays and the American film musical's
relationship to popular music (specifically swing and rock) are examined.
He includes a selective discography and bibliography.

PC 549. MORELLA, JOE and EDWARD Z. EPSTEIN. <u>Rebels</u>: <u>The Rebel Hero in</u>
<u>Films</u>. New York: Citadel Press, 1971. 210 pp.
Morella and Epstein define the rebel hero as a sensitive individual, lacking ambition, who has dropped out of society yet maintains a certain nobil-
ity. Through the rebel hero Hollywood's normally sharp distinction between
good and evil becomes muddled. This book traces the evolution of the
rebel hero from his first appearance with John Garfield's role in <u>Four</u>
<u>Daughters</u> (1938) through the 1960s, and concludes with speculations on
the future of the rebel hero.

PC 550. MORIN, EDGAR. <u>The Stars</u>. New York: Grove Press, 1960.
191 pp.
Morin's broad discussion of the star system, with emphasis on Hollywood,
examines viewer attitudes toward stars and stars' influences on films.
He includes a general description of the evolution of the star system
from the 1920s to the 1960s. Placing particular emphasis on Charlie
Chaplin as a comic hero and James Dean as a mythological hero, Morin examines the audience's attraction to stars. As expresser of ritual, admired
object, and subject of advertising, the star, for Morin, plays a major
role in helping people shape their own personalities.

PC 551. MURRAY, EDWARD. <u>The Cinematic Imagination</u>: <u>Writers and the Motion</u>
<u>Picture</u>. New York: Ungar, 1972. 317 pp.
Murray finds the motion picture to be the most popular form of art in
the 20th century and examines the influence of movies on both plays and
novels. Although he does not deal exclusively with American artists,
most of the playwrights, filmmakers, and novelists whose work he discusses
are American. He notes that the demand for visual realism ("the cinematic
imagination") transformed 19th-century plays and novels even before the
invention of the cinematic apparatus. Murray finds that the possibilities
created by cinematic techniques (such as montage, parallel editing, fast
cutting, etc.) were appropriated by writers and increased the visual bias
in 20th-century literary art.

PC 552. MURRAY, EDWARD. <u>Nine American Film Critics</u>: <u>A Study of Theory</u>
<u>and Practice</u>. New York: Ungar, 1975. 248 pp.
Beginning with James Agee, Murray explicates the "guiding principles"
of American film critics who have mirrored and shaped the motion picture's
respectability as an art form since W.W. II. He also evaluates how the
application of these principles has encouraged or stunted an increasingly
educated audience's cinematic literacy and insight. In terms of "practical
criticism," Murray proves to be a stern critic of excess, the unwarranted
devotion to a single-minded method or enthusiasm: he remains skeptical
of "sociological criticism" (Robert Warshow), auteur theory (Andrew Sarris),
"psychoanalytic-mythological" approaches (Parker Tyler), sarcastic poses
(John Simon), the undisciplined adulation of "trash" (Pauline Kael).
Murray reserves his greatest praise for the moderates--in his estimate,
Stanley Kauffmann, Vernon Young and Dwight Macdonald--for those who maintain a balanced view of individual directors, film history and the "human
condition" while contributing to the cinematic renaissance of the postwar
era.

PC 553. MURRAY, JAMES P. <u>To Find an Image</u>: <u>Black Films from Uncle Tom</u>
<u>to Superfly</u>. Indianapolis, Ind.: Bobbs-Merrill, 1973.
205 pp.
Murray surveys the history of the portrayal of blacks in film and examines
the political and social significance of that depiction. He examines
the image of the black man as portrayed in white films and analyzes the
reactions of black audiences to these frequently inaccurate, one-sided
images. Along with an assessment of the cultural significance of the
black film, the author includes a collection of interviews with prominent

black filmmakers (including Gordon Parks and Ossie Davis) who have broken
into the predominantly white film industry to make such successful films
as Shaft and Cotton Comes to Harlem.

PC 554. NACHBAR, JACK, ed. Focus on the Western. Englewood Cliffs, N.J.:
Prentice-Hall, 1974. 150 pp.
This anthology of essays proposes that the Western is an artifact not
of history, but of the American idealization of its history. Nachbar
has gathered fourteen essays that support Frederick Jackson Turner's 1893
hypothesis that the central myth of American history is the existence
of a limitless American frontier. This collection explores four areas
of Western studies: origins and development of the genre, definition
of the Western, the Western as a cultural artifact, and the contemporary
Western. John Cawelti's "Savagery, Civilization and the Western Hero"
and Robert Warshow's "Movie Chronicle: The Westerner" are included in
the anthology. Cawelti defines the Western as "the epic moment" when
the settler confronts, struggles with, and ultimately tames the frontier.
Warshow's 1954 essay presents the Western hero as the last gentleman who
acts primarily out of a sense of personal honor. The collection contains
a chronology of historically significant and influential films and events,
and a bibliography of books, articles, and journals that deal with the
Western as a genre.

PC 555. NAVASKY, VICTOR S. Naming Names. New York: Viking Press, 1980.
482 pp.
Navasky examines the House Committee on Un-American Activities' investigation into the allegations of Communist influence in Hollywood and contends that the Committee chose Hollywood because its members felt that
the film industry provided an ideal apparatus for producing and distributing Communist propaganda. Citing the strongly anti-Communistic theme
and content of many American movies, Navasky attempts to show the extent
that Hollywood fought Communism in its films. The author explores the
impact HUAC's investigations had on Hollywood, the role of informers such
as Larry Parks and Elia Kazan, and the decision of the Hollywood Ten and
others to risk imprisonment rather than respond to the Committee's questions. Finally, Navasky writes about what he sees as the tragedy of the
blacklist years. While Hollywood never posed a threat to the nation's
well-being, the investigation caused actors, writers, and directors to
"name names" and thus to fall into a moral and psychological trap.

PC 556. NESTEBY, JAMES P. Black Images in American Films, 1896-1954.
Washington, D.C.: University Press of America, 1982. 281 pp.
Nesteby's historical and cultural survey of black images in American film
describes censorship arising from economic conditions, as minority viewpoints were suppressed in an attempt to make films that could reach the
widest possible audience. The author notes that Afro-American roles
reflect cultural attitudes of the times in which films were made and traces
the origins and evolution of black film stereotypes. Nesteby chronicles
the largely unsuccessful attempts made by Civil Rights workers to replace
negative stereotypes with positive role models, and white audiences'
gradual acceptance of black screen stars despite their continued failure
to acknowledge Afro-Americans as equals.

PC 557. NICHOLS, BILL. Ideology and the Image: Social Representation
in the Cinema and Other Media. Bloomington: Indiana University
Press, 1981. 334 pp.
Nichols makes use of a variety of approaches (including psychoanalysis,
Marxism, structuralism, semiotics, theories of perception, and communications theory) to explore the relationships between images, aesthetics,
and ideology. He considers how the cinema, as a sign system, can perpetuate a society's set of values and discusses both the pleasure provided

by the cinema and the relationship between that pleasure and the capitalist economic system. Through detailed discussions of Blonde Venus, The Birds, and the documentary films of Frederick Wiseman, Nichols examines how ideology informs film images and explores the potential links between perception and the ideology implicit in film style.

PC 558. NICHOLS, BILL, ed. Movies and Methods: An Anthology. Berkeley: University of California Press, 1976. 640 pp.
This collection of essays reveals the range of critical methods used in film scholarship. The theoretical underpinnings and practical applications of generic, auteurist, structuralist, formalist, and semiological approaches to film are revealed as Nichols groups these essays to portray the evolution of, or debate surrounding, these various methodologies. He includes essays from classical film theory which these newer approaches have expanded upon. Individual essays address questions on the nature of the cinema, the extent to which film is like a language, the ways technique and style are manipulated, and the ways in which films relate to their historical and ideological context.

PC 559. NOBLE, PETER. The Negro in Films. London: Knapp, Drewett, 1948. 288 pp.
Noble explores the ways in which the depiction of blacks in films contributed to their continued segregation in American society. He characterizes the images of blacks found in American movies as an attempt to justify their exploitation and sees film portrayals as nurturing feelings of contempt for blacks among white audiences. He discusses the depiction of blacks in silent and European films, the black musical genre, the portrayal of blacks in independent and government films as well as in specific American sound films. Included are a bibliography on "Blacks in American Life" and a list of films from 1902-48 which featured black performers or contained racial themes.

PC 560. NORTH, JOSEPH H. The Early Development of the Motion Picture (1887-1909). New York: Arno Press, 1973. 313 pp.
North outlines the evolution of film production, distribution, and exhibition from 1887 to 1909, writing in response to what he sees as the absence of film histories regarding the contributions of filmmakers, technicians, and businessmen prior to D. W. Griffith. Rather than discussing the controversy over who actually invented the cinematic apparatus, this book begins with the invention of Thomas A. Edison and William Kennedy Laurie Dickson's Kinetograph and follows the development of film technology from an apparatus designed for a single viewer, through the invention of screen projection, and the rise of the nickelodeon theater. North describes the development of early film exchanges and discusses their importance as the first economical and efficient method of film distribution. This volume describes the establishment of an industry structure which predated the mass production of motion pictures and the beginning of Griffith's directorial career at Biograph.

PC 561. O'CONNOR, JOHN E. The Hollywood Indian: Stereotypes of Native Americans in Film. Trenton: New Jersey State Museum, 1980. 80 pp.
This work examines the portrayal of Native Americans in ten popular films. O'Connor has researched the production of these films and determined that the negative stereotypes used by Hollywood are not the result of a purposeful distortion but rather were due to technical and business related production decisions. He cites the commercial and collaborative nature of Hollywood studio filmmaking along with dramatic considerations of the Western formula such as the need to satisfy audience expectations, the demand for high action scenes, and the desire to limit moral ambiguity, as combining to shape Hollywood's inaccurate portrayal of Native Americans

and their culture. Among the films discussed by O'Connor are America (1924), Drums Along the Mohawk (1939), They Died with Their Boots On (1941), Broken Arrow (1950), Cheyenne Autumn (1964), and Little Big Man (1970).

PC 562. O'CONNOR, JOHN E. and MARTIN A. JACKSON, eds. American History/ American Film: Interpreting the Hollywood Image. New York: Ungar, 1979. 290 pp.
This anthology consists of essays by various authors describing how fourteen films prove an effective mirror of the political, social, and psychological condition of America at the time of their release. Films are selected from throughout the history of American filmmaking and are examined in light of how they reflect such topics as the new woman in the 1920s, gangsters and the Depression, Russia as a W.W. II ally, the Cold War, 1960s youth culture, and the rebirth of optimism during the Bicentennial. Among the films discussed are: Way Down East, The Big Parade, Steamboat 'Round the Bend, Drums Along the Mohawk, Red River, Dr. Strangelove, and Rocky.

PC 563. PAINE, JEFFERY MORTON. The Simplification of American Life: Hollywood Films of the 1930's. New York: Arno Press, 1977. 305 pp.
Paine discusses the tendency of 1930s Hollywood films to retain a pre-Depression optimism, refusing to portray the harsh realities of 1930s America. The author describes Hollywood's reaction to the Depression as obscured by the simplification of genres. To illustrate this position, Paine offers an in-depth consideration of the Western genre. In addition, he cites specific characteristics of film practice, such as the medium's documentary realism and various editing styles, as well as developments in film technology, including deep focus cinematography and panchromatic film stock, as making this simplification acceptable and in some ways inevitable. The study concludes with a discussion of how criticism attempts to fit films into an established definition of culture.

PC 564. PARKS, RITA. The Western Hero in Film and Television: Mass Media Mythology. Ann Arbor, Mich.: UMI Research Press, 1982. 197 pp.
Parks investigates "the generic constants and the artistic variables" of the Western hero's portrayal in film and television. She traces the Westerner's evolution from historical figure (Daniel Boone, Billy the Kid, Kit Carson, Buffalo Bill) to mass media myth (Roy Rogers, The Man Who Shot Liberty Valance, Stagecoach, The Plainsman). This cultural folk hero (for example, Tom Mix, William S. Hart, John Wayne, Gary Cooper) often crosses the line between fact and fiction, history and myth, to "create a reality more genuine than the facts can hope to produce." Parks indicates that the West, even during its heyday, was aware of its own legends and that the subsequent development of the Western in movies and television has been in part to "demythologize" the region and lend it more human characteristics.

PC 565. PEARY, DANNY and GERALD PEARY, eds. The American Animated Cartoon: A Critical Anthology. New York: Dutton, 1980. 310 pp.
This anthology describes American cartoon animation outside of the Walt Disney Studio. The careers and films of independent cartoonists unaffiliated with studios (such as Winsor McCay, George Griffin, and John and Faith Hubley), and non-Disney industry animators (such as Paul Terry, Ralph Bakshi, Walter Lantz, Hanna-Barbera, and J. R. Bray), are discussed. Several essays on the Warner Brothers Studio reveal its challenge to the Disney Studio's artistic hegemony since the 1930s. Also included are a feminist critique of cartoons, a historical report of the 1937 strike at the Fleischer studio, a transcript of Walt Disney's testimony before HUAC alleging Communist activity in Hollywood, and an essay on the International Tournee of Animation. Though this collection concentrates on

contributions to the American cartoon made by animators not affiliated
with Walt Disney's studio, several essays do discuss Disney's animation.

PC 566.   PEARY, GERALD and ROGER SHATZKIN, eds.   The Classic American Novel
          and the Movies.   New York: Ungar, 1977.   356 pp.
This collection of essays examines the film adaptations of various American
novels published before 1930.   Essays discuss film versions of the novels
of James Fenimore Cooper, Nathaniel Hawthorne, Herman Melville, Mark Twain,
Henry James, Stephen Crane, Theodore Dreiser, F. Scott Fitzgerald, Ernest
Hemingway, William Faulkner, and others.   Individual essays analyze the
transformations these novels underwent during their adaptation to the
screen.   The process of adaptation is described by film historians and
literary critics who reveal how filmmakers reduce the scope of novels,
create a cinematic narrative structure, and introduce or alter the ideological content of the novels they take as sources.   This anthology
includes several interviews with screenwriters and filmmakers describing
specific adaptations of American novels.

PC 567.   PEARY, GERALD and ROGER SHATZKIN, eds.   The Modern American Novel
          and the Movies.   New York: Ungar, 1978.   461 pp.
This collection of essays on major American novels and their film versions
from 1930-75 examines how a novel becomes a film and the problems of theme,
content, and ideology that are confronted in the process of adaptation.
The contributors agree on the importance of the novel's author, but also
examine the role of the film's director in translating the novel to the
screen.   This process is studied in thirty-two films, including The Big
Sleep, The Old Man and the Sea, Deliverance, All the King's Men, Catch-
22, The Grapes of Wrath, To Have and Have Not, and Miss Lonelyhearts.
Essays on the politics of adaptation examine ideological choices that
are made when adapting novels to film.   The contributors include scholars,
prominent film critics, and novelists examining film adaptations of their
own work.

PC 568.   POTAMKIN, HARRY ALAN.   The Compound Cinema: The Writings of Harry
          Alan Potamkin.   Edited by Lewis Jacobs.   New York: Teachers
          College Press, 1977.   646 pp.
Jacobs reprints Potamkin's contributions to a variety of avant-garde and
political magazines in order to spotlight this film critic's intellectual
journey from the "aesthetic ferment" of the 1920s to the "social consciousness" of the Depression decade.   Part I, "Film as Art (1926-1930)," emphasizes Potamkin's role as New Critic, preoccupied with cinematic "unity"
and fastidious craftsmanship.   Part II, "Film and Society (1930-1933),"
documents his growing belief that any work of art represents an "ideological statement of the social group that produced it"--a perspective illustrated in his treatment of film cults, children's films, Soviet art and
politics, and the distinctive national attributes of the American and
other Western cinemas.   Part III gives greatest prominence to Potamkin's
columns for the New Masses, but also includes his analysis of "bourgeois
film critics" and a proposal for a multidisciplinary film school.

PC 569.   POWDERMAKER, HORTENSE.   Hollywood: The Dream Factory.   Boston:
          Little, Brown, 1950.   342 pp.
Powdermaker's model of "applied anthropology" proposes to investigate
Hollywood as a "social system," subjecting it to an analysis typically
reserved for preindustrial cultures.   Emphasizing Hollywood's role as
an institution of production, Powdermaker's observations are based on
her 1946-47 fieldwork, consisting of 300 interviews, attendance at meetings
of the Screen Writers' Guild, visits to studio sets, and close scrutiny
of the industry's trade papers and censorship codes.   Assuming that Hollywood represents "a caricature of selected contemporary tendencies"--in
particular the "manipulation of people through mass communications"--she

reports on the high degree of "frustration" to be found among executives, scriptwriters, directors, and actors and actresses. She largely perceives Hollywood as symptomatic of democracy's flirtation with the forces of totalitarianism, as an institution where "humiliation," "animistic thinking," and the denial of mature decision-making persist.

PC 570. PYE, MICHAEL and LYNDA MYLES. The Movie Brats: How the Film Generation Took Over Hollywood. New York: Holt, Rinehart & Winston, 1979. 273 pp.
Pye and Myles discuss Hollywood after the collapse of the studio system and expose the changed relationship between the six major distribution companies and individual filmmakers. In examining the filmmaking careers of Steven Spielberg, Martin Scorsese, John Milius, Brian DePalma, George Lucas, and Francis Coppola, the authors find a new generation of filmmakers who have inherited the power of the old movie moguls to reach a large audience but who operate under a system of financing and production which is vastly different from that of their predecessors. Most of the filmmakers studied in this book are the products of film schools; Pye and Myles document the tendency of their films to reveal a scholar's knowledge and appreciation of the cinema.

PC 571. RANDALL, RICHARD S. Censorship of the Movies: The Social and Political Control of a Mass Medium. Madison: University of Wisconsin Press, 1968. 280 pp.
Randall examines the historical and social significance of movie censorship in America. Beginning with a discussion of the laws governing movie content and the legal procedures involved, he describes the roles played by both state and federal authorities in censoring films. The importance of private citizen groups, criminal prosecution, and Hollywood's practice of self-censorship is explored in relation to how these forces affect motion picture content. Randall concludes with an evaluation of the status of free speech in America and its application to the motion picture industry.

PC 572. RENAN, SHELDON. An Introduction to the American Underground Film. New York: Dutton, 1967. 318 pp.
Renan discusses American films of personal statement that are oppositional in form, technique, or content, specifically those films which have come to be known as the New American Cinema. In part arising out of the tradition of personal filmmaking established by the avant-garde movements of the 1920s and 1940s, in part out of certain technological innovations which made filmmaking equipment more accessible, these films represent a rebellion against the domination of Hollywood and the American commercial cinema. Renan includes a brief history of the underground film in America and a discussion of twenty-four of the most widely recognized American oppositional filmmakers. He also describes the development of the underground film's own system of finance, production, distribution, publicity and exhibition, and includes both a discussion of the multi-media "Expanded Cinema" and an extensive list of films and their availability for purchase or rental.

PC 573. RICHARDS, JEFFREY. Visions of Yesterday. Boston: Routledge & Kegan Paul, 1973. 391 pp.
Richards examines cinema of the political right, attempting to show that the mythologies presented and ideologies implicit in certain films exemplify and dramatize aspects of 20th-century right wing political movements. He sets out to prove this thesis by documenting the relationship between film and three political movements: British imperialism, American populism (as seen in the films of John Ford, Frank Capra, and Leo McCarey), and German national socialism. Richards concludes with a discussion of Nazi cinema, its themes, and its most prominent filmmaker, Leni Riefenstahl.

Included are a filmography of the principal films discussed throughout
the book and a bibliography listing books and periodicals which examine
the historical and cultural significance of film.

PC 574. ROBINSON, DAVID. Hollywood in the Twenties. New York: Barnes,
1968. 176 pp.
Robinson chronicles the history of Hollywood filmmaking from the end of
W.W. I to the introduction of talking pictures and relates films and filmmakers to American life and culture of the time. Approximately seventy
filmmakers who the author feels were most significant to the evolution
of filmmaking in the 1920s are discussed. He describes the structure
and operation of the industry, the contributions of Europeans in Hollywood
(including Ernst Lubitsch, Zoltan Korda, and several Swedish, German,
Russian, and French directors), the role played by creative producers
like Thomas Ince and Mack Sennett, and the status of the great silent
film stars as actors and idols. Six major figures (Charlie Chaplin, Buster
Keaton, Erich von Stroheim, Joseph von Sternberg, John Ford, and Robert
Flaherty) are singled out for their important contributions to the evolution of the medium. Robinson concludes with a look at the special techniques and language of silent film and a survey of the impact of sound
on the existing film industry and its conventions.

PC 575. RODDICK, NICK. A New Deal in Entertainment: Warner Brothers
in the 1930s. London: British Film Institute, 1983. 332 pp.
Although Roddick observes that many of Warner Brothers' productions
reflected the New Deal by possessing a social conscience and by maintaining
a reassuring tone about the abilities of American institutions, the major
thrust of this book is the description of the classical style of filmmaking
associated with Hollywood in the studio era. The author's examination
of Warner Brothers from the time of the stock market crash to the beginnings of U.S. involvement in W.W. II describes the hegemony of the Hollywood studio stystem. Roddick portrays the assembly-line style of studio
filmmaking through an analysis of profit and loss figures on a number
of feature films. He includes a detailed case history of the production
of Anthony Adverse to demonstrate the collaborative quality of the work
within this system.

PC 576. ROFFMAN, PETER and JIM PURDY. The Hollywood Social Problem Film:
Madness, Despair, and Politics from the Depression to the Fifties.
Bloomington: Indiana University Press, 1981. 364 pp.
In this examination of films from the 1930s through the 1950s, Roffman
and Purdy find that certain Hollywood films reflect the predominant attitudes of their times. Section I, devoted to films from 1930-33, contains
a contrast between films with right-wing themes (advocating temporary
extremism to combat the Depression) and those with leftist orientations
(such as Warner Brothers' I Am a Fugitive from a Chain Gang). The authors
characterize films from 1933-41 as upholding the American system through
its treatment of such themes as the ex-convict or juvenile delinquent
in society and the nature of rural problems. The third section is centered
on W.W. II and the portrayal of American fascists, "super-shysters,"
and plutocrats. The volume concludes with a discussion of minorities,
HUAC, and post-war labor problems in relation to Hollywood films produced
after W.W. II.

PC 577. ROLLINS, PETER C., ed. Hollywood as Historian: American Film
in a Cultural Context. Lexington: University Press of Kentucky,
1983. 276 pp.
This collection of thirteen essays explores the various aspects of Hollywood's relationship to history. Analyses of individual films demonstrate
how movies have influenced cultural change. Several wartime movies and
documentaries influenced by the New Deal are discussed to show how they

shaped public attitudes and thus influenced history. The capacity for film to act as a historical document and to reveal unconscious attitudes of its time is explored through analyses of The Snake Pit and Dr. Strangelove. Birth of a Nation and Wilson are considered as examples of historical reconstruction. Three Chaplin films, The Grapes of Wrath, and Apocalypse Now are used to examine the relationship between aesthetics and ideology.

PC 578. **ROSEN, MARJORIE.** Popcorn Venus: Women, Movies and the American Dream. New York: Coward, McCann & Geoghegan, 1973. 416 pp.
This chronological study of American films examines Hollywood's influence on the values of American audiences, especially American women. Rosen exposes thematic trends over the years and reveals how these trends shaped women's perceptions of themselves. Throughout the book, Rosen links the changing portrayals of women to concurrent social, cultural, and economic events in America. She links the early days of motion pictures to the emergence from Victorianism, noting the morally controlling influence of most early films. Rosen traces the effect of the Depression and W.W. II on Hollywood's depiction of women and also the effect this changing portrayal had on American audiences. She concludes by chronicling the evolution of the portrayal of domesticity and sexuality from the 1950s into the early 1970s.

PC 579. **ROSENTHAL, ALAN.** The Documentary Conscience: A Casebook in Film Making. Berkeley: University of California Press, 1980. 436 pp.
Rosenthal's case studies of individual documentary films made during the 1970s examine the work of socially committed filmmakers in light of their beliefs, personal backgrounds, and social visions. By looking at various problems overcome during production (from fund-raising to censorship), he describes the documentary filmmaking process and questions the ability of films to bring about social change. One criterion used in selecting films and filmmakers for this study was Rosenthal's desire to compare documentaries made both inside and outside of institutions (for example, broadcasting networks). The first three sections of this book are discussions of historical films made for television, investigative filmmaking, and documentary films. Other sections examine feminist films, documentaries about Vietnam, and leftist concerns such as Attica, Native Americans and labor unions.

PC 580. **ROSENTHAL, ALAN.** The New Documentary in Action: A Casebook in Film Making. Berkeley: University of California Press, 1971. 287 pp.
Rosenthal uses case studies of individual nonfiction films to emphasize the practical problems of documentary filmmaking. Through extensive interviews with filmmakers, this volume follows specific films from conception through exhibition in an attempt to examine the working methods of documentary filmmaking. Factors beyond the control of the filmmaker which determine the final look of the film are also illuminated. Rosenthal concentrates on certain types of documentary film such as cinema verite, reconstructions, sponsored films, and television journalism to identify obstacles specific to each. Occasionally Rosenthal includes interviews with specific people associated with a film to demonstrate the collaborative nature of filmmaking. Among the filmmakers interviewed are: Allen King, Frederick Wiseman, Albert Maysles, Peter Watkins, D. A. Pennebaker, George Stoney, and Allen Funt.

PC 581. ROSOW, EUGENE. Born to Lose: The Gangster Film in America.
New York: Oxford University Press, 1978. 422 pp.
Rosow looks to the American myth of success and our fascination with romantic criminal figures to find the sources of the gangster film genre.
Finding movie genres to be myths which are particularly responsive to
changing social tensions, he surveys the development of the gangster film
as it reveals the changing self-image of America's advanced capitalist
society. Through analyses of recurring characters, themes, and iconography,
the author traces the rise of the gangster movie in the 1920s and observes
the evolution of the genre during the Depression, as gangsters were transformed into G-men under the influence of the New Deal. Rosow follows
the genre through the 1940s as Hollywood's wartime gangsters helped to
defeat the Nazis. The post-war shift to criminal syndicates in the movies
is linked to investigations in the 1950s which revealed large criminal
organizations in America. He concludes that the Hollywood gangster film
symbolizes many of the values and beliefs of American society.

PC 582. ROSS, LILLIAN. Picture. New York: Rinehart, 1952. 258 pp.
In this narrative account of the production of MGM's The Red Badge of
Courage, Ross provides an insight into the Hollywood studio system during
the early days of television. She traces the development of this feature-
length motion picture from preproduction meetings between the director,
screenwriter, and the studio, through principal shooting, post-production
editing, and the development of publicity strategies, to the distribution
and critical reception of the film. Ross describes the roles played by
producers, directors, studio officials, and production personnel, as well
as the personalities of notable Hollywood figures such as Louis B. Mayer,
Dore Schary, and John Huston. Forces shaping the final version of the
film, such as the Production Code Administration's review of the script
prior to production and the disastrous audience response to early sneak
previews, are described to reveal how they changed Huston's original conception of the screen version of Stephen Crane's novel.

PC 583. ROSS, MURRAY. Stars and Strikes. New York: Columbia University
Press, 1941. 233 pp.
In this chronicle of the unionization of Hollywood film studios, Ross
attempts to reveal the economic, political, social, and psychological
forces that combined in the trade union movement and how these forces
affected the entire motion picture industry. Noting that the International
Alliance of Theatrical Stage Employees and the American Federation of
Musicians pre-dated the motion picture industry, he explains how film
exhibition became the first section of the motion picture industry to
unionize. He analyzes the impact of the NRA period and the National Labor
Relations Act, concluding that they helped to push film production
employees toward trade unionism. He also examines the creation and operation
of film producers' organizations such as the Association of Motion Picture
Producers and the Academy of Motion Picture Arts and Sciences, and
describes the response of these industry groups to the growing power of film
trade unions.

PC 584. ROSS, T. J., ed. Film and the Liberal Arts. New York: Holt,
Rinehart & Winston, 1970. 419 pp.
This collection of essays by filmmakers, critics, and theorists is designed
to examine the cinema's relationship with other art forms and its role
in society. Ross has divided the volume into six sections, each concentrating on a particular aspect of the film medium. The essays in "Film
and Rhetoric" describe the language of film and develop a communications
model for the cinema. The sections on "Film and Literature," "Film and
the Visual Arts," and "Film and Music" describe various elements shared
by the cinema and these other art forms. "Film and Society" explores
the relationship of cinema to social values. The final section, "Film

and Esthetics," looks at the critical evaluation of movies and film's status as an art form. Each essay is followed by questions designed to elicit from the reader comparisons between his or her experience of the cinema and that of the essayist.

PC 585. **ROSTEN, LEO C.** Hollywood: The Movie Colony, the Movie Makers. New York: Harcourt, Brace, 1941. 436 pp.
Using the results of several thousand questionnaires and hundreds of interviews with Hollywood professionals, Rosten characterizes Hollywood as an index of American society and culture. His study is a description of the values, politics, and practices of Hollywood, as well as of the night life, marriage patterns, and legends surrounding America's filmmaking community. Through a discussion of the impact of Hollywood on American speech, dress, and consumption, Rosten examines how American movie content both reflects and reinforces public tastes and morality. Appendices include industry economic data, Hollywood marriage and divorce statistics, a study of the geographical distribution of fan mail, and copies of the questionnaires circulated by Rosten.

PC 586. **RUBIN, STEVEN JAY.** Combat Films: American Realism 1945-1970. Jefferson, N.C.: McFarland, 1981. 233 pp.
Rubin examines eight films made between the end of W.W. II and 1970, focusing on their attempts to portray warfare without the artificial glory or heroics of previous war films. Through information gleaned from extensive interviews with the makers of these films, he traces the frustrations encountered during the making of A Walk in the Sun (1945), Battleground (1949), The Longest Day (1962), The Great Escape (1963), Twelve O'Clock High (1949), The Bridge on the River Kwai (1957), Hell Is for Heroes (1962), and Patton (1970).

PC 587. **RUSSO, VITO.** The Celluloid Closet: Homosexuality in the Movies. New York: Harper & Row, 1981. 276 pp.
In this historical survey of homosexuality and lesbianism in films, Russo maintains that homosexuality has been a minor, but nonetheless significant theme explored in the movies, despite the claims of film studios that they did not make films about the subject. He observes that when Hollywood did portray homosexuality, it was done in a degrading manner, often depicting gays as social and psychological misfits. Russo praises television for honest and objective approaches to homosexuality; he believes that television depicts homosexuals with warmth and sensitivity, and that its attempts to understand homosexuality often prove more successful than Hollywood's stereotypical depictions.

PC 588. **SALT, BARRY.** Film Style and Technology: History and Analysis. London: Starword, 1983. 408 pp.
This history of the formal features of film style, and the developments in film technology which shaped them, is based on Salt's examination of several thousand films dating from 1895-1970. Salt analyzes the history of film technique in terms of the construction of individual films and the distribution of certain cinematic qualities (such as shot length). Salt finds that the existence of an individual filmmaker's style can be established by a formal, stylistic analysis of that director's films. He includes one such study of the films of Max Ophuls. Salt chronicles the technological evolution of the cinematic apparatus through descriptions of innovations in cameras, lenses, film stocks, lighting, projection, sound, color and wide screen processes, and editing techniques.

PC 589. SAMPSON, HENRY T. Blacks in Black and White: A Sourcebook on
          Black Films. Metuchen, N.J.: Scarecrow Press, 1977. 333 pp.
This historical survey of independent black film production from 1910-50
describes the organization of film companies and the production of motion
pictures. Sampson bases this narrative account on reviews, quotations,
and memoirs of persons in the industry. The accomplishments of The Lincoln
Motion Picture Company, the first black-owned company to produce black
films and distribute them nationally, and the twenty-year career of Oscar
Micheaux are highlighted as examples of successful black American film
production. Over one third of this book is devoted to film synopses which
show the evolution of film themes. As most of these films are unavailable
to the general public, Sampson includes descriptions, a filmography, and
a list of credits.

PC 590. SANDERSON, RICHARD ARLO. A Historical Study of the Development
          of American Motion Picture Content and Techniques Prior to 1904.
          New York: Arno Press, 1977. 234 pp.
Attempting to identify trends in early film content and technique,
Sanderson examined over 680 films in the Library of Congress Paper Print
Collection. This book contains the conclusions drawn from that research.
The author found that the earliest films were predominantly "actualities"
made by filmmakers who pointed their cameras at everyday life. A later
development was the story film, which he classifies into four types:
documentary, travelogue, entertainment, and sports. Sanderson chronicles
the gradual evolution of such film techniques as pans, tilts, fades, dis-
solves, and stop motion effects, all of which were found in the films
he studied.

PC 591. SANDS, PIERRE N. A Historical Study of the Academy of Motion
          Picture Arts and Sciences, 1927-1947. New York: Arno Press,
          1973. 262 pp.
Sands traces the history of the Academy of Motion Picture Arts and Sciences
and its attempt to stimulate movie attendance, in part, by encouraging
the development of techniques of film production. He discusses the
Academy's contribution to education, military filmmaking during W.W. II,
and technical activities within the motion picture industry, placing particular emphasis on the founding of the "Oscar" award system. He also
describes the organization of the Academy, its founding, by-laws, officers,
and branches.

PC 592. SARRIS, ANDREW. The American Cinema: Directors and Directions,
          1929-1968. New York: Dutton, 1968. 387 pp.
Sarris introduces eleven categories for ranking Hollywood directors.
This typology, which is based on an application of auteur theory, "converts
film history into directorial autobiography" in order to remedy the
excesses of "sociologically oriented" movie historians. These categories
include what Sarris calls "Pantheon Directors"--Howard Hawks, Alfred
Hitchcock, Charles Chaplin, D. W. Griffith and others--who have "transcended
technical problems" with a "personal vision" of the world. Sarris's discussion of the remaining ten categories covers the careers and works of
over 100 other directors, including Vincente Minelli, Douglas Sirk, Otto
Preminger, Nicholas Ray, John Huston, William Wyler, and Fred Zinnemann.
According to Sarris, scholars have traditionally perceived American
directors as "artisans" functioning within a mass medium, rather than recognizing their "performance under pressure"--the coherence they achieve under
difficult circumstances in a "money-oriented environment."

PC 593. SAYRE, NORA. Running Time: Films of the Cold War. New York:
          Dial Press, 1982. 243 pp.
Sayre's broad cultural history of 1950s films examines how Hollywood
addressed American anxieties regarding the Cold War, McCarthyism, and fears
of nuclear holocaust. She surveys important 1950s film themes including:
anti-Communism, the American family in conflict, delinquent behavior,
sexuality, science fiction and extraterrestrial threats, and anti-Semitism.
Citing specific genre films such as The Day the Earth Stood Still, The
Thing, High Noon, The Bridge on the River Kwai, and Paths of Glory, Sayre
reveals how films of this period transcended their generic conventions
to expose the problems and tensions that plagued America in the 1950s.

PC 594. SCHATZ, THOMAS. Hollywood Genres: Formulas, Filmmaking, and
          the Studio System. Philadelphia: Temple University Press, 1981.
          297 pp.
Schatz maintains that a generic study of American film is the most effective way of understanding and analyzing the cultural and psychological
relationship between Hollywood and its audience. All Hollywood genres
develop through cooperation between film studios and audiences, consti-
tuting a form of contemporary mythmaking which reinforces American ideologies. This study focuses on the "classic era" of the Hollywood studio
system from 1930-60 and is divided into two sections. Part I discusses
the theoretical concerns of genre films, emphasizing the cultural role
of genre filmmaking. Part II contains chapters that analyze such Hollywood genres as the Western, the gangster film, musicals, melodramas, the
screwball comedy, and the hardboiled detective film. Included in each
chapter is an examination of one or more films which typify that genre.

PC 595. SCHICKEL, RICHARD. The Disney Version: The Life, Times, Art
          and Commerce of Walt Disney. New York: Simon & Schuster, 1968.
          384 pp.
Schickel, responding to the portrayals of Walt Disney as a Horatio Alger
figure, attempts to present a more realistic biography of Disney. He
traces Disney's film career from his early animated short films to the
production of feature-length live-action and animated productions. The
construction of the Walt Disney Studio and Disneyland, and Walt Disney's
personal fascination with new technologies (such as Technicolor and the
multiplane camera), are viewed in relation to what Schickel calls Disney's
obsessive personality. He characterizes Disney's career as shaped by
a drive for success which is peculiar to Midwesterners, and cites evidence
of this drive found in Disney's films. These films are considered in
terms of the values and assumptions shared by Disney and the American
middle class.

PC 596. SCHICKEL, RICHARD. His Picture in the Papers: A Speculation
          on Celebrity in America Based on the Life of Douglas Fairbanks,
          Sr. New York: Charterhouse, 1973. 171 pp.
Schickel describes the life and career of Douglas Fairbanks, Sr., in an
attempt to examine the cultural phenomenon of celebrity in America.
Fairbanks's career began as the Hollywood star system was in the initial
stages of development. Unlike many of his contemporaries, he flourished
under public attention, exhibiting a temperament and an intuition perfectly
suited for stardom. According to Schickel, Fairbanks embodied, and built
a career on, certain traits commonly identified at that time as components
of the American character (optimism, youthfulness, belief in the success
ethic, luck, and self-confidence). As a whole, Schickel takes Fairbanks's
life to be the "archetypal celebrity drama" exhibiting the rapid rise
and tragic fall that have become part of our expectations for public
figures.

PC 597. SCHUMACH, MURRAY. The Face on the Cutting Room Floor: The Story of Movie and Television Censorship. New York: Morrow, 1964. 305 pp.

Schumach describes the changing role of censorship in American film production. Among the subjects discussed are censorship and the courts, the appointment of Will Hays as head of the Motion Picture Producers and Distributors Association of America, and the impact of various pressure groups on the film industry's practice of self-censorship. Schumach examines individual films which tested the acceptable limits on the depiction of sex and violence in their day. He also includes a copy of the Motion Picture Production Code, samples of foreign censorship standards, and a description of how some other countries classify films.

PC 598. SCHWARTZ, NANCY LYNN. The Hollywood Writer's War. New York: Knopf, 1982. 334 pp.

Schwartz uses diaries, newspaper clippings, and interviews with writers who belonged to the Screen Writers Guild to construct this history of the Guild and its confrontation with the forces of McCarthyism in the late 1940s and early 1950s. Chronicling the blacklist, Schwartz documents not only the struggle of the Guild as it faced opposition from the Right (especially the House Committee on Un-American Activities), but also the Screen Writers Guild's struggle for political independence as reflected in the films of the period. The book includes a filmography of writers (such as John Lee Mahin, Dalton Trumbo, John Howard Lawson, and Budd Schulberg) who had prominent roles in developing the Screen Writers Guild into one of the most powerful and influential unions in Hollywood.

PC 599. SHADOIAN, JACK. Dreams and Dead Ends: The American Gangster/Crime Film. Cambridge, Mass.: MIT Press, 1977. 366 pp.

Shadoian maintains that the gangster film genre reflects the American dream of success and the often desperate and tragic lengths that Americans go to in pursuing that dream. To support this thesis, Shadoian examines forty-five gangster films from 1930-75, concentrating on such films as Public Enemy, The Killers, Kiss of Death, White Heat, Kiss Me Deadly, and The Godfather. In explaining why the gangster film genre has frequently proven unpopular with audiences and critics, he points to the tendency for the gangster/crime film to reveal unpleasant aspects of American society. The book concludes with a selected bibliography of books and articles which explore the cultural and historical significance of the gangster/crime film.

PC 600. SHALE, RICHARD. Donald Duck Joins Up: The Walt Disney Studio During World War II. Ann Arbor, Mich.: UMI Research Press, 1982. 185 pp.

Shale examines the wartime activities of the Walt Disney Studio and the consequent shift in emphasis from entertainment to educational films. The production of military and government films for, among others, the Treasury Department provided an opportunity to test Walt Disney's personal belief in the ability of the cinema to function as a teaching tool and also provided a period of experimentation with the capabilities of the medium. Shale discusses such films as Saludos Amigos, Three Caballeros and Victory Through Air Power (a feature length propaganda film), as well as the health and agricultural films made for the Coordinator of Inter-American Affairs. He also examines the impact of W.W. II on the content of the entertainment short subjects which the studio continued to produce.

PC 601. **SHINDLER, COLIN.** Hollywood Goes to War: Films and American Society 1939-1952. Boston: Routledge & Kegan Paul, 1979. 152 pp.
This work examines Hollywood's role in W.W. II in providing both entertainment and propaganda. Relating events in Europe and the Pacific with American films and filmmaking, Shindler discusses Hollywood from 1939-52. Pre-war films with preparedness themes, combat films, portrayals of the home front, and the impact of shortages and rationing on the motion picture industry are among the topics addressed in this book. Stereotypical portrayals of Japanese and Germans in propaganda films are matched against the stereotypes of Americans in melting-pot combat films. Shindler concludes with a discussion of McCarthyism and the strong anti-Communist bias of films produced immediately after the war.

PC 602. **SHORT, K. R. M.,** ed. Feature Film as History. Knoxville: University of Tennessee Press, 1981. 192 pp.
This volume explores the ways in which motion pictures produced as entertainment can function as historical documents which mirror the economic, social, and psychological states of the culture in which they are produced. Three American films, Casablanca, Tennessee Johnson, and The Negro Soldier, are used to examine the relationship between Hollywood liberals and W.W. II. Short includes a discussion of Hollywood's campaign against anti-Semitism during 1945-47. While the remainder of this book deals with European films, the methodology used and the issues raised (film and reality, cinema's depiction of national consciousness, censorship, and the portrayal of ideological consensus) can be applied to American feature films.

PC 603. **SIMON, JOHN.** Private Screenings. New York: Macmillan, 1967. 316 pp.
This volume begins with Simon's "critical credo" in which he discusses the responsibilities of the critic. He continues with a chapter devoted to his personal favorites, including directors Federico Fellini and Akira Kurosawa and several American and foreign films. Devoting a chapter to each year between 1963-66, he offers reprints of previously published reviews and a commentary on the New Wave films of this period. The penultimate chapter is focused on the career and films of Jean-Luc Godard. The volume concludes with a chapter on the portrayals of women in contemporary film, with an emphasis on the development of "stereotyped" actresses.

PC 604. **SITNEY, P. ADAMS.** Visionary Film: The American Avant Garde. 1974; Rev. ed. New York: Oxford University Press, 1979. 463 pp.
Sitney discusses American avant-garde films and filmmakers from the 1940s through the 1970s. He describes how young American filmmakers in the 1940s, unable to gain entrance to the Hollywood film industry because of its long apprenticeships, turned to the European avant-garde tradition. Their "film poems" were produced without financial reward and for limited audiences. Sitney chronicles the rise of both the "New American Cinema" and the "underground film" which developed out of the increased social awareness of some filmmakers. Concerns of the American avant-garde filmmakers are connected with American post-Romantic poets and the Abstract Expressionist painters. Sitney identifies a historical pattern in American avant-garde cinema and has invented the terms "trance films," "mythopoeic films," "structural films," and "participatory films" to define this pattern. This book is a description of a network of film production and distribution isolated from commercial American cinema.

PC 605. SITNEY, P. ADAMS, ed. Film Culture Reader. New York: Praeger,
         1970. 438 pp.
Sitney's introductory remarks consider the history of Jonas Mekas's Film
Culture—its progression from being a "general intellectual review" in
the mid-1950s to its "quasi-official" status as an apologist for the avant-
garde in the late 1960s. Sitney's selection of representative pieces
documents the magazine's transition from unfocused elitism to underground
sponsorship. Part I, "The Formative Years, 1955-58," indicates that,
while the journal applauded the European screen and Hollywood nonconform-
ists, it also sought a catholicity of taste by introducing "film history,
theory, sociology and economics." Part II, devoted to the New American
Cinema from 1959 to 1963, suggests that the success of the French and
British New Waves had led to hopes that an independent film movement might
be nourished in the United States. After a brief section spotlighting
Andrew Sarris and the "auteur" theory, Sitney reprints appreciations of
specific experimental artists—for example, Stan Brakhage, Kenneth Anger,
Andy Warhol, Jordan Belson—and their contributions to world cinema.

PC 606. SKLAR, ROBERT. Movie-Made America: A Social History of American
         Movies. New York: Random House, 1975. 340 pp.
Film is treated as an art form, an entertainment medium, and a product
of a complex industry in this historical narrative of the cinema in America.
Information on the evolution of film censorship, the development of moviemaking technology, and the changing psychological and sociological make-
up of film audiences is presented in relation to the cultural significance
of films in America and abroad from the early silent film period to the
mid-1970s. Sklar also includes profiles of D. W. Griffith, Frank Capra,
Walt Disney, Adolph Zukor and other prominent film figures who were instrumental in developing the motion picture into one of the most important
and influential forms of communication and entertainment in American history.

PC 607. SLIDE, ANTHONY. Aspects of American Film History Prior to 1920.
         Metuchen, N.J.: Scarecrow Press, 1978. 161 pp.
Surveying the history of the American film from the turn of the century
to 1920, Slide documents such aspects of American film as the Tannhouser
and Paralta film companies, the early evolution of the star system, and
the first child movie actors. He also includes profiles of directors
such as Colin Campbell, J. Searle Dawley, and Victor Heerman. A chapter
descibes the little-known film career of Katherine Anne Porter, including
her appearance in Chaplin's Shanghaied (1915). Slide concludes with a
section surveying research material on American film prior to 1920.

PC 608. SMITH, JULIAN. Looking Away: Hollywood and Vietnam. New York:
         Scribner, 1975. 236 pp.
Smith attempts to identify reasons why Hollywood evaded the cultural,
historical, and moral significance of U.S. involvement in the Vietnam
War. Examining the evolution of the American war film, he establishes
a background against which Hollywood's failure to portray Vietnam is
explored. For Smith, an analysis of various anti-establishment films of
the 1960s and 1970s such as Dr. Strangelove (1964), Patton (1970), and
Slaughterhouse-Five (1972) reveals Hollywood's disdain for U.S. military
involvement in Southeast Asia; yet, at the same time, these films equally
demonstrate Hollywood's reluctance or inability to confront directly the
issue of the Vietnam War.

PC 609. SNYDER, ROBERT L. Pare Lorentz and the Documentary Film. Norman:
         University of Oklahoma Press, 1968. 232 pp.
Snyder surveys the history of the documentary film in American cinema,
concentrating on filmmaker Pare Lorentz's contributions during the 1930s
and 1940s. He describes the formation of the U.S. Film Service, an organi-

zation under Lorentz's supervision that produced major documentaries in
the 1930s and 1940s, including The River, The Plow That Broke the Plains,
and The Fight for Life. The author raises questions about the U.S. government's role in the production of documentary films, particularly the use
of the film medium as an instrument for disseminating information and
propaganda. Also included in this book are a filmography listing Lorentz's
and the U.S. Film Service's achievements, and a bibliography listing books,
pamphlets, and articles concerned with the history of the American documentary film.

PC 610. **SOBCHACK, VIVIAN**. The Limits of Infinity. New York: Barnes,
1980. 246 pp.
The primary focus of this discussion of American science fiction films
is on their capacity to reveal insights into man's culture, morality, and
psyche. Beginning with Destination Moon (1950), and continuing through
the 1950s, 1960s, and 1970s to include recent films such as Close Encounters of the Third Kind and Star Wars, Sobchack documents ways in which
science fiction films have recorded the frustrations and hopes of Americans
as they entered the nuclear age. She suggests that science fiction films
proved an effective means of dealing with McCarthyism, racism, sexual
deviance, and political corruption.

PC 611. **SOLOMON, STANLEY J.** Beyond Formula: American Film Genres. New
York: Harcourt Brace Jovanovich, 1976. 310 pp.
Solomon begins with a theory of film genres in which the defining aspect
of each genre is a mythic structure rather than the more obvious shared
iconography. He attempts to make this book a discussion of major narrative
patterns instead of a description of the characteristic images of film
genres. He discusses such American genres as Westerns, musicals, horror
movies, crime films, detective stories, and war films.

PC 612. SORLIN, PIERRE. The Film in History: Restaging the Past. Totowa,
N.J.: Barnes & Noble Books, 1980. 226 pp.
Sorlin explores the capacity for films to act as documents of social history. Acknowledging both the usefulness and inherent distortions of newsreels, this book concentrates on films of historical reconstruction, proposing a method of study that attempts to find the political logic underlying a film's production and structure. This method rejects comparison
of fiction films with the period they depict, looking instead at how historical fiction films demonstrate a culture's understanding of its own
history. Although this methodology is applied to Soviet and Italian films,
Sorlin's primary focus is on D. W. Griffith's Birth of a Nation.

PC 613. **SPATZ, JONAS**. Hollywood in Fiction: Some Versions of the American
Myth. The Hague: Mouton, 1969. 148 pp.
In his study of Hollywood as a mythmaker, Spatz defines the images that
make up the American Dream and then considers their relationship to the
symbols embodied in the Hollywood mystique. He examines Hollywood as
both a literary and a social symbol, the total meaning of which is a combination of its popular and intellectual images. Spatz contends that
the Hollywood film functions as an instrument of art, education, social
reform, and propaganda. Hollywood itself acts as both an active force
in American culture and a powerful and ambiguous symbol. Focusing on
such literary figures as W. D. Howells, F. Scott Fitzgerald, and Budd
Schulberg, the author identifies three themes that emerge in novels with
a Hollywood background: the myths of success, utopia, and democratic
art.

PC 614. **SPEARS, JACK.** The Civil War on the Screen and Other Essays.
New York: Barnes, 1977. 240 pp.
Spears discusses Hollywood's frequent use of the American Civil War as
a subject despite the Hollywood contention that such productions are doomed
to financial failure. He writes in depth about three specific films:
Birth of a Nation, Gone with the Wind, and The General. Spears also considers the popularity of the Civil War as a topic of early silent films,
the portrayal of Abraham Lincoln and other Civil War figures, and the
inaccurate portrayals of blacks and Southern society. Also included in
the book are essays on character actor Louis Wolheim, director Edwin S.
Porter, and actress Nazimova.

PC 615. **SPOTO, DONALD.** Camerado: Hollywood and the American Man. New
York: New American Library, 1978. 238 pp.
This study focuses on the cinema's reflection of changing images of the
American man. Spoto examines the film hero in comedy, Western, romance,
adventure, and crime films, and the hero's relation to images of masculinity held by film audiences. The author surveys the screen hero over
the past fifty years, discussing characters, stars, films, and directors.
He divides the heroes into types ("regular guy," comic, "romantic suf-
ferer," outlaw, and strong man), and for each type discusses actors who
best represent it. Spoto analyzes specific films in detail to show these
types at work.

PC 616. **STODDARD, KAREN M.** Saints and Shrews: Women and Aging in American
Popular Film. Westport, Conn.: Greenwood Press, 1978. 174 pp.
Stoddard investigates images of aging women in American sound motion pictures in an attempt to identify the cultural myths these images reinforce.
She looks at incidental roles, characters with limited time on-screen,
claiming that the visual shorthand needed to give the audience an instant
sense of a character can be highly indicative of what a culture believes
and wishes to legitimize. Between 1930-45 the dominant Hollywood image
of the aging woman was that of a source of love and nurture. Film images
of older women from the late 1940s to the 1960s reflected a growing popular
awareness of psychology (especially mother/child relationships). The
films Stoddard discusses from the late 1960s primarily employed major
stars and had aging as an important theme. She also considers negative
stereotypes of aging women and how they reinforce negative connotations
associated with growing older in America.

PC 617. **SUID, LAWRENCE H.** Guts and Glory: Great American War Movies.
Reading, Mass.: Addison-Wesley, 1978. 357 pp.
Suid reveals audiences' changing attitudes toward war films by surveying
the portrayal of the American military in Hollywood feature films from
D. W. Griffith's Birth of a Nation (1915) to Ted Post's Go Tell the Spar-
tans (1978). Specific films are described in detail and are grouped according to common themes and concerns. Chapters address early films, the
portrayal of W.W. II, the revised image of war during the Korean conflict,
and Hollywood and Vietnam. Movies which portray the military in an unfavorable light such as Seven Days in May and The Bedford Incident are also
discussed, as are John Wayne and Hollywood's portrayal of Marines. Film
productions which received military assistance are compared with those
which receive no such assistance to reveal the complex relationship between
Hollywood and the Pentagon.

PC 618. **TALBOT, DANIEL,** ed. Film: An Anthology. 1959; Rev. ed. Berkeley:
University of California Press, 1966. 404 pp.
Talbot's anthology demonstrates the wide-ranging impact of the motion
picture industry on "ethics, public behavior, clothes, and even our food."
The volume begins with a section devoted to the motion picture as a "social
instrument." In this context, Pauline Kael describes the current plight

of the industry, Parker Tyler discusses Hollywood's "surrealist eye,"
James Agee treats the silent comedies, and Gilbert Seldes diagnoses Hollywood's timid portrayal of human sexuality. For the second section, Talbot
has reprinted classic definitions of the medium by well-known European
filmmakers and aestheticians. The volume concludes with a focus on prominent personalities and events of film history. This section includes
anecdotal essays by Terry Ramsaye, Ben Hecht, and Henry Miller, a socio-
historical analysis (Lewis Jacobs on D. W. Griffith), and a psychoanalytic
interpretation of The Cabinet of Dr. Caligari by Siegfried Kracauer.

PC 619. THOMAS, SARI, ed. Film/Culture: Explorations of Cinema in Its
         Social Context. Metuchen, N.J.: Scarecrow Press, 1982.
         275 pp.
Thomas is skeptical of the scholarly preoccupation with aesthetics and
stresses the motion picture's role as "social interaction" by dividing
her anthology into the classic communication model of Sender-Message-
Receiver. The first section, "The Industry," includes discussions of Hollywood as a business susceptible to economic and institutional analysis.
"Form and Content," the second section, offers analyses of how a film
works or "means" as a language, as a document of everyday life (home
movies), and as a ritual and "sociodrama." The concluding section, "The
Audience," offers an account of the medium's psychological and behavioral
effects as manifested in the spectator's identification with movie stars
and in formulaic plots, the influence on sexual attitudes, and the dynamics
of conversing about the merits of individual films.

PC 620. THOMSON, DAVID. America in the Dark: Hollywood and the Gift
         of Unreality. New York: Morrow, 1977. 288 pp.
Thomson describes the relationship between Hollywood films and their American audiences and discusses what the relationship has meant to American
culture. He identifies as a major force in American society, and in American films, the simultaneous craving for both the real and the imaginary.
Thomson discusses how Hollywood as an American institution addresses this
craving. Chapter-long discussions of Orson Welles and Citizen Kane, the
portrayal of women, and the depiction of the "common man" include examples
from individual American films.

PC 621. THORP, MARGARET FARRAND. America at the Movies. New Haven, Conn.:
         Yale University Press, 1939. 313 pp.
In this early attempt at describing the relationship between American
audiences and Hollywood films, Thorp discusses how Hollywood addressed
audience desires by offering subjects with universal appeal, such as
escapes through excitement or luxury. She analyzes the industrial nature
of American motion pictures, the distribution practices of block booking
and blind buying, as well as exhibitors' attempts to increase audiences
through give-aways, promotions in theaters, and double bills. Discussing
Better Film Councils, the National Board of Review and the Hays Office,
Thorp examines censorship and the attempts which have been made to reform
the cinema.

PC 622. TOEPLITZ, JERZY. Hollywood and After: The Changing Face of Ameri-
         can Cinema. Translated by Boleshaw Sulik. London: Allen &
         Unwin, 1974. 280 pp.
Toeplitz describes the state of the American motion picture industry in
the post-studio filmmaking era. He describes the changing nature of the
major studios: their absorption by major corporations, and their liqui-
dation of real estate, film libraries, and other assets. Through a discussion of the portrayal of Vietnam, blacks, and the ideal of freedom,
the author explores the political content of mid-1970s films. Toeplitz
also discusses the changing portrayal of violence and sex in American
films, as well as the rebirth in the 1960s and 1970s of an active under-

ground cinema. The relationship between television and filmmaking, and the early prospects for cable delivery systems and home video cassettes are also examined.

PC 623. TUDOR, ANDREW. Image and Influence: Studies in the Sociology of Film. New York: St. Martin's Press, 1974. 260 pp.
Tudor's sociological consideration of the movies examines the cinema's role as a common forum for a population's beliefs, goals and concerns. Noting that moviegoing once was the dominant leisure activity of Americans, Tudor develops a communications model for the cinema, commenting on existing research similar to his own and speculating on the directions future work should take. Growing out of this communications model are discussions of film language and of Hollywood's role in American culture. Tudor develops a theory of popular genres based on his observations regarding the Western, gangster, and horror film genres.

PC 624. TUSKA, JON. The Detective in Hollywood. Garden City, N.Y.: Doubleday, 1978. 436 pp.
This volume is a comprehensive introduction to the conventions and creators of detective films. Tuska follows the changes in depiction and perspective of the screen detective from 1900 (Sherlock Holmes in Baffled) to 1974 (Roman Polanski's Chinatown). General topics addressed include popular detectives, the authors who created them, changes in literary detectives as they were adapted to the screen, and the lives and personalities of actors, writers, and directors of detective films. Detective films are surveyed by theme in roughly chronological order. Themes include: the classic detective, detectives in fantasy worlds, secret societies, marriage and murder, detective series in the 1940s, the books and films of Raymond Chandler, the detective as victim of the corrupt social order, the film noir of the 1940s and 1950s, and contemporary detectives.

PC 625. TYLER, PARKER. The Hollywood Hallucination. New York: Creative Age Press, 1944. 246 pp.
Contending that Hollywood represents the "industrialization of the mechanical worker's daylight dream," Tyler finds the American movie to be "monstrous and pernicious," and yet one of the few remaining repositories of "classical-humanist" traditions--a contradiction which he admits may possess an "intrinsic social hope" for a Western culture at war with itself. However, he abandons literary criteria to engage in an appreciation of the medium's oblique, child-like, and narcissistic relationship to reality. In particular, Tyler stresses the "hopelessly compromised" concepts of good and evil in American films through an analysis of the plots of films such as Gone with the Wind and Meet John Doe, the ambiguous image of women conveyed by Greta Garbo and Mae West, and the phenomenon of the "good villain" from Sam Spade and Charles Foster Kane to Charlie Chaplin as Adolph Hitler.

PC 626. TYLER, PARKER. Magic and Myth of the Movies. New York: Holt, 1947. 283 pp.
In this sequel to The Hollywood Hallucination, Tyler finds that Hollywood's apparent focus—its "lust to display the obvious, and sure-fire, the sensational"--makes the American movie open to "psychoanalytic-mythological investigation." He explores the "latent presence of the most venerable stereotypes of emotions" through discussions of the clown (for instance, Charlie Chaplin and Danny Kaye), the Hollywood productions of James M. Cain's novels (Double Indemnity and Mildred Pierce), and the innuendos of contemporary screen comedy (as in Arsenic and Old Lace). Other topics include the trivialization of supernatural experience (in The Song of Bernadette), and the simplistic translation of both psychological awareness (Alfred Hitchcock's Spellbound) and social consciousness (John Ford's The Grapes of Wrath).

PC 627. VOGEL, AMOS. Film as a Subversive Art. New York: Random House, 1974. 336 pp.

Vogel emphasizes the power of the cinema to release humanity from artificially imposed cultural, psychological and moral constraints. Locating this power in the process of film viewing and the unlocking of the audience's unconscious, he finds the movies singularly suitable for such subversion. Vogel discusses early Soviet experiments with film as well as the impact of Expressionism, Surrealism, and Dadaism on the cinema. Films that destroy normal notions of time and space, or of plot and narrative, as well as those which eliminate realistic representation, the image, the camera, the artist, or the screen are all considered. Films that exploit taboos governing nudity, pornography, homosexuality, birth, death, and anticlericalism are discussed with numerous examples cited for each type of cinematic subversion.

PC 628. WAGENKNECHT, EDWARD. The Movies in the Age of Innocence. Norman: University of Oklahoma Press, 1962. 280 pp.

This book, written from the perspective of a movie fan, is a description of what early motion pictures looked like to their audiences, especially to the first generation of children to grow up with the movies and to make them a part of their lives. Wagenknecht's personal reminiscences, admittedly subjective in their selection of films, stars, and directors, involve silent movies both before and after the appearance of feature-length motion pictures. He provides a historical survey of the beginnings of the film industry and discusses the important contributions made by such individuals as Thomas Edison, George Melies, Edwin S. Porter, and Mack Sennett and such early movie studios as Biograph and Vitagraph. The book contains chapter-long discussions of actress Mary Pickford, director D. W. Griffith, and the careers of several lesser-known silent film actresses.

PC 629. WALKER, ALEXANDER. The Celluloid Sacrifice: Aspects of Sex in the Movies. New York: Hawthorn Books, 1966. 241 pp.

In this work, Walker concentrates on three issues of the portrayal of sex in American movies: the nature of female sexuality on the screen, how the portrayal of sex drives is controlled through censorship, and the depiction of male heroes as victims of female domination in Hollywood sex comedies. Walker discusses the careers and screen personae of Clara Bow, Theda Bara, Mary Pickford, Mae West, Greta Garbo, Marlene Dietrich, Jean Harlow, and Marilyn Monroe.

PC 630. WALKER, ALEXANDER. The Shattered Silents: How the Talkies Came to Stay. New York: Morrow, 1979. 218 pp.

Beginning with radio's contribution in paving the way for the new sound technology, Walker uses a chronological model to describe the events leading to the appearance of sound motion pictures. He discusses the collaboration among Bell Telephone Laboratories, Western Electric, and Warner Brothers (resulting in the development of the Vitaphone system) in relation to competitive systems like Fox's Movietone and RCA's sound film production unit (RKO). The chaotic nature of the early days of sound films initially led the other major producers and distributors to enter into an agreement delaying sound production until one standardized system became dominant. Walker examines the obstacles to developing that system and the ways in which the film industry accomplished the conversion of theaters, the transition from recording on wax discs to optical sound tracks, and the invention of the boom microphone which freed productions from being staged around a single, fixed micophone.

PC 631. **WALKER, ALEXANDER.** Stardom: The Hollywood Phenomenon. New York: Stein & Day, 1970. 392 pp.
This introduction to the Hollywood star system concludes that Hollywood films reflect general social and economic forces, and that stars are direct or indirect reflections of the needs, drives, and dreams of American society. The author relates stars to society in general and to the film industry in particular, and summarizes various films and performances. He discusses the star as an individual and as an image or icon, examining the interaction of individual and image off screen. Among the topics discussed are the creation of stars, stage stars in films, talking pictures, Hollywood scandals, television, and the decline of the star system. Walker reviews the careers and images of many stars, omitting those he feels are adequately surveyed in other books.

PC 632. **WARSHOW, ROBERT.** The Immediate Experience: Movies, Comics, Theatre and Other Aspects of Popular Culture. Edited by Sherry Abel. 1960; Rev. ed. Garden City, N.Y.: Doubleday, 1970. 282 pp.
Lionel Trilling's introduction and Part I of this posthumous collection provide a portrait of Robert Warshow as a New York Jewish intellectual and a Commentary editor who maintained diverse allegiances to Henry James and Humphrey Bogart, was troubled by both Joseph McCarthy and the Rosenbergs, and sought balanced critiques of comic books, the New Yorker, and the movies. Skeptical of traditional aesthetic and socio-psychological approaches to film, Warshow argues that the critic should communicate "the immediate experience of seeing and responding to the movies as most of us see and respond to them." This compilation includes his chagrin over compromises in The Best Years of Our Lives, his discomfort with heavy-handed reactionary (My Son John) and liberal (Arthur Miller) stances, his appreciation of an aging Chaplin, and his reviews of Italian neo-realism and 1920s Russian montage.

PC 633. **WASKO, JANET.** Movies and Money: Financing the American Film Industry. Norwood, N.J.: Ablex, 1982. 247 pp.
Wasko offers an examination of "the historical relationship between the American movie industry—the production, distribution, and exhibition of theatrical motion pictures—and banks." Discussing the chronological history of film financing from 1919 through the 1970s, she provides detailed case studies (D. W. Griffith, The Bank of America, Walt Disney Productions, Warner Communications, among others) to focus on the issue of control, namely the power that the financial institutions possess over the ultimate product. Because commercial banks, investment bankers, insurance companies, and venture capitalists have aligned themselves with the various sectors of the film industry, they have helped to influence the way the movie business conducts itself, what products are made, how they are made, and the messages conveyed to the American public.

PC 634. **WELSCH, JANICE R.** Film Archetypes: Sisters, Mistresses, Mothers and Daughters. New York: Arno Press, 1978. 373 pp.
Welsch draws on post-W.W. II Hollywood to clarify America's contradictory images of women. She discusses the careers and major roles of Elizabeth Taylor, Audrey Hepburn, Grace Kelly, Doris Day, Debbie Reynolds, Marilyn Monroe, and Kim Novak to illuminate the polarities of mother and whore, and to consider the cinematic treatment of archetypal daughters, sisters, and mistresses. Welsch justifies her focus on the 1950s on-screen image by noting the uniqueness of the era: while the monopolistic nature of the studio system began to deteriorate, the movie stars proved to be "an important part of the film industry as well as a significant factor in the fantasies of the people." The appendix not only identifies each actress's major films but also offers details concerning facets of the individual roles (that is, social and marital status) and the film's production (the studio, the director, and the male lead).

PC 635. WHITE, DAVID MANNING and RICHARD AVERSON. The Celluloid Weapon:
         Social Comment in the American Film. Boston: Beacon Press,
         1972. 271 pp.
White and Averson assert that Hollywood films do not simply provide escapist entertainment but that they also have the capacity to reveal the hopes
and problems of American society. This social vision is most prominent
in certain message films which go beyond mass entertainment to include
social commentary. In surveying the history of seventy years of message
films, this book focuses on certain specific filmmakers such as D. W.
Griffith and Frank Capra, as well as the social climate surrounding such
films as Birth of a Nation, All Quiet on the Western Front, The Grapes
of Wrath, On the Waterfront, and Cheyenne Autumn. The major themes
addressed by the Hollywood message film and discussed by White and Averson
are Prohibition and the gangster, Hollywood mobilization and post-war
adjustment, anti-Communism, the Civil Rights movement, and the drug culture.

PC 636. WILLIAMS, CAROL TRAYNOR. The Dream Beside Me: The Movies and
         the Children of the Forties. Rutherford, N.J.: Fairleigh Dickin-
         son University Press, 1980. 304 pp.
Williams examines the relationship between films and their audiences in
the 1940s, distinguishing between the nostalgic response of today's film
buffs and the reception of films at the time of their release. She
addresses the potential of American films to influence the values and attitudes of audiences, finding this influence at its strongest during the
war years when moviegoing became something of a communal rite. Williams
examines the roles of men and women in 1940s character types and Hollywood's influence on popular conceptions of glamour and beauty. Films
such as Gone with the Wind, Casablanca, The Best Years of Our Lives, Since
You Went Away, and Cover Girl, are discussed in light of their influence
on American behavior, manners, and taste. This work includes Williams's
own recollections of her relationship to 1940s movies and an admittedly
"subjective typology" of actors and actresses.

PC 637. WOLFENSTEIN, MARTHA and NATHAN LEITES. Movies: A Psychological
         Study. Glencoe, Ill.: Free Press, 1950. 316 pp.
This volume reflects the interest in national character studies (for example, Margaret Mead) and psychoanalytic approaches to film (Siegfried
Kracauer) favored by the wartime and early postwar generation of the 1940s.
Placing particular emphasis on the contemporary Hollywood melodrama--and
making frequent reference to recent British and French films for comparative purposes--Wolfenstein and Leites analyze numerous plots and themes
as symptomatic of the "recurrent day-dreams which enter into the consciousness of millions of movie-goers." Contending that popular movies do not
suggest escape but the "working-over of emotional problems," the authors
diagnose the "aspirations, fears and wishes" found in the American cinematic treatment of love, familial relations, violence, and voyeurism.
Summarizing "distinctive plot configurations," the authors conclude that
while the British often indulge in self-accusation, and the French reflect
on the inevitable restrictions inhibiting human desire, the American screen
suggests a people who place great priority on winning against tough, external odds.

PC 638. WOLL, ALLEN L. The Hollywood Musical Goes to War. Chicago:
         Nelson-Hall, 1983. 186 pp.
Woll discusses the status of the movie musical as the dominant film genre
of wartime Hollywood and develops the thesis that the American musical
thrives during the most critical periods of American history. He looks
beyond the escapism of musicals, attempting to link elements of the genre
to cultural attitudes prevalent at the time of production. The author
discusses the Latin American musical and its relationship to the "Good
Neighbor Policy," the portrayal of blacks in the musical in connection

with the notion of "separate but equal," Hollywood's interventionist stance as it appears in musicals with preparedness themes and the negative reaction of Congress to that stance.

PC 639. WOLL, ALLEN L. The Latin Image in American Film. 1977; Rev.
         ed. Los Angeles, Calif.: UCLA Latin American Center, 1980.
         128 pp.
Woll traces the changing depiction of Latins and Latin culture in American films and finds that, unlike the revision of negative portrayals of blacks, Orientals, and Native Americans, there has not been a significant attempt to counter Latin stereotypes. According to Woll, American films of the silent era depicted Central and South America as a uniform culture, largely populated by murderous bandits and submissive women. The war years of 1939-45 featured a softening of Latin stereotypes and an influx of Latin actors and themes into Hollywood. The more sympathetic portrayal of Latins and the acknowledgment of various Latin cultures continued during the 1945-60 period of post-war realism in Hollywood. The mid-1960s saw a return of the old abuses as Latins were depicted as excessively violent or as the targets for comedic scorn. Woll discusses individual films and performers such as Viva Villa, Viva Zapata, Salt of the Earth, Ramon Novarro, Carmen Miranda, Lupe Velez, Delores Del Rio and their relationship to the Latin image in American films.

PC 640. WOLLEN, PETER. Signs and Meaning in the Cinema. 1969; Rev.
         ed. Bloomington: Indiana University Press, 1972. 175 pp.
Wollen proposes to bring cinematic analysis into the larger realm of ideas "to sharpen perceptions of the American screen." The first section is devoted to the career and cross-cultural milieu of Sergei Eisenstein. Section II is concerned with a reassessment of the reputation of such Hollywood directors as Howard Hawks and John Ford. Wollen devotes his third section to a treatment of the general concept of film as language and discusses semiotics in relation to film criticism. His 1972 conclusions advocate the modernist interrogation of a medium's components and the adoption of a perceptive neutrality to enhance the critical understanding of Hollywood and foreign films.

PC 641. WOOD, MICHAEL. America in the Movies. New York: Basic Books,
         1975. 206 pp.
Wood discusses ways in which films reflect and visualize certain aspects of American society. He examines the capacity of movies to reveal tensions and fears that individuals would often rather ignore, and believes that films can enable audiences to confront their fears in entertaining and enlightening ways. Thus, for Wood, the movies can act as a gauge against which audiences judge their actions and confront their anxieties. This thesis is explored through discussion of films such as Touch of Evil, The Hustler, The Ox-Bow Incident, and The Wild One, of the genre that each film belongs to, and of the ways that film genres can reflect changing views of a culture.

PC 642. WRIGHT, WILL. Sixguns and Society: A Structural Study of the
         Western. Berkeley: University of California Press, 1975.
         217 pp.
In this survey of Western films, Wright tries to explain the popularity of the genre and to reveal what Westerns tell audiences about their society. He uses a structuralist method of criticism derived from Kenneth Burke's work on the social structure of literature, Claude Levi-Strauss on the conceptual structure of tribal myths, and Vladimir Propp on the narrative structure of Russian folktales. Discussing the mythic deep structures on which Westerns are based, and the Western as a particular variety of myth, the author relates film plots to American institutions, attitudes, and values and demonstrates how changes in the plot types reveal new con-

ceptions of society. The approach is used to analyze films in four subgroups: the classical Western, Westerns with themes of vengeance, transitional Westerns, and Westerns portraying professionalism. Films studied
include Shane, Duel in the Sun, Stagecoach, High Noon, Broken Arrow, Rio
Bravo, The Wild Bunch, and Butch Cassidy and the Sundance Kid. The plot
of each film is examined in some detail to identify the elements that
give it a unique meaning.

PC 643. YOUNGBLOOD, GENE. Expanded Cinema. New York: Dutton, 1970.
432 pp.
Youngblood's volume, based on articles originally contributed to the Los
Angeles Free Press, celebrates those experimental moviemakers who have
borne witness to the 20th century's transformation from the Industrial
to the Cybernetic Age. After applauding the mythopoeic vision of Stan
Brakhage and the Buddhist-inspired "cosmic consciousness" of Jordan Belson,
Youngblood posits how art may benefit from technology as demonstrated
in John Whitney's computer-made movies and in Nam June Paik's exploitation
of the television medium. The volume concludes with a discussion of the
holographic cinema, to Youngblood the most persuasive symbol of "man's
ongoing historical drive to manifest his consciousness outside of his
mind, in front of his eyes."

PC 644. ZHEUTLIN, BARBARA and DAVID TALBOT. Creative Differences: Profiles of Hollywood Dissidents. Boston: South End Press, 1978.
370 pp.
The authors discuss the careers of sixteen people from various levels
of the American film industry, all of whom are significant for their substantial creative differences with the film industry. Running from the
pre-blacklist era to the 1970s, these profiles portray the frustration
of attempting to merge oppositional political thought with mainstream
film practice. Zheutlin and Talbot examine some of Hollywood's occasional
successes at fulfilling cinema's potential by transcending stereotypes
and conservative modes of representation.

VI.   MEDIA

GENERAL

PC 645. ABEL, ELIE, ed. What's News: The Media in American Society.
San Francisco: Institute for Contemporary Studies, 1981.
296 pp.
The essays in this anthology examine the social and cultural impact of
mass media in America. Individual essays discuss economic factors that
shape the media, the monopolistic structure of publishing and broadcasting
industries, and the development of media "baronies." Abel includes four
content analyses that examine the news as entertainment, the reporting
of business news in America, the selection of "newsworthy" events, and
the images of political candidates of network news. Also included are
evaluations of new communications technologies and speculations on how
those technologies will change society. Essays consider the use of the
First Amendment by the press, and the potential violations of individual
rights posed by the current structure of mass media.

PC 646. BAGDIKIAN, BEN H. The Information Machines: Their Impact on
         Men and the Media. New York: Harper & Row, 1971. 359 pp.
Bagdikian speculates on the future structure of mass media and predicts
a more complex relationship between media and information systems. Identifying the technologies which are likely to be of greatest importance
in the late 1970s and beyond, he discusses the probable content of news,
its mode of distribution, and the effect reporting will have on news events
and the lives of consumers. Bagdikian's speculations are placed in the
context of the social, economic, and technological forces which were determining the form of the news at the time of his study.

PC 647. BARBER, JAMES D. The Pulse of Politics: Electing Presidents
         in the Media Age. New York: Norton, 1980. 342 pp.
Barber examines the current role played by the media in the presidential
campaign process. Examining specific presidential campaigns, he analyzes
the new power of the media. This analysis is presented within the framework of what Barber sees as a general historical pattern of presidential
campaigns, characterized by three themes which dominate campaign years:
politics as conflict, politics as conscience, and politics as conciliation.
For Barber, the media have emerged as a powerful political force controlling the process of elections and shaping the electorate's perception
of candidates and issues.

PC 648. BRAESTRUP, PETER. Big Story: How the American Press and Tele-
         vision Reported and Interpreted the Crisis of Tet 1968 in Vietnam
         and Washington. 1977; Rev. ed. New Haven, Conn.: Yale Univer-
         sity Press, 1983. 613 pp.
Braestrup evaluates the performance of major press and television news
organizations during the Tet Offensive, providing a description of the
economic, and organizational limitations of the news media. Judging media
coverage of the Tet offensive to be a distortion, Braestrup, the Washington
Post Saigon Bureau Chief at the time, seeks to illuminate the causes and
effects of that distortion. Discounting the ideology of reporters as
a factor, he faults the tendency of reporters to seek "themes" or "story-
lines" which offer drama at the expense of information, and further points
to President Johnson's failure to provide a frame of reference upon which
reporters could base their coverage. For Braestrup, a combination of
sins of commission and sins of omission resulted in the media's portrayal
of Tet as a defeat of American forces while historians agree that precisely
the opposite was true.

PC 649. CARPENTER, EDMUND and MARSHALL McLUHAN, eds. Explorations in
         Communication: An Anthology. Boston: Beacon Press, 1960.
         208 pp.
The essays in this anthology were collected from the journal Explorations,
published between 1953 and 1959, and address such broad concerns as the
role played by literacy in the development of Western culture and the
impact of electronic mass media on modern society. The editors seek to
prepare readers for the clash between new and old technologies and to
maximize the educational potentials of each. Individual essays examine
print media, television, and newspaper journalism, the "language" used
by each, and their ability to shape and distort ideas.

PC 650. COHEN, STANLEY and JOCK YOUNG, eds. The Manufacture of News:
         Social Problems, Deviance and the Mass Media. Beverly Hills,
         Calif.: Sage, 1973. 383 pp.
With this collection of twenty-six articles, the editors intend to direct
research away from the emphasis on the effect of mass media on values
and behavior, and toward the identification of the conceptions of deviance
and social problems (and the views of society implicit within those conceptions) that are revealed in the media. Several of the selections are

fiction excerpts; most are scholarly essays, some prepared especially
for this volume. In addition to a general introduction, the editors provide substantial introductory notes for each of the book's three sections:
"The Process of Selection"; "Modes and Models," the largest section, consisting of case studies of "modes of presentation and underlying models
of deviance and social problems" employed in the media; and "Effects and
Consequences." The volume is international in scope; half of the selections deal primarily with media in the United Kingdom. Those relevant
to the American scene include a reading of Mickey Spillane's fiction,
an analysis of the portrayal of minority Americans in magazine fiction,
and a survey of crime reporting in Colorado newspapers from 1948 to 1950.

PC 651. CZITROM, DANIEL J. Media and the American Mind: From Morse to
McLuhan. Chapel Hill: University of North Carolina Press, 1982.
254 pp.
Czitrom examines the cultural and historical significance of modern media
in American society, with a particular focus on the assimilation of the
telegraph, the motion picture, and the radio into everyday life. Exploring
the notion that American culture and communications have become virtually
synonymous in the 20th century, the author discusses the significance
of modern media from a variety of theoretical perspectives, including
those of progressive theorists concerned with mass media's power
to raise levels of social consciousness, those of empiricists interested
in scientific aspects of communications study, and those of formalists
who concentrate upon the changes in sensory awareness brought about by
the media.

PC 652. DALEY, CHARLES V., ed. The Media and the Cities. Chicago: University of Chicago, Center for Policy Study, 1968. 90 pp.
In the wake of race riots and the Kerner Commission's Report on Civil
Disorders, thirty-three observers--scholars, members of Congress, and
representatives of the media--assembled in Chicago to evaluate what responsibility the media bore. Working sessions produced these essays on the
white-controlled media, editorial responsibility, television coverage
of urban violence, and the role of public television. Though their views
are divided, the contributors recognize that the media are owned by and
shaped for whites, a factor which mars the objectivity of reporting on
the origins and consequences of civil disorders. Aware of these failures,
participants consider issues like the "credibility gap" between media
and minority groups, the imposition of editorial guidelines, and the
media's responsibility in covering issues of poverty, urban decay, and
the polarization of the races.

PC 653. DAVIS, ROBERT E. Response to Innovation: A Study of Popular
Argument about Mass Media. New York: Arno Press, 1976.
725 pp.
Davis studies the rhetorical strategies employed by both advocates for
and opponents of new mass media from 1891 to 1955. Drawing almost exclusively on magazine articles, he reveals that the arguments of both factions
revolved around the same issues and proceed through the same persuasive
strategies. Advocates argued that the media reinforce the institutionalized conventions and values of education, religion, law, and entertainment,
while opponents argued that they undermine these conventions. Davis groups
the arguments according to various rhetorical strategies: cause (analyzing
the effects of the media), comparison (comparing the new media with older
media forms like theater or dime-novels), association (detailing the types
of people who operate and support the new media), and definition (emphasizing a particular capacity of the new media over others).

PC 654. DENNIS, EVERETTE E. The Media Society: Evidence About Mass Communication in America. Dubuque, Iowa: Brown, 1978. 166 pp.
Drawing on a substantial amount of media research, Dennis assesses both
the power of the media as a force in society and the internal organization
of media institutions. His review includes material on media's actual
ability to influence individual behavior and on various methodologies
of media research. In evaluating the means by which the media generate
the messages they produce, he analyzes the social structure of the press,
the social status of journalists, the content of the material produced,
and the role of the press as a social institution. Last, Dennis looks
at media criticism, focusing on the various means for criticizing the
press, the works of particular critics, and the question of how the media
can serve the public interest. He closes with an assessment of the value
of media research, favoring a healthy relationship between researchers
and media professionals.

PC 655. DENNIS, EVERETTE E. and JOHN C. MERRILL. Basic Issues in Mass
         Communication: A Debate. New York: Macmillan, 1984. 201 pp.
Dennis and Merrill present thirteen of the most controversial issues in
media studies in a pro-and-con format to generate further debate on these
subjects among students and media professionals. On each issue, one of
the authors assumes an extreme position and the other vehemently argues
the opposing side. The arguments serve to clarify the fundamental issues
of the controversies. Topics addressed include freedom of the press,
public access to media and to the news, the influence of media on society,
ethics in reporting, and U.S. journalistic imperialism.

PC 656. DIAMOND, EDWIN. Good News, Bad News. Cambridge, Mass.: MIT
         Press, 1978. 263 pp.
Diamond draws on the results of a "press watch" conducted by the News
Study Group at the Massachusetts Institute of Technology between 1975
and 1977. From M.I.T.'s analysis of newspapers, magazines, and television
news, he examines the relationship between the press and politicians during
the 1976 campaign. Diamond focuses on media images of the primaries,
the ways candidates used the media, the presidential debates, and the
television advertising strategies of Presidents Ford and Carter. The
second section of this book uses audience popularity surveys and the M.I.T.
study to analyze the sensationalism of television news as a result of
new technologies and perceived changes in audience demographics. In the
final section, Diamond looks at national magazines and metropolitan newspapers to examine the effects of Watergate on print journalism, the
"celebrification of the news," and the coverage of the Boston busing story.

PC 657. FARRAR, RONALD T. and JOHN D. STEVENS, eds. Mass Media and the
         National Experience: Essays in Communications History. New
         York: Harper & Row, 1971. 196 pp.
Farrar and Stevens have assembled eleven diverse articles on various themes
and historical topics in the field of mass media studies. Subjects
addressed include new issues surrounding freedom of expression, the benefits
and costs of technological advance, regional studies, the growing academic
interest in black journalism, photojournalism and the importance of visual
communication, and tools for media research. All of the essays are general,
emphasizing need for further study in the areas addressed and evaluating
different theoretical and methodological approaches to their subjects.

PC 658. GANS, HERBERT J. Deciding What's News: A Study of CBS Evening
         News, NBC Nightly News, Newsweek and Time. New York: Pantheon
         Books, 1979. 393 pp.
Gans studied various journalists in these four news organizations to determine how and why news stories are selected and reported. He seeks to
identify similarities in news coverage rather than differences in the

two media forms and to illuminate the values and ideology of journalism professionals. The first section of this book employs content analyses to reveal the structure and content of news reporting. The second section reports Gans's observations on the operation of news-gathering agencies, their methods of news selection, and their responses to economic, editorial, and censorship pressures. The final section includes Gans's critique of news reporting and his suggestions for and speculations on its future.

PC 659.   GITLIN, TODD. The Whole World Is Watching: Mass Media in the Making & Unmaking of the New Left. Berkeley: University of California Press, 1980. 327 pp.
Gitlin examines mass media coverage of the New Left from 1965 to 1971, charting the various perspectives from which the media viewed the movement as well as the subsequent strategies employed by the New Left (primarily the SDS) to combat media distortion. His dual purpose is to prove his theory that the governing political elite effects ideological control through the media, and to provide an accurate history of a certain segment of the New Left. He concludes by exploring the implications of his theory for countercultural movements in the 1980s.

PC 660.   GRABER, DORIS A. Mass Media and American Politics. Washington, D.C.: Congressional Quarterly Press, 1980. 304 pp.
Graber analyzes the political power of the media--primarily print and video--and seeks to go beyond election coverage to determine what role the media play in a wide range of political situations. She explores the mutually productive relationships between the media and public institutions, and the ways in which organizations try to control the news, arguing that relatively few people, most of whom have a big-business orientation, control the means by which public political perceptions are shaped. She also discusses how political socialization by the media operates differently for different sectors of the populace, and evaluates the impact of media coverage on public understanding of elections, political operations, natural and man-made disasters, and foreign affairs. Graber concludes with a look at alternatives to the mass media, recent technological developments, and possible future regulatory policies to deal with these technological advances.

PC 661.   GREENBERG, BRADLEY S. and BRENDA DERVIN. Use of the Mass Media by the Urban Poor: Findings of Three Research Projects with an Annotated Bibliography. New York: Praeger, 1970. 251 pp.
Greenberg and Dervin respond to the absence of information available on poverty and mass communications systems by describing three research projects which focus on a wide range of media-related behavior (including media use and availability, and audience preferences and attitudes), a number of media forms (radio, TV, films, and print), and various demographic groups. They also attempt to develop a comprehensive analysis of the communications behavior of the poor. Among the topics discussed are: content preferences and TV and newspaper use in adults, the uses of leisure time and media by adolescents, and the functions performed by TV for poor children.

PC 662.   GROSSMAN, MICHAEL B. and MARTHA J. KUMAR. Portraying the Media: The White House and the News Media. Baltimore, Md.: Johns Hopkins University Press, 1981. 358 pp.
This is a sourcebook of commentary and analysis on contemporary interactions between the President and the media. The information is gathered from Washington journalists and Presidential staff members, as well as analyses of the print and TV media. The authors argue that the prestigious news organizations persistently put out favorable stories about the Presidency, that there are recurring patterns of coverage from administration to administration, and that there are similarities in the kinds of stories

that appear about the Presidency. The authors also provide case studies
which illustrate these arguments, and describe how the White House tries
to manipulate the press and how it processes publicity operations.

PC 663. HADDEN, JEFFREY K. and CHARLES E. SWANN. Prime Time Preachers:
The Rising Power of Televangelism. Reading, Mass.: Addison-
Wesley, 1981. 217 pp.
This examination of the "electronic church" not only discusses syndicated
religious television programs in the context of the history of religious
radio and TV broadcasts, but also discusses the use of direct mailings,
recordings, publications, and telephone banks by large religious organizations. Hadden and Swann identify the major television evangelists, discuss
how they came to power, and speculate on the scope and implications of
their impact in the U.S. Their study is based upon the authors' observation of the production, administration, and content of religious programming. Audience data from Arbitron are used in an attempt to identify
the size and nature of audiences of syndicated religious programs.

PC 664. HALBERSTAM, DAVID. The Powers That Be. New York: Knopf, 1979.
771 pp.
Halberstam traces the growth of the national press and its influence on
Americans' perceptions of national events beginning with the Roosevelt
administration and concluding with Watergate. Four media institutions--
CBS, Time, The Washington Post, and the Los Angeles Times--are examined
in detail, and their ability to mold public thought concerning such subjects as Presidential elections, the McCarthy hearings, Vietnam, the Civil
Rights Movement, and, especially, Watergate is traced. Biographical
sketches of prominent media figures provide the background for the analysis
of these four media powers.

PC 665. INNIS, HAROLD A. The Bias of Communication. Toronto: University
of Toronto Press, 1951. 226 pp.
Innis here surveys the historical "interface" of communications and society
as technology has shaped cultures and political power has become more
organized. He begins by examining the early oral traditions that were
superseded by writing in Egypt and Greece, a technological shift which
he traces in Roman Law, the Byzantine Empire, the Renaissance and Reformation, the American colonies, and the contemporary U.S. Innis discovers
that the psychic and social structure of a culture derives from the dis-
torting power of its dominant technology. He argues that freedom of
thought is threatened by the "mechanization of knowledge," even as Western
culture returns to an aural tradition through electronic technology.

PC 666. JACOBS, NORMAN, ed. Culture for the Millions: Mass Media in
Modern Society. Princeton, N.J.: Van Nostrand, 1961. 200 pp.
This is a collection of papers by communications scholars, journalists,
social scientists, historians, philosophers, and artists presented at
a national seminar sponsored jointly by the Tamiment Institute and
Daedalus--The Journal of the American Academy of Arts and Sciences at
Tamiment-in-the-Poconos in June 1959. In addition to formal essays, the
volume includes panel discussions on a general theory of mass culture,
the mass media, mass culture and the creative artist, and the ideals and
dangers of mass culture. In the keynote address, Edward Shils focuses
on the fate of high-brow culture in a mass society, especially when
increased leisure time encourages the growth of a middle-brow culture and
a "mediocre intelligentsia." Other self-styled "cultural crusaders" emphasize the reception of mass media, some lamenting the deterioration of
elite standards, others applauding the democratization of culture by the
mass media.

PC 667. KEY, WILSON BRYAN. _Media Sexploitation_. Englewood Cliffs, N.J.:
Prentice-Hall, 1976. 234 pp.
Key investigates the techniques used in advertising and film to deceive
the eyes, ears, and nose. Concentrating upon particular products like
cigarettes, and films like _The Exorcist_, his study includes examination
of the commercial appropriation of the unconscious, subliminal rock, and
cultural conditioning for addiction. With demographic and psychological
studies in hand, advertisers most perniciously direct buying behavior,
Key argues, by employing subliminal stimuli. These "sexploitation" techniques, he insists, have been cleverly and extensively adapted for mass
merchandising, which relies upon the media's overwhelming ability to manipulate the public.

PC 668. KIRBY, JACK TEMPLE. _Media-Made Dixie: The South in the American
Imagination_. Baton Rouge: Louisiana State University Press,
1978. 203 pp.
Writing within the context of the historiographical theories developed
since 1900, Kirby investigates popular historical images of the South
in "non-historical" sources. Using marketplace success as his standard
in this basically chronological study, he discovers various "generic"
styles in these images, such as Neo-Confederate, Gothic, and Neo-Abolition-
ist. Kirby sees academic historians as part of a "circle" of influence,
defining the course of history for the "masses." He claims that the changing social environment, new empirical evidence, and Hollywood's recurring
demand for entertainment have all contributed to shifts in Southern stereotypes.

PC 669. KUHNS, WILLIAM. _The Electronic Gospel: Religion and Media_.
New York: Herder & Herder, 1969. 173 pp.
Kuhns explores the parallels between the functions of religion and entertainment media and focuses on our desire to understand the nature and
ploys of fantasy. Postulating that the entertainment media may be usurping
the functions once performed exclusively by religion, he discusses the
church's use of the media as pulpit, and the importance of fantasy in
media and religion. He also notes the church's moralizing criticism of
film, radio, and television.

PC 670. LEWELS, FRANCISCO J., Jr. _The Uses of the Media by the Chicano
Movement: A Study in Minority Access_. New York: Praeger, 1974.
185 pp.
Lewels focuses on the problems of stereotyping Mexican-Americans in the
mass media. After assessing the demographics of the Mexican-American
community, he examines the relationship between Mexican-Americans, the
media, the Chicano Media Movement, its challenges to the broadcasting
industry on the coverage of minority issues, agreements implemented, CATV,
and the future of the Movement. Recognizing that the white majority owns
and operates the communications network in America, Lewels points to the
"systematic discrimination" in the ways in which Mexican-Americans--like
blacks before them--have been portrayed or ignored. Intent on debunking
the melting-pot myth, he approves the accomplishments of public interest
group activity, dialogue at the local level, and cable TV. He notes that
there have been significant gains in programming, coverage, and foundation
grants, though dissatisfaction within the Chicano community is still
present.

PC 671. MacKUEN, MICHAEL BRUCE and STEVEN LANE COOMBS. More Than News:
         Media Power in Public Affairs. Beverly Hills, Calif.: Sage,
         1981. 231 pp.
Applying sophisticated communications research to social science issues,
MacKuen and Coombs appraise mass media's impact on American voting behavior.
In separate studies, MacKuen surveys social communication and the mass
policy agenda, and Coombs evaluates editorial endorsements and electoral
outcomes. Both find that the media influence the electoral process in
analytically discernible and politically significant ways. With the help
of survey data, elaborate codification, and multivariate analysis, MacKuen
distinguishes between "real" and "media" events, while Coombs encourages
diversity in the editorial opinions the media offer.

PC 672. MADDOX, BRENDA. Beyond Rebel: New Directions in Communications.
         New York: Simon & Schuster, 1972. 288 pp.
Maddox looks toward the "revolution" that two-way communications will
soon bring about, a "liberating technology" that will extend communications
control. Setting video cassettes and electronic video recording aside,
she concentrates instead on satellites, cable television, and telephones,
each of which she assesses after a historical introduction. Maddox argues
that two-way communications--cheap, portable, and instantaneous--will
transcend national boundaries, undermine centralized control, and promote
a wider sense of community and greater exchange. To counter resistance,
she calls upon consumers and civil libertarians to demand revised rate
schedules and a coherent international policy.

PC 673. McLUHAN, HERBERT MARSHALL. The Mechanical Bride: Folklore of
         Industrial Man. New York: Vanguard Press, 1951. 157 pp.
This work analyzes the manipulation and control exercised by the press,
radio, movies, and advertising. It is these media, McLuhan asserts, and
not the people themselves, who have created the "folklore of industrial
man." Full-page reproductions of ads and copy are followed by questions
and commentary which challenge the reader to reflect on familiar images
in American life. Subjects include: comic book characters (Blondie,
Tarzan, Superman, L'il Abner), the front page of the New York Times, self-
improvement texts, hosiery ads, Emily Post, Nielsen ratings, deodorant
ads, seductively designed book jackets, and "the Mechanical Bride."

PC 674. MENDELSOHN, HAROLD. Mass Entertainment. New Haven, Conn.: Col-
         lege & University Press, 1966. 203 pp.
Mendelsohn examines the sociological effects of mass entertainment in
America and, in so doing, discusses the historical impact of the devalua-
tion of entertainment in Western culture, the role of entertainment in
various social classes, the impact of the theoretical works of Skinner,
Hebb-Olds, Freud, and Lessing in the realm of mass entertainment psychology,
and the sociological functions of the media. He discusses the interrelationships between aesthetics, culture, and entertainment in light of communications saturation in the 20th century.

PC 675. PATTERSON, THOMAS. The Mass Media Elections: How Americans Choose
         Their President. New York: Praeger, 1980. 203 pp.
Patterson studies the ways in which voters respond to media presentations
of campaigns. He examines election coverage by the press, focusing on
the ability of mass media to attract, educate, and influence the audience.
Patterson uses empirical evidence to identify a parallel between the
response of voters to a campaign and the coverage of that campaign in the
media. He also describes the shape of campaign coverage and documents
the differences between print and broadcast coverage.

PC 676. PALETZ, DAVID L. and ROBERT M. ENTMAN. Media, Power, Politics.
New York: Free Press, 1981. 308 pp.
The authors provide a journalistic account of how the structure of the
media influences the political thinking and behavior of Americans who
possess power. They explore the media-manipulating activities of politicians, judges, interest groups, and other elites. They also look at
how media content--news and entertainment alike--socializes the majority
of Americans into accepting the legitimacy of the social system. Finally,
Paletz and Entman consider how public opinion on both domestic and foreign
issues is strongly affected by the media and their powerful manipulators,
and how the media often undermine the attempts of ordinary citizens to
participate in politics.

PC 677. PEI, MARIO. Weasel Words: The Art of Saying What You Don't Mean.
New York: Harper & Row, 1978. 208 pp.
Using a term popularized by Theodore Roosevelt, Pei explores the tendency
to use words of convenient ambiguity or depleted meaning, principally
in commercial advertising and politics. He examines the customary channels
of transmission--radio and television, Hollywood, the press, books--and
then considers the use of language in pornography, the women's liberation
movement, science, and education. Pei intends first to inform and educate
readers and to recognize "weasels" when they appear, especially in media
that exploit sensationalism and are driven by the profit motive. He then
argues for improvement in the use of language, recommending a middle course
between restricting sex and violence through Federal legislation and relying on the industry to govern itself responsibly.

PC 678. PHELAN, JOHN M. Mediaworld: Programming the Public. New York:
Seabury Press, 1977. 169 pp.
Phelan offers a strongly stated critique of "the marriage of bureaucracy
and entertainment," which has produced a manufactured culture that erodes
traditional standards and local heritage. He dissects the conditioned
assumptions that mass communications enforce, the predictable formulas
that the entertainment bureaucracy perpetuates, and the passive audience
reception that "mediaworld" encourages. Phelan argues that the media
have linked public issues and celebrities in a "star system," in which
both are packaged for a mass market. He claims that the new regionalism
and resurfacing ethnic concerns will counteract the media-induced spiritual
malaise, and predicts that media excess will plant the seeds of its own
destruction.

PC 679. POOL, ITHIEL DE SOLA, ed. The Social Impact of the Telephone.
Cambridge, Mass.: MIT Press, 1977. 502 pp.
Originally presented in a series of MIT seminars to celebrate the telephone's centennial, the papers in this collection investigate whether
the invention has had a social impact. Social scientists, historians,
economists, and Bell System engineers consider alternative paths of development in the telephone's early years, the changes in lifestyle it introduced,
its impact on the city, influence on human interaction, and social uses.
Uniformly concerned with the sociology of science, the contributors note
that the telephone has been a "facilitating" rather than an active device,
and that its immediate effects are hard to trace. Nevertheless, Pool
concludes, its social impact is profound and liberating if the technology
can be understood, especially now that telecommunications make national
isolation difficult and a global network more probable.

PC 680. POOL, ITHIEL DE SOLA, ed. Talking Back: Citizen Feedback and
Cable Technology. Cambridge, Mass.: MIT Press, 1973. 325 pp.
This collection of essays examines the nature and social effects of "interactive on-demand telecommunications." Aiming to understand the process
in process, various observers--political scientists, engineers, and com-

munications consultants among them—explore what cable can bring, what
options its technology can offer, and what possibilities two-way communications suggest. They suggest that broadband two-way communications will
restructure communities and community interaction, most significantly
among medium-sized groups of people, reversing the current trend toward
individual alienation; but, Pool remarks, it is uncertain whether homogeni-
zation or increasing diversity will result.

PC 681. READ, WILLIAM H. _America's_ _Mass_ _Media_ _Merchants_. Baltimore,
Md.: Johns Hopkins University Press, 1976. 209 pp.
In the wake of recent protest against transnational media monopolies,
Reed considers their effect on foreign political dynamics and cultural
identities. Beginning with an overview of America's transnational mass
media, he then considers visual media, print media, their influence, and
the foreign relations controversies they have generated. Read argues
that American mass media are ubiquitous but not totalitarian: they can
only contribute to decisions abroad since they engage foreign audiences
in an open marketplace. Separating the issues relating to national exports,
multinational operations, and foreign imitations, he cautions the buyer
to beware, but supports the free flow of information and posits that
national identity will be supplemented by rather than submerged in the
process.

PC 682. RIVERS, WILLIAM L., THEODORE PETERSON, and JAY W. JENSEN. _The_
Mass _Media_ _and_ _Modern_ _Society_. 1965; Rev. ed. San Francisco:
Rinehart Press, 1971. 342 pp.
This study provides a critical analysis of the media in their historical,
intellectual, economic, political, and social contexts. Focusing on newspapers, magazines, broadcasting, films, and books, the authors consider
a variety of subjects such as regulation, persuasion, entertainment, audiences, and the future. They see mass media as a social institution, one
in which rapid technological development has blurred the distinction
between personal and mass communication, has made the private public, and
has sharply limited analysis as information has burgeoned. Although the
media have not taken responsibility for these effects, the authors argue
that they must accept the crucial role of evaluating and interpreting
the news, particularly if information and its power are to be wielded
intelligently.

PC 683. RIVERS, WILLIAM L., WILBUR SCHRAMM, and CLIFFORD G. CHRISTIANS.
Responsibility _in_ _Mass_ _Communication_. 1957; Rev. ed. New York:
Harper & Row, 1980. 378 pp.
Weighing criticism of the media against human imperfectibility, Rivers,
Schramm, and Christians consider how a mass communications system with
vast potential can build an information base responsibly. After a brief
overview of the communication process, they evaluate three concepts of
responsibility, the effects of government and business pressures, the
depictions of minorities in the news, and media's function as popular
art. Emphasizing that standards should evolve from a series of local
decisions, the authors downplay the media's power to manipulate the public,
and call instead for a discriminating audience and for codes of media
conduct. Where these codes fail, they warn, government is likely to exercise a regulatory power that could only damage a free society.

PC 684. ROBINSON, GLEN O., ed. _Communications_ _for_ _Tomorrow:_ _Policy_ _Per-_
spectives _for_ _the_ 1980s. New York: Praeger, 1978. 526 pp.
This collection of essays explores major issues in communications policy
that are likely to emerge over the next two decades. Representatives
of the government, public interest groups, and the communications industry
examine general trends and facilities, the structure and regulatory boundaries of the industry, government roles and institutional capabilities,

and applications of the "new electronic media." Robinson observes that global well-being hangs on communications as never before, although the quality of their content lags behind their technological advances. The collection offers no single conclusion, but it focuses on creating just policies, based on the traditional American freedoms.

PC 685. ROBINSON, MICHAEL J. and MARGARET A. SHEEHAN. Over the Wire and on TV: CBS and UPI in Campaign '80. New York: Russell Sage, 1983. 332 pp.
The authors use journalism's own criteria of excellence to measure CBS and UPI for objectivity, seriousness, fairness, and comprehensiveness during their coverage of the 1980 campaign. They quantitatively and qualitatively compare the performances of print and network broadcast journalism when covering the same event. Using the results of that comparison, Robinson and Sheehan speculate on the potential consequences for citizens who have shifted from print to broadcast media as their primary source of campaign information. The authors also consider how the American political process has been changed by the new methods of reporting.

PC 686. RUBIN, RICHARD L. Press, Party, and Presidency. New York: Norton, 1981. 246 pp.
This book addresses the changing relationship between mass communication media, political parties, and the Presidency from the country's beginnings to the present. Rubin demonstrates how changes in mass communication have produced critical changes in key American political institutions. He begins with a look at the early relationship between newspapers and party leaders and the media's role in shaping American politics and public opinion; he also examines how the growing independence of the press in the 19th century led to political reform movements. According to Rubin, contemporary mass communication has allowed political journalism to penetrate the electoral system as a whole. This has brought about the decline of the political party and separated the President from his party organization.

PC 687. RUCKER, BRUCE W. The First Freedom. Carbondale: Southern Illinois University Press, 1968. 322 pp.
Rucker focuses on freedom of the press as "America's democratic keystone," initially ratified to combat 18th-century totalitarianism but since threatened by the contemporary focus on economic concerns. He examines today's newspapers, television, AM/FM radio, and magazines, and how these media have either become part of monopolistic chains or fostered alternatives to them. Rucker argues that free "competition of thought" is disappearing: as financial concerns intrude, mass media avoid scrutinizing the interests of their own owners and advertisers. The best alternatives for reclaiming a free press, he declares, are weekly newspapers and grass-roots operations.

PC 688. SCHILLER, HERBERT I. Mass Communications and American Empire. New York: Kelley, 1969. 170 pp.
Relying upon diverse governmental and industrial sources, Schiller outlines the structure and policy of mass communications in the U.S. and their economic and political functions. After charting the rise of commercial broadcasting, he analyzes the relationship between the domestic communications complex and the military, the application of electronics to counterrevolution, and Comsat and Intelsat, before concluding with suggestions for a democratic restructuring of mass communications. Schiller argues that mass media are dominated by national interests and commercial monopolies which reinforce the power of the ruling classes and suppress weak developing countries. He calls upon the American public sector, universities, and the black social movement to combat the status quo with aggressive popular pressure, before entrenched powers in space communications provoke international disruption.

PC 689. SCHRAMM, WILBUR, ed. Communications in Modern Society. Urbana:
         University of Illinois Press, 1948. 252 pp.
This collection offers fifteen early studies of the mass media, prepared
when television was emerging and communications research was a new discipline. Contributors survey contemporary communications and the problems
of control, extent and supply, process and channels, audiences, new media,
social effect, and responsibility. Acknowledging that typical American
communities are now heterogeneous, massive, and dependent on mass communications, Schramm recommends a better understanding of communications operations and their maximum use for the public good. To reach that understanding, this collection of essays asks basic questions about control, responsibility, and freedom in the media.

PC 690. SCHRAMM, WILBUR, ed. Mass Communications. 1949; Rev. ed. Urbana:
         University of Illinois Press, 1960. 695 pp.
In this collection of essays on mass communications, various authors from
the social sciences trace the development of mass communications, their
structure and function, their control and support, their content, audiences,
effects, and responsibility, as well as the communications process. Mass
communications are treated as an integral part of modern society, important
to those who study society or are interested in social change. Scholars
in anthropology, psychology, sociology, political science, and economics
evaluate mass media as organizations with a discernible effect on audiences,
an impact on the economy through advertising, and a public responsibility
to uphold.

PC 691. SCHRAMM, WILBUR and DONALD F. ROBERTS, eds. The Process and
         Effects of Mass Communication. 1954; Rev. ed. Urbana: University
         of Illinois Press, 1971. 997 pp.
This collection of essays replaces the "bullet theory" of direct impact
with more dynamic models of mass communication's effect. Various writers
examine the messages, audience, attitudes, social effects, public opinion,
innovations, and the technological future of the media, after introductory
essays review recent changes in each arena. Revising previously held
views of the relationship between mass and interpersonal communication,
this collection renders a more complex concept of mass audience, the result,
in part, of studies of political campaigns and TV's effect on children.
Schramm and Roberts conclude that the images projected by the media and
the behavior of the audiences are gradually becoming more homogeneous.

PC 692. SCHWARTZ, TONY. Media: The Second God. New York: Random House,
         1981. 206 pp.
Drawing upon a background in advertising and political communication,
Schwartz provides a personal insight into how media achieve impact on
audiences. His account includes strategy in commercials, social uses
of the media, political communication, and electronic technology in the
classroom. Schwartz presents the media as ubiquitous and omniscient,
capable of insuring a community of knowledge and of functioning as organized religion once did. People have more control over media operations
than they think, Schwartz maintains, but they have yet to exercise it
or to comprehend the promise of mass communications.

PC 693. SELDES, GILBERT. The Great Audience. New York: Viking Press,
         1951. 299 pp.
Seldes explores three popular arts--movies, radio, and television. These
giant entertainment industries are analyzed and assessed in terms of their
products, their enormous business organizations, and their pervasive influence on the standards and tastes of the mass audience. Seldes, the author
of The Seven Lively Arts (see PC 59) recants his earlier statement "that
popular entertainment could be accepted and criticized on the same basis
as the fine arts." He now argues that the popular arts are "machine-made"

products created by people who are "virtually forbidden to express their own profoundest feelings about the meaning of life." Admittedly prejudiced in favor of the democratic arts, he has put aside his aesthetic preoccupations to concentrate on the effects of the entertainment media on society at large. His ultimate purpose is "to make the popular arts serve free men trying to secure a free society."

PC 694. SERVAN-SCHREIBER, JEAN-LOUIS. The Power to Inform; Media: The Information Business. New York: McGraw-Hill, 1974. 297 pp. Servan-Schreiber assesses the present and anticipated problems of the information industry, technological progress, and the effect of the industry on its practitioners as well as on readers, observers, and citizens. Concentrating on the American press and television, he considers money-making in the press empire, the power of the pen, electronic overinformation, and what he calls "freedom reinvented." Observing that the power of such agencies as government and political parties is inevitably curbed by public resistance, Servan-Schreiber argues that only the power to inform goes unchecked and fuels all other power blocs. Though the media should never be controlled in a free society, he nevertheless contends that ethical vigilance should be renewed, and public demands for access, equality in information, participation in media, and privacy should be honored.

PC 695. SMITH, ANTHONY. The Geopolitics of Information: How Western Culture Dominates the World. New York: Oxford University Press, 1980. 192 pp. Observing that the ideological Cold War between East and West has been replaced by an "information" struggle between nations of the prosperous North and developing South, Smith describes the controversy and suggests possible remedies. Guided by the MacBride Commission's report to UNESCO, he begins with a historical overview of reigning Western news agencies and examines how their dominance is giving way, as new technologies and Third World countries emerge. Charges of imperialism have tilted the "disposition of power" to the South, Smith argues, though Third World countries have been accused of disguising internal repression in the process. To reduce havoc and foster real interdependence, Smith calls for freedom from restraints everywhere, greater attention to press ethics, and the intervention of governments and of companies with long-range vision.

PC 696. SNOW, ROBERT P. Creating Media Culture. Beverly Hills, Calif.: Sage, 1983. 261 pp. Snow concentrates on the language of media and their strategies for selecting and interpreting contemporary events. After examining the media's perspectives and grammar, he looks closely at newspapers, novels and magazines, radio, television, and film, and then investigates the source of media power. Observing that the media channel more and more information, Snow analyzes the linguistic and interpretative strategies that continuously reshape culture. He argues that mass communication is a two-way process, one in which audiences are accountable for their own behavior and the media must encourage a broader socialization and sense of community.

PC 697. SOBEL, ROBERT. The Manipulators: America in the Media Age. Garden City, N.Y.: Anchor Press, 1976. 458 pp. Sobel evaluates the traditional American tension between mass and elite cultures, and between equality and liberty, in light of the emergence of the "mass intellectual" and decline of high culture in the 20th century. He traces the genesis of mass society from the American Revolution to the 1920s and radio, its development in the 1930s and 1940s through film and in the 1950s through TV, and its maturation as the media have consolidated power. Sobel describes a new urbanized, middle-class culture which turns information into entertainment--where Watergate is a drama of manners--which conforms to the formulas of show business. Catering to numbers rather than excellence, the media have created a mass society that "goes along," Sobel argues, and passively allows reality to be replaced by manipulated images.

PC 698. STANLEY, ROBERT H. and CHARLES S. STEINBERG. The Media Environment: Mass Communications in American Society. New York: Hastings House, 1976. 306 pp.
This study examines the content, structure, and control of America's mass media in an effort to assess their social impact. Emphasis falls on newspapers, motion pictures, radio, and television as they have developed over the years and led to new technologies. Reviewing recent communications theories, Stanley and Steinberg opt for an eclectic approach to the "mediacracy" of the 20th century, which has produced a move from insularity to mass culture and a gap between scientific achievements and sociology. They aim to reduce this "cultural lag" so that technological developments like television can foster international cooperation and rapprochement.

PC 699. STEIN, ROBERT. Media Power: Who Is Shaping Your Picture of the World? Boston: Houghton Mifflin, 1972. 265 pp.
Pointing to the extraordinary power that the media have acquired, Stein investigates how mass images are produced, by whom, under what conditions, and for what purpose. After assessing the recent increase in information and the impact of new media, he considers the effect of social change upon the corporate atmosphere, the transformation of traditional processes and forms, the New Journalism, the underground press, the newsroom revolt, future technology, and freedom of expression. While technological advances have reduced government control in Stein's view, they have also made the media more powerful than elected officials in shaping what ordinary people think. With power comes more responsibility than publishers and broadcasters yet admit, and Stein calls upon them to set aside packaging and encourage genuine human response.

PC 700. STEINBERG, CHARLES S., ed. Mass Media and Communication. 1966; Rev. ed. New York: Hastings House, 1972. 686 pp.
This collection, which emphasizes communications media as socio-cultural forces, connects the study of personal communication with the study of contemporary media systems. After reviewing the structure and development of mass communications, the essayists analyze public opinion, mass media (newspapers, magazines, motion pictures, broadcasting, books) and their effects, international communications, the motivation of assent, and media freedom and responsibility. Characterizing the 20th century as the age of mass communications, Steinberg looks beyond the technology and discovers a new social milieu created by mass media, whose symbols offer new ways for people to communicate. Steinberg's anthology identifies media collectively as a constructive force, the very power of which limits its irresponsible use.

PC 701. STROUSE, JAMES C. The Mass Media, Public Opinion, and Public Policy Analysis: Linkage Explorations. Columbus, Ohio: Merrill, 1975. 279 pp.
Enlisting communications theory as "the first testable paradigm" for political science, Strouse examines the role of mass media in bringing public opinion to bear on government policy making. After assessing the impact of policy, he considers political campaigning, the President and the press, blacks and the media, and cable television. Strouse argues that mass media galvanize latent opinion and therefore influence political behavior, but they do not control voting nor did they cause race riots. Instead, he claims, mass media have become potent weapons in political protest and may well reduce, through CATV, the expense of running a campaign.

PC 702. TEBBEL, JOHN. The Media in America. New York: Crowell, 1974.
422 pp.
In this work Tebbel surveys the history of books, newspapers, magazines, and broadcasting against a political and social backdrop. He moves chronologically from the beginnings of the press in the American Colonies and the First Amendment, to the flourishing of magazines and newspapers in the 19th century, the advent of the mass market, and the increasingly activist role of the press, radio, and TV, before concluding with a defense of their liberal bias. Fundamentally anti-authoritarian, Tebbel emphasizes the value of freedom and the extent to which the American press has traditionally been defined by its insistence upon its freedom of expression..

PC 703. THAYER, LEE, ed. Ethics, Morality and the Media: Reflections on American Culture. New York: Hastings House, 1980. 302 pp.
This collection of twenty-seven essays examines the major ethical and moral issues of today's mass media. After Thayer's introduction, journalists, academics, writers, advertising executives, and television professionals offer formal "points of view," as well as several "conversations." They address the moral dilemma of what should be done if free people choose "badly" how to spend their leisure time, particularly once local traditions have lost their hold. Thayer observes that it is difficult to accept science as the ultimate authority or to separate "media" from its "users," and he replaces a one-way model of "transmission" with a more dynamic paradigm for the interaction of producers and consumers.

PC 704. TUCHMAN, GAYE, ARLENE KAPLAN DANIELS, and JAMES BENET, eds. Hearth and Home: Images of Women in the Mass Media. New York: Oxford University Press, 1978. 333 pp.
This collection of contributions from media analysts and sociologists is an attempt to redress the failure of most media researchers to examine the images of women in American media and the impact of these images on American girls and women. Although there are sections on women's pages in newspapers and on women's magazines, the volume focuses in particular on television. Two related concepts are central to the discussion and lend the book thematic unity: the reflection hypothesis, which characterizes mass media as an undiscerning "mirror" of dominant cultural values, and the concept of symbolic annihilation, the systematic derogation and underrepresentation of women in the mass media. In general, the researchers find that women's magazines are less stereotyped and more receptive to change than television, and that newspapers still tend to marginalize women, presenting traditional roles and issues in their women's pages.

PC 705. TUCKER, FRANK H. The Frontier Spirit and Progress. Chicago: Nelson-Hall, 1980. 371 pp.
This study explores national life and culture in four countries to discover models of human accomplishment prevalent in each. Aided by economic and social data from U.N. publications, Tucker considers the U.S., the Soviet Union, Germany, and Japan, focusing on the media which reach young people: textbooks, magazines and comics, motion pictures, and television. He argues that in all four countries person freedom and individualism are valued. Noting that carelessness is also criticized and sacrifice approved for the collective good, Tucker maintains that flexibility, courage, and cautious progress are consistently affirmed.

PC 706. TUNSTALL, JEREMY. The Media Are American. New York: Columbia University Press, 1977. 352 pp.
Tunstall examines "media imperialism" historically, claiming that after 1945, the British Empire and other countries began emulating the forms and content of the American media. His study covers various media, a considerable stretch of time, and most larger countries in and out of the West. Tunstall argues that imported American media have fixed patterns

in consumption, format, and perceived political realities, many of which
are copied even when inappropriate to the political and social situations
in other countries. Lately, however, new technologies have permitted
challenges from the Middle East and Mexico, which encourage Tunstall to
predict that these countries will soon gain media self-sufficiency.

PC 707. **WHITE, DAVID MANNING** and **RICHARD AVERSON**, eds. Sight, Sound,
    and Society: Motion Pictures and Television in America. Boston:
    Beacon Press, 1968. 466 pp.
The editors have collected essays of nonevaluative criticism which emphasize the relationship between media and such American institutions as
government, business, education, and the arts. The contributors--film
and TV producers, educators, government officials, critics, and scholars--
explore the premise that mass communication forms offer insights into
how American society communicates with itself. One section of this work
consists of a discussion of the relationship between movies or TV and
American audiences. Other sections connect the content of mass communications messages with aesthetic concerns and include essays on the originators of these messages. Such media controversies as censorship, the
depiction of violence, the potential political impact of mass communication
systems, and government regulation are considered.

PC 708. **WINICK, CHARLES**, ed. Deviance and Mass Media. Beverly Hills,
    Calif.: Sage, 1978. 309 pp.
Winick has assembled fourteen studies concerning the relationship between
the portrayal of antisocial behavior in the mass media and subsequent
deviance in society. The essays discuss a variety of media representations
and a number of forms of deviance. The volume includes content-oriented
studies dealing with the representations of subjects such as drug abuse,
obesity, and mental and physical illness; comparative studies such as
the depiction of rape in British and American films; and examples of media
inventions of and contributions to deviance.

PC 709. **WOOD, JAMES PLAYSTED**. The Great Glut: Public Communication in
    the United States. Nashville, Tenn.: Nelson, 1973. 192 pp.
Wood provides a historical account of the contemporary media onslaught.
He focuses on the emergence of the American press, from Colonial newspapers
through 19th-century giants, to 20th-century mass media in various forms,
and the ways in which they barrage the public. Wood quarrels with the
one-way nature of mass communications, their inevitable distortion of
information, and the inability of mass audiences to respond to high culture.
Favoring competition over government control, however, he points out that
individuals may still choose to ignore the surfeit of communications or
to examine, at least, the sources of what they receive.

PC 710. **WRIGHT, CHARLES R.** Mass Communication: A Sociological Perspective.
    1959; Rev. ed. New York: Random House, 1975. 179 pp.
Wright examines the process by which mass communications affect social
structure and influence culture. His study identifies the characteristics
of mass communications, their role as social institutions, their impact
on work and the professions, the links between interpersonal and mass
communications, contributions to mass culture, and empirical research
on social effects. After surveying the theoretical field, Wright argues
that mass communications register a complex social effect, not a simple
impact. Employing functional analysis as the most useful sociological
orientation, he moves toward questions rather than answers about the process he considers and the implications of its effects.

PC 711. **ADAMS, WILLIAM C.**, ed. Television Coverage of the 1980 Presidential Campaign. Norwood, N.J.: Ablex, 1983. 197 pp.
In the first chapter of this collection, Adams reviews current issues
in academic research on campaign coverage. Various contributors then
discuss in detail numerous aspects of the coverage of the 1980 campaign.
For example, one essay contrasts the reporting by CBS and UPI of identical
campaign events. Individual chapters examine the use of opinion polls,
the reporting of energy issues throughout the campaign period, and television's coverage of the primaries, national conventions, candidates'
debates, and election night.

PC 712. **ADLER, RICHARD P.**, ed. "All in the Family": A Critical Appraisal.
New York: Praeger, 1979. 322 pp.
Adler has collected material from sources which considered "All in the
Family" from a number of perspectives. The scripts from three of the
show's episodes are included, as are samples of critical reviews which
reveal the controversy provoked by Archie Bunker's bigotry. Several
research studies chronicle the impact of the show on audiences, and longer
analytical essays place "All in the Family" in cultural and historical
contexts. Adler includes a "Symposium" in which TV critics, members of
the show's production team, and TV industry executives explore the significance of the series.

PC 713. **ADLER, RICHARD** and **DOUGLASS CATER**, eds. Television as a Cultural
Force. New York: Praeger, 1976. 198 pp.
This collection of essays, by attempting to apply serious criticism to
the television medium, explores television's ability to function as a
cultural document. Individual essays discuss such topics as the narrative
aspects of TV news, the relationship between prime time medical programs
and morality, and the status of television melodrama as our culture's
most characteristic aesthetic form. Also included are an evaluation of
television criticism, an essay declaring that television functions for
American society the way dreams function for an individual, and a selected
reading list on television as a cultural force.

PC 714. **ADLER, RICHARD P.**, **GERALD S. LESSER**, **LAURENE KRASNEY MERINGOFF**,
THOMAS S. ROBERTSON, **JOHN R. ROSSITER**, and **SCOTT WARD**. The Effects
of Television Advertising on Children. Lexington, Mass.: Lexington Books, 1980. 367 pp.
This book examines television's role in acculturation by summarizing available data on the amount and conditions of children's television viewing
habits. The authors present surveys on issues concerning TV advertising's
effect on children including: children's ability to distinguish commercials from entertainment programs, the influence of various commercial
techniques on children's perception of messages, the role played by advertising in shaping attitudes about food and nonprescription drugs, advertising's role in "consumer socialization," and the effect of TV advertising
on parent-child relationships. Available research evidence is reviewed
and evaluated, and recommendations for future research or reform efforts
are made. Appendices include the TV industry's self-regulatory codes
and guidelines governing advertisements during children's television programming.

PC 715.   ALLEY, ROBERT S.   Television: Ethics for Hire? Nashville, Tenn.:
          Abingdon, 1977. 192 pp.
Alley draws upon interviews with over forty television writers, directors,
producers, and actors in his discussion of the medium's ability to echo
the moral assumptions of society. His questions concern, among other
things, the extent of television's responsibility to its audience. Alley
examines the moral messages of television comedy, focusing on "M*A*S*H"
and programs produced by Norman Lear. The widely held belief that television has usurped parental roles and contributed to a loss of authority
in the home is critically examined. In his discussion of violence and
TV drama, Alley focuses on individual shows (such as "Police Story,"
"Kojak," and "The Streets of San Francisco") to explore television's images
of law and order, and its emphasis on aggression and retributive violence.
Also discussed are such nonviolent alternatives to these dramas as "The
Waltons" and "Little House on the Prairie."

PC 716.   ANDERSON, KENT.   Television Fraud: The History and Implications
          of the Quiz Show Scandals. Westport, Conn.: Greenwood Press,
          1978. 226 pp.
This discussion of the television quiz show scandals illuminates the corporate structure of television and the roles played by advertisers and
government regulatory agencies within that structure. Anderson places
the initial popularity of the TV quiz show within the historical context
of the television industry and American postwar society. The game show
form is linked to elements of the American self-image (the work ethic,
notions of upward mobility and self-help, and the value of knowledge).
Part business history, part social history, this work focuses on the public
reaction to the scandals and what that reaction reveals about Americans
at the time.

PC 717.   ARLEN, MICHAEL J.   Living-Room War. New York: Viking Press,
          1969. 242 pp.
This collection contains essays on television coverage of the Vietnam
War, the 1968 Republican and Democratic national conventions, athletes,
politicians, riots, and assassinations, as well as conventional programming.
Rather than criticize different programs Arlen looks at the phenomenon
of television-watching, treating it "as something we are doing to ourselves." He analyzes how it transforms events—how it reconstitutes the
way our perceptual apparatus receives the world. Articles span the years
1966 through 1969.

PC 718.   BARNOUW, ERIK.   The Golden Web: A History of Broadcasting in
          the United States, Volume II—1933 to 1953. New York: Oxford
          University Press, 1968. 391 pp.
Barnouw discusses radio programming and broadcasting from 1933 to the
beginnings of the McCarthy era. He traces the rise of American broadcasting networks, noting the increased importance of advertisers and the battles between newspapers and radio. Among the topics which Barnouw discusses are: the establishment of the Federal Communications Commission
and the implications of its licensing power, early "equal time" provisions,
the introduction of FM radio, wartime regulations, and the early struggles
for standardization of television technology. Barnouw also examines radio
broadcasting's relationship to politics, focusing on Huey Long, Father
Coughlin, and the medium's role in political campaigns.

PC 719.   BARNOUW, ERIK.   The Image Empire: A History of Broadcasting in
          the United States, Volume III—from 1953. New York: Oxford
          University Press, 1970. 396 pp.
This volume of Barnouw's history of broadcasting looks at U.S. broadcasting
as a world phenomenon and explores the implications of international distribution of American programming. Barnouw also focuses on themes and

events in domestic broadcasting history such as McCarthyism and the effects of the Blacklist, the involvement of film studios in the production of TV programming, the quiz show scandals, and the Kennedy-Nixon debates. Throughout this study, Barnouw looks at the relationship of broadcasting to politics, focusing on such areas of concern as the roles played by television in elections and the Civil Rights movement, and the coverage of Vietnam and the antiwar movement. He also traces trends in prime-time programming and places them in a social and historical contexts.

PC 720. **BARNOUW, ERIK.** The Sponsor: Notes on a Modern Potentate. New York: Oxford University Press, 1978. 220 pp.
Barnouw examines the roles played by programming sponsors in modern media systems. He traces the increasing importance of programming underwriters throughout the history of radio and television, and describes the shift in sponsorship from individual merchants to corporate entities. Barnouw also outlines the extent of sponsor impact on media industries, on media audiences, and on American society.

PC 721. **BARNOUW, ERIK.** A Tower in Babel: A History of Broadcasting in the United States, Volume I--to 1933. New York: Oxford University Press, 1966. 344 pp.
This narrative account of the early history of broadcasting describes the shift in power from print media to radio and the growth of radio as an industry and as a means of expression. Barnouw begins with an account of early broadcasting experiments and chronicles the roles played by telephone and telegraph companies, universities, the makers of electrical equipment, the military, and independent inventors in refining broadcasting applications. He reveals the mutual concerns that connected the marketing of receivers and the formation of broadcasting. The early history of broadcast regulation is described, including the Navy's demand for regulation during W.W. I, the Radio Acts of 1912 and 1927 (which appear in Barnouw's appendices), and the establishment of the Federal Radio Commission.

PC 722. **BARNOUW, ERIK.** Tube of Plenty: The Evolution of American Television. New York: Oxford University Press, 1975. 520 pp.
This volume presents condensed and revised material from Barnouw's historical trilogy, A History of Broadcasting in the United States (see PC 718, PC 719, and PC 721). Barnouw's historical account of TV's role in American life places the technological origins and economic evolution of the medium in the context of American social and cultural history. He surveys programming highlights, chronicles the medium's rise in popularity, and evaluates TV coverage of news events throughout the medium's development.

PC 723. **BERGER, ARTHUR ASA.** The TV-Guided American. New York: Walker, 1976. 194 pp.
Berger analyzes several American television programs to establish their cultural significance and to determine what they reveal about the American character. He describes television as a medium which reinforces American values, sex roles, and notions of heroism. Virtually all types of television programming are discussed as Berger examines such TV commercials as advertisements for Levi's and McDonalds, such situation comedies as "All in the Family," "Rhoda," and "Chico and the Man," such dramatic programs "Mission Impossible," "Kung Fu," "Ironside," and "Star Trek," such children's programs as "Batman," television news, and sports programs.

PC 724. BLUEM, A. WILLIAM. Documentary in American Television: Form,
     Function, Method. New York: Hastings House, 1965. 311 pp.
Bluem establishes a context for his historical and critical examinations
of television documentary by discussing still photography, radio and film
documentary, and naturalism and realism in the theater. Against this
background he describes trends in TV documentary, tracing the development
and proliferation of such "prestige documentary series" as "CBS Reports,"
"NBC White Papers," and their supposedly impartial examinations of social
issues; "theme documentaries" which function as a mode of expression rather
than as reporting; "compilation documentaries" such as "Victory at Sea"
and filmed biographies; and locally originated documentaries. Bluem
describes specific programs, places them in historical and social contexts,
and includes reflections by their creators. Throughout the volume, he
explores how the technology of television (especially editing) necessarily
transforms filmed events, often introducing unintended emotional effects.

PC 725. BOGART, LEO. The Age of Television: A Study of Viewing Habits
     and the Impact of Television in American Life. 1956; Rev. ed.
     New York: Ungar, 1972. 515 pp.
Bogart here assembles the results of research on television as of 1958,
in which television is presented as a neutral medium with both positive
and negative aspects. He portrays the psychological phenomenon of TV's
appeal to its audience, and describes the social aspects of viewing by
establishing the conditions under which audiences watch it. Information
on TV's relationship to other media and to advertising, and its impact
upon politics and children, are included. Bogart examines television's
sense of reality by exploring the content, the characters, and situations
of its images.

PC 726. BOWER, ROBERT T. Television and the Public. New York: Holt,
     Rinehart & Winston, 1973. 205 pp.
This book is a follow-up to the survey of 1960s television audiences
reported in Gary Steiner's The People Look at Television: A Study of Audience Attitudes (see PC 825). Bower seeks to identify how audience attitudes toward television have changed since Steiner's survey. Changes
in programming are connected with changing attitudes of audiences, and
Bower compares what was seen as positive or negative about television
in the early 1970s with the results of Steiner's survey. Bower's study
also describes the viewing practices of families, the discrepancy between
survey responses and actual viewing behavior, and includes data on how
the age, race, education, and social and economic conditions of viewers
shape their response to television. Bower concludes that from the 1960s
to the 1970s there was a declining enthusiasm about television, although
audiences were watching TV more than ever.

PC 727. BRAUER, RALPH. The Horse, the Gun, and the Piece of Property:
     Changing Images of the TV Western. Bowling Green, Ohio: Bowling
     Green University Popular Press, 1975. 246 pp.
Beginning with a definition of the Western genre and a discussion of critical literature on the Western, Brauer examines the transition from Western
movies to TV Westerns. He traces thematic trends within the genre, identifying three main phases: "the phase of the horse" featured loner heroes
defending what was morally right; "the phase of the gun" saw lawmen defending society; and in "the property Western" there was an increased emphasis
on land ownership. The identification of these phases facilitates Brauer's
description of the evolving iconography of the Western, wherein he assigns
cultural significance to various manifestations of the Western formula.
Included in this book are a lengthy discussion of "Gunsmoke" and a chapter
concerning the portrayal of minority groups in the Western. Brauer also
analyzes the rhetoric of Richard Nixon's Manson speech and the lyrics
of Bob Dylan's "John Wesley Harding" album to demonstrate the influence
of Western myths.

PC 728. BRINDZE, RUTH. Not To Be Broadcast: The Truth About the Radio.
         New York: Vanguard Press, 1937. 310 pp.
Brindze voices concern about several threats or potential threats to freedom of speech on the radio. She contends that advertisers and "bank-
dominated monopolies" control American radio, that station editorial views
are determined by class—not public—interest, and that the listening
public is either uninformed about or oblivious to who controls radio.
Citing the use of radio as an instrument of control by European fascists,
Brindze warns against both big business and government involvement in
American radio. She concludes with several reform proposals, including
the placing of limits on the number of affiliates a major broadcasting
corporation may have, full disclosure of corporate stockholders and their
holdings, and development of a government-supported station to air electoral debates and other public interest programs.

PC 729. BROWN, LES. Television: The Business Behind the Box. New York:
         Harcourt Brace Jovanovich, 1971. 374 pp.
In January 1970, Brown began a twelve-month detailed observation of how
American commercial television works. This book represents the results
of his exploration into the structure and philosophy of American broadcasting. He describes the dominance of the three major networks to demonstrate
how their competition shapes television's seasonal schedules, dictates
the relationship between networks and individual production companies,
and controls network-affiliate relations. The debut of the Public Broadcasting Service is chronicled, and Brown examines its status as a fourth
network, influenced by similar economic realities, despite its position
as the purveyor of alternative programming.

PC 730. BROWN, LES and SAVANNAH WARING WALKER. Fast Forward: The New
         Television and American Society. New York: Andrews McMeel Parker,
         1983. 264 pp.
The term "new television" refers to the proliferation of channels made
possible by such new communications systems as two-way cable, interactive
video discs, satellite-to-home broadcasting, electronic mail, and pay-
per-view TV. These essays were collected from the magazine, Channels
of Communication, and represent a critical approach which attempts to
interpret technological developments and their social implications rather
than make evaluative aesthetic judgments. Individual essays explore the
commercial and social potential of cable TV, and evaluate the status of
the three major networks, questioning their commercial viability in light
of the new technologies. Other issues discussed include political content
in network news, the impact of the Nielsen ratings, TV's impact on children,
the portrayal of blacks on TV, and the guilt audiences feel when viewing
television.

PC 731. BROWN, RAY. Children and Television. Beverly Hills, Calif.:
         Sage, 1976. 368 pp.
Brown breaks this study into three sections which focus on children as
an audience, factors which shape their viewing experience, and the effects
on children of exposure to TV. The first section examines the viewing
habits of children, identifies which TV characters they find memorable,
and compares producers' assumptions about programming with audiences'
reactions to it. The second section offers a general psychology and sociology of young people's viewing by exploring the social context of TV
use and the characteristics of audience members which influence their
experience of television. Brown examines the effects of TV viewing by
describing the relationship of social learning and imitation to TV, the
medium's impact on children's leisure activities, the effects of TV advertising on youths, and the results of studies of TV violence which contradict the findings of the Surgeon General's Report.

1365

PC 732. BRYSON, LYMAN. Time for Reason: About Radio. New York: Stewart,
1948. 127 pp.
This book contains transcripts of a series of informal radio talks sponsored by the Columbia Broadcasting System in 1946-47; the talks were
intended to respond to public confusion about radio and to inform public
criticism of the medium. Among the subjects covered are network and station organization, and radio's response to varying audience characteristics
such as age, tastes, and the size of the audience. Several guest commentators address the role of the Federal Communciations Commission, public
service broadcasting, and the respective responsibilities of broadcasters,
advertisers, and listeners. Bryson concludes by considering radio's potential as an "instrument of enlightenment." He argues that radio has interspersed such events as a program on juvenile delinquency among regular,
popular programs; and that the challenge is to persuade local stations
to carry special programs and to persuade the public to listen to them.

PC 733. BUNCE, RICHARD. Television in the Corporate Interest. New York:
Praeger, 1976. 150 pp.
Bunce examines the economic, legal, and administrative factors that maintain the hegemony of the current American broadcast structure and prevent
alternative broadcasting systems from developing. He describes the process
whereby the industrial and economic structures of the radio industry are
"superimposed" onto the new television technology, thus insuring the maintenance of a broadcast structure that maximizes the purchase of individual
receivers and insures that the medium remain a one-way information distribution system. The histories of local ownership and newspaper-
broadcasting cross-ownership are discussed in light of attempts to halt
monopolistic business practices. Bunce examines the willingness and ability of the corporations that control American broadcasting to represent
the diverse interests of American society. Also discussed are the corporate practices of media conglomerates and television's relationship to
American military and industrial interests.

PC 734. CANTOR, MURIEL G. Prime-Time Television: Content and Control.
Beverly Hills, Calif.: Sage, 1980. 141 pp.
This discussion of the various forces that combine to shape television
content focuses on the prime-time dramatic programming of the major networks. Cantor describes the structural, political, legal, and creative
conditions that provide the context within which television programs are
produced. A description of the relationship between the networks, their
affiliates, sponsors, and rating services reveals the economic and organizational structure of the medium. Legal and regulatory controls of broadcasting such as the First Amendment, the Fairness Doctrine, and the influence of various pressure groups are also described. Cantor also examines
less formal controls on television, such as the social and cultural norms
that shape TV drama. A chapter detailing the production process of a
television drama is included to reveal the power relationships among the
creative staff of a TV production.

PC 735. CANTRIL, HADLEY and GORDON W. ALLPORT. The Psychology of Radio.
New York: Harper, 1935. 276 pp.
Cantril and Allport assert that radio ushered in a "new mental world"
and that, while technical and managerial aspects of broadcasting have
been the subject of extensive comment, the "human factors" of radio have
been neglected. The first part of the book considers radio's influence
on listener habits and attitudes, the implications of private ownership
for programming, and issues of propaganda and censorship. The second
part discusses the findings of five experiments which studied the effect
of such different variables as sentence rhythm, speaking speed, and sex
of broadcaster upon listener response. The third part looks at educational

uses of radio and ways of expanding social participation in programming. While praising the general excellence of broadcasting, Cantril and Allport express concern for possible abuses of radio, particularly its exploitation for political ends. They warn that a "dictatorship of private profits" may be damaging to radio's goals for the social and intellectual growth of society.

PC 736. CARNEGIE COMMISSION ON THE FUTURE OF PUBLIC BROADCASTING. A Public Trust: The Report of the Carnegie Commission on the Future of Public Broadcasting. New York: Bantam Books, 1979. 401 pp.
This Carnegie Commission report on the future of public broadcasting establishes objectives for broadcasters in the 1980s, calling upon them to be more flexible in their service to the public and to expand programming options. Finding the financial, organizational, and creative structures of public broadcasting flawed, the Commission advocates a structural reorganization designed to free public broadcasting from its dependence upon the government and other institutions for funding. Detailed proposals outlined in the report include: the use of audience measurement data to determine programming needs, a renewed commitment to the educational possibilities of broadcasting, revisions of the structure and goals of public radio, and the establishment of alternative program funding methods.

PC 737. CASS, RONALD A. Revolution in the Wasteland: Value and Diversity in Television. Charlottesville: University of Virginia Press, 1981. 238 pp.
Cass examines the criticism that television lacks diversity and value and finds it to be a reasonable assessment of TV's shortcomings. He presents an overview of the television industry in the early 1980s, describing the motives and operation of regulatory principles, the status of public broadcasting, and the structural limitations of commercial television which prevent it from functioning in the public interest. Cass looks to several new technologies, and finds that videocassettes and discs, satellite and cable distribution systems, and subscription television offer the best alternatives to TV's lack of diversity and its inability to function in the public interest.

PC 738. CATER, DOUGLASS and RICHARD ADLER, eds. Television as a Social Force: New Approaches to TV Criticism. New York: Praeger, 1975. 171 pp.
Cater's introductory essay to this anthology speculates on why thinking people rarely apply their critical faculties to television, and establishes the need to increase viewer awareness of the medium through social and cultural analyses of TV. The essays that follow are examples of this kind of critical analysis. Essays by Michael Novack and David Littlejohn examine the qualities of the medium that determine its impact on viewers and their society. Paul H. Weaver compares the journalistic practices of newspapers with those of television, while Michael J. Robinson focuses on broadcast journalism, finding it responsible for the public's loss of confidence in government. Other essays include a speculation on the cultural impact of future communication technologies, and a survey of literature which has attempted to view TV as a social force.

PC 739. CATER, DOUGLASS and STEPHEN STRICKLAND. TV Violence and the Child: The Evolution and Fate of the Surgeon General's Report. New York: Russell Sage, 1975. 167 pp.
Cater and Strickland describe the process which led to the formation of the Committee on Television and Social Behavior and its report to the Surgeon General on the effects of television violence. Outlining the disagreement about the meaning of the Report, they chronicle the numerous misinterpretations of the Committee's findings. The responses of the public, press, TV industry, Federal Communications Commission, and scien-

tific community are described. The authors critically evaluate the Committee's research and results and find American institutions ill-equipped
to undertake such a study. They describe the time constraints placed
on the Committee and the difficulty of recruiting social scientists.
Included is a proposal for future studies which would facilitate cooperation between the government, TV industry, and scientists, thus allowing
for more concrete results.

PC 740. CHARREN, PEGGY and MARTIN W. SANDLER. Changing Channels: Living
         (Sensibly) with Television. Reading, Mass.: Addison-Wesley,
         1983. 272 pp.
This broad survey of television begins with a defense of the medium and
data that describe how pervasive a presence it is in American life.
Charren and Sandler discuss how the world is portrayed on television, looking at the depiction of women, the family, the elderly, minorities, crime,
and celebrities. The economic realities of the television industry are
described through analyses of the corporate structure of major broadcasters
and the relationships between networks and their affiliates. Charren
and Sandler look at new communication technologies, including cable, pay
TV, videocassettes, and interactive cable, and discuss their potential
impact on American broadcasting.

PC 741. CHESTER, EDWARD W. Radio, Television and American Politics.
         New York: Sheed & Ward, 1969. 342 pp.
Chester's historical overview of the relationship between broadcast media
and the American political process measures the extent to which broadcasting transformed American political campaigns, conventions, and the creation
of candidate images. Chester specifically discusses TV's role in Presidential campaigns from 1952-1968 and the methods used by state and local
candidates to manipulate broadcasting's capabilities. Attempts at broadcast regulation made by Congress and the FCC are examined, with particular
focus on the Fairness Doctrine, the concept of equal time, and their impact
on television's and radio's relationship to politics. In evaluating television's performance, Chester finds that the medium has not always furthered the democratic process as economic considerations often precluded
the presentation of minority points of view.

PC 742. COGLEY, JOHN. Report on Blacklisting Volume II Radio-Television.
         n.p.: The Fund for the Republic, 1956. 287 pp.
This portion of Cogley's two-volume study (see PC 440) focuses on the
institutionalization and expansion of the blacklist into the radio and
television industries. Cogley discusses the impact of the blacklist on
journalists and the process of "clearance" through which those who were
blacklisted could become employable by recanting their previous "subversive" ideological positions. He explores the complex relationship between
union activity and blacklisting, concentrating on Actors Equity Association
and the American Federation of Television and Radio Artists. Cogley
includes excerpts from interviews with network executives, producers, agents,
directors, advertising executives, and members of labor organizations
who describe their individual experiences with the blacklist.

PC 743. COLE, BARRY G., ed. Television: A Selection of Readings from
         TV Guide Magazine. New York: Free Press, 1970. 605 pp.
This collection of articles from TV Guide was designed to provide an overview of the content, regulation, audience, and significance of American
television. A section devoted to television news includes discussions
of the quality of TV journalism and the coverage of Vietnam, civil disorders, and political conventions. Insights into network programming
decisions and articles on TV content are contained in a section on television programming. Reflections on regulatory issues, the First Amendment,
and sex and violence on television make up a chapter on censorship. Also

included are articles concerning television's audience, its effects, and speculations on the future of the medium.

PC 744. COMSTOCK, GEORGE A. Television in America. Beverly Hills, Calif.: Sage, 1980. 155 pp.
From Comstock's perspective, television programming is simultaneously news and entertainment. When discussing television news, the author describes how the economic structure of the television industry and various technological considerations shape the coverage of news events and audience experience of that coverage. Comstock explores the overall impact of television on American society by looking at the medium's influence on children, its ability to affect how viewers spend their time, and the extent to which prime-time entertainment can function as informative programming by presenting unfamiliar experiences to viewers.

PC 745. COPPA, FRANK J., ed. Screen and Society: The Impact of Television upon Aspects of Contemporary Civilization. Chicago: Nelson-Hall, 1979. 217 pp.
This collection of essays attempts to measure and report the extent of television's effect on viewers and social institutions. Essays discuss the medium's impact on viewer interests, leisure activities (especially sports and movie attendance), family life, and social relationships. The manipulation of the medium by politicians is documented, as is the extent to which sports have been changed by television. The differences between public and commercial television are analyzed to reveal how the source of program funding (government or corporate) shapes television form and content.

PC 746. CROSS, DONNA WOOLFOLK. Media-Speak: How Television Makes Up Your Mind. New York: Putnam Publishing Group, 1983. 288 pp.
Cross coins the term "mediaspeak" to describe the language of television and its method of portraying reality. She reveals how the structure of the television broadcasting industry determines the form that "mediaspeak" takes, thereby reflecting the goals of major corporate advertisers and conditioning audiences to accept the social and political structure while dismissing criticisms of consumer society. For Cross, television serves a repressive function. In a broad discussion of television, she analyzes American advertising, describes how the language of TV news determines what is newsworthy, and explores the ways in which entertainment programs perpetuate American attitudes. Also examined are the importance of celebrities to American society and the political uses of television.

PC 747. CULBERT, DAVID H. News for Everyman: Radio and Foreign Affairs in Thirties America. Westport, Conn.: Greenwood Press, 1976. 238 pp.
Culbert details the radio broadcasting careers of six of the most prominent foreign affairs commentators during the years leading up to American involvement in W.W. II. For each commentator he provides biographical detail, an assessment of radio mannerisms, detail on notable broadcasts, attitudes toward the Roosevelt administration and foreign affairs, and suggestions about the commentator's impact on American foreign policy. The immediacy and drama of radio in covering distant events counteracted America's isolationism, as, for the first time, serious journalism captured a mass audience. Thus, Culbert argues, although the commentators may not have influenced policy decisions directly, they helped create a political climate favorable to an interventionist foreign policy. The commentators discussed are Boake Carter, H. V. Kaltenborn, Raymond Gram Swing, Elmer Davis, Fulton Lewis, and Edward R. Murrow.

PC 748. DeLUCA, STUART M. Television's Transformation: The Next 25 Years.
San Diego, Calif.: Barnes, 1980. 287 pp.
In spite of the book's title, DeLuca concentrates almost exclusively on
the history of television, reserving the final chapter for prognostication.
His major emphasis is on the technological, legal, and business developments that have brought the television industry to where it is now. He
shows how these three elements have always been intermingled in television
history, each technological development producing legal battles which,
when resolved, generate the business policies which have determined the
structure of the industry as we know it. The survival of public television
and the explosive growth of cable and home video equipment, he feels,
will ultimately lead toward greater diversification of programming than
the networks, reliant upon sponsors who want only mediocre, mass-market
fare, have been able to provide. He also predicts greater small-scale
use of television in education, medicine, industry, and the private sector.

PC 749. DIAMOND, EDWIN. Sign Off: The Last Days of Television. Cambridge,
Mass.: MIT Press, 1982. 273 pp.
Diamond analyzes TV as a "mature institution"--one that is in its prime--
as he discusses the status of the medium at the time when new technologies
are changing the shape of American commercial television. Writing with
the belief that media reflect ideology, he focuses on how TV presents
American institutions. In a discussion of TV news, Diamond examines the
"story-telling" model of news reporting, the practice of advertising the
news, the alternative offered by CNN, and the coverage of such events
as the radioactive leak at Three Mile Island, the conflicts in the Middle
East, and the seizure of American hostages in Iran and their return.
Other topics explored include: religious television, the depiction of
sexuality on TV, and the effects of audience research information.

PC 750. DIAMOND, EDWIN. The Tin Kazoo: Television, Politics, and the
News. Cambridge, Mass.: MIT Press, 1975. 269 pp.
Diamond contends that most journalism in America inadequately covers daily
news events. The first section of the book documents these inadequacies
and explores their implications for American society by describing the
pervasiveness of the medium and that audience for whom it is the primary
source of information. The second part of Diamond's book consists of
case studies of broadcast and print news coverage of important events
of the 1960s and 1970s, including Vietnam, Watergate and the Nixon presidency, political campaigns, and the Pentagon Papers story. From these
case studies, Diamond draws general conclusions about the status of the
media in America and formulates recommendations for changes in the functioning of broadcast journalism.

PC 751. EBERLY, PHILIP K. Music in the Air: America's Changing Tastes
in Popular Music, 1920-1980. New York: Hastings House, 1982.
406 pp.
This history of musical taste in America explores the relationship between
the notion of "popular music" and mass media forms, specifically radio.
Eberly traces fads in American music--including jazz, swing, rock and
roll, and disco--and makes note of the ways in which these popular music
trends helped define particular eras in American history. He examines
business and programming developments in music radio, outlines the technical evolution of the medium, and speculates on the future relationship
between American music and broadcasting industries.

PC 752. ELIOT, MARC. American Television: The Official Art of the Arti-
          ficial. Garden City, N.Y.: Anchor Press, 1981. 301 pp.
Eliot illuminates the various forces that combine to shape American network
television. He includes a television writer's description of the process
of producing a program to reveal the economic and creative restrictions
and the structural limitations of the television medium. Analyses of
the structures that shape American television make up the balance of this
book as Eliot discusses the implicit cooperation between networks on prime-
time scheduling; the structuring quality of daily, weekly, and seasonal
network schedules; and the roles played by corporate advertisers, the
federal government, and ratings systems. Eliot uses the term "format"
(a combination of genre, program length, and scheduling) to describe individual programs and program types throughout the thirty-five year history
of network broadcasting, and analyzes these "formats" to reveal the existence and evolution of programming trends in prime-time network scheduling.
Included are selective breakdowns of these scheduling "formats" (with
descriptions of individual shows and discussions of their success or failure), and the complete fall network schedules from 1946-1980.

PC 753. ELLISON, HARLAN. The Glass Teat: Essays of Opinion on the Subject
          of Television. 1970; Rev. ed. New York: Jove, 1977. 319 pp.
This collection contains fifty-two of Ellison's critical essays which
were written for the Los Angeles Free Press from 1968-1970. The tone
of these reviews shifts from aggressive attacks on the medium to outright
apoligies as Ellison considers such issues as the widespread appeal of
banal programming, the abundance of depictions of violence but not sex
on network TV, and the debate surrounding the accuracy of television news.

PC 754. EPSTEIN, EDWARD J. News from Nowhere: Television and the News.
          New York: Random House, 1973. 321 pp.
Epstein bases this study of television news and newsgathering on six months
of direct observation of network news departments, interviews with journalists and news executives, and contacts with advertising agencies, the
FCC, network executives, and local affiliates. He describes government
regulations, the economic realities of network and affiliate relations,
and internal editorial procedures as forces which shape the form and content of television news. The author attempts to identify the values of
individual journalists and to determine whether those values are modified
to coincide with the values and concerns of the networks. Included are
examinations of specific network news stories and Epstein's attempts to
relate those stories to the organizational factors which help to shape
them.

PC 755. ESSLIN, MARTIN. The Age of Television. San Francisco: Freeman,
          1982. 138 pp.
Esslin describes what he sees as the international cultural revolution
brought about by television through its pervasive presentation of an alternative "reality" with elements of both the real and the fictional. Esslin
analyzes the structure of television dramas (their recurring character
types, cycles of myths, and different kinds of dramatic structure) to
reveal how these elements illuminate the self-image of our technological
culture. Included are a discussion of the ability of television to unify
audiences by offering a shared experience and speculations on the psychological and sociological effects of the television medium. Finding a
need to allow a greater access to television and to provide a greater
variety of programming, the author describes potential alternatives to
the current structure of American broadcasting.

PC 756. FESHBACH, SEYMOUR and ROBERT D. SINGER. Television and Aggression:
An Experimental Field Study. San Francisco: Jossey-Bass, 1971.
186 pp.
Feshbach and Singer studied the effects television's portrayal of violence
had on preadolescent and adolescent boys to determine whether it stimulated
aggressive behavior, or whether violent programming allowed the vicarious
release of hostility through the presentation of acceptable fantasies.
This field study of youths in private schools and boys' homes used the
number and type of aggressive acts engaged in by the experimental group
as an indication of aggressive attitudes. The study found that a significant number of the participants did not become more aggressive as a result
of exposure to an "aggressive TV diet," and that some participants
exhibited reduced aggression, lending credence to the hypothesis that TV
viewing, by allowing for vicarious involvement in violence, can serve
to safely release hostility.

PC 757. FORNATALE, PETER and JOSHUA E. MILLS. Radio in the Television
Age. Woodstock, N.Y.: Overlook Press, 1980. 212 pp.
Fornatale and Mills argue that, though radio is "the most ubiquitous of
the mass media," radio's impact on American literature has received little
examination. They seek to remedy this neglect by presenting a consideration of radio in the period 1950-80, notably noncommercial radio, radio
news, and the effect on the medium of an emerging teen culture. They
also treat such current issues as AM stereo, all-channel legislation,
and satellite transmission of broadcasts. Fornatale and Mills believe
that the industry is generally optimistic about the continued growth and
development of radio. They conclude by urging several reforms: a streamlined FCC, more diversified music programming, expanded noncommercial
stations, limits on commercial station multiple ownership, and creation
of government offices of media studies and public advocacy.

PC 758. FRANK, ROBERT SHELBY. Message Dimensions of Television News.
Lexington, Mass.: Lexington Books, 1973. 120 pp.
Frank's "message analysis" is an attempt to classify and describe communicated messages by looking not only at the content of TV news, but also
at its use of film language. A discussion of the political importance
of TV news establishes the framework within which Frank's observations
are reported. After outlining his methodology for TV news analysis, Frank
includes a study undertaken during the 1972 campaign period which examines
not only the events covered by TV news, but also the serial order of
stories, and the use of various camera angles and close-ups. Also included
is a parallel study of The New York Times, providing a means of comparison
between print and electronic journalism.

PC 759. GILBERT, ROBERT E. Television and Presidential Politics. North
Quincy, Mass.: Christopher, 1972. 335 pp.
This evaluation of television's impact on the Presidency and Presidential
power discusses the political implications of television and the ways
in which the medium was used as a campaign instrument from 1952-68.
Eisenhower's television "spot" campaign in 1952 and Stevenson's 1956 attempt
to use television to establish a Democratic coalition are examined.
Gilbert also describes the important role played by the candidates' visual
images in the 1960 Nixon-Kennedy debate. Included are critical evaluations
of Goldwater's television advertising campaign in 1964 and the Democratic
response. The role of television in the 1968 election is examined through
analyses of the TV campaigns of Nixon, Humphrey, and Wallace, and television's coverage of the Democratic National Convention in Chicago.

PC 760. GOETHALS, GREGOR T. The TV Ritual: Worship at the Video Altar.
Boston: Beacon Press, 1981. 164 pp.
This book examines the symbolic function of television images within
America's technological society. Though acknowledging that television
informs, entertains, and sells, Goethals is primarily concerned with television's role as a social symbol. Connecting TV programming with "iconic"
and "iconoclastic" motifs in American culture, he identifies three functions of television's role as a "public symbol." The patterns of news
broadcasts are cited as examples of television's function as ritual.
The medium's ability to act as an icon and identify America's institutional
order is linked by Goethals to the depiction of the family, nature, and
machines; finally, he points to documentaries and comedy as examples of
TV's "iconoclastic" questioning and criticism of institutions.

PC 761. GOLDSEN, ROSE K. The Show and Tell Machine: How Television Works
and Works You Over. New York: Dial Press, 1977. 427 pp.
Goldsen describes what she sees as the "cultural revolution" brought about
by television. The nature of the television medium is defined through
discussions of the medium's organization of time and attraction of attention, the potential for desensitization and behavior modification of the
audience, and the corporate structure that links networks with advertising
and public relations agencies. Goldsen examines the cultural significance
of individual programs ("Sesame Street" and "The Mickey Mouse Club") as
well as recurring themes (the family in prime time programming), and genres
(the evolution of the television crime fighter). Behavioral conditioning
techniques used in commercials are linked to the importance of the image
in advertising. Goldsen examines other external forces that shape American
television, including the Federal Communications Commission, the Nielsen
rating system, and other audience measurement methods. Appendices include
Goldsen's observation of the content of television images and examples
of Nielsen Market Section Audience Reports.

PC 762. GREENBERG, BRADLEY S. Life on Television: Content Analyses of
U.S. TV Drama. Norwood, N.J.: Ablex, 1980. 204 pp.
Greenberg's content analyses are drawn from prime time fictional series
on commercial television from 1975-77. Attempting to isolate the themes
and values of TV by analyzing patterns of representation, he focuses on
the depiction of four specific areas with potential social implications:
antisocial and "pro-social" behavior, black Americans, the American family,
and sex roles. Greenberg makes further observations about TV's portrayal
of relationships between the sexes, its sex-typing of behaviors, the demographic characteristics of fictional TV characters, and television's depiction of the elderly and of all racial minorities. By combining his observations and conclusions Green is able to define the features of the artificial reality created by the images of network television.

PC 763. HAMMOND, CHARLES MONTGOMERY, Jr. The Image Decade: Television
Documentary: 1965-1975. New York: Hastings House, 1981.
285 pp.
Hammond describes the evolution of television documentaries at the three
major networks from 1965-75 by isolating individual producers and reporters
who created innovative broadcast documentaries during this period. "Theme
documentaries," which expressed a point of view, are discussed in light
of their potential to function as social commentary. Individual programs
from three modes of documentary television (investigative reporting, TV
news magazines, and news specials) are examined, as are the portrayals
of such important news stories as urban violence, the Vietnam War, Watergate, 1968 politics, and U.S. relations with China.

PC 764. HAZARD, PATRICK D., ed. TV as Art: Some Essays in Criticism. Champaign, Ill.: National Council of Teachers of English, 1966. 221 pp.
These papers, commissioned by the Television Information Office for the National Council of Teachers of English, were assembled in an attempt to stimulate new approaches to television and to explore the educational potentials of the medium. Hazard includes an essay which places the television writing of Rod Serling and Paddy Chayevsky in the context of American literature; a discussion of the relationship between dramatic programming and American culture; and an analysis of ABC's "The Making of a President" and the political implications of mass communications in America. Three essays focus on children and television. Hazard also includes a proposed lesson plan to accompany the TV program "The Story of a Newspaper Man" to demonstrate the educational possibilities of the medium.

PC 765. HERSCHENSOHN, BRUCE. The Gods of Antenna. New Rochelle, N.Y.: Arlington House, 1976. 155 pp.
This critical appraisal of television stresses the negative cultural effects of the medium. Herschensohn traces the increased social and political importance of TV in the 1960s, declaring that characteristics of the medium shaped what was broadcast and created a "visual bias" in news coverage. This "visual bias," and what Herschensohn sees as liberal attitudes in the major networks, are blamed for television's "distorted view" of such important political events as the Vietnam War and Watergate. Herschensohn includes an "alphabet of visual and audio television news techniques" which, he claims, documents potential distortions inherent in the "langauge" of television news.

PC 766. HETTINGER, HERMAN S. A Decade of Radio Advertising. Chicago: University of Chicago Press, 1933. 354 pp.
In this early study of radio advertising, Hettinger draws contrasts between the structure of American radio and that of European and Canadian broadcasting systems. He argues that these foreign systems suffer from overly intrusive government regulation (or, in Canada's case, from insufficient financing), that foreign radio tends to be less tolerant of free speech, more conventional and restricted in programming, and less successful in its coverage of events, and that the American system is clearly preferable. Hettinger argues against government control of radio on grounds of excessive cost, and, as a further argument, warns against the possibility of federal-state disputes. While he faults American radio for several inadequacies, notably a lack of originality in programming, he believes these may be remedied without a fundamental change in the system's structure. Hettinger calls for uniform trade practices throughout the industry, research and evaluation, and improved self-government of American broadcasting.

PC 767. HIMMELSTEIN, HAL. On the Small Screen: New Approaches in Television and Video Criticism. New York: Praeger, 1981. 207 pp.
This book analyzes the status of television and video criticism in the early 1980s by placing it in the context of other modes of art criticism. Himmelstein finds television to be a unique phenomenon for the critic because of its status as an economic institution, its potential to effect social change, and its role as the dominant culture's disseminator of information. Attempting to identify existing critical approaches to television and suggest new critical directions, Himmelstein focuses on five critics and their responses to questions about critical discourse, the role of these critics, and the nature of their readership. John O'Connor of the New York Times and Bernie Harrison of the Washington Star are pointed to as examples of "popular critics." Horace Newcomb is cited as an example of an "academic critic." Museum video curator David Ross, and video artist Douglas Davis are used to compare video and television critics.

PC 768. HOFSTETTER, C. RICHARD. Bias in the News: Network Television
         Coverage of the 1972 Election Campaign. Columbus: Ohio State
         University Press, 1976. 213 pp.
This study of weekday nightly news programs begins with the first day
of the 1972 Democratic National Convention and continues through the Republican National Convention to the eve of the elections. The author analyzes
the content of these broadcasts in an attempt to identify patterns of
campaign news coverage, to demonstrate how those patterns relate to individual candidates, issues, or networks, and to determine whether any bias
is observable. Hofstetter finds that the trends in coverage of specific
issues were uniform across the three major networks, and that, though
considerably greater coverage was devoted to the Democratic Party, it
was not clear that either party was favored. This book concludes that
while coverage of the two parties was by no means equal, partisan bias
did not dominate network news coverage.

PC 769. JOHNSON, NICHOLAS. How to Talk Back to Your Television Set.
         Boston: Little, Brown, 1970. 228 pp.
Johnson describes the ways in which television influences American society
and the lives of individual Americans. He examines the growing concentration of media ownership and the potential implications such a concentration may have on the content of television. He also speculates on
the development of new communication technologies, including cable, as
alternatives to "over-the-air" broadcasting. Finding a need to reform
television before America can progress in other areas of its national
agenda, Johnson proposes reforms of the medium that Congress or the FCC
could enact, as well as describing avenues for individual involvement
in media reform.

PC 770. KAHN, FRANK J., ed. Documents of American Broadcasting. 1968;
         Rev. ed. Englewood Cliffs, N.J.: Prentice-Hall, 1978.
         638 pp.
Kahn provides a source book of forty-nine documents in broadcasting's
history, regulation, and public policy. Arranged chronologically and
occasionally abridged, these documents include the U.S. Constitution,
the Radio Act of 1912, "War of the Worlds," the Fairness Doctrine, and
the Criminal Code. Kahn observes that the radio and television industries
have evolved as products of shifting values and needs, which these materials document. He describes the democratic methods through which values
have been applied and needs met as broadcasting developed into one of
the most powerful social, educational, economic, journalistic, and political instruments in America.

PC 771. KAPLAN, MILTON ALLEN. Radio and Poetry. New York: Columbia
         University Press, 1949. 333 pp.
Kaplan traces the broadcasting of poetry and verse plays on radio from
its fitful beginnings in the 1930s to its substantial popularity in the
1940s. He pays particular attention to the radio play, seeing it as a
"new literary form" and considering ways in which the medium and time
format of radio affects playwriting technique. Kaplan contends that radio
has encouraged popular appreciation of poetry and secured a large audience
for poets. Among other topics, he treats the influence of radio on "common
speech" poetry, the interplay of the verse and the emotions of the audience,
and the use of radio for propaganda and morale-building during W.W. II.
Kaplan concludes with a call for greater boldness and initiative within
the radio industry, and for greater support of radio poetry among listeners,
critics, and the government.

PC 772. KEELEY, JOSEPH. The Left-Leaning Antenna: Political Bias in Television. New Rochelle, N.Y.: Arlington House, 1971. 320 pp.
Keeley echoes the charge against the leftist-liberal bias of television made by Spiro Agnew in his speech of November 13, 1969. In a broad discussion of the content and structure of American television, Keeley purports to document that bias. Appendices include the text of Agnew's speech, excerpts from the National Association of Broadcasters Code, an FCC notice on the Fairness Doctrine, a proposal to counteract leftist and liberal thought on television, excerpts of House Sub-Committee hearings on CBS's documentary "Hunger in America," and the Code of Broadcast News Ethics of the Radio Television News Directors Association.

PC 773. LABUNSKI, RICHARD. The First Amendment Under Siege: The Politics of Broadcast Regulation. Westport, Conn.: Greenwood Press, 1981. 184 pp.
Labunsky looks at the major issues raised by Federal regulation of electronic communication and at the environment in which regulation takes place. He begins by considering whether it is damaging to First Amendment principles to continue to maintain that the electronic and print media are not constitutionally equal, especially in light of the decline of newspapers and the growth of the electronic media. The author then discusses the evolution of broadcasters' First Amendment rights. This is followed by a discussion of the concepts of public interest, diversity, and access as they apply to the regulation of broadcasting, as well as to the present reforms that are underway in these areas.

PC 774. LANG, KURT and GLADYS ENGEL LANG. Politics and Television. Chicago: Quadrangle Books, 1968. 315 pp.
This collection of sociological studies of televised events explores television's ability to shape public impressions of politicians and political activities. The Langs use content analyses, controlled observations, and audience surveys to determine the response of viewers to such events as McArthur Day in Chicago in 1951 (contrasting TV coverage with the experiences of on-the-scene observers), the Republican and Democratic conventions of 1952, the Kennedy-Nixon debates (measuring their effect on the voting intentions of viewers), and the 1964 Presidential election (exploring the impact of outcome projections on late voters). Also included is a chapter on television portrayals of political personalities. From the results of these studies, the authors conclude that TV content and its effects are not dependent on the qualities of the medium, but instead arise from the application of the medium by human agents.

PC 775. LAZARSFELD, PAUL F. The People Look at Radio. Chapel Hill: University of North Carolina Press, 1946. 158 pp.
Lazarsfeld presents the results of a 1945 survey undertaken to identify Americans' attitudes about radio. The book includes audience opinions on advertising, a description of listening habits, and opinions on news and entertainment programming. Throughout his analysis of survey results, Lazarsfeld emphasizes the social responsibility of radio.

PC 776. LEINWOLL, STANLEY. From Spark to Satellite: A History of Radio Communication. New York: Scribner, 1979. 242 pp.
Beginning with Marconi's invention of wireless telegraphy, Leinwoll describes the invention of vacuum tubes and the superheterodyne circuit which made radio and television possible. He discusses the growth of domestic and international broadcasting, including the founding of RCA, the development of ham radio, and the rise of shortwave. The exploration of space is discussed, from early radar and semiconductor experiments to earth-orbiting satellites. A final chapter explores the laser as a potential communication device.

PC 777. LESHER, STEPHAN. Media Unbound: The Impact of Television Jour-
          nalism on the Public. Boston: Houghton Mifflin, 1982. 285 pp.
Lesher concentrates on the inherent limitations of journalistic "truth"
and their consequences. Focusing more on such television programs as
"60 Minutes" than on print media, he examines the coverage of specific
episodes, like the Tet offensive in Vietnam, and the fallout that reporting
produced. Distinguishing between what is informative and what is need-
lessly confrontational in such presentations, Lesher emphasizes how unavoidably human imperfection skews reports which thus misinform a national
audience. He insists upon legal constraints to correct the problem and
suggests that his readers recognize the shortcomings of media coverage.

PC 778. LESSER, GERALD S. Children and Television: Lessons from "Sesame
          Street". New York: Random House, 1974. 290 pp.
Lesser, an educational psychologist involved with the Children's Television
Workshop, describes the creation of "Sesame Street" and its role, not
simply as a series designed for broadcast, but also as an experiment connecting academicians, educators, and television creators. He delineates
the objectives of "Sesame Street," the establishment of curriculum goals
tailored to the television medium, and the attempt to balance entertainment
with education. Exploring the relationship of children to the television
medium, Lesser outlines the Children's Television Workshop's methods of
attracting the young audience's attention. He provides suggestions for
improving children's television and includes the results of tests designed
to determine the impact of "Sesame Street" on children as well as a description of the initial critical response to the show.

PC 779. LEVIN, HARVEY J. Broadcast Regulation and Joint Ownership of
          Media. New York: New York University Press, 1960. 219 pp.
Levin uses standard economic analysis to explore the question of whether
the FCC's joint ownership policy—favoring owners of exclusively broadcast
media over owners of non-broadcast as well as broadcast media—promotes
competition and superior programming. While the policy seeks to avoid
"private restraint on the flow of ideas" which might result from joint
ownership among the media, it also has the power to damage the media's
ability to operate in the public interest by reducing financial stability
within the industry. He weighs these two factors against one another—
competition versus financial stability—and decides that in the long run
the joint ownership policy probably improves the performance of all media,
despite temporary setbacks to certain newspapers or radio stations. It
also protects the First Amendment rights of broadcasters, not from government suasion, but from the control of oligarchic private owners.

PC 780. LEVIN, HARVEY J. Fact and Fancy in Television Regulation: An
          Economic Study of Policy Alternatives. New York: Russell Sage,
          1980. 505 pp.
Levin illuminates the assumptions and goals which underlie current broadcasting regulatory strategies. Providing an overview of the television
industry's economic structure and methods of broadcast regulation, he
goes on to evaluate the success of regulatory policy and to measure its
effects on programming and industry economics. This evaluation leads
to a critique of current policy regarding the diversity of station ownership, crossownership, and the prime-time access rule. Levin examines
alternative regulatory strategies including quantitative programming
requirements and alternative methods to fund public broadcasting.

PC 781. LINSKY, MARTIN, ed. Television and the Presidential Elections:
         Self Interest and the Public Interest. Lexington, Mass.: Lexing-
         ton Books, 1983. 137 pp.
This book describes the proceedings of a symposium on network television's
influence on Presidential elections held at the Institute of Politics
at Harvard's John F. Kennedy School of Government. The participants,
including executives from the three major networks, members of the academic
community, and representatives from PBS, BBC, and CNN, respond to a hypothetical election in their discussion of the ways in which candidates
and networks interact. Among the issues explored are the effect that
exit polls and forecasts have on the outcomes of elections, the possible
relationship between decreased voter turnout and the declining audience
for network campaign coverage, and the problems faced by campaign managers
and politicians in dealing with the television industry.

PC 782. LITMAN, BARRY RUSSELL. The Vertical Structure of the Television
         Broadcasting Industry: The Coalescence of Power. East Lansing,
         Mich.: Division of Research, Graduate School of Business Adminis-
         tration, Michigan State University, 1979. 172 pp.
Litman argues that the vertically integrated structure of the television
industry prevents the medium from offering diversified programming, since
the three television networks have succeeded in eliminating a high percentage of potential competition. Tolerant of such network practices as the
purchase of independent stations, forced station-network affiliation,
and network-sponsored production, the FCC has largely ignored the problems
created by vertical integration and thus has remained ineffectual in its
attempts to establish a wider range of television fare. Litman views
divestiture of owned and operated stations as a necessary step in any
attempt to redress the balance of power within the TV industry.

PC 783. MacDONALD, J. FRED. Blacks and White TV: Afro-Americans in Tele-
         vision Since 1949. Chicago: Nelson-Hall, 1983. 288 pp.
Noting the distorted image of blacks in American popular culture, MacDonald
judges television's role in reinforcing or correcting that image. He
characterizes the relationship between Afro-Americans and TV as "ambivalent" and observes that the medium clings to negative stereotypes, often
ignores black performers, and employs few blacks in production positions.
This analysis divides television history into three time periods.
MacDonald notes that blacks initially appeared quite frequently on TV and
he finds that the years from 1948-57 can be characterized by a movement
from "honesty to duplicity." He chronicles the influence of the Civil
Rights movement on TV from 1957-70 and observes an evolution toward a
fair treatment of blacks in the industry. Finally, MacDonald notes that
while blacks were more visible than ever on TV during the 1970s and early
1980s, traditional stereotypes continued to dominate.

PC 784. MACY, JOHN W., Jr. To Irrigate a Wasteland: The Struggle to
         Shape a Public Television System in the United States. Berkeley:
         University of California Press, 1974. 186 pp.
Macy explores the design and development of public broadcasting in the
U.S. He discusses the critical, political, financial, artistic, and organizational difficulties encountered during attempts to provide a nonpolitical
and independent public system. Appendices include: legislation governing
public television and radio, sources of funding and public television
station type, and locations and call numbers of public television licencees.

PC 785. MAHONY, SHEILA, NICK DeMARTINO, and ROBERT STENGEL. Keeping PACE
with the New Television: Public Television and Changing Technology. New York: Carnegie Corporation of New York/VNU Books
International, 1980. 281 pp.
This book updates the recommendations and projections of the Carnegie
Commission's study of public broadcasting reported in A Public Trust (PC
736). Reviewing new developments in regulatory policy, industry economics,
and technology, the authors examine what opportunities the new technologies
provide for public broadcasting. They outline a proposed nonprofit cable
TV network for performing arts, culture, and entertainment called PACE.
The first portion of this book provides a detailed proposal for PACE,
while the remainder contains reports on the status of and future implications for public broadcasters of satellite communications, cable TV, pay
TV, home video, and videotext services.

PC 786. MANDER, JERRY. Four Arguments for the Elimination of Television.
New York: Morrow, 1977. 371 pp.
This negative appraisal of the television medium finds the problems of
television inherent in the technology itself. Denying that technologies
are neutral, Mander sees TV as a dangerous force in American society,
one that is ultimately irredeemable. His first argument asserts that
modern society alienates individuals by limiting direct human experience
and that television limits our experience still further. The second argument describes technological and economic factors which insure that the
medium will be dominated by corporate powers to the exclusion of citizen
input. Mander further declares that the psychological and physiological
effects of television on audience members benefit those who control the
medium by "amounting to conditioning for autocratic control." The author's
final argument states that technology precludes the possibility that TV's
democratic potential will be fulfilled by insuring a bias toward advertising. Mander combines his personal impressions, based on a fifteen-
year career as a public relations and advertising executive, with reference
to studies of the physiological and psychological effects of television.

PC 787. MANKIEWICZ, FRANK and JOEL SWERDLOW. Remote Control: Television
and the Manipulation of American Life. New York: New York Times
Books, 1978. 308 pp.
Mankiewicz and Swerdlow explore television's impact on American individuals
and institutions. They use the establishment of TV's "Family House" as
a case study to examine the politics of TV and to illuminate the roles
played by public opinion, the Legislative branch, government regulatory
agencies, and the press in shaping the medium. Television's ability to
raise or lower the national consciousness is established through an analysis of the medium's role in the feminist and Civil Rights movements.
A summary of existing studies reveals TV's role in the education and
socialization of young viewers, and a discussion of politics, TV news,
and the medium's ability to set a national agenda establish the power
of the medium. Mankiewicz and Swerdlow include an analysis of the economic
structure of television and a discussion of the controversy surrounding
violent programming.

PC 788. MEEHAN, DIANA M. Ladies of the Evening: Women Characters of
Prime-Time Television. Metuchen, N.J.: Scarecrow Press, 1983.
190 pp.
In this description and interpretation of the images of women presented
on American television from 1950-80, Meehan explores the attitudes and
values expressed by those images. Based on an examination of specific
episodic dramas and situation comedies and on interviews with fifteen
television writers, Meehan identifies a series of recurring female character types. These types are discussed in light of their social and historical contexts, the degrees of vulnerability or strength they exhibit,

and the interaction of specific female television characters. Meehan concludes that socially and culturally prescribed sex roles are apparent in TV programming and that these depictions, despite offering a distorted picture, create certain expectations for the behavior of American women.

PC 789. MEHLING, HAROLD. The Great Time Killer. New York: World, 1962. 352 pp.
This book, written for viewers who were dissatisfied with television's failure to live up to their expectations, finds the structure of the broadcasting industry (specifically the relationship between advertising agencies and networks) to be the primary cause of television's inadequate service to the public. Mehling examines the industry structure, discussing the roles played by advertisers in censorship, the connection between Hollywood and television production companies, and the impact of audience ratings and Federal regulations on the industry. In a discussion of the quiz show scandals Mehling concludes that they are indicative of more widespread corruption involving the medium as a whole.

PC 790. MELODY, WILLIAM. Children's Television: The Economics of Exploitation. New Haven, Conn.: Yale University Press, 1973. 164 pp.
Melody responds to a proposal by Action for Children's Television that would eliminate commercials from children's television programming. He discusses the economic aspects of children's television to determine whether special regulations are required to prevent the exploitation of young viewers and whether the current programming and advertising practices were necessitated by the economic structure of TV. Melody looks to the future of television to determine whether the "problems" identified by ACT would eventually correct themselves and whether the adoption of ACT's proposal would lead to the eventual disappearance of children's programming. Based on his findings, Melody outlines a plan to eliminate advertising in children's television without negative effects on the existing TV industry structure.

PC 791. MINOW, NEWTON N., JOHN BARTLOW MARTIN, and LEE M. MITCHELL. Presidential Television. New York: Basic Books, 1973. 232 pp.
This discussion of politics and the power of television explores the relationship between the Executive branch and the major broadcasting networks. Television's power, not only to enhance a President's personal image but also to determine which issues receive national attention, is discussed in light of the potential for abuse of that power. The authors include a historical discussion of past abuses, a description of the role played by the Federal Communications Commission in regulating Presidential use of television, and proposed reforms to give the Legislative and Judicial branches and the opposition party improved access to broadcasting.

PC 792. MOODY, KATE. Growing Up on Television: The TV Effect. New York: Times Books, 1980. 242 pp.
Moody examines the cumulative effects of television viewing on children, focusing on the effects on our culture as well as on individuals. Documenting shifts in familial ritual and social structure, she demonstrates how viewing patterns usurp family rules and rituals and have brought about a change in our sources of information, entertainment, and education. She describes the physiological impact of prolonged TV viewing and explores its impact upon perception, reading, and learning, as well as its promotion of aggressive behavior. Moody proposes methods to mediate TV's effect in the home, the school, and society as a whole. Appendices include a list of recommended books for parents and children to share, and a list of local and national children's television reform groups.

PC 793. MORRIS, NORMAN S. Television's Child. Boston: Little, Brown, 1971. 238 pp.
Observing that television viewing makes up a significant portion of children's leisure-time activity, Morris discusses TV's impact on children's values, education, and reading habits. Concerned with television's effect beyond the controversy surrounding the depiction of violence, Morris consulted clinical psychologists, psychiatrists, educators, network executives, advertisers, and parents in an attempt to establish guidelines for parental supervision of children's TV use. He provides a broad overview of many of the issues raised in discussions of children's programming, including the amount of credibility TV images have for children, the medium's effect on children's view of the world, the potential policy-making power of citizen's groups, the impact of advertising on children, and changes in teaching methods in reaction to the influence of television.

PC 794. MOSCO, VINCENT. Broadcasting in the United States: Innovative Challenge and Organizational Control. Norwood, N.J.: Ablex, 1979. 153 pp.
This historical overview of American broadcasting focuses on technological developments that had the potential to revolutionize the structure of commercial broadcasting. Mosco explains why the structure of American media remained the same despite technological innovations and efforts to reform the FCC. In describing the evolution and eventual fates of FM radio, UHF-TV, cable TV, and subscription TV, Mosco reveals how the broadcast regulatory system works and the combination of forces (broadcasting networks, Congressional Commerce Committees, Executive and Judicial branches of government, and consumer groups) that have preserved the broadcasting status quo. The book concludes with Mosco's proposed reforms of American broadcasting which include a call for a review of the FCC.

PC 795. NEWCOMB, HORACE. Television: The Critical View. 1976; Rev. ed. New York: Oxford University Press, 1982. 549 pp.
This anthology contains a variety of critical perspectives on television. Essays collected in a section on television programming are largely descriptive and include discussions of viewers' responses to such individual programs as "The Waltons," "Star Trek," "M*A*S*H," and "Roots" as well as such popular TV genres as soap operas, situation comedies, and detective dramas. Newcomb's second section explores TV's effect on American culture and the role of the medium in contemporary society. Individual essays offer general conclusions on such topics as the negative consequences of the medium's influence, TV's symbolic content, its replacement of other forms of communication, and its blurred distinction between fantasy and reality. Essays in the final section examine the industrial, economic, cultural, and political structures which shape television.

PC 796. NEWCOMB, HORACE. TV: The Most Popular Art. Garden City, N.Y.: Anchor Books, 1974. 272 pp.
Newcomb focuses on TV's role as a popular art form and examines the various formats of TV programming. The medium's ability to create such new entertainment forms as situation and domestic comedies is paired with television's manipulation of traditional formulaic elements in such popular entertainment as Westerns and mystery stories. Newcomb considers television formulas, including medical shows, soap operas and adventure shows, and their power to assert American values and explore contemporary problems. He discusses news, sports, and documentary programming and the process whereby TV entertainment formulas shape nonfiction programming. Newcomb defines an aesthetic approach to understanding television, based upon what he sees as the medium's "intimacy, continuity, and history."

PC 797. NOBLE, GRANT. Children in Front of the Small Screen. Beverly Hills, Calif.: Sage, 1975. 256 pp.
Noble believes that television plays a positive role in industrial society and he develops a theoretical position explaining television's popularity. Noble finds that a regularly appearing group of fictional characters acts as an extended kin group for the TV viewer, thus expanding the viewer's contact with society beyond his immediate family. TV provides behavior models and allows for both escape from society and a simultaneous involvement with it. Noble applies this theoretical perspective to television viewing and child development, and explores the extent to which TV creates children's understanding of social roles. He reviews the evidence on televised violence and its effect on children and includes a study of the relationship between television viewing and deviant behavior. Also included is a study of the producers of children's programming which describes their values and objectives. Noble concludes that television makes society accessible to increasingly isolated audience members.

PC 798. NOLL, ROGER G., MERTON J. PECK, and JOHN J. McGOWAN. Economic Aspects of Television Regulation. Washington, D.C.: Brookings Institution, 1973. 342 pp.
The authors trace the effect of government policies on the American television industry and critically evaluate the regulatory goals and methods of government policymakers and the FCC from an economic perspective. They examine the possibility for a better television system, exploring the prospect of increasing television diversity in the early 1970s through expansion within the economic structure of the commercial television industry. FCC regulatory policies designed to facilitate diversity are discussed in light of their implications for the development of public television, subscription, pay, and cable TV, and direct satellite-to-home broadcasting.

PC 799. O'CONNOR, JOHN E., ed. American History/American Television: Interpreting the Video Past. New York: Ungar, 1983. 420 pp.
This collection of fourteen essays explores the role played by television in recent history and the medium as a source of research material for social, political, and cultural historians. Four basic approaches are used by the essayists included in this anthology: television news and documentaries are used as primary evidence of historical events; dramatic television programs are considered as interpreters of history; the history of television as both an industry and an art form is discussed; and the impact of television programs on social and cultural history is examined. Essays are devoted to individual dramatic programs such as "Brian's Song" and "Marty"; documentary programming such as "The Selling of the Pentagon" and news coverage of Watergate; and broader subjects, such as Richard Nixon's television image, and the role of TV in Edward Kennedy's attempt at the 1980 Presidential nomination. Also included are an extensive bibliography and a guide to archive and manuscript sources for the study of television.

PC 800. OWEN, BRUCE M., JACK H. BEEBE, and WILLARD G. MANNING, Jr. Television Economics. Lexington, Mass.: Lexington, 1974. 218 pp.
Owen stresses the disproportionate economic influence exerted by the three major broadcasting networks over the entire television industry in this discussion of the interrelated functions of television stations, networks, viewers, advertisers, and broadcast regulators. Modifications of the present structure of TV operations are proposed, with a particular focus on the lax regulatory guidelines which have permitted the construction of an unmanageable network power base. The potential for new technologies to assist in the restructuring of the current system of TV operations is regarded as an essential consideration in any plan to establish a less rigid, more diversified television market.

PC 801. PALMER, EDWARD L. and AIMEE DORR, eds. Children and the Faces
of Television: Teaching, Violence, Selling. New York: Academic
Press, 1980. 360 pp.
This anthology reviews the issues involved in determining the effect of
television viewing on children. Essays are divided into three sections
which focus on separate dimensions of the debate over television's potential and actual impact: television as an instrument of education, the
effects of televised violence, and the effects of TV advertising. Each
section begins with a historical discussion of the particular issue.
The essays which follow discuss such topics as TV production methods,
patterns of consumption, results of previous research, strategies used
to bring about change in the medium, and speculations on future research,
practice, and policy.

PC 802. PATTERSON, THOMAS E. and ROBERT D. McCLURE. The Unseeing Eye:
The Myth of Television Power in National Politics. New York:
Putnam, 1976. 218 pp.
Patterson and McClure examine television's influence on voters through
its roles in creating and presenting a candidate's image and in informing
citizens about issues and events. The authors interviewed over 2,000
voters, contacting them several times during the 1972 Presidential campaign
to determine the effects of television on their opinions of candidates
and issues throughout the campaign. From a content analysis of television
network news and paid political broadcasts, Patterson and McClure conclude
that television news fails in its responsibility to inform viewers of
candidate stances on issues and that political advertisements are incapable
of manipulating viewers, but do fulfill an informative function.

PC 803. POWERS, RON. The Newscasters. New York: St. Martin's Press,
1977. 243 pp.
Powers chronicles what he sees as the transformation of American newscast-
ing into "show business," and observes that the informative function of
TV news has been usurped by its entertainment function. Powers attributes
this transformation in the form and content of TV news to sales-oriented
station management and their habit of pandering to audience desires rather
than following sound journalistic principles. Included in this book are
the results of interviews with such newscasters and news personalities
as Barbara Walters, Walter Cronkite, Mike Wallace, Tom Snyder, Dan Rather,
and Geraldo Rivera, who discuss the shift from issue-oriented news to
people-oriented news/entertainment.

PC 804. RANNEY, AUSTIN. Channels of Power: The Impact of Television
on American Politics. New York: Basic Books, 1983. 207 pp.
Ranney argues that the nature of American political reality shaped by
television is antiestablishment and even adversarial, that there exists
within television news a strong bias against politicians and political
establishments. The transmission of this bias to the general public,
he asserts, has led to the fragmentation of the political system. Furthermore, the importance of television forces politicians to consider constantly how their political activity will be presented in the nightly
news; image is a greater concern than substance. Television, Ranney concludes, has weakened the ability of Presidents and Congressmen to govern,
and the industry's inattention to bureaucratic politics has helped
unelected officials to fill the resulting policy-making vacuums.

PC 805. REEL, A. FRANK. The Networks: How They Stole the Show. New
York: Scribner, 1979. 208 pp.
Reel, observing that the American television industry functions as a monopoly, explores the relationship between the economic structure of the TV
industry and television programming. A historical discussion of the economic development of commercial television describes how this monopolistic

structure arose, while examinations of the relationships between networks, rating systems, local affiliates, and independent producers illuminate how the present network system is perpetuated. Reel reveals the influence of TV networks in such areas as station ownership, syndication, and merchandising. He attributes the shortcomings of American TV to the corporate structure of commercial television and speculates on the possibilities for reform offered by new technologies and the influence of government regulatory agencies.

PC 806. **ROSEN, PHILIP T.** The Modern Stentors: Radio Broadcasters and the Federal Government 1920-1934. Westport, Conn.: Greenwood Press, 1980. 267 pp.
This book is a chronicle of American broadcasting from the era prior to Federal regulation to the establishment of the Federal Communications Commission by the Communications Act of 1934. Rosen discusses the interplay of broadcasting technology, the government, and business interests, and how these forces determined the shape of broadcasting in America. He exposes the conflict between the need for broadcasting regulation and the freedoms guaranteed by the First Amendment, and he describes how that conflict was resolved by various regulatory efforts including the Interdepartmental Radio Advisory Committee, the Federal Radio Commission, and the Radio Act of 1927. He focuses on the process by which these early regulatory efforts led to the establishment of the modern broadcasting industry structure.

PC 807. **ROWLAND, WILLARD D., Jr.** The Politics of TV Violence: Policy Uses of Communication Research. Beverly Hills, Calif.: Sage, 1983. 320 pp.
This discussion of research on the effects of violence in TV programming is concerned with how that research is used in policy-making decisions within the TV industry and governmental regulatory agencies. Rowland focuses on the relationship between four forces active in the TV violence dispute: governmental policy-makers, the broadcasting industry, citizens' groups, and the academic research community. The first portion of this book examines the early history of mass communications research, placing it in the context of American social science research. Rowland then focuses on the period from 1927-72 and the interaction between communications research and broadcast public policy-making. He also discusses the status of more recent research (1972-81), its relationship to changes in broadcast technologies, and its political implications.

PC 808. **SALDICH, ANNE RAWLEY.** Electronic Democracy: Television's Impact on the American Political Process. New York: Praeger, 1979. 122 pp.
Saldich critiques commercial television's misuse of its power, especially in light of television's impact on American politics and government. Finding a "similarity between tyranny and television" (in both, a highly centralized minority shapes the experience of the majority), she re-evaluates Marshall McLuhan's theories of media and examines television coverage of events in Vietnam, in Wounded Knee, and in Chicago in 1968 to reveal what that coverage demonstrates about television's misuse of its power. Saldich concludes that broadcasting has usurped certain governmental powers, yet TV is without the system of checks and balances necessary in a democracy. She finds that television executives function like political gatekeepers, determining the national political agenda. In measuring TV's impact on governmental processes, Saldich finds that the medium has personalized power, increased the expense of the election process, weakened political parties, and diminished the significance of their conventions.

PC 809. SARSON, EVELYN, ed. Action for Children's Television. New York:
Avon Books, 1971. 127 pp.
This collection of essays on the status of children's television in the
early 1970s was prepared from the First Symposium of Effect on Children
of TV Programming and Advertising. The contributors--politicians, academicians, and children's television production personnel--discuss television's ability to communicate to children and the ways young viewers
interact with the medium. Included are suggested methods to improve children's programming, proposals to eliminate commercialism in children's
television, and discussions of new methods to acquire financial support
for children's TV.

PC 810. SCHRAMM, WILBUR. Responsibility in Mass Communication. New York:
Harper & Row, 1957. 391 pp.
Schramm argues that the vast changes being made in the field of communications must be attended by a reevaluation of ethical responsibility.
This reevaluation, in turn, will lead to a "new philosophy" of mass communication. Schramm divides his study into four parts. The first discusses the nature of the changes in communications. The second outlines
four theories, the last of which, the theory of "social responsibility,"
Schramm proposes as the "new philosophy." In the third section, Schramm
discusses the moral problems in communications. In the final part, he
asserts that these problems are the mutual responsibility of the government,
media, and public.

PC 811. SCHWARTZ, TONY. The Responsive Chord. Garden City, N.Y.: Anchor
Press, 1973. 173 pp.
This discussion of the powers of television is shaped by Schwartz's extensive background in radio and television advertising and by the communications theory of Marshall McLuhan. Schwartz begins by summarizing existing communications theories, identifying their strengths and weaknesses.
He discusses the historical transition from print-based communication
modes to the auditory-based modes of broadcasting and builds his own theory
around the "resonance principle" which he uses to examine how the television medium can be manipulated to transmit a particular message. He
also discusses television and radio commercials within their communications
environment and television's role in the political process and examines
the extent to which TV has shaped the education of children.

PC 812. SCHWARZ, MEG, ed. TV & Teens: Experts Look at the Issues. Reading, Mass.: Addison-Wesley, 1982. 222 pp.
The contributors to this anthology explore the relationship between adolescents and television, identifying the medium's shortcomings and proposing
modifications to programming and advertising practices. Essays examine
the current role models and career options presented by television and
formulate suggested improvements. Included is a discussion of programs
depicting drug abuse, alcoholism, and suicide. The essays examine the
potential of television to have a positive effect on adolescents. The
products and methods of advertising directed at teens are examined in
light of their influence on sex-role stereotyping and contribution to
the adolescent's self-perceptions.

PC 813. SHAYON, ROBERT LEWIS. The Crowd-Catchers, Introducing Television.
New York: Saturday Review Press, 1973. 175 pp.
Considering TV as an institution, Shayon describes the history of the
medium, its technical operations (including programming decisions), and
TV's relationships with the Legislative and Judicial branches of the FCC.
He reveals how the medium disguises itself from its audience, and questions
the medium's ability to function in the public interest. He also speculates on the role that new technologies will play in the future of television.

PC 814. SHAYON, ROBERT LEWIS, ed. The Eighth Art. New York: Holt,
         Rinehart & Winston, 1962. 269 pp.
Most of the essays contained in this volume were commissioned by the CBS
TV Network in 1960 for a proposed quarterly magazine on the subject of
television. The contributors, writing from a variety of perspectives,
discuss a range of media-related issues. Included are an analysis of
TV's impact on American politics, an essay on the status of TV criticism,
and several discussions of the medium's relationship to other arts (literary adaptations, ballet, theater). Several contributors explore the informative qualities of the medium as they discuss television and education,
the effects of TV viewing on children's reading habits, and the medium's
potential as a facilitator of international communication.

PC 815. SIEPMANN, CHARLES ARTHUR. Radio, Television and Society. New
         York: Oxford University Press, 1950. 410 pp.
Siepmann reviews the history of broadcasting in the U.S. and surveys what
is known about broadcasting's effect on the outlook and behavior of its
consumers. He describes the organizational and economic systems under
which broadcasting operates and the role played by broadcasting in modern
society. Using radio as a frame of reference, Siepmann examines propaganda,
issues of free speech, and the relationship between education and the
mass media.

PC 816. SIMMONS, STEVEN J. The Fairness Doctrine and the Media. Berkeley:
         University of California Press, 1978. 285 pp.
Simmons focuses on the policy developed by the FCC in 1959 to address
the problem of equal media time for opposing views, a policy that has
been difficult to administer. He reviews its early history and present
application, its relationship to advertising, personal attack and political
editorial rules, and the problem of defining an "issue." Recognizing
that mass media can now exclude voices that were once protected by the
First Amendment, Simmons supports controls but severely criticizes the
current administration of the fairness doctrine. He points out areas
for reforms and recommends that airwave access be expanded in order to
curtail the need for regulation.

PC 817. SKLAR, ROBERT. Prime-Time America: Life on and Behind the Tele-
         vision Screen. New York: Oxford University Press, 1980.
         200 pp.
Sklar views television as a medium which creates and transmits "cultural
products" to its viewers. He examines the product that television provides,
the process by which TV programming is created, and the critical reception
of television. Observing that television provides a kind of "legitimized
tastelessness," Sklar discusses the portrayals of sex, violence, and the
American class structure on TV. He also chronicles the controversy surrounding the effects of TV violence, and various advertising strategies
used on television. Sklar provides insight into the production of television programming by profiling TV director Jay Sandrich and the Children's
Television Workshop, and by examining the production of the "Dick Cavett
Show" and the competition between networks.

PC 818. SKORNIA, HARRY J. Television and the News: A Critical Appraisal.
         Palo Alto, Calif.: Pacific Books, 1968. 232 pp.
Skornia's evaluation of television news identifies the co-existence of
journalistic and commercial demands as an inherent weakness in TV reporting.
He documents the shortcomings of television journalism, finding that time
and budget allocations limit the effectiveness of TV news departments
and that certain qualities of the medium have the tendency to change the
events television depicts. Skornia observes that television news coverage
is characterized by an overemphasis on immediacy of coverage and highly
visual stories, a preoccupation with celebrities, and the presence of

fragmented, discontinuous stories. He finds a probusiness, anti-labor bias in TV news and describes the existence of other forms of editorial censorship. Calling for increased professionalism, an end to multiple ownership, and the isolation of news departments from public relations and advertising sales departments, Skornia concludes with recommendations for the improvement of television journalism, an effort urgently needed as more and more people use television as their primary news source.

PC 819. SLOAN COMMISSION ON CABLE COMMUNICATIONS. On the Cable: The Television of Abundance. New York: McGraw-Hill, 1971. 256 pp.
This report explores the implications of the growth of cable communications systems and their potential to revolutionize media in ways beyond the simple provision of more programs and better television reception. Noting that cable communication has had no established regulatory structure, the Sloan Commission draws attention to the opportunity for citizens to become involved in determining the future shape of this medium and thus insure that it would operate in "the public interest." Included are proposals on the form cable regulation could take and predictions and recommendations for the next ten to fifteen years of cable use. A brief description of the technology and history of cable reveals its potential for revolutionizing the broadcasting industry and increasing the democratization of media.

PC 820. SMALL, WILLIAM. To Kill a Messenger: Television News and the Real World. New York: Hastings House, 1970. 302 pp.
Small's defense of television news reporting praises the medium's immediacy, accessibility, and accuracy and examines the conflict between commercial and journalistic concerns. Small begins by surveying the historical highlights of TV news coverage and goes on to examine social and political events in which TV played a significant role, including the Civil Rights Movement, Nixon's Checkers Speech, and the 1968 Democratic National Convention. He is able to reveal different aspects and uses of the television medium through discussions of television and urban disorders, news coverage of Vietnam and the antiwar movement, such regulatory concerns as the Fairness Doctrine, and such political uses of the medium as the coverage of political conventions, the relationship between the Executive branch and television networks, and Congressional coverage.

PC 821. SMEAD, ELMER E. Freedom of Speech by Radio and Television. Washington, D.C.: Public Affairs Press, 1959. 182 pp.
This study is concerned with the competing definitions of public interest offered by the FCC, Congress, the Judicial branch, and radio and television broadcasters. Smead analyzes the competition—and frequent conflict— between these interests by looking at a range of issues, such as broadcasting of offensive or defamatory material, political campaign coverage, control and censorship of news reporting, and the relative merits of government regulation and industry self-regulation. He finds that the FCC, while theoretically objective in the exercise of its administrative authority, is in fact quite susceptible to Congressional pressure; furthermore, contrary to broadcasters' claims, the FCC has been reasonably restrained in its use of regulatory sanctions.

PC 822. SMITH, ANTHONY. The Shadow in the Cave: The Broadcaster, His Audience and the State. Urbana: University of Illinois Press, 1973. 351 pp.
This history of broadcasting in the U.S. and Britain attempts to demonstrate how broadcast media came to possess such extensive control over the knowledge and desires of citizens, and how the tensions between broadcasters and national leaders developed. Tracing the ideology of impartiality which governs journalists, he argues that broadcasters have always

had to weave a narrow path between potential sedition and utter insipidity. This has led them, at times, to satisfy no one in reporting news except those members of the audience who desire cheap drama. Smith argues for the development of courageous programming founded on the actual shared values of the broadcaster and the audience.

PC 823. SPRAGENS, WILLIAM C. The Presidency and the Mass Media in the Age of Television. Washington, D.C.: University Press of America, 1978. 425 pp.
Primarily concentrating on the administrations since FDR, Spragens analyzes the important relationship between the Presidency and mass media, and the importance of television and "image" politics in nearly all political relationships. He focuses special attention on the White House press secretaries and the White House press office, as well as on the way in which television networks, metropolitan daily newspapers, wire services, magazines, and other components of the mass media handle news about the Presidency. Both the media and the Presidency are analyzed as institutions; Spragens examines the current relationship between them and predicts the future course of this relationship.

PC 824. STAVINS, RALPH L., ed. Television Today: The End of Communication and the Death of Community. Washington, D.C.: Institute for Policy Studies/Communication Service Corp., 1969. 292 pp.
The performance of Washington, D.C. TV stations is used as a case study to examine the concept of "broadcasters' responsibility." Essays discuss how "operating in the public interest" is defined by the FCC, its relationship to broadcast license renewal, and the attempts made by local stations to fulfill their responsibility to the community within which they operate. Five essays make up a theoretical discussion of TV which establishes the conflict between commercial and community interests, identifies the relationship of television to various groups within the viewing audience, analyzes TV programs and potential alternatives, and explores several definitions of "public interest." Stavins uses a chapter which contains quantitive research on broadcasting in the mid-Atlantic states and a chapter which attempts to establish the programming needs of Washington, D.C.'s black community as the bases for this negative evaluation of Washington local stations' performance in the public interest. Also included are excerpts of documents relevant to presenting a FCC license challenge.

PC 825. STEINER, GARY A. The People Look at Television: A Study of Audience Attitudes. New York: Knopf, 1963. 422 pp.
Steiner attempts to describe the "average American viewer" through a lengthy survey of television audiences. Measurement of audience attitudes toward the medium identifies the dependence of Americans on television—and the guilt they feel while watching it. Factors such as educational level, amount and degree of satisfaction, and favorite types of programs are connected to give an overall picture of TV audience demographics and viewer attitudes in 1960. Other information reported by Steiner includes audience reactions to various kinds of commercials, the relationship of program selection to what is offered, television's relation to leisure activities (especially within the family), and the degree of correspondence between what people say about television and their actual behavior. Steiner includes copies of the questionnaires used and a description of his methodology.

PC 826. TAYLOR, SHERRIL W., ed. Radio Programming in Action: Realities and Opportunities. New York: Hastings House, 1967. 183 pp.
Taylor believes that radio is in the process of expanding into a medium of greater proportions than ever before. Radio, he argues, is capable of reaching a wide variety of specialized audiences not available to television. He has amassed twenty-seven papers by radio professionals address-

ing potential developments in news and public service programming, music, sports, and entertainment in large and small radio markets.

PC 827. TUCHMAN, GAYE, ed. The TV Establishment: Programming for Power and Profit. Englewood Cliffs, N.J.: Prentice-Hall, 1974. 186 pp.
The essays included in this anthology are based on the premise that television content reflects society's values, ideals, and socioeconomic perspective. Several authors explore American commercial television's legitimization of the status quo and the limits subsequently imposed upon the kinds of ideas presented on TV. Individual essays analyze the ownership and regulation of the industry to reveal how the structure and organization of American television influences news, public affairs, and entertainment programming so that the long range effects of television support American consumerism and the limiting of dissent and to some extent control political and intellectual discourse.

PC 828. TUROW, JOSEPH. Entertainment, Education, and the Hard Sell: Three Decades of Network Children's Television. New York: Praeger, 1981. 153 pp.
Turow examines television programming designed for children that appeared on the three commercial networks from 1948-78 in an attempt to chart the shape of that programming and to place it into the context of developments within the TV industry. The author divides the period of his study into three sections (1948-59, 1960-69, 1970-78). In each section he traces the changing shape of children's programming, describes its content, characters, themes, and scheduling, and places this description in the context of television economics and regulation at the time. Turow concludes by examining the implications of his observations for future children's programming.

PC 829. UDELSON, JOSEPH H. The Great Television Race: A History of the American Television Industry 1925-1941. University: University of Alabama Press, 1982. 197 pp.
Udelson notes that most histories of the development of television severely understate events in the medium's development that occurred prior to W.W. II. He begins his study with the invention of the first workable television techniques in 1925 and follows developments in the engineering, programming, and marketing of early television. Udelson describes the first television boom (lasting roughly from 1925-33), the variety of programs offered, the marketing of commercially manufactured receivers, and the subsiding of this boom due to the low quality of image reception. He then examines patent disputes between alternative television systems and the FCC's refusal to officially authorize the television medium until uniform, industry-wide standards could be established, in part through the efforts of the National Television System Committee. Udelson concludes with a discussion of the commercialization of the medium in the late 1930s and early 1940s.

PC 830. WERTHEIM, ARTHUR F. Radio Comedy. New York: Oxford University Press, 1979. 439 pp.
Setting his history in the context of the role of humor in the American character, Wertheim traces the development of radio comedy as a distinct form of entertainment. While concentrating on specific performers such as Freeman Gosden, Charles Correll, Jack Benny, and Fred Allen, as well as on various character types culled from the iconography of traditional American humor, he emphasizes the comedian's relation to the public, especially with regard to such historical calamities as the Depression and W.W. II. Noting that radio comedy developed in response to the needs of an unhappy nation, Wertheim begins with the earliest examples of humor on the radio--quick jokes by musicians--and then analyzes the comedy of

the Depression, the maturing of radio comedy in Benny's routines of the late 1930s and the small town and middle-American shows like <u>Fibber McGee and Molly</u>, the dressy, slick performers of the 1940s such as Fred Allen and Edgar Bergen, and the final subsidence of the genre with the advent of television in the early 1950s.

PC 831. **WHITE, LLEWELLYN.** <u>The American Radio: A Report on the Broadcasting Industry in the United States from The Commission on Freedom of the Press</u>. Chicago: University of Chicago Press, 1947. 260 pp.

White traces the development of radio from Marconi's early experiments to the advent of television. He looks at a range of topics, including advances in radio technology, the evolution of network broadcasting, competition and monopoly-building within the industry, and government regulation of radio in the areas of licensing, antitrust, and free speech. White is particularly concerned with the harmful effects of advertising's domination of radio, arguing that product sales take precedence over programs of social and educational value to the listening public. The report recommends that the industry separate advertising from programs and devote prime listening hours to public-interest broadcasts, that the Federal government adopt policies to promote new local and non-commercial stations, and that radio listeners organize to evaluate and shape the policies of stations and industry groups.

PC 832. **WINN, MARIE.** <u>The Plug-In Drug</u>. New York: Viking Press, 1977. 231 pp.

This work illuminates the psychological, cultural, and social effects of television. Winn bases her conclusions on various scientific studies of the psychological and physiological effects of TV viewing, as well as interviews with parents, children, teachers, social workers, television executives, and psychologists. The concept of "TV addiction" is examined in light of the physiological effects of TV viewing and the extent to which the medium induces a change in consciousness. Winn explores the differences in concentration involved in TV viewing and reading and discusses the results of prolonged exposure to television violence. Television's effect on children is the focus of much of this book as Winn considers television's effect upon a child's perception of the world, its impact on the play activities of children, and its influence on child-rearing strategies.

PC 833. **WITHEY, STEPHEN B.** and **RONALD P. ABELES,** eds. <u>Television and Social Behavior: Beyond Violence and Children</u>. Hillsdale, N.J.: Lawrence Erlbaum, 1980. 356 pp.

These essays explore the relationship between television and viewer behavior. They examine such methodological and conceptual problems of TV research as the ability to isolate television's influence from other factors and the difficulty of using new research perspectives and directions. Included in this volume is a description of the psychological effects of black stereotypes on both black and white viewers. Several essays discuss television and children, covering such areas as the effect of TV viewing on cognitive development, TV's ability or inability to provide models of effective decision-making, and the limits of children's understanding of TV. Other essays discuss the organizational and economic context of the TV industry and the relationship between TV, audiences, the industry, and researchers.

PC 834. WILLIAMS, FREDERICK, ROBERT LaROSE, and FREDERICK FROST. Children, Television and Sex-Role Stereotyping. New York: Praeger, 1981. 161 pp.
Observing that sex roles are heavily stereotyped on television, the authors explore the prospect of reforming these stereotypes and using TV to bring about "more balanced social attitudes." Williams, LaRose, and Frost examine how children learn about social roles from television by reviewing and summarizing previous research on the subject. Studies of sex-role biases in children and of the results of exposure to nonstereotypic TV characters are included. A chapter is also devoted to outlining a theory on the processes whereby television-viewing shapes children's attitudes and behavior.

PC 835. WOLF, FRANK. Television Programming for News and Public Affairs: A Quantitative Analysis of Networks and Stations. New York: Praeger, 1972. 203 pp.
Wolf assumes that TV acts as an "agent of political socialization" and seeks to identify factors which determine the amount of news and public affairs programming on commercial television. His findings are based upon interviews, questionnaires, and a survey of program schedules undertaken between 1966 and 1971. Finding the structure of television ownership to be much less significant in determining programming than is widely assumed, Wolf analyzes the impact of FCC regulations and finds that they too have very limited actual effect. The organizational relationship between networks and their local affiliates is also discounted as a factor. Wolf concludes that the economic structure of television as an industry is the primary factor in determining the quantity of public affairs programming.

NEWSPAPERS/JOURNALISM

PC 836. ARGYRIS, CHRIS. Behind the Front Page. San Francisco: Jossey-Bass, 1974. 305 pp.
Argyris, a behavioral scientist, analyzes the organizational health of American newspapers in order to discover what must be done to create self-examining, self-regulating newspapers in an industry known for its stolidity, hypersensitivity to criticism, and conservatism. Argyris's three-year "multi-research" case study of a newspaper he calls The Daily Planet "focuses on the internal processes by which one newspaper maintains itself as a system." His intention is to understand and help excise those forces that "lead to organizational dry-rot and inhibit self-examination." The book is divided into three parts. The first sets forth Argyris's theoretical framework, and presents a detailed diagnosis of The Daily Planet's organizational ills and their consequences. The second part describes attempts to address those ills from within through the establishment of a mechanism for self-examination. The author analyzes the results of those attempts, and their reception within the company. In the final part of the book he discusses the implications of these results.

PC 837. BABB, LAURA LONGLEY, ed. Of the Press, by the Press, for the Press (and Others, too): A Critical Study of the Inside Workings of the News Business. Washington, D.C.: Washington Post Writers Group, 1974. 246 pp.
This collection of writings by members of the Washington Post staff is an attempt at self-criticism; the journalists criticize both their own paper and the press in general. In the introduction, Philip Geyelin discusses the establishment of a critical mechanism at the Post. This mechan-

ism partly consisted of "F.Y.I."--For Your Information--editorials that "praised and censured" developments at the Post, at other papers, and in other media.   In addition, the Post established an ombudsman whose responsibilities were to monitor and criticize the Post's performance, to answer reader complaints, and to contribute regularly to an editorial column called "The News Business" that "served as a vehicle for commentary by other staff members and by outsiders" on the operation of the Post and other news-disseminating organizations. This book is a compilation of "F.Y.I." editorials, News Business columns, and internally circulated critical memos written by the Post's first ombudsman, Richard Harwood.

PC 838. BAGDIKIAN, BEN H. The Effete Conspiracy and Other Crimes by the
         Press. New York: Harper & Row, 1972. 159 pp.
The fifteen essays collected in this volume, most of which originally appeared in the Columbia Journalism Review between 1962 and 1971, cover a variety of topics. Bagdikian examines, often with sarcasm, the Du Pont family's enduring control over two Delaware dailies; Senator J. William Fulbright's 1963 investigation into how public relations concerns representing foreign governments and companies influence news coverage in the U.S.; the issues raised when the subsidiary of a corporate conglomerate happens to be a newspaper; and the printing of the Pentagon Papers. Seven of the essays deal with the relationship of the press with the Presidency, under the Kennedy, Johnson, and Nixon administrations in particular. One theme persists: Bagdikian's belief that the daily press is conservative, contrary to the accusations (most energetically pursued by the Nixon-Agnew administration) that the press is involved in a "liberal conspiracy"-- the "effete conspiracy" of the title--to wreck traditional values.

PC 839. BALK, ALFRED. A Free and Responsive Press: The Twentieth Century
         Fund Task Force Report for a National News Council. New York:
         Twentieth Century Fund, 1973. 88 pp.
Concerned with preserving the freedom of the press and improving its performance, the Twentieth Century Fund (a research group that studies major social, political, and economic institutions) established a task force in 1971 to consider the feasibility of creating a press council in the U.S. This volume includes a short overview of the decision reached by the task force--that a national news council is necessary--and a lengthy background paper presented to the task force by the author. Balk describes the crisis of credibility that has threatened the press, noting the recent intensity and abundance of press criticism from the government, the courts, within the press itself, and in public opinion surveys. He discusses the British Press Council as well as local press councils in the U.S. He also emphasizes the need for journalists to realize expanded consumer participation in, and a growing humanization of, the press as an institution. His conclusions helped influence the task force to call for a national press council that would receive and examine complaints concerning news reporting and that would initiate its own studies and reports on issues involving freedom of the press.

PC 840. BENT, SILAS. Newspaper Crusaders: A Neglected Story. New York:
         McGraw-Hill, 1939. 313 pp.
Since its inception in America, the newspaper has operated not only as a disseminator of information but also as a medium of political ideas and ethics. In its latter function, according to Bent, it has served as an energetic, often powerful crusader. Bent surveys the intentions and accomplishments of the foremost crusaders--Joseph Pulitzer, William Randolph Hearst, E. W. Scripps--and the foremost crusades, including the establishment of a Constitution, the Alien Sedition Acts, corruption in Tammany Hall, child labor laws, and organized crime.

PC 841. BESSIE, SIMON MICHAEL. Jazz Journalism: The Story of the Tabloid
         Newspapers. 1939; Rev. ed. New York: Russell & Russell, 1969.
         247 pp.
Bessie surveys the rise of tabloid newspapers in the late 19th century
and describes the enthusiastic popular response and the equally fervent
negative response of the established press, the church, and the "upper
ranges of the social ladder." He discusses the way Americans characteristically reach moral judgment, contending that denunciations of the tabloids are a function of the "spectacular" contrast between the national
moral attitudes and the facts of national life. Bessie is concerned with
the reasons the tabloid appeared and prospered, and argues that it was
part of a pattern that included speakeasies, jazz, movie-star worship,
and other "gigantic exaggerations" of the time, all of which signaled
deeper forces operating in "the heart of a post-war America."

PC 842. BLEYER, WILLARD G. Main Currents in the History of American Jour-
         nalism. Boston: Houghton Mifflin, 1927. 464 pp.
Bleyer traces the influences that shaped the course of the American press
and the problems it faced in the early years of the 20th century. Rather
than try to present a complete history in a single volume, he discusses
only the most influential newspapers and editors, treating at length their
role in the development of the American press from an assortment of crude
handbills to the vast, highly sophisticated, internationally influential
major newspapers of the 20th century. Because British journalism was
important in shaping American journalism before 1800, the work's first
chapter sketches the evolution of the British press.

PC 843. BOGART, LEO. Press and Public: Who Reads What, When, Where,
         and Why in American Newspapers. Hillsdale, N.J.: Erlbaum, 1981.
         285 pp.
The author analyzes the recent history of the American newspaper industry.
Newspapers enjoyed a long period of power and prosperity, but in the 1970s
and the early 1980s circulation growth dropped off. The ascendancy of
newspaper chains and "media conglomerates" threatens the local independent
press, and the industry is challenged by the technology of home communication systems, which provide access to huge volumes of information and
news. In order for newspapers to maintain a "folk awareness," to record
and be the voice of community life, and to maintain individuality within
the community, those who run newspapers must adapt to a changing public.
Bogart focuses his analysis on this public and its demands. He discusses
reading habits among different age groups and across different economic
and regional backgrounds, the reasons that readers select particular newspapers, and the effects of these habits and choices on editorial policy.
Bogart contends that newspapers are not only compatible with change and
public demand, they are indispensable: no other medium can provide "the
newspaper's command of big ideas, its traditions of inquiry, sweeping
synthesis, and inspired advocacy."

PC 844. BRIGHAM, CLARENCE S. History and Bibliography of American News-
         papers 1690-1820. 2 vols. Worcester, Mass.: American Antiquar-
         ian Society, 1947. 1508 pp.
Brigham's plan is to "write a brief historical account of each newspaper,
with exact dates of changes of titles and names of publishers, followed
by a checklist of all files located." He does this for 2120 newspapers
spanning twenty-nine states and the District of Columbia. He also provides
an alphabetical listing of newspapers by state with information about
the printers and current holdings, and an index of titles and printers.

PC 845. BRIGHAM, CLARENCE S. Journals and Journeymen: A Contribution
to the History of Early American Newspapers. Philadelphia:
University of Pennsylvania Press, 1950. 114 pp.
This set of lectures concerning various features of early American news-
paper history is arranged topically, and contains historical information
Brigham gathered while compiling his lengthy Bibliography of American
Newspapers. Brigham devotes his short "memoranda" to such topics as late
Colonial and early 19th-century circulation rates, advertising (including
the advent of headlines), the delay in receiving news of world events,
inflammatory editorializing, and women newspaper publishers.

PC 846. BROWN, LEE. The Reluctant Reformation: On Criticizing the Press
in America. New York: McKay, 1974. 244 pp.
In this study of the press and press criticism, Brown contends that the
press has often been slow to heed its critics and reluctant to adopt
reforms. In the first chapter, Brown discusses the responsibility of the
press toward the public interest, and elucidates theories of press criticism on the basis of this responsibility. In subsequent chapters he argues
for the necessity of press criticism, surveys its history, and treats
in detail the newer attempts by the press at self-criticism, especially
in the form of a national press council. He includes six appendices that
"suggest the ethical basis for press criticism" and that describe the
results of a variety of monitoring activities and experiments in criticism
conducted in recent years.

PC 847. BRUCKER, HERBERT. Communication Is Power: Unchanging Values
in a Changing Journalism. New York: Oxford University Press,
1973. 385 pp.
Brucker's evaluation of the press is based on his contention that the
U.S. "must strive constantly . . . to democratize its communications."
The focus of this work is on who, in fact, directs the enormous power
of the press in this country. Recent government attempts to circumscribe
or manipulate the press are, Brucker asserts, a threat to the nation:
only when the press is free to accurately report news, acting as the agent
of the people and giving them a voice, does a democracy function effectively. While acknowledging that journalism is a business, Brucker decries
the growing corporate involvement in the press and other media. He argues
for greater access to and for the press, less partisan and self-aggrandizing reporting, and the necessity for press councils.

PC 848. BULLOCK, PENELOPE L. The Afro-American Periodical Press: 1838-
1909. Baton Rouge: Louisiana State University Press, 1981.
330 pp.
Bullock discusses the cultural origins, functions, and influence of ninety-
seven black periodicals published between 1838 and 1909. She begins with
a short overview of the social and political background of these periodicals, and then conducts a longer examination of their evolution. She
concludes with an analysis of the major trends and recurrent themes.
Three appendices--publications data and selected "finding" list, a chronology, and a geographic distribution chart--provide bibliographic material.

PC 849. CASEY, RALPH D., ed. The Press in Perspective. Baton Rouge:
Louisiana State University Press, 1963. 217 pp.
This collection of lectures, delivered between 1947 and 1963 at the University of Minnesota, focuses on the need for the press to give greater
attention to the meaning and interpretation of news and, more generally,
on its need continually to upgrade its performance as a trustee of the
public interest. Casey includes lectures by professional journalists--
among others, James Reston on the conservatism and reticence of the press
in foreign affairs and Eric Sevareid on the intellectually arid "one-
dimensionality" of most news reporting--and he includes lectures by such

observers of the American media as Henry Steele Commager, who speaks on government violation of the civil liberties of the press, and Reinhold Niebuhr, on the "moral obligations" of newspapermen. Other lecturers include Herbert Block, Pierre Salinger, Joseph Alsop, Jr., and Elmer Davis.

PC 850. CATER, DOUGLASS. The Fourth Branch of Government. Boston:
         Houghton Mifflin, 1959. 194 pp.
Cater believes that publicity is "uniquely indispensable to the American system of government," and that Washington correspondents therefore function as "middlemen" in the formulation of policy, often mediating between a mutually antagonistic Congress and President. Though he provides a chapter-long historical account of Washington news coverage, Cater gathers most of the evidence for his notion of "government by publicity" from the Federal bureaucracy under the Truman and Eisenhower administrations and its simultaneous efforts to maintain secrecy and to leak information to the public. In individual chapters he examines the Question Period in the British House of Commons (and compares it with the Presidential press conference in the U.S.), and the Soviet press and its relationship to government.

PC 851. CLARKE, PETER and SUSAN H. EVANS. Covering Campaigns: Journalism
         in Congressional Elections. Stanford, Calif.: Stanford Univer-
         sity Press, 1983. 151 pp.
Clarke and Evans describe and explain political reporting and editorializing by newspapers during Congressional elections. They discuss the knowledgeability of journalists covering elections, the manner in which these journalists select their information, and whether their treatment of a candidate varies with the candidate's influence. The authors also describe how voters are affected by newspaper coverage of election campaigns. They conclude that journalists are neither activists nor conspirators; rather, journalists generally approach their work in an even-tempered, even routine manner; this attitude often leads to conservatism and retrenchment. Finally, Clarke and Evans ask journalists, candidates, and campaign aides to evaluate their findings and to make suggestions for improving the current state of affairs.

PC 852. COHEN, BERNARD C. The Press and Foreign Policy. Princeton, N.J.:
         Princeton University Press, 1963. 288 pp.
Cohen investigates the impact of newspapers on the U.S. government's foreign policy. First, he discusses the press as observer, focusing on the search for foreign policy news, and the presentation of that news. Second, he discusses the press as participant, concentrating on the reciprocal influence of foreign policy coverage and policy-making. Finally, he discusses the press as catalyst, describing the ways the public uses the press to satisfy its interest in foreign affairs, and the impact of this interest on foreign policy coverage. The overarching issue, Cohen states, involves the "competing demands of diplomacy and democracy on the organization and conduct of foreign affairs reporting." He believes that these demands are incompatible, that a new set of reportorial practices is in order, and offers a number of suggestions in his conclusion.

PC 853. CROUSE, TIMOTHY. The Boys on the Bus. New York: Random House,
         1973. 383 pp.
Crouse's insider's account of the press coverage of the 1972 Presidential campaign begins during the Democratic primaries and continues through President Nixon's re-election and Watergate. Crouse's focus is on the inner workings of "pack journalism," a term describing the way groups of reporters must follow a single candidate for weeks or months, "like a pack of hounds sicked on a fox." The reporters travel together on buses (hence the title) and planes, eat together, drink, gamble, and compare notes together. With few exceptions, caution and toeing the line are

the rule, the stories published are almost identical, and making waves
or trying for any kind of big scoop is generally frowned upon. Crouse
recounts in anecdotal form the "camaraderie, hardship, and luxury" of
life on the campaign trail, describing the many events (most of which
never made the news) and personalities that combined to make 1972 an especially chaotic, influential, and disturbing year for journalists and for
the press as an institution.

PC 854. DEEDY, JOHN G., Jr., ROBERT LEKACHMAN, MARTIN E. MARTY, and
         DAVID WOLF SILVERMAN. The Religious Press in America. New York:
         Holt, Rinehart & Winston, 1963. 184 pp.
This study of the nature and aims of the religious press and its interaction with the society at large is divided into four essays. Marty writes
on the Protestant press, Deedy on the Catholic press, Silverman on the
Jewish press, and Lekachman on what he calls "the secular uses of the
religious press." The latter urges the various religious presses to maintain a rigorous self-criticism and to describe--not merely emphasize--
the relevance of their tradition to the problems all people share. Each
of the four contributors discusses the audiences of these presses and
their interests, the intellectual and emotional assumptions of the audiences, the nature of news in a religious publication, the practice of
interpreting religiously political situations, and the influence or "effectiveness" of the publications.

PC 855. DENNIS, EVERETT E. and WILLIAM L. RIVERS. Other Voices: The
         New Journalism in America. San Francisco: Harper & Row, 1974.
         218 pp.
New Journalism is the name Dennis and Rivers apply to the journalistic
styles that, finding their impetus in the turbulence of the 1960s, are
premised on a "dissatisfaction with existing values and standards," with
the colorlessness of traditional journalism, and with the wrongheaded
and impossible struggle for objectivity. The authors treat at length
the nature and practice of the seven fundamental expressions of New Journalism: new non-fiction, which emphasizes scene and style in an attempt
to color the objective reality of journalism with the subjective reality
of novels; alternative journalism, which generally aims to be controversial
and unfriendly to centers of power and to what alternative journalists
consider a debilitated traditional press; journalism reviews, which are
newspapers or magazines written by journalists that criticize improper
journalistic practices; advocacy journalism, which is clearly partisan
writing; counter-culture journalism, which includes the underground press
and underground news services; alternative broadcasting, which takes the
form of alternative TV and radio stations; and precision journalism, which
uses sophisticated technological and statistical tolls to make reporting
as purely scientific as possible.

PC 856. DETWEILER, FREDERICK G. The Negro Press in the United States.
         Chicago: University of Chicago Press, 1922. 274 pp.
Detweiler's early study of the black press helped introduce little-known
but durable and ardent press to mainstream white culture. This survey
begins with black self-expression during the period of slavery. These
efforts include folk songs, spirituals, and oration. During this time,
two free black men in the North, Samuel Cornish and John B. Russell, published the first black periodical, Freedom's Journal, in 1827. Although
Freedom's Journal died three years later due to a lack of funds, other
periodicals (twenty-four altogether in the antebellum era), as well as
pamphlets and tracts, began circulating. Detweiler traces the histories
of these publications through the Emancipation and Reconstruction and
into the first three decades of the 20th century. He discusses recurrent
themes, the efforts made by this press to eliminate racial oppression
and prejudice, operational details, and content, including editorials,

poetry, and advertising, and the way they reflect and criticize black life in America in the early part of the 20th century.

PC 857. DOWNIE, LEONARD, Jr. The New Muckrakers. Washington, D.C.: New Republic Book, 1976. 269 pp.
In Downie's opinion, the great surge of investigative reporting in the early 1970s "considerably influenced" the course of the nation. The author approaches this modern investigative reporting, or muckraking, by discussing the efforts and objectives of several of its most well-known practitioners. Woodward and Bernstein, whose legendary successes unleashed a torrent of investigative reports around the country, are discussed at length, as are, among others, Seymour Hersh, who "turned around" public opinion on the Vietnam War by uncovering the atrocities at My Lai; Jack Anderson, whose column on corruption and duplicity in Washington has been for several years "the cutting edge" of American investigative reporting; and I. F. Stone, who for nearly two decades decried the ills and excesses of American government in his newsletter, I. F. Stone's Weekly. Downie also discusses New Journalism, the alternative press, and public response to and the future prospects for the muckraking approach to reporting.

PC 858. EMERY, EDWIN. The Press and America: An Interpretive History of the Mass Media. 1954; Rev. ed. Englewood Cliffs, N.J.: Prentice-Hall, 1978. 574 pp.
Emery's history of the American press emphasizes the correlation between journalism and the political, economic, and social trends of each era. He begins in Europe, from whose roots American journalism grew. The first part of the book establishes the journalistic principles which arose out of and were shaped by historical forces up to the time of the Civil War. The remaining chapters treat developments in the modern media and, in this newest edition, contain detailed discussions of the broadcast media. Included are chapters devoted to the press and the Vietnam War, the Pentagon Papers, the black press, and the underground press. The volume is amply illustrated and includes annotated bibliographies after each chapter.

PC 859. EMERY, EDWIN and EDWIN H. FORD. Highlights in the History of the American Press. Minneapolis: University of Minnesota Press, 1954. 398 pp.
Emery and Ford describe this collection of articles, produced over the course of a century, as a "supplement to the established histories of journalism." While admitting that a compilation lacks the continuity, "the singleness of purpose," found in the work of a single writer, the authors point out that it makes possible a "catholicity" of viewpoints that one writer could not hope to achieve. Emergy and Ford organize the selections into six historical periods, beginning with the rise of the English press, continuing through the Colonial, Revolutionary, Jacksonian, and Reconstruction eras into the age of mass circulation and "press giants." Because less is known about the early decades of the press, the essays in the first sections of the book, with the exception of considerations of Daniel Defoe by John Dos Passos and of Benjamin Franklin by Albert Henry Smyth, discuss general trends. Essays concerning later developments generally focus on particular editors and publishers who were representative of their age. The subjects of these essays include Horace Greeley, Joseph Pulitzer, and Adolph Ochs.

PC 860. EPSTEIN, EDWARD J. Between Fact and Fiction: The Problem of Journalism. New York: Random House, 1975. 232 pp.
In this collection of essays written during the late 1960s and early 1970s, Epstein takes as his subject the inherent inability of journalists to establish the truth about issues they report. Unlike legal authorities, they cannot compel information from a witness; instead, they are dependent upon and cannot afford to alienate self-aggrandizing sources who may lie

or distort the truth. In addition, journalists for the most part "lack the technical competence to evaluate evidence with any authority" and, faced with the daily pressure of printing a newsworthy story, must proceed without verification. The only alternative to merely recapitulating the possibly fraudulent testimony of a source is for journalists to recast the testimony into their own version of the story. In either case, the public learns of "news"--the "signalizing" of an event, as Walter Lippman says--rather than truth, "the hidden facts." Epstein discusses the nature and implications of journalism as news reporting rather than as truth-seeking, examining press coverage of, for example, the Black Panthers, the Pentagon Papers, and Watergate.

PC 861. EPSTEIN, LAURILY KEIR, ed. Women and the News. New York: Hastings House, 1978. 144 pp.
This collection of essays is the product of a conference on "Women and the News" held at Washington University in St. Louis in 1977. The essays are based on the premise that the media play "an important role in defin-ing women's status." Three essays address the effect upon women and women's issues of the media's function as a personal "agenda-setter"--that is, the way those stories emphasized in the news become emphasized by the reader in his or her personal list of urgent issues. In addition, several essays are devoted to the inability of women and other "disadvan-taged" or "marginal" groups to receive equitable news coverage, a problem that is exacerbated by imprecise and often self-justifying definitions of news and newsworthiness on the part of editors, producers, and pub-lishers.

PC 862. FINKLE, LEE. Forum for Protest: The Black Press During World
War II. Rutherford, N.J.: Fairleigh Dickinson University Press,
1975. 249 pp.
Finkle contends that the black American press has historically, with few exceptions, argued for social change only within existing institutions and in the name of white America's ideals. This conservatism became most apparent and was most deeply challenged when America was involved in W.W. II. Many of the nation's blacks, alienated by discrimination, were apa-thetic about the war. Black newspaper editors, already convinced that an "exemplary war record would aid the black community in gaining equal-ity," began to adopt increasingly militant language to encourage blacks to "'fight for the right to fight.'" This study focuses on the aims and rhetoric of black newspapers during the war, as well as the reaction to these papers and their editorial views among blacks and whites. Finkle focuses this study on the largest black papers. The author elucidates their positions toward the Japanese and the Axis powers and on a variety of wartime issues, including racial proscription in the selective service, black life in army camps and in war theaters, and the agenda for social change on the homefront during the war.

PC 863. FISHMAN, MARK. Manufacturing the News. Austin: University of
Texas Press, 1980. 180 pp.
Fishman contends that the way a society comes to know itself receives little scholarly attention despite the fact that the process of self-learning is also one of self-shaping. Fishman's focus is on the social construction of "the public reality of mass media news." He is interested in the formative role the media play in constructing "large-scale social phenomena," such as mental illness or crime. He investigates the process whereby news accounts are produced so as to "create and recreate" those phenomena they report.

PC 864. FORSYTH, DAVID P. The Business Press in America: 1750-1860.
Philadelphia: Chilton Books, 1964. 394 pp.
Unlike popular magazines or the daily press, the business newspaper, which
is devoted to "the specific interests of a specific industry, trade, profession, or occupational group," makes its readers proficient in their
field by disseminating new, specifically relevant information. Though
it wields enormous influence, often greater than that of other media,
its history has not received much attention. Forsyth's book focuses on
the first 115 years of business paper publishing in this country, ranging
from its "embryonic" phase to the period preceding its greatest growth.
After briefly surveying the history of business communications from ancient
Egypt to Colonial America, Forsyth proceeds to describe the establishment
and growth of the business press against the backdrop of economic developments. He devotes chapters to papers in all the major publication classifications, including the railroad, mining and metalworking, printing, and
petroleum.

PC 865. GERALD, J. EDWARD. The Social Responsibility of the Press.
Minneapolis: University of Minnesota Press, 1963. 214 pp.
Gerald's purpose is to describe the "market place" of information and
entertainment, along with its "journalistic products," and to analyze
the influence these products have now and can have in the future upon
the social institutions necessary to "self-government." The responsibility
of the press is, in his opinion, to exist symbiotically with these institutions, thereby perpetuating and strengthening the nation's health.
Gerald's analysis incorporates elements of social and economic history,
political theory, and social and behavioral science.

PC 866. GLESSING, ROBERT J. The Underground Press in America. Bloomington:
Indiana University Press, 1970. 207 pp.
Glessing's survey of the history, nature, aims, and implications of the
underground press was written around the height of that movement. He
describes the history of underground newspapers as "largely a chronicle
of youthful reaction to the technical, political, and cultural conditions
in the American society." The perspective and aspirations of these newspapers were divorced from, and committed to subverting, established values
and practices. Glessing describes the often unorthodox (and unprofitable)
economic operations of the newspapers, their editorial practices, their
readership, and their impact. He concludes with an optimistic, if guarded,
appraisal of their future.

PC 867. HARRISON, JOHN M. and HARRY H. STEIN, eds. Muckraking: Past
Present, and Future. University Park: Pennsylvania State University Press, 1973. 165 pp.
With the rise of investigative journalism in the 1960s and 1970s, the
practices and larger purposes of so-called muckraking journalism have
enjoyed a new respect. Harrison and Stein have collected a set of essays
that re-examine—and for the most part vindicate—early 20th-century muckrakers, and trace muckraking efforts in contemporary journalism. The
essays establish, from a variety of perspectives, the stimulating,
generally therapeutic role of muckrakers in 20th-century American life.
Among the issues addressed are the relationship between muckrakers and
the middle class; the muckrakers' effect upon race relations; law, justice,
and the muckrakers; and the muckrakers' aesthetics.

PC 868. HESS, STEPHEN. The Washington Reporters. Washington, D.C.:
Brookings Institution, 1981. 174 pp.
Hess investigates the attitudes of Washington journalists toward politics,
politicians, and co-workers, as well as the nature of their assignments
and the kinds of stories they produce. He discovers that many members
of the Washington press corps feel that they ought to do more "in-depth"

reporting, but resist becoming specialists. Furthermore, Hess discovers that few have strong political beliefs. What draws journalists to Washington, he believes, is not an interest in the political process, but rather the excitement and attraction of proximity to powerful personalities.

PC 869. HESS, STEPHEN and MILTON KAPLAN. The Ungentlemanly Art: A History of American Political Cartoons. 1968; Rev. ed. New York: Macmillan, 1975. 252 pp.

From Benjamin Franklin, who originated American political cartooning with his famous serpent cartoon in 1754, to Jules Feiffer's caricatures of Nixon, American political cartoonists have served as representatives of their age and as voices of protest. Often men with no artistic training, they developed the political cartoon from a simple lithograph disseminated in handbills and tracts to elaborate illustrations that exercise enormous influence on readership rates and on the sensibilities of readers. Hess and Kaplan survey the evolution of the American political cartoon in newspapers and in such humor magazines as Judge and Puck. They present over 300 cartoons spanning 200 years, including numerous examples of the work of Thomas Nast, who conducted an extensive and highly damaging campaign against William "Boss" Tweed; Bill Mauldin, who gained widespread fame for his "G.I. Joe" W.W. II cartoons; and Herbert Block, perhaps the most influential 20th-century cartoonist, who attacked McCarthyism, the Atom bomb, and Watergate.

PC 870. HOHENBERG, JOHN. A Crisis for the American Press. New York: Columbia University Press, 1978. 316 pp.

Hohenberg argues that freedom of the press and the full exercise of First Amendment rights are being threatened by rising public antipathy, increasingly unfavorable judicial rulings, and the restricting efforts of a number of powerful political figures. He acknowledges the press' abuses, its self-righteousness, its fondness for provocation, "its violence and partisanship and other glaring imperfections," but he laments that these abuses have caused a crisis of confidence so pervasive and an antagonism and suppressiveness so energetic that the very notion of "an independent press in a democratic society will have to be fought out in the public arena again." Hohenberg contends that it is vital for all citizens in a democracy that the press wins this battle and retains its independence; compromise or defeat would be a subversion of the founding principles of the nation and would ultimately undercut the rights of free expression of all Americans.

PC 871. HUDSON, FREDERICK. Journalism in the United States, From 1690 to 1872. 1873; Reissued New York: Harper & Row, 1969. 789 pp.

Hudson divides U.S. journalism history into five eras, ranging from "The Beginning in Massachusetts" (1690-1704) to "The Independent Press" (1835-72). He discusses the gradual sophistication of the Colonial press, the press in the Revolutionary era, and the press as a vehicle for politically partisan rhetoric in the first half of the 19th century. His especially extensive discussion of the mid- to late-19th-century press includes overviews of such varied topics as female journalists, newspapers on the Pacific coast, the major New York City papers, war correspondents, comics, advertisements, and libel.

PC 872. HULTENG, JOHN L. The Messenger's Motives: Ethical Problems of the Mass Media. Englewood Cliffs, N.J.: Prentice-Hall, 1976. 262 pp.

The author argues that, although journalists face a barrage of ethical questions so complex and far-ranging that they "would tax a Solomon," the established guideposts and restraints within the media for answering these questions are "blurred, indistinct, or nonexistent." External restraints are also infrequent, and there are no monitoring agencies with any real authority. The degree to which a journalist adheres to ethical standards, finally, depends upon what he perceives those standards to be and upon his own integrity. Hulteng's objective is to raise a variety of these questions and to evaluate the different ways they have been addressed. His intent is to enable those in the media and those who study the media to begin offering solutions to these ethical questions.

PC 873. HYNDS, ERNEST C. American Newspapers in the 1980s. 1975; Rev. ed. New York: Hastings House, 1980. 383 pp.
This revision of his American Newspapers in the 1970s was necessitated, Hynds argues, by the ongoing "revolution" in media caused by technological advances and the changing needs of readers. Hynds's premise is unchanged: he believes other media can complement the newspaper, but that none can replace it; that the newspaper is essential to the functioning of individuals in a complex world and to the maintenance of "the democratic system." Hynds's aims also remain the same: he wants to help readers make the most of newspapers by describing what newspapers are, what they should be, and how they operate. He also wants to assist newspapers in "realizing more of their potential," and to this end discusses what they have done successfully in the past and what some plan to do in the future. Besides providing a brief history of the press in America, he describes the roles and responsibilities of newspapers, various aspects of their operation, and different types of papers. In his concluding chapter, he notes a number of the pacesetting newspapers throughout the U.S.

PC 874. JOHNSON, MICHAEL L. The New Journalism: The Underground Press, the Artists of Nonfiction, and Changes in the Established Media. Lawrence: University Press of Kansas, 1971. 171 pp.
In exploring the broad changes in journalism in the 1960s, Johnson considers not only the style and techniques of New Journalists such as Truman Capote, Norman Mailer, and Tom Wolfe, but he also discusses rock journalism, underground radio, and what he calls the New Muckrakers. He notes the limitations of established media and contends that the new forms of journalism have done a more thorough and honest job of responding to the profound political and social changes of the 1960s. The New Journalism emphasizes three categories of written journalism: underground publications; New Journalistic books; and examples of the established media's use of New Journalistic approaches. Johnson provides a brief history of the underground press and concludes with a chapter speculating on the future of New Journalism.

PC 875. JOHNSTONE, JOHN W. C., EDWARD J. SLAWSKI, and WILLIAM W. BOWMAN. The News People: A Sociological Portrait of American Journalists and Their Work. Urbana: University of Illinois Press, 1976. 257 pp.
Johnstone and his co-authors base this study on the contention that while there have been a number of analyses of various subgroups of journalists, no previous inquiry has "examined the full range of journalistic manpower in the American news media, and no study has focused simultaneously on backgrounds, careers, attitudes, and work." While demographically based, the authors' broad "frame of reference" also incorporates elements of social psychology and behavioral science. They describe the social background, training, and recruitment of journalists, their career histories, professional aspirations, on-the-job behavior and values, and job satisfaction, as well as working conditions, financial remuneration, and hierarchies and divisions of labor in the industry as a whole and at individual newspapers. The study is based on a national probability sample involving over 1300 interviews conducted in the fall of 1971.

PC 876. KAROLEVITZ, ROBERT. Newspapering in the Old West: A Pictorial History of Journalism and Printing on the Frontier. Seattle, Wash.: Superior, 1965. 191 pp.

The trailblazers and early settlers in the Old West craved news; they longed to know of affairs "back East" and they were anxious for the latest intelligence about the wilderness ahead of and around them. Karolevitz traces the adventures and accomplishments of the editors and publishers who established presses in the West to meet this demand and to make their own fortunes. This pictorial overview spans developments in the West from the first crude hand presses of pioneering publishers in the early decades of the 19th century, through the establishment of regular newspapers in the 1840s and 1850s and the advent of the age of mechanization at the end of the century. Karolevitz discusses newspapers in all the Western states, describing the effects of such forces as economic fluctuations in the mineral industries, technological developments in communications and transportation, Mormonism, crime, and natural phenomena. He hopes that the combination of his anecdotal narrative style and the vast selection of photographs will "recreate the flavor and the atmosphere of newspapering on the frontier."

PC 877. KERN, MONTAGUE, PATRICIA W. LEVERING, and RALPH B. LEVERING. The Kennedy Crises: The Press, the Presidency, and Foreign Policy. Chapel Hill: University of North Carolina Press, 1983. 290 pp.

The authors study the day-to-day coverage by five major newspapers of President Kennedy's foreign policy. They focus on four crises--Laos, Berlin, Cuba, and Vietnam--and on the way in which the President interacted with the press during these crises. The authors discuss how Kennedy successfully manipulated the press and tried to use his personality and power to control it, especially during times of anxiety and upheaval. However, between foreign policy crises, the press coverage of public opinion and of his political adversaries pushed Kennedy to adopt more aggressive policies. The authors conclude that though political factions defined the issues, press scrutiny tended to intensify them.

PC 878. KOBRE, SIDNEY. Foundations of American Journalism. Westport, Conn.: Greenwood Press, 1958. 362 pp.

Kobre's sociological survey focuses on the larger trends in American journalism during the 18th and 19th centuries. The crude sheets and handbills of the early Colonial period evolved into the comprehensive and highly sophisticated newspapers of the Civil War and Reconstruction. Kobre fixes his analysis on how this communication revolution reflected and affected American life. The press in America has been a highly dynamic and reactive institution propelled by rapid and chaotic social change and by the editors and publishers who respond both to this change and to the constant public demand for news. After briefly surveying ancient attempts at news communication and the rise of the European newspaper, Kobre treats at length the rise of the press in the Colonies, its role in the War for Independence, Federalist and Republican papers in the early Republic, newspapers and westward expansion, democracy and mass communications in Jacksonian America, Southern newspapers, the rise of magazines, and the press and the Civil War.

PC 879. KRIEGHBAUM, HILLIER. Pressure on the Press. New York: Crowell, 1972. 248 pp.

Krieghbaum maintains that an adversarial relationship between government figures and the press has existed since print first emerged as a channel for public information. However, the infighting has escalated significantly in degree and in kind during the past decades, especially during the Nixon Administration. He asserts that attacks on the media as a social force, the gratuitous use of subpoenas, and suppressive court injunctions generate fear in the minds of sources and could further damage--perhaps irreparably--the already clouded image of the media.

PC 880. LEE, ALFRED McCLUNG. The Daily Newspaper in America: The Evolution of a Social Instrument. New York: Macmillan, 1937. 798 pp.
The author asserts that the American newspaper industry owes its development primarily to the influence of "blind" social forces and only in a secondary, reactive way to Horace Greeley, William Randolph Hearst, and other great publishers. His treatment of the history and operation of American newspapers takes as its subject the way the press adjusts to and expresses, through editorial policy, these social changes. By editorial policy Lee means "the criteria of the selective process which [editors] exert on news sources and news, and . . . the treatment to which they subject material prior to publication." Lee analyzes editorial policy trends, which he sees as the "qualifying features" of the newspaper as a social instrument, and as expressions of "folkways," mores, and current social practices. In this context, Lee discusses all aspects of the daily American newspaper, including labor, production, management, advertising, foreign news, and syndicates.

PC 881. LEE, JAMES MELVIN. History of American Journalism. Boston: Houghton Mifflin, 1917. 462 pp.
This study was the first history of American journalism written in the 20th century. It is a comprehensive catalogue of information, surveying the birth and development of the newspaper in America with particular emphasis on the 19th century. Although in the final chapter he offers personal impressions of contemporary journalism, Lee otherwise keeps "strictly to facts and to documents quoted"; he attempts a fair, thorough, and unsensationalistic account of a press that was criticized for its apparent subservience to the reader's most prurient instincts and to monied and political interests.

PC 882. LIEBLING, A. J. The Press. 1961; Rev. ed. New York: Ballantine Books, 1964. 293 pp.
In this volume Liebling compiles articles on the press he wrote for The New Yorker during the 1940s, 1950s, and 1960s. He is concerned with the way the press perceives and treats the news and with the way the press itself is perceived and treated by political interests, monopolistic and self-aggrandizing publishers, and the public. When he feels that his articles need explanation or updating, he includes comments, and, though he calls himself "an incorrigible optimist," and his intent is remedial, the tone of both the articles and the commentary is sardonic and highly critical.

PC 883. LOFTON, JOHN. The Press as Guardian of the First Amendment. Columbia: University of South Carolina Press, 1980. 358 pp.
Lofton argues that the press has not been an effective guardian of free expression, especially of unpopular views. His study shows that historically the press has taken sides on political issues, especially those that concern their own ideological and regional interests. This partisanship is evident in incidents such as the Southern press attacks on the Abolitionist press, lack of support for the radical labor press, and the press' submission to government restrictions on free speech during W.W. I that were clearly unconstitutional. Lofton concludes by calling for newspapers to be strong champions of free expression. He argues that they should allow substantial access to those with conflicting viewpoints and to those with no other means of public expression.

PC 884.   MARBUT, F. B. News from the Capital: The Story of Washington
          Reporting. Carbondale: Southern Illinois University Press,
          1971. 304 pp.
Marbut surveys the "evolving" history of government news reporting, beginning with the tenure of Thomas Jefferson, during which time Washington
was made the nation's capital. He asserts that the press has always been
deeply involved in Washington's governing process. Marbut emphasizes
the historical context that the journalists and journalism of each period
reflected. Among the issues Marbut discusses are Jacksonian Democracy
and the press, Congress and the press, political columnists and the press,
and the impact on the press of the telegraph and later of radio, television,
magazines, and 20th-century wars.

PC 885.   MERRILL, JOHN C. The Elite Press. New York: Pitman, 1968.
          336 pp.
Merrill describes forty of the most important newspapers in the world,
five of which are American: The Baltimore Sun, The Christian Science
Monitor, St. Louis Post-Dispatch, Los Angeles Times, and The New York
Times. He also discusses at length those factors that make a newspaper
widely read and influential. Merrill defines two classes of elite papers:
the "free" paper of the open society, which offers ideas the reader may
consider, and the "restricted" paper of the closed society, which gives
its readers what they must know in order to be "well-integrated" in their
culture. Although both classes are "serious, concerned, intelligent,
and articulate," Merrill is more concerned with free or "quality" papers
("courageous, independent, news-view-oriented") than with restricted or
"prestige" papers ("the voice of some authoritarian institution"). The
author describes himself as an optimist, believing that the great newspapers attack prejudice and superannuated tradition and unify their readers
in a "world community of reason."

PC 886.   MERRILL, JOHN C. and RALPH D. BARNEY, eds. Ethics and the Press:
          Readings in Mass Media Morality. New York: Hastings House,
          1975. 338 pp.
This compilation of thirty-five essays from such contributors as Michael
Novak, Jacques Ellul, Chet Huntley, Barry Goldwater, and Nat Hentoff
addresses the theoretical underpinnings and ethical implications of journalism as well as the ethical questions journalists encounter every day.
The first part of the work, "Ethical Foundations," is a venture into the
ethical philosophy of journalism, and includes such essays as "Instinct
and Ethics" by Edmund A. Opitz, "Masscomm as Guru" by W. H. Perry, and
"The 'Apollonysian' Journalist" by John C. Merrill. The lengthier second
section, "Ethical Problems," delineates a number of problems, including
"A Few Frank Words About Bias" by Thomas Griffiths, "Responsibility for
'Self-generating' News" by J. K. Hvistendahl, and "Objectivity and the
Tactics of Terrorists" by Eugene Methvin. The purpose of these essays
is to study the motivations and consequences of journalistic practice,
rather than its methodology.

PC 887.   MERRILL, JOHN C. and HAROLD A. FISHER. The World's Great Dailies:
          Profiles of Fifty Newspapers. New York: Hastings House, 1980.
          399 pp.
This description of fifty of the world's most influential newspapers is
a completely rewritten and expanded version of Merrill's The Elite Press
(see PC 885). Unlike the earlier work, this book does not attempt to
rank the newspapers it describes. Merrill and Fisher reiterate the
former's earlier contention in The Elite Press that there are two classes
of "elite" dailies: the free paper of the open society and the restricted
paper of the closed society. Greatness becomes a matter of context, and
Merrill and Fisher discuss contextual issues at length. They include
descriptions of ten newspapers that did not appear in The Elite Press,

including several American dailies: The Washington Post, the Louisville Courier-Journal, The Miami Herald, The Wall Street Journal, and The Atlanta Constitution.

PC 888. **MITFORD, JESSICA.** Poison Penmanship: The Gentle Art of Muckraking. New York: Knopf, 1979. 277 pp.
Mitford bases this work on the premise that America needs "a new generation of muckrakers" who will spur the country to address and correct a host of "morally 'unsavory' or 'scandalous'" conditions and misdeeds. She collects in chronological order magazine articles she wrote over a twenty-year period (1957-79) in order to "demonstrate . . . the development of investigative techniques" and to reconstruct her efforts to acquire those qualities essential to muckraking journalistic success: "'ratlike cunning, a plausible manner, a little literary ability' . . . plodding determination, and an appetite for tracking and destroying the enemy." Most of Mitford's subjects are "odd pockets of American enterprise," including the American funeral industry; TV censorship; Elizabeth Arden's Main Chance, an Arizona health farm retreat for wealthy women; the Famous Writers' correspondence school; and The Sign of the Dove, a high-priced Manhattan restaurant/ tourist trap. She includes a comment with each story explaining why she wrote that story, how she investigated it, and how it was received.

PC 889. **MOTT, FRANK LUTHER.** American Journalism: A History, 1690-1960. 1941; Rev. ed. New York: Macmillan, 1962. 901 pp.
Originally published as American Journalism: A History of Newspapers in the United States Through 250 Years, 1690-1940, this work is a histori-cal narrative and a reference book. Mott gives an overview of the begin-nings of American journalism; the Revolutionary press; the partisan press of the early Nationalist period; the Reconstruction press; the rise of the independent press; "yellow journalism"; and the modern mass circulation newspaper. For those requiring additional information, Mott provides bibliographical notes on further sources at the end of each chapter.

PC 890. **PARK, ROBERT E.** The Immigrant Press and Its Control. New York: Harper, 1922. 488 pp.
Language and tradition, Park argues, unite Americans: "Our great cities . . . are mosaics of little language colonies, cultural enclaves, each maintaining its separate communal existence within the wider circle of the city's cosmopolitan life." Each of these communities has a press, and Park discusses the sentiments and needs that led to the development of so varied and extensive an immigrant press, tracing these forces to traditions in the home country and to conditions and assimilating tenden-cies in the U.S. He treats in detail the formative influence of the papers in immigrants' lives, the content of the papers, and their stance on such issues as W.W. I, capitalism, and nationalism. He also devotes several chapters to the powers that control the press, including advertisers, the government, and local political interests. While the social conditions and trends that Park studies do not, for the most part, still exist, the work remains a comprehensive, carefully documented study of a segment of America's press in the first decades of the 20th century.

PC 891. **PAYNE, GEORGE HENRY.** History of Journalism in the United States. New York: Appleton, 1920. 454 pp.
Payne traces the varying influences of American newspapers, ranging from Benjamin Harris's early Public Occurances (sic) (1690) to the "yellow press" of Joseph Pulitzer and William Randolph Hearst. He focuses both on newspapers (Boston Gazette, New York Times, New York Sun) and on jour-nalists (the Bradfords, Peter Zenger, Samuel Adams, Horace Greeley). An appendix of nine important documents and a thirty-page bibliography are included.

PC 892. POLLARD, JAMES E. The Presidents and the Press. New York: Macmillan, 1947. 866 pp.
Pollard describes the relationship between the press and each U.S. President up to and including Franklin D. Roosevelt. In the first thirty or forty years of the Presidency, newspapers were strongly partisan, and Presidents like Andrew Jackson wielded enormous power over what was printed and who printed it. Gradually, the era of "personal journalism" emerged, with such powerful editors as Horace Greeley and Charles Dana. These were men who "talked to Presidents as they would to equals and sometimes worse." After Lincoln, who was clearly aware of the importance of public relations, the dynamic between press and Presidents grew relatively calm. With the ascendancy of Theodore Roosevelt, however, a new trend developed. The press began to have a "direct and regular" relationship with Presidents. The White House press conference became "a national sounding board" for the dissemination and discussion of information; these conferences reached the height of their influence under Franklin Roosevelt. Pollard considers them a unique "democratic agency," an important developer and shaper of American and world opinion.

PC 893. POLLARD, JAMES E. The Presidents and the Press: Truman to Johnson. Washington, D.C.: Public Affairs Press, 1964. 125 pp.
In this supplement to his The Presidents and the Press (see PC 892), Pollard discusses the public relations activities of Harry S. Truman, Dwight D. Eisenhower, John F. Kennedy, and Lyndon B. Johnson. According to the author, advances in news coverage since 1945 which were made possible by technological developments in the media, especially television and radio, have altered the relationship between the White House and the American public. Presidential news conferences are discussed as a major instrument in the creation of the public image of Presidents during the last forty years.

PC 894. PORTER, WILLIAM E. Assault on the Media: The Nixon Years. Ann Arbor: University of Michigan Press, 1971. 320 pp.
Porter describes this account as "an informal history" of one aspect of the relationship between President Nixon's administration and the media: "the government's offensive," its campaign to "intimidate, harass, regulate, and in other ways damage the news media." Except for the first and last chapter, the book proceeds chronologically, each chapter corresponding to roughly a year. The first chapter surveys Nixon's increasingly unpleasant relationship with the press early in his political life--a relationship that shaped his later attitudes. In the final chapter, Porter speculates on the effects of the White House's "assault." He argues that while every President has felt some measure of antagonism toward the press, President Nixon was the first to attack the credibility not of a single journalist or newspaper, but of journalism itself. His crusade, Porter contends, resulted in unparalleled damage to free expression in this country. Porter appends a section entitled "Documents of Significance" that consists of previously confidential White House memoranda, speeches, and excerpts from court decisions. These documents make clear the Administration's antipathy toward the press and describe its strategy of attack.

PC 895. REGIER, C. C. The Era of the Muckrakers. Chapel Hill: University of North Carolina Press, 1932. 254 pp.
In 1906 Theodore Roosevelt named the aggressive reformers in American journalism "muckrakers"; some thirty years earlier, the rise of industrial empires and their neglect of workers created the need for these reformers. Regier examines the popular muckraking magazines of this period (1900-10 in particular), authors and publishers (including Lincoln Steffens, Charles Edward Russell, Benjamin O. Flowers, and S. S. McClure), and the objects of their criticism (state and national governments, big business, the church, and urban problems).

PC 896. RESTON, JAMES. The Artillery of the Press: Its Influence on
American Foreign Policy. New York: Harper & Row, 1967.
116 pp.
Reston describes this work as "an attempt to define and illustrate the
problems of conducting American foreign policy in the last third of the
20th century with a press and a Constitution whose traditions were formed
in the last third of the 18th century." Focusing on the problematic nature
of the relationship between the government and the press, Reston argues
that the ascendancy of the U.S. in the world arena demands not a more
"compliant" press but one that is more critical and meticulous. A controlled press may be more efficient and may meet certain obligations to
one's country, but finally the obligation to truth and the reporting of
facts are more important. Even those government officials whose careers
and policies have been damaged by the press agree with this contention--
at least after they have left office. Reston describes at length relations
between the President and the press, the influence of the press on public
policy, the ramifications of printing the truth, and other issues pertaining to the behavior and responsibilities of a free press in "the changing
and convulsive world in which American policy must operate."

PC 897. RICHSTAD, JIM and MICHAEL H. ANDERSON, eds. Crisis in International News: Policies and Prospects. New York: Columbia University Press, 1981. 473 pp.
These collected essays focus on "a serious, emerging crisis over news
collection, dissemination, and policy-making within and between
nations. . . ." Richstad and Anderson have selected essays that
reflect the political and cultural pluralism of the New International Information Order, a predominantly Third World multi-national
movement regulating information flow that has drawn criticism from
Western free-flow traditionalists. These essays represent "the
many viewpoints and value systems at operation" in international
news circulation, expressing both scholarly and "'real life'" perspectives. All the essayists consider information to be a resource,
like oil or gold, effective use and control of which closely correlates with national and international power. Their foremost
concern is achieving "global equity" in existing information communication systems.

PC 898. RIVERS, WILLIAM L. The Adversaries: Politics and the Press.
Boston: Beacon Press, 1970. 273 pp.
Rivers contends that the relationship between government officials and
journalists should be adversarial. On the one hand, the press needs rigorous and exact criticism in order to "live up to its best possibilities,"
and, on the other hand, democratic government works only if people are
informed, critically and at length, about its aims and operation. Rivers
includes investigations conducted by him and his students that examine
the history and nature of the relationship between the press and the government. Topics include Nixon and the press, the public relations efforts
of the Executive branch, reporters and their sources, and government newsletters and periodicals. Rivers also describes a number of measures the
press should take in order to function more efficiently and with more
integrity.

PC 899. RIVERS, WILLIAM L. The Opinionmakers. Boston: Beacon Press,
1965. 207 pp.
This examination of modern political journalism is concerned primarily
with the Washington press corps, and with how it interacts with members
of Congress, Presidential administrations, television journalists, and
news magazines (Time in particular). Rivers asserts that an elite group
of correspondents exerts considerable influence, both on government policy
and on the style and substance of much of the nation's political reporting.
Walter Lippmann and James Reston are singled out as two such figures,

and Rivers provides chapter-long biographical sketches for each. The author's recurrent theme is that information policy has always been at the core of governing the U.S. His introductory survey of the party press, as it existed under Washington, Jefferson, and Jackson, establishes the historical backdrop for the numerous examples he gives of efforts made by the Eisenhower, Kennedy, and Johnson administrations to control information and shape the news.

PC 900. RIVERS, WILLIAM L., WILLIAM B. BLANKENBURG, KENNETH STARCK, and
         EARL REEVES. Backtalk: Press Councils in America. San Francisco:
         Harper & Row, 1972. 146 pp.
During 1967 and 1968, the authors designed and established press councils in five dissimilar communities. In his introductory chapter, Rivers briefly recounts the history of the press council idea, its European forms, and its relative unpopularity among American newspapers. He asserts that escalating social tensions since 1960 exacerbated the conflict between newspapers and their audience, and that editors and publishers, facing attacks from both poles of the political spectrum, felt the need to invent new ways to communicate with their readers. The rest of the book records the experiences of the councils: in St. Louis, Missouri, and Cairo, Illinois, where individuals from black communities met with editors, publishers, and reporters to discuss--often acrimoniously--ways to improve the coverage of issues they considered important; in Redwood City, California, where council members were drawn from an occupational cross-section; in Bend, Oregon, where the council was a "blue-ribbon" group of local leaders; and in Sparta, Illinois, where the editor and publisher of a small-town weekly was criticized for not assuming a leadership role in the community.

PC 901. ROSHCO, BERNARD. Newsmaking. Chicago: University of Chicago
         Press, 1975. 160 pp.
By "newsmaking" Roshco means that news content is "the end-product of a social process" in which some information is published while other information is "ignored or discarded." This inquiry into how society affects and is affected by the organizational structure of the news media and its products is premised on the contention that "seemingly autonomous labors . . . actually are attuned to influences and concerns that emanate from the way the overarching society is structured." Roshco analyzes the relationships the news media maintain with other social institutions and how these relationships determine what media professionals define as news, as well as where they seek news and how they present it. He also discusses the processes whereby dominant social values shape news content. In considering these issues he treats such questions as "why the . . . press developed a definition of 'objectivity' that encourages distorted reportage"; "why most news is 'managed' and why the fact of 'news management' becomes a news story only under special circumstances"; and "why conflict between the press and presidents always lurks beneath the surface. . . ." News performance has itself become "'newsworthy,'" Roshco states, and in the final chapter he "abandons analysis for advocacy," discussing the kinds of standards the press should be aiming for.

PC 902. ROSTEN, LEO C. The Washington Correspondents. New York: Harcourt,
         Brace, 1937. 436 pp.
Rosten undertakes his survey of Washington political journalists with the conviction that "what the newspaperman tells, what he considers worth telling, and how he tells it are the end products of a social heritage, a functional relationship to his superiors, and a psychological construct of desire, calculation and inhibition." He examines the Washington social milieu; the changing character of Presidential press conferences, from Theodore Roosevelt to Franklin D. Roosevelt; the role of the press associations; and the various sources for news available in the capital. The responses to two questionnaires Rosten designed, and which he distribu-

ted to 127 correspondents, form the basis for his portrait of the corps. Rosten details their social and economic backgrounds, education, professional training, reading habits, and political leanings. Statistical data generated by the questionnaires are included among the book's appendices.

PC 903. RUTLAND, ROBERT. The Newsmongers: Journalism in the Life of
the Nation 1690-1972. New York: Dial Press, 1973. 430 pp.
"The press helped make America independent," Rutland writes. "Since then, the constant struggle has been to determine whether the many experiments launched by the American Revolution will have a lasting value." This volume chronicles the "experiment" of free journalistic expression in America. The developments Rutland surveys and analyzes include the rise of the printing press in Colonial America; the "ink-stained revolutionaries" of 1776 who used the press as a trumpet and a sword; newspapers as a political force so potent they were able to "catapult" Andrew Jackson into the White House; newspapers' culpability in the making of the Civil War, as well as their role in 20th-century wars; rise of sensationalism; muckrakers; and the ascendancy of television. In surveying this panorama of journalistic activity, Rutland concludes that the press has only partly fulfilled the hopes of the founding fathers, who championed a free press in order to insure that the active citizen would receive a "free and helpful flow of information"; that while technological progress has been the most striking feature of American journalism, the side effects have been an increasingly "impersonal and institutionalized" press; that the business community's close alliance with the press has too often determined a paper's survival and shape, and that business interests and the machinations of politicians, especially Presidents, have seriously hampered free expression.

PC 904. SCHILLER, DAN. Objectivity and the News: The Public and the
Rise of Commercial Journalism. Philadelphia: University of
Pennsylvania Press, 1981. 222 pp.
Schiller examines notions of press objectivity in the context of the vast social and economic changes of the Jacksonian and later antebellum periods, and the rise, during this time, of the penny press. He argues that the success of this press, which originated in its appeal to a burgeoning class of urban tradesmen, was a result of "its remarkably fluent use of the idiom and ideology" of the common person. In a time of upheaval, the penny press seemed to many to champion those rights and values most essential to the cause of equality and to the Republic. The commitment of these papers to "cheap, value-free information--to objective fact" became an expression of the belief that private, privileged interests could not monopolize or manipulate channels of communication and the dissemination of knowledge. Schiller focuses on the National Police Gazette and its coverage of crime news as a particularly potent example of the way objectivity came to represent a fundamental expression of the democratic impulse.

PC 905. SCHUDSON, MICHAEL. Discovering the News. New York: Basic Books,
1978. 228 pp.
Before 1830, as Schudson explains in this study of the idea of objectivity in American journalism, newspapers were considered vehicles of partisan rhetoric and were read by those interested in that rhetoric, not in news. The idea of "news" was invented in the Jacksonian era. By the end of the century, despite the ascendancy of sensationalism, such major newspapers as The New York Times had committed themselves to purveying "nonpartisan, strictly factual" news. Most journalists, though, had not yet made the full division of facts from values that is the hallmark of contemporary notions of objectivity. That "segregation," the result of a growing distrust in values, occurred only around W.W. I. Concurrently,

1409

however, the belief that "facts are not human statements about the world but aspects of the world itself" began to be undermined by the cataclysms of war, and by the duplicity of war propagandists and of postwar public relations professionals. Confronted with the subjectivity of perception, newspapers institutionalized it, establishing personal forms of reporting, such as political and opinion columns. Meanwhile, rules and procedures were being established to provide guidelines for reporting. To the extent that one's statements were verified by a consensus of professionals—the rulemakers—those statements were factual, or objective. Schudson analyzes the compulsion to be objective. This compulsion, he argues, is the expression of moral philosophy, "a declaration of what kind of thinking one should engage in," and a tacit political commitment to the groups one acknowledges as morally authoritative.

PC 906. SHAW, DONALD L. and MAXWELL I. McCOMBS. The Emergence of American Political Issues: The Agenda-Setting Function of the Press. St. Paul, Minn.: West, 1977. 211 pp.
The authors argue that the American press plays an "agenda-setting" function for American political issues. Their intention is to discover what audiences actually learn from the press, as well as the conditions under which they learn. Shaw and McCombs begin by defining agenda-setting and discussing its implications for the community. They then look at how the news, advertising, and public opinion establish competing issue agendas for the voters. They proceed to examine what sorts of people are susceptible to agenda-setting and to determine what voters are likely to learn from the press about issues. The book concludes with a discussion of agenda-setting within the larger political process.

PC 907. SIGAL, LEON V. Reporters and Officials: The Organization and Politics of Newsmaking. Lexington, Mass.: Heath, 1973. 221 pp.
Sigal's investigation of the relationship between the press and the government focuses on how and why news gets made. The news the press prints may alter the perceptions of policy-makers, limit or shape their options and arguments, and thereby affect the actions of the government, yet the actual nature of news is not easily defined. "One big trouble with news," Sigal writes, "is that nobody knows what it is. The other trouble is that nobody knows what it means." Sigal discusses how two newspapers in particular, The New York Times and the Washington Post, make and understand news. He describes the constraints that organizational structure places upon journalists; the nature and implications of the "beat" and the selection of news sources; the nature and effects of the reporter's self-concept and approach to protocol; and the ways government officials use and understand the news.

PC 908. SMITH, ANTHONY. Goodbye Gutenberg: The Newspaper Revolution of the 1980s. New York: Oxford University Press, 1980. 367 pp.
Propelled by social trends and technological opportunities, the newspaper is undergoing a revolution comparable in scale to the advent of printing. Smith contends that computerization and other electronic advances rescued the newspaper in the 1960s when it seemed on the point of being overwhelmed by more information than the technology could process, and by industrial relations problems, rising costs, internecine competition, and demographic changes in its audience. "Like a deus ex machina" the computer solved these growing difficulties, but its extraordinary impact introduced an entirely new set of issues. These concern "the social control of information, the nature of the individual creative function, the ways in which information interacts with human memory." According to Smith, these "completely new relationships between man and knowledge" require different intellectual skills than those that have been traditionally valued, so

established roles within the information industry are being eliminated or drastically revised. Smith foresees the evolution of the journalist into an "information technician" depending more upon the skills of information research than on those of composition.

PC 909. TEBBEL, JOHN. The Compact History of the American Newspaper. New York: Hawthorn Books, 1963. 286 pp.
Tebbel's history of the American newspaper traces the ongoing efforts of the "Establishment" to control what is printed and the countervailing efforts of private individuals to print news freely. He begins his survey in 1690 with Benjamin Harris, who published the New World's first newspaper. Tebbel discusses the expansion and increasing independence and authority of the newspaper throughout the 18th and 19th centuries, as well as the propagandistic function it often served, especially in war, public controversy, and political elections. For the rich and powerful, like Joseph Pulitzer and William Randolph Hearst, the newspaper became an instrument for personal gain. Finally, in the last section of the book, Tebbel describes "the transition from propaganda and personal journalism to the conservative newspapermaking of a new generation of business publishers" in the 20th century. In this context he discusses jazz journalism, or tabloids; the ascendancy of newspaper chains; the demise of rural newspapers; the dangers of monopoly; and the crisis of purpose afflicting the contemporary media.

PC 910. THOMAS, DANA L. The Media Moguls. New York: Putnam, 1981. 237 pp.
Thomas discusses the achievements of the most powerful figures in newspaper and magazine publishing in the 20th century. Taking into account the "teeming variety" of journalistic experiences, he treats publishers as diverse as Abraham Cahan, who founded the New York Daily Forward in 1897, an ethnic paper for Jewish immigrants; DeWitt Wallace, who launched the relentlessly moral and optimistic Reader's Digest in the early 1920s, an age of "rampant skepticism"; and Bob Guccione, who sensed in the 1960s that the pornography market could support Penthouse, a magazine even more sexually explicit than Playboy. In addition, Thomas considers founding figures in the underground press, business press, and at a number of the nation's major dailies. He describes several ironies involved in the ascendancy of these moguls: Joseph Patterson, for instance, founder of the "unflinchingly conservative" Daily News, began as a "firebrand socialist who preached the overthrow of the capitalist system," while Katherine Graham's Washington Post, renowned for its crusade against corruption in government, was "for most of its history . . . a mouthpiece of crooked politicians." Thomas concludes with a discussion of the threat that TV and new technologies pose for the traditional newspaper and its hegemony as the foremost disseminator of information.

PC 911. THOMAS, ISAIAH. The History of Printing in America. 2 vols. 1810; Reissued New York: Burt Franklin, 1967. 1063 pp.
This classic study, the first of its kind in the U.S., surveys not only newspapers in the Colonies and in the early years of the Republic, but also the history of printing, dating back to the origin of books, with the main emphasis on America. Thomas's comprehensive description of the nature and development of the press and the practice of newsmanship in 18th-century America treats the rise of newspapers in each of the Colonies, delineating the methods and materials of printing, the contents of the papers, their physical appearance, editorial aims, and the public responses.

PC 912. TUCHMAN, GAYE. Making News: A Study in the Construction of Real-
         ity. New York: Free Press, 1978. 244 pp.
Tuchman bases her argument on the notion that "the act of making news
is the act of constructing reality itself rather than a picture of reality." When we perceive, consider, and discuss public events, we do so
within a context the media have established, and that context shapes our
perceptions, considerations, and discussions. The author asserts that
the news is "first and foremost" a social institution embedded in relationships with other institutions, and is the product of professional news-
workers whose practices serve organizational needs. Tuchman gathered
data over a ten-year period, studying newspapers and TV, and she presents
field observations to substantiate the historical context of the "invention" and development of news and news organizations and professionalism:
the "invention" of news as a response to the challenges that 19th-century
capitalism posed to Colonial mercantilism, and its development in the
context of the emergence of corporate capitalism. These historical considerations further buttress her contention that news is a "legitimating
ideology," and that what it legitimates, finally, is the status quo.

PC 913. UDELL, JON G., et al. The Economics of the American Newspaper.
         New York: Hastings House, 1978. 160 pp.
Udell explores from a variety of perspectives "the role that business
and economic considerations play in assuring the free public a free press."
After establishing the way fundamental economic rights and responsibilities
underlay press freedom in particular and the First Amendment in general,
Udell focuses on the economic life of the newspaper in post-W.W. II American society. Its dual nature as a business and a trustee of the public
interest generates questions of enormous range and importance. The author
asks if the pursuit of profit undermines or enhances a newspaper's integrity, and whether publishers and editors can remain market- or product-
oriented without vitiating the basic values of dispassionate truth-seeking
newsmanship. To answer these questions Udell analyzes both the role of
the newspaper in the economy and economic issues within the industry itself.
The latter include the capital requirements of new technologies, circulation, and advertising; revenue and cost analysis; cost controls; and
labor relations.

PC 914. WEBER, RONALD, ed. The Reporter as Artist: A Look at the New
         Journalism Controversy. New York: Hastings House, 1974.
         312 pp.
In these articles, reviews, book chapters, and interviews, contributors
such as Tom Wolfe, Gay Talese, Nat Hentoff, Norman Podhoretz, George
Plimpton, and Dwight Macdonald discuss New Journalism from varying perspectives. By New Journalism Weber means the general "awareness of the literary and journalistic potential of nonfiction writing," an issue that has
engaged all the authors here in "sharp criticial controversy." Weber
divides the material into four parts. Part I, "Personal Journalism,"
includes essays that describe the development and characteristics of New
Journalism. Pieces in Part II, "The Article as Art," argue that the literary essay or magazine article is the journalistic art form commensurate
with the age, while Part III, "Fact in the Fiction Void," extends this
argument, emphasizing the artistic or aesthetic potential of journalism.
Finally, Part IV, "Dissent and Qualification," contains works that denounce,
call into question, or express serious reservations about New Journalism.

PC 915. WEISBERGER, BERNARD. The American Newspaperman. Chicago: Uni-
         versity of Chicago Press, 1961. 226 pp.
Weisberger's premise, as stated by Daniel Boorstin in the preface, is
that "the American newspaperman is a touchstone of American civilization."
The recording and dissemination of news is also the recording and recapitulation of the concerns of an era. The best journalists have also played

a part in shaping public life: they are "beacon[s] for public desires."
In this light, the history of the American newspaperman "cannot fail to
be a history of what has interested the American people." Weisberger
surveys American newspaper history beginning in the Colonial period and
proceeding to the mid-20th century. He focuses on how historical developments and advances within the industry have changed the nature of the
profession and how such varied, powerful, and culturally representative
figures as Ben Franklin, Horace Greeley, and Joseph Pulitzer have changed
the industry and shaped history.

PC 916. WOLSELEY, ROLAND E. The Black Press, U.S.A. Ames: Iowa State
University Press, 1971. 362 pp.
In this treatment of the history and nature of the black press in America,
Wolseley aims to make known "a heretofore neglected and subordinated"
force and to set that force in the context of those social movements that
have a special attraction for blacks. By black press, Wolseley means
a press that blacks own and manage, one that is intended for black consumers, and one that must "serve, speak, and fight for the black minority." Wolseley surveys the history of the press as well as its current
status, discussing such topics as the problems facing black owners and
publishers, the impact of mainstream ideologies, the training and educational problems of black journalists, and the professional possibilities
open to them.

VII. SPORTS

PC 917. ANGELL, ROGER. The Summer Game. New York: Viking Press, 1972.
303 pp.
Angell's essays on baseball, which first appeared individually in The
New Yorker, are collected here and in two later volumes, Five Seasons
(1977) and Late Innings (1982). Together, these essays survey important
news and trends in the game since 1962 and also offer personal tributes
to the people and the environment of baseball. Angell's books include
his annual "state of the game" pieces that appeared every November, as
well as articles that appeared while the season was in progress. He
describes a world of remarkable athletes made complex by the intrusion
of such forces as commercialization. Angell ponders the excitement and
subtleties of baseball from the standpoint of an appreciative spectator.

PC 918. ASINOF, ELIOT. Eight Men Out. New York: Holt, Rinehart & Winston,
1963. 302 pp.
Asinof provides a comprehensive history of the events surrounding the
World Series of 1919, in which eight members of the Chicago White Sox
were permanently suspended from baseball for their role in fixing the
outcome to the benefit of professional gamblers. He traces the individual
careers of the players involved, discusses economic conditions in baseball
in 1919, describes the trial at which the players were acquitted and the
proceedings within the baseball establishment that brought about their
suspensions, and follows each player's post-baseball history. The image
of baseball as a game and a business receives considerable attention here,
and Asinof surveys the public shock at "the fix," as well as the attempts
to clean up the sport by Commissioner of Baseball Judge Kenesaw Mountain
Landis.

PC 919. ATWELL, ROBERT H., BRUCE GRIMES, and DONNA LOPIANO. The Money
Game: Financing Collegiate Athletics. Washington, D.C.: American Council on Education, 1980. 56 pp.
Atwell, Grimes, and Lopiano argue that, while fewer than 5% of American
college students participate in intercollegiate athletics, and expenditures
for athletic programs account for only about 1% of the nation's overall
college and university budget, the attention lavished on college sports
far outstrips these participation levels and expenditures. Intercollegiate
athletics has become big business, especially at schools that enjoy television revenues and sizeable gate receipts from competition. The authors
analyze the structure of the athletic establishment at a number of colleges,
discuss the methods by which sports are financed, and consider the ways
in which sports budgets are spent.

PC 920. AXTHELM, PETER. The City Game: Basketball in New York from the
World Champion Knicks to the World of the Playgrounds. New York:
Harper's Magazine Press, 1970. 210 pp.
Baseball may be the American pastime, and football may command millions
of viewers, but basketball, played on a narrow strip of asphalt by those
"without cars or allowances," is the game of the cities. Athletes in
suburbs and small towns learn basketball; city athletes "live" it. Axthelm
discusses "basketball life" in New York--"the most active, dedicated basketball city of all"--on both the playground and professional levels. In
the ghetto community especially, basketball provides moments of order
and achievement, a means of "defining identity and manhood in an urban
society that breeds invisibility." Axthelm relates the stories of a number
of great New York players, the playground legends, the very few who made
it professionally and the many who could not escape the cycle of poverty,
drugs, and crime. On the other end of the spectrum is the 1970 National
Basketball Association Champion New York Knicks, who captured the affection
of the city and awakened the national media to the excitement of professional basketball. Axthelm discusses these two worlds in "an attempt
to describe the magic they share . . . a mutual appreciation of a game
that projects a significance . . . to those who have known it, understood
it, lived it."

PC 921. BALL, DONALD W. and JOHN W. LOY, eds. Sport and Social Order:
Contributions to the Sociology of Sport. Reading, Mass.: Addison-
Wesley, 1975. 574 pp.
Consulting editor Loy considers this collection of essays by sports sociologists a methodologically diverse and thematically comprehensive guidebook
to issues of "general sociology" within the context of sports. Loy and
co-editor Ball have included twelve essays, generally "analytical reviews"
or "micro-research monographs." These essays discuss such topics as the
connections between sports and social inequality, geography, politics,
and violence, the occupational experiences of coaches and athletes, and
the theoretical underpinnings of sports sociology.

PC 922. BARBER, RED. 1947: When All Hell Broke Loose in Baseball. Garden
City, N.Y.: Doubleday, 1982. 380 pp.
Barber, a long-time baseball announcer, writes that in 1947, "baseball
. . . became a force, not only in sports, but also in the overall history
of this country." The year was marked by relentless and sometimes vicious
personal conflict among the game's power brokers: Happy Chandler, Commissioner; Branch Rickey, president and general manager of the Brooklyn
Dodgers; and Larry MacPhail, owner and president of the New York Yankees.
Rickey was responsible for bringing Jackie Robinson, baseball's first
black player, into the league that year. At the same time, baseball's
popularity was reaching its highest level ever, and media attention, including the emergence of television, grew correspondingly. Barber recounts
the way the Yankees and Dodgers overcame these often chaotic forces to

meet in one of the most exciting and widely followed World Series in baseball history.

PC 923. BEISSER, ARNOLD R. The Madness in Sports. New York: Meredith,
1967. 231 pp.
Beisser perceives in American attitudes toward sports a growing seriousness
manifested in the wealth of rituals, relationships, and norms that develop
in and around contemporary athletic activity. The author, a psychiatrist,
uses a series of case studies to examine the psychological meaning and
symbolism of sports. He finds that for some the athletic arena provides
a socially sanctioned outlet for asocial and anti-social desires, while
for others it serves as a haven of rules and structures, a shelter from
a "forbidding world."

PC 924. BENAGH, JIM. Making It to #1: How College Football and Basketball
Teams Get There. New York: Dodd, Mead, 1976. 302 pp.
Benagh investigates the structure of contemporary collegiate athletics
and the ways in which teams are built and maintained. He takes a close
look at the realities of college football and basketball, particularly
recruiting procedures. He examines the corruption and the self-perpetuating nature of this system and contends that the value system of collegiate
sports is being undermined by increasingly harsh economic pressures that
competitive athletic departments must confront. Noting the college athlete's growing dissatisfaction with the exploitative nature of collegiate
sports, the author concludes with advice for the college-bound athlete,
including tips on how to win a scholarship.

PC 925. BETTS, JOHN RICKARDS. America's Sporting Heritage: 1850-1950.
Reading, Mass.: Addison-Wesley, 1974. 428 pp.
Betts's study details the emergence of sports as a major element of American society, "an important factor in the development of national character." He is concerned with the way sports have been influenced by historical change and how they have in turn "penetrated our language, literature, arts, educational philosophy, city planning, and other facets of
American civilization." The book divides into two parts, "The Rise of
Class Sport" and "The Rise of Mass Sport." "The Rise of Class Sport"
treats developments from 1860-1920, a period in which the technological
revolution transformed sports from a rural diversion to a highly organized,
urban form of entertainment. "The Rise of Mass Sport" focuses on the
way the social stratifications which had previously typified sports involvement gradually eroded between 1920 and 1950.

PC 926. BOUTILIER, MARY A. and LUCINDA SAN GIOVANNI. The Sporting Woman.
Champaign, Ill.: Human Kinetics, 1983. 307 pp.
Women have entered the traditionally male realm of sport during the 1970s
and 1980s in greater numbers than ever before and occasionally with great
fanfare. However, the authors question whether this movement actually
signifies progress toward equality between the sexes, as some observers
have claimed. Drawing from diverse interdisciplinary sources, Boutilier
and San Giovanni argue that contemporary sport remains a patriarchal institution. Male values and male power remain intact because women's involvement has not significantly affected prevailing conceptualizations of sport.
In this context Feminism is ineffective; no alternative derived from and
embracing women's experiences and consciousness has surfaced.

PC 927. BOUTON, JIM. Ball Four Plus Ball Five. New York: Stein & Day,
1981. 457 pp.
This volume provides the complete version of the original Ball Four (1970),
and some reflections on baseball and the impact of Ball Four from the
perspective of 1980. Bouton's book, edited by Leonard Shecter, offers
a glimpse of the life of professional baseball players as well as personal

ruminations on the ups and downs of Bouton's pitching career. Bouton's
day-to-day chronology of the end of his playing career reveals the workings
of baseball as a business, the pressures on players and their families
inherent in the professional game, and the relationship of players to
management. The book also discusses what many of the players mentioned
in the original Ball Four were doing a decade later.

PC 928. **BOYLE, ROBERT H.** Sport: Mirror of American Life. Boston: Little,
        Brown, 1963. 293 pp.
Boyle argues that sports "gives form and substance" to a great deal of
American life and that this influence is not the product of any "national
flaw" but rather of a combination of social and psychological factors.
He surveys a number of these factors, including technological growth,
urbanization, increased leisure time, aggression, and egoism. His overview
indicates how the shaping of sports closely reflects the shaping of society.
He then turns his attention to the actual practice of sports in America.
He analyzes the ways in which sports are affected by race and class distinctions, devoting chapters to the Negro baseball leagues, the hot-rod cult,
country clubs, and the Harvard-Yale weekend.

PC 929. **CADY, EDWIN.** The Big Game: College Sports and American Life.
        Knoxville: University of Tennessee Press, 1972. 254 pp.
The Big Game, Cady contends, is the consummate sporting scene, a clash
between two college teams that is imbued with an intensity and glamor,
for both participants and spectators, unsurpassed anywhere else in the
world, and by any other sporting event in the U.S. Invoking such disparate figures as Emerson, Jefferson, and Santayana, Cady probes the nature
of the Big Game, the needs it serves, and its evolution and implications.
He discusses its aesthetic and mythic resonances, and analyzes its constituent parts: recruiting, regionalism, the role of blacks and women,
the status of amateurism, and the media. Acknowledging and denouncing
the many pernicious elements involved in sports at this level, Cady argues
nonetheless that the Big Game should not, as some suggest, be eliminated.
Through a liberation from the most harmful and manipulative aspects of
commercial and media interests, through a "fresh reconciliation with academe," and through other such "untiring acts of daily renewal," the Big
Game can continue to serve the culture it symbolizes.

PC 930. **COFFIN, TRISTRAM POTTER.** The Illustrated Book of Baseball Folklore.
        New York: Seabury Press, 1975. 166 pp.
In this study of the origin and history of baseball in America, Coffin
examines the folklore that has developed about the sport. He contends
that America needs a national game to bolster its pride, meet the demands
of its self-image, and transmit its culture to other countries. He points
out how baseball stimulates a fan's loyalty toward and identification
with a city. Utilizing anecdotes and player profiles, Coffin discusses
the legendary nature of baseball heroes. He considers the evolution of
baseball language and the role of the sportswriter as mythmaker. He also
devotes a section to baseball art, including literature and film. The
survey contains over 200 drawings and photos.

PC 931. **COHEN, STANLEY.** The Game They Played. New York: Farrar, Strauss
        & Giroux, 1977. 245 pp.
This study of the college basketball scandal of the early 1950s, involving
several members of New York's highly successful City College basketball
team, is a reflection on morality in American culture. Writing in a personal narrative style, Cohen considers the subject in terms of the fall
of the American hero. He focuses on the individuals involved in the incident and provides information on their backgrounds and the impact of the
scandal on their personal lives. In chronicling this event, he casts
light on the operation of the legal system in the U.S. and reveals the

repressive political climate of the period. He then relates this event
to a similar college basketball scandal which occurred a decade later.

PC 932. COLE, LEWIS. A Loose Game. New York: Bobbs-Merrill, 1978.
          198 pp.
Cole's account examines the "unique and determining factors" of the "peculiarly American institution" of basketball. His discussion ranges over
a wide variety of topics, from his own experience on the playgrounds to
the predominance of black players in the professional ranks to the impact
of television and the merger of the American Basketball Association with
the National Basketball Association in 1976. The title of the book refers
to what Cole perceives to be the essence of basketball; it is ever-changing,
highly creative and spontaneous, a "loose" game which continually enthralls
both spectators and participants in new ways.

PC 933. CREPEAU, RICHARD C. Baseball: America's Diamond Mind, 1919-1941.
          Orlando: University of Florida Press, 1980. 228 pp.
Baseball reigned as the national pastime during the years between W.W.
I and W.W. II. Using sports sections of newspapers as indications of
how most Americans viewed major league baseball, Crepeau examines how
American cultural values and baseball were interconnected in the "golden
age" of the sport in the 1920s and 1930s. The baseball literature of
the years between the wars expressed notions of democracy, fair play,
patriotism, nationalism, and opportunity. Crepeau addresses the impact
on the baseball world not only of the wars, but also of the transformation
of a rural agrarian society into an urban-industrial one; the emergence
of baseball superstars and heroes; commercialization and the corporate
player; and a variety of other changes in American culture. He contends
that the baseball world, like the larger society, responded to the social
changes between the wars by retaining some of the values of the rural
past while embracing the new pattern of urban life in America.

PC 934. DIZIKES, JOHN. Sportsmen and Gamesmen. Boston: Houghton Mifflin,
          1981. 350 pp.
Dizikes profiles the careers and contributions of eleven individuals
involved in the emergence and development in America of such activities
as horse racing, sports publishing and writing, gambling, chess, and yachting. Dizikes places each of the men he discusses within the social context
of the 19th century, under the cultural shadow of President Andrew Jackson,
one of America's first prominent sportsmen and gamesmen.

PC 935. DOLSON, FRANK. Beating the Bushes. South Bend, Ind.: Icarus
          Press, 1982. 278 pp.
Dolson's affectionate study highlights the unglamorous, unpredictable,
and often hilarious nature of life in baseball's minor leagues. As opposed
to many big league stars, most players in the minors have not become
obsessed with their public images or contracts; for them, "the game is
still the thing." Dolson's account ranges from lighthearted anecdotes--
players living in clubhouses, managers driving buses, day-long triple-
headers--to serious discussions of alcoholism, racism, and failure.

PC 936. DURSO, JOSEPH. The All-American Dollar: The Big Business of
          Sports. Boston: Houghton Mifflin, 1971. 294 pp.
Durso analyzes the professional sports "boom" that occurred in the 1950s.
He analyzes football's growth, emphasizing the importance of administrators
like Pete Rozelle and Sonny Werblin, and such player-personalities as
Joe Namath and O. J. Simpson. His discussion of baseball is framed by
his analysis of other fast-growing sports: he notes that as football,
basketball, and hockey increase the length of their season and their share
of the sports market, baseball is challenged to maintain its supremacy
as "America's national pastime." Durso examines the impact on sports

competition of gambling, both state-sponsored and illicit, and devotes
considerable attention to the role and the cost of sports advertising.
Throughout this work, the emphasis is on the economic explosion in professional sports.

PC 937. DURSO, JOSEPH. The Sports Factory. New York: Quadrangle Books,
          1975. 207 pp.
Durso's investigative expose condemns a college sports system which has
grown more sophisticated but which remains guilty of many of the charges
contained in the Carnegie Foundation report of 1929. This report decries
a system which rewarded varsity athletes at the expense of the values
of higher education. Durso discusses such figures as Paul "Bear" Bryant,
Butch Lee, and Jerry Tarkanian. Other stories include the growing television market, Nebraska football, and the 1974 Hanford Report. Durso
includes an extract from the Carnegie document, and the NCAA bylaws regarding recruiting.

PC 938. DWORKIN, JAMES B. Owners Versus Players: Baseball and Collective
          Bargaining. Boston: Auburn House, 1981. 306 pp.
Dworkin examines the impact of free agency on mobility and salaries in
professional baseball. He focuses briefly on early attempts within the
sport to organize players, and he devotes attention to the Major League
Baseball Players Association, the union that was successful in challenging
baseball's reserve clause and instituting a system of free agency for
experienced players. He provides charts to indicate how well the 201
players who opted for free-agent status between 1976 and 1980 performed,
and he reports on the results of salary arbitration of 115 players between
1974 and 1980. In his later chapters, Dworkin compares the contract and
free-agency situation in baseball to that in other major American sports.

PC 939. EDWARDS, HARRY. The Revolt of the Black Athlete. New York:
          Free Press, 1969. 202 pp.
Edwards chronicles his personal struggle and organizational efforts to
expose racism in American sports and to gain justice for black athletes
and citizens. His work analyzes and defines the goals and tactics underlying the organized protests of black athletes during the 1960s. Edwards
discusses the political, economic, and social implications of black activism in athletics, as well as its local, national, and international repercussions. He shows how black athletes left behind "the facade of locker
room equality" to assume their place in the larger "Black Liberation Movement."

PC 940. EDWARDS, HARRY. Sociology of Sport. Homewood, Ill.: Dorsey
          Press, 1973. 395 pp.
Edwards describes this study as a "comprehensive analytical profile" of
"what has happened and is happening in and to American sport." Edwards
is concerned with sport's integral role in contemporary life, and with
its future possibilities as a significant agent or index of social change.
The book is divided into three parts. Part I is an overview of the study
of American sports. Edwards surveys important writings in the field,
differentiates between sports, play, games, and other forms of leisure,
and develops an "operational" definition of sports. In Part II, he probes
what he calls "the dominant American sports creed," examining its social,
political, and economic complexities as well as the ethical values which
inform it. Finally, Part III is an analysis of the interrelationship
of sports and social change in which Edwards articulates the dynamic
between sports, democratic ideals, and social dissent.

PC 941. EITZEN, D. STANLEY, ed. Sport in Contemporary Society: An Anthology. New York: St. Martin's Press, 1979. 467 pp.
While most Americans are interested in sports, few understand sports.
Lack of attention from academics and generally superficial, unanalytic
coverage by journalists have perpetuated "sports illiteracy" and its by-
product: an untempered, quasi-mythological glorification of sports and
sports heroes. Eitzen aims to rectify this problem by compiling an anthology of essays--drawn from both sports sociology and journalism sources--
that consider sports from a variety of perspectives and sensibilities.
The essays address such issues as racial discrimination in sports; violence
in sports; sports and sex-role stereotyping; the role of sports in socializing young people in American values; and sports and social or economic
mobility. Contributors include Eitzen, Frank Deford, Pete Rozelle, Michael
Novak, and Spiro Agnew.

PC 942. FRANK, LAWRENCE. Playing Hardball: The Dynamics of Baseball
Folk Speech. New York: Peter Lang, 1983. 126 pp.
The language of baseball is a product of the distinct community of ballplayers and of the relations between that community and mainstream American
culture. Frank, who played and observed professional minor league baseball, describes and analyzes the vernacular among and about pitchers,
hitters, fielders, and umpires. Baseball "folk speech derives from the
particular environments, tasks, and features of the game itself, but it
reflects the anxieties and values of the broader culture."

PC 943. GALLNER, SHELDON M. Pro Sports: The Contract Game. New York:
Scribner, 1974. 231 pp.
Gallner, an attorney, interviewed athletes and studied court cases for
this volume in which he analyzes the relationships between professional
athletes and their employers. He discusses sports as a business investment
for owners, as well as the often controversial role played by agents and
attorneys in the business process. Gallner analyzes scouting, player
drafts in various sports, and contract negotiating. He devotes considerable attention to salary structures, league organization, and the dilemma
of players in deciding whether or not to play out their options. His
last sections, written in a more personal vein, question whether players
and fans are getting "a fair shake" in the present system. The appendix
offers specific documents related to sports contracts, and the notes give
detailed citations of sources for future research.

PC 944. GERBER, ELLEN W., JAN FELSHIN, PEARL BERLIN, and WANEEN WYRICK.
The American Woman in Sport. Reading, Mass.: Addison-Wesley,
1974. 562 pp.
This work offers a "multi-disciplinary analysis of the problems, patterns,
and processes associated with the sport involvement of women" in American
culture. The authors' analyses of women in sports reflect their "cogni-
zance of the changing trends in both education and society at large, with
particular attention to current feminist ideas." The authors include
an historical survey of women's participation in sports, an analysis of
the implications of institutional sports for sportswomen, a "presentation
of a psychological profile," a "motivational analysis of the woman athlete," and an examination of "performance capacities of the sportswoman."

PC 945. GOLDSTEIN, JEFFREY H., ed. Sports Violence. New York: Springer-
Verlag, 1983. 223 pp.
Goldstein has compiled essays from various perspectives and approaches--
historical, sociological, and psychological--about violence in sport.
Never an easily isolated or independent phenomenon, violence in sport--
both legitimate and illegitimate forms of excessive physicality or
brutality--has been and remains tied to the culture in which it appears.
As evidenced in many countries and throughout history, sports violence
manifests basic social problems.

PC 946. GOLDSTEIN, RICHARD. Spartan Seasons: How Baseball Survived the
        Second World War. New York: Macmillan, 1980. 290 pp.
This work studies the impact of W.W. II on major league baseball. The
war affected everything from spring training (travel restrictions disal-
lowed trips south) to the quality of play (only those too young or somehow
unfit for service remained in the league) to the composition of the ball
itself (natural rubber was reserved for military use). Despite steady
and good-natured support by fans, the very existence of the major leagues
was threatened by "intimations [that] the sport was a frivolity that might
well be dispensed with." Goldstein discusses the measures players, coaches,
and owners took in order to meet the exigencies that the war forced upon
them.

PC 947. GUTTMANN, ALLEN. From Ritual to Record. New York: Columbia
        University Press, 1978. 198 pp.
Convinced that sports are among "the most discussed and least understood
phenomena of our time," Guttmann elucidates the nature of modern sports
in general and American sports in particular. In the first chapter he
constructs a paradigm that distinguishes the abstract forms of play, games,
contests, and sports from one another. Basing his analysis of sports
upon this paradigm, Guttmann describes the development of ancient forms
of sports into modern forms as an evolution from sacred ritual to a secular
obsession with quantifiable achievement, or "records." He also discusses
the economic and religious underpinnings of the rise of modern sports.
The rest of the book is concerned with sports in America. He discusses
baseball--the "quantified pastoral"--as a fundamental expression of the
"American spirit," the national fascination with football, and America's
preference for team rather than individual sports.

PC 948. HALBERSTAM, DAVID. The Breaks of the Game. New York: Knopf,
        1981. 362 pp.
This account of the activities of a professional basketball team, and
the impact of the sport on team members, families, fans, and the press,
is the product of an entire season (1979-80) Halberstam spent living and
traveling with the Portland Trailblazers. He provides team history and
demography, including much information on players who were acquired from
other teams or traded away, and his portraits of individual players offer
biographical information on the player's origins, education, and pre-
basketball experience. Halberstam also discusses team management and coaching, taking into account the range of National Basketball Association
franchises, as well as ownership attitudes on such issues as salaries,
agents, and the unionization of players.

PC 949. HARDY, STEPHEN. How Boston Played. Boston: Northeastern Uni-
        versity Press, 1982. 272 pp.
Basing his study on the notion that "Bostonians have long been at the
forefront of America's sports history," Hardy analyzes the "intertwining"
of sports and recreation with social, cultural, economic, and political
developments in Boston during the fifty years following the Civil War.
The rapid ascendancy of sports to respectability and institutionalism
created new patterns of community life. These patterns reflected the
greater social movements of the period. The transition from a rural-
agricultural to an urban-industrial society on the one hand nurtured "industry, innovation, and opportunity" out of which formalized and sophisticated
athletics grew, and on the other hand deepened a feeling of restlessness
and suffocation from which sports and games served as a release. Playing
baseball or bicycling in the park after work or on the week-end satisfied
the need for outdoor life, evoking the sense of the frontier and pastime
that were threatened "by the stultifying regime of the machine age."
Hardy is not wholly satisfied with this thesis, however, and argues that
sports were also an integrating force in a "modern city culture" fragmented

by money, occupation, language, and race, that they provided sources of identity, moral invigoration, and, for spectators, vicarious triumph in a symbolic "struggle of life." He analyzes the "circumstances, events, and personalities" of the age, discussing among other topics sporting clubs, parks and playgrounds, bicycle crazes, and a variety of athletic heroes.

PC 950. HARRIS, JANET C. and ROBERTA J. PARKS, eds. Play, Games and Sports in Cultural Contexts. Champaign, Ill.: Human Kinetics, 1983. 521 pp.
This anthology explores from an anthropological perspective the meanings of play, games, and sports for people engaging in these activities. The papers presented in this volume focus on diverse historical and geographical topics, and the analysis of games, play, and sports divides into five parts: games, sports, and interpretations of cultures; sports and rituals; play and interpretations; socialization and enculturation through play, games, and sports; and acculturation, cultural pluralism, games, and sports. Contributors include Clifford Geertz, Richard Lipsky, David Q. Voigt, Victor Turner, Michael A. Salter, Helen B. Schwartsman, Kendall Blanchard, J. R. Fox, and others.

PC 951. HART, M. MARIE and SUSAN BIRRELL, eds. Sport in the Socio-Cultural Process. 1972; Rev. ed. Dubuque, Iowa: William C. Brown, 1981. 721 pp.
Hart intends this anthology of thirty-eight essays and excerpts to be an investigation of the "intricate mutual interdependence" between sports and culture. In the first part of the book, Hart chooses works which establish the cultural coordinates of sports; she includes essays on the definition of sport, on its social organization, and on the influence of technology. The second part of the book concerns those involved in the sporting "process"; essays treat the way Americans, both as a whole and in various ethnic, social, sexual, and age groupings, take part in sports. In the third part of the book, the selected essays describe the way the "social systems" of media, economics, and politics affect the practice, organization, and viewing of sports.

PC 952. HENDERSON, EDWIN B. The Black Athlete: Emergence and Arrival. Cornwells Heights, Pa.: The Publishers Agency, 1976. 306 pp.
This survey of the black athlete in American sports, written by Henderson in conjunction with the editors of Sport Magazine, begins before W.W. II when organized sports practiced de facto if not official segregation. The success of black athletes in boxing and track and field, however, along with Jackie Robinson's breakthrough and the social changes brought about by the war led to a huge influx of black athletes in almost all major American sports. Henderson charts these developments primarily by recounting the struggles and accomplishments of the great black athletes in each sport. These include boxers Jack Johnson, Joe Louis, and Muhammad Ali; sprinters Jesse Owens and Wyomia Tyus; jockey Major Taylor; Jackie Robinson, Satchell Paige, and Willie Mays in baseball; Kareem Abdul-Jabbar and Wilt Chamberlain in basketball; football player Jim Brown; decathlete Rafer Johnson; golfer Lee Elder, and Arthur Ashe and Althea Gibson of tennis. Numerous photographs accompany the text.

PC 953. HIGGS, ROBERT J. and NEIL D. ISAACS, eds. The Sporting Spirit: Athletes in Literature and Life. New York: Harcourt, Brace, Jovanovich, 1977.
American society is "pervaded by the awareness, the values, and the spirit of sports." In order better to understand the meaning of sports in American culture, Higgs and Isaacs compile from a wide variety of sources essays and excerpts that reflect or explain the profound exchange between sports and society. The work is organized into four parts. Part I is an intro-

duction to athletes and athletic themes in literature. Higgs and Isaacs select passages from such ostensibly anomalous sources as Virgil, Gregory Corso, and John Updike. Part II contains the first person accounts of such athletes as Jesse Owens, Diana Nyad, and Gene Tunney. Part III offers essays of social and cultural criticism, again drawn from an extraordinarily varied range of sources, including Xenophanes arguing for "Wisdom over Strength," selections from Castiglione's "The Book of the Courtier," and Norman Mailer on the death of boxer Benny Paret. Finally, Part IV consists of historically or philosophically based inquiries into sports. Excerpts from the well-known works of Veblen and Huizinga are included, as are Rilke's poem "To Nike" and writings from Damon Runyon, Arnold Toynbee, and Howard Slusher.

PC 954. HOCH, PAUL. Rip Off the Big Game: The Exploitation of Sports by the Power Elite. Garden City, N.Y.: Anchor Books, 1972. 222 pp.

Hoch analyzes sports in terms of its power relationships and the exploitation of athletes for purposes other than glory on the field. He questions whether professional sports still retain the quality of "play" common to the activities of children and participants in pre-industrial sports and games. In addition, Hoch analyzes the ownership structure in professional sports, the relationship of the sports ethos to ideas of militant nationalism, and the extent to which sports in colleges are used to promote a big-time athletic image rather than academic excellence.

PC 955. HOLWAY, JOHN. Voices from the Great Black Baseball Leagues. New York: Dodd, Mead, 1975. 363 pp.

In this oral history, Holway interviews seventeen black ballplayers who participated in the Negro leagues. His argument, elucidated in the introduction, is that the ability of players in the Negro leagues was equal to, if not superior to, that of major league white players. Holway provides statistical tables for each of his interviewees which reflect that player's performance against major league all-star teams. In addition to discussions of baseball heroics, these interviews include information on the education and occupations of the men interviewed.

PC 956. ISAACS, NEIL D. All the Moves: A History of College Basketball. Philadelphia: Lippincott, 1975. 319 pp.

This study, illustrated with more than 200 black-and-white photos, chronicles the history of college basketball from its invention in 1891 by James Naismith to the 1973 NCAA champion North Carolina State team. Isaacs describes the gradual refinement of the game in terms of rules and style of play, and its growth in popularity. He focuses on the significant coaches, teams, and players who have contributed to the evolution of the modern college game; he also includes a section on the impact of black players on basketball--not only on its style but on its role as a social institution. In addition, Isaacs reflects on the state of the contemporary college game, especially on the dangers of pressurized recruiting and on the need for further rule modifications.

PC 957. ISAACS, NEIL D. Jock Culture, USA. New York: Norton, 1978. 221 pp.

This work, which examines the role of sports in American society, asserts that sports have become a principal means of instructing and inculcating values. Isaacs focuses on the modern athlete as the primary source and standard for the American hero today and as a reservoir of American artistic expression. Isaacs employs a personal perspective in this study, utilizing interviews with sports personalities and his own anecdotes. He contends that American institutions reflect the values of the contemporary sports structure, and he considers the ways in which the ethic of competition has subverted the political and educational institutions in American culture. He also analyzes the way sports in literature reflect distinctly American themes.

PC 958. IZENBERG, JERRY. How Many Miles to Camelot: The All-American Sport Myth. New York: Holt, Rinehart & Winston, 1972. 227 pp.
In this first-person narrative, Izenberg decries the excesses and inequities of sports in America. His childhood vision of sports as Camelot was debunked by the racism, politics, and win-at-any-cost extremism that he became familiar with as a sportswriter. The particular injustices he attacks include the vicious reaction to Muhammad Ali's Islamic and pacifist beliefs, the immense pressure placed on little league ballplayers by their adult coaches, gambling, and bloodthirsty and bigoted fans cheering for injuries and for the defeat of black athletes.

PC 959. JOHNSON, WILLIAM O., Jr. Super Spectator and the Electric Lilliputians. Boston: Little, Brown, 1971. 238 pp.
Johnson is concerned with the "intense absorption of grand masses of people," disengaged both from each other and from all social responsibility, "watching all at once the transmission of electronic signals from afar." His treatment of TV and sports in the late 1960s and early 1970s focuses on the way the "American Television Establishment" has become "the entire energy, the very id of Super Spectator," the way it has remade sports, spectators, and the dynamic between the two. The TV revolution in sports has transformed every athlete into "a walking corporation," as well as inspired an immense proliferation of new sports, new events in old sports, and geographical, organizational, and rules changes. TV unifies families, communities, countries, and the world at the same time that it atomizes them. It determines the survival of every sport, controls allegiances, heightens costs and rewards, symbolizes, and determines values. Johnson discusses all of these aspects using anecdotes and extended, generally colloquial analyses from his perspective as a highly critical but equally culpable spectator.

PC 960. KAHN, ROGER. The Boys of Summer. New York: Harper & Row, 1971. 442 pp.
Kahn writes about the Brooklyn Dodgers in the 1950s and the later experience of some of their most famous stars after their baseball careers had ended. Of the team in the 1950s, Kahn writes that they were "outspoken, opinionated, bigoted, tolerant, black, white, open, passionate: in short, a facinating mix of vigorous men. They were not, however, the most successful team in baseball." In fact, the Dodgers lost in the World Series to the New York Yankees in both 1952 and 1953, the two years Kahn covered the team as a sportswriter. His heroes of these years, whose defeats and triumphs he traces into the 1960s, include Jackie Robinson, Roy Campanella, Duke Snider, Carl Erskine, Billy Cox, and Carl Furillo.

PC 961. KOPPETT, LEONARD. A Thinking Man's Guide to Baseball. New York: Dutton, 1967. 319 pp.
This study of organized baseball in America analyzes the working conditions, living habits, customs, and personalities that make up major league baseball. Topics of discussion include finances, the press, baseball owners, umpires and fans, and such significant baseball figures as Casey Stengel, Mickey Mantle, and Willie Mays. Koppett contrasts modern baseball with the earlier era of the game and observes that the themes of interaction, human fallibility, and unpredictability that appear in baseball are evident in life as well. This work contains six appendices, describing the ballpark employees, a chronology of major rule changes, scorekeeping and standard averages computation, the baseball hierarchy, and roster regulations.

PC 962. KOWET, DON. The Rich Who Won Sports. New York: Random House, 1977. 271 pp.

Kowet attempts to unmask the little-known owners of professional sports franchises in the U.S. He notes that the activities of the very rich are usually "concealed by towering gates around palatial estates and frosted-glass portholes of expensive yachts. The rich who own sports have to surrender some of this gold-plated privacy." Team ownership, he argues, only demonstrates the basic eccentricity of many of America's richest people, particularly as their teams seldom provide much profit and can be viewed simply as expensive toys. Kowet portrays owners who have inherited their wealth, those who have made their own fortunes and branched out into sports team ownership, and those who have made team, franchise, and league investment their personal path to wealth. He also considers the relationship of politics to team ownership and the ways in which owners have been able to take advantage of municipal pride for their personal gain.

PC 963. LARDNER, JOHN. White Hopes and Other Tigers. New York: Lippincott, 1951. 190 pp.

Lardner chronicles the history of boxing from 1919 to 1929. He describes how, during this period, prizefighting appealed to a new and larger variety of fans and became a million-dollar business. Reflecting the conditions of its social and economic context, Lardner notes that boxing placed a premium on "individual luster" and ingenuity. The glory of fighters and fights transcended the ring, pervading such "other social arts of man" as politics, motion pictures, popular fiction, and propaganda. Boxers such as Luis Firpo and Gene Tunney and promoters like Jimmy Johnston captured the imagination of the American public.

PC 964. LINEBERRY, WILLIAM P., ed. The Business of Sports. New York: Wilson, 1973. 220 pp.

Lineberry presents a collection of magazine essays from sources as diverse as Ebony, Vogue, The Wall Street Journal, and Business Week, along with his own introductory essays to each of the book's six sections. "Sports as an Investment" (Section I) analyzes the emergence of a number of professional sports as major money-making enterprises. "Commercialism" (II) considers the interaction of sports and advertising, off the field in the form of player promotion of products and on the field as owners use a variety of non-sports gimmicks to lure fans to their particular form of entertainment. "The Promoters" (III) discusses the people who make money from sports without ever engaging in athletic competition. "The Players" (IV) discusses the relationship of athletes to the economic aspects of sports, while "All That Glitters" (V) hints at difficulties in maintaining profitability in sports. "Regulation, Reform, and Redemption" (VI) examines the actual and potential role of government in regulating professional sports.

PC 965. LIPSKY, RICHARD. How We Play the Game. Boston: Beacon Press, 1981. 189 pp.

Lipsky proposes a political theory of American sport. He contends that the "sportsworld exists as a dramatic, symbolic universe that generates emotional impact and creates meaning" for the 70% of Americans who claim they are fans as well as for others. Drawing on personal experiences, journalistic and impressionistic accounts, and psychological and philosophical interpretations, Lipsky interprets this universe founded on play as functioning in two major ways: as a transmitter and socializer of dominant values, and as a symbolic refuge. These functions accrue from the way the game (a ritual drama) symbolizes life but exists as a counterpoint to the larger bureaucratic and machine-dominated world. Lipsky develops his theme by exploring sporting events, team allegiances, heroes, and language.

PC 966. LIPSYTE, ROBERT. Sports World: An American Dreamland. New York: Quadrangle Books, 1975. 292 pp.
Depicting sports as a microcosm of American life, Lipsyte contends that sports have so pervaded the American consciousness that a sports mentality and sports values figure significantly in the ways our culture operates. Lipsyte writes from a personal perspective based upon his experiences with athletes and teams as a reporter for The New York Times. He considers the character and popularity of specific sports as expressions of American culture (football as the sport of the 1960s, basketball as the dominant sport of the 1970s) and investigates the concept of the sports hero in America, focusing upon Muhammad Ali, who attained a "royal" status as heavyweight champion of the world.

PC 967. LOWENFISH, LEE and TONY LUPIEN. The Imperfect Diamond: The Story of Baseball's Reserve System and the Men Who Fought to Change It. New York: Stein & Day, 1980. 258 pp.
Lowenfish and Lupien present a historical chronicle of the contract system in professional baseball in which a player, in effect, became the property of his team; he had no right to negotiate freely once he was signed. The authors analyze the Players League rebellion of 1890, David Fultz and the Baseball Players Fraternity of 1912-18, the reign after the Black Sox scandal of Commissioner Kenesaw Mountain Landis, and the players who played outside of the U.S. rather than submit to the reserve system. They also discuss the victory of the Major League Baseball Players Association and Marvin Miller against the baseball establishment in achieving fundamental changes in the reserve system. Lupien offers his reflections on his fifty years in baseball as player, scout, and college coach, and some speculations on the future of major league baseball.

PC 968. LOY, JOHN W., GERALD S. KENYON, and BARRY D. McPHERSON, eds. Sport, Culture and Society: A Reader on the Sociology of Sport. 1969; Rev. ed. Philadelphia: Lea & Febiger, 1981. 376 pp.
This collection of essays, first published when the fields of sports history and sports sociology were relatively new, considers a variety of specific sports and athletes, as well as the more abstract phenomena of "sport" and its relationship to society. The editors offer an essay on "The Sociology of Sport," and other authors contribute such pieces as "The Structure and Classification of Sport" (Reger Callois) and "Team Competition, Success, and the Adjustment of Group Members" (Albert Myers). The book also contains essays on specific sports, ranging from rifle teams to professional basketball to Pueblo baseball, and other essays on spectators, college sports, and the technological revolution in sports.

PC 969. LUCAS, JOHN. The Modern Olympic Games. South Brunswick, N.J.: Barnes, 1980. 242 pp.
Lucas traces the evolution of the modern Olympic Games from 1896 to 1980. He focuses on the Olympic ideal and the philosophy of amateur sport. The Olympic Games have as their "sole reason for existence, the brotherhood of man, the physical health of mankind, and the joy of international athletic competition." Attention is given to the need for reform to preserve the Olympic Games as a means for achieving significant international communication between nations and people. Lucas also examines the influence on the Olympic movement of the three presidents of the International Olympic Committee—Baron Pierre de Coubertin, Avery Brundage, and Lord Killain.

PC 970. LUCAS, JOHN A. and RONALD A. SMITH. Saga of American Sport. Philadelphia: Lea & Febiger, 1978. 439 pp.
Arguing that sports reflect the dominant social themes in American society, the authors chronicle the history of American sports from its Colonial and early American manifestations to the present. Lucas and Smith examine

how social milieu dictated the sporting activities in which Americans
participated. They trace the changes in sports that accompanied the country's transition from agriculture to industry, as well as English and
immigrant influences, and the effects of the Civil Rights and women's
rights movements. They maintain that such national characteristics as
cultural unity through diversity, the spirit of adventure, competitiveness,
success and mobility, pragmatic materialism, violence, and humanitarianism
have filtered into "the deepest membranes" of the American sporting scene.

PC 971. LUDWIG, JACK. The Great American Spectaculars: The Kentucky
    Derby, Mardi Gras, and Other Days of Celebration. Garden City,
    N.Y.: Doubleday, 1976. 247 pp.
Ludwig focuses on five major events in American culture: the Kentucky
Derby, the Indianapolis 500, the Rose Bowl, the Masters Tournament, and
the Mardi Gras. He juxtaposes his own impressions of each event with
political and social events, observing that the "American Spectacular"
is a circus intended to divert the attention of the masses from the realities of contemporary American life.

PC 972. MANCHESTER, HERBERT. Four Centuries of Sport in America: 1490-
    1890. New York: Derrydale, 1931. 245 pp.
In this history of sports in America, Manchester relies upon original
sources to trace the evolution of specific sports from 1490 to 1890.
Contending that sports are in large measure an outgrowth of the life of
the age, he considers developments in sports in light of changes in American culture. The introduction of the horse to America by the colonists,
for example, altered the Indian sport of hunting. Similarly, the growth
of the cities was responsible for the origin of team games, although with
the evolution of urban life the role of sport has shifted to one of exercise and escape from the city. The work is illustrated with black-and-
white drawings.

PC 973. MERCHANT, LARRY. . . . And Every Day You Take Another Bite.
    Garden City, N.Y.: Doubleday, 1971. 191 pp.
Merchant satirizes both professional football and recent books that have
revealed "inside stories" of professional sports. Arguing that such characters as the biblical David, Napoleon, Sitting Bull, Crazy Horse, and
Charles Darwin speak in "footballese," he illustrates the broad use to
which sports cliches can be put. He also offers his own reflections on
the game as it is played today, the impact of television and advertising,
and the personalities who play, coach, and promote the game as an American
passion. Finally, he offers his own fanciful contribution to the new
literature of athlete-authors with "Stop Action: An Intimate Football
Diary by a Nobody."

PC 974. MERCHANT, LARRY. The National Football Lottery. New York: Holt,
    Rinehart, & Winston, 1973. 325 pp.
In this work Merchant discusses the intricacies of the professional sports
gambling establishment. He discovers that sports gambling is a weekly
activity for twelve to fifteen million football fans, and his contacts
range from the man who sets the weekly point spread to a former player
who admits his involvement in fixing games.

PC 975. MICHENER, JAMES A. Sports in America. New York: Random House,
    1976. 466 pp.
Michener writes from the perspective of a sports fan and advocate who
is concerned about sports as an institution in American life. The work
is both a reflection on the value of sports in everyday life and a look
at the structure of modern professional and collegiate athletics. Michener
enumerates the ways in which people can participate in sports, furnishing
information on physical education and training. He also looks at the

role of sports in the emotional and physical development of children and investigates the business of sports in America, particularly financing, the media network, and government control.

PC 976. MROZEK, DONALD. Sport and American Mentality: 1880-1910. Knoxville: University of Tennessee Press, 1983. 284 pp.
Between 1880 and 1910, Mrozek contends, sports in America evolved from an infrequent spectacle, haphazard and somewhat disreputable, into a national institution characterized by a vast participation generally free of class demarcations. Mrozek argues that such late 19th-century cultural forces as national unification, the increase of leisure time, a growing concern with physical health, a nascent youth culture, and changing attitudes about women and sexuality precipitated an unprecedented interest in sports. The games and spectacles of the past began to take on modern features; sports' new respectability and emerging institutionalism were reflected in such developments as the standardization of rules and the rise of predetermined schedules. By the second decade of the 20th century, sports had acquired "a measure of . . . permanence and autonomy" which presaged its later prominence in the national consciousness.

PC 977. NOLL, ROGER G., ed. Government and the Sports Business. Washington, D.C.: Brookings Institution, 1974. 445 pp.
The eleven essays included in this work focus upon the operation of professional team sports in America. These essays devote particular attention to the effects of governmental policy on the financial performance of sports teams. Authors from government, the private sector, sports management, and the academy address such topics as social theory, attendance and price setting, taxation, labor relations, discrimination, broadcasting, subsidized stadiums and arenas, self-regulation, and Federal anti-trust laws. The essays present conclusions on the factors involved in a team's performance, and the potential influence of government policy on competition.

PC 978. NOVAK, MICHAEL. The Joy of Sports: End Zones, Baskets, Balls and the Consecration of the American Spirit. New York: Basic Books, 1976. 337 pp.
Novak examines sports as a form of religion in America and contends that for the fan, sports express metaphysical beauty, excellence, imagination, and vitality--all qualities that Novak considers central to human existence. Each of his expository chapters is followed by a "Sportsreel" section that illustrates Novak's observations through anecdotes and portraits of individual performers. He investigates the impact of sports on America, observing that sport functions as a universal language that unifies our nation. The work contains a section on women in sports and an examination of the role of the writer in the world of sports.

PC 979. NOVERR, DOUGLAS A. and LAWRENCE E. ZIEWACZ. The Games They Played: Sports in American History, 1865-1980. Chicago: Nelson-Hall, 1983. 423 pp.
Limiting their discussion to those sports "that have experienced their unique development and major evolution in the United States" (baseball, basketball, boxing, golf, tennis, and track and field), Noverr and Ziewacz attempt to establish sports' "overall historical and cultural context" in this country. They argue that sports have an expansiveness and malleability that allow them to provide a "focus" for the aspirations, efforts of self-definition, and iconographies of each new generation. Noverr and Ziewacz emphasize this unique and exalted status of sport as they survey its role and practice beginning in the Gilded Age and continuing through the 1970s.

PC 980. OGLESBY, CAROLE A., ed. Women and Sport: From Myth to Reality. Philadelphia: Lea & Febiger, 1978. 256 pp.
The essays in this collection examine the relationship among women, sports, and society. The contributors review the established literature of the field of women in sports from a feminist perspective. They seek fresh insights into women's sports problems and offer feminist definitions and descriptions of sport. The first section, entitled "Women's Sport, Society and Ourselves," considers among other topics the interrelationship of sports, societal views of women and the female body, and sexuality. The second section deals with myth, reality, and social change in women's sports. In the epilogue, Oglesby concludes that American society must support women's sports programs in international competition, but must also create an environment that encourages the efforts of all women to realize their athletic potential.

PC 981. PETERSON, ROBERT. Only the Ball Was White. Englewood Cliffs, N.J.: Prentice-Hall, 1970. 406 pp.
In this work about black baseball players, Peterson analyzes the hostility toward blacks in early major league baseball. This hostility led to the formation of a variety of leagues that provided a source of income and an outlet for the talents of black players. Peterson describes the structure and management of various Negro leagues as well as barnstorming life on the road. Detailed appendices provide information on year-by-year league standings, East-West all-star games, and a register of all players and officials.

PC 982. PLIMPTON, GEORGE. Paper Lion. New York: Harper & Row, 1966. 362 pp.
Plimpton's stint with the Detroit Lions was one of a series of athletic "experiments" he conducted in the 1960s (he also boxed with Archie Moore and pitched in a baseball all-star game, among other ventures). He wanted to describe "what happened to someone with the temerity to climb the field-box railings and try the sport oneself . . . to play out the fantasies, the daydreams that so many people have." His self-deprecatory and anecdotal account of life as a "last-string" quarterback in the Lions' 1963 summer training camp tries to capture the flavor of professional football life. Plimpton wants to get beyond the allure of public adulation and explore what sets apart the player from the spectator, to probe from within the nature of the "fantasy."

PC 983. RADER, BENJAMIN G. American Sports: From the Age of Folk Games to the Age of Spectators. Englewood Cliffs, N.J.: Prentice-Hall, 1983. 376 pp.
Rader's chronological history of sports in America begins with a discussion of the importance of folk games and popular pastimes in the Colonies and the new U.S. He then describes the developing ideology of a "sporting youth" between about 1850 and 1920. His last major section focuses on the period from 1920 to the present, which he calls "The Age of the Spectator." He provides the historical context for a discussion of the modern sports hero, the development of team sports, the emergence of television as a primary medium for transmitting sports information, college sports, the status of professional athletes, and new pressure within sports and in the society as a whole for more participation at the professional level by women and members of minority groups. Rader concludes with the notion that sport has supplanted church, family, and community as an institution that holds modern society together.

PC 984. RADER, BENJAMIN G. In Its Own Image: How Television Has Transformed Sports. New York: Free Press, 1984. 228 pp.
Rader surveys the developments off the field that have influenced the
character and ethos of professional sports. His main concern is the impact
of television broadcasting and reporting. He argues that the demands
of the electronic medium and its system of commercial sponsorship have
wrought changes in athletic competition itself, ranging from rules which
are stretched or changed to accommodate broadcast crews to the on-camera
behavior of athletes. He examines the rating wars among the major television networks, sportscasters' jargon, and the impact of media hype on
amateur sports. Rader contends that television has changed competitive
contests into entertainment spectacles.

PC 985. REIDENBAUGH, LOWELL. Take Me Out to the Ball Park. St. Louis,
Mo.: Sporting News, 1983. 288 pp.
Reidenbaugh provides textual, photographic, and cartoon illustration portraits (the latter drawn by Amadee Wohlschlaeger) of thirty-five present
and former major league ball parks. Each portrait presents the history
and important highlights of that field or stadium. The personalities
of owners and their families, as well as players, managers, and fans emerge
here. Reidenbaugh writes favorably of the triumph of new clubs and their
domed, multi-purpose stadiums.

PC 986. RIBALOW, HAROLD U. The Jew in American Sports. 1948; Rev. ed.
New York: Bloch, 1966. 414 pp.
Ribalow chronicles the contributions of particular Jewish athletes to
American sports in the first half of the 20th century. Using interviews
as well as traditional research techniques, Ribalow not only profiles
each athlete's athletic accomplishment, he also sketches that athlete's
family and community background. His subjects include boxers Benny Leonard
and Barney Ross, baseball players Hank Greenberg and Al Rosen, Dolph
Schayes in basketball, Sidney Franklin, the "bullfighter from Flatbush,"
golfer Herman Barron, and chess masters Emanuel Lasker and Bobby Fischer.

PC 987. RIESS, STEVEN A. Touching Base: Professional Baseball and American Culture in the Progressive Era. Westport, Conn.: Greenwood
Press, 1980. 268 pp.
Riess connects baseball to larger themes in American culture during the
period around the turn of the 20th century. He discusses the ideology
of baseball, which contributes to a mythology of the sport as an all-
American pastime open to any member of society. Riess notes that in this
period most fans were white and middle class and that all major league
players were white. The popular notion that baseball was a sport for
working people is also untrue. Most working-class Americans did not have
leisure time for baseball, except on Sundays, and most local communities
banned the playing of the game on that day according to long-standing
blue laws. Riess also debunks the notion that baseball players came from
rural areas and used baseball as a path to middle-class respectability
or wealth.

PC 988. RITTER, LAWRENCE S. The Glory of Their Times: The Story of the
Early Days of Baseball Told by the Men Who Played It. New York:
Macmillan, 1966. 300 pp.
Ritter's oral history approach to the subject of major league players
in the early 20th century focuses on individual players. Interviewees
range from Sam Crawford (who played from 1899 to 1919) to Paul Waner (1926-
45), and include such personalities as Bill Wambsganss (1914-26), Lefty
O'Doul (1919-34), and Heinie Groh (1912-27). Ritter cites Jacques Barzun's
contention that "whoever wants to know the heart and mind of America had
better learn baseball" in arguing that his oral history of baseball is
also a chronicle of America. To this end, Ritter asks his subjects not

only about what it was like to be a baseball player "but also about what
it was like just to be alive then."

PC 989. ROBERTS, RANDY. Papa Jack: Jack Johnson and the Era of White
         Hopes. New York: Free Press, 1983. 274 pp.
In this biography of Jack Johnson, boxing's first black heavyweight champion, the author describes Johnson's challenge to "the standards of white
America," both in and out of the ring. Roberts highlights Johnson's resistance to racial barriers during his boxing career, in his later stage acts,
and in his private life. The author outlines Johnson's confrontations
with authority and the law, uncovering the "invisible scars" that hid
beneath the boxer's "flawless control" in the ring, but that manifested
themselves in Johnson's "reckless and disorderly" private life.

PC 990. ROONEY, JOHN F. The Recruiting Game: Toward a New System of
         Intercollegiate Sports. Lincoln: University of Nebraska Press,
         1980. 204 pp.
This volume is a response to what Rooney calls the recent "explosion of
criticism concerning big-time collegiate sports." He argues that the
present system creates many student athletes who "[don't] care about,
or [aren't] capable of obtaining, a baccalaureate degree." In addition
to describing the abuses of recruiters in college football, the deification
of athletes on campus, and the ramifications of a system that uses players
for their ability on the field with little regard for their education
or post-football future, Rooney offers a comprehensive alternative based
on regional sports affiliations of colleges in a semi-professional relationship that would create a system which would more accurately reflect
what he sees as college football's role in American society.

PC 991. RUST, ART, Jr. "Get That Nigger Off the Field!": A Sparkling,
         Informal History of the Black Man in Baseball. New York: Dela-
         corte Press, 1976. 228 pp.
In his history of black baseball players, Rust observes that our national
pastime has reflected the racial attitudes of American culture. This
work contains an introduction by Bill White, features profiles of prominent
black baseball players from the segregated Negro leagues, and provides
portraits of black players who have broken the color line in major league
baseball. Written from a personal perspective, the book presents the
black ballplayer as a role model for the young black fan, and includes
commentary by various baseball figures. In the three appendices, Rust
cites the contributions of black men to baseball since the integration
of the Major Leagues in 1947, and describes the discrimination that still
exists in the big leagues. The book is illustrated with over 100 black-
and-white photos.

PC 992. SCOTT, JACK. The Athlete Revolution. New York: Free Press,
         1971. 242 pp.
Scott discusses the volatile world of college athletics during the late
1960s and early 1970s. The conservative and traditional nature of sports,
sports coaching, and sports administration was being challenged by the
increasing--and increasingly strident--radicalism of young people, and
by the critical demands of minorities, women, and a number of concerned
educators. In other words, Scott states, "the highly political nature
of competitive athletics" was becoming clear. In addition, drug abuse
had become widespread, and commercialism, with all the abuses that accompany it, had skyrocketed. Many felt that the notion of amateurism was
a sham, and some decried all forms of competitive athletics. Scott
describes and condemns the various abuses in and of amateur sports, but
he does not renounce competition itself. He calls instead for a renewed
commitment to educating athletes, a decommercialization of college sports,
and an increased voice for athletes and students in administrative policy
decisions.

1430

PC 993. **SEYMOUR, HAROLD.** Baseball: The Early Years. New York: Oxford
University Press, 1960. 373 pp.; Baseball: The Golden Age.
New York: Oxford University Press, 1971. 492 pp.
Seymour's two-volume history of baseball in America traces the sport as
pastime and a symbol of America from its origins as an amateur contest
for young gentlemen to the sport's "golden age" that ended around 1930.
Both volumes discuss baseball's great personalities and consider the
behind-the-scenes operation of clubs which, by the 20th century, had become
business enterprises as well as purveyors of athletics and entertainment.
Seymour examines the scandals within the game, including the 1919 Chicago
Black Sox World Series, an event that thrust the professional game into
a new era of centralized control under a commissioner. He also analyzes
the emergence of the minor league farm system and its role in developing
professional talent in the 20th century.

PC 994. **SHECTER, LEONARD.** The Jocks. Indianapolis, Ind.: Bobbs-Merrill,
1969. 278 pp.
A former sports journalist, Shecter offers a warning to readers otherwise
inclined to accept at face value American sports' self-advertisement.
His book is an expose of hucksterism and cynicism in and toward sports.
Through a series of vignettes supported by analysis, Shecter assesses
the debasing impact of team owners, promoters, individual athletes, sports'
governing bodies, and the media on sports.

PC 995. **SMITH, LEVERETT T., Jr.** The American Dream and the National Game.
Bowling Green, Ohio: Bowling Green University Popular Press,
1970. 285 pp.
In the late 19th century, sports in general and baseball in particular
were popularly considered either irrelevant, and to some degree immoral,
or as manifestations of the dynamic quality of 19th-century American life.
By the second half of the 20th century, however, sports had achieved a
wholly different aspect; they were now esteemed by most as a "repository
for [the] values" threatened in the perplexing and chaotic modern world,
a stay against loss and confusion. Moreover, critics and anthropologists
had begun to regard the practice of sports as an undertaking fundamental
to psychological health and as a metaphor or model useful for understanding
behavior. Smith analyzes these evolving attitudes toward sports, locating
them in the broader contexts of national and personal self-definition
and of unifying social values. He draws extensively from fiction, social
criticism, and sports journalism, and from both high cultural and popular
sources; Huizinga, Hawthorne, Ring Lardner, and The Sporting News are
among the wide variety of authorities cited. Although Smith is concerned
with the idea of the "national" game and therefore primarily treats baseball, he devotes his final chapter to football, which has seen such a
great ascendancy since W.W. II that it now has at least an equal claim
to that title.

PC 996. **SOMERS, DALE A.** The Rise of Sports in New Orleans: 1850-1900.
Baton Rouge: Louisiana State University Press, 1972. 320 pp.
Developments in New Orleans' sporting life during the second half of the
19th century are representative of the larger leisure revolution that
was occurring across the country at that time. Somers details the ascendancy of sports as a permissible and later praiseworthy urban recreational
habit, tracing from their antebellum origins the institutionalizing and
commercializing of such sports as baseball, horse racing, yachting, and
boxing. He also discusses spectator sensibilities, the proliferation
of athletic clubs, the role of blacks in the new sporting scene, and the
birth of amateur/professional distinctions.

PC 997. TELANDER, RICK. Heaven Is a Playground. New York: St. Martin's Press, 1976. 282 pp.
To examine the function of play in the life of the individual and community, Telander chronicles his experiences on a New York City playground for one summer and provides insight into the role that basketball plays in a black ghetto culture. He relies upon profiles of players and community figures to show the significance of basketball in the social structure of the neighborhood. Not only is basketball predominant as an activity but language and status are also defined by the sport. The author points out that basketball is regarded as a means of attaining personal and professional success, which to some degree explains how environment has contributed to black dominance in basketball.

PC 998. TUNIS, JOHN. The American Way in Sport. New York: Duell, Sloan & Pearce, 1958. 180 pp.
Tunis is concerned with the attitudes that make sports such a pervasive phenomenon in American society. Examining patterns and cycles of change in major American sports, he describes the tremendous growth of spectator interest, the concomitant rise of various individual sports, and the introduction of the profit motive into the sporting world. Among other topics, Tunis discusses the role of the frontier in sports development, early baseball, "industrialized" football, the heroes of the 1920s, Indiana's hysteria over basketball, and the government's role in sports.

PC 999. TWIN, STEPHANIE L., ed. Out of the Bleachers: Writings on Women and Sports. Old Westbury, N.Y.: Feminist Press, 1979. 229 pp.
Twin has compiled a volume of essays that aims to analyze and champion women athletes, as well as to destroy the prejudices hindering them. The essays are divided into three sections. In the first section, contributors discuss physiology and social relations. To what extent, if any, are women physically less developed than men or incapable of rigorous athletic participation? How do the myths about a woman's physical abilities, as well as the actual nature of those abilities, shape her own and popular conceptions concerning her social and athletic status and aspirations? The second section offers reflections on the lives of such sportswomen as long jumper and sprinter Willye B. White, tennis star Althea Gibson, and swimmer Gertrude Ederle. The last section includes works that evaluate the future prospects of women's athletics. These works denounce the organization and operation of the sports structure at present, but they argue that it can be rehabilitated and humanized. Contributors to this volume include Ann Crittenden, Frances Willard, Paul Gallico, Louise Bernikow, Jack Scott, and Harry Edwards.

PC 1000. TWOMBLY, WELLS. 200 Years of Sport in America: A Pageant of a Nation at Play. New York: McGraw-Hill, 1976. 287 pp.
This pictorial history is an "impressionistic look" at sports in America rather than a comprehensive survey. The work seeks to capture the drama of the sporting spectacle as well as the spirit of its time, and by rendering these colorfully to understand the appeal of a sport or athlete at a particular time, as well as the general appeal of sports and athletes. Twombly's text is therefore popular and discursive, focusing on especially dramatic events and charismatic personalities. The text is divided into four chronological sections: The Pastoral Age, 1776-1865; The Passionate Age, 1866-1919; The Golden Age, 1920-1945; and The Electronic Age, 1946-1976. Each section is illustrated with prints and photographs, many in color.

PC 1001. TYGIEL, JULES. Baseball's Great Experiment: Jackie Robinson and His Legacy. New York: Oxford University Press, 1983. 291 pp.

Tygiel discusses the process of integration in the Major Leagues. He begins his discussion with Branch Rickey signing Jackie Robinson to play with the Brooklyn Dodgers' minor league club in 1946, and continues through the 1959 season when the Boston Red Sox signed Pumpsie Green and became the last team to add a black player to its line-up. Tygiel emphasizes the larger historical and social context of baseball's integration, detailing its impact upon American society. He analyzes the response of fans and players, of non-fans, and of racist and Civil Rights groups. Tygiel is also interested in the black player's evaluation of his own experience, and he includes accounts of Larry Doby, Satchell Paige, Willie Mays, and a number of other black stars.

PC 1002. VINCENT, TED. Mudville's Revenge: The Rise and Fall of American Sport. New York: Seaview Books, 1981. 346 pp.

This "popular" sports history addresses the development of American sport and the changing nature of people's involvement with sport. Vincent asserts that American sports have been "Romanized," transformed, that is, from a pastime with a communal emphasis into a spectacle and a big business. The rise of sports popularity is represented in three cases--track and field, baseball, and basketball. The author maintains that it is now time for "Mudville's Revenge"; people ought to become sports contestants and participants rather than viewers of sports on television, an activity which he contends is merely a form of empty mass entertainment. The increasing number of Americans now engaging in mass participatory sports may indicate a return to the strong association of Americans with sports. The book ranges over such topics as "the democratic age of sport," the growth of the professional sports organization, and the commercialization of sports.

PC 1003. VOIGT, DAVID Q. American Baseball: From Gentleman's Sport to the Commissioner System. Norman: University of Oklahoma Press, 1966. 336 pp. American Baseball: From the Commissioners to Continental Expansion. Norman: University of Oklahoma Press, 1970. 350 pp. American Baseball: From Postwar Expansion to the Electronic Age. University Park: Pennsylvania State University Press, 1983. 384 pp.

Voigt's three-volume history of baseball investigates, as Allan Nevins notes in the foreword, all aspects of the subject: the game's origins and evolution, "the professionalism that grew out of it, and the big business that was reared upon it." Voight emphasizes the interpenetration of baseball and American culture, and treats not only the important players, moments, and organizational and rule developments, but also the game's sociological and psychological significance. Volume I charts the development of baseball from its rural, leisurely, partly cricket-inspired roots in the first half of the 19th century through its spectacular rise as a part of the larger leisure revolution of the closing decades of the 19th century and the early part of the 20th century. Volume II begins with an extended treatment of the "deadball dynasties" in the first few decades of the 20th century, and traces developments through the 1919 Black Sox scandal, the introduction of a livelier ball, and the popularity of players like Babe Ruth and Joe Dimaggio, up to the expansion of teams to the West coast, the growing impact of TV coverage and new technologies, intimations of a salary revolution, and other aspects of the "mid-century upheaval" in the sport. Volume III chronicles developments since W.W. II, including the reception of black players by other players and by fans, continued expansion, the impact of the players' union and the reserve clause, and the ever-increasing influence of the media.

PC 1004. VOIGT, DAVID Q. America Through Baseball. Chicago: Nelson-
Hall, 1976. 221 pp.
Voigt synthesizes aspects of baseball's history and the history of the
U.S. in his attempt to demythologize both. He treats in depth the founding
of major league baseball in 1871 as well as the origins of two of the
sport's oldest teams, the Cincinnati Reds and the Boston Red Sox. He
considers developments in baseball as they have illuminated, supported,
or contradicted traditional American beliefs in a national purpose, a
work ethic, and notions of "fair play." Voigt also analyzes the ways
in which baseball has been refracted through the prism of various media
from the early days of sports newspapers to the present era of televised
sports entertainment.

PC 1005. WEAVER, ROBERT B. Amusements and Sports in American Life. Chicago: University of Chicago Press, 1939. 195 pp.
Weaver surveys the evolution of play in America during the last 300 years
and describes the types of recreational activities practiced in different
regions of the country throughout American history. He reveals that while
amusements were officially discouraged in early America, some Colonial
amusements and sports were enjoyed by the Puritans. Weaver further
describes sport and amusement after the Revolutionary War, on the frontier,
and after the Civil War. He traces the origin and growth of specific
American sports, emphasizing the importance of recreational activities
in American society.

PC 1006. WHORTON, JAMES C. Crusaders for Fitness: The History of American
Health Reformers. Princeton, N.J.: Princeton University Press,
1982. 359 pp.
Whorton surveys the history of American health reformers from the Jacksonian to the Progressive periods of American history. He examines the
major themes of health reform, or "hygienic religion," focusing on those
individuals who were central to the evolution of its ideology. He discusses such topics as Christian physiology, physical education, hygiene,
muscular vegetarianism, uric acid and other fetishes, physical culture,
and the bicycle craze. The health crusaders he discusses include Sylvester
Graham, William Alcott, Mary Gove Nichols, Horace Fletcher, John Harvey
Kellog, Dioclesian Lewis, Dudley Sargent, and Bernarr Macfadden. Whether
"running, gymnastics or vegetable diet has been the key," Whorton contends,
"the kingdom of health has in the final analysis been the world of maximum
human performance."

PC 1007. WOLF, DAVID. Foul! The Connie Hawkins Story. New York: Holt,
Rinehart & Winston, 1972. 400 pp.
Wolf contends that his story of Connie Hawkins's implication in a basketball fixing scandal, Hawkins's blacklisting by the National Basketball
Association, his performances with the Harlem Globetrotters and other
professional teams, and his eventual reinstatement to the NBA after his
name was cleared is more than just the saga of a uniquely talented athlete.
It is, Wolf argues, "also a chronicle of the corruption, racism, hypocrisy,
and exploitation that are realities in modern, big-time athletics." Wolf
attacks the criminal justice system that pressured the young Hawkins into
making false confessions, the NBA for its hypocritical attitudes, and
sports entrepreneurs and administrators who believe "that ownership of
a franchise places them above the law." A previous article by Wolf in
Life helped to clear Hawkins's name, and this book ends with Hawkins beginning a new career as a member of the Phoenix Suns.

1434

PC 1008. WOOLF, BOB. Behind Closed Doors. New York: Atheneum, 1976.
300 pp.
Woolf examines recent developments in professional sports from his perspective as a sports attorney and representative for more than 300 major
athletes in contract negotiations. Woolf discusses his successful negotiations with team ownership in an age when the notion of players as team
property was being challenged for the first time. As a solution to the
difficulties and endless court battles that have arisen from the conflict
between players' desire for independence and management's intransigence,
Woolf offers the notion of a Sports Regulatory Board established by
Congress--even though, as he notes, "government control is repugnant to
many Americans, who do not trust anyone in Washington . . . ."

PC 1009. YAEGER, ROBERT C. Seasons of Shame: The New Violence in Sports.
New York: McGraw-Hill, 1979. 278 pp.
Yaeger bases his study of violence in sports on the notion that sports
are a teaching tool and that the growing atmosphere of brutality in sporting events fosters brutality in the general social sphere. This trend
is particularly evident in its effects on young people who are most impres-
sionable and are therefore susceptible to the concept that one must win
at any cost. Yaeger surveys the origins of contact sports, analyzing
the emotional and psychological underpinnings of these sports, and he
describes the ways in which commercial interests perpetuate and intensify
violent trends in sports today. He spends several chapters discussing
the culpability of everyone involved--players, coaches, rulemakers, the
media, and fans--and he treats in detail the effects of violence on all
of these groups, as well as on children. Finally, he offers a number
of suggestions for improvement--including rule and equipment changes,
substantial penalties for violation, and forcing parents and high school
coaches to take responsibility--in order that good sportsmanship might
be reestablished.

VIII. MATERIAL CULTURE

PC 1010. BECHER, FRANKLIN D. Housing Messages. Stroudsburg, Pa.: Dowden,
Hutchinson & Ross, 1977. 142 pp.
Becher considers how physical forms communicate values to those who see
and use the physical environment, particularly human habitats. His early
chapters look at the role of the physical environment as a communication
medium. Becher explores the preferences people have regarding housing
environments, such as free standing, recycled, and hand-built units; these
environments generally reflect the values of those who create them. The
middle chapters address the question of who should or can create appropriate images for a setting's occupants, by what processes, and for whose
benefit. The final chapters discuss environmental messages associated
with specific components such as high crime territories and planned playgrounds. Becher also looks at the physical environment as part of a social
change process. The book is illustrated with drawings and black-and-white
photos.

PC 1011. BELASCO, JAMES WARREN. Americans on the Road: From Autocamp
to Motel. Cambridge, Mass.: MIT Press, 1979. 212 pp.
Belasco examines the social impact of the automobile in this study of
the American motel industry. Describing the motel as "a revealing interface between business and culture" and "a material embodiment of tourist
dreams of communication, independence, equality, and spontaneity," the
author divides his account into three phases: the age of autocamping

(1910-20) as a vacation alternative for the comfortable middle classes;
the rise of municipally sponsored autocamps in the 1920s; and early experiments with privately owned cabin camps, cottages, and auto courts that
gave rise to the modern motor hotel.

PC 1012. BENES, PETER. Two Towns: Concord and Wethersfield, a Comparative
Exhibition of Regional Culture 1635-1850. Concord, Mass.:
Concord Antiquarian Museum, 1982. 176 pp.
The catalogue of an exhibit of the same name, the book compares matching
artifacts of domestic life from Concord, Massachusetts, and Wethersfield,
Connecticut, in an attempt to discover cultural similarities and differ-
ences between the two communities. This book is an illustrated listing
of the artifacts considered.

PC 1013. BERGER, MICHAEL L. The Devil Wagon in God's Country: The Automobile and Social Change in Rural America, 1893-1929. Hamden,
Conn.: Archon Books, 1979. 269 pp.
Berger explores the effects of the automobile on the shape of life in
rural America. The pejorative label referred to in the title reflects
the hostility the automobile originally encountered in rural areas. Automobiles changed family and community life, bringing access to goods and
services previously available only to urban dwellers. This change in
mobility not only changed the shape of rural life; it transformed ideals
and attitudes. The book deals with the auto as a symbol for and means
of change.

PC 1014. BROWNE, RAY B. and MARSHALL FISHWICK, eds. Icons of Popular
Culture. Bowling Green, Ohio: Bowling Green University Popular
Press, 1970. 128 pp.
This collection of twenty-three articles defines icons as external expressions of internal convictions. The contributors argue that the icon,
often an artifact, reveals basic social attitudes, assumptions, and needs.
Each icon is an admired object to which the public responds on an emotional
level. The book includes articles on political buttons, historic sites,
school houses, postage stamps, pinball machines, popular fashions, and
human icons such as George Washington, the Beatles, and Shirley Temple.
Throughout, iconography is considered as a methodology for understanding
popular culture.

PC 1015. BURLINGAME, ROGER. The March of the Iron Man: A Social History
of Union Through Invention. New York: Scribner, 1938. 500 pp.
Burlingame's history of the early U.S. examines the technologies which
assisted the development of the nation. The author traces technological
innovation from the printing press and industries of the Colonial era
to the Pennsylvania rifle of the Revolutionary period, the development
of the steamboat and cotton gin, and the railroad, telegraph, and Yankee
Clippers of the age of expansion and industrialization. Burlingame sees
machines as democratizing and equalizing forces, and finds in them a metaphor for defining the national character.

PC 1016. BUSH, DONALD J. The Streamlined Decade. New York: Braziller,
1975. 214 pp.
In this illustrated survey of the architecture and decorative arts of
the 1930s, Bush traces the principle of streamlining, its development
from science, and its relationship to contemporary sculpture. He sees
streamlining as a symbol of optimism during a time of social turbulence;
its forms are emblematic of speed, efficiency, and the elimination of
extraneous detail. Streamlining became an expression of the national
mood and of citizen interests, reflected in useful products, art objects,
automobiles, architecture, and home furnishings. The author traces analogies in swing music, film and stream-of-consciousness literature, and
in the technocrat political movement.

PC 1017. CLAY, GRADY. Close-Up: How to Read the American City. New
           York: Praeger, 1973. 192 pp.
Clay looks at the hidden meanings of common American urban architecture
and geography. He shows how to discern the development of the city and
to read the conflicts embodied in various urban assemblages. He also
shows how to recognize such forms as fixes (perceptions), epitome districts (those areas full of symbolic meaning), fronts (dividing lines),
and strips (linear developments), naming those for which no common name
exists. Clay concentrates on the contemporary, with some references to
the historical. The book includes illustrations as guides to identification.

PC 1018. DEETZ, JAMES. An Invitation to Archaeology. Garden City, N.Y.:
           Natural History Press, 1967. 150 pp.
In this introductory text, Deetz defines the field, and covers dating,
how material is analyzed, the determinants of space and time, and how
human behavior is extrapolated from physical evidence. The book includes
examples from New World, Old World, and historical archaeology.

PC 1019. DEETZ, JAMES. In Small Things Forgotten: The Archeology of
           Early American Life. Garden City, N.Y.: Anchor Press, 1977.
           184 pp.
In this book, which primarily concentrates on the historical archaeology
of Colonial New England, Deetz demonstrates how the study of artifacts
yields information about culture. Examples include gravestones, buildings,
ceramics, and furniture. Deetz also shows how changes in domestic and
cultural activities, such as like cutting meat and playing musical instruments, are part of material culture. One chapter discusses findings at
an Afro-American site.

PC 1020. FITCHEN, JOHN. The New World Dutch Barn. Syracuse, N.Y.: Syra-
           cuse University Press, 1968. 178 pp.
Fitchen offers a technical account of the all-wood New World barn, including drawings, a detailed description and analysis of its structural system,
and some conjecture on its construction. The book is based entirely on
material evidence found in Fitchen's research area of east central New
York state.

PC 1021. GIEDION, SIEGFRIED. Mechanization Takes Command: A Contribution
           to Anonymous History. New York: Oxford University Press, 1948.
           743 pp.
Giedion's concept of "anonymous history" is designed to connect the ordinary details and artifacts of an epoch with its general guiding ideas.
This account focuses on the rise of mechanization in agriculture, breadmaking, meat-packing, furniture production, and household labor. Beginning with the Middle Ages, Giedion traces a developmental line through
the 15th, 18th, 19th, and 20th centuries in England, France, and the U.S.
American contributions to mechanization include the assembly line, the
production of patent furniture, the development of mechanical production
of the lock (the subject of a lengthy discussion in this volume), and
the implementation of several mechanical processes in factories and households. It is through this particular history of mechanization that the
author demonstrates the impact of technology on cultural self-definition.

PC 1022. HALL, BEN M. The Golden Age of the Movie Palace: The Best Remain-
           ing Seats. New York: Potter, 1961. 266 pp.
This history of movie theaters in America focuses on luxury theaters and
considers the way in which the physical theater and its decoration affect
the total movie experience. Hall argues that, like the films produced
during the period when most of these theaters were built, ornate theaters
satisfied a public taste for illusion and fantasy; when tastes changed

during the 1930s and after W.W. II, these theaters declined in popularity. To defend this claim, Hall considers the design, architecture, finishing, style, and location of famous theaters, as well as advertising, programs, films, live attractions, and orchestras. A chapter is devoted to an analysis of theater organs and organ music; surveys of management techniques and theater chains are also included.

PC 1023. HART, JOHN FRASER. The Look of the Land. Englewood Cliffs, N.J.: Prentice-Hall, 1975. 210 pp.
Hart examines the rural landscape and the influences on it, looking at plant cover, land division systems, farm size, farm buildings, house types, and the influence of mining, forestry, and recreation. Historical geography treats the entire landscape and human modifications of it as a large and complex artifact, and Hart reads the landscape for cultural clues including regional differences in North America, and the influences of European traditions.

PC 1024. HINDLE, BROOKE, ed. The Material Culture of the Wooden Age. Tarrytown, N.Y.: Sleepy Hollow Restorations Press, 1981. 394 pp.
This volume of ten essays examines the influence of wood technology on American material environment in the 18th and 19th centuries. The essays describe the use of wood on the farm, in home building, in transportation (as the basic material in shipbuilding, road building, and bridges), as an energy source, and finally as raw material for potash, naval stores, and charcoal. The authors explain how these varied uses of wood made the American material environment different from Europe and how the dominance of wood and the ease of working it encouraged both technological change and personal mobility.

PC 1025. HORN, MARILYN. The Second Skin: An Interdisciplinary Study of Clothing. Boston: Houghton Mifflin, 1975. 435 pp.
Horn's study of clothing accounts for its evolution and historical importance to individuals and society. Examining American culture and clothing from the perspectives of a number of disciplines (anthropology, art, economics, physiology, psychology, and sociology), Horn argues that clothing choices manifest an individual's self-image and cultural participation. Her discussion addresses a number of issues: the symbolism of clothing; the way in which clothing reflects as well as defines differences in social roles and status; the function of clothing in mass culture; the relation between changes in society and changes in fashion; and the connection between clothing choices and the individual's preference for conformity or individuality. Moreover, some of the chapters focus on particular topics: "Aesthetics and Dress" examines standards of taste and beauty, the interaction between culture and art, and clothing choice as a mode of expression as well as a physical experience; "Clothing and the Physical Self" takes up issues of comfort and appearance; "Clothing in the Economy" treats consumption patterns, the American clothing industry, and the international clothing market; and "Acquisition and Care of Clothing" discusses clothing decisions and the responsibilities of the consumer.

PC 1026. HORNUNG, CLARENCE. Treasury of American Design. 2 vols. New York: Abrams, 1972. 846 pp.
Hornung has assembled a selection of renderings of American artifacts and draft works made by artists employed by the Works Progress Administration during the Great Depression; this index comprises more than 17,000 renderings housed at the National Gallery of Art. Hornung's selection is topically arranged and includes maritime objects, signs, furniture, decorative arts, toys, cooking equipment, and folk art. Essays introduce each section and many illustrations are in color.

PC 1027. KIDWELL, CLAUDIA and MARGARET C. CHRISTMAN. Suiting Everyone:
The Democratization of Clothing in America. Washington, D.C.:
Smithsonian Institution Press, 1974. 208 pp.
Kidwell and Christman's historical and sociological study traces what
the authors call the clothing revolution in America. Their thesis is
that the spirit of egalitarianism and the techniques of skilled craftsmanship created a new kind of "store clothes." They explore the numerous
elements that came together in the 19th century to spur the progress of
this new industry, and they conclude that by the end of the century the
common qualities of American dress served almost to obliterate evidence
of ethnic origins and to blur social distinctions.

PC 1028. KUBLER, GEORGE. The Shape of Time: Remarks on the History of
Things. New Haven, Conn.: Yale University Press, 1962.
136 pp.
This book draws on the structuralist concepts of linguists to explain
the form of objects. Although Kubler speaks in terms of art, he looks
at the set of all human-made things. Kubler proposes that instead of
looking at "style" we should think in terms of "prime objects"--true origi-
nals and the succession of their early and late replications. Kubler
feels that the thought patterns of the makers can be determined through
the patterns of these prime objects.

PC 1029. LEY, SANDRA. Fashion for Everyone: The Story of Ready-to-Wear,
1870-1970. New York: Scribner, 1975. 153 pp.
Ley presents a chronological examination of the growth of ready-to-wear
clothes for men and women. One of the major innovations in fashion, ready-
to-wear originated in Europe, England, and America as tailors realized
that they could market rejected made-to-order clothes. Following this
discovery in the late 19th century, a number of forces, according to Ley,
combined to popularize ready-to-wear: the rise of women's magazines (particularly the illustrated magazines); the advent of the great department
and specialty stores; the development of the factory method of production;
the invention of the sewing machine and the sized or graded pattern (But-
terick); and the formation of the International Ladies Garment Workers
Union. Throughout her study, Ley identifies the major fashions in ready-
to-wear by decade and considers how particular styles emerged in response
to the economic, social, and political concerns of a particular period
in American history. She explains, for example, how the Depression produced a "cheaper look" in fashion, and how W.W. II inspired originality
in American fashion as designers were denied access to Parisian styles.
Ley closes her study by looking at the "Jackie" (Kennedy) fad as well
as at stylistic freedom inherent in the fashion of the 1970s; she argues
that ready-to-wear has had a democratizing effect insofar as it blurs
social and class distinctions.

PC 1030. MEIKLE, JEFFREY L. Twentieth Century Limited: Industrial Design
in America, 1925-1939. Philadelphia: Temple University Press,
1979. 249 pp.
Meikle's illustrated history of industrial design during the Depression
era of 1925-39 seeks to relate this design to America's "faith in a future
of limitless technological plenty." Meikle looks at the subject through
the works of individual industrial designers in product design, architecture, transportation, and planning.

PC 1031. MEINIG, D. W., ed. The Interpretation of Ordinary Landscapes.
New York: Oxford University Press, 1979. 255 pp.
These nine essays by several leading geographers are an introduction to
reading the landscape as an indicator of cultural values and as a companion to social history in the interpretation of the lives of ordinary
people. The book begins with two general essays on reading the landscape,

then offers six essays on the symbolic meanings of landscape and a final essay in appreciation of W. G. Hoskins and J. B. Jackson, the leading proponents of landscape geography.

PC 1032. MONTGOMERY, CHARLES F. American Furniture in the Henry Francis du Pont Winterthur Museum: The Federal Period. New York: Viking Press, 1966. 497 pp.
This is an extensive catalog of the Federal period furniture in the collections of the Henry Francis du Pont Winterthur Museum. Montgomery follows the art historical approach to material culture scholarship. A brief history of the cabinet-making business during the period is followed by detailed descriptions of each piece which concentrate on stylistic matters. Montgomery includes biographies of known cabinet-makers and a bibliography.

PC 1033. NOEL HUME, IVOR. A Guide to the Artifacts of Colonial America. New York: Knopf, 1970. 323 pp.
This is a guide to the types of objects found in 17th and 18th century archaeological sites in British Colonial America. Noel Hume presents an illustrated history of the major classes of artifacts, and in the introductory essay, "Signposts to the Past," gives his thoughts on the uses of artifacts as a means of interpreting history.

PC 1034. NOEL HUME, IVOR. Here Lies Virginia: An Archaeologist's View of Colonial Life and History. New York: Knopf, 1963. 316 pp.
This is a social history of Colonial Virginia interpreted largely through historical archaeology and artifacts. Noel Hume proposes that historical archaeology can fill in the gaps of recorded history and makes his case by using examples from many archaeological projects, particularly National Park Service work and his own work in Williamsburg.

PC 1035. NOEL HUME, IVOR. Historical Archeology. New York: Knopf, 1969. 355 pp.
Although this is primarily a textbook on the practice of historical archeology, Noel Hume's theories of site analysis are of primary interest for students of material culture. Practical lessons on site selection, excavation techniques, and record-keeping are supplemented by discussions on the meaning of archeological sites and artifacts.

PC 1036. PIKE, MARTHA V. and JANICE GRAY ARMSTRONG, eds. A Time to Mourn: Expressions of Grief in Nineteenth Century America. Stony Brook, N.Y.: Museums at Stony Brook, 1980. 192 pp.
This is a catalogue for an exhibit of the same name. Essays by several authors on custom and change, cemeteries, and mourning customs precede the illustrations and catalogue of objects and art works in the exhibit. The exhibit and the book focus primarily on the 19th century, but some early and later examples are shown.

PC 1037. POULSEN, RICHARD C. The Pure Experience of Order: Essays on the Symbolic in the Folk Material Culture of Western America. Albuquerque: University of New Mexico Press, 1982. 172 pp.
Focusing on the implicit symbolism behind social action, Poulsen explores the representation of meanings in objects of material culture used by 18th and 19th century Anglo-Americans in the Western U.S. Poulsen employs structuralist and psychological theories to analyze the structure of symbolic systems and to examine their devolution under conditions of cultural change, a process he terms vernacular regression. Concentrating on the history of Scandinavian emigrant colonies in Utah, the author analyzes their cultural orientation as revealed by architectural design, tombstone motifs, patterns of spatial organization, and territorial boundary markers. Throughout the work, Poulsen emphasizes the different forms which symbolic patterning assumes in the sacred and secular domains of culture.

PC 1038. PULOS, ARTHUR J. American Design Ethic: A History of Industrial
    Design to 1940. Cambridge, Mass.: MIT Press, 1983. 441 pp.
Pulos relates the history of formal and informal design from the Colonial
period to W.W. II and describes the growth of the field of industrial
design. He explores the effects of industrial design on products and
their users, as well as the way in which interest in industrial design
has affected the American educational system. The text is supplemented
by illustrations.

PC 1039. QUIMBY, IAN M. G., ed. Material Culture and the Study of American
    Life. New York: Norton, 1978. 250 pp.
This volume consists of eleven essays originally presented at the 1975
Winterthur Conference, which was convened to establish the study of decorative and functional objects as a legitimate historical research mode.
Topics include: the visual and psychological impact of objects on society;
the growth of historical archaeology; artifacts as a source of historical
ideas; artifacts in college American Studies program; Indian artifacts
of the Southwest; vernacular architecture; historic preservation of buildings; museums as arbiters of popular taste; museum exhibits and what they
communicate to the general public; historical and educational films and
their use of material culture; and the care of museum objects.

PC 1040. QUIMBY, IAN M. G. and POLLY ANNE EARL, eds. Technological Inno-
    vation and the Decorative Arts. Charlottesville: University
    Press of Virginia, 1974. 373 pp.
This collection of papers originally prepared for a conference at the
Henry Francis du Pont Winterthur Museum in 1973, deals with technological
change in the 18th and 19th centuries and its relationship to the development of home furnishings. It provides art history and history of technology perspectives on material culture in America and on the changes
brought about by the Industrial Revolution. The essays deal with various
aspects of American taste, new contributions to the decorative arts, the
rise of a consumer society, and the role of museums in art study. The
collection includes essays on the jewelry and silver trades, iron castings,
pressed glass, fine furniture, calico printing, printed textile styles,
wall-paper, the furniture industry, technological utopianism, and the
role of the American museum in encouraging innovation in the decorative
arts. The consensus of the authors is that the period was one of sweeping
technological change and of the evolution of a truly American standard
of taste in decoration, no longer imitative of European traditions.

PC 1041. ROONEY, JOHN F., Jr., WILBUR ZELINSKY, and DEAN R. LOUDER, eds.
    This Remarkable Continent: An Atlas of United States and
    Canadian Society and Cultures. College Station: Texas A & M
    University Press, 1982. 316 pp.
This book is an anthology of maps and drawings illustrating the cultural
and social geography of the U.S. and Canada. Each section includes an
introductory essay and a brief bibliography. Topics include cultural
regions, settlement, structures, social organization, language, ethnicity,
religion, politics, foodways, music and dance, sports and games, place
perception, and land division patterns.

PC 1042. SCHLERETH, THOMAS J., ed. Artifacts and the American Past.
    Nashville, Tenn.: American Association for State and Local
    History, 1980. 294 pp.
This collection includes ten essays concerning several topics involved
in the study of material culture: photography, trade catalogues, maps,
museums and historic sites, and landscape studies. The editor's purpose
is to suggest ways of teaching and exploring American history both inside
and outside of the classroom. Moreover, Schlereth encourages research
on artifacts which goes beyond descriptive cataloguing and concentrates
on analysis and interpretation.

PC 1043. SCHLERETH, THOMAS J., ed. Material Culture Studies in America.
          Nashville, Tenn.: American Association for State and Local
          History, 1982. 419 pp.
Schlereth has collected and edited twenty-five essays on material culture
studies by leading scholars in the field. In his introduction he traces
the development of material culture studies and outlines nine approaches:
symbolist, environmentalist, functionalist, structuralist, behavioralist,
national character, cultural history, social history, and art history.
The remaining essays, all of which have been published previously, explore
material culture research in theory and in practice.

PC 1044. VAN RAVENSWAAY, CHARLES. The Arts and Architecture of German
          Settlements in Missouri: A Survey of a Vanishing Culture.
          Columbus: University of Missouri Press, 1977. 533 pp.
This book examines the German settlements in Missouri, particularly in
the 19th century, through the vernacular arts, crafts, and architecture.
Van Ravenswaay includes funerary art, weaving, basketry, and pottery,
and provides extensive illustrations. The work serves as a regional model
for the examination of material culture evidence for social history.

PC 1045. WARWICK, EDWARD, HENRY C. PITZ, and ALEXANDER WYCKOFF. Early
          American Dress: The Colonial and Revolutionary Periods. New
          York: Benjamin Blom, 1965. 428 pp.
The authors present a descriptive and analytic history of early American
dress from the Colonial period to 1800. Their illustrated study combines
pictorial evidence and historical fact to show what people wore and to
explain how their dress reflected their daily lives, their personalities,
and the morals, tastes, and economic situation of the nation. One section
of the book covers dress by geographic location: Virginia (1607-75),
New England (1620-75), New York (1623-1675), Pennsylvania, and the frontier. In these chapters, the writers show how rank, occupation, and family
tradition affected dress within the geographical locales. Another portion
of the study demonstrates that changes in the Colonies which occurred
between 1675 and 1775 are reflected in the dress of men and women. The
authors note that as cities and towns emerged, an aristocracy developed
that demanded a fashion similar to that prevalent in high European society.
The study also looks briefly at the clothing worn by children between
1585 and 1790, and the authors emphasize that differences in national
origin and class produced negligible differences in children's fashion.

PC 1046. WILCOX, R. TURNER. Five Centuries of American Costume. New
          York: Scribner, 1963. 207 pp.
Wilcox presents a catalogue of the styles which have characterized American
dress and a survey of American attitudes toward clothing. Filled with
sketches, the book considers the clothing worn between the 16th and 20th
centuries by Native Americans, early settlers, the military, civilians,
and children. Wilcox points first to the opposing and competing stylistic
forces in Native American dress: Native Americans preferred simplicity
in clothing, yet they also valued ornamentation of the body as their affinity for reshaping body parts and tattooing suggests. While this desire
for simplicity and decoration has prevailed in American clothing throughout
the ages, a way of dressing has emerged which is purely American: simple,
comfortable, smart, and appropriate for any hour of the day or evening.
According to Wilcox, casualness is the predominant note of contemporary
dress.

PSYCHOLOGY

Research in the field of psychology is generally published in journal rather than in book form. Consequently, psychologists produce a massive amount of research data in the form of journal articles. The volumes that do appear, often as collections of papers presented at conferences or in previously published articles, can be found through the same bibliographic sources as the articles.

Psychological Abstracts is the most general bibliographic source for research in psychology. Published annually, the Abstracts provide brief, non-evaluative descriptions of journal articles, books, and dissertations. The volume is divided into separate sections for the various schools of psychology, as well as for the various subjects they address.

Further published studies can be found in the journals themselves, most devoted to specialized research, which usually include book review sections. Such volumes as the Social Sciences Index include research conducted by psychologists, as well as by other social scientists. Separate bibliographies are available in such areas as gerontology, homosexuality, drug abuse, parapsychology, behavior modification, mental retardation, and child language. More general bibliographies in psychology are scarce. One such volume, Bibliographic Guide to Psychology, has been compiled from the resources of the New York Public Library.

The Bibliographic Guide to Psychology is published annually by G. K. Hall and has appeared since 1975. This guide provides comprehensive annual bibliographies of international book and serial publications. It includes subject headings for sensation; cognition; emotion; will; applied, comparative, genetic, and child psychology; personality; phrenology; graphology; and parapsychology.

Lloyd de Mause has edited A Bibliography of Psychohistory (New York: Garland Reference Library of Social Science, Vol. 6, 1975), which lists psychohistorical studies. Other sources provide background to contemporary psychology; these include the National Research Council's 1927 publication, A Bibliography of Bibliographies in Psychology, 1900-1927, which is useful for a survey of early 20th-century work in American psychology.

Since serials are the major source for the dissemination of information in psychology, researchers can consult the Library of Congress's monthly publication produced by the Joint Committee on the Union List of Serials. This listing has been issued since January 1, 1950. Margaret Tompkins and Norma Shirley have expanded and revised their volume, Serials in Psychology and Allied Fields (New York: Whitson, 1976). This volume provides an annotated listing of social science periodicals giving publication and subscription information as well as brief descriptions of the materials covered by each serial.

Because this bibliography has been designed to provide examples of work reflecting on American culture as a whole, no theoretical studies have been included, although there are some volumes which address American contributions to psychological theory in general. The focus has been on those studies which concern the history of American psychology, racial and ethnic variables, sexual behavior, children in America, drinking and drug abuse, and the interrelationship between the individual, at various stages of life, and American society. Cross-cultural studies, offering a comparative analysis of psychological variables in differing cultures, have also been included as they reflect on cultural differences between the U.S. and other Western and non-Western cultures.

While no particular school of psychology is favored, several have been excluded due to their emphasis on empirical and quantitative studies; this includes much of the work done by behaviorists, cognitive, experimental, and developmental psychologists, psychopharmacologists, and clinicians. Some areas, such as that of mental test measurement and development, a prominent part of American psychology, have been represented by general treatments rather than by the specific volumes which describe mental test development and statistics.

J. Jordan Sullivan
Columbia University

PSY 1. ABRAMSON, PAUL R. The Political Socialization of Black Americans:
        A Critical Evaluation of Research on Efficacy and Trust. New
        York: Free Press, 1977. 195 pp.
This volume examines the phenomenon of black schoolchildren having less
political efficacy than their white counterparts. Abramson's explanations
derive from the work of political and social scientists. The first explanation, political education, focuses on differences in political education
in American schools. The social-deprivation explanation examines social-
structure conditions which reduce black self-confidence. The intelligence
explanation posits racial differences in intelligence, and the last, political reality, centers on differences in black and white political reality.
In a comparative evaluation, Abramson rejects only the intelligence explanation.

PSY 2. ALBIN, MEL and DOMINICK CAVALLO, eds. Family Life in America,
        1620-2000. New York: Revisionary Press, 1981. 345 pp.
The twenty-four contributions to this volume form a portrait of the American experience from the perspective of the family. The purpose is to
examine everyday experiences of family life in terms of intersecting socio-
economic and cultural contexts; the multi-perspective approach is intended
to undercut the tendency among social scientists to ascribe a single meaning to family life. Contributors explore relations within the family
and between the family and the social environment. The volume is divided
into five sections: "Family Structure in America," "Sexuality and the
Family," "The Family and Socialization," "Families in Crisis," and "Social
Mobility and the Family." Contributors include John Demos, Howard
Feinstein, Linda Gordon, Edward Shorer, and Christopher Lasch.

PSY 3. ALLPORT, GORDON W. The Nature of Prejudice. Cambridge, Mass.:
        Addison-Wesley, 1954. 496 pp.
Allport investigates the psycho-social dynamics of racial and ethnic prejudice in modern societies. His analysis explores the relationships between
"in-groups" and "out-groups," socio-cultural factors in the development
of prejudice, and the psychological dynamics of the prejudiced personality.
He goes on to suggest various legislative and educational approaches for
the reduction of intergroup tensions.

PSY 4. ALTMAN, IRWIN and MARTIN M. CHEMERS. Culture and Environment.
        Monterey, Calif.: Brooks-Cole, 1980. 337 pp.
The authors treat people, culture, and physical environment as three interdependent variables. The book is divided into three parts. The first
treats environmental orientation and cognitions, the world-views generated
in a particular environment, and how that environment is perceived. The
second part treats behavioral processes related to the environment in
chapters concerning privacy, personal space, and territoriality. The
final part is concerned with the sense of place in the environment and
includes chapters on the American home, communities and cities. The book
concludes with a consideration of the future of Culture/Environment studies.

PSY 5. ARMSTRONG, LOUISE. The Home Front: Notes from the Family War
        Zone. New York: McGraw-Hill, 1983. 252 pp.
This study focuses on wife battering and child abuse. It is not so much
about family violence as it is a study of the public response to the pub-
licizing of these issues, and the effect of efforts to resolve them through
therapeutic rather than legal means. Armstrong argues that the medicalization of family violence reduces the credibility of the family as the
locus of caring relationships. She takes issue with policy makers who
have decriminalized acts of violence that occur in the home (acts that,
if directed against strangers, would be illegal). Armstrong explores
the historical, psychological, legal, and therapeutic background of family
violence, using case histories. She argues that equal rights protection
under the law must be extended to the realm of the family.

PSY 6. AUSTIN, GILBERT R. and HERBERT GARBER, eds. The Rise and Fall
of National Test Scores. New York: Academic Press, 1982.
270 pp.
This book addresses the controversial issue of changing standards in test
scores. The contributors seek to explicate the complexities of these
changes as well as to advance causal explanations. Trends in college
admission test scores, performance of ethnic minorities, effects of class
differences, and achievement trends of high school students are examined.
The test process itself is reviewed, with particular attention to test
construction, test validity and relevance, and the effects of revisions
in the school curriculum. Problems associated with data interpretation
are discussed and the author compares test score trends in Britain and
the Republic of Ireland, and the U.S.

PSY 7. BARCUS, F. EARLE. The Images of Life on Children's Television:
Sex Roles, Minorities, and Families. New York: Praeger, 1983.
217 pp.
Barcus evaluates some of the primary images of life mediated to children
through television using a sample of fifty hours of network and independent
station programs directed at a child audience. The data base is analyzed
in terms of the frequency of appearance and the status and prestige
afforded the television characters. Value orientation, behavioral patterns,
and personality traits of the characters are also analyzed. Barcus's data
show that in children's programs female characters are overwhelmingly
underrepresented and are generally in traditional, passive, and nurturing
roles. Barcus concludes that the television image distorts the changing
status of women in society. Minorities are also vastly underrepresented
in the sample, and although black characters have reached higher levels
of status and behavior, they are so outnumbered that they are virtually
absent. Other minority groups also receive inadequate recognition and
respect. The survey also demonstrates that the family on television is
portrayed in a traditional and stereotypical manner, with clearly defined
parental roles and little input from the children in family decision making.

PSY 8. BARDWICK, JUDITH M. Psychology of Women: A Study of Bio-Cultural
Conflicts. New York: Harper & Row, 1971. 242 pp.
Bardwick argues against traditional psychoanalytic views of women. She
discusses the biological bases of sex differences in the infant and the
mature adult, and inquires into the origin and development of differences
in personality and skills between the sexes. Bardwick explores the female
ego, self-esteem, dependence, passivity, and aggression in the sexes,
and examines changing roles and achievement motives at various stages
of the lives of men and women. Bardwick concludes that in early developmental stages sex is a positive source of identity for both boys and girls,
but that at later stages anxiety about sexual identity begins, often continuing throughout childhood to adulthood.

PSY 9. BARDWICK, JUDITH M., ed. Readings on the Psychology of Women.
New York: Harper & Row, 1972. 335 pp.
This collection focuses on female psychological development in modern
America. Part I addresses the development of sex differences, including
the biological determinants of sexual differentiation. Part II, which
discusses socialization and cultural values, includes Matina Horner's article
"The Motive to Avoid Success and Changing Aspirations of College Women"
as well as selections by Peter J. Weston, Alice S. Rossi, and Shirley
S. August. Part III deals with the qualifications, frustrations, and
stresses of the traditional female roles. Part IV looks at the Women's
Movement from a psychological perspective; Part V presents some intercultural role comparisons; Part VI deals with women in relationship to their
bodies; and the final section discusses women and the criteria of mental
health.

PSY 10. **BARKER, PHILIP.** Basic Family Therapy. Baltimore, Md.: University
          Park Press, 1981. 214 pp.
Barker outlines the development of family therapy during the last thirty
years, and discusses normal family development, theoretical issues concerning family systems, and practical ways of inducing therapeutic change.
He gives detailed descriptions of assessment techniques, common family
problems, and various therapeutic approaches and methods. Finally, the
termination process, the results of family therapy, and how to learn and
teach the subject are discussed. Barker seeks to provide a wide-ranging
guide to approaches and techniques. His own theoretical model is based
on general systems theory and on the McMaster model of family functioning.

PSY 11. **BARNES, HENRY ELMER.** Psychology and History. New York: Century,
          1925. 195 pp.
Barnes begins with the developments in psychology and psychiatry which
have had an impact on the historian in the exploration of man and human
culture. The first half of the book provides an overview of the development of key psychological concepts and their relation to history, social
theory, and sociology. Barnes explores the contributions of major theorists who helped to shape social psychology. Among those examined are
William James, Edward Lee Thorndike, and John B. Watson. He also refers
to the pioneering work of several 18th-century theoreticians. The second
half of the book examines the historical background of the psychological
interpretation of history. In elucidating attempts to integrate psychology
and history, Barnes focuses in particular on the work of Karl Lamprecht
and James Harvey Robinson.

PSY 12. **BARON, AUGUSTINE,** ed. Explorations in Chicano Psychology. New
          York: Praeger, 1981. 222 pp.
The contributors to this volume argue that Chicano psychology must be
recognized as a special field of study and not be subsumed under mainstream
psychology. The contributions are divided into three sections: "Community
and Social Psychology," including papers on the heterogeneous forms of
the Chicano family, the elderly, sex role stereotyping, and the concept
of acculturation; "Counseling and Educational Psychology," which explores
aptitude testing, admissions selection procedures, and the characteristics
of minority college students; and "Mental Health Issues and Research,"
discussions of rates of utilization of mental health services by the Chicano population, the efficacy of culturally sensitive milieu treatment
for Mexican-American psychotic patients, and coping patterns among Anglo
and Chicano university students.

PSY 13. **BARRETT, ROSALYN C.** and **GRACE K. BARUCH.** The Competent Woman.
          New York: Irvington Press, 1978. 184 pp.
Barrett and Baruch discuss the circumstances which lead women to aspire
toward professional or nontraditional careers, and those which preclude
the vast majority of women from articulating or pursuing such goals.
While the authors document advantages which accrue for women who seize
opportunities, they also point to the high price which these new opportunities for advancement exact. The authors draw on statistical and psychological data to critically examine the socialization process that historically has directed women away from the sphere of public competence
and achievement and toward traditional roles which frequently prove unful-
filling. They evaluate the social recognition and rewards which accompany
success, and draw a socioeconomic profile of successful women.

PSY 14. BAUM, ANDREW, JEROME SINGER, and STUART VALINES, eds. Advances
in Environmental Psychology, Vol. I: The Urban Environment.
Hillsdale, N.J.: Erlbaum, 1978. 204 pp.
This book, a collection of papers concerned with different aspects of
city life, represents cognitive psychology, social psychology, and environmental psychology. Among the topics examined are the effects of stress
in terms of cognitive overload; the effects of mass transportation, population density, and crowding; the interdependence of city dwellers as
it is affected by the amount of environmental information to be processed;
and the development of appropriate models for future environmental studies.

PSY 15. BELL, LELAND V. Treating the Mentally Ill: From Colonial Times
to the Present. New York: Praeger, 1980. 245 pp.
This book is an account of the major developments in American mental health
care and attitudes toward the treatment of mental illness since Colonial
times. The author believes that there are patterns evident in a history
of American mental health care: persistent societal rejection and fear
of the mentally ill; the discomforting anonymity of patients and their
acquiescence to any form of treatment; the isolation of the mentally ill
from normal life, a situation popularly expressed and condoned by the
phrase "out of sight, out of mind." Another significant historic characteristic has been disagreement among professionals about treatment of
the mentally ill, with the result that modes and types of therapy have
remained in a state of flux.

PSY 16. BELLE, DEBORAH, ed. Lives in Stress: Women and Depression.
Beverly Hills, Calif.: Sage, 1982. 246 pp.
This book chronicles the major research findings of the Stress and Families
Project, funded by the National Institute of Medical Health, and is
designed to explore the causes and consequences of women's depression.
The text is based on quantitative and qualitative research data from a
pilot study of a small number of women. Each chapter represents the work
of individuals or small groups who designed and conducted research on particular topics. An introductory chapter titled "Research Methods and
Sample Characteristics" explains how the study of forty-three women and
their families was conducted. "The Ecology of Poverty" explores, through
a consideration of the life experiences of the respondents, the thesis
that poverty in America has become increasingly feminized. Part III looks
at the lives of women in the context of the broader social institutions
and environments with which they interact. Part IV examines the personal
relationships of the women and the importance of these relationships to
their emotional well-being. The final section deals with the way in which
stress and physical problems undermine mental health. Follow-up interviews
with the families are contained in an epilogue.

PSY 17. BERCERRA, ROSINA M., MARVIN KARNO, and JAVIER I. ESCOBAR, eds.
Mental Health and Hispanic Americans: Clinical Perspectives.
New York: Grune & Stratton, 1982. 232 pp.
This volume is devoted to institutional and cultural values affecting
the mental health care available to Hispanic-Americans. The first section
treats the Hispanic patient within a sociocultural perspective, examining
the influence of religious and cultural values, and the impact of available
social networks. Section two treats schizophrenia, substance abuse, and
depression as the major syndromes in the Hispanic-American population.
The third section is devoted to subgroups within the community and assesses
the special circumstances and needs of Hispanic women, gang members, children, and Vietnam veterans. The volume concludes with discussions of
health care services within the Hispanic-American community. Topics
include group therapy, the relationship between the Anglo psychiatrist
and the Hispanic patient, and issues of clinical services management.

PSY 18. BERRY, GORDON L. and CLAUDIA MITCHELL-KERNAN, eds. Television
and Socialization of the Minority Child. New York: Academic
Press, 1982. 289 pp.
This is a collection of contributions from specialists in education, psychology, psychiatry, and sociology. Based on research which suggests
that minority socialization may be negatively affected by television viewing,
the contributors and editors assume that television is a significant socializer in the minority child's experience. This assumption is tested on
such developmental issues as cognitive, language, and moral development;
identity formation; and self-concept areas chosen for their relevance
to the minority groups studied. The ethnic groups under consideration
in this study are American Indians, Asian Americans, Afro-Americans, and
Hispanics. Chapters treating the role of television and ethnic identity,
minority groups and the media, and research perspectives are included.

PSY 19. BETTELHEIM, BRUNO. Freud and Man's Soul. New York: Knopf, 1983.
112 pp.
Bettelheim argues that the Standard Edition of the Complete Psychological
Works of Sigmund Freud, translated by James Strachey, frequently distorts
the original German text. According to Bettelheim, this translation,
the version which most English-speaking psychoanalysts and therapists
use, favors a more scientific and objective language than the original.
The author supports his claim with examples of mistranslation. Bettelheim
believes that the work should be retranslated to avoid the medicalization
of psychoanalysis, particularly in America, and to recover a humanistic
dimension of Freud's thought not accurately presented in the existing
translation.

PSY 20. BJORK, DANIEL W. The Compromised Scientist: William James in
the Development of American Psychology. New York: Columbia
University Press, 1983. 221 pp.
This volume traces early details of William James's life that were later
to have impact on the development of American psychology. James's early
interest in art was opposed by his father, who wanted James to be a scientist. The compromise suggested by this book's title is the development
of scientific psychology as a middle ground between art and hard science.
The latter part of the book discusses James's relationship with his academic contemporaries.

PSY 21. BLOS, PETER. The Adolescent Passage: Developmental Issues. New
York: International Universities Press, 1979. 521 pp.
This book deals with the departure of the adolescent, at the onset of
physical maturation, from the family into the broader social milieu.
Blos explores the problems associated with the psychic instability and
vulnerability of the adolescent during this transition. Each chapter
examines a particular theoretical or technical issue in the psychoanalytic
theory of adolescence. Employing a developmental framework, Blos examines
the mutual influence of the adolescent and his environment in discussing
the generation gap, aggression, and the syndrome of prolonged adolescence.
A section on "Normative Stages of Male and Female Adolescence" examines
character formation. Delinquency—its causes and consequences—and psychic
structure formation are among other topics reviewed. The penultimate
section deals with body image and the interrelatedness of psychic problems
and physical disorders.

PSY 22. BLUM, HAROLD P., ed. Psychoanalytic Explorations of Technique:
Discourse on the Theory of Therapy. New York: International
Universities Press, 1980. 468 pp.
This is a representative selection of papers which deal with the theoreti-
cal underpinnings of current psychoanalytic techniques. The contributions
by Blum and Anna Freud discuss the psychoanalytic pursuit of insight in

both child and adult analysis. Other papers focus on therapeutic alliance, transference and interpretation, object relations theory, and Mahler's separation-individuation theory. A paper by Mark Kazer critically evaluates recent work on psychoanalytic techniques by Charles Brenner, Ralph R. Breenson, Karl Menninger, and Philip Holzman. An essay by K. R. Eissler explores the nature of the relationship between psychoanalytic theory and practice. The three final papers center on the work of earlier analysts and shed some light on current controversies within the field.

PSY 23. BLUMSTEIN, PHILIP and PEPPER SCHWARTZ. American Couples: Money, Work, Sex. New York: Morrow, 1983. 655 pp.
The authors have focused on couple-relationships in this study of American lifestyles. Their interest lies in exploring issues of power, gender, and diversity. They include data and case studies on live-in heterosexual couples, homosexual and lesbian couples, and conventional married couples. The first section presents the authors' findings in the areas of money, work, and sex. The second part of the book contains case studies representing each type of couple studied.

PSY 24. BORING, EDWIN G. A History of Experimental Psychology. 1929; Rev. ed. New York: Appleton-Century-Crofts, 1950. 777 pp.
Boring focuses on the psychology developed between 1860 and 1910 in Europe and the U.S., and traces its roots in 18th-century philosophical speculation. He includes extensive biographical information on psychologists such as Pierre Flourens, Gustav Theodor Fechner, Wilhelm Wundt, as well as the Americans William James and G. Stanley Hall. The volume covers the gradual development of physiological, behavioral, functional, gestalt, and dynamic psychology and concludes with an assessment of the state of the field of experimental psychology.

PSY 25. BOYER, L. BRYCE. Childhood and Folklore: A Psychoanalytic Study of Apache Personality. New York: Library of Psychological Anthropology, 1979. 205 pp.
Boyer's analysis of the "expressive culture" of the Chiricahua and Mescalero Apaches begins with an overview of the affinity between psychoanalytic and anthropological study in the interpretation of folklore. The author then offers a brief history of the two groups as well as an account of their social structures. Subsequent topics include childrearing and personality organization, symbology in Apache folklore, and folk-tale variation in the service of psychological defense mechanisms. A lengthy chapter discusses the special significance of the bat in Apache folklore. In the penultimate chapter the author treats the use of folklore knowledge in understanding the psychiatric patient and includes an analysis of a case history.

PSY 26. BOYKIN, A. WADE, ANDERSON J. FRANKLIN, and J. FRANK YATES, eds. Research Directions of Black Psychologists. New York: Russell Sage Foundation, 1979. 440 pp.
This volume is the product of two conferences of black psychologists held at the University of Michigan, Ann Arbor in 1974 and at Teachers College, Columbia University in 1975. The meetings were convened with the aim of facilitating in-depth exchange among black psychologists engaged in research on the black community. This volume explicitly seeks to "provide psychologists and educators with the perspective of black research psychologists on facets of the multitude of scholarly issues in psychology and education in general and their implications for the black community in particular." At the same time, the editors aim to encourage black psychologists to share their resources and knowledge to improve the black community. The introduction attempts to place black psychology in a historical context and subsequent chapters explore the primary issues in black psychology under the headings of methodology, identity and adjustment, cognitive abilities, motivational issues, and problems for further research.

PSY 27. BRISLIN, RICHARD, WALTER J. LONNER, and ROBERT M. THORNDIKE.
         Cross-Cultural Research Methods. New York: Wiley, 1973.
         351 pp.
The authors divide the treatment of cross-cultural research into two sections. The first addresses "Substantive Issues" such as questionnaire
wording and translation, survey methods, the conduct of experiments, and
cross-cultural use of psychological tests. In the second section specific
techniques are examined in an inventory of particular instruments. Factor
analysis and other multivariate techniques are discussed in the concluding
chapters.

PSY 28. BRODY, EUGENE B., ed. Behavior in New Environments: Adaptation
         of Migrant Populations. Beverly Hills, Calif.: Sage, 1970.
         479 pp.
This volume evolved from a set of papers prepared for a conference on
"Migration and Behavioral Deviance" held under the auspices of the National
Institute for Mental Health, at Dorado Beach, Puerto Rico in 1968. The
unifying theme is a concern with the human consequences of migration--
the social and behavioral changes it engenders, the opportunities it
affords, the vulnerabilities it exposes, and the radical adaptation which
it requires. The process of migration is examined from two interrelated
perspectives: the intrapsychic, which focuses on the individual, and
the interpersonal, which focuses on the interplay between the individual
and his environment. The contributors explore a host of issues such as
migration in terms of deprivation and the involuntary migration of refugees,
the transition from rural to urban environments, and the social, cultural,
and individual behavior adaptations of migrants, looking in particular
at problems associated with ethnicity, adolescence, and mental health.
The final part of the book is devoted to an examination of program planning
and research on the urban socialization process, using illustrative case
studies and simulated models.

PSY 29. BROMBERG, WALTER. Psychiatry Between the Wars, 1918-1945: A
         Recollection. Westport, Conn.: Greenwood Press, 1982.
         184 pp.
Bromberg combines historical perspectives and personal recollection to
examine psychiatric history. The period between the two wars saw the
development of "neuropsychiatry" and Bromberg traces the social and historical forces that shaped this development. The book is specifically
devoted to American work during this period and includes an assessment
of contemporary traditions in neurology, the functions of state hospitals,
and the role of psychiatry in criminology. He concludes with a brief
account of psychiatry in W.W. II.

PSY 30. BROWN, HOWARD. Familiar Faces--Hidden Lives. New York: Harcourt
         Brace Jovanovich, 1976. 246 pp.
This book details one individual's experience of being gay--the discovery
of homosexuality, the search for friends and lovers, and the legal, psychiatric, and religious barriers to the acceptance of gay people. In
1966 Brown was appointed New York City's first Health Services Administrator. A year later, he resigned his position, fearful that his homosexuality might be exposed and damage his career as a top ranking public
official. Beginning with the Stonewall riots in 1969, Brown chronicles
his journey from a life of concealment toward increased politicization
and his decision to "come out" publicly in 1973. Brown also documents
the particular difficulties which homosexuals in small rural towns experience and the pervasive problems which gay men in America face.

PSY 31. BROWNING, DON S. Pluralism and Personality: William James and
         Some Contemporary Cultures of Psychology. Lewisburg, Penn.:
         Bucknell University Press, 1980. 280 pp.
In Browning's view, Jamesian psychology and philosophy are significant
tools for understanding the rapid-paced and pluralistic society of contemporary America. He places James's work in the context of subsequent
psychology, in particular the Freudian and Behavioral schools. Browning
explores James's ideal of the "strenuous mood" (a balance of religious,
mystical, and ethical sensibilities) and its relationship to such issues
as the empirical self, will, freedom, care, and the individual's relation
to a culture of detachment and instinctual pluralism.

PSY 32. BROWNMILLER, SUSAN. Against Our Will: Men, Women, and Rape.
         New York: Simon & Schuster, 1975. 472 pp.
This is an analysis of the psychology of rape and its historical, cultural,
and institutional manifestations. "From prehistoric times to the present,"
Brownmiller declares, "rape has played a critical function. It is nothing
more or less than a conscious process of intimidation by which all men
keep all women in a state of fear." The blame, the author argues, cannot
be placed on either victim or rapist but rather on a society that "con-
dones" rape through its legal system, its institutions, its wars, its
social sanctions. For Brownmiller, rape is not a crime committed upon
the woman, but rather one committed by man against man through the defile-
ment and disgrace of women, who are seen as man's personal property.

PSY 33. BRUGGER, ROBERT J., ed. Our Selves/Our Past: Psychological
         Approaches to American History. Baltimore, Md.: Johns Hopkins
         University Press, 1981. 416 pp.
This anthology by a representative sample of historians includes both
individual and group studies, employing a variety of psychological, historical, and theoretical approaches by historians to the American past.
Selections range from essays on American Puritan figures to contemporary
cultural events (such as Lifton's account of "America's New Survivors")
and traits.

PSY 34. BULLOUGH, VERN and BONNIE BULLOUGH. The Subordinate Sex: A His-
         tory of Attitudes Toward Women. Urbana: University of Illinois
         Press, 1973. 375 pp.
The authors, drawing on historical documents, employ an interdisciplinary
perspective to examine attitudes toward women from the earliest society
through contemporary societies. They discuss changes in attitudes toward
women as related to a variety of influences including Christianity, Islam,
and Hinduism, as well as socioeconomic variables, and the effects of role
changes and urbanization. The penultimate chapter provides a treatment
of attitudes toward women in America.

PSY 35. BURHAM, JOHN C. Psychoanalysis and American Medicine 1894-1918.
         New York: International Universities Press, 1967. 249 pp.
The author focuses on the effect of psychoanalysis on American medicine
at the turn of the century, the ways in which psychoanalytic propositions
were assimilated into American medical practice, and the effect of American
medical practice on psychoanalysis. Burham sketches the history of the
psychoanalytic movement from 1894 to 1918: the major European developments,
the diffusion of psychoanalytic propositions in the U.S., the emergence
of a small coterie of American psychoanalysts, and the influence on psychoanalysis of its early American practitioners. The author focuses on the
general cultural context, American scientific thinking, the medical profession itself and the early 20th-century psychotherapy movement. In
addition he details fin-de-siecle controversies which provided the backdrop
for the importation of psychoanalysis. The fate of Freud's teachings,
and the agents and agencies through which psychoanalysis was transmitted

are discussed. Burham concludes that Freud's theories had influence well beyond the field of psychotherapy and were a harbinger of ideational and cultural change.

PSY 36. BURR, WESLEY, RUBEN HILL, and F. IVAN NYE, eds. Contemporary Theories About the Family. Vol. I. New York: Free Press, 1979. 668 pp.
This collection of contributions from leading writers on the family attempts to evaluate recent theoretical formulations on family phenomena. The aim is to stimulate further research and theory building in this field. The introduction explores the historical and developmental context of the volume and explains the impetus behind its preparation. Among the principal topics surveyed are family and change, including discussions on fertility, working mothers and familial organization; family interaction, which focuses on social class and its effects on socialization, disciplinary techniques, and the family and recreation; and family problems—a section which discusses violence, stress, and deviance in the family.

PSY 37. BURR, WESLEY, RUBEN HILL, and F. IVAN NYE, eds. Contemporary Theories About the Family. Vol. II. New York: Free Press, 1979. 226 pp.
The focus of the work in Volume I is on the construction of family theory at a macro level. Volume II elucidates general sociological and sociopsychological theories, which the editors aim to integrate with the more specific approaches outlined in Volume I. The family is examined in light of the following theories: Choice and Exchange, Symbolic Interaction, the Systems Approach, Conflict Theory, and Phenomenological Approaches. Given the disparity of orientations and the multidimensional structure of current theory, a synthesized approach to the subject is difficult. The editors see this volume as a step in the development of a clearly explicated and empirically testable family theory.

PSY 38. BUSS, ALLAN R., ed. Psychology in Social Context. New York: Irvington, 1979. 407 pp.
This collection of essays on topics ranging from paradigms of psychological thought to social, developmental, and personality psychology is presented as an introduction to the "emerging field of the sociology of psychological knowledge." Through a critique of current research and the historical sources of psychological thought, the collection emphasizes psychology's need to attend to metatheoretical, methodological, and substantive theoretical issues with an understanding of the discipline's social context. The contributors advocate the development of a "dialectical psychology."

PSY 39. CAMPBELL, ANGUS, PHILIP E. CONVERSE, and WILLARD L. RODGERS. The Quality of American Life: Perceptions, Evaluations, and Satisfactions. New York: Russell Sage Foundation, 1976. 583 pp.
This volume is an analysis of the data collected in a national sampling of Americans' self-reports of satisfaction or dissatisfaction in various domains such as marriage, jobs, and housing. The volume is divided into three parts. The first treats methodological and measurement issues and reports the results of the national sample. The authors examine previous research and measurement scales developed to assess the individual's perception of his/her life's quality and problems associated with self-reporting and differing types of defining "satisfaction" are discussed at length. Part two offers a discrete analysis of the results reported in part one. This section is divided into chapters which consider how various factors contribute to an overall satisfaction or dissatisfaction within domains. Part three offers a similar disaggregation of the results, through its focus on the situation of women and blacks. The volume concludes with a discussion of the implications of perceived quality of life in terms of what the authors call a "structure of gratification."

PSY 40. CARD, JOSEFINA J. Lives After Vietnam: The Personal Impact of
         Military Service. Lexington, Mass.: Lexington Books, 1983.
         184 pp.
The author presents a critical path analysis of a cohort of men who were
finishing high school at the time of America's escalating involvement
in Vietnam in the early 1960s. Card culled her sample from Project TALENT,
an exhaustive longitudinal study of career aspirations and achievements
conducted first in 1960 on high school students with a follow-up survey
fourteen years later. Using a stratified sample of 1500 (divided between
Vietnam veterans, non-Vietnam veterans, and those who did no military
service), Card surveyed the men, now thirty-six years old, once again.
The study sketches a psychological profile of the three groups and examines
the social, economic, and personal consequences of their experiences.
The effects of military service and combat on veterans' subsequent educational attainment, occupational status, health, and family and personal
life are examined in detail.

PSY 41. CARTER, ELIZABETH and MONICA McGOLDRICK, eds. The Family Life
         Cycle: A Framework for Family Therapy. New York: Gardner,
         1980. 468 pp.
The Family Life Cycle discusses the development of American middle-class
families. The book is divided into five sections, each focusing on an
aspect of the family life cycle and relevant theories. Part two offers
a developmental perspective which divides family development into separate
stages. The third part focuses on special issues within the family.
Some issues discussed are death, separation and divorce, remarriage, and
the present roles of women in families. Part four discusses variations
within the family life cycle. The concluding section treats the family's
attitudes toward ceremonies and rites within the life cycle.

PSY 42. CATH, STANLEY H., ALAN R. GURWITT, and JOHN MUNDER ROSS, eds.
         Father and Child: Developmental and Clinical Perspectives. Boston:
         Little, Brown, 1982. 636 pp.
This volume is devoted to the relationship between fathers and their children. Section one provides a historical overview of the role fathers
have played in the development of individuals and, in particular, cases
such as "Father-Son Themes in Freud's Self-Analysis." Section two treats
the father's impact from a developmental perspective and ranges from discussions of fathers and newborn infants to fathers and adolescents. The
third section pursues the role of fathers in the lives of post-adolescent
children. Section four is a series of essays which discuss the role of
the father as it is translated into a cultural code. This section includes
discussions of the patriarchal tradition in the Bible, in 19th-century
fiction, and as it has changed over time. The final section discusses
clinical problems arising out of father-child interactions. Topics
included in this section are divorce, child abuse, incest, homosexuality,
and the effect of the father's death on young children.

PSY 43. CENTERS, RICHARD. The Psychology of Social Classes: A Study
         of Class Consciousness. Princeton, N.J.: Princeton University
         Press, 1949. 244 pp.
Centers analyzes and interprets empirical data on the question of class
consciousness as reflected in public attitude surveys conducted in 1945-
47. He brings a psychological perspective to the "interest group theory"
of class structure and social stratification. The author addresses the
social and theoretical context of class structure, analyzes the political
and economic factors which affect class stratification, and examines the
relationship between class consciousness or class identification and the
American class structure, outlining the psychological differences between
social class and social strata.

PSY 44. CHAPMAN, ARTHUR H. The Treatment Techniques of Harry Stack
         Sullivan. New York: Brunner/Mazel, 1978. 235 pp.
Drawing on Sullivan's published works, transcripts of lectures and seminars,
and accounts by former students of his theories, Chapman sketches a profile
of the treatment techniques of one of America's foremost psychiatrists.
The main body of the book is devoted to an explication of Sullivan's theoretical positions and his innovative treatment methods. Using the method
of participant observation, Sullivan explored the concepts of awareness,
language, and nonverbal communication in the therapeutic process; he was
also deeply interested in the structuring of the interview situation.
In the final chapter Chapman offers a brief biography of Sullivan and
presents an overview of his important works.

PSY 45. CHESLER, PHYLLIS. Women and Madness. Garden City, N.Y.:
         Doubleday, 1972. 359 pp.
Chesler presents a feminist analysis of the psychological problems of
women. The author explains that "this is a book about the dramatically
increasing numbers of American women of all classes and races, who are
seen, or who see themselves, as 'neurotic' or 'psychotic,' and who seek
psychotherapeutic help and/or are physically hospitalized." Chesler examines female mental illness within the context of patriarchal value systems
and structures. The study examines why women seek help, what behavior
is viewed as requiring help, and how the women studied are or are not
helped. Chesler discusses the psychological dimensions of women's personality in American culture, presents psychiatric histories of female
patients, and suggests that sex is a significant factor in how clinicians
treat such women. She found that most of the subjects studied "were simply
unhappy and self-destructive in typically (and approved) female ways.
Their experiences made it clear to one that help-seeking or help-needing
behavior is not particularly valued or understood in our culture."

PSY 46. CHESLER, PHYLLIS and EMILY JANE GOODMAN. Women, Money, and Power.
         New York: Morrow, 1976. 259 pp.
In this psychological analysis of the attitudinal and motivational forces
that keep women "in their place," the authors explore the types of power
attainable in society and suggest a variety of reasons why women have
not gained it: the psychodynamics of beauty, the psychology of total
commitment to motherhood, the psychology of volunteerism, marital security,
and the myth of alimony. Chesler and Goodman argue that even money, the
most powerful source, is frequently not turned into power in the hands
of women. Moreover, women who are successful in a "man's world" merely
get caught up in the "machinery that keeps this a man's world." The
authors describe their book as "about the psychoeconomic condition of women"
and "an exploration into impotence and power, myth and reality."

PSY 47. CHILD, IRVIN L. Italian or American? The Second Generation in
         Conflict. New Haven, Conn.: Yale University Press, 1943.
         208 pp.
Child studies the phenomenon of acculturation at the level of individual
behavior and attitudes in order to illuminate the phenomenon at the level
of societal process and cultural pattern. Using male, second-generation
Italians in New Haven as his subjects, Child devotes several chapters
to the general psychological significance of the acculturative situation,
laying out the fairly uniform conditions. The remainder of the book is
an analysis of the typical ways in which his subjects reacted to these
conditions. He finds three basic types of reaction: the rebel reaction,
the in-group reaction, and the apathetic reaction. Child suggests that
this problem is a classic example of a "double approach-avoidance conflict" in which either alternative (Italian or American) had its pros
and cons. In addition, Child asserts that while the social situation
affects the frequency of one type of reaction over another, these types
of reaction in turn have a profound effect on the social situation.

PSY 48. CHILDS, ALAN W. and GARY B. MELTON, eds. Rural Psychology. New York: Plenum Press, 1983. 442 pp.
This book examines the meaning of "ruralness" and attempts to establish whether or not particular behaviors and experiences may be attributed to life in a rural milieu. Although the book is largely psychological in orientation, an early chapter presents a sociological overview of the demographics of the contemporary rural setting in the U.S. The contributors deal with behaviorist issues such as familial interaction and cognitive, linguistic, and social development, paying particular attention to the rich cultural context of the study. Previous examinations of rural life are criticized for presenting a distorted vision of reality because analysis was shaped by a model of cultural deprivation. Other issues discussed include: quality of life, social services in rural communities, isolation and its relationship to child abuse, education policy, crime, and energy and waste problems.

PSY 49. CHILMAN, CATHERINE, ed. Adolescent Sexuality in a Changing American Society: Social and Psychological Perspectives for the Human Services Professions. 1978; 2nd ed. New York: Wiley-Interscience Press, 1983. 320 pp.
Chilman presents "an analytic overview and summary of the available research related to the social and psychological aspects of adolescent sexuality." Chilman critically evaluates some of the major research done in the field, focusing in particular on methodological drawbacks. The theoretical context of adolescent sexuality in the fields of biology, sociology, and psychology is documented. The societal context of American adolescents is also sketched. Chilman discusses adolescent sexuality under the following subject headings: "Heterosexual Behavior and Attitudes and Adolescents," "Contraceptive Use," "Abortion Among Adolescents," "Illegitimate Births to Adolescents," "Adolescent Marriage and Childbearing Within Marriage." The final chapters concern the policy and research implications of these discussions. Throughout the author attempts to link scientific and humanistic paradigms in her interpretation of the literature.

PSY 50. CLARK, REGINALD. Family Life and School Achievement: Why Poor Black Children Succeed or Fail. Chicago: University of Chicago Press, 1983. 249 pp.
Clark attempts to establish a causal link between the dynamics of family life and the achievement of poor black students in the school system. He argues that a child's success or failure is influenced not so much by demographic factors such as family size, employment, and educational background, but by parental disposition and relationships within the family. Through a detailed analysis of ten case studies, Clark documents the attitudes, knowledge, skills, and behaviors with which parents equip the child who is successful at school. He emphasizes that it is the family's overall "cultural style" which is a determinant of academic development and classroom preparedness. Clark contrasts two different parental styles: the first, found in the homes of high school achievers, is characterized by frequent interaction with interest in children, encouragement, sponsored independence, and authoritative parenting. The second style, associated with families of low achievers, features loose social ties between parent and child, less involvement, unsponsored independence, and authoritarian style parenting.

PSY 51. COHEN, RAQUEL E. and FREDERICK L. AHEARN. Handbook for Mental Care of Disaster Victims. Baltimore, Md.: Johns Hopkins University Press, 1980. 143 pp.
This handbook, directed mainly at health administrators and practitioners, outlines the key planning processes which are essential for the provision of post-disaster services to victims. The main mental disorders associated

with disaster victims—stress, crisis, loss, and mourning—are examined together with a discussion on coping and adaptation strategies. The authors suggest some models for disaster-related intervention. This involves development of a plan for the implementation of a mental health service after a disaster, the mobilization of all available resources and the employment of the most appropriate intervention techniques. The final chapters suggest specific strategies to be applied at different stages of the disaster.

PSY 52. COMSTOCK, GEORGE, STEVEN CHAFFEE, NATHAN KALZMAN, MAXWELL McCOMBS, and DONALD ROBERTS. Television and Human Behavior. New York: Columbia University Press, 1978. 581 pp.

The volume opens with a concise review of the literature followed by a survey of the scientific data available on television content: type of program, theme, portrayal, news coverage, and violence. Succeeding topics which are explored and evaluated include: changes in audience character associated with viewing times and types of programs; the make-up and size of the audience for news and violent drama; racial differences between audiences; and the public view of television performance. The next series of papers deals with television in everyday life, television's influence on other activities, including the consumption of other media, the proportion of leisure time devoted to viewing, and decision-making about program choice. Children's consumption patterns, and the effects of age, sex, ethnicity, and class are examined, as are television's implications for American politics. The book concludes with an examination of the role of social and behavioral sciences in television policy making, the identification of key issues which require further scientific study, and tentative solutions to problems associated with the study of television and human behavior.

PSY 53. CONRAD, JOHN P. and SIMON DINITZ, eds. In Fear of Each Other: Studies of Dangerousness in America. Lexington, Mass.: Lexington Books, 1977. 141 pp.

This book forms part of a series undertaken by Conrad and Dinitz to investigate "the problem of the identification, treatment and control of the dangerous offender." The authors contend that until public fear about the dangerous offender can be allayed there will be no pressure for or support of policy reform in adjudication and detention processes. This book is an overview of the central elements of the Dangerous Offenders Project which explores ways of reconciling the offender with society. Case studies of dangerous offenders are presented and critically discussed in terms of the system's capacity to prevent, contain, or rehabilitate the perpetrators of serious crimes. Another case study at a hospital for the criminally insane documents the way in which "dangerous" is defined and applied to particular patients. The psychological and social implications of dangerousness are explored, as is the biological perspective on the labeling of the dangerous offender. The efficacy of a rehabilitation-reform intervention strategy is reviewed by the editors. The final chapter summarizes the ethical issues raised in the treatment of the dangerous individual, particularly in regard to the tension between the individual's rights and the interest of society.

PSY 54. CRESTER, G. A. and J. J. LEON, eds. Intermarriage in the United States. New York: Hayworth Press, 1982. 111 pp.

These articles examine the incidence of intermarriage within specific ethnic groups. The groups studied include black Americans, Chinese Americans, Japanese Americans, Koreans, and Mexican Americans. Ernst Porterfield, in his paper on black American intermarriage, argues that as intermarriage increases it will be increasingly legitimized by society and a concomitant decline in racial discrimination will occur. In her study of marriage

and divorce in Hawaii, Margaret M. Schewetfeger suggests that where intermarriage is a well-established practice, ethnicity becomes less important
a factor in the choice of spouse and the prospects for marital stability.
John N. Tinker argues that Japanese-Americans have followed a model of
progressive cultural, structural and marital assimilation in their three-
generation history in the U.S. In the final contribution Kris Jeter argues
that a combination of factors including immigration policy and the American
ideology of individual freedom have helped to effect a small but significant increase in intermarriage.

PSY 55. DANA, RICHARD H., ed. Human Services for Cultural Minorities.
         Baltimore, Md.: University Park Press, 1981. 366 pp.
This anthology is divided into four sections, each of which focuses on
a single minority culture: Native American, Afro-American, Hispanic American, and Asian American. The contributors explicate the predispositions
and values which influence utilization of human services among these cultural groups. The discussions demonstrate the problems which arise when
human services and social programs aimed at these groups are conceived
and implemented by professionals who are primarily middle class and white.
The exploration of the specificity of culture, class, and race suggests
that a radical revision of services is in order to render them more effective
and accessible to those with special needs. The section on Native Americans includes a discussion of the failure of conventional treatment strategies and the comparative success of incorporating Shamanism into a therapeutic program. The focus is on ways of combining traditional cultural
strategies with human services to address problems such as family conflict
and suicide. The section on Afro-Americans concentrates on the issue
of racial identity and how the pervasive racism in society affects the
provisions of services to the black community. Folk healers and other
indigenous therapeutic methods are examined in regard to Hispanic Americans,
with a special emphasis on intervention strategies for the Hispanic child
and the treatment of juvenile drug abusers. The dichotomy between the
stereotypical view of Asian Americans and the reality of their experience
is discussed, together with the issues of cultural identity, conflict,
and the process of acculturation.

PSY 56. DAVID, DEBORAH S. and ROBERT BRANNON, eds. The Forty-Nine Percent
         Majority: The Male Sex Role. Reading, Mass.: Addison-Wesley,
         1976. 338 pp.
The authors argue that in the wake of increased attention to the situation
of women in American society, the male has been ignored. The editors
of this collection of essays seek to remedy this imbalance. In their
introduction, they outline American culture's "Blueprint of Manhood,"
proposing a conceptualization of the male sex role. The readings in part
one present various dimensions of that role, the "core requirements" of
"no sissy stuff," the "Big Wheel," the "sturdy oak," and "Give 'Em Hell."
The second section illustrates the ways in which American men learn their
roles. The final part offers articles examining the challenges to these
roles presented by women's liberation and more general "human liberation,"
and explores the normative changes that may take place in the future.

PSY 57. DECKARD, BARBARA SINCLAIR. The Women's Movement: Political,
         Socioeconomic, and Psychological Issues. 1975; Rev. ed. New
         York: Harper & Row, 1983. 512 pp.
Deckard compares old and new assessments of women. Part one describes
and analyzes the status of women in the U.S., and offers a critique of
psychological theories about women, sex role socialization, the family,
working women, and laws affecting women. Part two presents a history
of the status of women throughout the 19th century and the women's movement
in the U.S. in relation to social, economic, and political factors. This
section concludes with an examination of the contemporary women's movement.
The volume concludes with an analysis of three major ideological positions

in the women's movement: socialist, radical feminist, and women's rights feminist.

PSY 58. DEMPSEY, JOHN J. The Family and Public Policy: The Issue of the 1980s. Monterey, Calif.: Brooks Cole, 1981. 169 pp.
This book traces the emergence of the family as a subject of public policy making, from the Colonial era through industrialization to the late 20th century, when the family came to concern both the political and scientific/professional communities. In particular, Dempsey analyzes the explosion of political interest in and commitment to the family which began in the mid-1960s and culminated in 1980 with a White House Conference on Families. The principal recommendations of that conference are contained in the Appendix. Public policy making is explored in the context of such issues as abortion, unwanted pregnancy, disability, poverty, home mortgage rates, and self-sufficiency. Dempsey argues that the momentum generated by the WHCF will make the family the central policy issue of the 1980s. In addition, he looks at general theories of goal attainment, intervention strategy, systems analysis, and more specific approaches such as child welfare and normalization principle models.

PSY 59. DEUTSCH, FRANCINE. Child Services: On Behalf of Children. Monterey, Calif.: Brooks/Cole, 1983. 287 pp.
Deutsch divides the volume into three sections: the first treats historical, philosophical, and ideological frameworks for child services. Section two is devoted to specific issues of child care and includes examinations of day care programs, child protection services, early childhood education, and services for developmentally dysfunctional children. The third section discusses several topics including the development of a social policy of child and family advocacy; the role of social science professionals in society; and prospective designs for future action and social change. The volume includes extensive references to the role of culture in determining child services practice and theory.

PSY 60. DEUTSCH, HELENE. The Psychology of Women: A Psychoanalytic Interpretation. 2 vols. New York: Grune & Stratton, 1944. 877 pp.
Psychoanalysis traditionally has sought to explain "feminine behavior" on the basis of biologic, anatomic, and psychic factors, thus largely ignoring the educational and cultural factors and the socialization process in female character formation. Deutsch incorporates Freud's behavioral theories into her own in a discussion of puberty, adolescence, menstruation, feminine passivity, masochism, the masculinity complex, homosexuality, and other archetypical aspects of "feminine development." Deutsch also considers the influence of environment in her final chapter and acknowledges its importance.

PSY 61. DUMONT, RICHARD G. and DENNIS C. FOSS. The American View of Death: Acceptance or Denial? Cambridge, Mass.: Schenkman, 1972. 117 pp.
Dumont and Foss present an overview of the literature on American attitudes toward death summarizing the frequently-stated paradox that Americans accept death and that they also deny it. After examining the two views, the authors review the methodological and conceptual issues and problems of death-attitude research and present evidence that Americans display a great deal of attitudinal variability toward death and dying. They conclude that Americans are in fact ambivalent about death.

PSY 62. EDWARD, JOYCE, et al. Separation-Individuation Theory and Application. New York: Gardner Press, 1981. 232 pp.
This volume is an introduction to the contributions of Margaret Mahler to the field of psychoanalysis. The authors summarize her studies on developmental psychology, focusing in particular on the separation-individuation axiom, and demonstrating the applicability of the axiom

in clinical practice. This book is divided into two sections. The first section offers a theoretical discussion of the separation-individuation concept and describes the four stages of the process: differentiation, practicing, rapprochement, and consolidation. Section two is devoted to an analysis of five case studies. The authors emphasize the crucial role of the parents in making a success of the separation-individuation process, and call for the mobilization of social, legal, and community resources to strengthen the family unit.

PSY 63. ERIKSON, ERIK. Childhood and Society. New York: Norton, 1950. 397 pp.
In Erikson's theory, the stages of personality development are inseparable from the process of socialization. The eight stages identified begin with the development of basic trust versus mistrust, a major conflict during the oral-sensory state of early infancy. The second stage is the development of autonomy versus shame and doubt, which is the major result of how the muscular anal stage is handled by the parents. The third is that of initiative versus guilt, the crisis of the phallic stage; the fourth is industry versus inferiority, when the child learns to obtain recognition through productivity. Stage five is that of identity versus role confusion, the crisis of adolescence; six is intimacy versus isolation, during young adulthood; seven is generativity versus stagnation, during adulthood; and finally ego integrity versus despair, during maturity and later life. Erikson's approach is psychoanalytic and he ties his micro-analytic concerns to the broader cultural and political concerns of macro-analysis.

PSY 64. ERIKSON, ERIK. Identity and the Life Cycle. New York: International Universities Press, 1959. 171 pp.
These papers deal with the dynamics which characterize the developmental and socially organized aspects of the human life cycle. Erikson's special focus is the stage of adolescence marked by the formation of ego identity. He demonstrates how his clinical observations and "applied" work lead to a fundamental rethinking of the central tenets of the psychological theories underlying psychotherapeutic practices. These papers on ego development and historical change, growth and crisis of the healthy personality, and the problem of ego identity chronicle the author's growing dissatisfaction with the established paradigm in clinical psychology, and his eventual reformulation of life cycle theory to include the crucial psycho-social stage of adolescence.

PSY 65. ERIKSON, ERIK. Identity, Youth and Crisis. New York: Norton, 1968. 336 pp.
This volume, a collection of papers written by Erikson over a twenty-year period, is an attempt to address the broad concept of Identity in a philosophical and psychological context. In particular, Erikson describes the development of his concepts of identity and identity formation through clinical observation and developmental data. Topics discussed include the life cycle and identity confusion in both case and life histories. Erikson also discusses identity in broader social contexts in addition to the roles of womanhood and race in the psychology of identity formation.

PSY 66. EWING, JOHN A. and BEATRICE A. ROUSE, eds. Drinking: Alcohol in American Society, Issues and Current Research. Chicago: Nelson-Hall, 1978. 443 pp.
This volume is comprised of contributions from a wide range of perspectives. It begins with a section devoted to the history of drinking behavior in the U.S. The second section is devoted to discussions on the medical, social, psychiatric, and safety problems associated with drinking. In the third section special populations such as teenagers and college students are the focus of discussions of personal and sociocultural aspects

of alcohol use. The next section treats past, present, and future attempts
to control alcohol use and abuse and the effects of legal intervention
on drinking behavior. The fifth section, a summation, presents a review
of both drinking behavior and social policy. The editors, in their final
chapter, offer a conceptual model for indicating the "major influences
and consequences of drinking behavior."

PSY 67. FEAGANS, LYNNE and DALE CLARK FARRAN, eds. The Language of Chil-
         dren Reared in Poverty: Implications for Evaluation and Inter-
         vention. New York: Academic Press, 1982. 286 pp.
The papers presented here grew out of a 1980 conference on children's
language development and poverty. Language functions as a crucial form
of social interaction as it links the individual with his environment
in a two-way interactive process. Impoverished language skills will affect
a child's communication with the world around him. The contributors examine the subject from both theoretical and applied perspectives. Part
one explores the effects on language development of verbal and behavioral
interactions of mothers with their children. Data are drawn from studies
conducted in both the U.S. and abroad. Part two shifts the focus to the
school environment. The papers in this section attempt to locate the
relationship between language skills and school performance and suggest
interactive strategies to help children to succeed in school. A third
section on language evaluation questions the appropriateness of I.Q. tests
for measuring language proficiency and points to alternative methods of
evaluation. Part four critically assesses language intervention strategies,
focusing in particular on two special programs for preschool poverty children. The final part of the book focuses on the implications of particular
theoretical positions on the issue of poor children's language.

PSY 68. FERRISS, ABBOTT L. Indicators of Change in the American Family.
         New York: Russell Sage Foundation, 1970. 145 pp.
This book is a compilation of time series data on the family originally
collected by the U.S. Bureau of the Census and the Division of Vital Statistics, National Center for Health Statistics. The book is intended
as a data resource for researchers and others as well as a point of departure for the examination of social change. The statistical time series
are presented and organized topically: marriage, marital status, households, fertility, dependency, divorce, work, income, and poverty. Each
set of data is illustrated by a table or graph and is accompanied by a
brief commentary.

PSY 69. FIELD, TIFFANY M., ANITA M. SOSTEK, PETER VIETZE, and P. HERBERT
         LEIDERMAN, eds. Culture and Early Interactions. Hillsdale, N.J.:
         Erlbaum, 1981. 266 pp.
This volume is a collection of studies by psychologists, anthropologists,
pediatricians, and psychiatrists on interactions and cultural influences
in infancy and childhood among Hispanic, Hopi, and Navaho cultures within
the U.S., as well as cultures of Europe, Africa, South America and the
islands of the South Pacific. The investigators interpreted their filtered
observations of face-to-face, feeding and play interactions in the light
of varying cultural contexts, such as the public/private context of early
interactions, varying cultural values regarding the roles of interaction
partners (mothers, fathers, siblings), and social behaviors such as eye
contact. The chapters have been arranged according to the major variables
studied: cultural contexts, cultural and socioeconomic status, cultural
values, growth and developmental status of infants, and methodological
considerations.

PSY 70. FIGLEY, CHARLES R. Stress Disorders Among Vietnam Vets: Theory, Research and Treatment. New York: Brunner/Mazel, 1978. 326 pp.

The volume consists of several essays organized in an effort to define and discuss disorders related to experience in Vietnam. There is first an attempt to define the construct of long-term combat-related stress disorders among veterans. Secondly the contributions identify the theoretical and clinical importance of these disorders for the helping professions. The third focus is on the long-term effects of the residue of combat stress. Other essays examine the research implications of both the lack of awareness of the stress problem and methodologies to deal with it; specific treatment questions; and the effect of stress disorders on military and postmilitary life. Among the topics considered in relation to stress disorders are drug use, psychiatric syndromes, the POW experience, and the issue of the delayed stress response syndrome.

PSY 71. FORREST, GARY G. Alcoholism and Human Sexuality. Springfield, Ill.: Thomas, 1983. 395 pp.

Applying behaviorist, psychodynamic, and family therapy perspectives, Forrest explores the interrelation between alcoholism and sexual dysfunction and deviation. In the first part of the book he uses research, clinical evidence, and case studies to illustrate the different sexual dysfunctions associated with alcohol abuse, which include frigidity, impotence, and loss of sexual desire. Part two also draws on clinical data to demonstrate the sexual deviations which often characterize the psychologically disturbed alcoholic. The author pays particular attention to the problems of rape and incest. Strategies for intervention and treatment of alcohol-related sexual problems through sex therapy and psychotherapy are referred to throughout the book. Forrest argues that the focus must be primarily on the addiction and that the sexual problem be treated secondarily.

PSY 72. FRIENZE, I., J. PARSONS, P. JOHNSON, D. RUBLE, and G. ZELLMAN. Women and Sex Roles: A Social Psychological Perspective. New York: Norton, 1978. 444 pp.

In this volume five American psychologists write about theory and research on the psychology of women and the psychology of sex roles. Methods of psychological research are covered with a sensitivity to the historical background of sexism in the field. Views of classic theories of sex role socialization and of the feminine personality are presented. A section is devoted to the changing roles of women in America and focuses on such areas as women's participation in the family and labor force, women's adult development, the biosocial aspects of reproduction, sexual roles of women, achievement and non-achievement in women, and psychological disorders in women as indices of social strain.

PSY 73. FROSCH, JOHN. The Psychotic Process. New York: International Universities Press, 1983. 521 pp.

Frosch attempts an integration of the various components that enter into the psychotic process and in doing so characterizes the process structurally and distinguishes it from neurotic processes. Three frames of reference for the psychotic process are proposed: the nature of the danger and conflict, the modes of dealing with this danger, and the specific disturbances in the ego and ego functions. These are discussed in the context of the early and recent psychoanalytic theories of the topographic model of the mind, the libido, the dual instinct, and the structural model of the mind. Frosch compares his formulations with those of Melanie Klein, W. R. Fairbairn, M. S. Mahler, H. S. Sullivan and their followers. The book's penultimate section offers special considerations of etiology, the direct-defense controversy, adaptation, and the differences between neurosis and psychosis. It concludes with a consideration of the value of psychoanalysis in the therapeutic treatment of psychoses.

PSY 74. FULLER, ROBERT C. Mesmerism and the American Cure of Souls.
Philadelphia: University of Pennsylvania Press, 1982. 227 pp.
Fuller explores the popular psychology of mesmerism which gained prominence
as a healing science in the revivalist years of 19th-century America.
The emergence of mesmerism as a psychological means of expression is
attributed to the vicissitudes of a rapidly changing society in which secularism was increasingly superseding religious faith. Fuller argues that
"in its doctrines (beliefs) and therapeutic practices (ritual), mesmerism
framed symbolic processes through which individuals might learn to participate in some ultimate reality." Mesmerism was not so much a secular
departure from religious practice as many other popular psychologies were,
but rather an attempt to lead the individual beyond the exigencies of
his daily experience to a greater health-bestowing power which transcends
the structures of ecclesiastical and scriptural forms. The author presents
a historical analysis of the doctrine from its inception in Europe through
its importation to America, and ends with an account of its demise.

PSY 75. GARBARINO, JAMES et al., eds. Children and Families in the Social
Environment. New York: Aldine, 1982. 296 pp.
This collaborative effort between Garbarino and his graduate students
attempts to understand the developing child in terms of the risks and
opportunities which characterize his or her milieu. Both psychodynamic
and systems approaches are brought to bear in this study of the family
and its social environment. The focus of the book is primarily on the
web of affiliations which link the child, the family, and the social
environment. Apart from the intrafamily examination of childbearing and
child-rearing practices, the broader contextual environment of the neighborhood and the community are surveyed. Social services and support services for children are reviewed as are the ideological, cultural, and
institutional roots of social policy making in the family realm. In conclusion, an attempt is made to critically evaluate some of the major issues
concerning children, family, and social environment raised by the study,
setting them against the backdrop of social history and the future.

PSY 76. GEDO, JOHN E. Beyond Interpretation: Toward a Revised Theory
for Psychoanalysis. New York: International Universities Press,
1979. 280 pp.
Gedo's treatment of psychoanalytic theory is primarily directed toward
revision of clinical procedures. The revision is based on the author's
belief that the human personality is organized around a hierarchy of personal aims. These aims begin with the biological needs of the infant.
The entire hierarchy—including conscious and unconscious wishes—forms
the person's primary identity, the "self-organization." The discussion
includes three detailed narratives and incorporates the post-Freudian
metapsychology developed and extended by such psychologists as Arnold
Goldberg and Heinz Kohut. The first half of this study is devoted to
laying the clinical grounds for the subsequent theoretical chapters which
form the concluding half of the book.

PSY 77. GERSONI-STAVN, DIANE, ed. Sexism and Youth. New York: Bawher,
1974. 468 pp.
Gersoni-Stavn examines how the socialization process instills sexist attitudes into the child during his or her psychic development. Part I
explores how society constructs the "Second Sex," delving into indoctrina-
tion to sex roles in America. Part II looks into sexism as it is manifest
in the American educational system. The third part deals with the ways
in which children's storybooks and schoolbooks stereotype the sexes and
contribute to the socialization of what the author sees as another "sexist
generation." The final part offers readings on the influence of children's
television and children's toys on the development of sexual identity and
the perpetuation of sex role stereotypes.

PSY 78. GIFFORD, GEORGE E., ed. Psychoanalysis, Psychotherapy and the
New England Medical Scene, 1894-1944. New York: Science History
Publications, 1978. 483 pp.
Almost all the papers published in this collection were presented at the
symposium "Psychoanalysis, Psychotherapy and the New England Medical Scene,
1894-1944" which was held in Boston on April 12-14, 1973. The purpose
of the symposium was to examine the forces that affected the acceptance,
rejection, and final assimilation of the psychodynamic paradigm into the
New England medical scene. The contributors and participants include
medical, intellectual, and social historians; historically oriented psychiatrists, psychologists, and social workers; and historians with personal
recollections of the period. There are discussions of the work of William
James, G. Stanley Hall, and others during the late 1890s; of the New
England medical tradition of medical psychotherapy; of social, cultural,
and religious trends and the social and intellectual background of New
England; and of the coincidence of psychotherapy movements with medical
psychotherapeutic schools during the fifteen years before W.W. II. Each
section is followed by records of discussions, and the book ends with
a panel discussion, "Early Psychoanalysis in Boston."

PSY 79. GILGEN, ALBERT R. American Psychology Since World War II: A
Profile of the Discipline. Westport, Conn.: Greenwood Press,
1982. 272 pp.
Gilgen provides an overview of pre-W.W. II American psychology prior to
his more detailed discussion of the period between 1945-75. The impetus
for the book, a series of studies indicating convergence within an apparently fragmented discipline, leads the author to conclude that American
psychology is more closely unified than may appear. The major events
within the field, the rise and fall of Clark Hull's influence as well
as that of B. F. Skinner, are accompanied by a parallel increase in attention to cognitive psychology through the 1960s and 1970s. Throughout
the period treated, developmental psychology became steadily more comprehensive as it drew on the theory and practice of other subdivisions of
applied (or professional) psychology. This process involves a dramatic
rise in the numbers of clinical psychologists and their shift from psycho-
diagnostics to psychotherapy. The author includes appendices which rate,
separately, psychologists, events, and influences on the discipline since
1945.

PSY 80. GILLIGAN, CAROL. In a Different Voice: Psychological Theory
and Women's Development. Cambridge, Mass.: Harvard University
Press, 1982. 190 pp.
Gilligan's thesis, that psychological theory to date has persistently
misunderstood women, is discussed through a review of the literature and
through an interpretation of three separate studies which demonstrate
tangible differences between men and women not adequately reflected in
existing research. A study of college students examines issues of identity
and moral development in early adulthood, and an abortion-decision study
examines the relation between experience and thought and the role of conflict in development. The third study, a rights and responsibilities
study, explores and refines issues of morality and the individual's relation to different views of self which emerged from the previous studies.
Gilligan uses results of these studies to demonstrate the inadequacy of
the understanding of human development which omits women's experience
from theory construction.

PSY 81. GLAZER, NONA Y. and CAROL F. CREEDON, eds. Children and Poverty: Some Sociological and Psychological Perspectives. Chicago: Rand McNally, 1968. 328 pp.
The first part of this five-part volume addresses the issue of theoretical models appropriate to poverty and assesses current institutional interest in poverty. Part two uses the works of novelists and poets and transcripts of conversations with the poor to represent the experience of poverty. The third section is devoted to the causes of poverty and the character-istics of the poor. In part four, the contributors evaluate the impact of poverty on personality development, learning ability, and the ability to perform demanding tasks. The volume concludes with an analysis of the role of social organizations in the continuance of poverty. The empha-sis throughout is on an interdisciplinary understanding of factors which create and maintain the pervasive poverty in American society.

PSY 82. GLENN, JULES and MELVIN A. SCHARFMAN, eds. Child Analysis and Therapy. New York: Aronson, 1978. 759 pp.
This extensive survey of child analysis and therapeutic practice employs two complementary perspectives, one derived from the developmental model of child maturation and the other premised upon the analytic process itself. Among the topics treated are general principles of child analysis; the assessment of patients; child analysis at different developmental stages; aspects of the analytic process; and special problems in the psychoanalysis of adopted children. While each subject is explored in an explicit theo-retical context, the theses are substantiated by extensive references to clinical data and experience.

PSY 83. GOLDBERG, ARNOLD, ed. Advances in Self Psychology. New York: International Universities Press, 1980. 562 pp.
This volume contains chapters and discussions by many of the leading authors of the recently formed school called Self Psychology. Several major topics are considered, including developmental issues, the concept of mental health, clinical applications, and the science of man. The volume concludes with reflections by Heinz Kohut in which he comments on the preceding papers and on the current status of Self Psychology in relation to classical psychoanalysis and other schools.

PSY 84. GONSIOREK, JOHN C. Homosexuality and Psychotherapy: A Practi-tioner's Handbook of Affirmative Models. New York: Haworth Press, 1982. 212 pp.
Gonsiorek has assembled contributions from leading psychiatrists, psycholo-gists, and social workers who have pioneered therapeutic and mental health practices which are supportive of people involved in or seeking to build homosexual relationships. This volume constitutes a broad-ranging and in-depth analysis of some of the central issues relating to homosexuality and lesbianism in contemporary society. Conscious of the need to depatholo-gize homosexuality, each of the contributors advances affirmative models from which to view the subject of homosexual counseling and mental health. Drawing on behaviorist and systems theory, the contributors explore such topics as diagnostic concepts in working with male and female popu-lations, sexual orientation of the therapist, the coming-out process, homophobia, gay men involved in heterosexual marriages, sexual dysfunction, counseling for parents, sexual assault, and religious and moral issues in working with homosexual clients.

PSY 85. GOODWIN, LEONARD. Causes and Cures of Welfare: New Evidence on the Social Psychology of the Poor. Lexington, Mass.: Lexington Books, 1983. 199 pp.
Goodwin examines whether or not perceptions of the poor living on welfare correspond to the realities of their lives. Concomitantly, he questions the extent to which present welfare policies address the needs of the poor. Specifically, the author raises the following questions with regard to the Aid to Families with Dependent Children program and the Work Incentive Program: Do welfare recipients stay outside the work force because they reject work or because they prefer to live on welfare? Why do some recipients become economically independent while others do not? These and other questions are addressed in an analysis of research--questionnaires and interviews--conducted in New York City and Chicago in 1978. Psychological attitudes shaped by work background, nature of the job market, and Federal intervention were viewed as key to the achievement of economic independence in the analysis of the research data.

PSY 86. GORDON, MICHAEL, ed. The American Family in Social-Historical Perspective. New York: St. Martin's Press, 1973. 428 pp.
This collection of papers is designed as an introductory text to the social history of the family from the Colonial era to the 20th century. While the emphasis is mainly on the American family, reference is made to European and English material to provide historical background and to allow for comparison. The concept of modernization and the emergence of the family in its modern form provides the unifying link of this anthology. The five parts of the book treat different aspects of the family: the first section focuses on aspects of domestic life in preindustrial households in both Europe and America and traces the family into the urban industrialized environment of the 19th century. Part II, containing contributions by John Demos, deals with childhood and adolescence in historical perspective. Women, in particular their roles and relationships in the 19th and early 20th centuries, constitute the subject matter of the third section. Sexual behavior and sexual ideology in America are critically examined in Part IV. Edward Shorter contributes a paper on illegitimacy, sexual revolution, and sexual change in Modern Europe. The final section contains an abstract of the Grabhill, Kiser, and Whelpton study on The Fertility of American Women which traces the demographic transition which led to a decline in both mortality and fertility rates in the 19th century.

PSY 87. GOULD, ROGER. Transformations. New York: Simon & Schuster, 1978. 343 pp.
Gould's book is a study of adult life cycles--the various stages of emotional development or the psychic phases of adult life. The "stages" of adult life identified by Gould are as follows: from age sixteen to twenty-two youngsters are "condensed energy looking for direction, breaking away from parental control; age twenty-two to twenty-eight is a period of optimism and determination of one's expectations; from twenty-eight to thirty-four life becomes more complicated and disillusionment and soul searching are more characteristic; from thirty-four to forty-five there is a rise in emotional awareness that "time is running out"; over forty-five life becomes more settled, more inner-directed, and there is an acceptance of life as it has been and will be.

PSY 88. GRAFF, HARVEY and PAUL MONACO, eds. Quantification and Psychology: Toward a New History. New York: University Press of America, 1980. 526 pp.
The papers collected in this volume amount to a concerted attempt on the part of a number of scholars to integrate quantitative methodology and psycho-historical propositions within the realm of history. Psychologists have been propelled toward questions of collective behavior and social processes which cannot be addressed through individual case studies.

The papers presented in this volume, ranging from studies of political violence in Nazi Germany, to Victorian rectitude, and to personality characteristics of the children of the Great Depression, point to ideas and concepts which may serve as a basis of common understanding between the two approaches. The integration of the quantitative and psychohistorical approaches hinges on the interplay between quantifiable psychological factors and the effects of critical historical events.

PSY 89. GREEN, ROBERT J. and JAMES L. FRAMO, eds. Family Therapy: Major Contributions. New York: International Universities Press, 1981. 564 pp.

Among the principal concepts explored in this volume are family stability and change, family and social organization, communication, individuality and family conflict, marital conflict and parental alliances in well-functioning families, dysfunction and unresolved conflict, the involvement of children in the resolution of family conflict, and affective expression. These concepts cannot be viewed as solitary processes but must be understood in terms of their enmeshment in the form and function of the family. The contrasting approaches to family therapy in this book derive their unity of intent from shared basic aims; the emphasis throughout is on the social context of psychological distress.

PSY 90. GREENBERG, JAY R. and STEPHEN A. MITCHELL. Object Relations in Psychoanalytic Theory. Cambridge, Mass.: Harvard University Press, 1983. 437 pp.

The authors present a discussion of psychoanalytic theory from Freud's original postulation through current theoretical models. The discussion is centered on the concept of "object relations" and incorporates various theoretical models originating in Freud's theory. Greenberg and Mitchell discuss the major theorists in Western psychology with a particular emphasis on Freud and H. S. Sullivan in the first part of the volume. Part two, dealing with alternative theoretical models, discusses the work of Melanie Klein, W. R. D. Fairbairn, and others. The third section treats attempts to accommodate various theoretical models and includes discussions of the work of Heinz Hartmann and Margaret Mahler. In the concluding section the authors evaluate the "mixed model strategies" of more recent theorists such as Heinz Kohut and Joseph Sandler.

PSY 91. GRUBB, W. NORTON and MARVIN LAZERSON. Broken Promises: How Americans Fail Their Children. New York: Basic Books, 1982. 368 pp.

This volume is devoted to a discussion of the ways in which parents affect their children indirectly through their own difficulties as well as through more overt actions such as child abuse. The primary focus is on the ways in which American society ignores its responsibility toward its children. The volume is divided into three sections. The first two focus on the child and the state, public responsibility toward the child, the relation between social class and the child's experience, and institutions devoted to child care and children's issues. Additional topics include conflicts within the educational system, welfare policy, and child care and parent education. The last section focuses on family policy and the reconstruction of state attitudes toward its responsibility to both the child and the family.

PSY 92. GRUNEBAUM, HENRY and JACOB CHRIST, eds. Contemporary Marriage: Structure, Dynamics and Therapy. Boston: Little, Brown, 1976. 506 pp.

These essays by psychologists, psychiatrists, sociologists, and marriage counselors explore the interplay of social, psychological, and biological forces that shape American marriages. The book begins with articles on myths and realities in the history of American family life, changing sex roles and the future of marriage, and the legal and psychological dimen-

1471

sions of divorce. The second section focuses on psychological dimensions, the physiology of maleness and femaleness, theories of marital choice, and power distributions within the family. The final part is aimed at the therapist and deals with prevention, diagnosis, and treatment of marital problems.

PSY 93. HABER, CAROLE. Beyond Sixty-Five: The Dilemma of Old Age in America's Past. New York: Cambridge University Press, 1983. 181 pp.
Haber examines the creation of formal "scientific" classifications of aging and the effect these categorizations have on the care of the elderly. Haber finds changes in treatment of and attitudes toward the elderly throughout American history. By the 19th century, social categorization had become rigid enough to increase the likelihood of the elderly being seen as unproductive and useless. These attitudes, reflected in social policy, are based on a transformation in the way society attempted to eliminate disease and dependence. The study examines the ideas of early gerontology specialists such as doctors, sociologists and welfare advocates, as well as business and government planners.

PSY 94. HALE, NATHAN G. Freud and the Americans: The Beginnings of Psychoanalysis in the United States, 1876-1917. New York: Oxford University Press, 1971. 574 pp.
Hale discusses the developments in American psychology in the decades preceding Freud's visit to Clark University in 1909. These developments, leading to functional psychology and behavioral theory, also paved the way for an American acceptance of psychoanalytic theory. The author examines the origins of American psychoanalytic organizations and the works of various founding members with respect to their divergence from orthodox analytic thought and to their compliance with and development of psychoanalytic theory and practice.

PSY 95. HEELAS, PAUL L. F. and ANDREW J. LOCK, eds. Indigenous Psychologies: The Anthropology of the Self. New York: Academic Press, 1981. 322 pp.
Heelas and Lock present a collection of essays meant to be a systematic, interdisciplinary investigation of what people take themselves to be. Their book is a union of psychological and anthropological analyses, and the material is organized in three sections. Introductory essays by the editors comprise the first section, "The Indigenous and the Universal." "Anthropological Perspectives" includes essays by Ruth Padell and Jean Smith which respectively discuss the psychologies of ancient Athens and the Maoris. Section three, "Psychological Perspectives," includes chapters which analyze the development of Western psychologies.

PSY 96. HELMER, JOHN. Bringing the War Home: The American Soldier in Vietnam and After. New York: Free Press, 1974. 346 pp.
Helmer assesses the political consciousness among American servicemen who served in Vietnam. The study is based on interviews with working class Vietnam veterans who are evenly divided among "straights" (members of Veterans of Foreign Wars), "addicts" (opium addicts), and "radicals" (members of the Vietnam Veterans Against the War). The study explores pre-service characteristics and attitudes, recruitment into the military, the soldier's war experiences, and "homecoming." In a concluding chapter, Helmer develops the relationship between rebellion, alienation, and class consciousness and draws implications from the study for the broader impact of the war on American society.

PSY 97. HILGARD, ERNEST R., ed. American Psychology in Historical Perspective: Addresses of the Presidents of the American Psychological Association, 1892-1977. Washington, D.C.: American
Psychological Association, 1978. 558 pp.
Hilgard has reprinted twenty-one addresses of APA presidents, several
from each of three periods. There is a background chapter on the history
of the APA, and introductory materials on the periods themselves. Biographical sketches of all APA Presidents through 1977 as well as synopses
of their work are provided. The addresses indicate the dominant research
and theoretical trends of both academic and applied psychology in America
in areas of testing, physiological psychology, learning theory, social
psychology and theory construction.

PSY 98. HIPPLE, JOHN L. and LU B. HIPPLE. Diagnosis and Management of
Psychological Emergencies: A Manual for Hospitalization. New
York: Thomas, 1983. 182 pp.
Hipple and Hipple present a systems approach as a framework within which
professionals may evaluate people who are in psychological crises and
make decisions regarding the advisability of hospitalizing them. In deciding on the degree of psychological crises and the appropriate treatment
intervention in each case, the authors argue that the system and subsystem
of the client's social milieu must be taken into account. These systemic
factors include: spouse, family, workplace, available living arrangements,
neighborhood resources, and community facilities. Institutional systems
such as hospitals, law enforcement agencies, the judiciary, and other
referral services also combine to influence the client's social conditions.
However, the immediate task facing the professional mental health worker
is to cope with psychological crises and instigate a follow-up treatment
program after the initial crisis has passed. Apart from exploring the
legal and medical ramifications, Hipple and Hipple examine specific cases
which required evaluation by professionals and outline strategies for
intervention.

PSY 99. HITE, SHERE. The Hite Report: A Nationwide Study in Female Sexuality. New York: Macmillan, 1976. 438 pp.
This study of the social and psychological dimensions of female sexuality
is based on interviews with a nationwide sample of over 1,800 American
women. Hite presents excerpts from these interviews as well as her own
findings about female attitudes toward masturbation, orgasm, intercourse,
clitoral stimulation, lesbianism, sexual slavery, and the sexual revolution.
The book presents an extremely candid picture of what sexuality means
to American women.

PSY 100. HOFLING, CHARLES K. and JERRY M. LEWIS, eds. The Family: Evaluation and Treatment. New York: Brunner/Mazel, 1980. 324 pp.
This volume from the American College of Psychiatrists provides a handbook
on contemporary research and intervention in family practice. Part I
focuses on the psychological issues and includes discussions of the role
of the family in individual development, making the distinction between
family interviews and family therapy. Part II treats the general living
systems theory and emphasizes such aspects as evolutionary and biological
perspectives in relation to family behavior and development. The final
section is devoted to specific treatment issues involving families and/or
individuals. The volume concludes with a lecture by Yrjo O. Alanen which
discusses the interactional origin of schizophrenia.

PSY 101. HUNTER, EDNA J. Families Under the Flag: A Review of Military
Family Literature. New York: Praeger, 1982. 337 pp.
This review is divided into three sections. The first, consisting of essays
on the military family, discusses the effects of frequent separations
and family reunions in the creation of "flipflop" family roles, the hazard-

ous duty assignments with the constant threat of injury and/or death of a loved one, and the role of institutional support in the place of the extended family. The second section is devoted to mobility and stress of adjustment to foreign cultures and alienation from the civilian community. The third part is an extensive annotated bibliography of work to date on the military family.

PSY 102. JACOBY, RUSSELL. Social Amnesia: A Critique of Conformist Psychology from Adler to Laing. Boston: Beacon Press, 1975. 191 pp.

Rather than offering a history of the origin of psychoanalysis, Jacoby traces the developments in analytic thought since its establishment by Freud. The focus is on what Jacoby calls the forgetting of the ideas upon which psychoanalysis was based. He discusses the theoretical interplay between psychoanalysis, Marxism, and "critical theory." The author argues that our current "enlightenment" is, in fact, a willful repression of what we already know, namely, a forgetting of psychoanalysis because of its disturbing theories. He locates the development of a "negative psychoanalysis" in the 1920s, compounded by the translation of Freud into English and the relocation of members of the Frankfurt School to America in the late 1920s and 1930s. In effect, Jacoby argues, Freudian ideas have been lost or "repressed" as a result of assimilation into the English and American tradition of positivism.

PSY 103. JENKINS, ADELBERT H. The Psychology of the Afro-American: A Humanistic Approach. New York: Pergamon Press, 1982. 213 pp.

Jenkins eschews traditional approaches to the study of black Americans, which he maintains are characterized by a persistent racist cultural bias and an overemphasis on instinctual drives and environmental factors as shapers of behavior. These theories, he claims, seek to explain social disadvantage by looking within the black community and black people themselves. The psychological functioning of black Americans is frequently couched in negative terms, which has tended to highlight social and personal deficiencies and to direct attention away from the positive, creative, and self-directed aspects of the psyche. Jenkins aims to refocus the study of black American psychology by supplanting the mechanistic-behaviorist approach with a humanistic perspective. He casts the individual in the role of agent--not victim--of society. The thrust of his thesis is to construct meanings and the possibilities of being both effective and productive in life. In an introductory chapter, Jenkins outlines the theoretical framework of his study and acknowledges the influence of Robert White and Joseph Rychlak on his views. In the chapters that follow, he employs a humanistic perspective to critically evaluate the literature on the psychology of black Americans. The central question which is addressed throughout this volume is how psychology can make a contribution to a changed conception of Afro-Americans.

PSY 104. JENSEN, ARTHUR R. Bias in Mental Testing. New York: Free Press, 1980. 786 pp.

In Jensen's view, the most widely used standardized tests--I.Q., scholastic aptitude, and achievement tests--are not biased against "any of the native-born English speaking, minority groups" for which sufficient data are available. Most work on test bias has focused on black Americans and sufficient data are lacking for other minorities such as Asian-Americans. Jensen's approach is essentially psychometric rather than theoretical in regard to the careful use of mental tests. The author's objective is to determine the psychometric methods necessary to discern test bias and to use tests fairly insofar as they are applicable to a given group. The volume concludes with a summary chapter on uses and abuses of tests, and includes the author's personal recommendations for fair usage.

PSY 105. JONES, ENRICO E. and SHELDON J. KORCHIN, eds. Minority Mental
       Health. New York: Praeger, 1982. 406 pp.
This volume is divided into two parts. The first treats issues of theory
and research in the field of minority psychology. The editors divide the
existing theories into historical and cross-cultural perspectives and
there are contributions from both. Proposals for theoretical and research
paradigms are offered in the areas of stress, ethnicity, social class,
adaptive strategies in U.S. minorities, and for work in the Japanese and
Chinese-American communities. The second part consists of essays treating
direct intervention strategies. Among the topics considered are family
therapy with black families, changing norms of Hispanic families, and
psychopathology, psychotherapy, and the Mexican-American patient. The
volume calls for an understanding of minority function and dysfunction
on its own terms as well as for greater numbers of bicultural and bilingual
helping professionals.

PSY 106. JONES, REGINALD L., ed. Black Psychology. New York: Harper
       & Row, 1972. 432 pp.
This volume is a selection of writings by black psychologists, social
scientists, and behavioral scientists. Essays range from the empirical
to the philosophical. The collection is organized into seven sections.
The first deals with the issue of black psychology as a discipline in
its own right. Part II focuses on the psychological assessment of blacks;
Part III is devoted to issues of personality and motivation; Parts IV
and V are oriented toward applied psychology, with an emphasis on counseling and educating blacks. Part VI offers a series of essays with differing
perspectives on racism and, finally, Part VII treats the role of the black
psychologist and black psychology in the black community and outside of
it.

PSY 107. KAMIN, LEON J. The Science and Politics of I.Q. Potomac, Md.:
       Erlbaum, 1974. 183 pp.
Kamin addresses the central issues of the heritability of I.Q. levels.
After a detailed analysis of empirical evidence Kamin concludes that the
assumption of heritability is unwarranted. He then addresses the relationship between I.Q. test use in America and the social view expressed or
endorsed by those using such tests. The author demonstrates the role
I.Q. tests have played as instruments of oppression against the poor.
He traces the development of I.Q. testing in America, the relation between
psychology and the immigrant, I.Q. tests and separated identical twins,
kinship correlations, studies of adopted children, and the accuracy of
available secondary sources. Throughout the discussion there is a twofold
emphasis on the science and politics of I.Q. test development and use.

PSY 108. KAPLAN, BERT, ed. Studying Personality Cross-Culturally. New
       York: Harper & Row, 1951. 687 pp.
This book of readings contains articles on theory and research in special
problems of personality study. The volume presents an extended historical
account of the major issues in the field of culture and personality; a
series of theoretical papers analyzing the role of personality and motivational processes in societal functioning; a discussion of the development
of personality as it involves socialization and preparation for societal
participation; a series of methodological papers that clarify problems
of cross-cultural research; a survey of relationships between linguistics
and cross-cultural personality study; an attempt to develop a framework
for assessing the influence of cultural factors in personality study; discussions of projective techniques, dreams, and psychiatric interviewing;
a discussion of the problem of interpreting psychic symbolism across cultures; an analysis of the role of myth and artistic productions; and
finally, a discussion of methodological issues in the cross-cultural study
of mental illness. An integral part of this volume is a series of case
studies of national and subnational populations that illustrate some
of the issues discussed.

PSY 109.   KATZ, SEDELLE and MARY ANN MAZUR.   Understanding the Rape Victim:
A Synthesis of Research Findings.   New York: Wiley, 1979.
340 pp.
This book is a review and synthesis of the empirical literature on rape
and the rape victim. The authors explore a wide range of issues in rape
victimology studies. Prominent among these is the issue of "victim pre-
cipitation"--the extent to which the victim, consciously or unconsciously,
plays a role in and has some responsibility for the crime. Another issue
concerns the effects of rape on the victim's subsequent adjustment; the
authors are especially concerned with the connection between rape and
psychiatric illness. The book contains three major sections. First the
authors review the social, sexual, and personality characteristics of
rape victims. Second, they examine the rape situation, including the setting, who the rapist is and the victim's relation to him, and what happens
during the rape. Finally, the authors explore the aftereffects of rape
from the victim's perspective.

PSY 110.   KAUFMAN, DEBRA R. and BARBARA L. RICHARDSON.   Achievement and
Women: Challenging the Assumptions.   New York: Free Press,
1982. 188 pp.
Kaufman and Richardson study the motivations, goals, performance and feelings of women about achievement in an academic, historical, and social
context. In particular, the authors explore the interplay between the
public and private roles assumed by men and women. The lack of attention
paid to the specific experiences and achievements of women in academia
is a particular focus of this book. Explanations of female subordination
that focus exclusively on socialization patterns are eschewed in favor
of a broader approach which acknowledges the influence of cultural values,
understanding and experience of history, and the parameters set by social
structures. In the analysis of achievement, the authors move from intrapsychic motivation to achieve to the social and historical forces which
condition and define achievement. Specifically, they examine "how academic
models of achievement have contributed to the popular interpretation of
women's capabilities and how in general social science models of human
behavior have focused on rather narrow and male-specific criteria regarding
the relationship of ability, ambition, personality, achievement and worldly
success." The analysis traces women's experiences in two dimensions:
the public and private spheres and over the life cycle.

PSY 111.   KAZDIN, ALAN E.   History of Behavior Modification: Experimental
Foundations of Contemporary Research.   Baltimore, Md.: University
Park Press, 1978. 468 pp.
This volume, third in a series commissioned by the Committee on Brain Sciences of the National Research Council, focuses on the contributions of
basic laboratory research in psychology and physiology to the development
of behavior modification. Kazdin begins by tracing the emergence of behavior modification as a departure from traditional psychiatric and clinical
approaches; in particular, behavior modification departs from the "medical
model" of mental illness in its formulation of a psychological rather
than a disease-based model. He traces the development of behaviorism
from the work of John B. Watson to contemporary applied behavior analysis.
The volume covers a wide variety of contrasting philosophical assumptions,
and relates the development of behavior modification to other developments
in the helping professions over the course of the 20th century. Although
the focus is principally on the work done in the U.S., developments in
behavioral analysis from other cultures are also considered.

PSY 112. KERCKHOFF, ALAN C. Ambition and Attainment: A Study of Four
Samples of American Boys. Washington, D.C.: American Sociological Association, 1974. 106 pp.

Kerckhoff's study of motivation is based on data collected in 1969 from
samples of sixth-, ninth-, and twelfth-grade boys and from a 1963 sample
of high school graduates in a middle-size American city. He explores
social psychological factors in status mobility within the American
stratification system. Central factors analyzed are ability, opportunity,
performance, sanctions, understanding, and ambition. Kerckhoff found
that much of the variance in educational and occupational outcomes results
from differences in academic performance, extracurricular participation,
and peer relationships. These factors were juxtaposed to background variables such as family socioeconomic status and IQ scores.

PSY 113. KESSLER, SUZANNE J. and WENDY McKENNA. Gender: An Ethnomethodo-
logical Approach. New York: Wiley, 1978. 233 pp.

Kessler and McKenna studied the issue of gender from social, psychological,
cultural, and biological perspectives. Their book represents the results
of gender research and theory construction. Included are discussions
of gender attribution as a scientific endeavor for psychoanalytic, social
learning, and cognitive developmental researchers. The final chapter
treats gender attribution in everyday life with a focus on the trans-
sexual's experience.

PSY 114. KETT, JOSEPH. Rites of Passage: Adolescence in America, 1790
to the Present. New York: Basic Books, 1977. 327 pp.

Kett examines the economic and social relationship between adults and
youth as it has developed since the American Revolution. Changing perspectives on the role of the adolescent in family and social life are
reflected in chapters which discuss education, religion, and work habits.
In Part two, Kett demonstrates the development of "The Age of Adolescence"
in the later half of the 19th century through changes in educational and
professional expectations for the young. Part three, 1900 to the present,
is identified as the "era of adolescence," which emerges with the development of modern psychology in America, England and Germany. G. Stanley
Hall's early text, Adolescence, is discussed at length in regard to the
modern American understanding of adolescence, which is identified both
romantically and scientifically.

PSY 115. KIRKPATRICK, MARTHA, ed. Women's Sexual Development: Explorations of the Inner Space. Vol. I. New York: Plenum Press,
1980. 298 pp.

The fifteen contributions by authors from all fields of the social sciences
in this volume explore the issue of female sexual development. The diversity of the contributions reflects the multifaceted nature of the topic.
The general psychological and physiological aspects of female sexuality
are discussed, as is the history of sexuality in America and the intriguing
representation of women in American folklore. Sexual practices and experiences, lesbian relationships, father/daughter relationships, the sexual
revolution and its implications for today's generation of American women,
and sexual and psycho-sexual health issues constitute the principal themes
explored.

PSY 116. KIRKPATRICK, MARTHA, ed. Women's Sexual Experience: Explorations
of the Dark Continent. Vol. II. New York: Plenum Press, 1982.
328 pp.

The contributions to Volume Two are drawn from a wide range of sources:
academic, experiential, journalistic, and personal. Female sexuality
is viewed in two dimensions: first, the changing experiences of women
over the life cycle, with particular focus on mid-life and beyond, and
second, the specific experiences of women of color, in particular, American

Indian and black women. Universal problems which women experience in the world of the home--incest and domestic violence--are discussed. The implications of permissiveness in society are examined through papers on prostitution and the vulnerability of women to sexually transmitted disease. Childbirth, teenage motherhood, and childlessness are also addressed.

PSY 117. KIRMAN, WILLIAM J. Modern Psychoanalysis in the Schools. Dubuque, Iowa: Kendall/Hunt, 1977. 218 pp.
The author asserts that the process of psychoanalysis, one devoted to emotional reeducation, is an important tool for contemporary education. Research findings indicate a relationship between "emotional education" and improved intellectual performance. The classroom should adopt the ideal home as its paradigm for classroom interaction and should encourage integrated learning experiences. Kirman discusses the role of counselors and counseling in assisting classroom teachers with the implementation of analytically gained insights.

PSY 118. KLUCKHOHN, CLYDE and H. A. MURRAY, eds. Personality in Nature, Society, and Culture. New York: Knopf, 1953. 701 pp.
These readings inquire into the interdependence of personal characteristics, culture, and the social milieux in which people live. The following questions are posed: Does a people's way of raising children develop a particular type of personality common to that society? How much is personal lifestyle influenced by a society's "traditional designs for living," or culture? Articles also deal with the constitutional (genetic, physiological), the group-membership (social class, race, culture), the role (age, sex), and the situational (education and acculturation) determinants of personality as well as with the interrelations among these determinants. The volume includes summaries of many studies which focus on Americans in general and subgroups within this society.

PSY 119. LAMB, MICHAEL E. and ABRAHAM SAGI, eds. Fatherhood and Family Policy. Hillsdale, N.J.: Erlbaum, 1983. 276 pp.
The volume arises from the attention addressed to the family as a result of the women's movement, and stresses the need for institutional, economic, legal, and attitudinal reevaluation of the role of men and women in the family. The editors delineate the major concerns of the volume as (1) the factors limiting male involvement in child care, (2) the ways in which these factors can be changed, and (3) the effects of change on traditional concepts of the family. The editors combine both scholarly literature and contemporary theory to define the changing role of fatherhood, and social policy toward the family. Contributions include discussions of cross-cultural research in fatherhood and social policy, the gender dilemma in social welfare, the father's perspective on participation in the family and its outcome for child development, and the societal perspective of costs and benefits of increased paternal participation.

PSY 120. LENDER, MARK EDWARD and JAMES KIRBY MARTIN. Drinking in America: A History. New York: Free Press, 1982. 222 pp.
Lender and Martin unite historical and social science investigations to increase the available information on the role of drinking (and nondrinking) behavior in American society. The authors find that drinking behavior and popular reactions to it both mirror and shape national responses to a variety of issues. The Republican ideology of the American Revolutionary period is the starting point, providing a secular approach to the Temperance movement, which has been more commonly viewed from evangelical or religiously conservative perspectives.

PSY 121. LETTIERI, DANIEL J. Drugs and Suicide: When Other Coping Strategies Fail. Beverly Hills, Calif.: Sage, 1978. 303 pp.
Using research studies conducted across the U.S., Lettieri organized a
collection of essays establishing the link between drug use and suicide.
The volume is divided into four parts. The first section examines various
theoretical perspectives addressing the question of drug use and abuse.
In the second section the essays discuss behavioral and symptomatic alternatives. Section three is concerned with developing research and strategies to further study the problems of both drug abuse and suicide. The
volume concludes with a section concerned with the social issues surrounding the central questions of the book.

PSY 122. LETTIERI, DANIEL J., MOLLIE SAYS, and HELEN WALLENSTEIN PEARSON,
eds. Theories on Drug Abuse: Selected Contemporary Perspectives.
Rockville, Md.: National Institute on Drug Abuse, 1980. 488 pp.
The editors have compiled a broad-ranging collection of essays devoted
to the etiology and treatment of drug abuse. The essays reflect an interdisciplinary approach, and are drawn principally from the biomedical and
social sciences. The volume is divided into two sections. Section one
is concerned with theoretical perspectives and overviews of substance
abuse, including interactive models of nonmedical drug use, an existential
theory of drug dependence, and drug use as a protective system. This
section continues with several essays treating the role of social interactions in drug use. Topics include psychological, social, and epidemio-
logical factors in juvenile drug use, and the Iowa theory of substance
abuse among hyperactive adolescents. Other topics are drug abuse as
learned behavior, a psychosocial theory of drug abuse, and a national history of drug abuse. The second part is devoted to the relation between
theories and clinical practices in intervention and treatment.

PSY 123. LeVINE, ROBERT A. Culture, Behavior, and Personality: An Introduction to the Comparative Study of Psychosocial Adaptation.
1973; Rev. ed. New York: Aldine, 1982. 335 pp.
The author's conceptualization of "the pragmatics of interpersonal communication" is indicative of his psychosocial approach, which functions
as a critique of existing practices in the field of psychology. LeVine
uses an interdisciplinary approach, emphasizing psychoanalytic and anthropological perspectives, in the analysis of psychosocial development and
adaptation. The relationship between the individual and culture is
stressed, with a critique of those personality theories and testing methods
which lack a social context. LeVine's goal is to "lay the basis for a
new psychoanalytic anthropology focused on the accessible surface rather
than the hidden depths."

PSY 124. LEVINSON, DANIEL J. The Seasons of a Man's Life. New York:
Knopf, 1978. 363 pp.
The study is based on forty intensive, long-term interviews with selected
men from various backgrounds and occupations. Levinson describes specific
developmental periods and a general developmental sequence identified
with typical ambitions, successes, failures, and anxieties from Early
Adult Transition (ages seventeen to twenty-two) to Mid-Life Transition
(forty to forty-five) to the Age Fifty Transition (fifty to fifty-five)
and beyond. The author raises several questions about the basic issues
of adult life for American men, including essential problems and satisfactions, the sources of disappointment, grief, and fulfillment, and the
effects of life events on the predictable cycles he describes.

PSY 125. LIFTON, ROBERT J. The Broken Connection: On Death and the
Continuity of Life. New York: Basic Books, 1983. 495 pp.
In the first section of this book, Lifton presents what he calls an "open
system" aimed at developing an adequate understanding of the psychological
relation between death and the flow of life. Lifton discusses general
principles concerning death imagery and struggles for continuity, then
applies these to explorations of the individual life cycle, the varieties
of psychiatric disorder, and aspects of the historical process. In addition, there is a focus on the consequences of the contemporary image of
destruction, for Lifton the "nuclear image." In part two, Lifton addresses
concepts of fundamental emotions, classical neuroses, and the phenomenon
of suicide in the context of the system developed in part one. In the
third section, Lifton discusses broader historical issues concerned with
the theme of death and continuity such as victimization and mass violence,
"nuclear distortions" and "nuclearism," which Lifton defines as "the passionate embrace of nuclear weapons as a solution to death and a way of
restoring a lost sense of immortality."

PSY 126. LIFTON, ROBERT J. The Life of the Self: Toward a New Psychology.
New York: Basic Books, 1983. 190 pp.
Lifton argues that the focal point of psychological theorizing ought to
be a concern with the "fundamental psychological paradigm," which, he proposes, takes death and life-continuity as its focus. Lifton views death
as a complex psychological symbol which is (1) inevitable, (2) present
in life, as in the case of psychic numbing, and (3) a formative or con-
stitutive symbol or an element of creativity and renewal. The author
contrasts his position with those of Freud and Erikson. Among the arguments Lifton uses to support his theory are those stemming from his extensive work with survivors, both of Hiroshima and the Vietnam experience.
He argues for a psychology which rests on a psycho-historical approach
in combination with the formative-symbolic approach and which produces
a holistic sense of the person within the psychological paradigm.

PSY 127. LOEHLIN, JOHN C., GARDNER LINDZEY, and J. N. SPUHLER. Race Differences in Intelligence: San Francisco: Freeman, 1975.
380 pp.
The authors' analysis of the relation between intelligence and race hinges
on their goal of a "sober, balanced and scholarly examination of the evidence that bears upon the role of genetic and environmental factors in
the determination of group differences in ability in the U.S." For the
purposes of this study "intelligence" is understood as performance on
conventional intelligence tests and "race differences" as the difference
between racial-ethnic groups in the U.S. The authors present a historical
account of the literature and indicate the moral and political ramifications of the work in this field.

PSY 128. MACCOBY, ELEANOR EMMONS, ed. The Development of Sex Differences.
Stanford, Calif.: Stanford University Press, 1966. 351 pp.
This collection of essays by noted behavioral psychologists presents a
comprehensive view of early research conducted in the field of sex role
differentiation. Articles deal with the influence of sex hormones on
behavior, sex differences and intellectual functioning, "social learning"
and sex differences and behavior, cognitive-developmental analysis of
sex-role concepts and attitudes in children, and the impact of cultural
institutions on sex differences. This anthology includes a classified
summary of the research conducted on sex differences.

PSY 129. MACCOBY, ELEANOR EMMONS and CAROL NAGY KACKLIN. The Psychology of Sex Differences. Stanford, Calif.: Stanford University Press, 1974. 634 pp.

The authors present an extensive body of evidence about how the sexes do and do not differ in terms of intellectual performance and social behavior. Maccoby and Kacklin examine intellect and achievement in men and women, achievement motivation and self-concept, and abilities and cognitive styles. They inquire into male and female temperament, social approach-avoidance, and societal power relationships. They also deal with the origins of psychosexual differences as evidenced by sex-typing and modeling in child development, and examine the differential socialization of boys and girls.

PSY 130. MALCOLM, JANET. Psychoanalysis: The Impossible Profession. New York: Random House, 1981. 192 pp.

Malcolm offers an assessment of the training of psychoanalysts and the practice of the profession in this account of an analyst who was trained in New York and who maintains his practice there. Although the identity of the analyst is not revealed, the volume offers a view of the people and politics of one of America's leading analytic training institutes. The author, through interviews, offers insights into the effects of psychoanalytic training and practice on both personal and professional levels.

PSY 131. MANASTER, GUY J. and RAYMOND J. CORSINI. Individual Psychology. New York: Peacock, 1982. 322 pp.

This book provides a general introduction to the extensive literature on Individual Psychology. The central tenets of the theory are explicated through a wide range of case histories drawn from clinical practice. The introductory chapter introduces the reader to the central tenets of Adlerian theory, a theory of personality which amounts to a general philosophy of life. Adler's theory is holistic, phenomenological, teleological, and social interactionist in orientation. The individual is perceived as a unique, indivisible unit: integrated, self-directed and in control of self. Chapter two deals with the history and current status of the Adlerian paradigm. Succeeding chapters deal with the dynamics of personality, biological factors, social aspects, the creative self and its structures, the development and maintenance of personality, personality types, education, psychotherapy and counseling in both the familial and group contexts. In the penultimate chapter the authors, both Adlerians, present their personal views of Individual Psychology. Employing an approach which combines humanistic and scientific elements, the authors have presented a concise and clearly argued exegesis of the theory and practice of Adlerian Psychology.

PSY 132. MANN, PHILIP A. Community Psychology: Concepts and Application. New York: Free Press, 1978. 339 pp.

Mann's concern is to further define the parameters of community psychology, which emerged in response to the challenges laid down by community-based social policies initiated in the 1960s. The book is divided into three parts: the first part explores the historical origins of the community-oriented approach and seeks to delineate the conceptual framework of community psychology. Moving from the general to the specific, part two deals with the four main models which have been advanced by psychologists working in this field--the mental health model, the organization model, the social action model, and the ecological model. Mann examines the theoretical propositions underlying these models and describes the intervention strategies and research particular to each. Special emphasis is placed on the model's conceptualization of the community context. Part three critically evaluates and compares the different models focusing on the integrative element of their approach to community problems. The author derives a series of concepts and considerations from his exegesis of the models, which inform intervention strategies, research, and training in community psychology. The book was prepared with the intent of bringing some coherence to prior work done in the field and establishing guidelines for continued research and practice.

PSY 133. MARSELLA, ANTHONY J. and PAUL B. PEDERSON, eds. Cross-Cultural Counseling and Psychotherapy. New York: Pergamon Press, 1981. 358 pp.
This collection is concerned with the foundations, past research, evaluation, and future of cross-cultural counseling and psychotherapy. The volume is the result of a conference held at the East-West Center in Honolulu in June 1979. Among the topics considered are pluralistic counseling and psychotherapy for Hispanic-Americans, Afro-Americans, Japanese-Americans, and American Indians. In each case, the papers attempt to provide a sense of the history of counseling and psychotherapy with these various minority cultures and to provide suggestions for future reseach and development of intervention and treatment strategies which respect cultural differences.

PSY 134. MARTIN, DEL and PHYLLIS LYON. Lesbian/Woman. New York: Bantam, 1972. 283 pp.
"At a time when women, the forgotten sex, are voicing their rage and demanding their personhood, it is fitting that a book on the lesbian be written." Lesbian feminist writers Del Martin and Phyllis Lyon undertook that task and analyze the lives, roles, conflicts, and struggles of women who love women. They discuss the self-images of lesbians, their sexuality and sex roles, their lifestyles, and the problems sometimes faced by lesbian mothers. The authors talk about what it is like to grow up gay, about lesbian paranoia, and about real and imagined fears. They discuss lesbian support groups, the role of lesbianism within the feminist movement, and the possibilities and hopes for "lesbian liberation." "Like her heterosexual sister, the Lesbian has been downtrodden, but doubly so: first, because she is a woman, and second, because she is a Lesbian."

PSY 135. McCONNEL-GENET, SALLY, RUTH BARKER, and NELLY FURNAM, eds. Women and Language in Literature and Society. New York: Praeger Press, 1980. 352 pp.
This book focuses on women and their use of language. It explores the way in which language shapes and gives meaning to women's lives and how in turn women constitute themselves in literature and society through language. Building on the theories of language which have evolved since de Saussure's pioneering work on semiotics, the contributors to this volume attempt to synthesize more recent feminist scholarship with linguistic theory and research. The focus of the contributions alternates between language within the text and the broader context of women's lives. The power of language as both a mediator and a structuring process is emphasized throughout. The book is divided into four parts: The first section reviews the feminist theories and analyses which have emerged within anthropology, linguistics, and literature, and shows how the introduction of the women's perspective is helping to reformulate these disciplines. Part two explores the impact of male social and cultural hegemony on women's language. The third part examines the contextual factors which affect and are affected by language such as education, economics, membership of social groups, environment, ideology, and historical period. The final part presents a variety of methodological and theoretical viewpoints for "reading" women's writing and expanding the scope and context of inquiry into women's literature.

PSY 136. McCUBBIN, HAMILTON I., BARBARA B. DAHL, and EDNA J. HUNTER, eds. Families in the Military System. Beverly Hills, Calif.: Sage, 1976. 393 pp.
Although this volume focuses on the military family, the collection indicates the growing parallels between military and civilian family experiences, in particular in the areas of paternal absence and geographic mobility. Topics covered range from the adolescent's experience of the military to the treatment of women as "dependents," and include alienation, mobility, and the effects of prolonged family separation. In addition, the transitional aspect of military family life is stressed with discussions of divorce and family dissolution, problems arising from retirement, and the efforts to begin a second career after retirement. The volume concludes with an annotated bibliography of research on the military family.

PSY 137. MILVASKY, J. RONALD. Television and Aggression. New York: Academic Press, 1982. 505 pp.
This research monograph reports the findings of an extensive panel study involving 3200 young people over a three-year period in two Midwestern cities. The study assesses the impact of television viewing on the behavior of elementary schoolchildren and teenage boys. The researchers conclude that there is a statistically significant association between exposure to violent television and aggressive behavior at specific points in time. Other findings suggest that there is no evidence of a causal relationship between television exposure and levels of aggression among elementary schoolchildren. While girls are considerably less aggressive than boys, the actual cross-sectional correlations between aggression and violent television exposure are higher for girls than boys. With regard to personal, property, or teacher-directed aggression, no causal link between television viewing and behavior could be established on the basis of the study. Similarly, with regard to teenage delinquency and television viewing, no significant association could be proven.

PSY 138. MOWRER, O. HOBART. Psychology of Language and Learning. New York: Plenum Press, 1980. 294 pp.
This collection of essays includes papers written over the course of twenty-five years. The first section consists of papers originally published between 1945 and 1961 which attempt to establish connections between Pavlov's First Signal System (conditioning) and his Second Signal System (language and prediction). Mowrer explores the process of thinking and vocalization in animals, the Autism theory of speech development, and the forms of language learning. The second part of the book contains a psycho-linguistic critique of Noam Chomsky's work. During the 1960s, Mowrer's research focused on the analysis of communication and the phenomena of lying and deception. Papers on these and related topics appear in the third and final section of the book, titled "Language Abuse and Psychopathology."

PSY 139. MUSTO, DANIEL F. The American Disease: Origins of Narcotic Control. New Haven, Conn.: Yale University Press, 1973. 354 pp.
This volume is the result of work begun in 1968 in the investigation of the history of drug abuse in America. The historical documents discussed reveal a dichotomy between "medical" and "political" approaches. The author finds that the latter histories appear to be political party platforms rather than direct descriptions of U.S. narcotics control. The study traces both the legal and medical approaches as they developed in the early 20th century. Topics treated include the Federal response to addiction maintenance programs, the narcotic clinic era, the "troubled twenties," and Federal support of the medical approach. The study was conducted at the request of the National Institute of Mental Health.

PSY 140. NEURINGER, CHARLES and JACK L. MICHAEL, eds. Modification in
          Clinical Psychology. New York: Appleton-Century-Crofts, 1970.
          261 pp.
This volume is based on the proceedings of the Ninth Annual Institute
for Research in Clinical Psychology held at the University of Kansas in
April 1967. The theme of the conference was the role and place of behavior
modification techniques in clinical psychology. The ten papers presented
reflect the diversity of concerns of students of behavior modification
within psychology. Subjects dealt with include behavior modification
in the preschool setting, rehabilitation, human aggression and research,
and self-regulation. The final paper by Jack L. Michael summarizes the
principal foci of the conference, including some topics raised but not
included in this publication. The theme which emerges is the preference
for a direct approach to the application of reinforcement and punishment
to modify behavior, over the traditional learning theory model which was
popularly used by clinical psychologists to address abnormal behavior
in the 1940s and 1950s.

PSY 141. OBERNDORF, C. P. A History of Psychoanalysis in America. New
          York: Grune & Stratton, 1953. 280 pp.
Oberndorf examines the 19th-century precursors of Freudian psychology
and the "anticipations" of Freud's thinking by New England novelists (such
as Nathaniel Hawthorne). The remainder of the book is an account of the
development of psychoanalytic practice in America, starting with the psychoanalytic psychiatry of the Manhattan State Hospital in 1908. Oberndorf
discusses the growth and development of formal training methodologies
and deviations in psychoanalytic concepts, especially following W.W. II.

PSY 142. OPLER, MARVIN K. Culture and Mental Health: Cross-Cultural
          Studies. New York: Macmillan, 1959. 533 pp.
The controlling perspective of this volume is that of social psychiatry,
which Opler defines as a complex combination of disciplines. Accordingly
the contributors include psychiatrists, psychoanalysts, public health
workers, anthropologists, social psychologists, and sociologists. Each
contributor "has worked in close association with psychiatry for a considerable period of time." The central theme is the variable effect of
culture or culture stress on mental health and the authors present several
appropriate methods of study. Opler provides an introduction which discusses the cultural backgrounds of mental health. The volume continues
with a section devoted to American Indian cultures (North and South),
people of the South Pacific, Asians, Africans, and Anglo-Americans. The
last two sections are devoted to modern problems, chiefly oriented toward
ethnic difference within a single culture, and world perspectives such
as transcultural psychiatry.

PSY 143. PASTEUR, ALFRED B. and IVORY L. TOLDSON. Roots of Soul: The
          Psychology of Black Expressiveness. Garden City, N.Y.: Anchor
          Press, 1982. 324 pp.
The purpose of this book is to present a new and highly innovative account
of the nature and characteristics of black expressiveness. The authors
argue that black expressiveness is founded upon vibrant emotionalism and
a deep-rooted sense of rhythm, and that its impact has spread beyond the
black community and into the popular culture of Western society. The
central thesis contends that black expressiveness helped to shape psychological problems such as stress, depression, and frustration. To substantiate their thesis the authors have drawn on a wide variety of sources
including black music, dance, athletics, graphic arts, sculpture, styling,
and self-expression. Black literature is also explored, using such writers
as W. E. B. DuBois, Ntozake Shange, and James Baldwin. The authors demonstrate the universality of black expressiveness and its contribution to
the enrichment of life. The final part of the book includes suggestions
for the adaptation of black expressiveness as a therapeutic process.

PSY 144. PEPLAU, LETITIA ANNE and DANIEL PERLMAN, eds. Loneliness: A Sourcebook of Current Theory, Research, and Therapy. New York: Wiley, 1982. 430 pp.
This book had its genesis in collaborative research undertaken by the authors, which culminated in a Conference on Loneliness held at UCLA in 1979. A number of papers delivered at the conference have been incorporated in this volume together with additional papers especially commissioned. Peplau and Perlman characterize loneliness as a widespread and often life-threatening problem of contemporary life. The book is divided into six parts, each of which investigates a different theme: aloneness, conceptual and methodological issues in studying loneliness, theoretical approaches to loneliness, loneliness in adulthood, developmental perspectives on loneliness, and therapy for loneliness. Among the principal topics covered are: the nature of loneliness, the cause and consequences of loneliness, its distribution in society, and the pattern of loneliness across the life cycle. The book is intended to have interdisciplinary appeal to practitioners in psychiatry, counseling, social work, gerontology, psychology, and sociology.

PSY 145. PERRUCCI, ROBERT and MARC PILISUK. The Triple Revolution: Social Problems in Depth. Boston: Little, Brown, 1968. 689 pp.
This collection of essays deals with three revolutions. The technological revolution is the development of elaborate nuclear and ballistic missile technology, which has had far-reaching social and psychological effects on American life. The cybernation revolution is reflected in the use of computers and automated machinery, largely (though not exclusively) as they are applied to the processes of production. Lastly, the human rights revolution is evident in the growing demand for full economic, political, and social equality by millions of people in the U.S. and other nations. According to the essayists, the problems generated by these revolutions cannot be met by the civilian and military institutions that have so far evolved in our society.

PSY 146. PETERSON, DONALD R., ed. Educating Professional Psychologists. New York: Transaction Books, 1982. 192 pp.
This volume is a report of a conference on education in professional psychology held at Virginia Beach in April 1978. The focus of the conference was the practitioner-model program of education within clinical psychology, its development, and the impact of new technologies. The book is divided into four parts. The first of these is concerned with the emergence of professional psychology as a discipline and sketches the background to the Virginia Beach conference. The second part focuses on the development of the Doctor of Psychology concept and such basic educational process issues as entrance requirements, assessment, professional training, curriculum design, and the accreditation process. The third section examines existing program models and discusses their relation to the various settings in which they are found. The final section concludes with a survey of the issues raised and resolutions adopted at the conference, and a critical overview of recent issues within the discipline.

PSY 147. PETERSON, MARK A., HARRIET B. BRAIKER, and M. SUZANNE POLICH. Who Commits Crimes: A Survey of Prison Inmates. Cambridge, Mass.: Oelgeschlager, Bunn & Hain, 1981. 267 pp.
This volume reports and analyzes a research project conducted in California's prison system. A survey conducted with 624 incarcerated men is discussed in terms of the data it yielded with respect to psychological, social, and legal implications. The main emphasis is on self-reports of criminal activity. The authors divide the respondents into relative high and low criminal activity categories. The differences in social background, psychological profile, drug history, as well as self-concept and motivation, are discussed and analyzed. Among their findings are

issues reflecting broader social questions such as racism, the relatively high crime rate of the young, and drug abuse. The authors argue for a more appropriate use of information in criminal justice.

PSY 148. PHILLIPS, E. LARKIN. *Stress*, *Health* and *Psychological* *Problems* *in* *the* *Major* *Professions*. Washington, D.C.: University Press of America, 1982. 462 pp.

Phillips explores the physical, psychological, and stress-related health problems which assail people who work in major professions and advances some explanations for these problems. The professions surveyed include medicine, dentistry, nursing and other health occupations, teaching, the clergy, university teaching, business, and the legal profession. Phillips also includes a chapter on women, whose stress, tension, and anxiety problems result not so much from overt discrimination by men but rather from the myriad of economic and professional constraints on their achievement potential. High stress, tension, and anxiety levels are in general attributed to increased materialism, selfishness, and the pervasive aggressiveness which characterizes contemporary living patterns.

PSY 149. QUEN, JACQUES M. and ERIC T. CARLSON, eds. *American* *Psychoanaly-sis*: *Origins* and *Development*. New York: Brunner/Mazel, 1978. 216 pp.

This is a collection of twelve articles with an introduction by the editors on the germination, flowering, and recent relative decline of Freudian theory in America. Several of the entries are on the major analytic institutes, their theories and orientations, and are written by past or present officials of the institutes. Other articles concern intellectual, economic, and political factors that influenced the readiness for acceptance of psychoanalysis. John Brunbaum's article discusses the converse, namely, the influence of psychoanalysis on America.

PSY 150. REEVES, CLEMENT. *The* *Psychology* *of* *Rollo* *May*. San Francisco: Jossey-Bass, 1977. 326 pp.

Reeves's analysis of Rollo May's psychology begins with May's first book *The* *Art* *of* *Counseling* (1939). Using this early work, Reeves shows that the existential-ontological theorizing and practice of May's later career inform even this early book. The central concepts of May's psychology, Anxiety, Will, and Love, are discussed and critiqued chronologically. The author finds May's work to be in the forefront of contemporary psychological theorizing and demonstrates May's use of classic psychoanalytic theory as well as the less conventional existential and ontological philosophy which shapes his major work. The volume concludes with an afterword by Rollo May.

PSY 151. REISS, IRA L. *Family* *Systems* *in* *America*. 1971; Rev. ed. New York: Holt, Rinehart & Winston, 1980. 538 pp.

Reiss attempts to provide a synthesized account of the family system in America, making use of previous research in the field. The introductory chapter offers an overview of major developments in the study of the family in the 20th century. Some of the principal themes discussed in the book include: changes in gender roles and their effect on the family, sexuality, the causes and consequences of pre-marital sexuality, power relations, communication and commitment within marriage, and divorce and remarriage. This edition contains a chapter on gender role changes in Sweden and a chapter on the gender equalization policy in the Peoples' Republic of China.

PSY 152. ROSENBAUM, MAX and ALVIN SANDOWSKY. The Intensive Group Experience. New York: Free Press, 1976. 210 pp.
The authors justify their focus on the group experience by tracing the
development of social (group) change over the course of the 1950s and
1960s. The intensive group experience is seen as representative of group
behavior in general, and the book attempts to assess the changes in the
group experience in recent years. Several kinds of group experience are
focused on, including group psychotherapy, personal growth, encounter
and self-awareness groups, and problem-oriented groups. In each discussion
the existence of the group is related to relevant sociocultural pressures
or conditions in American society.

PSY 153. RUSSIANOFF, PENELOPE. Women in Crisis. New York: Human Sciences
Press, 1981. 319 pp.
This volume is a collection of papers presented at the first conference
on "Women in Crisis," held in New York in May 1979. The contributors
include psychiatrists, psychologists, and social workers from the U.S.
and abroad. The focus of the volume is on the "double discrimination"
faced by women. The women at the center of this volume are those who
are discriminated against first on the basis of their sex and secondly
for the "crisis"--drug abuse, alcoholism, mental illness, or involvement
in the criminal justice system. The volume is divided into three parts:
(1) "Women in Crisis: The Issue," (2) "Intervention: Problems and
Approaches," and (3) "Making Changes." Topics covered include learned helplessness; the double bind faced by minority women; sexism in treatment;
rape; the efforts to change the situation with postintervention and support
systems; the establishment of interdisciplinary treatment networks; and
the utilization of Federal monies to assist women in crisis.

PSY 154. RYAN, WILLIAM. Blaming the Victim. New York: Vintage Books,
1976. 299 pp.
Ryan's study in social psychology examines the tendency of the American
middle class to place the blame for poverty on the poor rather than on
the structural inequalities within "the American system." The author
discusses the myths and folklore surrounding victim-blaming, and identifies
the ideological underpinnings of contrasting approaches to the analyses
and solution of various social problems confronting American society.
Ryan examines the dynamics of class, status, power, and social change
and concludes with some recommendations for overcoming the problem of
victim-blaming through public policy and private action.

PSY 155. SABINI, JOHN and MAURY SILVER. Moralities of Everyday Life.
New York: Oxford University Press, 1982. 238 pp.
In this examination from a social psychology perspective, the authors
examine such commonplace phenomena as envy, gossip, and procrastination
rather than focusing on aggression to assess their relationship to other
social phenomena. The method used is a linguistic analysis of social
behavior and the use of "ideal type" explanations of behavior. Chapter
topics include a socio-psychology of the Holocaust, a plea in defense of
gossip, anger and the subjective, the objective and the ambiguous, and
New York social psychologists.

PSY 156. SAGER, CLIFFORD J. Marriage Contracts and Couple Therapy: Hidden
Forces in Intimate Relationships. New York: Brunner/Mazel,
1976. 335 pp.
Sager examines the dynamics of the unwritten and unspoken contracts between
partners which form an integral part of any committed relationship.
Sager's thesis centers on the nature of the marriage contract. The individual contract refers to each person's conscious and unconscious perceptions of the obligations and rewards attached to the marital relationship.
Sager explores the processes through which the two individuals grow toward

a marital system wherein their two separate contracts become a single operational, interactional contract. The author draws on case studies to develop his thesis that the central goal of marital therapy should be the attainment of the interactional contract. This book is intended to equip both the professional therapist and the couple with useful tools and techniques for examining marriage both within and outside of the context of marital therapy. Additional topics include the proposed integration of the "contractual concept" into the theoretical basis of the professional therapist's work, and the possibility of applying the concept in educational and marital breakdown prevention programs.

PSY 157. SCHAFER, ROY. A New Language for Psychoanalysis. New Haven, Conn.: Yale University Press, 1981. 394 pp.
This book is a reconceptualizataion of psychoanalysis in terms of action language. Schafer presents different aspects of the views of existence, experience, and personal change that are inherent in psychoanalytic interpretation. Schafer also deals with the theoretical writings of Heinz Hartmann, conducting a critical examination of the presuppositions, lines of development, and the inescapable problem of the traditional language of psychoanalytic theory. Lastly, Schafer identifies the mechanistic and anthropomorphic modes of thought that are essential and correlative aspects of measurement conceptualizations.

PSY 158. SCHRAMM, WILBUR, JACK LYLE, and EDWIN PORTER. Television in the Lives of Our Children. Stanford, Calif.: Stanford University Press, 1961. 324 pp.
The authors base their research on an earlier study based in the United Kingdom. For this study, focusing on American and Canadian children, the authors have used 6000 children. They stress that the important variables are in what the child brings to television rather than what it brings to them. Topics considered include how a child uses television and learns from the television, television and social relationships, and the effects of television. The volume concludes with a postscript by psychiatrist Lawrence Z. Freedman.

PSY 159. SCHULTZ, DUANE P. A History of Modern Psychology. New York: Academic Press, 1969. 346 pp.
Schultz concentrates on the last 100 years of development of the discipline, with an emphasis on individual theorists responsible for the development of various schools of psychology. Systems are discussed in relation to both precursors and followers, with an emphasis on developmental continuity. Schultz identifies four areas—learning, perception, motivation, and personality—as central to American psychology and places these in the context of current developments of humanistic psychology.

PSY 160. SERBAN, GEORGE. New Trends of Psychiatry in the Community. Cambridge, Mass.: Ballinger, 1977. 305 pp.
How do community mental health programs impact the prevention and treatment of mental dysfunction in the community? This is the question posed by the contributors to this book, each of whom confronts a different aspect of mental health care. The book is largely based on the proceedings of the Fourth International Symposium of the Kitty Scientific Foundation, entitled "A Critical Appraisal of Community Psychiatry" held March 28-29, 1976 in New York City. The first chapter is a critical evaluation of the rationale for community health care, a history of programs, and the basic premises of the approach. Chapter two explores the epidemiology of mental illness, focusing in particular on mental disorders in children. A comprehensive evaluation of Community Health Services is presented in chapter three, with special emphasis on ethnicity and culturally conditioned patterns of health care. The final chapter deals specifically with the disorder of schizophrenia and its manifestation and treatment in the community context.

PSY 161. SHEEHY, GAIL. Passages: Predictable Crises of Adult Life.
          New York: Bantam, 1977. 393 pp.
Sheehy examines the "inevitable" personality and sexual changes Americans
experience at various stages of adult emotional development. She identifies the "trying twenties," the decade that confronts adults with "the
question of how to take hold in the adult world"; the "catch thirties,"
when most illusions are shaken and life requires deepening commitments
and increasing compromise; the "forlorn forties," the "dangerous years"
in which goals and aspirations are reassessed; and finally, the "refreshed"
or "resigned" fifties, a time that can be the best if one has successfully
redefined old roles and goals and gained new purpose. The author uses
examples to describe life crises and what she sees as opportunities for
creative change in adulthood.

PSY 162. SLATER, PHILIP E. The Pursuit of Loneliness: American Culture
          at the Breaking Point. 1970; Rev. ed. Boston: Beacon Press,
          1976. 206 pp.
Philip Slater revised the earlier edition of this book which was largely
a product of the 1960s. His objective is to provide a less esoteric
account of his ideas by setting them in a more permanent context, one which
would not be so easily affected by changing political and social moods.
His concern is the alienated individual in contemporary American life.
Slater attributes the prevalence of alienation, manifested in tension,
frustration, and a general disorientation in the quality of life, to a
lack of correspondence between what the individual "believes" life should
be and what it really is. The individual is cast in the role of accomplice
in his own oppression, a theme which resonates in Slater's examination
of such issues as the media, violence, contemporary culture, and the economy.
Slater sets out the fundamental goals of society: safety, survival, beautiful and healthy surroundings, and freedom to pursue personal goals.
It is the conflict between the fourth goal and the other three which generates the tension and frustration endemic in contemporary American society.
If these goals are to be united or brought into more harmonious relation
with each other, society will first have to set about the task of establishing real, fundamental cooperation.

PSY 163. SPRAFKIN, JOYCE N., CAROLYN SWIFT, and ROBERT HESS, eds. Rx
          Television: Enhancing the Preventive Impact of TV. New York:
          Haworth Press, 1983. 139 pp.
The thematic unity of this book rests in the argument that television
can be harnessed to produce programs that teach prosocial behavior, promote
good health, and help to change stereotypical attitudes. The authors
maintain that the level of violence has been reduced on the television
screen as a result of public pressure. However, they point out that successful action like this requires sustained vigilance in order to avoid a return
to more violent programming. One essay, on the effects of commercials
on children's values and habits, recommends that parents and teachers
help students to understand the pervasive techniques employed by the media
and to encourage them to develop critical viewpoints. Other essays discuss
the internalization of the television program content by children, and
the pervasive, inaccurate and unrepresentative sex, race, and age stereotypes on the screen.

PS 164.   STAATS, ARTHUR W. Psychology's Crisis of Disunity: Philosophy
          and Method for a United Science. New York: Praeger, 1983.
          391 pp.
In Staats's view, psychology has yet to become a fully developed science.
The author uses Thomas Kuhn's theory of scientific development as a starting point for his analysis of psychology-as-science. The argument calls
for a major theoretical and meta-theoretical interest in the unification
of psychology. Staats believes that potentially monumental progress may

be attained if the problems of the disorganization of knowledge within psychology are solved. The disorganization can be remedied through efforts aimed at experimental, theoretical, methodological, philosophical, and organizational unity.

PSY 165. **STEINMANN, ANNE** and DAVID J. FOX. The Male Dilemma: How to Survive the Sexual Revolution. New York: Aronson, 1974. 324 pp.

"The United States in the 1960s saw the beginning of a profound and sweep-ing sexual revolution . . . sexual relationships and roles as we have known them in this country, including marriage and child-raising, seem to be shaken to their very roots." The Male Dilemma examines how that "revolution" has affected the average American man and woman. The result, the authors argue, has been a new dimension within the "battle of the sexes," a new sex role ambivalence in both sexes. The book explores the conflict and confusion that has arisen as a result of changing demands and personal expectations and proposes ways in which American men and women might begin to revise "anachronistic and unworkable patterns of sexual behavior" so that they may achieve "psychological and social stabil-ity and mutual sexual satisfaction in the future."

PSY 166. **STEWART, ABIGAIL J.**, ed. Motivation and Society. San Francisco: Jossey-Bass, 1982. 379 pp.

Stewart has collected a series of papers which discuss and critique the theories of Motivation and Achievement developed by David McClelland. The volume includes an examination of motivation in individuals, an explo-ration of fundamental social motives, and finally, there is a section devoted to the role of motives as they operate in society. An end note by McClelland provides a personal review of the impact of motivation research on McClelland's life and work as a theorist and educator.

PSY 167. **SZASZ, THOMAS S.** The Ethics of Psychoanalysis: The Theory and Method of Autonomous Psychotherapy. New York: Basic Books, 1965. 226 pp.

This volume begins with a preface by the author in which he reaffirms his commitment to his radical position toward psychoanalysis. Szasz believes that the fields of therapeutic interaction have an ethos which is neither medical nor mental in orientation. For Szasz, the moral, politi-cal, and scientific significance of the psychoanalytic situation is that it is "a model of the human encounter regulated by an ethics of individ-ualism and personal autonomy." Psychoanalysis is described in terms of social action rather than as a healing process. As such, Szasz's position characterizes psychoanalytic treatment as aimed at increasing the patient's self-knowledge and ultimately his freedom of choice in the conduct of his life. This is achieved through the analysis of communications, rules, and games. Szasz stresses a "contractual" rather than "therapeutic" rela-tionship between analyst and analysand. His overall emphasis lies on the social context of this contractual relationship.

PSY 168. **SZASZ, THOMAS S.** The Manufacture of Madness: A Comparative Study of the Inquisition and the Mental Health Movement. New York: Harper & Row, 1970. 383 pp.

Szasz traces the development of what he calls "Institutional Psychiatry" from its roots in Christian theology to its current practices which he finds to be couched in medical rhetoric and enforced by police power. His analysis is based on the analogy between witchcraft and mental illness. Szasz focuses on the parallels between the consequences of being labeled a witch and those of being labeled, by institutional psychiatry, as men-tally ill. Among the examples he cites are American servicemen who are classified as mentally ill for marrying Asian women, and the example of the model psychiatric scapegoat—the homosexual, which is for Szasz, analogous to the heretic in the 17th-century society. The volume emphasizes that the power of institutional psychiatry has direct social and cultural consequences.

PSY 169. SZASZ, THOMAS S. The Myth of Mental Illness: Foundations of a Theory of Personal Conduct. 1961; Rev. ed. New York: Harper & Row, 1974. 297 pp.
For this revision of the 1961 edition, Szasz has included a new preface and summary and has made substantial changes in the text. The fundamental argument—that involuntary psychiatric interventions are intolerable—remains the same. The author discusses the growth and structure of the myth of mental illness, which he defines as "whatever the therapist needs it to mean." As an example of the myth in operation Szasz analyzes the clinical and theoretical use of the diagnosis of hysteria. In part two he offers a "semiotical analysis of behavior" which includes analysis of behavior based on language and protolanguage rule-following and game-model analyses of behavior. The last chapter is devoted to the ethics of psychiatry.

PSY 170. TAGESON, C. WILLIAM. Humanistic Psychology: A Synthesis. Homewood, Ill.: Dorsey Press, 1982. 286 pp.
This book attempts to provide a synthesized account of the various theoretical perspectives which have emerged in the field of humanistic-existential psychology. Tageson examines the work of some of the major authors in the field including Joseph Nuttin, Carl Rogers, Abraham Maslow, Victor Frankl, Amedeo Giorgi, Sidney Jourard, Frederick Perls, Rollo May, Ludwig Binswagner. The principal topics covered include the Phenomenological Approach, Holism, the Actualizing Tendency, Self Determination, the Ideal of Authenticity, Self Transcendence, and Person-Centeredness. His approach is axiomatic in that he identifies the uniquely human attribute of self-reflective awareness as the source of thematic unity among these various humanistic authors. The application of humanistic principles both within and outside of the psychological domain is explored. In conclusion, the author addresses critics of the movement and suggests directions for its future development.

PSY 171. TSENG, WEN-SHENG and JOHN F. McDERMOTT. Culture, Mind and Therapy: An Introduction to Cultural Psychiatry. New York: Brunner/Mazel, 1981. 304 pp.
Interest in the field of cultural psychiatry began in the 19th century when missionaries, explorers, and later psychiatrists first encountered strange behavior and practices in "primitive societies." In the 20th century Kraepelin, Freud, and Jung all showed interest in cross-cultural analysis of the experience of psychiatric illness. In the 1940s and 1950s studies focused on the cultural aspects of the expression of psychiatric illness; more recent studies concentrate on variations in therapeutic practices. In this book, Tseng and McDermott argue that cultural psychiatry must not focus exclusively on the experience of minority or marginal groups in society, but rather must project its research further to include the behavior disorders and treatment approaches. This book is an attempt to integrate much of the scholarly work done in cultural psychiatry to date. It also endeavors to go beyond mere description of cultural differences and to consider the implications of those cultural differences for the field of cultural psychiatry itself. A wide range of psychiatric disorders are examined in a cross-cultural context. In the final section of the book, the authors draw up some directions for the future under the headings of Research, Training, and Therapy.

PSY 172. TURNER, SAMUEL M. and RUSSELL T. JONES, eds. Behavior Modification in Black Populations: Psychological Issues and Empirical Findings. New York: Plenum Press, 1982. 330 pp.
The editors seek to address the paucity of literature relating black populations and behavior modification techniques and research. The material is intended to identify what a behavioral approach is and to determine the effectiveness of its use with black populations. Chapter topics include behavioral therapy, a brief history of the treatment of black patients by the mental health professions as well as discussions of specific mental health issues. Among these are "Psychiatric Symptoms in Black Patients," "The IQ Controversy and Academic Performance," "Rational Behavior Therapy," "Substance Abuse," and "Sexual Disorders." The volume concludes with a chapter on the implementation of community programs and discusses the black population in behavioral community psychology.

PSY 173. UNGER, RHODA KESSLER and DENMARK, FLORENCE L., eds. Women: Dependent or Independent? New York: Psychological Dimensions, 1975. 828 pp.
Psychology has begun to look at women from a fresh perspective, one not defined by nor oriented toward men. In this volume a number of behavioral scientists discuss the relevant issues of this "new" psychology. The principal focus of the book is "not whether biological or social factors produce sex-characteristic behavior, but how much of such behavior is affected by each variable." The editors intend to provide an interactional viewpoint on sex roles in modern America. Articles discuss sex-role stereotypes, how therapists look at women, the development of sex differences and sex roles, sex differences in cognitive functions, the question of psychosexual neutrality at birth, menstruation and pregnancy, and the internal and external barriers to female achievement.

PSY 174. VALLIANT, GEORGE E. The Natural History of Alcoholism. Cambridge, Mass.: Harvard University Press, 1983. 370 pp.
Alcoholism plays a major role in American society and is generally involved in the four major causes of death for males between twenty and forty: suicide, accidents, homicide, and cirrhosis of the liver. As many as one-third of all American families are affected by this disease. The present volume reflects the results of Harvard Medical School's Study of Adult Development which followed 660 men from 1940 to 1980. The volume is divided into four parts. The first attempts to define alcoholism; part two discusses various patterns of recovery as seen in the longitudinal study. The third section discusses methodological issues such as sample measurement. The volume concludes with a section devoted to the lessons for treatment learned through analysis of the study.

PSY 175. VERHOFF, JOSEPH, ELIZABETH DOUVAN, and RICHARD A. KULKA. The Inner American: A Self Portrait from 1957 to 1976. New York: Basic Books, 1981. 647 pp.
The authors conducted a replication of the 1957 study on American help-seeking patterns. They find that, along with an increase in the percentage of educated Americans and the growth of community and social resource programs, help-seeking is increasing. However, they caution that the increase is not uniform and, for some groups, there is less reliance on professional resources in 1976 than in 1957. The study involves nearly 5000 adult Americans, predominantly white, and from all areas of the country. Topics covered in an overview of help-seeking include feelings and sources of well being, self-perceptions, marriage, parenthood, work and symptoms of stress. Appendices include the interview questionnaire and statistical analysis comparing the results of the 1957 and 1976 studies.

PSY 176. VERHOFF, JOSEPH and SHEILA FELD. Marriage and Work in America: A Study of Motives and Roles. New York: Van Nostrand Reinhold, 1970. 404 pp.
The authors selected three relatively specific personality characteristics for the focus of their discussion—the motives for affiliation, for achievement, and for power based on the work of Henry Murray, David McClelland, and John W. Atkinson—and relate these to a study of overall psychological adjustment and the forces affecting mental health and illness. The specific concerns of this volume are work, marriage, and parenthood: that is, how men and women with different personal motivation react to these important social demands. Following chapters that discuss motives and work, marriage, and parenthood, the authors devote a chapter to a comparative discussion of roles in American marriage, parenthood, and work.

PSY 177. WATTS, THOMAS D. and ROOSEVELT WRIGHT, Jr., eds. Black Alcoholism: Toward a Comprehensive Understanding. Springfield, Ill.: Thomas, 1983. 242 pp.
This book is divided into four sections. Section one discusses the etiological factors of black alcoholism. Section two, titled "Treatment," includes articles which investigate issues of treating alcoholism and the consequences of various methodologies. The third section provides methods for the prevention of alcoholism in the black community. The volume concludes with discussions of research methodologies, as well as public policy and practice in intervention and prevention of black alcoholism.

PSY 178. WAX, MURRAY. Indian Americans: Unity and Diversity. Englewood Cliffs, N.J.: Prentice-Hall, 1971. 236 pp.
This book offers an orientation to the contemporary situations and problems of American Indian peoples. It is at the same time an effort to provide information about the Indian population and to direct the interested reader to a wider range of material and sources. Wax's concern is to equip the reader with a basic knowledge of historical and present-day realities of the Indian people, particularly those readers involved with developing programs of assistance. The book is divided into three parts: historical development and comparative relationships; contemporary U.S. Tribal Communities; and Indians and the greater society. The book contains a bibliography and extensive reference material on Federal expenditure on American Indians, Indian population, education, and health.

PSY 179. WEBER, G. H. and L. M. COHEN, eds. Beliefs and Self-Help: Cross-cultural Perspectives and Approaches. New York: Human Sciences Press, 1982. 359 pp.
This volume focuses not on the psychological motivations of those who constitute a self-help group but rather on the self-help group as a particular form of association. Twelve contributors examine the social context in which groups emerge, the process by which they become institutionalized and the cultural beliefs and values shared by those who associate themselves with the group. Empirical analysis of self-help groups at work is based on observations in the U.S., Mexico, Kenya, and South Africa. The papers present specific case studies and relate these to beliefs, ethnicity, and associated group processes and dynamics. The concepts of culture and cross-cultural comparison provide the unifying themes of this work.

PSY 180. WEXLER, PHILIP. Critical Social Psychology. New York: Routledge & Kegan Paul, 1983. 176 pp.
In this critique of liberal social psychology, Wexler views Capitalism as problematic and focuses on the relationship among ideological practices and meanings, class relations, and mode of production. The author generates a set of categories for examining ideology and cultural processes

that responds to the power of economic relations. Essentially, this work is concerned with the interplay of culture, ideology, and mode of production, and the extent to which they reproduce a particular set of social and economic relations. Wexler argues for a framework of social psychology which is founded in the social reality of contemporary society.

PSY 181. WILCOX, ROGER. The Psychological Consequences of Being a Black American: A Sourcebook of Research Black Psychologists. New York: Wiley, 1971. 492 pp.
Wilcox has assembled articles and speeches which reflect research and theoretical trends in black psychology. The emphasis of the collection is on education, with special focus on the issues of learning, intelligence testing, and achievement testing. In addition to research and theoretical articles, Wilcox has included essays of historical significance within the psychological research literature for the problems of being a black American.

PSY 182. WILLERMAN, LEE. The Psychology of Individual and Group Differences. San Francisco: Freeman, 1979. 531 pp.
As an advocate of an interdisciplinary approach, Willerman stresses the links--and potential links--between a psychology of individual and group differences and the fields of biology and genetics. The emphasis of the book, in its survey of areas of difference, is on behavior genetics. Where relevant, environmental factors are also discussed. Willerman provides a historical context for his discussion of differences in intelligence, personality, psychopathology, mental retardation, and the gifted, as well as sex, age, and racial and ethnic differences among groups.

PSY 183. WILLIAMS, RICHARD H. and CLAUDINE G. WIRTHS. Lives Through the Years: Styles of Life and Successful Aging. New York: Atherton, 1965. 298 pp.
Williams and Wirths's book studies life cycles and adult development in America. Based on the results of extensive interviews conducted in Kansas City over a five-and-a-half year period, this micro-sociological work describes and analyzes the general pattern and course of an individual's life. The authors identify and define "success" and use their analysis of "lifestyle" to produce a theoretical framework from which to view individual differences in the aging process. They conclude that there are six principal styles of life, all of which can lead to successful old age.

PSY 184. WITKIN, H. and D. GOODENOUGH. Cognitive Styles: Essence and Origins. New York: International Universities Press, 1981. 141 pp.
The cognitive style of Field Dependence-Independence expresses the extent of differentiation of an individual's psychological structures. In this monograph Witkin and Goodenough assign a pivotal role in conceptualizing perception-personality relationships to central adapting, regulating personality structures. The proliferation of research in the area of field dependence-independence is attributed by the authors to its strong theoretical framework and its suitability for empirical analysis. The authors' task is twofold: first to review the later knowledge on field dependence-independence and to propose revisions and extensions of field-dependence theory in the light of that knowledge, and second, to review evidence on the origins of the field-dependent and field-independent cognitive styles. They examine such diverse influences as genetic and endocrine factors, special training, child-rearing, and cultural and ecological effects.

PSY 185. WOODRUFF, DIANA S. and JAMES E. BUREN, eds. Aging: Scientific Perspectives and Social Issues. New York: Van Nostrand, 1975. 421 pp.
This volume surveys the processes and problems of aging. The first section provides a brief history of gerontology in the U.S. Subsequent sections offer sociological, psychological, and biological perspectives on aging, discussing changes in the psychological and physiological make-up of older Americans as well as the changing nature of social interactions as people age. The editors present readings on planned environments for the elderly and on the economic and public policy implications of the increasing proportion of older Americans in the population.

PSY 186. WORTIS, HELEN and CLARE RABINOWITZ. The Women's Movement: Social and Psychological Perspectives. New York: AMS, 1972. 151 pp.
In this volume behavioral scientists discuss issues prominent in the earlier years of the women's movement. Contributing authors examine the changing role of women, the impact of the women's movement on child development, and the concept of the maternal role. The essays inquire into the implications of equality between the sexes for the modern American family and for the single woman. An article by Jean Baker Miller and Ira Mothner deals with the psychological consequences of sexual inequality. The volume also includes a comprehensive resource bibliography.

PSY 187. ZILBERGELD, BERNIE. The Shrinking of America: Myths of Psychological Change. Boston: Little, Brown, 1983. 307 pp.
Zilbergeld's central question, "are we really capable of making significant psychological change in ourselves?" is addressed from the perspective of the American desire for perfectability. Zilbergeld uses national history and cultural values to demonstrate the attractiveness of the "therapeutic sensibility" for contemporary Americans, for whom nearly all elements of life are psychologized and therapy is generally encouraged as a solution for most problems. Actual therapies are discussed and evaluated, ranging from traditional psychoanalysis to more popular and less obviously "therapeutic" systems. In addition, the author examines the effects of marginal success on the therapy consumer, whose dissatisfaction with therapy is seen to actually worsen rather than improve the client's sense of well-being. Zilbergeld argues for a change in existing expectation of the ease of individual change and of the efficacy of psychotherapy for producing permanent change.

PSY 188. ZINBERG, NORMAN E. and I. KAUFMAN, eds. Normal Psychology of the Aging Process. 1963; Rev. ed. New York: International Universities Press, 1978. 285 pp.
In a series of twelve papers and formal discussions, this book seeks to explicate the psychodynamics of older people's lives. Part one contains the proceedings of the First Annual Scientific Meeting of the Boston Society for Gerontologic Psychiatry, a group committed to the study of the aged in terms of dynamic psychiatry. The earlier essays are characterized by an emphasis on the nature and functions of the ego. The new chapters in this edition veer toward a preoccupation with object relations and narcissism. The subjects treated in this volume include: psychological responses to the physical phenomenon of aging; changes in the theoretical mental structures of id, ego, and superego with aging; vicissitudes of sexuality and aggression; interpersonal relations; social and cultural implications of aging; and psychopathology.

RELIGION

In putting together the section on American religion, my aim has been to keep the listing sufficiently brief in length to serve as a manageable guide for the nonspecialist and sufficiently comprehensive in scope to remain of some use to those more familiar with the field. The resulting 300 and some odd selections are representative of work on religion that would be of interest to the Americanist. In this case the Americanist angle amounts principally to a preference for scholarship that takes on the complicated interplay between American religious development and the broader currents of American culture. Such interplay would include both the "Americanization" of religion and the role of religion in the shaping of American culture.

Organization of the bibliography falls into three main divisions. The first contains works which offer an overview of American religious history in some comprehensive manner—either in a survey, a thematic interpretation, a collection of source material with commentary, or a series of essays. Generally here is where one would start any investigation. Especially recommended are Ahlstrom (1972) and Hudson (1981). The remaining two divisions separate the scholarship into historical and topical treatments of American religion, and each division comes with its own subdivisions. Naturally the entire apparatus of categorization is merely a device of convenience, and readers should be prepared to follow paths that cut across established divisions.

Other bibliographies of American religion, more general in focus, can be consulted in order to supplement and complement the broadly Americanist perspective of this section. For sheer comprehensiveness Nelson Burr's A Critical Bibliography of Religion in America, Vol. IV of Religion in American Life (Princeton, N.J.: Princeton University Press, 1961), remains uncontested. Burr later went on to update and abridge his earlier work in the Goldentree bibliography, Religion in American Life (New York:

Appleton–Century–Crofts, 1971). For a bibliography moderate in length and scope, try Ernest R. Sandeen and Frederick Hale, American Religion and Philosophy: A Guide to Information Sources (Detroit, Mich.: Gale Research, 1978), which is notable for its pithy annotations. Periodical literature, absent in this section, is given exclusive and thorough attention in Robert deV. Brunkow, Religion and Society in North America: An Annotated Bibliography (Santa Barbara, Calif.: ABC-Clio Information Services, 1983). Biographical information, downplayed here, can be found in Henry Warner Bowden, Dictionary of American Religious Biography (Westport, Conn.: Greenwood Press, 1977). Also of interest for reference purposes is Edwin S. Gaustad, Historical Atlas of Religion in America, Rev. ed. (New York: Harper & Row, 1976). Finally, many of the works listed under the first division of this section contain very helpful bibliographies and suggestions for further reading. Ahlstrom (1972), Handy (1976), and Gaustad (1982, 1983) are cases in point.

James Wetzel
Columbia University

I. COMPREHENSIVE SURVEYS, ENCYCLOPEDIC ACCOUNTS, AND THEMATIC INTERPRETATIONS OF AMERICAN RELIGIOUS HISTORY

R 1. AHLSTROM, SYDNEY E. A Religious History of the American People. New Haven, Conn.: Yale University Press, 1972. 1158 pp. Throughout this work Ahlstrom remains attentive to how American religious movements have been shaped by influences from abroad and the social and historical situation at home. While respecting and relating the radical diversity of the American religious scene, he highlights Puritanism and its legacy. The final section of the book, "Toward Post-Puritan America," discusses the end of the Puritan epoch and the contemporary challenges to American Protestant hegemony.

R 2. ALBANESE, CATHERINE L. America: Religions and Religion. Belmont, Calif.: Wadsworth, 1981. 389 pp. The organizing theme of this wide-ranging survey is the dialectic that exists between the rich religious pluralism of America's peoples and regions and the one public religion of America. The focus throughout is on popular religion, with Part One being devoted to the multifaceted equation (here Albanese uses a history of religions approach) and Part Two on the oneness (here a more topical approach). Suggested readings are included at the end of each chapter.

R 3. CLEBSCH, WILLIAM A. From Sacred to Profane America: The Role of Religion in American History. New York: Harper & Row, 1968. 242 pp. "This book contends that the chief features of the American dream were formed by people's religious concerns and that they came into realization outside the temple." Clebsch observes a complex pattern in American history whereby aspirations generated in a religious setting achieve their fruition in the society at large, turning the achievements of the saints into the property of the citizens. In this way the contribution of religion to American life has been tied ironically to a process of profanation or disassociation from religious institutions. Clebsch maps out this thesis for six "programs" involved in shaping the American dream—education, pluralism, social amelioration and personal morality, novelty, participation of diverse peoples in an open society, and nationality.

R 4. GAUSTAD, EDWIN S. Dissent in American Religion. Chicago: University of Chicago Press, 1973. 184 pp. Religious dissent is an elusive quarry in a society diverse and flexible in its character, having neither stalwart orthodoxy nor national church. In this study, Gaustad recounts the story of American religion's loyal opposition amid a shifting consensus. Organized topically, his study gives attention to three main species of dissenter: the schismatic, the heretic, and the misfit. In an epilogue, he discusses new directions in religious dissent.

R 5. GAUSTAD, EDWIN S., ed. A Documentary History of Religion in America. 2 vols. Grand Rapids, Mich.: Eerdmans, 1982, 1983. 1145 pp. These two volumes provide a sampling of documentary sources covering the full spectrum of American religious history. Emphasis has been placed on voices spoken from within the religious traditions. Volume One covers the period up to the Civil War, and Volume Two continues the story to recent times.

R 6. **GUNN, GILES,** ed. New World Metaphysics: Readings on the Religious Meaning of the American Experience. New York: Oxford University Press, 1981. 464 pp.
Gunn offers this anthology as a counterargument to the treatment of American religion and American culture as autonomous worlds. He locates their intersection in a common concern for the symbolic meaning of America itself. A parade of voices from many eras and cultural camps attest to a variegated process of sacralization, whereby the meaning of America has evolved into the religion of American culture.

R 7. **HANDY, ROBERT T.** A Christian America: Protestant Hopes and Historical Realities. 1971; Rev. ed. New York: Oxford University Press, 1984. 269 pp.
Beginning with colonial times, but concentrating on the 19th and early 20th centuries, Handy follows the Protestant quest for a Christian America. He devotes attention to the connection evangelicals drew between the spread of Christianity and the progress of civilization, to Protestant commitment to religious freedom and voluntary persuasion, and to the fading of the dream in contemporary America. In a section added to the 1984 edition, Handy reflects on whether the resurgence of religious fundamentalism may realize the quest after all.

R 8. **HANDY, ROBERT T.** A History of the Churches in the United States and Canada. New York: Oxford University Press, 1976. 471 pp.
The Christian outposts in the North American wilderness represented the interests of six nations contending for possessions in the New World. In this history, Handy brings together the Canadian and American churches into one narrative. Beginning with the early Colonial period, he explores the Old World seeds of New World church development. With the onset of boundary disputes, war, and cultural conflict, the church histories diverge and are given separate treatment. The narrative comes together again after W.W. II, when the Canadian and U.S. religious scene become subject to the same problems and opportunities of a declining Christian culture.

R 9. **HILL, SAMUEL S.,** ed. Religion in the Southern States: A Historical Study. Macon, Ga.: Mercer University Press, 1983. 423 pp.
The sixteen state histories that make up this volume were originally assigned to become part of the forthcoming Encyclopedia of Religion in the South. Smith has decided to publish them as a set in the belief that the South as a geographical region has displayed an identifiable and distinct cultural and social unity. The final essay of the collection, by Smith himself, summarizes Southern religious history.

R 10. **HILL, SAMUEL S.,** Jr. The South and the North in American Religion. Athens: University of Georgia Press, 1980. 152 pp.
Hill's contrapuntal rendering of two cultures coexisting within the same culture centers on Northern and Southern interaction in three epochs: 1795-1810, 1835-1850, and 1885-1900. Topics of discussion include the dominant events and types of development peculiar to each region, dialogue between cultures, and the relationship between religious and regional identity. The approach is sociological, with attention also given to historical development and the dynamics of religious belief.

R 11. **HUDSON, WINTHROP S.** Religion in America: An Historical Account of the Development of American Religious Life. 1965; Rev. ed. New York: Scribner, 1981. 486 pp.
Hudson's concise history of religion in America keeps an eye toward the commonalities that run through "the seemingly rampant pluralism." The revised third edition incorporates recent scholarship and adds a section on the turn to religious conservatism in the 1970s and 1980s.

R 12. **MARTY, MARTIN E.** Righteous Empire: The Protestant Experience in America. New York: Harper & Row, 1970. 295 pp.
Marty's history covers two centuries of the American Protestant experience, beginning with the birth of the new nation. Part I, "The Evangelical Empire, 1776-1877," concentrates on the efforts of a relatively homogeneous group of Protestant evangelicals in creating the kingdom of God in America. Part II, "From Evangelical Empire to Protestant Experience, 1877-," recounts the challenges to the old empire from non-Protestant peoples and forces.

R 13. **McLOUGHLIN, WILLIAM G.** Revivals, Awakenings, and Reform: An Essay on Religion and Social Change in America, 1607-1977. Chicago: University of Chicago Press, 1978. 239 pp.
"Revivals alter the lives of individuals; awakenings alter the world view of a whole people or culture." With this distinction made, McLoughlin examines how the revivalistic impulse has panned out into five distinct awakenings spanning the entire breadth of American history. His essay draws out the common cultural assumptions that are behind and have given shape to the recurring patterns of ideological and social change showcased in awakenings. Taken as a whole, he contends, awakenings indicate that American history is best understood as a millenarian movement.

R 14. **MEAD, SIDNEY E.** The Lively Experiment: The Shaping of Christianity in America. New York: Harper & Row, 1963. 220 pp.
Once transplanted to American soil, the European churches and sects fragmented and fanned out under the influences of the frontier and religious freedom. Denominationalism, democracy, and the unbroken continuum of Christian church history obscured by plurality in America are all motifs of Mead's interpretation of American Christianity. The nine essays contained in The Lively Experiment span two centuries of American church development, but they are not intended to be a comprehensive account of American Protestantism.

R 15. **MELTON, J. GORDON.** The Encyclopedia of American Religions. 2 vols. Wilmington, N.C.: McGrath, 1978. 1203 pp.
Melton's Encyclopedia gives brief descriptions of the origins, membership, and beliefs of some 1,200 churches, including lesser-known sects and cults. Organization is by "families" of churches (e.g., The Reformed-Presbyterian Family, The Pentecostal Family), which are individually introduced by Melton in essays on their heritage, thought, world, and lifestyle.

R 16. **MOSELEY, JAMES G.** A Cultural History of Religion in America. Westport, Conn.: Greenwood Press, 1981. 183 pp.
With an understanding of religion indebted to Clifford Geertz and a respect for variety reminiscent of William James, Moseley describes new cultural forms of religion in nine different episodes of American life, ranging from the Puritans of New England to the new religious movements of the 1970s. The remarkable feature of his study is that he employs as many interpretive approaches as he takes on topics. For instance, American Puritanism gets a history of religious approach, while Transcendentalism is billed as "the religion of nature in the form of literature."

R 17. **MULDER, JOHN M. and JOHN F. WILSON, eds.** Religion in American History: Interpretive Essays. Englewood Cliffs, N.J.: Prentice-Hall, 1978. 459 pp.
These essays run the gamut from New England Puritanism to radical theology in the 1960s. The range and quality of the essays attest to the recovery of American religious history and supply the reader with a set of readings on central issues in the interpretation of American religion. Detailed notes accompanying each article facilitate further research.

1503

R 18. NIEBUHR, H. RICHARD. The Kingdom of God in America. New York:
       Harper & Row, 1937. 215 pp.
A seminal interpretation of American Christianity, Niebuhr's book posits
the idea of the kingdom of God as the unifying force of a pluralistic
tradition. The concern throughout is with American Christianity as a
movement able to shape culture rather than merely be shaped by it.

R 19. PIEPKORN, CARL ARTHUR. Profiles in Belief: The Religious Bodies
       of the United States and Canada. 4 vols. New York: Harper & Row,
       1977-1979. 777 pp.
Piepkorn's unfinished magnum opus offers concise descriptions of a large
cross-section of the religious traditions in the U.S. and Canada. As
the title indicates, emphasis is on doctrine. Volume One covers Roman
Catholic, Old Catholic, and Eastern Orthodox traditions; Volume Two takes
on Protestant Denominations; and Volumes Three and Four, which are printed
together, detail Holiness and Pentecostal movements (III), and Evangelical,
Fundamentalist, and Other Christian Bodies (IV).

R 20. RICHEY, RUSSELL E., ed. Denominationalism. Nashville, Tenn.: Abing-
       ton, 1977. 288 pp.
Ten essays by distinguished scholars of American Religion explore the
pervasive and enduring phenomenon of denominationalism. The collection
is divided into five sections: "The Denominational Theory of the Church";
"Evangelical Denominationalism"; "Ethnic Denominationalism"; "Transformation"; and "Perspective." Emphasis tends to fall on the 19th century,
with attention limited to Protestantism and mainly evangelical Protestantism. Overall, the collection is designed to speak to the question of
the origins and essence of denominationalism.

R 21. SMITH, H. SHELTON, ROBERT T. HANDY, and LEFFERTS A. LOETSCHER. Ameri-
       can Christianity: An Historical Interpretation with Representative
       Documents. 2 vols. New York: Scribner, 1960, 1963. 1249 pp.
This massive work, written by three leading church historians, serves
as both an interpretive exposition of the major developments in American
Catholicism and Protestantism and as a primary reference source for those
developments. Approximately two-thirds of the work is devoted to primary
sources, which include selections of substantial length. Volume One
covers the period from 1607-1820; Volume Two from 1820-1960.

R 22. SMITH, JAMES WARD and A. LELAND JAMISON, eds. Religious Perspectives
       in American Culture. Princeton, N.J.: Princeton University Press, 196
       427 pp.
This second volume of the Religion in American Life series consists of
essays on the influence and expression of religion in contemporary American
life. The impact of religion is assessed with regard to education, law,
politics, fiction, poetry, music, and architecture.

R 23. SMITH, JAMES WARD and A. LELAND JAMISON, eds. The Shaping of American
       Religion. Princeton, N.J.: Princeton University Press, 1961. 514 pp.
This collection of essays—the first volume in the Religion in American
Life series—offers a look at the internal dynamics of America's religions,
especially their institutional structures and intellectual life. Part
One consists of separate essays on Protestantism, Catholicism, Judaism,
and the new religions. The next part takes on special topics in the intellectual history of American religion. Among the scholars contributing
are H. Richard Niebuhr, Oscar Handlin, Sydney Ahlstrom, and Perry Miller.

R 24. STROUT, CUSHING. The New Heavens and New Earth: Political Religion in America. New York: Harper & Row, 1974. 400 pp.
Strout takes his cue from Tocqueville's observation that religion and liberal democracy have been complementary forces in America. He describes the historical manifestation of a particular style of religion, "a democratic and republican religion," with an eye toward the tensions produced by the religious diversity of times more contemporary than Tocqueville's. Strout's account begins with the Puritans, ends with the "new pluralism" of the 1960s, and is concerned broadly with the articulation between American religious ideas and values and political concepts of liberty, equality, community, and justice.

II. HISTORICAL BREAKDOWN OF AMERICAN RELIGIOUS HISTORY: COLONIAL BEGINNINGS, HIGHLIGHTING NEW ENGLAND PURITANISM

R 25. ADAIR, JOHN. Founding Fathers: The Puritans in England and America. London: Dent, 1982. 302 pp.
Adair's retelling of the history of Puritanism, spanning two centuries in England and America, is in large part an effort to acclimate the reader to the Puritans (as evidenced by his concluding chapter, "The Puritan Within Us"). The emphasis he assumes therefore downplays whatever doctrinal peculiarities the movement has to concentrate instead on the broad contours of Puritanism as shaped by its Reformation and Renaissance parentage. A recurring theme in the narrative is the prophetic stance Puritans in the Old World and the New World take toward England.

R 26. BOYER, PAUL and STEPHEN NISSENBAUM. Salem Possessed: The Social Origins of Witchcraft. Cambridge, Mass.: Harvard University Press, 1974. 231 pp.
Salem showcased tensions common to late 17th-century New England society—conflict between landed farmers and commercial capitalists, demographic shifts, changing loci of authority. Geographic isolation exacerbated these tensions, and the witchcraft outburst proceeded along lines of existing factional conflicts. Such is the thesis of Boyer and Nissenbaum, who meticulously reconstruct a social portrait of the Salem community using the extensive records of the village and its church.

R 27. DEMOS, JOHN PUTNAM. Entertaining Satan: Witchcraft and the Culture of Early New England. New York: Oxford University Press, 1982. 543 pp.
Demos's major study of witchcraft in early New England society offers four angles of vision on the topic: (1) biography, revealing what sorts of people were most vulnerable to accusations of witchcraft, (2) psychology, revealing what sorts of internal stress were likely to prompt accusations, (3) sociology, relating witchcraft to the shapes and structures of community life, and, finally, (4) history, explaining why witchcraft trials occurred in some places but not in others. All told, these perspectives illuminate how witchcraft "belonged to the regular business of life in premodern times."

R 28. ELLIS, JOHN TRACY. Catholics in Colonial America. Baltimore, Md.: Helicon, 1965. 486 pp.
The exhaustive treatment Ellis offers of Catholic missions in North America from the time of Columbus to the American Revolution falls into three divisions—The Spanish Missions, The French Missions, and The English Missions. While he is generally sympathetic to European efforts at Christianizing the Indians, Ellis does not fail to consider the darker side

of the enterprise: "the white man's cruelty to the native Indians, the latter's barbarous retaliations, and the exhaustive wars between European rivals for mastery of the new world."

R 29. ERIKSON, KAI T. Wayward Puritans: A Study in the Sociology of Deviance. New York: Wiley, 1966. 228 pp.
The level of deviance in any stable society is a constant that enables the society to define its own boundaries. In times of external conflict, such as war, internal conflict or "crime" is at a minimum. Periods devoid of external challenge, on the other hand, witness an increase in internal tension. Erikson plays out this sociological hypothesis in an examination of three Puritan "crime waves"--the Antinomian Controversy, the Quaker invasion, and the Witches of Salem Village.

R 30. GANNON, MICHAEL V. The Cross in the Sand: The Early Catholic Church in Florida, 1513-1870. Gainesville: University of Florida Press, 1965. 210 pp.
The Catholic Church in Spanish Florida represented the oldest establishment of the Christian faith in the New World. Gannon's straightforward history of the Church spans the period from the voyages of Ponce de Leon in the early 16th century to Civil War and Reconstruction in the U.S. Much attention is devoted to Florida's Indian missions, whose activities were impeded by the conflict between English and Spanish interests and finally stopped entirely when the territory was ceded to England in 1763. Whenever possible, Gannon introduces primary source material into his narrative.

R 31. HALL, DAVID D. The Antinomian Controversy, 1636-1638: A Documentary History. Middletown, Conn.: Wesleyan University Press, 1968. 447 pp.
The Antinomian Controversy has long been recognized by historians as a turning point in New England Puritanism. In a single volume, Hall has assembled the major primary documents essential for an understanding of the episode. Included are exchanges between John Cotton and other ministers, John Wheelwright's Fast-Day sermon, John Winthrop's short history of antinomianism, and the transcript of Anne Hutchinson's trial. Hall's introduction contains a brief history of the Controversy and a discussion of the theological issues involved.

R 32. HALL, DAVID D. The Faithful Shepherd: A History of the New England Ministry in the Seventeenth Century. Chapel Hill: University of North Carolina Press, 1972. 301 pp.
Through three generations of the New England ministry, Hall follows the cultural rite of passage whereby a European institution assumed an American identity. This development, he argues, did not proceed in a straightforward evolution. As the second generation passed into the third, a weakening of Puritan self-identity resulted in fewer differences between the American ministry and Old World models. For each generation, Hall is attentive to how the complex interplay of ideas and social situations shaped definitions of the ministry.

R 33. HAMBRICK-STOWE, CHARLES E. The Practice of Piety: Puritan Devotional Disciplines in Seventeenth-Century New England. Chapel Hill: University of North Carolina Press, 1982. 296 pp.
"Historians have long treated New England Puritanism as an intellectual and a social movement. At its heart, however, Puritanism was a devotional movement, rooted in religious experience." Taking this less developed tack in Puritan scholarship, Hambrick-Stowe discusses the character of worship and private devotional activity for 17th-century New Englanders. In addition to diaries, spiritual autobiographies, and meditative poetry, he pays special attention to the devotional manuals introduced into Puri-

tanism from the late 16th century onward. Qualifying the picture of the early American community as one of rationalists hostile to "technique" and passive in their spirituality, he argues that devotional and meditational disciplines have been central to Puritan practice from the start.

R 34. HANSEN, CHADWICK. Witchcraft at Salem. New York: Braziller, 1969. 252 pp.
Departing from traditional views of the Salem witchcraft trials as a mixture of fraud and fanaticism, Hansen argues for the reality of witchcraft in 17th-century New England, where its malefic influence produced tangible effects in a community that believed in the power of the demonic. Much documentary evidence is marshalled to support this thesis.

R 35. HOLIFIELD, E. BROOKS. The Covenant Sealed: The Development of Puritan Sacramental Theology in Old and New England, 1570-1720. New Haven, Conn.: Yale University Press, 1974. 248 pp.
Literally hundreds of sermons, meditations, and polemical treatises on baptism and the Lord's Supper attest to the keen interest Puritans had in the sacraments. Focusing on 17th-century Puritanism, Holifield describes the emergence of a vital sacramental piety shaped from within a Reformed theology. He contends that sacramental discussions reveal many of the fundamental presuppositions of Puritan thought: "Implicit in the debates and devotional manuals were crucial assumptions about finitude and infinity, spirit and flesh, reason and the senses."

R 36. LUCAS, PAUL R. Valley of Discord: Church and Society Along the Connecticut River, 1636-1725. Hanover, N.H.: University Press of New England, 1976. 275 pp.
Lucas examines ecclesiastical controversy in the Connecticut Valley in order to demonstrate, contra much current historiography, that Puritan ideals and practice were often at odds. The story he recounts involves a debate among clergy expanding to a debate encompassing the laity and finally evolving into two separate factions struggling for control of the church. He concludes that "the legacy of those early Puritans was one of drift, dissension, and institutional instability."

R 37. MORGAN, EDMUND S. Visible Saints: The History of a Puritan Idea. New York: New York University Press, 1963. 159 pp.
The Puritans who settled the Bay Colony in the 1630s and 1640s sought to establish a community of the elect, free from the corruption of the Church of England they had left behind. In a concise history of the ideal of visible sainthood, Morgan describes the origins, consequences, and decline of a uniquely American ecclesiastical innovation--the requirement that all candidates for church membership attest to an experience of saving grace.

R 38. PETTIT, NORMAN. The Heart Prepared: Grace and Conversion in Puritan Spiritual Life. New Haven, Conn.: Yale University Press, 1966. 252 pp.
Pettit's study of the Puritan conversion experience centers on preparationism, or the doctrine that sinners could prepare themselves for regenerative grace. The "heart prepared," an image Puritans drew from scriptural exegesis, marked a significant departure from Reformed predestinarian theology and contributed to a distinctly Puritan piety. After discussing the Continental and English background, Pettit concentrates on American preparationism and contends that this doctrine was at issue both in the Antinomian Controversy and the Half-Way Covenant.

R 39. POPE, ROBERT G. The Half-Way Covenant: Church Membership in Puritan
New England. Princeton, N.J.: Princeton University Press, 1969.
321 pp.
By 1640 it had become established practice for most Puritan churches to
require all candidates for church membership a testimony of heartfelt
conversion. By 1669 so few members of the second generation could meet
this requirement that church leaders were forced to effect a compromise
to check flagging admissions. Children of unregenerate parents were
allowed to own the covenant "half-way," an arrangement granting them bap-
tismal but not communion privileges. Pope's analysis of the Half-Way-
Covenant challenges its standard interpretation as a falling off in Puritan
piety. Instead he reads the compromise as part of American Puritanism's
transformation from a sect to a church (terms borrowed from Ernst
Troeltsch).

R 40. RUTMAN, DARRETT B. American Puritanism. New York: Norton, 1977.
135 pp.
Rutman's monograph on American Puritanism seeks to establish a middle
ground between intellectual and social history, or as he puts it, between
"New England as a Puritan idea" and "New England as a society." Given
this ecumenical task, he articulates an understanding of Puritanism which
situates the rhetoric of its religiosity within the social settings where
rhetoric had its impact. On the whole, his efforts are directed more
toward conceptualization than exposition.

R 41. SOLBERG, WINTON U. Redeem the Time: The Puritan Sabbath in Early
America. Cambridge, Mass.: Harvard University Press, 1977.
406 pp.
Until well into the 20th century, Sabbath observance was a distinguishing
national characteristic of Americans. Solberg traces the roots of this
practice in the first major historical account of the development of the
Puritan Sabbath, beginning with the 16th-century English inheritance and
ending with the Great Awakening. The central issue of his study concerns
"how a new and powerful Sabbatarian impulse emerged in England on the
eve of colonization and proved so significant in molding the United States
in its most formative years."

R 42. STOEVER, WILLIAM K. 'Faire and Easie Way to Heaven': Covenant
Theology and Antinomianism in Early Massachusetts. Middletown,
Conn.: Wesleyan University Press, 1978. 251 pp.
In 1636, the orthodox consensus in Boston received a jolt that shook the
very foundations of the New England Way. Anne Hutchinson, inspired by
the preaching of John Cotton, led a sizable portion of the community in
protest against what she and her followers perceived to be a return to
the legality of a covenant of works, calling in its stead for justification
based on an experience of grace. Stoever's complex analysis of the controversy, focusing on ministerial debates, examines antinomianism in light
of "a theological dialectic that was the common property of Reformed
divines in the 16th and 17th centuries." He frames the controversy as
one episode in a long-standing Puritan effort to relate nature and grace
in such a way that neither is abrogated.

R 43. SWEET, WILLIAM WARREN. Religion in Colonial America. New York:
Scribner, 1942. 367 pp.
Sweet's comprehensive account of the beginnings of organized religion
in America highlights the evolution of religious liberty. Early chapters
discuss the establishment of European religious groups in the New World
and the maintenance of the European church-state tradition in America
until about 1660. In subsequent chapters following late 17th- and 18th-
century developments, Sweet notes the rise in importance of left-wing
groups, the beginnings of a church-state separation, and the gradual Americanization of Christianity.

HISTORICAL BREAKDOWN: LATER COLONI-
AL RELIGION AND THE EARLY NATIONAL
PERIOD

R 44. BALDWIN, ALICE M. The New England Clergy and the American Revolution.
       Durham, N.C.: Duke University Press, 1928. 222 pp.
The central thesis of Baldwin's investigation is that the rights of life,
liberty, and property at issue in America's struggle for independence
had their ideological roots in a Puritan theology that lent them the status
of religious convictions. After detailing the connection between Puritan
and republican ideals, she goes on to argue that the New England clergy
were great popularizers of political philosophy, making the principles
of resistance to unjust authority and natural rights available to the
church-going populace long before the battles of the American Revolution.

R 45. BOLTON, S. CHARLES. Southern Anglicanism: The Church of England
       in Colonial South Carolina. Westport, Conn.: Greenwood Press,
       1982. 220 pp.
Bolton's thorough history of the Anglican Church in Colonial South Carolina
challenges the stereotypical rendering of the Anglican clergy as overbear-
ing and self-seeking allies of British imperialism. He shows that the
Anglican establishment was by and large favorably disposed toward colonial
interests, espoused religious moderation, and allowed for considerable
exercise of lay prerogative. Nevertheless, the Church remained tied to
a financial and social aristocracy, and this proved its undoing with the
birth of the Republic.

R 46. BRIDENBAUGH, CARL. Mitre and Sceptre: Transatlantic Faiths: Ideas,
       Personalities, and Politics, 1689-1775. New York: Oxford Univer-
       sity Press, 1962. 354 pp.
"The purpose of this work," Bridenbaugh writes, "is to discover what
Englishmen and Americans thought about the relation of church to state,
where they acquired their opinions, what they did with and about these
ideas, and finally, how their outlook and actions affected the long course
of history." Bridenbaugh's period of interest is between 1689 and 1775,
and he concentrates on the ecclesiastical struggle between Anglicans and
dissenters over the establishment of an American episcopate. His account
illuminates how religious controversy contributed to a nascent American
sense of nationality and became a cause of the American Revolution.

R 47. BUSHMAN, RICHARD L. From Puritan to Yankee: Character and the
       Social Order in Connecticut, 1690-1765. Cambridge, Mass.: Harvard
       University Press, 1967. 343 pp.
During the period from 1690 to 1765, Connecticut underwent the transition
from an homogeneous Puritan community bound by religious sanction to a
more heterogeneous society of Yankees prepared to fight for their liberty
by the eve of the Revolution. Bushman examines the social changes behind
this transformation and argues that the law and authority of Puritan tradition lost out to economic ambitions and the religious impulses of the
Great Awakening.

R 48. GAUSTAD, EDWIN SCOTT. The Great Awakening in New England. New
       York: Harper, 1957. 173 pp.
Gaustad offers a general account of the Great Awakening and its theological
and institutional ramifications. He couches the event primarily as a
struggle between the forces of Enlightenment rationalism and Pietistic
emotionalism, with attention given to how this battle took on a Puritan
cast. His account devotes separate attention to the Northampton revivals
that foreshadowed the main event, the traveling itinerant preachers, the
height of the revival, the debate between Jonathan Edwards and Charles
Chauncy, and the legacy of this watershed event.

R 49. GEWEHR, WESLEY M. The Great Awakening in Virginia, 1740-1790.
        Durham, N.C.: Duke University Press, 1930. 292 pp.
In this study of the Great Awakening in Virginia, the author "endeavors
to show the far-reaching effects of the series of evangelical revivals
which swept the colony in wave after wave during the thirty or forty years
preceding the American Revolution, and then again after the war." Gewehr
discusses a revolution in personal religion and a social revolution linked
to the rise of political democracy and 19th-century humanitarian and educational reforms.

R 50. GOEN, C. C. Revivalism and Separatism in New England, 1740-1800:
        Strict Congregationalists and Separate Baptists in the Great Awaken-
        ing. New Haven, Conn.: Yale University Press, 1962. 370 pp.
The Great Awakening occasioned not only an outburst of religious enthusiasm
but also widespread religious dissent against the standing Congregationalist order in New England. Goen's systematic study of the separatist
churches formed during the revival attempts to determine "the location,
circumstances and characteristics of every discoverable separatist congregation."

R 51. GREVEN, PHILIP. The Protestant Temperament: Patterns of Child-
        rearing, Religious Experience, and the Self in Early America.
        New York: Knopf, 1977. 431 pp.
In an attempt to get at the Puritan piety behind the Puritan intellect,
Greven sets forth a typology of temperaments which he applies across generations and denominations in 17th and 18th century New England. He delineates three essential types--the "evangelical," preoccupied with self-
abasement and given to marked conversion experiences; the "moderate," avoiding excesses of any kind and concerned with self-control; and the "genteel," suffering from no spiritual anxiety and prone to self-assertion.
Greven documents how these temperaments and their concomitant notions
of selfhood were inculcated through child-rearing practices.

R 52. GRIBBIN, WILLIAM. The Churches Militant: The War of 1812 and Ameri-
        can Religion. New Haven, Conn.: Yale University Press, 1973.
        210 pp.
Speaking of the period on and about the War of 1812, Gribbin remarks,
". . . if the American mind of that era is to be fathomed, one might begin
by observing America's churches in the laboratory setting that the war
provided." Using sermons as data, Gribbin attempts to reconstruct the
popular religious ideology of warring Americans. In mapping the variety
of religious responses to the war, he offers the reader a unique glimpse
of the complex dynamics of ecclesiastical life in the early years of the
Republic.

R 53. HARLAN, DAVID. The Clergy and the Great Awakening in New England.
        Ann Arbor, Mich.: UMI Research Press, 1980. 172 pp.
Historians of the Great Awakening have, by and large, accepted the judgment
of its great protagonists, Jonathan Edwards and Charles Chauncy, in viewing
the event as dividing all of New England's clergy into opposed camps of
enlightened rationalists and evangelical revivalists. Harlan seeks to
qualify this polarity by describing the response of ministers who maintained a middle ground between Calvinism and Liberalism.

R 54. HEIMERT, ALAN. Religion and the American Mind: From the Great
        Awakening to the Revolution. Cambridge, Mass.: Harvard University
        Press, 1966. 668 pp.
Heimert explores the mind of religious America as it was shaped by the
watershed events of Awakening and Revolution. Of the Great Awakening,
he notes the division of American Protestantism into evangelical and ration-
alist camps and follows the indigenous expressions of these two strains

of thought within the evolution of Puritanism. Of the revolutionary period,
he describes how the two intellectual options coming out of the Awakening--
liberalism and evangelical Calvinism--contributed in distinctive ways
to the political ideology of the new Republic. He argues, contrary to
the usual assumptions, that liberalism's spokesmen tended to be more conservative and reticent about revolution than their Calvinist counterparts.

R 55. HEIMERT, ALAN and PERRY MILLER, eds. The Great Awakening: Documents
      Illustrating the Crisis and Its Consequences. Indianapolis, Ind.:
      Bobbs-Merrill, 1967. 663 pp.
Due to the death of Perry Miller this anthology is largely the work of
Alan Heimert, who made selections that would reflect the Awakening "as
both a significant progression of events and a crisis in the history of
the American mind." A generous number of important texts are represented,
including in their entirety Gilbert Tennent's Nottingham sermon, Charles
Chauncy's warning against enthusiasm, and the Harvard faculty's rebuke
of George Whitefield. In the introduction Heimert supplies a general
overview of American intellectual life in the era of the Awakening.

R 56. ISAAC, RHYS. The Transformation of Virginia, 1740-1790. Chapel
      Hill: University of North Carolina Press, 1982. 451 pp.
Isaac's history traces a half-century of religious and political revolutions in Virginia. The guiding theme throughout is that of religion and
the changing roles of ecclesiastical authority; the approach is one of
social history informed by ethnography.

R 57. JAMES, SIDNEY V. A People Among People: Quaker Benevolence in
      Eighteenth-Century America. Cambridge, Mass.: Harvard University
      Press, 1963. 405 pp.
James's study of Quaker benevolence is concerned broadly with how self-
isolated sectarians entered into the American religious mainstream via
humanitarian endeavor. He traces the process whereby Quakers expanded
their social relations among fellow Friends to take in the entire society
around them, including blacks, Indians, and other dispossessed groups.
An important thesis of the book is that by the second half of the 18th
century, the Quakers' practice of disinterested benevolence placed them
in harmony with the ideals current among many Americans in the Revolutionary era.

R 58. LIPPY, CHARLES H. Seasonable Revolutionary: The Mind of Charles
      Chauncy. Chicago: Nelson-Hall, 1981. 179 pp.
The common rendering of Charles Chauncy in the historiography is that
of a foil to the theological brilliance of Jonathan Edwards. Seeking
to give Chauncy a fairer shake, Lippy portrays a man "whose impact extended
to virtually every dimension of life in eighteenth century Massachusetts."
As the "seasonable" Puritan, or one whose opinions reflected whatever
the current controversy happened to be, Chauncy's contentious career illuminates many facets of later colonial religion.

R 59. LOETSCHER, LEFFERTS A. Facing the Enlightenment and Pietism:
      Archibald Alexander and the Founding of Princeton Theological Semi-
      nary. Westport, Conn.: Greenwood Press, 1983. 303 pp.
Soon after its founding in 1812, Princeton Seminary became the home base
for a conservative theology that was to have significant impact on religious
attitudes in the Southern and Middle States. Loetscher's recounting of
the story of the Seminary's founder, Archibald Alexander, weaves together
biographical and institutional history with the larger social and cultural
movements of Pietism and Enlightenment rationalism.

R 60. LOVEJOY, DAVID S. Religious Enthusiasm and the Great Awakening.
Englewood Cliffs, N.J.: Prentice-Hall, 1969. 115 pp.
In the 17th and 18th centuries, the term "enthusiasm" was a term of
reproach, indicating an emotional outburst unconnected either with revelation
or religious inspiration. As such, it was used by detractors of the Great
Awakening to stigmatize the revival. On the other side, the revival's
proponents argued that the Awakening marked the greatest outpouring of
the Spirit yet to be witnessed in America. Lovejoy's book, as part of
the American Historical Sources series, offers an introductory essay on
the nature and consequences of the Great Awakening debate together with
the original documents illustrating the event. Selections include the
major historical figures, such as Jonathan Edwards, Charles Chauncy,
Gilbert Tennent, and George Whitefield.

R 61. MARINI, STEPHEN A. Radical Sects of Revolutionary New England.
Cambridge, Mass.: Harvard University Press, 1982. 213 pp.
Marini's intricate study of sectarianism in revolutionary New England
follows the emergence of three sects into indigenous religious cultures,
later known as the Shakers, the Universalists, and the Freewill Baptists.
He singles these out for special treatment because they represent the
first popular rejection of New England Calvinism. Once these sectarian
movements had evolved into full-blown religious alternatives, Calvinism
could no longer contain native religious energies. Marini concludes that
the success of the sects marks the first expression of an American pluralism rooted in revolutions of the spirit.

R 62. McLOUGHLIN, WILLIAM G. Isaac Backus and the American Pietistic
Tradition. Edited by Oscar Handlin. Boston: Little, Brown, 1967.
252 pp.
Isaac Backus, a convert to the Baptist Church during the great revival
of 1741, spent the better part of his life fighting for a principle of
voluntarism in religion at odds with the privileged and state-supported
position of the Congregationalist Churches. McLoughlin's recounting of
Backus's life and times reflects on pietistic efforts at separating church
and state in the years prior to the American Revolution. The vision Backus
had of a Christian America free from state encroachment, McLoughlin points
out, predominated in America until very recently.

R 63. MILLS, FREDERICK V. Bishops by Ballot: An Eighteenth Century Ecclesiastical Revolution. New York: Oxford University Press, 1978.
367 pp.
The years immediately following the American Revolution witnessed in the
political and constitutional arena many concrete expressions of the principle of popular sovereignty. Looking at the Church of England in America
during this period, Mills notes an analogous development in the ecclesiastical arena. More specifically he details the developments leading up
to the adoption of a republican-type ecclesiastical constitution by the
Protestant Episcopal Church in 1789, a settlement which granted laity
and clergy the right to elect their own bishops. Mills sees this democratization of the church as one prominent example of the influence of republican ideals on church development in the early national period.

R 64. TANIS, JAMES. Dutch Calvinistic Pietism in the Middle Colonies:
A Study in the Life and Theology of Theodorus Jacobus Frelinghuysen.
The Hague: Martinus Nijoff, 1967. 203 pp.
As one of the first Colonial ministers to emphasize experiential religion
over theological dogma, Frelinghuysen became a seminal figure in the shaping of American pietism, particularly in the Middle Colonies. His ministry
in the Raritan Valley marked an important prelude to the Great Awakening.
Tanis offers an account of Frelinghuysen's life and theology as a way
into Dutch Reformed pietism and its impact on the American religious scene.

R 65. TRACY, PATRICIA J. Jonathan Edwards, Pastor: Religion and Society in Eighteenth-Century Northampton. New York: Hill & Wang, 1980. 270 pp.
An abundant scholarship exists for the philosophical and theological thought of Jonathan Edwards, yet comparatively little attention has been paid to the pastoral implications of his ideas and activities. Tracy seeks to correct this deficiency, while opening up at the same time a window on the great Awakening as a social movement. Her explanation of Edwards's success in tapping into the social energies of the Northampton congregation suggests some of the dynamics at work in the broader revival.

R 66. TRINTERUD, LEONARD J. The Forming of an American Tradition: A Reexamination of Colonial Presbyterianism. Philadelphia: Westminster Press, 1949. 352 pp.
Trinterud's study of the Presbyterian Church covers a century of its history, from its colonial roots to its place in the fledgling republic. The first part of the book concerns the formative years of the church (1706-1758), when it forged its American identity amid shifting allegiances and spiritual awakening. The remaining half picks up the story of how the American church conceived its purpose and direction in the turbulent years surrounding the American Revolution.

R 67. YOUNGS, J. WILLIAM T., Jr. God's Messengers: Religious Leadership in Colonial New England, 1700-1750. Baltimore, Md.: Johns Hopkins University Press, 1976. 176 pp.
Congregational ministers living in New England during the first half of the 18th century were challenged to meet the religious needs of a burgeoning mercantile society. In recounting their story, Youngs develops the themes of growing professionalism among the clergy, revivalism, and the changing role of the minister in Colonial New England.

HISTORICAL BREAKDOWN: REVIVALISM AND WESTWARD EXPANSION IN NINETEENTH-CENTURY AMERICA

R 68. BOLES, JOHN B. The Great Revival, 1785-1805: The Origins of the Southern Evangelical Mind. Lexington: University Press of Kentucky, 1972. 236 pp.
Boles seeks to explain how the great revival that swept across the South in the beginning of the 19th century came about. He does this by reconstructing the religious world-view of Southern evangelicalism and by suggesting ways in which that world-view contributed to widespread expectations for a new dispensation. The evangelicals discussed are mainly white Baptists, Methodists, and Presbyterians in the six states of Virginia, North Carolina, South Carolina, Georgia, Kentucky, and Tennessee.

R 69. CARWARDINE, RICHARD. Transatlantic Revivalism: Popular Evangelicalism in Britain and America, 1790-1865. Westport, Conn.: Greenwood Press, 1978. 249 pp.
The revivalism central to American cultural development retained even throughout the 19th century a transatlantic character that linked together the British and American evangelical Protestant communities. Carwardine illuminates the nature of this revivalism by exploring its manifestation on both sides of the Atlantic. He begins with the great American revivalists active during the Second Great Awakening, turns to a consideration of their influence on popular British evangelicalism, and concludes with whatever can be gleaned from the work of American revivalists in a culture different from though related to their own.

R 70. CROSS, WHITNEY R. The Burned-over District: The Social and Intellectual History of Enthusiastic Religion in Western New York, 1800-1850. Ithaca, N.Y.: Cornell University Press, 1950. 383 pp.

The Burned-over District refers to western New York during the first half of the 19th century, a time of repeated religious upheaval for that area. In a close analysis of this district, Cross demonstrates how town and urban centers were as much a part of revivalism as was the frontier. Moreover, as the storm center of uncontained religious enthusiasm, The Burned-over District illuminates many of the religiously motivated social movements of the 19th century.

R 71. DOLAN, JAY P. Catholic Revivalism: The American Experience, 1830-1900. Notre Dame, Ind.: University of Notre Dame Press, 1978. 248 pp.

Dolan's main thesis is that the revivalism so obviously an important part of American Protestant experience during the second half of the 19th century also played a vital role in the shaping of Catholic piety. At the heart of Catholic revival efforts was the parish mission, which involved touring Catholic preachers who would urge their assembled listeners to revitalize their spiritual lives. Dolan discusses the European antecedents of the parish mission, its indigenous American expression, its preachers and their audience. A final chapter draws out the parallels between Protestant and Catholic revivalism.

R 72. FINDLAY, JAMES F., Jr. Dwight L. Moody: American Evangelist, 1837-1899. Chicago: University of Chicago Press, 1969. 440 pp.

Findlay's biography of Moody offers an inroad to the urban evangelicalism of the post Civil-War era. "Through Moody," writes Findlay, "one learns of premillennialism, dispensationalism, and the revival of 'holiness,' or schemes of sanctification within Protestant circles in America." As a member of both evangelical Protestantism and the secular world of the Gilded Age, Moody reflected in his life and work an evangelicalism beset by external pressures from industrialization and internal pressures from theological disputes.

R 73. FOSTER, CHARLES I. An Errand of Mercy: The Evangelical United Front, 1790-1837. Chapel Hill: University of North Carolina Press, 1960. 320 pp.

"The power of American Victorianism as a conservative counterpoise to native radicalism," argues Foster, "is obvious to any thoughtful observer of the American scene in the nineteenth century." In his study of the evangelical united front, Foster describes how this Victorian morality came to the States via evangelical Protestantism. Part one of his book deals specifically with the rise of the United Front in Great Britain and its activities abroad. The next part takes up the Front's establishment, naturalization, and eventual dissolution in the American environment.

R 74. GOODYKOONTZ, COLIN BRUMMITT. Home Missions on the American Frontier: With Particular Reference to the American Home Missionary Society. Caldwell, Idaho: Caxton, 1939. 460 pp.

From the late 18th century up through the decades following the Civil War, Goodykoontz discusses the efforts and motivations of eastern-based Protestants involved in fostering the westward advancement of religion and education. In particular he concentrates on the joint work of Congregationalists and Presbyterians in the Home Missionary Society, which he argues supplied "the chief means through which the missionary spirit of New England was made effective in the West." The influence of his teacher, Frederick Jackson Turner, is readily apparent throughout the work.

R 75. JOHNSON, CHARLES A. The Frontier Camp Meeting: Religion's Harvest
        Time. Dallas, Tex.: Southern Methodist University Press, 1955.
        325 pp.
"Among all of the weapons forged by the West in its struggle against lawlessness and immorality," writes Johnson, "few were more successful than
the frontier camp meeting." His study of this notable feature of American
frontier revivalism discusses the camp meeting's institutional growth,
flowering, and decline in the trans-Allegheny West during the first four
decades of the 19th century. While setting out the impact of these meetings on humanitarian reform movements and frontier culture, he attempts
to create the atmosphere of the "Camp Meetin' Time."

R 76. JOHNSON, PAUL E. A Shopkeeper's Millennium: Society and Revivals
        in Rochester, New York 1815-1837. New York: Hill & Wang, 1978.
        210 pp.
Johnson attempts to explain why the revival of 1830, spearheaded by Charles
G. Finney, inspired hundreds of thousands of middle-class Americans "to
make society in God's name." Using Rochester as an illustrative case,
he assesses the impact of migration, boom-town economics, and temperance,
Sabbatarian, and antimason crusades on community relations. He contends
that the revival served the interests of ruling economic groups and "provided a solution to the social disorder and moral confusion that attended
the creation of a free-labor economy."

R 77. SIZER, SANDRA S. Gospel Hymns and Social Religion: The Rhetoric
        of Nineteenth-Century Revivalism. Philadelphia: Temple University
        Press, 1978. 222 pp.
Sizer's study is an "historical reconstruction of revivals and gospel-
hymn rhetoric" informed methodologically by the anthropology of Clifford
Geertz and Claude Levi-Strauss and the literary criticism of Kenneth Burke.
Chapter One spells out her theoretical debts, while the remaining text
explores the language of popular hymnody in the context of revivalism
and evangelicalism from the Finney period onward. She proposes to show
how the metaphors and symbols found in the gospel hymns articulated a
world and simultaneously created a community identity.

R 78. SMITH, TIMOTHY L. Revivalism and Social Reform in Mid-Nineteenth-
        Century America. New York: Abingdon Press, 1957. 253 pp.
In his study of the revivalism and perfectionist aspirations that flourished between 1840 and 1865 in all major Protestant denominations, Smith
describes how a democratized Christian faith became the common possession
of the evangelical populace and fostered widespread efforts at purging
society of its ills. "The quest of personal holiness," he contends,
"became in some ways a kind of plain man's transcendentalism, which geared
ancient creeds to the drive shaft of social reform." It is in this ferment
of perfectionist energies, emanating primarily from the cities, where
Smith finds the antecedents for the Christianity that later became known
as the social gospel.

R 79. SWEET, WILLIAM WARREN. Religion in the Development of American
        Culture, 1765-1840. New York: Scribner, 1952. 338 pp.
Sweet links the impulse for expansion and religious experimentation evident
in the English colonies with the pioneering spirit that won the West:
"It was in the great new west that the 'heretic,' the individualist par
excellence, found opportunity for self-expression, and the story of experimentation in organized religion on the frontier constitutes one of the
most significant and important aspects of a new Western civilization and
culture." His study of the impact of religion on the formation of this
culture concerns primarily the role of Protestant nonconformity in fostering the westward migration of American civilization.

HISTORICAL BREAKDOWN: THE ANTEBEL-
LUM RELIGIOUS SCENE

R 80. CLARKE, ERSKINE. Wrestlin' Jacob: A Portrait of Religion in the
     Old South. Atlanta, Ga.: John Knox Press, 1979. 207 pp.
Clarke's portrait of the Old South depicts the encounter of white preachers
and black slaves in two settings--the plantation and the city. Part One
is devoted to the plantation and focuses specifically on Liberty County,
Georgia, a Puritan community bent on cultivating blacks who would be both
good Christians and obedient slaves. The next part switches to Charleston,
South Carolina, the cosmopolitan city that produced Denmark Vesey. Highlighted in Clarke's portrait is the ability of black slaves to find spiritual resources for resistance against those who considered themselves benevolent.

R 81. CONFORTI, JOSEPH A. Samuel Hopkins and the New Divinity Movement:
     Calvinism, the Congregational Ministry, and Reform in New England
     Between the Great Awakenings. Grand Rapids, Mich.: Christian
     University Press, 1981. 241 pp.
Friend and disciple of Jonathan Edwards, Samuel Hopkins rose to prominence
as the guiding light of the New Divinity movement within New England Congregationalism, America's first indigenous school of Calvinism. Conforti's
account of his public life and religious thought reveals much about both
the character of Hopkins and his contributions to the theological trends
of the time. The major emphasis of the book is on the development of
New Divinity under Hopkins's leadership into the New England theology.

R 82. HOOD, FRED J. Reformed America: The Middle and Southern States,
     1783-1837. University: University of Alabama Press, 1980.
     254 pp.
"The Reformed of the middle and southern states have been interpreted
as adjuncts to other important and, significantly, functionally dissimilar
religious groups when in reality they developed their own patterns of
thought and action with regard to the American nation." Seeking to give
a fairer characterization of the Reformed churches, which by 1780 had
come to form the largest religious sector in the country, Hood describes
the role they played in shaping the ethos and morals of the new nation.
Focusing primarily on Presbyterians and Dutch Reformed groups, he stresses
how their leaders sought to use religion to impose a particular moral
vision upon the country.

R 83. HUTCHISON, WILLIAM R. The Transcendentalist Ministers: Church
     Reform in New England Renaissance. New Haven, Conn.: Yale Uni-
     versity Press, 1959. 240 pp.
Focusing on those transcendentalists who remained within the Christian
fold, Hutchison takes up the question of whether transcendentalist religion
was "anything more than a tendency to appraise the universe through the
spectacles of an intuitive faith." His period of interest falls between
1830 and 1860, a time marked by pronounced theological controversy and
the founding of transcendentalist religious societies. The central controversy for transcendentalist ministers was their debate with conservative
Unitarians, an exchange Hutchison portrays without drawing the usual caricature of dreamy nature-lovers facing bloodless rationalists. His concluding chapter discusses the relevance of the transcendentalist controversy for the subsequent development of liberal Protestantism in America.

R 84. GRIFFIN, CLIFFORD S. Their Brothers' Keepers: Moral Stewardship
in the United States, 1800-1865. New Brunswick, N.J.: Rutgers
University Press, 1960. 332 pp.
Griffin examines the trustee tradition in American Protestantism as it
came to bear on the numerous social and moral crusades of the antebellum
era. Members of this tradition traced their roots back to a Calvinistic
heritage, where saints accepted the responsibility for reforming the behavior of their fellow citizens. By 1840 the moral persuasion of the Protestant trustees had evolved into a wave of political activity that encompassed antislavery, temperance, and anti-immigrant movements. "At the
end of the Civil War," notes Griffin, "morality by persuasion and morality
by compulsion were permanent characteristics of American life."

R 85. KUYKENDALL, JOHN W. Southern Enterprise: The Work of National
Evangelical Societies in the Antebellum South. Westport, Conn.:
Greenwood Press, 1982. 188 pp.
Kuykendall examines the campaigns of five major voluntary societies to
establish missions in the Old South, where denominational loyalties were
strong and suspicion of Northerners growing. These interdenominational
societies formed the large part of a "benevolent empire" that flourished
in the first third of the 19th century and sought to evangelize the entire
nation. The ultimate failure of its millennialist enterprise reveals
how the philosophy of voluntary societies came into conflict with an emerging Southern religiosity.

R 86. LOVELAND, ANNE C. Southern Evangelicals and the Social Order 1800-
1860. Baton Rouge: Louisiana State University Press, 1980.
293 pp.
"Southern evangelicals saw themselves as guardians of the religious and
moral purity of the southern people and felt that it was their duty to
concern themselves . . . with issues and problems relating to the social
order." Loveland draws out the ideological basis of this self-perception
by detailing the common world-view of Baptist, Methodist, and Presbyterian
clergymen in the Old South. Through a close consideration of major controversies, such as temperance, slavery, and religious education of blacks,
she illustrates how Southern evangelicals maintained some measure of autonomy from the dominant ideology of the Old South.

R 87. LYNN, ROBERT W. and ELLIOT WRIGHT. The Big Little School: Two
Hundred Years of the Sunday School. 1971; Rev. ed. Birmingham,
Ala.: Religious Education Press, 1980. 178 pp.
"The Sunday School at its height was the symbol of the most enduring religious movement in American history." In their chronicle of this movement,
Lynn and Wright cover the period from the late 18th century up to the
1970s. Emphasis is on the heyday of the Sunday School—the antebellum
period—when it was linked strongly to revivalism and served as an integral
part of evangelical education. In their concluding chapter, the authors
suggest reasons for the durability of the Sunday School movement and assess
both its strengths and weaknesses.

R 88. MATHEWS, DONALD G. Religion in the Old South. Chicago: University
of Chicago Press, 1977. 274 pp.
"This essay," writes Mathews, "suggests in broad outline how and why Evangelical Protestantism became the predominant religious mood of the South."
It is important to note the word "mood" here, as Mathews is concerned
neither with doctrine, theology, nor denominational history but rather
with the subtle fusing of religious and societal allegiances in a distinctly Southern ethos. His argument runs along two related directions:
one concerns how Evangelical Protestantism in the Old South shaped the
identity of a rising middle class, while the other explores how the inclusion of blacks in this process can serve as the measure by which Southern
Evangelicalism can be judged.

1517

R 89.   MILLER, RANDALL M. and JON L. WAKELYN, eds.   Catholics in the Old
        South: Essays on Church and Culture. Macon, Ga.: Mercer Univer-
        sity Press, 1983.   260 pp.
This collection of essays on Catholicism fills an important lacuna in
the expanding literature on religion in the Old South. A wide variety
of approaches and angles have been brought to bear on the evolution of
the Church in the Old South and the shaping of a minority culture in the
midst of the Protestant majority. Conflict between religious and regional
identities is a recurring theme.

R 90.   ROSENBERG, CARROLL SMITH.   Religion and the Rise of the American
        City: The New York City Mission Movement, 1812-1870.   Ithaca,
        N.Y.: Cornell University Press, 1971.   300 pp.
Following a description of the city and its social needs in early 19th-
century America, Rosenberg assesses the impact of the Second Great Awaken-
ing on urban reform and mission activities, such as those of the Female
Moral Reform Society and the Protestant Episcopal City Mission Society.
She argues that these activities were "the product of an optimistic, truly
'Jacksonian' belief in the perfectibility of man." The second half of
her book takes on the variety of missions operating in post Panic-of-1837
New York.

HISTORICAL BREAKDOWN: SLAVERY, CIV-
IL WAR, AND RECONSTRUCTION

R 91.   BARNES, GILBERT HOBBS.   The Antislavery Impulse, 1830-1844.   New
        York: Appleton-Century, 1933.   298 pp.
Beginning with the Great Revival of 1830 and ending with the moment when
slavery was openly and successfully denounced in the House, Barnes narrates
the ever-broadening power of the antislavery movement. He argues against
traditional economic and social interpretations of opposition to slavery
and proposes instead "a more significant tale of a religious impulse which
began in the West of 1830, was translated for a time into an antislavery
organization, and then broadened into a sectional crusade against the
South." In his reading, the movement of the 1830s figures heavily in
leading the nation to civil war.

R 92.   DRAKE, THOMAS E.   Quakers and Slavery in America.   New Haven, Conn.:
        Yale University Press, 1950.   245 pp.
Drake's narrative begins with George Fox's visit to Barbados in 1671 and
ends with Lee's surrender in 1865. Using extensive manuscript records,
he examines the religious motivations that led Quakers to progressively
increase their role in opposing slavery in the North, the South, and the
West Indies. Special attention is given to the uneasy ideological relationship between Quakers, the Anti-Slavery Society, and other radical aboli-
tionists.

R 93.   ESSIG, JAMES D.   The Bonds of Wickedness: American Evangelicals
        Against Slavery, 1770-1808.   Philadelphia: Temple University Press,
        1982.   208 pp.
Rather than consider evangelical attacks on slavery either as dependent
on natural rights theory or as isolated denominational movements, Essig
attempts to show how the same religious impulse motivated Baptist, Methodist, Presbyterian, and Congregationalist thinkers to become antislavery
crusaders. He seeks "to relate the genesis of evangelical antislavery
commitment to attitudes, values, and tensions within evangelicalism itself,
while taking developments within denominations into account when they
appeared relevant." David Barrow, Samuel Hopkins, Francis Asbury, David

Rice, William McKendree, and James O'Kelly figure prominently in this study.

R 94. FARISH, HUNTER DICKINSON. The Circuit Rider Dismounts: A Social
History of Southern Methodism, 1865-1900. Richmond, Va.: Dietz
Press, 1938. 400 pp.
Farish's account of the Methodist Episcopal Church in the aftermath of
the Civil War follows the evolution of the Church's social consciousness.
He describes how, in the decade immediately following the war, Southern
Methodism maintained its traditional aversion to political involvement
and concentrated its energies on fending off absorption into her northern
sister Church. Hence its impact on social relations during Reconstruction
remained at the level of personal morality. Farish goes on to discuss
the broadening of the Church's social concerns after about 1876 into humanitarian reforms. Still, he concludes, southern Methodism never developed
a social critique that aimed at "institutional" change.

R 95. FRIEDMAN, LAWRENCE J. Gregarious Saints: Self and Community in
American Abolitionism, 1830-1870. New York: Cambridge University
Press, 1982. 344 pp.
The abolitionism that receives Friedman's attention is that first-
generation immediatist variety practiced by Northern whites. In an engag-
ing investigation of the social psychology of these "gregarious saints,"
Friedman analyzes the combination of convivial sociality and Wesleyan
personal piety at work in the abolitionist psyche. He reads the movement
as part of a general American missionary crusade and as reflective of
Northern middle-class values.

R 96. JONES, DONALD G. The Sectional Crisis and Northern Methodism:
A Study in Piety, Political Ethics, and Civil Religion. Metuchen,
N.J.: Scarecrow Press, 1979. 341 pp.
Jones calls into question the standard historiography that equates Northern
Methodist ethics with personal piety and accuses Protestantism in general
of political and social quietism in the aftermath of Civil War. Instead
he portrays a socially vital Methodism which during the third quarter
of the 19th century assumed a prophetic and social role that went far
beyond the usual renditions of "frontier religion," "pietistic individualism," and "evangelical moralism." Underlying his account is the suggestion that the tragedy of the War and the challenge of reconstruction
compelled churchmen to broaden their notions of moral good and evil to
include social and political expressions.

R 97. MATHEWS, DONALD G. Slavery and Methodism: A Chapter in American
Morality, 1780-1845. Princeton, N.J.: Princeton University Press,
1965. 329 pp.
Mathews uses the Methodist Episcopal Church as an illustration of American
attitudes toward slavery and abolition in the period from 1780 to 1845.
Methodism is a good choice, he notes, owing to its large size, geographical
distribution, ability to reflect the opinions of its lay members, and
active role in antislavery and colonization movements and in mission to
the slaves. Overall Mathews intends his study of Methodism to shed light
on the fate of antislavery thought in the South, the relationship between
early and later antislavery movements, and the character of the abolitionist crusade.

R 98. WILSON, CHARLES REAGAN. Baptized in Blood: The Religion of the
Lost Cause, 1865-1920. Athens: University of Georgia Press, 1980.
256 pp.
With the fall of the Confederacy in 1865 went the dream of Southern politi-
cal autonomy, but the dream of a separate cultural identity lived on.
Wilson's investigation of the religion of the Lost Cause describes the

blending of history and religion in a post-Civil War Southern civil religion. Originating in antebellum times and baptized in the blood of war, Southern religion stressed chivalric and agrarian values and the enduring importance of Southern culture.

HISTORICAL BREAKDOWN: THE GILDED AGE AND THE PROGRESSIVE ERA

R 99. ABELL, AARON I. The Urban Impact on American Protestantism, 1865-1900. Cambridge, Mass.: Harvard University Press, 1943. 275 pp.
By the turn of the century, Protestants, pressured by an increasing urban labor force, "had measurably Christianized their social and economic attitudes, formulated and developed a far-flung system of social service, and sacrificed sectarian concerns to basic religious needs." Abell explores the multitude of Protestant social programs operating during the Gilded Age, including the American Christian Commission, the Salvation Army, and the W.C.T.U. He also examines the contribution of such influential reformers as Washington Gladden, Richard Ely, and William J. Tucker.

R 100. CARTER, PAUL A. The Spiritual Crisis of the Gilded Age. DeKalb: Northern Illinois University Press, 1971. 295 pp.
In an attempt to define the crisis of belief and doubt during the period from 1865 to 1895, Carter argues that even though no single trend of growth or decline in faith can be traced, there were "recurrent rhythms" of response to the central pressures of the time: Darwinianism, industrialization, and mass education. Some of the topics he addresses include changing concepts of sin and freedom, the career of Henry Ward Beecher, and the theology of Social Christianity.

R 101. FURNISS, NORMAN F. The Fundamentalist Controversy, 1918-1931. New Haven, Conn.: Yale University Press, 1954. 199 pp.
Furniss presents a "factual account of men and events" during a period when "the Fundamentalist . . . found his basic beliefs challenged and rose to their defense." He defines the controversy as simply that twofold threat to fundamentalism of higher Biblical criticism and theories of evolution. The Scopes Trial is highlighted.

R 102. GATEWOOD, WILLARD B., Jr., ed. Controversy in the Twenties: Fundamentalism, Modernism, and Evolution. Nashville, Tenn.: Vanderbilt University Press, 1969. 459 pp.
The conflict between fundamentalists and modernists over evolution was but one, albeit central, element in the crusade against "the new infidelity." This collection of documents and commentaries lays out the nature and consequences of the famous clash within American Christianity and relates the debate to the cultural and psychological milieu of the 1920s. Classic statements of fundamentalist and modernist thought are followed by literary, political, and educational statements attesting to the wide-ranging impact of the controversy.

R 103. HOPKINS, CHARLES HOWARD. The Rise of the Social Gospel in American Protestantism. New Haven, Conn.: Yale University Press, 1940. 352 pp.
In the first major history of the social gospel in American Protestantism, Hopkins sets out the movement's origin and development during the gilded age. His study devotes separate attention to each of the movement's major phases: "1865-1880, The Birth of Social Christianity"; "1880-1890, A Youthful Movement"; "1890-1900, The Social Gospel Comes of Age"; and, finally, "1900-1915, Maturity and Recognition." Overall he reads the social

gospel as American Protestantism's response to the challenge of modern industrial society and highlights its critique of capitalism and laissez-faire economics.

R 104. HUTCHISON, WILLIAM R. The Modernist Impulse in American Protestantism. Cambridge, Mass.: Harvard University Press, 1976. 347 pp.
Hutchison's intellectual history of the emergence of Protestant liberalism in America takes the reader from Unitarianism after the heyday of Transcendentalism to liberalism's encounter with neo-orthodoxy in the first quarter of the 20th century. Key liberal theological motifs are explored in the face of fundamentalist and humanist critiques and scientific and hermeneutical advances of the time. Central to Hutchison's account is the concept of "modernism," a theological construct he holds to be at the heart of liberalism's progressivist ideology.

R 105. JORDAN, PHILIP D. The Evangelical Alliance for the United States of America, 1847-1900: Ecumenism, Identity, and the Religion of the Republic. New York: Edwin Mellon Press, 1982. 277 pp.
Jordan depicts the Evangelical Alliance's Eriksonian search for identity and their advancement of a conservative but basically democratic social program. He also analyzes the ecumenical movement as a whole, tracing its theology and political ideology from the Great Awakening to the social gospel. His central thesis is that "Alliance activities throughout the nineteenth century laid the basis for the twentieth century Federal Council, subsequent National Council of the Churches of Christ in America, and even the National Association of Evangelicals, while simultaneously attempting to foster a national evangelical and democratic faith."

R 106. MacKENZIE, KENNETH M. The Robe and the Sword: The Methodist Church and the Rise of American Imperialism. Washington, D.C.: Public Affairs Press, 1961. 128 pp.
MacKenzie begins by asserting that Methodism, because it provided order when the government could not, became the most powerful Protestant denomination on the frontier. To support this observation, he examines Methodist influence on public policy during the extra-territorial expansion of 1865-1900. MacKenzie seeks to prove "that while the Methodist Church did not in itself instigate American imperialism, either consciously or unconsciously, it did help to develop a rationale which would make this type of venture more palatable to individuals who might ordinarily have been exceedingly critical."

R 107. MAGNUSON, NORRIS. Salvation in the Slums: Evangelical Social Work, 1865-1920. Metuchen, N.J.: Scarecrow Press, 1977. 299 pp.
Magnuson, in an attempt to rectify the mistaken association of revivalism with reactionary conservatism, portrays "the sizeable body of Christians whose extensive welfare activities and concern sprang from their passion for evangelism and personal holiness." Making use of previously unexamined magazines such as the Christian Herald, he discusses the origins, methods, and contributions of the Salvation Army, the Volunteers of America, the urban rescue missions, the rescue mission homes for women, and the Christian and Missionary Alliance.

R 108. MAY, HENRY F. Protestant Churches and Industrial America. New York: Harper, 1949. 297 pp.
With an eye toward the "articulate, urban middle-class section of American Protestantism," May charts the response of the church to the forces of industrialization at work in 19th-century America. Since his focus is on the impact of Christian social thought upon the American mainstream—particularly its critique of social determinism and advancement of pro-

gressivism under the banner of the Social Gospel--he downplays theology
in favor of social thought. In the introduction to the second edition,
May assesses the limitations and strengths of his perspective and responds
to some of his critics.

R 109. McLOUGHLIN, WILLIAM G., Jr. Billy Sunday Was His Real Name.
        Chicago: University of Chicago Press, 1955. 324 pp.
Billy Sunday, the famous baseball player turned evangelist, combined fundamentalist theology and ardent Americanism to produce a revival of startling
proportions. McLoughlin offers his biography of Sunday as a study both
of Sunday's career and the revivalism of his era. Specifically, McLouglin
tries to account for the historical circumstances that made the American
public particularly receptive to Sunday's message in the years from 1908
to 1918.

R 110. MOORE, JAMES R. The Post-Darwinian Controversies: A Study of
        the Protestant Struggle to Come to Terms with Darwin in Great
        Britain and America, 1870-1900. New York: Cambridge University
        Press, 1979. 502 pp.
Moore seeks to revise the prevailing historiography on the post-Darwinian
controversies "by describing its polemical origins and baneful effects
and by offering an interpretation of Protestant responses to Darwin that
shows their affinities with the metaphysical and theological traditions
from which Darwinism and post-Darwinian evolutionary thought derives."
In short, Moore rejects the common tendency to couch Protestant reaction
in warfare metaphors and expounds the thesis that Christian theology was
not antithetical to evolutionary theory.

R 111. SPAIN, RUFUS B. At Ease in Zion: Social History of Southern Bap-
        tists, 1865-1900. Nashville, Tenn.: Vanderbilt University Press,
        1967. 247 pp.
Using the reports of the Southern Baptist Convention, state conventions,
and the weekly denominational papers, Spain argues that although Southern
Baptists openly defended the status quo, they "nonetheless modified their
denominational program to accommodate in many practical ways the new emphasis on socialized religion." Contrasted with the pervasive activity of
the Northern Social Gospel movement, the Southern Baptists must appear
reactionary. But Spain insists that the largest Southern Protestant denomination accommodated to a changing society while still trying to administer
to the spiritual needs of the individual.

R 112. SZASZ, FERENC MORTON. The Divided Mind of Protestant America,
        1880-1930. University: University of Alabama Press, 1982.
        196 pp.
Szasz reads the fifty-year period between 1880 and 1930 as a watershed
in main-line Protestant church history. A fundamental realignment along
liberal and conservative lines, cutting across denominations and forged
in the raging controversies over evolution and higher criticism, heralded
a new religious pluralism for the nation. This era marked the end of
Protestant domination of American life.

R 113. THOMPSON, JAMES J. Tried As By Fire: Southern Baptists and the
        Religious Controversies of the 1920s. Macon, Ga.: Mercer Uni-
        versity Press, 1982. 224 pp.
In 1919 Southern Baptist leadership perceived a world on the verge of
major transformation, where religion would be "tried as by fire." Thompson
explores these postwar religious attitudes and focuses especially on the
disputes among Baptists over interdenominational cooperation and the church-
union issue. He depicts the 1920s as a time ripe for a complex, sometimes bitter debate concerning how the church should respond to the surrounding society. Issues receiving detailed treatment include evolution,

biblical criticism, social action, Roman Catholicism, and the decline
of rural America.

R 114. WHITE, RONALD C. and C. HOWARD HOPKINS. The Social Gospel and
Reform in Changing America. Philadelphia: Temple University
Press, 1976. 306 pp.
White and Hopkins seek to enlarge--biographically, topically, and
geographically--the traditionally defined dimensions of the social gospel.
The authors argue that the social gospel never solidified into a single
movement: "Rather it was a network of movements operating in different
contexts." They present primary sources (writings by Rauschenbusch figure
prominently) linked by critical explication and historical narrative to
illustrate the complexity and diversity of the social gospel.

HISTORICAL BREAKDOWN: DEVELOP-
MENTS SINCE WORLD WAR I

R 115. BAILEY, KENNETH K. Southern White Protestantism in the Twentieth
Century. New York: Harper & Row, 1964. 180 pp.
The legacy of slavery, Civil War, and Reconstruction has been felt in
virtually every southern institution, including religion. Bailey seeks
to delineate Southern identity, specifically from the point of view of
its Protestantism, which he considers unique "for its piety and for its
commitment to old-fashioned Scriptural literalism." He examines the
South's three major denominations--Baptists, Methodists, and Presbyterians--
at the end of the century and up through the early 1960s.

R 116. CARTER, PAUL A. The Decline and Revival of the Social Gospel:
Social and Political Liberalism in American Protestant Churches,
1920-1940. Ithaca, N.Y.: Cornell University Press, 1956.
265 pp.
The guiding question of Carter's study is whether the social gospel continued to make an impact on American Protestantism following the Progressive era. What he observes is a series of remarkable transformations:
"the relativizing of the social gospel's ethic through the experiences
of Prohibition and pacifism, the supernaturalizing of its religious sanction through the experience of the European theological critique, the
broadening of its social horizon through the experience of the ecumenical
movement." He concludes that these changes came as an evolution rather
than an abdication of the original social gospel.

R 117. DOUGLAS, MARY and STEVEN M. TIPTON, eds. Religion and America:
Spirituality in a Secular Age. Boston: Beacon Press, 1983.
290 pp.
Modern American religion undergoes critical assessment at the hands of
a diverse group of specialists--anthropologists, historians, theologians,
sociologists, and philosophers. Some important themes of this essay collection include the place or lack of a place for religion in a secular
culture, problems with the paradigm of secularity, the conversations
between theology and tradition and theology and science, and the dynamics
of the contemporary religious scene.

R 118. HERBERG, WILL. Protestant, Catholic, Jew: An Essay in American
Religious Sociology. 1955; Rev. ed. New York: Anchor Books,
1960. 309 pp.
Herberg's study focuses on the religious scene in mid-20th-century America,
perceived by many to be a time of paradox, when in the midst of growing
secularism Americans still insisted on describing themselves in religious

terms. The answer Herberg proposes to the paradox is that Judaism, Catholicism, and Protestantism have become alternative validations of the American way of life.

R 119. HILL, SAMUEL S., Jr. Southern Churches in Crisis. New York: Holt, Rinehart & Winston, 1967. 234 pp.
Smith describes what he perceives to be a crisis in Southern Christianity, where traditional values have come into conflict with the region's new social and cultural ethos. He addresses this crisis in an examination of "popular southern religion"--the South's peculiar brand of Protestant evangelicalism. As part of his analysis, he gives an overview of Southern religious history and the current social revolution, delineates distinctive Southern religious patterns, and classifies their popular expression using a church-sect typology.

R 120. HILL, SAMUEL S., Jr. and DENNIS E. OWEN. The New Religious/ Political Right in America. Nashville, Tenn.: Abingdon, 1982. 160 pp.
A new religious/political conservative cause and crusade entered visibly into the American scene in the campaigns leading up to the fall election of 1980, when the Moral Majority gained increasing notoriety. Hill and Owen seek to delineate and understand the New Religious/Political Right (NRPR) on its own terms. Though the authors wish to be as fair as possible to their subject, they do not refrain from making evaluative judgments: "The NRPR is neither biblical nor Constitutional enough to recommend itself as a constructive element. Rather than calling us to a putative heritage and destiny, it threatens to divert us by creating a new one, one that does not do profound justice to our religion or to our politics, and in any event,is not edifying."

R 121. JORSTAD, ERLING. Evangelicals in the White House: The Cultural Maturation of Born Again Christianity, 1960-1981. New York: Edwin Mellen Press, 1981. 171 pp.
Jorstad takes a close look at the evangelical revival of the 1970s in light of its immediate historical background and its cultural maturation in the national political campaign of 1980. His main interest concerns the impasse created within evangelical ranks by the revival. Two opposing camps have emerged--one holding to a conservative position, where Christian truths are maintained as immutable and sufficiently self-interpreting to serve each generation, the other holding to a forward-looking position, where doctrines are revised to meet the exigencies of the contemporary world. That this division has precipitated down to the popular level, Jorstad argues, indicates that American evangelicalism will no longer play its traditional role of a nonpolitical yet doctrinally unified spiritual force in American culture.

R 122. JORSTAD, ERLING. The Politics of Moralism: The New Christian Right in American Life. Minneapolis, Minn.: Augsburg, 1981. 128 pp.
The outspokenness of the New Christian Right came to the fore in the national election of 1980, when evangelicals used political influence to promote a moral vision. Coming on the heels of that election, Jorstad's book offers a fresh impression of their "politics of moralism," by which he means the tendency of conservative evangelicals to advance their political and moral opinions as unarguable commands of God. He assesses the impact of moralism on the American religious scene in light of the Right's skillful use of advanced communications technology.

R 123. KATER, JOHN L., Jr. Christians on the Right: The Moral Majority in Perspective. New York: Seabury Press, 1982. 157 pp.
Kater offers a twofold perspective on the Christian Right. Historically, he links the movement with populist and millennialist impulses that have been evident throughout American religious history. Theologically, he examines critically whether the claims of the New Right are consistent with the affirmations of traditional Christian belief. Here he contends that their theology is more an ideological justification of a political vision of America than a genuine outgrowth of the Christian faith. Despite his criticisms of the movement, Kater maintains a balanced approach to the Christian Right and its import for American culture.

R 124. MARTY, MARTIN E. A Nation of Behavers. Chicago: University of Chicago Press, 1976. 239 pp.
Marty takes on the delicate task of recounting the contemporary history of American religion, using an approach which he describes as "mapping group identity and social location." The religious geography of mid-20th-century America divides into six zones--Mainline Religion, Evangelicalism and Fundamentalism, Pentecostal-Charismatic Religion, the New Religions, Ethnic Religion, and Civil Religion. This organization is based on the visible loyalties of religious groups, as reflected in their beliefs, behavior, and self-understanding.

R 125. MARTY, MARTIN E. The New Shape of American Religion. New York: Harper, 1959. 180 pp.
"The new shape of American religion is the result of the erosion and corrosion worked in by the American environment on the religions which have thrived in it." Marty looks at American Protestantism at mid-century and concludes that its accommodation to a pluralistic and open society has exacted a heavy price--the loss of religious content. After analyzing how this has come to pass, he advances an alternative to the further leveling of religious distinctiveness. Protestants, he urges, ought to adopt a "cultural ethic," where renewed forms of Christian communal existence center on the parish.

R 126. MEYER, DONALD B. The Protestant Search for Political Realism, 1919-1941. Berkeley: University of California Press, 1960. 482 pp.
Meyer focuses on the minority of Protestant ministers who between the two World Wars sought to revive the social gospel by linking political and social activism with religious commitment. This fusing of religion and social concern, he contends, ultimately precipitated a crisis within American Protestantism, since what began as a social critique soon ended up as a critique of religion itself. Special attention is accorded to the thought and politics of Reinhold Niebuhr.

R 127. MILLER, ROBERT MOATS. American Protestantism and Social Issues, 1919-1939. Chapel Hill: University of North Carolina Press, 1958. 385 pp.
Miller examines the social attitudes of major Protestant churches in the decades of prosperity and then depression between World Wars. Under "social" he includes fundamental issues of civil liberties, labor, race relations, war, and the relative merits of capitalism, socialism, and communism. His study rests upon the assumption that the social stances taken by the Protestant churches at this time played a formative role in modern American history.

R 128. QUEBEDEAUX, RICHARD. By What Authority: The Rise of Personality Cults in American Christianity. San Francisco: Harper & Row, 1982. 204 pp.

Quebedeaux investigates a recent development in the religion of popular culture: the rise to celebrity status of religious leaders through skillful use of the mass media. Specifically, his main concern is with "the social impact of the mass media and technological advance on modern American religion—from Falwell's Moral Majority . . . to Schuller's technology of salvation." In addressing this issue, Quebedeaux is able to suggest the broad contours of popular religion in America, including both its nature and sources of authority.

R 129. SCHNEIDER, HERBERT WALLACE. Religion in 20th Century America. Cambridge, Mass.: Harvard University Press, 1952. 244 pp.

Schneider's survey is an assessment of American religion at mid-century in light of a half-century of religious revolution. His professed focus is "religious experience itself—not the American religious traditions, not the churches as social institution, not the currents of philosophical theology, but the religious life." The style he employs to render this life is unique, combining personal reminiscence with the standard disciplines of the social sciences, history, and philosophy.

III. TOPICAL BREAKDOWN OF AMERICAN RELIGIOUS HISTORY: AMERICAN RELIGIOUS THOUGHT AND THEOLOGICAL DEVELOPMENT

R 130. AHLSTROM, SYDNEY E., ed. Theology in America: The Major Protestant Voices from Puritanism to Neo-Orthodoxy. Indianapolis, Ind.: Bobbs-Merrill, 1967. 630 pp.

"It has been widely believed," notes Ahlstrom, "that a substantial American theological tradition simply does not exist." To challenge this perception, he has assembled an anthology of American religious thinkers—including Puritans, Transcendentalists, Romantics, Pragmatists, Social Gospelers, and Neo-Orthodox theologians. Emphasis has been placed on periods rather than denominations, with the most attention given to theological activity stemming broadly from the Reformation experience in Great Britain. Each selection is prefaced by a brief introduction.

R 131. ALBANESE, CATHERINE L. Corresponding Motion: Transcendental Religion and the New America. Philadelphia: Temple University Press, 1977. 210 pp.

Albanese attempts to draw out the relatively unexplored religious dimension of the Transcendentalist movement. Specifically, she is concerned with how transcendentalism served as the vehicle for the unique expression of an American religion. As a way into its religiosity, she explores in depth the language common to the six charter members of the Transcendentalist Club, a group including Ralph Waldo Emerson and Bronson Alcott. Her approach here, as in her other major works, is that of history of religions.

R 132. BOWDEN, HENRY WARNER. Church History in the Age of Science: Historiographical Patterns in the United States, 1876-1918. Chapel Hill: University of North Carolina Press, 1971. 269 pp.

Bowden explores how American religious thinkers, such as Ephraim Emerton, Frank Hugh Foster, Arthur Cushman McGiffert, Walter Rauschenbusch, Philip Schaff, John Gilmary Shea, and Williston Walker conceived of and practiced historical writing. His discussion hangs together through his efforts to delineate major historiographical issues as they were debated in an intellectual climate suffused with the language of scientific empiricism.

R 133. BOZEMAN, THEODORE DWIGHT. Protestants in the Age of Science: The Baconian Ideal and Antebellum American Religious Thought. Chapel Hill: University of North Carolina Press, 1977. 243 pp.
Bozeman contends that science, and the Baconian ideal in particular, was a significant influence on American religious thinkers during the romantic period. After locating the Baconian ideal in the Scottish common-sense philosophy in vogue at the time, he uses Old School Presbyterianism as a case study in the prehistory of the conflict between Darwinism and religion. The yoking together of the Bible and Bacon in the minds of religious thinkers supports his larger thesis that "the nation's Protestant leadership tended to assimilate the gospel of Christianity to concepts of the nature of American civilization."

R 134. CHERRY, CONRAD. Nature and the Religious Imagination: From Edwards to Bushnell. Philadelphia: Fortress Press, 1980. 242 pp.
From the early 18th century until the middle of the 19th century, American theological thought displayed a fascination for natural imagery as symbolic of spiritual truths. Cherry charts the complex development of this theological vein in New England, a journey that takes the reader from Jonathan Edwards to Horace Bushnell. Characteristic of this line of thought is the tension between moralism and imaginative symbolism.

R 135. CLEBSCH, WILLIAM A. American Religious Thought: A History. Chicago: University of Chicago Press, 1973. 212 pp.
The history Clebsch offers of American religious thought consists of substantial essays on Jonathan Edwards, Ralph Waldo Emerson, and William James, connected by brief "interludes" that get the reader from one thinker to the next. Rather than chronicle a multitude of theological positions, Clebsch chooses to draw out the distinctly American element in the spirituality common to these three thinkers. In a phrase, that spirituality "is not to feel but to be, not comfortable but at home, not in one's particular world but in the universe."

R 136. EDWARDS, REM B. A Return to Moral and Religious Philosophy in Early America. Washington, D.C.: University Press of America, 1982. 275 pp.
Responding to what he feels is a neglect of the early period of American philosophical thought, Edwards focuses attention on our Puritan, Enlightenment, and Transcendentalist heritage. The account is purposefully selective, taking Jonathan Edwards, Thomas Jefferson, and Ralph Waldo Emerson as representative figures.

R 137. FERM, DEANE WILLIAM. Contemporary American Theologies: A Critical Survey. New York: Seabury Press, 1981. 182 pp.
Ferm summarizes the major trends in contemporary American Christian theology, points out representative literature, and suggests ways in which theology could best address the demands of the contemporary situation. After a brief summary of American Protestant theology from 1900 to 1960, he goes on to devote separate treatment to the secularism of the 1960s, black theology, South American liberation theology, feminist theology, evangelical theology, Roman Catholic theology, and the future of American theology.

R 138. FIERING, NORMAN. Jonathan Edwards's Moral Thought and Its British Context. Chapel Hill: University of North Carolina Press, 1981. 391 pp.
Fiering's analysis of Edwards's moral thought places Edwards in dialogue with the British moral sense theorists, Schaftsbury and Hutcheson. In general Fiering calls for a greater sensitivity to the pluralistic intellectual climate influencing Edwards and challenges, pace Perry Miller, strong Lockean readings of Edwards. The overall aim of the study is to

spell out Edwards's understanding of the contribution of religion and grace to moral conduct.

R 139. FIERING, NORMAN. Moral Philosophy at Seventeenth-Century Harvard: A Discipline in Transition. Chapel Hill: University of North Carolina Press, 1981. 323 pp.
Fiering uses Harvard as a pretext for investigating the evolution of moral philosophy in 17th-century New England. After a relatively brief account of the history of the subject as part of the university curriculum, he addresses two major themes: the rejection of Scholastic-Aristotelian ethics in the face of the Cartesian revolution, and the development of a new psychology of the passions as the necessary prelude for sentimentalist ethical theory.

R 140. FROTHINGHAM, OCTAVIUS BROOKS. Transcendentalism in New England: A History. New York: Putnam, 1876. 386 pp.
Frothingham takes a sympathetic look at the movement of which he was once a member. Published not long after the eclipse of Transcendentalism in America, his book sets Transcendentalist ideas in the history of ideas and examines the movement's central message, practical aims, and major leaders.

R 141. HANDY, ROBERT T., ed. The Social Gospel in America, 1870-1920: Gladden, Ely, Rauschenbusch. New York: Oxford University Press, 1966. 399 pp.
In his introduction to the writings of three major figures of the Social Gospel movement within liberal Protestantism, Handy argues that these men contributed to the culture's adjustment to urbanization using, as a basis, a Christocentric, historical, and synthetic theology. The movement both benefited from and stimulated middle-class idealism, as its political ideals fell between the extremes of Protestant orthodoxy and militant political socialism. "It should be added," says Handy, "that the whole liberal mood was strongly influenced by . . . romantic, monistic, idealism."

R 142. HARLAND, GORDON. The Thought of Reinhold Niebuhr. New York: Oxford University Press, 1960. 298 pp.
Harland locates Niebuhr's central theological concern in his attempt to "relate redemptively Christian faith and social responsibility, agape and the struggle for social justice." After expounding Niebuhr's mature theological ethic, Harland examines its concrete expression in Niebuhr's attitudes toward American foreign policy, democracy, communism, the atomic bomb, economic philosophy, and race.

R 143. HAROUTUNIAN, JOSEPH. Piety versus Moralism: The Passing of the New England Theology. New York: Holt, 1932. 329 pp.
The advent of capitalism, with its valorization of the self-sufficient, enterprising individual, mitigated the theocentric piety of Calvinism and threatened it with anachronism. Haroutunian's study of the decline of Calvinism in New England begins with the revival of its theology in the hands of Jonathan Edwards and then goes on to consider the fate of Calvinism with Edwards's less-gifted successors, who turned piety into moralism. Careful attention is given to the interplay between theology and social change.

R 144. HOLIFIELD, E. BROOKS. The Gentlemen Theologians: American Theology in Southern Culture, 1795-1860. Durham, N.C.: Duke University Press, 1978. 262 pp.
Taking Christian rationalism as the dominant mode of theological reflection in early 19th-century America, Holifield explores its manifestation in the Old South. By linking Southern orthodoxy with attempts to ground

the truths of revelation in human reason, he calls in question the one-sided image of Southern religion as "ubiquitous religious feeling and unremitting biblicism." An important focus of Holifield's investigation is on the relationship between theology and urbanity, particularly the efforts of prominent urban clergymen to demonstrate the reasonableness of the Christian faith to an educated and aspiring class of Southerners.

R 145. HOWE, DANIEL WALKER. The Unitarian Conscience: Harvard Moral
        Philosophy, 1805-1861. Cambridge, Mass.: Harvard University
        Press, 1970. 398 pp.
With their social consciousness founded upon their confidence in the moral goodness of human nature, Unitarian clergy were commonly known for their benign optimism. As a way into the mindset prevailing at antebellum Harvard, where most Unitarian ministers received their education, Howe examines the philosophy behind the Harvard moral consensus. While recognizing that moral philosophers in Cambridge, Massachusetts, were the spokesmen for a socially and culturally distinct class, centered on Boston, he contends that a study of their thought is of more than parochial interest: "A close examination of Unitarian moral philosophy sheds considerable light upon the general outlook of Western man as he adjusted his inherited Christian views to the modes of thought of the Enlightenment."

R 146. HUTCHISON, WILLIAM R., ed. American Protestant Thought: The
        Liberal Era. New York: Harper & Row, 1968. 243 pp.
Hutchison's selections cover a century of liberal Protestantism in America, with emphasis placed on the heyday of liberalism, roughly the period from the mid-1870s to the mid-1920s. In his introduction, Hutchison supplies a brief historical overview of the development of liberal Protestant thought in America.

R 147. IRISH, JERRY A. The Religious Thought of H. Richard Niebuhr.
        Atlanta, Ga.: John Knox Press, 1983. 121 pp.
Irish shapes his systematic presentation of Niebuhr's thought around three questions that were recurrent motifs in Niebuhr's own life and theology: "Who am I? What shall I do? How is faith in God possible?" These questions lead Irish to an analysis of Niebuhr's concept of selfhood, his account of God and Jesus Christ, and finally "what Niebuhr describes as a permanent revolution of mind and heart initiated and sustained by revelation."

R 148. KEGLEY, CHARLES W. and ROBERT W. BRETALL, eds. Reinhold Niebuhr:
        His Religious, Social, and Political Thought. New York: Macmillan,
        1956. 486 pp.
This volume is structured as a dialogue. It begins with an intellectual autobiography of Niebuhr, after which follow twenty critical essays by such figures as Emil Brunner, Paul Tillich, and Abraham Heschel. As a group, these essays explore Niebuhr's role as social critic and ethicist, his relationship as a liberal to the political world, and the nature of his Christian philosophy. Niebuhr concludes the volume with a detailed reply to his interpreters.

R 149. LEVINSON, HENRY SAMUEL. The Religious Investigations of William
        James. Chapel Hill: University of North Carolina Press, 1981.
        311 pp.
Levinson presents a comprehensive account of James's reflections on religion, which he sets in the context both of James's own religious milieu and of James's philosophical and psychological thought. A large portion of the book is devoted to an examination of James's Gifford Lectures, now known as The Varieties of Religious Experience.

R 150. MEAD, SIDNEY E. Nathaniel William Taylor, 1786-1858: A Connecticut
Liberal. Chicago: University of Chicago Press, 1942. 259 pp.
The working assumption behind Mead's biography of Nathaniel Taylor is
that theology develops out of the answers a theologian offers to questions
rooted in his or her own religious situation. Hence the life of Taylor
becomes an avenue for exploring Taylorism, that "offspring of the forced
marriage of New England Calvinism with revivalism" which paved the way
for progressive orthodoxy and liberalism. A revisionist aspect of Mead's
account is his association of Taylor with the pre-Revolutionary Old Cal-
vinists rather than with the Edwardians.

R 151. MILLER, PERRY. Jonathan Edwards. New York: Sloane, 1949. 348 pp.
The life that concerns Miller in the case of Jonathan Edwards is, as he
puts it, "the life of his mind." Whatever Miller chooses to include of
Edwards's career as a minister is therefore secondary to the engaging
story of Edwards's intellectual maturation. Most of the text describes
how Edwards secured himself a place as an original interpreter of the
American experience by virtue of his creative synthesis of Puritanism
with Locke's empiricism and Newton's science.

R 152. NICHOLS, JAMES HASTINGS. Romanticism in American Theology: Nevin
and Schaff at Mercersburg. Chicago: University of Chicago Press,
1961. 322 pp.
In mid-19th century America, the college and seminary of the German
Reformed Church at Mercersburg played an important dissenting role in reaction to mainline evangelical Protestantism. Mercersburg's greatest voices
were those of John Nevin, the theologian, and Philip Schaff, the historian.
Both men represented the concerns of the traditionalist, sacramental movement, which had captivated much of European Christendom. Nichols describes
their importance for introducing the American religious mind to the fecund-
ity of German idealism and the need for historical consciousness.

R 153. ROTH, JOHN K. and FREDERICK SONTAG. The American Religious Experience: The Roots, Trends, and Future of American Theology. New
York: Harper & Row, 1972. 401 pp.
The presentation Roth and Sontag offer of major currents in American
religious thought rests on two assumptions. One is that an American tradition of theological thinking exists, and the other is that this tradition
has something to do with what it means to be an American. The authors
depict a diverse group of thinkers, ranging from Puritans to death-of-
God and black liberation theologians, in an overall effort to define the
nature and direction of the modern American spiritual quest.

R 154. SMITH, JOHN E. The Spirit of American Philosophy. 1963; Rev.
ed. Albany: State University of New York Press, 1983. 253 pp.
The spirit of American philosophy is embodied by the group of thinkers
who brought us the "golden age" in American philosophy—Charles Peirce,
William James, Josiah Royce, John Dewey, and Alfred North Whitehead.
At the heart of this spirit is a conception of philosophy which keeps
it in touch with the important issues of metaphysics, ethics, and religion.
Smith portrays sensitively the religious dimension of each man's thought.

R 155. WHITE, MORTON. Science and Sentiment in America: Philosophical
Thought from Jonathan Edwards to John Dewey. New York: Oxford
University Press, 1972. 358 pp.
The unifying theme of White's analysis of the development of American
philosophy concerns how noted luminaries came to terms with science and
the scientific method. Each philosopher in question decides what applications and inherent limitations scientific method has with regard to
a wide variety of epistemological, metaphysical, aesthetic, and ethical
problems. All of the figures White chooses to examine have taken pains

to keep their technical conclusions in conversation with the main spiritual problems of their time. Students of religion should note especially the chapters on Jonathan Edwards, Ralph Waldo Emerson, William James, and Josiah Royce.

R 156. WILMORE, GAYRAUD S. and JAMES H. CONE, eds. Black Theology: A Documentary History, 1966-1979. Maryknoll, N.Y.: Orbis Books, 1979. 657 pp.
This collection of fifty-six essays and documents chronicles the origin, development, and program of black theology. Divided into six sections, each prefaced by an introduction by one of the editors, the anthology covers such topics as the transition from civil rights to black power, the critiques of white theology and the responses of white theologians, and the complex relationship of black theology with the black church, black women, and third world theologies. The volume includes an annotated bibliography.

R 157. WRIGHT, CONRAD. The Beginnings of Unitarianism in America. Boston: Starr King Press, 1955. 305 pp.
An important precursor to liberal Protestantism in America can be found in the 18th-century Arminian movement within New England congregationalism, which sought to supplant traditional Calvinistic patterns of thought. Wright follows this movement from the Great Awakening to the Unitarian controversy at the beginning of the 19th century. Arminianism, as opposed to Calvinism, held to the ability of human beings to play an active role in their redemption.

TOPICAL BREAKDOWN: AMERICA'S OTHER MAJOR FAITHS: JUDAISM AND CATHOLICISM

R 158. ABELL, AARON I., ed. American Catholic Thought on Social Questions. Indianapolis, Ind.: Bobbs-Merrill, 1968. 571 pp.
This sourcebook of thirty-nine essays written by Catholics between 1856 and 1963 illustrates responses to newly industrialized America and to conflicts within the Church. In his introduction Abell places the selections in historical context and highlights the salient issues involved with the growth of the Church, the increased concern about social issues, and the "new pluralism."

R 159. BLAU, JOSEPH L. Judaism in America: From Curiosity to Third Faith. Chicago: University of Chicago Press, 1976. 156 pp.
"The wandering Jew may be only a legend, but wandering Judaism is a fact." Such is Blau's colorful way of indicating a tradition that varies with each change of cultural scene. His attempt to characterize Judaism in the American scene relies on identifying motifs rather than fixed dogmas or sources of authority. These include "voluntarism," or the permissibility of more than one conclusion, "pluralism," or the view that all starting points are equally valid, and finally "moralism," or the tendency to emphasize the practical consequences of religious commitment.

R 160. CROSS, ROBERT D. The Emergence of Liberal Catholicism in America. Cambridge, Mass.: Harvard University Press, 1958. 328 pp.
The last decades of the 19th century found the American Catholic Church situated in a modern industrialized democracy committed to public education, the separation of church and state, and the advancement of secular knowledge. Seeing the modern scene as an opportunity rather than a threat, the Church's liberal leadership—John Ireland, John Keane, and James Gibbons especially—began a campaign to reconcile the Catholic tradition

with American-style democracy. Their efforts are what Cross describes
as the emergence of liberal Catholicism, "a major attempt to improve the
often unhappy relation between Catholics and American culture."

R 161. CURRAN, ROBERT EMMETT. Michael Augustine Corrigan and the Shaping
of Conservative Catholicism in America, 1878-1902. New York:
Arno Press, 1978. 547 pp.
Curran's warrant for this study is that "the conservative, authoritarian,
monolithic stance that Corrigan symbolized became the dominant one in
the American Church in the first half of the twentieth century." Combining
biography and traditional historical narrative, Curran explains the process
whereby Corrigan gathered and then abused power. He places this process
within the larger context of the Americanist issue and of the attempts
by Catholics to establish an acceptable relationship between church and
state.

R 162. DAWIDOWICZ, LUCY S. On Equal Terms: Jews in America, 1881-1981.
New York: Holt, Rinehart & Winston, 1982. 194 pp.
"Between 1881 and 1981," writes Dawidowicz, "the Jews underwent the greatest dispersion of their millennial history in a mass migration without
parallel in any people's history." Taking the migration of East European
Jewry as her starting point, Dawidowicz recounts a century of Jewish life
in America, highlighting the difficulties of adjustment, anti-Semitism,
war and holocaust, Zionism, Jewish political, educational and social activity, and religiosity. In her epilogue, she concludes that the period
has been one of overall prosperity and spiritual health for American Jews.

R 163. EISEN, ARNOLD M. The Chosen People in America: A Study in Jewish
Religious Ideology. Bloomington: Indiana University Press, 1983.
237 pp.
Opportunities for the large-scale assimilation of Jews into American society have raised the question of Jewish self-identity. Eisen's study follows two generations of theological and rabbinical reflections on the
concept of chosenness. Mutations of this concept indicate how American
Jews have faced the challenge of preserving a tradition while participating
in a non-Jewish society.

R 164. ELLIS, JOHN TRACY. American Catholicism. 1956; Rev. ed. Chicago:
University of Chicago Press, 1969. 322 pp.
Ellis's general survey of American Catholicism offers a concise chronological sketch of the Church's development from the days of colonial missions to recent times. The revised edition adds a chapter on the 1960s,
"the most eventful and tumultuous decade in the 20th-century history of
the Catholic Church."

R 165. FEINGOLD, HENRY L. A Midrash on American Jewish History. Albany:
State University of New York Press, 1982. 241 pp.
Feingold's wide-ranging essay on the Jewish experience in America is con-
cerned mainly with whether American Jewry can stave off dissolution into
the pluralistic solvent of secular American culture. Whether it can,
Feingold contends, hangs on its ability to identify itself with Klal
Yisrael (the universal community of Jewry) in the face of America's many
challenges to ethno-religious enterprises. Each chapter presents a dif-
ferent angle on Jewish survival by taking on a distinct historical episode.
Among those episodes covered are the colonial period, the Reformed movement,
Yiddish theatre, Zionism, Orthodox Judaism, anti-Semitism during the 1920s,
and the Holocaust.

R 166. FEINGOLD, HENRY L. Zion in America: The Jewish Experience from
        Colonial Times to the Present. 1974; Rev. ed. New York: Hippo-
        crene Books, 1981. 367 pp.
Feingold's synthesis of the Jewish experience in America rests on the
assumption that, despite certain similarities with other immigrant groups,
Jews constitute a unique case within the framework of American ethnic
history. This exceptionalism stems from Judaism's bonds to a distinctive
civilization that has resisted absorption into any host culture. What
Feingold finds in America, then, is the interaction of two separate historical traditions--one Jewish, the other American--each borrowing from
one another yet both retaining their independence.

R 167. GLAZER, NATHAN. American Judaism. 1957; Rev. ed. Chicago: Uni-
        versity of Chicago Press, 1972. 210 pp.
The updated version of Glazer's study of American Judaism describes within
the context of American religious history how Jews have acclimated themselves to an environment of manifest religious pluralism and underlying
spiritual homogeneity. Important in this regard is Judaism's character
as a "national" religion, whose organic links between ethnicity and religiosity have made assimilation into the American mainstream problematic.
An additional theme of Glazer's investigation is the confrontation of
Judaism with the modern challenges to faith that all religions encounter.

R 168. GLEASON, PHILIP. The Conservative Reformers: German-American
        Catholics and the Social Order. Notre Dame, Ind.: University
        of Notre Dame Press, 1968. 272 pp.
In his case study of German-American Catholic immigrants, Gleason seeks
"to show how the assimilation of the group was shaped by its distinctive
heritage and by various historical contingencies, and in particular to
show how the interest of the group in social reform was related to the
process of Americanization." He discusses these issues in depth for one
German society, the Central-Verein, as it came to face the challenges
of the American environment especially during the early part of the 20th
century.

R 169. HALPERN, BEN. The American Jew: A Zionist Analysis. 1956; Rev.
        ed. New York: Schocken Books, 1983. 196 pp.
Unlike more traditional Zionists, Halpern argues that the problems of
Diaspora Jewry are endemic to Jewish history and therefore survive even
the creation of a Jewish state. His penetrating examination of assimilation and anti-Semitism in the U.S. has in many ways set the agenda for
contemporary American Jewish intellectuals. The 1983 postscript of the
revised edition consists of Halpern's assessment of his own position more
than twenty-five years later.

R 170. HALSEY, WILLIAM M. The Survival of American Innocence: Catholicism
        in an Era of Disillusionment, 1920-1940. Notre Dame, Ind.: Uni-
        versity of Notre Dame Press, 1980. 230 pp.
Halsey discusses the efforts of Catholic intellectuals to defend a brand
of American idealism and innocence during a period of general disillusionment and cultural decline. Ingredients of this innocence, he notes, trace
back to a 19th-century faith in a rational universe, moral progress, and
a "genteel" culture. After describing the Catholic literary and philosophical expressions of this optimistic faith, Halsey concludes with
a brief history of its subsequent demise in the decades following
W.W. II.

R 171. HENNESEY, JAMES. American Catholics: A History of the Roman Catholic Community in the United States. New York: Oxford University Press, 1981. 397 pp.

This is a comprehensive account of the history of Catholicism in America, from its Colonial beginnings to the present time. As the title suggests, the emphasis is on the history of a people, though not to the exclusion of either institutional development or ecclesiastical leadership. Hennesey also gives attention to the secular context of the church's history, as well as to the complex relationship between the American church and the Vatican.

R 172. JICK, LEON A. The Americanization of the Synagogue, 1820-1870. Hanover, N.H.: University Press of New England, 1976. 247 pp.

The decade of the 1820s marked the beginning of a progressive increase in the number of immigrants to the U.S. Of the Jewish population arriving, a significant portion originated from the provinces that were later to become part of the German empire. Jick describes the rapid economic advance and acculturation of these German Jewish immigrants and offers a sociological analysis of their attempts to enter American society without sacrificing their Jewish identity. "Their experience," he writes, "constitutes a unique chapter in the annals of American-Jewish history and provides significant insights into the ongoing process of social adaptation."

R 173. LIEBMANN, CHARLES S. The Ambivalent American Jew: Politics, Religion, and Family in American Jewish Life. Philadelphia: Jewish Publication Society of America, 1973. 215 pp.

Liebmann believes that integration into American society and Jewish group survival are two incompatible values held by American Jews. This observation leads him to argue "that the behavior of the American Jew is best understood as his unconscious effort to restructure his environment and to reorient his own self-definition and perception of reality so as to reduce the tension between these values." In drawing out this thesis, Liebmann considers American Judaism's European roots, its subgroups, and its political liberalism. The concluding section offers speculations about the future of Judaism in America.

R 174. McAVOY, THOMAS T. The Great Crisis in American Catholic History, 1895-1900. Chicago: Regnery, 1957. 402 pp.

In the last decade of the 19th century, the Catholic Church in the U.S. found itself divided over whether Catholic practices should be adapted to the American milieu. Those favoring adaptation were the Americanists, and those opposing were conservatives, often of foreign birth. "The differences," writes McAvoy, "were basically between democracy and monarchism--between the Catholic leaders of the young pragmatic United States, which was dominantly Protestant, and the churchmen of the old Catholic countries of southern Europe, who regarded republican governments as opposed to religion." McAvoy tells the story of this conflict and explains how it was that something called "Americanism" could come under papal censure. The study was reprinted in 1963 under the title, The Americanist Heresy in Roman Catholicism (University of Notre Dame Press).

R 175. McAVOY, THOMAS T., ed. Roman Catholicism and the American Way of Life. Notre Dame, Ind.: University of Notre Dame Press, 1960. 248 pp.

Most of the essays in this collection come out of two Notre Dame symposia on the difficulties of adaptation and acculturation faced by the Catholic minority in the U.S. as it enters the second part of the 20th century. The first group of essays situates Roman Catholicism within the contemporary American religious scene and addresses some of its outstanding problems. The next group deals specifically with Catholic immigrants in an urban setting.

R 176. MOORE, DEBORAH DASH. At Home in America: Second Generation New
        York Jews. New York: Columbia University Press, 1981. 303 pp.
"As early as 1900," writes Moore, "Jewish observers characterized New
York City as the heart of American Jewry." As a step toward characterizing
the Jews inhabiting this city, Moore focuses on the second generation,
whose members have by and large successfully wedded Jewishness with a
New York urban culture. She explores along the way Jewish middle-class
ethnicity, neighborhoods, education, and liberalism.

R 177. NEUSNER, JACOB. American Judaism: Adventure in Modernity. Engle-
        wood Cliffs, N.J.: Prentice-Hall, 1972. 170 pp.
Neusner's basic question is the following: "What happens to archaic
religions in modern American civilization?" The answer he suggests depends
on his use of American Judaism as a case-study for the experience of modernity. His inquiry proceeds topically, giving attention to the modern renderings of five traits associated with archaic religions: holy way, holy
man, holy people, holy land, and holy faith.

R 178. NEUSNER, JACOB. Stranger at Home: "The Holocaust," Zionism, and
        American Judaism. Chicago: University of Chicago Press, 1981.
        213 pp.
The creation and maintenance of a Jewish state and the destruction of
the Jews in Europe during W.W. II are the key events in what Neusner calls
"the myth of Holocaust and redemption." His essays, fifteen in all,
explore this myth and address how it shapes the perception and experience
of American Jews. Taken together, they advance the thesis that the appropriation of this particular myth by American Jews has rendered American
Judaism "a system removed from participation in the world, a detached
and noncathectic way of living in the world."

R 179. O'BRIEN, DAVID J. American Catholics and Social Reform: The New
        Deal Years. New York: Oxford University Press, 1968. 287 pp.
Catholics attempting to face difficult social issues from a Catholic point
of view refer to papal encyclicals for guidance. O'Brien's study of American Catholicism during the New Deal years--a period witnessing the beginnings of Catholic activism--concerns "the manner in which American Catholics in the 1930's interpreted and applied the social teaching of the
Church to American problems." By detailing this "process of referral,"
O'Brien offers the reader a case study in the interaction of American
and Catholic tradition.

R 180. PIEHL, MEL. Breaking Bread: The Catholic Worker and the Origin
        of Catholic Radicalism in America. Philadelphia: Temple Univer-
        sity Press, 1982. 296 pp.
Piehl explores the beginnings of American Catholic radicalism in a nuanced
history of the Catholic Worker movement founded by Dorothy Day and Peter
Maurin during the early 1930s. An important issue for Piehl is the seeming
incongruity between traditional Catholic religiosity and a radical social
vision. Special attention is given to Dorothy Day, in so far as her life
captures the complexities of the movement she started.

R 181. PLESUR, MILTON. Jewish Life in Twentieth-Century America: Chal-
        lenge and Accommodation. Chicago: Nelson-Hall, 1982. 235 pp.
The prelude to 20th-century Jewish history, Plesur argues, is founded
in the 1890s--a watershed decade witnessing the large-scale immigration
of East European Jews and the shift in the American economy from an agricultural base to one of urban-centered industry. He goes on to describe
how Jews shaped and were shaped by urban America. Notable personalities
are also given their due.

R 182. **RISCHIN, MOSES.** The Promised City: New York's Jews, 1870-1914.
        Cambridge, Mass.: Harvard University Press, 1962. 342 pp.
Rischin narrates the transformation of the diverse multitude of East European Jews into urban Americans. Specifically he traces the physical,
economic, and spiritual effects city life exerted on small-town Jews who
were attempting to build a community within New York City. Special attention is devoted to the cooperation between the immigrant Jewish labor
force and social reformers, both of whom worked to rid the city of social
ills. While anti-Semitism was not a major presence during this time period,
Rischin claims that "the attitudes which conditioned the later anti-
Semitism already had taken place."

R 183. **SARNA, JONATHAN D.** Jacksonian Jew: The Two Worlds of Mordecai
        Noah. New York: Holmes & Meier, 1981. 233 pp.
"The Mordecai Noah of this book," writes Sarna, "is a highly significant
figure on the American scene, a leader of the American Jewish community,
and most important, the first man in history to confront and grapple boldly
with the tensions between these two distinct roles." Sarna presents his
account of Noah's career as an inroad into American Jewish experience
in general. He contends that Noah's unfulfilled quest for an adequate
synthesis of Jewishness and Americanness still calls for resolution thirteen decades after his death.

R 184. **SHANABRUCH, CHARLES.** Chicago's Catholic: The Evolution of an
        American Identity. Notre Dame, Ind.: University of Notre Dame
        Press, 1981. 296 pp.
Shanabruch's history of the response of the Archdiocese of Chicago to
the ethnic diversity of its members between 1833 and 1924 provides an
excellent case study of American Catholicism in an urban environment.
By focusing on Chicago, the most cosmopolitan and eventually the largest
see in the U.S., Shanabruch hopes to reveal some of the dynamics of religio-
ethnic influences on the development of American cities. Throughout the
investigation, he explores the response of the Church to the dual pressures
of immigrant nationalism and indigenous nativism.

R 185. **SKLARE, MARSHALL.** Conservative Judaism: An American Religious
        Movement. 1955; Rev. ed. New York: Schocken Books, 1972.
        330 pp.
Sklare's sociological analysis of Conservative Judaism frames the movement's internal development against the backdrop of Jewish interaction
with the broader American community. After a general discussion of the
changing needs and values of the American Jewish community, he proceeds
to address the strains with Orthodoxy, the development of the conservative
synagogue, the training and role of the conservative rabbi, the nature
of conservative ideology, and recent developments within the movement.
He argues that Conservatism's most outstanding contribution has been its
ability to offer for many East European Jews an acceptable means of acculturation, but he notes as well challenges posed to its authority by the
Orthodox resurgence and the alienation of young conservatives from American
culture.

TOPICAL BREAKDOWN: UNCONVENTIONAL SPIRITUALITY IN AMERICA

R 186. ADLER, MARGOT. <u>Drawing Down the Moon: Witches, Druids, Goddess-Worshippers, and Other Pagans in America Today</u>. Boston: Beacon Press, 1979. 455 pp.
"The modern Pagan resurgence includes the new feminist goddess-worshipping groups, certain new religions based on the visions of science-fiction writers, attempts to revive ancient European religions--Norse, Greek, Roman--and the surviving tribal religions." The theoretical scaffolding of this depiction of modern paganism is supplied in the first part of Adler's book, where she attempts to define "pagan" and "witch" and also to elucidate the pagan world-view. The sections that follow take on the witchcraft revival, other neo-pagan expressions, how members of pagan groups have been interpreted and misinterpreted in the scholarship, and finally how pagans orient themselves to the world at large.

R 187. ANDREWS, EDWARD DEMING. <u>The People Called Shakers: A Search for the Perfect Society</u>. New York: Oxford University Press, 1953. 309 pp.
Andrews's study is a rich account of the culture, evolution, and decline of the American Shaker community. Among the aspects of Shaker life he details are their economic practices, modes of worship, internal order, and relations with the world. Appendices include the millennial laws governing Shaker existence and a statistical breakdown of Shaker communities.

R 188. ARRINGTON, LEONARD J. and DAVIS BITTON. <u>The Mormon Experience: A History of the Latter-day Saints</u>. New York: Knopf, 1979. 404 pp.
Availing themselves of unrestricted access to Mormon archives, Arrington and Bitton have composed an "analytical, interpretative, topical history designed for a broad readership." This introduction to the Church of Jesus Christ of Latter-day Saints divides into three parts: The Early Church, The Kingdom in the West, and The Modern Church. A bibliographical essay is included.

R 189. BESTOR, ARTHUR EUGENE, Jr. <u>Backwoods Utopias: The Sectarian and Owenite Phases of Communitarian Socialism in America, 1663-1829</u>. Philadelphia: University of Pennsylvania Press, 1950. 288 pp.
Bestor's study focuses on the ideal of communitarian socialism or the belief that systematic social reform can be accomplished through the establishment of special communities. The communitarian ideal, Bestor argues, exerted its greatest appeal in the middle decades of the 19th century, when its message of social harmony and voluntary action "found ready echo in a nation of experimenters." He devotes special attention to the Owenite experiment at New Harmony.

R 190. BRADEN, CHARLES S. <u>Spirits in Rebellion: The Rise and Development of New Thought</u>. Dallas, Tex.: Southern Methodist University Press, 1963. 571 pp.
Around the middle of the 19th century, the Portland healer, P. P. Quimby, supplied the impetus for two strains of popular religious movements centered on the healing of disease. One developed under the leadership of Mary Baker Eddy and became Christian Science. The other, a much looser confederation of individuals and institutions, went under the name of New Thought. Braden's history of New Thought describes its nature and sources, groups in America, outreach programs, and following abroad.

R 191. BRADEN, CHARLES S. These Also Believe: A Study of Modern Cults and Minority Religious Movements. New York: Macmillan, 1949. 491 pp.
This study examines thirteen minority religions which originated or had their major development in America. Personal interviews with group leaders coupled with the group's published documents explore group background, tenets, hierarchy, practices, motivation and current concerns. The groups surveyed include Father Divine's Peace Movement, Psychiana, New Thought, the Unity School, Christian Science, Theosophy, the "I Ams," the Liberal Catholic Church, Spiritualism, Jehovah's Witnesses, Anglo-Israelis, the Oxford Group, and Mormonism.

R 192. BRIDGES, HAL. American Mysticism: From William James to Zen. New York: Harper & Row, 1970. 208 pp.
Bridges explores the history of American mysticism in the 19th century, holding that it "shows striking similarity to mystical patterns of experience and thought throughout the world's history." After setting out the primary intellectual influences on the American scene, he goes on to examine James's Varieties, the mysticism of the Quakers, the philosophy of Wallace Thurman, Abraham Heschel, and Thomas Merton, the impact of Vivekananda and Zen, and the LSD experiments of Timothy Leary.

R 193. BROMLEY, DAVID G. and ANSON D. SHUPE, Jr. "Moonies" in America: Cult, Church, and Crusade. Beverly Hills, Calif.: Sage, 1979. 269 pp.
Bromley and Shupe offer a sociological analysis of the origin, organization, and development of the Unificationist movement along with the fervent opposition it has engendered. They frame the Unification Church as an illustrative case of a world-transforming movement that "aims at total change of the social structure through employing persuasion as its primary strategy." In this way they attempt not only an explanation of the Moonie phenomenon but also the construction of a theoretical model capable of handling analogous movements.

R 194. BROMLEY, DAVID G. and ANSON D. SHUPE, Jr. Strange Gods: The Great American Cult Scare. Boston: Beacon Press, 1981. 249 pp.
Bromley and Shupe challenge the conventional wisdom that depicts American religious cults as mysterious, unprecedented, and growing by leaps and bounds. While the authors believe that a "cult hoax" has been fabricated by cultists and their opponents and perpetuated by the media, they nonetheless identify the very real sources of conflict evident in the emergence of cults. The nature of this conflict is explored with regard to historical context, cult organization, and the response to cult activity from the church, family, and government.

R 195. CAMPBELL, BRUCE F. Ancient Wisdom Revived: A History of the Theosophical Movement. Berkeley: University of California Press, 1980. 249 pp.
The early history of the Theosophical movement, founded in 1875, was marked by its antagonistic stance toward American culture, which proved unreceptive to Theosophy's championing of Oriental religious thought and its initial anti-Christian attitudes. With recent American interest in the East, however, Theosophy has gained new respectability. Campbell contends that the change in the movement's relation to the general culture has made the time ripe for an account of its development that avoids the usual poles of accusation and apologetics. His work purports to be an historically and sociologically informed analysis of Theosophy's problems, inner conflicts, and contributions to American society.

R 196. **CARDEN, MAREN LOCKWOOD.** Oneida: Utopian Community to Modern Corporation. Baltimore, Md.: Johns Hopkins University Press, 1969. 228 pp.

The Oneida community, founded by John Humphrey Noyes in 1848, was one of the most significant and long-lived utopian communities ever attempted in America. Carden's study follows Oneida's transformation from a perfectionist community dedicated to utopian ideals to an "ideological" community where cooperation became tied more to economic stability than to perfectionist hopes. The central question of the investigation concerns "how Oneida, and later ideological Oneida, managed to keep alive an unusual set of ideals, or values, among a small group of people over a long period of time."

R 197. **DESROCHE, HENRI.** The American Shakers: From Neo-Christianity to Presocialism. Translated by John K. Savacool. Amherst: University of Massachusetts Press, 1971. 357 pp.

"Shakerism has a double claim on our interest, for its story comes to us as one of the last chapters in the history of sectarian Christianity and as one of the first chapters in the prehistory of modern socialism." Such is the thesis of Desroche, whose study of Shakerism locates the movement's pulse in an intersection of millenarian motivations and social drives. Desroche explores historically and sociologically the Shaker decision to defect from the established church and an entire civilization.

R 198. **ELLWOOD, ROBERT S., Jr.** Alternative Altars: Unconventional Spirituality in America. Chicago: University of Chicago Press, 1979. 192 pp.

Ellwood's study of American religions outside the Judeo-Christian mainstream concentrates on methodology and foregoes the usual historical and sociological survey. In the first part of the book, "Perspectives," he lays out a theoretical model drawing from contemporary sociology, anthropology, and phenomenological psychology. Following this is a section entitled, "Histories," where the model is applied to three case examples—Spiritualism, Theosophy, and American Zen.

R 199. **ELLWOOD, ROBERT S., Jr.** Religious and Spiritual Groups in Modern America. Englewood Cliffs, N.J.: Prentice-Hall, 1973. 334 pp.

Borrowing a term from Max Weber, Ellwood characterizes a large American religious subculture as representing an "exemplary" religious style—a faith based on mystical or shamanistic experiences. Included under this rubric are Theosophy, UFO cults, Spiritualism, Eastern religious movements, neo-paganism, and "initiatory" groups. Ellwood's goal is one of empathetic understanding, where the reader gets some feel for what it would be like to belong to one of these groups. Selected primary source readings supplement the exposition.

R 200. **EVANS, CHRISTOPHER.** Cults of Unreason. New York: Delta Books, 1973. 247 pp.

This book by an experimental psychologist delves into the background, founders, and followers of contemporary atypical belief systems. Topics covered include Scientology and Dianetics, flying saucers, the Aetherians (who communicate with superior beings in outer space), the Atlanteans, biofeedback, Yoga, Eastern religions, and "black boxes." Evans contends that attraction to these unconventional cults lies in mankind's failure to find strength, comfort and a sense of community in traditional religion and the "cold" world of science. Such cults incorporate technological advances within a theological framework.

R 201. FOSTER, LAWRENCE. Religion and Sexuality: Three American Communal
        Experiments of the Nineteenth Century. New York: Oxford Univer-
        sity Press, 1981. 363 pp.
Foster looks at the radically new models of marriage and the nuclear family
advocated by three controversial religious groups during the turbulent
decades prior to the Civil War. The Shakers, the Oneida Perfectionists,
and the Mormons proposed communities founded on principles as diverse
as celibacy, group marriage, and polygamy. Rather than treat these communitarian movements as an "American sideshow," as has often been the
custom, Foster addresses the questions that call for a deeper understanding
of the relation between religion and sexuality: Why should thousands
of Americans have been so dissatisfied with conventional marriage and
sex-roles as to form separate communities; what did it mean in personal
terms to pursue alternative models; and finally, how did the new alternatives become institutionalized?

R 202. FULLER, ROBERT C. Mesmerism and the American Cure of Souls. Phila-
        delphia: University of Pennsylvania Press, 1982. 227 pp.
In the first complete history of 19th-century American Mesmerism, Fuller
argues that Mesmerism went beyond popular psychology to become a psychologized faith for many Americans. The main question the book takes on is
how Mesmerism achieved its large following. Using sociological analysis
indebted to Max Weber, Fuller links the rise of Mesmerism with the displacement of traditional religious authority.

R 203. GOTTSCHALK, STEPHEN. The Emergence of Christian Science in American
        Religious Life. Berkeley: University of California Press, 1973.
        305 pp.
Since its founding by Mary Baker Eddy in 1879, the Church of Christ (Scientist) has emerged as one of the two major indigenous religions in America--
the other being Mormonism. Gottschalk focuses on the movement's formative
years, roughly 1885 to 1910, in an attempt to portray its mature religious
expression. His account, proceeding broadly chronologically, addresses
five important aspects in Christian Science's development: its prophetic
self-understanding as addressing an age in spiritual crisis, its central
teachings as compared to other religious alternatives of the time, its
encounter with rival movements, the reaction of mainstream Protestantism,
and the impact of Christian Science on individual lives. A concluding
chapter explores the relation between Christian Science and the broader
patterns of American culture.

R 204. HANSEN, KLAUS J. Mormonism and the American Experience. Chicago:
        University of Chicago Press, 1981. 257 pp.
Hansen's history of Mormonism follows its progression from a profoundly
anti-American movement, whose founder sought to establish an independent
Mormon kingdom outside the influence of the U.S. government, to a highly
respectable middle class religion in the 20th century. Hansen brings
many disciplinary perspectives to bear in his attempt to explain this
seemingly miraculous transformation.

R 205. HOLLOWAY, MARK. Heavens on Earth: Utopian Communities in America,
        1680-1880. 1951; Rev. ed. New York: Dover, 1966. 246 pp.
The utopian impulse has had a long and varied history in the Western imagination. In America, particularly during the first half of the 19th century,
many blueprints for the perfect community were put to the test. Holloway's
survey of several dozen of the most important and typical American communities assesses their successes and failures and their contributions
to American life. Detailed treatment is accorded to Shakers, New Harmony,
Brook Farm, Fourieristic phalanxes, and Oneida.

R 206. JACKSON, CARL T. The Oriental Religions and American Thought: Nineteenth-Century Explorations. Westport, Conn.: Greenwood Press, 1981. 302 pp.

Jackson offers his study of 19th-century American interest in Oriental religions on the supposition that Eastern religious imports have been more than a passing fad in American culture. He concentrates most on Buddhism and Hinduism, religions that captured the attention of a diverse group of philosophers, scholars, missionaries, and popular religious leaders. Throughout his study he is attentive to "the strange transformations that Asian conceptions undergo when introduced into a new environment."

R 207. KASHIMA, TETSUDEN. Buddhism in America: The Social Organization of an Ethnic Religious Institution. Westport, Conn.: Greenwood Press, 1977. 272 pp.

Kashima's social history of the Japanese Buddhist Church in America spans from 1899 to the present. Watershed events in this narrative include the establishment of the first temple, the passing of the Oriental Exclusion Act, the internment of Japanese citizens during W.W. II, and the creation of the Institute for Buddhist Studies. In setting out this history, Kashima also examines the internal structure of the Buddhist Church as it has evolved and speculates about its future. Looking forward to the completion of the "Americanization" process, he envisions greater ethnic diversity within Buddhist ranks.

R 208. LAYMAN, EMMA McCLOY. Buddhism in America. Chicago: Nelson-Hall, 1976. 342 pp.

Layman's survey begins with an overview and definition of Buddhism and continues with a brief history and characterization of every major sect found in America. Topics she addresses include the contributions of Buddhism to psychology, its relation to Western religious traditions, and the distinctive life-styles and motivations of American Buddhists. In speculating about the potential Buddhist influence on the American religious scene, she notes the appeal meditation has for both psychologists and Christian churches: ". . . the influence of Buddhism in America has been and will continue to be greater than membership figures would lead us to expect."

R 209. LEVI, KEN, ed. Violence and Religious Commitment: Implications of Jim Jones's People's Temple Movement. University Park: Pennsylvania State University Press, 1982. 207 pp.

This collection of essays examines the People's Temple Movement as an example of modern cult violence and its various facets. Separate sections discuss the religious and historical context surrounding Jonestown, the appeal and methods of cult extremism during the 1970s, and the public, philosophical, and theological reaction to Jonestown. A final essay offers an insider's view of life in the violent cult.

R 210. MELTON, J. GORDON and ROBERT L. MOORE. The Cult Experience: Responding to the New Religious Pluralism. New York: Pilgrim Press, 1982. 180 pp.

Seeking to correct the myths propagated by anti-cult groups, Melton and Moore take a critical look at the rise of nontraditional religious alternatives, first noticed during the 1960s. They reject both a new religious model, which overlooks the historical roots of the new movements, as well as the cult model, which too simplistically reads the new movements as a threat to society. Instead the authors locate the newness of the nontraditional religions in the social situation that has given birth to a radical religious pluralism.

R 211. MEYER, DONALD. The Positive Thinkers: Religion as Pop Psychology from Mary Baker Eddy to Oral Roberts. 1965; Rev. ed. New York: Pantheon Books, 1980. 396 pp.

First issued in 1965, Meyer's book offers a comprehensive sweep of popular religious psychologies designed to secure health and peace of mind. Part one deals with the late 19th-century phenomenon of mind cure, and the remaining two sections give attention to psychologies after 1900 that display structures analogous to that of mind cure. Meyer links the rise of mind cure and related movements with a reaction against the Old Protestant establishment. In the postscript to the 1980 edition, he speculates about whether the current strength of evangelicalism marks a return to the "Old-time Positive Religion."

R 212. MEYERS, MARY ANN. A New World Jerusalem: The Swedenborgian Experience in Community Construction. Westport, Conn.: Greenwood Press, 1983. 217 pp.

Since the 1890s when the founders of the General Church of the New Jerusalem removed their congregation from Philadelphia to a rural setting, Swedenborgians in America have preserved their distinctive religious subculture outside the interference and influence of the American mainstream. The success this sect has demonstrated in justifying and preserving its eschatological outlook to its largely upper-middle class contingency is the subject of Meyers's study. Most of her conclusions are drawn from ethnographic research done in and around Bryn Athyn, the episcopal seat of the General Church.

R 213. MOORE, R. LAURENCE. In Search of White Crows: Spiritualism, Parapsychology, and American Culture. New York: Oxford University Press, 1977. 310 pp.

Belief in the possibility of communication with spirits through mediums (spiritualism) and in the existence of extraordinary mental powers (parapsychology) have enjoyed large audiences in 19th- and 20th-century America respectively. In his history of these phenomena, Moore notes especially the appeal of their practitioners to the tools and methods of scientific empiricism for legitimation. When trying to determine the place of spiritualism and parapsychology in American culture, he goes beyond the usual platitudes about popular yearnings for mystification to argue that each movement in its time offered a resolution to the conflict between religious and scientific interests.

R 214. NEEDLEMAN, JACOB. The New Religions. Garden City, N.Y.: Doubleday, 1970. 245 pp.

What Needleman designates as "new" concerns those forms of spirituality emerging from the movement away from Western traditions toward Eastern religions and mysticism first witnessed in California during the late 1960s. He explicates these new religious sensibilities--drawing from Zen, Meher Baba Subud, Transcendental Meditation, Krishnamurti, and Tibetan Buddhism--by examining their doctrines (or lack of doctrines) within the context of an American search for new sources of spiritual value. He concludes that the new religions will influence American society by "reviving the idea of the psycho-spiritual instrumentality of moral behavior."

R 215. NEEDLEMAN, JACOB and GEORGE BAKER, eds. Understanding the New Religions. New York: Seabury Press, 1978. 314 pp.

"What is the place and significance of new religions in the context of American history? . . . What is the religious significance of cultural change? . . . What is the outer and inner sociology of spiritual life?" Each of three sections, totaling twenty-four essays, addresses one of these three questions in an attempt to portray the dynamics and impact of the new religions.

R 216. O'DEA, THOMAS. The Mormons. Chicago: University of Chicago Press, 1957. 289 pp.
O'Dea's sociological analysis of Mormonism, the fruit of both library research and field work in a rural Mormon village, offers a sympathetic rendering of the Mormon world-view by a non-Mormon. Roughly the first third of the book is devoted to the historical background of the religious movement, while the remainder presents topical treatments of Mormon values and social institutions. Throughout the study, O'Dea pays careful attention to the social and political pressures that worked to shape Mormon practice and belief.

R 217. PAVLOS, ANDREW J. The Cult Experience. Westport, Conn.: Greenwood Press, 1982. 209 pp.
Pavlos examines the emergence of religious cults in recent times, considers their effect on society, and speculates on their future. Using a broadly psychological approach, he addresses a number of important questions-- how alienated youth become susceptible to conversion and commitment to a cult religion and ideology, what goes on in the extralegal work of deprogramming, and how readjustment proceeds for those who leave cults. A large spectrum of groups are discussed, ranging from well-known organizations such as the Unification Church and the Krishna Consciousness Society to smaller communities such as the Lake City organization and the Church of the True World.

R 218. PREBISH, CHARLES S. American Buddhism. North Scituate, Mass.: Duxbury Press, 1979. 220 pp.
Prebish's examination of American Buddhism divides into three sections, covering respectively the origins and acculturation of American sects, case illustrations, and what the future may hold for Buddhism's development in America. He contends that the Eastern import will fail to make a significant cultural impact until it becomes fully American and responsive to American religious needs, and that remains to be seen.

R 219. SESSIONS, GENE A. Mormon Thunder: A Documentary History of Jedediah Morgan Grant. Urbana: University of Illinois Press, 1982. 413 pp.
Sessions takes Grant (1816-1856), mayor of Salt Lake City and second counselor to Brigham Young, as a representative figure of early Mormonism. Grant's biography reveals a prophetic figure and powerful preacher, who combined personal piety with otherworldly radicalism. In his narrative account of Grant's life, Sessions makes generous use of sermons and letters.

R 220. TIPTON, STEVEN M. Getting Saved from the Sixties: Moral Meaning in Conversion and Cultural Change. Berkeley: University of California Press, 1982. 364 pp.
"Sixties youth have joined alternative religious movements basically," argues Tipton, "to make moral sense of their lives." He uses case studies drawn from Zen, millenarian Pentecostalism, and EST to explore how a new ethic emerges and is appropriated by youth who have experienced the moral vertigo of cultural dislocation. He concludes with a consideration of how generalizable these solutions may be given changes in the American religious scene since the 1970s. Overall Tipton offers his study as an elucidation of the social nature of moral ideas and how they change.

R 221. ZARETSKY, IRVING I. and MARK P. LEONE. Religious Movements in Contemporary America. Princeton, N.J.: Princeton University Press, 1974. 837 pp.
This volume of essays offers, from the perspective of the social and historical sciences, descriptive and methodological pieces on contemporary marginal religious movements in America. Eight sections take on the legal, ritualistic, social, psychological, and historical aspects of these move-

ments with particular attention given to how alternative religions interact
with the society at large. Speaking of these movements as a whole, the
editors note: "They can be looked at as an index of the personal and
communitarian needs of segments of the American population, the success
and failure of established institutions in meeting these needs, and the
sources, mechanism, and direction of social and religious evolution."

TOPICAL BREAKDOWN: THE AFRO-AMERI-
CAN RELIGIOUS EXPERIENCE

R 222. FAUSET, ARTHUR HUFF. Black Gods of the Metropolis: Negro Religious
        Cults in the Urban North. Philadelphia: University of Pennsyl-
        vania Press, 1944. 128 pp.
Fauset's ethnographic study of urban blacks attempts to unravel the complicated combination of socio-economic conditions, white Christianity,
and African religious sensibilities informing cult religious expression.
The central question of his investigation is whether an observed predisposition of blacks toward religion is more the result of limitations
imposed on them by racism and poverty or the result of lingering ties to
an African cultural heritage.

R 223. FRAZIER, E. FRANKLIN and C. ERIC LINCOLN. The Negro Church in
        America/The Black Church Since Frazier. New York: Schocken Books,
        1974. 216 pp.
In this Schocken edition, Frazier's classic sociological analysis of the
Negro Church first published in 1964, spanning the period from slavery
to the urban migrations following W.W. II, is appended and updated by
C. Eric Lincoln's monograph on the struggle of the Black Church during
the 1960s. Frazier argues that the determining factor in the evolution
of the Negro Church was the social inequality and relative isolation of
blacks in American society. Lincoln speaks of the death of the Negro
Church and the emergence of the Black Church, which seeks to be the symbol
and instrument of a new freedom founded on racial inclusiveness.

R 224. JOHNSON, CLIFTON H., ed. God Struck Me Dead: Religious Conversion
        Experiences and Autobiographies of Ex-slaves. Philadelphia:
        Pilgrim Press, 1969. 172 pp.
These fifty accounts of religious conversion as told by ex-slaves were
selected from a hundred interviews taken over the years from 1927 to 1929
by anthropologists Paul Radin and A. P. Watson, who respectively provide
a Foreword and an Essay to the volume. The original language has been
preserved except for minor modifications of dialect. Though the experience
of conversion is a highly individualistic affair, the editor notes that
a common pool of visions, symbols, and rituals cut across the variety
of experiences and open a window on black religious and folk culture coming
out of the days of slavery.

R 225. LEVINE, LAWRENCE W. Black Culture and Black Consciousness: Afro-
        American Folk Thought from Slavery to Freedom. New York: Oxford
        University Press, 1977. 522 pp.
In the century spanning from the antebellum era to the 1940s, Levine traces
the contours of black folk thought as it evolved under the influences
of slavery and then freedom. Seeking to correct the ideal construct of
a "pure victim," he argues that a remarkably vital and self-conscious
black culture existed amid racial injustice and brutality. His folk
sources are extensive and comprehensive, shedding light on religious as
well as other important aspects of black folk culture.

R 226. LINCOLN, C. ERIC. The Black Muslims in America. 1961; Rev. ed.
        Boston: Beacon Press, 1973. 302 pp.
In this study, Lincoln sets out the origins and rationale of the Black
Muslim movement led by Elijah Muhammad. He reads the movement's racial
ideology, where "white" by definition is evil, as symptomatic of social
conflict. Specifically, he advances Black Muslims as a case illustration
of a broad sociological thesis: "Whenever there is an actual or a felt
discrepancy in the power relations of discrete systems or subsystems,
a condition of social anxiety will emerge." Feeling totally disenfran-
chised from the prevailing culture of white Christian America, the Muslims
have opted for an alternative set of values.

R 227. LINCOLN, C. ERIC, ed. The Black Experience in Religion. Garden
        City, N.Y.: Anchor Press, 1974. 369 pp.
This anthology divides into five sections, each of which is introduced
by the editor. General topics of discussion include the worship style
of the black church, black preaching and theology, the relation between
black protest and black religion, black sects and cults, and finally,
the varieties of black religion in Africa and the Caribbean. The emphasis
of the articles is on contemporary experience, i.e., the 1960s and early
1970s, with some attention given to historical background.

R 228. LITWACK, LEON F. Been in the Storm So Long: The Aftermath of
        Slavery. New York: Knopf, 1979. 651 pp.
"To describe the significance of freedom to four million black slaves
of the South is to test severely our historical imagination." With this
precautionary note issued, Litwack chronicles the experience of emancipated
blacks in the aftermath of Civil War. From abundant sources of ex-slave
testimony, he seeks to capture the diverse perceptions of freedom professed
by black men and women born into servitude.

R 229. MAYS, BENJAMIN ELIJAH and JOSEPH WILLIAM NICHOLSON. The Negro's
        Church. New York: Institute of Social and Religious Research,
        1933. 321 pp.
Looking at the Negro church of the early 1930s, Mays and Nicholson assess
its membership, ministry, institutions, finances, worship life, and social
programs from sociological data culled from 609 urban and 185 rural
churches widely distributed in twelve cities and four country areas. Overall
the authors present a bleak picture of a church whose development has
been retarded by racism, but they end on an upbeat note with their discussion of the genius or "soul" of the Negro church.

R 230. NELSEN, HART M. and ANNE KUSENER NELSEN. Black Church in the Six-
        ties. Lexington: University Press of Kentucky, 1975. 172 pp.
The avowed purpose of the Nelsens' sociological investigation of the black
church is "to assess the character of black religiosity as basically otherworldly and an opiate of civil rights militancy or as temporal and an
inspiration of militancy." After a preliminary overview of previous
studies on the black church, the Nelsens use data from the Gallup poll
to discuss black orientations and attitudes toward the church and what
relationship exists between militancy and black religious institutions,
both orthodox and sectarian.

R 231. RABOTEAU, ALBERT J. Slave Religion: The "Invisible Institution"
        in the Antebellum South. New York: Oxford University Press,
        1978. 382 pp.
Raboteau's is the first study to make full use of available slave narratives, black autobiographies, and black folklore in an effort to present
a composite picture of black religious experience in the antebellum South.
His investigation covers issues of the African influence on slave religious
expression, the nature of the Christianity presented to the slaves, the

process of conversion and evangelization, and the distinctiveness, if any, of religion in slave quarters.

R 232. SERNETT, MILTON C. Black Religion and American Evangelicalism: White Protestants, Plantation Missions, and the Flowering of Negro Christianity, 1787-1865. Metuchen, N.J.: Scarecrow Press, 1975. 320 pp.
"Negro Religion before the Civil War," writes Sernett, "did not represent a fourth American faith after Protestantism, Judaism, and Catholicism." It drew instead from the white evangelical heritage of American Protestantism and grafted onto that tradition its own unique folk experience. In order to capture this complex fusing of cultures, Sernett portrays Christianity from the point of view of both the white evangelicals with their plantation missions and the slaves who converted. The progression of the narrative is from white to black, from American evangelicalism to the Negro churches.

R 233. SIMPSON, GEORGE EATON. Black Religions in the New World. New York: Columbia University Press, 1978. 415 pp.
Simpson is concerned with "the African Diaspora" in North America, the West Indies, and Latin America--those black descendants of sub-Saharan Africans who were dispersed throughout the New World via the Atlantic slave trade. Taking a sociological approach, he surveys the variety of religions that have influenced these peoples over the past five hundred years. Students of black religion in North America will find his last two chapters particularly illuminating.

R 234. WALKER, CLARENCE E. A Rock in a Weary Land: The African Methodist Episcopal Church During the Civil War and Reconstruction. Baton Rouge: Louisiana State University Press, 1982. 157 pp.
The primary focus of Walker's book is on the missionary efforts of the African Methodist Episcopal Church directed toward freedmen. Convinced of both the spiritual need for the saving message of the Gospel and the temporal need for good, productive citizens, A.M.E. missionaries sought to elevate poor and oppressed blacks to social and economic equality while Christianizing them. Walker argues that the combination of temporal and spiritual purpose under the canopy of Methodism provided the rationale for the emergence of a black middle class.

R 235. WASHINGTON, JOSEPH R., Jr. Black Religion: The Negro and Christianity in the United States. Boston: Beacon Press, 1964. 308 pp.
In a theological and historical assessment of black Christianity in the U.S., Washington argues that segregation has diminished the spiritual resources of both black and white churches, leaving American Christianity in a generally impoverished state. To remedy this situation, he calls for the assimilation of the black church into the Christian mainstream. Four sections make up his analysis: "Religion and the Protest Movement," "Folk Religion and Negro Congregations," "Response to Protestant Paternalism," and "Challenge to Negro and White Christians."

R 236. WASHINGTON, JOSEPH R., Jr. Black Sects and Cults: The Power Axis in an Ethnic Ethic. Garden City, N.Y.: Doubleday, 1972. 176 pp.
Rather than delineate the multitude of black sects and cults, Washington chooses to concentrate on highly representative sect and cult types in an effort "to reveal the universal and particular emphases of these disinherited black folk." The common core he seeks is that of an ethnic ethic, which he finds exemplified across the board, in Methodists and Baptists as well as Pentecostals and cult members. Linking black sectarianism to a black ethos, he concludes that the cult and sect impulse is indicative of a desire for community and the power for self-determination.

R 237. WILLIAMS, MELVIN D. Community in a Black Pentecostal Church:
        An Anthropological Study. Pittsburgh, Pa.: University of Pitts-
        burgh Press, 1974. 202 pp.
Williams's case study of a black Pentecostal community centers on the
Zion Holiness Church in Pittsburgh. After having spent three years there
as an observer (beginning in 1969), he offers an account of "the distinctive quality of social relations, communal ideology, and social behavior
within the group." Religion, he argues, serves as a system of symbols
capable of sustaining group identity within a separate urban subculture.
Topics of discussion include the history of Zion, its membership, church
activity, distinctive style, design for living, and status hierarchy.

R 238. WILMORE, GAYRAUD S. Black and Presbyterian: The Heritage and
        the Hope. Philadelphia: Geneva Press, 1983. 142 pp.
Wilmore explores the challenges of black membership within the Presbyterian
church, where blacks are a minority and often worship in segregated congregations. His inquiry leads him to reflect on the larger issues of
black identity within American Christianity and the complexities of interracial worship.

R 239. WILMORE, GAYRAUD S. Black Religion and Black Radicalism: An Inter-
        pretation of the Religious History of Afro-American People. 1972;
        Rev. ed. Maryknoll, N.Y.: Orbis Books, 1983. 288 pp.
In the revised and enlarged edition of his study of the black church,
Wilmore argues that a prophetic tradition of black radicalism has remained
essential to black religious experience. Identifying contours of this
radical tradition are the quest for freedom from white hegemony, a renewed
appreciation for the image of Africa, and the understanding of protest
as a theological prerequisite for the liberation of an oppressed people.
At the same time, Wilmore points to reactionary tendencies within the black
church, and he sensitively draws out the paradoxical coexistence of the
church's radical and reactionary faces.

TOPICAL BREAKDOWN: WOMEN AND RELI-
GION IN AMERICA

R 240. BEAVER, R. PIERCE. American Protestant Women in World Mission:
        History of the First Feminist Movement in North America. 1968;
        Rev. ed. Grand Rapids, Mich.: Eerdmans, 1980. 237 pp.
First issued under the title All Loves Excelling: American Protestant
Women in World Mission, Beaver's book chronicles the activities of women
in overseas missions, beginning with the founding in 1800 of the Boston
Female Society of Missionary Purposes under the leadership of Mary Webb.
His narrative emphasizes the structures and institutions through which
the missionary movement developed. The revised edition includes a chapter
on the 1970s, where Beaver discusses missionary activity in light of contemporary feminism.

R 241. BOYD, LOIS A. and R. DOUGLAS BRACKENRIDGE. Presbyterian Women
        in America: Two Centuries of a Quest for Status. Westport, Conn.:
        Greenwood Press, 1983. 308 pp.
Making extensive use of archival and documentary sources, Boyd and
Brackenridge present a detailed account of the changing roles of women in
Presbyterian church life from 1789 to 1981. Some of the topics addressed
by the authors include the uses of Scripture by church leaders to justify
the subordination of women, the ordination of women, the involvement of
women in missions and education, and ministers' wives.

R 242. GODFREY, KENNETH W., AUDREY M. GODFREY, and JILL M. DERR. Women's
        Voices: An Untold History of the Latter-day Saints, 1830-1900.
        Salt Lake City, Utah: Deseret Book, 1982. 448 pp.
Women's Voices is a collection of twenty-five documents ranging over the
course of the 19th century and written by first-generation Mormon women.
Selections reflect on aspects of Mormon experience as a whole and also
on issues peculiar to women's subculture within Mormon society. Source
material is drawn from letters, journals, diaries, and autobiographies
and is prefaced by introductions which situate the women authors biographi-
cally and historically.

R 243. JAMES, JANET WILSON, ed. Women in American Religion. Philadelphia:
        University of Pennsylvania Press, 1980. 274 pp.
This collection of thirteen essays on the history of women in American
religion is comprehensive in terms of periods covered, and an attempt
is made to consider Catholic and Jewish women as well as Protestant.
After the editor's useful overview of the topic, more narrowly focused
essays explore women's roles with regard to the social status of the clergy,
congregational life, lay leadership, social outreach, missionary efforts,
and notions of piety and religious knowledge.

R 244. PORTERFIELD, AMANDA. Feminine Spirituality in America: From Sarah
        Edwards to Martha Graham. Philadelphia: Temple University Press,
        1980. 238 pp.
In making her case for an identifiable tradition of feminine spirituality
in America, Porterfield follows the lead of her teacher, William Clebsch,
who argued that a uniquely American religious sensibility hinges on the
notion of being at home in the universe. Porterfield advances a feminine
variation: "The feminine spirituality that is the subject of this book
differs from the manly spirit of being at home in the universe only, but
significantly, in how concretely the metaphor has been experienced."
She leaves the precise characterization of this spirituality to concrete
illustrations.

R 245. RUETHER, ROSEMARY RADFORD and ROSEMARY SKINNER KELLER, eds. Women
        and Religion in America/Volume One: The Nineteenth Century.
        San Francisco: Harper & Row, 1981. 353 pp.
Seven women historians under the editorial guidance of Keller and Ruether
offer analytical essays and illustrative documents on the role of women
in American religion during the 19th century. It was during this formative
century that women's participation in the nation's religious life expanded
beyond hearth and home to leadership positions in social movements and
religious institutions. Each essay stands on its own, and together they
bring out the many-faceted story of the influence of religion in the lives
of 19th-century women, including both its liberating and oppressive aspects.

R 246. RUETHER, ROSEMARY RADFORD and ROSEMARY SKINNER KELLER, eds. Women
        and Religion in America/Volume Two: The Colonial and Revolutionary
        Periods. San Francisco: Harper & Row, 1983. 434 pp.
Departing from more well-trodden historiographical paths, Ruether and
Keller present 17th- and 18th-century America as the scene of a complex
intercultural drama of conflicting religious visions. In this second
volume of their documentary history, they have assembled nine essays introducing primary source material bearing on the role of women in the multi-
farious religious environment of early America. Women and religion are
discussed with regard to the following: American Indian life, Spanish
and colonial French settlements, New England Puritanism, the South, the
experience of Colonial blacks, sectarian and utopian groups, revivalism,
civil religion, and the American Revolution.

R 247. SKLAR, KATHRYN KISH. Catherine Beecher: A Study in American Domes-
        ticity. New Haven, Conn.: Yale University Press, 1973. 356 pp.
Catherine Beecher was the daughter of Lyman Beecher, the prominent spokesman for a resurgent evangelicalism, and like her father she was concerned
with influencing society and interpreting American culture. But Beecher's
female identity, Sklar writes, "excluded her from the main vehicle of
contemporary social influence, the church, and it persistently relegated
her to a marginal social status when she sought a central one." Beecher's
attempt to create an alternative channel of cultural influence in the
home and family is the main focus of Sklar's study of domesticity in 19th-
century America.

R 248. SWEET, LEONARD I. The Minister's Wife: Her Role in Nineteenth-
        Century American Evangelicalism. Philadelphia: Temple University
        Press, 1983. 327 pp.
Nineteenth-century revivalism bore witness to the emergence of the minister's wife as an institutional leader of church women. Sweet organizes
his historical study around models that illustrate the roles available
to ministers' wives--the Companion, the Sacrificer, the Assistant, and
the Partner--and considers as well the kind of spirituality associated
with each. The typology is a heuristic convenience, and Sweet avoids
the temptation of turning models into "ideal types."

TOPICAL BREAKDOWN: ENCOUNTERS WITH NATIVE AMERICANS

R 249. AXTELL, JAMES, ed. The Native American People of the East. West
        Haven, Conn.: Pendulum Press, 1973. 126 pp.
Axtell's book is part of The American People series, collections of primary
source material on the everyday lives of people in a variety of historical
eras. Making use of the reports of European colonists and explorers,
Axtell has assembled information on many facets of Indian life in Eastern
America--birth, growth, love and marriage, work and play, right and wrong,
heaven and earth, death.

R 250. BEAVER, ROBERT PIERCE. Church, State, and the American Indians:
        Two and a Half Centuries of Partnership in Missions Between Protes-
        tant Churches and Government. St. Louis, Mo.: Concordia, 1966.
        230 pp.
Beaver's period of interest extends from the missionary work of the Mayhews
and John Eliot around 1641 to Indian policy during the Grant and Hayes
administrations. His theme is the establishment, maintenance, and eventual
dissolution of a unique cooperation between the government and Christian
missionaries in the conversion of Indians--a cooperation manifestly at
odds with an ideal church-state separation.

R 251. BERKHOFER, ROBERT F., Jr. Salvation and the Savage: An Analysis
        of Protestant Missions and American Indian Response, 1787-1862.
        New York: Atheneum, 1972. 186 pp.
Combining anthropology and history, Berkhofer uses Protestant missionary
activity and Indian response as a case study for acculturation. His basic
thesis is that once Indians lost their political autonomy they were no
longer able to distance themselves from an encroaching alien culture.
Acculturation therefore proceeded in a manner defined by the dominant
white culture: "The Americans called the tune to which the Indians danced
regardless of tribal culture." To demonstrate this thesis, Berkhofer
employs a comparative approach ranging over a wide variety of Protestant
denominations and Indian tribes.

R 252. BOWDEN, HENRY WARNER. American Indians and Christian Missions:
        Studies in Cultural Conflict. Chicago: University of Chicago
        Press, 1981. 255 pp.
The year 1492 marked the beginning of nearly 500 years of cultural conflict
between native Americans and European explorers and settlers. In a balanced account of the religious dimension of this conflict, Bowden follows
Christian missionary and Indian interaction through various regions and
time periods. Using ethnographical and historical material, he describes
the ethos of native American religion and shows how the missionaries'
efforts at conversion were wittingly or unwittingly destroying the culture
of the very people they wished to aid. An extensive bibliographical essay
is included.

R 253. KELLER, ROBERT H., Jr. American Protestantism and United States
        Indian Policy, 1869-82. Lincoln: University of Nebraska Press,
        1983. 359 pp.
Ulysses S. Grant initiated the Peace Policy toward Native Americans when
he turned over the Indian Office to the control of Christian missionary
boards. This compromise of church/state separation, following along the
lines of a long-standing cooperation between the government and missionaries, allowed in Keller's words "evangelicals, Friends, philanthropists,
and other Christians a bedrock of experience to test their beliefs through
performance." The burden of Keller's tale is the failure of Christian
fortitude and good intentions to overcome the myth of racial superiority
and the overwhelming desire of whites for ownership, control, and use'
of the land.

R 254. MILNER, CLYDE A., II. With Good Intentions: Quaker Work Among
        the Pawnees, Otos, and Omahas in the 1870s. Lincoln: University
        of Nebraska Press, 1982. 238 pp.
Milner focuses on the work of Quaker missionaries under Grant's Peace
policy in the 1870s. Using case studies of Quaker interaction with the
Pawnee, Oto, and Omaha peoples, Milner concludes that though the Quakers
were well-motivated, their ethnocentrism rendered them no less damaging
in their assaults on Indian culture than other humanitarians and Indian
reformers of this period. He also discusses the efforts made by Indian
peoples to protect their heritage despite the "help" of Quaker missionaries.

R 255. SEGAL, CHARLES M. and DAVID C. STINEBACK. Puritans, Indians, and
        Manifest Destiny. New York: Putnam, 1977. 249 pp.
Segal and Stineback have assembled forty-five primary source documents
illustrating the basic issues and attitudes involved in Puritan and Indian
contact during the 17th century. Their anthology is divided into five
sections, each with an introduction by the authors: "Land and Trade,"
"Government Relations "The Pequot War," "Christianizing the Indians,"
and "King Philip's War." The readings as well as the accompanying narrative are offered in support of the thesis that "the history of Puritan
and Indian relations is best seen as a cultural conflict with a philosophical (or theological) basis."

R 256. SHEEHAN, BERNARD. Savagism and Civility: Indians and Englishmen
        in Colonial Virginia. New York: Cambridge University Press,
        1980. 257 pp.
Sheehan discusses the inability of white colonists to understand the
Indians in any terms other than those of a preconceived mythology of Indian
savagism. This primal myth of Western Christendom proved impervious to
revision even in the face of Indian-settler contacts that contradicted
its presuppositions. By dogmatically casting Indians as immature and
bestial savages, Sheehan argues "Englishmen reconciled the presence and
character of the native people with their own interests."

R 257. VAUGHAN, ALDEN T. and EDWARD W. CLARK, eds. Puritans Among the
        Indians: Accounts of Captivity and Redemption. Cambridge, Mass.:
        Harvard University Press, 1981. 275 pp.
Puritans who endured and eventually escaped captivity among the Indians
tended to interpret their experience soteriologically as one of punishment
and redemption. Vaughan and Clark have selected and edited the best New
England accounts available of captivity among the Indians, offering the
reader a first-hand look at an "important expression of Puritan theological
and social thought." In their introduction the editors discuss the literary, historical, and religious significance of the captivity narratives.

TOPICAL BREAKDOWN: NATIVISM AND
RACISM IN AMERICAN RELIGION

R 258. BILLINGTON, RAY ALLEN. The Protestant Crusade, 1800-1860: A Study
        of the Origins of American Nativism. New York: Macmillan, 1938.
        514 pp.
Fear of the immigrant in mid-19th-century America joined with a long-
standing antipapal tradition to produce a nativistic political action that
culminated in the Know-Nothing party. Billington traces the roots of
anti-Catholic sentiment and concentrates on its expression in the first
half of the 19th century. He goes on to analyze the political power of
Protestant organizations swelled by xenophobic Americans and suggests
reasons for the ultimate failure of nativists to produce anti-Catholic
and anti-foreign legislation.

R 259. CHALMERS, DAVID M. Hooded Americanism: The History of the Ku
        Klux Klan. 1965; Rev. ed. New York: Franklin Watts, 1981.
        477 pp.
The Klan, Chalmers explains, "is a secret, oath-bound society that draws
its members from rural and working class strata, or subcultures, which
are socialized to establish reputation, social space, and often personality
by fighting." From the lynchings of the Reconstruction to the Greensboro
murders, the Klan has worked to purge society of what it considers undesirable people while revitalizing its mission through an appeal to traditional values. Chalmers traces Klan activity state by state and chronologically, classifying the four periods of Klan history as Reconstruction,
pre-W.W. I to pre-W.W. II, Cold War to the late 1960s, and finally the decade
of the seventies.

R 260. DOBKOWSKI, MICHAEL N. The Tarnished Dream: The Basis of American
        Anti-Semitism. Westport, Conn.: Greenwood Press, 1979. 291 pp.
In an effort to suggest an alternative to the consensus historiography
of Oscar Handlin, John Higham, and Richard Hofstadter, Dobkowski marshals
evidence of negative imagery of Jews and Jewry between 1877 and 1927.
Arguing that anti-Semitism of an ideological nature was widespread, he
demonstrates that stereotypes "invaded a cross-section of American intellectual and cultural life, and that their use increased significantly
in the Gilded Age and lasted well into the Progressive era."

R 261. HARRELL, DAVID EDWIN, Jr. White Sects and Black Men in the Recent
        South. Nashville, Tenn.: Vanderbilt University Press, 1971.
        161 pp.
Harrell's study of sectarianism in the recent South centers on the issue
of racial attitudes and offers an angle of vision on religious groups
largely neglected by scholars. He argues that racial views among Southern
sects are more a product of class structure than theology, which serves
primarily as a convenient rhetoric. Before arriving at this conclusion,

Harrell explores the complex social structure of a diverse and large white sect-and-cult community in the South.

R 262. HIGHAM, JOHN. Strangers in the Land: Patterns of American Nativism, 1860-1925. 1955; Rev. ed. New York: Atheneum, 1963. 431 pp.
Higham believes that recurring patterns of nativism can be found in anti-Catholic, anti-radical, and Anglo-Saxon traditions within American culture. In his period of focus, 1860 to 1925, xenophobic feelings reached an unusually high pitch, a phenomenon Higham links with a strident and dogmatic brand of nationalism. Proponents of this nationalism advanced religious and ethnic prejudice in a crusade for Americanization.

R 263. KINZER, DONALD L. An Episode in Anti-Catholicism: The American Protective Association. Seattle: University of Washington Press, 1964. 342 pp.
Kinzer's narrative, based on the files of the "patriotic press," memoirs, Catholic newspapers, records of state legislatures, and other sources, tells both the story of the A.P.A. and of the larger A.P.A. movement of the 1890s. After highlighting the various strains of anti-Catholic sentiment, he concentrates on the origins, successes, internal struggles, and ultimate decline of the A.P.A. His history shows how "the organization was the beneficiary of its era, and an instrument, which both its supporters and its opponents used to gain political support and to mold public opinion."

R 264. MURRAY, ANDREW A. Presbyterians and the Negro: A History. Philadelphia: Presbyterian Historical Society, 1966. 270 pp.
Murray's history of the Presbyterian church's treatment of blacks from colonial times to the early 1960s attempts to discern the denomination's recurring patterns of behavior on issues of race. He concludes that, despite its share of prophetic figures, the church generally "has been shaped of prevailing American racial patterns rather than taking the lead in shaping them." The one notable exception to this has been the role of Presbyterians in educating blacks.

R 265. OSBORNE, WILLIAM A. The Segregated Covenant: Race Relations and American Catholics. New York: Herder & Herder, 1967. 252 pp.
In 1958 the American Catholic hierarchy denounced segregation as morally and religiously unacceptable. Nevertheless de facto segregation remained within the Church. Osborne surveys the extent of segregated congregations in each of the country's major geographical regions in order to assess the Church's real commitment to integration and racial equality. He concludes that while no official sanction exists for discrimination of any kind, American bishops need to take a more active and visible role in civil rights causes.

R 266. REIMERS, DAVID M. White Protestantism and the Negro. New York: Oxford University Press, 1965. 236 pp.
Focusing on the period from the early 19th century to the early 1960s, Reimers examines how Protestant churches have historically dealt with issues of race and integration especially within their own organizations. Under white Protestantism he includes the major denominations and interdenominational groups such as the National Council of Churches. He argues that the actual practices of the churches fell short of their social pronouncements and that their attitudes toward blacks generally mirrored those of the surrounding society.

R 267. ROY, RALPH LORD. Apostles of Discord: A Story of Organized Bigotry and Disruption on the Fringes of Protestantism. Boston: Beacon Press, 1953. 437 pp.

Roy's polemical depiction of the forces of intolerance and bigotry who use Protestantism as a source of authority is intended "to warn Americans, and Protestants in particular, of the ominous threat to Christian values and to democracy which these fringe groups represent." His straightforward presentation of religiously organized racism, nativism, and extremism gives the reader some sense of the underbelly of American religion during the Cold War.

R 268. SMITH, H. SHELTON. In His Image, But . . .: Racism in Southern Religion, 1780-1910. Durham, N.C.: Duke University Press, 1972. 318 pp.

Imago Dei is the biblical doctrine of the equality of all human beings in the sight of God. Nevertheless the majority of Southern church leaders interpreted Genesis anthropology to allow for the supremacy and domination of whites over blacks. Smith traces the history of the anti-Negro movement in Southern religion from its inception in antebellum times to its role in opposing the political and social equality of freedmen. In addition to the theological inconsistencies of racism, Smith considers its impact on human relations.

TOPICAL BREAKDOWN: VARIETIES OF EVANGELICALS

R 269. ABELL, TROY D. Better Felt Than Said: The Holiness-Pentecostal Experience in Southern Appalachia. Waco, Tex.: Markham Press, 1982. 206 pp.

Abell's book is the result of one year's field work in Southern Appalachia, where he regularly attended Holiness-Pentecostal worship services in two different mountain communities. Rich in descriptive material, Abell's assessment of Appalachian religion borders on the impressionistic, though he does offer analyses of the Holiness-Pentecostal system of causation and certainty, glossolalia, locus of control, and personality.

R 270. ANDERSON, ROBERT MAPES. Vision of the Disinherited: The Making of American Pentecostalism. New York: Oxford University Press, 1979. 334 pp.

Anderson explores the social history behind the genesis and early development of Pentecostalism, which he identifies as "a movement that emerged on the world scene in 1906 during a Los Angeles revival in which speaking in tongues was regarded as a sign of Baptism in the Spirit for the individual, a sign of a Second Pentecost for the Church, and a sign of the imminent Second Coming of Christ." He limits his investigation to the movement's formative years, the period from the late 19th century to the early 1930s.

R 271. BLOESCH, DONALD G. The Future of Evangelical Christianity: A Call for Unity Amid Diversity. Garden City, N.Y.: Doubleday, 1983. 202 pp.

As one of the leading voices in evangelical theology, Bloesch examines the state of contemporary evangelicalism, weighing its historical development and assessing its future prospects. He locates the movement's theological unity in its ties with the Reformed tradition, which emphasizes the revelation of God through Jesus Christ. With this tradition seen as fundamental, Bloesch charts a course for evangelicalism that avoids its association with either a rigid fundamentalism or an empty liberalism.

R 272. DIETER, MELVIN ESTERDAY. The Holiness Revival of the Nineteenth
Century. Metuchen, N.J.: Scarecrow Press, 1980. 356 pp.
As a reform movement within American Protestantism, the holiness revival
of the 19th century sought to combine the prevalent mood of revivalism
with Wesleyan perfectionism, producing in Dieter's words "as widespread
a popular quest for the beatific vision as the world had known." In his
account of the development of this variegated movement, Dieter traces its
evolution from a fluid creative force in the decades prior to the Civil
War to a number of holiness churches and institutions during the Gilded
Age.

R 273. HARRELL, DAVID EDWIN, Jr. All Things Are Possible: The Healing
and Charismatic Revivals in Modern America. Bloomington: Indiana
University Press, 1975. 304 pp.
Harrell's account of faith healing and charismatic revivalism concentrates
on the numerous independent evangelistic associations founded after WW
II by charismatic ministers. He describes how these individuals broke
off from the control of smaller pentecostal churches and rose to affluence
and public notoriety. Attention is given to notable individuals, such
as Oral Roberts and Gordon Lindsay, and to the general features of the
healing revival (1947-1958) and the related charismatic revival (1958-
1974).

R 274. HUNTER, JAMES DAVISON. American Evangelicalism: Conservative
Religion and the Quandary of Modernity. New Brunswick, N.J.:
Rutgers University Press, 1983. 171 pp.
Using a sociology of knowledge approach indebted to Peter Berger and Walter
Luckmann, Hunter examines the success of contemporary evangelicalism in
confronting modern challenges to traditional religious belief. He shows
precisely where evangelicals have compromised with modernity (e.g., their
downplaying of sin and damnation) and where they have held their ground
(e.g., their moral vision). As background to this discussion, Hunter
spells out what he means by modernity and the evangelical tradition.

R 275. MARSDEN, GEORGE M. The Evangelical Mind and the New School Presbyterian Experience: A Case Study of Thought and Theology in
Nineteenth-Century America. New Haven, Conn.: Yale University
Press, 1970. 278 pp.
As an inroad into the outlook of American evangelicalism, Marsden focuses
on the thought of New School Presbyterianism in mid-19th century America.
He argues that the ideology of this denomination, as representative of
the mainline Protestantism of its day, dovetailed with prevailing American
values concerning morality, human nature, and national mission. Throughout
the book Marsden interprets intellectual developments in the context of
popular revivalism.

R 276. MARSDEN, GEORGE M. Fundamentalism and American Culture: The Shaping of Twentieth-Century Evangelicalism, 1870-1925. New York:
Oxford University Press, 1980. 306 pp.
"Fundamentalism was a loose, diverse, and changing federation of co-
belligerents united by their fierce opposition to modernist attempts to
bring Christianity in line with modern thought." With this understanding
of fundamentalism in mind, Marsden recounts the general history of its
rise, focusing specifically on the degree to which the movement was shaped
by the surrounding culture. He argues that fundamentalists assumed an
ambivalent posture toward their culture, indicative of their profound
transformation from "respectable" evangelicals in the 1870s to ridiculed
reactionaries in the 1920s.

R 277. McLOUGHLIN, WILLIAM G., ed. The American Evangelicals, 1800-1900:
An Anthology. New York: Harper & Row, 1968. 213 pp.
Twelve selections from American evangelicalism's major spokesmen lay out
the ideology that played a formative role in the 19th-century American
culture of rugged individualism, laissez faire economics, democratic politics, the Protestant ethic, and manifest destiny. Included are selections from Lyman Beecher, Charles G. Finney, Horace Bushnell, Dwight L.
Moody, and Josiah Strong, among others. In his introduction, McLoughlin
briefly describes the nature of 19th-century evangelicalism with regard
to its philosophy, theology, and social history.

R 278. McLOUGHLIN, WILLIAM G., Jr. Modern Revivalism: Charles Grandison
Finney to Billy Graham. New York: Ronald Press, 1959. 551 pp.
With a mind toward correcting the false stereotype of revivals as "orgies
of mass hysteria" and of revivalists as "grim or theatrical prophets of
hellfire and damnation," McLoughlin examines the important role revivalism
played in shaping the intellectual, social, and religious life of America.
Modern revivalism is taken to begin circa 1825 with the efforts of Charles
Finney and the narrative is continued up to the end of the 1950s. Throughout the study, the author is attentive to how revivalist preaching often
mirrors and reinforces the presumptions of American popular culture.

R 279. O'CONNOR, EDWARD D. The Pentecostal Movement in the Catholic Church.
Notre Dame, Ind.: Ave Maria Press, 1971. 301 pp.
From a Catholic perspective, O'Connor sets forth a phenomenological account
and theological assessment of the emergence of Pentecostal spirituality
within American Catholic ranks. He begins with the movement's origin
and growth in and around the University of Notre Dame and then takes up
topics of a more general and theoretical concern. Of particular concern
for O'Connor is how a charismatic outlook meshes with the institutional
setting of the Church.

R 280. QUEBEDEAUX, RICHARD. The New Charismatics II. 1976; Rev. ed.
San Francisco: Harper & Row, 1983. 272 pp.
In a world plagued by social fragmentation, economic inequality, spiritual
uncertainty, and widespread prejudice and intolerance, the Gospel promise
for a new life in the present seems either hopeless or false. It is in
the light of modern dehumanization that Quebedeaux explores the Charismatic
Renewal as a potential church revitalization movement. He argues that
the strength the renewal has demonstrated since the early 1960s marks
it as more than just a fad. Thorough revisions and corrections have been
made to the original text, documentation, and bibliography, to the point
where Quebedeaux can refer to the new edition as "in some respects an
altogether new book."

R 281. QUEBEDEAUX, RICHARD. The Worldly Evangelicals. San Francisco:
Harper & Row, 1978. 189 pp.
"Evangelical Christianity has finally emerged from its anticultural ghetto
into the mainstream of American life. It is a new force to be reckoned
with." Who these evangelicals are, what they believe, and where they
may be heading are all questions Quebedeaux addresses. In general his
concern is more with the identification of trends and movements than with
the defense of any particular thesis.

R 282. SANDEEN, ERNEST R. The Roots of Fundamentalism: British and American Millenarianism, 1800-1930. Chicago: University of Chicago
Press, 1970. 328 pp.
Fundamentalists gained notoriety during the 1920s for their impassioned
critiques of evolutionary theory and the new biblical criticism. Consequently many historians have located the distinctiveness of fundamentalism
in its antagonistic stance toward modernism rather than in any specific

theological content. Sandeen challenges this reading by linking the movement to a tradition of millennial speculation that well preceded the 1920s.
He argues that "fundamentalism ought to be understood partly if not largely
as one aspect of the history of all millenarianism."

TOPICAL BREAKDOWN: THE AMERICAN
PURSUIT OF THE MILLENNIUM

R 283. CHERRY, CONRAD, ed. God's New Israel: Religious Interpretations
      of American Destiny. Englewood Cliffs, N.J.: Prentice-Hall, 1971.
      381 pp.
"The presupposition underlying this volume is that any vital myth does
not hide in the hinterland of a 'realm of ideas' but impinges upon the
life of a people as a spring of their action." The myth Cherry illustrates
with thirty selected readings is that of America's divinely ordained mission to lead the world into a new age. Each of the book's seven sections
explores how the myth has evolved in changing historical circumstances.
John Winthrop, Thomas Jefferson, Walt Whitman, Lyman Beecher, Washington
Gladden, Reinhold Niebuhr, and Elijah Muhammad are among the figures presented.

R 284. DAVIDSON, JAMES WEST. The Logic of Millennial Thought: Eighteenth-
      Century New England. New Haven, Conn.: Yale University Press,
      1977. 308 pp.
Rather than a historical account of millennialism, Davidson's book is
an analysis of a peculiar way of thinking; that is, he argues that millennial thought possesses a logic of its own. Half of his study is devoted
to mapping out that logic using the case of 18th-century New England.
The other half traces some of its historical ramifications. Throughout
the investigation, Davidson explores how eschatology shapes social perception.

R 285. GILPIN, W. CLARK. The Millenarian Piety of Roger Williams. Chicago:
      University of Chicago Press, 1979. 214 pp.
For the eschatologically minded Puritan of the 17th century, millenarianism
supplied the key for understanding both one's religious vocation and one's
place in history. The central claim of Gilpin's study of Roger Williams
is that Williams's famous opinions about religious liberty are best understood in light of the millenarian piety that animated all of his life
and thought. As Gilpin is careful to read Williams in close relation
to his historical setting, the reader gains insight as well into the
religious motivations behind the New England settlement.

R 286. HATCH, NATHAN O. The Sacred Cause of Liberty: Republican Thought
      and the Millennium in Revolutionary New England. New Haven, Conn.:
      Yale University Press, 1977. 197 pp.
Focusing on the period between 1740 and 1800, Hatch describes the attempts
of the New England clergy to reconcile their identities as members of
the Kingdom of God and patriots of a new nation. His central thesis is
that ministers progressively interpreted the civil order in religious
symbols to the point where "the cycles of republican history and the linear
perspective of Christian eschatology became indivisible, the joining of
separate traditions in mutually supportive union." Hatch advances this
marriage of politics and religion as the unifying ideology of the New
England ministers.

R 287. KRAUS, CLYDE NORMAN. Dispensationalism in America: Its Rise and
Development. Richmond, Va.: John Knox Press, 1958. 156 pp.
The historical study Kraus offers of dispensationalism traces the inner
development of the American Bible and Prophetic Conference movements and
distinguishes them from other forms of premillennialism. Beginning with
the teachings of John Darby and the Plymouth Brethren and ending with
the publication in 1909 of the Scofield Reference Bible, he seeks to
explain how the various dispensational movements, without becoming escapist,
attempted "to redefine certain traditional theological concepts in order
to strengthen [their] position against liberalizing tendencies." His
last chapter focuses on C. I. Scofield's doctrine and how it encapsulated
dispensational theology.

R 288. MOORHEAD, JAMES H. American Apocalypse: Yankee Protestants and
the Civil War, 1860-1869. New Haven, Conn.: Yale University
Press, 1978. 278 pp.
"What makes the 1860s especially interesting is the sheer intensity and
virtual unanimity of Northern conviction that the Union armies were hasten-
ing the day of the Lord—indeed that the war was not merely one sacred
battle among many but was the climactic test of the redeemer nation and
its millennial role." As his statement indicates, Moorhead uses the Civil
War and Reconstruction to illustrate a long-standing tradition within
American Protestantism of reading watershed events within an apocalyptic
framework of universal history. The uniqueness of the Civil War situation
stems from the confusion of America's mission—believed for seventy years
prior to secession to be one of moral persuasion—with the military might
of the North.

R 289. TUVESON, ERNEST LEE. Redeemer Nation: The Idea of America's Millennial Role. Chicago: University of Chicago Press, 1968.
238 pp.
Tuveson contends that religion played a central role in the development
of America's self-image as a "redeemer nation," and he analyzes the significance of millennialism for creating the idea of a nation "chosen"
to lead the world into a new utopian order. This ideology of chosenness,
lying behind much of American expansionism and nationalism, comes as part
of an apocalyptic refrain within American Protestantism, having spokesmen
as diverse as John Adams, Jonathan Edwards, Timothy Dwight, Lyman Beecher,
and Woodrow Wilson.

R 290. WEBER, TIMOTHY P. Living in the Shadow of the Second Coming:
American Premillennialism, 1875-1925. New York: Oxford University
Press, 1979. 232 pp.
A persistent feature of American religious life has been an interest in
Biblical prophecy, most notably in contemporary evangelicals. Weber
explores the historical roots of this phenomenon in the premillennialism
of the late 19th and early 20th centuries. Among the questions he attempts
to answer are what practical consequences proceeded from the expectation
of an imminent Second Coming and how premillennialists dealt with the
tensions inherent in their eschatology. The focus throughout is on
religious behavior.

TOPICAL BREAKDOWN: CIVIL RELIGION

R 291. ALBANESE, CATHERINE L. Sons of the Fathers: The Civil Religion
of the American Revolution. Philadelphia: Temple University
Press, 1976. 274 pp.
One of the most interesting debates in American religious historiography
continues to be over the nature and existence of a common civil faith
that cuts across denominational loyalties. In Sons of the Fathers,
Albanese argues that a great many of the symbols involved with the civil
faith evident in the 20th century were forged in the period of Enlightenment, Revolution, and nation-building. She also draws out the continuities between colonial, especially New England, religion and the civil
religion of the American Revolution.

R 292. BELLAH, ROBERT. The Broken Covenant: American Civil Religion
in Time of Trial. New York: Seabury Press, 1975. 172 pp.
Bellah wishes to articulate the present in terms of the past in order
to speak to what he perceives as the moral and religious erosion of contemporary society--America's current time of trial. He hopes to show
that the contemporary utilitarian morality of self-interest has not been
the prevailing conception throughout American history. On the contrary,
the fundamental religious and moral conception of America in the 17th
and 18th centuries involved "a much broader range of social, ethical,
aesthetic, and religious needs than the utilitarian model can deal."
Only if Americans draw from the resources of their past, Bellah contends,
will they avoid either the destruction of their society or a "technical
tyranny."

R 293. BELLAH, ROBERT N. and PHILIP E. HAMMOND. Varieties of Civil Religion. San Francisco: Harper & Row, 1980. 208 pp.
Bellah and Hammond attempt to broaden the scope of the civil religion
debate by placing it in a comparative religious context. A large portion
of the book is devoted to the American case, which is explicitly covered
in four of the book's eight chapters: "Religion and the Legitimation
of the American Republic"; "The Japanese and American Cases"; "The Conditions for Civil Religion: A Comparison of the United States and Mexico";
and "Pluralism and Law in the Formation of American Civil Religion."

R 294. CUDDIHY, JOHN MURRAY. No Offense: Civil Religion and Protestant
Taste. New York: Seabury Press, 1978. 232 pp.
Cuddihy adds a new twist to the civil religion debate by taking Robert
Bellah's original concept and turning it on its head. Taking civil religion to mean "the religion of civility," Cuddihy goes on to challenge
two "myths"--that civil religion is a theology rather than an attitude
manifested in rites and practices and that civil religion is in fact civil,
knowing its place and steering clear of church religion. On the contrary,
Cuddihy's study argues that the code of religious etiquette at the heart
of civil religion, with its demand of benign inoffensiveness, is mostly
at odds with sectarian sensibilities.

R 295. HUDSON, WINTHROP S., ed. Nationalism and Religion in America:
Concepts of American Identity and Mission. New York: Harper
& Row, 1970. 211 pp.
"No one can understand American national self-consciousness without taking
into account the religious heritage of the American people." In support
and illustration of this claim, Hudson has selected many short readings--
spanning from New England Puritanism to 20th-century civil religion--that
draw out the basic ingredients of American identity, sense of mission,
and destiny. The volume is divided into five sections that are interlaced
with Hudson's explanatory comments.

R 296. MEAD, SIDNEY E. The Nation with the Soul of a Church. New York:
Harper & Row, 1975. 158 pp.
This collection of essays spans a decade of Mead's reflections on American
religion. The common theme which unites them is identified by Mead as
"an unresolved tension between the theology that legitimates the constitutional structure of the Republic and that generally professed and taught
in a majority of the religious denominations of the United States." Mead's
prose is animated by his concern about the "anxious misery" produced by
this tension.

R 297. MEAD, SIDNEY E. The Old Religion in the Brave New World: Reflections on the Relation Between Christendom and the Republic.
Berkeley: University of California Press, 1977. 189 pp.
In these Jefferson Memorial Lectures, Mead takes up a favorite theme:
the divided loyalties of American citizens/church members, split between
traditional Christian orthodoxy on the one hand and the antithetical constitutional principles of the Republic on the other. Baleful effects
of this conflict include sectarian confusion, the irrelevance of Establishment religion to common life, and the general undermining of inclusive
society. Mead's prognosis is for the eventual hegemony of the Republic's
theology, indicated by the retreat of sectarian religious expression into
the private lives of individuals.

R 298. MOREY-GAINES, ANN-JANINE. Apples and Ashes: Culture, Metaphor,
and Morality in the American Dream. Chico, Calif.: Scholars
Press, 1982. 196 pp.
Morey-Gaines tracks the variations and metamorphoses of an elusive yet
pervasive metaphor of American culture--the American Dream. Her approach
is by and large literary, focusing primarily on works of 19th- and 20th-
century fiction. The study proceeds as an examination of the dream idea
as it appears in characteristically American expressions of religion,
individualism, and fascination for the frontier. Students of religion
will be especially interested in the author's discerning discussion of
civil religion.

R 299. WILSON, JOHN F. Public Religion in American Culture. Philadelphia:
Temple University Press, 1979. 198 pp.
The fruit of a decade's reflection on civil religion, Wilson's monograph
aims at clarifying the concept and stressing its usefulness as an interpretation of American religious history. Rather than a chronicle of cultural expressions of Public Religion (his preferred term of art), Wilson's
is a theoretical work, concerned as much with explanatory models as with
the "data" of Public Religion. He gains a novel perspective on civil
religion scholarship by reading its predominant motif--that civil religion
functions as an independent tradition--as part of a program to promote
civil religion as a source of cultural revitalization.

TOPICAL BREAKDOWN: CHURCH AND STATE

R 300. BLAU, JOSEPH L., ed. Cornerstones of Religious Freedom in America.
1949; Rev. ed. New York: Harper & Row, 1964. 344 pp.
In his introduction Blau states that his thirty-five selections "are
intended to serve as a reminder that the interpretation which has been
given to freedom of religion in the United States has been the separation
of church and state." After beginning with a brief background of writers
before 1940, he goes on to devote the rest of the volume to the recent
opinions of the Supreme Court and of various religious organizations,

such as the American Ethical Union, the United Synagogues of America, and the National Council of the Churches of Christ.

R 301. CORD, ROBERT L. Separation of Church and State: Historical Fact and Current Fiction. New York: Lambeth Press, 1982. 307 pp.
Cord seeks "to prove beyond reasonable doubt that no 'high and impregnable wall' between Church and State was in historical fact erected by the First Amendment nor was one intended by the Framers of that Amendment." In a continuous debate with Leo Pfeffer (see R 309), Cord examines important historical documents with an eye toward exceptions to what he calls Pfeffer's "absolutist" position. He further argues how precedent-setting cases have been based on inaccurate historical analysis, and in a final sustained polemic he calls for resolution of the church-state issue via the political process.

R 302. DRINAN, ROBERT F. Religion, The Courts, and Public Policy. New York: McGraw-Hill, 1963. 261 pp.
Drinan begins by observing that any analysis of church-state controversies must first take into account the symbiotic relationship between the two institutions. With this understanding presupposed, he goes on to discuss three major "anxieties" confronting Jews, Protestants, and Catholics: conducting business on Sundays, introducing religion into public education, and supporting church-related private schools with public money. He advances general recommendations for all parties involved as to how one can "guarantee the preservation of a free society" and implies that solutions to controversies ought to arise from the will of the people rather than strictly from the courts.

R 303. HOWE, MARK DeWOLFE. The Garden and the Wilderness: Religion and Government in American Constitutional History. Chicago: University of Chicago Press, 1965. 180 pp.
In this series of collected lectures, Howe advances the thesis that Supreme Court decisions on the separation of church and state have manifested a failure on the part of the Court to comprehend the theological roots of the First Amendment. He returns to American social and intellectual history in an effort to frame a more adequate theory of church and state separation. Discussed are the writings of Roger Williams, the formation of Protestant institutions, the bonds between religious and civil liberty, and the interplay of the evolving concepts of neutrality and equality within constitutional doctrine.

R 304. HUDSON, WINTHROP S. The Great Tradition of the American Churches. New York: Harper, 1953. 282 pp.
From John Cotton to Walter Rauschenbusch, Hudson discusses the balance major preachers have sought to achieve between church and state. Infused throughout the string of biographies is an urgent call for churches to assume more responsibility for the molding of society. Hudson argues that the decades before the 1890s, which was a time of abdication, can serve as an appropriate model for morale-building and the reinstigation of the "voluntary principle in religion."

R 305. McLOUGHLIN, WILLIAM G. New England Dissent, 1630-1833: The Baptists and the Separation of Church and State. 2 vols. Cambridge, Mass.: Harvard University Press, 1971. 1324 pp.
McLoughlin advances his massive study of New England dissent and especially its Baptist expression as a corrective to the common understanding of church and state separation as having either rationalistic or pietistic roots--i.e., that its origins are found either in the Enlightenment or in the radical Reformation. While emphasizing the pietistic tradition in America, McLoughlin is careful to point out how it interacted with rationalism and nationalistic ideology after 1770. Through this inter-

action, he contends, came a shift in the cultural myth that defined church and state relations: "The old religious myth of the errand in the wilderness, the city upon the hill, the Bible Commonwealth which was an outpost looking backward toward Europe, was rejected for the new nationalist myth of divinely directed manifest destiny."

R 306. MILLER, GLENN T. Religious Liberty in America: History and Prospects. Philadelphia: Westminister Press, 1976. 156 pp.
Miller argues that religious liberty was not the fixed result of the American Revolution but instead had to be won and developed through a series of American revolutions marked by strident debate and even bloodshed. Throughout Miller attempts to portray religious liberty as "the way in which our society has chosen to order its life," rather than as some ideal construct projected onto American history.

R 307. MORGAN, EDMUND S. Roger Williams: The Church and the State. New York: Harcourt, Brace & World, 1967. 170 pp.
In addition to being one of the most celebrated religious dissenters in early America, Roger Williams was a formidable intellectual engaged openly with "the hidden conflicts that tormented every Puritan." Morgan braves the convoluted polemics of Williams's voluminous writings in an effort to reveal the symmetry of ideas behind the impassioned rhetoric. In particular, Morgan sets out the issues that most captivated Williams--the church, the state, and the relationship between them.

R 308. O'NEILL, CHARLES EDWARDS. Church and State in French Colonial Louisiana: Policy and Politics to 1732. New Haven, Conn.: Yale University Press, 1966. 315 pp.
O'Neill's analysis of church-state relations in French Colonial settlements supplements the more numerous studies on the same topic for the English Colonies. Concentrating on the religious policy of the French monarchy, O'Neill considers theory and practice from the beginning of the Colony until its retrocession to the king by the Company of the Indies. While intended to be neither a general nor an ecclesiastical history of the territory, his study does supply sufficient details to establish the context for the "interrelated attitudes of civil and religious officials in Paris, Quebec, and Louisiana."

R 309. PFEFFER, LEO. Church, State, and Freedom. 1953; Rev. ed. Boston: Beacon Press, 1967. 832 pp.
Pfeffer's study explores the evolution of church and state separation in the United States and considers as well what import this separation has for a democracy. In Part One he traces the history leading up to the adoption of the first amendment, including in this discussion both Old World antecedents and a comparative look at other cultures and political systems. The next two parts take on the dynamics of church-state relations and the preservation of religious liberty, highlighting in each case legal angles.

R 310. SMITH, ELWYN A. Religious Liberty in the United States: The Development of Church-State Thought Since the Revolutionary Era. Philadelphia: Fortress Press, 1972. 386 pp.
Focusing on the national period and its immediate antecedents, Smith seeks "to analyze the thought of Americans whose social leadership and intellectual work have proved consequential in fashioning the laws and customs that institutionalized religious liberty." As his main concern is with the elucidation of ideas, Smith dips into actual controversies only to serve this end.

R 311. **STOKES, ANSON PHELPS** and **LEO PFEFFER.** Church and State in the United States. 1950; Rev. ed. New York: Harper & Row, 1964. 660 pp.

In this edition, Pfeffer has updated and compressed into one volume Anson Stokes's landmark three-volume history of the church and state in the U.S. Shortening of the original was effected primarily through the summarizing of much primary source material that Stokes had presented in full. The present edition falls into three divisions: "The Foundations of American Church-State Separation and Religious Freedom"; "The Establishment and Adjustment of Churches Independent of the State"; and "Modern and Contemporary Problems and Their Solution."

SCIENCE, TECHNOLOGY, AND MEDICINE

PREFACE

Any discussion of major library and archival sources in the fields
of American science and technology properly begins with consideration
of various Federal libraries and repositories. The Library of Congress
has unparalleled collections of published materials in these fields.
Its holdings of archival materials that relate to science and technology,
as well as business, governmental, and other kinds of activities related
to science and technology, probably constitute the largest single collection of such materials in the U.S. Important too are the holdings of
the Smithsonian Institution. Medicine and agriculture have often played
an important role in the development of science and technology. The
National Library of Medicine has extensive holdings of published works,
as well as an excellent rare book and archival collection, in the history
of medicine and public health. The National Agricultural Library has
vast holdings of printed materials relating to agriculture, including
agricultural science, technology, enterprise, and public policy. The
National Archives contain many of the records of Federal agencies which
have had a scientific or technological mission or component (e.g., the
Children's Bureau).

There are other significant repositories of archival materials for
the history of science and technology. Several leading universities,
notably Pennsylvania, Harvard, Yale, Columbia, and the Bancroft Library
of the University of California at Berkeley, have important collections.
In addition, since the 1960s many universities and colleges have established institutional archival collection programs to preserve the papers
of prominent faculty, alumni, and benefactors. Often the institutional
records of the institution itself, such as the minutes of the trustees
or the official papers of the presidents and other key administrators,
or even the files of important research institutes, will have been preserved. In other instances, such materials exist but the local archival

program has not had the support necessary to acquire and process them. Also to be mentioned in this regard are the many oral history interviews of the Oral History Collection of Columbia University, which contains a small but significant number of interviews with Columbia faculty, scientists, and policy makers; see Elizabeth B. Mason and Louis M. Starr, eds., The Oral History Collection of Columbia University (New York: Oral History Research Office, 1979). New interviews are being deposited all the time, and presumably there will be updated guides published from time to time.

Unfortunately there is no general composite guide to archival holdings in the fields of history of science and technology in America. It is more likely that scientists or doctors who taught at academic institutions would have their papers preserved than such individuals as inventors and engineers. The researcher may have to pore over the massive volumes of the National Union Catalog of Manuscript Collections to find collections. Since reporting to NUCMC is necessarily voluntary, and since many repositories are seriously underfunded, given their responsibilities, the researcher should not interpret the lack of an entry for a particular individual as meaning there are no papers. They may be in private hands (especially if the individual was an entrepreneur or worked in the private sector) or they may be in a repository but not yet reported. The best technique, which is time-consuming, is to trace the individual's life history and inquire at likely institutions, and if necessary, contact the person's living family members. Such biographical directories as American Men of Science (1906-) may help, but often more useful is Who's Who. Researchers interested in inventions and inventors should also use U.S. patent applications. Scholars working in the field may also be able to help.

This does not exhaust the list of significant repositories in the field. The Library of the American Philosophical Society, Philadelphia, has rich collections for the history of science in general before 1900 as well as numerous major collections in the history of genetics. The

Rockefeller Archive Center, Pocantico Hills, North Tarrytown, New York
has wonderfully rich collections relating to the history of Rockefeller
philanthropy and the sciences those philanthropies supported. Other
noteworthy repositories include the Center for the History of Chemistry,
University of Pennsylvania, which has major collections of archival materials and books; the Center for the History of Electrical Engineering,
Institution of Electrical and Electronic Engineers, 345 E. 47th Street,
New York, New York, 10017; and the Center for the History of Physics,
American Institute of Physics, 335 E. 45th Street, New York, New York,
10017. It is often difficult to find archival materials of business corporations and engineers, but the Eleutherian Mills-Historical Library
has many collections and other materials relating to the economic, business
and technological history of the Mid-Atlantic region, including the papers
of many key corporations and national trade associations. The Library
is associated with the doctoral program at the University of Delaware.
The Archives of the History of American Psychology, University of Akron,
Akron, Ohio is a significant repository in a specialized field, as is
the Archives of Psychiatry, Oscar Diethelm Historical Library, of the
Department of Psychiatry at the New York Hospital-Cornell Medical College
in New York City.

The secondary literature of the history of science and technology
is so vast as to be considered virtually unmanageable. No guide can be
comprehensive, although Eugene S. Ferguson's Bibliography of the History
of Technology (Cambridge, Mass.: MIT Press, 1968) covers a wide variety
of works including bibliographies, biographies, encyclopedias, periodicals,
and guides to manuscripts. Researchers should be aware of the large "practitioner literature," that is, historical or quasi-historical accounts
of the sciences and technologies written by leading figures in the respective fields. This genre is of widely varying quality and utility for
researchers. Chaff abounds. Researchers should not ignore, however,
some of the "life and letters" volumes, which often preserve facts and

points of view difficult to obtain elsewhere, especially for the 19th century, but they must be read with a critical eye. Sometimes the practitioners wrote reasonably substantial efforts, as, for example, economist Joseph Dorfman's The Economic Mind in American Civilization (New York: Viking, 1947-56), E. G. Boring's History of Experimental Psychology, 2nd ed. (New York: Appleton-Century-Crofts, 1950), or Robert R. Sears, Your Ancients Revisited: A History of Child Development (Chicago: University of Chicago Press, 1975). Often such works have bibliographies as well which contain references not easily found elsewhere.

Bibliographical guides exist. The official journal of the History of Science Society, Isis (1913-), publishes an annual critical bibliography issue. Technology and Culture (1959-), the official journal of the Society for the History of Technology, publishes a current bibliography, by year, for the history of technology. The National Library of Medicine publishes a very useful annual Bibliography of the History of Medicine (1964-). All of these have an "international" focus. Such guides cannot be complete, given the enormous quantity of material published every year, and researchers may wish to consult a variety of other guides, including the appropriate sections of such journals as the Journal of American History; the Journal of Southern History; America: History and Life; Biological Abstracts; Index Medicus; and Chemical Abstracts, among others.

In the last two decades the history of American science and technology has attracted growing numbers of historians, and a modern monographic literature has emerged. Researchers may find the following historiographical volume of interest: Sally Gregory Kohlstedt and Margaret W. Rossiter, eds., Historical Writing on American Science: Perspectives and Prospects, Osiris, Second Series, Volume 1, August 1985. Osiris is the now-revived monograph journal of the History of Science Society. No comparable historiographical volume exists for American technology. Researchers may be interested in three publications of the Agricultural History Center, University of California, Davis: G. Terry Sharrer, comp.,

1568

<u>1001 References for the History of American Food Technology</u> (1978); Vivian
B. Whitehead, comp., <u>A List of References for the History of Agricultural
Technology</u> (1979); and Margaret W. Rossiter, comp., <u>A List of References
for the History of Agricultural Science in America</u> (1980).

Finally, there is no substitute for reading what the scientists
and engineers themselves wrote about their work. Fortunately for
researchers, much can be done with the various scientific and technological
journals published in the United States; many of these are located in
academic libraries and in major public libraries. In turn many such journals carried information about the individuals in their technical communities, and published "state of the art" essays from time to time. Among
journals of general interest are <u>Scientific American</u> (1845-), which carried
much information about technology in the 19th century; <u>Science</u> (1880-),
which attempted to speak for the scientific and technical community in
society more generally; and, for the late 19th century, <u>Popular Science
Monthly</u> (1871-1915) was a remarkable guide to the "religion" of science
and technology in American civilization and culture. The history of science and technology in America, as a field or fields of self-conscious
professional study, is still quite new as compared with other areas of
interest to American Studies and American history. Hence many of the
tools and conveniences that older fields possess do not yet exist; often
researchers must improvise as they proceed.

Hamilton Cravens
Program in History of
Technology and Science
Iowa State University

STM 1. ABRAHAMS, HAROLD J. and MARION B. SAVIN, eds. Selections from
        the Scientific Correspondence of Elihu Thomson. Cambridge, Mass.:
        MIT Press, 1971. 569 pp.
In 1880 Elihu Thomson (1853-1937) and his colleague Edwin J. Houston
founded a company to market an arc lighting system of generators, lamps,
and accessories. The Thomson-Houston Electric Company became a leading
manufacturer in the nascent electric lighting industry and merged with
the Edison General Electric Company in 1892 to form the General Electric
Company, with Thomson remaining as consultant. Drawing mainly from the
Thomson Correspondence at the American Philosophical Society Library,
Abrahams and Savin have selected and annotated over 300 letters which
provide a sense of Thomson's role in electrical invention and the electrical industry in the late 19th and early 20th centuries. Thomson's
wide-ranging correspondence with physicists, electrical engineers, industrial scientists, fellow inventors, and business associates illustrates
the diverse technical interests of a major American inventor-entrepreneur.

STM 2. ACHENBAUM, W. ANDREW. Old Age in the New Land: The American Experi-
        ence Since 1790. Baltimore, Md.: Johns Hopkins University Press,
        1978. 237 pp.
Achenbaum argues that there have been marked shifts in perceptions of
the elderly as well as in elderly life since 1790, but he suggests that
responses of and toward the aged in America occur in direct response to
cultural attitudes. He discusses rhetorics which valorize old age as
well as those which denigrate it, and also presents discussions of demographic and socioeconomic aspects of old age in America. He describes
how in the 20th century Social Security was created as a response to the
"problem" of old age, and discusses changes in the conditions of the
elderly since Social Security.

STM 3. AITKEN, HUGH G. J. Syntony and Spark: The Origins of Radio.
        New York: Wiley, 1976. 347 pp.
Aitken's history of radio in America begins with the contributions of
Clerk Maxwell in the 1860s, discusses those of Hertz and Sir Oliver Lodge,
and concludes with Marconi's work. He surrounds his technical history
with essays that discuss the interrelationship of science, technology,
and economic affairs.

STM 4. AITKEN, HUGH G. J. Taylorism and the Watertown Arsenal: Scientific
        Management in Action, 1908-1915. Cambridge, Mass.: Harvard Uni-
        versity Press, 1960. 269 pp.
In 1909 the Ordinance Department of the U.S. Army decided to introduce
at its Watertown, Massachusetts arsenal Frederick Taylor's comprehensive system of scientific management, which, Aitken emphasizes,
included a rational and systematic approach to production problems, new
tools and machinery, new factory organization, new cost accounting techniques, and time studies of work. Between 1909 and 1911, Taylor's col-
laborator, Carl Barth, and the Ordinance Department introduced mechanical
improvements into the machine shop and set the stage for time studies,
but failed to prepare the foundry workers for the time studies. Resistant
to change and especially to a speed-up, the workers spontaneously went
out on strike. This produced a Congressional investigation and a ban
on time studies and incentive pay in government contracted work. In investigating the goals and perceptions of all parties to the controversy,
Aitken provides a case study of the reaction to scientific management
in America.

STM 5. **AKIN, WILLIAM E.** Technocracy and the American Dream: The Technocrat Movement, 1900-1941. Berkeley: University of California
Press, 1977. 227 pp.
Akin, unlike previous historians, attributes the origins of technocracy
to the emphasis of Americans of Progressive persuasion upon efficiency,
expertise, and centralized planning and administration, and also to the
engineering profession's search for an occupational identity, the scientific management movement, and the ideas of Thorstein Veblen. After discussing origins and several leading personalities, Akin traces the movement
from its peak years in 1932 and 1933, when it offered an alternative social
organization, through its period of fragmentation and subsequent decline.
Some adherents turned to Keynesian economics or to radical political movements, while others joined Howard Scott's Technocracy, Inc. Akin argues
that the movement declined because it lacked a viable theory of political
action. However, he notes that the modern centralized post-industrial
state, administered by a meritocratic elite of trained experts, bears
a striking resemblance to the Progressive conception from which technocracy
evolved.

STM 6. **ALLEN, GARLAND E.** Life Science in the Twentieth Century. New
York: Wiley, 1975. 258 pp.
Allen provides an introduction to some of the major recurrent ideas in
the discipline of the life sciences in America during the 20th century,
including the elaboration of "classic" Mendelism, population genetics,
and conceptions of DNA. The book focuses on theories of embryonic development, inheritance, evolution, biochemistry, and molecular biology. Allen's
primary theme is that there has been a shift in biological scientific
ideas from the 19th to the 20th centuries: descriptive natural history,
speculative evolutionary theory, and mechanistic physiology have been
influenced by physical and chemical theories.

STM 7. **ALLEN, GARLAND E.** Thomas Hunt Morgan: The Man and His Science.
Princeton, N.J.: Princeton University Press, 1978. 447 pp.
In this biography, Garland Allen assesses the personal life and professional career of Thomas Hunt Morgan (1866-1945), a major figure in the
history of modern American biology. Allen uses Morgan's career as a vehicle to analyze the naturalist-experimentalist dichotomy in the history
of modern biology. He also describes the variety of institutional settings
in which Morgan worked, including the Naples Zoological Station; the Marine
Biological Laboratory at Woods Hole; the famous "fly room" at Columbia
University, where Morgan and his colleagues studied Drosophila to establish
the principles of the Mendelian-chromosome theory of heredity; and the
Division of Biological Sciences at the California Institute of Technology,
which Morgan organized in 1928. Morgan is portrayed as the leading expon-
ent of a new experimental, quantitative approach to biology. Allen argues
that this methodology was an important element of later research in bio-
chemical and molecular genetics.

STM 8. **ANDERSON, OSCAR E.**, Jr. The Health of a Nation: Harvey Wiley
and the Fight for Pure Food. Chicago: University of Chicago
Press, 1958. 332 pp.
Harvey Washington Wiley (1844-1930) was Chief Chemist of the U.S. Department of Agriculture from 1883 to 1912 and a central figure in the political
struggle for the first Federal Pure Food and Drug Act (1906). Anderson
presents Wiley as the archetypal government scientist, a man equally adept
at dealing with professional colleagues, industrial clients, and congressional committees. Wiley's contributions to the domestic sugar industry and his campaign against food adulterants during the 1880s and 1890s
are discussed against the background of Washington politics. Anderson
details Wiley's role in the Progressive campaign against food adulteration.
He concludes with a discussion of Wiley's career after resigning from

public service in 1912 to become a "propagandist for pure foods" in Good
Housekeeping magazine.

STM 9. ANDERSON, OSCAR E., Jr. Refrigeration in America: A History
of a New Technology and Its Impact. Princeton, N.J.: Princeton
University Press, 1953. 344 pp.
Anderson provides a history of refrigeration technology in the U.S.,
relates it to general American history, and describes its social, agricultural, and industrial impact. Americans began exporting natural ice to
the Caribbean in the 1790s, but significant changes in the industry came
only after 1830, when changed eating habits increased demand. Urbanization
in the period from 1860 to 1890 stimulated a search for practical mechanical methods of producing ice, and these methods began to prevail after
1890. Mechanical refrigeration enabled the transportation and storage
of foods needed by growing urban centers, but there was substantial opposition to the cold storage of food before W.W. I. After the war, marked diet
changes helped popularize individual home refrigerating units. Anderson
also discusses refrigerated transportation, frozen foods, rural refrigeration, and various uses of refrigeration in industry.

STM 10. ARCHER, GLEASON L. History of Radio to 1926. New York: American
Historical Society, 1938. 421 pp.
Archer surveys early long-distance communications systems, then details
the evolution of radio. He describes pre-W.W. I technical developments, patent litigation, and attempts to arouse public interest. The
entrance of the U.S. into W.W. I brought Navy control of all American wireless stations and removed patent infringement barriers
impeding radio development. Archer describes the wartime and postwar
struggle for American predominance in wireless communication and the formation in 1919 of the Radio Corporation of America (RCA) to unify American
radio communications, to pool patents held by American Telephone and Telegraph, General Electric, and Westinghouse, and to act as a sales agency
for their radio equipment. He then describes the radio boom of the early
1920s, the development of radio broadcast stations and programming, and
the struggle for control of the industry. Archer ends his account in
1926, when the industry was on the verge of crisis and in great need of
national regulation.

STM 11. ARMSTRONG, DAVID A. Bullets and Bureaucrats: The Machine Gun
and the United States Army, 1861-1916. Westport, Conn.: Greenwood Press, 1982. 239 pp.
Armstrong begins his study of the U.S. Army's failure to put the
machine gun to effective use prior to W.W. I by observing that
"organized development of new weapons and methods of employing them is
a recent phenomenon." He challenges the assertion made by some that the
American Civil War led to innovations in military technology: inventions
(with the exception of the Gatling gun) were not utilized, he claims.
Congressional statutes limiting the size and finances of the Army
during the period after the Civil War, Armstrong argues, inhibited military
exploitation of the machine gun. Only W.W. I, he continues, forced
the Army's bureaucracy to recognize that technology had changed the nature
of battle and to develop a "doctrine and organization" for using the
machine gun.

STM 12. BADASH, LAWRENCE. Radioactivity in America: Growth and Decay
of a Science. Baltimore, Md.: Johns Hopkins University Press,
1979. 327 pp.
Badash describes the European origins of the history of radioactivity,
its reception in America, and the development of the concept by chemists
Bertram Boltwood and Herbert McCoy. He then describes how the study of
radioactivity has moved in two directions: toward the development of

1573

radiochemistry and to atomic and nuclear physics. His study covers the period between 1900 and 1920.

STM 13. BAIER, KURT and NICHOLAS RESCHER, eds. Values and the Future: The Impact of Technological Change on American Values. New York: Free Press, 1969. 527 pp.
This collection of seventeen essays represents a philosophical approach to questions of value-related technological innovations (such as computers), the social trends they can affect, the economic trends which influence and are influenced by technology, and the changing values of social groups affected by technological change. Contributors include Kenneth Boulding, John Kenneth Galbraith, Alvin Toffler, and David Lewis.

STM 14. BALDWIN, RICHARD S. The Fungus Fighters: Two Women Scientists and Their Discovery. Ithaca, N.Y.: Cornell University Press, 1981. 212 pp.
Baldwin describes the discovery of nystatin, an anti-fungal agent, at the Albany laboratory of the New York State Department of Health. Elizabeth Hazen, a microbiologist, enlisted organic chemist Rachel Brown in her efforts to extract and chemically define the substance from soil samples. Baldwin's case study in medical research emphasizes the two women's self-lessness in putting the proceeds of their work into the further development of nystatin (named for New York State).

STM 15. BANNISTER, ROBERT C. Social Darwinism: Science and Myth in Anglo-American Social Thought. Philadelphia: Temple University Press, 1979. 292 pp.
Bannister's study of Social Darwinism in America and England argues that Darwinism was not widely used by conservative reformers, and that most thinkers rejected the concept as unreliable and misguided. The "myth" of Social Darwinism arose in response to a cultural need for an explanation of 19th-century rampant individualistic and economic growth.

STM 16. BARITZ, LOREN. The Servants of Power; A History of the Use of Social Science in American Industry. Middletown, Conn.: Wesleyan University Press, 1960. 273 pp.
Baritz offers a study of the uses of social science in American industry. His general theme is that social scientists who work for industry have begun to learn how to control the conduct of employees. Chapters discuss such issues as the development of industrial psychology in the early 20th century, the growing interest of business managers in the new social sciences (particularly Ford Motor Company officials), and the function of intelligence and personality tests. Also considered are the activities of such "applied" social scientists as Hugo Munsterberg and Walter Dill Scott, the famous Hawthorne experiments, and the contributions of such social scientists as Elton Mayo to the development of "managerial sociology."

STM 17. BATES, RALPH S. Scientific Societies in the United States. 1945; Rev. ed. Cambridge, Mass.: MIT Press, 1965. 326 pp.
Bates presents the collective history of scientific and technical societies in the U.S., stressing the role these organizations have played in the coordination and stimulation of research. Bates deals with the 18th-century foundations (chiefly the American Philosophical Society and the American Academy of Arts and Sciences), the establishment of state and local academies of science and early specialist societies in the ante-bellum period, and the first attempts at centralizing science through national institutions. Bates views the proliferation of national societies in the late 19th century as the "triumph of specialization." The final chapters treat the coordination of scientific and technological activities in the 20th century through national scientific councils and government

agencies, as well as U.S. participation in international bodies like UNESCO. The book concludes with a chronology of U.S. science and technology and a comprehensive bibliography of sources on American scientific societies.

STM 18. BATHE, GREVILLE and DOROTHY BATHE. Oliver Evans: A Chronicle of Early American Engineering. Philadelphia: Historical Society of Pennsylvania, 1935. 362 pp.
The authors discuss Evans's improvements in milling, his efforts at building steam engines, and his involvement in lawsuits over patent rights. Evans was, the Bathes argue, the first engineer who believed that people could be transported by steam engines, though he was unable to pursue the development of the steam locomotive because of lack of funds. This biography also includes many documents and letters.

STM 19. BAXTER, JAMES PHINNEY, III. Scientists Against Time. Boston: Little, Brown, 1946. 473 pp.
Baxter's book is a history of the U.S. Office of Scientific Research and Development (OSRD), established by President Roosevelt in June 1941 to coordinate American defense research. Directed by MIT electrical engineer Vannevar Bush, OSRD facilitated contacts between military planners, government laboratories, and university and industrial scientists and engineers. OSRD was responsible for the mobilization of civilian scientists and, on the advice of the National Defense Research Committee and the Committee on Medical Research, contracted with university and industrial laboratories for the development of new weapons and medicines. Aided by the unprecedented amount of funds available for war research, OSRD made rapid breakthroughs in radar, proximity fuses, chemical warfare, anti-malarials, and penicillin. OSRD activities culminated in the Manhattan Project and the development of the atomic bomb. Baxter treats the role science and technology played in strategic decisions, the administrative tensions between civilian scientists and the military, and the technical contributions of physics, chemistry, and medical research to the war effort.

STM 20. BEALL, OTHO T., Jr., and RICHARD HARRISON SHRYOCK. Cotton Mather: First Significant Figure in American Medicine. Baltimore, Md.: Johns Hopkins University Press, 1954. 241 pp.
Beall and Shryock aim not only to reclaim Mather as a founder of American medicine but to examine pre-Enlightenment medical thought in the Colonies. Drawing significantly on Mather's one explicitly medical work, The Angel of Bethesda (selections of which are reprinted in an appendix), the authors find that Mather's work derived inspiration from both science and Christianity, and contains many prescient ideas, particularly in the area of preventive medicine.

STM 21. BEARDSLEY, EDWARD H. Harry L. Russell and Agricultural Science in Wisconsin. Madison: University of Wisconsin Press, 1969. 237 pp.
This biography of Harry L. Russell illuminates the development of agricultural science in America during the 20th century. According to Beardsley, Russell exemplifies the abrupt shift in the late 19th century away from a combination of laboratory and field testing in agricultural science to a reliance on laboratory studies in conjunction with the land-grant experimental station. At the University of Wisconsin, Russell and his associates and students conducted experiments dealing with animal nutrition and vitamins, and were at the forefront of such discoveries as bovine tuberculosis and the butterfat test for Wisconsin cheeses.

STM 22. BEARDSLEY, EDWARD H. The Rise of the American Chemistry Profession, 1850-1900. Gainesville: University of Florida Press, 1964. 76 pp.
This short monograph is the only available survey of the social and institutional history of the 19th-century American chemical community. Beardsley begins his account with the expanding educational opportunities for chemists in America from the mid-1840s to the late 1870s, after the establishment of scientific schools and land-grant colleges. He then discusses the German training of a generation of American chemists and their attempts to organize laboratories and scientific studies on the German model after their return. The next two chapters deal with the development of chemical journals and chemical societies, two important elements of professional culture. The final chapter illustrates the varied occupational niches available by the turn of the century for chemists in government, industry, and academe.

STM 23. BEAVER, DONALD deB. The American Scientific Community, 1800-1860: A Statistical-Historical Study. New York: Arno Press, 1980. 379 pp.
Beaver begins by describing the new historiographic method he has devised and then proceeds to apply this method in an analysis of the American scientific community during the early 19th century. Beaver explains that although the scientific community barely existed in the U.S. at the beginning of this period, it grew rapidly and became organized—scientific journals and societies were established. Beaver, by tabulating the number of papers published in scientific journals by different scientists, creates a hierarchical ordering of scientists—a list which he claims can be used not only to study changes within the scientific community but also to compare that community to other professions or the population in general. He discovers "a correlation between the writing of many papers and scientific eminence."

STM 24. BEDINI, SILVIO A. The Life of Benjamin Banneker. New York: Scribner, 1972. 434 pp.
Benjamin Banneker (1731-1806) was a famous member of the community of "mathematical practitioners" in Colonial America. A landed freeman and tobacco planter, Banneker was introduced to astronomy and surveying during the 1780s, learning from the popular Newtonian texts of the period with the help of his neighbor George Ellicott. Banneker mastered methods for the calculation of ephemerides and incorporated his results in a series of almanacs published in Philadelphia, Baltimore, and other Eastern cities between 1791 and 1796. During 1791 he served as astronomical assistant on the survey of the District of Columbia directed by Andrew Ellicott. Using all extant records concerning Banneker's life and a wide variety of other sources, Bedini has reconstructed the intellectual and social environment in which Banneker worked.

STM 25. BEDINI, SILVIO A. Thinkers and Tinkers: Early American Men of Science. New York: Scribner, 1975. 520 pp.
Bedini concentrates on the neglected accomplishments of the "little men of science" whose practical achievements in new instruments and techniques were important contributions to early American scientific culture. Bedini has constructed a detailed account of the mathematical practitioners movement in 17th- and 18th-century America, a diverse community of mapmakers, surveyors, navigators, makers of mathematical instruments, part-time science teachers, and philomaths. The emergence of formal technical training in the lectures, academies, museums, and other new scientific institutions of the Federal and Jacksonian periods helps to explain the demise of the movement.

STM 26. BELL, WHITFIELD J., Jr. The Colonial Physician and Other Essays.
New York: Science History, 1975. 229 pp.
This volume is a collection of fifteen of Bell's essays and notes on medical historiography and the history of early American medicine, originally
published between 1940 and 1973. Two widely cited papers in the volume
are the title essay, "A Portrait of the Colonial Physician" (1970), and
"Philadelphia Medical Students in Europe, 1750-1800" (1943). These essays
portray the structure of medical practice in Colonial America and the
educational route--apprenticeship followed by sojourns in Edinburgh and
London--taken by ambitious recruits to the medical profession at that
time. The Colonial Physician also includes biographical sketches of the
medical men John Redman (1722-1808), Thomas Parke (1749-1835), and James
Hutchinson (1752-1793), and an account of how Bell tracked down documents
for his biography of John Morgan, Continental Doctor (Philadelphia: University of Pennsylvania Press, 1965).

STM 27. BELL, WHITFIELD J., Jr. Early American Science: Needs and Opportunities for Study. Williamsburg, Va.: Institute of Early American History and Culture, 1955. 85 pp.
In this monograph, Bell surveys the history and historiography of early
American science and points to areas for further research. He suggests
that biographical studies of American men of science should include the
physicians, amateurs, patrons, and European correspondents who contributed
to the pursuit of science in early America. Bell notes the need for
studies of individual sciences, including surveying and exploration; scientific education before 1820; the relations of science and government; and
the diffusion of scientific knowledge through publications, learned societies, and museums. The book includes an extensive bibliography of general
history of science, the history of science in America to 1820, and works
relating to fifty early American scientists from Benjamin Smith Burton
to James Woodhouse.

STM 28. BEZILLA, MICHAEL. Electric Traction on the Pennsylvania Railroad,
1895-1968. University Park: Pennsylvania State University Press,
1980. 233 pp.
Bezilla has attempted to integrate "the diverse technological, economic,
political, social, and, yes, romantic elements of railway electrification
into a coherent, readable account." The Pennsylvania was one of a dozen
American railroads which converted portions of their lines from steam
to electrical operation in the late 19th century. The bulk of the text
deals with cost and other factors which caused most other railroads to
avoid electrification up until the introduction of diesel-electric locomotives before W.W. II.

STM 29. BILLINGTON, DAVID P. The Tower and the Bridge: The New Art of
Structural Engineering. New York: Basic Books, 1983. 306 pp.
Billington proposes that structural art--an engineering art form which
is, like photography, an Industrial Revolution art form--is "parallel
to and fully independent of architecture." The history of structural
art, he claims, has two major periods: The first begins with the Iron
Bridge (1779) and ends with the Eiffel Tower (1889); the second period
is marked by developments arising out of the use of steel-reinforced concrete from the late 19th century to the present. Drawing his examples
not only from the U.S. but also from France, England, Scotland, Switzerland,
and Italy, Billington concentrates upon those pioneering engineers who,
he states, combined economy with elegance. He also claims that structures
of metal and concrete (such as the Eiffel Tower and the Brooklyn Bridge)
are democratic rather than autocratic, exhibiting a "lightness . . . which
parallels the essence of a free and open society."

STM 30. BILSTEIN, ROGER E. Flight Patterns: Trends of Aeronautical
Development in the United States. Athens: University of Georgia
Press, 1983. 236 pp.
Bilstein's general thesis is that the 1920s formed a watershed in the
advance of aviation in the U.S. Discussed in this context are the first
air mail flights, government regulation of aircraft, and the development
of aeronautical technology. In addition, Bilstein demonstrates how aviation was integrated into the music, art, literature, film, and Feminism
of the 1920s.

STM 31. BIRR, KENDALL. Pioneering in Industrial Research: The Story
of the General Electric Research Laboratory. Washington, D.C.:
Public Affairs Press, 1957. 204 pp.
Although industrial research laboratories have become increasingly important in the 20th century, Birr's remains one of the few histories of the
subject. Birr provides an institutional history of one of the first and
most successful research laboratories in American history. After describing the roots of industrial research in the 19th century, Birr traces
the development of the General Electric Research Laboratory from its establishment in 1901 to its post-W.W. II reorganization. He presents a
detailed history of the laboratory's organization and administration which
so effectively shifted scientific interests and produced scientific discoveries and technical inventions.

STM 32. BLAKE, JOHN B. Public Health in the Town of Boston, 1630-1822.
Cambridge, Mass.: Harvard University Press, 1959. 278 pp.
The author begins with an overview of public health and the 17th century.
He then discusses such issues in Boston public health as the inoculation
controversy of 1721-2, the impact of yellow fever and the development
of quarantine, and the city's later struggles with smallpox at the end
of the century. By 1822, the beginnings of the sanitary reform movement
were in place. Blake argues that the history of Boston's public health
is significant for the whole of the American experience.

STM 33. BLANTON, WYNDHAM BOLLING. Medicine in Virginia in the Eighteenth
Century. Richmond, Va.: Garrett & Massie, 1931. 449 pp.
Blanton's survey of medical history in Virginia argues that the end of
the 18th century saw the rise of a truly American medicine, as hospitals
and medical societies developed and Americans made contributions to the
knowledge of inoculation and the behavior of certain epidemic diseases.
Blanton discusses such topics as plantation medicine, medical care during
the Revolutionary War, medical quackery, and health legislation.

STM 34. BONNER, THOMAS N. American Doctors and German Universities:
A Chapter in International Intellectual Relations, 1870-1914.
Lincoln: University of Nebraska Press, 1963. 210 pp.
This book examines the migration of American medical men to Germany and
the German-speaking universities of Switzerland and Austria-Hungary before
W.W. I. Attracted by the atmosphere of Lernfreiheit and unparalleled
opportunities for laboratory research and clinical training, an estimated
15,000 American medical students attended twenty-eight German-speaking
universities between 1870 and 1914. Bonner discusses patterns of migration
and American medical student life in Germany; the state of clinical specialties such as dermatology, ophthalmology, and obstetrics in the medical
communities of Vienna and Berlin; and the impact of German models and
practices on the development of the basic medical sciences in the U.S.
By the 1890s, American research facilities and postgraduate medical education had become competitive with German institutions, a point acknowledged by the visiting German physicians whose opinions are considered
in Bonner's penultimate chapter.

STM 35. BONNER, THOMAS N. Medicine in Chicago 1850-1950. Madison, Wis.:
     American History Research Center, 1957. 302 pp.
The author argues that the medical history of Chicago is important for
the history of the city, and that it is useful for studying medical development as well. He addresses such issues in the history of medicine, using
Chicago as an example, as the cost of medical care, the relation of disease
to environment, medical education, the medical profession as a political
force, and public health issues.

STM 36. BOORSTIN, DANIEL. The Republic of Technology: Reflections on
     Our Future Community. New York: Harper & Row, 1978. 105 pp.
This historian's essay argues that scientific innovation has created an
international community that he calls the Republic of Technology. Using
such examples as television, he argues that technology has a universally
democratizing tendency, and can lead to "a world where experience will
be created equal." Boorstin discusses the Constitution as an example
of "political technology," and describes the contributions of American
immigrants in the 1930s and 1940s to the technological revolution.

STM 37. BOSK, CHARLES L. Forgive and Remember: Managing Medical Failure.
     Chicago: University of Chicago Press, 1979. 236 pp.
Bosk, a sociologist, acted for eighteen months as participant/observer
of the surgical training program at Pacific Hospital in order to study
the reactions of individual surgeons and the medical community to surgical
failure, the institutional structure of surgical training, and the professionalization of the surgeon in his or her training. He found that
moral failures were treated more seriously than technical ones, and that
responses to failure play a large part in the surgeon's definition of
self and profession. Although a sociological study, Bosk's book is descriptive of the American medical profession, its training, and its institutional structure.

STM 38. BOYD, THOMAS ALVIN. Professional Amateur: The Biography of
     Charles Franklin Kettering. New York: Dutton, 1957. 242 pp.
Charles Kettering invented the electric cash register, the modern system
of battery ignition, and the electric self-starter, and he directed industrial research for General Motors. Thomas Boyd, a long-time member of
Kettering's research staff, first recounts Kettering's childhood, early
work experience, and education as background to his inventive activity.
Kettering worked until 1909 in the National Cash Register Company's development department and then founded his own research company, Delco, which
concentrated on inventions for the automotive industry. Boyd describes
several of Kettering's important automative innovations before and during
W.W. I. Finally, Boyd describes Kettering's work after 1920 as vice-
president of research for General Motors, where he presided over the
development of tetraethyl lead and "Ethyl" gasoline, high compression
engines, and the two-cycle Diesel engine.

STM 39. BOZEMAN, THEODORE D. Protestants in an Age of Science: The Bacon-
     ian Ideal and Antebellum American Religious Thought. Chapel
     Hill: University of North Carolina Press, 1977. 243 pp.
This study of the impact of natural science on religious thinking concentrates on the Protestant American proponents of Baconianism in the 19th
century. The author argues that the Scottish strain in American
Protestantism—or Presbyterianism—was as influential as Transcendentalism,
and that 19th-century Americans were comforted by the links between science
and religion that the Baconian approach offered.

STM 40. BRANCA, PATRICIA, ed. The Medicine Show: Patients, Physicians, and the Perplexities of the Health Revolution in Modern Society. New York: Science History, 1977. 280 pp.
This collection of essays is representative of the various methodological approaches historians of medicine have taken, a topic Gerald Grob explores in the first essay; generally, however, the essays are social histories of such topics as 18th-century hospitals, middle-class women and health reform in the 19th century, and mortality among slave children. Contributors include Paul Starr, Regina Morantz, Charles Rosenberg, and Arthur Imhof.

STM 41. BRANDON, RUTH. A Capitalist Romance: Singer and the Sewing Machine. Philadelphia: Lippincott, 1977. 244 pp.
Brandon's biography of Singer not only traces the course of his life and his founding of the I. M. Singer Co., but documents as well the social history of the era, describing the "sewing machine wars" between Hunt, Howe, and Singer, and the social effects of the machine. She argues that Singer's success was representative of the immigrant rags-to-riches story, and that he was viewed by the public as a capitalist hero.

STM 42. BRIEGER, GERT H., ed. Medical America in the Nineteenth Century: Readings from the Literature. Baltimore, Md.: Johns Hopkins University Press, 1972. 338 pp.
This volume is a selection of source documents on the history of the medical profession and public health in the U.S. during the 19th century. Drawn from both medical journals and the general periodical press, they range from Benjamin Rush's "On the Causes of Death in Diseases That Are Not Incurable" (1811) to the "Announcement of the Johns Hopkins Medical School (1893)," the harbinger of a new era in American medicine. The readings are grouped under the headings of medical education, medical literature, the medical profession, medical practice, surgery, psychiatry, hospitals, and hygiene. Brieger has added introductory notes to each section, as well as editorial notes on each selection.

STM 43. BRIEGER, GERT H., ed. Theory and Practice in American Medicine. New York: Science History, 1976. 272 pp.
This is a collection of essays from the Journal of the History of Medicine and Allied Sciences. Included are essays by Charles Rosenberg on the dispensary, Gerald Grob on the mental hospital, Phyllis Allen Richmond on germ theory, and John B. Blake on Colonial smallpox inoculation. In his introduction, Brieger discusses historiographical issues raised by work in this field.

STM 44. BRIGHT, ARTHUR AARON, Jr. The Electric-Lamp Industry: Technological Change and Economic Development from 1800 to 1947. New York: Macmillan, 1947. 526 pp.
Bright provides an account of the evolution of the electric lighting industry by focusing on the lamp, the most important variable in lighting quality. First, he surveys lighting from 1800 to 1880. Then he provides a more detailed account of the commercial and technological events from 1880 to 1896, the formative period of the industry. He also analyzes technological and structural changes during the years from 1896 to 1912 when electric lighting gained predominance over its arc-lighting and gas competitors. Bright analyzes the monopolistic forces operating from 1912 to 1947 in the industry, the economic and commercial effects of electric lamp patents, new technological developments, such as electric-discharge light sources, and the production and marketing of fluorescent lighting. Finally, he draws conclusions concerning the record of technological progress and argues that General Electric's use of patents to preserve its leading position produced some of the industry's technological inadequacies.

STM 45. BRIGHT, CHARLES D. The Jet Makers: The Aerospace Industry from
         1945 to 1972. Lawrence: Regents Press of Kansas, 1978.
         228 pp.
Bright discusses how Americans managed to emerge in the technological
forefront in the jet industry in the face of great odds. He concentrates
on the "giants" of the industry, those who pioneered in the manufacture
of fixed-wing aircraft: Boeing, Curtiss-Wright, Grumman, Lockheed, and
McDonnell. The Cold War presented a technological challenge to which
the aerospace industry vigorously responded.

STM 46. BROOKS, COURTNEY G., JAMES M. GRIMWOOD, and LOYD S. SWENSON, Jr.
         Chariots for Apollo: A History of Manned Lunar Spacecraft.
         Washington, D.C.: National Aeronautics and Space Administration,
         1979. 538 pp.
The authors begin their well-illustrated history of manned space flight
with the creation of NASA (1958) and the decision to land men on the moon
(1961). Although there were subsequent trips to the moon, they end their
history with Apollo II (1969), the flight during which astronauts visited
the lunar surface for the first time. Their focus is on the spacecraft--
the command, service, and lunar modules--of the Apollo program. The history covers three stages: the definition and design of the vehicles,
their development and certification, and their operation. The authors
pay particular attention to two major problems that faced the Apollo team:
the question of which "mode" (route) ought to be employed and the development of an adequate rocket launching vehicle.

STM 47. BROWN, E. RICHARD. Rockefeller Medicine Men: Medicine and Capi-
         talism in America. Berkeley: University of California Press,
         1979. 283 pp.
Brown's book argues that corporate Capitalism and 20th-century medicine
worked to produce a medical system that is economically discriminatory,
largely inaccessible, and socially irresponsible. He bases his argument
on a historical examination of the development of modern medicine in
America, with its beginnings in the philanthropic and progressive goals
of corporate America and the corresponding impact of these goals on the
medical profession. He contends that Capitalism inevitably shaped the
growth of "scientific medicine," medical education, and public policy.

STM 48. BRUCE, ALFRED W. The Steam Locomotive in America: Its Development
         in the Twentieth Century. New York: Norton, 1952. 443 pp.
Bruce's technical history of steam locomotive design and construction
concentrates on the years between 1901 and 1950, the great age of the
steam locomotive. He is interested in technical details of how the locomotive developed, with specific reference to the transition from steam
cylinder to rails. An introductory chapter on the history of railroads
and a description of the locomotive-building industry are included. Extensive use is made of tables, charts, and other statistical data.

STM 49. BRUCE, ROBERT V. Bell: Alexander Graham Bell and the Conquest
         of Solitude. Boston: Little, Brown, 1973. 564 pp.
Bruce examines Bell's life and especially his invention of the telephone.
Although other accounts stress the electrical aspects of the telephone,
Bruce argues that Bell's understanding of vocal physiology and acoustics
was fundamental to the process of invention. Bell's father and grandfather
taught speech, and Bell used his father's system of phonetic signs to
teach speech to the deaf. After coming to the U.S., Bell attempted in
the 1870s to develop a harmonic multiple-telegraph system to send several
messages over a single wire. While involved in this project, his understanding of the science of sound led him to invent the telephone. Although,
as Bruce points out, Bell was mainly a teacher of the deaf, not a professional inventor like Thomas Edison, he worked on inventions to improve
aircraft, kites, space frame architecture, hydrofoils, and sheep breeding.

STM 50. BRUCE, ROBERT V. Lincoln and the Tools of War. Indianapolis,
         Ind.: Bobbs-Merrill, 1956. 368 pp.
Especially in the early years of his presidency, Abraham Lincoln's enthusiasm for new or improved weapons embraced small arms, light and heavy
artillery, rockets, projectiles, explosives, flame throwers, submarines,
naval armor, and mines. Bruce recounts Lincoln's involvement in the
development of weapons and munitions and describes the struggle over new
weapons between Lincoln and General James W. Ripley, Chief of Army Ordinance, who was more interested in standardizing and regularizing old weapons
and ammunition than procuring new ones. Against the background of the
Civil War, Bruce describes Lincoln's relations with a number of inventors
and his important role in promoting weapons research and development.
Lincoln's powers were not great enough to secure adoption of all his ideas,
but, as Bruce notes, he played an important role in introducing the breech-
loading rifle and the machine gun, to mention only the most important
innovations.

STM 51. BUCK, PETER. American Science and Modern China, 1876-1936. New
         York: Cambridge University Press, 1980. 283 pp.
This comparative history of the introduction of American science into
China in the late 19th and early 20th centuries describes the ways modern
science was promoted in China and those who promoted it. Buck argues
that the conflicts involved in the transmission of scientific principles
reveal misunderstandings about differences in social structure between
the two countries. Buck also discusses the views held by Chinese students
of American science.

STM 52. BURGER, EDWARD J., Jr. Science at the White House: A Political
         Liability. Baltimore, Md.: Johns Hopkins University Press,
         1980. 180 pp.
Burger, a physician and scientist drawing on his experiences as a member
of the supporting staff for the Presidential Science Adviser during the
early 1970s, argues that the relationship between science and the public
policy-making process is fraught with difficulty because scientists and
politicians view things differently: scientists are interested in the
far-reaching implications; politicians, in current and highly visible
issues. He describes the two functions of the presidential science advisory apparatus: "policy making for science" (allocating money for various
kinds of reserach); and "science for policy making" (applying scientific
information, methods, or judgments to decisions about government policy).
This second function, Burger notes, becomes problematic in a democratic
society: the electorate feels threatened by scientific "planning." Burger
illustrates his thesis by examining four "substantive issues": national
health policy, health-related research and development, the environment,
and population control.

STM 53. BURLINGAME, ROGER. Engines of Democracy: Inventions and Society
         in Mature America. New York: Scribner, 1940. 606 pp.
In the first volume (see STM 56) of his survey history of American technology, Burlingame describes technological forces prior to 1865 that tended
to unify the nation. He focuses in this second volume on the social
aspects of several categories of late 19th- and 20th-century American inventions. Improved and new technical systems, such as the telegraph, telephone, railroad, urban water supply, construction techniques, high-speed
rotary printing, and electric power and lighting, helped consolidate American society. Other inventions, such as photography, the phonograph, and
sound films, had a more immediate cultural impact, while new transportation
and communication technologies increased the pace of American life.
Finally, Burlingame discusses the social movements and personalities working to conserve natural resources. He concludes with a discussion of
his central theme--the propensity for technological change to cause social
change.

STM 54. **BURLINGAME, ROGER.** Inventors Behind the Inventor. New York: Harcourt, Brace, 1947. 211 pp.
Burlingame is interested in those little-known inventors whose inventions made other famous inventions possible. Benjamin Franklin, he argues, was "behind them all," and the book begins with a portrait of him. Other inventors discussed include John Fitch, whose steamboats anticipated Fulton's, Joseph Henry, whose developments in telegraphs preceded Morse's; and those people who made Edison's moving pictures possible by the development of celluloid and nitro-cellulose film.

STM 55. **BURLINGAME, ROGER.** Machines that Built America. New York: Harcourt, Brace, 1953. 214 pp.
Burlingame explores what he argues is the uniquely American democratization of technology. Though this is commonly credited to "Yankee ingenuity," the author argues that American inventors often worked against great odds. He believes that mass production, however, could have originated only in America. This general history of technological progress shows how innovation often arose from necessity.

STM 56. **BURLINGAME, ROGER.** March of the Iron Men: A Social History of Union Through Invention. New York: Scribner, 1940. 500 pp.
In this first volume of his survey history of American technology, Burlingame traces the development of invention in the U.S. from the early Colonial period to 1865 and stresses the central role invention played in creating the social patterns of American life. Americans first formed small communities and tried to transplant old world culture. Soon developing skills, Americans produced inventions, such as the Pennsylvania rifle, which enabled them to win both political and technological independence. Burlingame describes a number of American inventions, such as the cotton gin, the Yankee clipper, revolvers, and sewing machines; and he argues that steam power, railroads, and the telegraph played crucial roles in the formation of an expanding American society. Burlingame also sees technology by the 1860s as a dynamic force overwhelming the separation manifest in the Civil War.

STM 57. **BURROW, JAMES G.** AMA: Voice of American Medicine. Baltimore, Md.: Johns Hopkins University Press, 1963. 430 pp.
The small group of physicians who established the American Medical Association (AMA) in 1847 were concerned with improving the standards of medical education and contending with competition from sectarian practitioners. However, the AMA was not politically effective at the national level until after 1900, when internal organizational reforms designed to increase the AMA's influence as a pressure group were instituted. Burrow's history concentrates on AMA response to issues of social policy and public health in the 20th century. He relates the AMA's role in the pure food and drug campaign, 1901-1921; the struggle for a Federal health department during the Progressive Era; and reactions to schemes for compulsory health insurance just before and after W.W. I. Burrow describes changing patterns of medical care and AMA attitudes toward voluntary health insurance, medical education, and other national health policy issues from the 1920s through the 1960s.

STM 58. **BURROW, JAMES G.** Organized Medicine in the Progressive Era: The Move Toward Monopoly. Baltimore, Md.: Johns Hopkins University Press, 1977. 218 pp.
Burrow's study of changes in the medical profession in the Progressive Era argues that physicians, who shared the basic goals of Progressivism, organized in these years and developed a cohesive sense of their profession. The profession began its life as a political force, and developed a public image that was extremely potent, while at the same time it contributed significantly to Progressive crusades for reform.

STM 59. CALHOUN, DANIEL HOVEY. The American Civil Engineer: Origins
and Conflict. Cambridge, Mass.: MIT Press, 1960. 295 pp.
Calhoun describes the development of civil engineering in the period from
the 1770s to 1850s. He argues that the engineering profession hardly
existed before the post-1816 development of large, hierarchically organized
public works such as the New York canal system, in which civil engineers
learned professional skills and roles. Calhoun traces the history of
various canal and railroad projects and the careers of important 19th-
century civil engineers. He shows that the economic panic and depression
of the 1840s raised doubts about the status, work, and professional activities of civil engineers, but that their organizational roles were by then
so well established that reform was difficult. Finally, Calhoun describes
the attempt to found a national association which culminated in 1867 with
the establishment of the American Society of Civil Engineers.

STM 60. CALVERT, MONTE A. The Mechanical Engineer in America, 1830-1910:
Professional Cultures in Conflict. Baltimore, Md.: Johns Hopkins
University Press, 1967. 296 pp.
Calvert, in this widely cited contribution to the history of engineering,
describes the development of the mechanical engineering profession from
its origins in small machine shops to its confrontation with large scale
production technology in bureaucratic business structures in the late
19th century. Calvert describes the social, cultural, and occupational
milieu in which mechanical engineering developed and then analyzes its
growth through engineering schools and professional associations. Finally,
Calvert turns to the changing relationships among mechanical engineers,
other engineers, the public, business, and the bureaucratic industry that
replaced the early, small all-purpose machine shops run by engineer-
entrepreneurs. The central conflict in Calvert's study is between the older
"shop culture" composed of shop-trained gentlemen engineers and the newer
"school culture" made up of engineering school-trained corporate employees.
This was a pioneer sociological study of the profession.

STM 61. CARSON, RACHEL. Silent Spring. Boston: Houghton Mifflin, 1962.
368 pp.
Carson's famous book, which originally appeared serially in The New Yorker,
has been credited with spearheading an international environmentalist
movement. Carson details the pollution of the earth's environment by
pesticides, the most potent and prevalent of which was DDT. She describes
the chemical properties of major pesticides and eloquently details their
effects on water, air, soil, vegetation, and living organisms.

STM 62. CHANDLER, ALFRED D., Jr. The Visible Hand: The Managerial Revolution in American Business. Cambridge, Mass.: Harvard University Press, 1977. 608 pp.
The "visible hand" of Chandler's title stands for management which, he
argues, has replaced Adam Smith's "invisible hand" of market forces as
the force that coordinates the production and distribution of goods within
American modern business enterprise. The shift from financial capitalism
to managerial capitalism became possible, according to Chandler, when
the volume of economic activity reached the point at which administrative
coordination became more efficient than market coordination. In this
history of modern business management (which begins with the era of traditional enterprise before the 1840s and ends with the period following
W.W. II), Chandler also examines the role of technological advances
(cheaper coal, the railroads, the telegraph) without which the managerial
revolution could not have occurred.

STM 63. CHILDS, HERBERT. An American Genius: The Life of Ernest Orlando
Lawrence. New York: Dutton, 1968. 576 pp.
This authorized biography of E. O. Lawrence (1901-1958) emphasizes the
American context of Lawrence's career. Educated in the Midwest, Lawrence
took his Ph.D. at Yale in 1925. Three years later he moved to the University of California, where in 1932, with the help of his student
M. S. Livingston, he constructed a cyclotron capable of accelerating parti-
cles to 1,000,000 electron volts. Lawrence's Radiation Laboratory soon
became an international center for high energy physics, and in 1939 he
received the Nobel Prize for his contributions. Lawrence explored the
medical and industrial applications of artificial radioisotopes, as he
sought foundation support to build bigger and bigger cyclotrons. During
W.W. II, Lawrence directed work on the electro-magnetic separation of
uranium isotopes for the Manhattan Project. In the postwar years, he
was involved in the administrative affairs of the new world of "big science" which his cyclotrons helped to create. Childs provides an account,
based on hundreds of interviews and archival sources, of Lawrence's personal and professional activities.

STM 64. CLARK, MARGARET. Health in the Mexican-American Culture: A Community Study. Berkeley: University of California Press, 1959.
253 pp.
Based on a study of Spanish-speaking persons in San Jose, California,
this work provides "sociocultural information" for health professionals
working with Mexican-Americans. Noting that curing practices are a function of beliefs about the nature of health, Clark states that any medical
system must be understood in relation to other cultural categories--
economics, religion, social relationships, education, family structure,
and language--which she proceeds to examine. Clark concludes that medical
beliefs and practices are gradually changing, folk remedies gradually
giving way, within the Mexican-American community.

STM 65. COCHRANE, REXMOND C. Measures for Progress: A History of the
National Bureau of Standards. Washington, D.C.: National Bureau
of Standards, U.S. Department of Commerce, 1966. 703 pp.
Drawing on the models of the Physikalisch-Technische Reichsanstalt in
Germany and the National Physical Laboratory in Britain, Congress created
the National Bureau of Standards (NBS) in 1901. Under the aggressive
direction of Samuel Wesley Stratton (1901-1922), the NBS was soon conducting fundamental research into physical constants and the properties of
materials and providing thermometric, optical, electrical, and other standards for government agencies, scientific laboratories, and industrial
concerns. Cochrane's official history discusses the Bureau's administration and scientific accomplishments from 1901 to the early 1960s, including
early work on standardization in electricity, railroads, automobiles,
and radio; the 1920s campaign for the elimination of waste in industry;
and military research during W.W. I and W.W. II. Among the appendices
are a biographical sketch of Stratton; a record of NBS appropriations
and other supporting funds, 1902-1955; a roster of NBS administrative,
scientific, and technical staff chiefs, 1905-1960; and a bibliography
of selected publications by NBS staff members.

STM 66. COCHRANE, REXMOND C. The National Academy of Sciences: The First
Hundred Years, 1863-1963. Washington, D.C.: National Academy
of Sciences, 1978. 694 pp.
The National Academy of Sciences (NAS) was created in 1863 as an elite
organization which would provide expert advice to the Federal government
on technical problems. During the 19th century government officials asked
for advice on coinage, weights and measures, the purity of whiskey and
other relatively minor matters. The need for technological mobilization
during W.W. I changed this tentative relationship, and the Federal govern-

ment turned to the newly established National Research Council of the Academy. Since then, the NAS and its members have become increasingly involved in questions of science and public policy. Cochrane's official history details the organizational development and advisory activities of the NAS under successive leaders from Alexander Dallas Bache (1863-1867) to Frederick Seitz (1962-1969). The author also surveys European antecedents of the NAS and earlier American efforts to form a central scientific society. Among the appendices are lists of NAS members, foreign associates, officers, and council members, 1863-1963.

STM 67. COHEN, I. BERNARD. Franklin and Newton. Philadelphia: American
Philosophical Society, 1956. 657 pp.
The purpose of this work is to view the "interaction between the creative scientist and his scientific environment" in order to reveal the nature of scientific thought. Cohen views Newton not for his accomplishments but for his influence on future scientific inquiry, particularly those of Franklin. Though Franklin is rarely viewed as Newtonian, by bringing to light the experimental aspects of Newton's work, Cohen illustrates the influence Newton had on Franklin's work in electricity. Throughout this work the two scientific approaches--the theoretical and the experimental--are contrasted. This work is divided into four sections: part one views the personalities of these two scientists in relation to their scientific thought; part two exposes the contribution of Newton's work to experimental science; part three views the Newtonian works studied by 18th-century scientists and the influence this had on Franklin's concepts on electricity; and part four provides information on these concepts--their reception, use and later influence.

STM 68. COHEN, PATRICIA CLINE. A Calculating People: The Spread of Numer-
acy in Early America. Chicago: University of Chicago Press,
1982. 271 pp.
Cohen points out that Americans began to use statistics and numbers in their customary cultural discourse after the 1820s. The rise of various kinds of counting and statistics in commerce, census reports, politics, and medicine are discussed, together with explanations as to why some counting (for example, the problem of "insanity" among blacks in the 1840 Federal census) was spurious. Ultimately, statistical evaluations inundated both governmental and business spheres, thus reflecting the emergence of a new aspect of American culture.

STM 69. COLE, JONATHAN R. Fair Science: Women in the Scientific Community.
New York: Free Press, 1979. 336 pp.
Cole's study of women in science is based on the premise that the scientific profession is extremely stratified in an inequitable fashion, and that women have suffered from this implicit stratification as well as from overt sex discrimination. He explores gender differences in patterns of scientific productivity, IQ and achievement, employment, and research success. He concludes with a discussion of affirmative action policies.

STM 70. COLEMAN, WILLIAM. Biology in the Nineteenth Century: Problems
of Form, Function, and Transformation. New York: Wiley, 1971.
187 pp.
In this introduction to the development of biology during the 19th century, Coleman concentrates more on the achievements of Europe than on those of the U.S. The contributions of both institutions and individuals are discussed. Specific chapters consider the development of theories about cells, transformation (e.g., evolution), the human sciences, animal physiology, and the rise of Experimentalism in the closing decades of the 19th century.

STM 71. CONDIT, CARL W. American Building Art: The Twentieth Century.
New York: Oxford University Press, 1961. 427 pp.
Condit considers "American building techniques. . . . The chapters correspond to the division of building art into its basic structural types
and the primary structural materials in which they are embodied." He
theorizes that both are the logical and "organic" results of the 19th-
century methods and materials. Condit also discusses the social and economic factors that lie beneath 20th-century innovations and their relevance
to such comparatively recent constructions as concrete dams and "The Metropolitan Parkway." Also included are over 130 plates and extensive notes.

STM 72. CONDIT, CARL W. Chicago, 1910-1929: Building, Planning, and
Urban Technology. Chicago: University of Chicago Press, 1973.
354 pp.
Condit traces the continuing evolution of the physical city of Chicago
in the years between 1910 and 1929. He discusses the Chicago Plan of
1909--the Burnham Plan--which was a landmark in urban history. He argues
that the example of Chicago presents the paradox of a well-planned city
that fails to meet the needs of its inhabitants.

STM 73. CONDIT, CARL W. Chicago, 1930-1970: Building, Planning, and
Urban Technology. Chicago: University of Chicago Press, 1974.
351 pp.
Condit followed his earlier study of urban technology in Chicago with
this work, which details the turning point in urban planning marked by
the Depression and the following war. Condit describes the Century of
Progress exposition in 1933-4, building under the New Deal, the renewal
and reconstruction that followed the war years, and the efforts at transportation reform. This thoroughly illustrated study addresses aspects
of urban planning, public policy and city politics, as well as elements
of urban technology.

STM 74. CONDIT, CARL W. The Port of New York: A History of the Rail
and Terminal System from the Beginnings to Pennsylvania Station.
Chicago: University of Chicago Press, 1980. 456 pp.
Condit's book approaches the issue of the interdependence of transportation
and urban life. He argues that New York City has been uniquely shaped
by its urban "circulation system." This study concentrates on the metropolitan railroad system, and provides detailed studies of Pennsylvania
Station and Grand Central Terminal. The author argues that corporate
structure is less important to the history of the railroad than is the
railroad's relation to the city.

STM 75. CONE, THOMAS E. History of American Pediatrics. Boston: Little,
Brown, 1979. 278 pp.
Cone provides an overview of a neglected area in the history of medicine.
For the period before 1850, when pediatrics emerged as a specialty, he
describes child care and child health with attention to such topics as
the feeding of Colonial children and their common diseases. As pediatrics
developed in the 19th century, infant feeding became a primary concern.
Cone follows the history of pediatrics to the present, and discusses such
contemporary problems as the battered child and sudden infant death syndromes.

STM 76. CONOT, ROBERT. A Streak of Luck. New York: Seaview Books, 1979.
565 pp.
Conot's Edison biography is the first to exploit systematically the vast
collection of material maintained at the old Edison laboratory at West
Orange, New Jersey. Conot examines Edison in a highly critical light,
and focuses upon his personality and personal relations rather than on
his technical achievements. The book is divided into two parts. The

first deals with Edison's childhood and early inventive career, including his work on the telegraph, telephone, phonograph, and electric light and power system. The second part traces his less innovative career after the opening of the Pearl Street central station in the early 1880s until his death in 1931. An appendix contains a list of Edison's patents and an Edison chronology. Conot also provides a reference guide and illustrates his text with two portfolios of photographs.

STM 77. CONSTANT, EDWARD W., II. The Origins of the Turbojet Revolution. Baltimore, Md.: Johns Hopkins University Press, 1980. 311 pp. Constant provides an analysis of the emergence of jet-powered aircraft. The focus of his book is international, not simply American. Early sections consider the general process of technological innovation and change, discussing the so-called "normal technology" of T. S. Kuhn from a non-deterministic point of view. Constant then discusses how reciprocating propeller engines were replaced by turbojet engines, pointing out that a variety of factors were responsible.

STM 78. COOPER, GRACE ROGERS. The Sewing Machine: Its Invention and Development. 1968; Rev. ed. Washington, D.C.: Smithsonian Institution, 1977. 238 pp. The sewing machine—the first widely advertised consumer appliance—revolutionized the ready-made clothing industry. Cooper describes the development of sewing machine components prior to 1845 and the marketing of the first commercial machines after 1845. Although historians generally give Elias Howe, Jr. full credit for inventing the sewing machine, Cooper mentions other notable contributors. She then recounts the litigation that plagued the industry in the 1850s and its resolution through the first significant American patent pooling arrangement. She also details the development in the late 1850s of a less expensive machine for the average family. The appendices trace related economic developments, list over 150 19th-century sewing machine companies and all of the Smithsonian's sewing machine patent models, and provide biographical sketches of leading inventors.

STM 79. CORN, JOSEPH J. The Winged Gospel: America's Romance with Aviation, 1900-1950. New York: Oxford University Press, 1983. 177 pp. In this contribution to the social and cultural history of technology Corn explores the fascination of Americans with airplanes in the first half-century of mechanical flight. This enthusiasm often took on a quasi-religious quality, perceiving in aviation not only technology's promise of progress but also a freedom from earthbound constraint and corruption and an ability to effect change in society and even in human nature. Corn includes case studies of three groups of aviation enthusiasts—the women pilots who gave a more domesticated image to flying, those who envisioned a future in which everyone would own and fly a plane, and those who sought to instill this enthusiasm in the next generation. The author has examined much of the popular literature of aviation written during the years addressed.

STM 80. CORNER, GEORGE W. A History of the Rockefeller Institute, 1901-1953: Origins and Growth. New York: Rockefeller Institute, 1965. 635 pp. The independent research institute has been an important new institutional niche for American science in the 20th century. One of the first and most successful of these was the Rockefeller Institute for Medical Research (RIMR), founded by John D. Rockefeller, Sr., in 1901. Under the direction of Simon Flexner from 1902 to 1935, the RIMR quickly established a reputation for first-rate work in experimental medical research. Organized in semi-autonomous divisions headed by scientists like Flexner, Phoebus

A. T. Levene, Alexis Carrel, and Jacques Loeb, RIMR staff had made major contributions to general physiology, organic and physical chemistry, and the biology of infectious diseases by the 1930s. Corner's detailed narrative of the RIMR's first half-century is in three sections. The first describes its foundation, organization, and activities through W.W. I; the second summarizes major research areas from 1918 to 1935; and the third deals with the Institute under Flexner's successor, neurophysiologist H. S. Gasser. Among Corner's appendices are Frederick Gates's account of the origins of the RIMR and a list of Institute trustees, scientific directors, and staff from 1901-1953.

STM 81. COURTWRIGHT, DAVID T. Dark Paradise: Opiate Addiction in America Before 1940. Cambridge, Mass.: Harvard University Press, 1982. 270 pp.
Courtwright notes, as others have, the transformation of the stereotype of the opiate addict--from the middle-aged, middle-class matron in 1895 to the lower-class, urban (criminal) male in 1935. He accounts for the transformation differently than others have: he claims that changes in medical practice, not just laws making narcotics illegal (the anti-maintenance policy of the early 20th century), caused this transformation. Courtwright documents both the decline in addiction which occurred even before the narcotic laws and the reasons for the decline: although opiates were always a part of the underworld scene, they became associated solely with the underworld when doctors stopped turning "respectable" patients into opiate addicts. While denying the theory that narcotic laws turned addicts into criminals, he concedes that these laws were probably harsher than they would have been had the stereotype of the addict not changed. He includes statistics as well as interviews with addicts and those who deal with addicts.

STM 82. COWAN, RUTH SCHWARTZ. More Work for Mother: The Ironies of Household Technology from the Open Hearth to the Microwave. New York: Basic Books, 1983. 257 pp.
Cowan begins by noting that, although historians have begun in the past few decades to study work, most of them focus on market labor. She proposes to study housework, which is like work performed in the marketplace insofar as it has become industrialized but unlike market labor insofar as it is unpaid and performed in isolated workplaces by unspecialized workers. Cowan begins with a brief discussion of housework in America during the pre-industrial era (before 1860), then proceeds chronologically with her history of the dialectical relationship between housework (a work process) and household technology (part of a complex technological system). She contends that advances in technology do not necessarily mean "less work for mother," although if properly understood and controlled they could.

STM 83. CRAVENS, HAMILTON. The Triumph of Evolution: American Scientists and the Heredity-Environment Controversy, 1900-1941. Philadelphia: University of Pennsylvania Press, 1978. 351 pp.
Cravens investigates the heredity-environment controversy among American natural and social scientists between W.W. I and W.W. II. He begins with the intellectual and institutional history of hereditarian thought in American biology and psychology from 1890-1920, emphasizing research in mutation theory, eugenics, instincts, and intelligence testing. Cravens contrasts the search for a science of social control by biologists and psychologists with the theories of culture adopted by anthropologists and sociologists during the same period. He then discusses debates within the scientific community over eugenics and race, instinct and human behavior, and mental testing between 1915 and 1941. By the late 1930s, most natural and social scientists had adopted the view that nature and nurture were interdependent variables for explaining human behavior. At the same

time, concepts of biological evolution were joined with new theories of cultural evolution.

STM 84. CROUCH, TOM D. A Dream of Wings: Americans and the Airplane, 1875-1905. New York: Norton, 1981. 349 pp.
In his discussion of how American technologists managed to work out the practicalities of flight, Crouch points out that by 1885 a community of technologists interested in the problem had been established. Among its most important members were Octave Chanute (a prominent civil engineer who made many important flights with gliders), Samuel P. Langley (a pioneer of solar astronomy who designed several powered airplane models), and the Wright brothers. America's rising technological competence by the late 19th century facilitated its efforts in this new industry, as did its success in getting like-minded technologists to cooperate on common problems in applied research.

STM 85. DAIN, NORMAN. Clifford W. Beers: Advocate for the Insane. Pittsburgh, Pa.: University of Pittsburgh Press, 1980. 392 pp.
This is a biography of Clifford Beers, whose autobiographical account of his own mental breakdown and recovery, A Mind That Found Itself (1908), was the foundation of Beers's reform efforts. Beers was the founder of the National Committee for Mental Hygiene (now the National Mental Health Association) and the American Foundation for Mental Hygiene. Dain places Beers in the context of the social history of care for the mentally ill in America.

STM 86. DAIN, NORMAN. Concepts of Insanity in the United States, 1789-1865. New Brunswick, N.J.: Rutgers University Press, 1964. 304 pp.
The author addresses the problems confronting early Americans who wanted to bring the treatment of the insane within the realm of medical care. The work is arranged chronologically; Dain documents the late 18th-century use of "moral treatment," the development in the early 19th century of psychiatry as a specialty and a generally optimistic attitude toward the mentally ill. From the 1860s to W.W. II, Dain argues, the insane were ill-treated and the profession generally despaired of helping them.

STM 87. DANIELIAN, N. A.T. & T.: The Story of Industrial Conquest. New York: Vanguard Press, 1939. 460 pp.
Danielian argues that American Telephone and Telegraph formed a "state within a State." Attributing its origins to Alexander Graham Bell's patents, he then describes its initial growth in Boston, the transfer of authority to New York control by 1907, the rapid expansion in W.W. I, and its reactions to the Depression. Recognizing the importance of patent development and control, corporate leaders organized an engineering department in 1881 and an industrial research laboratory in 1911 to develop patents as a basis for economic power. After 1925, the Bell Laboratories conducted specialized research in a number of areas, but Danielian stresses the central role this research played in gaining market domination. A.T. & T. also used patent pooling arrangements, particularly in radio and sound motion pictures, to establish a position of dominance. Danielian also provides information on corporate ownership, managerial structures, labor relations, technological unemployment, profits, and strategies for public relations.

STM 88. DANIELS, GEORGE H. American Science in the Age of Jackson. New York: Columbia University Press, 1968. 282 pp.
American Science in the Age of Jackson is a history of the generation of scientists and "friends of science" active between 1815 and 1845. George Daniels analyzes the work of a sample of fifty-six practicing scientists during that period (drawn from prolific publishers in national jour-

nals). He details the emergence of a professional scientific community
in antebellum America, with its own journals, societies, and a recognized
position in American intellectual life. Daniels suggests that the scientific thought of the day was characterized by a blend of Baconian Empiricism, Scottish common-sense philosophy, and Protestant theology. The
"reign of Bacon," he argues, explains the lack of American achievements
in abstract science during the 19th century.

STM 89. DANIELS, GEORGE H. Science in American Society: A Social History.
New York: Knopf, 1971. 390 pp.
Daniels does not claim comprehensiveness for his social history of science,
but rather states that he attempts to "provide an outline" for the study
of scientific themes. He discusses such topics as New World science,
the transmission of scientific ideas, the reception of evolution, the
rise of professionalization in science and medicine, and the relation
of science to progress.

STM 90. DANIELS, GEORGE H., ed. Darwinism Comes to America. Waltham,
Mass.: Blaisdell, 1968. 137 pp.
Noting that Darwinism posed a major threat to old ways of thinking, Daniels
selects and presents passages from the writings of 19th-century Americans
who attempted to accommodate the new theory to those older ways of thinking.
He provides substantial introductions to each section in which he places
the writings in context. Among those authors whose thoughts on Darwinism
he presents are Asa Gray (the earliest champion of Darwinism in America);
the Rev. Joseph P. Thompson (who recognized the threat to traditional
religion posed by Darwinism); William North Rice, J. Lawrence Smith, D.
R. Goodwin (scientists who rejected Darwinism); Joel A. Allen, Edward
Drinker Cope, Joseph LeConte (who subscribed to a Neo-Lamarckian rather
than a Darwinian theory); James McCosh, C. B. Warring, John Fiske (who
attempted to accommodate Darwinism to religion); John Wesley Powell (who
accommodated Darwinism to social thought); and Alexander Winchell (a prominent geologist who first rejected and then accepted evolutionary theory).

STM 91. DANIELS, GEORGE H., ed. Nineteenth-Century American Science:
A Reappraisal. Evanston, Ill.: Northwestern University Press,
1972. 274 pp.
This book contains the proceedings of a Northwestern University conference
devoted to the reassessment of 19th-century American science. The first
group of papers, dealing with the historiography of American science,
includes Edward Lurie's review of the field, Nathan Reingold's reappraisal
of "American indifference to basic research," Robert Bruce's statistical
profile of American scientists, 1846-1876, and Howard Miller's analysis
of the political character of scientists' laments about lack of financial
support. The second group, on American scientists and their research
roles, includes Mark Beach's provocative argument that the scientific
Lazzaroni did not exert the influence other historians have claimed, and
Daniel Kevles's study of the institutional base of American physics.
The final category contains papers on science, technology, and entrepreneurship in 19th-century America. Charles Rosenberg's piece on agricultural
experiment station scientists and Edwin Layton's characterization of the
communities of science and technology as "mirror-image twins" are the
most widely cited articles in the volume.

STM 92. DAVID, PAUL A. Technical Choice, Innovation, and Economic Growth:
Essays on American and British Experience in the Nineteenth Century. New York: Cambridge University Press, 1975. 334 pp.
This economic historian examines 19th-century American technological innovations with an emphasis on micro-economic phenomena. The four technical
essays that make up this book discuss labor scarcity and the problem of
technological progress, tariff protection and the textile industry, the

mechanization of reaping in the antebellum Midwest, and railroad innovations.

STM 93. DAVIES, JOHN D. Phrenology, Fad and Science: A Nineteenth-Century
American Crusade. New Haven, Conn.: Yale University Press,
1955. 203 pp.
Davies argues that while phrenology may appear a piece of quackery today,
in the 19th century its proponents and practitioners were convinced of
its rootedness in scientific principle and rigorous in their research
and application of phrenological theory. The author believes that phrenology provides the historian with a "case study in the movement and influence
of ideas," and places phrenology within the context of 19th-century intellectual and scientific history.

STM 94. DAVIS, NUELL PHARR. Lawrence and Oppenheimer. New York: Simon
& Schuster, 1968. 384 pp.
The contrast in the personalities and professional lives of the protagonists provides dramatic counterpoint for Nuell Pharr Davis's Lawrence and
Oppenheimer. Ernest O. Lawrence, a zealous Midwesterner, was, according
to the author, an experimentalist obsessed with building bigger and more
powerful particle accelerators. Ironically, it was Oppenheimer, the ascetic, cerebral theoretician, who presided over the mission-oriented research
at Los Alamos which designed the atomic bomb in W.W. II. (Lawrence worked
on methods of electromagnetic separation of uranium isotopes for the Manhattan Project.) After the war, both Lawrence and Oppenheimer remained
active in the high politics of American science. Nuclear research prospered at Lawrence's Radiation Laboratory in Berkeley, California.
Oppenheimer, after serving on the General Advisory Commission of the new
Atomic Energy Commission, became involved in a regrettable imbroglio over
his security clearance during the McCarthy years.

STM 95. DeVOLPI, A., G. E. MARSH, T. A. POSTAL, and G. S. STANFORD. The
Progressive Case and National Security. Elmsford, N.Y.: Pergamon
Press, 1981. 304 pp.
The four authors of this volume--all physicists at the Argonne National
Laboratory--present the history of the Progressive case, a lawsuit which
arose out of the Federal government's unsuccessful attempt to suppress
Howard Morland's 1979 article on the H-bomb. His article, developed from
information available to the public, eventually appeared in the liberal
periodical, Progressive. The authors attempt to elucidate the technical,
social, and legal issues that underlie the case. They claim the case
is not just an isolated dispute but a paradigmatic confrontation between
concerned citizens and the government, between the democratic process
and the governmental policy of secrecy. The outcome of the Progressive
case, they conclude, is ambiguous, giving neither side a clear victory.
They further conclude that the public's right to know does not necessarily
pose a threat to national security--that, in fact, an informed citizenry
may promote national security.

STM 96. DIAMOND, SIGMUND, ed. The Nation Transformed: The Creation of
an Industrial Society. New York: Braziller, 1963. 528 pp.
The editor provides a long introduction to this collection of selections
from original sources in which he provides an overview of the history
and transforming influences on American industrialization. The book contains selections about the city and the factory by Jacob Riis, Mary Antin,
and Samuel Gompers; about the role of education by Jane Addams and John
Dewey; about manifest destiny by John Fiske and Mark Twain.

STM 97. DIXON, BERNARD. Beyond the Magic Bullet. New York: Harper &
          Row, 1978. 249 pp.
The "magic bullets" Dixon refers to are specific therapies--treatments
developed in keeping with the theory of "specific aetiology" (the theory
that particular diseases have particular causes). The spectacular success
medical scientists operating under the theory have had during the past
century has, he argues, caused that theory to overshadow the other equally
important element in medicine (alleviating the patient's disease, his
overall ill health, not just eliminating discrete diseases). After a
brief examination of the development of scientific medicine, Dixon documents the historic breakthroughs made by 19th-century "microbe hunters"
such as Pasteur and Koch. He then turns his attention to the failures
of the specific aetiology theory: its failure to allow fully for the
body's ability to fight germs on its own; its failure to explain psycho-
somatic illness or "placebo" cures; the way the theory focuses on the
individual and ignores the community; its preoccupation with the treatment of disease rather than the maintenance of health; and the way in
which it leads to a highly technological medicine which benefits only
those in affluent countries. Dixon finds the theory inadequate for dealing
with today's health problems: cancers, coronary disease, and mental illness in wealthy countries--as well as basic sanitation and nutrition in
the Third World.

STM 98. DONEGAN, JANE B. Women and Men Midwives: Medicine, Morality,
          and Misogyny in Early America. Westport, Conn.: Greenwood Press,
          1978. 316 pp.
Donegan questions the "paradox" of women's abandonment of midwives in
favor of male physicians in her history of American midwivery, which concentrates on leisure-class women in Philadelphia, New York, and Boston
between the mid-18th century and the Civil War. She examines the response
of the orthodox medical community to midwives, stating that physicians
claimed that obstetrical competence demanded education. In the 1840s
and 1850s, Donegan argues, pioneering medical women, often with the help
of male feminist reformers, sought to expand women's medical sphere.

STM 99. DOWLING, HARRY F. City Hospitals: The Undercare of the Under-
          privileged. Cambridge, Mass.: Harvard University Press, 1982.
          245 pp.
Dowling's study of publicly-owned general hospitals in American cities
is divided into four historical periods: the poorhouse period, up to
1860, when the hospital was a subordinate part of the almshouse; the practitioner period, from 1860 to 1910, when medical care was dispensed in
hospitals largely by physicians with their own practices; the academic
period, ushered in by the Flexner Report in 1910, which saw the integration
of the hospitals with medical schools; and the community period, beginning
in 1965 as Social Security began to take effect, a transition Dowling
argues is still in progress.

STM 100. DOWLING, HARRY F. Fighting Infection: Conquests of the Twentieth
          Century. Cambridge, Mass.: Harvard University Press, 1977.
          339 pp.
Dowling, a practicing physician and medical researcher, documents the
rapid development of specific cures for infectious diseases that has
occurred during the first seventy-five years of the 20th century. After
a brief historical account of the beginnings of bacteriology (especially
of Pasteur's contribution to this new science), Dowling turns his attention
to medical breakthroughs which led to various serums, vaccines, sulfona-
mides, and antibiotics. Focusing on the U.S., he takes into account not
just the activities of medical researchers but also society's increasing
concern for human health, which led to more active public health agencies,
the public's increasing acceptance of both medical professionals and sani-

tary procedures, and the advances in industrial technology which aided
the fight against infectious diseases.

STM 101. DUFFY, JOHN. The Healers: The Rise of the Medical Establishment.
New York: McGraw-Hill, 1976. 385 pp.
The Healers is an account of American medicine "in its social setting,"
ranging from traditional Indian folk medicine before European settlement
to the dilemmas of the contemporary health care industry. John Duffy
describes the conditions of public health, the state of medical education,
and the structure of medical practice and professional life at successive
periods in American history. Other chapters deal with such topics as
medicine in the Revolutionary and Civil Wars; Benjamin Rush, the "American
Hippocrates"; sectarian medicine; the rise of American surgery; the emergence of organized public health; and women and minorities in medicine.

STM 102. DUFFY, JOHN. A History of Public Health in New York City, 1625-
1866. New York: Russell Sage, 1968. 619 pp.
This detailed account of public health in New York City illuminates an
important theme in the social history of medicine--the impact of urbanization on public health. Beginning with the Dutch settlement of the 17th
century, Duffy analyzes changing health conditions in the city and the
efforts of politicians, medical men, and civic reformers to create mechanisms for safeguarding public health. He discusses mortality patterns
and the incidence of epidemic disease; quarantine measures; the problems
of sewage disposal, street cleaning, and water supply; the introduction
of food and market regulations; tenement house conditions in the mid-19th
century; changes in the medical profession; and the role of hospitals.
Duffy also describes early attempts to create organizations to deal with
the threats to public health and concludes with the reform movement leading
to the passage of the Metropolitan Health Act of 1866.

STM 103. DUFFY, JOHN. A History of Public Health in New York City, 1866-
1966. New York: Russell Sage, 1974. 619 pp.
In the second volume of his history of public health in New York City,
Duffy concentrates on the institutional history of public health agencies
in the city beginning with the Metropolitan Board of Health established
in 1866. He describes the administrative mechanisms set up to deal with
the complex health problems of a major urban center, and explores the
interactions of politics and medical expertise which characterized the
development of public health in New York. Duffy also examines trends
in maternal and child health, problems of environmental pollution, measures
for the control of communicable disease, and efforts to curb venereal
disease. A concluding chapter summarizes trends in public health in New
York City over the entire period from 1625 to 1966.

STM 104. DUNLAP, THOMAS R. DDT: Scientists, Citizens, and Public Policy.
Princeton, N.J.: Princeton University Press, 1981. 318 pp.
Dunlap offers a history of the use of DDT in America. After a discussion
of the slow evolution of chemical insecticides from the late 19th century
to W.W. II, the account then focuses on DDT which was introduced for civilian
use in 1946, and finally banned in 1972. According to Dunlap, the debate
over DDT's use began in government agencies and eventually spread into
the public sector. The last sections of the book discuss the emergence
of the public campaign to ban the chemical, devoting particular attention
to the Wisconsin DDT hearings of 1968-1969.

STM 105. DUNWELL, STEVE. The Run of the Mill: A Pictorial Narrative of the Expansion, Dominion, Decline and Enduring Impact of the New England Textile Industry. Boston: Godine, 1978. 299 pp.
Tracing its history from the early 19th century to the present, Dunwell claims that textile manufacturing--the first craft to be successfully mechanized--represented all industry in its early years. He focuses on the New England mill town where the themes of industrialization (themes such as the machine as ally and tyrant, the exploitation of a permanent factory class, the monopoly, even the American Dream itself) were, according to him, first introduced. The first half of the book provides a historical account; the second consists of selections from interviews with millworkers and photographs Dunwell himself has taken. He notes how not only the physical layout of the mill towns but also the "logic, ethic, and history" of the people were (and are) determined by the mills.

STM 106. DUPRE, J. STEFAN and SANFORD A. LAKOFF. Science and the Nation: Policy and Politics. Englewood Cliffs, N.J.: Prentice-Hall, 1962. 181 pp.
Science and the Nation deals with American science policy and the involvement of scientists in politics in the years after W.W. II. Dupre and Lakoff begin with a brief historical overview of science and government in the U.S. After W.W. II, the national goals of military security and economic growth lent impetus to Federal support of research and development in universities, industry, and government agencies such as the Atomic Energy Commission and the Department of Defense. The authors, both political scientists, stress the importance of government contracts and grants as mechanisms for the subvention of extramural research during the 1940s and 1950s. This system altered the traditional relationships of the public and private sectors and fostered an increasing reliance upon Federal funds for research and development in American industries and universities. In the second half of the book, the focus shifts to the roles of scientists in providing policy advice in the arms race and debates over the control of atomic energy.

STM 107. DUPREE, A. HUNTER. Asa Gray, 1810-1888. Cambridge, Mass.: Harvard University Press, 1959. 505 pp.
Asa Gray, a pioneer in plant geography and Darwin's chief defender in America, is the subject of this biography by Hunter Dupree. Though educated as a physician, Gray's interests turned early to botany. Called to Harvard in 1842, he soon became the leading botanist in the U.S., establishing an herbarium and extensive botanical library, and training a new generation of botanists. Gray's chief antagonist in the debate over Darwinism, Harvard colleague Louis Agassiz, was also his adversary in the realm of the politics of science. Agassiz was a leader of the Lazzaroni, a group whose elitist goals for American science (exemplified in the National Academy of Sciences) clashed with those of Gray, William Barton Rogers, and others. By the late 1860s, these conflicts had been mediated, and Gray returned to botany and his public support of Darwinism. Gray's acceptance of evolution did not shake his religious faith, a factor which made his moderate stance appealing to a wide spectrum of scientific and religious men. Dupree succeeds in weaving Gray's scientific biography into the broader context of social, political, and intellectual life in 19th-century America.

STM 108. DUPREE, A. HUNTER. Science in the Federal Government: A History of Policies and Activities to 1940. Cambridge, Mass.: Harvard University Press, 1957. 460 pp.
This volume is a survey of Federal patronage of scientific activity in the U.S. Beginning with the Lewis and Clark Expedition (1803) and the Coast Survey (1807), science was used as a tool of exploration and national expansion. After the Civil War, the Federal scientific establishment

expanded into agriculture, geology, forestry, public health, and other areas as government concerns shifted from the settlement of the frontier to the problems of urbanization, industrialization, and natural resources conservation. The mechanism for this expansion was the scientific bureau, an organizational form which combined the conflicting demands of scientific research and political accountability. The contributions of science and technology to W.W. I (orchestrated by new agencies like the National Research Council) and the increased importance of scientific research in the national economy insured a close relationship between science and government during the 1920s and 1930s. Dupree blends institutional history with commentary on broader historical trends. One example is the quest for central scientific organization, a theme Dupree develops in his discussion of the Smithsonian Institution (1848), the National Academy of Sciences (1863), and other institutions.

STM 109. ELLIS, JOHN. The Social History of the Machine Gun. New York: Pantheon Books, 1975. 186 pp.
Though Ellis's study is not restricted to American uses of and responses to the machine gun, he discusses such topics as the first use of machine guns in the Civil War, the development of the Gatling gun, and the use of the machine gun as a standard weapon in battles between management and labor in the late 19th and early 20th century. He discusses as well the symbolic function of the machine gun in American gangster films.

STM 110. ELSNER, HENRY. The Technocrats: Prophets of Automation. Syracuse, N.Y.: Syracuse University Press, 1967. 252 pp.
Elsner, a sociologist and former member of Technocracy Inc., provides a history of the technocracy movement from its post-W.W. I origins in Thorstein Veblen's short-lived Technical Alliance to the 1960s. Howard Scott, a member of the alliance and later director of Technocracy Inc., shared Veblen's belief that only overall planning and coordination could overcome the waste and inefficiency inherent in business control of industry. In 1932, Scott and others interested in problems of technological growth and economic change began meeting in New York City. Elsner describes the sudden national attention this group and their ideas gained in 1932 and 1933 and the subsequent organization of the movement into two factions, the Continental Committee on Technocracy Inc. and Technology Inc. The latter group enjoyed greater organizational success, and Elsner describes its activities before and during W.W. II, its post-war reorganization, and its decline in the 1950s. Finally, Elsner provides a sociological and political interpretation of the movement.

STM 111. EMME, EUGENE M., ed. The History of Rocket Technology: Essays on Research, Development, and Utility. Detroit, Mich.: Wayne State University Press, 1964. 320 pp.
In his introduction, Emme contends that the essays collected in this volume show the history of rocketry to be a complex interaction of science, engineering, and industry within a political, economic, and strategic context. He argues that accelerating technical development of rocket propulsion has produced political and economic tensions on both the national and international level. The initial essays trace rocketry from Robert H. Goddard's first liquid-fuel rocket fired in 1926 and discuss early U.S. satellite proposals. The next group describes the major American rocket programs, directed by the military, while the third section deals with American manned-flight projects, including rocket-research airplanes and the first American manned space venture, Project Mercury. The final two sections discuss the development of space telemetry, a technology necessary for rocket flight, and the Soviet Union's rocket program. There is also an extensive bibliography.

STM 112. **EMME, EUGENE M.**, ed. <u>Impact</u> <u>of</u> <u>Air</u> <u>Power</u>: <u>National</u> <u>Security</u>
<u>and</u> <u>World</u> <u>Politics</u>. Princeton, N.J.: Van Nostrand, 1959.
914 pp.
Rapid technological changes associated with the evolution of air power
have had important consequences for national policy and security. Essays
collected in this volume and written by military leaders, statesmen, social
scientists, historians, physicists, and engineers deal with this important
relationship. Selections in Part I describe the history of air power
and investigate its nature. Part II concerns air power's effect on strategy and tactics and contains essays on classical theories of air war,
the role of air power in W.W. II and later wars, and the military lessons
drawn from W.W. II. Concerned with post-W.W. II policy, selections in Part
III describe American and Soviet air policies, European and Asian air
power, and more general problems of defense and diplomacy. Emme's introductions for each chapter provide continuity and state salient assumptions.
A prefatory statement for each selection gives its source and a biography
of the author.

STM 113. **ENGLISH, PETER C.** <u>Shock</u>, <u>Physiological</u> <u>Surgery</u>, <u>and</u> <u>George</u>
<u>Washington</u> <u>Crile</u>: <u>Medical</u> <u>Innovation</u> <u>in</u> <u>the</u> <u>Progressive</u> <u>Era</u>.
Westport, Conn.: Greenwood Press, 1980. 271 pp.
The surgical complication of shock, when it came to be seen as important
in the 1880s, led to the development of "physiological surgery," surgery
in which experiments were conducted to develop safer techniques. George
Washington Crile was a leader in physiological surgery; English's book
studies his career from 1888 to 1918, concentrating on his work with shock.
English also discusses Crile as a representative Progressive reformer.

STM 114. **ENOS, JOHN LAWRENCE.** <u>Petroleum</u> <u>Progress</u> <u>and</u> <u>Profits</u>: <u>A</u> <u>History</u>
<u>of</u> <u>Process</u> <u>Innovation</u>. Cambridge, Mass.: MIT Press, 1962.
336 pp.
Enos analyzes the nature of technological progress as revealed in several
waves of innovations that increased gasoline production to meet the needs
of the expanding American transportation network. He traces the development of the major thermal cracking methods--the Burton, the Dubbs, and
the Tube and Tank processes--and the major catalytic cracking methods--
the Houdry, the Houdry flow, the TCC, and the Fluid Catalytic Cracking
processes. For each process, Enos demonstrates the need for the innovation,
identifies people involved, describes the research and development effort,
identifies barriers to progress, calculates the innovation's economic
advantages, and determines its effect upon the industry. Enos also draws
general conclusions concerning the individual innovators, the effects
of the economies of scale, the changes in productivity resulting from
the innovations, and the consequences of institutionalizing innovation.

STM 115. **ESTES, J. WORTH.** <u>Hall</u> <u>Jackson</u> <u>and</u> <u>the</u> <u>Purple</u> <u>Foxglove</u>: <u>Medical</u>
<u>Practice</u> <u>and</u> <u>Research</u> <u>in</u> <u>Revolutionary</u> <u>America</u> <u>1760-1820</u>. Han-
over, N.H.: University Press of New England, 1979. 291 pp.
Estes's study details how digitalis--the foxglove--came to be used for
the treatment of congestive heart failure--dropsy--in America. Dr. William
Withering, a British doctor, discovered the drug and reported his findings
in 1785; Hall Jackson, a physician in Portsmouth, New Hampshire, wrote
Withering for foxglove seeds. Estes examines Jackson's career, the state
of Portsmouth's health, and the knowledge of dropsy at the time, attempting
to illustrate the nature of medical research and the communication of
its results in the 18th century.

STM 116. **ETHERIDGE, ELIZABETH W.** The Butterfly Caste: A Social History
of Pellagra in the South. Westport, Conn.: Greenwood Press,
1972. 278 pp.
Pellagra was endemic in the South during the early part of the 20th century.
Often a lethal disease, pellagra caused its victims to develop a skin
rash known for its shape which resembled a butterfly. According to
Etheridge, pellagra was not recognized as a distinct disease until 1907
when an epidemic broke out in an asylum in Alabama. Usually affecting
poor communities, the disease soon became identified as occurring in
regions beset with hookworm. The cause of pellagra was attributed to a
variety of sources, including spoiled corn, insect-borne bacteria, and
spring heat and sunshine. Some individuals blamed Italian immigrants
and the emancipation of slaves. Vitamin deficiency was finally identified
as the real cause of pellagra.

STM 117. **ETTLING, JOHN.** The Germ of Laziness: Rockefeller Philanthropy
and Public Health in the New South. Cambridge, Mass.: Harvard
University Press, 1981. 263 pp.
Ettling's study of the Rockefeller Sanitary Commission for the Eradication
of Hookworm Disease, established in 1909 at the height of the Progressive
movement, is a social history of medicine and public policy. Ettling
argues that it is necessary to look at the activities of those involved
in the Commission, like Frederick T. Gates and Wickliffe Rose, in order
to understand how the reform movement was at once scientific and "modern"
in nature yet deeply rooted in the evangelical sentiment of the 19th century.

STM 118. **EZELL, EDWARD CLINTON** and **LINDA NEWMAN EZELL.** The Partnership:
A History of the Apollo-Soyuz Test Project. Washington, D.C.:
National Aeronautics and Space Administration, 1978. 560 pp.
On July 17, 1975, the American Apollo and the Russian Soyuz spacecraft
successfully tested an international docking system and joint flight procedures for orbital rendezvous. The Apollo-Soyuz project began officially
in the summer of 1972 after the Nixon-Kosygin summit conference produced
an agreement on cooperation in space. In recounting the project's history,
the Ezells concentrate on the National Aeronautics and Space Administration
(NASA) side due to the scarcity of information on the Soviet space program.
Arguing that the project can only be understood within an international
context, they describe Cold War competition and early efforts at cooperation before recounting the divergent evolution of American and Russian
manned space craft. They then detail efforts to create a viable test
project, particularly after the 1972 summit. They also discuss technical
solutions arrived at through numerous conferences between NASA and Soviety
Academy engineers, the selection and training of crews, and the nearly
flawless flight in July 1975.

STM 119. **FAGEN, M. D.,** ed. A History of Engineering and Science in the
Bell System: The Early Years (1875-1925). New York: Bell
Telephone Laboratories, 1975. 1073 pp.
This volume, first in a projected series on communications technology,
commemorates the fiftieth anniversary of Bell Laboratory's founding and
the centennial of the telephone's invention. Bell personnel researched
and wrote this volume. The approach is highly technical. Two opening
chapters discuss Alexander Graham Bell's invention of the telephone and
the Bell System's corporate history to 1925. Following chapters detail
aspects of communications technology: the telephone transmitter and
receiver; transmission by wire and radio; switching and signalling systems
to establish direct communications between telephone users; telegraph
and other non-voice services; special materials and components; and quality
assurance. Finally, there is an account of basic research in three areas:
electrical communications theory; speech, hearing, and sound; and the

nature of materials. The volume also provides a bibliography of historically important technical papers.

STM 120. FAGEN, M. D., ed. A History of Engineering and Science in the
Bell System: National Service in War and Peace (1925-1975).
New York: Bell Telephone Laboratories, 1978. 757 pp.
The second volume (see STM 119) on Bell System engineering and science
is the work of many active and retired members of the Bell Laboratory's
technical staff. Divided into two sections, it details Bell System
contributions to national defense, first in the period before and
during W.W. II, then in the Cold War and subsequent missile crisis.
Topics in the first section concern gunfire-control systems, acoustics
systems for locating and destroying submarines, and military wire and
radio communications systems. Post-war topics include air defense,
further work on underwater acoustics and radar, radio-inertial guidance
for missiles, military control and communications systems, and systems
engineering and research for military weapons. The final chapter
details two examples of special government projects for which the Bell
System created subsidiaries: the Sandia Corporation working on atomic
weapons, and Bellcomm working with NASA on the Apollo lunar-exploration
project.

STM 121. FARRELL, JAMES J. Inventing the American Way of Death, 1830-
1920. Philadelphia: Temple University Press, 1980. 297 pp.
The author argues that what he calls "the dying of death"--the removal
of death from cultural consciousness--occurred between 1830 and 1920,
and that it continues to shape American attitudes toward death today.
He first chronicles the intellectual history of this phenomenon and then
moves to social history, examining cemetery organization and the history
of funerals. His study concludes with an analysis of funerals and burials
in an Illinois county.

STM 122. FELLMAN, ANITA CLAIR and MICHAEL FELLMAN. Making Sense of Self:
Medical Advice Literature in Late Nineteenth-Century America.
Philadelphia: University of Pennsylvania Press, 1981.
198 pp.
Examining medical advice literature of the period 1870 to 1890, the
Fellmans discover an "interest approaching obsession in the self," which,
although not new to late 19th-century America, certainly reflected the
concerns and ideology of that time and place. These domestic medical
guides were, they argue, less optimistic that individual well-being would
be accompanied by social perfection than guides of the 1830s and 1840s.
Sticking to rules of hygiene and instructions for emergency measures,
and including no cures for cancer or other serious diseases, they were
also less "anti-physician" than the earlier guides. But the emphasis
in late 19th-century medical advice literature was still on self-
improvement and positive thinking. The Fellmans note that this belief
in positive thinking--a belief in individual will--was an ideological
response to personal and social "illness."

STM 123. FISHER, MARVIN. Workshops in the Wilderness: The European
Response to American Industrialization, 1830-1860. New York:
Oxford University Press, 1967. 238 pp.
Pre-Civil War European visitors have provided some of the best accounts
of the development in the U.S. of a distinct system of manufacture.
Fisher provides a short overview of industrialization from 1800 to the
Civil War, then draws on travelers' accounts to investigate American industrialization in the years from 1830 to 1860, its impact on American character and imagination, and its divergence from European methods. Surprised
by the extent of American technological development, Europeans developed
contradictory images of America as "garden" and as "workshop." They

reported a distinct American attitude toward industrial design, and many attributed American industrialization to American character, natural abundance, and lack of class and craft restraints. Although most saw in manufacturing the possibility of increasing opportunities for the nation as a whole, some, nevertheless, betrayed ambivalence and even pessimism concerning machine technology and its place in nature and their "garden" image of America.

STM 124. FLACK, J. KIRKPATRICK. Desideratum in Washington: The Intellectual Community in the Capital City, 1870-1900. Cambridge, Mass.: Schenkman, 1975. 192 pp.
In the decades after the Civil War, groups of scientists, educators, and literati established cultural coteries in Washington in an attempt to raise the tone of intellectual life in the capital. Due to the expansion of government science and the consequent growth of Washington's scientific population during the 1870s and 1880s, there was also an increase in the number of local scientific societies. These organizations are the focus of Flack's book. He argues that learned associations and clubs like the Philosophical Society of Washington (1871), the Cosmos Club (1878), and the Washington Academy of Sciences (1898) are best understood as part of the broader intellectual community of Gilded Age Washington. These scientific institutions served the dual purpose of promoting professional scientific activity while advancing national culture.

STM 125. FLEMING, DONALD. William H. Welch and the Rise of Modern Medicine. Boston: Little, Brown, 1954. 216 pp.
William H. Welch (1840-1934) was one of the most influential scientist-administrators of late 19th- and early 20th-century America. Trained in medicine in New York and Germany during the 1870s, Welch returned to Europe in 1884-1885 to study bacteriology with Robert Koch and Max von Pattenkofer. He introduced the tradition of laboratory research in pathology and bacteriology into American medicine, first at the Bellevue Hospital Medical School in New York and after 1884 at Johns Hopkins. In the late 1880s and early 1890s, Welch organized the Johns Hopkins University Medical School, stressing the importance of scientific research and clinical observation to medical practice. The Hopkins program became a model for the reform of American medical education. After 1900 Welch was active in the administration of new scientific foundations, research institutes, and the councils of the national scientific community. Fleming discusses Welch's education, research, and his importance as an institutional entrepreneur.

STM 126. FLEXNER, JAMES T. Steamboats Come True: American Inventors in Action. New York: Viking Press, 1944. 406 pp.
Starting with the apparent paradox that the steamboat was developed in agricultural America and not in industrial England, Flexner investigates the invention of the steamboat through biographies of three early steamboat inventors: John Fitch, James Rumsey, and Robert Fulton. He describes Fitch's childhood, early work experience, priority conflicts with Rumsey, his remarkably successful boat of 1790, and subsequent failures and death from drinking. Fulton's major interest was submarine warfare, but he also developed in 1806 a steamboat that was somewhat inferior to Fitch's. Flexner argues, however, that Fulton invented the steamboat. Unlike Fitch, Fulton grasped basic principles and improved his design as problems arose and built effective steamboats. A partially realized aspiration before Fulton, the steamboat was so well established after 1806 that its use and development continued without break.

STM 127. **FLINK, JAMES J.** America Adopts the Automobile, 1895-1910. Cambridge, Mass.: MIT Press, 1970. 343 pp.
Between 1890 and 1910, Americans developed attitudes and institutional contexts that subsequently made the automobile industry a significant force for change in America. Flink describes the social and cultural factors that structured the American automotive industry in this formative period. He believes that the end of the period came when Henry Ford introduced a high-performance, low-priced automobile. After discussing methods used by manufacturers to gain public acceptance of the automobile, Flink describes government responses (both as potential customer and as a regulator of automobile use) and the development of automobile clubs, roads, and mechanical expertise. Flink also provides an account of changing automobile design and business structures, both of which allowed production for a mass market by 1910.

STM 128. **FLINK, JAMES J.** The Car Culture. Cambridge, Mass.: MIT Press, 1975. 260 pp.
Flink argues that the motor vehicle, automobile industry, and highway system have played such a central role in American life that they provide the basis for a new technical and economic synthesis of American history. To support this position, Flink investigates American automobile culture from the 1850s to the present. He first discusses the automobile's reception before W.W. I, competitive structure of the nascent car industry, the rise of several dominating firms, and the careers of Henry Ford and William Durant, the founder of General Motors. Flink then argues that the "car culture" had become national in extent by the 1920s and that the car, auto industry, and highway formed the backbone of the new consumer goods oriented society and economy. In his conclusion, however, Flink claims that the car industry is now on its death bed. For corroboration he points to American disenchantment with large, expensive, and energy-inefficient cars, and the increasing recognition of the social and environmental problems that road, car, and auto industry produce.

STM 129. **FORD, DANIEL.** The Cult of the Atom: The Secret Papers of the Atomic Energy Commission. New York: Simon & Schuster, 1982. 273 pp.
This economist's account of the creation of the Atomic Energy Commission in 1946 and its subsequent growth details the AEC's gradual acquisition and suppression of knowledge of the dangers of nuclear energy. Ford, a member of the Union of Concerned Scientists, argues that the 1979 Three Mile Island nuclear reactor accident represented the culmination of this major technological venture, basing his claims on investigation of AEC archives.

STM 130. **FOSTER, MARK S.** From Streetcar to Superhighway: American City Planners and Urban Transportation, 1900-1940. Philadelphia: Temple University Press, 1981. 246 pp.
Foster's thesis is that city planners acted optimistically in planning cities around the automobile and the trolley in the early 20th century. In the case of the trolley, they could not foresee the corruption of trolley operators; in the case of the automobile, they could not foresee universal use of the automobile and attempted to respond to outward migration from the cities. The study documents the failed efforts of well-intentioned American city planners.

STM 131. **FOX, RICHARD W.** So Far Disordered in Mind: Insanity in California, 1870-1940. Berkeley: University of California Press, 1978. 204 pp.
Fox's study of the social and cultural meaning of insanity in California in the 20th century documents the restructuring of attitudes toward the mentally ill, the rise of the psychiatric profession, and the universali-

zation of therapy. Essentially a study of deviance, Fox's book explores
changing attitudes toward the abnormal and the normal.

STM 132. FURNER, MARY O. Advocacy & Objectivity: A Crisis in the Pro-
        fessionalism of American Social Science, 1865-1905. Lexington:
        University Press of Kentucky, 1975. 357 pp.
Furner traces the process of professionalization in American social science
from 1865 to 1905, concentrating on the disciplines of economics, sociology,
and political science. From common origins in moral philosophy, these
disciplines emerged as specialized areas of study in the research universities of late 19th-century America. Furner uses the academic freedom cases
of the 1880s and 1890s to explore emerging patterns of professional conduct
and the establishment of boundaries for appropriate behavior for academic
social scientists. The conflict between social advocacy and academic
objectivity as the primary role for professional social scientists and
its implications for the political uses of technical expertise are dominant
themes of Furner's history.

STM 133. GALISHOFF, STUART. Safeguarding the Public Health: Newark,
        1895-1918. Westport, Conn.: Greenwood Press, 1975. 191 pp.
Galishoff limits his discussion to measures taken by the Newark Board
of Health that "best typify [its] response to the major health problems
of that period [1895-1918]." Although focusing on Newark, he suggests
there may be similarities between Newark's development of public health
policy and developments in other American cities. Galishoff notes that
Newark's leaders paid little attention to industrialization's effects
on public health during the post-Civil War era. This changed, however,
in the 1890s when the Newark Board of Health founded a bacteriological
laboratory, which aided greatly in battling the contagious diseases that
plagued the city. He demonstrates how cooperation between medicine and
society and increasing governmental involvement in public health led to
the following reforms: a purer water supply, a sewer system, extermination
of malaria-causing mosquitoes, a more sanitary milk supply (which helped
to lower the infant mortality rate), a program for treating tuberculosis,
legislation to improve industrial hygiene and safety, and improvements
in conditions within tenements.

STM 134. GIEDION, SIGFRIED. Mechanization Takes Command: A Contribution
        to Anonymous History. New York: Oxford University Press, 1948.
        743 pp.
By "anonymous history," the author means that he believes it is important
to explore the impact of mechanization, to study industrial methods, that
is, from the outside. Mechanization's fullest expression, he argues,
is the assembly line, which he describes in detail. He also describes
aspects of mechanization in soil treatment, breadmaking, and meat packing;
the development of the chair, table, upholstery, and railroad cars; and
the impact of mechanization on all aspects of housework. He concludes
his study with a fully detailed account of the mechanization of the bath.

STM 135. GIES, JOSEPH and FRANCIS GIES. The Ingenious Yankees: The Men,
        Ideas, and Machines That Transformed a Nation. New York:
        Crowell, 1976. 376 pp.
The authors describe technological innovations in America from 1776 to
1876. Dividing the period into four chronological parts, they discuss
in the first section such topics as Oliver Evans and Eli Whitney's cotton
gin; in the second, steamboat and bridge development; in the third, the
rise of the railroads and the development of the telegraph, sewing machine,
and reaper; and in the fourth, the invention of the typewriter, telephone,
and industrial laboratory.

STM 136. GILPIN, ROBERT. American Scientists and Nuclear Weapons Policy. Princeton, N.J.: Princeton University Press, 1962. 352 pp. This book deals with the involvement of science policy makers and physical scientists (including James Killian, Robert Oppenheimer, Linus Pauling, Edward Teller, and Eugene Rabinowitch) in debates over American nuclear weapons policy after W.W. II. Beginning with the General Advisory Committee of the Atomic Energy Commission, Gilpin discusses the issues of the hydrogen bomb, tactical nuclear weapons, ballistic missiles, and the nuclear test-ban debates of 1958-1962. He analyzes conflicts among the nuclear scientists and examines their roles in the formulation of national security policy during the 1950s and early 1960s. Gilpin's major concerns are the "emergence of scientists as men of political power" and the role of scientific expertise in public debates over policy questions of technological complexity. He emphasizes the important point that scientists are not neutral participants in the political arena, despite their assertions to the contrary.

STM 137. GOLDSTINE, HERMAN H. The Computer from Pascal to von Neumann. Princeton, N.J.: Princeton University Press, 1972. 378 pp. Goldstine provides first a brief account of attempts to automate computing from the 17th century to the differential analyzers of the 1930s. The remainder of the book is a scientific autobiography in which Goldstine describes the computer projects on which he worked. Throughout he concentrates on ideas and people, although he provides the technical detail necessary to understand computer hardware.

STM 138. GOULD, STEPHEN JAY. The Mismeasure of Man. New York: Norton, 1981. 344 pp. Gould provides an account of the rise of hereditarian and racist approaches to human science since the mid-19th century. Topics covered include the American polygenist school of racial anthropology (e.g., S. G. Morton and L. Agassiz); the uses and abuses of Binet's "mental test" as reinterpreted by such American psychologists as H. H. Goddard and Lewis M. Terman; and the Cyril Burt scandal. Gould, a paleontologist, criticizes these and various other scientific experiments which suffered from insufficient positivism.

STM 139. GREEN, CONSTANCE. Eli Whitney and the Birth of American Technology. Boston: Little, Brown, 1956. 215 pp. Arguing that the American Revolution made necessary a new economic system based on native resources, Green portrays Eli Whitney as an inventor and manufacturer who contributed significantly to the solution of this problem. Whitney, Green believes, invented the cotton gin and mass production techniques for manufacturing rifles, which laid the bases, respectively, for the cotton kingdom of the South and the industrialism of the North. In describing the economy of the new nation, Green stresses its need for a commodity that could be traded on British markets. Cotton filled this requirement after Whitney invented a cotton gin in 1793 to clean cotton of its seed. After experiencing losses from manufacturing problems and from ruinous competition with his gin, Whitney turned in 1798 to the manufacture of government muskets. Green argues that Whitney developed not a new musket, but a new system of manufacture substituting machinery for scarce labor and representing the first large-scale American experiment in the mass-production methods that became the basis for the nation's industrial growth.

STM 140. GREENBERG, DANIEL. The Politics of Pure Science. New York: New American Library, 1967. 303 pp. This book by a former news editor of Science details the vested interests, shifting alliances, and advisory elites involved in the politics of pure science in the U.S. since W.W. II. Greenberg begins with an outline of

1603

hierarchies within the scientific community in the mid-1960s and an analysis of the ideological commitments of basic scientists in the postwar period. The second section of the book contrasts prewar support of scientific research with the increasing importance of Federal (especially military) patronage in the decades after W.W. II. After tracing the evolution of new organizations and networks in the government of science, Greenberg turns to case studies such as the Mohole fiasco and debates over high energy particle accelerators in the late 1950s and early 1960s to illustrate the continuing tension between the scientists' desire for autonomy and political demands for accountability. Accustomed to privileged political status and continual growth in Federal funds for science, scientists in the late 1960s were reluctant to accept new political priorities which afforded them no more access to power and government patronage than other interest groups.

STM 141. GREENE, MOTT T. Geology in the Nineteenth Century: Changing Views of a Changing World. Ithaca, N.Y.: Cornell University Press, 1982. 324 pp.

Greene focuses on the development of geological science during the 19th century: from the Neptunist-Plutonist debate of the early 1800s to the early 20th century and the rise of dynamic theories of the earth. Greene departs from the traditional emphasis on British geologists and their interest in stratigraphy and paleontology. He stresses instead the importance of those geologists on both sides of the Atlantic who developed ideas of the planet's major landforms. This interpretation, Greene insists, culminated in Alfred Wegener's theory of continental drift, which was congruent with the new indeterminist ideas of the early 20th century.

STM 142. GROB, GERALD N. Edward Jarvis and the Medical World of Nineteenth-Century America. Knoxville: University of Tennessee Press, 1978. 300 pp.

Edward Jarvis was an eminent psychiatrist in the years between 1840 and 1880; he was a prominent figure in the growing public health movement, a founder of the modern census, and a promoter of the recording of vital statistics. Grob argues that Jarvis was a representative figure of the professional response to the increased need for public health policy in 19th-century America.

STM 143. GROB, GERALD N. Mental Illness and American Society, 1875-1940. Princeton, N.J.: Princeton University Press, 1983. 428 pp.

Grob's purpose is to analyze the experiences of American society in dealing with mental illness as a medical and social problem. He describes the complex interrelationships among patients, psychiatrists, institutions, and government in an attempt to understand the shift from a supportive attitude (before W.W. II) to an antipathetic attitude toward mental institutions (after W.W. II). Grob arrives at five major conclusions about the period 1875-1940: first, despite shortcomings, mental hospitals did provide minimum care to people who could not care for themselves; second, psychiatry became increasingly an "administrative" specialty; third, the patient population—mostly acute patients to begin with—changed to a population of mostly chronic patients; fourth, policy decisions often grew out of professional or political concerns rather than concern for patient needs; and fifth, the central issue was not therapeutic effectiveness but rather humane care for those who could not care for themselves.

STM 144. GROB, GERALD N. Mental Institutions in America: Social Policy to 1875. New York: Free Press, 1973. 458 pp.

Grob followed his study of mental hospitals and public policy in Massachusetts with this description of American responses to mental illness before 1875. Conscious of the mental institution as a social phenomenon revealing of attitudes toward dependent groups such as the mentally ill,

Grob examines the mental institution in America in terms of definitions of disease, public policy and decision-making, and socioeconomic differentials in care; he also describes the beginnings of American psychiatry.

STM 145. GROB, GERALD N. The State and the Mentally Ill: A History of the Worcester State Hospital in Massachusetts, 1830-1920. Chapel Hill: University of North Carolina Press, 1966. 399 pp.
Grob argues that, in the first half of the 19th century, mental institutions were in fact extremely effective in their treatment of patients, and that generally state hospitals have responded to cultural changes with institutional change. He finds representative the history of Worcester State Hospital—the prototype for state hospitals—and the history of Massachusetts' policy-making in regard to the care of the insane.

STM 146. GROUEFF, STEPHANE. Manhattan Project: The Untold Story of the Making of the Atomic Bomb. Boston: Little, Brown, 1967. 372 pp.
Most historians of the Manhattan Project focus on scientists building the first uranium pile in Chicago and the experimental plutonium and uranium bombs in Los Alamos. However, between 1942, when the Chicago pile went critical, and 1945, when the bomb was tested, Americans also built mammoth industrial plants to produce fissionable material, which had previously existed only in microscopic laboratory quantities. This is the story Groueff tells. He focuses on plutonium production in Hanford, Washington, and on uranium-235 production in Oak Ridge, Tennessee, and he provides a detailed account of the almost insurmountable engineering problems involved. Groueff describes the intensive efforts of the engineers and scientists who simultaneously explored several avenues of production and transformed laboratory techniques and concepts into industrial methods.

STM 147. GURALNICK, STANLEY M. Science and the Ante-Bellum American College. Philadelphia: American Philosophical Society, 1975. 326 pp.
Traditional interpretations of the antebellum American college depict a stagnant curriculum emphasizing classical knowledge and moral philosophy, but sadly neglecting scientific studies. Guralnick dispenses with this misconception by demonstrating the expansion of science teaching and financial support for science at fifteen Northeastern colleges from about 1820 to 1860. Mathematics, astronomy, physics, and chemistry all found their places in the colleges as subjects with intellectual utility for administrators committed to an educational philosophy of mental discipline. Indeed, through the continual addition of new subjects, science had saturated the college curriculum by the 1840s and 1850s. Instead of seeing the Lawrence Scientific School, Sheffield Scientific School, and others as institutional responses in a college climate hostile to practical knowledge, Guralnick views them as administrative solutions to the demand for new areas of study which could no longer be accommodated within the already overcrowded college course. (An appendix provides brief biographies of fifty-nine professors who taught science or mathematics for at least five years between 1828 and 1860 at one of Guralnick's institutions.)

STM 148. HABAKKUK, H. J. American and British Technology in the Nineteenth Century: The Search for Labour-Saving Inventions. New York: Cambridge University Press, 1962. 222 pp.
English visitors to the U.S. in the first half of the 19th century noted in several industries a distinct American emphasis on mechanization, standardization, and mass production. Habakkuk, an economic historian, provides a theoretical analysis and an interpretive history of technological change in both England and the U.S. to explain the greater acceptance in the U.S. of capital intensive methods. He argues that the scarcity of labor in the U.S. and the relatively rapid expansion of investment

resulted in a propensity to solve manufacturing problems by introducing new mechanical means of production. England's abundance of labor, particularly after 1815, and slower rate of investment prevented it from following the same path. Although he focuses on the period before 1850, Habakkuk devotes his final chapter to a discussion of technological development in the half century before W.W. I. Again he stresses differences in labor and capital supply and market expansion.

STM 149. **HABER, SAMUEL.** Efficiency and Uplift: Scientific Management in the Progressive Era, 1890-1920. Chicago: University of Chicago Press, 1964. 181 pp.

In this study of scientific management and Progressivism, Haber discusses Frederick Winslow Taylor's ideas and the division of his followers into three ideological groups following his death. The author also describes the efficiency mania provoked by Louis Brandeis's insistence in 1910 that scientific management could save railroads millions of dollars. Subsequently, several leading Progressives adopted scientific management in a political reform program that gave a crucial role to an educated elite of experts. The major successes of the Taylorites and Progressives came in W.W. I when expert administration became for a time more important than politics and legislation, and efficiency became a patriotic duty. Finally, Haber discusses the brief alliance between scientific management and radical groups in the post-war period, and the Taylor Society's eventual return in the late 1920s to a more conservative pro-business orientation.

STM 150. **HALL, R. CARGILL.** Lunar Impact: A History of Project Ranger. Washington, D.C.: National Aeronautics and Space Administration, 1977. 450 pp.

Hall's history of Project Ranger from 1959 to 1965 describes the organizations, personalities, and technology which produced the first successful American lunar exploration. Sponsored by the National Aeronautics and Space Administration (NASA), the project was executed by the Jet Propulsion Laboratory at California Institute of Technology. He details the project's origins in the Sputnik era and describes its nine spacecraft launches-- the first six of which were failures. Hall also analyzes conflicts between different groups associated with the project: space scientists versus planetary scientists, scientists versus engineers, launch versus payload engineers, Air Force versus Army rocketeers, and NASA Headquarters versus field centers. President Kennedy's decision in 1961 to send a man to the moon provoked, Hall argues, a major change in the project: a multipurpose space and planetary science program became a narrowly focused probe to evaluate landing sites for the Apollo lunar module. In evaluating the Ranger legacy, Hall points out that the project provided technical and administrative models for subsequent NASA projects, both manned and unmanned.

STM 151. **HALLER, JOHN S., Jr.** American Medicine in Transition, 1840-1910. Urbana: University of Illinois Press, 1981. 457 pp.

Haller discusses several aspects of American life and medicine that transformed American medical care in the 19th century: the removal of practice from the home to the office or hospital, innovations in surgery, the growth of specialism, and germ theory, among others. He discusses physicians' reactions to these changes, and claims that most were "profoundly self-conscious" about their professional roles.

STM 152. HALLER, JOHN S., Jr. Outcasts from Evolution: Scientific Attitudes of Racial Inferiority, 1859-1900. Urbana: University of Illinois Press, 1971. 228 pp.

Haller's book is a study of intellectual thought on the nature of race from 1859--when Darwin's The Origin of Species appeared--to 1900--when Mendel's law of inheritance was rediscovered. During this period, commentators turned with relief to "science" to justify their views of the inferiority of the black race. He traces the "scientific" basis of 19th-century racism, examining such traditions as anthropometrical rationalizations, neo-Lamarckian theory, Social Darwinism, and Spencer's sociological applications of Darwinism.

STM 153. HALLER, JOHN S., Jr. and ROBIN M. HALLER. The Physician and Sexuality in Victorian America. Urbana: University of Illinois Press, 1974. 331 pp.

The authors describe how Victorian Americans increasingly turned to their physicians for sexual advice and how the Victorian physician accordingly became an arbiter of public morality, gradually replacing the minister in moral influence. They discuss the Victorian Era as a transitional stage in the development of middle-class morality, and argue that many Victorian women challenged traditional sexual roles in their new attention to sexuality within marriage.

STM 154. HALLER, MARK H. Eugenics: Hereditarian Attitudes in American Thought. New Brunswick, N.J.: Rutgers University Press, 1963. 264 pp.

Haller's history of the American eugenics movement is divided into three phases. Before 1905, many of those charged with the care and treatment of the feeble-minded, insane, epileptics, paupers, and criminals began to attribute their condition to heredity and to search for ways to improve the race by restricting their propagation. These hereditarian views were coupled with an incipient public reaction against the wave of immigrants. The eugenics movement, most influential between 1905 and 1930, offered a solution to the problem of "dependents and delinquents." Programs of sterilization, permanent custodial care, and immigration restriction were designed to prevent the "unfit" from breeding, thereby alleviating social problems. Initially a melioristic movement related to other Progressive reforms, eugenics became increasingly racist and conservative after W.W. I. The movement declined in the 1930s due to the excesses of Nazi eugenics and improved understanding of the complexity of human heredity, which undermined the purported scientific basis for eugenic measures. Haller examines the intellectual background of the movement and analyzes the views of American eugenists as diverse as Charles Benedict Davenport and Madison Grant.

STM 155. HAMMOND, JOHN W. Charles Proteus Steinmetz: A Biography. New York: Century, 1924. 489 pp.

Hammond's authorized biography of Charles Steinmetz remains the only full-length account of this important mathematician and electrical engineer. Hammond describes Steinmetz's ancestors, education, engineering work, and political ideals and activities. Because of his socialist affiliation in Breslau, Steinmetz fled Germany in 1888 and came to the U.S. Barely escaping deportation, Steinmetz worked first for Rudolf Eickemeyer, an electrical manufacturer and inventor in Yonkers, New York, and then for General Electric after it bought Eickemeyer's firm in 1892. Starting in the 1890s, Steinmetz made major engineering contributions by analyzing such problems as hysteresis (the loss of power due to the alternating magnetism of electric motors), providing mathematical calculations for alternating current systems, and investigating the effects of lightning on electrical systems. While at General Electric, Steinmetz functioned as a consulting engineer, taught at the local university in Schenectady, New York, and held public office as a socialist.

STM 156. **HAMMOND, JOHN W.** Men and Volts: The Story of General Electric.
Philadelphia: Lippincott, 1941. 424 pp.
Hammond describes the development of the General Electric Company as an
example of the history of the process of electrical invention and its
many commercial, industrial, and consumer uses and benefits. The work
also describes the corporation's advances concerning lighting, motors,
large-scale electrical systems, steam turbines, and applied research.
Hammond further traces the development of General Electric Company as
a vast organizational enterprise and as an increasingly important institution in American society.

STM 157. **HANLE, PAUL A.** Bringing Aerodynamics to America. Cambridge,
Mass.: MIT Press, 1982. 184 pp.
As air flight was being developed in the early years of this century,
most advances were made by German scientists, particularly those at Gottingen and Aachen. When Caltech's center for theoretical aerodynamics,
based on the Gottingen model, was established at Pasadena, Harry Guggenheim
saw the potential to develop national air supremacy, and sought to attract
German scientists to this country. This book details the efforts to bring
aviation pioneer Theodore von Karman to the U.S. in the 1920s and 1930s,
and discusses the establishment of the Caltech lab as the foremost center
for theoretical aerodynamics in the world.

STM 158. **HANSON, DIRK.** The New Alchemists: Silicon Valley and the Micro-
electronics Revolution. Boston: Little, Brown, 1982. 364 pp.
Hanson offers an account of the rise of the electric and electronic "hardware" industries which led to the development of computers, and especially
the new generation of computers from contemporary "Silicon Valley." The
work emphasizes developments since the late 1930s, including the very
large computing machines of W.W. II, the rise of solid state physical
technology, the development of silicon chips, and the implications of
these developments. Hanson expresses concern with whether the U.S. can
maintain its lead in technology over the other industrialized nations
of the world.

STM 159. **HARTLEY, EDWARD NEAL.** Ironworks on the Saugus: The Lynn and
Braintree Ventures of the Company of Undertakers of the Ironworks
in New England. Norman: University of Oklahoma Press, 1957.
328 pp.
Hartley, historian for the Saugus Ironworks Restoration from 1949 to 1954,
provides an account of this mid-17th century enterprise, which was the
first effective, sustained, and integrated ironworks producing cast and
wrought iron in Colonial America. First, he describes the origins of
the enterprise and the relationship between its promoters and government
at both local and English levels of authority. After examining the management of the ironworks, Hartley describes the technology involved, the
design of the works, the life of the workers, and the continuing economic
problems. The original owners of the works went bankrupt in the early
1650s, but the enterprise continued to operate until 1670. Its trained
workers went to other ironworks operating on a smaller scale and these
also proved unsuccessful. Hartley blames the failures upon inadequate
capitalization, high wages, and, above all, competition from imported
iron.

STM 160. **HARVEY, A. McGEHEE.** Adventures in Medical Research: A Century
of Discovery at Johns Hopkins. Baltimore, Md.: Johns Hopkins
University Press, 1976. 464 pp.
Harvey's study addresses the contributions physicians have made to clinical
research and medical education at Johns Hopkins University and Medical
School since the Hospital opened in 1889. He discusses William Welch's
role in bringing scientific methods to the practice of medicine, the impor-

tant contributions to surgery made by William Halsted and Hugh Young, and the introduction of new methods in open heart surgery in the last decades. His aim is not only to detail the work done at Johns Hopkins, but to explore the question of medical research in this country.

STM 161. HARVEY, A. McGEHEE. Science at the Bedside: Clinical Research in American Medicine, 1905-1945. Baltimore, Md.: Johns Hopkins University Press, 1981. 554 pp.

In his examination of the "evolution of clinical research" in the U.S., Harvey answers basic questions about who the clinical scientists were and what motivated them, what techniques they used, what facilities and training they had, how their research was supported and its results disseminated, and how clinical research was influenced by medical societies. His book has four parts. In the first, Harvey discusses formative influences on U.S. clinical research--the British, French, and finally, the German (specialization). In the second, he documents the development of facilities and institutions (notably Johns Hopkins Medical School and the Rockefeller Institute) which fostered clinical research. The third section relates the positive effect on research of professionalization--the establishment of full-time positions in clinical departments. The fourth section contains brief accounts of the development of research at fifteen geographically diverse U.S. medical centers.

STM 162. HASKELL, THOMAS L. The Emergence of Professional Social Science: The American Social Science Association and the Nineteenth-Century Crisis of Authority. Urbana: University of Illinois Press, 1977. 276 pp.

The American Social Science Association (ASSA), founded in 1865, was a pioneer effort of professional men, natural scientists, and university reformers to institutionalize social inquiry and to establish their authority as arbiters of intellectual and moral issues in American society. By the 1890s, the ASSA had spawned such diverse groups as the National Conference of Charities and Correction, the civil service reform movement, and specialist societies of economists, historians, and sociologists. Haskell's book focuses on the institutional history of the ASSA as a means of examining the transition from amateur to professional social science. He argues that the ascendancy of a younger generation of professionals in the 1890s may be explained by the reorientation of social thought which replaced older modes of social explanation by an outlook which stressed the interdependence of social groups in industrial society. Haskell's analysis relates the specialization of scholarship to broad official trends in late 19th-century America.

STM 163. HENRY, JOSEPH. The Papers of Joseph Henry. Vol. I: December 1797-October 1832: The Albany Years. Edited by Nathan Reingold, Stuart Pierson, Arthur P. Molella, James M. Hobbins, and John R. Kerwood. Washington, D.C.: Smithsonian Institution Press, 1972. 496 pp.

As the first Secretary of the Smithsonian Institution from 1846 to 1878, Joseph Henry (1797-1878) was a central figure in the American scientific community. The Henry Papers project, jointly sponsored by the Smithsonian, the National Academy of Sciences, and the American Philosophical Society, will provide extensive documentation on Henry's research and professional career. This volume, the first of a projected fifteen, covers Henry's years in Albany, New York, where he studied and taught before going to Princeton, New Jersey, in October 1832. Faced with a paucity of direct evidence about Henry's education and early career, the editors present a portrait of scientific culture in Albany during the 1820s, concentrating on the Albany Academy and the Albany Institute. Henry's relationships with local scientific men like T. Romeyn and L. C. Beck; his initial experiments in electricity and terrestrial magnetism; his correspondence with

Benjamin Silliman and others; and his interest in the applications of
science to technology are among other topics covered in this volume.

STM 164.   HENRY, JOSEPH. The Papers of Joseph Henry. Vol. II: November
           1832-December 1835: The Princeton Years. Edited by Nathan
           Reingold, Arthur P. Molella, Michele Aldrich, James M. Hobbins,
           and Kathleen Waldenfels. Washington, D.C.: Smithsonian Insti-
           tution Press, 1975. 524 pp.
This volume of the Henry Papers (the first of five on his Princeton years)
begins with his move from Albany in late 1832. Drawing on correspondence,
lecture notes, and other documents, the editors describe Henry's activities
as the new professor of natural philosophy at the College of New Jersey
(later Princeton University). During the early 1830s, Henry was preoccupied with his teaching and research. This volume shows him preparing
experimental demonstrations for his lectures; equipping a laboratory with
induction coils, galvanic batteries, magnets, and other apparatus for
his research in electro-magnetism; and making pilgrimages to Philadelphia,
where he became involved in an active scientific community. Henry fre-
quented Peale's Museum, the Franklin Institute, and the American Philosophical Society in Philadelphia, and discussed his work with Alexander
Dallas Bache, Robert Hare, and other new colleagues. Henry continued
his experimental investigations at Princeton; the latter part of the volume
details his work on self-induction (begun in August 1834) and the subsequent priority dispute with Michael Faraday.

STM 165.   HEWLETT, RICHARD G. and OSCAR E. ANDERSON, Jr. A History of
           the United States Atomic Energy Commission. Vol. I: The New
           World, 1939-1946. University Park: Pennsylvania State Univer-
           sity Press, 1962. 766 pp.
In this first volume of the U.S. Atomic Energy Commission's (AEC) official
history, Hewlett and Anderson describe the war-time atomic bomb project
and the post-war legislative battle that led to the establishment of the
AEC. Concentrating on the highest level of decision-making, the authors
explain effects technological development had on national and international
policy decisions. For each stage of the atomic bomb's development, they
provide a detailed account of seemingly insurmountable technical problems
and the complex interrelationship of science, industry, and government.
Hewlett and Anderson then examine the origins of the Atomic Energy Commission Act of 1946 and attempts to gain international control of atomic
energy. They describe the political infighting and scientists' lobby
which blocked military control of atomic energy. Their history ends on
January 1, 1947, when the new Commission took over control of atomic energy
from the military.

STM 166.   HEWLETT, RICHARD G. and FRANCIS DUNCAN. A History of the United
           States Atomic Energy Commission. Vol. II: Atomic Shield, 1947-
           1952. University Park: Pennsylvania State University Press,
           1969. 718 pp.
This second volume of the U.S. Atomic Energy Commission's official history
begins in January 1947, when the Commission assumed responsibility for
the remnants of the W.W. II project that produced the first atomic bomb
and ends with the detonation in November 1952 of the first thermonuclear
bomb. By 1952, the Commission supported hundreds of nuclear scientists
working in national and other laboratories and presided over a nuclear
weapons arsenal, giant production facilities, and twelve experimental,
or research, reactors. To explain this transformation, the authors investigate the Commission's administrative history and the relationship of
scientific research, public policy, and national defense during the Cold
War. A major development described is the shift from the initial anticipation of the peaceful use of atomic energy to an increasing stress on
weapons after the Soviet Union in 1949 detonated its first atomic bomb.

For reasons of national security, Americans then built, according to the authors, an atomic shield against their former ally.

STM 167. HEWLETT, RICHARD and FRANCIS DUNCAN. Nuclear Navy, 1946-1962. Chicago: University of Chicago Press, 1974. 477 pp.
Hewlett and Duncan provide an administrative history of the U.S. Navy's nuclear propulsion program, which during the Cold War revolutionized the design first of submarines and then of other Naval vessels. The key figure in the study is Hyman G. Rickover, a Naval engineering officer who, when named head of the Navy's reactor project, turned it into a crusade for a nuclear fleet. First, the authors provide an historical context for Rickover's project; then they focus on Rickover and analyze his particular style of technological innovation. Rickover built a practical industrial engineering organization and kept close control over all aspects of the project. He set up an informal organization of technical specialists and engineers rather than relying on the usual hierarchy of Navy administrators. The authors recount the difficulties Rickover faced, his methods for maintaining administrative control over all aspects of nuclear energy in the Navy, and his close collaboration with and even control of civilian contractors.

STM 168. HINDLE, BROOKE. David Rittenhouse. Princeton, N.J.: Princeton University Press, 1964. 394 pp.
In a eulogy for David Rittenhouse (1732-1796), Benjamin Rush hailed him as "one of the luminaries of the eighteenth century." Based on extensive manuscript resources, Brooke Hindle's biography deals with the varied aspects of Rittenhouse's career in science and politics. A Philadelphia manufacturer of orreries, telescopes, and surveying instruments, Rittenhouse's primary scientific interests were closely related to his instrument making. He was centrally involved in American observations of the transit of Venus in 1769 and published a number of papers on astronomical calculations. Like many of his contemporaries, Rittenhouse investigated a wide range of subjects in natural philosophy, including meteorology, optics, and magnetism. As president of the American Philosophical Society, he was influential in the institutional life of early American science. Rittenhouse was also active in politics during the American Revolution and early Republic, serving as treasurer of Pennsylvania (1777-1789) and first director of the U.S. Mint (1792-1795).

STM 169. HINDLE, BROOKE. Emulation and Invention. New York: New York University Press, 1981. 162 pp.
Hindle's book has two major concerns: the inventiveness and creativity at the center of mechanical technology, and the American environment which encourages such inventiveness. Regarding the first of these concerns, Hindle argues that inventions come out of the practice of emulation, which he defines as the urge "to equal or surpass the work of others." Emulation, according to him, grows out of traditional ways of instructing in the practical and fine arts and relies upon "spatial thinking" (that is, non-verbal conceptualizing). Regarding the second major concern, Hindle notes that the American Revolution and Industrial Revolution overlap in time and states that American leaders were "responsive to the opportunities [technology] offered the new nation." He focuses on two "conceptually new technologies"--the steamboat (which put the new steam engine to use) and the telegraph (which utilized electromagnetism).

STM 170. HINDLE, BROOKE. The Pursuit of Science in Revolutionary America, 1735-1789. Chapel Hill: University of North Carolina Press, 1956. 410 pp.
This monograph deals with the role of science in American society from the 1730s through the Revolutionary War and the establishment of the new nation. Hindle begins with a description of the cultural circles of natu-

ral historians, physicians, clergymen, and natural philosophers who established intercolonial networks for the dissemination of scientific information. Informal contacts were institutionalized in scientific societies, medical schools, and other organizations during the 1760s and 1770s, and observations of the transit of Venus in 1769 brought American science to European attention. Hindle surveys the spectrum of scientific investigation during this period, from the work of David Rittenhouse and Benjamin Franklin to the less recondite realms of surveying, exploration, and natural history. Hindle argues that the American Revolution lent impetus to the growth of scientific institutions as an expression of cultural nationalism. Faith in the benefits of scientific progress prompted continued activity in medicine, natural history, and natural philosophy during the early Republic, while utilitarian interests in economic improvement motivated the practical application of science to agriculture, commerce, and industry.

STM 171. HINDLE, BROOKE. Technology in Early America: Needs and Opportunities for Study. Chapel Hill: University of North Carolina Press, 1966. 145 pp.
This bibliography of the history of American technology covers the period prior to 1850. By way of introduction, Hindle provides a short interpretive essay, in which he evaluates existing approaches to the history of technology, stresses the need to study the things built and the men who built them, and considers key problems in the history of American technology. In his critical bibliographic essay, Hindle treats both recent and contemporary guides, sources, surveys, and studies of American technology. He provides an outline for the history of American technology and identifies key figures. Finally, Lucius Ellsworth surveys the literature on artifact collections and describes collections owned by various museums, sites of historical reconstruction, and historical societies in the U.S.

STM 172. HINDLE, BROOKE, ed. America's Wooden Age: Aspects of Its Early Technology. Tarrytown, N.Y.: Sleepy Hollow Restorations, 1975. 218 pp.
Few have investigated the wood technology that pervasively conditioned American society prior to the 1850s. This volume contains six essays on different aspects of this subject and an introduction, in which Hindle describes the wide uses wood found in early America. Three authors examine the relationships between wood and historical events and trends: Charles F. Carroll describes the effect abundant forests had on settlers in Colonial New England; Nathan Rosenberg traces the development of wood-working machines between 1800 and 1850 and argues that Americans sought resource-intensive methods of manufacture; Louis C. Hunter recounts the central role water power, based on wood technology, played in American industrialization. In the remaining essays, Charles E. Peterson explains lumbering through a pictorial essay, Silvio A. Bedini treats the use of wood in a variety of scientific instruments, and Charles Howell describes water-powered Colonial grist mills.

STM 173. HINDLE, BROOKE, ed. Early American Science. New York: Science History, 1976. 213 pp.
This volume contains reprints of twenty-two Isis articles originally published between 1925 and 1973. Three-fifths of the articles first appeared between 1950 and 1961, a period when studies of early American science flourished, for reasons discussed in Hindle's introduction. The collection begins with important historiographic essays by George Sarton, Arthur M. Schlesinger, and Richard H. Shryock. Benjamin Franklin looms large: eight selections concern aspects of his scientific interests. Scientific biographies of Thomas Robie, James Logan, Thomas Clap, and John Lining are also included, as well as studies in the history of scientific ideas, such as the American reception of mechanical philosophy and phlogiston

theory. In the final section, articles by Brooke Hindle and John Greene address the wider social meanings of science in Colonial Philadelphia and Jeffersonian America.

STM 174.   HINSLEY, CURTIS M., Jr. Savages and Scientists: The Smithsonian Institution and the Development of American Anthropology, 1846-1910. Washington, D.C.: Smithsonian Institution Press, 1981. 319 pp.
The work traces the development of anthropological studies done under the Federal government's aegis from the founding of the Smithsonian Institution in 1846 to 1910, when the power and prestige of the professional academic movement, led by Franz Boas, overshadowed "government anthropology." Hinsley pays considerable attention to various government anthropologists, including John Wesley Powell, William Henry Holmes, and James Mooney. He emphasizes the intellectual history of the leading anthropologists at the Smithsonian Institution, and develops an analysis of 19th-century "scientific professionalism" which differs from much of the recent literature on the topic.

STM 175.   HIRSHFELD, DANIEL S. The Lost Reform: The Campaign for Compulsory Health Insurance in the United States from 1932 to 1943. Cambridge, Mass.: Harvard University Press, 1970. 221 pp.
Hirshfeld's chronological study begins in 1900, when the foundations for compulsory health insurance were laid in reform movements which extended into the health field. With the Depression and the emergence of the Social Security system in 1935, the efforts of health reformers seemed to have been rewarded. Hirshfeld's book details the failure of Federal health insurance in the context of other reform efforts. By 1943, however, advocates of Federal health insurance changed tactics, and began to work for a single centralized national program, and progress again began to be made.

STM 176.   HOFFMAN, WILLIAM and JERRY SHIELDS. Doctors on the New Frontier: Breaking Through the Barriers of Modern Medicine. New York: Macmillan, 1981. 207 pp.
The authors discuss recent breakthroughs in medical research, among them Norman Shumway's work with heart transplants, Noguchi's developments in forensic medicine, and Nathan Kline's research on tranquilizers. They discuss as well sensationalistic and controversial research such as cloning, brain-freezing, and the thalidomide disaster.

STM 177.   HOFSTADTER, RICHARD. Social Darwinism in American Thought. 1944; Rev. ed. Boston: Beacon Press, 1955. 248 pp.
This monograph deals with the impact of Darwinian evolution on American social thought during the late 19th and early 20th centuries. Hofstadter carefully distinguishes between the influence of Darwin's work and the writings of Herbert Spencer, whose doctrines were in vogue in the U.S. By analyzing the views of William Graham Sumner and Lester Frank Ward, Hofstadter demonstrates how evolutionary metaphors were used to support both conservative and reform social ideologies. Later chapters trace these alternative versions of social Darwinism through debates on ethics, politics, and other areas of social theory, and assess the influence of Darwinism on the social gospel and pragmatist movements. Finally, Hofstadter explores how social Darwinism was invoked by American expansionists during the 1890s to justify racist and imperialistic visions of national purpose.

STM 178. HOLLINGER, DAVID. _Morris R. Cohen and the Scientific Ideal._
Cambridge, Mass.: MIT Press, 1975. 262 pp.
Morris R. Cohen, a Russian-Jewish immigrant who was a principal founder
of the discipline of the philosophy of science, is the subject of this
book. Cohen was one of the first to study the growing "scientific culture"
of 20th-century America, and yet remained critical of crudely empiricist
or behavioristic pseudoscientific views of human behavior. This study
attempts to place Cohen's contributions to 20th-century intellectual
thought in America.

STM 179. HORWITCH, MEL. _Clipped Wings: The American SST Conflict._ Cambridge, Mass.: MIT Press, 1982. 473 pp.
Conflict over the building of commercial supersonic transports began in
the 1960s, and culminated in the shutdown of all efforts to build American
SSTs in 1971. Horwitch's book details how the SST debate involved not
only issues of technological innovation and its economics, but how it
grew into an environmental issue, attracting widespread societal concern.
The SST conflict is placed in a larger context of increased suspicion
toward technological change in the 1960s, and the consequences public
opinion have had on governmental decision-making on technological issues.

STM 180. HOVENKAMP, HERBERT. _Science and Religion in America, 1800-1860._
Philadelphia: University of Pennsylvania Press, 1978. 273 pp.
Most American Protestants in the early 19th century shared a belief that
nature presented incontrovertible evidence of the existence and sovereignty
of God. Natural theology thus provided common ground between orthodox
religion and Baconian science. Using a variety of religious periodicals,
natural theological treatises, biblical tracts, and scientific literature,
Hovenkamp explores the relationships of science and religion in antebellum
America. He discusses the attempts of theologians to construct a science
of religion which utilized Baconian methodology to demonstrate the validity
of religious belief. The efforts of natural scientists to reconcile
religion with science are examined through the analysis of debates over
uniformitarian geology, interpretations of Genesis, the species question,
the unity of the human race, and biological evolution.

STM 181. HUGHES, THOMAS PARKE. _Elmer Sperry: Inventor and Engineer._
Baltimore, Md.: Johns Hopkins University Press, 1971.
348 pp.
Sperry was a major figure in the history of control engineering and founder
of the company that became the giant Sperry Rand Corporation. Spanning
the years from 1880 to 1930, Sperry's career encompassed the era of heroic
independent inventors and the transition to organized research and development. Hughes traces Sperry's career from his first inventions in arc
lighting to his later work in gyroscopic closed loop, or feedback, controls,
when he directed engineers, inventors, and industrial scientists in his
own research and development companies. Hughes investigates through Sperry
the inventive process and characterizes him as an inventor-entrepreneur
presiding over technological change. However, the course of Sperry's
career also enables Hughes to shed light on the rise of American industrialism and finance capitalism, early military-industrial contracts,
and other important aspects of the history of American technology.

STM 182. HUGHES, THOMAS PARKE. _Networks of Power: Electrification in
Western Society, 1880-1930._ Baltimore, Md.: Johns Hopkins
University Press, 1983. 474 pp.
Hughes states that, although historians and social scientists have paid
much attention to the impact of technology on society, few have examined
the effect of society, or culture, on the "shape of technology." He limits
his history of the electric power systems to various regional power systems
in three countries: the U.S., Great Britain, and Germany. Declaring

that power systems are cultural artifacts, Hughes finds that the decision-makers behind the power systems in these three countries--even though they had the same pool of technology to draw upon--created different kinds of systems because "geographical, cultural, managerial, engineering, and entrepreneurial" factors differed from region to region. In spite of these differences, Hughes proposes a four-phase model for the growth of power systems during this era: invention and development, technology transfer from one place to another, growth, and substantial momentum.

STM 183. HUGHES, THOMAS PARKE, ed. Changing Attitudes Toward American Technology. New York: Harper & Row, 1975. 340 pp.
Hughes has collected recent selections on attitudes toward technology as well as historical responses by such writers as Henry David Thoreau, Henry Adams, and newspaper editors. Chronologically arranged, the essays reveal overwhelming optimism in the 19th century about the technological future, a growing belief that a technological society was imminent, and finally disillusionment during W.W. I and the Depression. The study is preceded by a section of essays about current attitudes by such writers as Barry Commoner and Perry Miller.

STM 184. HUNTER, LOUIS C. A History of Industrial Power in the United States, 1780-1930. Vol. I: Waterpower in the Century of the Steam Engine. Charlottesville: University Press of Virginia, 1979. 606 pp.
Hunter traces the introduction and extension of the use of machinery in production. He also examines the advances in the generation and distribution of power, as well as the development of supporting facilities. He places these developments within the context of economic history. Hunter also analyzes machine power within its social context: that is, how machines affected the people using them and their relations with each other. He makes frequent comparisons to the process of industrialization in Europe, especially in England and France; and includes chapters on water-driven mills, mill and factory villages, and the first industrialized cities. The work also includes numerous illustrations.

STM 185. HUNTER, LOUIS C. Steamboats on Western Rivers: An Economic and Technological History. Cambridge, Mass.: Harvard University Press, 1949. 684 pp.
Hunter provides an account of the economic, technological, and business aspects of the American steamboat on Western rivers from its rapid rise in the 1820s and 1830s to its even more rapid decline after the Civil War. First, he describes the introduction and expansion of steamboat traffic in the West and the slow evolution of flimsy, shallow draft, fresh-water vessels, well adapted to navigational requirements and Western economic and technological resources. Next, he analyzes the business organization of steamboat manufacture and operation and explains the antebellum prevalence of small-scale individualistic enterprise. Finally, Hunter describes the decline of the steamboat. After 1850 railroads provided faster and more reliable service and replaced the long-standing East-West trade through New Orleans and up the Mississippi. Hunter compares railroads and steamboats and explains the economic and trade factors that first encouraged, then undermined the steamboat.

STM 186. IMERSHEIN, ALLEN W., ed. Challenges and Innovations in U.S. Health Care. Boulder, Colo.: Westview Press, 1981. 154 pp.
The essays collected in this volume describe or analyze various recent attempts to change the state of health care in America. Imershein differs, in his introduction, with other critics of the health care system who conclude that there is "little potential for significant change." Topics covered include the potential of nonphysician primary care, health maintenance organizations, the confusion arising out of legislation that estab-

lished agencies for planning and organizing health services, the shortcomings of neighborhood health centers established as part of the "Great
Society" program, the Veterans Administration, changing physician ideology
with regard to communication with dying patients, chiropractic (the outside
challenge to medicine), suggestions for better promoting healthy lifestyles,
ineffective consumer involvement in organizing health care, and the more
effective self-care movement.

STM 187. JAFFE, BERNARD. Men of Science in America. 1944; Rev. ed.
          New York: Simon & Schuster, 1958. 715 pp.
Jaffe selects twenty American scientists who conducted pioneering research,
more in the field of pure than applied science, and argues that, contrary
to opinion, America has made significant contributions in this field.
He provides biographical portraits of, among others, Benjamin Franklin,
Louis Agassiz, Thomas Hunt Morgan, Edwin Powell Hubble, and Enrico Fermi.

STM 188. JENKINS, REESE V. Images and Enterprise: Technology and the
          American Photographic Industry, 1839-1925. Baltimore, Md.:
          Johns Hopkins University Press, 1975. 371 pp.
In this study of the American photographic industry, Jenkins demonstrates
the central role technical change played in the formulation of business
strategies and the industry's organizational structure. He identifies
distinctive product technologies as fundamental for explaining marketing
changes and the general history of the industry and divides his book into
five sections corresponding to periods dominated by different photosensi-
tive carrier bases or forms of photography. The initial chapters focus
on the daguerreotype and the wet collodion periods, but the major portion
of the book deals with the period after 1880 and the development of dry
gelatin on glass plates, the gelatin on celluloid film in the amateur
roll film system, and cinematographic film which became economically important after 1909. Focusing on the central role of technology, Jenkins
provides a history of the industry from a reliance on empirical methods
in the early decentralized, draft-based industry to the period of institutionalized technological innovation in a highly centralized industry.

STM 189. JEREMY, DAVID J. Transatlantic Industrial Revolution: The Dif-
          fusion of Textile Technologies Between Britain and America,
          1790-1830. Cambridge, Mass.: MIT Press, 1981. 296 pp.
Jeremy deals with the problems inherent in the transfer and diffusion
of technology from one culture to another by using as an example the transit of British textile technology to America in the early 19th century.
The larger economic and social conditions which made the transfer of technology possible are stressed. Jeremy argues that industrialization of
the textile industry occurred earlier in America than has been previously
believed, and that by the early 19th century technology was crossing the
Atlantic in both directions. The four specific industries dealt with
are cotton spinning, power-loom weaving, calico printing, and woolen manufacturing.

STM 190. JEWKES, JOHN, DAVID SAWERS, and RICHARD STILLERMAN. The Sources
          of Invention. 1958; Rev. ed. New York: Norton, 1969. 372 pp.
The authors of this study explore the conditions under which modern industrial inventions have arisen in modern times, seeking to pinpoint the
nature of invention rather than development. Portraits of individual
inventors and studies of corporation research precede case histories of
such technological inventions as the safety razor, insulin, the Moulton
bicycle, and xerography.

STM 191. JOHNSON, ARTHUR MENZIES. The Development of American Petroleum
Pipelines: A Study in Private Enterprise and Public Policy,
1862-1906. Ithaca, N.Y.: Cornell University Press, 1956.
307 pp.
Johnson examines the relationship of private enterprise to public policy
by tracing the development of petroleum pipelines between the Civil War
and the early 20th century. Pipelines were significant because they were
more efficient as overland oil carriers, there was no direct public contact
with them, and they developed within a free enterprise economy. Hence,
there was little effective public policy to regulate them. Indeed, public
policy was used as a "competitive weapon" in intra-oil industry struggles,
and also between railroad and oil corporations. Standard Oil capitalized
on public indifference and ignorance to fight off any attempts by state
governments to regulate it. By 1906, Johnson argues, the regulation
of pipelines had become a national problem, and the Federal government
interceded in an attempt to regulate interstate pipeline transport. Public
indifference and corporate power, however, had largely set the patterns
of conflict, and would limit the effectiveness of the government's efforts.

STM 192. JOHNSON, THOMAS C., Jr. Scientific Interests in the Old South.
New York: Appleton-Century, 1936. 217 pp.
Johnson discusses Southern contributions to American technology; Southerners played a large role in the development of the steam railway, the
improved cotton-gin, the reaper, the Atlantic cable, and photography.
He discusses scientific education in Southern schools and the support
of scientific work by political leaders. His study consists in large
part of descriptions of the careers of individuals.

STM 193. JONAS, STEVEN. Medical History: The Training of Doctors in
the United States. New York: Norton, 1978. 426 pp.
Jonas analyzes problems in health care delivery in America, concluding
that the underlying fault is in medical education. He provides a brief
history of medical education and evaluates its current status, and proposes a new system of medical education that he calls "health-oriented
physician education," emphasizing the importance of preventive measures
in health care.

STM 194. JONAS, STEVEN, ed. Health Care Delivery in the United States.
1977; Rev. ed. New York: Springer, 1981. 492 pp.
This collection of essays describes the various elements of health care
delivery in America and their interactions. The essays address the economics and politics of health care in nursing, ambulatory care, mental
health services; the role of government in health care; and National Health
Insurance.

STM 195. JONES, JAMES H. Bad Blood: The Tuskegee Syphilis Experiment.
New York: Free Press, 1981. 272 pp.
Jones's study describes the infamous Tuskegee Syphilis Experiment, a forty-
year experiment in which Southern black men with syphilis were left
untreated in order to study the unchecked evolution of the disease. Told
they had "bad blood," the black men cooperated with the Federal program
they believed was helping them. Jones attempts to explain how the public
health officials who initiated and continued the study had good intentions
and yet allowed the experiment to go on until the story was broken in
1972.

STM 196. JOSEPHSON, MATTHEW. Edison: A Biography. New York: McGraw-
Hill, 1959. 511 pp.
In this biography, Josephson focuses on Edison's inventive activity from
the 1860s to the 1890s. He argues that Edison's style of invention
included surveys of relevant scientific literature, an emphasis on practical

inventions to meet market demands, and the systematic application of scientific methods. Born in 1847, Edison worked as a tramp telegraph operator in the 1860s and devoted most of his early inventive activity to telegraphic apparatus. Josephson argues that Edison established the world's first industrial research laboratory in 1876 at Menlo Park, New Jersey, where he invented a system of electric lighting. Josephson details Edison's promotion of this lighting system in the 1880s and his shifting interest to areas such as ore separation, motion pictures, and the nickel storage battery in the 1890s. An underlying theme is Edison's continuing conflicts with his financial backers. In the final chapters Josephson discusses Edison's friendship with Henry Ford, his later years, and his death in 1931.

STM 197. JUNGK, ROBERT. Brighter Than a Thousand Suns: A Personal History of the Atomic Scientists. New York: Harcourt, Brace, 1958. 360 pp.
The work is an account of the development of the atomic bomb, along with its profound implications. It includes a discussion of non-American developments, such as the German effort during W.W. II, in order to place the American effort in perspective. Jungk discusses the Manhattan Project in some detail, as well as post-war developments, with particular regard to the development of the U.S.S.R.'s atomic program. The study also describes, at length, American concerns over "disloyalty" and "espionage" as part of the overall policy regarding nuclear warfare.

STM 198. KAKAR, SUDHIR. Frederick Taylor: A Study in Personality and Innovation. Cambridge, Mass.: MIT Press, 1970. 221 pp.
Kakar's psychohistorical study of Frederick Taylor places the inventor of scientific management in his cultural and historical context and investigates the relation between personality and innovative drive. Kakar describes Taylor's parents, early childhood, and social and economic milieu and identifies recurring themes and conflicts in Taylor's personality. Next, he describes Taylor's apprenticeship and career at Midvale Steel Works. During this period, Taylor through his work temporarily resolved basic conflicts in his personality and achieved most of his innovations in engineering and scientific management. Finally, Kakar discusses Taylor's activities after Midvale, his dismissal from Bethlehem Steel, and his years, until his death in 1915, as prophet of scientific management. Kakar points out that Taylor's resolution through scientific management of his neurotic anxieties about authority and subordination addressed important problems of industrial management in a period when traditional methods of management were fast becoming obsolete.

STM 199. KARGON, ROBERT H. The Rise of Robert Millikan: Portrait of a Life in American Science. Ithaca, N.Y.: Cornell University Press, 1982. 205 pp.
Robert Millikan (1868-1953), the first American-born physicist to win the Nobel Prize, is the subject of this self-described "essay" in the history of American science. Millikan was particularly noted for his work on the electron and cosmic rays; he was instrumental too in the development of the California Institute of Technology as a major innovative force in American science and technology. Kargon's portrait places Millikan in the context of a technocratic trend in the 20th century.

STM 200. KARGON, ROBERT H., ed. The Maturing of American Science: A Portrait of Science in Public Life Drawn from the Presidential Addresses of the American Association for the Advancement of Science 1920-1970. Washington, D.C.: American Association for the Advancement of Science, 1974. 256 pp.

This selection of AAAS presidential addresses illuminates the changing relations of science and society in the U.S. from 1920 to 1970. Kargon's introduction, "The New Era: Science and American Individualism in the 1920's," discusses the efforts of leading scientists and engineers (like George Ellery Hale, Robert A. Millikan, Gano Dunn, J. J. Carty, and Frank B. Jewett) to obtain public and private support for scientific research after W.W. I. Kargon focuses on the National Research Council, the growth of industrial research, science in government (especially Herbert Hoover's Department of Commerce), and the ill-fated National Research Fund. The fifteen presidential addresses which follow are divided into four groups, corresponding to periods Kargon sees in the recent history of American science. From 1920 to 1940, the importance of science to economic growth was a characteristic theme. The second phase (1940-1957) was one of wartime reorganization of science and the expansion of research and development in the Federal bureaucracy. From 1958 to 1965, the problems of managing science and the need for a national science policy gained priority. Finally, public criticism of science during the late 1960s was accompanied by retrenchment in Federal support. The increasing dependence of the American scientific establishment on public funds is a major theme in The Maturing of American Science.

STM 201. KASSON, JOHN. Civilizing the Machine: Technology and Republican Values in America, 1776-1900. New York: Grossman, 1976. 274 pp.

Kasson argues that technological development and republican values, like human freedom, political and moral purity, and social responsibility and harmony, shaped one another throughout the 19th century. He focuses on several cases that exemplify this interaction. He begins with the debate during the Revolutionary Era over the introduction of domestic manufacturers and the attempt to build a model Republican factory town in Lowell, Massachusetts, to avoid the factory problems found in Europe. By the 1830s and 1840s political and economic problems became evident at Lowell, and Ralph Waldo Emerson began asking if technology would be a liberating or deadening force on culture and individual imagination. Kasson also describes the aesthetic responses to, and claims for, machinery and investigates the crisis of American Republicanism in an urban-industrial age through several utopian and dystopian novels of the 1880s and 1890s.

STM 202. KAUFMAN, MARTIN. American Medical Education: The Formative Years, 1765-1910. Westport, Conn.: Greenwood Press, 1976. 208 pp.

Kaufman surveys the history of American medical education from the founding of the University of Pennsylvania Medical School in 1765 to the Flexner Report of 1910. He focuses on calls for medical reform in the 19th century and argues that Jacksonian pressures to liberalize licensing laws paved the way to increased competition between regular physicians and sectarian doctors during the antebellum period. The lack of standards for medical schools at the time led also to the proliferation of unregulated proprietary institutions. The efforts of the American Medical Association (AMA) and other reform groups were unsuccessful until late in the century, when the Johns Hopkins University Medical School provided an institutional model based on scientific research and thorough clinical training. Organizations like the American Association of Medical Colleges (1890) and the AMA Council on Medical Education (1905) exerted increasing control over professional training.

STM 203. **KELLY, FRED C.** The Wright Brothers. New York: Harcourt, Brace, 1943. 340 pp.

Kelly's biography was authorized by Orville Wright; it offers a complete profile of both brothers but does not document Orville's scientific work after Wilbur's death. Kelly describes their early experiments and the first flights, and goes on to detail as well their involvement in developing airplanes in America and abroad. The volume also contains several early photographs.

STM 204. **KELLY, PATRICK and MELVIN KRANZBERG**, eds. Technological Innovation: A Critical Review of Current Knowledge. San Francisco: San Francisco Press, 1978. 390 pp.

Kelly and Kranzberg maintain that technological innovation is an important component of economic growth. In this volume, "technological innovation" includes a range of activities from initial problem definition, through research and development, to the diffusion of new technical devices, processes, and products. An interdisciplinary research team of six scholars, the Georgia Tech Innovation Project group, had overall responsibility for this study of our knowledge of innovation. In the initial five chapters, the group investigates general themes and argues for a holistic, "ecological" approach transcending disciplinary bounds. The following nine chapters deal with such topics as the role of inventors, innovation and natural resources, innovation in industry, diffusion of innovations, technological forecasting, and innovation and economic growth. There is also an extensive bibliography of works on technological innovation.

STM 205. **KENNEDY, DAVID M.** Birth Control in America: The Career of Margaret Sanger. New Haven, Conn.: Yale University Press, 1970. 320 pp.

Kennedy chronicles Sanger's role in the birth control movement from 1912 to W.W. II; he argues that Sanger's temperament both informed and responded to the changing fortunes of the movement in those years, when birth control was first advocated and officially rejected and then, finally, more broadly accepted. Sanger retired from the movement as birth control became acceptable. Kennedy also places Sanger's work in a social and cultural context.

STM 206. **KENNEDY, GAIL,** ed. Evolution and Religion: The Conflict Between Science and Theology in Modern America. Boston: Heath, 1957. 114 pp.

This collection of essays, preceded by an introduction by the editor, illustrates the American response to Darwinism, particularly in reference to religion. Seminal essays by William Jennings Bryan and Henry Ward Beecher represent accommodationist responses; an essay by Arthur Garfield Hays discusses the Scopes trial, and Sidney Hook's "The New Failure of Nerve" is included. The editor argues that four responses were available to Americans: "fundamentalism, humanism, modernism, and the new orthodoxy."

STM 207. **KETT, JOSEPH F.** The Formation of the American Medical Profession: The Role of Institutions, 1780-1860. New Haven, Conn.: Yale University Press, 1968.

Kett discusses the attempts of medical societies, licensing boards, and medical schools to regulate the medical profession in Maryland, Massachusetts, New York, Ohio, and South Carolina before the Civil War. He contrasts the organization of Colonial medical practice with earlier European traditions, but emphasizes professional developments between 1820 and 1860. Case studies of Thomsonianism (a medical sect based on botanic remedies) and homeopathy provide Kett with a perspective for analyzing the role of institutions in transforming the American medical profession. He argues that the decline of Thomsonianism after 1845 reflected the increased status of trained medical advisers over domestic practitioners.

The debate between regular physicians and homeopaths in the 1850s was one between two types of educated physicians. By the eve of the Civil War, the prevalence of medical degrees and public demands for physicians with scientific training tightened requirements for entering the medical profession more effectively than antebellum licensing laws and the efforts of medical organizations.

STM 208. KEVLES, DANIEL J. The Physicists: The History of a Scientific Community in Modern America. New York: Knopf, 1978. 489 pp.
The Physicists is an account of the transformation of American physics from a provincial backwater in the late 19th century to world leader by the 1940s. In this study, Daniel J. Kevles traces the networks of elites and institutions--academic, industrial, and governmental--that linked physics to its social environs and conditioned the opportunities and expectations of successive generations of practitioners. By constructing a rich context for his treatment of the physics community, Kevles also provides a guide to the social history of modern American science in general. Two major themes run through his narrative. Leading physicists espoused an ideal of "science for its own sake," yet found their patrons among big business and the military, who were interested less in the advance of knowledge than in the utilities of science for economic benefit and military might. The same leaders adhered to a political philosophy of "best science" elitism, which conflicted with American democratic traditions of geographic and institutional pluralism. The tensions generated by these contrasts had important implications for the power and status of the physics community.

STM 209. KILLIAN, JAMES R., Jr. Sputnik, Scientists, and Eisenhower: A Memoir of the First Special Assistant to the President for Science and Technology. Cambridge, Mass.: MIT Press, 1977. 315 pp.
In November 1957, President Eisenhower created the President's Science Advisory Committee (PSAC) and appointed MIT President James R. Killian, Jr., as his first special Assistant for Science and Technology. Killian and PSAC were to provide advice to the White House on space and defense research and on ways to strengthen American science and technology. Based on personal recollections and contemporary documents, this memoir deals primarily with Killian's service in the Eisenhower Administration. He begins with the public reaction to Sputnik and the discussions which led to his appointment. Killian places PSAC in the context of earlier science advisory groups in the executive branch of the U.S. government and decribes the White House milieu in which he worked. Next, he outlines the membership and organization of PSAC from 1957 to 1959, and PSAC's role in debates over the organization of the National Aeronautics and Space Administration, defense missile programs, arms limitation negotiations, the coordination of government scientific research, and Federal support for science education. Killian also discusses his relationship with Eisenhower and the continuing need for science advice in the White House.

STM 210. KISTIAKOWSKY, GEORGE B. A Scientist at the White House: The Private Diary of President Eisenhower's Special Assistant for Science and Technology. Cambridge, Mass.: Harvard University Press, 1976. 448 pp.
George Kistiakowsky, Harvard chemist and veteran of Los Alamos, succeeded James Killian as Eisenhower's Special Assistant for Science and Technology on July 15, 1959. On that day he began a private journal of entries about his White House activities until his appointment ended in 1960. Besides heading the President's Science Advisory Committee, Kistiakowsky was involved in the technical aspects of arms control negotiations, bureaucratic rivalries over defense research and development and the space race, and in establishing priorities for the cultivation of American science.

Though necessarily limited in perspective, the diary documents the practical politics of science policy advising in the post-Sputnik years. Kistiakowsky has added explanatory notes to the text of the diary, and Charles S. Maier's introduction places it in historical context.

STM 211. KOHLSTEDT, SALLY GREGORY. The Formation of the American Scientific Community: The American Association for the Advancement of Science 1848-1860. Urbana: University of Illinois Press, 1976. 414 pp.

This detailed account of the creation and early years of the American Association for the Advancement of Science (AAAS) focuses on internal politics and institutional history. Kohlstedt examines American responses to the model provided by the British Association for the Advancement of Science (1831) and discusses precursors like the American Association of Geologists and Naturalists (1840). During the 1840s and 1850s, continuing tension existed between amateur and professional AAAS members who placed differing emphases on the relative value of original research and the dissemination of scientific knowledge. Kohlstedt discusses the efforts of the Lazzaroni and other leaders to control American science by establishing and enforcing standards for research and publication. As a national scientific congress, the AAAS became the arena for debates between amateur and professional factions in antebellum science. Kohlstedt also presents a collective biography of the AAAS leadership and other members, over 2,200 persons who constitute a "profile of the active scientific community from 1848 to 1860."

STM 212. KOPPES, CLAYTON R. JPL and the American Space Program: A History of the Jet Propulsion Laboratory. New Haven, Conn.: Yale University Press, 1982. 299 pp.

This history of the Jet Propulsion Laboratory in Pasadena, California, describes the JPL's beginnings in 1936, when a group of Cal Tech researchers began building rockets. While the JPL's original function was to develop missile technology, in the late 1950s the JPL became a major force in the American space program and planetary exploration. Koppes traces the role of a technological research program in relation to national military and scientific policy, exploring tensions that can develop between the goals of government and the goals of research.

STM 213. KRANZBERG, MELVIN, ed. Ethics in an Age of Pervasive Technology. Boulder, Colo.: Westview Press, 1980. 246 pp.

This book provides an account of the 1974 Wunsch Conference on technology in which the participants considered the moral problems attendant upon the application of modern technology. Part I includes essays by Daniel Bell on religion and culture in the post-industrial age, by Isaiah Berlin on the incompatibility of certain values, and by Gershon Scholem. All contributors to this section agree that the problems of our technological age are unique in terms of their magnitude, the interconnectedness of effects, and the possibility of unintentional effects of certain technological changes. In Part II the contributors assert that a holistic and moderate approach needs to be taken to construct the new ethics needed for this age of pervasive technology. The final two parts deal with the problems inherent in translating these ethics into action; contributors include Walter Rosenblith, Jacques Ellul, Hans Jonas, and Abraham Kaplan. The book concludes with the "Mount Carmel Declaration on Technology and Moral Responsibility."

STM 214. KRANZBERG, MELVIN and CARROLL W. PURSELL, Jr., eds. Technology in Western Civilization. Vol. II: Technology in the Twentieth Century. New York: Oxford University Press, 1967. 772 pp.
Kranzberg and Pursell edited a two-volume set treating the history of technology in the West. Volume II focuses on American technology in the 20th century because, as they argue, industrial leadership passed to the U.S. in this century. The editors prepared both volumes as teaching texts and have divided the second volume into twelve sections, some of which deal with important technical topics such as rationalization, transportation, materials and structures, energy, and food. A number of general sections treat topics such as "Technology and the State," "Technology in War," and "Scientific Research, Technology, and Automation." Historians and social scientists conversant with 20th-century technical developments in this volume have written the history of technology not as "how things are made," but as social history with technology as the material aspect of culture.

STM 215. KROEBER, A. L. and CLYDE KLUCKHOHN. Culture: A Critical Review of Concepts and Definitions. Cambridge, Mass.: Peabody Museum of American Archaeology and Ethnology, Harvard University, 1952. 223 pp.
The work offers a highly theoretical examination and review of the concepts of "culture" and "civilization," and traces their historical development, as well as describing the controversial, contemporary debates surrounding them. Kroeber and Kluckhohn describe, as a point of departure, European notions of culture, dealing particularly with English and German writers. They then describe the multiplying uses, meanings, and implications of "culture" in the American social sciences, especially after the 1910s, in trying to arrive at a working synthesis for social scientists in general. Although it is essentially a secondary work, the section on the definitions of culture can also serve as a primary source.

STM 216. KUEHN, THOMAS J. and ALAN L. PORTER, eds. Science, Technology, and National Policy. Ithaca, N.Y.: Cornell University Press, 1981. 530 pp.
The editors warn that the twenty-five essays they have gathered are only a sampling of the rich literature about the relationships among technological change, society, and the American government. They note that technology has, in the last century, advanced more rapidly than society's ability to manage it. The essays discuss various topics: technology's effect on society and the new social organization's technology demands; how political systems deal with technology; technology's effect on the economy; American science and technology in relation to the science and technology of the world as a whole; the role of Federal government (Executive, Legislative, and Judicial branches) in managing technology; state and local governments and the control of technology; educating citizens so they can make informed decisions about technological policies, thereby making technology more responsive to human needs; and various methods of involving the average citizen in the management of technology.

STM 217. LAKOFF, SANFORD A., ed. Knowledge and Power: Essays on Science and Government. New York: Free Press, 1966. 502 pp.
This collection of essays deals with the broad theme of science and government in the U.S. since W.W. II. Lakoff's introduction surveys science and social thought from Francis Bacon to Herbert Marcuse. The first section is devoted to case studies in science and public policy, for example, Enid C. B. Schoettle's analysis of "The Establishment of NASA." She discusses conflicts among scientists, government administrators, politicians, and military men over the control of space exploration in the aftermath of Sputnik. The second section, on governing science, contains essays on the pluralism of the U.S. scientific establishment and the organi-

zation of the President's Science Advisory Committee. The final section includes essays on the role of scientists in national policy and suggestions for new programs and priorities in Federal support of basic research.

STM 218. LAYTON, EDWIN T., Jr. The Revolt of the Engineers: Social Responsibility and the American Engineering Profession. Cleveland, Ohio: Case Western Reserve University Press, 1971. 286 pp.
Layton argues that the clash between two versions of professionalism, one stressing professional loyalty, the other bureaucratic or business loyalty, was central to the development of the engineering profession. He discusses the balance between the two loyalties found in engineering societies prior to 1900. Then he turns to the small group of progressive engineers who based their concept of professional loyalty on their visions of social reform. These engineers tried to link the profession to the national Progressive movement and partially achieved their goal in 1920 when the various engineering societies joined in the Federated American Engineering Societies (FAES) under Herbert Hoover. When the FAES recommended the application of engineering methods to several important issues of the day, however, it succeeded only in arousing a conservative, business reaction that crippled engineering progressivism. Finally, Layton traces the decline of professional loyalty and the rise of business loyalty among engineers in the 1920s and 1930s.

STM 219. LAYTON, EDWIN T., Jr., ed. Technology and Social Change in America. New York: Harper & Row, 1973. 181 pp.
Layton has reprinted ten essays mainly on 19th-century American technology and provided a short, interpretive introduction and annotated bibliography. The section on the origins and nature of technological change includes: Eugene S. Ferguson, "On the Origin and Development of American Mechanical 'Know How'"; "The Invention of the Western Steamboat" by Louis C. Hunter; Robert S. Woodbury's "The Legend of Eli Whitney and Interchangeable Parts"; "At the Turn of a Screw: William Sellers, the Franklin Institute and a Standard American Thread" by Bruce Sinclair; and "Technology and Democracy, 1800-1860" by Hugo A. Maier. The second section contains essays assessing technology's impact on society: "Bursting Boilers and Federal Power" by John G. Burke; Leo Marx's "The Machine in the Garden"; "Sullivan's Skyscrapers as the Expression of Nineteenth Century Technology" by Carl Condit; "Veblen and the Engineers" by Edwin Layton; and "Human Values and Modern Technology" by Herbert Muller.

STM 220. LEAVITT, JUDITH WALZER. The Healthiest City: Milwaukee and the Politics of Health Reform. Princeton, N.J.: Princeton University Press, 1982. 294 pp.
Using case studies that represent the three major areas of public health reform in Milwaukee--infectious diseases, sanitation, and food control-- Leavitt analyzes the major components of public health efforts in American cities. Focusing on government's role in improving its constituents' health, Leavitt shows how Milwaukee overcame the overwhelming health threats posed by the rapid growth of the American city. Between 1846 and 1910, Milwaukee health officers, with the growing support of the community, effected control of infectious disease; established mechanisms to oversee garbage collection and disposal, sewage systems and water supply; and developed means to control the production and sale of food.

STM 221. LECHEVALIER, HUBERT A. and MORRIS SOLOTOROVSKY. Three Centuries
           of Microbiology. New York: McGraw-Hill, 1965. 536 pp.
This book is a history of the origins and development of microbiology.
Beginning with Girolamo Francastoro and continuing through Louis Pasteur
and Robert Koch, the authors discuss the impact of microbiology on scientific research in both Europe and America. In particular, they consider
the role played by discoveries in microbiology in such fields as mycology,
immunology, protozoology, chemotherapy, and genetics.

STM 222. LEHMAN, MILTON. This High Man: Life of Robert Goddard. New
           York: Farrar, Strauss, 1963. 430 pp.
Reading H. G. Wells's War of the Worlds in 1898 stimulated Robert Goddard's
lifelong interest in space travel and exploration. His biographer, Milton
Lehman, describes Goddard's family and educational background and then
details his rocket researches while professor of physics at Clark University in Worcester, Massachusetts. First working with smokeless powder
propellants, Goddard switched to liquid fuel in the 1920s and flew the
world's first liquid-fuel rocket in 1926. His military work during W.W. I
and W.W. II led to such rocket-related military devices as the "bazooka"
and rocket-assisted take-off units for airplanes. Although receiving
support in the 1920s and 1930s from the Smithsonian Institution, the
Carnegie Institution, and the Guggenheim Foundation, Goddard remained a
little-known and solitary rocket scientist. His 214 patents proved so
fundamental to rocketry that the U.S. Government bought them all after
Goddard died in 1945.

STM 223. LESSING, LAWRENCE. Man of High Fidelity: Edwin Howard Armstrong,
           A Biography. Philadelphia: Lippincott, 1956. 320 pp.
Edwin Howard Armstrong (1890-1954) made three basic contributions to the
radio: the regenerative or feedback circuit in 1912, which initiated
the era of amplified sound; the superheterodyne circuit in 1918, which
underlies modern radio and radar reception; and wide-bank frequency modu-
lation (FM radio) in 1933. A fourth invention in 1922, superregeneration,
earned him a great deal of money but was technically impractical unless
channels were widely spaced. Portraying Armstrong as one of the last
of the lone inventors, Lessing describes his decision at fourteen to become
a radio inventor, his education in electrical engineering at Columbia
University, and his early inventive activity. He then recounts Armstrong's
radio work in W.W. I for the Army Signal Corps and in the post-war period,
when he became one of the few millionaire inventors. Lessing investigates
Armstrong's inventive activity and details the bitter and protracted patent
infringement suits that eventually depleted his resources, broke up his
marriage, and led him to commit suicide.

STM 224. LEVENTHAL, HERBERT. In the Shadow of the Enlightenment: Occult-
           ism and Renaissance Science in Eighteenth-Century America.
           New York: New York University Press, 1976. 330 pp.
The author argues the importance of studying those aspects of 18th-century
scientific thought that were not new products of the Enlightenment but
rather continuations of the Elizabethan "world picture." He describes
the continuing influence of such ideas as the "four humors," astrology,
witchcraft, and alchemy in popular and scientific thought in 18th-century
America.

STM 225. LEVIN, BEATRICE S. Women and Medicine. Metuchen, N.J.: Scare-
           crow Press, 1980. 257 pp.
The author of this overview of women and medicine has a dual focus: she
discusses such women's health care issues as breast cancer, abortion,
birth control, and thalidomide and DES, often uncovering sexist treatment
of women by the profession. She also provides biographical studies of
such American women physicians as Elizabeth Blackwell, Elizabeth Garrett
Anderson, and Mary Putnam Jacobi.

STM 226. LEY, WILLY. Rockets, Missiles, and Men in Space. 1944; Rev.
ed. New York: Viking Press, 1968. 557 pp.
Ley's book first appeared in 1944 under the title Rockets; he has updated
it since to cover the American space program. Both a technical description
of various missile and rocket systems and a history of American aeronautical development, this overview attempts a comprehensive portrayal of the
American space effort. Extensive appendices describe technical characteristics of various rockets, missiles, and satellites and several foreign
space programs.

STM 227. LITOFF, JUDY BARRETT. American Midwives: 1860 to the Present.
Westport, Conn.: Greenwood Press, 1978. 197 pp.
Litoff's history of midwifery since 1860 discusses briefly Colonial midwifery and the distinction between midwifery and obstetrics which arose
in the 19th century. The focus of the book is on the midwife debate of
the early 20th century, with most of the opposition coming from obstetricians and the support from public health officials concerned with infant
and maternal mortality. Litoff also discusses the development of nurse
midwifery as a specialty, which grew out of this debate, and the recent
appearance of lay midwives.

STM 228. LOMASK, MILTON. A Minor Miracle: An Informal History of the
National Science Foundation. Washington, D.C.: National Science
Foundation, 1976. 285 pp.
President Truman established the National Science Foundation (NSF) in
May 1950 as an independent Federal agency for the support of basic scien-
tific research. Lomask's episodic account deals with the legislative
history of the NSF Act of 1950, the establishment of the first National
Science Board, and the appointment of physicist Alan T. Waterman as first
NSF director. Lomask discusses the role of Waterman and his successors
in setting NSF policies and indicates the continuing tension between NSF
officials and government bureaucrats over NSF responsibility for the coordination of government research and development activity. He also
describes some of the educational projects and institutional programs sponsored by the rapidly growing NSF in the late 1950s and 1960s, including
the recent program for Research Applied to National Needs. Lomask's official account illuminates the important role that the NSF has played in
national science policy since W.W. II.

STM 229. LUDMERER, KENNETH M. Genetics and American Society: A Historical
Appraisal. Baltimore, Md.: Johns Hopkins University Press,
1972. 222 pp.
Ludmerer begins his social history of genetics in the U.S. with a discussion of the American eugenics movement from 1905-1930. He describes the
role of human genetics in the eugenists' programs for racial improvement
and contrasts the involvement of geneticists like Charles B. Davenport
in the eugenics movement with the opposition of others like L. C. Dunn
and Herbert Spencer Jennings, who denounced eugenics as an abuse of science.
Ludmerer also analyzes the political use of genetics and hereditarian
ideas as tools for legitimating social policies such as eugenic sterilization and the Immigration Restriction Act of 1924. Later chapters deal
with the effects of social and political events on the study of genetics.
During the early 1930s, Nazi eugenics caused a negative reaction to
eugenics in America and, according to Ludmerer, inhibited research on human
genetics. This situation prevailed until after W.W. II, when public concern over the genetic hazards of radiation fostered renewed interest in
human genetics.

STM 230. LURIE, EDWARD. Louis Agassiz: A Life in Science. Chicago: University of Chicago Press, 1960. 449 pp.
As a leader of the Lazzaroni and director of the Museum of Comparative Zoology, the Swiss naturalist Louis Agassiz (1807-1873) was one of the leading men of science in mid-19th-century America. Lurie discusses Agassiz's research in geology, paleontology, and zoology in Switzerland and America; his acceptance by the elite social circles of antebellum Boston after his arrival in 1846; the establishment of the Museum of Comparative Zoology at Harvard; and Agassiz's role in promoting American science during the 1850s and 1860s. Agassiz became Darwin's principal American opponent, and his 1859 debate with Asa Gray over biological transmutation reflected the increasingly conservative tone of his scientific views.

STM 231. MABEE, CARLETON. The American Leonardo: A Life of Samuel F. B. Morse. New York: Knopf, 1943. 420 pp.
This biography of Morse portrays the inventor as a Renaissance man; Morse not only invented and promoted the telegraph, but also was a well-known portrait painter and a founder of the National Academy of Design, a poet, a businessman, and a politician who ran for mayor of New York. Mabee details Morse's scientific innnovations but insists that Morse be remembered as a man of many talents and achievements.

STM 232. MacLAURIN, W. RUPERT. Invention and Innovation in the Radio Industry. New York: Macmillan, 1949. 304 pp.
MacLaurin analyzes the process of invention and innovation in the radio industry from its 19th-century European scientific background to American entry into W.W. II. He focuses on the historical relation between scientific research, invention, and innovation (the creation from an invention of a marketable, new or improved product). First, he investigates the characteristics of several important radio inventors, some of whom were also successful innovators. After recounting the role that large established firms and new firms played in promoting technical change, MacLaurin reviews the patent disputes of the 1920s and describes the development of industrial research in radio and television. Finally, MacLaurin considers the relationship from 1900 to 1941 between government regulation and technical progress and draws conclusions concerning the process of invention and innovation and its relationship to the business cycle.

STM 233. MANNING, KENNETH. Black Apollo of Science: The Life of Ernest Everett Just. New York: Oxford University Press, 1983. 397 pp.
Manning's biography of Just reveals the racial prejudice that kept Just tied to Howard University and denied significant research money for his important biological work. Manning describes Just's work in cell biology at Howard University and Woods Hole, his belief in the importance of the ectoplasm in development, and his theories of evolution and heredity.

STM 234. MANNING, THOMAS G. Government in Science: The U.S. Geological Survey, 1867-1894. Lexington: University of Kentucky Press, 1967. 257 pp.
Government in Science explores the interaction of geological knowledge and research with Congressional politics and legislation in post-Civil War America by focusing on the U.S. Geological Survey--the central scientific bureau of the Federal government in the late 19th century. Manning first discusses contributions to geology, paleontology, and topography resulting from the rival King, Hayden, and Powell surveys of the trans-Mississippi West mounted after 1865. He then turns to the political machinations surrounding the establishment of the Geological Survey in 1879. Manning details Survey activities during the tenures of the first two directors, Clarence King (1842-1901) and John Wesley Powell (1834-

1902). King, responding to keen contemporary interest in exploiting land resources, steered the Survey toward economic geology. Powell, who succeeded King in 1881, broadened the scope of Survey activities and used his considerable entrepreneurial talents to obtain increasing support for pure science as part of the Survey's mission. Two recurrent themes in Manning's account are the tension between military and civilian control over Geological Survey work and the incessant demands from Congress for useful knowledge in exchange for continued financial patronage.

STM 235. MARK, JOAN. Four Anthropologists: An American Science in Its Early Years. New York: Science History, 1980. 209 pp.
Mark traces the careers of the four 19th-century anthropologists, F. W. Putnam, Alice Fletcher, Franklin Hamilton Cushing, and William H. Holmes, in order to describe the professionalization of the discipline. Putnam brought to the study of ancient man the techniques of natural history and contemporary natural science theory. Fletcher and Cushing respectively studied the Omaha and Zuni tribes as users of artifacts, thus broadening anthropology from its mere concern with material culture. And Holmes, of the Smithsonian Institution, extended this line of inquiry and discovered the importance of stratigraphy in archaeology, as well as contributing to the study of "primitive" art.

STM 236. MARKS, GEOFFREY and WILLIAM K. BEATTY. Women in White. New York: Scribner, 1972. 238 pp.
While the authors discuss women in ancient and medieval medicine, the focus of their study is on the struggle for women's rights in medicine in America. This overview includes a discussion of women and nursing, midwifery, and the relationship of the work of such reformers as Dorothea Dix and Jane Addams to women and medicine. The careers of individual women in health care, such as Elizabeth Blackwell and Mary Putnam Jacobi, are discussed as well.

STM 237. MAYNARD, AUBRE de L. Surgeons to the Poor: The Harlem Hospital Story. New York: Appleton-Century-Crofts, 1978. 258 pp.
Maynard's book details what he has called the first "honest venture" in integrating the professional staff of a major American hospital, the Harlem Hospital; the author himself was a surgeon on the staff for over forty years. Around 1920, the Hospital first allowed blacks on its staff. Maynard discusses attitudes toward black patients, prejudice among white doctors, and the staff's treatment of Martin Luther King after the attempt on his life in 1958.

STM 238. MAZLISH, BRUCE, ed. The Railroad and the Space Program, An Exploration in Historical Analogy. Cambridge, Mass.: MIT Press, 1965. 223 pp.
This volume uses historical analogy to evaluate the probable impact of the space program on American society. The authors chose the railroad as the best analogy, because it had far-reaching, fundamental effects on society. In his introduction, Mazlish discusses the concept of historical analogy, summarizes the specified investigations into the railroad contained in the volume, discusses analogies with the space effort, and makes suggestions for further study. Mazlish argues that the most significant analogy is one that treats technological systems as complex social inventions involving technological, economic, political, sociological, and intellectual factors. The essays include an analysis of the railroad's effect on the technological frontier between nature and the man-made world, investigations of the railroad's economic and political impacts, its role in creating modern forms of industrial administration, and its effect on the 19th-century American imagination.

STM 239. McCALLUM, HENRY D. and FRANCES T. McCALLUM. The Wire that Fenced
          the West. Norman: University of Oklahoma Press, 1965. 285 pp.
The McCallums detail early efforts to build effective fences and the forerunners of barbed wire. They describe the three inventors of practical
barbed-wire fencing--one of whom turned out a crude barb with a coffee
mill--and its subsequent manufacture and distribution. In discussing
its application and effects, they relate many infamous feuds among cattle-
men and comment on the public response to this "barbaric" new device.

STM 240. McCULLOUGH, DAVID. The Great Bridge. New York: Simon & Schuster,
          1972. 636 pp.
The Brooklyn Bridge, built between 1869 and 1883, links lower Manhattan
with downtown Brooklyn. Now dwarfed by surrounding skyscrapers and other
bridges, its graceful span across the East River was an engineering project
of unequalled magnitude. McCullough begins with the engineering vision
of John A. Roebling, whose design for the structure drew on his earlier
contributions in civil engineering. Washington Roebling assumed responsibility for the project in 1869 after his father's death. McCullough
explains the technical problems Roebling and his colleagues faced in constructing a suspension bridge across a turbulent tidal strait--the difficulties of structural design, the use of caissons for digging the underwater foundations, and the logistics of organizing a large labor force
and obtaining sufficient quantities of steel and stone. The Brooklyn
Bridge was also a political project, and McCullough describes the currents
of civil competition and political influence which plagued Roebling:
recalcitrant trustees, straitened finances, local and state politicians
vying for political advantage, and the corrupt Tweed Ring, who saw the
bridge as a lucrative source of patronage for their allies.

STM 241. McCULLOUGH, DAVID. The Path Between the Seas: The Creation
          of the Panama Canal, 1870-1914. New York: Simon & Schuster,
          1977. 698 pp.
Opened to traffic in 1914, the Panama Canal was an engineering triumph
which embodied ideals of national pride, imperial power, and technical
progress. David McCullough discusses these overtones in his account of
the construction of the Canal, which draws on an array of archival sources.
Like his earlier book on the Brooklyn Bridge (see STM 240), this volume
weaves the technical history of the Canal with its broader social and
political dimensions. Beginning with abortive French attempts to build
an Isthmian crossing, McCullough places negotiations for the Canal in
the context of U.S. foreign policy and details the political maneuvers
which cleared the way for the project to begin. Engineers John Stevens
and George Washington Goethals presided over the building of the Canal,
which involved engineering problems of unparalleled magnitude. The locks
alone were only a small part of the fifty-mile Canal, but they required
new expertise in the structural properties of concrete and the design
of a novel electrical control system. McCullough also describes William
Gorgas's fight against yellow fever, and the daily lives of the thousands
of engineers and laborers who lived in tropical Panama while constructing
the Canal.

STM 242. McDONALD, FORREST. Insull. Chicago: University of Chicago
          Press, 1962. 350 pp.
In providing Chicago with electric power in the years between 1892 and
the early 1930s, Samuel Insull developed one of the more economically
and politically complex technological systems of the day. Through Insull's
career, McDonald provides an account of the origins and expansion of the
electric power industry from the early 1880s--when Thomas Edison first
employed Insull--to Insull's downfall in the early 1930s. After describing
Insull's childhood and early education, McDonald turns to Insull's work
with Edison and his contribution to the founding of the Edison General

Electric Company, precursor of General Electric. When he moved to Chicago, Insull helped develop technical methods for combining the newer AC system with the older DC one, and was instrumental in introducing steam turbines into power generation. McDonald describes Insull's managerial, marketing, and financial innovations, then devotes the final chapters to the financial collapse of Insull's utility holding company and his indictment and acquittal on charges of fraud.

STM 243. McDONALD, FORREST. Let There Be Light: The Electric Utility in Wisconsin, 1881-1955. Madison, Wis.: American History Research Center, 1957. 404 pp.
The evolution of the electric power industry was a dynamic element in the 20th-century revolution in energy utilization, industrial production, communications, and transportation. In providing a history of Wisconsin's electric utilities from the 1880s to the post-W.W. II period, McDonald focuses on technological, managerial, and financial aspects of local companies and identifies state and national trends. He describes the personalities and electrical manufacturing companies which introduced central power stations in the 1880s and 1890s, the rapid growth of electric traction and hydroelectric stations in the first years of this century, and the reorganization and rationalization of the industry after W.W. I. By providing financial, engineering, and managerial assistance, holding companies helped create in the 1920s the institutional structure that faced economic and political challenges in the 1930s. McDonald evaluates the industry's response to this crisis and describes its post-W.W. II development.

STM 244. McGRAW, THOMAS K. TVA and the Power Fight, 1933-1939. Philadelphia: Lippincott, 1971. 201 pp.
Since the turn of the century, the power industry has been marked by a struggle between a private tradition, which built most of the network of generators and high tension lines, and a public tradition, which tried to curb the financial and political excesses it perceived among private utilities. These two traditions clashed between 1933 and 1939 over the attempt to develop a publicly-owned electric-utility system in the Tennessee Valley (TVA). McGraw traces the development of these two traditions, describes the personalities involved, and recounts initial efforts to reach an accommodation when the TVA was established in 1933. Then he provides an account of the major court fights between the TVA and the private utilities and the collaboration between the TVA and the Public Works Administration to force the sale and integration of the private utilities into the TVA network. Finally, McGraw evaluates the success of the TVA and explains why other river systems were not developed according to the TVA model.

STM 245. McLAUGHLIN, LORETTA. The Pill, John Rock, and the Church. Boston: Little, Brown, 1983. 243 pp.
McLaughlin's book details the career of John Rock, a leading figure in the development of the oral contraceptive. Known as the "Father of the Pill," Rock was a Roman Catholic whose work with infertility led to the development of the pill. When the FDA approved the pill in 1960, and the Catholic Church mobilized efforts against its use, Rock insisted that it was not an unnatural form of birth control; he continued to hope that the Church would approve it. McLaughlin's study places Rock's career and the pill's discovery in a social context of the history of reproductive medicine, Church politics, clinical research, and Feminism.

STM 246. MEIKLE, JEFFREY L. Twentieth Century Limited: Industrial Design
in America, 1925-1939. Philadelphia: Temple University Press,
1979. 249 pp.
This study of industrial design between the wars argues that American
designers borrowed from such foreign sources as the Bauhaus movement and
the 1925 Paris Exposition to create a uniquely American design idiom.
This illustrated history examines designs of household appliances, furniture, and industrial architecture in light of what they can tell us
about the optimism of American culture in the 1930s toward the new "modern"
future.

STM 247. MELOSH, BARBARA. "The Physician's Hand": Work Culture and Conflict in American Nursing. Philadelphia: Temple University
Press, 1982. 260 pp.
Melosh begins by noting that nursing, originally a domestic duty, has
"always been a woman's job": the medical division of labor--whereby women
are paid less than men, perform menial tasks, and defer to male
authorities--replicates a larger sexual division of labor within society.
Her study covers the period from the 1920s, when the specially trained
nurse had become an established part of medical care, to the 1970s. Melosh
discusses not only the professionalization of nursing but also the resistance to professionalization among nurses themselves and the less official
"occupational culture" developed on the job (a culture composed of lore,
anecdotes, and practical suggestions for managing relations with doctors,
supervisors, and hospital administrators). She also examines the history
and culture of hospital schools and discusses nursing within each of its
three major settings: private duty nursing, public health nursing (nursing
at its most autonomous), and institutional nursing.

STM 248. MERRILL, GEORGE P. The First One Hundred Years of American
Geology. New Haven, Conn.: Yale University Press, 1924.
773 pp.
Merrill's study reviews the work of the pioneers of geology in 19th-century
America. It includes detailed information on geologists, the various
state geological surveys, the Federal surveys, the rise of paleontology,
the various schools of geological theory, as well as the distinctly American contribution to geology--physiography. Merrill touches upon the personal characteristics and the methods of work of these early pioneers,
and the conditions under which they worked. He also evaluates the validity
of their conclusions by measuring them against the standards of the period
in which they were done.

STM 249. MERRITT, RAYMOND H. Engineering in American Society, 1850-1875.
Lexington: University Press of Kentucky, 1969. 199 pp.
Merritt explores the 19th-century origins of American technological and
industrial leadership by investigating the engineering profession in the
decades before and after the American Civil War. During this period engineering became an institutionalized and scientific profession, with engineers playing central roles in rationalizing industry (both technically
and managerially) and in physically improving American cities. In focusing
on these themes, Merritt provides information on technical education,
technical expertise as the basis of social standing, and the growing cosmopolitan orientation of engineers. Engineers, Merritt believes, were
functional intellectuals using knowledge to transform industry, the organization of business, and the physical basis of civilization, motivated
by a vision of a harmonious future. Merritt demonstrates his theses by
examining individual careers through memoirs, personal papers, periodicals,
and society transactions.

STM 250. MEYER, STEPHEN, III. The Five Dollar Day: Labor Management and Social Control in the Ford Company 1908-1921. Edited by Elizabeth Pleck and Charles Stephenson. Albany: State University of New York Press, 1981. 249 pp.

Meyer seeks to reinterpret "Ford's place in the evolution of the American social and economic system." He limits his discussion to the period beginning with the appearance of the Model T (1908), continuing with the evolution of mass production (1910-14) and the introduction of the famous Five Dollar Day (1914), which was an attempt to solve attitudinal and behavioral problems among the workers, and concluding with the termination of Ford's unique "sociological" management program (1921). Meyer focuses on the Highland Park factory where virtually all of these technical and managerial innovations were developed.

STM 251. MILLER, HOWARD S. Dollars for Research: Science and Its Patrons in Nineteenth-Century America. Seattle: University of Washington Press, 1970. 258 pp.

Dollars for Research is a study of the patronage of science in the U.S. from the Smithson bequest of 1838 to the foundation of the Carnegie Institution in 1902. Miller begins with the generation of the 1840s—including Alexander Dallas Bache, Joseph Henry, and Louis Agassiz—and their entrepreneurial activities in securing financial support for scientific research. He contends that informal mechanisms of private philanthropy for observatories, laboratories, and scientific schools established during the 1840s and 1850s created an institutional legacy which structured patterns of patronage for science after the 1880s. Miller analyzes both the diverse motivations of 19th-century benefactors of science and the arguments scientists advanced for the endowment of research. In the concluding chapters, Miller examines the new institutional forms of the research university and the philanthropic foundation, and contrasts their relationship to the scientific community with the public patronage of the Federal government. He uses the Cope-Marsh fossil controversy and Allison Commission investigation as a case study.

STM 252. MILLER, LILLIAN, FREDERICK VOSS, and JEANNETTE M. HUSSEY. The Lazzaroni: Science and Scientists in Mid-Nineteenth Century America. Washington, D.C.: Smithsonian Institution Press, 1972. 121 pp.

The Lazzaroni were an elite network of American scientists who banded together informally to establish high professional standards in the mid-19th-century American scientific community. Led by Alexander Dallas Bache, Superintendent of the U.S. Coast Survey, the "Cambridge-Washington clique" included Joseph Henry, Benjamin Peirce, Louis Agassiz, James Dwight Dana, Charles Henry Davis, C. C. Felton, John Fries Frazer, Benjamin A. Gould, and Wolcott Gibbs. Through frequent correspondence, personal visits, and joint membership on the committees of leading scientific societies, the Lazzaroni lobbied for increased patronage of pure science. Members of the group were influential leaders in the early years of the American Association for the Advancement of Science (1848), Harvard's Lawrence Scientific School (1847), and the movement for a National Academy of Sciences (1863). Opponents of the Lazzaroni—who included Asa Gray, William Barton Rogers, Matthew Fontaine Maury, and Charles W. Eliot—objected to their self-appointed status as guardians of quality in public and private scientific institutions. In this volume, which originated as a companion to a 1972 National Portrait Gallery exhibition, Miller and her colleagues have compiled a series of biographical sketches of the Lazzaroni, their chief antagonists, and allies.

STM 253. MISHLER, ELLIOT G., et al. Social Contexts of Health, Illness, and Patient Care. New York: Cambridge University Press, 1981. 277 pp.
The authors of this collection are interested in the contributions they, as social scientists and behavioral scientists, can make to the biomedical model of clinical care. Essays address such topics as the relation of economic change to illness, the social construction of illness, the physician/patient relationship, and the machine metaphor in medical care; all essays address issues of context in American health care.

STM 254. MITROFF, IAN I. The Subjective Side of Science: A Philosophical Inquiry into the Psychology of the Apollo Moon Scientists. New York: Elsevier, 1974. 329 pp.
Mitroff attempts to discover fundamental principles about the nature of scientists by a philosophical and social science investigation into the attitudes and scientific beliefs of forty scientists involved in the Apollo projects. He argues that a tension exists between those who consider scientists objective and disinterested observers and those who see them as committed, often partisan, participants. The study finds a broad range of attitudes among scientists.

STM 255. MOHR, J. C. Abortion in America: The Origins and Evolution of National Policy 1800-1900. New York: Oxford University Press, 1978. 331 pp.
Mohr's study of abortion in 19th-century America seeks to determine why and how abortion, legal in America in 1800, became uniformly illegal by 1900. He explores physicians' responses to abortion, changing public opinion on the issue, the nature of anti-abortion legislation, and the ultimate legitimation of anti-abortion as national policy.

STM 256. MOORE, HARRY H. American Medicine and the People's Health. New York: Appleton, 1927. 647 pp.
Moore describes his book as "a tentative formulation of the problem of medical organization." The first section treats the development and organization of American medicine (c. 1927). Part II treats maladjustments in the medical establishment, the shortage and inaccessability of personnel and equipment in private practice, and the lack of interest among practitioners in preventive medicine. Part III describes efforts of the state to provide more adequate medical service, and treats the issue of health insurance, community health organizations and clinics, and the issue of public health in general. The study concludes with a discussion of the future of organized medicine.

STM 257. MORANTZ, REGINA, CYNTHIA POMERLEAU, and CAROL FENICHEL, eds. In Her Own Words: Oral Histories of Women Physicians. Westport, Conn.: Greenwood Press, 1982. 271 pp.
The editors gathered oral histories from nine women physicians, including a public health advocate, an Indian Health service doctor, a medical administrator, and an opthalmologist; the doctors are from three generations of women, and the editors discuss changes in the careers of these women over the century. The collection is preceded by a long essay by Regina Morantz, "From Art to Science: Women Physicians in American Medicine, 1600-1980."

STM 258. MORGAN, H. WAYNE. Drugs in America: A Social History, 1800-1980. Syracuse, N.Y.: Syracuse University Press, 1981. 233 pp.
Morgan's study is primarily of opiate use in America. He argues that, especially by the late 19th century, Americans have opposed and legislated against drug use because it implies a threat to social and economic order. He also explores the relationship of racial imagery to certain drugs in the cultural imagination.

STM 259. MORGAN, JOHN S. Robert Fulton. New York: Mason, Charter, 1977. 235 pp.
Morgan's biography of Robert Fulton argues that, much as Fulton might have wanted to be remembered as a gentleman who ran shipping lines, he was in fact one of American society's first "technologists." Fulton not only developed the steamboat but persisted in improving and promoting it—in contrast to James Watt, who retired after inventing the steam engine. In development and application Fulton's career distinguished itself from that of the pure scientist.

STM 260. MORISON, ELTING E. From Know-How to Nowhere: The Development of American Technology. New York: Basic Books, 1974. 199 pp.
Morison describes the evolution of American engineering, then criticizes the present approach to designing new technologies. First he recounts American engineering practice before the Erie canal project of the 1820s and establishes the importance of that project in bringing together existing practice and training a generation of engineers. Without the benefit of theory, these engineers working in canals, railroads and iron mills in the 1850s reformed existing practice to produce methods often startlingly new. He then argues that the process of innovation changed when General Electric founded in 1901 a laboratory in which groups of engineers used scientific ideas to systematically improve the light bulb. This new approach produced new designs, rather than mere rearrangements of old practice, and dramatically increased man's power over nature. Finally, Morison argues that no vision guides this new style of engineering and that a human dimension is missing from it.

STM 261. MORISON, ELTING E. Men, Machines, and Modern Times. Cambridge, Mass.: MIT Press, 1966. 235 pp.
Morison investigates the effects of change in mechanical systems on the men working with them. In this collection of his essays, he focuses on four aspects of change: conditions at point of origin; the character of the agents of change; the nature of resistance; and means to facilitate accommodation to change. Most of his examples come from military history: the introduction of continuous-aim naval gunfire in the U.S. Navy after 1900; the unsuccessful attempt to replace sail with steam just after the Civil War; and the introduction of land-based aircraft as the basis of anti-submarine warfare in W.W. II. There are also essays on the nature of bureaucracy with anecdotes drawn from Army and Navy history, the use of the computer, and the introduction and development in the late 1860s of Bessemer steel. Finally, Morison draws on these essays to make suggestions for organizing and managing to accommodate to the human scale the constantly changing, complex, and large modern systems of ideas, energies, and machinery.

STM 262. MOYER, ALBERT E. American Physics in Transition: A History of Conceptual Change in the Late Nineteenth Century. Los Angeles, Calif.: Tomash, 1983. 218 pp.
Granting that the period between 1905 and 1950—during which Planck's quantum hypothesis and Einstein's special relativity theory were introduced—was a period of upheaval in science, Moyer questions the assumption that physics was in a state of conceptual calm prior to that. He focuses on American physical scientists and their intellectual commitments during the period 1870 to 1905. Moyer begins by discussing the argument and reception of a book on modern physics written by John Stallo, a layman. He then proceeds to a discussion of certain representative physical scientists: Alfred Mayer, Amos Dolbear, John Trowbridge, Henry Rowland, Albert Nichelson, and Edwin Hall—atomo-mechanists; Simon Newcomb, J. Willard Gibbs, Samuel Langley, and Francis Hipher—men who did not subscribe to the mechanical view of the universe. Moyer's concluding section examines the younger generation of American physicists who attended the 1904 Congress of Arts and Science.

STM 263. MULHOLLAND, JAMES A. A History of Metals in Colonial America.
          University: University of Alabama Press, 1981. 215 pp.
Mulholland contends that the method of extraction and use of metals in
Colonial America followed a three-stage pattern of development. Prospect-
ing activities characterized the early Colonial Period; early settlers
were primarily interested in precious metals but also showed some interest
in iron and tin. A period of entrepreneurship followed when British financing assisted colonists in setting up iron works such as the Principio
Company in Maryland. Finally, during the 18th century, an indigenous
iron trade developed in response to a series of Iron Acts which fostered
the industry. These domestic enterprises were of vital importance to
Americans during the Revolutionary War.

STM 264. NASH, RODERICK, ed. The American Environment: Readings in the
          History of Conservation. Reading, Mass.: Addison-Wesley, 1968.
          236 pp.
Nash's collection of essays describes the history of the reform movement
of conservation in America from its beginnings. He includes early essays
by "conservationists" like Henry David Thoreau, Carl Schurz, and Frederick
Law Olmsted to illustrate what he sees as the beginnings of American conservation efforts; essays by members of the Progressive conservation movement; representative pieces describing conservation measures under the
New Deal; and essays from the environmental crusades of the 1960s.

STM 265. NELSON, WILLIAM R., ed. The Politics of Science: Readings in
          Science, Technology, and Government. New York: Oxford Univer-
          sity Press, 1968. 495 pp.
The editor argues that with the increased appropriation of Federal funds
to science since W.W. II, a veritable new area of study has opened up:
the politics of decision-making in regard to scientific research and allocation of resources. He notes that the collected essays reveal a governmental emphasis on the physical rather than the biological sciences.

STM 266. NEVINS, ALLAN. Ford: The Times, the Man, the Company. New
          York: Scribner, 1954. 688 pp.
In his initial volume on the Ford Motor Company, Nevins intertwines the
history of the company and the industry with Henry Ford's biography.
First, he provides a short account of early automobile developments and
pioneers in Europe and America. Ford's childhood on his family's farm
and early work experiences provide a background for the account of Ford's
first experiments in the 1890s with small engines, his first horseless
carriage, early racing experiences, and establishment in 1903 of the Ford
Motor Company. Nevins describes Ford's development of several different
automobile models in his effort to produce a light, low-cost model with
broad market appeal. These efforts led to the Model T and the opening
in Highland Park, near Detroit, in 1910 of a plant using mass production
techniques. Finally, Nevins analyzes the characteristics of the Ford
Motor Company's success, describes its relations to workers and the high
wages paid, and identifies personal and structural weaknesses that later
seriously threatened the company.

STM 267. NEVINS, ALLAN and FRANK ERNEST HILL. Ford: Decline and Rebirth
          1933-1962. New York: Scribner, 1962. 508 pp.
The volume completes the three-volume history of the Ford Motor Company
(see STM 266 and STM 268). Nevins and Hill describe the company's decline
during the 1930s, which was associated with Henry Ford's individualist
style of management, and detail the reorganization and rebuilding of the
company after 1944, when Henry Ford II took charge with a new and vigorous
style of management involving teamwork and mobilization of quality personnel. The authors treat a number of topics within this framework:
competition with other firms, ongoing labor problems, administrative deci-

sion making, overseas operations, and war production. They also discuss Ford's creation in 1936 of the Ford Foundation to reduce Federal taxation of the family fortune. The Foundation eventually received 95 percent of the stock owned by Edsel, Henry, and Clara Ford, and the sale of this stock in the 1950s gave control for the first time to public stockholders. Finally, the authors evaluate the development of the company and its position in the early 1960s.

STM 268. NEVINS, ALLAN and FRANK ERNEST HILL. Ford: Expansion and Challenge 1915-1933. New York: Scribner, 1957. 714 pp.
By 1915, the Ford Motor Company was doing more than all other American automobile manufacturers combined to make the automobile an integral part of American life. Beginning with the company's advanced position of 1915, this second volume of Ford Motor Company history details the war years, the period of expansion and crises in the 1920s, and the first Depression years. Nevins and Hill discuss issues that at times made Ford a national political figure and describe Ford's labor problems and conflicts. Another theme concerns the factors driving war-time and post-war expansion of the company, both in the U.S. and abroad, and construction of a giant vertically-integrated plant at River Rouge. The authors also investigate Ford's attempts to maintain his control over the company and his resistance to change and retention of the Model T into the mid-1920s, when increasing competition mandated the development of a new model. Finally, Nevins and Hill consider the Depression's impact on the Ford Motor Company and evaluate the Ford Motor Company and the Ford legend.

STM 269. NOBLE, DAVID F. America by Design: Science, Technology, and the Rise of Corporate Capitalism. New York: Knopf, 1977. 384 pp.
In this study of the interconnected development of modern American science, technology, and corporate Capitalism, Noble explicitly rejects any form of technological determinism and argues that engineers subordinated technology to corporate interests in the first three decades of the 20th century. Engineers created a scientific mode of production, but prevented the social revolution that Noble believes this new mode implied. Noble traces the central role chemical and electrical engineers played in science, technology, and corporate management. These engineers were instrumental in reforming the patent system in the interests of corporations, establishing uniform standards necessary for smoothly functioning industrial production, institutionalizing research and invention within corporate laboratories, subordinating education to industrial Capitalism, and developing social control through personnel management.

STM 270. NOVOTNY, ANN and CARTER SMITH, eds. Images of Healing: A Portfolio of American Medical & Pharmaceutical Practice in the 18th, 19th, & Early 20th Centuries. New York: Macmillan, 1980. 144 pp.
Consisting of photographs accompanied by explanatory captions, this volume provides a record of the "people, artifacts, documents, institutions and techniques of the healing professions" in the U.S. from 1730 to 1930. The photographs and introductory essays attempt not only to provide history but also to place American medical practice within a social context—to gauge the effects of events such as the Civil War or the New Deal on medical care. The editors also provide a chronology for the era which takes note of important happenings within medicine as well as of larger historical events.

STM 271. **NUMBERS, RONALD L.** Almost Persuaded: American Physicians and Compulsory Health Insurance 1912-1920. Baltimore, Md.: Johns Hopkins University Press, 1978. 158 pp.
Numbers's study of the first American debate over compulsory health insurance documents the formation of a Committee on Social Insurance by the American Association for Labor Legislation to devise a health insurance bill, and discusses how this led to serious consideration of health insurance bills in the years between 1916 and 1920. Numbers finds that initial support for the bill among the medical profession shifted, with the result that these early attempts at reform failed.

STM 272. **NUMBERS, RONALD L.** Creation by Natural Law: Laplace's Nebular Hypothesis in American Thought. Seattle: University of Washington Press, 1977. 184 pp.
Numbers's study of the nebular hypothesis in America argues that the hypothesis, which was developed by Laplace in 1796, and which posited the creation of the solar system by natural law, thrived in America well before Darwin's The Origin of Species appeared in 1859. Like Darwin's hypothesis, this too was a naturalistic cosmogony which had to be accommodated to biblical theology much as Darwin's did.

STM 273. **NUMBERS, RONALD L.,** ed. Compulsory Health Insurance: The Continuing American Debate. Westport, Conn.: Greenwood Press, 1982. 172 pp.
Numbers's collection of essays provides a historical context for the long debate over compulsory health insurance. It includes an essay by Numbers on the medical community's opposition; by Arthur Viseltear on public health reform efforts from 1920-1950; by Gary Land and Theodore Marmor on foreign systems; by Paul Starr, Monte Poen, and Roy Lubove on the economic, political, and ethical issues, respectively. Lobbyist Wilbur Cohen concludes with a view of the future of compulsory health insurance.

STM 274. **NUMBERS, RONALD L.,** ed. The Education of American Physicians: Historical Essays. Berkeley: University of California Press, 1980. 345 pp.
Lloyd Stevenson argues in an introductory essay that American medical education became increasingly important in the 19th century. The essays collected discuss issues in the history of medical education in terms of medical specialties; James Whorton writes on the changes in the teaching of chemistry, Gert Brieger on surgery, and Judith Walzer Leavitt on public health. The volume was intended as a festschrift for William Norwood, the first historian of medical education.

STM 275. **NUMBERS, RONALD L.** and **JUDITH W. LEAVITT,** eds. Sickness and Health in America: Readings in the History of Medicine and Public Health. Madison: University of Wisconsin Press, 1978. 454 pp.
This collection is preceded by an overview, with statistics, of sickness and health in America. Part I of the collection includes essays on medical practice and institutions: Barbara Sicherman on diagnosis and neurasthenia, Regina Morantz on women doctors, Morris Vogel on mid-Victorian hospitals, and Richard Shryock on essays by Martin Pernick on a yellow fever epidemic, John Duffy on the social impact of disease in the late 19th century, and Daniel Fox on tuberculosis reporting in New York City. A pictorial essay is also included.

STM 276. NUMBERS, RONALD L. and JUDITH W. LEAVITT, eds. Wisconsin Medicine: Historical Perspectives. Madison: University of Wisconsin Press, 1981. 212 pp.
This collection of essays covers such aspects of medicine in Wisconsin as frontier medicine, medical societies, hospitals, and medical education. The editors acknowledge that their attempt is to document the history of Wisconsin health care, but admit that state divisions are perhaps arbitrary and that their collection may be representative of the history of medicine in the Midwest.

STM 277. OEHSER, PAUL H. Sons of Science: The Story of the Smithsonian Institution and Its Leaders. New York: Henry Schuman, 1949. 220 pp.
In 1838, the U.S. received a bequest of over $500,000 from James Smithson, an English chemist, to establish an institution "for the increase and diffusion of knowledge among men." Smithson's unprecedented gift sparked Congressional debate over what form the new organization should take, and the 1846 legislation creating it contained elements of competing proposals for a national university, library, and museum. Physicist Joseph Henry, the first Secretary of the new Smithsonian Institution, had his own clear conception of the institution's purpose, however, and he devoted its resources to the promotion of original scientific research and publication. Under the direction of Henry and his successors, the Smithsonian became one of the most important sources of patronage for scientific research in 19th-century America. Oehser's Sons of Science is an anecdotal history of the Smithsonian's first century organized around the biographies of the first seven Secretaries.

STM 278. OLESON, ALEXANDRA and SANBORN C. BROWN, eds. The Pursuit of Knowledge in the Early American Republic: American Scientific and Learned Societies from Colonial Times to the Civil War. Baltimore, Md.: Johns Hopkins University Press, 1976. 372 pp.
Evidence of growing interest in the institutional history of American science, the essays in this volume examine the role of learned academies, literary and philosophical societies, organizations for promoting useful knowledge, mechanics institutes, and other scientific associations in the pursuit of knowledge in America before the Civil War. John Greene and Hunter Dupree delineate regional and national patterns of scientific organization, while Nathan Reingold discusses the diversity of roles within the 19th-century American scientific community. Studies of particular societies include the Royal Society of London and its American members, the Albany Institute, the Academy of Natural Sciences and the Franklin Institute in Philadelphia, and the American Association for the Advancement of Science. Another set of papers investigates scientific societies in selected cities and regions, including New York, Boston, the southeastern U.S., the Ohio Valley, and Canada. Other essays deal with humanistic, medical, and agricultural organizations in early America. Two concluding essays by Richard Storr and Barbara Rosenkrantz suggest areas for further research on the social functions of learned societies in early American science.

STM 279. OLESON, ALEXANDRA and JOHN VOSS, eds. The Organization of Knowledge in Modern America, 1860-1920. Baltimore, Md.: Johns Hopkins University Press, 1979. 478 pp.
The specialization characteristic of modern scholarship is a relatively recent phenomenon. These essays examine the general historical problem of the organization of knowledge in America from 1860 to 1920. Edward Shils suggests that the university was the center of the movement, joined by a variety of other institutions for the pursuit of knowledge, such as the National Academy of Sciences and the Carnegie Institution of Wash-

ington. Louis Galambos considers economic aspects of the reorganization
and utilization of knowledge at the turn of the century, and two essays
are devoted to the organization of industrial and agricultural science.
Daniel Kevles provides a comparative institutional analysis of the physics,
mathematics, and chemistry communities in the late 19th century. Other
case studies explore the intellectual disciplines of biology, the humanities, and the social sciences. Museums and libraries aided in disseminating knowledge to a wider public, a growing problem as professionalization
restricted learning to an audience of experts. In the concluding chapter,
Charles Rosenberg focuses on the social functions of disciplines, and
calls for an historical "ecology of knowledge" in modern America.

STM 280. **OLTON, CHARLES S.** Artisans for Independence: Philadelphia
　　　　　Mechanics and the American Revolution. Syracuse, N.Y.: Syracuse
　　　　　University Press, 1975. 172 pp.
Olton's book is a case study of Philadelphia's master craftsmen between
1765 and 1790. Olton argues that an understanding of these "middle-class"
artisans can tell us much about class experience in revolutionary America.
He is interested accordingly in such matters as artisans' guilds, artisans'
role in city politics, their importance to the war effort, and, in turn,
the war's impact on the manufacturing economy. He concludes with a discussion of their support of Republican efforts.

STM 281. **OWEN, MARGUERITE.** The Tennessee Valley Authority. New York:
　　　　　Praeger, 1973. 275 pp.
The Tennessee Valley Authority (TVA) is the only American agency that
systematically controls and develops a river system, its watershed area,
and resources. The Federal government created the TVA in 1933 to develop
the valley by providing for flood control, the generation of electricity,
year-round navigation, and fertilizer production and utilization. Owen
follows the history from the construction during W.W. I of a hydroelectric
works for nitrate production at Muscle Shoals, Alabama, to the extensive
TVA system of the 1960s. She identifies the distinguishing feature of
this unique Federal agency, describes its activities, indicates methods
used to achieve its goals, and summarizes its accomplishments. Although
the TVA faced stiff political opposition from private utility companies
and other groups, Owen argues that it was a non-partisan agency working
to improve the resources and beauty of the region.

STM 282. **PACKARD, FRANCIS R.** History of Medicine in the United States.
　　　　　2 vols. 1901; Rev. ed. New York: Hoeber, 1931. 1323 pp.
The first volume of this survey of American medicine begins with Colonial
medicine, early hospitals and medical schools, and the role of the medical
profession in the Revolutionary War. Volume II discusses the rise of
medical education and the beginnings of specialization, as well as the
development of medical journals and societies.

STM 283. **PARKER, GAIL THAIN.** Mind Cure in New England: From the Civil
　　　　　War to World War One. Hanover, N.H.: University Press of New
　　　　　England, 1973. 197 pp.
Parker's intellectual history of the mind cure movement--the 19th-century
tradition of belief in the power of mind over body--traces the use of
such mind curists as Mary Baker Eddy and Henry Wood of the works of
Swedenborg, Emerson, and William James. She outlines the reasons for widespread acceptance of New Thought and Christian Science movements and argues
that they represented a "strategy of living that worked" for many 19th-
century believers.

STM 284. **PARTRIDGE, BELLAMY.** Fill 'er Up!: The Story of Fifty Years of Motoring. New York: McGraw-Hill, 1952. 235 pp.
The first auto race, which took place in Chicago in 1893, marked the beginning of the golden age of the motorcar and established the automobile as a viable mode of transportation in what had been until then an agricultural society. Partridge devotes a section to Henry Ford and the national reaction to the automobile; describes the first auto show, the advent of the Automobile Association, automobile racing, and the rise of tourism; details the growth of roads in the U.S.; relates stories of personal excursions he took during the early days of the automobile; and concludes with a speculative chapter on the future of motoring in America. Illustrated with fifty-six black-and-white illustrations, this work also includes a chronology of the motorcar.

STM 285. **PENICK, JAMES L., Jr., CARROLL W. PURSELL, Jr., MORGAN B. SHERWOOD,** and **DONALD C. SWAIN.** The Politics of American Science 1939 to the Present. 1965; Rev. ed. Cambridge, Mass.: MIT Press, 1972. 453 pp.
The editors have selected documents dealing with changing relationships between science and the Federal government since 1939. The first section surveys the politics of science in 20th-century America. The next treats wartime institutional administrative innovations in Federal support of science and technology. In the postwar period, central problems included the creation of the National Science Foundation, military versus civilian control of atomic energy, and the administration of medical and military research. Section four treats the 1950s, when managing the burgeoning Federal science system became an important problem. After Sputnik, space and scientific manpower training became crucial issues, resulting in the creation of the National Aeronautics and Space Administration (1958) and passage of the National Defense Education Act (1958). The final section concerns threats to the social system of science resulting from environmental pollution, the Vietnam War, and domestic crises.

STM 286. **PETERSON, JULIA J.** The Iowa Testing Programs: The First Fifty Years. Iowa City: University of Iowa Press, 1983. 260 pp.
Beginning in the late 1920s, professors of education at the University of Iowa developed various batteries of academic achievement tests for pupils in the state's public and parochial schools. According to Peterson, the tests were initially designed to discover talent in the manner of statewide sports and music contests. In the 1930s, however, a different notion developed, namely that the "average" American represented many different but interrelated types. In response to this notion, the achievement of tests became oriented toward national standardization, thus setting a trend in the whole field of educational measurement and social sorting. Peterson discusses the construction of these tests, the values of the testers, the problems of persuading the public to accept the beneficial aspects of testing, the invention of various mechanical and electronic scoring and record-keeping technologies, and the relationship between academic institutes and the larger world of private enterprise.

STM 287. **POEN, MONTE N.** Harry S. Truman Versus the Medical Lobby: The Genesis of Medicare. Columbia: University of Missouri Press, 1979. 260 pp.
Truman's advocacy of compulsory health insurance did not see results during his administration, as Poen's study illustrates, and his attempts were labeled socialistic and un-American by the AMA medical lobby; Medicare, inaugurated under Johnson, provided less comprehensive coverage than Truman had sought. Poen's study details the powerful opposition met by Truman's reform efforts, exploring the medical community's mobilization and organization.

STM 288.   POOL, ITHIEL de SOLA, ed. The Social Impact of the Telephone.
Cambridge, Mass.: MIT Press, 1977. 502 pp.
The editor notes, in the introduction, that few sociologists of science
have turned their attention to the telephone, a piece of technology which
has become ubiquitous in modern society, even though a wave of "technology
assessment" began as early as the 1930s. Originally presented at a series
of seminars celebrating the 100th anniversary of the telephone's invention,
the twenty-one essays in this collection--written by writers, engineers,
economists, historians, geographers, sociologists, psychologists, political
scientists, and one architect--approach the question of the telephone's
social impact in a variety of ways. The first essays examine various
telephone systems proposed during the telephone's early history. They
are followed by essays on the telephone's effects on daily life, on the
shape of cities ("human ecology"), and on human interaction. The final
group of essays takes a look at novel uses of the telephone: crisis intervention (hotlines), and instructional communication.

STM 289.   POST, ROBERT C. Physics, Patients, and Politics: A Biography
of Charles Grafton Page. New York: Science History, 1976.
227 pp.
Post uses the biography of a now-forgotten scientist to investigate the
interrelationships between scientists, inventors, politicians, and bureaucrats in antebellum Washington. Post argues that Charles Grafton Page
(1812-1868) was widely recognized in the 1830s and 1840s as Joseph Henry's
equal in electrical science. In 1842 Page became a patent examiner in
the recently reorganized Patent Office, then an important niche for non-
academic scientists. Post discusses Page's electrical experiments and
inventions, places them in the context of contemporary science and technology, and examines Page's career as patent examiner and patent agent.
Page's exclusion from the scientific community in the two decades preceding
his death reveals a shift in the relationship between the Patent Office
and the scientific community: inventors gained a privileged position.
His practical bent and political involvements further alienated Page from
the scientific community which was defining key precepts of professional
decorum in this formative period.

STM 290.   PRICE, DON K. Government and Science: Their Dynamic Relation
in American Democracy. New York: New York University Press,
1954. 203 pp.
Price's series of essays discusses the influence of the work of the scientist on American public policy, a process he believes has been at work
since the Revolutionary War. He argues that democratic controls must
work with scientific professional consensus to influence governmental
policy and administration.

STM 291.   PROUT, HENRY G. A Life of George Westinghouse. New York: American Society of Mechanical Engineers, 1921. 375 pp.
George Westinghouse is best known for his air-brake and his introduction
of alternating current, which dramatically improved the distribution and
application of electric power. Nevertheless, Henry Prout finds Westinghouse's business career and technical activities too diverse to present
chronologically. In the course of one day, Westinghouse often dealt with
financial, administrative, commercial, and engineering aspects of numerous
companies from San Francisco to St. Petersberg. Throughout his career,
Westinghouse averaged one new patent every forty-five days. Therefore,
after a short introduction discussing Westinghouse's ancestry, education,
and early experience, Prout treats Westinghouse's career topically with
chapters devoted to the air-brake, alternating-current, Niagara Falls
power, electric traction, steam and gas engines, and natural gas, among
other subjects. Finally, he discusses Westinghouse's European enterprises,
financial methods, administrative abilities, relations to employees, and
personality.

STM 292. PUPIN, MICHAEL. From Immigrant to Inventor. New York: Scribner, 1923. 396 pp.
Michael Pupin (1858-1935) was a Serbian immigrant whose productive career as a professor and electrical inventor exemplified the opportunities available to enterprising physicists in late 19th- and early 20th-century America. After graduating from Columbia College in 1883 (nine years after arriving in New York), Pupin obtained advanced training at Cambridge and Berlin, two European centers of electrical science. In 1889 he returned to Columbia to join the new Department of Electrical Engineering, where he taught until his retirement in 1931. Pupin's most important contribution was the introduction of spaced inductance coils in telephone networks, an innovation which reduced attenuation and distortion in the lines and helped to make long-distance phone service possible. Pupin's activities in applied science--which coincided with the establishment of industries based on electrical technology--illustrate the evolving relationships between academic inventors and industrial patrons.

STM 293. PURCELL, EDWARD A., Jr. The Crisis of Democratic Theory: Scientific Naturalism and the Problem of Value. Lexington: University Press of Kentucky, 1973. 331 pp.
Purcell examines the spread of Pragmatism and Scientific Naturalism and its impact on developments in law, philosophy, and social science in the five decades after 1910. He suggests that in the 1920s there was far more excitement about what Scientific Naturalism could do to create a new science of society than the disillusionment some historians have attributed to the era. This new naturalistic social science, the author insists, challenged and undermined traditional democratic theory and such hoary precepts as the essential rationality of man. Ironically, these new naturalistic interpretations helped to strengthen the arguments of those who thought that democratic government is impractical. By the 1940s, thanks to the rise of European totalitarianism, a new belief system was created wherein democracy and Naturalism were supposedly reconciled.

STM 294. PURSELL, CARROLL W., Jr. Early Stationary Steam Engines in America: A Study in the Migration of a Technology. Washington, D.C.: Smithsonian Institution Press, 1969. 152 pp.
Pursell provides a short account of the introduction and diffusion of stationary steam engines in the U.S. before the Civil War. He identifies those responsible for bringing the steam engine to Colonial America, characterizes the early inventors, and explains why New York and Philadelphia rose early to predominance in steam engine manufacture. Due to the population movement Westward after 1812, Pittsburgh, Louisville, and Cincinnati also became centers for steam engine production. By the 1830s, Pursell argues, steam engines found numerous applications in the South, the West, and even in New England, a region many believe relied on water power. Pursell evaluates the contributions American engine builders made to the development of steam engine technology and argues that before the Civil War steam engines removed limits on the location and the energy supply of American industry, introduced a system of uniform parts, and contributed to coal and iron production.

STM 295. PURSELL, CARROLL W., Jr., ed. Readings in Technology and American Life. New York: Oxford University Press, 1969. 470 pp.
Pursell provides seventy-four selections from various primary sources and arranges them in fourteen topical and chronological chapters from the Colonial period to the post-W.W. II era. He breaks with the traditional emphasis on great men and inventions and stresses instead the social history of technology. Reflecting this approach, several chapter headings recall categories common to American history texts, such as "Winning the West," "The Progressive Era," or "The Great Depression." Pursell also includes readings on various important technical institutions,

the social ideas of technologists, and policy issues. For each chapter and selection there are short introductions providing a broad historical framework for the readings. There is also a brief bibliography.

STM 296. PURSELL, CARROLL W., Jr., ed. Technology in America: A History of Individuals and Ideas. Cambridge, Mass.: MIT Press, 1981. 264 pp.
The twenty essays in this collection--roughly half of them dealing with the 19th century and the other half with the 20th--examine the lives of Americans who contributed significantly to technological advances. But according to the editor, the biographical format is not meant to imply that only great men and women were involved; rather, these lives are presented as "windows" through which we can see "the interplay of ideas and institutions that combined to shape the tools of their time." Those individuals include Thomas Jefferson, Eli Whitney, Cyrus McCormick, Alexander Graham Bell, Thomas Edison, Henry Ford, Enrico Fermi, and Robert H. Goddard.

STM 297. PYNE, STEPHEN J. Fire in America: A Cultural History of Wildland and Rural Fire. Princeton, N.J.: Princeton University Press, 1982. 654 pp.
Pyne's book chronologically studies the history of fire in America. After describing basic principles of fire, its behavior and control, he discusses the use of fire by American Indians, as well as the ways fire affected their history. Attentive to regional history, Pyne describes the fire history of most areas of the country. He details the development of fire control, fire policy, and the forest service.

STM 298. QUIMBY, IAN M. G. and POLLY ANNE EARL, eds. Technological Innovation and the Decorative Arts. Charlottesville: University Press of Virginia, 1974. 373 pp.
This collection of papers originally prepared for a conference at the Henry Francis du Pont Winterthur Museum, deals with technological change in the 18th and 19th centuries and its relationship to the development of home furnishings. It provides art history and history of technology perspectives on material culture in America and its changes with the Industrial Revolution. The essays deal with various aspects of American taste, new contributions to the decorative arts, the rise of a consumer society, and the role of museums in art study. The collection includes essays on the jewelry and silver trades, iron castings, pressed glass, fine furniture, calico printing, printed textile styles, wallpaper, the furniture industry, technological utopianism, and the role of the American museum in encouraging innovation in the decorative arts. The consensus of the authors is that the period was one of sweeping technological change and the evolution of a truly American standard of taste in decoration, no longer imitative of European traditions. Several authors view this as the beginning of strong American leadership in some aspects of decorative art.

STM 299. RAE, JOHN B. American Automobile Manufacturers, the First Forty Years. Philadelphia: Chilton, 1959. 223 pp.
Rae argues that technically trained business leaders were essential for the growth of the American automobile industry because they successfully harmonized technological and business considerations in building the industry. This study identifies the New England and Midwestern mechanics as well as the bicycle, carriage, and wagon manufacturers who originated the industry. Also discussed are the unsuccessful attempts to control manufacturing through the Seldon patents and the first mergers, including the formation of General Motors Company in 1908. Rae evaluates Henry Ford's important role in the development of mass production and the quickening effect of W.W. I on the trend to large-scale firms that mass production

introduced. In the 1920s the growth of the giant corporations and the decline of the independents continued, and the Depression completed the process. Throughout his book, Rae concentrates on the business leaders and finally summarizes their common characteristics.

STM 300. RAE, JOHN B. Climb to Greatness: The American Aircraft Industry, 1920-1960. Cambridge, Mass.: MIT Press, 1968. 280 pp.
Rae details the development of the American aircraft industry from its post-W.W. I crisis to the late 1950s, when missile manufacturing transformed the industry. He describes the personalities involved, military influences, business developments, and the important technological innovations of the period. Not until the late 1920s did the military have a clear policy toward airplane manufactures, but then the steady volume of military orders provided some stability to the industry. Rae believes that military procurement policies produced intense technological competition among privately-owned firms and a pace of development which forced even the most successful to reinvest much of their income in research. Rae devotes almost a third of the book to explaining the mobilization of industry resulting in its remarkable production achievements during W.W. II. Finally, he recounts postwar developments including helicopters and jets.

STM 301. RAE, JOHN B. The Road and the Car in American Life. Cambridge, Mass.: MIT Press, 1971. 390 pp.
Rae's study of the interaction between the roadway system and the mass-produced automobile in America focuses on events since 1930. He first provides a short account of the highway in history and of attempts in the 1890s and early 1900s to improve American roads. During these years, the automobile revolution inaugurated a new era in highway transportation and greatly increased the demand for a new and comprehensive highway policy. Rae then investigates the economic and social impact after the 1920s of the increasing volume of traffic and improved road systems, which contributed to American mobility and eased the transportation of goods. In the third section, Rae details the effects cars and roads have had on the city by promoting suburban development and the dispersion of business and industry. He also describes urban streets, freeways, and transport options and surveys potential future transportation problems.

STM 302. RAFFEL, MARSHALL W. The U.S. Health System: Origins and Functions. New York: Wiley, 1980. 639 pp.
Raffel studies health care as an industry in this work--an industry that in 1978 represented 9.1% of the Gross National Product. His text covers such topics as medical education, allied health professions, the history of American hospitals, health costs and health insurance, and issues in public health.

STM 303. REED, JAMES. From Private Vice to Public Virtue: The Birth Control Movement and American Society Since 1830. New York: Basic Books, 1978. 456 pp.
Reed begins his study of birth control in America by examining how 18th- and 19th-century demographics began shifting and a need for birth control became more pressing. By the 1870s, legislation was necessary to suppress birth control. Reed concentrates on the individual efforts of Margaret Sanger, Robert Dickinson, and Clarence Gamble. He concludes with an extensive discussion of American recognition of a global population explosion, which had the effect of making birth control a "public virtue," "a moral imperative in a crowded world."

STM 304. REINGOLD, NATHAN, ed. Science in America Since 1820. New York: Science History, 1976. 334 pp.
Science in America Since 1820 is a collection of twenty-one articles published in Isis between 1954 and 1975. These papers present an eclectic array of topics and approaches in the history of American science. Among articles dealing with the broad cultural setting are George Daniels's discussion of the process of professionalization in American science from 1820 to 1860, and Stanley Guralnick's revisionist critique of standard notions of the role of science in the antebellum college curriculum. Many of the contributions deal with questions of intellectual history in American geology, natural history, genetics, physics, and astronomy. Another group of articles focuses on scientific institutions, including the National Institute (1944), Midwestern academies of science, state geological surveys, the Permanent Commission of the Navy Department (1863), and the National Research Council (1916). In his introduction Nathan Reingold offers some reflections on the recent historiography of American science.

STM 305. REINGOLD, NATHAN, ed. Science in Nineteenth-Century America: A Documentary History. New York: Hill & Wang, 1964. 339 pp.
Reingold uses contemporary documents and interpretive commentary to present a picture of 19th-century American science as dominated by natural history and a "geophysical tradition." Geographical sciences like taxonomic natural history, geology, meteorology, and oceanography were suited to the exploration and mapping of an uncharted continent. Mathematics and astronomy were pursued as tools for navigation and surveying. Reingold discusses the work of natural historians William Maclure and Constantine Rafinesque; physical scientists Joseph Henry and William C. Redfield; and the Wilkes Expedition (1838-1842). Other documents indicate the growing self-consciousness of the American scientific community, focusing on Lazzaroni activities in scientific organizations such as the Coast Survey and the National Academy of Sciences. The relationship of American to European science is illustrated in the contributions of Asa Gray and others to evolution and paleontology. Finally, through the work of Henry Rowland, J. Willard Gibbs, A. A. Michelson, and others, Reingold analyzes the rise of physics in America and suggests its connections with the earlier geophysical tradition.

STM 306. REINGOLD, NATHAN, ed. The Sciences in the American Context: New Perspectives. Washington, D.C.: Smithsonian Institution Press, 1979. 399 pp.
This is a collection of papers presented at a bicentennial conference, the February 1976 meeting of the Association for the Advancement of Science. The editor argues that the collection reveals an increased trend toward a merger of intellectual and social history of science. Essays by historians of science such as Charles Rosenberg, Steven Pyne, Stanley Cohen, and Carroll Pursell are included.

STM 307. RETTIG, RICHARD A. Cancer Crusade: The Story of the National Cancer Act of 1971. Princeton, N.J.: Princeton University Press, 1977. 382 pp.
Rettig's study of the National Cancer Act of 1971 is divided into three parts: a description of previous efforts at legislation and cancer research, a legislative history of the Act itself, and the administration and implementation of the Act. Rettig argues that cancer played a large part in the presidential politics of 1971-1972, and places cancer legislation in a larger context of public policy decision-making, agenda setting, and implementation.

STM 308. REVERBY, SUSAN and DAVID ROSNER, eds. Health Care in America: Essays in Social History. Philadelphia: Temple University Press, 1971. 275 pp.

Consisting of thirteen essays, this work examines the social relations involved in health care. The editors, in their introductory essay, argue that until recently medical history was written mostly by physicians and therefore documented the "unfolding of medical science" rather than health care and its social context. The essays treat three major concerns: first, the tension between medical and lay or social groups regarding control of health care (in particular, childbirth and vaccination); second, the social and economic consequences of shifting the locus of health care from the home to the health care institution; and third, the relationships among medical professionals (doctors and nurses), nonprofessional medical workers, and health care institutions.

STM 309. RISSE, GUENTER B., RONALD L. NUMBERS, and JUDITH WALZER LEAVITT, eds. Medicine Without Doctors: Home Health Care in American History. New York: Science History, 1977. 124 pp.

Risse's introductory essay explores the tradition of self-help in America. The editors have collected five papers delivered at a 1975 symposium at the University of Wisconsin: an essay by John B. Blake on self-help manuals, James Cassedy on factors promoting self-help, Ronald Numbers and Regina Morantz on sectarians and women, home practitioners of self-help, and James Harvey Young on patent medicines.

STM 310. ROPES, HANNAH ANDERSON. Civil War Nurse Diary and Letters. Edited by John R. Brumgardt. Knoxville: University of Tennessee Press, 1980. 149 pp.

Brumgardt has edited and provided an introduction for Hannah Ropes's diary and letters. Ropes was a New England reformer and abolitionist whose expertise was described in Louisa May Alcott's Hospital Sketches. Brumgardt's introduction puts Ropes's career in the social context of 19th-century reform and the history of American nursing.

STM 311. ROSE, MARK H. Interstate Express Highway Politics, 1941-1956. Lawrence: Regents Press of Kansas, 1979. 169 pp.

This study of highways in America describes efforts at highway-building as early as 1890, though Rose concentrates on the post-W.W. II years. He describes Congress's authorization of construction of the National System of Interstate Highways in 1944, which was largely ineffectual, and the Interstate Highway Act of 1956, under which the American interstate system developed. Rose devotes attention to the politics of economic policy-making, urban planning, and the development of transportation facilities.

STM 312. ROSEN, GEORGE. Madness in Society: Chapters in the Historical Sociology of Mental Illness. New York: Harper & Row, 1968. 330 pp.

Rosen's central theme is that conceptions of madness in Western society have resulted from sociocultural forces. Accordingly, Rosen does not focus on the observations of medical men in dealing with the phenomena of mental illness, but rather on the status of the mentally afflicted in societies during different historical periods, and on the psychological, cultural, and social forces which have determined this status. Mental illness in America is discussed in the context of the Western world.

STM 313. **ROSEN, GEORGE.** The Structure of American Medical Practice 1875-1941. Edited by Charles Rosenberg. Philadelphia: University of Pennsylvania Press, 1983. 152 pp.
This volume is a collection of lectures delivered by George Rosen of Yale University for the inaugural Richard H. Shryock Lectures at the University of Pennsylvania in 1976. Conscious of medical practice as a social function, Rosen examines such trends in American medicine as the growth of office practice and professional group practices, and discusses such topics as licensing, insurance, and the role of the AMA. Rosen's social history looks at the changes in the economics of American medical practice.

STM 314. **ROSENBERG, CHARLES E.** The Cholera Years: The United States in 1832, 1849, and 1866. Chicago: University of Chicago Press, 1962. 257 pp.
Cholera was the classic epidemic disease of the 19th century. Rosenberg's social history of the public response to three major cholera outbreaks in the U.S. between 1832 and 1866 analyzes changes in social thought, medical knowledge, and public health reform during the period. As the pietistic character of American social values became increasingly critical and empiricist, cholera was transformed from a moral dilemma into a problem which could be solved through social action. Focusing on New York City, Rosenberg examines changing theories of disease causation and the role of the medical profession in the response to cholera, efforts to combat the epidemics by improving water supply and sanitation, and the establishment of the Metropolitan Board of Health in 1866. Using a wide variety of contemporary newspapers, periodicals, and medical sources, Rosenberg explores the interaction of medicine and society in mid-19th-century America.

STM 315. **ROSENBERG, CHARLES E.** No Other Gods: On Science and American Social Thought. Baltimore, Md.: Johns Hopkins University Press, 1976. 273 pp.
This collection of essays explores the interactions of science and social thought in American history. Rosenberg examines the ideological uses of scientific images and ideas in rationalizing such social realities as the role of women, male sexual identity, and 19th-century views on heredity. The connections between social values and the scientist's perception of his or her role are illustrated in studies of Charles Davenport's eugenics and George Beard's work on neurasthenia. Science also served as a source of authority in social thought, as Rosenberg demonstrates in essays on the pietistic motivations of early public health reformers and the spiritual function of science in Sinclair Lewis's Arrowsmith. Rosenberg then turns to the development of agricultural experiment stations and analyzes the interaction of social priorities and the disciplinary commitments of experiment station scientists in structuring the new institutions. Rosenberg also shows the relationship between scientific institutions and the production of knowledge by investigating the social context of scientific innovations like hybrid corn and vitamin A, and the structure of the genetics discipline in the U.S.

STM 316. **ROSENBERG, NATHAN.** Perspectives on Technology. New York: Cambridge University Press, 1976. 353 pp.
The collection of essays written by Rosenberg in the 1960s and 1970s stems from his interest in long-term economic growth and the characteristics of industrializing societies. In the initial essays, Rosenberg discusses the key economic sectors of machine tools and woodworking machinery and the distinct features of 19th-century American technology. Rosenberg then delineates the manner in which economists have analyzed the relationship between technological change and economic growth. An important aspect of this relationship is the speed of adaptation and extent of diffusion of technology, a theme Rosenberg follows in the next group of essays

devoted to developing economies, 19th-century mechanisms of technology transfer, and the transfer from England to the U.S. of steam and iron-working technologies. Finally, Rosenberg discusses various aspects of the relationship between natural resources and technological change and innovation.

STM 317. ROSENBERG, NATHAN. Technology and American Economic Growth. New York: Harper & Row, 1972. 211 pp.
Rosenberg presents a conceptual framework and related information to explain the relationships between technology and long term economic growth in the U.S. After analyzing social and economic factors underlying innovation and diffusion of technology, Rosenberg describes 19th-century America as borrower in steam power and metallurgy, and innovator in interchangeable parts and mass production. For Rosenberg the unifying theme for 19th-century America is the widening scope of mechanization and the diffusion of machine technology. The unifying theme in the 20th century is diversity and an increasing proportion of technological change resulting from prior advances in science. Rosenberg emphasizes the important change from machine-based technologies to technologies based on chemistry, electricity, and biology. Finally, Rosenberg examines technology and social options and surveys important issues arising from technology's social and environmental impact.

STM 318. ROSENBERG, NATHAN, ed. The American System of Manufactures: The Report of the Committee on the Machinery of the United States 1855 and the Special Reports of George Wallis and Joseph Whitworth 1854. Edinburgh: Edinburgh University Press, 1969. 440 pp.
This volume contains three reports that together constitute an account of mid-19th-century American manufacturing. Since the British Board of Ordinance faced great difficulties acquiring new firearms in the early 1850s, Parliament sent the Committee on the Machinery of the U.S. to investigate and purchase American equipment for producing standardized firearms with interchangeable parts. Two other visitors, Joseph Whitworth, a machine tool manufacturer, and George Wallis, an industrial designer, had the expertise necessary to evaluate American manufacturing and wrote accounts of their visits to the New York Exhibition of 1853 and manufacturing sites in the Northeast. Rosenberg's introduction provides historical context. He describes the problems the British Board of Ordinance faced in a period of impending war and the steps taken to solve these problems by transferring the American system of arms manufacture to the Enfield Armoury. Rosenberg also provides a short history of the American system of manufacture.

STM 319. ROSENKRANTZ, BARBARA GUTMAN. Public Health and the State: Changing Views in Massachusetts, 1842-1936. Cambridge, Mass.: Harvard University Press, 1972. 259 pp.
The Massachusetts State Board of Health, established in 1869, was the first state institution in the U.S. with broad responsibilities for preventing disease and promoting the public health. Rosenkrantz discusses the work of Lemuel Shattuck and others who campaigned for sanitary reform in antebellum Massachusetts; the origins of the State Board of Health; and its investigations of poor housing conditions, water supplies, sanitation, and other public health problems after the Civil War. Rosenkrantz also analyzes changing concepts of the etiology of disease and the shifting relationship of sanitary science to social reform. As specific medical prophylaxis and new therapies were adopted in public health work after the 1880s, the sanitary engineers and reformers of an earlier generation were displaced by laboratory scientists, chemists, and physicians who viewed public health as a science. In her last chapter, Rosenkrantz considers the implications of this redefinition for public health policies after W.W. I.

STM 320. ROSNER, DAVID. A Once Charitable Enterprise: Hospitals and
Health Care in Brooklyn and New York, 1885-1915. New York:
Cambridge University Press, 1982. 234 pp.
Rosner's study argues that the organization of health service is reflective
of cultural values. His book chronicles the transformation of the older
charity hospitals into the modern "scientific" versions, with attention
to issues in hospital financing, patients' social class, and the relation
of politics to hospital administration.

STM 321. ROSSITER, MARGARET W. The Emergence of Agricultural Science:
Justus Liebig and the Americans, 1840-1880. New Haven, Conn.:
Yale University Press, 1975. 275 pp.
Focusing on the careers of three of Liebig's most illustrious American
students--Eben Horsford, John P. Norton, and Samuel W. Johnson--Rossiter
relates the history of the transformation of American agricultural science
and the importation of German chemical research laboratories and agricultural experiment stations into the U.S. from 1840 to 1880. During the
1840s Eastern farmers were distressed about "worn-out soil," and Liebig's
new agricultural chemistry was given an enthusiastic reception. At the
same time, several of Liebig's American students undertook the task of
building new institutions at home to carry out a program of scientific
research adapted to practical needs. But, as Rossiter's account shows,
economic obstacles and a reaction in the 1850s and 1860s against the vogue
of soil analysis hindered their attempts. Horsford's plan to create a
"Giessen on the Charles" in Cambridge, Massachusetts, foundered on the
high overhead costs connected with his laboratory. Johnson's later efforts
to create a research-oriented agricultural experiment station met with
aggressive demands for immediate practical results from Connecticut farmers
and government patrons. While their ambitions were realized only in the
next generation, the activities of Rossiter's agricultural chemists were
an important prelude to the success of the later scientist-entrepreneurs.

STM 322. ROSSITER, MARGARET W. Women Scientists in America: Struggles
and Strategies to 1940. Baltimore, Md.: Johns Hopkins University Press, 1982. 439 pp.
Rossiter argues that women emerged as important figures in science as
higher education and greater employment opportunities became available
to them and as science and technology themselves developed in America.
She describes the resistance met with by women scientists in the 19th
and 20th century and the strategies they developed to overcome it, in
academics and government, in industrial employment, and among the scientific community.

STM 323. ROTHMAN, DAVID J. Conscience and Convenience: The Asylum and
Its Alternatives in Progressive America. Boston: Little, Brown,
1980. 464 pp.
Rothman's book is a study in reform, he states in his introduction. Progressive reformers worked out of ideological formulations of idealism--
thus "conscience"--and the administrators of criminal justice responded
to their reforms, which enlarged their spheres of authority, with alacrity--
thus "convenience." He argues that the failure and misguided nature of
these reforms are suggestive for contemporary policy concerns.

STM 324. ROTHSTEIN, WILLIAM G. American Physicians in the Nineteenth
Century: From Sects to Science. Baltimore, Md.: Johns Hopkins
University Press, 1972. 362 pp.
Rothstein analyzes the relationships of private practitioners, medical
societies, medical schools, and the licensing system in 19th-century American medicine, and relates changes in medical institutions to trends in
medical knowledge and the economic interests of physicians. Competition
among medical schools and rival therapies in the antebellum period fostered

the institutionalization of medical sects like Thomsonianism and homeopathy. Rothstein discusses therapeutic nihilism and other developments in medical practice after the Civil War, as well as the increasing stratification and specialization of the medical profession. Advances in scientific medicine (especially anesthesia, antisepsis, and bacteriology) together with the reform of medical education and more stringent licensing regulations ensured the hegemony of regular physicians and the demise of sectarian medicine by the early 20th century.

STM 325. RUDISILL, RICHARD. Mirror Image: The Influence of the Daguerrotype on American Society. Albuquerque: University of New Mexico Press, 1971. 342 pp.
The author explores the daguerrotype's influences in America from 1840 to 1860, arguing that the new invention encouraged nationalistic impulses, allowed Americans to adjust to a technological rather than an agrarian self-image, and, most important, seemed to confirm Transcendentalist views of God in nature. The daguerrotype, argues Rudisill in this broad cultural history, was completely assimilated into the American consciousness, more so than most inventions, precisely because it met many of the culture's spiritual and emotional needs.

STM 326. RUSSETT, CYNTHIA EAGLE. The Concept of Equilibrium in American Social Thought. New Haven, Conn.: Yale University Press, 1966. 203 pp.
Russett discusses the influence of equilibrium and biological sciences on the social sciences. After a brief discussion of the different models of equilibrium theory used in physics and biology, the author then traces the steps whereby the notions of equilibrium became established in American social sciences by leading figures in the field, including Albion W. Small, John Dewey, Vilfredo Pareto, and Talcott Parsons.

STM 327. RUSSETT, CYNTHIA EAGLE. Darwin in America: The Intellectual Response, 1865-1912. San Francisco: Freeman, 1976. 228 pp.
Russett surveys the impact of evolutionary theory on American culture in the late 19th and early 20th centuries through a series of "intellectual portraits" of prominent thinkers. After a brief discussion of the scientific reception of Darwin's The Origin of Species and the introduction of Herbert Spencer's ideas to American intellectual circles, Russett turns to the efforts of Protestant theologians to reconcile Darwinism and religion. The issues of moral freedom and the divinity of nature also exercised Cambridge Metaphysicians like John Fiske, William James, C. S. Peirce, and Chauncey Wright, who worried about the implications of evolution for Determinism and Positivism. Russett also explores trends in social thought, concentrating on the Social Darwinism of William Graham Sumner and Lester Frank Ward, John Dewey and Pragmatism, Henry Adams's search for an evolutionary science of history, and Thorstein Veblen's social theory. Finally, Russett examines the Naturalism of novelists Jack London, Frank Norris, and Theodore Dreiser as a reflection of new evolutionary attitudes.

STM 328. SAVITT, TODD L. Medicine and Slavery: The Diseases and Health Care of Blacks in Antebellum Virginia. Urbana: University of Illinois Press, 1978. 332 pp.
Savitt's book, which focuses on conditions in Virginia from the Revolution to the Civil War, begins with a discussion of 19th-century attitudes toward blacks and disease. Savitt discusses health conditions among slaves, and the related considerations of food, clothing, and work, as well as white responses to diseases among slaves, and the ways in which self-interest dictated these responses, which were of varying efficacy.

STM 329. **SCHMOOKLER, JACOB.** <u>Invention</u> and <u>Economic Growth</u>. Cambridge, Mass.: Harvard University Press, 1966. 332 pp.
This work describes factors that foster technological innovation. Using patent statistics and studies of 900 specific inventions in railroading, agriculture, petroleum refining, and papermaking, Schmookler analyzes relationships between invention and economic growth. Variations in issued patents are, Schmookler argues, linked to investment in inventive activity and are reasonably good indicators of changes in investment patterns over time in a given industry and of investment differences between industries at a point in time. Schmookler's major theme is that the production of new technology is primarily an economic activity and that the pattern of demand for both goods and services explains both short and long range changes in the direction of inventive effort. He also discusses individual and corporate inventors, reasons for the postwar decline in the ratio of the number of patents to that of scientists and engineers, patent performance of big and small companies, and the closing of fields of inventive activity when markets are saturated.

STM 330. **SCHNEER, CECIL J.**, ed. <u>Two</u> Hundred <u>Years</u> of <u>Geology</u> in <u>America</u>. Hanover, N.H.: University Press of New England, 1979. 385 pp.
These essays are the published proceedings of the New Hampshire Bicentennial Conference on the History of Geology. They concentrate on two kinds of themes, argues the editor in his introduction. The first methodological theme is the tension between those approaches which are concerned with the origin and evolution of ideas and those which argue that science must be placed in its social context. The second theme addressed concerns the major concepts intrinsic to the science, such as the geosynclinal hypothesis and its relation to isotasy and plate tectonics. The essays are arranged chronologically, and address topics in the history of geology from the geology of the Colonies to contemporary theories of continental drift.

STM 331. **SCHON, DONALD A.** <u>Technology</u> and <u>Change</u>: <u>The New Heraclitus</u>. New York: Delacorte Press, 1967. 248 pp.
Schon directly examines the concept of technological innovation and the notion of "research and development," and discusses how they have become corporate virtues. He concentrates on technological change within American industry, arguing that it constitutes "a metaphor for change in our society as a whole."

STM 332. **SCHUYLER, HAMILTON.** <u>The Roeblings</u>: <u>A Century of Engineers, Bridge-Builders</u>, and <u>Industrialists</u>. <u>The Story of Three Generations of an Illustrious Family</u>, 1831-1931. Princeton, N.J.: Princeton University Press, 1931. 425 pp.
The author concentrates less on the material structures built by the Roeblings--including the Brooklyn Bridge and the George Washington Bridge-- than on the lives of John Roebling, his son Washington, and his grandsons Ferdinand and Charles. Technical descriptions of the cable-making industry and the suspension bridge are included in this illustrated biography.

STM 333. **SCHWABE, CALVIN W.** <u>Cattle</u>, <u>Priests</u>, and <u>Progress</u> in <u>Medicine</u>. Minneapolis: University of Minnesota Press, 1978. 277 pp.
Schwabe describes the relationships between veterinary medicine and advancements in knowledge about human health. He bases his arguments on three premises: first, medical progress consists of an increase in the number of effective means of combating disease and in <u>factual</u> knowledge about biological processes, not in unfounded theories; second, veterinary medicine relates directly to human well-being because it is related to food production, maintenance of environment, and the understanding and treating of disease; and third, there were three major breakthroughs in the approach to medicine--all intimately connected to animal medicine--amassing of

facts, comparative biology, and rigorous comparative medical research as it was conducted in the first veterinary schools. In the first four chapters, Schwabe traces historically the extent to which animal medicine has improved human medicine, and in the last chapter he urges greater cooperation between the two disciplines.

STM 334. SEARS, ROBERT R. Your Ancients Revisited: A History of Child Development. Chicago: University of Chicago Press, 1975. 70 pp.

Sears provides a brief interpretive introduction to the history of sciences related to children in 20th-century America. Among the topics discussed are the origins of child-oriented inquiries in psychology, medicine, dentistry, physical growth, and psychology, the involvement of philanthropists in child science in the 1920s, the child guidance movement, child welfare institutes, the impact of the Depression and W.W. II on child science, and Federal support of research after 1950. A substantial discussion of the intellectual history of child development is also included. Sears's major theme is that child science has been influenced by social and cultural circumstances more than most sciences have been; tension between its "pure" and "applied" scientific traditions has resulted.

STM 335. SELLERS, CHARLES COLEMAN. Mr. Peale's Museum: Charles Willson Peale and the First Popular Museum of Natural Science and Art. New York: Norton, 1980. 370 pp.

Sellers, a descendant and biographer of Charles Willson Peale, traces the history of his ancestor's museum from its beginning in 1784 to its dispersal (purchased by P. T. Barnum, the collection was divided and scattered between 1845 and 1854). Sellers reports that Peale, a painter with a modest portrait gallery open to the public, received encouragement to convert the gallery into a natural history museum from the American Philosophical Society, presided over at the time by Benjamin Franklin. He asserts that Peale's museum, which spawned numerous "tawdry and specious" imitations, played a "strong supportive role in the development of science in this country." He also notes the triple function of the museum: the systematic arrangement and documentation of actual specimens, the promotion of research, and the "diffusion of knowledge."

STM 336. SHAFER, HENRY BURNELL. The American Medical Profession, 1783 to 1850. New York: Columbia University Press, 1936. 271 pp.

Shafer argues that the period his book covers saw the medical profession transformed by modern methodologies. The book contains an extensive survey of medical education, its substance, requirements, and efficacy, and discussion of medical practice, ethics and fees, medical literature, and medical regulations and societies.

STM 337. SHERWIN, MARTIN J. A World Destroyed: The Atomic Bomb and the Grand Alliance. New York: Knopf, 1975. 315 pp.

Sherwin examines the wartime roots of the postwar atomic diplomacy. He analyzes political relations among the scientists, politicians, military leaders, and diplomats concerned with the use of the atomic bomb against the Japanese. Sherwin discusses the attempts of scientists such as Niels Bohr to alert political leaders to the revolutionary political implications of nuclear weapons and the need for international control. These proposals were rejected, Sherwin argues, because Roosevelt and Churchill hoped to maintain the Anglo-American atomic monopoly as a diplomatic counter against the Soviet Union's postwar ambitions. According to Sherwin, Roosevelt was far from conciliatory toward the Soviet Union. His attitude laid the foundation for the atomic diplomacy which Truman followed after coming to office in April 1945. Thus, wartime and diplomatic maneuvers arising from science policies set the stage for the Cold War.

STM 338. **SHINE, IAN** and **SYLVIA WROBEL.** Thomas Hunt Morgan: Pioneer of
Genetics. Lexington: University Press of Kentucky, 1976.
160 pp.
This biography of Morgan, the first Nobel laureate in genetics, places
him in the context of the development of biological sciences in the early
20th century. Originally a zoologist, Morgan made significant contributions to embryology as well as genetics, the authors argue. His genetic
work at Columbia University with the fruit fly established Mendelian laws
and their exceptions, and formed the foundation of all subsequent genetic
work.

STM 339. **SHRYOCK, RICHARD HARRISON.** American Medical Research, Past and
Present. New York: Commonwealth Fund, 1947. 350 pp.
This account of American medical research begins with formative foreign
influences and goes on to trace the historical development of American
research. He brings forward such important factors in that development
as the influence of Johns Hopkins Medical School, the role of publications
and support for research, and the relation of research to teaching.

STM 340. **SHRYOCK, RICHARD HARRISON.** The Development of Modern Medicine.
1936; Rev. ed. New York: Knopf, 1947. 472 pp.
This book, a revision of the 1936 version, is not exclusively about American medicine, but it provides a broad overview of the history of medicine
since the 16th century and includes much discussion of American contributions. Making the general argument that society and medicine interact
and influence each other, Shryock argues specifically that measurement,
experiment, and the development of instruments—quantitative gains—
transformed modern medicine. He closes with two chapters on the then-
contemporary American medicine.

STM 341. **SHRYOCK, RICHARD HARRISON.** Medicine and Society in America,
1660-1860. New York: New York University Press, 1960.
182 pp.
Medicine and Society in America is an account of selected topics in the
social history of American medicine before the Civil War. Shryock begins
with the origins of the medical profession and surveys its social structure, trends in early medical education, and the establishment of medical
societies and journals. In the next chapter, on medical thought and practice, 1660-1820, Shryock explains changing views on disease causation,
concentrating on the work of Cotton Mather and Benjamin Rush. He then
discusses public health in early America, relates patterns of disease
to such factors as diet, climate, and social conditions, and describes
public response through sanitation, quarantine, and other precautionary
measures. The final chapter traces developments in medical research and
medical education from 1820-1860. In addition to an emphasis on the social
context of medical practice, one of Shryock's recurrent motifs is the
comparison of American developments with European traditions.

STM 342. **SHRYOCK, RICHARD HARRISON.** Medicine in America: Historical
Essays. Baltimore, Md.: Johns Hopkins University Press, 1966.
346 pp.
This volume is a selection of essays on American science and medicine
originally published between 1930 and 1962, to which Shryock has added
a summary of "The Medical History of the American People." Among the
historiographic contributions are two early articles drawing attention
to the importance of medical sources and the history of science for American historians, an analysis of "The Interplay of Social and Internal
Factors in Modern Medicine," and Shryock's paper on "American Indifference
to Basic Science During the Nineteenth Century" (first published in 1948).
Other chapters deal with medical practice in the antebellum South; medicine
and the Civil War; the public health and tuberculosis movements; medicine

in early 19th-century Philadelphia; the history of the medical profession
and the role of women; and studies of such diverse figures as Cotton Mather,
Benjamin Rush, Sylvester Graham, and William Charles Wells. These essays
relate the history of medicine to trends in American social and intellectual history.

STM 343. SINCLAIR, BRUCE. A Centennial History of the American Society
of Mechanical Engineers, 1880-1980. Toronto: University of
Toronto Press, 1980. 226 pp.
Sinclair offers a history of the American Society of Mechanical Engineers
(ASME) from 1880 to 1980. According to Sinclair, the founders of the
ASME envisioned two distinct but interrelated goals for the society:
those interested in social ramifications sought to define the role of
mechanical engineers as a progressive agent in America; those concerned
with the technical aspects of the profession were more interested in the
formulation of a specialized body of knowledge. Conflicts over the original social and technical visions of the founders as well as later efforts
to redefine the society's aims shaped and refined ASME's institutional
form. Such disagreements led ASME to create geographical and technical
divisions, encouraged participation in the standardization of materials
testing and in the rationalization of factory processes, prompted disorganization due to the allegation that mechanical engineers were in part
responsible for the Depression, and ultimately reaffirmed the mechanical
engineer's contribution to national life in post-W.W. II America.

STM 344. SINCLAIR, BRUCE. Philadelphia's Philosopher Mechanics: A History
of the Franklin Institute 1824-1865. Baltimore, Md.: Johns
Hopkins University Press, 1974. 353 pp.
Like other mechanics institutes, the Franklin Institute in Philadelphia
began with the rhetoric of democracy, social improvement, and the virtues
of philosophically informed artisans. It soon moved away from the original
democratic ideas, assumed the mantle of national leadership, and developed
an active program of teaching, research, and publication. During the
antebellum period, the Franklin Institute functioned as a national technical institute and served as a focal point for those who believed that
technology was the basis of America's future. Sinclair's history of this
important institute focuses on the interrelations of science, technology,
and culture in an urban and institutional context. He discusses important
personalities, financial problems, scientific research, and the Institute's
organization and economic roles. Sinclair also includes four pictorial
essays illustrating persons and apparatus of Philadelphia's technological
culture.

STM 345. SKOLNIK, HERMAN and KENNETH M. REESE, eds. A Century of Chemistry:
The Role of Chemists and the American Chemical Society. Washington, D.C.: American Chemical Society, 1976. 468 pp.
With over 115,000 members, the American Chemical Society (ACS) is one
of the world's largest scientific societies. This centennial volume provides information on the history and current activities of the ACS. Topics
discussed include chemical education, professional relations, government
service, chemistry and public affairs, and ACS governance and publications.
A series of individual sections covers developments in each of the ACS
specialty divisions, ranging from agricultural and food chemistry to computers in chemistry. The book concludes with a listing of ACS national
and local officers, committee members, journal editors, meetings, and
membership statistics from 1876 to 1975.

STM 346. SMITH, ALICE KIMBALL. A Peril and a Hope: The Scientists' Move-
          ment in America: 1945-47. 1965; Rev. ed. Cambridge, Mass.:
          MIT Press, 1970. 591 pp.
Smith provides an account of the campaign of scientists to influence the
control of atomic energy during and just after W.W. II and to make science
serve the cause of peace. First, she traces their unsuccessful wartime
efforts to affect the use of the atomic bomb, and their reactions in August
and September 1^45 to the bombing of Japan. Then she details the scientists' actions in late 1945 as lobbyists and publicists campaigning against
the War Department bill sponsoring military control of atomic energy.
They offered instead a plan for international control. She recounts the
founding of the Federation of Atomic Scientists and the Federation of
American Scientists to organize the effort to shape public policy. The
latter sections deal with the scientists' effort to educate the public,
their campaign for the MacMahon bill (providing civilian control of atomic
energy), various schemes for international control, and the eventual
decline of their active political participation.

STM 347. SMITH, ALICE KIMBALL and CHARLES WEINER, eds. Robert Oppenheimer,
          Letters and Recollections. Cambridge, Mass.: Harvard University
          Press, 1980. 376 pp.
Smith and Weiner have collected the letters of Robert Oppenheimer from
his entrance to Harvard in 1922 until he left his post as director of
the nuclear weapons laboratory at Los Alamos. The editors provide excerpts
from an interview with Oppenheimer conducted by Thomas Kuhn, and an epilogue chronicling Oppenheimer's career after Los Alamos. The editors'
goal is to trace Oppenheimer's scientific beginnings, before he became
a controversial public figure.

STM 348. SMITH, MERRITT ROE. Harpers Ferry Armory and the New Technology:
          The Challenge of Change. Ithaca, N.Y.: Cornell University
          Press, 1977. 363 pp.
Smith focuses on the national armory at Harpers Ferry, Virginia, and its
resistance to the introduction of machines to manufacture small arms and
interchangeable parts, a change that took place with ease at the Springfield armory in New England. Until the mid-1830s, the labor-intensive
system of manufacture at Harpers Ferry remained economically competitive
with the increasingly mechanized system at Springfield. Smith demonstrates
the central role that the Federal government and the Army Ordinance Department played in promoting the development, before the economic value became
evident, of labor-saving machinery and a new system for relating men and
machines. Although important inventors such as John Hall and Thomas
Blanchard worked at Harpers Ferry, its local culture and isolation prevented
technological change, even in the face of pressure from the Ordinance
Department. Smith investigates this resistance through a narrative of
Harpers Ferry from its founding in 1798 to its destruction in 1861.

STM 349. SMITH, ROBERT A. A Social History of the Bicycle: Its Early
          Life and Times in America. New York: American Heritage Press,
          1972. 269 pp.
Smith's illustrated history of the bicycle industry begins with the production of early bicycles in the 1890s--which anticipated methods of automobile production--and describes the bicycle craze of the 1890s, when
the introduction of the bicycle had effects even on the American economy.
He discusses early debates over the bicycle and health and morality, bicycle daredevils, the growth of bicycle racing, and attempts to introduce
cycling divisions into the U.S. Army at the decade's end.

STM 350. SONNEDECKER, GLENN. Kremers and Urdang's History of Pharmacy.
          1940; Rev. ed. Philadelphia: Lippincott, 1976. 571 pp.
Parts One and Two of this history trace the rise of pharmacy in the ancient
and medieval worlds and the social history of the profession in Italy,
France, Germany, and Great Britain. Parts Three and Four, the major portion of the book, deal with pharmacy in the U.S. from its Colonial beginnings to the structure of the contemporary pharmaceutical industry. Among
the topics discussed are military pharmacy in the Revolutionary War, medical sects in early 19th-century America, and the history of the pharmacy
profession in the U.S. Separate chapters focus on the organization of
local, state, and national associations; the setting of legal standards
for pharmaceutical practice; the establishment of schools of pharmacy;
and the publication of professional literature such as pharmacopoeia,
dispensatories, textbooks, and journals. Sonnedecker's history traces
the changing social roles of pharmacists in the American health care system.

STM 351. SPENCE, CLARK C. Mining Engineers and the American West: The
          Lace-Boot Brigade, 1849-1933. New Haven, Conn.: Yale University
          Press, 1970. 407 pp.
Spence describes American mining engineers, their problems, roles, accomplishments, and influence on the American West from the 1840s to the Great
Depression of the 1930s. They received advanced training first in
European--mainly German--mining schools and then, after the 1860s, increasingly in American schools. Before becoming mining consultants--their
most important 19th-century role--graduates of mining schools worked in
various capacities in mines and on state or national geological surveys.
Although known for versatility, mining engineers became increasingly specialized as technical change and increased scale of operations made mining
more complex. With much improved technical education and extensive experience in deep mining, American mining engineers traveled and transferred
American technology throughout the world from the 1890s to W.W. I.

STM 352. SPENCER, FRANK, ed. A History of American Physical Anthropology,
          1930-1980. New York: Academic Press, 1982. 495 pp.
This volume contains the papers from a symposium held in 1981 which com-
memorated the fiftieth anniversary of the founding of the American Association of Physical Anthropology. The authors of these papers, all experts
in various aspects of physical anthropology, have provided "state of the
art" essays on the progress of their fields in the last half-century.
Many of the essays discuss intellectual and institutional developments;
all have extensive bibliographies listing the major works in their fields.
Among the topics addressed are paleontology, early man, physical growth,
biological variation, primate research, and race concept in physical anthropology.

STM 353. STAGE, SARAH. Female Complaints: Lydia Pinkham and the Business
          of Women's Medicine. New York: Norton, 1979. 304 pp.
Stage addresses as a social phenomenon the immense success of Lydia
Pinkham's Vegetable Compound, a nostrum for female complaints, in the late
19th century. She argues that women chose the patent medicine over care
by a physician because of its accessibility and price, and discusses how
advertising for the compound reflected the role of Victorian American
women. Stage provides a full history of the Pinkham business as well.

STM 354. STANTON, WILLIAM. The Great United States Exploring Expedition
          of 1838-1842. Berkeley: University of California Press, 1975.
          433 pp.
The U.S. Exploring Expedition from 1838 to 1842 was the first systematic,
publicly-financed American attempt at scientific exploration. Often called
the Wilkes expedition after its Navy commander, Charles Wilkes (1798-1877),
it circumnavigated the globe, made the first official sighting of the

Antarctic continent, examined several Pacific island groups, and explored the Pacific coast from Puget Sound to San Francisco. These activities established American interest in the Pacific and supported claims for the intellectual maturity of American science. Stanton provides a narrative of the scientific, commercial, and nationalistic motives for the expedition, the decade of preparation and controversy preceding it, and the expedition itself with its scientific work.

STM 355. **STANTON, WILLIAM.** The Leopard's Spots: Scientific Attitudes Toward Race in America, 1815-59. Chicago: University of Chicago Press, 1960. 248 pp.
In The Leopard's Spots, Stanton recounts the antebellum controversy over the issue of the unity of the human race and focuses on the polemics of the "American school" of ethnology, which included George R. Gliddon, Samuel G. Morton, Josiah C. Nott, and Ephraim G. Squier. The members of the American school adopted a polygenist view of the races of man, arguing for separate creations and against the orthodox biblical account. They rejected monogenist interpretations and any suggestion that the species of the human race had changed over time. Stanton relates their ideas on race to prevailing liberal conceptions of scientific progress and suggests that their anti-clerical stance was an important factor in the reception of polygenist theories. Stanton argues that the doctrine of diverse origins was not used by Southerners as a justification of slavery due to its unpalatable implications for the biblical account of creation. Their arguments against biblical chronology also put the American school in the paradoxical position of preparing the way for Darwinism. Stanton's book is also a case study in the interaction of American science, religion and social thought before the Civil War.

STM 356. **STEARNS, RAYMOND P.** Science in the British Colonies of America. Urbana: University of Illinois Press, 1970. 766 pp.
Stearns provides a survey of scientific activity in the American Colonies from about 1520 to 1770. He stresses the overwhelming importance of natural history in early Colonial science. The role of the Royal Society of London in promoting science in New England, Virginia, and the other British Colonies is examined in detail. Stearns discusses the emergence of scientific communities in Boston, New York, Philadelphia, Williamsburg, and Charlestown. This trend culminated in the establishment in 1769 of the American Philosophical Society, an institution modeled on the Royal Society of London. By the 1770s, Stearns concludes, Colonial science had become American science.

STM 357. **STERN, NANCY.** From ENIAC to UNIVAC: An Appraisal of the Eckert-Mauchly Computers. Bedford, Mass.: Digital Press, 1981. 286 pp.
In the 1940s and 1950s, J. Presper Eckert and John W. Mauchly developed four electronic digital computers, the first of which was a product of the ENIAC project at the University of Pennsylvania. Stern discusses the gap between these two engineers' technical expertise and their entrepreneurial naivete. Also considered are the resistance of the scientific community to their inventions, the narrowness of business corporations in the 1950s with regard to funding research and development in this area, and the full support these "whiz kids" received from the Federal government, especially the National Bureau of Standards.

STM 358. **STEVENS, ROSEMARY.** American Medicine and the Public Interest. New Haven, Conn.: Yale University Press, 1971. 572 pp.
Rosemary Stevens examines the effects of specialization in medicine on the organization and politics of health care in 20th-century America. In the first section, the author surveys trends in the medical profession and medical science to 1900, focusing on the beginnings of specialties

and the role of the American Medical Association in improving medical education. Parts Two and Three deal with the establishment of specialty boards, new educational mechanisms, and licensing arrangements in the medical care system from 1900 to 1950. The final two sections discuss political aspects of specialization in both the public and professional arenas. Stevens examines the impact of medical specialization on recent trends in professional education and the roles of physicians, politicians and the public in establishing efficient and equitable means of organizing and financing American health care services.

STM 359. STILGOE, JOHN R. Metropolitan Corridor: Railroads and the American Scene. New Haven, Conn.: Yale University Press, 1983. 397 pp.
The title for this book highlights the main points of the author's thesis: that in the years between 1880 and 1930, the railroad industry reshaped the American landscape; combined elements of rural, suburban, and urban culture; and created a fourth distinctive built environment which he calls the Metropolitan Corridor. Focusing less on the industry than its physical presence and infrastructure, Stilgoe has drawn on a wide range of sources-- novels, photographs, films, and memorabilia--to show the powerful impact of railroads on American life and imagination.

STM 360. STOCKING, GEORGE W., Jr. Race, Culture, and Evolution. Essays in the History of Anthropology. New York: Free Press, 1968. 307 pp.
Stocking offers a history of "scientific racism" as seen from the vantage point of the science of anthropology. The bulk of the essays in his book discuss anthropology in America in the late 19th and early 20th centuries, with Franz Boas and his disciples cast in the role of those anthropologists who undercut "scientific racism."

STM 361. STOVER, JOHN F. American Railroads. Chicago: University of Chicago Press, 1961. 302 pp.
Stover illustrates the many ways in which railroads have affected American life; he concentrates largely on the role of government and the economy on railroad history. The overview begins with a discussion of the first railroads, continues with their transformation of the West, and moves into a discussion of the legal and economic battles both among the railroads and between the railroads and the states. The railroad "problem," Stover concludes, was "political rather than technical."

STM 362. STOVER, JOHN F. Iron Road to the West: American Railroads in the 1850s. New York: Columbia University Press, 1978. 266 pp.
Stover surveys the development of American railroads during a major period of their growth, marked by a three-fold increase in track mileage, the linking of short East Coast trunk routes, and the emergence of a new rail system in the Old Northwest and Upper Mississippi valley. The account focuses on rail lines in respective regions (Northeast, Midatlantic, South, and West), stressing the impact of rail service on hinterland areas and as a binding force in the national economy.

STM 363. STOVER, JOHN F. The Life and Decline of the American Railroad. New York: Oxford University Press, 1970. 324 pp.
Stover examines the role the railroad has played in all facets of American culture. He begins with the building of the B. & O., discusses the railroads and the frontier and the role of railroads in the Civil War, goes on to explore the diminishing attraction of the railroad for passenger travel, and discusses the competition among railroads and Federal regulation of them. He argues that railroads transformed America from an agrarian to an industrial state.

STM 364. STRASSMANN, WOLFGANG PAUL. Risk and Technological Innovation:
          American Manufacturing Methods During the Nineteenth Century.
          Ithaca, N.Y.: Cornell University Press, 1959. 249 pp.
Strassmann is concerned mainly with the interaction of business enterprise
and technological change during the 19th-century American industrial revolution. He defines innovation as all actions taken to bring a device
or process into commercial use and risk as the significant and sometimes
unpredictable chance of loss. Using these concepts, Strassmann investigates four fields of 19th-century manufacturing: iron and steel, textiles,
machine tools, and electric power generation and use in manufacturing.
He discusses the characteristics and trends of American economic history
and reformulates them to explain the high incidence of success and the
low riskiness of technological innovation in these fields during the 19th
century. Finally, he draws general conclusions and finds that American
innovators generally were cautious and that successful innovation in manufacturing was fairly predictable long before the advent of giant corporations and their laboratories.

STM 365. STRICKLAND, DONALD A. Scientists in Politics: The Atomic Scien-
          tists Movement, 1945-46. Lafayette, Ind.: Purdue University
          Press, 1968. 149 pp.
Strickland investigates the political activism of atomic scientists after
W.W. II, which he regards as the first major confrontation of scientists
and politicians in American history. He concentrates on factionalism,
conflict, and ideological divisions. He argues that the Scientists Movement consisted of two phenomena: reactions of Manhattan Project scientists
to the Truman administration's atomic energy bill in the fall of 1945,
and attempts to mobilize support in the scientific community and liberal
groups in early 1946 for Senator MacMahon's atomic energy bill to establish
civilian control of atomic energy. Strickland describes earlier political
organizations of scientists, the evolution of the Scientists Movement,
and the scientists' dialogue concerning their proper political role.
He also discusses the scientists' lobbying activities and their publicity
campaign to inform the public about atomic energy.

STM 366. STRICKLAND, STEPHEN P. Politics, Science, and Dread Disease:
          A Short History of United States Medical Research Policy. Cam-
          bridge, Mass.: Harvard University Press, 1972. 329 pp.
Strickland examines government support of cancer research from the late
1920s through the National Cancer Act of 1971 as a case study in the formulation of national policy for biomedical research. He discusses the rise
of the National Institute of Health as a center of government biomedical
research in the 1930s and 1940s; the tensions among politicians, administrators, and scientists over control of the pace and direction of cancer
research; and the role of Congressional leaders in obtaining legislative
support for medical research. He also recounts the activities of two
important constituencies in the politics of medicine: professional organizations such as the American Medical Association and the medical research
lobby founded by Mary Lasker in the mid-1940s. Strickland's analysis
of the political strategies and the bureaucratic struggles in the evolution
of a major national research enterprise illustrates the interaction of
science, politics, and public opinion in modern America.

STM 367. STRUIK, DIRK J. Yankee Science in the Making. 1948; Rev. ed.
          New York: Collier Books, 1962. 544 pp.
Struik's survey of the relationship of science and technology to the social
and industrial development of New England before the Civil War is based
on the premise that the "history of science . . . must include its sociology." After a brief account of the Colonial period, Struik relates science
and invention from 1780-1830 to the practical needs of New England navigators, the construction of canals and turnpikes, and early attempts

to mass produce guns and textiles. The last section, on the period from
1830-1860, deals with the diffusion of scientific knowledge through public
lectures and colleges; geological surveys and government support of science;
medicine and public health; technological improvements in steam power
and water supply; science and religion; and the pursuit of natural history
and astronomy. Struik concludes with a discussion of developments in
agricultural and technical education during the 1840s and 1850s.

STM 368. SWAIN, DONALD C. Federal Conservation Policy: 1921-1933.
Berkeley: University of California Press, 1963. 221 pp.
Swain traces the struggle within the Federal bureaucracy over conservation.
He maintains that Federal scientists and civil servants concerned with
conservation policy were able to keep the impetus toward progressive conservation alive, thus preparing the way for the New Deal in spite of the
conservative domination of the White House. Ideological debates within
the Federal conservation "establishment" over the future direction of
conservation policy are considered (for example, the conflict between
the National Park Service and the Forest Service). Also discussed are
the development of Federal policies concerning soil erosion in the Department of Agriculture and the evolving concern, manifested by Hoover and
the bureaucrats for multiple-purpose planning of resource management.

STM 369. SWENSON, LOYD S., Jr., JAMES M. GRIMWOOD, and CHARLES C.
ALEXANDER. This New Ocean: A History of Project Mercury.
Washington, D.C.: National Aeronautics and Space Administration,
1966. 681 pp.
Established in October 1958, Project Mercury, the first American manned-
spaceflight program, produced two suborbital ballistic flights and four
orbital missions before its termination was announced in June 1963. The
space race with the Soviet Union transformed it into the first step in
the voyage to the moon. In this first volume of official National Aeronautics and Space Administration (NASA) history, each author was responsible for one chronological segment. Alexander details research in
rocketry and space medicine from W.W. II to 1958 and describes the roles
played by the military and the National Advisory Committee for Aeronautics,
which formed the core of NASA. Arguing that most of the basic and applied
research for the project was completed by 1958, Swenson examines development problems and emphasizes the complexity of modern government-managed
technological programs. Grimwood recounts Project Mercury's operations
from Alan B. Shepard, Jr.'s suborbital flight in May 1961 through the
manned orbital missions of 1962 and 1963.

STM 370. TEMIN, PETER. Taking Your Medicine: Drug Regulation in the
United States. Cambridge, Mass.: Harvard University Press,
1980. 274 pp.
Temin's book is at once a historical study of the development of drug
regulation in America and a discussion of the shortcomings of drug policy
as it has evolved. The author traces drug regulation from the Pure Food
Act of 1906; he discusses the extension of the FDA's mandate to distinguish
between prescription and other drugs in 1938, the discovery of antibiotics
and the drug boom in the post-W.W. II era, and the 1962 Kefauver hearings
in which new drug amendments were created in response to the thalidomide
tragedy. He discusses as well drug trials and clinical decision-making
in regard to prescribing.

STM 371. THOMPSON, FRANK J. Health Policy and the Bureaucracy: Politics
and Implementation. Cambridge, Mass.: MIT Press, 1981.
334 pp.
Thompson's study of American health policy analyzes its three major aspects:
policy itself, implementation, and scorekeeping, concentrating especially
on the political issues involved in implementing Federal policy. He argues

that the statutory language of health policy bills can have effect on
their implementation, as can political circumstances. Thompson discusses
such programs and policies as Medicaid and Medicare, the VA Medical Program,
and the Occupational Safety and Health Act (OSHA), and analyzes as well
American health care institutions.

STM 372. THOMPSON, ROBERT LUTHER. Wiring a Continent: The History of
the Telegraph Industry in the United States, 1832-1866. Princeton, N.J.: Princeton University Press, 1947. 544 pp.
Thompson describes the profound impact the telegraph had on the nation's
political, economic, and social life and details its growth between 1846
and 1866 into America's first nationwide, industrial monopoly. He
describes Samuel F. B. Morse's invention of the telegraph and eventual
success in gaining a Congressional grant to construct a line from Baltimore
to Washington, D.C. Congress allowed control of the telegraph to pass
in 1846 into private hands, and Thompson recounts the subsequent enthusiastic, uncoordinated founding of dozens of small companies. He shows how
ruthless competition, bad management, and poorly-constructed lines took
their toll of these early companies and then describes the emergence in
the late 1850s of six powerful companies that divided the industry and
the nation into six sovereign territories. Finally, Thompson describes
how the Civil War enabled one of these six, the Western Union Telegraph
Company, to buy its largest competitors and gain by 1866 monopoly control.

STM 373. TOBEY, RONALD C. The American Ideology of National Science,
1919-1930. Pittsburgh, Pa.: University of Pittsburgh Press,
1971. 263 pp.
A belief in the effectiveness of centralized administration of science
and a Progressive faith in scientific method as a guarantor of social
progress were the basic tenets of what Ronald Tobey terms the "national
science" movement of the 1920s. His analysis focuses on the ideology
of influential spokesmen like George Ellery Hale, Robert A. Millikan,
and science popularizer Edwin E. Slosson, and their campaign to gain public
support for pure science in the post-W.W. I period. Tobey argues that
four factors explain the demise of the movement in the 1930s: public
confusion over Einstein's theories of relativity "denied science the power
of revelation"; the breakdown of consensus on issues of social reform
and scientific expertise undermined an important plank in the national
science platform; attempts to obtain financial support from big business
placed scientists in an essentially conservative political position; and
the practical solutions of engineers and technocrats allayed public anxieties during the Depression more readily than abstract appeals to the cultural value of science.

STM 374. TOBEY, RONALD C. Saving the Prairies: The Life Cycle of the
Grasslands School of Ecology, 1895-1955. Berkeley: University
of California Press, 1981. 315 pp.
Tobey traces the rise and subsequent fall of the grasslands school of ecology whose central research center was at the University of Nebraska.
According to Tobey, the seeds of the school's fall were contained in its
early success which bound it to a fixed paradigm of ecology (the grasslands) that did not apply to ecological developments in the 1930s, such
as the Great Drought. In discussing this case study of the grasslands
school, Tobey documents the shift of biological science from 19th-century
natural history approaches to 20th-century experimental and statistical
modes of inquiry.

STM 375. **TRESCOTT, MARTHA MOORE**, ed. Dynamos and Virgins Revisited:
Women and Technological Change: An Anthology. Metuchen, N.J.:
Scarecrow Press, 1979. 280 pp.
Trescott has collected essays that focus on two subjects. The first series
examines women's role as participants in technological change--as opera-
tives and workers in various industries and as inventors and scientists.
The second series of essays covers some of the effects technology has
had on women's lives: on childrearing and childbearing, women's work
and the home, and sex role socialization. A prefatory essay by Ruth Cowan,
"From Virginia Dare to Virginia Slims: Women and Technology in American
Life" provides an overview for this collection.

STM 376. **TUNIS, EDWIN.** Colonial Craftsmen and the Beginnings of American
Industry. Cleveland, Ohio: World, 1965. 159 pp.
This volume describes the nature of various Colonial crafts, dividing
them into five categories: "country work," which includes, among others,
the crafts of weaving, milling, and tanning; "town shops," which include
those of baking and hatting, "bespoke work," those of pewtering, cabinet-
making, and plumbing; "group work," those of shipbuilding and potting;
and "manufactories," those of papermaking and glassblowing. An introductory essay on the general structure of the New World craftsmanship precedes
this study.

STM 377. **VAN HEYNINGEN, W. E.** and **JOHN R. SEAL.** Cholera: The American
Scientific Experience, 1947-1980. Boulder, Colo.: Westview
Press, 1983. 343 pp.
The authors begin with a brief history of cholera outbreaks in the 19th
century. Of these six outbreaks, only two reached the U.S. By the 20th
century, cholera was no longer a health problem in the U.S.; but
Americans--in particular American military medical researchers--became
involved in studying the disease, first in Cairo (1947) and later in Bang-
kok (1958-59). Van Heyningen and Seal discuss the establishment and operations of the various Naval Medical Research Units (NAMRUs). They also
document the roles in cholera research played by the U.S. Department of
State (through its connection to the Southeast Asia Treaty Organization),
by Johns Hopkins University's Center for Medical Research and Training
in Calcutta (established in 1962), and by the U.S.-Japan Cooperative Medical Science Program (established in 1965). The authors conclude their
history with the founding of an international organization for studying
the disease--the International Centre for Diarrhoeal Disease Research
at Bangladesh.

STM 378. **VAN TASSEL, DAVID D.** and **MICHAEL G. HALL**, eds. Science and Society in the United States. Homewood, Ill.: Dorsey Press, 1966.
360 pp.
This collection of essays provides an introduction to the history of science and social institutions in the U.S. The editors' introduction
sketches in the background of intellectual developments in European science,
and social and political conditions affecting the progress of science
in the U.S. This is followed by a series of essays tracing the connections
of American science and industry, agriculture, medicine, social thought,
higher education, private agencies, government agencies, and the military.

STM 379. **VOGEL, MORRIS J.** The Invention of the Modern Hospital: Boston
1870-1930. Chicago: University of Chicago Press, 1980.
171 pp.
Vogel credits the development of the "modern" hospital in the years between
1870 and 1930 not only to the 19th-century revolution in medical knowledge--
the discovery of antisepsis, for instance, and improved surgical technique--
but more so to the sociological shifts in urban life which, for example,

prompted physicians to try to centralize their practices around the hospital. The public image of the institution, Vogel argues, changed as well, and was associated less commonly with charity and dependency.

STM 380. VOGEL, MORRIS J. and CHARLES E. ROSENBERG, eds. The Therapeutic Revolution: Essays in the Social History of American Medicine. Philadelphia: University of Pennsylvania Press, 1979. 270 pp.
Vogel points out in his introduction that because modern medicine is "the most completely fulfilled of all the promises of the twentieth century," its story has often been presented uncritically. Recently, though, medicine has been subject to "shrill complaints" which obscure its history as much as the earlier panegyrics did. The essays in this collection, he claims, avoid both extremes and examine 19th- and 20th-century medicine within its multiple contexts. The title essay, by Rosenberg, documents the shift from a holistic to a mechanistic understanding of the body. Three essays challenge the assumption that medical practitioners welcomed scientific medicine. Other topics covered include the birth control controversy, the mental hospital, the public municipal hospital, the health insurance controversy, the professionalization of nursing, and the dilemmas of contemporary medicine.

STM 381. VOGEL, VIRGIL J. American Indian Medicine. Norman: University of Oklahoma Press, 1983. 605 pp.
Vogel's book is a historical survey of American Indian medical practices in North America. Focusing on Indian theories of disease and treatment and their contributions to white civilization, Vogel also provides an overview of white reactions to Indian medicine. Though he discusses shamanistic and ritualistic aspects of Indian medicine, Vogel is more interested in the theoretical and specific contributions Indians made, particularly in the area of botanical pharmacology.

STM 382. WACHHORST, WYN. Thomas Alva Edison: An American Myth. Cambridge, Mass.: MIT Press, 1981. 328 pp.
The author offers not only a traditional biography of Edison but an examination of Edison as a cultural myth, "a vehicle for every major American cultural theme." The Edisonian hero embodies the ideals of technological progress, the work ethic, the Horatio Alger success story, a sense of world mission, and self-made individualism. Wachhorst traces the changing response to the figure of Edison in 20th-century America.

STM 383. WALLACE, ANTHONY F. C. Rockdale: The Growth of an American Village in the Early Industrial Revolution. New York: Knopf, 1978. 553 pp.
Wallace uses cultural anthropology methods to investigate changes wrought from 1825 to 1865 by the Industrial Revolution in the social, economic, political, and cultural life of Rockdale, a small textile manufacturing community in Pennsylvania. He describes the evolution of manufacturing technology, analyzes family patterns, class structure and conflict, and recounts the ideological debates concerning control of the new machine technology. "Enlightenment utopians" promoted cooperative control of industry, while "Evangelical Christian Capitalists" argued that private ownership and a stratified society were part of a divine plan. In defeating their opponents, Evangelical Capitalists developed a concept of "Christian Stewardship," binding owners to care for workers, and established churches and Sunday schools to teach acceptance of class stratification as necessary for Christian Capitalism. Finally, Wallace describes the effect of the Civil War in uniting manufacturers and workers against a common external foe.

STM 384. WALTERS, RONALD G. Primers for Prudery: Sexual Advice to Victorian America. Englewood Cliffs, N.J.: Prentice-Hall, 1974. 175 pp.

Walters studies American sexuality as a cultural indicator, tracing the history of sexual attitudes as manifested in advice literature in the 19th century. He finds that these manuals were adamant in prescribing sexual restraint, but argues that it would be wrong to characterize 19th-century thinking about sexuality as naive and repressive. Walters provides an afterword containing case studies of 19th-century people.

STM 385. WANGENSTEEN, OWEN H. and SARAH D. WANGENSTEEN. The Rise of Surgery: From Empiric Craft to Scientific Discipline. Minneapolis: University of Minnesota Press, 1978. 785 pp.

The authors do not discuss American contributions to the history of surgery exclusively, but they do address such American developments as the discovery of anesthesia in the mid-19th century, Lister's contributions in antisepsis, and Alexander Fleming's and Paul Ehrlich's discoveries about wound infection and wound management.

STM 386. WEISS, HARRY B. and HOWARD R. KEMBLE. The Great American Water Cure Craze: A History of Hydropathy in the United States. Trenton, N.J.: Past Times Press, 1967. 236 pp.

Weiss and Kemble describe the introduction of hydrotherapy into this country by homeopathic practitioners who studied the cure abroad. They discuss the standing of hydropathy in the medical and lay communities, the growth of hydropathic colleges, and such successful water-cure doctors as Dr. Schieferdecker, whose efforts led to a scandal surrounding a patient's death, and Dr. Joel Shew, author of the Water-Cure Manual of 1847.

STM 387. WHITE, JOHN H., Jr. American Locomotives: An Engineering History, 1830-1880. Baltimore, Md.: Johns Hopkins University Press, 1968. 504 pp.

While English engineers carefully graded their railroad beds, laid substantial track, and built massive viaducts and tunnels, Americans constructed cheap lines, often with sharp curves, around and over hills to avoid expensive tunnels, cuts, and fills. In the first half of the 19th century, Americans built for these tracks more flexible, simple, and powerful locomotives with low initial costs and ease of maintenance. White divides his comprehensive technical history of this pioneering period into three sections. He first describes conditions influencing locomotive design, locomotive manufacturers, and materials. He next considers components such as boilers, smokestacks, pumps, gauges, running gears, and cowcatchers. In the third section, White details the characteristics of representative locomotives, most built before 1865, and provides numerous photographs, illustrations, and engineering drawings. The appendix includes biographical sketches of many early locomotive designers and builders.

STM 388. WHITE, JOHN H., Jr. The American Railroad Passenger Car. Baltimore, Md.: Johns Hopkins University Press, 1978. 699 pp.

White's history of American railroad cars concentrates on standard car models. Emphasizing the formative period during the 19th century, White writes about manufacturers, materials, production methods, and interior design. He first describes the characteristics of common day coaches from 1830 to 1910, when they were made of wood, and in the subsequent period, when metal became the rule. He then details the evolution of parlor, dining, private, and sleeping cars as well as utility cars for baggage and mail. These cars became quite complex due to the slow improvement of their conveniences, sanitation, safety, and decoration. White also addresses component parts of the cars such as trucks, bearings, wheels, and couplers and devotes a chapter to self-propelled cars and motor trains

used in sparsely populated regions. The appendices contain biographical
sketches of car designers and builders, and general statistical information.
The text is also supplemented with photographs, illustrations, and engineering diagrams.

STM 389. WHORTON, JAMES C. Before Silent Spring: Pesticides in Pre-DDT
America. Princeton, N.J.: Princeton University Press, 1974.
288 pp.
Technological changes in agricultural production and food distribution
in late 19th-century America created unprecedented problems in the control
of insect pests. Economic entomologists and agriculturalists turned to
new chemical pesticides to solve the "insect emergency," a decision which
had unexpected consequences for public health. In the first section of
Before Silent Spring, Whorton discusses public indifference and the ambivalent attitude of the medical profession to chronic arsenic poisoning from
pesticide residues on agricultural products during the late 19th century.
He then turns to the Federal regulation of spray residues after the Pure
Food and Drug Act of 1906 and the activities of government chemists and
toxicologists who wrestled with the enforcement of uncertain standards.
Whorton analyzes the administrative struggles and pressure group politics
involved in the passage of more stringent regulations for pesticide spray
residues on foods during the 1920s and 1930s. This episode illustrates
the difficulties of balancing the benefits of improved agricultural technology with the potential hazards of chemical pollutants.

STM 390. WHORTON, JAMES C. Crusaders for Fitness: The History of American
Health Reformers. Princeton, N.J.: Princeton University Press,
1982. 359 pp.
Focusing on the years between 1830 and 1920, Whorton examines the serious
side of what has been called "health faddism," suggesting that health
reform movements be viewed as hygienic ideologies revealing of cultural
aspirations and anxieties. Whorton discusses the religious nature of
these ideological movements, many of which presented good hygiene in terms
of moral obligation, and examines as well the reasoning of particular
health crusaders. Finally, Whorton discusses the not inconsequential
public impact of health reform efforts: if health reform followers did
not attain spiritual perfection, they often did benefit from the practical
common sense of many hygienic reform messages.

STM 391. WIK, REYNOLD M. Henry Ford and Grass-Roots America. Ann Arbor:
University of Michigan Press, 1972. 266 pp.
In this study of Henry Ford's impact on rural America, Wik asserts that
Ford's greatest contribution was mass producing a practical automobile
and demonstrating the feasibility of motor transport on the farm. Wik
discusses the pervasive impact the Model "T" and the Fordson tractor had
on rural America and the resulting popularity Ford achieved from 1908
to 1929 among "grass-roots" Americans. With the Tin Lizzie and the tractor
as background, Wik evaluates Ford's ideas about science, agriculture,
politics, and education and investigates the way rural Americans came
to believe that Ford, himself a product of rural society, epitomized their
values. Using correspondence from farmers to Ford, Wik describes the
great political influence Ford had among farmers. The Depression dis-
credited Ford's ideas, however, and farmers turned to the Federal government for solutions to their problems. Finally, Wik suggests an explanation
for Ford's profound influence on American life.

STM 392. WIK, REYNOLD M. Steam Power on the American Farm. Philadelphia:
University of Pennsylvania Press, 1953. 288 pp.
Steampower on 19th-century farms played a crucial role in making large-
scale farming possible and paved the way for the even more influential
internal combustion tractor. Wik provides an account of the stationary

steam engines of the early 1800s, the portable engines of the 1840s, and the self-propelled engines widespread in the 1870s. The major portion of the book is about the steam-engine boom lasting from the mid-1880s until 1910 and bringing in the steam-powered threshers, combines, and plows in the major grain-growing regions of the U.S. Wik also discusses the manufacturing, distribution, and financing of steampowered equipment and portrays the threshermen who used the equipment. Finally, he evaluates the role manufacturers of steam equipment played in the rapid introduction of gasoline tractors after 1913.

STM 393. WILLIAMSON, HAROLD F., RALPH L. ANDREANO, ARNOLD R. DAUM, and GILBERT C. KLOSE. The American Petroleum Industry: The Age of Energy 1899-1959. Evanston, Ill.: Northwestern University Press, 1963. 928 pp.

The authors describe the American petroleum industry's shift from producing primarily illuminants to supplying energy to an expanding industrial economy. They discuss technical advances, cycles of scarcity and overproduction, the growth of government influence, changes in the industry's structure from near monopoly to multi-firm competition, and American development of foreign resources. The study falls into four chronological periods. The authors first outline factors prior to 1914 making petroleum primarily a source of energy, describe forces promoting new firms, and recount the industry's contributions to W.W. I. They then treat the expansion of the industry in the 1920s and the drive toward vertical integration by major oil companies. In part three they detail the industry's Depression experience and subsequent recovery, the emergence of catalytic cracking, and competition in the domestic market. Finally, the authors review the industry's response to W.W. II and post-war readjustments.

STM 394. WILLIAMSON, HAROLD F. and ARNOLD R. DAUM. The American Petroleum Industry: The Age of Illumination 1859-1899. Evanston, Ill.: Northwestern University Press, 1959. 864 pp.

Williamson and Daum's history of the American petroleum industry covers the period when its main products were lubricating oils and illuminants. They survey early uses of petroleum, discuss the pioneers who established the industry in the late 1850s, and describe the intense industrial competition and establishment of domestic and foreign markets during the industry's formative years from 1862 to 1873. The success of John D. Rockefeller's plan to dominate the refining and transportation segments of the industry through his Standard Oil Company changed the industry's corporate structure by the mid-1880s. Finally, the book recounts the expansion during the 1890s of crude oil production into Ohio and Indiana, the growth of independent oil companies, the increased competition in foreign markets, and the first signs of the turn from illuminants to energy as the primary product of the oil industry. Other topics include general business and economic developments, drilling and refining techniques, transportation methods, and early attacks on the oil trust.

STM 395. WISELY, WILLIAM H. The American Civil Engineer 1852-1974: The History, Traditions and Development of the American Society of Civil Engineers. New York: American Society of Civil Engineers, 1974. 464 pp.

Wisely's history of American civil engineering discusses early 19th-century engineering and the various false starts at forming a professional organization before the founding of the American Society of Civil Engineers in 1867. He describes the activities of the Society, provides extensive appendices detailing its activities and membership, and broadly sketches the history of civil engineering as a profession.

STM 396. WRIGHT, HELEN. Explorer of the Universe: A Biography of George
Ellery Hale. New York: Dutton, 1966. 480 pp.
George Ellery Hale (1868-1938) is an important figure in the history of
American science. His scientific contributions included the invention
of the spectroheliograph and discoveries concerning the temperature and
magnetic fields of sunspots. His institutional contributions included
the founding of the Yerkes, Mount Wilson, and Palomar observatories; the
Astrophysical Journal; the American Astronomical Society; the International
Union for Cooperation in Solar Research; and what became the International
Council of Scientific Unions. Hale was instrumental in reviving the
National Academy of Sciences and organizing the National Research Council,
which coordinated American scientific research during and after W.W. I.
He also played a significant role in building the Throop Polytechnic Insti-
tute into the California Institute of Technology. Wright follows the
thread of Hale's scientific work and describes his entrepreneurial activities separately.

STM 397. YORK, HERBERT. The Advisors: Oppenheimer, Teller, and the Superbomb. San Francisco: Freeman, 1976. 175 pp.
The explosion of a Soviet atomic bomb in 1949 provoked a secret debate
within the American nuclear community between proponents of the hydrogen
fusion (or "super") bomb, led by physicist Edward Teller, and their opponents, led by J. Robert Oppenheimer, Chairman of the General Advisory Committee (GAC) of the Atomic Energy Commission. Fearing an unwarranted
escalation of the arms race, the GAC in October 1949 advised against
developing the superbomb. (Their report is reproduced in an appendix.)
President Truman decided to proceed with the superbomb, however, and by
1955 both the U.S. and the Soviet Union had developed thermonuclear weapons.
In this history of the debate, Herbert York, first director of the Lawrence
Livermore Laboratory (where research for the H-bomb was carried out),
considers the technical, strategic, and moral issues involved. He discusses American and Soviet research on the superbomb prior to 1949, the
debate itself, and subsequent programs to build the superbomb. York also
analyzes the GAC's advice, arguing that their recommendations would not
have upset the nuclear balance of power, but might have had a moderat-
ing effect on the Cold War arms race.

STM 398. YOUNG, JAMES HARVEY. The Medical Messiahs: A Social History
of Health Quackery in Twentieth-Century America. Princeton,
N.J.: Princeton University Press, 1967. 460 pp.
The Medical Messiahs is a sequel to Young's earlier book, The Toadstool
Millionaires (see STM 399). Despite advances in medical knowledge and
the educational level of the public, health quackery still flourishes.
In this volume Young presents case histories of 20th-century medical char-
latans who promoted "miracle" drugs or set up bogus clinics to treat hap-
less patients. He also analyzes the sophisticated mass-market advertising
used by modern quacks to peddle their nostrums. Federal regulatory agencies armed with legal sanctions to combat quackery are a central focus
of the book. The Food and Drug Administration was directly responsible
for policing harmful remedies, the Post Office Department prosecuted for
mail fraud, and the Federal Trade Commission attacked dishonest advertisers.
The American Medical Association, the American Cancer Society, and the
National Better Business Bureau also figured prominently in the campaign
to protect consumers from the "medical messiahs." Their efforts will
continue to be necessary, Young points out, since promoters of quack remedies use the alluring promise of good health as a potent psychological
weapon.

STM 399.   YOUNG, JAMES HARVEY. The Toadstool Millionaires: A Social His-
           tory of Patent Medicines in America Before Federal Regulation.
           Princeton, N.J.: Princeton University Press, 1961. 282 pp.
This book is an account of the history of the patent medicine trade in
America from Colonial origins to the passage of the first Federal Pure
Food and Drug Act in 1906. James Harvey Young discusses the purveyors
of proprietary remedies and their marketing methods, the continuing criticism of physicians and pharmacists, and the varieties of public response
to the numerous nostrums available in the 19th century. His final chapters
describe the mobilization of public opinion against patent medicines at
the turn of the century, and the passage of legislation designed to protect
consumers against unscrupulous quacks.

STM 400.   ZUCKER, PAUL. American Bridges and Dams. New York: Greystone
           Press, 1941. 46 pp.
In Zucker's "technical book," he "proposes to show explicitly the artistic
appearance and beauty of American bridges and dams." In brief essays,
he treats the following subjects: the bridge as landmark, the bridge
as functional form, wooden and stone bridges, iron and steel bridges,
concrete and reinforced concrete bridges, bridges in interstate traffic
and city planning, and dams. The body of the book is comprised of photographs and explanatory captions.

STM 401.   ZUCKERMAN, HARRIET. Scientific Elite: Nobel Laureates in the
           United States. New York: Free Press, 1977. 335 pp.
Nobel laureates form a highly visible cadre within the scientific elite.
In this volume, Harriet Zuckerman presents a sociological portrait of
the ninety-two Nobel laureates between 1901 and 1972 who did their prize-
winning work in the U.S. After introductory chapters on scientific elites
and the sociology of the Nobel Prize, Zuckerman focuses on the biographical
sketches of her sample, drawing on personal interviews with forty-one
Nobel laureates. By tracing their social and educational backgrounds
and comparing their careers to those of other members of the scientific
elite and rank-and-file, she demonstrates how the process of cumulative
advantage selects future laureates for recognition. Zuckerman discusses
master-apprenticeship relations among Nobel laureates, their upward mobility within the research system, and the social context within which their
prize-winning research was done. She also examines the effect of the
Nobel Prize on the subsequent careers of laureates. In portraying the
complex interactions of intellectual merit and ascribed status which differentiate this ultra-elite from other members of the scientific community,
Zuckerman highlights the mechanisms of social stratification active in
contemporary American science.

SOCIOLOLOGY

A wide range of bibliographic aids are available for students interested in sociological approaches to the analysis of the American experience.
The best place to begin is <u>Sociological Abstracts</u>, "a collection of non-
evaluative abstracts which reflects the world's serial literature in sociology and related disciplines." Published five times a year, this comprehensive review includes the major sociology journals as well as journals
in related social science fields (e.g., anthropology, education, political
science), in the humanities, and those of general interest that contain
articles addressing sociological issues. Each issue contains a subject
index, a source index, an author index, and cross-references to documents
previously listed. Some supplements also include abstracts of conference
papers. Articles are organized under the following subject categories:
methodology and research technology; history and theory of sociology;
social psychology; group interactions (including racial and ethnic relations); culture and social structure; complex organization; social change
and economic development; mass phenomena (including social movements,
public opinion, collective behavior, leisure, mass culture, and sport);
political interactions; social differentiation; rural sociology and agriculture; urban structures and ecology; the arts; education; religion;
social control; science; demography; family and socialization; health
and medicine; social problems and social welfare; knowledge; community
development; policy, planning, and forecasting; radical sociology; environmental interactions; poverty; violence; feminist studies; Marxist sociology;
clinical sociology; sociology of business; and visual sociology.

Although most of the major journals in sociology have book review
sections, the space available for book reviews is necessarily limited.
The major source for book reviews is <u>Contemporary Sociology</u>, the book review
journal of the American Sociological Association. In addition to reviews
of individual works, <u>Contemporary Sociology</u> frequently contains review

essays that focus on current issues in the field, and review symposia, in which two or more reviewers critically analyze an important new work in some depth.

Annual Review of Sociology provides interpretive and critical surveys of recent trends and developments in sociological theory and in research in specialized fields. For example, essays published in Volume 9 (1983) include: "America's Melting Pot Reconsidered," "Changing Family and Household: Contemporary Lessons from Historical Research," "Middletown III: Problems of Replication, Longitudinal Measurement, and Triangulation," and "The New History of Sociology." The essays are especially useful for the bibliographies they contain.

Additional general bibliographical sources include the Social Sciences Index, a quarterly, cumulative subject and author index of recent articles in the social sciences published in English. It also includes a listing of citations to book reviews. The Social Science Citation Index is a systematic annual index of the places in which previously published works and authors have been cited. Current Contents: Social and Behavioral Sciences is a weekly publication that reprints the tables of contents of a wide range of journals. Moreover, each issue contains abstracts of a small number of articles of general interest. The International Bibliography of Sociology, one of four annual volumes of the International Bibliography of the Social Sciences, claims to be "the most complete means to obtain global information about the previous year's publications in this domain from the entire world." It includes books, articles from scientific periodicals, and research reports.

In addition to these general research aids, there are several abstracts or bibliographies published in specialty areas. Urban Affairs Abstracts, published weekly by the National League of Cities, covers a wide range of political, economic, and social issues and problems concerning urban life, from animal control to land use to public safety to youth. The Sage Urban Studies Abstracts is a quarterly periodical that abstracts

1672

approximately 250 "books, articles, pamphlets, government publications, significant speeches, and legislative research studies." Although it is not restricted to material on the U.S., a substantial number of the items abstracted focus on American society.

Criminal Justice Abstracts is a quarterly that contains "hundreds of in-depth abstracts of current books, articles, dissertations, and reports published all over the world." Many issues also contain a review or bibliographical essay that synthesizes research on a particular subject. Abstracts on Crime and Delinquency, more inclusive than Criminal Justice Abstracts, includes abstracts of the National Council on Crime and Delinquency's comprehensive collection of "documents, books, pamphlets, journals, and unpublished materials" on all aspects of crime and criminal justice in the U.S.

The Sage Race Relations Abstracts is a quarterly journal that reviews literature on race relations. It provides abstracts of books, articles, and research reports from a wide range of sources, especially British and American. The Index to Periodicals by and About Blacks provides an annual review of Afro-American periodicals of "general and scholarly interest." The Hispanic American Periodicals Index is an annual index of "articles, documents, reviews, bibliographies, original literary works, and other items . . . which regularly contain information on Latin America . . . and Hispanics in the United States." Published quarterly, The Women's Studies Abstract includes a list of articles pertaining to women's studies, some of which are abstracted.

Sociologists use many different research methods and sources of data--observation, experiments, documentary analysis, and survey research--most of which are also employed by other academic disciplines. Reflecting American sociology's strong quantitative orientation, considerable data have been obtained through survey research. One of the most important sources of survey data is the Inter-university Consortium for Political and Social Research (ICPSR), a cooperative effort of over 240 educational

and research institutions around the world to obtain, maintain, and share
more than 5,000 data files on a wide variety of topics, subject areas,
and disciplines.

Another indispensable source of data is the United States Census
Bureau, which collects, processes, compiles, and disseminates a voluminous
amount of information on American society. Much of the data can be found
in published form in libraries designated as Federal depositories; some
of the data have been recorded on machine-readable computer tapes. In
addition to the decennial census and periodic sample surveys of the American population and its characteristics (which include categories such
as sex, race, age, marital status, education, place of birth, ancestry,
immigration, language, residence, marital history, employment status,
income, etc.), the Census Bureau also conducts censuses of housing, agriculture, business, construction industries, governments, manufacturers,
mineral industries, and transportation. It also tabulates and publishes
statistics on the foreign trade of the U.S.

In addition, the Federal government annually publishes an enormous
amount of material on American society. Government publications are
indexed in the Monthly Catalog of United States Government Publications
(Washington, D.C.: Government Printing Office). A more general index
may be found in Government Reference Books: A Biennial Guide to U.S.
Publications (Littleton, Colo.: Libraries Unlimited), "an authoritative
guide to atlases, bibliographies, catalogs, compendia, dictionaries, directories, guides, handbooks, indexes, manuals, and other reference publications issued by agencies of the United States government."

Scholarly journals, of course, are indispensable to research in
sociology. Among the journals of sociological interest are the following:
Adolescence; American Demographics; American Journal of Sociology; American
Sociological Review; Annals of the American Academy of Political and Social
Sciences; Comparative Studies in Society and History; Crime and Delinquency;
Daedalus; Demography; Ethnic and Racial Studies; Harvard Educational Review;

International Migration Review; Journal of Ethnic Studies; Journal of Gerontology; Journal of Marriage and the Family; Journal of Social History; Pacific Sociological Review; Sex Roles; Signs; Social Forces; Social Problems; Social Science History; Social Science Journal; Social Science Quarterly; Sociological Quarterly; Sociology and Social Research; Sociology of Education; Urban Affairs Quarterly; Work and Occupations.

Norman R. Yetman
University of Kansas

I. GENERAL STUDIES

SOC 1. BROGAN, DENIS W. The American Character. New York: Knopf, 1944.
168 pp.
This book was written by an Englishman in order to make certain American
principles and attitudes more intelligible to the British public. The
intention was that the British would better understand American traditions
and strive together with America toward creating a "world society." Brogan
describes the forces—geographic, biological, historical, economic, and
social—that came together in the years of America's development. The
author reviews the history of the concepts of unity and liberty in America
and stresses their emotional importance for the American people. Finally,
he describes the "American way in war" as a reflection of national character and a natural outgrowth of America's history.

SOC 2. CAMPBELL, ANGUS. The Sense of Well-Being in America: Recent Patterns and Trends. New York: McGraw-Hill, 1981. 263 pp.
"This is a book about the way people feel about their lives" and the
changes that have occurred in the sense of psychological well-being of
the American people from the late 1950s to the late 1970s. Based on
national surveys obtained from a sample of the American people between
1957 and 1978, Campbell's study examines, in separate chapters, the relative significance of several dimensions of well-being; social status
(including income, education, and occupation), marital status, family and
friendship patterns, job satisfaction (for both men and women), residential
location, perceptions of life in the U.S., place in the life cycle, and
measures of health and sense of personal control. He identifies differences in the sense of well- or ill-being among different segments of the
population as well as changes over time for the population as a whole.
Among his most important findings was a generally weak relationship between
objective, material conditions of life and the experience of well-being;
more important is the surrounding social environment—social relationships,
especially marriage—in accounting for the subjective sense of well-being.

SOC 3. CHEEK, NEIL H., Jr. and WILLIAM R. BURCH, Jr. The Social Organization of Leisure in Human Society. New York: Harper & Row,
1976. 283 pp.
Cheek and Burch regard leisure as a product of both the bio-social and
the socio-cultural nature of human beings. The authors consider leisure
and recreation patterns common to contemporary adults in the U.S., which
are contrasted with patterns in other industrial societies. The authors
determine that leisure establishes and maintains bonds within a group
and between different groups. Cheek and Burch consider the interdependence
between group characteristics, the physical design of places, and behavior
regularities in society. The authors also analyze the role of myth in
the formation of social conduct and examine the social implications of
the emergence of recreation in our society.

SOC 4. COLEMAN, JAMES S. The Asymmetric Society. Syracuse, N.Y.: Syracuse University Press, 1982. 191 pp.
This book is based on lectures presented by Coleman at the Abrams Lecture
Series at Syracuse University in 1981. Its aim is "to present a conception
of the way society is coming to be organized, and to show some of the
implications for the lives of ordinary people." Coleman argues that there
are two kinds of persons: natural and corporate. The dominant trend
of the last half century in modern industrial societies has been the growing power of the latter. This power imbalance in favor of the corporate
has created a new social structure—the asymmetric society. Coleman
explores the implications of this and other themes in five chapters, each

of which contains Coleman's revised lecture at the beginning and concludes
with his response to comments and questions that followed it.

SOC 5. GREENWAY, JOHN. The Inevitable Americans. New York: Knopf, 1964.
        371 pp.
This analytical, comparative, historical, and anthropological approach
to the study of American national character was written in response to
the popular view that Americans are "rotten to the heart." Greenway's
thesis is that the American national character is an inevitable culmination
of its history. Several basic aspects of American life are examined
against the patterns established by other societies to illustrate the
unique disparities that together establish the culture of the U.S. The
"acquisitive," "dissident," and "playful" natures of Americans are examined
in the context of history, going as far back as the Anglo-Saxons. All
of the material is presented in a philosophical framework of cultural
determinism that argues that "Americans--like everyone else in the world--
were driven by their cultural genes to become what they are and what they
will be."

SOC 6. GURIAN, JAY P. and JULIA M. GURIAN. The Dependency Tendency:
        Returning to Each Other in Modern America. Lanham, Md.: Univer-
        sity Press of America, 1983. 176 pp.
"This is another book . . . telling Americans what is wrong with them."
The authors contend that in their quest for individualism and personal
independence, Americans have lost the "positive" features of dependency
and, as a consequence they have become afflicted by widespread "alienation,
rootlessness, anomie, and purposelessness." They argue that these traits
have become prominent as "dependency networks were devalued in the rush
to make the individual supreme over nature, society, family, and marriage."
Their book is a critical analysis of the sources of the tension between
independence and dependence and those factors in American society that
have contributed to the imbalance between the two that they find. It
is also a plea for the realization of a new sense of dependency and a
new social order.

SOC 7. HACKER, ANDREW. The End of the American Era. New York: Atheneum,
        1972. 239 pp.
According to Hacker, American society has been undergoing a steady decline
since the end of W.W. II. "Tensions and frustrations are bound to arise
when 200 million human beings demand rights and privileges never intended
for popular distribution. It is too late in our history to restore order
or re-establish authority: the American temperament has passed the point
where self-interest can subordinate itself to citizenship." The American
middle classes have overtaken the nation. People who do not belong to
this class will remain "superfluous" as the selfish, overriding middle
class will allow them no gains. An ideology of self-indulgence has made
for irreconcilable goals among American citizens. Writing in the early
1970s, Hacker claimed that the nation was becoming ungovernable.

SOC 8. HERBERG, WILL. Protestant-Catholic-Jew: An Essay in American
        Religious Sociology. New York: Doubleday, 1956. 309 pp.
In this study, Herberg espouses his "triple-melting pot" theory of ethnic
stratification in American society. He suggests that religion has ultimately superseded national origins in dividing American society into three
major religious groups that provide the major source of ethnic identification in America. After analyzing the dynamics of the three principal
religious communities in America, Herberg argues that "From the 'land
of the immigrants' America has, as we have seen, become the 'triple-melting
pot,' restructured in these great communities with religious labels,
defining three great 'communions' or 'faiths.' . . . The third generation,
coming into its own with the cessation of mass immigration, tries to

recover its 'heritage,' so as to give itself some sort of 'name' or context of self-identification and social location, in the larger society."

SOC 9. JANOWITZ, MORRIS. The Last Half-Century: Societal Change and Politics in America. Chicago: University of Chicago Press, 1978. 582 pp.

"This study deals with social control in advanced industrial society, especially the United States, and particularly the half-century after World War I." The Last Half-Century is a macro-sociological study of major trends in recent American society that focuses on political institutions and their inability "to produce effective and authoritative policies to manage economic and social tensions and political conflict." Janowitz identifies several master trends that have dramatically affected American society since the 1930s, and he cites a wide range of factors, including the growth of national mass media, an undermining of legal norms by the judiciary, and the decline of local community, that have created a situation in which traditional mechanisms of social control are no longer effective. After having diagnosed its weaknesses in the first two-thirds of the book, Janowitz devotes the final section to prescriptions of what might be done to reestablish social control in contemporary American society.

SOC 10. LARRABEE, ERIC and ROLF MEYERSOHN, eds. Mass Leisure. Glencoe, Ill.: Free Press, 1958. 429 pp.

This collection of articles considers leisure from sociological, anthropological and psychological perspectives. The contributors view leisure as a social phenomenon, and consider types of mass leisure, the development of leisure and leisure activities as affected by social changes, and the effects of leisure and leisure activities on mass culture. Many classic pieces are reprinted, including essays by Margaret Mead, Bertrand Russell, and Aldous Huxley. Other articles include definitions of leisure, social conditions and historical context, play, sports, holidays, hobbies, fads and habits, the future of leisure, and leisure and social change. All contributors consider leisure in its popular sense rather than as something reserved for the elite or aristocratic classes.

SOC 11. LAUER, ROBERT H. and JEANETTE C. LAUER. Fashion Power: The Meaning of Fashion in American Society. Englewood Cliffs, N.J.: Prentice-Hall, 1981. 275 pp.

This book is an analysis of the meaning of fashion--patterns of clothing, dress, and personal adornment--in American life over the past two centuries. The Lauers interpret fashion as an index of broader changes in American society and culture, and they characterize fashion as a "perplexing and elusive," albeit powerful, force. They review various explanations that have been advanced to interpret fashion and the social functions--as indicators of class position, gender, and national identity--that it performs. New styles, they contend, "involve the search for meaning and identity . . . , the struggle for status . . . , and economic considerations." They conclude by advancing a theory of fashion that seeks to explain why patterns of fashion change in the directions that they do.

SOC 12. LIPSET, SEYMOUR MARTIN. The First New Nation: The United States in Historical and Comparative Perspective. New York: Basic Books, 1963. 366 pp.

Lipset argues that America perceives the same "double vision" of itself as do peoples beyond its borders. The American nation projects two images, two faces: the affluent, egalitarian and progressive image; and the corrupt, morally lax, and grossly inegalitarian image. Lipset's book attempts to "reconcile these two pictures--to look at America in a comparative and historical context is to point up the fact that such contrasts have distinguished American society through its history. The contrasts, more-

over, are linked to two basic American values—equality and achievement."
It is the combination of these two seemingly or potentially incompatible
values that shapes the character, social structure, and institutions of
American society. Lipset discusses the bases for national authority and
national identity, explores the changing American character and values,
delves into the broader "meaning" of America as the first truly new nation,
and studies its implications for new nations of the 20th century.

SOC 13. LOUV, RICHARD. America II. New York: Penguin Books, 1983.
         328 pp.
This book is an attempt to interpret and to comprehend the social changes
permeating contemporary American society. Louv, a journalist, contends
that "the America we know is dying, but a second America is rising from
the body of the first." America II is divided into six sections, each
dealing with a different but related dimension of this "second America":
migrating patterns, new forms of urbanization, new forms of housing and
communities, the reversal of the rural-to-urban migration pattern, new
urban and work forms, and the implications of these several changes for
the future of American society. Louv focuses especially on what he terms
"the America II social agenda: the growing privatization of public services, residential separation by lifestyle and age, the widening wage
spread, the conflict between the right to migrate and the rights of people
in the attracting areas, and the potential despoliation of nature by those
seeking nature."

SOC 14. MEAD, MARGARET. And Keep Your Powder Dry. 1942; Rev. ed. New
         York: Morrow, 1965. 340 pp.
In this study Mead described the nation's character in the context of
W.W. II and discussed its strengths and weaknesses with the intention of
identifying the psychological equipment with which America could win the
war. Mead considered the implications of the social class structure,
the motive to achieve, and the American "success system." What is an
American? How does one become an American? Under what conditions can
an American display a full determination to fight and win the war? In
posing such questions, Mead explored the structure of the family, the
patterning of aggressive behavior in America, and the fundamental need
of Americans "to believe that they are right." In conclusion, she considered the possible role for such a character structure—after winning
the war—in "building the world anew."

SOC 15. NAISBITT, JOHN. Megatrends: Ten New Directions Transforming
         Our Lives. New York: Warner Books, 1982. 355 pp.
"As a society we have been moving from the old to the new. And we are
still in motion. Caught between eras, we experience turbulence. Yet,
amid the sometimes painful and uncertain present, the restructuring of
America proceeds unrelentingly." In separate chapters Naisbitt examines
ten critical restructurings—"megatrends"—characterizing American society
in the late 1970s and 1980s. The basic shift in American society is from
an industrial to an "information," highly technological, society in a
closely interwoven global economy. Other important changes include political and economic decentralization, increasing participatory democracy,
and a demographic shift from the industrial Northeast to the South and
the West. Naisbitt's tenth megatrend is from a "society with a limited
range of personal choices . . . into a free-wheeling multiple option society."

SOC 16.   PACKARD, VANCE.   A Nation of Strangers.   New York: McKay, 1972.
          368 pp.
Social alienation in America is the central topic of A Nation of Strangers.
Packard delves into the impact of rootlessness and the concomitant break-
down of modern American institutions and the social structure itself.
Americans, he argues, have lost their sense of community, a basic human
need.   "Personal isolation is becoming a major social fact of our time.
A great many people are disturbed by the feeling that they are rootless
or increasingly anonymous, that they are living in a continually changing
environment where there is little sense of community."   In his analysis,
Packard examines the causes of massive uprooting, problems of adjustment
to increased social fragmentation, and its impact on American lifestyles
and personalities.

SOC 17.   RIESMAN, DAVID, with REUEL DENNEY and NATHAN GLAZER.   The Lonely
          Crowd: A Study of the Changing American Character.   New Haven,
          Conn.:   Yale University Press, 1950.   386 pp.
This is an investigation into the nature and character of American society,
exploring "social character types" and manifestations of change in the
American's life-style and self-perception.   Riesman argues that, in contrast to his "inner-directed" predecessors, the American of the 1950s
was more a product of his peers, in the characterological sense.   Yet,
Riesman notes, he paradoxically remains a lonely member of the crowd
because he never comes really close to the others or to himself.   The author
delves into three "planes" of American social life.   The first part of
the book describes and evaluates modes of conformity throughout America's
history, examining changing roles and morality in America.   Part two is
a reassessment of the sphere of politics insofar as this represents a
characteristic field of emotional commitment for the American middle- and
upper-class man.   In the final section, Riesman proposes that adjustment
to social norms is not "autonomy" and that for "other-directed" Americans the quest for real autonomy in work and leisure is blocked by societal
norms.

SOC 18.   WILLIAMS, ROBIN M., Jr.   American Society: A Sociological Inter-
          pretation.   1951; Rev. ed.   New York: Knopf, 1970.   575 pp.
This book presents a sociological analysis of American social and cultural
life.   The author begins with an introductory chapter on basic sociological
approaches and concepts.   In chapters that follow Williams looks separately
at kinship and family structures, social stratification, economics and
politics, education, and religion, and he studies the interaction of these
social institutions.   Other sections deal with value systems, social organizations, integration, group interrelations, and social and cultural change
in American society.   This is a functional analysis of the U.S., and the
"consensus view" of American social institutions and structures.

SOC 19.   YANKELOVICH, DANIEL.   The New Morality: A Profile of American
          Youth in the 70's.   New York: McGraw-Hill, 1974.   166 pp.
This is a summary and analysis of a systematic study of the changing attitudes of American young people (ages sixteen to twenty-five) in the period
from 1967 to 1973.   Yankelovich's research was based on 3,522 one-to-two
hour interviews with both college and non-college youth.   The period,
the author explains, "stretches from the peak of the Vietnam War protest
movement to the disappearance of the war as an issue among young people.
It is also a period in which the women's movement has sought to raise
the consciousness of the nation. . . . We have seen sweeping changes in
sexual morality, work-related values . . . and other challenges to traditional beliefs and values."

SOC 20. YANKELOVICH, DANIEL. New Rules: Searching for Self-Fulfillment
in a World Turned Upside Down. New York: Random House, 1981.
278 pp.
Yankelovich uses a combination of personal interviews and survey research
to argue that American society is about to embark on a cultural revolution
that is "moving our industrial civilization toward a new phase of human
experience." He identifies numerous subtle shifts in American culture
that indicate among Americans a search for "self-fulfillment," for a "new
American philosophy of life." As any other cultural transformation, this
search for self-fulfillment and the social and economic forces that under-
.pin it create personal and societal predicaments. New Rules, therefore,
is about cultural change and how the search for self-fulfillment "expresses
itself in the lives of Americans, how inflation and other economic realities are shaping and being shaped by it, how seekers of self-fulfillment
pursued a self-defeating strategy in the seventies, and how Americans
in the eighties are learning to distinguish false and destructive strategies
from valid ones adaptive to a world that is just beginning to emerge."

II. URBAN, COMMUNITY, AND REGIONAL STUDIES

SOC 21. BALDASSARE, MARK. Residential Crowding in Urban America. Berkeley:
University of California Press, 1979. 250 pp.
This book disputes the widespread notion that household crowding and neighborhood density contribute to pathologies. Rather than rely on animal
studies of the effects of crowding, Baldassare derived his basic data
concerning family life and the perceived quality of and satisfaction with
neighborhood life from respondents' evaluations in national surveys.
He concludes that "the commonly expressed thoughts about a link between
density and well-being are not substantiated and . . . that the typical
treatment of pathology and crowding [based principally on animal studies]
should be replaced by a more comprehensive and complex view of humans
in crowded environments."

SOC 22. BERK, RICHARD A., C. J. LaCIVITA, KATHERINE SREDL, and
THOMAS F. COOLEY. Water Shortage: Lessons in Conservation from
the Great California Drought, 1976-1977. Cambridge, Mass.:
Abt Books, 1981. 209 pp.
A book providing illustrations of some practical difficulties in econometric studies, as well as the limits of quantitative analysis in complex
policy issues, Water Shortage reports the results of a study of the organization, behavior, strategies, and outcomes in fifty-seven public water
districts before, during, and after the California drought of 1976-77.
Water Shortage is a contribution to the quantitative development of an
emerging theory of conservation. Its data are drawn from communities
in only one state over a brief period, but the variety of conditions,
levels of preparedness, responses, and alternatives are diverse.

SOC 23. BOLLENS, JOHN C. and HENRY J. SCHMANDT. The Metropolis: Its
People, Politics, and Economic Life. 1965; Rev. ed. New York:
Harper & Row, 1982. 461 pp.
Bollens and Schmandt provide an overview of the American metropolis, with
attention paid primarily to the metropolitan community (the socio-economic
city) rather than to the municipality alone (the legally defined city).
The authors are especially concerned with "social characteristics and
trends, economic developments, physical and land use considerations, government and politics, and citizen roles." They also address the problems

created by rapid metropolitan growth and discuss possible organizational policy and planning strategies for the metropolis of the future.

SOC 24. BOWDEN, CHARLES and LEW KREINBERG. Street Signs Chicago: Neighborhood and Other Illusions of Big-City Life. Chicago: Chicago Review Press, 1981. 198 pp.
The authors' basic proposition is that there have never been any true "neighborhoods" in Chicago, and that the effort to think about the city's history and present conditions in those terms is at best misguided and at worst a tool of manipulation used by the people who exercise centralized power. Bowden and Kreinberg develop their argument along two lines: First, they suggest that Americans mistakenly talk about neighborhoods in terms of the European village, which never actually developed in the industrial cities of the U.S. Second, they demonstrate that Chicago's geography itself doomed the city to be a "way-station" to other areas of the nation. Thus no classic neighborhood could develop. Unless Americans as a culture change their assumptions of unlimited growth and mobility, the authors argue, all large American cities face the same future.

SOC 25. BRADBURY, KATHARINE L., ANTHONY DOWNS, and KENNETH A. SMALL. Urban Decline and the Future of American Cities. Washington, D.C.: Brookings Institution, 1982. 309 pp.
This study of urban decline arrives at conclusions roughly similar to those of the President's Commission for an Agenda for the 1980s, which traced the course of urban decline across the country. The authors are less confident than the commission that the unhindered operation of the national economy will eventually bring about a new and productive urban equilibrium. Urban Decline reinforces an emerging consensus that urban areas are declining in importance in American life and that trying to resist the trend is futile. It provides a searching examination of the causes of urban decline.

SOC 26. CASTELLS, MANUEL. The City and the Grassroots: A Cross-Cultural Theory of Urban Social Movement. Berkeley: University of California Press, 1983. 450 pp.
Castells focuses on the relationship between citizen action and urbanization in order to develop a theory of urban social movement. Such a relationship is most evident when people mobilize to change the city, thereby changing society as a whole. The main hypotheses of this study are: The city is a major social product resulting from conflicting social interests and values. Major innovations in the city's role, meaning, and structure tend to be the outcome of grassroots mobilization and demands. A theory of urban change must account for the transformation resulting both from the action of the dominant interest and from the grassroots resistance and challenge to such a domination. Such a theory must recognize sources of urban social change other than class relationships: the autonomous role of the state, gender relationships, and ethnic and national movements.

SOC 27. CASTLEMAN, CRAIG. Getting Up: Subway Graffiti in New York. Cambridge, Mass.: MIT Press, 1982. 191 pp.
"Getting up" refers to the marking and painting of New York City subway trains that has been occurring since the late 1960s. This study describes the graffiti, its writers, the social organization of the writers, the politics of graffiti, and the city, state, and subway efforts to eradicate it. Based primarily on interviews with graffiti writers, Getting Up includes many photographs of the most striking examples of subway graffiti.

SOC 28. CAUDILL, HARRY M. Night Comes to the Cumberlands: A Biography
         of a Depressed Area. Boston: Little, Brown, 1962. 394 pp.
"The mountaineer," Caudill writes, "can present no enigma to a world which
is interested enough to look with sympathy into the forces which have
made him." In his historical account of Appalachia, America's most economically and socially devastated region, Caudill examines the social, economic
and political forces that have shaped the region and its people. Caudill
describes the impact that national events--the Civil War, the Depression,
the two World Wars--had on the region, as well as the impact of local
phenomena, such as the feuds and "moonshiners." His greatest concern
lies in the relation of the land to the people; he discusses the ecological
devastation resulting from the timber industry, from unsophisticated agriculture techniques, and from the coal industry. In his final section,
he proposes a project similar to that of the Tennessee Valley Authority
to revitalize the region.

SOC 29. DOWNS, ANTHONY. Opening Up the Suburbs: An Urban Strategy for
         America. New Haven, Conn.: Yale University Press, 1973.
         219 pp.
America's "urban crisis," characterized by high unemployment, increased
welfare rolls, and deteriorating housing, is generally considered to be
the result of the movement of middle- and upper-class familes and of manufacturing concerns to suburban areas. Downs proposes a solution to this
crisis. He suggests that the suburbs be "opened up" to low-income families
by the provision of low-income housing in all suburban communities, and
the provision of moderate-income housing in newly growing suburban communities. Such opportunities should be provided by government subsidies
of low-cost housing and changes in current suburban housing codes and
standards.

SOC 30. ENGEL, J. RONALD. Sacred Sands: The Struggle for Community in
         the Indiana Dunes. Middletown, Conn.: Wesleyan University Press,
         1983. 352 pp.
This is a more analytic and conceptual book than its counterpart, Duel
for the Dunes: Land Use Conflict on the Shore of Lake Michigan (see Soc
34), but it is less detailed in the historical presentation of the conflicts over the Indiana Dunes. Engel's book places emphasis on social
movement organizations (the Prairie Club and Save the Dunes Council),
which are presented as Transcendentalist groups. Sacred Sands traces
the connections between the rise of physical and social ecology at the
University of Chicago, as well as concern for the working class on the
part of the Hyde Park SMO.

SOC 31. FEAGIN, JOE R. The Urban Real Estate Game: Playing Monopoly
         with Real Money. Englewood Cliffs, N.J.: Prentice-Hall, 1983.
         214 pp.
The Urban Real Estate Game relies on a vast amount of information gathered
from recent urban literature as well as from journalistic sources. The
book's purpose is not to provide new empirical knowledge, but to organize
available information to emphasize how capitalists are the key actors
in the production of urban forms. Much of Feagin's analysis ends with
the unchallenged domination of powerful coalitions of bankers, developers,
industrial corporations, public officials, and politicians.

SOC 32. FISCHER, CLAUDE S. To Dwell Among Friends: Personal Networks
         in Town and City. Chicago: University of Chicago Press, 1982.
         451 pp.
"This book is about how urban life changes personal relations and the
ways people think and act socially: such matters as friendship, intimacy,
involvement in the community, and lifestyle." Based on interviews with
1,050 adults in fifty Northern California communities, Fischer's study

is designed to test the traditional thesis that urban life is "socially, mentally, and morally unhealthy" by comparing residents of large cities with those in small towns. Fischer is concerned with the nature, role, and characteristics of personal networks, and he concludes that the quantity and quality of the social ties of urban dwellers and small town residents are similar but that the latter tend to be more involved with relatives, the former with non-kin.

SOC 33. **FISH, JOHN HALL.** Black Power/White Control: The Struggle of the Woodlawn Organization in Chicago. Princeton, N.J.: Princeton University Press, 1973. 356 pp.

The Woodlawn Organization (TWO), in an impoverished Chicago South Side community, was America's best-known grassroots community organization in the 1960s. Fish provides an account of the activity of this organization. In its early years, the aim of TWO was the control of community resources and decisions by the mass participation of community residents. Its accomplishments were impressive: TWO succeeded in attracting millions of dollars in funding from various sources; it gained some control over Woodlawn's economic base; and it fostered strong community leadership. But, as Fish describes, the continued deterioration and abandonment of the neighborhood have left TWO in a changed and somewhat powerless position. Decisions about the community are made elsewhere—by the City of Chicago or by the federal government. TWO has survived, but its goal of community control has not been realized. Fish provides a treatment of problems and possibilities encountered by mass-based organizations in ghetto communities.

SOC 34. **FRANKLIN, KAY and NORMA SCHAEFFER.** Duel for the Dunes: Land Use Conflict on the Shores of Lake Michigan. Urbana: University of Illinois Press, 1983. 320 pp.

This is a history of the conflict over the Indiana Dunes, on the southeastern shore of Lake Michigan. The first seven chapters are a chronicle of the changing interests in the Dunes, from the days of their initial survey in 1821 to the growing conflict between conservationist efforts to preserve them and those of the states of Illinois and Indiana and major steel corporations to develop them. In the final three chapters, Franklin and Schaeffer examine the shift of the conflict over the Dunes to the National Park Service, the bureaucracy responsible for the Dunes after the Indiana Dunes National Lakeshore was created in 1966.

SOC 35. **FRIEDLAND, ROGER.** Power and Crisis in the City: Corporations, Unions and Urban Policy. New York: Schocken Books, 1983. 248 pp.

Friedland proposes a complex causal model to explain the extent of urban renewal, social expenditures, public jobs creation, and fiscal strain in American central cities between 1964 and 1975. Friedland sees the state as implementing policies to accomplish both economic growth and social control. Friedland argues that two key variables—corporate power and labor union power—determine urban policies and policy outputs. Friedland classifies the 130 largest central cities in the U.S. by means of two dichotomies (corporate and union power). He then runs, for each city, a series of regressions between basic economic and demographic variables and the difference in the effect of each variable between the two sets of cities.

SOC 36. **GANS, HERBERT J.** The Levittowners: Ways of Life and Politics in a New Suburban Community. New York: Pantheon Books, 1967. 474 pp.

This book, the author writes, "is not a defense of suburbia, but a study of a single new suburb, Levittown, New Jersey, in which I lived as a 'participant-observer' for the first two years of its existence to find out

how a new community comes into being, how people change when they leave
the city, and how they live and politic in suburbia." Gans followed the
development of Levittown from its beginning in 1958, and focuses his
research on three major interrelated questions: the origin of the new community, the quality of suburban life, and the effect of suburbia on the
behavior of its residents. He also examines the political organization
and decision-making processes of the suburb, thus presenting a microcosmic
view of the process of change and the possibility of innovation in a social
system. His conclusions, based on observation and interviews and questionnaires administered to suburban residents, suggest that a community such
as Levittown is shaped by outside forces--organizations and institutions
usually founded by national bodies. He further found that suburbanites
are by and large pleased with the community that develops and that the
population mix of suburbia is the primary source of change within it.
The politics of suburbia, Gans concludes, are "no more distinctive than
the rest of its life," decision-making being directed mostly by experts
and outside agencies.

SOC 37. **GARDNER, HUGH.** The Children of Prosperity: Thirteen Modern American Communes. New York: St. Martin's Press, 1978. 281 pp.
Gardner's book chronicles the rural communes of the late 1960s and early
1970s. Gardner started his investigation with the understanding that
"the fate of the new communes would be determined by the extent to which
their members could commit themselves to what they were doing and build
new organizations that would reinforce this commitment--or by failing
to do so, choose to value their personal freedom over the roots and obligations of life in community." Gardner's study is a history of those years
on the rural communes.

SOC 38. **GAVENTA, JOHN.** Power and Powerlessness: Quiescence and Rebellion
in an Appalachian Valley. Urbana: University of Illinois Press,
1980. 267 pp.
In this book, Gaventa traces the history of the Appalachian region, showing
how mining corporations turned it into a kind of "internal colony" within
a larger industrial capitalist society and, despite its wealth, subordinated it to the economic needs of the larger social formation. Gaventa's
thesis is that students of political participation and conflict have
approached the problem in the wrong way, examining the outcomes of conflicts
when the real question should be: "Why do people fail to act upon their
interests?"

SOC 39. **GOETZE, ROLF.** Rescuing the American Dream: Public Policies
and the Crisis in Housing. New York: Holmes & Meier, 1983.
150 pp.
This is a study in the political economy of contemporary American housing.
The objective of Goetze's analysis is "to broadly identify the new forces
already reshaping urban neighborhoods, trace their linkages, and point
out opportunities in revitalization that are advantageous to both newcomers
as well as previous residents. . . ." The author contends that decent
housing--either in the form of homeownership or rentals--is beyond the
reach of increasing numbers of Americans. Although interest rates may
decline and housing starts increase, there is now--and will be in the
future--a housing crisis in American society. To meet this crisis more
effective means must be sought to adapt existing housing, and new urban,
taxation, and housing policies--at both Federal and local levels--will
have to be implemented.

SOC 40. GOLD, DIANE E. Housing Market Discrimination: Causes and Effects
         of Slum Formation. New York: Praeger, 1980. 304 pp.
Gold investigates the historical development of slum neighborhoods in
New York City. The research consists of field interviews with residents
and an econometric analysis of five slum and three non-slum areas. Gold's
thesis is that landlords exert virtually monopolistic control over the
housing market and, like capitalists generally, utilize that power to maximize private capital accumulation. The hypotheses she tests are: (1)
black neighborhoods have been adversely affected by the policies of financial and governmental institutions; (2) speculator real estate interests
have caused the decay of black neighborhoods; (3) the unequal distribution
of city services has contributed to the decline of black neighborhoods;
and (4) slum rents are higher in lower-quality neighborhoods while nonslum
rents are higher in higher-quality neighborhoods.

SOC 41. GOODMAN, CARY. Choosing Sides: Playground and Street Life on
         the Lower East Side. New York: Schocken Books, 1979. 200 pp.
Goodman begins his account of the rise of organized sports and play with
a historical overview of life in the streets of the Lower East Side of
New York during the 1890s and the first decade of the 20th century. He
discusses the streets as the site of life itself for the community largely
made up of recently immigrated Jews. The discussion includes the interplay
between politics, theater, and social reform before the author turns to
the phenomena of street games. Part one concludes with a chapter devoted
to the Playground Association of America. The second part, "The Decline
of the Jewish Immigrant Street Life," traces the gradual impact of playgrounds, vacation schools, and settlement houses on the street life of
the Lower East Side. Goodman analyzes the destructive elements of the
social and psychological suppression which accompanied these efforts at
socialization for the Jewish community at large and for its subgroups,
such as women, who became increasingly excluded from social activities.

SOC 42. GORO, HERB. The Block. New York: Vintage Books, 1970.
         186 pp.
Goro lived in a deteriorated ghetto area of the Bronx in New York City.
In this book, he combines photographs with the stories told by the people
living in one block of this area. "In this community," Goro begins, "there
is no community. . . . It seems to be just a stopping point. . . . It's
just a place where they stop over and just find a place to live--for a
temporary type of period." As residents tell their stories, a grim picture
of life for the very poor in urban America emerges. Goro provides a portrait of what it means to be excluded from American society--to be without
a job, to live in deteriorated and overcrowded housing, to lack decent
medical care, and to lack educational opportunities. Goro provides insight
into the enormity, complexity, and urgency of the problems facing the
very poor in America's large cities.

SOC 43. GOTTMAN, JEAN. Megalopolis: The Urbanized Northeastern Seaboard
         of the United States. Cambridge, Mass.: MIT Press, 1961.
         810 pp.
The Northeastern seaboard of the U.S. is covered by a nearly unbroken
sequence of urban and suburban areas. It begins in New Hampshire and
extends as far south as Virginia, as far west as the Appalachian foot-
hills. Gottman describes this enormous and unique region, focusing on
the forces of urbanization that gave rise to this megalopolis, and the
distinctive characteristics of the area. Gottman contends that many
accepted theories and concepts concerning the nature and structure of the
city, the organization of land use and development, must be abandoned
when studying this region. He begins with a discussion of the dynamics
of urbanization and the historical development of the region. In Part
II, he focuses on land use and the mixture of urban and rural areas.

The economic and social foundations of the society and the problems confronted are the topic of Part III. Gottman then discusses the complex interaction and interdependencies of the various areas of the region.

SOC 44. GREENBERG, STANLEY. Politics and Poverty: Modernization and Response in Five Poor Neighborhoods. New York: Wiley, 1974. 282 pp.

Five poor urban neighborhoods are the subject of this study. These neighborhoods are populated by Mexican-Americans, by migrants from Appalachia, and by blacks who migrated from the South. With industrialization and urbanization, the poor were forced out of rural areas and into the expanding cities; this was the origin of poor inner city neighborhoods, and a major focus of this study. The political response of the residents to the deteriorating conditions of their neighborhoods is Greenberg's second focus. "The naked trauma of modernization," Greenberg discovers, "does not produce an overriding political style." In some communities the response is a radical political style, in others a liberal style, while in others no consistent style of political action emerges at all.

SOC 45. HATCH, ELVIN. Biography of a Small Town. New York: Columbia University Press, 1979. 293 pp.

For much of American history the small town was one of the basic forms of social organization. Hatch is concerned with the changes in values and world view effected by the shift from a rural-agrarian society to an urban-industrial one and, especially, by the extent to which urban-industrial patterns have penetrated and altered the nature of small towns and the farming operations that support many of them. He attempts to examine these changes in microcosm by focusing on the community activities and the ideological assumptions that underlay these activities in a small town in California. Based on field work, interviews, and archival research, Hatch contrasts the nature of community life before 1940 and during and after W.W. II.

SOC 46. KILLIAN, LEWIS M. White Southerners. New York: Random House, 1970. 171 pp.

This book is part of a Random House Series entitled "Ethnic Groups in Comparative Perspective." The "White Southerners" whom Killian describes are a special part of multi-ethnic America, a regional minority with a distinct economic and cultural heritage that sets it apart from the national dominant majority. White Southerners is the "portrait of a region and a people." Killian's study examines the social and economic development of the South and the nature of its people. There are sections devoted to marginal white Southerners, such as Catholics and Jews, and to Southern migration. Killian suggests that white Southerners are a "quasi-minority," with a "minority-like subjective reaction to their status." Killian's study makes a significant contribution to the study of ethnicity in America and makes a strong case for his central thesis: "The reaction of the minority to discrimination, both real and imagined, may evoke increased hostility from the dominant group and lead to an intensification of conflict. This has been the experience of white Southerners."

SOC 47. LA GORY, MARK and JOHN PIPKIN. Urban Social Space. Belmont, Calif.: Wadsworth, 1981. 356 pp.

The authors, a sociologist and a geographer, are convinced that spatial structure provides an integrating framework that can produce coherent research and theory about the city. The book is organized around three major themes in the literature on urban space. The first is the question of how space is used and arranged in the city; the second deals with the static aspects of space without considering the question of how these spatial structures emerge in the community; the third provides a consideration of spatial arrangements as key variables in urban studies. The

authors stress that U.S. planning practice is regulative rather than normative. It is characterized by multiple levels of political control designed
to mediate private interests.

SOC 48. **LAKE, ROBERT W.** The New Suburbanites: Race and Housing in the
Suburbs. New Brunswick, N.J.: Rutgers University, Center for
Urban Policy Research, 1981. 303 pp.
As the black middle class expanded during the 1970s, so also did its demand
for suburban housing. Lake is concerned with the magnitude, direction,
and characteristics of the black suburban population and how the experiences of black suburban home buyers compare with whites. He delineates
the outlines of black suburbanization since 1970, the extent to which
it is dispersed throughout or concentrated in particular sections of the
suburbs, the social characteristics of black homebuyers, differences from
whites in housing search experiences and housing costs, and the pressures
confronting real estate brokers. He concludes with a discussion of the
policy implications of his findings.

SOC 49. **LEGGETT, JOHN C.** Class, Race and Labor: Working-Class Consciousness in Detroit. New York: Oxford University Press, 1968.
252 pp.
Class conflict is a significant factor in most American "inner cities"
and inner-city social relations. Leggett explores continuing class consciousness and the interrelated variables of racial and ethnic awareness.
This study of class conflict in Detroit, based on a series of in-depth
interviews with representatives of black and white minority groups, suggests an interplay of the variables of social class and race affecting
uprootedness, occupational security, marginality, and neighborhood conditions. After exploring the connection between class consciousness and
voting, Leggett also addresses the effects of plant location, automation,
and the rising expectations, opinions, and goals of militant racial and
ethnic groups in the urban ghettos of America.

SOC 50. **LYND, ROBERT S.** and **HELEN MERRELL LYND.** Middletown: A Study
in Contemporary American Culture. New York: Harcourt, Brace,
1929. 550 pp.
This work is the first ethnographic study of a U.S. community using methods
of participant-observation fieldwork. "Middletown," at the time of the
study, was a small Midwestern industrial city. The Lynds structured their
work around six major activities of the inhabitants of Middletown: earning
a living, making a home (including marriage, divorce, and child-rearing),
training the young (formal education), leisure and recreation, religion,
and community activities. The investigation covers the years 1885-1925
and the focus throughout is on revealing the interrelations between the
varying, often contradictory, institutional habits that comprise Middletown
life.

SOC 51. **LYND, ROBERT S.** and **HELEN MERRELL LYND.** Middletown in Transition:
A Study in Cultural Conflicts. New York: Harcourt, Brace, 1939.
604 pp.
This reappraisal of "Middletown" documents the changes that resulted from
the Great Depression of 1929-35. The book follows the same general plan
as the first study, and the data are presented in the same generalized
way. The authors respond to Middletown residents' own criticism of the
original study, especially those relating to the "objectivity" of social
science, the "coldness" of its analysis, and the problems of scope and
focus. In some cases, the Lynds have structured their study in ways which
react to these comments, giving a new perspective to the original work.

SOC 52. MANCINI, JANET K. Strategic Styles: Coping in the Inner City.
Hanover, N.H.: University Press of New England, 1981. 350 pp.
In Strategic Styles, Mancini presents five portraits of African-American
boys growing up in Roxbury, a poor section of Boston. In-depth interviews,
self-characterizations, and psychological tests are used to create a
taxonomy of "strategic styles," ways in which each of the boys copes with
his socio-cultural world. The result is five styles: "the conformist,
retreater, tough guy, actor, and the cool guy." Mancini compares Merton's
individual adaptations and Rainwater's strategies for living to her own
scheme. Included are an examination of the positive male role models
available to the boys, interviews with the boys' best friends, and a discussion of the importance of school, work, and money for these youths.

SOC 53. McNALL, SCOTT G. and SALLY A. McNALL. Plains Families: Exploring
Sociology Through Social History. New York: St. Martin's Press,
1983. 325 pp.
The authors use the Great Plains region of the U.S., from the 1860s to
the present, as a sociological laboratory--as a base to investigate how
and why the settlers came to the Plains, to examine the beliefs they and
their descendants held, how the economy and polity affected them, and
how all of these factors worked in concert. Through the use of diaries,
letters, and interviews, members of the Plains families themselves present
firsthand accounts of their day-to-day lives, and of the impact of local,
national, and world events.

SOC 54. MULLER, PETER O. Contemporary Suburban America. New York:
Prentice-Hall, 1981. 218 pp.
This book describes the physical, geographic, economic, and social processes by which "the" suburb has "evolved into a self-sufficient urban
entity" from having been an appendage to "the" central city. Muller gives
a short account of the past and present condition of once-suburban cities.
The "big city is not about to die because large numbers of people will
continue to prefer to live and work there, and the central business district will continue to service the innermost urban realm," but it should
not anticipate a mass return to it.

SOC 55. NORTON, R. D. City Life-Cycles and American Urban Policy. New
York: Academic Press, 1979. 182 pp.
"This book is an interdisciplinary study of differential urban development
in the United States since 1945. Its purpose is to place urban policy
choices in historical perspective." Norton, an economist, contrasts the
increasing concentration of minority poor in central cities with the accelerating decentralization of economic activity. These divergent trends are
at the root of structural unemployment. The author examines the economic
and political implications of two proposed responses to these conditions:
economic revitalization of central cities and dispersal of the urban underclass to areas of economic opportunity. He contends that the latter offers
the best opportunity for permanent improvement of the economic position
of the underclass.

SOC 56. PALEN, J. JOHN, ed. City Scenes: Problems and Prospects. Boston:
Little, Brown, 1977. 326 pp.
The essays in this volume address the contemporary urban scene, critical
urban problems, and urban prospects. Among the topics considered in section one are Chicago as an exemplar of modern urban crisis; the relationship between neighborhood, life-style, and power; and the growth of suburbia. Under the category of urban problems, the editor has collected papers
on ethnicity and race, security problems and issues in cities, poverty
in urban areas, and urban housing. In the concluding section, contributors
examine the monetary crises faced by large urban areas, the use of land
in the inner city, and policy considerations for the future of cities.

SOC 57. PHILLIBER, WILLIAM W. Migrants in Urban America: Cultural Conflict or Ethnic Group Formation? New York: Praeger, 1981. 138 pp.

The migration of more than 7 million people from the Appalachian region since W.W. II has been one of the most significant demographic changes in American society in the 20th century. This migration was usually to cities and frequently in migration streams that led from the South to the North. This study, based on survey data, focuses on Appalachians in Cincinnati. It discusses their social characteristics--housing patterns; occupational, educational, and income attainments; and the extent of welfare dependency--and the problems of adjustment Appalachians encounter. Philliber compares these problems to those of native white Cincinnatians and blacks. The author contends that Appalachians have become a distinct ethnic group in American society.

SOC 58. PHILLIPS, E. BARBARA and RICHARD T. LeGALES. City Lights: An Introduction to Urban Studies. New York: Oxford University Press, 1981. 540 pp.

City Lights shows the unique views of American urban life evident in different social sciences. The book covers urbanization, community social and spatial organization, and urban social norms. Consistent with a growing interest in economy and society, there are chapters on the urban political economy, urban work, the urban fiscal crisis, and municipal budgeting. City Lights is an introduction to American urban studies, an interdisciplinary tour of the field with the advantages as well as disadvantages of cross-disciplinary work.

SOC 59. REED, JOHN SHELTON. The Enduring South: Subcultural Persistence in Mass Society. Lexington, Mass.: Heath, 1972. 135 pp.

With increased modernization and industrialization, it has been argued, the South has become increasingly similar to the North. In The Enduring South Reed refutes this thesis and amasses survey data to demonstrate that a Southern "subculture" persists in modern America. He concentrates on three traits popularly considered to characterize Southerners: an attachment to locality and family; a fundamentalist religious attitude; and a tendency to favor private use of force and firearms. The use of survey data extending over the past few decades enables the author to demonstrate the persistence and prevalence of these attitudes. Reed's analysis provides a counter-perspective on the theme of modernization and cross-regional uniformity in modern American mass society.

SOC 60. REED, JOHN SHELTON. Southerners: The Social Psychology of Sectionalism. Chapel Hill: University of North Carolina Press, 1983. 157 pp.

This monograph was based on a 1971 survey of a sample of white North Carolinians that was designed to test the validity of conceiving white Southerners as an ethnic category. Reed adapted questionnaire items used in other studies of ethnic groups to provide this examination of "the fundamental nature and underlying dimensions of [Southern] regional identity." He concludes that recent economic and demographic changes that have in some respects transformed the South "have not rendered Southern identity useless and irrelevant, nor have they doomed it to extinction. . . . Southernness still remains important, in some ways more important than ever."

SOC 61. ROEBUCK, JULIAN B. and MARK L. HICKSON, III. The Southern Redneck: A Phenomenological Class Study. New York: Praeger, 1982. 210 pp.

In the social class structure of the South, which the authors contend has changed little since the antebellum period, "rednecks" are the poor, undereducated, disreputable whites--the poor farmers and blue collar workers. Roebuck and Hickson examine rednecks' historical experience, their position in Southern society, and the nature of their folk culture. The primary focus of their analysis, however, is a phenomenological understanding of the redneck world--an attempt, based on the authors' own experiences, participant observation, interviews, diaries, and folkore, "to reconstruct the contemporary social reality of the redneck in terms of his own actions, definitions, and interpretations."

SOC 62. SCHOENBERG, SANDRA PERLMAN and PATRICIA L. ROSENBAUM. Neighborhoods That Work: Sources for Visibility in the Inner City. New Brunswick, N.J.: Rutgers University Press, 1980. 179 pp.
This is a field study of inner-city working-class and lower-class neighborhoods in St. Louis. Its objective is to investigate the sources and levels of viability of such neighborhoods in a metropolitan area. Schoenberg and Rosenbaum found neighborhoods that were relatively successful and others that were not, and explain why these differences occurred. The authors define a neighborhood not as a community but as an ecological area. They determined the viability of a neighborhood by assessing how well it conformed to four propositions: (1) it has mechanisms to define and enforce shared agreements about public behavior; (2) it has an organization that provides for communication, leadership, and neighborhood identification; (3) it has linkages to private and public resource givers; and (4) it creates conditions for exchanges among conflicting groups for goal definition and goal support over time.

SOC 63. SIEGAL, HARVEY ALAN. Outposts of the Forgotten: Socially Terminal People in Slum Hotels and Single Room Occupancy Tenements. New Brunswick, N.J.: Transaction Books, 1978. 211 pp.
Based on an eighteen-month participant observation study of an area in the Upper West Side of Manhattan, Outposts of the Forgotten attempts to "make sense of [the] often incomprehensible and sometimes even malevolent world" of single-occupancy housing units, tenements, and hotels that are occupied by "the lonely, the wretched, and desperate . . . , society's rejects and discards." Siegal's research sought to "understand how people, drastically lacking in material resources, could construct a social world capable of satisfying their many, varied, and often exotic needs." He focuses on the mutual support networks and sense of community that develops in such circumstances and on the relations of SRO residents with an often hostile society and its primary representatives--social workers, the police, and landlords.

SOC 64. SUSSER, IDA. Norman Street: Poverty and Politics in an Urban Neighborhood. New York: Oxford University Press, 1982. 230 pp.
This is an ethnography of the dynamics of a white working class neighborhood in Brooklyn. Its specific concern is with how national economic and political changes affect the lives of working-class people. The author focuses especially on the ways in which deindustrialization and fiscally induced reductions in urban social services affect the quality of people's lives and the manner in which community residents respond to these forces. He explores community social organization and friendship networks, especially those among women, and relates such networks to the development of political organization. He also points to those factors, some of them inherent in the very structure of American political and economic institutions, that divide the community and preclude effective political mobilization.

SOC 65. TERKEL, STUDS (LEWIS). Division Street: America. New York: Pantheon Books, 1967. 381 pp.
"I had an idea of the kind of people I wanted to see: homeowners, homemakers, landladies, project dwellers, old settlers, new arrivals, skilled hands, the unskilled, the retired, the young, the haut monde, the demimonde,

1692

the solid middle monde—like Margaret Fuller, I was out to swallow the world. My world was my city." The results of Terkel's exploration of the city of Chicago are presented in this oral history of contemporary American urban society. The people speak for themselves; Terkel has compiled transcripts of his taped conversations with seventy Chicagoans from all strata of society. Virtually all facets of urban society are described here, as seen through the eyes of "real" Americans.

SOC 66. TREMBLAY, KENNETH R., Jr. and DON A. DILLMAN. Beyond the American Housing Dream: Accommodation to the 1980s. Lanham, Md.: University Press of America, 1983. 156 pp.
Tremblay and Dillman analyze the results of a study on housing preferences in order to project the range and nature of future housing alternatives. This study of 2,801 U.S. households reveals how Americans feel about living in a variety of housing environments, ranging from single-family houses to mobile homes. The authors believe that there are three major possibilities in the future: a growing number of Americans will most likely live in multiple family dwellings; the mobile home industry will continue to grow rapidly; and it will remain possible for some Americans to purchase conventional single-family detached homes.

SOC 67. UNDERWOOD, KENNETH WILSON. Protestant and Catholic: Religious and Social Interaction in an Industrial Community. Boston: Beacon Press, 1957. 484 pp.
This book is a study of the interaction of Protestants and Catholics in the industrial community of Holyoke, Massachusetts, in the 1950s. Religion is not examined exclusively but rather is seen as an all-pervasive social force that affects the political, economic, and cultural lives of the people. The first part of the book examines inter-religious community relations as illustrated in an incident that led to a conflict situation between Protestants and Catholics. Part two describes the institutional and organizational life of the two churches, and the final section examines the relations of the two churches to class and ethnicity in the community and to other social and political institutions. The study more particularly examines the effect of religio-ethnic minority-majority shifts in an American town. "Holyoke has in its short history shifted from a dominantly Protestant community, in terms of religious affiliation, to a dominantly Roman Catholic one," Underwood writes. "This study of it affords, therefore, some insight into what happens to an American community when 'it becomes Catholic.'"

SOC 68. VAN TIL, JON. Living with Energy Shortfall: A Future for American Towns and Cities. Boulder, Colo.: Westview Press, 1982. 209 pp.
Van Til presents a series of integrated futuristic scenarios depicting possible American ways of life, given various levels of energy supply and societal affluence. Section one presents a series of energy ideologies and relates them to three energy futures. An analysis of four institutional sectors provides for the connection. Historical, contemporary, and future spatial patterns are analyzed in section two. The final section considers co-production as a means by which community groups may control the production and consumption of energy.

SOC 69. VEYSEY, LAURENCE. The Communal Experience: Anarchist and Mystical Counter-Cultures in Twentieth Century America. New York: Harper & Row, 1973. 495 pp.
In a cultural history of 20th-century American communal ventures, Veysey identifies a tradition of cultural radicalism in America and attempts to demonstrate the relation of that tradition to the mainstream culture. He identifies two strands in the counter-cultural tradition: the mystical or inward-turning, and the anarchist or outward-turning forms. Comparing and contrasting the two strands, Veysey analyzes a number of communal

ventures, many not previously investigated, which represent some of the most successful of the communities in terms of longevity, stability, and dedication. He examines the types of people who participate in such communities, their internal organizations, and the positions held on nine general areas of ideological commitment (including God, property, authority, optimism/desperation). This work provides a cultural and intellectual history of the modern American communal experience, as well as a sociological analysis of the relations between ideas and the social order in voluntary radical communities.

SOC 70. WARREN, ROLAND L. The Community in America. 1963; Rev. ed.
Chicago: Rand McNally, 1972. 418 pp.
"If the concept of the community as a social entity has any inherent validity, there must be identifiable characteristics which all communities have in common, whatever the differences which may distinguish one from another." Warren presents a theoretical analysis of community, focusing on relations among people and institutions that arise because of their clustering in the same location. The book begins with a presentation of Warren's model of community; this model is expanded and applied in subsequent chapters as Warren explores the changes that American communities have undergone, interactions within and external to the community, the tasks performed by and for the community, and community action and development.

SOC 71. WHITT, J. ALLEN. Urban Elites and Mass Transportation: The Dialectics of Power. Princeton, N.J.: Princeton University Press, 1982. 231 pp.
Whitt is essentially concerned with the nature and distribution of power in contemporary American society—especially at the local and regional level, and how it is related to political processes at the national level. He compares three different models of political power (pluralist, elitist, and class-dialectical), derives a series of hypotheses from each model, and tests each model with evidence drawn from public policy concerning urban mass transportation. The author's central conclusion is that public mass transportation systems, such as BART in San Francisco and the METRO in Washington, D.C., "are not likely to solve the problems they were presumably designed to alleviate."

SOC 72. WILSON, ROBERT A. and DAVID A. SCHULZ. Urban Sociology. New York: Prentice-Hall, 1978. 368 pp.
It is the authors' intent to provide a book that "integrates a sociological frame of reference with the analysis of the problems of cities." The book discusses three basic ways in which the city has been viewed through the eyes of the sociologist. These include the city as an ecological system, as a system of social stratification, and as a system of social participation. The authors deal with the family as a basic unit of urban organization and focus on the neighborhood and community. They focus on housing, crime, and minority groups. The final section includes a discussion of the relationship of social science and public policy.

SOC 73. YIN, ROBERT K. Conserving America's Neighborhoods. New Brunswick, N.J.: Plenum Press, 1982. 195 pp.
Yin maintains that "the neighborhood constitutes a social unit, essential to our cultural fabric. Thus participation in neighborhood life is as fundamental as participation in American society as a whole. . . ." A compilation of the author's separate essays on the potential uses of public policy for preserving the social life of contemporary urban neighborhoods, Conserving America's Neighborhoods describes strategies—citizen actions, governmental actions, and research actions—for preserving neighborhoods as social units.

SOC 74. ZABLOCKI, BENJAMIN. Alienation and Charisma: A Study of Contem-
          porary American Communes. New York: Free Press, 1980. 455 pp.
A study of contemporary American communes in their formative years, the
overall aim of this research is to understand more clearly how consensus
is gained and lost among groups of people striving for similar ideological
goals. This book does not focus on the collective decision-making process
itself; instead it focuses on the problem of abstracting the dimensions
of consensual decision-making that are relevant to communal survival and
achievement.

SOC 75. ZICKLIN, GILBERT. Countercultural Communes: A Sociological Per-
          spective. Westport, Conn.: Greenwood Press, 1983. 198 pp.
This book is based on research that the author conducted in approximately
twenty countercultural communes between 1968 and 1971. The communes the
author studied were almost exclusively rural, straight (as opposed to
gay or lesbian), and located on either the East or the West Coast. The
first two chapters are concerned with ideology--the dominant themes, values,
and assumptions of the counterculture and their adaptation in the communal
movement. The next four chapters are concerned with the implementation
of ideology into practice. They are essentially ethnographic, analyzing
the social structural dilemmas that the author identified in his intensive
examination of five of the communes--achievement of solidarity, child
rearing, the organization and meaning of work, and financial arrangements.
In his final chapter Zicklin attempts to account for the rise of the
counterculture and draws some generalizations about the dynamics of communal
life.

SOC 76. ZUKIN, SHARON. Loft Living: Culture and Capital in Urban Change.
          Baltimore, Md.: Johns Hopkins University Press, 1982. 212 pp.
Zuckin, an occupant of a loft in a Greenwich Village building that had
originally housed a sweatshop in the garment industry, witnessed the conversion of her building from manufacturing to residential use. Skeptical
of boosters' claims that such conversions had long-term benefits, she
sought to study the political economy of loft living. Her primary focus
in this study is with "how an untested and unlikely sort of housing space--
a loft--becomes a hot commodity, [the] social forces [that] benefit from
the rise of the loft market, and how that form of real estate development
fits the general pattern of contemporary capitalism." She considers the
dynamics of loft living to reflect the broader phenomenon of deindustrialization and the transition from industrial to service economies that is
occurring throughout the U.S. and Western Europe.

III.   RACE AND ETHNICITY

SOC 77. ABRAMSON, HAROLD J. Ethnic Diversity in Catholic America. New
          York: Wiley, 1975. 207 pp.
This book provides an in-depth look at the sociological, religious, and
marital behavior of Catholic ethnic groups in America today. It is based
on a nationwide survey. Abramson argues that white Catholics have not
assimilated into an undifferentiated "Catholic" ethnic group as other
commentators would suggest; rather, ethnic diversity based on national
origins and social class remains strong within Catholic America. His
findings contradict the "Triple Melting Pot" theory, which proposes that
Americans have come to be divided into three principal groups, Protestant,
Catholic and Jew. Through integration of both empirical sociology and
social history, Abramson proposes a new set of theoretical tools with
which to view "religio-ethnic" systems.

SOC 78. ALMQUIST, ELIZABETH McTAGGART. Minorities, Gender, and Work.
Lexington, Mass.: Heath, 1979. 223 pp.
Almquist is concerned with explaining the market position of American
racial and ethnic minorities. She begins her analysis with a discussion
of several theories--human capital, dual labor market, and Marxist--that
have been used to explain the different socio-economic attainments of American ethnic groups. She then surveys the assimilation and socio-economic
status of eight American racial and ethnic groups--Native Americans, blacks,
Mexicans, Cubans, Chinese, Japanese, and Filipinos--assessing the factors
(especially the degree of assimilation) that have influenced their status,
as drawn from 1970 census data. Finally, Almquist focuses especially
on the employment experience of minority women.

SOC 79. ANDERSON, CHARLES H. White Protestant Americans: From National
Origins to Religious Group. Englewood Cliffs, N.J.: Prentice-
Hall, 1970. 188 pp.
Anderson looks at a special kind of "ethnic" group, white Protestants.
As other ethnic groups became increasingly incorporated into society,
the author contends, "white Protestants increasingly perceive that they,
too, constitute a definable group with distinctive social and familial
networks, and psychological and cultural moorings." He describes the assimilation process of Anglo-Saxons, Scots, Swedes, Norwegians, Finns, Germans,
and Dutch and their "amalgamation" into one religio-ethnic community.
He examines the white Protestants' familial and religious organization,
class structure, and structural or civic involvement. Anderson argues
for the "triple melting pot" theory of ethnicity, proposing that Protestantism or religion has superseded national origin as the primary nexus
of ethnic identification for disparate Protestants.

SOC 80. APOSTLE, RICHARD A., CHARLES Y. GLOCK, THOMAS PIAZZA, and
MARIJEAN SUELZLE. The Anatomy of Racial Attitudes. Berkeley:
University of California Press, 1983. 342 pp.
The objective of this study is to "comprehend the anatomy of white racial
attitudes." To undertake this task, which has been the subject of considerable previous research, the authors sought first to develop valid
social indicators of prejudice. Using survey data from in-depth interviews
of several samples from the San Francisco Bay area, they identify several
analytically distinct components of white racial attitudes: perceptions
of white-black differences, explanations for them, and prescriptions ("how
the deprived status of blacks is responded to"). The authors focus on
the explanations of perceived racial differences. They identify several
different "explanatory modes"--"which lie at the root of what is ordinarily
meant by prejudice"--and explore the social correlates of these explanations.

SOC 81. ASTIN, ALEXANDER W. Minorities in American Higher Education:
Recent Trends, Current Prospects, and Recommendations. San Francisco: Jossey-Bass, 1982. 263 pp.
This volume is an assessment of the status of blacks, Chicanos, Puerto
Ricans, and Native Americans in higher education. Astin examines trends
in minority enrollments by degree level, field of study, and type of institution. He notes that while there were substantial increases in the number
of minority students in higher education during the late 1960s and early
1970s, these increases have not continued during the late 1970s and early
1980s. Astin identifies several factors (e.g., relatively high dropout
rates in high schools, inadequate high school preparation in the natural
sciences, a high percentage of minority enrollments in community colleges)
that affect patterns of minority group enrollment and ultimate educational
success. Finally, Astin raises questions concerning the equality of educational opportunity, which, he maintains, should be defined not in terms
of access to some form of higher education but in terms of the financial

resources expended by the institutions that students attend. Minority students are likely to attend those institutions with fewest resources.

SOC 82. BALTZELL, E. DIGBY. The Protestant Establishment: Aristocracy and Caste in America. New York: Random House, 1964. 429 pp.
Baltzell contends that in order for an upper class to maintain a continuity of power and authority, especially in a mobile society, its membership must be representative of society as a whole. To gain insight into the future function of the Anglo-Saxon, Protestant upper-class in an ethnically and religiously heterogeneous democracy, Baltzell analyzes the conflicting attitudes and values of the old-stock upper-class Americans in the years between Theodore Roosevelt and John Kennedy.

SOC 83. BARRERA, MARIO. Race and Class in the Southwest: A Theory of Racial Inequality. Notre Dame, Ind.: University of Notre Dame Press, 1979. 261 pp.
Barrera merges historical and sociological analysis in this examination of the Chicano experience. He examines Chicano history to develop a model of racial inequality and in the process reinterprets that experience in a new theoretical framework. The book is divided into two parts, the first of which focuses on Chicano history from the Mexican War to the present. Here Barrera emphasizes the political economy of Anglo domination. Part two, more explicitly conceptual, has two chapters. The first deals with the role of the state in creating and perpetuating Chicano-Anglo inequalities in the Southwest. The concluding chapter presents the formal theory of racial inequality--what Barrera terms a "class differentiated colonial perspective"--that underlies his historical analysis.

SOC 84. BARRON, MILTON L. American Minorities. New York: Knopf, 1962. 525 pp.
Barron presents seven articles in social science literature on the problems of American minorities. In the first section of the book, Barron is concerned with problems of dominant group and minority group relations throughout the world. Section two covers religion, race, and nationality as group alliances, while the third section deals with prejudice and discrimination. The status of Native Americans and blacks is examined as well as religious stratification and minority reaction to prejudice and discrimination. Barron concludes with an examination of the principal techniques devised to reduce the problems of inter-group relations.

SOC 85. BARSH, RUSSEL LAWRENCE and JAMES YOUNGBLOOD HENDERSON. The Road: Indian Tribes and Political Liberty. Berkeley: University of California Press, 1982. 301 pp.
This book about Indian tribal rights "is addressed to a great riddle: the political relationship between these sovereign American tribes and the other American government, that is, the government of the United States." Barsh and Henderson examine the anomalous political status of the relatively powerless Native Americans, who, they maintain, have been deprived of the basic right to establish their own local governments and to govern themselves. After an analysis of the history of Indian-white relations and, in particular, the history of tribal-Federal law, the authors conclude that "a new conceptualization of the federal-tribal relationship, which we call the federal-tribal compact or treaty federalism, is necessary to reconcile the status of tribes with American society's essential social and political values."

SOC 86. BEE, ROBERT L. Crosscurrents Along the Colorado: The Impact
         of Government Policy on the Quechan Indians. Tucson: University
         of Arizona Press, 1981. 184 pp.
This book is a case study of the effects of Federal Indian policies on
Native Americans. Bee describes the impact on the Quechan (or Yuma)
Indians of the Lower Colorado of a century of Federal government efforts
to "improve" their economic and social status and the series of "adaptive
strategies" that the Quechans developed in responding to shifts in Federal
policies. In addition to ethnographic field notes, Bee utilizes community
and archival records, oral histories, and some survey research to delineate
the exploitative colonial "pattern of hostile dependency" that has characterized Federal-Quechan relations.

SOC 87. BILLINGSLEY, ANDREW. Black Families in White America. Englewood
         Cliffs, N.J.: Prentice-Hall, 1968. 218 pp.
This book presents an examination of the history, structure, aspirations,
and problems of the black family in America and, more importantly, attempts
to explain how this basic institution, the nexus of social behavior, functions within the larger black community. Billingsley traces the black
heritage, patterns of social mobility and achievement of the black family,
and its struggles within white-controlled society. Disagreeing with the
traditional treatment of the "Negro family" in American scholarship, which
tended to equate it with "problem family," the author advances his own
conception. While contending that the legacy of slavery and the societal
constraints of race and class have injured the black family, Billingsley
refutes studies that argue that the black family is disintegrating, in
grave danger, or ineffectual. "Negro families," Billingsley concludes,
"have shown amazing ability to survive in the face of impossible conditions.
They have also shown remarkable ability to take the barest shreds of opportunity and turn them into social capital of stability and achievement."

SOC 88. BLACKWELL, JAMES E. and PHILIP HART. Cities, Suburbs and Blacks.
         Bayside, N.Y.: General Hall, 1982. 228 pp.
This is an empirical study of the perceptions and attitudes of suburban
and urban black Americans. Utilizing survey data from five metropolitan
areas, the authors seek to determine whether there have been changes in
the priorities and concerns of blacks during the period since publication
of Myrdal's An American Dilemma in 1944. Blackwell and Hart find that
the major concerns voiced by blacks involve structural conditions--economic
conditions, education, justice, housing, and political power--the primary
determinants of which lie outside the black community.

SOC 89. BLAU, JOSEPH L. Judaism in America: From Curiosity to Third
         Faith. Chicago: University of Chicago Press, 1976. 156 pp.
Blau believes that an important influence on American Judaism has been
American religious "voluntaryism," the right not only to choose among
religions, but to choose no religion at all. He also asserts that American
Jews are "protestantized," referring not to Protestant Christianity,
but to the fact that there is no commanding authority which can impose
any theological decisions upon American Jewry. Religious "pluralism"
is the third aspect of American life which Blau feels has significantly
shaped American Judaic practices. Finally, he believes that the American
religious emphasis on morality rather than ritual has helped American
Jewry because Blau believes that moral concepts form the basis of the
Jewish historic vision. According to Blau, this last trait has helped
enlarge the American Jewish community because it has allowed greater
participation by those whose religious enthusiasm is limited.

SOC 90. BLAU, ZENA SMITH. Black Children/White Children: Competence,
         Socialization, and Social Structure. New York: Free Press,
         1981. 283 pp.
Blau's objective is "to identify the social processes that influence the
development of intellectual competence in black children and white children
in order to account for their differences in measured ability in the early
years of schooling." Blau obtained IQ and achievement scores of over
1000 black and white fifth and sixth graders from the Chicago area, and
also interviewed the mothers of these children in order to identify the
parents' social origins and the socialization practices they employed.
She concludes that her findings "provide strong evidence that the sources
of [the differences in measured ability between black and white children]
are social, not genetic, in origin."

SOC 91. BLAUNER, ROBERT. Racial Oppression in America. New York: Harper
         & Row, 1972. 309 pp.
Fundamental to Blauner's argument is the notion that "racial groups and
racial oppression are central features of the American social dynamic
. . . that racial minorities are internal colonies of American capitalism."
Part I presents the various theoretical perspectives of black sociology,
offering an alternative framework for the study of black ethnicity and
analyzing some of the major components of racism in America—white privilege, exploitation and control, the mechanisms of cultural domination,
restricted mobility, and dehumanization. Blauner then introduces his
"colonial paradigm." Part II consists of an analysis of the assimilationist bias in the study of race relations, discussing and examining the
anti-assimilationist posture of Mexican-Americans. In Part III, Blauner
presents various case studies of institutional racism, attempting to demonstrate the pervasiveness of racial inequality in the social, political,
and economic structure.

SOC 92. BOGARDUS, EMORY S. The Mexican in the United States. Los Angeles:
         University of Southern California Press, 1934. 126 pp.
Noting that Mexican immigration increases when the U.S. economy improves,
and anticipating both, Bogardus studies the problems of Mexican immigrants
in the U.S. Using life histories, interviews, and psycho-social analyses,
and describing experiences of Mexican-Americans and their views of these
experiences, Bogardus considers problems of racial adjustment and conflict.
Among the topics covered are labor, property, leisure, health, crime,
and community and family life of Mexican-Americans, as well as various
other dimensions of their social situation in the U.S.

SOC 93. BONACICH, EDNA and JOHN MODELL. The Economic Basis of Ethnic
         Solidarity: Small Business in the Japanese American Community.
         Berkeley: University of California Press, 1980. 290 pp.
The Economic Basis of Ethnic Solidarity examines the relationship between
class and ethnic solidarity. The substantive focus of the book is the
experience of the Japanese Americans, whom the authors characterize as
a "middleman minority," a conceptual category that Bonacich has been instrumental in developing. The authors use both secondary sources to reinterpret the Japanese experience through W.W. II, and interview data obtained
through the Japanese American Research Project at UCLA to examine the
dynamics of the Japanese American community in the post-War period. The
authors discuss the implications of the increasing integration of the
second (Nisei) and third (Sansei) generations into the mainstream of the
American economy for the maintenance or disintegration of ethnic solidarity.

1699

SOC 94. BOURNE, DOROTHY DULLES and JAMES R. BOURNE. Thirty Years of Change
         in Puerto Rico: A Case Study of Ten Selected Rural Areas. New
         York: Praeger, 1966. 411 pp.
In examining ten rural areas, the study describes thirty years of change
in Puerto Rico, from a traditional to a more modern society. The first
part of the work describes the governmental apparatus of Puerto Rico,
concentrating on those departments most concerned with rural affairs.
The second part looks at ten rural communities: their internal institutions for amelioration of rural life, especially the Second Unit Schools,
the subsequent change in social and economic conditions, and attitudes
of the populace. The Bournes claim that great progress has been made
since the 1930s in Puerto Rico in the spheres of labor conditions and
wages, public health and sanitation, nutrition, population control, and
education. The authors argue that change in Puerto Rico has been generated
by internal conditions and beliefs as much as by external assistance from
the central government and the U.S.

SOC 95. BRIGGS, VERNON M., Jr. Chicanos and Rural Poverty. Baltimore,
         Md.: Johns Hopkins University Press, 1973. 81 pp.
Briggs examines the contemporary situation of the Chicano population of
rural America. He argues that the lives and general welfare of a disproportionately high number of Chicanos are affected, mostly adversely, by
developments in the rural economy. He also claims that the high rate
of rural poverty among Chicanos has assumed a character distinct from
the poverty of other regions and groups. The public policy of the U.S.,
rather than alleviating the problem, is actually a major cause of the
condition of Chicanos today. And in order for the situation to improve,
the U.S. must change this policy, and Chicanos themselves must be encouraged to bargain collectively with their employers.

SOC 96. BROTZ, HOWARD. The Black Jews of Harlem: Negro Nationalism
         and the Dilemmas of Negro Leadership. New York: Free Press
         of Glencoe, 1964. 144 pp.
Brotz writes his work from a "black nationalist" perspective. He argues
that blacks have begun to embrace Judaism because, whereas Christianity
has always been a "white" religion, the roots of the Jewish religion can
be traced back to Ethiopia. By rejecting Christianity, "white man's
religion," Brotz asserts that blacks "express contempt for [the white man]
. . . and in doing so they assert a supreme independence of his moral
and religious principles."

SOC 97. BUELL, EMMETT H., Jr. and RICHARD A. BRISBIN, Jr. School Desegre-
         gation and Defended Neighborhoods: The Boston Controversy.
         Lexington, Mass.: Lexington Books, 1982. 202 pp.
Buell's School Desegregation and Defended Neighborhoods focuses on the
political events surrounding the implementation of court-ordered desegregation in Boston. Buell says "defended neighborhoods" are areas within
cities that maintain a separate identity and a sense of community, where
strong social networks exist among the inhabitants, and where violence
is acceptable as a means of preventing social change. Buell contends
that defended neighborhoods react differently to school desegregation
than do other neighborhoods.

SOC 98. CAFFERTY, PASTORA SAN JUAN, BARRY R. CHISWICK, ANDREW M. GREELEY,
         and TERESA A. SULLIVAN. The Dilemma of American Immigration:
         Beyond the Golden Door. New Brunswick, N.J.: Transaction Books,
         1983. 214 pp.
"Immigration may well be the thorniest and most ethically problematic
issue confronting America today and in the coming decades," contend the
authors. They examine the impact of changes in American immigration policy
since 1965. These policies have produced both a change in the places from

which immigrants have been drawn and an increase in the number of immigrants entering the country. The authors consider the social, economic, and political issues that this "new immigrant wave" has raised, and identify the different values and economic or political interests in the current debate over immigration policy. They conclude with a series of recommendations concerning future American immigration policy.

SOC 99. CARMICHAEL, STOKELEY and CHARLES V. HAMILTON. Black Power: The Politics of Liberation in America. New York: Vintage Books, 1967. 198 pp.
"This book is about why, where and in what manner black people in America must get themselves together. . . .--It is about black people taking care of business--the business of and for black people." Carmichael, one of the most prominent and militant leaders of the black protest movement of the late 1960s and early 1970s, and Hamilton, a political scientist, propose a framework for a new black unity, a new black consciousness, what "might be called a sense of peoplehood: pride, rather than shame, in blackness, and an attitude of brotherly, communal responsibility among black people."

SOC 100. CHENAULT, LAWRENCE R. The Puerto Rican Migrant in New York City. New York: Columbia University Press, 1938. 190 pp.
Chenault examines the conditions of Puerto Ricans in Puerto Rico and in New York City in order to show the effects of the mass migration of the 1920s. In Part I he looks at the social conditions of Puerto Ricans on their native island, and maintains that poverty is the main cause of emigration, as Puerto Ricans move to the U.S. to seek a better life. In looking at the employment, housing, and health of Puerto Ricans in Part II, Chenault argues that their living conditions in the U.S. are often equally as poor as in their native land. Indeed, because of linguistic, cultural, and economic barriers, the status of Puerto Ricans in America is worse than that of American blacks. Furthermore, the complete environmental change from a rural to an urban setting necessitates adjustments from which social problems arise. Chenault examines topics such as antisocial behavior, the effects of migration upon the family, and recreation and social activities.

SOC 101. CHURCHILL, CHARLES W. The Italians of Newark: A Community Study. New York: Arno Press, 1975. 173 pp.
Churchill's interviews with approximately 700 Italians, half of whom were born in Italy, form the core of this book. The first section of the book details the respondents' backgrounds in Italy, their emigration to Newark and their early life in that city. Work, family, religion, political life, organizations, education, and public opinion are also included in the interviews' scope. Section two contains a description of the respondents, including their occupations and political wards. An appendix on foreign language broadcast listeners and foreign newspaper readers is included.

SOC 102. CLARK, KENNETH B. Dark Ghetto: Dilemmas of Social Power. New York: Harper & Row, 1965. 251 pp.
Dark Ghetto combines the results of a study conducted by Harlem Youth Opportunities Unlimited (HARYOU) with Clark's own observations to present a social psychological view of life in the New York City black ghetto in the early 1960s. A prologue entitled "The Cry of the Ghetto" presents interviews with residents of the area. Clark defines "The Invisible Wall" of the slum area and examines the social dynamics within, looking at social and economic decay, housing conditions, under-employment, family instability, and social mobility of ghetto dwellers. Clark probes the psychology of the ghetto, dealing with sex and status in the community, the black matriarchy, the distorted masculine image, and the pathology of the ghetto:

mental illness, homicide, suicide, drug addiction, and other forms of
personal and social disorganization. He presents a picture of the "separate and unequal" public schools and the politics and power structure
of the ghetto, and concludes by proposing some strategies for change.

SOC 103. COHEN, NAOMI W. American Jews and the Zionist Idea. New York:
        KTAV, 1975. 172 pp.
Cohen asserts that the Zionist movement saw itself not as a uniquely Jewish
expression, but as one of the series of nationalist movements which swept
Europe in the late 19th and early 20th centuries. She sees Zionism as
a force which prevented American Jews from completely losing their Jewish
identities in America. She also believes that the movement moderated
the distinctive characteristics of American Jews. Cohen argues that the
affluence and security of American Jews made their response to the Zionist
movement a unique one.

SOC 104. COHEN, STEVEN M. American Modernity and Jewish Identity. New
        York: Methuen, 1983. 210 pp.
Based on data from two national sample surveys and two surveys of the
Boston Jews undertaken in 1965 and 1975, Cohen's study analyzes the social
and demographic characteristics of American Jews and the implications
of his findings for the future of American Jewry. He notes Jewish educational and socio-economic achievements, the extent of Jewish residential
mobility, and the characteristics of Jewish family life and political
behavior. Above all, he is concerned with how acculturation and assimilation are affecting religiosity and ethnic identity among four generations
of American Jews.

SOC 105. CONKLIN, NANCY FAIRES and MARGARET A. LOURIE. A Host of Tongues:
        Language Communities in the United States. New York: Free
        Press, 1983. 314 pp.
Conklin and Lourie explore the nature of "linguistic pluralism" in the
U.S., revealing the diverse origins of the American people. Although
comprised of peoples speaking many different languages and many varieties
of English, the U.S. has increasingly become a mono-lingual society. The
authors provide a review of non-English immigrant languages, the social,
economic, and political pressures whereby mono-lingualism developed, and
the resistance to monolingualism that some groups (for example, the
Germans) manifested. In addition to a history of the diversity of foreign-
language communities in the U.S., the authors consider how an American
standard English and the several regional dialects emerged. The final
sections of the book explore the implications of linguistic pluralism
for public and educational policy.

SOC 106. DAY, DAWN. The Adoption of Black Children. Lexington, Mass.:
        Heath, 1979. 156 pp.
Day studied twenty-four adoption agencies in the District of Columbia
and Baltimore area. She looks at how racial discrimination makes the
adoption system ineffective in ministering to the needs of black clients.
This book provides suggestions as to how social service agencies can be
made more responsive to the needs of black homeless children and potential
black adoptive parents. Day provides evidence that the problem of finding
black homes for black children is not the unwillingness of blacks to adopt.
She suggests that blacks have traditionally cared for homeless children
through informal adoptive methods and would respond to more formal agency
mechanisms if the mechanisms were effectively geared toward their needs.

SOC 107.   DENTLER, ROBERT A., D. CATHERINE BALTZELL, and DANIEL J. SULLIVAN.
            University on Trial: The Case of the University of North Caro-
            lina. Cambridge, Mass.: Abt Books, 1983. 192 pp.
This book analyzes the extension of the Supreme Court's 1954 decisions
in Brown v. Board of Education--namely, that racially segregated schools
are unconstitutional--to systems of higher education. As a result of
court orders initiated during the Johnson administration, the University
of North Carolina system was one of several Southern systems of higher
education mandated, either by court order or by the Department of Health,
Education, and Welfare, to desegregate its dual system of historically
white and black state institutions. This book is an analysis of UNC's
response to orders to implement integration and the complex conflicts
of interest that were manifested in efforts both to achieve and to resist
the desegregation sought by HEW. The authors, who are critical of UNC
efforts to forestall desegregation, statistically and descriptively note
the differences that exist between white and black components of the UNC
system, and propose ways in which UNC might more effectively implement
desegregation.

SOC 108.   DENTLER, ROBERT A. and MARVIN B. SCOTT. Schools on Trial: An
            Inside Account of the Boston Desegregation Case. Cambridge,
            Mass.: Abt Books, 1981. 244 pp.
This book is a participant's "clinical" view of the controversial 1974
Boston school desegregation case, Tallulah Morgan v. James W. Hennigan,
which led to extensive racial conflict in the city. The authors served
as consultants and advisors to Judge Arthur Garrity, who presided over
the case and ordered the city to implement busing to remedy the pervasive
segregation in the city's school system. They do not intend to write
a legal or educational history of the Boston case; rather their aim in
this book "is to present some parts of what we have learned in the course
of this unusual experience." They discuss the court's findings regarding
segregation in the Boston schools; describe how the court sought to remedy
the wrongs it identified; and evaluate the different methods used to
address the issue of quality and equality in the Boston school system.

SOC 109.   DINNERSTEIN, LEONARD, ed. Antisemitism in the United States.
            New York: Holt, Rinehart & Winston, 1971. 140 pp.
The first set of essays in this collection deals with the psycho-social
and economic roots of antisemitism. Another group of essays traces the
origins of antisemitic thought in the Progressive period. Other essays
include studies of the reaction in Georgia to the Dreyfus Affair and the
role of American Catholics in antisemitic movements. In the final section,
the persistence of black antisemitism is discussed.

SOC 110.   DINNERSTEIN, LEONARD and DAVID M. REIMERS. Ethnic Americans:
            A History of Immigration and Assimilation. New York: New York
            University Press, 1975. 184 pp.
This account of patterns of immigration and the integration of immigrants
into American life concentrates on non-British groups, with particular
emphasis on the post-1840 period. The book includes chapters on the "old"
immigration, the "new" immigration, the efforts to restrict immigration,
Spanish-speaking minorities (Mexicans, Puerto Ricans, Cubans, and South
Americans), and processes of ethnic mobility in modern America. The
authors' basic conclusion is that the pressures for assimilation are undermining the forces of ethnicity in American society.

SOC 111.   DRAKE, ST. CLAIR and HORACE T. CAYTON.   Black Metropolis: A
           Study of Negro Life in a Northern City. New York: Harcourt,
           Brace, 1945.   809 pp.
This study examines black-white relations in pre-W.W. II Chicago. It
probes the world the blacks constructed from their "separate subordinate
status" and reveals the impact of this societal bifurcation upon the people
and institutions of Chicago's black ghetto. Drake and Cayton provide
an extensive analysis of race relations in the city and of the class and
status stratifications within Chicago's black community. They argue that
"a study of Negro life in Chicago is important not only because it is typical of northern urban communities, but also because it involves one of
the cities in which change is taking place most rapidly and where in the
next decade friction, and even conflict, between capital and labor, Negroes
and whites, will probably reach its most intense form and where a new
pattern of race relations is most likely to evolve."

SOC 112.   DUFF, JOHN B.   The Irish in the United States. Belmont, Calif.:
           Wadsworth, 1971.   87 pp.
Duff examines the assimilation of the Irish into the American mainstream
and their numerous contributions to the cultural, political, and economic
life of America. This work looks at the Colonial beginnings of Irish immigration and the Great Migration during the mid-19th century when the "Great
Hunger" caused by the massive failure of the potato crop forced hundreds
of thousands to seek refuge in America. Duff recounts the Irish struggle
for acceptance in America, their eventual integration into the mainstream,
and their prominence in American politics.

SOC 113.   EISEMAN, ALBERTA.   Rebels and Reformers: Biographies of Four
           Jewish Americans. Garden City, N.Y.: Zenith Press, 1976.
           131 pp.
The first chapter of this work recounts the life of Uriah Levy, who became
the first Jewish officer in the U.S. Navy in 1817. The next figure treated
is Ernestine L. Rope, a Polish immigrant who actively advocated women's
rights in the antebellum period. Louis D. Brandeis, the active Zionist,
adviser to President Woodrow Wilson, and Supreme Court Justice, is discussed
next. The next chapter tells the story of Lillian D. Wald, who organized
the first visiting nurse service affordable to ordinary New Yorkers.

SOC 114.   EISINGER, PETER K.   The Politics of Displacement: Racial and
           Ethnic Transition in Three American Cities. New York: Academic
           Press, 1980.   223 pp.
This book began as a study of processes occurring in the 1970s of a "transition to black rule and the concomitant political displacement of whites
and white-defined interests" in the cities of Detroit and Atlanta.
Eisinger characterizes his book as a study of "losers" that describes the
adjustment of displaced elites to their loss of power to previously subordinated minority groups. He explores a general theory of ethno-racial
political transition. Eisinger describes this process as existing when
members of a previously subordinate ethnic group come to form a working
electoral majority that can "seize and retain the mayoralty." Eisinger's
focus is on displaced elites and he identifies five possible strategies
and psychological responses: cooperation, maintenance, subversion, contestation, and withdrawal.

SOC 115.   FALLOWS, MARJORIE R.   Irish Americans: Identity and Assimilation.
           Englewood Cliffs, N.J.: Prentice-Hall, 1979.   158 pp.
Fallows provides a socio-historical analysis of the Irish experience in
the U.S. One of her primary concerns is to assess the extent to which
the Irish have become assimilated into American life and the processes
whereby this occurred. She examines the forces that contributed to Irish
emigration and the continuities and contrasts between Irish and American

cultures, especially the institutions of the family, politics, and religion, which played crucial roles in determining Irish adaptation to American society. She suggests that Irish assimilation was not uniform across the nation but varied from city to city. However, by the late 1970s the Catholic Irish (upon whom the book focuses) had achieved substantial cultural, structural, and marital assimilation.

SOC 116. FERNANDEZ, JOHN P. Racism and Sexism in Corporate Life. Lexington, Mass.: Heath, 1981. 359 pp.
Based on interviews with over 4,000 corporate managers, Racism and Sexism in Corporate Life seeks to assess their attitudes toward relationships with work peers and superiors; performance evaluation procedures; and, most importantly, their company's Affirmative Action programs. A substantial part of Fernandez's analysis focuses on the differential impact on and reactions to Affirmative Action programs on the part of different groups--white males, white females, blacks, Hispanics, and Asians.

SOC 117. FISHER, SETHARD. From Margin to Mainstream: The Social Progress of Black Americans. New York: Praeger, 1982. 175 pp.
Fisher contends that "a new racial order is emerging and an old one dying. . . . The assault on racism continues--and with decisive success." His analysis is concerned with documenting the emergence of this "new racial order," which he characterizes as the transition of black America from a caste to a class situation. He includes a discussion of strategies and tactics that might be adopted in this new situation to ensure the realization of black equality in American society.

SOC 118. FISHMAN, PRISCILLA. The Jews of the United States. New York: Quadrangle Books, 1973. 302 pp.
Fishman is concerned with two aspects of the history of Jews in America in the past three generations. First, what has the Jewish presence meant in the formation of modern America? Second, is the American Jewish community different from all other Jewish communities which have existed in the past? Fishman also considers what America would have been like without Jewish contributions and what adjustments Americans have had to make because of the Jewish presence. Finally, she tries to discover what specifically Jewish ideals found in the U.S. would have been absent if the Jewish community had not been a group of consequence in the past century.

SOC 119. FRAZIER, E. FRANKLIN. Black Bourgeoisie. Glencoe, Ill.: Free Press, 1957. 264 pp.
Frazier looks at the "world of reality" and the "world of make-believe" of the black bourgeoisie--the former being the concrete reality of their economic condition and social status, the latter being the behavioral standards and values of the isolated social world of the black middle class in America. Frazier examines the forces and occupational differentiation responsible for the emergence of the black bourgeoisie, its economic basis and educational achievements, and its role within the larger black society. Frazier argues that the black middle class was unacceptable to the black and white worlds and therefore developed both a deep-seated inferiority complex and a fantasy world which "attempts to escape the disdain of whites and fulfills [the] wish for status in American life."

SOC 120. FRAZIER, E. FRANKLIN. The Negro Family in the United States. 1939; Rev. ed. New York: Dryden, 1951. 372 pp.
The black American family has undergone many radical transplantations in its history--from Africa to America, from slavery to freedom, and from the plantation to the urban metropolis. Frazier examines these transitions and the adjustments in the organization of the black family which they required. He argues that, depending on the social situation of the black

family, "the forms of sexual and familial relationships may vary from casual contacts to permanent association, from promiscuity to monogamy, and from patriarchal and matriarchal to the modern egalitarian organization of domestic relations." He examines the "natural history" of the black family during slavery, a period in which it was marked by matrifocality and a tenuous existence. After slavery, when the freed slaves found employment and owned land, the black family became traditionally patrifocal. However, the migration to the cities caused much social disorganization within the black family.

SOC 121. FRAZIER, E. FRANKLIN. The Negro in the United States. 1949; Rev. ed. New York: Macmillan, 1963. 769 pp.
Frazier explores the roots of black oppression in the slave experience. He goes on to analyze racial conflict and new forms of accommodation that arose with emancipation. Inquiring into the nature and structure of the black community in pre–Civil Rights America, the author examines social and economic stratification in rural and urban settings, and the role of the family, the church, fraternal organization, and business enterprise in shaping the black community. He explores education for black Americans, their literature and intelligentsia, their social movements and race consciousness; and he deals with physical and mental illness, unemployment, poverty, family disorganization and crime, concluding with some speculations as to the prospects for integration of blacks into American society.

SOC 122. FRYE, HARDY T. Black Parties and Political Power: A Case Study. Boston: G. K. Hall, 1980. 220 pp.
This is a case study of a black independent party, the National Democratic Party of Alabama, during the 1960s and 1970s. Frye examines the historical and social factors that contributed to the formation of the NDPA. He also assesses the party's effectiveness in challenging the dominance of the traditional Democratic Party of Alabama—which had virtually excluded blacks from political participation in that state—and in gaining recognition from the national Democratic Party. He uses his case study to evaluate the impact and prospects of a black political party, which he sees as "likely to be limited in success to miniscule areas of the American political arena"—primarily localities where blacks are in a majority, and racial tensions and political consciousness are high.

SOC 123. GALLO, PATRICK J. Ethnic Alienation: The Italian-Americans. Cranbury, N.J.: Associated University Presses, 1974. 254 pp.
Using the results of forty-five interviews, Gallo tries to determine whether the American political system tends to neutralize or sharpen an ethnic group's sense of exclusion from the dominant roles, values, and institutions, and results in types of behavior that differentiate ethnic groups from native whites. He chooses Italian-Americans as his sample ethnic group and finds that many of these immigrants brought with them predispositions that alienated them from the political system, and were reinforced by structural separation after arrival. This alienation decreases and political interest increases, however, as one moves along the three-generational span.

SOC 124. GANS, HERBERT J. The Urban Villagers: Group and Class in the Life of Italian-Americans. 1962; Rev. ed. New York: Free Press, 1982. 443 pp.
Gans's book is the result of a participant-observation study conducted in an inner-city Boston neighborhood called the West End in 1957 and 1958. Gans focuses on native-born Americans of Italian heritage and considers their life among other ethnic groups in the area. He provides an analysis of class and ethnic group behavior in Italian-American families, peer groups, and community organizations and also examines institutional life and educational and economic achievements. Gans finds that class super-

sedes ethnicity or national origin in defining the Italian-American subculture, which is in many ways similar to that of other ethnic working
class populations. Peer group society, Gans argues, is not solely an
ethnic phenomenon, but rather a working-class phenomenon. In the post-
scripts added to the revised edition, Gans tempers his initial hopes for
sociology and social policy as tools for social improvement and updates
his conclusions with recent scholarship.

SOC 125. GARROW, DAVID J. Protest at Selma: Martin Luther King, Jr.,
          and the Voting Rights Act of 1965. New Haven, Conn.: Yale
          University Press, 1978. 346 pp.
Garrow's work focuses on the strategy and dynamics of the Southern Christian
Leadership Conference under the leadership of Martin Luther King, Jr.
in organizing and implementing the 1965 non-violent protest against the
Jim Crow system in Selma, Alabama. He also considers the effect of this
protest on building support for the 1965 Voting Rights Act. Finally,
he assesses the impact of the Voting Rights Act in transforming the nature
of black political participation in the South and, ultimately, the nature
of Southern politics.

SOC 126. GLAZER, NATHAN. Affirmative Discrimination: Ethnic Inequality
          and Public Policy. New York: Basic Books, 1976. 248 pp.
Glazer argues that the racial and ethnic quotas, statistical requirements,
and differential treatment arising from Affirmative Action have had unfortunate social, economic, and political consequences. He claims that "this
course is not demanded by legislation--indeed, it is specifically forbidden
by national legislation--or by any reasonable interpretation of the Constitution." His study looks at Affirmative Action programs in employment,
education, and housing, and explores the moral and political pitfalls
of such programs. Racial and ethnic group consciousness, according to
Glazer, have assumed such a primary position in public policy decisions
that they have come to violate the individual merit ethic on which the
most basic institutions of this nation were founded. Glazer suggests
that anti-discrimination legislation, more strictly enforced, would be
in adherence to justice and equity.

SOC 127. GLAZER, NATHAN, JOSEPH L. BLAU, HERMAN O. STEIN, OSCAR HANDLIN,
          and MARY F. HANDLIN. The Characteristics of American Jews.
          New York: Jewish Education Committee Press, 1965. 290 pp.
This volume contains essays devoted to Jewish communal institutions in
America and the values they embody. The essays treat the current situation
of Jews in America and place a special emphasis on the nature and develop-
ment of Jewish social services. Essays address such topics as "Social
Characteristics of American Jews," "Jewish Social Work in the United
States," the "Spiritual Life of American Jewry," and the "Acquisition of
Political and Social Rights by the Jews in the United States."

SOC 128. GLAZER, NATHAN and DANIEL PATRICK MOYNIHAN. Beyond the Melting
          Pot: The Negroes, Puerto Ricans, Jews, Italians, and Irish
          of New York City. Cambridge, Mass.: MIT Press, 1963. 363 pp.
This study contends that "the notion that the intense and unprecedented
mixture of ethnic and religious groups in American life was soon to blend
into a homogeneous end product has outlived its usefulness, and also its
credibility." Glazer and Moynihan point to the persistence of ethnicity,
and to the maintenance of a distinct ethnic identity. They suggest, however, that the ethnic groups, while remaining distinct and identifiable,
are transformed by their American experiences. According to Glazer and
Moynihan, "the ethnic group in American society became not a survival
from the age of mass immigration but a new social force," a group linked
by interest, family, and fellow-feeling.

SOC 129. GLAZER, NATHAN and DANIEL PATRICK MOYNIHAN, eds. Ethnicity:
          Theory and Experience. Cambridge, Mass.: Harvard University
          Press, 1975. 512 pp.
Glazer and Moynihan have collected essays that focus on the persistence
of ethnicity as opposed to the "melting pot" theory. Ethnic groups are
not viewed as marginal subgroups at the edges of society which are expected
to disappear in time, but as major elements of the society. The book
contains purely theoretical essays as well as essays pertaining to specific
ethnic groups and the ways in which they distinguish themselves in different countries. Two of the essays deal specifically with ethnic groups
in America, one with the Irish and Italians and the other with blacks.

SOC 130. GLICK, CLARENCE E. Sojourners and Settlers: Chinese Migrants
          in Hawaii. Honolulu: University Press of Hawaii, 1980.
          408 pp.
This work is a historical, economic, and sociological examination of the
exceptional experience of the overseas Chinese in Hawaii. Glick contrasts
the Chinese integration into the Hawaiian economy and society with their
separation in the mainland U.S. In Hawaii the Chinese were imported primarily as contract agricultural laborers, but they reconstructed much
of their traditional social organization. After they had been replaced
in agriculture by other Asian immigrant groups, the Chinese moved to the
cities, where they became an integral component of the urban business and
professional community. Glick examines the nature and persistence of
traditional Chinese culture and social organization in defining the Chinese
community in contemporary Hawaii.

SOC 131. GOLDSTEIN, SIDNEY and CALVIN GOLDSCHNEIDER. Jewish Americans:
          Three Generations in a Jewish Community. Englewood Cliffs,
          N.J.: Prentice-Hall, 1968. 274 pp.
This statistical survey of trends in American Judaism is based on statistics gathered from 1,500 Jewish families in Providence, Rhode Island.
Geographic and occupational mobility are examined, as are residential
clustering and education. Occupational patterns of the Providence Jews
are studied, and another chapter deals with Jewish fertility patterns.
Mortality and life expectancy are compared among the generations, and
the effects of intermarriage and conversion to other religions upon the
Providence community are also analyzed.

SOC 132. GOODWIN, CAROLE. The Oak Park Strategy: Community Control of
          Racial Change. Chicago: University of Chicago Press, 1979.
          240 pp.
Goodwin conducted a participant-observation study on how her neighborhood
(Oak Park, Chicago) did not follow the racial succession pattern that
was the fate of a nearby community. She describes informal and formal
responses to the prospect and reality of black population movement as
products of distinctive forms of neighborhood social organization. Goodwin
argues that access to mechanisms of local political control--the village
municipal structure and a community relations commission--were instrumental
in enabling residents to maintain their commitment to a bi-racial neighborhood.

SOC 133. GORDON, ALBERT I. Jews in Suburbia. Boston: Beacon Press,
          1959. 264 pp.
Gordon gathers most of the information for his study from interviews with
rabbis and religiously active Jews, using the "participant-observer" technique. He concludes that Jews have flocked to suburbia to have the "best
of both worlds": professional success in the city, but "leisurely living"
in the country. He believes that because suburban families move so often,
less money and effort are devoted to creating permanent religious institutions in the suburbs. This deficiency is offset, though, by the impor-

tance such mobile living lends to the nuclear family in Jewish life; and Gordon asserts that the increasing significance of the family will counter-balance the decreasing importance of the synagogue in suburban Judaism.

SOC 134. GORDON, MILTON M. Assimilation in American Life: The Role of
          Race, Religion, and National Origins. New York: Oxford Uni-
          versity Press, 1964. 276 pp.
Gordon traces the history of the concept of assimilation, discussing the
three mainstream theories of assimilation in sociological thought: "Anglo-
conformity," "the melting pot," and cultural pluralism. He suggests that
assimilation is in fact a multi-dimensional process and that there are
several variables to be considered when examining the assimilation of any
given racial, religious, or national group. These "subprocesses" of assimilation are cultural, behavioral, acculturational, structural, marital,
identificational, attitude-receptional, behavior-receptional, and civic.
Acculturation precedes all other subprocesses. Ethnic groups achieve
the various "stages" of assimilation at different times, depending on
the social, political, and economic circumstances in which they find themselves. "Structural pluralism" is the resulting American reality. Gordon
also introduces the concept of "ethclass"--the conjunction of the horizontal layers of social class and the various ethnic group ties. Close,
intimate interaction, he argues, occurs within the ethclass.

SOC 135. GORDON, MILTON M. Human Nature, Class, and Ethnicity. New York:
          Oxford University Press, 1978. 309 pp.
This collection of essays introduces the variables of power and conflict
into Gordon's earlier assimilation model, developed in Assimilation in
American Life (Soc 134). Through an analysis of the psychology of human
nature, Gordon constructs a causal theory of racial and ethnic group relations which examines both dependent and independent variables in the assimilation process. The dependent variable consists of four subvariables:
(1) type of assimilation, with the principal distinction between cultural
and structural; (2) degree of total assimilation; (3) degree of conflict
between minority and majority groups; and (4) degree of access to societal
rewards in the economic, political, and institutional realms. The independent variables, derived through psycho-social analysis, are (1) bio-
social development variables; (2) interaction process variables; and (3)
societal variables. Gordon's essays on subsocieties, subcultures, ethnicity, assimilation, pluralism, social class, and marginality complement
this causal model of intergroup relations.

SOC 136. GREBLER, LEO, JOAN W. MOORE, and RALPH C. GUZMAN. The Mexican-
          American People: The Nation's Second Largest Minority. New
          York: Free Press, 1970. 777 pp.
According to the authors, this book provides a "comprehensive study of
the socio-economic position of Mexican-Americans in selected urban areas
of five Southwestern states." In order to "comprehend the nexus of interrelated factors that impinge on the experience and position of a minority
group," the authors use an interdisciplinary approach and consider issues
in the history, socio-economic conditions, relation of the individual to
the social system, role of churches, and political interaction, as pertaining to Mexican-Americans in the Southwest.

SOC 137. GREELEY, ANDREW M. Ethnicity in the United States: A Preliminary
          Reconnaissance. New York: Wiley, 1974. 347 pp.
In this volume, Greeley analyzes the demography of ethnic identification,
the religio-ethnic composition and distribution of the American population,
and the educational and economic differences among religio-ethnic groups.
He examines the importance of ethnicity versus religion and the significance of the ethnic factor as a predictor of political attitudes and behavior. Greeley summarizes these theories of assimilation: Anglo-conformity,

the melting pot, and cultural pluralism. His own "acculturation but not assimilation" perspective suggests that the experiential history of immigrant groups in this country as well as in the country of origin contributes significantly to the creation of distinct cultural systems and is in part responsible for the existence of distinct ethnic groups in America. He concludes that "under the influence of education, generation, and the experiences in American society both at the time of immigration and sub-sequently, the common culture grows larger. . . . Certain immigrant char-acteristics persist, but in addition, under the impact of the experience of American life, some traits become more rather than less distinctive."

SOC 138. GREELEY, ANDREW M. Why Can't They Be Like Us?: America's White Ethnic Groups. New York: Dutton, 1971. 223 pp.
Strength in diversity is the theme of Greeley's study of white ethnics, mainly Catholics and Jews in America. Why Can't They Be Like Us? defines ethnicity and its functions, outlines the steps in ethnic assimilation, and explores competition and alienation among ethnic groups—the persis-tence of the "we/they" relationship in intergroup relations. He also outlines the characteristics which delineate an ethnic group: who the white ethnics are, what their life situations are like, and how they differ from one another. For Greeley the salvation of America lies in the recog-nition by social scientists and policymakers of the rich cultural diversity of its white ethnics.

SOC 139. GURIN, PATRICIA and EDGAR EPPS. Black Consciousness, Identity and Achievement. New York: Wiley, 1975. 545 pp.
This book studies the higher education of black Americans during the intense decade of the 1960s. The data were gathered from ten broadly repre-sentative, historically black colleges. The results of a series of longi-tudinal and cross-sectional complementary studies extending from 1964 to 1970 are also documented. The authors examine the socio-psychological dimensions of the process of individual and group change during the racially turbulent 1960s. The central guiding question for the structure of the study was: "How did students integrate their collective commitment as blacks with their goals for individual achievement and personal ful-fillment?"

SOC 140. HALE, JANICE E. Black Children: Their Roots, Culture, and Learn-ing Styles. Provo, Utah: Brigham Young University Press, 1982. 191 pp.
This book is an effort to relate Afro-American culture to the realities of educating black American children. Hale contends that African cultures have left a substantial imprint on Afro-American culture, especially in the child-rearing practices that affect the learning styles of black Ameri-can children. The author seeks to demonstrate how Afro-American culture emphasizes values, practices, and cultural style (e.g., concepts of time, cooperation and sharing; religious styles; emphases on spontaneity) that frequently conflict with the demands of formal educational systems in the U.S.

SOC 141. HALL, RAYMOND L. Black Separatism in the United States. Hanover, N.H.: University Press of New England, 1978. 306 pp.
Hall's examination of black separatist movements in the American experience focuses on five movements in the late 1960s: the Congress of Racial Equal-ity, the Student Non-Violent Coordinating Committee, the Republic of New Africa, the Black Panthers, and the Black Muslims. Of these, only the Black Muslims experienced a modicum of organizational success. Lacking support—especially financial—from black Americans, subjected to govern-ment harassment, and plagued by authoritarian leadership and organiza-tional problems, each of the other movements has today virtually disap-peared. Hall concludes that, despite their demise, their militant rhetoric may have contributed to changes in American race relations.

SOC 142. HALPERN, BEN. Jews and Blacks: The Classic American Minorities.
New York: Herder & Herder, 1971. 191 pp.
Halpern begins his work by describing several conflicts between Jews and
blacks which took place in the late 1960s. These included the debate
over adding a black studies program at Brandeis University in 1968-9,
and a dispute over the control of the school board in the Ocean Hill-
Brownsville section of Brooklyn. He points out that in recent years, the
Jewish community has become splintered, while blacks have become more
united. He concludes that the Christianity of most American blacks will
make it easier for them to assimilate into the mainstream of American
culture, while the Jewish religion will make Jewish assimilation more
difficult.

SOC 143. HALSELL, GRACE. The Illegals. Briarcliff Manor, N.Y.: Stein
& Day, 1978. 216 pp.
The general phenomenon of illegal or "undocumented" immigrants has become
a volatile political issue. Halsell focuses on the largest group of
illegal aliens, Mexicans. She contends that there is a "war on our door-
step" as the U.S. seeks to hold back a tide of the "hungry and unemployed"
seeking the abundance of American society. This book is a journalistic
account of her efforts to comprehend the complexity of this phenomenon.
She concludes that the problem of illegal Mexican immigrants will be solved
only by improving the living conditions in the country of origin through
a global Marshall Plan.

SOC 144. HENTOFF, NAT, ed. Black Anti-Semitism and Jewish Racism. New
York: Baron, 1969. 237 pp.
Most of the contributors to this book argue that whatever black anti-
semitism may exist stems from the fact that blacks are the "Jews" of
America and face the same conditions in the U.S. that Jews faced in Europe.
They argue that American Judaism will fail to retain the support of Jewish
youth if it attempts to insulate itself behind a shield of "anti anti-
semitism." Two dissenting views are provided by Earl Raab and Rabbi Jay
Kaufman, the former arguing that the black "movement" of the 1960s is
"developing an anti-semitic ideology." James Baldwin's contribution fits
neither category, but argues that blacks are anti-semitic because they
are anti-white.

SOC 145. HIRSCH, HERBERT and ARONANDO GUTIERREZ. Learning to Be Militant:
Ethnic Identity and the Development of Political Militance in
a Chicano Community. San Francisco: R&E Research Associates,
1977. 146 pp.
This monograph on Chicano political socialization provides an empirical
analysis of the development of political militancy in the Mexican-American
community in the late 1960s. The authors focus on the history of the
Chicano movement in Texas and the emergence and development of La Raza
Unida, a radical political party organized in 1970. The authors examine
many central questions about ethnic and political mobilization, such as
the social and psychological determinants of militant ethnic identity,
the precipitants of political action among Chicano students, and the implications of militancy for the future of ethnic relations and social policy.

SOC 146. HSU, FRANCIS L. K. The Challenge of the American Dream: The
Chinese in the United States. Belmont, Calif.: Wadsworth,
1971. 160 pp.
Hsu discusses the different types of Chinese immigrants, Chinese language
and language barriers, family and kinship patterns (and their adaptation
to the American social context), community ties and organizations, the
religious factor and assimilation, and the institutional and personal
prejudice encountered historically by Chinese Americans. Finally, the
author examines Chinese identity, Chinese Americanization, and the combi-

nation of Asian and American values that resulted in the Chinese realization of the "American Dream."

SOC 147. JAFFEE, A. J., RUTH M. CULLEN, and THOMAS D. BOSWELL. The Changing Demography of Spanish Americans. New York: Academic Press,
1980. 426 pp.
Jaffee, Cullen, and Boswell use demographic data from the 1970s to assess
the differential rates of assimilation and demographic convergence with
non-Hispanic whites among the five major categories employed by the Census
Bureau to distinguish Hispanics: Mexicans, Puerto Ricans, Cubans, Central/
Latin Americans, and "other Spanish," which the authors treat as Hispanos.
The authors found that their three measures of assimilation--outmarriage,
use of English in the home, and non-Spanish surname--were positively
related to their chief convergence variable, fertility. Thus fertility
declines as assimilation increases. The authors conclude that recent
arrivals--Cubans and Central/Latin Americans--are experiencing greater
assimilation and demographic convergence with non-Hispanic whites than
the other groups.

SOC 148. JANOWSKY, OSCAR I., ed. The American Jew: A Composite Portrait.
New York: Harper, 1942. 322 pp.
Studies in this volume treat the relationship of American Jews to their
synagogues, the weaknesses of Jewish education, and the American Jewish
literary scene. A short essay examines the changing role of the Hebrew
language in American Jewish culture, while another focuses upon economic
trends within the Jewish community. American anti-semitism is examined,
as is the influence of Zionism in American Jewish life. The two final
essays evaluate the popular "portrait" of American Jews and their lifestyles.

SOC 149. JANOWSKY, OSCAR I., ed. The American Jew: A Reappraisal. Philadelphia: Jewish Publication Society of America, 1954. 468 pp.
Two statistical studies in this collection consider American Jewish demographics and Jewish economic status. Another piece studies Jewish relations with American "gentile" society, looking particularly at the Regents
Prayer Case which caused significant anti-semitic reaction. Another selection documents the "synagogue building boom" in the years following W.W.
II. Contributions by Jewish-Americans to art, music, and literature in
the U.S. are examined in separate articles.

SOC 150. JOHNSON, DANIEL M. and REX R. CAMPBELL. Black Migration in
America: A Social Demographic History. Durham, N.C.: Duke
University Press, 1981. 190 pp.
This is a study of the migration patterns and processes of black Americans
from the 15th century to the 1970s. The authors assess the historical
and socio-economic forces that in different eras affected black migration.
They examine the volume of migration, the characteristics and motivation
of the migrants, and the social consequences of black migration. The
authors devote the first four chapters to the Atlantic slave trade and
black migration during slavery, the Civil War, and Reconstruction. The
bulk of the work, however, is devoted to black migration during the 20th
century.

SOC 151. JORGENSEN, JOSEPH G. Western Indians: Comparative Environments,
Languages, and Cultures of 172 Western American Indian Tribes.
San Francisco: Freeman, 1980. 673 pp.
Western Indians is a comparative analysis that seeks to reconstruct life
among 172 Indian tribes of North America prior to their contact with Europeans. An interpretive synthesis of data from anthropology, archaeology,
cultural geography, and history, the book examines the environments, languages, and cultures of these Indian societies and seeks explanations

for them. Under the category of "aboriginal culture" Jorgensen devotes
separate chapters to technology, subsistence economy, economic organization,
social organization, political organization, ceremonialism, and spirits
and shamanism.

SOC 152. **KANTROWITZ, NATHAN.** Ethnic and Racial Segregation in the New
York Metropolis: Residential Patterns Among White Ethnic Groups,
Blacks and Puerto Ricans. New York: Praeger, 1973. 104 pp.
Using demographic statistics to document the prolonged residential segregation of ethnic groups in New York City, Kantrowitz challenges the concept
of immigrant assimilation. Each ethnic group, according to this study,
tries to distance itself from its own poor, yet the better-off of each
group do not integrate with each other; thus ethnic segregation is present
in both poverty and prosperity. Kantrowitz sees his study as an aid in
the consideration of social policies to modify segregation policies.
Quantitative information is detailed in the appendix.

SOC 153. **KARNIG, ALBERT K.** and **SUSAN WELCH.** Black Representation and
Urban Policy. Chicago: University of Chicago Press, 1980.
179 pp.
Karnig and Welch seek to interpret black urban political participation
from a broader conceptual framework than the several disparate perspectives
that have previously been advanced. From a review of the substantial
literature on black urban political participation, they posit nearly thirty
variables to explain why blacks are or are not elected to offices in city
governments. They then test these variables on data drawn from 184 large
cities, finding that Federal anti-poverty funds did not contribute to
black political representation. Moreover, black political success is
not negatively affected by the presence of large white ethnic populations
or positively affected by the presence of relatively large educated white
upper strata.

SOC 154. **KILLIAN, LEWIS M.** The Impossible Revolution? Black Power and
the American Dream: Phase II. 1968; Rev. ed. New York: Random
House, 1975. 198 pp.
In this analysis of "The Black Revolution" of the 1960s, Killian traces
the history of the black struggle for power and opportunity in America
and examines past strategies of protest. The Black Power strategy of
unity, angry protest, and violent change, Killian argues, alienated both
whites and blacks, produced ideological and actual discord among the black
community and black leadership, and generated a defensive white backlash.
Phase II updates and reevaluates the original 1968 volume, after the period
of black protest had declined. The violent phase subsided, Killian wrote,
not because the racial crisis passed, but because "white power has demonstrated that open black defiance was extremely dangerous and often suicidal.
The ranks of the most dramatically defiant black leaders were decimated
by imprisonment, migration and assassination." One significant strategy
that has gained appeal in the 1970s is the politics of group rights—
demands for the recognition of the black community as a political entity
with power that is not dependent on white goodwill.

SOC 155. **KIM, ILLSOO.** New Urban Immigrants: The Korean Community in
New York. Princeton, N.J.: Princeton University Press, 1981.
329 pp.
This analysis of the Korean community in New York is divided into four
parts. Kim first discusses the push factors—overpopulation, rapid urbanization, and a new class structure that have stimulated recent Korean emigration. Then he examines the economic adaptation of Korean immigrants
and their socio-economic success in the New York metropolitan area. The
third part of the book is devoted to the cultural characteristics of the
Korean community, the extent of their cultural and structural assimilation,

and their political relations with the Korean government. Finally, Kim
provides a historical analysis of the development of Korean society in
relation to Korean immigration to the U.S.

SOC 156. KITANO, HARRY H. L. Japanese Americans: The Evolution of a
        Subculture. 1969; Rev. ed. Englewood Cliffs, N.J.: Prentice-
        Hall, 1976. 231 pp.
Kitano presents a picture of the Japanese in the U.S. throughout the 20th
century. He surveys the experience of early Japanese immigrants and traces
the pattern of their occupational and educational achievements, and their
familial relationships and community organization. He devotes a chapter
to the wartime evacuation, and describes the current Japanese family,
community, and culture in Hawaii and on the mainland.

SOC 157. KNOLL, TRICIA. Becoming Americans: Asian Sojourners, Immigrants,
        and Refugees in the Western United States. Portland, Oreg.:
        Coast to Coast Books, 1982. 356 pp.
Since 1970 more than 2 million Asian immigrants have entered the U.S.
Knoll provides a description of several East Asian groups by their land
of origin, focusing on the most recent immigrants. The book has separate
chapters devoted to the experiences of Chinese, Japanese, Filipino, Korean,
Vietnamese, Laotian, Overseas Chinese, and Kampuchean immigrants to the
mainland West Coast. The author interweaves journalistic accounts,
scholarly secondary sources, census data, novels, personal accounts and
autobiographies, interviews, and photographs to convey the diverse experiences of these peoples.

SOC 158. KOBRIN, FRANCESE and CALVIN GOLDSCHNEIDER. The Ethnic Factor
        in Family Structure and Mobility. Cambridge, Mass.: Ballinger,
        1978. 257 pp.
Using survey data on the Rhode Island population, Kobrin and Goldschneider
examine patterns of family life and social mobility among Protestants,
Jews, and Catholics, and, among Catholics, French Canadian, Italian, Puerto
Rican, and Irish subcommunities. Their objective is "to examine ethnic
differentiation in the context of socio-economic and life cycle changes
so as to clarify the patterns of continuity and change characterizing
ethnic communities." They contend that ethnic pluralism continues to
be a crucial fact of American community life and that ethno-religious
identification is closely related to variations in marriage and family
patterns, socio-economic status and social mobility, and residential patterns and migration. For Kobrin and Goldschneider, ethnicity is a dynamic,
phenomenon: as the broader society changes, new forms of ethnic identity
and ethnic cohesiveness emerge.

SOC 159. KRAMER, JUDITH and SEYMOUR LEVENTMAN. Children of the Gilded
        Ghetto: Conflict Resolutions of Three Generations of American
        Jews. New Haven, Conn.: Yale University Press, 1961.
        228 pp.
This is a study of the social structure of the minority Jewish community
of North City, located in the Midwestern U.S. Historical data are provided
on the city and its Jewish inhabitants which suggest the restrictive
effects of local anti-semitism and the pressures for in-group participation
among Jews. One hundred male respondents from three generations of Jews
provided the sample for this survey, which was used to predict the
"stratification of life changes in the second generation and the changes
expected in the third generation." Samples were selected to test specific
hypotheses about the resolutions of conflict in a minority community,
rather than to permit generalizations about all American Jews.

SOC 160. LADNER, JOYCE. Mixed Families: Adopting Across Racial Boundaries.
          Garden City, N.Y.: Anchor Press, 1977. 290 pp.
Ladner's study, based on interviews conducted in seven American states,
focuses on the experiences and problems surrounding white American families
who adopt black children. Ladner examines the historical evolution of
adoption agencies and their role in cross-racial adoption. She discusses
the personal and political motivations of the adoptive parents, societal
reactions, and the possible consequences for the adopted child in the
estimated 15,000 annual transracial placements nationwide. The author
presents a sociological perspective on the probable impact of mixed families on American racist attitudes and on developing black pride, asserting
that neither black pride nor the black family institution will be negatively affected by the increase of interracial adoption in the 1970s.

SOC 161. LEVINE, GENE M. and ROBERT C. RHODES. The Japanese American
          Community: A Three Generation Study. New York: Praeger, 1981.
          238 pp.
A product of the Japanese American Research Project at UCLA, Levine and
Rhodes's study of three generations of Japanese Americans concentrates
on the Nisei (second generation) adaptation to American life and the relation between their socio-economic integration into American society and
the maintenance of the Japanese American community. The primary objective
of the study is "to attempt to discover how the Japanese American community
has managed to retain its solidarity as it has, considering all the contrary pressures toward acculturation and assimilation." The authors document the extensive cultural, structural, and marital assimilation of the
Sansei (third generation) and the consequent diminution of the classic
Japanese American community.

SOC 162. LEWIS, OSCAR. La Vida: A Puerto Rican Family in the Culture
          of Poverty--San Juan and New York. New York: Random House,
          1965. 669 pp.
This is a study of 100 Puerto Rican families from four slums in Greater
San Juan and their relatives in New York City. Through interviews and
field observation of the Rio family (an extended family with relatives
in New York), Lewis offers a portrait of urban slum life in San Juan,
the patterns and problems of adjustment for Puerto Rican immigrants to
New York City, and the concept of a culture of poverty. "The culture
of poverty (in modern nations)," Lewis writes, "is not only a matter of
economic deprivation, of disorganization or of the absence of something.
It is also something positive and provides some rewards without which
the poor could hardly carry on." Lewis's methodology incorporates empirical, theoretical, and subjective analyses.

SOC 163. LIEBERSON, STANLEY. A Piece of the Pie: Blacks and White Immi-
          grants Since 1880. Berkeley: University of California Press,
          1980. 419 pp.
Lieberson enters the cultural-structural debate concerning explanations
of ethnic group achievement: are the differential attainments of blacks
and new Europeans explained by the greater disadvantages blacks encountered
or by differences in the cultural characteristics that each group brought
to the urban experience? Utilizing statistical and qualitative data,
Lieberson compares the political and legal environments, educational opportunities, trends in residential segregation, and occupational opportunities
of blacks and new immigrants. Lieberson concludes that the basic difference between these two categories is that "blacks were victims of more
severe forms of discrimination than were the new Europeans."

SOC 164.   LIGHT, IVAN H.   Ethnic Enterprise in America: Business and Wel-
           fare Among Chinese, Japanese and Blacks.   Berkeley: University
           of California Press, 1972.   209 pp.
As recently as 1972, only a small number of black proprietors or black
small businessmen existed in America. Light seeks an explanation for
this perplexing phenomenon, noting that "Americans of Chinese and Japanese
descent offer empirical illustration of the manner in which poverty, discrimination and ethnic visibility stimulated business proprietorship among
some disadvantaged [and radically distinct] immigrants." After discussing
in detail the three ethnic groups' credit, banking, kinship, and community
structures, Light concludes that the key factor is the existence of unitary
organizations of community spokesmanship and community organization.
Voluntary associations and the creation of moral community within the
ethnic group prove critical in economic advancement. In this, according
to Light, Asian Americans have largely succeeded due to their cultural
heritage, but black America remains internally divided.

SOC 165.   LINCOLN, C. ERIC.   The Black Muslim in America.   1961; Rev.
           ed. Boston: Beacon Press, 1973.   302 pp.
This is an inquiry into the Black Muslim movement in America as it existed
in the 1950s. A separationist minority within a minority, Black Muslims
preach black supremacy and oppose integration efforts. They believe Christian religion has hindered black aspirations for dignity and equality
in America. Lincoln places the Black Muslim movement in its psychological
and sociological context, examining the dynamics of black nationalism
and the development of the Temple of Islam in America. He explores the
mass movement nature of the Muslim appeal and the members' attempts to
reach the black population. Lincoln concludes that the Black Muslim movement represents one attempt to break out of the bondage of discrimination
and despair which he argues "threatens the peace and casts a dark shadow
over the happiness and prosperity of all America."

SOC 166.   LIVINGSTON, JOHN C.   Fair Game? Inequality and Affirmative Action.
           San Francisco: Freeman, 1979.   281 pp.
"Without affirmative action," writes Livingston, "the struggle for racial
justice would be stalemated, at the price of both justice and social
peace." Appalled that proponents of affirmative action capitulated before
its critics, Livingston undertakes a defense of this controversial policy.
He examines the divergent meanings of equality that have been invoked
in the controversy, and explores some of the basic assumptions of American
culture--"the values underlying majority rule, the fundamental questions
of why men should obey laws, and the sources of political obligation and
legitimacy."

SOC 167.   LOPATA, HELENA ZNANIECKI.   Polish Americans: Status Competition
           in an Ethnic Community. Englewood Cliffs, N.J.: Prentice-Hall,
           1976.   174 pp.
Lopata deals with the differences between life in Poland and in America,
traces the development and maintenance of the Polish ethnic community,
and comments on Polish-Americans' relationships with other groups and
the degree of their structural assimilation into American institutions.
She concludes that stratification on the basis of class and social status
in America has resulted in companionate circles of elites and non-elites.

SOC 168.   LOPREATO, JOSEPH.   Italian Americans.   New York: Random House,
           1970.   204 pp.
Lopreato discusses the promise and problems of immigration, describes
in detail the immigrants' backgrounds, and explains the centrifugal and
centripetal forces that led to the great Italian migration. Italian Americans deals with the patterns of urban settlement that produced the closely
knit ethnic enclaves, or "little Italies," that were later transformed

1716

into Italian American communities. Lopreato also describes patterns of educational and occupational achievement, assimilation, intergroup conflict, and changing indigenous institutions, such as family and religious life. He offers the Italian immigrant experience as representative of the experience of "white immigrants" in America in the late 19th and early 20th century.

SOC 169. LYMAN, STANFORD M. The Black American in Sociological Thought: New Perspectives on Black America. New York: Capricorn, 1973. 220 pp.
In this work, Lyman presents a critique of the way in which many social scientists have dealt with black ethnicity. He contends that Robert E. Park, John Dollard, Gunnar Myrdal, Gordon Allport, T. W. Adorno, and Talcott Parsons never really understood "the American dilemma," for sociologists have tended to take the Aristotelian view "that science could only study that which behaves in accordance with slow, orderly, continuous and teleological movement" and thus were led "to make radical separation of events from processes." To Lyman, the sociology of black people has to address itself to existential matters and deal with the disjunctive, marginal, and often absurd position of those caught between two worlds, rather than continue the kind of liberal conservatism that has thus far characterized it.

SOC 170. LYMAN, STANFORD M. Chinese Americans. New York: Random House, 1974. 213 pp.
Lyman discusses the "Chinese diaspora," the background of Chinese community organization, its transplantation to the U.S., and the internal isolation of early immigrant communities of "Chinatowns." He gives a historical account of the anti-Chinese movement in America from 1785 to 1910 and the subtle forms of institutional racism that persist in many American cities. His study includes an examination of Chinese-American class structure and occupational achievement, a discussion of social problems encountered by the community, and alienation, rebellion, and the new Chinese-American consciousness. Lyman suggests that the Chinese example defies classical sociological classification and that a reevaluation of assimilation models is necessary when examining the Chinese-American experience.

SOC 171. MacDONALD, J. FRED. Blacks and White T.V.: Afro-Americans in Television Since 1948. Chicago: Nelson-Hall, 1983. 288 pp.
"This is a study of the relationship between television and blacks in the decades since the medium became popular." Based on extensive analysis of TV shows, MacDonald's study is divided into three periods. During the first period, 1948-1957, the TV industry "veered from honesty to duplicity in its depiction of Afro-Americans." The second period, 1957-1970, was the era of the black protest movement, during which TV "slowly, but undeniably, evolved toward a fairer stance toward blacks." Since 1970, the third period, blacks have become more prevalent in programming but still "remain vulnerable to racial ridicule."

SOC 172. MANGUM, GARTH L. and STEPHEN F. SENINGE. Coming of Age in the Ghetto: A Dilemma of Youth Unemployment. Baltimore, Md.: Johns Hopkins University Press, 1978. 114 pp.
What are the causes and consequences of the disastrous levels of unemployment and underemployment among black ghetto youths? This study examines that question from demographic, economic, and anthropological perspectives. The authors produce a "harsh picture" of ghetto youth employment, a portrait that "leaves little doubt that the basic causes are found in perverse population trends, deteriorating local economies, and dysfunctional life styles." They conclude with a discussion of the implications of their findings for U.S. public policy.

SOC 173. MARKIDES, KYRIAKOS S. and HARRY W. MARTIN. Older Mexican Americans: A Study in an Urban Barrio. Austin: University of Texas
Press, 1983. 139 pp.
This monograph is based on survey research on elderly residents of a mixed
Anglo and Chicano neighborhood in southwest San Antonio. The authors
contend that it is intended as a preliminary, not definitive, investigation
of the Chicano aged, but their analysis provides explicit comparison with
older Anglos as well. They emphasize the place of the older Mexican-
American in the family, and devote separate chapters to comparing psychological distress and life satisfaction, health and health-care utilization,
religious behavior, and the retirement experiences of men in the two ethnic
communities. The authors conclude their analysis by relating their findings to current literature in gerontology and by identifying possible
topics for new research.

SOC 174. MARX, GARY T. Protest and Prejudice: A Study of Belief in the
Black Community. New York: Harper & Row, 1967. 256 pp.
This study, based on 1,119 interviews with black Americans in 1964, treats
the nature of the "Negro mood" in the mid-1960s. "Our data suggest that
many people hold an overly sensational image of the Negro mood," the author
writes. "To be sure there is deep anger and frustration, as well as varying degrees of suspicion and resentment of whites. Yet, there is still
optimism about the possibility of change within the system. Most Negroes
favor integration in principle, are loyal to the United States, are opposed
to indiscriminate violence, and are not consistently anti-white or anti-
Semitic." Marx describes the climate of opinion on a number of Civil
Rights issues prominent in 1964 and cites "a measure of civil rights militancy." His analysis treats the social and psychological contexts of
militancy, the effects of religion on protest, and the nature of black
nationalism in the days just before "Black Power" was to supplant "We
Shall Overcome" as a rallying slogan. The second part of the book examines
black attitudes toward whites in general and Jews in particular, and the
factors affecting hostility in race relations. The concluding chapter
considers the connection between responses to the Civil Rights struggle,
attitudes toward whites, and the future of black protest.

SOC 175. MAYER, EGON. From Suburb to Shtetl: The Jews of Boro Park.
Philadelphia: Temple University Press, 1979. 196 pp.
The residential movement of American Jews during the 20th century has
been from the inner city, the "urban shtetl," to the suburbs. The Orthodox
Jews of Boro Park in Brooklyn contradict this ethnic-immigrant model of
dispersal and assimilation. The renaissance of American Orthodoxy has
forced a re-evaluation of earlier assimilationist theories. Most Jews
expected Orthodoxy to disappear within two to three generations after
arrival. Instead, this wing of American Jewry has grown stronger. By
adopting a bifurcated core value system compartmentalizing their institutions into the sacred and the secular, Orthodox Jews in Boro Park have
developed a cultural amalgam of traditional and modern values. Religion
for the Jews in Boro Park is thus easier to practice than ever before.

SOC 176. McADAM, DOUG. Political Process and the Development of Black
Insurgency, 1930-1970. Chicago: University of Chicago Press,
1982. 304 pp.
McAdam reviews and evaluates two dominant social movement models: classical
and resource mobilization. He proposes an alternative "political process"
model, in which he seeks especially to delineate the role of institutionalized political power in explaining social insurgency. He tests this perspective with an analysis of the roots and dynamics of the black protest
movement. He concludes that the "structure of political opportunities"
available to blacks improved from 1930 to 1954, that these opportunities
contributed to a growing sense of political efficacy among blacks, and

that the organizational growth of black colleges, churches, and the NAACP combined to provide the underlying conditions that led to black insurgency in the 1950s and 1960s.

SOC 177. McDONAGH, EDWARD C. and EUGENE S. RICHARDS. Ethnic Relations in the United States. New York: Appleton-Century-Crofts, 1953. 408 pp.
McDonagh and Richards have assembled a study of the status of various ethnic groups based on four criteria: social status, educational status, legal status, and economic status. Objective data and empirical findings are relied upon to determine the legitimate status of immigrant groups, and readings are included which indicate the problems confronted by specific immigrant groups in the U.S. The book is concerned with understanding, analyzing, and improving ethnic relations, and analyzes seven ethnic groups: blacks, Jews, Mexicans, Indians, Japanese, Chinese, and European immigrants.

SOC 178. McLAUGHLIN, JOHN B. Gypsy Lifestyles. Lexington, Mass.: Lexington Books, 1980. 105 pp.
Based on a reading of secondary sources (most of them written by non-gypsies) and on interviews with gypsies, this study seeks to convey gypsy origins, and the nature of gypsy social organization and occupational pursuits in American society. Characterized by transient lifestyles and lacking educational credentials, gypsies are found at the bottom of the economic and social scale. While he warns that gypsies should not be stereotyped as thieves and swindlers, McLaughlin devotes several chapters to analyses of such people and their activities.

SOC 179. McLEMORE, S. DALE. Racial and Ethnic Relations in America. 1980; Rev. ed. Boston: Allyn & Bacon, 1983. 445 pp.
This book employs what the author terms a "processual-historical" approach to examining the nature of race and ethnicity in American life. This involves combining the sociological analysis of intergroup relations and the history of American ethnic groups. McLemore begins with the earliest contact between Europeans and Native Americans and provides a chronological examination of ethnic group contacts, conflict, and assimilation that concludes with a discussion of the "ethnic revival" of the 1970s. Conventional sociological concepts, such as prejudice and discrimination, stereotyping, social distance, and race and ethnicity, are introduced in the course of the book. McLemore is especially concerned with assessing and comparing the degree of assimilation experienced by different American ethnic groups, and discusses the English, the colonial Irish and Germans, the 19th-century Irish and Germans, the Italians, and the Jews. Separate chapters are devoted to the experiences of Chicanos, Japanese, blacks, and American Indians.

SOC 180. MEIER, AUGUST B. and ELLIOTT RUDWICK. CORE: A Study in the Civil Rights Movement, 1942-1968. New York: Oxford University Press, 1973. 563 pp.
Combining sociological analysis with a historical perspective, Meier and Rudwick analyze an organization that helped mold the Civil Rights Movement in the U.S. The Congress of Racial Equality (CORE) was started in 1942 as a small interracial group advocating nondirect action. By the early 1960s it had become a major force in the movement for equality. The book describes the pioneering efforts of the black struggle in the 1940s and 1950s, recounting its origins in the radical Christian pacifist movement and its early sit-ins. Through a discussion of the ideological and structural changes within the organizations, the authors consider the reasons for the rise and decline of CORE within the context of the black struggle in America. They detail the "coming of age" of the organization in 1960 and outline its role in the drives for jobs, school integration, and better

housing in the North during the early 1960s, the zenith of the organization's power. The authors also show how, at the end of the decade, CORE's
effectiveness declined as it came to espouse the ideology and goals of
the rising Black Power movement.

SOC 181. MILLS, C. WRIGHT, CLARENCE SENIOR, and ROSE KOHN GOLDSON. The
Puerto Rican Journey: New York's Newest Migrants. New York:
Harper, 1950. 238 pp.
This study reports and analyzes the results of interviews conducted with
Puerto Rican immigrants to two core areas of New York City: Spanish Harlem
and the Morrisania section of the Bronx. The authors begin with a section
devoted to the history and development of Puerto Rico--especially since
it became a U.S. territory--and the characteristics of Puerto Rican
migrants. Section Two examines the motivations for migration and includes
an analysis of the migrant's economic expectations. Section Three concerns
the effects of Puerto Rican migration to New York City. Here the authors
discuss the general history of migrations to the city, the emerging Puerto
Rican community, its conflicts and solidarity, and its adaptation to a
new cultural environment. The authors append their survey questionnaire
and a discussion of Puerto Rican demographics in New York City.

SOC 182. MONTERO, DARREL. Japanese Americans: Changing Patterns of Ethnic
Affiliation Over Three Generations. Boulder, Colo.: Westview
Press, 1980. 171 pp.
Montero's study analyzes the socio-economic adaptation of a national sample
of three generations of Japanese Americans. He develops a historical
model to examine the effects of Japanese-American socio-economic mobility
and to explain the dynamics of the assimilation process the group experienced. He shows that their substantial socio-economic mobility eroded
the cohesiveness and solidarity of the Japanese-American community and
contributed to its increasing cultural and social assimilation.

SOC 183. MONTERO, DARREL. Vietnamese Americans: Patterns of Resettlement
and Socioeconomic Adaptation in the United States. Boulder,
Colo.: Westview Press, 1979. 218 pp.
Vietnamese Americans describes the flight of the more than 170,000 Indo-
chinese refugees who entered the U.S. between April 1975 and November
1979. Using data from a national sample of Vietnamese, Montero analyzes
the social, educational, and occupational characteristics with which they
entered the U.S. and their economic adaptation and resettlement in this
country. In order to place the Vietnamese immigration experience in a
broader socio-historical context, Montero advances a model of Spontaneous
International Migration, which attempts to account for the unique nature
of the Vietnamese flight and resettlement and to "predict the prospects
for future socioeconomic adaptation and cultural assimilation of the Vietnamese."

SOC 184. MOORE, JOAN W. with HARRY PACHON. Mexican Americans. 1970;
Rev. ed. Englewood Cliffs, N.J.: Prentice-Hall, 1976.
173 pp.
This volume offers a portrait of the Mexican-American community, providing
historical and sociological observations on the problems faced by this
American minority. The authors explore the impact of American institutions
on the Mexican tradition and examine the resulting changes in Mexican-
American family and community structure. They also address the clashes
of values encountered by Mexican Americans attributable to language and
culture. Finally, they trace the development of Mexican-American politics
and ethnic consciousness that in recent years has resulted in a new militancy and the Chicano movement.

SOC 185. MOSKOS, CHARLES C., Jr. Greek Americans: Struggle and Success. Englewood Cliffs, N.J.: Prentice-Hall, 1980. 162 pp.
Moskos provides a socio-historical analysis of the Greek experience in American life that focuses on the nature of Greek assimilation and the communal factors, especially the Greek church, press, and voluntary associations, that affected it. He devotes attention to the period of peak migration (1890-1920) to the U.S. and emphasizes the significance of the substantial percentage (about 40%) of immigrants who later returned to Greece and the impact of their presence there. He is most concerned, however, with analyzing the adaptation of Greeks to American life, which has been marked by their "embourgeoisement," which he maintains was a consequence of their participation in Greece in a "market rather than a subsistence economy," by the relative absence of a working class orientation, and their general social conservativeness.

SOC 186. MYRDAL, GUNNAR, with RICHARD STERNER and ARNOLD ROSE. An American Dilemma: The Negro Problem and Modern Democracy. New York: Harper, 1944. 1483 pp.
This book's central thesis is that there is a discrepancy between "creed and culture" in America's treatment of blacks. "From the point of view of the American Creed the status accorded the Negro in America represents nothing more and nothing less than a century-long lag in public morals; in practice the solution is not effectuated. The Negro in America has not yet been given the elemental civil and political rights of formal democracy . . . and this anachronism constitutes the contemporary 'problem' both to Negroes and to whites." An American Dilemma appraises the status and life situation of black Americans prior to W.W. II. Myrdal treats racial theory, populations, and migration patterns of the black population. He and his collaborators examine economic and political inequality, the long-term impact of slavery, the meaning of segregation, and the resulting social inequality and rigid stratification of American society. The book also contains an analysis of the black community, its leadership, institutions, and general structure.

SOC 187. NEE, VICTOR G. and BRETT DE BARY NEE. Longtime Californ': A Documentary Study of an American Chinatown. New York: Pantheon Books, 1972. 410 pp.
"What forces created Chinatown and continue to perpetuate its existence? What has been the source of its exceptional cohesiveness and resilience as an American ethnic community? What is the consciousness of its people?" These are the questions that occupy the authors in this study of San Francisco's Chinese community. By exploring the history of this community, the Nees were able to distinguish three separate societies in Chinatown, differentiated by the time and circumstances of their arrival in this country. Life in Chinatown is described by the residents themselves, as the authors weave their commentary around transcriptions of taped interviews with community members.

SOC 188. NEWMAN, WILLIAM M. American Pluralism: A Study of Minority Groups and Social Theory. New York: Harper & Row, 1973. 307 pp.
Newman applies conflict theory to an examination of contemporary American society and the character of minority group relations within it. The book offers an introduction to the concepts and basic theoretical issues of ethnic/race relations. It reviews and critiques the work of Robert Park, Louis Wirth, Nathan Glazer, Daniel Patrick Moynihan, and other prominent writers who have sought to explain the social processes of American pluralism. Newman extrapolates twenty-six basic propositions from the underlying assumptions of the theories reviewed. The final section addresses the bases and issues of prejudice and discrimination in America.

SOC 189. NIELSEN, GEORGE R. The Danish Americans. Boston: Twayne, 1981.
          237 pp.
This book is divided into four parts, which are devoted to the socio-
historical and cultural characteristics of Danish immigrants, the diversity
of their religious affiliations in the U.S., their patterns of geographical
distribution, and their contributions to and integration into American
life. Nielsen emphasizes the rapid cultural and structural assimilation
of Danish Americans, their religious diversity, and, in contrast to other
Scandinavian immigrant groups, their lack of geographical concentration
and their dispersion throughout the country.

SOC 190. NOVAK, MICHAEL. The Rise of the Unmeltable Ethnics: Politics
          and Culture in the Seventies. New York: Macmillan, 1972.
          321 pp.
Novak's study of Slavic, Italian, and Greek Americans places these ethnic
groups outside the American "melting pot." He labels these Americans
the unmeltable ethnics and details their lifestyles, aspirations and resent-
ments in American society as well as their cultural and political contributions to American life. Underlying Novak's study is the rejection of
the White Anglo-Saxon Protestant (WASP) conception of America as one ethnically unified nation. In its place Novak advances the concept of a
multi-faceted, ethnically diverse America.

SOC 191. O'CONNELL, BRIAN J. Blacks in White-Collar Jobs. Montclair,
          N.J.: Allanheld Osmun, 1979. 127 pp.
The primary focus of this study is the employment experience of inner-
city blacks and the manner in which they have been affected by and
responded to structural changes in the employment marketplace. The author
is especially concerned with the employment impact of major urban redevelop-
ment schemes. Using statistical analyses of U.S. census data, he demonstrates that the employment experience of black women and men in expanding
white collar jobs is different and that the income gap between blacks
and whites has declined among younger and better educated blacks. Nevertheless, he concludes that the prospects for long-term change in the occupational structure of the black community are "dismal."

SOC 192. PAP, LEO. The Portuguese Americans. Boston: Twayne, 1981.
          300 pp.
This book is divided into two parts. The first part is a history of Portuguese settlement in the U.S. from the discovery of North America to the
1980s, focusing especially on those areas of the country (e.g., the Northeast, California, and Hawaii) where the Portuguese have most heavily clus-
tered. Part II examines the nature of traditional Portuguese cultural
backgrounds and social and communal institutions and the impact that these
have had in affecting their cultural and socio-economic adaptation to American life.

SOC 193. PARENTI, MICHAEL J. Ethnic and Political Attitudes: A Depth
          Study of Italian Americans. New York: Arno Press, 1975.
          344 pp.
Parenti utilized interviews on political views and ethnic sentiments
and experiences to trace the relationship between ethnic and political
attitudes. Eighteen first, second, and third generation Italian Americans
living in New York City provided the field for Parenti's interviews.
Parenti's purpose is to explore how, why and when personal and ethnic
views influence political choices. Many of the findings are presented
in the form of case studies. Interview schedules and vitae of those questioned are included in an appendix.

SOC 194. PARKAY, FORREST W. White Teacher, Black School: The Professional
          Growth of a Ghetto Teacher. New York: Praeger, 1983. 212 pp.
White Teacher, Black School is Parkay's account of his reactions to eight
years of teaching at DuSable High School, on Chicago's South Side. Parkay
creates a typology of teachers—burnouts, altruists, and technicians—and
discusses the attitudes and behavior of each type. He creates a sixfold
typology of students, ranging from the most teachable—the conformists—
to the street-wise and aggressive marginals, who seem to use school as
little more than a convenient setting for displaying feelings of contempt
and rage for those in authority. This book includes Parkay's recommendations for teachers in schools like DuSable. Parkay tries to provide students with success experiences in order to bolster their self-esteem and
their positive feelings about school. He emphasizes general skills such
as learning how to learn and learning to judge the implications of one's
own behavior, rather than specific skills in grammar or composition.

SOC 195. PARSONS, TALCOTT and KENNETH B. CLARD, eds. The Negro American.
          Boston: Houghton Mifflin, 1966. 781 pp.
This collection of essays addresses the various structural causes of racial
prejudice and discrimination in the American social system around 1965.
The essays suggest that a series of structural and institutional changes
was under way in American society in the late 1960s that made possible
the powerful movement for the inclusion of black Americans in the mainstream of life. The contributing editors examine the various "diagnostic
factors" involved in the process of social change: demographic, economic,
familial and personal, identificational and attitudinal. They also analyze
the various sectors of society involved in the process of change and the
internal and external sources of pressure for it.

SOC 196. PATCHEN, MARTIN. Black-White Contact in Schools: Its Social
          and Academic Effects. West Lafayette, Ind.: Purdue University
          Press, 1982. 387 pp.
This study involves a test of the contact theory of race relations, which
posits that prejudice between two groups will be reduced when they possess
equal status and seek common goals. Patchen studied the effects of the
racial composition of the student body on interracial attitudes, behavior,
and academic achievement in twelve Indianapolis high schools of varying
degrees of racial intermixture. He examined a wide range of factors to
assess the impact of desegregation on academic performance. He concludes
that academic performance was less affected by interracial contact than
by other factors, such as IQ scores and types of curriculum.

SOC 197. PETERSEN, WILLIAM. Japanese Americans: Oppression and Success.
          New York: Random House, 1971. 268 pp.
Japanese Americans discusses Japanese migration to Hawaii and the U.S.
mainland and the racial discrimination they encountered there, which ultimately culminated in internment and internal exile. It also recounts
the Japanese-American success story, the story of a racially distinct group
which, despite severe discrimination, defied the majority's socially
ascribed status, overcame the social pathologies thought characteristic
of racial minorities, and rose to the top of the socio-economic ladder.
Petersen suggests that the Japanese are a "deviant case," an anomaly in
the sociology of ethnicity. He believes that the Japanese are in fact
a "subnation" within a nation. It is the Japanese-Americans' "basic group
identity" within that subnation and its socio-cultural standards that
have accounted for their success in the U.S.

SOC 198. PETTIGREW, THOMAS F. A Profile of the Negro American. Princeton,
          N.J.: Van Nostrand, 1964. 250 pp.
The central focus of this book is the frustration and demoralization of
the black personality and black community that result from American society's continual pattern of racial discrimination. Pettigrew argues that
if blacks "had not accepted American society, if they had just adopted
the larger group's values and aspirations, the pattern of discrimination
would not have had such a demoralizing effect. The frustration comes
of his accepting as valuable all that the rest of America treasures, but
being held back from achieving the very goals for which society urges
all citizens to strive." Pettigrew presents a profile of the burden of
being black in white America, delving into problems of health, crime,
and general social organization. The author discusses popular myths and
prejudices about blacks at mid-century and discusses the role of protest
as a response to those myths, prejudices, and patterns of discrimination.

SOC 199. POLL, SOLOMON. The Hasidic Community of Williamsburg: A Study
          in the Sociology of Religion. New York: Free Press of Glencoe,
          1962. 308 pp.
Poll studies the origins and the social and economic life of the New York
Hasidic community which seeks to separate itself not only from non-Jews
but also from more acculturated Jews. The Hasidim, the author notes,
cannot physically isolate themselves from the secular world and are not
ascetic. Instead, they use their own economic resources, and the resources
of the non-Hasidic world (e.g., autos, appliances) to maintain their insularity, to reinforce their religious norms and ritual, and to resist assimilation. The book makes use of Poll's fieldwork among the Williamsburg
Hasidim.

SOC 200. QUAN, ROBERT SETO and JULIAN B. ROEBUCK. Lotus Among the Mag-
          nolias: The Mississippi Chinese. Jackson: University Press
          of Mississippi, 1982. 162 pp.
The Chinese in Mississippi, primarily small grocery store owners, occupy
a social status between whites and blacks. Quan and Roebuck's study
focuses on the nature of the Chinese community in Mississippi and what
it means to be Chinese in such a context. The discussion is organized
around five categories within the Chinese community: the aged, businessmen,
younger professionals, college students, and children. The authors provide
quotations from interviews in order to convey a sense of the world of
the Mississippi Chinese.

SOC 201. RINGER, BENJAMIN B. The Edge of Friendliness: A Study of Jewish-
          Gentile Relations. New York: Basic Books, 1967. 272 pp.
The Edge of Friendliness assesses the Jewish experience in an affluent
Midwestern suburb by means of sociological method. Ringer's subject is
Jewish-Gentile interaction, the questions raised, for those of both faiths,
by the establishment of a significant Jewish presence in a traditionally
Protestant community. Ringer finds that there was resistance to the Jewish
influx, but that more open conflict was rare and that tolerance prevailed.
"Functional" relationships--those developed in businesses, community organizations, neighborhoods--brought the faiths together, creating opportunities
for more extensive and personal interaction. Yet, Ringer concludes, an
"air of uncertainty" remained in these relationships that was exacerbated
by the gentiles' general failure to confront Jewish desires to maintain
a distinctive identity while participating in the life of the community.

SOC 202. RINGER, BENJAMIN B. "We the People" and Others: Duality and
America's Treatment of Its Racial Minorities. New York:
Tavistock, 1983. 1165 pp.
In this study Ringer examines America's treatment of racial minorities
from Colonial English settlements to the present. He contends that race
relations in the U.S. have been characterized by a structural duality
between what he terms the "Domain of the People" (the economic and politically dominant white society) and the domain of blacks, Native Americans,
Asians, and Puerto Ricans. This duality is the legacy, he argues, of
the two processes of colonization and colonialization. The book focuses
primarily on the nation's legal and political institutions, and the manner
in which they have contributed to the exploitation of non-white racial
groups.

SOC 203. ROGG, ELEANOR MEYER. The Assimilation of Cuban Exiles: The
Role of Community and Class. New York: Aberdeen, 1974.
241 pp.
Rogg presents a picture of the 750,000 Cubans in the U.S. in the mid-1970s.
The Cubans have sought exile in America since the rise of Fidel Castro's
socialist regime in 1959. Their exile has assumed a permanence that few
of them ever desired or expected. Nonetheless, they have "adjusted" more
rapidly in their exile than any other immigrant group in American history.
Studying the tightly knit community of exiles in Western New York and
New Jersey, Rogg examines occupational and educational adjustment, patterns
of acculturation, and the functional and dysfunctional effects of social
class and community in the process of assimilation. She concludes that
"community may slow acculturation in the short-run but not stop it; at
the same time it reduces the adjustment problems of its members. The
strong ethnic community has been favorable in the assimilation process
of this group of Cubans by slowing it to a manageable pace."

SOC 204. ROSE, PETER I. They and We: Racial and Ethnic Relations in the
U.S. New York: Random House, 1964. 177 pp.
The principal aspects of racial and ethnic relations in the U.S. are the
subject of this book. Rose presents a summation of what social scientists
have learned about America's racial and ethnic minorities. Also discussed
are the nature of prejudice and the extent of discrimination in the U.S.;
the immigrant experience; and the reaction of minority groups to discriminatory treatment. Rose hopes that the facts he presents will dispel some
of the popular misconceptions surrounding this topic. A note on research
in the field is included.

SOC 205. ROSE, PETER I., ed. The Ghetto and Beyond: Essays on Jewish
Life in America. New York: Random House, 1969. 504 pp.
This book includes articles by such scholars and writers as S. M. Lipset,
Daniel Aaron, Marshall Sklare, Alfred Kazin, Daniel Bell, and Philip Roth.
Peter Rose introduces the collection with a brief history of the Jewish
community in America and the nation's image of the Jew. The essays that
follow consider Jews' attitudes toward American reality and ideals, and
their relations with other Americans, including blacks and the Protestant
elite. Examined, as well, are Jewish religious and intellectual life,
Jews' role in American culture, and their political involvement with socialism and Civil Rights.

SOC 206. ROSS, A. MICHAEL and WILLIAM M. BERG. "I Respectfully Disagree
with the Judge's Order": The Boston School Desegregation Controversy. Lanham, Md.: University Press of America, 1981.
746 pp.
Based primarily on media coverage, this is a chronicle of events surrounding the Boston school desegregation controversy from 1963 to 1975. The
case study raises general questions concerning the dynamics of school

desegregation. By examining the roles of elected and appointed leaders, it focuses on how the conflict was managed by city officials. Moreover, it considers the tension between the actions of local officials and the involvement of the Federal courts. Finally, the book discusses the implications of the role of the mass media in the Boston crisis and the prospects of preventing violence in other school desegregation situations.

SOC 207. SAMORA, JULIAN, ed. La Raza: Forgotten Americans. Notre Dame, Ind.: University of Notre Dame Press, 1966. 218 pp.
As Samora explains, "this collection of papers attempts an assessment of the status of a minority population of the Southwestern United States concentrated in California, Texas, New Mexico, Arizona, and Colorado." Topics and issues covered in the seven papers include: history, culture, and education; the role of the Christian church; leadership and politics; the migrant worker; Civil Rights and equal opportunity; community participation and the middle class; and demographic characteristics of Mexican-Americans.

SOC 208. SCANZONI, JOHN H. The Black Family in Modern Society. Boston: Allyn & Bacon, 1971. 353 pp.
Scanzoni's study examines certain assumptions about the black American family. The data presented were gathered from black households in Indianapolis in early 1968. Scanzoni focuses on structural background factors of the husbands and wives interviewed on parental functionality, on their identification with their own parents, and on their achievement and mobility. The final section, which focuses on their relationship with their children, presents Scanzoni's substantive, theoretical, and practical conclusions. Scanzoni writes that the book "tries to grapple with pivotal theoretical issues linking stratification, socialization, husband-wife interaction, marital stability, the opportunity system, along with acceptance, persistence, and change of family structures within modern society."

SOC 209. SCHOFIELD, JANET WARD. Black and White in School: Trust, Tension, or Tolerance? New York: Praeger, 1982. 255 pp.
This is a description and analysis of peer relations in Wexler School, a middle school. Heralded on its opening as a model of high quality education and racial integration, four years later, heavily black, it was characterized as "a racial timebomb ticking toward disaster." The study examines the internal dynamics of the school, focusing especially on the relationship between race and gender. It also explores the impact of external factors--the policies of the school board, the broader politics of the city, and the city's class structure--on the development, maintenance, and change in race relations in the school during its first three years. The author concludes with a discussion of some of the conceptual and policy implications of her findings.

SOC 210. SCHRAG, PETER. The Vanishing Americans: The Decline and Fall of the White Anglo Saxon Protestant. London: Gollancz, 1972. 255 pp.
"He was our man," writes Schrag, ". . . Part Leatherstocking, part Teddy Roosevelt, part John Wayne, with a little Ben Franklin thrown in for good measure--frontiersman, cowboy, soldier, entrepreneur--plus a lot of other things besides, . . . red, white, and blue, free white and twenty-one." This is the WASP--the White-Anglo-Saxon-Protestant--who made America and who was to be emulated by all who came here. Schrag points to the progressive decline of that prototypic American, and the attendant ethic of success and mobility within American society. "It happens gradually," the author comments, "but you can notice suddenly a new crowd, new faces, new styles, a new sound: un-WASP, non-WASP, anti-WASP." Schrag looks at what is happening to the life and self-image of the WASP as a consequence of displacement.

SOC 211. **SEGAL, GERALDINE R.** Blacks in the Law: Philadelphia and the
Nation. Philadelphia: University of Pennsylvania Press, 1983.
313 pp.
Two themes are presented in this book: first, that the law is a potent
instrument for promoting (or resisting) social change in American society,
and black participation in the legal system is of crucial importance;
second, that the civil rights movement prompted a significant increase
in the number of black lawyers. This study includes Segal's earlier study
of Philadelphia black lawyers as well as a national assessment of blacks
in the legal profession. It took the Brown vs. Board of Education Supreme
Court decision to stimulate white law schools to think of admitting more
black students, and it took the civil rights movement and the Federal
legislation it influenced to induce these schools to action. In 1980
Segal solicited information on black lawyers in fifteen cities, besides
Philadelphia, in which there was at least one law firm with ninety or
more lawyers. The author concludes that black lawyers in these cities
have made some progress but that blacks are still substantially underrepresented in the profession.

SOC 212. **SELZNICK, GERTRUDE J.** and **STEPHEN STEINBERG.** The Tenacity of
Prejudice: Anti-Semitism in Contemporary America. New York:
Harper & Row, 1969. 248 pp.
This study, conducted in the mid-1960s and based on a survey of the attitudes and practices of a cross-national representative sample of individuals, reveals some disturbing facts about the persistence of prejudice
against American Jews over the two decades after W.W. II. The first part
of the book examines anti-Semitism along three dimensions: the beliefs
about Jews, support of discriminatory practices, and susceptibility to
political anti-Semitism, and the social and demographic strata in which
anti-Semitism is most prevalent, through an examination of education,
occupation, income, age, sex, nation of origin, religion, region, and
race. The final section seeks an explanation for the tenacity of prejudice,
presenting a theoretical analysis of the impact of education and other
factors on the persistence of anti-Semitic and anti-black prejudice.
The researchers conclude that "anti-Semitism continues at significant
levels, and lack of education is the primary factor in its acceptance."

SOC 213. **SEXTON, PATRICIA CAYO.** Spanish Harlem. New York: Harper &
Row, 1965. 208 pp.
Sexton's account of life and culture in Spanish Harlem begins with a historical overview of the area and the various ethnic groups--German, Italian,
black, and Puerto Rican--which have inhabited it since the end of the 19th
century. The author devotes separate chapters to considerations of urban
renewal projects, the schools, the role of religion as "tranquilizers
and agitators," and power structures in the inner city. In addition,
Sexton discusses the emerging community organization, development, and
mobilization, and the function of local initiatives such as community
schools, study clubs, and cooperatives in effecting change. A separate
chapter devoted to issues of politics and policy examines the inequities
in distribution of Federal funds and work programs in Spanish Harlem,
and explores various policy alternatives for social and economic growth.

SOC 214. **SHANNON, LYLE** and **MAGDALINE SHANNON.** Minority Migrants in the
Urban Community. Beverly Hills, Calif.: Sage, 1973. 352 pp.
Racine, Wisconsin in 1960 provides the setting for this study on Mexican
and black migrants in a predominantly Anglo society. The book's basic
intent is to determine which factors facilitated or impeded the assimilation of immigrants who had left their rural origins in the South for
Racine. This work concentrates on measuring the extent to which each
group was assimilated into the industrial economy and urban society.
Included are tables, maps and statistical data.

1727

SOC 215.   SIDORSKY, DAVID, ed.   The Future of the Jewish Community in
           America.   New York: Basic Books, 1973.   324 pp.
This collection of scholarly articles explores issues which continue to
be raised by the Jewish community's historic urge both to integrate into
the American mainstream and to retain its distinctive identity.   The complex
nature of these issues is reflected in the broad range of topics and of
approaches employed.   These include demographic and sociological profiles
of the Jewish community, considerations of how that community has been
shaped by ideological movements such as Zionism, examinations of its chief
institutions, i.e., school and synagogue, and a grappling with the questions posed by the 1960s youth culture, by the nature of Jewish education,
and by decision-making within Jewish organizations.

SOC 216.   SILBERMAN, CHARLES E.   Crisis in Black and White.   New York:
           Random House, 1964.   370 pp.
The problem of the black in America, according to Silberman, consists
of more than can be solved by a civil rights bill, better education, better
housing, and better jobs.   The 350 years of oppression of blacks in America,
and the complete humiliation of a race, cannot be eradicated easily.
In this work, Silberman argues that efforts must be made to restore black
Americans' dignity and to incorporate them into the economic and political
power structure of America, for only then will they be able to move within
the mainstream of American society.   Silberman argues for affirmative
action, and for public policy efforts to provide black Americans with
access to positions of power which historically have been denied them.

SOC 217.   SIMON, RITA JAMES and HOWARD ALTSTEIN.   Transracial Adoption.
           New York: Wiley, 1977.   197 pp.
In 1971, when Simon and Altstein began their research on the adoption
of black, Indian, and Asian children by whites, such adoptions had contributed to a substantial diminution in the number of such children in
public institutions.   However, by the time they had finished their research
in 1976, transracial adoption had become so controversial that it had
almost disappeared.   This study provides a discussion of the issues
involved in transracial adoption, and of "the implications of decisions
and rules currently enacted that affect the destiny of these children."
Simon and Altstein describe the history, prevalence, and types of transracial adoption in the U.S., basing their work on survey data obtained
from 204 white families who adopted nonwhite children.   The authors treat
the characteristics of the adopting parents and families, the parents'
motivations for adoption, the nature of the children's social awareness,
and the ways in which the parents sought to influence this process.

SOC 218.   SIMON, RITA JAMES and HOWARD ALTSTEIN.   Transracial Adoption:
           A Followup.   Lexington, Mass.: Lexington Books, 1981.
           147 pp.
This is a "second installment" of a study on transracial adoption.   Simon
and Altstein located 71% of the parents in their original sample, and
describe what happened to the families in the intervening years.   This
volume "focuses on the parents' relations with their transracially adopted
child(ren), on the siblings' relations with each other, on the parents'
perception of the adopted child's future identity."   Simon and Altstein
also question whether the transracial adoption has "introduced special
strains or problems or provided them with quantifications," and discuss
the continuing debate over transracial adoption and the prospects of such
adoption in the future.

SOC 219. **SKLARE, MARSHALL**. America's Jews. New York: Random House, 1971. 234 pp.
Sklare seeks to provide an "alternative to other treatments of American-Jewish life." He discusses the social history, group identity, and social characteristics of American Jewry. He explores family and kinship patterns within the Jewish community as well as such mechanisms for "transmission" of Jewish identity as religion, community organizations, and social services. Discussing the educational locus of Jewish identity, he looks at American-Jewish education in afternoon school, Sunday school, day school, and adult study. He analyzes the social interaction of Jews and Gentiles, the ease of intermarriage, and the Jewish response. Finally, he discusses the American Jewish community's relationship to Israel.

SOC 220. **SKLARE, MARSHALL**, ed. The Jew in American Society. New York: Behrman House, 1974. 404 pp.
This book makes available writings of social scientists who have studied the American Jew. The compilation—a companion to Sklare's earlier reader, The Jews: Social Patterns of an American Group (see SOC 234)—presents a sociological treatment which assesses contemporary issues and their historical backgrounds. The introductory essay urges a closer link between contemporary Jewish studies and other academic disciplines; the remainder of the book is organized around broad topics such as social history, social characteristics, the family, and Jewish religion and identity. Articles include Lloyd P. Gartner's "Immigration and the Formation of American Jewry, 1840-1952"; Sidney Goldstein, "American Jewry 1970: A Demographic Profile"; and Seymour Martin Lipset and Everett C. Ladd, Jr., "Jewish Academics in the United States."

SOC 221. **SKLARE, MARSHALL**, ed. The Jews: Social Patterns of an American Group. Glencoe, Ill.: Free Press, 1958. 669 pp.
This reader in the sociology of the American Jewish community includes material from dissertations and unpublished research reports and surveys. The articles are grouped into sections devoted to historical background, demography and social mobility, community life, religion, the psychological experience and the culture and value of American Jewry. Topics addressed include the social composition of the Jewish community, participation in the larger American community, aspects of group identification, parent-child relations, mental health, and political behavior.

SOC 222. **SKLARE, MARSHALL** and **JOSEPH GREENBLUM**. Jewish Identity on the Suburban Frontier. 1967; Rev. ed. Chicago: University of Chicago Press, 1979. 437 pp.
This consideration of "Jewishness" and acculturation in American society is based on an examination of "Lakeville," a prosperous Midwestern suburb. This case study explores issues of Jewish identity as expressed in individuals' relationships to religion and religious institutions, to Israel, to Jewish organizations, to friends and kin. The bulk of the data was gathered in the late 1950s; this revised edition evaluates developments since that time, such as the transformation of "Lakeville" into a predominantly Jewish community.

SOC 223. **SLAWSON, JOHN**. Unequal Americans: Practices and Politics of Intergroup Relations. Westport, Conn.: Greenwood Press, 1979. 249 pp.
Unequal Americans analyzes the principles used by policy-makers, specialists, and practitioners dealing with intergroup conflict. It is concerned "primarily with clarifying the methodology in the field of intergroup relations. It seems to ascertain the kind of social change and alterations in mental attitude that might contribute to (1) improved relationships among racial, ethnic, and religious groups in the U.S., (2) the achievement of equality of opportunity for all groups, and (3) the improvement of

1729

the social quality of life within these groups." Based on tape-recorded interviews conducted in 1970 with intergroup relations specialists, the book seeks to determine the dynamics and processes for dealing with problems of intergroup relations and the most effective methods for alleviating and preventing intergroup conflict.

SOC 224. SLEEPER, JAMES A. and ALAN L. MINTZ, eds. The New Jews. New
York: Vintage Books, 1971. 264 pp.
This book consists of essays by young American Jews who identify with
the counterculture's perception of the shallowness of middle class life
in the U.S. They seek meaning and knowledge in Jewish tradition and
spirituality—a sense of identity, commitment, and community as remedies
to the alienation and rootlessness of mainstream society and mainstream
American Judaism. The articles address such topics as a new Jewish communalism; the Jewish contribution to contemporary radicalism; the state
of Israel; theology; Jewish education; and Jews and the arts.

SOC 225. SORKIN, ALAN L. The Urban American Indian. Lexington, Mass.:
Heath, 1978. 158 pp.
Today more than half of the Native American population lives in cities.
Sorkin provides a primarily economic analysis of the social and economic
status of urban Indians and the nature of the health, housing, educational,
and occupational services available (or unavailable) to them. He advances
a three stage model of the development of urban Indian institutions: (1)
bar culture; (2) Indian centers and friendship networks; and (3) pan-Indian
ethnic organizations. Sorkin is critical of the paucity of Federal assistance to urban Indians and uses statistical data to demonstrate their
extremely disadvantaged status.

SOC 226. STEINBERG, STEPHEN. The Ethnic Myth: Race, Ethnicity, and Class
in America. New York: Atheneum, 1981. 277 pp.
Steinberg rejects arguments that blacks or other racial minorities suffer
from a culture of poverty, that Catholics are anti-intellectual, that
Jews are ethnically favored to succeed in the professions, and that the
success or failure of any immigrant group derives principally from its
cultural values. In studying the mobility of Jews and blacks, why Irish
rather than Italian immigrant girls became domestic servants, the persistence of racial prejudice, the political agenda of the "New Ethnicity,"
and educational and employment patterns among several racial and ethnic
groups, Steinberg argues that class rather than culture determines social
and political loyalties and that the timing of a group's arrival in a
particular socio-economic situation largely determines that group's upward
mobility.

SOC 227. TAYLOR, PAUL S. Mexican Labor in the United States. 2 vols.
Berkeley: University of California Press, 1930, 1931.
748 pp.
The work is a series of monographic studies, mainly comparing and contrasting the social and economic status of Mexican immigrants in various regions
of the U.S. Taylor presents analyses of selected areas of California,
Colorado, and Texas, in light of the agricultural industry in those regions;
and also of Chicago and the Calumet region, Bethlehem, Pennsylvania and
Nueces County, Texas against the background of Eastern industry and Southwestern cotton culture. Topical essays include: a comparison of American
and Mexican official statistics of the mass immigration; and a statistical
analysis of racial aspects of California elementary schools. The studies
are heavily statistical, but are also based on personal interviews. Major
themes include: cultural, language, and class barriers which keep Mexicans
separate from the mainstream; urban, industrial versus rural, agricultural
conditions; and the role of racial prejudice in the status of Mexicans.

SOC 228. THOMAS, WILLIAM I. and FLORIAN ZNANIECKI. The Polish Peasant in Europe and America: Monograph of an Immigrant Group. 2 vols. Chicago: University of Chicago Press, 1918. 1114 pp.
The authors have taken the Polish peasants as the subject of this documentary book on immigration and immigrant life. Volume one contains a study of the organization of peasant society and an analysis of the class structure in Poland, as well as samplings of letters written between family members in Poland and America. Volume two is a continuation of these letter samplings, from which the dissolution of familial solidarity is noted by the authors. There is an introduction to each family whose letters are published detailing the family's particular circumstances in Poland as well as in the U.S. after their immigration.

SOC 229. THOMPSON, DANIEL C. Sociology of the Black Experience. Westport, Conn.: Greenwood Press, 1974. 261 pp.
Thompson believes that the "Black Experience" necessitates a new black sociology, as "white sociology" has frequently accepted white middle America as the sociological norm. Thompson hopes to further develop and refine the dynamic concept of the "Black Experience" within the broad context of American history and culture, focusing on the family, socialization, and social organization of the American black ghetto and also examining the education and mobility patterns of black Americans. To Thompson, "when the concept of Black Experience is systematically defined, it promises to open up new vistas of research, analyses, interpretation and understanding in the sociology of race relations. It will suggest dimensions of racial adjustments, dynamics, and changes that have been generally overlooked or under-emphasized by sociologists, particularly influential white sociologists."

SOC 230. THRASHER, FREDERIC M. The Gang: A Study of 1,313 Gangs in Chicago. Chicago: University of Chicago Press, 1927. 605 pp.
Thrasher seeks to show the gang as a particular "type" of human group and one that is spontaneous in origin. He studies the different types of gangs and then turns to the motivations of the gang members which brought them into association. He suggests that gangs crop up because of the abundance of unsupervised leisure time and the lack of proper social activities. The life of the gang, according to Thrasher, is the quest for new experience. He examines the issue of race and nationality in the gang but concludes that conflicts are more class-oriented than nationality-oriented. He also examines the place of sex in the gang, and the internal dynamics and leadership patterns of the gang. He concludes with a chapter in which he suggests ways to combat the "gang problem."

SOC 231. UHLMAN, THOMAS M. Racial Justice: Black Judges and Defendants in an Urban Trial Court. Lexington, Mass.: Heath, 1979. 121 pp.
Uhlman contends that the relationship between the legal process and race involves two interrelated dimensions: internal—the causes and consequences of black under-representation in the legal profession and the judiciary—and external—the racially discriminatory decisions of courts. Using a major urban trial court as his focus, he examines the backgrounds and behavior of sixteen black judges and the treatment of over 34,000 black felony defendants. His objective is to "determine whether 'race makes a difference' in this court and, if so, exactly what the differences are."

SOC 232. VARADY, DAVID P. Ethnic Minorities in Urban Areas: A Case Study of Racially Changing Communities. Boston: Martinus Nijhoff, 1979. 187 pp.

This study examines the characteristics and causes of racial change in a middle to upper-middle class, predominantly Jewish, residential neighborhood in Philadelphia. Employing a two-stage sample survey of neighborhood residents in 1969 and 1974, the author seeks to determine the factors influencing the move-stay decisions of white householders. The decision by whites to move was influenced by several factors: (a) unwillingness to live as part of a racial minority, (b) the perceived quality of one's home, (c) concern about street crime, and (d) attitude toward Jewish-gentile relations. The author concludes that Jewish identity affected the decision to remain or, if one moved, the choice of a new neighborhood. He concludes with several neighborhood stabilization policy recommendations.

SOC 233. WACKER, R. FRED. Ethnicity, Pluralism, and Race: Race Relations Theory in America Before Myrdal. Westport, Conn.: Greenwood Press, 1983. 114 pp.

Wacker examines the contributions and basic assumptions of the sociologists who analyzed American racial and ethnic relations before publication of Myrdal's An American Dilemma in 1944. Among them are Robert E. Park, W. I. Thomas, E. Franklin Frazier, Everett Hughes, Horace Kallen, and Charles S. Johnson. The author assesses their contributions, which recently have been the object of considerable criticism for their "unscientific" research procedures. However, Wacker contends that much of this recent criticism fails to recognize the objectivity and rigor of these early sociologists and, especially, that it fails to acknowledge the debt that contemporary research on racial and ethnic relations owes them.

SOC 234. WALLACE, PHYLLIS A., LINDA DATCHER, and JULIANNE MALVEAUX. Black Women in the Labor Force. Cambridge, Mass.: MIT Press, 1980. 163 pp.

This book provides information on the activity in the marketplace of black women. Black women are found to have a labor market experience that differs from that of white women or black males. A review is provided of the conflicting findings and major economic studies concerning black female employment. These data indicate that some of the economic theories that relate to working women with families cannot be directly applied to black women. The authors point to the negative effects of racial discrimination in the marketplace, the lower black male income, the deficiencies in human capital, and the impact of urban labor markets as factors that impinge upon black working women.

SOC 235. WASKOW, ARTHUR I. The Bush Is Burning! Radical Judaism Faces the Pharaohs of the Modern Superstate. New York: Macmillan, 1971. 177 pp.

This work evaluates the contemporary status of Judaism world-wide and presents Waskow's personal relationship to his own heritage. Waskow, a "Radical Jew," first describes his own awakening to Judaism and his involvement with the Jewish communities in America and Israel. In subsequent chapters he analyzes the contemporary, political-religious situation of international Jewish culture by relating it to the ancient scriptures, and warns that the Jewish people today face a profound religious crisis which must be addressed.

SOC 236. WAXMAN, CHAIM I. American Jews in Transition. Philadelphia: Temple University Press, 1983. 272 pp.

This is a socio-historical study of the generational processes of Jewish adaptation to American society with special focus on the social patterns of contemporary American Jewry. Writing from an "unambiguously survivalist" perspective, Waxman examines the internal and external developments between 1964 and 1975 which influenced the fourth generation of Eastern

European Jews, and he provides a collective portrait of the social characteristics of the contemporary American Jewish community. He concludes with an assessment of the future prospects for American Jewry, which "lead one, especially a survivalist, to wavering between optimism and pessimism."

SOC 237. WEED, PERRY L. The White Ethnic Movement and Ethnic Politics. New York: Praeger, 1973. 243 pp.
In this study Weed places the revival of interest in America's white ethnic groups into a historical perspective, concentrating on group action and ethnic politics. In examining the importance of ethnicity in American society, Weed contends that ethnicity is an "independent predictor variable as important as socio-economic class." Examined in the book are: the components of the white ethnic movement and its major institutional forces; the role of ethnicity in community organization movements; the emergence of ethnic politics in the 1960s; and the reactions of both the Democratic and Republican parties to white ethnic awareness and the political implications of those reactions. Weed concludes his study with a section on the prospects for ethnic politics in the 1970s.

SOC 238. WEISBORD, ROBERT G. and ARTHUR STEIN. Bittersweet Encounter: The Afro-American and the American Jew. New York: Schocken Books, 1972. 242 pp.
The ambivalent relationships between Jewish and black Americans have been characterized by both symbiosis and conflict; the authors of Bittersweet Encounter explore black anti-Semitism and Jewish racism and provide insight into the historically divergent experiences of the two groups which may have fostered the friction. Unequal status encounters during the 1960s are cited as the primary reasons for flare-ups of conflict. However, many leaders and activists in the black struggle for power were liberal and radical Jews, and many blacks had favorable or mixed reactions to Jews even during this period of increased antagonism.

SOC 239. WESTFRIED, ALEX HUXLEY. Ethnic Leadership in a New England Community: Three Puerto Rican Families. Cambridge, Mass.: Schenkman, 1981. 176 pp.
This study of ethnic leadership among Puerto Ricans in a New England community focuses on the life histories of four ethnic leaders. College educated professionals, they are confronted with the dilemma of "reconciling their ethnic norms of behavior with the demands of American society." Westfried combines participant observation and life history approaches in order "to show to what degree a Puerto Rican leader maintains his own cultural traditions, to what degree he modifies them in America, and what aspects of American culture he finds it useful to adopt."

SOC 240. WHYTE, WILLIAM FOOTE. Street Corner Society: The Social Structure of an Italian Slum. Chicago: University of Chicago Press, 1943. 284 pp.
Whyte analyzes the social structure of the typical Italian slum in an Eastern city through presentation of the various interactions in a neighborhood which he calls "Cornerville." Whyte presents the inhabitants as individuals, rather than as social-work clients or potential defendants in criminal cases—the latter being stereotypes adopted by the "outside world." The social structure is seen as based on a network of mutual obligations which encompass both familial and fraternal organizations. The slum, according to Whyte, does not lack organization, but the social organization fails to mesh with the structure of the society around it.

SOC 241. WILLIAMS, LORETTA J. Black Freemasonry and Middle-Class Realities. Columbia: University of Missouri Press, 1980. 165 pp.
This book is a socio-historical analysis of the role and significance of Prince Hall Freemasonry, which was founded over 200 years ago as a result of the exclusion of American blacks from the Masons, and subsequently became the first nationally organized black institution. Williams analyzes the creation, development, characteristics, and functions of Prince Hall Masonry, which she interprets as a microcosm of the societal pressures confronting middle class black males. Her study is based on an explanatory model of "status incongruity," in which the black middle class experiences "strains due to discrepancies in status related to their being, simultaneously, achievers occupationally and socioeconomically, and members of a group stigmatized due to racial ascription as being of a lower social status."

SOC 242. WILLIAMS, ROBIN M., Jr., with JOHN P. DEAN and EDWARD A. SUCHMAN. Strangers Next Door: Ethnic Relations in American Communities. Englewood Cliffs, N.J.: Prentice-Hall, 1964. 434 pp.
This book presents a summary and synthesis of the researches conducted by a number of participants in the Cornell Studies in Inter-group Relations from 1948 to 1956. It provides a synopsis of the various theories and empirical data about inter-ethnic relations in America in our recent past. Williams explores the sociological dimensions of ethnocentrism and its more injurious manifestation in racial/ethnic prejudice. He examines the relationships of personality factors to prejudice and looks at the consequences of prejudice, discrimination, segregation, conflict, and protest. The senior author and others treat the dynamics of social interaction and intergroup attitudes—situational variation, exemption, structure, and process—in a multigroup society.

SOC 243. WILLIE, CHARLES VERT. The Ivory and Ebony Towers: Race Relations and Higher Education. Lexington, Mass.: Heath, 1981. 173 pp.
"This book is a comparative analysis of the adaptations of black and of white students to each other and to their teachers and administrators in institutions of higher education." Among the topics considered are school desegregation, whites as a minority, recruitment, financial aid, standardized testing, the lives of black students on white campuses and white students on black campuses, and the moral and ethical responsibilities of campus administrators.

SOC 244. WILSON, WILLIAM JULIUS. The Declining Significance of Race: Blacks and Changing American Institutions. 1978; Rev. ed. Chicago: University of Chicago Press, 1980. 243 pp.
This book is an analysis of the changing relationship between race and class in the American experience. Wilson distinguishes among three major periods of black-white relations in American history: preindustrial, industrial, and modern industrial, each of which reflects changes in black America's relation to the country's economic and political institutions. The primary focus of the book is on the past quarter century, the modern industrial period, during which, Wilson argues, "class has become more important than race in determining black access to privilege and power." Educated blacks increasingly have experienced substantial economic and preoccupational gains while the status of the uneducated and unskilled black underclass has deteriorated. The second edition includes an essay in which Wilson responds to some of his critics and extends his discussion of race, class, and public policy.

SOC 245. WILSON, WILLIAM JULIUS. Racism and Privilege: Race Relations
in Theoretical Sociohistorical Perspectives. New York:
Macmillan, 1973. 224 pp.
History, theory, and comparative analysis are joined in this examination
of intergroup relations in the U.S. and South Africa. Wilson applies
the "power-conflict" model (explained in Part I of the book) and asserts
that "both historical patterns of overt conflict and processes of integration in [South Africa and the U.S.] are largely explained in terms
of a theoretical framework of power." He qualifies this conclusion by
affirming the role of the ideology of racism in defining the nature of
intergroup relations. However, racism itself, he suggests, can be considered a function of an unequal power relationship. The extent of restric-
tiveness of the social structure is also found to be a key variable.

SOC 246. WOLF, ELEANOR P. Trial and Error: The Detroit School Segregation
Case. Detroit, Mich.: Wayne State University Press, 1981.
372 pp.
Trial and Error addresses the issue of racial isolation in Northern metropolitan school systems—substantially black inner city schools surrounded
by white suburban school systems. A major legal and sociological source
of contention has been the extent to which this segregation has been the
result of deliberate state action. Wolf examines these issues in the
litigation over the case of Bradley v. Milliken, which involved the racial
segregation of the Detroit public schools. The initial judgment of this
case was that racial isolation in the Detroit metropolitan area derived
from state action, and the judicial remedy involved a massive exchange
of students between Detroit and fifty-two suburban school districts.
Although the case was ultimately overridden by a divided Supreme Court,
the issues arising from it are still crucial to understanding the dynamics
of race relations in contemporary America.

SOC 247. ZORBAUGH, HARVEY W. The Gold Coast and the Slum: A Sociological
Study of Chicago's Near North Side. Chicago: University of
Chicago Press, 1929. 287 pp.
Zorbaugh's main concern in this work is the lack of any sense of community
and the disintegration of traditional forms of local government and institutions in the North Side of Chicago. The lack of local feelings, consciousness, and action is equally as apparent in the Gold Coast, with
its social rituals and social climbing, as it is in the rooming-house
district and the slum areas. Zorbaugh discusses the various neighborhoods—
Irish, German, Sicilian, Swedish, and black—as well as bohemia and "hobo-
hemia." He suggests that the sense of community had become a territorial
expression and that this trend should be recognized by community institutions adapted to meet this change.

IV.   FAMILY, SOCIALIZATION, AND EDUCATION

SOC 248. ADKINS, DOUGLAS L. The Great American Degree Machine: An Economic Analysis of the Human Resource Output of Higher Education.
Berkeley, Calif.: Carnegie Council on Policy Studies in Higher
Education, 1975. 663 pp.
That the American university system produces more degree holders than
the various academic disciplines can hold is part of the conventional
wisdom. However, little hard data have been collected on the extent of
that overproduction. This study fills a gap in the literature. Combining
statistical methodology and interpretive discussion, Adkins provides estimates of the annual degree output in the U.S. from 1890 to 1971, the age

distribution of degree recipients in certain years, the transition fre-
quencies and time-lapse distributions for the attainment of higher degrees
by holders of lower degrees, and the characteristics of degree holders
from 1930 to 1971. The analysis provides a statistical overview of growth
trends in "degree production."

SOC 249.   ALBRECHT, STAN L., HOWARD M. BAHR, and KRISTEN L. GOODMAN.
           Divorce and Remarriage: Problems, Adaptations, and Adjustments.
           Westport, Conn.: Greenwood Press, 1983. 211 pp.
The subject of this study is the dramatically increasing rate of divorce
in the U.S. Using data drawn from a sample of divorced persons living
in the eight intermountain states (Arizona, Colorado, Idaho, Montana,
Nevada, New Mexico, Utah, and Wyoming), the authors focus on divorce from
the perspective of those who experience it. They are concerned with "how
the individual makes the decision to terminate an unsuccessful marriage,
the constraints that are imposed on this decision, how these constraints
are overcome, [and] the adjustment process following the divorce. . . ."
Moreover, they examine the question of remarriage and the adjustment of
those who remarry.

SOC 250.   BAHR, HOWARD M., SPENCER J. CONDIE, and KRISTEN L. GOODMAN.
           Life in Large Families: Views of Mormon Women. Lanham, Md.:
           University Press of America, 1982. 254 pp.
Large families have become an anomaly in recent American life. However,
the belief system of the Church of Jesus Christ of Latter-Day Saints
strongly encourages them. The data for this study of large families are
derived from interviews with forty-one women who had had at least seven
children. All of the women were college graduates married to college
graduates, and they all resided in a single Utah county. The authors
focus on the advantages and rewards of life in large families and on the
dynamics of large family life. In addition to examining why these women
had chosen to have large families, they explore how they organize household
life, their self-perceptions, their perceptions of their husbands, their
marriages, and their responses to current women's issues.

SOC 251.   BANE, MARY JO. Here to Stay: American Families in the Twentieth
           Century. New York: Basic Books, 1976. 195 pp.
Bane denies that the modern American family is in trouble; American families are "here to stay." She argues that there is little, if any, historical evidence that family life in the past was any more highly valued
or more stable than today. She claims that family structure and mobility
in modern America is not much different today from what it was in the
past: the extended family has not declined—it never existed; only the
cause of family disruption has changed—from death to divorce; today's
families do not have fewer neighbors and friends to call upon for help.
The second half of her book involves consideration of contemporary policy
issues concerning the family—day care, maternity and child care leaves,
financial support laws in divorce cases, the legality of marriage contracts,
children's rights. Her thesis is that there is a tension in American life
between the values of family life, privacy, and its role in raising children, on the one hand, and other social values—sexual equality, protection
of children against abuse and neglect, provision of equal opportunities
for children and adequate care for the aged—on the other.

SOC 252.   BECKER, HOWARD S., BLANCHE GEER, EVERETT C. HUGHES, and
           ANSELM L. STRAUSS. Boys in White: Student Culture in Medical
           School. Chicago: University of Chicago Press, 1961. 456 pp.
In this report of a study undertaken at the University of Kansas Medical
School in 1956 and 1957 by a team of social scientists, the authors examine student choices and expectations, the areas in which conflicts
arise for students, and the way these influence their later activities

as doctors. The authors show that students tacitly and collectively set their academic priorities through pragmatic day-to-day decisions related to their long-term career goals. They discuss the idea of a student culture and look at the ways in which a student's individual identity is overshadowed by his identity as a student.

SOC 253. BENSON, LEONARD G. Fatherhood: A Sociological Perspective. New York: Random House, 1968. 371 pp.
While much sociological research on marriage and family life deals with social and psychological theories of motherhood, little has been written on the American father's role. In his introductory chapter Benson reviews the findings of earlier research on fatherhood. He explores the psychosocial dimensions of fatherhood, the role interactions between fathers and mothers, and the "passing of the patriarch." Benson also provides a view of the "man as parent," focusing on the parental figure as a role model and stabilizing force and on the father as "the breadwinner." The demands of both of these roles result in extraordinary emotional and psychological pressures on the father. Benson concludes that, "In a sense, the family has become more important to father, even as he has become relatively less important to the family. Once father was the prime agent of family strength; now he is often reliant upon it, especially for emotional sustenance."

SOC 254. BERGER, BRIGITTE and PETER L. BERGER. The War over the Family: Capturing the Middle Ground. Garden City, N.Y.: Anchor Press, 1983. 252 pp.
The Bergers believe that families will act responsibly if government leaves them alone, and they direct their ire against the "knowledge class," or the vast educational system, the therapeutic "helping" complex, sizeable portions of the government bureaucracy, the media, and the publishing industries. From the Bergers' perspective, Feminism was from the first a demand for "freedom from the family," which developed into a huge outcry against being female and also fed into an anti-family mood created by sexual liberationists, gay rights activists, the human potential movement, and the New Left.

SOC 255. BERK, RICHARD A. and SARAH FENSTERMAKER BERK. Labor and Leisure at Home: Content and Organization of the Household Day. Beverly Hills, Calif.: Sage, 1979. 280 pp.
This study is concerned with a little studied, frequently mundane, but critical phenomenon--the nature of the routine activities people daily undertake in their homes, including child care, cleaning and maintenance of the home, and the preparation of meals. The authors maintain that "despite the fact that people invest enormous amounts of time and energy in their household lives, we have little empirical information on the nature of these dynamic allocations or the mechanisms by which they occur." They are not merely interested in how much time is allocated to various activities but the sequence in which activities are undertaken and how time is allocated for them. Thus Labor and Leisure at Home provides a detailed analysis of how the "typical" household day is organized. The data for the study are derived from a national sample of 750 heterosexual households in 1976 in which wives kept a twenty-four hour diary and husbands constructed a daily retrospective account of their household activities. The authors undertake a complex quantitative processual analysis of the household day, comparing especially the structure of activities for families in which the wife is employed outside the home with those in which she is not.

SOC 256. BERNARD, JESSIE. The Future of Marriage. New York: World, 1972. 409 pp.

As a result of changing sexual mores and sex roles in modern American society, the future of marriage as a basic social and cultural institution has come increasingly under question. Bernard explores the future of marriage and the possible changes and alternatives to it. Her study inquires into the nature and future of the commitment that transforms a relationship into a marriage. She looks for clues in the attitudes toward marriage of radical and middle-class youth in the late 1960s and the early 1970s and makes predictions about the future of marriage on the basis of historical trends, statistical curves, and human wishes and desires. "Marriage," Bernard writes, "is the best of human statuses and the worst, and it will continue to be." It is not the institution itself that is threatened but its substance, its traditional roles and its expectations.

SOC 257. BERNARD, JESSIE. The Future of Motherhood. New York: Dial Press, 1974. 426 pp.

Motherhood is more than a role assigned to women; it is an institution that is currently undergoing change and redefinition in modern America. "Mother is a role and women are human beings," Bernard argues, and the institutionalization of motherhood has been harmful and limiting both to the woman and to the child. Bernard discusses "the movement for non-motherhood," which strives to make motherhood "truly voluntary," and "the environmental movement," which advocates the "rationing" of motherhood for population control. The author also presents recent trends in child-rearing and discipline. Elsewhere, she discusses women's roles as workers, inside and outside the home, and examines how women deal with their dual roles of mother and worker. The last section examines the various "tech-nologies" of motherhood (physical, social, medical, pharmacological, and psychological) and looks at the "politics" and "economics" of mother-hood. Bernard concludes with an exploration into variations on childbear-ing and alternative "institutions," suggesting ways in which the new social order can keep motherhood from remaining a form of biological institutional bondage for women in modern societies.

SOC 258. BIRNBAUM, ROBERT. Maintaining Diversity in Higher Education. San Francisco: Jossey-Bass, 1983. 209 pp.

Birnbaum explores the nature and significance of the considerable diversity in American higher education. He asks how educational diversity can be measured, whether it is increasing or decreasing, and what public policies can be developed to enhance or restrict it. To answer these questions he empirically analyzes changes to institutions of higher education in eight selected states between 1960 and 1980. Utilizing the terminology of evolutionary biology, Birnbaum examines the evolutionary stages--variation, selection, and retention--and the organizational characteristics of different types of institutions. Birnbaum concludes that "while Ameri-can higher education is still diverse, the level of diversity has decreased over the past twenty years." He then considers public policy implications of these findings.

SOC 259. BRENTON, MYRON. The Runaways: Children, Husbands, Wives, and Parents. New York: Penguin Books, 1978. 239 pp.

"There is a genuine runaway subculture out there, huge and varied," claims the author. He attempts to describe the variety of runaways--adults as well as children, the stresses that impel them to leave their families, and the settings to which they flee. He also discusses ways of responding when family members threaten to run away, of coping when they actually do, and how to respond when a runaway returns. He also gives advice con-cerning agencies to whom one can turn in such a situation.

SOC 260. BRIDGE, R. GARY, CHARLES M. JUDD, and PETER R. MOOCK. The Determinants of Educational Outcomes: The Impact of Families, Peers,
Teachers, and Schools. Cambridge, Mass.: Ballinger, 1979.
357 pp.
This is a highly technical quantitative analysis that seeks to "synthesize
the findings of over fifteen years of input-output research in education."
The authors identify those inputs "that seem to make a difference in educational achievement." The book is directed primarily to school policy-
makers, students in courses dealing with the impact of schooling, and
researchers using input-output approaches.

SOC 261. BROADHEAD, ROBERT S. The Private Lives and Professional Identity
of Medical Students. New Brunswick, N.J.: Transaction Books,
1983. 128 pp.
This book seeks primarily to depict the general impact of medical student
life on the private lives of medical students. It discusses the various
aspects of the medical school experience as they affect and are shaped
by certain features and concerns of medical students. The book draws
on the theoretical perspectives and methodology of symbolic interactionism
as those have been applied specifically to the processes entailed in the
acquisition of professional medical identity. The Private Lives and Professional Identity of Medical Students constitutes an update of Howard
Becker's Boys in White (SOC 252) primarily because it adds to the discussion about "blacks in white," "women in white," and the intersection of
student life with private or home life, or both.

SOC 262. BRONFENBRENNER, URIE. Two Worlds of Childhood: U.S. and U.S.S.R.
New York: Russell Sage, 1970. 190 pp.
Bronfenbrenner explores the process of socialization in the Soviet Union
and the U.S., seeking to understand the way in which a child, born into
a given society, becomes a participating member of that society. In the
author's words, the tasks are to "examine what each country does for and
with its children both intentionally and, perhaps, unintentionally. Then,
drawing upon existing research and theory one asks what are, or might
be, the consequences of the modes of treatment we observe; that is, what
values and patterns of behavior are being developed in the new generation
in each society." Finally, he looks into the possibilities for introducing
constructive changes in the process as it is taking place in America.
In pursuing this last objective, the author draws extensively on available
resources of behavioral science to identify what is known of the forces
affecting the development of human behavior, the principles on which the
forces operate, and how these principles might be exploited by our social
institutions in a manner consistent with our values and traditions. Socialization is examined as it occurs in several social contexts. The family
is discussed first, then other settings, such as pre-school centers, children's groups, classrooms, schools, neighborhoods, communities, and "the
nation as a whole."

SOC 263. CAPLOW, THEODORE, HOWARD M. BAHR, BRUCE A. CHADWICK, and
MARGARET HOLMES WILLIAMSON. Middletown Families: Fifty Years
of Change and Continuity. Minneapolis: University of Minnesota
Press, 1982. 436 pp.
This study is based on the research of the Middletown III project, which
was undertaken between 1976 and 1981 as a sequel to Robert and Helen Lynd's
Middletown (SOC 50) and Middletown in Transition (SOC 51). Middletown
Families, "a book about continuity and change in the family life of one
American Community during two generations," is but one of the project's
six major topics. The authors conclude that in Middletown the family
"is in exceptionally good condition." When compared to family life in
the 1920s, Middletown families today are characterized by "increased family
solidarity, a smaller generation gap, closer marital communication, more
religion, and less mobility."

SOC 264. CARGAN, LEONARD and MATTHEW MELKO. Singles: Myths and Realities.
          Beverly Hills, Calif.: Sage, 1982. 286 pp.
This study compares and contrasts a representative sample of singles and
married persons. The authors address some of the stereotyped conceptions
of singles: deviant, immature, sexually deviant, self-centered, lonely,
workaholic. They examine the statistical trends on singles in 20th-century
American society, but their primary focus is on a sample of singles and
married persons drawn from the Dayton, Ohio metropolitan area. The
authors compare single and married lifestyles--relationships with parents,
uses of leisure time, and sexual relationships--and attitudes--feelings
of loneliness, illness, attitudes toward marriage, general happiness,
and the future.

SOC 265. CAUHAPE, ELIZABETH. Fresh Starts: Men and Women After Divorce.
          New York: Basic Books, 1983. 338 pp.
The objective of this book is "to discover the means by which men and
women rebuild their social worlds at mid-life after undergoing a divorce."
It focuses on "upwardly mobile professional men and women with origins
in the middle, lower-middle, and working classes." Most of her research
subjects had been "persistent strivers" who had achieved considerable
personal affluence. She places her discussion of the life transitions
of these people in the historical context of this particular cohort, which
had been born during the Depression years of the late 1920s and 1930s.
During the 1950s they had experienced considerable mobility and prosperity,
but they were jolted by the social changes of the 1960s and during the
1970s the effects of these changes, in sex roles, were felt in their marriages. Her central finding is that "divorced men and women can master
their circumstances and take power over their lives."

SOC 266. CHERLIN, ANDREW J. Marriage, Divorce, Remarriage. Cambridge,
          Mass.: Harvard University Press, 1981. 142 pp.
This book is the first in a series entitled "Social Trends in the United
States," sponsored by the Center for Coordination of Research on Social
Indicators. The first of four sections focuses on the trends in marriage
and divorce; the second on explanations of the trends; the third on the
consequences of these trends; and the fourth on differences in the trends
experienced by blacks and whites. Cherlin argues that current levels
of marriage and divorce are more in line with long-time changes than the
unusual swing that peaked in the 1950s. The research of Elder and
Easterlin are cited to explain recent trends in marriage cohort effects.
Cherlin's conclusion is that the rapidly rising employment rates of women
constitute a central factor in the growing sense of independence among
women that is associated indirectly with rising divorce rates.

SOC 267. COLEMAN, JAMES S. The Adolescent Society: The Social Life of
          the Teenager and Its Impact on Education. New York: Free Press,
          1961. 368 pp.
Coleman was among the first to detail the emergence of an adolescent subculture in Industrial America; he examines American high schools and the
teenage "status system" within them. His study, based on extensive questionnaires and informal interviews with students at ten high schools in
different communities of various sizes, reveals the nature of the adolescent culture. Coleman probes the "value climates" of each school, examining the source of value systems, the distribution of elites within the
institution, and their paths to success. He looks at the structures of
association and the psychological effects of the high school social system,
and considers the effect of adolescent culture on secondary education in
the U.S., proposing that the formal educational system is at odds with
American youth culture. He concludes that the young American was "no
longer a child, but will spend his energies in ways he sees fit. It is
up to adult society to so structure secondary education that it captures
this energy."

1740

SOC 268. EGERTON, JOHN. Generations: An American Family. Lexington:
          University Press of Kentucky, 1983. 263 pp.
Egerton characterizes his objective as an attempt to tell "a collective
tale of the evolution of a nation." He does so by reconstructing the
collective experiences of a four-generation American family, the Ledfords
of Garrard County, Kentucky. More than an individual family biography,
Egerton interprets their experiences as representing a microcosm of and
a link between American society from the 18th century to the present.
In 1978 Burnam Ledford, age 102, and his wife, Addie, age 93, had thirteen
children, thirty-two grandchildren, and thirty-nine great-grandchildren.
Diverse in their occupations, for Egerton these descendants of Burnam
and Addie Ledford "resemble familiar characters in the modern American
dream-myth--an upwardly mobile, geographically dispersed, conservative-
leaning, moderately religious family of job-holding, goods-buying, sports-
loving, television-watching people." Their significance resides in their
typicality. "Just ordinary folks, they had not made history. . . . But
they had seen history, and lived it, and participated, however indirectly,
in its shaping; inevitably, inescapably, they were both beneficiaries
and victims of their nation's history." This is the story of the Ledford
clan and their participation in the American experience.

SOC 269. ELDER, GLEN H., Jr. Children of the Great Depression: Social
          Change in Life Experience. Chicago: University of Chicago
          Press, 1974. 400 pp.
This book emphasizes the effects of the economic deprivation on adolescents
during the Great Depression. The work is an analysis of those born between
1916 and 1925 and is part of the 1931 Oakland Growth Study. The first
section lays out the research questions; "Coming of Age in the Depression"
explores the effects of deprivation on the family and the particular impact
of status/role shifts on adolescent personality; the third part, "Adult
Years," follows the subjects into vocation, family, and community roles.
A final section, "The Depression Experience in Life Patterns," summarizes
the important implications of deprivation and the life cycle for social
theory and social policy.

SOC 270. ENTWISLE, DORIS R. and SUSAN G. DOERING. The First Birth: A
          Family Turning Point. Baltimore, Md.: Johns Hopkins University
          Press, 1981. 331 pp.
The First Birth's two goals are (1) to describe in chronological sequence
the experience of 120 mothers and sixty fathers during the perinatal period
(from the sixth month of the pregnancy through the sixth month of the
infant's life); and (2) to analyze and link prenatal experiences, childbirth, and postpartum events. This study tests Janis's theory of stress
to examine husbands' and wives' responses to the critical event of the
first birth. Entwisle and Doering begin with a review and summary of
related research findings. They examine the degree to which social class
and level of childbirth preparation affect the couples throughout the
perinatal period. They note that mothering responses are affected by
prenatal factors, which, in turn, are influenced differently by social
class. The authors conclude that prior assumptions about the degree to
which childbirth preparation bears on long-term parenting behavior need
to be examined.

SOC 271. EVERHART, ROBERT B. Reading, Writing, and Resistance: Adoles-
          cence and Labor in a Junior High School. Boston: Routledge
          & Kegan Paul, 1983. 302 pp.
Based on two years of field work at Harold Spencer Junior High School,
this is a theoretically grounded ethnography of the school culture of
an American junior high school. "The study focuses upon everyday life
of junior high schools, and is a chronicle of the daily routine of students
and, to a much lesser degree, teachers." The author is concerned with

1741

examining how daily lives in this school are affected by the broader demands of advanced capitalist society, and he examines the process whereby the material, productive forces of capitalist society impinge upon and are ultimately responsible for preparing children for functional roles in that society. Equally important, however, he explores the dynamic, dialectical process whereby students themselves interpret these demands ("interpretive structures") and "build their own history." His broader theoretical interest is "the degree to which the culture of junior high school youth renews, re-creates, defends, or modifies [societally imposed] regularities."

SOC 272. FEIGELMAN, WILLIAM and ARNOLD R. SILVERMAN. Chosen Children: New Patterns of Adoptive Relationships. New York: Praeger, 1983. 261 pp.
The objective of this book is to examine "the transformations occurring in the realm of American adoptions," especially as these have been influenced by broader and more fundamental social changes in modern American society. Based primarily on responses to a nationwide sample survey of adoptive families conducted in 1974-76, the book analyzes the changing nature of adoption relationships in American society and evaluates the role of social service professionals in serving adoptees and adoptive parents. Although their sample included all major types of adoptions, the authors focus especially on what they characterize as typifying "newer and emerging adoptive patterns": hard-to-place children, transracial and international adoptions, fertile adoptive parents, and single parent adoptions.

SOC 273. FOWLKES, MARTHA R. Behind Every Successful Man: Wives of Medicine and Academe. New York: Columbia University Press, 1980. 223 pp.
Fowlkes relates differences in role segregation to the structures of the work setting of medical and academic men, and establishes a link between occupational and family arrangements. Medical men, who operate in their work in a relatively hierarchical structure where they are in command over nurses and patients, are likely to have a more rigidly patriarchal setting at home. Academic men, who have more flexible schedules and flexible work relationships where they must negotiate with colleagues and students, have more egalitarian relationships with their wives, engage more in common activities with them and their children, and generally have more of a "companionship" marriage.

SOC 274. FOX, ELAINE. The Marriage-Go-Round: An Exploratory Study of Multiple Marriage. Washington, D.C.: University Press of America, 1983. 198 pp.
Fox is concerned with the process by which persons become multiple marriers. Using a symbolic interactionist perspective, she conducted in-depth interviews with eighteen persons who had had two or more marriages and divorces. In addition to examining the childhood experiences of her informants, Fox focuses on their different perceptions and expectations of marriage and how these are altered as a consequence of their marital failures.

SOC 275. FRIEDENBERG, EDGAR. The Vanishing Adolescent. Boston: Beacon Press, 1959. 144 pp.
Predicting the social upheaval of the 1960s, Friedenberg addresses the issues of apathy and alienation among American youth. He contends that adolescence, a primarily social process whose fundamental task is clear and stable self-identification, is disappearing from American culture. The process is being "frustrated and emptied of meaning" by a society which stresses uniformity and whose purpose is to insure "domestic tranquility." He first examines the processes of personal and emotional growth and then the social processes bearing on adolescents as they are nurtured

in the American public school system. An analysis of the high school
includes an outline of its basic functions in society and an assessment
of its impact on the development of young people. In particular,
Friedenberg is interested in the effect of the school's guidance policies
on the development of self-esteem. Personality data collected from five
high school boys are analyzed. In conclusion, the author urges schools
to take responsibility for the nurturing of individuality and self-clarity.

SOC 276. GARBARINO, JAMES and C. ELLIOT ASP. Successful Schools and Competent Students. Lexington, Mass.: Heath, 1981. 170 pp.
Garbarino and Asp contend that schools can make a difference, and they
present a series of articles on school success, its meaning, causes, and
consequences. They reject academic excellence as a criterion of school
success in favor of one that is a better predictor of eventual social
status and income: educational attainment measured by the number of years
of schooling completed. The authors search the literature for clues as
to why some students succeed while others do not, and what schools can
do to maximize success. The authors discuss a number of shortcomings
in today's high schools that inhibit academic culture and promote anti-
social behavior among students. They believe size to be a major factor.
This book ends with policy implications relevant to the development of
an academic climate in schools.

SOC 277. GEERKEN, MICHAEL and WALTER R. GOVE. At Home and At Work: The
Family's Allocation of Labor. Beverly Hills, Calif.: Sage,
1983. 167 pp.
Given the sharp increase in the number of working wives, how do families
allocate responsibilities in the labor force and in the home, and how
does this allocation affect the quality of family life, in particular,
the quality and stability of the marital relationship? To investigate
this question, the authors advance a sociological-economic model of work
allocation based on the notion of "utility maximization" by the family
unit. The data for the study are a national sample of 1,225 married respondents who were interviewed at length in 1974-75. The authors assess the
various factors that contribute to and affect a wife's decision to enter
the labor force and the kind of work role she occupies. They also examine
how the wife's work role in the labor force affects the allocation of
responsibility for housework. Finally, they analyze the impact of the
wife's work role on marital quality in different family income and life-
cycle situations.

SOC 278. GREELEY, ANDREW M. Catholic High Schools and Minority Students.
New Brunswick, N.J.: Transaction Books, 1982. 117 pp.
This research analyzes data from a large-scale, longitudinal survey begun
by the National Center for Education Statistics in 1980. Sixty thousand
tenth and twelfth graders, their parents, siblings, teachers, and school
administrators were the subjects of the project. Greeley's report focuses
on the fate of minority students in Catholic schools. He concludes that
the Catholic school itself has a positive impact on minority students'
achievement, even when the effect of family influence is controlled.

SOC 279. GROSS, EDWARD and PAUL V. GRAMBSCH. Changes in University Organization, 1964-1971. New York: McGraw-Hill, 1974. 257 pp.
With the turbulent "revolution" of the 1960s in American institutions
of higher learning, one would expect that major changes in university organization would have occurred. However, this comparative analysis of surveys
conducted (in 1964 and in 1968) on faculty and administrators' attitudes
in sixty-eight major national universities reveals little change in the
ranking of both educational and organizational goals and goal preferences.
Through an examination of type of control, research and scholarly productivity, university prestige, and amount of student unrest, the authors
conclude that there was greater differentiation convergence among American

universities in 1971. They also explore the perceived university power structure as related to goal sets. The final section looks at faculty-administration relationships and finds greater congruence between the two groups in the later sample.

SOC 280. HALEM, LYNNE CAROL. Divorce Reform: Changing Legal and Social Perspectives. New York: Free Press, 1980. 340 pp.
Divorce Reform is a history of over 300 years of alterations in the concept of divorce, its judicial treatment, and efforts at social and legal reform. Halem begins with the doctrines of divorce in Colonial times and concludes with an assessment of the no-fault divorce reform movement of the 1970s. She explores three social perspectives: the moralistic-theological view dominant from Colonial times to the 19th century, the social-pathological perspective of the Progressive era, and the psycho-pathological of the 20th century. Halem argues that all three are premised on divorce as an index of personal weakness, and that aspects of each remain today. Halem's primary focus is on the judicial system, and how the social and behavioral sciences have influenced legal remedies for divorce, custody, and alimony.

SOC 281. HERMAN, JUDITH LEWIS and LISA HIRSCHMAN. Father-Daughter Incest. Cambridge, Mass.: Harvard University Press, 1981. 282 pp.
Part one of this volume is a theoretical analysis of father-daughter incest. Herman establishes that (1) father-daughter incest is a common occurrence, (2) it causes harm to the child, and (3) the father, not the child, is to blame. Emphasis is placed on analyzing why the parent-child incest taboo is broken in an asymmetrical way (i.e., by fathers). This asymmetrical lapse makes sense in one particular type of family: one dominated by the father, with a rigid division of labor by gender, when the mother cares for the children of both sexes, but the father does not. Part two reports on the author's research. The sample consists of forty women who had incestuous relationships with their fathers. The comparative sample consists of twenty women who had seductive, but not overtly incestuous, fathers. A picture of the incestuous fathers and their families is: conventional to a fault; rigid adherence to a traditional division of labor by gender; fathers who ruled without question, half of whom were described as violent; mothers who were often disabled and kept economically dependent, socially isolated, and encumbered with the care of many children; daughters who were alienated from their mothers and were expected to "keep daddy happy." Part three deals with intervention: treatment strategies and prevention.

SOC 282. HOLMSTROM, LYNDA LYTLE. The Two-Career Family. Cambridge, Mass.: Schenkman, 1973. 203 pp.
Holmstrom contends that, "Our society makes it very difficult to have two careers in the same family. It simply is assumed that in the middle-class couple only one spouse will have a serious profession." What happens to the nature and functioning of the family when both spouses have highly demanding careers? Holmstrom studies twenty-seven couples, twenty of which were "professional" and seven "traditional"--i.e., the wife has no career--and presents a detailed analysis of the personal and professional barriers encountered by "the two career family." Holmstrom examines stratification by sex in the division of labor in the family and job, the differential allocation of time, effort, and money, and competitiveness and colleagueship in male and female married professionals. "The traditional family structure, like the inflexible occupational structure, perpetuates the assumption that there will be only one career per family." The author concludes with some suggestions for structural change within the family and the professions which would allow women more "lifestyle flexibility."

SOC 283. HOOD, JANE C. Becoming a Two-Job Family. New York: Praeger, 1983. 240 pp.
This is a study of how the dynamics of family life are affected by the wife's entrance into the paid labor force. The book is based on data that Hood obtained from interviews with members of sixteen families in 1975-76 and in a follow-up study in 1982-84. Hood discusses what families were like before the wives began working outside the home, their motivations for entering the work force, and the consequences for the family-- including the husband's reactions and how each spouse's provider, companion, parent, and housekeeper roles changed. She employs a "role bargaining model" to interpret her data, and in her final chapters she explores the implications of these changes for such issues as equality, power, bargaining, conflict and its resolution, and haring of domestic and provider roles among spouses.

SOC 284. HUNTER, CARMAN ST. JOHN and DAVID HARMAN. Adult Illiteracy in the United States: A Report to the Ford Foundation. New York: McGraw-Hill, 1979. 206 pp.
A basic assumption of this study is that adult education is intimately interwoven with the broader social and economic system and that the issue of illiteracy can therefore be considered only in this broader context. Hunter and Harman use existing data to examine three different issues: first, changing concepts of literacy and illiteracy and the relation between changing demands placed on persons and their aspirations in American society; second, the groups for whom formal educational opportunities have been least effective and among whom illiteracy has been most widespread; finally, existing programs and services available to adults who wish to remedy their educational deficiencies. The authors conclude with a series of recommendations for addressing the problems that they have identified.

SOC 285. ITZKOFF, SEYMOUR W. A New Public Education. New York: McKay, 1976. 372 pp.
This book explains how the public schools took on the responsibility of national moral authority and how, according to the author, it has been lost. Itzkoff examines conditions that now necessitate the rethinking of America's educational needs. He describes the development of the educational system in the U.S. and addresses such issues as separation of religion and education, the teaching profession, minorities, and youth. He also discusses issues that have important global implications, such as the problem of unrestrained economic and demographic growth. He contends that, as a result of these international problems, cultural and community life is bound to change and that a wholly new context of social adaptation will evolve. The idea of the "cultural community" is presented as the ideal context within which the individual can emerge to serve the wider needs of the larger international community. Itzkoff concludes with a proposal for a new structure in public education: the voucher system.

SOC 286. JENCKS, CHRISTOPHER and DAVID RIESMAN. The Academic Revolution. Garden City, N.Y.: Doubleday, 1968. 508 pp.
This study of American higher education offers a historical and sociological analysis of the general theory of the development of American colleges and universities, their relationship to the larger society, and the particular interest groups that founded them. The authors examine the nature of the academic revolution, or what they see as "the rise to power of the academic profession." This study sheds light on social stratification and generational conflict within higher education, occupational preferences as manifested in graduate professional schools, coeducation and "special-interest" colleges (such as women's colleges and ethnic and regional institutions), and the rise of "anti-university" colleges in modern

America. Jencks and Riesman also discuss the financial, intellectual, and generational problems that face America's academic system and the impact of the student "revolution" on that system.

SOC 287. JOHNSON, ROBERT ALAN. Religious Assortative Marriage in the United States. New York: Academic Press, 1980. 235 pp.
Johnson presents new findings on patterns of inter-religious marriage in the U.S., that have implications for theories of religion. This book includes an introduction by Thomas Mayer about trends in religious history. The rest of the book's emphasis is on the influence of interreligious marriage on religious composition. Johnson analyzes intermarriage patterns among six broadly defined religious groups (Baptists, Methodists, "Liberal" Protestants, Lutherans, Catholics, and others) in terms of the influence of population composition, the social distance separating them, and their within-group tendencies toward endogamy.

SOC 288. JONES, FAUSTINE CHILDRESS. A Traditional Model of Educational Excellence: Dunbar High School of Little Rock, Arkansas. Washington, D.C.: Howard University Press, 1981. 222 pp.
Jones seeks to identify those factors that contributed to effective black public schools during the Jim Crow era. She uses Dunbar High School, which for twenty-five years (1930-1955) maintained a reputation as one of the South's leading black secondary schools, as a case study. Her analysis of Dunbar's academic effectiveness is based primarily on an attitude survey of Dunbar's far-flung alumni. In her discussion, Jones provides a historical sketch of the school's background and development, analysis of responses from alumni, former administrators, and teachers concerning their perceptions of the quality of their educational experiences at the school, and an assessment of the overall educational significance of the school.

SOC 289. KAHN, ALFRED J. and SHEILA B. KAMERMAN. Helping America's Families. Philadelphia: Temple University Press, 1982. 266 pp.
This book is concerned with family support systems. It seeks to identify and evaluate those individuals, institutions, and agencies—public, voluntary nonprofit, religious, and marketplace—that offer help to American families. The authors focus on the range and variety of personal social services available to families and the delivery of these services. Their professed goal is to "highlight the growing importance of the service sector in contributing to a better quality of life for all people, rich and poor alike."

SOC 290. KANTER, ROSABETH MOSS. Work and Family in the United States: A Critical Review and Agenda for Research and Policy. New York: Russell Sage, 1977. 116 pp.
Kanter's book summarizes recent research findings on the interaction of work and family roles and points to critical issues in need of further scholarly and policy attention. These include the influence of family structure on the sexual division of labor in the work place; the effects of occupational structure and organization on family life; the impact of women's work on family relations; and the interaction of family and work responsibilities for family and individual well-being.

SOC 291. KRIESBERG, LOUIS. Mothers in Poverty: A Study of Fatherless Families. Chicago: Aldine, 1970. 356 pp.
Kriesberg's book provides insight into the particular problems confronting single-parent families in the U.S. Kriesberg explains that his study "attempts explanations of the way of life of poor people and the possible role their way of life plays in the intergenerational transmission of poverty." The author delves into the two principal approaches to such explanations: "the subculture of poverty" and "contemporary circum-

stances." Kriesberg's study is based upon survey data, on personal interviews, and participants' observations. He focuses on both female-and
male-headed families in an American city. He finds no integrated subculture of poverty, but rather a variety of conditions (racism, sexism, poor
housing and education) and personal attitudes and beliefs associated with
poverty.

SOC 292. LADD, EVERETT CARL, Jr. and SEYMOUR MARTIN LIPSET. The Divided
Academy: Professors and Politics. New York: McGraw-Hill, 1975.
407 pp.
American academics are found to be predominantly left-of-center in their
politics. This is the principal finding of a study based on the results
of two surveys sponsored by the Carnegie Commission on Higher Education.
Over 60,000 interviews administered to academics in all sorts of academic
institutions and disciplines were analyzed. Social scientists were found
to be the most liberal, followed by lawyers and humanists; people in the
physical and biological sciences, education, and medicine were found to
be in the middle; engineering, those in business programs and in applied
professional schools were the most conservative. "There is a much higher
proportion of radicals among social scientists than among any other group
in American society that may be defined by occupational criteria," the
authors conclude. Of this group, psychologists, anthropologists, and
sociologists were found to be considerably to the left of political scientists and economists. Ladd and Lipset's research provides some insight
into the politics of academia, and suggests some implications of those
politics in the wider society.

SOC 293. LASCH, CHRISTOPHER. Haven in a Heartless World: The Family
Besieged. New York: Basic Books, 1977. 230 pp.
Lasch maintains that modern society has assumed many of the family's important functions, reducing both the family's power and its privacy. He
argues that Capitalism has largely co-opted the family and brought its
roles into the public sphere where social workers, schools, and courts
are taking on the traditional functions of the family. The author calls
for a return to a traditional family structure capable of supporting its
members and offering a genuine "haven" from the outside world. Discussions
of sociological and psychological theories of the family are included.

SOC 294. LAUER, ROBERT H. and JEANETTE C. LAUER. The Spirit and the Flesh:
Sex in Utopian Communities. Metuchen, N.J.: Scarecrow Press,
1983. 256 pp.
All societies have addressed the question of how sexual relationships should
be regulated. This book analyzes sexual ideologies and sexual behavior
in American utopian communities of the 19th and 20th centuries. The
authors identify five types of utopian societies: religious communistic,
secular communistic/socialist, joint stock, anarchistic, and modern, the
first four of which existed primarily before W.W. II. They seek to determine
the different sexual arrangements various utopian groups considered ideal:
what ideologies and controls maintained these arrangements; how satisfying
and effective the arrangements were; and what others can learn from the
utopians' experiences—in particular what these various communities contribute to an understanding of the nature of intimacy.

SOC 295. LAVIN, DAVID D., RICHARD D. ALBA, and RICHARD A. SILBERSTEIN.
Right Versus Privilege: The Open-Admissions Experiment at the
City University of New York. New York: Free Press, 1981.
340 pp.
In 1970 City University of New York (CUNY) opened its doors to all New
York City high school graduates. Right Versus Privilege is an empirical
study of the effects. Lavin, Alba, and Silberstein collected data on
entering freshmen between 1970 and 1975, and additional data at the end

of each semester through the fall of 1975. The data show that open admissions helped minority students to enter CUNY. By the fall of 1975, blacks and Hispanics accounted for 43% of CUNY freshmen, more than twice the 1969 figure. The authors found that "although the percentages of white (Jewish and Catholic) students receiving degrees was higher than black and Hispanic students the program more than doubled . . . the number of black baccalaureates," while the number of hispanic graduates was increased by two-thirds.

SOC 296. LEVITAN, SAR A. and RICHARD S. BELOUS. What's Happening to the American Family? Baltimore, Md.: Johns Hopkins University Press, 1981. 206 pp.
Levitan and Belous contend that, contrary to some very visible social trends—increasing divorce rates, declining marriage rates, increased numbers of single parent families, increased numbers of mothers in the paid labor market—the family is not disintegrating. "American families are changing, but they are not eroding." The social changes that have occurred have created a highly pluralistic family structure in modern American society. Moreover, changing work roles have led to the demand by many women for a more equal division of labor and a more equal partnership in family decision-making. However, as the American family evolves, it confronts new problems and strains. This book is an attempt to address and to propose solutions to some of these problems.

SOC 297. LIGHTFOOT, SARA LAWRENCE. Worlds Apart: Relationships Between Families and Schools. New York: Basic Books, 1978. 257 pp.
In this interpretive study, Lightfoot is concerned with the "dynamic intersection" of the family and the school, the two institutions with the primary responsibility for the acculturation and socialization of children in modern American society. She contends that the importance of the relationship between these two institutions has been largely ignored in previous social science literature. The objective of Worlds Apart is "to record some of the complex dimensions of family-school intersection by recognizing both the consonant and dissonant faces of the relationship and by exploring some of the microscopic, interpersonal dynamics as well as the more macroscopic, structural patterns of interaction." Accordingly, Lightfoot focuses both on the external institutional and structural forces that shape families and schools and on the internal interpersonal and intrapersonal factors that affect interaction between them.

SOC 298. McGINNIS, TOM. More Than Just a Friend: The Joys and Disappointments of Extramarital Affairs. Englewood Cliffs, N.J.: Prentice-Hall, 1981. 203 pp.
"This book attempts to explore the true nature and significance of extramarital affairs. It deals with both the positive and negative aspects of affairs, their healthy and unhealthy characteristics, the joys and heartaches. The focus is on what really happens in affairs." McGinnis, a marital and family therapist, draws on case histories of twenty-five couples involved in extramarital affairs. He examines the social and cultural changes contributing to the increase in affairs, dispels several of the widespread myths concerning their causes and consequences, and attempts to deal with them in the context of concerns for both individual growth and family and marital commitment.

SOC 299. O'NEILL, NENA and GEORGE O'NEILL. Open Marriage: A New Lifestyle for Couples. New York: Evans, 1972. 287 pp.
The O'Neills contend that changing lifestyles in the late 1960s and early 1970s appeared to be related to the increasing dissatisfaction with traditional marital relationships. Rigid sex-role guidelines and rigid expectations were causing increasing tensions between marriage partners. The authors propose a new form of marriage, which they argue has the necessary

"qualities and conditions that seemed most necessary for growth for a man and woman living togther in today's world." <u>Open Marriage</u> advocates independent lifestyles, non-monogamous relationships, and sexual and personal adventure. The concomitant requirements are open and honest communications between partners, role flexibility within the marriage, open companionship, equality, identity and trust. The book is an example of the experimental manifestations of the "social revolution" of the 1960s.

SOC 300. **ORTIZ, FLORA IDA.** <u>Career Patterns in Education</u>: <u>Women, Men and Minorities in Public School Administration</u>. New York: Praeger, 1982. 183 pp.
<u>Career Patterns in Education</u> reports on a five-and-a-half year study of the socialization processes affecting upward mobility in public school administration. Ortiz collected data from 350 administrators in thirty-one school districts in an effort to discover which administrative positions offer the greatest opportunity for career movement, and whether the opportunity within a position is the same for male and female, minority and majority holders. The first section deals with the positions of vice-principal, principal, and four types of central office administrators in light of organizational structure; the type of activity required and the potential for upward movement are determined. Ortiz discusses the socialization process that aspirants go through in trying to reach the superintendency and she contrasts the experiences of women and minorities with those of white males in terms of position and mobility.

SOC 301. **PACE, C. ROBERT.** <u>Measuring Outcomes of College</u>: <u>Fifty Years of Findings and Recommendations for the Future</u>. San Francisco: Jossey-Bass, 1979. 188 pp.
This series of essays involves an assessment of the impact of college experience on students. Reviewing and synthesizing the findings of numerous surveys of students, alumni, and different institutions during the past fifty years, Pace focuses on several issues: what these surveys reveal about American higher education, levels of student achievement and acquisition of knowledge during college, student achievement after college, and the nature of colleges and universities as organizations and environments.

SOC 302. **PARSONS, TALCOTT** and **GERALD M. PLATT.** <u>The American University</u>. Cambridge, Mass.: Harvard University Press, 1973. 463 pp.
This is a systematic theoretical analysis of the socio-structural dimensions of higher education. Parsons and Platt propose a four-function paradigm for their analysis: latent pattern-maintenance, adaptation, goal-attainment, and integration. The work is prefaced by an extensive theoretical discussion of this paradigm. The model is applied to examine the core sectors of the university: graduate training and research; general education and socialization in the undergraduate college; professional schools; and "intellectuals" and the university system. The analyses focus on the dynamic process of the American university system: implications of crisis, continuity, and change.

SOC 303. **PESHKIN, ALAN.** <u>Growing Up American</u>: <u>Schooling and the Survival of Community</u>. Chicago: University of Chicago Press, 1978. 256 pp.
From 1972 to 1974, Peshkin lived in the small rural midwestern town of "Mansfield," and participated as fully as possible in the life of the community. His primary objective in this book is to describe what an American high school is like and the integral role that the high school plays in such communities. Using his own observations, the results of questionnaires and interviews, and student diaries, he examines the content of the Mansfield High curriculum; the classroom experience; the roles of school board, administration, and teachers; and the importance of extra-curricular activities and romances in the life of Mansfield High School students.

SOC 304. PESHKIN, ALAN. The Imperfect Union: School Consolidation and
Community Conflict. Chicago: University of Chicago Press,
1983. 207 pp.
"This book is about conflict over schools in village communities." It
is the story of the relationship between the community grade school in
the rural Illinois village of "Killmer" and "Consolidated School District
Unit 110," the broader administrative unit in which Killmer was located.
A controversy was ignited by a decision of Unit 110 to close, for financial
reasons, the Killmer grade school. Killmer residents, however, perceived
the school closing as not merely an educational decision but as threatening
the survival of their community. Thus, he writes, "in troubled times,
schools may become battlegrounds as people perceive their school's communal
function to be jeopardized by local or state policies." Peshkin and his
research staff used documentary evidence, interviews, and attendance at
public meetings to explore the historical, sociological, and cultural
background and meanings of this case study. Peshkin sees the Killmer-
Unit 110 controversy as a microcosm of conflicts generated throughout
the country by the trend, largely since W.W. II, toward school consolidation, not merely of schools in remote and underpopulated rural areas but
in more heavily populated areas as well.

SOC 305. PIOTRKOWSKI, CHAYA S. Work and the Family System: A Naturalistic
Study of Working-Class and Lower-Middle-Class Families. New
York: Free Press, 1978. 337 pp.
"Does work affect the quality of emotional life in families, and, if so,
how?" This is the basic question that Piotrkowski addresses. Her research
is based on in-depth interviews that she conducted with thirteen "normal"
working- or lower-middle class families; half the book is a case study
of relationships between the emotional and household life of a single
family and how the external work system and household work system shape
family life. She dismisses the notion that work and family are "separate
worlds"; although the work world may not be actively discussed at home,
the "tensions and conflicts [it creates] are absorbed by families and
are expressed in intrapersonal and interpersonal strains."

SOC 306. RAVITCH, DIANE. The Troubled Crusade: American Education, 1945-
1980. New York: Basic Books, 1983. 384 pp.
"This book is a report on the state of the crusade against ignorance during
a particularly tumultuous time in American history. . . ." It is a narrative history of American education between 1945 and 1980. Ravitch
focuses on several factors that were integral to the transformation of
American education during this period: the progressive education movement;
the loyalty investigations of the McCarthy era; the impact of the racial
revolution on the schools; educational reforms such as the "new" math,
science, and social studies; campus unrest; and, above all, the changing
role of the Federal government in American education. Ravitch argues
that while the extraordinary changes that occurred did not necessarily
bring about the idealistic visions anticipated by their proponents, neither
had their accomplishments been so limited as critics of American education
have charged.

SOC 307. REISS, DAVID. The Family's Construction of Reality. Cambridge,
Mass.: Harvard University Press, 1981. 426 pp.
A central thesis of this book is that the behavior of the family toward
its members is guided by the family's own paradigm. The paradigm consists
of shared experiences; transmission of values over historic time; and
feelings, assumptions, and codes of meaning regarding the world and the
family's role within it. The paradigm, if not predictive, is at least
critical concerning the types of linkages and transactions the family
has with the social environment. Reiss's research is based on observations
of 400 families in laboratory and household settings. The family-paradigm

concept emerges from his work on adaptation and problem solving. Family crises are the setting for examining how paradigms are shaped and programmed for endurance. A major section of The Family's Construction of Reality focuses on the family's bond to its social environment, where the family-paradigm world linkage is established.

SOC 308. **RICHARDSON, RICHARD C.**, Jr., **ELIZABETH C. FISK**, and **MORRIS A. OKUN**. Literacy in the Open-Access College. San Francisco: Jossey-Bass, 1983. 187 pp.

This study is concerned with the nature of literacy in the curriculum of open-access colleges. Although some four year schools are open-access institutions, community colleges have been the prototype of such schools. Therefore, the authors undertook a three year study of "Oakwood" Community College in an effort to determine how an open-access college was involved with the issue of literacy. The authors found not only a lack of emphasis on traditional forms of reading and writing (e.g., term papers, essay exams, required reading lists), but, more important, a dearth of what they identify as critical literacy, which involves analysis, synthesis, and original expression. They attribute this dearth of literacy to several factors: lack of an integrated curriculum and effective student advising; student demand for "relevant courses"; and the part-time involvement in the college by students and faculty alike. The authors maintain that to promote critical literacy such colleges must institute extensive changes: in admissions policies, standards for academic progress, financial aid practices, and approaches to remediation. In essence, they question the effectiveness of universal higher education.

SOC 309. ROGERS, DAVID. 110 Livingston Street: Politics and Bureaucracy in the New York City Schools. New York: Random House, 1968. 584 pp.

110 Livingston Street is the address of the New York City Board of Education and thus of the New York City school system, the subject of Rogers's study. Rogers's principal concern is desegregation, which he believes "brought many benefits," not the least of which was the attention drawn to the inadequacies of the school system. A "politics of futility" surrounds the system, argues Rogers, but he offers strategies to deal with this problem. The New York City school system is offered as a case study in educational reform.

SOC 310. ROGERS, DAVID and NORMAN H. CHUNG. 110 Livingston Street Revisited: Decentralization in Action. New York: New York University Press, 1983. 241 pp.

This book is a sequel to Rogers's earlier study of the New York City school system. In this volume, the authors assess the results of the 1970 decentralization of the school system. Studying eight individual community school districts, the authors analyze their functioning under decentralization, particularly their response to New York's changing ethnic population. In an epilogue, they discuss some of the problems still remaining in the decentralized system: the quality of Community School Boards, integration and neighborhood stabilization, and marginal teacher quality.

SOC 311. ROSENTHAL, KRISTINE M. and HARRY F. KESHET. Fathers Without Partners: A Study of Fathers and the Family after Marital Separation. Totowa, N.J.: Rowman & Littlefield, 1981. 187 pp.

This book focuses primarily on the relationship between separated fathers and their children and its effects on life-styles and personal growth. The sample was obtained from court records, day-care centers, lawyers, and others: 129 fathers separated at least one year who took care of their children, seven years old and under, weekends to full time, were interviewed. The authors show that divorce involves not a breakup of the family but a redefinition: the role of the father is restructured, and co-parenting is an essential ingredient for intact marriages and post-divorce arrangements. The authors discuss issues relating to parenting as the boundaries separating the husband role from the post-divorce parent role, and the interdependence of divorced parents. Rosenthal and Keshet contend that the structural demands of child care force changes such that men's roles might look more like those of women.

SOC 312. RUBIN, LILLIAN B. Intimate Strangers: Men and Women Together. New York: Harper & Row, 1983. 222 pp.
Rubin contends that "there are differences between [male and female] that are not simply a product of role learning and socialization." In an analysis based on object relations theory as modified by Chodorow and Dinnerstein, Rubin sees distinct male and female personality structures to be a consequence of the fact that women nurture. This fact contributes to different problems of identification and separation for male and female children, the resolution of which, in turn, creates different adult personalities. These differences in adults affect such critical issues as intimacy, sexuality, dependency, work, identity, and parenting. In her concluding chapter Rubin explores the struggles of many parents today to alter the manner in which parenting and the creation of traditional sex roles takes place. However, she concludes that "the search for personal change without efforts to change institutions within which we live and grow will be met with only limited reward."

SOC 313. SCANZONI, JOHN H. Sex Roles, Life Styles, and Childbearing: Changing Patterns in Marriage and the Family. New York: Free Press, 1975. 259 pp.
How do sex role norms affect such things as family size, the age of marriage, the effective use of contraceptives, the employment of women? How are these norms related to age, race, religion, education, marital and economic satisfaction? From the results of a study of 3,100 husbands and wives in ten cities throughout the U.S., Scanzoni offers some answers to these critical questions. His study offers findings on various issues, including the kinds of roles that men and women want to play both in and out of marriage, influence on birth intentions, and attitudes toward family size. Scanzoni concludes that persons who hold more modern, egalitarian sex role norms do indeed behave in such a way as to have smaller families.

SOC 314. SPEROUNIS, FREDERICK P. The Limits of Progressive School Reform in the 1970's: A Case Study. Washington, D.C.: University Press of America, 1980. 276 pp.
Public alternative schools are the descendants of two educational movements that emerged during the 1960s and early 1970s: the "free school" movement and the movement for community control of schools. This book is a case study, based on field work and extensive interviews, of an alternative public school, the Cambridge Alternative Public School, from its inception in 1970 to 1978. The author seeks to assess how effectively such a school has realized its professed goals of (1) providing a learning environment that stimulates creativity, cooperation, curiosity, and a sense of self-worth among its students and (2) involving parents in decisions concerning their children's education. His objective is "to illustrate the problems and dilemmas which interfere with the creation of learning environments which are non-repressive, participatory, and potentially liberating."

SOC 315. STACEY, WILLIAM A. and ANSON SHUPE. The Family Secret: Domestic Violence in America. Boston: Beacon Press, 1983. 237 pp.
The authors characterize domestic violence as a "family secret" because of the sensitivity of the subject and the many ways in which it is concealed from public view and punishment. This study analyzed "the largest single collection of domestic violence cases ever assembled," including information on both the victims (children and women) and the perpetrators

of violence. A substantial amount of the data was obtained from shelters for physically abused women and their children, and the authors examine, in particular, a single shelter in Dallas. In separate chapters the authors discuss the scope and history of domestic violence in America, its effects on women and children, the characteristics of battering men, the options available to battered women, and the legal aspects of domestic violence and police responses to it.

SOC 316. **STACK, CAROL B.** All Our Kin: Strategies for Survival in a Black Community. New York: Harper & Row, 1974. 175 pp.
Based on participant observation, this study of black family networks reveals various adaptive techniques and strategies necessary for survival in an urban ghetto. Stack reveals "how people are recruited into kin networks; the relationship between household composition and residence patterns; and the relationship between reciprocity and poverty." Instead of revealing some underlying pathology within the family, Stack argues that in the face of grinding poverty, kin networks are "adaptive structural features" that aid survival at the cost of upward mobility and stable marriages.

SOC 317. **STAINES, GRAHAM L.** and **JOSEPH H. PLECK.** The Impact of Work Schedules on the Family. Ann Arbor, Mich.: Institute for Social Research, 1983. 186 pp.
Staines and Pleck assess how different types of work scheduling on the part of adult family members affect household behavior and subjective assessments of family organization and functioning. They deal with a subsample of 1,090 workers living with a spouse or a child under age eighteen, from the 1977 Quality of Employment Survey taken by the University of Michigan's Survey Research Center. The authors examine work scheduling in terms of four separate conceptions: the pattern of days worked during the week, the scheduling of hours during the day, the number of hours of paid employment weekly, and the degree of work schedule flexibility. The data substantiate expectations that men and women act and react in different ways to various aspects of the work situation.

SOC 318. **STRAUS, MURRAY A.**, **RICHARD J. GEILES**, and **SUZANNE K. STEINMETZ.** Behind Closed Doors: Violence in the American Family. Garden City, N.Y.: Anchor Books, 1981. 301 pp.
This book reports the results of a nationwide survey of 2,143 families, "the first comprehensive study of violence in the American family." Utilizing a survey instrument called the "Conflict Tactics Scale," the authors seek to measure the extent of family violence, the numerous forms it takes (e.g., shooting, stabbing, as well as spanking), what violence means to participants, what kinds of families are violent, and the causes of family violence. While the authors study a range of violence in families, their analysis focuses especially on child abuse, spouse abuse, and the relationship between the two.

SOC 319. **SWAN, L. ALEX.** Families of Black Prisoners: Survival and Progress. Boston: G. K. Hall, 1981. 163 pp.
The objective of this study is "to describe and identify a composite of black prisoners' families and determine the nature and extent of the problems these families face before, during, and after the imprisonment of a family member." Utilizing interviews with a sample of 200 black families from Tennessee and Alabama, the author assesses the responses of and effects on family members of each step of the process from arrest, arraignment, trial, and imprisonment to the adjustment of families after imprisonment has been completed.

SOC 320. TAFT, JOHN. Mayday at Yale: A Case Study in Student Radicalism. Boulder, Colo.: Westview Press, 1976. 224 pp.
This is a detailed chronology of the events at Yale University in the spring of 1970 during the trial of Black Panther leader Bobby Seale, a day-by-day account of the mobilization leading to the nationwide "Mayday Weekend." Aside from providing a close look at the internal dynamics and external manifestations of the movement at this major university, Taft suggests some possible reasons for the decline and fall of the student movement. The view that emerges from this vivid description is one of disorganization, fragmentation, violence, and irrationality in a movement that was hardly ever a well-structured political force—a movement that naturally extinguished itself before it could successfully reach out to other political sectors outside the university and become more coherent and more institutionalized.

SOC 321. THORMAN, GEORGE. Family Violence. Springfield, Ill.: Thomas, 1980. 184 pp.
The nature, extent, causes, and consequences of family violence are the subjects of this book, which is intended primarily for social welfare workers. The author provides a broad overview and synthesis of literature on the subject, focusing most of her discussion on child abuse and wife beating. She devotes separate chapters to the characteristics of abused children and the dynamics of families in which they are found, and to battered wives and the effects of such violence on the entire family. Moreover, in separate chapters she examines methods of intervention and alternatives that are available in work with abused children and battered wives. She concludes with a general discussion of various approaches to the prevention of family violence.

SOC 322. WEAVER, W. TIMOTHY. America's Teacher Quality Problem: Alternatives for Reform. New York: Praeger, 1983. 270 pp.
"The purpose of this book is to draw together the essential research on teacher quality and to examine it in terms of implications for new policy initiatives." Weaver contends that the problem of teacher quality is not a result of inadequate teacher requirements. Rather it has been affected more significantly by several market conditions: cyclical fluctuations in the teaching job market; shifts in student occupational preferences; variations in education-student and teacher test scores; and fluctuations in teacher compensation reflecting supply and demand factors. Weaver examines the effect of these factors on the talent pools entering and leaving the teaching profession. He concludes with a proposal for reform of the strategies of education schools.

SOC 323. WEISS, ROBERT S. Marital Separation. New York: Basic Books, 1975. 334 pp.
With more than one million divorces occurring in the U.S. in 1975, Weiss's book explores an ever more important aspect of American family dynamics: the dissolution of marriage and the breakup of the family unit. His study is based on open-ended interviews with members of two therapy groups organized by the author, "Seminars for the Separated" and "Parents without Partners." The author examines how adults cope with, describe, and define their marital breakups, the adjustments in self-identity and lifestyle that such separations require, and the impact of separation and divorce on children, kin groups, and the family's social network. This sociopsychological analysis of qualitative data provides a coherent and comprehensive insight into the problems presently affecting hundreds of thousands of American families.

SOC 324. WESTBY, DAVID L. The Clouded Vision: The Student Movement in the United States in the 1960's. Lewisburg, Penn.: Bucknell University Press, 1976. 291 pp.
Westby attempts to explain the structural conditions that generated the massive student and counter-cultural movements of the 1960s in the U.S. Examining the characteristics of student radicals and activists, Westby finds them to be individuals who were structurally and ideologically on the "periphery" of the American capitalist system. He argues that capitalist "disaccumulation," an intensifying crisis of employment throughout sectors of the labor force, was the key element in this peripheralization. The answer to the radicalization phenomenon, according to the author, lies primarily in the increasing contradictions between the educational and occupational systems. Westby concludes with a prognosis for future re-radicalization and a new progressive social mobilization of American students as capitalist contradictions continue.

SOC 325. WHITE, MARGARET B. Sharing Caring: The Art of Raising Kids in Two-Career Families. Englewood Cliffs, N.J.: Prentice-Hall, 1982. 246 pp.
The author's focus is the relatively recent phenomenon in American society of shared parenting. The data for the study are based both on questionnaires and extensive interviews with parents who had consciously chosen, from the birth of their first child, to share equally in the responsibilities of work and child care and had done so for more than economic reasons. The book has four basic emphases. First, it provides descriptions of those involved in shared parenting. Second, it discusses some of the psychological, cultural, and political reasons for why this mode of parenting was not previously more widespread in American society and the pressures that work against it now. Third, it identifies issues with which couples who wish to adopt such arrangements should be concerned. Finally, it discusses shared parenting as an issue for national family policy.

SOC 326. WILLIE, CHARLES VERT. The Sociology of Urban Education. Lexington, Mass.: Heath, 1978. 184 pp.
In the preface to this book Willie establishes his basic premises: "Education in a nation most of which is urban essentially is urban education. Because cities and metropolitan areas are places to which all sorts and conditions of people have come, pluralism is a central concern for urban education. Pluralism is either a liability or an opportunity. Whether it is one or the other depends largely on how well cultural and racial desegregation and integration are handled. Sooner or later desegregation and integration will affect all. Pluralism is the essence of urban society." The twenty-five essays that comprise this book are variations on this general theme and are intended to encourage development of a "conceptual approach to desegregation and integration."

SOC 327. YABLONSKY, LEWIS. Fathers and Sons. New York: Simon & Schuster, 1982. 218 pp.
Fathers and Sons discusses the emotional bonds, interactions, interdependencies, and conflicts between fathers and sons. Interviews are used from over a hundred men regarding their dual roles of father and son. Yablonsky examines the various prototypes of each—autocratic, egocentric, and distant fathers; compliant and rebellious sons—and explains how they develop and affect the quality of family life. He covers problems affecting father-son relations, including delinquency, drugs, deviance, homosexuality, divorce, and the difficulties arising from multiple-son situations.

V.   GENDER AND SEX ROLES

SOC 328. ANGRIST, SHIRLEY S. and ELIZABETH M. ALMQUIST. Careers and Con-
          tingencies: How College Women Juggle with Gender. New York:
          Dunellen, 1975. 269 pp.
This "pre-liberationist" study follows eighty-seven members of the class
of 1968 of a small women's college through their four years. The authors
attempt to assess the specific effects of college on the career and family
orientations of the women studied and on the role development of these
students. The researchers identified five types of students: "consistent
careerists," "consistent traditionalists," "converts to careers,"
"defectors to careers," and "constant shifters."

SOC 329. BARDWICK, JUDITH M. In Transition: How Feminism, Sexual Libera-
          tion and the Search for Self-Fulfillment Have Altered America.
          New York: Holt, Rinehart & Winston, 1979. 203 pp.
In Transition is about the conflicts women experience among their roles
as wife, mother, and business woman. However, Bardwick sympathizes with
those women who are committed to defending "traditionally female" values,
and she does not denigrate those who choose different ways of life. Her
assumption is that all women, regardless of their specific choices, must
feel ambivalent about them, and she offers support to all.

SOC 330. BEER, WILLIAM R. Househusbands: Men and Housework in American
          Families. New York: Praeger, 1983. 153 pp.
Beer's book is an empirical study of househusbands--men who significantly
participate in traditional tasks of housekeeping. Most of these men,
like many contemporary women, had two jobs: paid employment and housework.
Beer's findings on the multiple subjective meanings of housework comprise
a large part of the book. Beer studies what happens when men participate
in work previously defined as female. It complements recent studies of
women pursuing careers previously defined as male.

SOC 331. BERGER, RAYMOND M. Gay and Gray: Older Homosexual Men. Urbana:
          University of Illinois Press, 1982. 233 pp.
Berger used a questionnaire survey of 112 gay men over the age of forty
to write Gay and Gray. He found that those men appear very "well adjusted"
according to a series of psychometric inventories. He also found them
to be doing remarkably well, scoring higher on scales of general happiness,
life-satisfaction, guilt, therapy seeking, and self-disclosure, as well
as in their sexual activity. Berger's sample was drawn from an unnamed
"four county area."

SOC 332. BERNARD, JESSIE. The Female World. New York: Free Press, 1981.
          614 pp.
Bernard insists that a female world does exist, that "most human beings
live in single-sex worlds," and that the worlds of men and women are "sub-
jectively and objectively" different. Nearly half of the book is concerned
with "The Social Structure of the Female World" and "The Group Structure
of the Female World." Bernard discusses the demographic, socio-economic,
social class, kinship, groups, and associational characteristics of contemporary American women.

SOC 333. BIRD, CAROLINE. The Two-Paycheck Marriage: How Women at Work
          Are Changing Life in America. New York: Rawson, Wade, 1979.
          305 pp.
It was not until the decade of the 1970s that women began to feel comfortable working outside the home. Two-Paycheck Marriage discusses how people
manage to work and have a family; the negative as well as positive aspects

1756

of working; how a double paycheck influences the lives of a couple who
both work; and what a woman's job does to those other aspects of her life,
including marriage, home, children, and feelings she may have about herself.
The first section of this book recounts how people in the U.S. became
two-paycheck families and how this change is affecting present economics.
Part two explores how this, in turn, changes the marriage, home, money
management, and children. Part three discusses the different options
that two paychecks give such couples. The final section is a projection
on how economic independence of women will change the meaning of family
life and the meaning of work.

SOC 334. BOUTILIER, MARY A. and LUCINDA SanGIOVANNI. The Sporting Woman.
Champaign, Ill.: Human Kinetics, 1983. 289 pp.
This book provides an interpretive overview of women in American sport.
Combining interviews and personal observation with a broad range of
scholarly and lay materials, the authors organize their data "from the perspective of social science and feminism." For the latter they employ
Jagger and Struhl's classification of four variants of feminism to "identify, interpret, and resolve the many problems facing women as they enter
into sport." The book is divided into two parts of four chapters each.
The first part emphasizes theoretical issues, including chapters on the
history of American women in sport, the psychological dimension of female.
athletic participation, and the social content of women in sport. The
second part focuses on the relation of women to various institutions that
influence sport: the family, educational institutions, the mass media,
and the government.

SOC 335. BRAXTON, BERNARD. Women, Sex and Race: A Realistic View of
Sexism and Racism. Washington, D.C.: Verta, 1973. 227 pp.
According to Braxton, "racism and sexism, parallel evils, could be seen
emerging from similar malignant roots." He further explains that "racism
consisted of ignorance, prejudice, sick egos and warped mentalities, discrimination and oppression based on a mythology of race." Sexism, he
argues, was derived from the same social and personal pathology "based
on an unscientific belief in female inferiority-male superiority." The
author discusses the influence of the myths of "woman as witch" and black
sexuality upon white male hostility. He examines the changing sexism
and racism in "new politics." Braxton claims that the hostility of the
white male stems from a fear of the power of women and other races, and
is perpetuated in a "politics of repression and sadism" that enables men
to keep women and ethnics in subordinate positions within society.

SOC 336. CARDEN, MAREN LOCKWOOD. The New Feminist Movement. New York:
Russell Sage, 1974. 234 pp.
This work focuses on the institutional dimensions of Femininism in America
in the late 1960s and early 1970s. The movement, says Carden, has come
a long way from the much criticized and caricatured "women's libbers"
who allegedly burned bras and the locally based organizations that appeal
to numerous and diverse types of women. The author examines the structure
of the two principal branches of the Feminist movement: the women's
liberation-oriented groups and the women's rights-oriented groups. The
former groups focus on consciousness-raising and political action and
encompass the radical faction; the latter groups (like the National Organization for Women—NOW) focus on more economic issues such as work place
and child care and espouse "liberal" ideology. Carden's concluding chapter
is a statement on the origins, spread, and future of Feminism in American
society. The work features an extensive bibliography on women.

SOC 337. CARGAN, LEONARD and MATTHEW MELKO. Singles: Myths and Realities. Beverly Hills, Calif.: Sage, 1982. 287 pp.
The core of this book is an empirical analysis comparing single people over eighteen years of age with other "civil status" categories. The basic data for this comparative study of never-married, divorced, once-married, and remarried persons is based on questionnaires completed by a sample of 400 adults in the Dayton, Ohio metropolitan area. Comparisons are drawn between various categories of the unmarried and the married.

SOC 338. CHERNIN, KIM. The Obsession: Reflections on the Tyranny of Slenderness. New York: Harper & Row, 1981. 199 pp.
The Obsession begins with a definition of the problem concerning eating habits and one's body. Chernin describes the meaning and magnitude of food obsessions, analyzes certain eating disorders, and then provides an explanation. She argues that a large, voluptuous body symbolizes the female figure and that in American culture the power of the female is considered dangerous. She uses church documents and classical mythology to show fear of women as carnal, fecund, material (versus intellectual), and powerful. Chernin says that one way to control the female force is to reshape women's bodies into slender, adolescent forms. She discusses how anorexic and obese women share the same hostility, fear of sexuality, and uneasiness about women's roles.

SOC 339. COLE, JONATHAN R. Fair Science: Women in the Scientific Community. New York: Free Press, 1979. 336 pp.
How can science, an institution in which meritocratic standards are the primary source of status and rewards, have so few women? Why have those women who have entered science not received eminence and visibility comparable to men? These questions direct Cole's quantitative analysis of women's place in the academic scientific community. Among the obvious explanations for the paucity of women in science is discrimination, and a considerable portion of Cole's study is devoted to analyzing this explanation. In his final chapter he assesses the controversy over affirmative action as a means for rectifying the historic exclusion of women from the scientific community.

SOC 340. CONOVER, PAMELA JOHNSTON and VIRGINIA GRAY. Feminism and the New Right: Conflict over the American Family. New York: Praeger, 1983. 253 pp.
This book seeks to explain why the Equal Rights Amendment failed to be ratified. There is a discussion of groups that arose in the late 1970s to oppose the ERA as well as other Feminist movements. During this period the New Right also threatened existing legalized abortion. This book examines both ERA and abortion battles and the broader struggle over the place of the family within society. The last chapter examines the future of abortion and ERA as Conover and Gray perceive them.

SOC 341. CROSBY, FAYE J. Relative Deprivation and Working Women. New York: Oxford University Press, 1982. 268 pp.
Some of the aims of this book are (1) to contribute to the understanding of the dynamics of deprivation, (2) to describe reactions of women and men to their jobs, and (3) to analyze the home life and job situations of women in general. Relative Deprivation and Working Women is an attempt to bring an established social science theory to the question of working women. Crosby used quantitative data to establish attitudinal differences among employed women, employed men, and housewives. This book describes people's reactions to their jobs, and the job and home situations of women.

SOC 342. DELAMATER, JOHN and PATRICIA MACCORQUODALE. Premarital Sexuality:
     Attitudes, Relationships, Behavior. Madison: University of
     Wisconsin Press, 1979. 277 pp.
This is an effort to develop and test empirically an integrated model
of the social influences on premarital sexuality that combines sociological
and sociopsychological perspectives. The study is based on survey data
from a sample of student and nonstudent college age men and women. The
authors document a process of sociosexual development, the importance
of sexual ideology, the role that the nature of relationships plays, and
the significance of sociopsychological characteristics in affecting premarital sexuality. Finally, the authors compare the premarital sexual
activity of students and nonstudents and of men and women.

SOC 343. D'EMILIO, JOHN. Sexual Politics, Sexual Communities: The Making
     of a Homosexual Minority in the United States, 1940-1970. Chicago:
     University of Chicago Press, 1983. 257 pp.
D'Emilio shows that the modern movement for homosexual rights predates the
"Stonewall Riot" of 1969. Using interviews, letters, medical journals,
and newspapers, he chronicles the small, organized "homophile" movement
of the 1950s, centered in the Mattachine Society and the Daughters of
Bilitis. W.W. II plays a significant role in creating "something of a
nationwide coming out experience," for homosexuals learned by coming into
contact with others that they were not unique. The postwar Red Scare,
however, forced homosexuals to remain underground. The homosexual bar
served as a community center during these years and beyond. Encouraged
by the Black Power and Feminist movements, a new, far more open homosexual
rights movement was born in the late 1960s. D'Emilio's account pays more
attention to the movement itself than to individuals involved.

SOC 344. DUBERMAN, LUCILE, with HELEN MAYER HACKER and WARREN T. FARRELL.
     Gender and Sex in Society. New York: Praeger, 1975. 274 pp.
The authors attempt to bridge the knowledge gap about women in mainstream
American sociology. This work offers a brief historical overview of the
roles and statuses of women in America; it discusses the significance
of socialization in determining American attitudes about masculinity and
femininity, sex and sexuality, the personal interaction of men and women
within the context of changing roles, as well as inequality between men
and women in the political and economic spheres. Chapters by Hacker present the "sex-differential theme from the cross-class, cross-race and
cross-cultural perspectives." A final chapter by Farrell discusses the
impact of the women's movement on male consciousness, male attitudes,
and male egos.

SOC 345. EHRENREICH, BARBARA. The Hearts of Men: American Dreams and
     the Flight from Commitment. Garden City, N.Y.: Anchor Press,
     1983. 206 pp.
Ehrenreich states that "the fact that, in a purely economic sense, women
need men more than the other way round, gives marriage an inherent instability that predates the sexual revolution, the revival of Feminism, the
'me generation' or other well-worn explanations for what has come to be
known as the 'breakdown of the family.'" The Hearts of Men is a book
that discusses how, within the last thirty years, the ideology that shaped
the breadwinner ethic has not only changed--been challenged--but has col-
lapsed. The author says, "this is a book about ideas, images, perceptions,
opinions from various sources. . . ."

SOC 346. EHRENREICH, BARBARA and DEIRDRE ENGLISH. For Her Own Good:
150 Years of the Experts' Advice to Women. Garden City, N.Y.:
Anchor Press, 1978. 325 pp.
For Her Own Good discusses the historical changes of women from the persecution of witches in medieval Europe to the suppression of midwives
in America, the 19th-century epidemics of hysteria, and the mid-20th century
epidemic of frigidity. The authors gathered much of their information
firsthand from the women they were teaching in a course on "Women and
Health" at the State University of New York. They trace the different
paths that women have been allowed to choose. When women have fulfilled
their roles as society sees them, they have found themselves left with
a personal sense of unfulfillment. Some of the women have reacted by
going through phases of depression, paralysis, and inactivity. Many of
the women who experience these symptoms are highly educated and seemingly
well-motivated individuals.

SOC 347. EPSTEIN, CYNTHIA FUCHS. Woman's Place: Options and Limits in
Professional Careers. Berkeley: University of California Press,
1970. 221 pp.
The ideology of equality of the sexes proposed by the women's movement
has become widely accepted. Legal, educational, and formal barriers to
equality have theoretically disappeared. What remain to keep women in
"their place" are the cultural and societal barriers that are still as
pervasive as ever. Epstein looks at the ideology of women's roles in
American society and examines the socialization process, its consequences,
and woman's struggle to reconcile her professional and familial roles.
She also examines the structural impediments to the incorporation of women
into the academic, professional, and corporate worlds and the social impediments and pressures imposed on women who manage to enter those worlds.
Epstein concludes that "the woman who has proved her capabilities in training generally cannot count on society for encouragement or her colleagues
for fair treatment. She faces a difficult decision in weighing whether
to begin . . . a career that almost inevitably will involve . . . conflict
with traditional images of her place in society and, perhaps, with her
own images of personal fulfillment." In the final chapter of this volume,
the author predicts change within the professions.

SOC 348. EPSTEIN, CYNTHIA FUCHS. Women in Law. Garden City, N.Y.: Anchor
Press, 1983. 438 pp.
Epstein's Women in Law is an account of change and stability, the old
and new, pressures and cross-pressures, aspirations and frustrations.
With interviews and other data that span the critical decade and a half
between 1965 and 1980, Epstein shows the extent to which conditions for
women in the legal profession have--and have not--changed. This is a
descriptive work drawing on data collected by the American Bar Association
and Bureau of the Census, but it is based mainly on the interviews gathered
for Epstein's doctoral dissertation in the mid-1960s and on formal interviews and interactions in the 1970s.

SOC 349. EVANS, SARA. Personal Politics: The Roots of Women's Liberation
in the Civil Rights Movement and the New Left. New York: Vintage Books, 1979. 274 pp.
Based on archival materials and extensive personal interviews with women
actively involved in the development of the contemporary radical Feminist
movement, Personal Politics explores the origins of radical Feminism in
the Civil Rights Movement and the New Left of the 1960s. Drawing parallels
with the 19th-century women's rights movement, Evans contends that white
Southern women who had become involved in the Civil Rights Movement were
the first to stress the similarities of racial and sexual oppression.
She emphasizes especially the impact of participants' involvement in the
New Left on the organizational form and ideology of radical Feminism.

SOC 350. FRIEDAN, BETTY. <u>The Feminine Mystique</u>. New York: Norton, 1963.
410 pp.

Based on the responses of 200 members of the Smith College Class of 1942
to questions posed fifteen years after their graduation, this book was
a cultural catalyst for the new Women's Movement in America in the mid-
1960s. Friedan argues that "there was a strange discrepancy between the
reality of our lives as women and the image to which we were trying to
conform, the image that I came to call the feminine mystique." She discovered that women were overwhelmingly dissatisfied with their lives--
betrayed by a "happy housewife" myth that had been invented by society
and the media in an effort to keep women in their place. The first to
uncover the subtle and not-so-subtle structural and cultural barriers
imposed upon American women, Friedan called for a recognition and resolution to the problem that "lay buried, unspoken, for many years in the
minds of American women."

SOC 351. FRIEDAN, BETTY. <u>It Changed My Life</u>: <u>Writings on the Women's
Movement</u>. New York: Random House, 1976. 388 pp.

Friedan, ideological leader and founder of the National Organization for
Women, chronicles her own Feminist development. She describes the experiences that led to and from the writing of <u>The Feminine Mystique</u> (see SOC
350), a book that sparked the Women's Movement in America. Part II deals
with Friedan's involvement in the movement her words helped create, and
with the many important issues encountered by NOW and other newly formed
Feminist organizations in the late 1960s. Part III, which is composed
of selections from the personal notebooks Friedan kept from 1971 to 1973,
brings to light many of the personal and ideological conflicts that arose
during this period between the women's rights-oriented Feminist and the
radical Feminists. Part IV discusses the new questions emerging from
the sex-role revolution of the mid-1970s. Finally, in "An Open Letter
to the Women's Movement" Friedan points to the need for continued organized
struggle to counter the reactionary forces (which she outlines). Despite
statistical gains in education and employment and attitudinal change,
women must continue to work toward a total incorporation into all aspects
of political and economic life. In Friedan's view, the movement must
seek institutional allies and work more actively toward structural as
well as attitudinal reform.

SOC 352. FULENWIDER, CLAIRE KNOCHE. <u>Feminism in American Politics</u>: <u>A
Study of Ideological Influence</u>. Edited by Gerald M. Pomper.
New York: Praeger, 1980. 165 pp.

<u>Feminism in American Politics</u> focuses on beliefs about women's roles and
the policies that affect them. Fulenwider begins with a discussion of
the complex relationships among political ideology, social movements,
and social change. The remaining chapters address the origins of citizens' ideas about political and social life in socially structured experiences, and the impact of those ideas upon political behavior. Fulenwider
uses data from the 1972 and 1976 American National Election Studies conducted by the Center for Political Studies at the University of Michigan,
and investigates the links between attitudes on Feminist issues and demographic characteristics such as race and sex, on the one hand, and political orientations such as trust and efficacy on the other. She then evaluates the impact of each variable upon political participation.

SOC 353. GIELE, JANET ZOLLINGER. <u>Women and the Future</u>: <u>Changing Sex
Roles in Modern America</u>. New York: Free Press, 1978.
386 pp.

This book has two primary foci. First, it is an examination of sex roles
in contemporary American society. The author presents chapters on population, politics, economics, family, and education that describe changes
taking place in each of these spheres. <u>Women and the Future</u> is also

Giele's attempt "to present the nature of what the world would be if the values for which women have traditionally stood were given larger place." Thus she delineates the structure of a future egalitarian society and the changes in roles, rewards, and cultural values necessary to effect it. She identifies two major strategies of change: affirmative action, or the redistribution of persons throughout the system, and more fundamental structural change, in which rewards are more equitably distributed. She sees the implications of the Women's Movement leading ultimately to a radical reordering of values and a diminution of contemporary American society's hierarchical structure.

SOC 354. GILDER, GEORGE F. Sexual Suicide. New York: Quadrangle Books, 1973. 308 pp.
The creation of an androgynous and sexually free society, the elimination of social and perhaps even biological differences between men and women, according to Gilder, would be synonymous with "sexual suicide." His controversial book seeks to uncover the myths of open marriage and sexual equality, the perils of "androgyny," institutional child care, and other such "feminist-fangled" ideas. In the same "male backlash" tradition as Steven Goldberg's The Inevitability of Patriarchy (SOC 357), Gilder argues that as a consequence of "the alliance between women's liberation and technology" (which detracts importance and status from motherhood and the family) America may come to face a procreation crisis. Unlike Goldberg, he does not argue for the inherent superiority of the male but rather for the societal necessity of the traditional female role. In the process he formulates a theory about the new societal forces that are leading America.

SOC 355. GOFFMAN, ERVING. Gender Advertisements. Cambridge, Mass.: Harvard University Press, 1979. 84 pp.
Goffman examines how men and women--primarily women--are represented in advertisements and what these representations reveal about conceptions of appropriate sex roles and relations between the sexes in American society. The book begins with brief theoretical essays on the ways in which gestures, expressions, and postures--human "displays"--reflect underlying conceptions of the sexes. The empirical data for his perceptive analysis are primarily advertisements using human subjects, drawn from newspapers and popular magazines. Goffman considers such issues as the relative size of males and females, the quality of women's hands, instructions between the sexes, the directions in which the eyes are looking, and, in general, the reflections of dominance and submissiveness depicted in these ads.

SOC 356. GOLDBERG, HERB. The Hazards of Being Male: Surviving the Myth of Masculine Privilege. New York: Nash, 1976. 200 pp.
Goldberg argues that the male role in American society carries with it as many weighty burdens and crippling restrictions as that of the female. He feels that the "male has paid a heavy price for his masculine 'privilege' and power. He is out of touch with his emotions and his body. Only a new way of perceiving himself can unlock him from old, destructive patterns and enrich his life." Goldberg attempts to demonstrate how the American male "denies and destroys himself daily." The demands and restrictions placed on his societal role are oppressive. He cannot be sensitive; he must be aggressive in order to achieve and succeed; he must support a wife and family. Goldberg advocates a kind of male liberation, a self-assertion on the part of men to be free human beings, unbound by societal roles or standards. Men, he argues, cannot expect to achieve "meaningful growth simply by piggy-backing the changes that are occurring in women's attitudes."

SOC 357. GOLDBERG, STEVEN. The Inevitability of Patriarchy. New York: Morrow, 1973. 256 pp.
Goldberg's theoretical investigation into the anthropological and biological bases for the universality of male dominance constitutes a "male backlash" to Feminist theory and the Women's Movement. Goldberg argues against the proposition basic to all the claims and theories of the Feminist movement: that there is "nothing inherent in the nature of human beings or of society that necessitates that any role or task (save those requiring great strength or ability to give birth) be associated with one sex or the other." The author sets out to demonstrate that anthropological and biological data show otherwise, that the weight of evidence demonstrates that the male is superior both physically and intellectually, is more aggressive, and is therefore destined to rule. Women have "complementary" virtues that allow them to deal with men on "equal" terms. "The central fact," Goldberg concludes, "is that men and women are different from each other from the game to the thought to the act and that emotions that underpin masculinity and femininity, that make reality as experienced by the male eternally different from that experienced by the female, flow from the biological natures of man and woman."

SOC 358. GREER, GERMAINE. The Female Eunuch. New York: McGraw-Hill, 1971. 349 pp.
"Hopefully, this book is subversive," Greer writes in her introduction. "The conventional moralist will find much that is reprehensible in the denial of the Holy Family, in the denigration of sacred motherhood, and the inference that women are not by nature monogamous. The political conservatives ought to object that by advocating the destruction of the patterns of consumption carried out by the chief spenders, the housewives, the book invites depression and hardship. . . ." The book does indeed invite criticism from most "liberal" thinkers, for it is an angry, inflamed, and heavily rhetorical essay examining society's "castration" of women. Greer looks at woman's body and soul and at the social mythologies and socialization processes that mold them. Looking at women and love, she examines the middle-class myth of love and marriage, which she contends was designed to keep women at home and out of the competitive job market. She looks at the hate and rebellion emerging from woman's oppression and the prospects for a women's "revolution."

SOC 359. GUTTENTAG, MARCIA and PAUL F. SECORD. Too Many Women? The Sex Ratio Question. Beverly Hills, Calif.: Sage, 1983. 277 pp.
Too Many Women examines the effect of the sex ratio on social organization. Guttentag died in 1977, and Secord redrafted her five chapters and wrote four more. The book stems from the idea that the number of opposite sex partners potentially available to women or men profoundly affects sexual behavior, marriage, divorce, childrearing, family stability, and structural aspects of society itself. The authors contend that adequate interpretation requires the use of an interdisciplinary approach involving anthropology, biology, history, psychology, and sociology.

SOC 360. HAMILTON, ROBERTA. The Liberation of Women: A Study of Patriarchy and Capitalism. Boston: Allen & Unwin, 1978. 117 pp.
The Liberation of Women explains how women were kept immobile by their biological differences. These differences included the dependence of women after childbirth and during nursing. This kept women dependent on men for most of women's adult lives. In the last several years women have been able to overcome their biological limitations with the help of birth control, abortion and test-tube babies. A Marxist analysis differs from biological thought in that the Marxists believe women's dependence stemmed from private property belonging to the man, which left the women's role as that of producing heirs for their husbands' wealth and

property. Hamilton believes both of these ideas to be partially valid
and she also discusses how they each fall short of explaining the differences among women as well as the differences between men and women.

SOC 361. HARRY, JOSEPH. Gay Children Grown Up: Gender Culture and
Gender Deviance. New York: Praeger, 1982. 269 pp.
"This is the story of the ugly duckling who grows up to be a beautiful
gay swan. It is a description of virtues acquired through adversity in
pre-adulthood." Harry contends that alienated pre-gay boys, "ugly duck-
lings," develop feminine preferences and homosexual orientations early
in childhood and that these differences from heterosexual boys force them
to devise or invent creative responses that are useful during adulthood.
His research is based on survey data obtained from samples of homosexual
and heterosexual men in the Chicago area in which the author asked respondents to recall certain features of childhood and adolescence. Homosexual
respondents were much more likely to remember childhood effeminacy and
to have experienced academic success, and they were much less likely to
report adolescent violence, interest in sports, or in heterosexual dating
than heterosexual males. The author then develops a theoretical explanation for the development and social reinforcement of homosexual identity.

SOC 362. HOWE, LOUISE KAPP. Pink Collar Workers: Inside the World of
Women's Work. New York: Putnam, 1977. 301 pp.
Occupational segregation by sex pervades the work force in contemporary
America despite statistical gains in actual female participation in the
labor force. Howe's study demonstrates that women are still relegated
to what she calls "pink collar occupations." While more women have gained
access to higher status, higher paying jobs, the overwhelming majority
of American women are still working in the traditionally or stereotypically
female occupations. The most common occupation remains unpaid housework,
and the largest proportion of women in the paid labor force are in the
"pinkest" categories--clerical service, and sales jobs. Howe interviewed
several hundred female workers--beauticians, salesworkers, nurses, dental
assistants, teachers, and others in female-dominated jobs (all categories
were over 90% female in 1975).

SOC 363. HUBER, JOAN and GLENNA SPITZE. Sex Stratification: Children,
Housework, and Jobs. New York: Academic Press, 1983.
278 pp.
This book proposes and tests a theory on how Americans respond to social
and economic changes and how these then affect sex stratification. "The
theory's central proposition holds that patterns of sex stratification
are shaped by the way a given subsistence technology enables women to
combine pregnancy and lactation with valued work." Huber and Spitze examine the changing roles of women, deriving their data from a telephone
survey of U.S. residents conducted in 1978. The main variables analyzed
in Sex Stratification include morality, education, fertility, and women's
participation in the work-force. Changes in women's roles were affected
by increased education, decreasing mortality, and fertility decline, but
economic conditions also had changed.

SOC 364. IGLEHART, ALFREDA P. Married Women and Work: 1957 and 1976.
Lexington, Mass.: Heath, 1979. 107 pp.
This book examines the intrapersonal changes among wives whose roles have
been challenged by changes in traditional sex-role ideology. The data
on which the study is based are personal interviews obtained for a 1957
national survey of mental health and its replication in 1976. The author
considers the impact of several demographic variables (e.g., age, education,
occupation, family income, age of youngest child) on several attitudinal
factors (e.g., attitudes toward working wives, preferences for housework,
job satisfaction). Among the noteworthy changes in married women's atti-

tudes toward work during the period were an increase in noneconomic commitment to work, a decline in the idealization of the homemaker role, and, among those who remained homemakers in 1976, a decided ambivalence about their role.

SOC 365. KRIEGER, SUSAN. The Mirror Dance: Identity in a Women's Community. Philadelphia: Temple University Press, 1983. 199 pp.

This study is based on seventy-eight lengthy interviews obtained by the author during her participation in a lesbian community in a Midwestern university town. The Mirror Dance "focuses on problems of merger and separation and on conflicts surrounding identity." Krieger examines the dynamics of this stigmatized, ideologically committed, and relatively new community of women and the ways in which members of the community sought to find new ways of protecting and defining their sense of self and controlling their personal sense of identity.

SOC 366. LADNER, JOYCE A. Tomorrow's Tomorrow: The Black Woman. Garden City, N.Y.: Doubleday, 1971. 304 pp.

Ladner spent almost four years interviewing, testing, and observing the thirty young black women from a St. Louis slum whose lives form the basis for this study. Ladner begins by presenting their life histories and the attitudes and behavior that are associated with approaching womanhood. She explains that black women can be seen as representative of the black community: "The total misrepresentation of the black community and the various myths which surround it can be seen in microcosm in the black female adolescent. Her growing up years reflect the basic quality and character of life in this environment; as well as anticipations for the future."

SOC 367. LEGHORN, LISA and KATHERINE PARKER. Woman's Worth: Sexual Economics and the World of Women. Boston: Routledge & Kegan Paul, 1981. 356 pp.

According to Leghorn and Parker, the economic structure of society "institutionalizes and sustains the value system of the society." All economies have a hierarchical family-based sexual division of labor dominated by men and men's values. The authors state that sex is the basic and historically most ancient form of stratification, and that other forms, such as class, race, or Colonialism, are modeled on that of "women doing menial, subservient work for men who have more power, resources, leisure time, and a higher standard of living."

SOC 368. LESERMAN, JANE. Men and Women in Medical School: How They Change and How They Compare. New York: Praeger, 1981. 239 pp.

The focus of this book is the patterns of change of 341 medical students. This includes the comparative effects of medical school socialization on women, who constituted 25.8% of the sample. Four problem areas of medical care delivery are focused upon in the assessment of "Professional orientation": (1) doctor-patient relationship; (2) political and economic organization of the medical profession; (3) prejudicial treatment of women physicians and patients; and (4) physician maldistribution.

SOC 369. LOTT, BERNICE. Becoming a Woman: The Socialization of Gender. Springfield, Ill.: Thomas, 1981. 463 pp.

Lott explains the theory behind Becoming a Woman in Simone de Beauvoir's words that "one is not born, but rather becomes a woman." The focus of Lott's work is the shared experiences of contemporary women and girls. She reviewed information about women's lives from biographies, fiction, newspaper accounts of current events, observations, statistical summaries of quantitative data, and from psychological laboratories and clinics. Becoming a Woman concerns itself with women's lives, but at times contrasts

the two genders. Lott believes that "all human behavior . . . can ultimately be explained by means of one set of general and interrelated principles. Anchoring this belief is the assumption that human behavior,
beyond molecular physiological responses and innate reflex mechanisms,
is learned. While the content of what is learned in diverse situations
may be almost infinite in its variety, the process is always the same."

SOC 370. MacKINNON, CATHARINE A. Sexual Harassment of Working Women:
          A Case of Sex Discrimination. New Haven, Conn.: Yale University
          Press, 1979. 312 pp.
MacKinnon began her work on sexual harassment in 1974. She developed
the argument that sexual harassment in the workplace does in fact constitute unlawful sex discrimination within the meaning of the Equal Protection
Clause of the Fourteenth Amendment. MacKinnon argues that there are two
distinct concepts of discrimination, the "difference" approach and the
"inequality" approach. The "difference" approach focuses on whether different treatment of the sexes is arbitrary and thus illegal, or rational
and therefore not unlawful. The "inequality" approach recognizes that
the sexes are socially unequal, and would prohibit all practices that
subordinate women to men.

SOC 371. MANDLE, JOAN D. Women and Social Change in America. Princeton,
          N.J.: Princeton Book, 1979. 228 pp.
Mandle reviews literature on the changing condition of women and documents
alterations in women's labor force participation, education, marital status,
birth rates, and death rates. She explains why the women's movement
started when it did. She describes the process as follows: (1) long-term
economic development changed women's relationship to the economy; (2)
this new relation produced and was tempered by changes in women's roles
in the family; (3) as a result of these processes a new "collective personality," together with economic and family sphere changes, produced a
social movement; (4) the social movement reinforced and encouraged further
change in women's economic situation, family life, and personalities.

SOC 372. MARET, ELIZABETH. Women's Career Patterns: Influences on Work
          Stability. Lanham, Md.: University Press of America, 1983.
          173 pp.
This is a study of patterns of women's labor market participation. Maret
provides a historical overview of trends in women's employment and how
these patterns differ from those of men. The primary thrust of her study
is a systematic analysis of the career patterns of 5,000 women. She identifies differences in the distinctive features of the career work patterns
of women. Moreover, she distinguishes between supply and demand explanations for these differences in the career work patterns of men and women.

SOC 373. MATTHEWS, SARAH H. The Social World of Old Women: Management
          of Self-Identity. Beverly Hills, Calif.: Sage, 1979.
          192 pp.
Matthews's thesis is that society and "gerontolized" professionals perpetuate a negative self-identity for the elderly and define old age as
post-adulthood. Matthews first introduces the problem of how older widowed
women attempt to retain a positive self-identity. She interviewed thirty-
one older widowed women. Her second chapter presents the societal context
of old age. The third chapter discusses oldness as a stigma. The next
four chapters deal with coping strategies which Matthews discovered in
situations in which an older woman finds similarities between herself
and the stereotypical old woman. The final chapter discusses negotiating
identity in the senior citizens center where Matthews was a participant
observer.

SOC 374. **MEDNICK, MARTHA TAHARA SHUCH, SANDRA SCHWARTZ TANGRI**, and **LOIS WLADIS HOFFMAN**. Women and Achievement: Social and Motivational Analyses. Washington, D.C.: Hemisphere, 1975. 447 pp.
The essays in this volume focus on the changing patterns of achievement and accomplishment for women as a group in American society from a socio-psychological perspective. The first section presents theoretical material concerning sex roles and social change, the implications for personality theory, research in understanding women, and current appraisals of sex-role stereotypes. It also examines these basic questions from a cross-cultural perspective. The second section explores achievement motives as they relate to such factors as early childhood experiences, sociali-zation, women's expectations for and causal attributions of success and failure, achievement-related conflicts in women, race, social class, and sex-role attitudes. The final section deals with achievement patterns and the effects of sex-labeling in the job market and with sex discrimina-tion in employment practices; it also explores the changing image of the career woman in the America of the mid-1970s.

SOC 375. **PITCHER, EVELYN GOODENOUGH** and **LYNN HICKEY SCHULTZ**. Boys and Girls at Play: The Development of Sex Roles. New York: Praeger, 1983. 207 pp.
This is a contribution to the growing literature on sex-role learning and behavior. For three years the authors recorded their systematic obser-vations of the play of three- to five-year-old children in preschools in the Boston metropolitan area. They examined the developmental progression of sex differences in the children's play, identified the striking ways in which boys' play differed from girls', and assessed the influences, especially from peers, that shaped these differences. Finally, the authors discuss the implications of their findings and whether it is possible to change the nature and course of traditional sex role development.

SOC 376. **PLECK, JOSEPH H.** The Myth of Masculinity. Cambridge, Mass.: MIT Press, 1981. 229 pp.
In this book Pleck critiques the paradigm underlying past and present male sex-role research, which he labels the male sex role identity paradigm. Drawing on the pattern of scientific "progress" described by Kuhn, Pleck's central thesis is that the sex-role strain paradigm is a far more unbiased and fruitful way to organize research on sex roles. Pleck examines the research both stemming from and used as confirmation of each of eleven propositions.

SOC 377. **READ, KENNETH E.** Other Voices: The Style of a Male Homosexual Tavern. Novato, Calif.: Chandler & Sharp, 1980. 212 pp.
This book on contemporary American homosexuality examines the social dynamics and structure of a male homosexual bar in a modern American city. Read constructs an anthropological theory of homosexuality, indicating the diversity of lifestyles embraced by the umbrella term "homosexuality." He applies the insights of the Existentialist writer Jean Genet to show the ways in which, symbolically, homosexual and heterosexual lifestyles mirror each other, and in reality, are often intermeshed.

SOC 378. **ROSENBERG, JAN.** Women's Reflections: The Feminist Film Movement. Ann Arbor, Mich.: UMI Research Press, 1983. 143 pp.
Rosenberg examines the world of Feminist filmmaking by providing a behind-the-scenes look at both contemporary and historical Feminist filmmakers. The basic themes of Feminist films—the emphasis on personal life and interpersonal relations, marriage conflicts, motherhood, and sexuality, as well as political concerns and the tension between private and public aspects of a woman's life, are discussed in the context of an ever-changing women's movement that is shown to provide a specialized audience for Femin-ism's unique film messages.

SOC 379. ROTHMAN, BARBARA KATE. In Labor: Women and Power in the Birthplace. New York: Norton, 1982. 320 pp.
The "medical model," according to Rothman, defines pregnancy as an abnor-
mality, the fetus as a foreign parasite, and birth as a surgical phenomenon.
She feels American obstetrics lost touch with nature some time in the
19th century. Another model of pregnancy and birth places the mother
in control not only of her body, but of the birth process as well. Rothman
labels this alternative, natural model the "midwifery model" in honor
of the centuries of midwives who assisted nature. The author's thesis
is that the medical model is not scientifically or socially appropriate
for most births; it serves the interests of medicine but not of families
or children.

SOC 380. RUZEK, SHERYL BURT. The Women's Health Movement: Feminist Alternatives to Medical Control. New York: Praeger, 1979. 351 pp.
This book traces the emergence and development of the women's health movement. Using fieldwork, interviews, and documents, Ruzek develops a typology of four obstetrical and gynecological "health care worlds," ranging
from the traditional-authoritarian to the radical Feminist. She also
discusses contradictory relationships between Feminist health activists
and the state, and strains relating to the movement's efforts to cope
with class and race divisions. This book deals with the organization
of health care and movements for change.

SOC 381. SCHREIBER, CAROL TROPP. Changing Places: Men and Women in Transitional Occupations. Cambridge, Mass.: MIT Press, 1979.
244 pp.
Schreiber explores the personal meaning of the movement of men and women
into jobs previously held predominantly by members of the opposite sex.
She is concerned with the motives, expectations, feelings, and experiences,
both of those who have entered previously sex-typed jobs and of their
peers and supervisors as well. Her study was carried out in a large work
organization that had sponsored such changes in the composition of traditionally sex-typed departments. Schreiber places her study in the tradition of "action research," which "seeks to combine social usefulness
with scientific meaning," and her discussion of the implications of this
approach is an important component of this book.

SOC 382. SCULLY, DIANA. Men Who Control Women's Health: The Miseducation
of Obstetrician-Gynecologists. Boston: Houghton Mifflin, 1980.
285 pp.
This study of obstetricians and gynecologists and their control over
women's health was based on Scully's extended field research in two settings:
"Elite Medical Center" and "Mass Hospital." The major focus of the book
is on obstetric and gynecologic surgery. In addition, the author examines
"how the practice of medicine and physicians' professional goals interact
to influence the development of attitudes and skills that are at variance
with the health care needs of women." Finally, based on her observations
in a teaching hospital, where many of the patients were poor, the author
addresses issues concerning inequities in health care delivery in America.

SOC 383. SOKOLOFF, NATALIE J. Between Money and Love: The Dialectics
of Women's Home and Market Work. New York: Praeger, 1980.
299 pp.
Sokoloff contends that one cannot understand women's labor market positions
without analyzing women's position in the home and the political and economic conditions in which these workplaces are embedded. She examines
the socialization process and sex roles and how they both relate to women's
experiences in the work force. After undertaking a critique of several
diverse models used to explain women's position in the work force, she
turns to a discussion of Marx and 20th-century theorists of monopoly Capi-

talism to understand women's disadvantageous position in modern capitalist societies. She concludes that "any attempt to analyze women's occupational attainment without fully incorporating her familial tasks in a patriarchal capitalist society would be analyzing less than half the picture."

SOC 384. STANLEY, LIZ and SUE WISE. Breaking Out: Feminist Consciousness and Feminist Research. Boston: Routledge & Kegan Paul, 1983. 202 pp.
Stanley and Wise critique the "grand theory" approaches of Marxism, Structural Functionalism, and contemporary Feminist theory for being overly abstract and jargonistic. They start from a premise that women's experiences constitute a separate ontology, or way of making sense of the world. The book does not discuss alternative methodological techniques and strategies but it examines explicitly and contextually the complex interrelationships underlying the production of knowledge.

SOC 385. STAPLES, ROBERT. Black Masculinity: The Black Male's Role in American Society. San Francisco: Black Scholar Press, 1982. 182 pp.
This is a sequel to Staples's earlier book, The Black Woman in America (see SOC 386) which focuses on the sexual, marital, and familial roles of black women. Staples's basic objective in Black Masculinity is "to examine the multiple dimensions of the role of black males in American society." He seeks to explain the sources of and the reality behind the "stereotypical [and] superficial images of black men as macho, hypersexual, violent and exploitative." Based on a conflict model that includes elements of Marxist, Pan-Africanist and internal Colonialist perspectives, his thesis is that black males are in conflict with the dominant American norms of masculinity, which imply autonomy over and mastery of one's environment. Because black males are more likely to be undereducated, unemployed, in prison, and excluded from participation in American society than black women, he contends that "in the black community, it is the men who need attending to."

SOC 386. STAPLES, ROBERT. The Black Woman in America: Sex, Marriage, and the Family. Chicago: Nelson-Hall, 1973. 269 pp.
Staples argues that black women have been oppressed as blacks and as females, a "dual dilemma." He reviews each role of the black woman from a historical perspective, and discusses such issues as black prostitution, blacks as wives and as mothers, black female sexuality, and the relationship between black women and Feminism. Attacking white racism, Staples concludes that "Black liberation is seen as Black women's liberation," and that black men will need to be "resocialized" in their attitudes toward black women.

SOC 387. STAPLES, ROBERT. The World of Black Singles: Changing Patterns of Male/Female Relations. Westport, Conn.: Greenwood Press, 1981. 259 pp.
Staples's book is about the worlds of middle-class, single black men and women. Staples's portrait of black single lifestyles includes an historical and social overview; the processes and places where singles meet, date, and sometimes mate; love and sex among singles; the extent and viability of interracial relationships; the importance of friendships; the emotional problems of loneliness; and the difficulties for single parents and those pursuing alternative lifestyles. Most of the data for the book came from 100 in-depth interviews in the San Francisco Bay area.

SOC 388. STEWART, DEBRA W. The Women's Movement in Community Politics in the U.S.: The Role of Local Commissions on the Status of Women. Elmsford, N.Y.: Pergamon Press, 1980. 147 pp.
This is an analysis of the impact and consequences of the creation of the Presidential Commission on the Status of Women (PCSW) by President Kennedy in 1961 and, more generally, an assessment of the motivations for and effects of advisory commissions on social movements. Created by Kennedy as a means of resolving certain political dilemmas, the PCSW nevertheless dramatized the unfavorable condition of women in American society and provided the organizational framework (in the form of state commissions on the status of women) for the development of the women's movement. Stewart's study examines the institutions that emerged at the local political level as a result of the creation of such local commissions. Her study is based on quantitative data on forty-eight local commissions throughout the country as well as on an intensive examination of five successful commissions. She seeks to identify those factors that contribute to the effective performance of a local commission in mobilizing women's interests and advancing women's movement ends.

SOC 389. STOLL, CLARICE STASZ. Female and Male: Socialization, Social Roles and Social Structure. Dubuque, Iowa: Brown, 1974. 228 pp.
"We have no choice over our bodies, only over our culture's evaluation of our particular body type," writes Stoll. "In America," she continues, "the evaluations attached to gender affect individual men and women in every area of life and throughout its course." Her book examines the consequences of being female and being male—the roles, costs, rewards, and identities that accompany rather simple biological differences. Stoll looks at sex differences as determined by nature and by culture, presents a statistical picture of sexism in America, and examines sexism as she sees it manifest in social science research. She discusses the processes of "becoming" male or female, maintaining those roles, and coping with consequences, and she concludes with a discussion of the "policies of gender."

SOC 390. WAGNER, JON. Sex Roles in Contemporary American Communes. Bloomington: Indiana University Press, 1982. 242 pp.
Sex Roles discusses six communes that have not been accorded a prominent place in socio-anthropological literature. The data support the contention that the communal movement is far from dead, and add a pertinent dimension to the controversial problems of sex roles. Sex Roles contains accounts of the Black Hebrew Israelites, the New Age Brotherhood, the Levites of Utah, the Shiloh Community, The Farm, and Haran. All but the first are located in the mainland U.S.

SOC 391. WEINBERG, MARTIN S. and COLIN J. WILLIAMS. Male Homosexuals: Their Problems and Adaptations. New York: Oxford University Press, 1974. 316 pp.
The majority of research on homosexuality has been conducted by psychologists and psychoanalysts, and thus homosexuality is often defined as pathological. The authors of this study reject such assumptions and instead attempt to provide a sociological view, which is guided by the sociology of deviance and by societal reaction theory. "In the context of this perspective, we conceptualize the homosexual situation according to three parameters: relating to the heterosexual world, relating to the homosexual world, and psychological problems." Weinberg and Williams's data were collected through a series of interviews with homosexual men in New York, San Francisco, and, for purposes of cross-cultural contrast, Amsterdam and Copenhagen. Concluding chapters discuss the implications of the data for future sociological research on homosexuality.

SOC 392. WEINBERG, THOMAS S. Gay Men, Gay Selves: The Social Construction of Homosexual Identities. New York: Irvington, 1983. 329 pp.
This is a detailed study of the processes whereby men form and maintain a homosexual identity. The primary data are thirty in-depth interviews conducted during the 1970s with men in an Eastern city. Utilizing a symbolic interactional model, the author fashions a three-stage sequence (a period that ranged in length from three to six years) in the development of a homosexual identity: suspecting that one may be a homosexual, self-labeling as a homosexual, and engaging in homosexual sexual behavior. The author also describes the respondents' views of homosexuality prior to their self-suspicions and their responses to their homosexual identity.

SOC 393. WOLGAST, ELIZABETH H. Equality and the Rights of Women. Ithaca, N.Y.: Cornell University Press, 1980. 176 pp.
The basic premise of Wolgast's philosophical examination of women's rights is that "justice requires men and women to be treated differently, not in all areas but in some important ones. . . . A good society will acknowl- edge the [biological] differences [between women and men], treating them with respect and fairness and accommodating institutions to the human condition." She therefore considers it essential that the appropriateness of the concept of equality for ensuring justice for women be assessed. She urges an alternative to egalitarian reasoning "that distinguishes between the interests of men and the interests of women," and she explores the political, social, legal, and societal implications of such a recon- ceptualization for American society.

SOC 394. YATES, GAYLE GRAHAM. What Women Want: The Ideologies of the Movement. Cambridge, Mass.: Harvard University Press, 1975. 230 pp.
This book examines American Feminism as ideology from sociological and historical perspectives. The focus is on ideological developments in American Feminism since 1963, or the "new Feminism." Yates discusses the three major currents of thought that have evolved in the movement. The first discussed is the classical Feminist perspective, which posits that women should be equal to men. The second, mostly identified with the more radical Feminism of the late 1960s and early 1970s, is the women's liberationist perspective: "women over against men"--a call for the superiority and supremacy of women. Of more recent origin is the third current, the androgynous perspective, which incorporates the ideology of the other two, yet posits that women and men should be equal to each other and calls for a non-sex-role defined society.

SOC 395. YORBURG, BETTY. Sexual Identity: Sex Roles and Social Change. New York: Wiley, 1974. 227 pp.
This book offers an interdisciplinary look at masculinity and femininity, the socially defined concepts of sexual identity. Yorburg examines the biological basis for sex differences, looks at sexual identity from a historical perspective, discusses cross-cultural variations on sexual identity, and then focuses on America, discussing male and female personal- ity and life cycle differences, and class and ethnic differences between the sexes. The author concludes on a positive note, asserting that the notion of cultural pluralism will eventually extend to the functions and activities of men and women: "The terms masculinity and femininity will disappear from modern languages because they will no longer reflect stand- ards that guide thought, emotion, and behavior," Yorburg asserts. "The primary source for such standards will be the individual and his or her temperament and abilities."

VI.   LIFE COURSE

SOC 396. BECKER, GAYLENE. Growing Old in Silence. Berkeley: University
          of California Press, 1980. 148 pp.
The purpose of this volume is to provide perspectives on the aged deaf
for practitioners who offer services to the disabled population. Becker
first notes that old age itself is treated as a disability; she then discusses the role played by age peers throughout the life of deaf individuals,
and the nature of community membership held by older deaf people and its
import for their collective identity. Also under consideration are the
overall adaptive behavior of the deaf in old age and the range of factors
which determine the success of such adaptation.

SOC 397. BERGHORN, FORREST J., DONNA E. SCHAFER, GEOFFREY H. STEERE,
          and ROBERT F. WISEMAN. The Urban Elderly: A Study of Life Satis-
          faction. Montclair, N.J.: Allanheld Osmun, 1978. 183 pp.
This book represents an interdisciplinary approach to gerontology. It
focuses upon the well-being of elderly citizens of a large Midwestern
city. The study is based on extensive interviews and includes analyses
of economic, social, and attitudinal variables that affect the life satisfaction of older people. It also integrates several social theories of
aging in order to explain the relationship found in the study between
the ability to cope with everyday problems and life satisfaction. The
authors draw policy implications from their findings that bear on the
welfare of the burgeoning population of elderly Americans in the later
20th century.

SOC 398. BRAIN, JAMES LEWTON. The Last Taboo: Sex and the Fear of Death.
          Garden City, N.Y.: Anchor Press, 1979. 256 pp.
Brain's analysis of the relationship between sex and the fear of death
takes the form of an anthropological and psychological study of sexual
behavior and language across several cultures. He finds that seemingly
universal fears and anxieties about sex and incest are rooted in the categorization abilities afforded by language. The author finds that associations between putrefaction and spiritual weakening link sex and death;
psychologically, this is paralleled by the psychic connections between
the perception of feces and death. Among the topics discussed in this
study are "dirty" jokes, initiation rites, obscenity and euphemism, womb
envy, and ritual pollution and sex roles.

SOC 399. BUTLER, ROBERT N. Why Survive? Being Old in America. New York:
          Harper & Row, 1975. 496 pp.
Over 10% of the American population are currently over sixty-five years
of age and the number of elderly Americans is on a steady increase. However, American society does not adequately provide for its older citizens
so that "old age in America is often a tragedy." "We talk earnestly
about our 'senior citizens,' but we do not provide them enough to eat.
We become angry with them for being burdens, yet we take for granted the
standard of living that their previous work has made possible for us.
Neglect in the treatment of choice, with medicine failing to care for
their physical needs, mental-health personnel ignoring their emotional
problems, communities neglecting to fill their social expectations."
Butler argues that elders often grow poor in this "affluent society,"
that their pensions are inadequate, yet public policy denies them the
right to work. He examines the conditions of housing for the elderly
community, the psychiatric neglect of the "political pacification" of
America's senior citizens (who comprise a significant portion of the voting
population) and calls for recognition of the problems of the aging.

SOC 400. CALHOUN, RICHARD B. In Search of the New Old: Redefining Old Age in America, 1945-1970. New York: Elsevier, 1978. 280 pp.
This book chronicles how "various interest groups worked to institutionalize a new, more positive concept of the aging process." The author hails this change as a "triumph of the public relations approach" that altered the image of America's elderly population. The primary focus of the book is the effort to redefine "retirement" from a sign of incapacity to a period of deserved personal freedom. Calhoun contends that the positive image has improved the status of older people.

SOC 401. CHARMAZ, KATHY. The Social Reality of Death: Death in Contemporary America. Reading, Mass.: Addison-Wesley, 1980. 335 pp.
The author looks from a sociological perspective at both earlier assumptions and current issues about death and dying. The major source of her theoretical perspective is symbolic interactionism. She attempts to demonstrate relationships between wider cultural values on which the social structure rests, and thoughts and actions of individuals who confront death in their daily lives. The author believes that the problems and dilemmas facing those who confront death (including the dying, suicidal, or bereaved) are not so different in kind from those experienced in more ordinary circumstances. This work seeks to review, synthesize, and extend current thought on death and dying.

SOC 402. CLARK, ROBERT L. and DAVID T. BARKER. Reversing the Trend Toward Early Retirement. Washington, D.C.: American Enterprise Institute, 1981. 64 pp.
Part of the conservative attack on the Social Security System, this monograph summarizes the recent economic literature on the increasing trend toward early retirement. The authors concentrate on the "retirement decision" and explain it as an individual rather than structural phenomenon that is precipitated by a rational decision based on an assessment of the impact of retirement on one's future financial status. The authors recommend raising the age of eligibility for full Social Security benefits as well as reducing the financial "incentives" to retire early.

SOC 403. CRYSTAL, STEPHEN. America's Old Age Crisis: Public Policy and the Two Worlds of Aging. New York: Basic Books, 1982. 323 pp.
Placing his analysis of old age policy within the context of demographic changes and the changing political economy, Crystal examines both the formal and informal support systems of the aging population. Crystal argues that "existing old age policies are inequitable, inefficient, and ineffective," leading to the division of the elderly population into haves and have nots. On the basis of an examination of the potentials and limitations of family assistance, Crystal concludes that the ability of the family to meet the basic needs of the elderly population has been "considerably oversold." He recommends the creation of a coherent old age policy that matches programs with needs instead of the current safety net through which the most needy portion of the elderly population slips.

SOC 404. DAVIS, PATRICIA A. Suicidal Adolescents. Springfield, Ill.: Thomas, 1983. 89 pp.
The recent rise in adolescent suicides is characterized in the foreword to this volume as an "epidemic crisis." This book reviews over 100 primarily psychological studies of adolescent suicide. The author begins by examining historical changes in societal attitudes toward suicide and by providing a general overview of the subject. She then devotes separate chapters to motivation, etiology (e.g., impulsiveness, drug abuse, social isolation, academic problems, family problems, loss of a loved one, etc.), prodromal clues, treatment, prevention, intervention, postvention for

the victim's family, and recommendations for those who live and work with adolescents.

SOC 405. DOWD, JAMES J. Stratification Among the Aged. Monterey, Calif.: Brooks/Cole, 1980. 153 pp.
In this book, a sociological explanation about aging is suggested; the author's thesis is that the greater the relative power of the individual older person, the greater the likelihood he or she will be able to negotiate a favorable situation in old age. The "Social Problem" of aging is that the elderly possess, relative to other age groups, lower status in the sense of negotiable power, privilege, and prestige; they are in an unfavorable exchange position. To understand either the process of aging or life in old age, according to Dowd, it is necessary to explicate the relationship between age and the possession of resources, stratification, and the mechanisms of exchange.

SOC 406. ECKERT, J. KEVIN. The Unseen Elderly: A Study of Marginally Subsistent Hotel Dwellers. San Diego, Calif.: San Diego State University Press, 1980. 243 pp.
This study of a single-room occupancy hotel (SRO) in San Diego is an ethnographic account of the lives of its elderly residents. Eckert characterizes the predominant values of the residents as utilitarianism, privacy, and freedom. The author identifies three life trajectories evident among the residents: the marginally socially adjusted, the late isolate, and the lifelong loner. Eckert concludes that the tenants' stubborn desire to remain independent leads to underutilization of social services even when severely ill.

SOC 407. ESTES, CARROLL L. The Aging Enterprise. San Francisco: Jossey-Bass, 1979. 283 pp.
Estes presents a critique of social policies and services for the aged, which she believes are failing to address the social and economic needs of that group. She discusses the way in which society thinks about the old and how these attitudes are conditioned by taken-for-granted assumptions and expectations. Working from the premise that reality is socially constructed, she argues that social scientists have for too long placed emphasis on individualist theories which locate problems with old age exclusively within the aged cohort, thus diverting attention away from the political, social, and economic structures and processes which shape our perceptions of the aged. Focusing attention on these structural determinants, Estes argues that a radical rethinking of our public policy with regard to the aged is required. She maintains that pluralist bargaining among vested interests in government bureaucracies has produced public policy which is of little benefit to the aged. Among the topics discussed are: the socio-political influences on the development of the Older American Act, pluralism, interest group politics and policy ambiguity, review of Federal programs for the elderly, decentralization, and citizen participation of the aged in policy and program implementation. Estes explores the origins and politics surrounding social policies for the aged, while at the same time exposing the "aging enterprise" which has been created by those very policies.

SOC 408. FARRELL, MICHAEL P. and STANLEY D. ROSENBERG. Men at Midlife. Dover, Mass.: Auburn House, 1981. 242 pp.
This is a comparative study based on the results of a 1973 survey of 300 working and middle class men aged thirty-eight to forty-eight and another sample of 200 men between twenty-five and thirty. The authors offer a typology of men's experience at midlife based on the person's satisfaction or dissatisfaction with his roles, and the denial or ability to express the perceived conflicts. The authors find that only 12% of their sample fit the expressive-dissatisfied stereotype of the male midlife crisis,

although another 30% of their sample are dissatisfied but deny expressing the conflict. The authors also reveal important social-class and rural-urban differences in the way males experience midlife.

SOC 409. FONER, ANNE and KAREN SCHWAB. Aging and Retirement. Monterey, Calif.: Brooks/Cole, 1981. 132 pp.
This book deals with both social and individual aspects of retirement in American society. The authors focus on "the retirement process and on people's lives in retirement--that is, the reasons people retire when they do, their activities as retirees, their reactions to retired life, and the individual and social factors associated with either a good or an unsatisfactory life in retirement." Foner and Schwab provide information about the social security system and profile the financial, health, and marital status of the retired population. The authors examine early retirement and conclude that both push and pull factors have influenced this trend.

SOC 410. FRENCH, JOHN R. P., Jr., STEVEN R. DOEHRMAN, MARY LOU DAVIS-SACKS, and AMIRAM VINOKUR. Career Change in Midlife: Stress, Social Support, and Adjustment. Ann Arbor, Mich.: Institute for Social Research, 1983. 143 pp.
This brief research report is part of a larger University of Michigan project investigating the effects of social environment on adjustment and health. It examines "how family stresses and social support affect the adjustment of enlisted men who are undergoing a stressful life event--leaving the Navy after twenty years of service and returning to civilian life." The empirical study, which compares a group of enlisted men leaving active service with a control group who remained in the Navy, is presented primarily as a test of the theory of "person-environment fit."

SOC 411. FUCHS, VICTOR. How We Live. Cambridge, Mass.: Harvard University Press, 1983. 293 pp.
Fuchs argues that the nature of society is fashioned by personal choices both in the domain of the family and in the public domain with regard to the issues of work, health, and education. This volume focuses on the nature of these choices and the ways in which they are affected by external circumstances and by the particular stage of an individual's life cycle. Writing from an economic perspective, Fuchs suggests that a better understanding of how choices change over time and differ with regard to socioeconomic class will lead to improved private choices and enhance the efficacy of public policy in this sphere. Change in external circumstances is explored through an examination of family life, work, health, and education. Three principal issues emerge during the course of this study: the decline in the importance of the family as a primary institution in American society; the demographic trends in fertility and mortality which have transformed the population structure; and the prevalence of deferred gratification as a criterion upon which to base choices. Fuchs concludes with some suggestions for public policy initiatives to address the changing needs of American society.

SOC 412. GEORGE, LINDA K. Role Transitions in Later Life. Monterey, Calif.: Brooks/Cole, 1980. 159 pp.
George explores the most common transitions experienced during later life and assesses their impact on individual well-being, which she defines as identity and social adjustment. Personal resources, coping skills, and social status are among the most important factors that influence well-being. She offers a model of adjustment to social stress and examines major role transitions associated with work, family life, and residential relocation, including retirement, part-time work, the empty nest, grandparenthood, widowhood, and remarriage.

SOC 413. GOODMAN, PAUL. Growing Up Absurd: Problems of Youth in the
Organized Society. New York: Random House, 1960. 296 pp.
In this analysis of American youth culture, Goodman examines the organized
system of semi-monopolies and the resulting disaffection of a growing
generation of Americans who found themselves on the inside of a "closed
room" trying to get out (or, contrariwise, who wanted to get into the
mainstream). Goodman was one of the first to inquire into America's "problem youth" of the late 1950s and early 1960s--the "Beatniks" and the rising
number of juvenile delinquents. The problems of youth, he argues, serve
as a kind of social indicator. "Such problems, by their form and content,"
Goodman writes, "test and criticize the society in which they occur.
The burden of proof, as to who is 'wrong,' does not rest with the young
but always with the system of society." This study sheds light on the
societal forces that led to the student revolution in the late 1960s and
early 1970s.

SOC 414. GOTTLIEB, DAVID. Babes in Arms: Youth in the Army. Beverly
Hills, Calif.: Sage, 1980. 172 pp.
This study had its genesis in the author's interest in the processes by
which youth enter the Army. The study peruses the lives of young army
volunteers, who were given free rein to talk openly and frankly about
themselves, their peers, their country and their army experiences. The
interviews were conducted with 115 enlistees stationed at Fort Sill, Oklahoma. A profile of the volunteers is sketched in the opening chapters
of the book. Gottlieb proceeds to examine the major reasons why youth
enlist (mainly the perceived educational benefits and the chance to escape
unemployment and home); the nature of army recruiters and the recruiting
process; the volunteers' first sojourn in the Army; social facets of life
in the Army; job assignment and work experience; and future expectations.
He finds that those interviewed were frequently critical of the Army,
mainly because of the discrepancies between their expectations and the
reality of Army life.

SOC 415. HAMERMESH, DANIEL S. Unemployment Insurance and the Older American.
Kalamazoo, Mich.: W. E. Upjohn Institute for Employment Research,
1980. 117 pp.
This is an inquiry into the distributional effects of the Federal legislative change in 1980 which required a dollar-for-dollar reduction of
Unemployment Insurance payment to recipients of Social Security benefits.
It also examines the legislation's effects on labor market participation
and consumption-behavior of the aged. The study's premise is that growing
numbers of aged in the population will increasingly affect Federal transfer
programs. Hamermesh employs an economic perspective to analyze the provisions of Unemployment Insurance; the effects of insurance and pensions
on income distribution; the role of Unemployment Insurance in the labor
market for older workers; Unemployment Insurance and consumption patterns;
and the function of Unemployment Insurance as a work incentive or disin-
centive. The author argues that reform is only possible through the imposition of a more discriminating set of job-search requirements on older
claimants.

SOC 416. HARRIS, CHARLES S., ed. Fact Book on Aging: A Profile of
America's Older Population. Washington, D.C.: National Council
on the Aging, 1978. 263 pp.
Drawing on a variety of Federal sources, this book assembles information
on the demographic composition, income, employment, physical and mental
health, housing, transportation, and criminal victimization of people
over sixty-five years old. Major themes include variations within the
older population, myths and prejudices, documentation of their real problems, aging as a process, and the difference between objective conditions
and subjective perceptions of those conditions. References to statistical
information assist the reader in locating more detailed information.

SOC 417. HARRIS, LOUIS, et al. The Myth and Reality of Aging in America.
        Washington, D.C.: National Council on the Aging, 1976.
        331 pp.
This is an investigation of public attitudes toward the aged and aging;
it examines the views and attitudes of older Americans about themselves
and documents their individual experiences of growing old in the U.S.
The study reveals that "most of the older people of this country have
the desire and the potential to be productive, contributing members of
our society," but also uncovers some disturbing facts about poverty among
the aged and about the "politics" of old age and retirement in American
public policy.

SOC 418. HARVEY, CAROL D. H. and HOWARD M. BAHR. The Sunshine Widows:
        Adapting to Sudden Bereavement. Lexington, Mass.: Heath, 1980.
        151 pp.
This book is based on a longitudinal study of the effects of sudden widowhood brought about by a mining accident. The authors suggest that a
widow's ability to adjust depends upon the resources available to her (such
as income, health, employment, or youth) rather than the comfort of family
and friends. Loneliness and dealing with children were two major short-
term problems.

SOC 419. HECHINGER, GRACE and FRED HECHINGER. Teenage Tyranny. New York:
        Morrow, 1963. 259 pp.
This work is a critique of the American cult of adolescence and an indictment of the producers who fuel it. The authors evoke the problems of
the teenager beset by peer pressure and by fads projected through the mass
media. In a chapter on rock 'n' roll, the Hechingers describe popular
singers as untalented assembly-line performers, and the music itself as
low-quality entertainment. Such defenders of an earlier popular culture
as Mitch Miller, Frank Sinatra, and Dwight McDonald are cited. The authors
acknowledge the attraction, however, of the music and the singers for
teenagers who desire their own culture in opposition to one identified
with their parents.

SOC 420. HICKEY, TOM. Health and Aging. Monterey, Calif.: Brooks/Cole,
        1980. 192 pp.
Hickey reviews the literature on the relationship between health and aging,
and dispels a number of commonly held myths. Using a life-span perspective,
Hickey documents changes in health and health-care needs and examines
the social, psychological, political, and economic context of health and
aging. Special attention is given to the long-term care patient in both
community and institutional settings.

SOC 421. HOCHSCHILD, ARLIE RUSSELL. The Managed Heart. Berkeley: Uni-
        versity of California Press, 1983. 307 pp.
Hochschild's interest is in the increased commercialization of human feelings in contemporary society. She argues that emotions are socially engineered and sold in a variety of exchanges which take place in both private
and public life. These exchanges are grounded in a set of "feeling rules"
which define the parameters of the emotions market. Furthermore,
Hochschild explores the idea "that emotion functions as a messenger from
the self, an agent that gives us an instant report on the connection
between what we are seeing and what we had expected to see, and tells us
what we feel ready to do about it." This relationship between the self
and the signal emotions becomes distorted by the commercialization of
private emotion through its transformation into emotional labor for
exchange. Much of the analysis is based on field observation of trainee
flight attendants and bill collectors whose jobs necessitate the management
of private emotions in the public realm.

SOC 422. JACOBS, RUTH HARRIET. Life After Youth: Female Forty. What
          Next? Boston: Beacon Press, 1979. 165 pp.
Jacobs's analysis of the lives and life choices facing middle-aged women
in contemporary American society is based on research interviews and workshops held throughout the country. The author argues that these middle-
aged women are subject to two forms of discrimination: sexism and agism.
Middle-aged women are treated with ridicule, fear, and disrespect in society, both in the myths created about them (for example, witches) and in
the reality of their ignominious existence on the periphery of mainstream
American life. Jacobs argues that "older women are underpaid, underutil-
ized, under recognised and underloved," even by themselves. In her pursuit
of the American middle-aged woman, the author has constructed a typology
of the older woman; each type is treated in a separate chapter in the
book: the nurturer, unutilized nurturer, re-engaged nurturer, chum net-
worker and leisurer, careerist employed and unemployed, seeker, faded
beauty, doctorer, escapist and isolate, and advocate and assertive older
woman. This typology attempts to account for the major role identifica-
tions of a large group in society which social science has tended to ignore.

SOC 423. JONES, LANDON Y. Great Expectations: America and the Baby Boom
          Generation. New York: Random House, 1981. 452 pp.
"No single generation has had more impact on us than the baby boom, and
no single person has been untouched. The baby boom is, and will continue
to be, the decisive generation in our history." Jones has produced an
encyclopedic social history of the baby boom generation. Although he
denies his is a demographic determinism, Jones sees the size of the cohort
born between 1946 and 1964 as affecting every aspect of American life.
This volatile generation--the "pig in the [demographic] python"--was the
first to grow up with suburbia, TV, rock music, mass affluence and consumerism, declining SAT scores, Vietnam, and mass college attendance.
He contrasts two demographic explanations for the baby boom itself:
Easterlin's cyclical "relative income" thesis that sees such dramatic population increases as the result of a small prosperous cohort, and Westorff's
modernization thesis that sees the baby boom as a historical aberration
amid general social and economic trends that have led to a general decline
in fertility in the West.

SOC 424. JORGENSEN, JAMES. The Graying of America: Retirement and Why
          You Can't Afford It. New York: Dial Press, 1980. 245 pp.
This is a guide to both private and government retirement plans. Jorgensen
presents an overview of the American retirement system, together with a
brief history and summary of the principles underpinning retirement plans.
He argues that retirement plans have become increasingly unworkable in
their current form; and explores the theory behind pensions, the effects
of inflation on the economy and the retirement system, and the protection,
guarantees and government insurance available to all private retirement
plans. He points to ways of beating inflation and the problems associated
with pensions sponsored by private companies. The history and growth
of Social Security are presented, and Jorgensen critically appraises the
future of that system, pointing to the need to change the system in order
to "save it from itself."

SOC 425. KALISH, RICHARD. Late Adulthood: Perspectives on Human Develop-
          ment. Monterey, Calif.: Brooks/Cole, 1975. 133 pp.
Kalish provides a brief introduction to social gerontology, including the
theoretical and practical issues involved in growing old in America.
Early chapters introduce methodological problems of psychological gerontology and the demography of aging. Also discussed are cognitive processes,
personality and role changes, and agencies and organizations that provide
services for elderly Americans. Kalish's book places late adulthood within
the context of the larger human life cycle, providing insights into the

various emotional, motivational, and attitudinal problems confronting
adults in the after-fifty stages of adult development.

SOC 426. KEITH, JENNIE. Old People as People: Social and Cultural Influences on Aging and Old Age. Boston: Little, Brown, 1982.
130 pp.
Keith takes as her starting point the idea that old people are not a separate cohort in society deserving differential treatment, but rather are
part of that society, which as a whole is subject to the liberating and
constraining effects of the aging process. The social and cultural contexts of "the idea of old age" are examined from a cross-cultural perspective. Keith investigates the dimensions of age differentiation, using
anthropological data gathered from a range of cultural contexts. In summarizing, Keith argues that her cross-cultural analysis demonstrates that
the aging process and the experiences of the elderly cannot be understood
without reference to the cultural context of a particular society and
to the fact that cultural norms and values are socially transmitted.
Age differentiation, in particular cultural settings, must first be elucidated before we can begin to come to terms with the physical and social
aspects of old age.

SOC 427. LARKIN, RALPH W. Suburban Youth in Cultural Crisis. New York:
Oxford University Press, 1979. 259 pp.
This is an ethnographic study of the student subcultures in a suburban
New Jersey high school. Larkin identifies "jock/rah-rahs," "politicos,"
"intellectuals," "freaks," "blacks," and "greaser" subcultures, in addition
to an undifferentiated mass. Larkin sees the school as a controlling
appendage of monopoly Capitalism, and is critical of the middle-class
values and lifestyles in evidence at "Utopia High."

SOC 428. LOFLAND, LYN H. A World of Strangers. New York: Basic Books,
1973. 223 pp.
Lofland begins this volume with an exploration of the nature of public
space in an effort to address the question of how city life is possible.
In the first part, she characterizes the preindustrial city and the early
industrial city, whose historical transformation gave rise to the modern
city (ordered according to spatial definitions) with which we are familiar
today. The author proceeds in part two to demonstrate how people actually
live in cities, specifically how they acquire the knowledge and skills
necessary to understand the urban environment. She focuses on the devices
employed by city dwellers to avoid or encourage interaction with the "world
of strangers," the dominant image of modern urban environments. Two major
themes emerge in this analysis: First, living in a world of strangers
is only possible because society has developed a way of ordering which
makes possible the identification of personally unknown others with some
accuracy. The social and psychological consequences of living as a complete stranger, Lofland believes, would be intolerable. Second, the city
creates a new kind of human being—a person who is able to relate to others
in new ways necessitated by city living. The cosmopolitan learns to know
the people who surround him only categorically.

SOC 429. LOPATA, HELENA ZNANIECKI. Widowhood in an American City. Cambridge, Mass.: Schenkman, 1973. 369 pp.
Lopata's work is a contribution to the study of life-cycles, women's roles,
and the aged in America. The author interviewed 301 widowed women (82%
white and 18% black) in sixty neighborhoods in the Chicago area. The
study probes the interviewees' lives before and after the death of their
husbands, emphasizing the role changes the women underwent. The author
identifies four basic types of widows: (1) the self-initiator who becomes
assertively independent; (2) the widow who continues her previous societal
involvements with little change; (3) the social isolate; and (4) women
with a high frequency of social contact.

SOC 430. **LOPATA, HELENA ZNANIECKI**. Women as Widows. New York: Elsevier, 1979. 485 pp.
This survey of widows in the metropolitan area of Chicago focuses on the resources available to widows and their use of those resources in constructing economic, social and emotional support systems for themselves. Historical, demographic and comparative perspectives on widowhood are presented in chapter one. Chapter two profiles Chicago and the kinds of resources available to widows in the greater metropolitan area. Chapters four through seven deal with the experiences of widows: their feelings about their dead spouses; their relationships with men; the support of children, friends, extended family, neighbors, and other social and religious organizations; and the changes which widowhood engenders in their way of life. Chapter eight focuses on the importance of self as a personal resource and the differences in self-identity and assurance which arise because of differences in educational background and race. Women and work—the job as a source of economic support—constitutes the subject matter of chapter nine. In summary, Lopata sketches a typology for classifying women according to particular adaptive types; the implications of widowhood for both younger and older women are reviewed.

SOC 431. **MALINCHAK, ALAN A**. Crime and Gerontology. Englewood Cliffs, N.J.: Prentice-Hall, 1980. 207 pp.
This book investigates the relationship between the elderly and the criminal justice system. Major portions of the book are devoted to the elderly as victims of crime, crime prevention programs designed to reduce victimization, and the elderly as criminals. Malinchak discusses the reasons why the elderly are more vulnerable to crime than other age groups, and shows how this sometimes leads to self-imprisonment. Malinchak concludes with recommendations for reforms, including educational programs for the elderly and better techniques for reporting victimization.

SOC 432. **MARSHALL, VICTOR W**. Last Chapters: A Sociology of Aging and Dying. Monterey, Calif.: Brooks/Cole, 1980. 227 pp.
Drawing on the theoretical perspective evolved by Berger and Luckman, Marshall sees the individual as the producer of his own reality. That reality in turn takes on an independent existence and is experienced and internalized by the individual. Thus, a dialectic is established between the individual and the social, with each to some degree determining and shaping the other. Marshall focuses first on aging and dying as they are experienced at the societal level by posing the question of how human mortality affects social organization. This is followed by an exploration of the individual who himself is experiencing aging or dying. The early chapters explore the changing demographic patterns in contemporary Western society, cross-cultural differences in dealing with death, and the increasingly universal patterns of bereavement associated with the transformative forces of industrialization and modernization. Marshall examines some of the foremost theories of gerontology, arguing that they are often problematic and unhelpful. The issue of mortality, the social organization of death and dying, and the environmental and community contexts of death are also discussed. The final chapter focuses on the meaning of death and how people try to make sense of it; Marshall speculates about future changes in patterns of death and dying and calls for more research in this area.

SOC 433. **MOSS, FRANK E**. and **VAL J. HALAMANDARIS**. Too Old, Too Sick, Too Bad: Nursing Homes in America. Germantown, Md.: Aspen Systems, 1977. 326 pp.
This study examines the moral, political, economic, and psycho-social problems involved in the adequate care of elderly, infirm persons in America. The authors describe and discuss these matters in great detail, presenting data on nursing home organization, patient care and patient neglect, intern-

ment and at-home care, costs, and Federal and state regulations for such institutions. Moss and Halamandaris identify the probable sources of problems characteristic of American nursing homes and suggest some possible public policy solutions and the implications for reform.

SOC 434. OLSON, LAURA KATZ. The Political Economy of Aging: The State, Private Power and Social Welfare. New York: Columbia University Press, 1982. 272 pp.
Olson examines how the availability and adequacy of income, pensions, health care, housing, and the whole array of human services is determined within the context of the problems of a capitalist political economy in which the state intervenes to mitigate only the worst consequences of capitalist production. In each of the policy areas discussed, Olson reveals how the state, through limited and generally inadequate services in relation to the needs of the aging population, acts to redistribute wealth from wage workers to private enterprise through mandatory programs based on regressive taxation.

SOC 435. OLSON, LAWRENCE, CHRISTOPHER CATON, and MARTIN DUFFY, eds. The Elderly and the Future Economy. Lexington, Mass.: Lexington Books, 1981. 195 pp.
In light of the vastly increased numbers of older Americans in the population, the authors set out to examine the nature of the changing relationship between the elderly and the economy. The book opens with a review of the major academic studies conducted on the status of the elderly in a changing society and the economic implications of their increased numbers in the population. The focus of the book, however, is on a simulation study of the economy and the income of the elderly over a projected twenty-five year period. Using this experimental design, the effects of pursuing a variety of policy strategies may be gauged with regard to the public needs of the elderly. Some of the policies examined include: increased labor force participation, income guarantees, and increases in personal savings and investment-oriented tax cuts. The editors conclude that, while all of the strategies examined benefit the elderly to some degree, only those options directed specifically at the elderly really make an impact on the problems of the poverty-stricken elderly. In fact, it is suggested that a combination of these options would improve the economy and safeguard the livelihood of America's older generation.

SOC 436. PALMORE, EDMARE. Social Patterns in Normal Aging: Findings from the Duke Longitudinal Study. Durham, N.C.: Duke University Press, 1981. 135 pp.
This multi-disciplinary, longitudinal study of the aging process demonstrates the complexity of interactive biomedical, behavioral and social factors in aging. This is the first in a projected series of monographs which will systematically examine the principal findings of the Duke Longitudinal Study from a variety of perspectives, encompassing biomedicine, behaviorism, and social sciences. Palmore advances a sociological perspective on normal aging, relying heavily on multivariate statistical analysis. His data on patterns of activity, life satisfaction, and sexual behavior provide insights into the experience of non-institutionalized adults. The issues of retirement, widowhood, and illness, and how older adults come to terms with them are examined in detail. Theories reviewed include: disengagement, activity and continuity theories, age stratification, life events and stress theory, and homogeneity versus heterogeneity theory.

SOC 437. PAMPEL, FRED C. Social Change and the Aged. Lexington, Mass.: Lexington Books, 1981. 212 pp.
Working within a structural perspective which emphasizes the significance of age stratification in determining patterns of social organization, Pampel analyzes the socio-economic position of the aged in the U.S. over

a thirty-year period. This analysis attempts to examine the effects of social change on the aged at both the individual and social levels. Most of the empirical findings are presented in multivariate quantitative analyses. Among the principal indicators examined are trends and causes of aggregate labor force participation and income of the aged population; compositional and processural effects on changes in the labor force participation of aged males; cohort change and retirement among aged females; changes in income inequality; age, race and sex as determinants of income; the effect of increases in personal income on living arrangements of unmarried aged persons; and the effects of income levels on the general financial satisfaction and good health of the aged population.

SOC 438. PARKER, STANLEY. Work and Retirement. Boston: Allen & Unwin, 1982. 203 pp.
Parker introduces his study of work and retirement with a brief overview of the history of retirement in Britain and the U.S. He proceeds to identify the major theoretical tenets that underlie our understanding of retirement and the elderly. In an effort to come to terms with the dynamics of old age and the retirement process, Parker examines the preparations made for retirement, the physical and psychological capacity of old people to work, and their experiences of retirement. Specifically, he questions how older and retired people spend their leisure time, why people retire early, and what kinds of adjustments must be made in order to maintain health, morale, and identity among retired people. In conclusion, Parker presents a number of policy alternatives which would lead to a more flexible framework for work and retirement, and smooth the transition from active working lives into active, participation-oriented, leisure lives.

SOC 439. PEGELS, C. CARL. Health Care and the Elderly. Rockville, Md.: Aspen, 1980. 225 pp.
Pegels presents a critical overview of health care facilities and programs directed at the elderly. The book is organized into three parts: Part I treats the historical development of long term health care; explores the effects of cost, expenditure and inflation on the provision of health care; assesses the quality of services available to the elderly; and suggests some cost-benefit alternatives to health care. Home Health Care Programs designed for the impaired elderly are also discussed. Part II shifts the focus of analysis to the institutionalized care of the old and in particular the nursing home industry. Pegels covers conditions and attitudes in the homes, medical direction, regulations and controls, and the advantages and disadvantages of developing a national health policy. Part III examines specific issues within the range of health care available to the aged: Vision, Hearing and Dental Care; Medicare and other forms of Health Insurance; the quality of care versus health care costs; Health Manpower; and Terminal Care.

SOC 440. RHODES, COLBERT and CLYDE B. VEDDER. An Introduction to Thanatology: Death and Dying in American Society. Springfield, Ill.: Thomas, 1983. 135 pp.
Rhodes and Vedder investigate the major causes of death in American society, together with the social, psychological and cultural ramifications surrounding human mortality. In particular, changing attitudes toward death over the life cycle are analyzed with a special emphasis on the factors which socialize Americans into a deep-rooted fear of death. The incidence of homicide and suicide, the death process, and the ritual surrounding funeral arrangements are also explored. The authors have included a section on bereavement and the different forms it takes when the death is sudden or expected, and when the deceased is a spouse, parent, or child. The issue of euthanasia and the living will is discussed. Moving from a practical to a more esoteric vein, the final chapter explores the issue of life after death by presenting those "belief positions" which advocate

immortality: Christianity, near-death experiences, and the Esoteric tradition.

SOC 441. RUBIN, LILLIAN. Women of a Certain Age. New York: Harper &
Row, 1979. 309 pp.
This study focuses on women at mid-life who have taken marriage and motherhood as their primary life tasks. Rubin's findings are based on lengthy
interviews with 160 women who range in age from thirty-five to fifty-four.
The author examines the ways in which women come to terms with that period
of their lives when the exigencies imposed by motherhood no longer pre-
dominate. In her interviews, she repeatedly found that the women were
ill-equipped to define themselves, their hopes, and plans for the future
without reference to the men in their lives: "For women family is at
the core of their lives, for men it is at the periphery." Rubin notes
that gender is more significant than social class in determining the quality of women's lives. Marriage and motherhood define a woman in the world
and provide her with a social identity. Among the issues discussed are:
men, work, family, sex, menopause, divorce, re-entering the labor force,
and returning to school.

SOC 442. SHAW, LOIS BANFILL, ed. Unplanned Careers: The Working Lives
of Middle-Aged Women. Lexington, Mass.: Lexington Books, 1983.
149 pp.
The papers in this collection are based on data gathered over a ten-year
period in a National Longitudinal Survey of the Work Experience of Mature
Women, conducted by the U.S. Bureau of Census under the auspices of the
Center for Human Resources Research at Ohio State University. The introductory chapter sketches the historical background to, and the impetus
behind, the study. The broad changes in women's family circumstances,
attitudes, and employment over the ten-year interview period (1967-77)
are described. The succeeding chapters treat specific issues which arose
from the study, such as problems with labor market re-entry, causes of
irregular employment patterns, occupational atypicality, attitudes toward
women working, economic consequences of poor health in mature women, and
mid-life changes wrought by changes in marital status.

SOC 443. STUB, HOLGER R. The Social Consequences of Long Life. Springfield, Ill.: Thomas, 1982. 277 pp.
This book explores the social consequences of increased longevity in modern,
industrialized society. The introductory chapter sketches the historical
background to the present study and highlights the pervasiveness of factors
such as disease, hunger, and starvation which served to keep mortality
rates high well into the 19th century. Stub examines both the sociological
and socio-psychological aspects of long life. The social aspects of
aging, family education, class and status, work, and retirement are
explored in light of increased longevity. The effects of long life are
also examined with regard to changing responses toward death, future orientation and achievement, changing perspectives on life cycle stages, and
the personal experience of loneliness, friendship, intimacy, and control.

SOC 444. UNRUH, DAVID R. Invisible Lives: Social World of the Aged.
Beverly Hills, Calif.: Sage, 1983. 198 pp.
Unruh's study is based on empirical observation of the activities of older
citizens, as they participate in a plurality of social worlds. The term
"social world" is defined sociologically as "an extremely large, highly
permeable, amorphous, and spatially transcendent form of social organization wherein actors are linked cognitively through shared perspectives
arising out of common channels of communication." Unruh begins his study
by examining the broader issue of social integration in old age, and how
the level of social-world integration changes as the individual progresses
along the life cycle. Social worlds are characterized according to par-

ticular age parameters: youthful, age-mixed, and older groups. Unruh develops a typology of social types for locating people along an integrative axis in the social world, moving from peripheral to core integration: consuming, collecting, creating, performing, marketing, organizing, representing, and evaluating. The four main social types are: strangers, tourists, regulars, and insiders. Social integration is viewed as a dynamic concept, in the sense that the aged are seen as a cohort capable of moving in and out of a variety of social worlds. Unruh's study is an attempt to gain fresh insight into the lives of the aged by developing the notion of social integration within gerontology.

VII.   SOCIAL INEQUALITY AND SOCIAL CLASS

SOC 445. AULETTA, KEN. The Underclass. New York: Random House, 1982.
        348 pp.
Auletta, a professional journalist, has undertaken an intensive analysis of the American underclass, its characteristics, and its social, behavioral, and psychological correlates. The focus of his analysis is the lives and personalities of twenty-six trainees attending the Wildcat Skills Training Center in Manhattan, a nonprofit employment training organization that was targeted to reach the hard-core unemployed. He provides personality profiles and analyses of the lives of his subjects that contradict fashionable prescriptions of either the right or the left. But his primary concern is for public policy and devising ways to deal with the burgeoning underclass. He is critical of Reagan budget cuts that dismantled the supported work programs that he maintained were, on balance, successful in enabling their participants to lead productive lives.

SOC 446. BALTZELL, E. DIGBY. The Protestant Establishment: Aristocracy
        and Caste in America. New York: Random House, 1964.   429 pp.
In this study conducted in the late 1950s, Baltzell argues that the White-Anglo-Saxon-Protestant establishment has been "gradually losing its power and authority in the course of the twentieth century." The "Establishment," however, seems reluctant to relinquish that power, to share and improve their upper-class traditions and cultures by "absorbing" the more educated and talented members of racial and ethnic minority groups, especially Jews. The focus of Baltzell's book is the persistence of patterns of exclusion and prejudice within what has come to be known colloquially as America's WASPs (White-Anglo-Saxon-Protestants). The author suggests that the separatist attitude of the white "Anglo" community is fostering its own destruction. His central thesis is that "in order for an upper class to maintain continuity of power and authority, especially in an opportunitarian and mobile society such as ours, its membership must, in the long run, be representative of the composition of society as a whole."

SOC 447. BEEGHLEY, LEONARD. Living Poorly in America. New York: Praeger,
        1983. 211 pp.
This book "is intended to correct some of the myths about poverty, to describe how those with very little money live, and to explain the correlates and causes of impoverishment." Beeghley examines the extent of poverty in America, the nature of the country's public assistance system, and the contradictions within that system. He also analyzes the relationships among poverty, public assistance, and work; the school correlates (e.g., crime, health) of poverty; and the culture and values of those in poverty. He concludes with a structural analysis of the characteristics of American society that create and maintain poverty.

SOC 448. BENSMAN, JOSEPH and ARTHUR J. VIDICH. The New American Society:
          The Revolution of the Middle Class. Chicago: Quadrangle Books,
          1971. 306 pp.
In this work of practical sociology, the authors argue that the changes
in the structure of American society which have occurred since W.W. II
"constitute virtually a social revolution." Rapid changes are taking place
which tend to obliterate older institutions and lifestyles from even the
memory of the "average American." The authors identify the newly emerging
groups of the changed social order and examine the major causes and trends
which reveal the origins and directions of the newly emerging society.
They examine increased bureaucratization and the rise of giant corporations,
the rise of the new middle class, their rebellious youth, and the lifestyles of the new classes. Bensman and Vidich are also concerned with
the absorption of immigrants and their descendants by American institutions
and organizations.

SOC 449. BLUMBERG, PAUL. Inequality in an Age of Decline. New York:
          Oxford University Press, 1980. 290 pp.
Blumberg maintains that Pax Americana, the era of American global economic
and political power, lasted only thirty years--from the end of W.W. II
to the mid-1970s. He is primarily concerned with explaining the diminished
American economic power since the mid-1970s and the dynamics of class
and income distribution during this period. He contrasts four different
perspectives on the nature of American class relations, income distribution,
and relative equality within the American class system. Convergence theory
interprets American society as increasingly affluent and marked by greater
income equality. Class stability theorists accept the notion of increasing
affluence in American society but deny that the gap between the classes
has narrowed. Blumberg contends that since 1972 neither of these models
is appropriate. He suggests two alternatives: a class stagnation model,
in which the classes are not gaining in affluence nor is the gap between
them narrowing, and a class divergence model, in which there is an actual
widening of the gap between different strata in the American class system.

SOC 450. CAPLOVITZ, DAVID. The Poor Pay More: Consumer Practices of
          Low-Income Families. New York: Free Press of Glencoe, 1963.
          225 pp.
A report of the Bureau of Applied Social Research of Columbia University,
this book explores the relationship of merchants to the low-income consumer,
the buying and shopping patterns of low-income families, credit patterns,
and family finances. Caplovitz also examines low-income consumer problems
such as unscrupulous sales practices and missed payments and their consequences. The study reveals the predicament of low-income families,
helpless victims of an amoral marketing system. Sales practices of merchants of high-cost durables in low-income areas and the consumer behavior
and problems of the families with which they deal are also examined.
Caplovitz concludes his analysis with some practical recommendations for
public policy actions and consumer education in low-income areas.

SOC 451. COLEMAN, RICHARD P. and LEE RAINWATER, with KENT A. McCLELLAND.
          Social Standing in America: New Dimensions of Class. New York:
          Basic Books, 1978. 353 pp.
Social class can be measured along many dimensions: income, wealth, occupation, education, and life style are traditional determiners of class.
In this volume, Coleman and Rainwater examine some of the long-standing
conceptions of social class in America to determine whether these conceptions have changed in the last generation. Approaches to social class
identification have traditionally focused on either quantitative or qualitative approaches, but in this work, the authors attempt to merge the
two approaches. Also, the interrelations between subjective and objective
indicators of class are explored. With this study, Coleman and Rainwater

have made an important attempt to bridge the gap between sociological theories of "prestige" and socio-economic models of class.

SOC 452. COLES, ROBERT. Privileged Ones: The Well-Off and the Rich in America. Boston: Atlantic Monthly Press, 1977. 583 pp.
According to Coles, the children of the upper classes in America must learn the ways of the ruling class at a very early age. They experience a class-specific socialization process in the same way that disadvantaged and minority children do. Coles analyzes the developmental patterns of such privileged children. He presents various psychological portraits of the children of the rich in different areas of the country, offering a look at their schools and social environments and at the conflicts and pressures they experience in growing up.

SOC 453. COOPER, MARK N., THEODORE L. SULLIVAN, SUSAN PUNNETT, and ELLEN BERMAN. Equity and Energy: Rising Energy Prices and the Living Standards of Lower Income Americans. Boulder, Colo.: Westview Press, 1983. 302 pp.
This book focuses on the deterioration in living standards of lower-income households that resulted from American energy price policies in the 1970s. The authors present detailed empirical assessments of trends that adversely affected lower income households between 1973 and 1983. First, the share of household energy expenditures as a percentage of household income increased, and income transfer programs failed to offset losses in purchasing power. Second, increases in energy-related rental costs contributed to a decline in the quality of lower-income housing. Finally, increases in energy-related costs strained the resources of local governments and led to a cutback in the provision of redistributive services (such as health, education and welfare) and a shift toward regressive taxes.

SOC 454. DAVIS, KAREN and CATHY SCHOEN. Health and the War on Poverty: A Ten Year Appraisal. Washington, D.C.: Brookings Institution, 1978. 230 pp.
The authors of this study examine programs of health care for the poor—including Medicare, Medicaid, the comprehensive health center program, and expanded maternal and child health programs—that arose from Lyndon Johnson's War on Poverty and Great Society. They evaluate the strengths and weaknesses of these health care services, which among Great Society programs "receive the largest and most rapidly growing share of budgetary resources," during the ten-year period from 1965 to 1975. Their study, based largely on governmental statistical data and secondary analyses, includes public policy recommendations for ways in which to improve health care delivery so that it might be universally available in American society.

SOC 455. DOLLARD, JOHN. Caste and Class in a Southern Town. New Haven, Conn.: Yale University Press, 1937. 502 pp.
This study in the social psychology of race relations was conducted in 1935-36. Dollard offers a psychoanalytic ethnography of "Southerntown," a community of some 2,500 inhabitants, attempting to "reveal the main structure of white-Negro adjustment in Southerntown from the standpoint of emotional factors." Social adjustment of the two races in Southerntown, Dollard found, had taken the form of "caste accommodation," and caste was determined by biological rather than cultural characteristics—that is to say, by racial characteristics. Dollard examines "caste patterning" in education, politics, and religion and looks at class factors as they manifest themselves within the caste order in terms of economic, sexual, and prestige gains. Caste and Class in a Southern Town is one of the few works on the subject combining Freudian and Marxian principles in aspects of its assessment.

SOC 456. DOMHOFF, G. WILLIAM. The Higher Circles: The Governing Class in America. New York: Random House, 1970. 367 pp.
The Higher Circles is an investigation into social stratification and the upper echelons--the men and women who wield tremendous power and essentially govern America. By means of a series of empirically based essays that establish the upper class through social indicators, Domhoff attempts to add strength to his earlier arguments. He exposes how the "power elite" make foreign policy, shape social legislation, and generally act to control the minds of the masses. The author disagrees with the pluralist perception of the power structure as presented in the works of Rose, Dahl, Banfield, and others, and argues instead for what he claims is the reality and persistence of an American power elite who manipulate and control the workings of the larger society.

SOC 457. DOMHOFF, G. WILLIAM. Who Rules America? Englewood Cliffs, N.J.: Prentice-Hall, 1967. 184 pp.
Through an examination of America's principal institutions, associations, foundations, and government agencies, Domhoff demonstrates how power and control are distributed in the American population. The author offers evidence that America's upper class, through its domination of private and corporate wealth, exerts a disproportionate amount of pressure in social and political, as well as economic, circles. He describes the power elite's mechanisms of control in the corporate economy, the shaping of the American policy, control of Federal, state and local government, the military establishment--even the FBI and the CIA. He concludes that the power elite may or may not be members of the upper class but that their power is ultimately based within it. According to Who Rules America?, the upper class in America, contrary to the myths of economic and political balance of power, constitutes a governing class within the society.

SOC 458. DOMHOFF, G. WILLIAM. Who Rules America Now? A View for the '80s. Englewood Cliffs, N.J.: Prentice-Hall, 1983. 230 pp.
This is a 1980s sequel to Domhoff's 1967 Who Rules America (see SOC 457), which examined the structure of class and power in the U.S. during the 1960s. Domhoff's focus is the distribution, characteristics, and dynamics of national class and power--the power elites and ruling class that govern, win the major domestic and foreign policy political battles, and benefit most from these policies. His objective is "to present systematic evidence that there is a ruling class by virtue of its dominant role in the economy and government. . . . This ruling class is cohesive, has its basis in the large corporations and banks, plays a major role in shaping the social and political climate, and dominates the federal government through a variety of organizations and methods."

SOC 459. FRIED, MARC. The World of the Urban Working Class. Cambridge, Mass.: Harvard University Press, 1973. 410 pp.
The data for Fried's statistical analysis were taken from surveys of residents of Boston's West End, a deteriorated working-class neighborhood in the central city. Classifying respondents as occupying high, medium, and low status levels, Fried examines their differential attitudes toward community life, the family, work, ethnicity, class and other variables. He argues that status level is the most important determinant of "role functioning," and is the essential cause for the working-class life style. The existence of the working-class community is explained by "the denial of acceptance and esteem by the larger society." Fried thus offers a situational explanation of poverty. By locating his results in a historical framework, he manages to enhance his presentation of empirical evidence with theoretical significance. This study represents a substantial addition to the theory of American social stratification.

SOC 460. GILBERT, DENNIS and JOSEPH A. KAHL. The American Class Structure:
A New Synthesis. Homewood, Ill.: Dorsey Press, 1982. 386 pp.
The authors contend that this book is not merely an updated version of
Kahl's 1957 American Class Structure (see SOC 474). However, it retains
some features of the earlier volume, especially its focus on scrutinizing
the methods and conclusions of the "most essential empirical studies"
of social stratification in the U.S. in a conceptual framework of classical
theory. The authors examine Weberian and Marxian models of stratification
and then isolate nine theoretically relevant variables by which stratification can be measured: occupation, income, wealth, personal prestige,
association, socialization, power, class consciousness, and mobility.
They then use these variables to construct their portrait of the American
class structure.

SOC 461. GORDON, MILTON M. Social Class in American Sociology. New York:
McGraw-Hill, 1963. 280 pp.
This study provides a basic theoretical framework from which to analyze
social and economic stratification in America. Gordon traces the development of social class analysis throughout the history of American sociological thought. The book attempts to classify and systematize class
analysis, emphasizing that economic factors alone do not suffice to explain
social stratification in modern industrial societies. The author examines
the structural and dynamic relationships between such variables as economic
power, status-group participation, and politico-community power in the
actual life of a society. "Economic factors," Gordon writes, "do not
operate in a vacuum. They function within a particular political and
community power context which they, in turn, condition. They are associated with particular occupational specializations. They have the effect
through time of producing a status order, and this status order in turn
plays a role in determining economic rewards in the current society."

SOC 462. GRONBJERG, KIRSTEN, DAVID STREET, and GERALD D. SUTTLES. Poverty
and Social Change. Chicago: University of Chicago Press, 1978.
284 pp.
This book is concerned with the nature of welfare in the U.S., which the
authors contend "is addressed through a mixed bag of programs scattered
across various public and private institutions and levels of government."
They seek to explain the absence of an effective American welfare system
and to identify the forces that "resist the movement toward comprehensive
[welfare] planning and programming. . . ." They provide a historical
examination of welfare and efforts to reform the welfare system. They
focus their analysis primarily on the manner in which the welfare system
and efforts to reform it are related to ideology, particularly the American
commitment to the idea of laissez-faire Capitalism, and to social
structure--especially industrialization and government, which they see as
the major sources of the ineffectiveness of welfare in American society.

SOC 463. HAMILTON, RICHARD F. Class and Politics in the United States.
New York: Wiley, 1972. 589 pp.
In this critique of mainstream theories of political sociology, Hamilton
argues that American society fits neither the pluralist nor mass-society
theories. Rather, social groups with stable political traditions transmit
their political attitudes to succeeding generations. With this "group
theory" of political society, Hamilton describes the characteristic political attitudes and demands of social class groupings and explores the question of the effect of social mobility on political attitudes. He finds
the most decisive break in attitudes between the lower- and upper-middle
classes and argues that religious subdivisions in the upper-middle class
have inhibited class polarization. Some attention is given to Lipset's
thesis of working-class authoritarianism and to the extent of support
for liberal politics in America. Hamilton has provided an interesting

theoretical perspective on the relations between political attitudes and
class in American society.

SOC 464. HERTZ, SUSAN HANDLEY. The Welfare Mothers Movement: A Decade
of Change for Poor Women? Lanham, Md.: University Press of
America, 1981. 193 pp.
This is a case study of the Welfare Mothers Movement, which "tried to
develop new options for welfare mothers, change the public stereotype of
the welfare recipient, and . . . bring about changes in the local and
national welfare systems." Hertz combines informal interviews, participant
observation, and survey research to examine the activities of the Welfare
Mothers Movement in Minnesota between 1969 and 1972. She analyzes the
various factors that intruded upon and contributed to the organization
and effectiveness of the movement.

SOC 465. HOCHSCHILD, JENNIFER L. What's Fair?: American Beliefs About
Distributive Justice. Cambridge, Mass.: Harvard University
Press, 1981. 345 pp.
Hochschild seeks to answer Sombart's famous question: Why is there no
socialism in the U.S.? She contends that part of the answer is that the
American poor do not seek to alter the substantial inequalities of wealth
that exist in American society. But why do the poor not support redistribution of wealth? This is the basic question her research is designed
to examine. The main thrust of her study is a comparison of the beliefs
concerning income redistribution derived from a series of intensive, qualitative interviews with a "small set of people" (twenty-eight randomly
selected working adults in New Haven, Conn.--twelve wealthy and sixteen
poor). From these interviews she identifies several constellations of
beliefs about distributive justice that explain why the American poor
do not seek the downward redistribution of wealth.

SOC 466. HOLLINGSHEAD, AUGUST B. Elmtown's Youth, the Impact of Social
Classes on Adolescents. New York: Wiley, 1949. 480 pp.
This volume, the author states, is "an analysis of the way the social
system of a Middle Western Corn Belt community . . . organizes and controls
the social behavior of high-school aged adolescents reared in it." He
studies the behavior of 735 adolescents in seven areas: the school, the
job, the church, recreation, cliques, dates, and sex. He concludes that
there is a direct correlation between adolescent behavior and the parental
place in the community structure, a conclusion that leads him to question
what he sees as the success-dominated ideology of American culture.

SOC 467. HOLLINGSHEAD, AUGUST B. Elmtown's Youth and Elmtown Revisited.
New York: Wiley, 1975. 395 pp.
This study is an attempt to update and revise the author's previous study,
Elmtown's Youth (SOC 466). The new volume incorporates the findings of
the earlier research with data collected in the early 1970s about how
the social class system organizes and controls the general behavior of
adolescents in a Midwestern community. The first four sections of the
book, which are revised versions of the original study, consider the community setting, status structure, and cultural characteristics of Elmtown,
and the jobs, religious behavior, recreation, and peer group structure
of high-school students and of Elmtown dropouts from different social
classes. The final chapter provides a look at Elmtown today. The author
argues that little has affected the basic class structure. According
to Hollingshead, "The relationship between class position and behavior
is a product of learning by the participants in social situations," and
adolescents assume the class status behavior of the parents quite early
in life.

SOC 468. HOLLINGSHEAD, AUGUST B. and FREDERICK C. REDLICH. Social Class
          and Mental Illness: A Community Study. New York: Wiley, 1958.
          442 pp.
Is mental illness related to social class? Does an individual's position
in the social status system affect his mental health and psychiatric treatments? Hollingshead and Redlich provide some tentative answers to these
and other questions. In a combined psychiatric and sociological study
of the distinct class structure of New Haven, Connecticut, the authors
found that members of different social classes exhibited definite types
of mental disorders. They found, moreover, that in each class mental
illness is perceived and treated quite differently. The book discusses
how members of the various classes became mentally ill, how their family
and peers react to their illness, and the type of treatment that is available to members of each class. The authors conclude with a series of
recommendations as to how American society might overcome the class-linked
shortcomings of mental illness and psychiatric treatment.

SOC 469. HOUSE, JOHN W. Frontier on the Rio Grande: A Political Geography
          of Development and Social Deprivation. New York: Oxford Uni-
          versity Press, 1982. 281 pp.
House offers a political geography of the Rio Grande, a riverline international boundary. He grounds his analysis of the potentially unifying
and divisive qualities of such a boundary on the principles of private
and public international law. This examination of the effects of the
frontier on both development and social deprivation is based on an operational model which analyzes the transactional flows of workers, services,
and capital across the Rio Grande. Central to the dynamics of this model
is the management of tension in a complex, interacting socio-political
system.

SOC 470. HOUSEMAN, GERALD L. The Right of Mobility. Port Washington,
          N.Y.: Kennikat Press, 1979. 111 pp.
Houseman begins his account of American mobility (ranging from interstate
travel to immigration) with an examination of the legal and social ramifications of mobility as a right. The author finds that the "overwhelming
thrust of technological developments, combining with the social phenomenon
of the closing of the frontier" has brought the U.S. to an alarming point
at which mobility is severely threatened. In addition, Houseman demonstrates the weak position of the right of mobility in public policy, American legal traditions, and constitutional interpretations. He details
several arguments for and against the development of a Constitutional
amendment to assure this right. The volume concludes with an appendix
listing Constitutional provisions on mobility from such nations as Japan,
Mexico, and the German Federal Republic.

SOC 471. JACKMAN, MARY R. and ROBERT W. JACKMAN. Class Awareness in the
          United States. Berkeley, Calif.: University of California
          Press, 1983. 231 pp.
"This book is an attempt to reorient the analysis of social class." The
authors contend that, following Marx and Weber, respectively, sociologists
have employed two distinct conceptions of class: an economically based
and dichotomous model, on the one hand, and a multiple criteria, multiple
hierarchy model, on the other. The authors seek to transcend the assumptions of both models by building on Centers's subjective interest-group
model of social class in the U.S., which emphasizes popular conceptions
of class. The authors suggest that there are five widely used categories
of class in American society: poor, working class, middle class, upper-
middle class, and upper class. Utilizing data from a national survey
conducted by the Survey Research Center at the University of Michigan
in 1975, their study is an effort to determine the extent to which people
place themselves in one of these five categories and to explore the objec-

tive (e.g., education, occupation, income) correlates of their personal conceptions and the implications of people's class identities for their social and political perspectives.

SOC 472. JENCKS, CHRISTOPHER, et al. Inequality: A Reassessment of the Effect of Family and Schooling in America. New York: Basic Books, 1972. 399 pp.
The authors begin by examining inequality in the schools, then turn to the book's main subject: inequality between blacks and whites in cognitive skills and the effect of racial factors on test scores, factors the authors feel are genetic. Detailed studies of such topics as the "hereditability" of IQ scores are presented.

SOC 473. JENCKS, CHRISTOPHER, et al. Who Gets Ahead?: The Determinants of Economic Success in America. New York: Basic Books, 1979. 397 pp.
Who Gets Ahead? is a sequel to Jencks's Inequality (see SOC 472), which concluded that differences in adult occupational status and earnings were not primarily a function of differences in family background, cognitive skills, and amount of schooling. Here Jencks and his co-authors undertake elaborate statistical analyses of eleven different social surveys to assess the impact of social origins, cognitive ability, noncognitive personality traits, and years of schooling as determinants of individual economic success among American males aged twenty-five to sixty-four. After presenting their findings, which emphasize the role of family background factors, personality differences, and the effects of schooling, the authors compare them with the conclusions reported in Inequality seven years earlier.

SOC 474. KAHL, JOSEPH A. The American Class Structure. New York: Rinehart, 1957. 310 pp.
This volume presents summaries of the results of empirical research on the American class system. Kahl begins by reviewing the dimensions of class according to Marx and Weber, and looks at studies by W. Lloyd Warner on Yankee City and by the Lynds on Middletown. Kahl examines interaction between groups, the relationship of class consciousness to political ideology, ethnic and racial barriers between classes, and social mobility. Kahl finds that the school system is the institution most often determinant of class.

SOC 475. KATZ, JACK. Poor People's Lawyers in Transition. New Brunswick, N.J.: Rutgers University Press, 1982. 273 pp.
This book is both a history of legal services to the poor from the Progressive era to the present and a case study of the professional staffs and organizations specializing in providing legal services to the poor in the Chicago area. Although Katz does not minimize the influence of external economic and political events on legal assistance for the poor, his analysis is primarily institutional--that is, he explores the internal and processural dynamics of such programs. He focuses primarily on the professionalization of legal services and the effect of this process on the character of reform. "Although Legal Services lawyers originally were styled 'antipoverty' warriors, their reform activities increasingly appeared to have less success in eliminating poverty than in legalizing the state's definition, organization, and maintenance of the poor as a segregated economic class."

SOC 476. KERCKHOFF, ALAN C. Socialization and Social Class. Englewood Cliffs, N.J.: Prentice-Hall, 1972. 170 pp.
Kerckhoff reexamines the empirical findings of research done in the 1950s and 1960s in order to "review our knowledge of the socialization process within the context of the stratification system of the United States."

The result is a summary of studies of the relations between social class
and socialization. Kerckhoff analyzes the differences of social class
in relation to the goals of socialization, the nature of the process itself,
and its outcomes. The influence of peers, parents, and teachers is given
close attention. Kerckhoff's theme is that "socialization experiences
vary by social class, [and] these experiences lead to the development
of different social classes . . . ultimately leading them to assume different adult positions."

SOC 477. KOHN, MELVIN L. Class and Conformity: A Study in Values. Home-
     wood, Ill.: Dorsey Press, 1969. 316 pp.
The focus of this study is the relation between social class and values.
Data are taken from three studies conducted in Washington, D.C., Turin,
Italy, and the U.S. nation-wide. In the Washington study, social class
and parent-child relations were investigated with a focus on parent values
as a function of class. In the comparative Turin study, it was found
that, as in the Washington study, middle-class parents stressed self-
direction while working-class parents placed value on conformity. In the
national study, the cause for these differential values was found to lie
in the experience of occupational self-direction.

SOC 478. KOMAROVSKY, MIRRA. Blue-Collar Marriage. New York: Random
     House, 1964. 397 pp.
This study attempts to fill an information gap about the working class
family unit in America. Based on a sample of fifty-eight families from
one small American community, this investigation examines the premarital
and marital socialization of the couples, expectations and realities of
working class marriage, interpersonal competence, sex, and marital satisfaction between the spouses. Working wives, kinship relations, the influence of work on the family unit, and the social life and leisure of the
couples are also analyzed. Insofar as marriage patterns vary from class
to class, Komarovsky's study attempts to eliminate some of the sociological
handicaps created by the preponderance of studies of middle class, educated
families.

SOC 479. KORNBLUM, WILLIAM. Blue Collar Community. Chicago: University
     of Chicago Press, 1974. 260 pp.
As a participant-observer in Chicago's South Side, a steel community,
Kornblum provides a description of patterns of interaction in a working-
class American community. His analysis centers on two significant factors
in community relationships: the formation and manipulation of ethnic
coalitions by local politicians; and the effects of work relationships
in the steel mills on community interaction. He then discusses ethnicity
and work relationships as they affect union and ward politics. His perspective is unusual in that he does not adhere to the conventional view
of American ethnic groupings as static and primary. Rather, he focuses
on local political leaders and their role in creating politically powerful
coalitions by use of ethnicity as symbol.

SOC 480. LAUMANN, EDWARD O. Prestige and Association in an Urban Community:
     An Analysis of an Urban Stratification System. New York: Bobbs-
     Merrill, 1966. 218 pp.
Although an abundance of studies of stratification in rural and small-
town America have been conducted, as well as a wealth of research on patterns of income, consumption, and residence in urban settings, this study
by Laumann attempts to fill a gap in our knowledge of the urban stratification system and other institutional subsystems. His model includes
parameters of subjective and objective social distance. This empirical
study is aimed at the advanced student of American stratification in urban
settings.

SOC 481. LEVISON, ANDREW. The Working Class Majority. New York: Coward,
          McCann & Geoghegan, 1975. 319 pp.
Levison attempts to shatter the "myths about the shrinking numbers, increasing affluence, and political extremism of blue-collar workers" in this
investigation of America's working-class. He argues that a vast gulf
separates the workers from the affluent American middle class, and that
a fundamental inequality persists. Popular conceptions about the conservative political attitudes of the working-class are likewise unfounded,
Levison claims; rather, "in certain vital respects, blue-collar workers
are still a largely liberal, not conservative, force in American politics."
Such popular misconceptions about the blue-collar worker, Levison asserts,
are "politically dangerous to any rational strategy for progress in America
in the seventies."

SOC 482. LEVITAN, SAR A. and RICHARD S. BELOUS. More Than Subsistence:
          Minimum Wage for the Working Poor. Baltimore, Md.: Johns
          Hopkins University Press, 1979. 179 pp.
Levitan and Belous contend that welfare, training, and other governmental
programs have done little to improve the situation of the working poor.
However, the controversial minimum wage has been "the most direct and
impressive policy tool designed to help improve their lot." This study
examines the role of the minimum wage in relation to the working poor
and the welfare state. It traces the history of minimum wage legislation
and evaluates the quantitative evidence on its effects. The authors argue
that the minimum wage has served a "highly beneficial function," that
it has not exacerbated youth unemployment, and that "there is no proof
that the minimum wage has caused massive problems."

SOC 483. LEWIS, MICHAEL. The Culture of Inequality. Amherst: University
          of Massachusetts Press, 1978. 207 pp.
"This book is about the manner in which many Americans interpret the existence of social and economic inequality. It is about their beliefs concerning such inequality and the consequences of these beliefs for the
human serviceability of the American experience." In the first part of
the book the author argues for the existence of an individualistic culture
of inequality in American society and discusses its implications for American life. He then tests his theoretical assertion in an illustration
of the culture of inequality as it manifests itself in a middle-sized
community's response to the pressures for change in the nature of race
relations and the character of existing relationships between the poor
and the rich of society. "The culture of inequality," Lewis concludes,
"makes victims of all but a few of us. It victimizes the disinherited
by mandating the persistence of their lowly estate. It victimizes many
of the rest of us by threatening our sense of self-worth, forcing us into
a demeaning struggle against a specter of self-denigration which threatens
us with despair."

SOC 484. LISTON, ROBERT A. The American Poor: A Report on Poverty in
          the United States. New York: Delacorte, 1970. 191 pp.
In this concise work, Liston discusses the extent of poverty in America,
its causes, and the quality of life of poor Americans. Statistics on
various facets of poverty are interwoven with the narrative. Liston begins
with the questions "What is poverty? Who are the poor?" and goes on to
discuss such issues as family planning, education, and job-training.
The final chapters are devoted to a report and evaluation of Federal government efforts to reduce poverty.

SOC 485. MILLS, C. WRIGHT. The Power Elite. New York: Oxford University
          Press, 1959. 423 pp.
The most controversial of Mills's major works, The Power Elite focuses
on the structure of power in post-W.W. II America. Mills contends that,
through a conjunction of historical circumstances, a concentration of
power unprecedented in American history has emerged. The "power elite"
refers to the interlocking and mutually dependent interests of the leaders
of the political, economic, and military orders. Mills argues that American foreign policy is dictated by vested economic interests. Moreover,
a permanent war economy has become established, and the military-industrial
complex has become so integral a part of American economic life that disarmament negotiations induce stock market fluctuations--"peace scares";
economic slumps are addressed by increased military spending. This interdependence among the institutional elites is reflected by the exchange
of roles among business leaders, politicians in powerful Washington posts,
and high ranking military men. Mills's analysis of the structure of power
contrasted sharply with the pluralist conception prevailing in the 1950s
and proved a harbinger of much of the radical critique of American society
that emerged during the turbulent 1960s.

SOC 486. MILLS, C. WRIGHT. White Collar: The American Middle Classes.
          New York: Oxford University Press, 1951. 378 pp.
This volume is a study of the new American middle classes. "The white-
collar people," Mills writes, "slipped quietly into modern society."
They have risen in numerical importance and perform the major routines
of life in modern America. According to Mills, they are a social class
alienated from their jobs and their lives, caught up in the impersonal
world of bureaucracy and business. Mills looks at the new middle class,
the managerial demiurge, the bureaucrat, the technician, the salesperson,
and the clerical workers of mass society. He analyzes the work attitudes,
status aspirations, and general psycho-social make-up of the white collar
worker in America and suggests various ways in which the middle class
might regain some power and control over their own life situations.

SOC 487. MILNER, MURRAY, Jr. The Illusion of Equality: The Effect of
          Education on Opportunity, Inequality, and Social Conflict.
          San Francisco: Jossey-Bass, 1972. 172 pp.
Milner characterizes American society as overcome by a weariness resulting
from endless striving with lack of expected level of satisfaction. This
is attributed to "status inflation," a generally neglected phenomenon
in stratification studies, which Milner defines as "the social process
through which the status value of any absolute amount of individual
resources decreases as the average level of these resources increases."
Status inflation results from a contradiction in American values, the
value of equality versus the value of achievement, which is partially
reconciled by the doctrine of equality of opportunity. In later chapters,
Milner discusses the egalitarian educational system in America and argues
that racial inequality will be reduced while class inequality will most
likely persist. Milner also relates the expansion of secondary education
to political stability; however, the increase in college education, he
argues, has fostered social conflict.

SOC 488. MYERS, JEROME K. and LEE L. BEAN. A Decade Later: A Follow-
          up of Social Class and Mental Illness. New York: Wiley, 1968.
          250 pp.
Another volume in the New Haven study of social class and mental illness,
this book explores the social class differences in what happened to the
original patients in the ten years following an earlier study conducted
by Hollingshead and Redlich. Here Myers and Bean examine the patients'
treatment experience and its outcome, social class and the patients' adjustment in the larger community. They also report their findings relating

to psychological factors, economic role performance, and social participation. They confirm earlier findings that social class is inextricably
related to the patients' general adjustment patterns after treatment and
to the success or failure of that treatment.

SOC 489. MYERS, JEROME K. and BERTRAM H. ROBERTS. Family and Class
    Dynamics in Mental Illness. New York: Wiley, 1959. 295 pp.
This study constitutes the second part of the analysis of social stratification and mental illness initiated in Hollingshead and Redlich's Social
Class and Mental Illness (see SOC 468). Myers and Roberts investigate
the social and psycho-dynamic factors in the development of mental illness
as they relate to a psychiatric patient's position in the class structure
of American society and the relationship between social mobility and the
development of psychiatric illnesses. The authors study fifty patients
and their families from different classes and cite the family relationships,
community pressures, and other class factors that manifested themselves
in the patients' mental disorders. Their work points to the necessity
of including social class variables in the study of psychiatric illness
in American society.

SOC 490. NELSON, JOEL I. Economic Inequality: Conflict Without Change.
    New York: Columbia University Press, 1982. 280 pp.
Nelson has two major objectives in this book. First, he examines trends
in economic inequality among Americans since 1960 and discovers relative
stability in "institutional" inequalities—that is, the relative positions
of business and labor in American society. Second, he uses these empirical
data to evaluate the efficacy of conflict (Marxist) and consensus (functionalist) theoretical perspectives concerning economic inequality. He
contends that neither model of modern American Capitalism adequately interprets the realities of contemporary American society. He devotes separate
chapters to case studies of the relative economic status of black Americans
and small businessmen, respectively, to document his basic thesis of stability in basic institutional inequalities during the past quarter century.
In his final chapter Nelson tests his hypotheses concerning the lack of
utility of conflict and consensus models to a postindustrial society by
examining the service economy, which he characterizes as "the central
thread of continuity in America's past and future." He concludes that
the absence in American society of a strong ideological commitment to
economic inequality leads to situational rather than institutional conflict
and thus to the perpetuation of these institutional inequalities.

SOC 491. PACKARD, VANCE. The Status Seekers: An Exploration of Class
    Behavior in America and the Hidden Barriers that Affect You,
    Your Community, Your Future. New York: McKay, 1959. 376 pp.
"In the early 1940's," Packard writes, "an era of abundance began which
by 1959 had reached proportions fantastic by any past standards." In
this study, Packard seeks to understand what happened to social class
in America as a consequence of this new-found affluence. Did America,
in fact, become a classless society? Were rigid old class distinctions
maintained, altered, or simply redefined? The result, Packard proposes,
was that Americans became involved in a rigorous, unrelenting process
of rating and status striving which resulted in distress, anxiety, feelings
of inferiority, and strain in the daily lives of average Americans. The
author examines the marks of status "snob-appeal" evidenced in housing,
job prestige, fashionable clothing, friends, clubs and civil associations,
religious affiliation, and the general behavior of "The Status Seekers."
This study of the "upgrading urge" of Americans today constitutes an examination of personality and national character in America in the immediate
post-W.W. II years.

SOC 492. PARKER, RICHARD. The Myth of the Middle Class: Notes on Affluence & Equality. New York: Liveright, 1972. 233 pp.
The mythmakers would have it that the poor and the very rich have disappeared from the American scene, that America has become a monolithic and
happy middle class society, and that power in that society is therefore
evenly distributed. Parker challenges such a view in an analysis of the
American socio-economic structure. "This myth of the Affluent Society,"
Parker writes, "still enjoys wide popularity. The effect has been a myopia
which ignores or distorts serious issues of social justice." Parker looks
at "America the Beautiful" of the post-W.W. II era, America before the
fifties, "The Affluent Fifties," and the rise of a "New Class" in the
1960s; he then examines the rich, the upper-middle class, and the lower-
middle class in an empirical analysis.

SOC 493. PIVEN, FRANCES FOX and RICHARD A. CLOWARD. The New Class War:
Reagan's Attack on the Welfare State and Its Consequences.
New York: Pantheon Books, 1982. 163 pp.
This book critically examines the efforts of "business-oriented leaders
who came to power with the election of Reagan in 1980 [to try] to dismantle" the protections of the welfare state against the "insecurities and
hardships of an unrestrained market economy." Approaching the topic from
a historical examination of periods of expansion and retraction of government relief and welfare programs, Piven and Cloward analyze the social
and political forces that they contend will preclude scuttling such programs today. They argue that efforts at retrenchment will fail primarily
because many subsistence programs have become permanent income-maintenance
entitlement programs and because American attitudes concerning the right
to basic subsistence have become deeply ingrained.

SOC 494. POMER, MARSHALL I. Intergenerational Occupational Mobility in
the United States: A Segmentation Perspective. Gainesville:
University Presses of Florida, 1981. 106 pp.
This monograph reanalyzes data on intergenerational mobility that formed
the basis of Blau and Duncan's 1967 American Occupational Structure (see
SOC 522), which minimized the role of inheritance in accounting for the
socio-economic position of American males. Pomer criticizes the procedures
and statistical methods employed by Blau and Duncan and proposes a "segmentation" perspective to replace the "individualistic" perspective that
underlies the reliance on father-son correlation in socio-economics that
the previous authors found. Pomer concludes that the data provide "clear
evidence that a person's socio-economic destination is affected by his
socio-economic origin. A person's probability of being in any occupation
is sensitive to the similarity of that occupation to his father's occupation."

SOC 495. REIMAN, JEFFREY H. The Rich Get Richer and the Poor Get Prison:
Ideology, Class, and Criminal Justice. Portland, Oreg.: Wiley,
1979. 214 pp.
"Acts that are not treated as crimes [e.g., occupational deaths and illnesses, price-fixing, consumer deception] pose at least as great a danger
to the public as acts that are, and often a considerably greater danger."
The former are committed by the affluent, while the latter are committed
primarily by the poor. Reiman contends that the crimes of the rich enable
them to get richer, while those of the poor get them prison. Arguing
from a structuralist perspective, he attempts to interpret the dimensions,
mechanisms, causes, and moral implications of the American criminal justice
system's failure to combat crime. His basic thesis is that the failure
of the criminal justice system in America to reduce crime actually benefits
the powerful and privileged. After delivering his indictment of the injustices of the American system of criminal justice, the author advances
suggestions for rehabilitating that system.

SOC 496. REISSMAN, LEONARD. _Inequality in American Society: Social Stratification_. Glenview, Ill.: Scott, Foresman, 1973. 137 pp.

Reissman establishes the link between the way in which social inequality is conceptualized and the extent to which it must be considered problematic. Taking a stand against the views of "poverty as a culture" and "inequality as class," Reissman demonstrates how these conceptualizations define poverty and inequality as non-problematic. The poor and the blacks are the two groups that Reissman cites as most seriously affected by social inequality; when indicating possible solutions to the problem of inequality for these two groups, he points out some important differences between them. America has two possible solutions to the dilemma posed by social inequality: "Either we can begin to revise our values concerning equality, or we begin to alter the structure of opportunities so as to enhance the search for equality."

SOC 497. ROTHMAN, ROBERT A. _Inequality and Stratification in the United States_. Englewood Cliffs, N.J.: Prentice-Hall, 1978. 243 pp.

This book is a systematic theoretical inquiry into structural inequality in American society. Rothman explores the economic, political, prestige, and discretionary characteristics of occupational, sexual, and racial/ethnic inequality. He examines the life chances and life experiences of various societal groups and social strata in the U.S. The author concludes with a chapter focusing on American definitions of achievement, and the processes and consequences of intra- and inter-generational mobility. Rothman's work provides a framework from which to analyze the dynamic elements of social stratification in the U.S.

SOC 498. RUBIN, LILLIAN BRESLOW. _Worlds of Pain: Life in the Working-Class Family_. New York: Basic Books, 1976. 268 pp.

Based on in-depth interviews with fifty white working-class couples, this study probes the personal life experiences of ordinary Americans and particularly the way in which life experiences are "intimately connected . . . with the work people do, their place in the class structure." A picture of the nearly desperate state of family life emerges as Rubin documents the sense of alienation, emptiness, and betrayal that these working-class couples express.

SOC 499. SANGER, MARY BRYNA. _Welfare of the Poor_. New York: Academic Press, 1979. 180 pp.

During the 1960s and 1970s, a substantial body of literature on the characteristics, behavior, and attitudes of the welfare poor was undertaken. Sanger's book is a review and evaluation of this research, focusing primarily on Aid to Dependent Children (AFDC), the largest and most controversial program to aid the welfare poor. She argues that because AFDC is the "most significant national income assistance program," its "impact on recipients is likely to reveal important dimensions of the entire poverty population." She examines the status of welfare families in relation to the major institutions of the labor market, the family, the health care system, and the educational system. She also assesses the political and methodological weaknesses of the prevailing models in poverty research, identifies several fundamental policy issues for welfare reform, and suggests several questions that previous research on the welfare poor has not considered.

SOC 500. SCHNAIBERG, ALLAN. _The Environment: From Surplus to Scarcity_. New York: Oxford University Press, 1980. 464 pp.

Schnaiberg examines the relationship between environmental quality and social justice. He maintains that "social inequalities are interwoven with each environmental concern." Therefore, "this book is not merely about saving the environment: It is about making our social and physical environment a fit place for both the powerless and the powerful to live and work in." He contends that the etiology of environmental problems can be located in the structure of socio-cultural production and that present and future environmental problems are rooted in the "creation and distribution of social surplus." In the first chapter, "the social problems of the environment," he analyzes the relationships between social and environmental structures. In the second part of the book, he critically evaluates the problems (e.g., through population growth, technological imperatives, the consumption demands of an affluent society, and the organizational characteristics of capitalist producers). After examining several recent environmental issues, the author considers some future options.

SOC 501. SEGALMAN, RALPH and ASOKE BASU. Poverty in America: The Welfare Dilemma. Westport, Conn.: Greenwood Press, 1981. 418 pp.
The authors contend that two competing conceptions of equality--equality of opportunity and equality of results (what they term "delivered equality") are central to debate over social policies for alleviating poverty in American society. They argue that the notion of delivered equality is the basic premise of much social welfare legislation and merely perpetuates poverty by denying the responsibility of the poor to act on their own behalf. A policy based on delivered equality, they write, "fosters a life-long delivered dependency that could seriously erode the democratic order." Their study examines the contours of social welfare and poverty in America, from a history of British and early American poor law to a consideration of contemporary social welfare policy alternatives.

SOC 502. SENNETT, RICHARD and JONATHAN COBB. The Hidden Injuries of Class. New York: Knopf, 1972. 275 pp.
Sennett and Cobb argue that a new form of class conflict is developing in America as a result of increased economic and social pressures on the working class. It is the internal conflict of the American blue-collar worker, whose dignity and self-esteem are threatened by his interpretation of his own position in the status hierarchy. Through a series of intensive informal interviews with working-class Americans, Sennett and Cobb examine the societal forces and attitudes that lead the working class to measure its own worth against the lives and work structures of those whom society seems truly to value. The authors argue that personal ability and personal dignity have become inseparably linked.

SOC 503. SILK, LEONARD and MARK SILK. The American Establishment. New York: Basic Books, 1980. 351 pp.
The authors seek to describe and analyze the impact of the sometimes amorphous entity known derisively as the "Establishment." They contend that it operates as a "Third Force," in addition to Business and Government, in the American polity. Its distinguishing characteristic is that its aims, in contrast to business and politics, are disinterest and public morality: "It worries not only about the whole nation but about all humanity." In separate chapters the authors examine the most influential and prominent institutional sectors in which the Establishment's political influence is manifested: Harvard University, The New York Times, the Ford Foundation, the Brookings Institution, the Council on Foreign Relations, and the Committee for Economic Development. In his two final chapters Silk discusses the links between the Establishment and Business and Government.

SOC 504. SLAWSON, JOHN. Unequal Americans: Practices and Politics of Intergroup Relations. Westport, Conn.: Greenwood Press, 1979. 249 pp.

Unequal Americans analyzes the principles used by policy-makers, specialists, and practitioners dealing with intergroup conflict. It is concerned "primarily with clarifying the methodology in the field of intergroup relations. It seeks to ascertain the kind of social change and alterations in mental attitude that might contribute to (1) improved relationships among racial, ethnic, and religious groups in the U.S., (2) the achievement of equality of opportunity for all groups, and (3) the improvement of the social quality of life within these groups." Based on tape-recorded interviews conducted in 1970 with intergroup relations specialists, the book seeks to determine the dynamics and processes for dealing with problems of intergroup relations and the most effective methods for alleviating and preventing intergroup conflict.

SOC 505. STASZ, CLARICE. The American Nightmare: Why Inequality Persists. New York: Schocken Books, 1981. 233 pp.

What happened to the "equality revolution" of the 1960s? In a critique of the ensuing conservative and neo-conservative drift Stasz seeks to revive the social criticism of that decade and to generate a "new criticism" that transcends today's conservative, liberal, and radical orthodoxies. Her basic objective is to understand how the American dream of economic success achieved by meritocratic effort has, because of persistent discrimination, been transformed into a nightmare for racial minorities and women. She identifies those values (especially individualism), ideologies (e.g., the characterization of affirmative action as "reverse discrimination"), and social policies that have characterized what she sees as a retreat from the vision of the 1960s. Finally, she outlines some "fresh social and economic policies—some mundane, some outrageous—but all practical and practicable, with promise of drawing the country closer to our founding ancestors' ideals."

SOC 506. THOMAS-LYCKLAMA a NIJEHOLT, G. On the Road for Work: Migratory Workers on the East Coast of the United States. Boston: Martinus Nijhoff, 1980. 211 pp.

This book seeks to provide a comprehensive understanding of migratory farm workers by combining statistical data analysis with descriptive reports on the lives and work of a sample of migratory and non-migratory workers in East Coast states. It examines the issue of migratory farm labor primarily as a problem "which is inherent in the agricultural production structure of the United States, and not as a migration problem." In particular the author uses survey data to compare the socio-economic status, mobility patterns, job security, and job opportunities of migratory and non-migratory farm workers. His findings provide the basis for a critique of existing government policies dealing with farm labor. In the final chapter he advances several policy recommendations to improve the quality of farm workers' lives.

SOC 507. TUCKER, WILLIAM. Progress and Privilege: America in the Age of Environmentalism. Garden City, N.Y.: Anchor Press, 1982. 314 pp.

Tucker seeks to interpret the "Age of Environmentalism," the period from the late 1960s to the present, in which the environmental movement emerged and "environmentalism [has] come close to being a national religion." He identifies what he perceives as contradictions in the environmentalist mentality, which is pervaded by a perverse satisfaction over the ecological damage that they have publicized. His book "is an attempt to save environmentalism from environmentalists," who, generally drawn from the privileged classes in American society, have been critics of progress and the protectors of their own interests. Environmentalism, according to Tucker, represents a rejection of progress and "has become an extremely conservative doctrine--fearful of the future, despairing of human effort, worried about social change, and wedded to the status quo."

SOC 508. WARREN, DONALD I. The Radical Center: Middle Americans and the Politics of Alienation. Notre Dame, Ind.: University of Notre Dame, 1976. 260 pp.

Middle America, the members of the working class, have divided into two groups, Warren asserts: "In one camp is the more content and secure portion" while in the other is "a more militant, more aggressively dissatisfied segment." This study attempts to define the Middle American population and investigates the sources of its dissatisfaction and the reasons behind its mobilization. Middle American radicalism, Warren writes, "has come far from its beginnings in the later 1960s. With the seismograph-like instruments of survey research we have charted its course." The results of that research are presented and analyzed here, and the implications of these empirical findings for public policy are explored.

SOC 509. WRIGHT, ERIK OLIN. Class Structure and Income Determination. New York: Academic Press, 1979. 271 pp.

This book, part of the Institute for Research on Poverty Monograph Series, is an empirical and quantitative analysis of inequality in American society from a Marxist perspective. Rather than employing occupation and education to measure inequalities, Wright emphasizes class, which he defines in terms of "common positions within the social relations of productions." He explores the manner in which different kinds of occupations--those involving supervision, supervising, or being one's own boss--affect economic outcomes. His basic theme is that class "plays a central role in mediating income inequality in capitalist society." He concludes that class position has a "significant and consistent impact on income," and that this is especially apparent in explaining income inequality between races and sexes. "Differential returns to education between blacks and whites and between men and women, which have been found in virtually every study of race and sex effects on income, disappear almost entirely when class position is held constant."

VIII. POLITICAL ECONOMY, OCCUPATIONS, AND WORK

SOC 510. ADLER, JUDITH E. Artists in Offices: An Ethnography of an Academic Art Scene. New Brunswick, N.J.: Transaction Books, 1979. 165 pp.

This is a study in the sociology of culture, in particular, of the organizational setting within which the arts are produced. Adler examines the dynamics of institutional change in the life of the California Institute of the Arts, an avant-garde school for the arts founded in the late 1960s with funds from Walt Disney. The author focuses on the manner in which the utopian ideology on which the school was founded ultimately became a casualty of the school's organizational--political, economic, and bureaucratic--requirements. The author's central argument is that "in coming to understand how artists are forced to adopt the manners demanded by a historically specific work setting we may learn how they come to work in the manner which is later associated with it."

SOC 511. AGASSI, JUDITH BUBER. Comparing the Work Attitudes of Women and Men. Lexington, Mass.: Lexington Books, 1982. 336 pp.

This is a follow-up study of the author's previous book, Women on the Job (see SOC 512). Two basic problems are dealt with in this volume: the problem of workers who are alienated from their work, its content, and its purpose; and the question of the difference between the sexes in various work attitudes. Agassi finds that no such distinction is sex-specific in the sense that no difference holds regardless of occupational differences. She also discovers that the quality of the content of work is the single important factor influencing women's active concern with the limitations of their current jobs.

SOC 512. **AGASSI, JUDITH BUBER.** Women on the Job: The Attitudes of Women to Their Work. Lexington, Mass.: Lexington Books, 1979. 263 pp.

This empirical study examines the validity of two groups of theories: one concerns women's attitudes toward work, and the other concerns factors that influence such attitudes. The findings indicate that the present shift toward more egalitarian views and values among employed women can be expected to continually diminish supposedly sex-specific differences in interest in advancement and promotion, and in attachment and commitment to work. All the results are based on a study of samples of employed women in three countries and three occupational clusters of jobs that are below the semi-professional level.

SOC 513. **ANDREW, ED.** Closing the Iron Cage: The Scientific Management of Work and Leisure. Montreal: Black Rose Books, 1981. 205 pp.

Andrew's primary goal is to explore "the leisure-as-compensation thesis found in contemporary literature on leisure." This work is based on empirical sociology and uses time-budget studies to look at the "evidence of words as well as deeds." In his examination, Andrew first looks at the ideas behind "leisure," including perspectives from Max Weber, from whom he takes his title, Frederick Winslow Taylor's time-motion studies, and other varying sociological thoughts about leisure. He then discusses the data that contemporary sociology has discovered, and endeavors, in his final analysis, to make "the possibilities of our civilization of leisure open to us."

SOC 514. **APPELBAUM, EILEEN.** Back to Work: Determinants of Women's Successful Re-entry. Boston: Auburn House, 1981. 141 pp.

This empirical study focuses on the generation of women who were born in the 1920s and 1930s and who first swelled the ranks of the labor force. The author tries to explain why so many women now work outside the home, and feels that an answer to this question "requires re-examination of the assumptions underlying the traditional view of sex roles within the family." She pays special attention to the interaction between the family as a social institution and the changing economic environment, as well as analyzing working wives' job satisfaction, factors contributing to women's successful re-entry into the job market, and the trends and prospects for the employment of married women.

SOC 515. **BAGDIKIAN, BEN H.** The Media Monopoly. Boston: Beacon Press, 1983. 282 pp.

This is an exploration of the institutional bias that controls the dissemination of information by the media. Bagdikian argues that through their failure to report on certain issues (in the private and corporate sector), the media are effectively denying the public an opportunity to understand the reality of their world. Two thousand five hundred of the leading newspapers, magazines, radio and T.V. stations, book publishers, and movie companies in the U.S. are owned by fifty corporations. This centralization of control constitutes, in Bagdikian's opinion, a new Private Ministry of Information and Culture. In his view, the fifty corporations set the national media agenda. This book describes the impact of concentrated control of the U.S. media by these corporations and the impact of mass advertising on the form and content of the advertising-subsidized media--newspapers, magazines, and broadcasting.

SOC 516. BARTH, PETER S. with H. ALLAN HUNT. Workers' Compensation and
Work-Related Illnesses and Diseases. Cambridge, Mass.: MIT
Press, 1980. 391 pp.
The authors, in introducing this volume, trace the background to the present
system of worker compensation and review the historical development of
the recognition of occupational diseases as a health problem. The incidence of occupational disease is recorded and the etiological and diagnostic issues relating to occupational diseases are explored. The authors
describe the legal and administrative milieu which provides the legal
framework for the workers' compensation scheme. Quantitative data on
occupational diseases and the payment of worker compensation benefits
are presented for the U.S. as well as for eight foreign jurisdictions.
This book attempts to understand how workers' compensation deals with
the multi-faceted problems of persons suffering from occupational illnesses
or diseases.

SOC 517. BERCH, BETTINA. The Endless Day: The Political Economy of Women
and Work. New York: Harcourt Brace Jovanovich, 1982. 212 pp.
Berch states that "the point of this book is to explain to you how our
economic system in America operates and how it structures the economic
life of women." Her work details the economic incentives controlling
women "behind the appearance of free choice" and the complex nature of
the woman's three productive roles in the market, in housework, and in
childbearing. Berch traces and analyzes the history of women's labor
in the U.S. She devotes two chapters to describing women's labor market
work, a chapter each to housework and childbearing, and three chapters
to how the government, business, and the unions respond to women. Two
remaining chapters present a worldwide perspective on women's work and
a discussion of the prospects for the future of the woman's place in free
enterprise.

SOC 518. BERGERSON, FREDERIC A. The Army Gets an Airforce: Tactics of
Insurgent Bureaucratic Politics. Baltimore, Md.: Johns Hopkins
University Press, 1980. 216 pp.
In the early 1970s, the U.S. Army possessed the third largest aviation
fleet in the world, after the U.S. Air Force and the Air Force of the
U.S.S.R., respectively. This study is an attempt to understand the bureaucratic political milieu and its members. Bergerson's analysis is based
on more than twenty interviews with officers and enlisted men in both the
Army and the Air Force. He examines the Army's historical acquisition
and subsequent loss of an air division, the reorganization and controversy
about domains which followed W.W. II, the advent of helicopter technology
and its political consequences, and the dynamics of insurgency, among
other topics.

SOC 519. BERKOWITZ, EDWARD and KIM McQUAID. Creating the Welfare State:
Political Economy of Twentieth-Century Reform. New York:
Praeger, 1980. 185 pp.
Berkowitz and McQuaid attempt a synthesis of "private" and "public"
approaches to social welfare in 20th-century America. Their work bases
its efforts on a theory of bureaucracy that holds that the structure of
an organization follows from its strategy and objectives. From this foundation, social welfare history becomes less a story of individual reformers
and more a reflection of governmental bureaucratic abilities. Berkowitz
and McQuaid's social welfare history follows the evolution of welfare
programs as their administration shifted from business to the government
at the end of the 19th century, in the early years of the 20th century,
and through the Depression to W.W. II.

SOC 520. BERMAN, RONALD. Advertising and Social Change. Beverly Hills, Calif.: Sage, 1981. 159 pp.

Berman provides an overview of the sociological dimensions of advertising. The five chapters indicate the scope of the book: "Advertising and the Rational State," "Advertising and Social Control," "Marketplace and Social Change," "Advertising and Mass Society," and "Advertising and Imposed Change." This volume focuses on the major criticisms of advertising and provides an introduction to some of the major sources that address these issues.

SOC 521. BERNARD, JESSIE. Academic Women. New York: World, 1964. 331 pp.

This work outlines the situation of academic women in American universities in the early 1960s. Combining systematic data and autobiographical, biographical, and personal documentary materials, Bernard presents a view of the theory and practice of discrimination against women, the differences between academic men and women, and career patterns of women within the academy. Bernard discusses the subject areas where women are most prevalent and the quality of role performance among academic women. She also deals with women's relationships with male colleagues—the conflicts and academic competition they encounter. One of Bernard's central findings is that: "As a whole, women who receive the doctor's degree are, no doubt because of the greater selectivity involved, superior insofar as test-intelligence is concerned." Yet she found they tend to be less "productive," as measured by published work, than male colleagues. Bernard attributes this difference to women's greater interest in teaching over pure research.

SOC 522. BLAU, PETER M. and OTIS DUDLEY DUNCAN. The American Occupational Structure. New York: Wiley, 1967. 520 pp.

In this study, based on an empirical survey of over 20,000 working American men, Blau and Duncan explore the dynamics of stratification in the U.S. Occupation is considered a major determinant of social class. This systematic analysis of American occupational structure and the opportunities it offers for occupational mobility contributes to the study of stratification in modern society. Such factors as race, migration, family, marital status, and fertility are considered in their relation to mobility patterns; the relations among occupational groups and their historical transformations are analyzed in a structural context. In a concluding chapter, the authors indicate the theoretical importance of their empirical findings.

SOC 523. BURAWOY, MICHAEL. Manufacturing Consent: Changes in the Labor Process Under Monopoly Capitalism. Chicago: University of Chicago Press, 1979. 267 pp.

Burawoy abstracts a number of points from the dominant sociological perspectives and integrates them with a Marxist approach to the study of the labor process. Drawing on data collected while working as a machine operator at Allied Corporation, Burawoy attempts to construct a theoretical framework for understanding the capitalist labor process. In tracing the Geer company of 1945 to the Allied Corporation of 1975, Burawoy notes two important changes in the labor process: (1) a greater individualism promoted by the organization of work, and (2) the demise of hierarchical conflicts and their redistribution in a number of different directions. He explores the rise of internal labor markets, the labor process in a recession, worker consciousness, class struggle and capitalist competitors, and the movement from competitive to monopoly Capitalism. For comparative purposes, a chapter on continuity and change in the Zambian Mining Industry is included.

SOC 524. BURRIS, BEVERLY H. No Room at the Top: Underemployment and Alienation in the Corporation. New York: Praeger, 1983. 330 pp.

Burris's general concern is with the relationship between education and work in the U.S. More precisely, her study examines the phenomenon of overeducation and employment. She describes the history of overeducation, its distribution among different demographic groups and occupational sectors, and, most importantly, the effects of overwork. Placing her analysis in a theoretical framework that emphasizes the contradictions of contemporary capitalist society, she uses empirical data drawn from in-depth interviews with thirty-two clerical workers, some college and some high school graduates, in a financial services corporation. She contends that the relation between the educational system and the labor market "is not a static disjunction between two societal sectors but a dynamic and developing contradiction." She concludes that "it is not overeducation but underemployment that plagues us, an underemployment that is rooted in our present economic and social structure."

SOC 525. BUSCH, LAWRENCE and WILLIAM B. LACY. Science, Agriculture and the Politics of Research. Boulder, Colo.: Westview Press, 1983. 303 pp.

This examination of the factors that influence the choice of research problems by agricultural scientists focuses in particular on the process and context in which public agricultural research is conducted in the U.S. In their critique of the research milieu, Busch and Lacy raise various economic, social, political, and philosophical considerations. They explore the social world of the scientist, the organizational structure of agricultural research, scientific communication, and the influence of scientific research outside of the academic domain. The study is based on in-depth interviews with scientists from various institutions, 1,400 mail questionnaires, and extensive documentary analysis.

SOC 526. BUSS, TERRY F. and F. STEVENS REDBURN. Shutdown at Youngstown: Public Policy for Mass Unemployment. Albany: State University of New York Press, 1983. 219 pp.

Buss and Redburn describe the Lykes Corporation's steel mill shutdown in terms of its impact on the workers, their families, and the community. Their work is primarily a case study with conclusions that are set in the larger context of research on individual employees and the community during economic distress. Buss and Redburn's data include interviews with 146 families, interviews with members of the political and business community, and evaluations of the efforts made by human service administrators. This work is supplemented by brief profiles of twelve of the workers interviewed.

SOC 527. BUTLER, STUART M. Enterprise Zones: Greenlining the Inner Cities. New York: University Books, 1981. 175 pp.

Butler explores the concept of the Enterprise Zone, which is intended to resolve the economic difficulties of inner city areas through reduced taxation and encouragement of entrepreneurial innovation and development. This study first addresses the problem of industrial and urban decline and critiques the various governmental responses to the crisis. Butler then discusses the theoretical origins of the Enterprise Zone, and analyzes the relative success of various Zones that have been created in metropolitan areas of both Britain and the U.S.

SOC 528. BUTTON, JAMES W. Black Violence: Political Impact of the 1960s Riots. Princeton, N.J.: Princeton University Press, 1978. 248 pp.

An analysis of the political effects and consequences of the black urban civil disorders of the 1960s, this study is particularly concerned with the responses of the Executive Branch of the Federal government to this violence. In general terms, it is an attempt to assess the utility or inutility of collective violence "as a strategy for dispossessed minorities." Button examines the pattern of Federal policy responses to ghetto riots by three agencies--the Office of Economic Opportunity, the Department of Housing and Urban Development, and the Department of Justice in three time periods: 1963-66, 1967-68, and 1969-72. In addition to his quantitative analysis, he held interviews with Federal officials concerning their perceptions of urban violence and its after-effects. Finally, Button presents case studies of the impact of riots in two medium-sized cities: Rochester and Dayton.

SOC 529. CALHOUN, DANIEL. Professional Lives in America: Structure and Aspiration, 1750-1850. Cambridge, Mass.: Harvard University Press, 1965. 231 pp.

This examination of professionalism in America focuses on the New England clergy; lawyers in the Nashville, Tennessee area; and the New York medical community. Calhoun describes the behavior and experience of these professional groups in the context of the tension between individual creativity and group responsibility. He argues that by 1850 these groups had moved toward bureaucracy and impersonality, achieving some degree of order while at the same time avoiding outright coercion of the members of the professional group.

SOC 530. CASPER, BARRY M. and PAUL DAVID WELLSTONE. Powerline: The First Battle of America's Energy War. Amherst: University of Massachusetts Press, 1981. 314 pp.

Casper and Wellstone detail the battle over the CU powerline that runs for 470 miles from North Dakota to Minneapolis and St. Paul. On one side of the controversy were its constructors, the Cooperative and the United Power Associations, and the democratic principles behind the necessity for individuals to sacrifice for the good of the nation. On the other side were the individuals who were asked to sacrifice: the farmers whose irrigation, aerial spraying, seeding, and lives would be changed by the construction of the lines. The book traces the controversy from legal protest to the guerrilla warfare and vandalism that continued even after the powerline was completed.

SOC 531. CHINOY, ELY. Automobile Workers and the American Dream. Garden City, N.Y.: Doubleday, 1955. 139 pp.

Chinoy's study of blue-collar workers in an American automobile factory is based on sixty-two in-depth interviews conducted in the early 1950s. The author outlines the basic tenets of the "American Dream," the ideology that success will come to those who strive for it. He examines the role of that dream in the attitudes, aspirations, and life cycles of automobile workers and considers the nature of the goals toward which these American workers strive. In comparing the reports of those he studied, Chinoy observed a chronology or hierarchy of aspirations of the workers throughout their work experience. He notes that workers begin to "shuffle the hierarchy of values which govern their behavior. In defensive efforts to prevent frustration and self-depreciation they assign to success a less prominent, less overriding place in their scheme of things." Conversely, Chinoy concludes, while success may have been relegated to a more realistic level in their value hierarchy, the ideal of "advancement," occupational and social, has not been abandoned.

SOC 532.   COSER, LEWIS A., CHARLES KADUSHIN, and WALTER W. POWELL. Books:
           The Culture and Commerce of Publishing. New York: Basic Books,
           1982. 411 pp.
This is a discussion of the various aspects of the publishing industry.
Beginning with the history of publishing, the authors explain the sociological reason for the changes in the publishing business--the change from
the cottage-publisher/patron system to the modern mass market system.
The reasons given for this change are essentially tied to the rise of
the middle class. Changes in middle-class education, economics, and reading popularity account for the shift in publishing focus. Besides the
history of publishing, the authors discuss marketing, editors, authors,
literary agents, book reviewers, distribution, and academics. Both the
individual roles of these factors and the interrelationship among these
factors are dealt with.

SOC 533.   COX, ALLAN. The Cox Report on the American Corporation. New
           York: Delacorte Press, 1982. 451 pp.
This study of thirteen corporations headquartered in the U.S. attempts
to build a profile of the corporate executive, the company he works for,
and the relationship between the two. Cox offers detailed data on what
corporations value in employees and perspective employees, how corporations
function, and why they succeed or fail. The family, educational and marital background of the corporate executive are examined together with an
account of how executives succeed. Cox points to the crucial role played
by attitude, image, luck, management style, brilliance, training studies
and advancement, mentors, and bosses.

SOC 534.   DAVIDSON, STEPHEN M., THEODORE R. MARMOR, et al. The Cost of
           Living Longer: National Health Insurance and the Elderly.
           Lexington, Mass.: Heath, 1980. 144 pp.
Davidson and Marmor analyze the probable impact of national health insurance on health supports for the elderly, concentrating on the implications
for eligibility, benefits, and administration. The authors consider the
differences that might emerge between states in a national plan, examine
various implementation issues, and pointedly ignore money estimates in
order to highlight other topics. Davidson and Marmor present an overview
of the need and use of medical benefits, discuss how Medicare and Medicaid
currently operate, describe three prototypical national health proposals,
and conclude by comparing the present benefit system with possible future
programs.

SOC 535.   DEAUX, KAY and JOSEPH C. ULLMAN. Women of Steel: Female Blue-
           Collar Workers in the Basic Steel Industry. New York: Praeger,
           1983. 197 pp.
Using records of employment, hiring and termination, and interviews with
both male and female employees, Deaux and Ullman analyze the volume and
permanence of women's entrance into high-paying, prestigious blue-collar
positions in the steel industry. The authors offer a brief history of
women's employment in the U.S., an account of the "psychological and social
factors that influence women's employment," and a description of the glorious past and recent decline of the American steel market as a prelude
to a discussion of how women in the basic steel industry represent a trend
in female employment. The work explores the interface of governmental
action and female employment, seeking to discover the influence of public
policy employment patterns in general and on women's employment in particular.

SOC 536. DeBRIZZI, JOHN A. Ideology and the Rise of Labor Theory in
          America. Westport, Conn.: Greenwood Press, 1983. 196 pp.
DeBrizzi locates the development of early labor theory in America within
the broader development of sociological thinking toward the end of the
19th century. He argues that the work of John A. Commons, one of the
early labor theorists, gained prominence not because of the explanatory
value of the theory itself but rather because of the particularly appealing
form which that explanation took. Commons argued that American society
was unique or exceptional when compared to other European societies.
DeBrizzi in contrast argues that the emergence of labor theory was closely
related to the increase of class conflict in America: this he demonstrates
through a historical analysis of the development of political economy
in 19th-century America. DeBrizzi presents a critique of the work of
Commons, Carter Adams, and Richard Ely and analyzes the development of
labor theory as a social activity which is subject to the influence of
class interests, culture, and the social conflicts that exist in society
at large.

SOC 537. DENKER, JOEL. Unions and Universities: The Rise of the New
          Labor Leader. Montclair, N.J.: Allanheld, Osmun, 1981.
          177 pp.
Denker explores the history of the relationship between unions and universities, suggesting that, traditionally, labor unions and universities
were antagonistic toward each other. As time has progressed, this hostility has changed; increasingly, labor related subjects are being studied
in universities, and college-educated people are more frequently finding
their way into the unions. Denker discusses the rise and evolution of
labor studies and the necessity of training in labor union management.

SOC 538. DOBELSTEIN, ANDREW W. Politics, Economics, and Public Welfare.
          Englewood Cliffs, N.J.: Prentice-Hall, 1980. 255 pp.
This book discusses public welfare policy as it has developed in political
response to growing expectations for increased Federal government authority.
The interaction of various branches and units of government provide a
framework for Dobelstein's discussion of public welfare expansion and
the process of policy making. The author argues that it is in the interactions of these parts of the governmental process that public expectations
are worked into the final public welfare programs which are used by a
growing number of Americans.

SOC 539. EISENSTEIN, SARAH. Give Us Bread But Give Us Roses. Boston:
          Routledge & Kegan Paul, 1983. 207 pp.
This study of working women's consciousness in the U.S., from 1890 to
W.W. I, examines the attitudes of young American working women to the experience of employment outside the home, and the changed relationship between
work and family. Eisenstein demonstrates how working-class women refused
to be undermined by the prevailing middle class ethos that women workers
were somehow improper and unwomanly. The focus is on the women workers
who filled the stores and factories of New York City, Philadelphia, Boston,
Chicago and other cities at the turn of the century. The emergence of
a working-class women's consciousness is contrasted with the persistent
commitment among many working women to the Victorian ideals of marriage
and family. This study places the relationship between women's changing
position in industry and older class and family cultures at the center
of analysis.

SOC 540. FITE, GILBERT C. American Farmers: The New Minority. Blooming-
          ton: Indiana University Press, 1981. 265 pp.
Fite's work attempts to explain how the number of farmers who have been
the nation's principal producers of food has decreased. He discusses
the technological, economic, and social developments that have affected

agriculture since the 1920s. His work traces the history of farm life from before the Depression up to the present, concentrating on the economic and political position of farmers and how they have responded to their declining influence. Fite also discusses the difficulty of uniting the members of this "new minority," and speculates as to the nature of the economic and political influence farmers may exert in the future.

SOC 541. FREEMAN, RICHARD B. The Over-Educated American. New York: Academic Press, 1976. 218 pp.
Freeman's basic argument is that though a college education has tradition- ally been viewed as a principal route for social and economic advancement, access to higher education by greater numbers of people in the 1960s and 1970s has meant that such education is no longer enough even for those with Ph.D.'s (often among the hardest hit). "The Over-Educated American," the author writes, "analyzes . . . the turnaround in the college job market and seeks to determine whether it constitutes a relatively long-term or merely a temporary change in the economic status of the graduates." Over- educated, in the context of Freeman's analysis, means that the type of college training does not correlate with available positions in the Ameri- can labor market. Freeman discusses increasing lack of academic job oppor- tunities and responses thereto, the "end of the Golden Age for teachers and researchers," the decreasing job market for professionals of all kinds, and declining advantages for white college men in light of affirmative action and other social policy programs.

SOC 542. FRIEDMAN, SAMUEL R. Teamster Rank and File: Bureaucracy and Rebellion at Work in a Union. New York: Columbia University Press, 1982. 302 pp.
The author examines the rank-and-file effort of a Los Angeles Local of the International Brotherhood of Teamsters to democratize their union. Genuine worker participation at Local 208 began in the 1950s, and many of the workers became activists in the social movements of the late 1960s. However, the higher echelons of the Teamsters, representing "the most corrupt, most gangster-ridden, and most undemocratic large union in the United States and Canada," successfully quelled worker activism. Friedman sees not only class conflict in the worker's struggle but also organiza- tional conflict within the "labor bureaucracy." The author believes that Local 208 serves as proof that worker agitation for decentralization can initiate social change in America.

SOC 543. GANS, HERBERT J. More Equality. New York: Pantheon Books, 1973. 261 pp.
In this collection of essays, Gans deals primarily with economic inequali- ties and economic policy. His assumption is that greater equality in income and power is desirable, and he predicts a growing concern in America with these issues. Essays included in this collection analyze the problems of contemporary American society, discuss the conflict between equality as a goal and other American values and practices, and the useful functions performed by poverty in this society. Gans also envisions an egalitarian society and speculates on the social and institutional effects of greater equality.

SOC 544. GARRISON, DEE. Apostles of Culture: The Public Librarian and American Society, 1876-1920. New York: Free Press, 1979. 319 pp.
Garrison deals with elite ideology, popular culture, individual leadership, and feminization in her study of public librarians, based on recent scholar- ship and printed sources. Early genteel and generally male American Library Association leaders are profiled statistically and in brief biogra- phies in an appendix. Their moral reform ideals lost out to "pleasing the public" between the 1890s and 1920, a change exemplified by the accept-

ance of popular fiction, some of which is analyzed at length. Their emphasis on liberal arts and breadth of knowledge was supplanted by training in standardization and mechanization, the methods of Melvil Dewey, who is treated in a seventy-page biography. These trends contributed to feminization, although the greatest inducement to employ women probably was their willingness to accept low pay. Garrison demonstrates that professionalization where females dominated did not lead to status and power.

SOC 545. GIBBS, LOIS MARIE. Love Canal: My Story. Albany: State University of New York Press, 1982. 174 pp.
Love Canal is the story of one community living in the vicinity of a toxic waste dump, at Niagara Falls, New York. Gibbs, as the leader of a community threatened by dangerous environmental pollutants, took on Federal and state bureaucracies in an effort to have the plight of her community recognized. She succeeded in convincing the authorities to relocate all those who lived in the area surrounding the Love Canal toxic waste dump. This volume chronicles the politicization of a group of citizens, fired by a common cause and determined not to be side-stepped by the government bureaucracies. The author traces the history, effects, impact on human lives and struggle of the Love Canal Home Owners Association in its quest for a remedy to a problem which she asserts is becoming increasingly international in its dimensions.

SOC 546. GOLDBERG, ROBERTA. Organizing Women Office Workers: Dissatisfaction, Consciousness and Action. New York: Praeger, 1983. 152 pp.
This study of consciousness and dissatisfaction among women workers is based on empirical research conducted at the Baltimore Working Women organization, a constituent of the larger Working Women's Movement. In particular, the focus of the investigation is on the type of consciousness of women who occupy clerical roles, regarding the issues of class and gender. Goldberg's findings point to the specificity of women's experience and to the contradictions between family obligations and the economic necessity to work. The study is introduced with an overview of clerical work in the 19th century and the feminization of office work which continued throughout the 20th century. The goals, structure, and organization of the Baltimore Working Women are outlined together with an analysis of the conditions which create worker dissatisfaction and the rise of a working consciousness.

SOC 547. HADWIGER, DON F. The Politics of Agricultural Research. Lincoln: University of Nebraska Press, 1982. 230 pp.
This account of the politics of U.S. agricultural research addresses the current state and goals of the research, and questions the genesis of particular agricultural research policies and the stated goals of the policy makers. Research undertaken by private industries and foundations as well as that pursued by international research centers is surveyed. Hadwiger also devotes some attention to the research conducted under the auspices of the National Institute of Health and the National Science Foundation. He includes case studies on cooperative extension services which are linked with agricultural research institutions by their history, budgetary controls, and policy processes.

SOC 548. HAYANO, DAVID M. Poker Faces: The Life and Work of Professional Card Players. Berkeley: University of California Press, 1982. 205 pp.
Hayano investigates the careers of professional poker players, while he attempts to define the "pro" as a sociological type. Hayano distinguishes four types of "hustlers": "the career professional," "the subsistence professional," "the outside supported professional," and "the worker professional." He explores the social hierarchy, career mobility, and life-

style of those in the gambling subculture and includes common misconceptions of the professional gambler as a social deviant. The author bases his analysis on observation and participation in the gamerooms of Gardena, California.

SOC 549. HEINZ, JOHN P. and EDWARD O. LAUMANN. Chicago Lawyers: The Social Structure of the Bar. New York: Russell Sage Foundation, 1983. 470 pp.
Heinz and Laumann's work describes and analyzes the legal profession in a major city in pursuit of three objectives: to understand the nature and differentiation within the profession; to describe how differentiation is converted into inequality in income, organizational resources, access to leadership positions, and honor or deference; and to examine the kinds and degree of social bonds among Chicago lawyers. To reach these objectives Heinz and Laumann have arranged their study in sections that focus on varying aspects of a lawyer's professional life, including the fields of law, the backgrounds, values, and career mobility of individual lawyers, and the relationships between attorneys.

SOC 550. HILL, STEPHEN. Competition and Control at Work: The New Industrial Sociology. Cambridge, Mass.: MIT Press, 1981. 280 pp.
In this book, the author attempts to reconstruct industrial sociology. He focuses on the social relations involved in production and employment and their ramifications both inside and outside organizations. A major theme is the precarious nature of industrial peace given the ineradicable opposition of certain interests; this feature is characteristic of the dominant forms of modern economic organization.

SOC 551. HOPKINS, ANNE H. Work and Satisfaction in the Public Sector. Totowa, N.J.: Rowman & Allanheld, 1983. 144 pp.
This book is an empirical assessment of the nature of workers' responses to their employment in a public sector setting. Its purpose is "to explore the interrelationships among the individual and the working environment, including unions, in a more comprehensive manner and in the context of the public sector." Utilizing a model that links job satisfaction with the nature of employees' jobs, their working environments, and "broadly based individual orientations," the author surveyed by mail-questionnaire a random sample of state employees in Nebraska, New York, Oregon, Tennessee, and Wisconsin. After drawing several conclusions concerning those factors that contribute to job satisfaction for public employees, the author discusses the broader implications of her findings.

SOC 552. HOWSDEN, JACKIE L. Work and the Helpless Self: The Social Organization of a Nursing Home. New York: Lanham, 1981. 164 pp.
This work sets out "to lend sociological understanding to the negotiated process through which elderly persons in nursing homes, along with the staff, come to meaningfully define place, self and interaction." Howsden presents an analysis of "observations, conversations, interviews, chart data, events and impressions" of the social organization of the "Wheatland" nursing home. Engaged in "observant participation" of all facets of life in the nursing home, the author seeks to contribute to sociological theory in the substantive area of aging and to present qualitative interpretations about a specific setting wherein "oldness" is managed.

SOC 553. KANTER, ROSABETH MOSS. Men and Women of the Corporation. New York: Basic Books, 1977. 348 pp.
Kanter's ethnography of the modern corporation traces the organization's place in the creation of male and female roles at work--roles which are often attributed to innate differences based on sex. She examines the roles and images dictated by a large, bureaucratic organization, paying particular attention to the masculine ethic of management and the femini-

zation of low paying, low status, clerical work. The social control mechanisms wielded over secretaries and corporate wives are critically examined. Kanter also discusses the structures and processes of organizational opportunity, distribution of power, and social differences, all of which help to legitimate and perpetuate the present system. In conclusion, Kanter suggests practical policies and programs which would enhance opportunity, empower more people, and balance the numbers within corporate structures.

SOC 554. KARSTEN, PETER. Soldiers and Society: The Effects of Military Service and War on American Life. Westport, Conn.: Greenwood Press, 1978. 339 pp.
Karsten explores the effects of military service on the soldier himself and on the wider community. He examines the recruitment process which precedes induction into the army; training; tour of duty and combat; homecoming; adjustment to civilian life; and the veteran's status. In Part Two, the author discusses the effects of war and the military on those not directly involved (the G.I. family), on the economy, and on social and political values. He develops three general categories of effects which unify the personal and social contexts of the study: physical injuries; alterations in socio-economic status or geographic location; and effects on value and personality formation.

SOC 555. KAUFMAN, H. G. Professionals in Search of Work: Coping with the Stress of Job Loss and Underemployment. New York: Wiley, 1982. 359 pp.
This volume addresses the psychological consequences of unemployment and underemployment among professionals in America. However, the perspective is not exclusively psychological and the analysis draws on a diversity of information from health, labor economics, sociology, social work, counseling, management, education, and public policy. The authors describe the four stages through which many jobless professionals pass and how these stages operate in accordance with many theories of stress. Other issues discussed include: the barriers and facilitators to finding work, the job search methods, improving employability and adjustment, and societal responses to unemployment. In addition, the authors outline the options for institutional change by government, professional societies, employers, and academic institutions.

SOC 556. KEELER, THEODORE E. Railroads, Freight and Public Policy. Washington, D.C.: Brookings Institute, 1983. 180 pp.
One in a series of studies on the regulation of economic activity, this book presents an analysis of the economic effects of regulation in the freight transportation industry before and after the 1976 and 1980 legislative reforms. Keeler examines the financial viability of the railroads in historical context and presents a brief history of railroad regulation. He introduces comparative data and economic models to assess the efficacy of rail freight regulation. The economic effects of deregulation, subsidies, taxation policies toward railroads, and competing forms of surface transport are analyzed, as are antitrust policies toward rail mergers, management, and labor. In conclusion, Keeler argues for policy changes which would ensure a profitable role for railroads in the U.S. economy.

SOC 557. KLAUSNER, SAMUEL Z. and EDWARD F. FOULKS. Eskimo Capitalists, Oil Politics and Alcohol. Montclair, N.J.: Allanheld, Osmun, 1982. 343 pp.
This study assesses the historical, socio-cultural, economic, and political factors contributing to the increase of alcohol-related violence on the North slope of Alaska and suggests some policy options available to the Eskimo government for dealing with the problem. Methods of data collection include participant observation, interviews with a representative sample, and documentary analysis. The research findings document the changes

brought about in an Eskimo community suddenly thrust into the American market economy and its Federal political system after the discovery of commercially viable oil. The authors argue that the increased use of alcohol by the Inupiat is an indicator of wider issues of social and cultural change and other attendant problems associated with the onset of sudden wealth. In conclusion, they suggest a number of recommendations for the Eskimos of the North Borough, and Federal and state government in order to stem the flow of alcohol.

SOC 558. KNOKE, DAVID and JAMES R. WOOD. Organized for Action: Commitment in Voluntary Associations. New Brunswick, N.J.: Rutgers University Press, 1981. 263 pp.
The authors argue that voluntary citizen groups constitute important corporate actors at all levels of democratic government. Like political parties, they specialize in aggregating and articulating the interests and needs of their members. This study analyzes the internal structure and function of mass-membership associations with social influence. Two questions guided the research conducted in thirty-two local chapters of various social information associations: which organizational conditions enable some groups to generate high levels of membership commitment to the collective endeavor, and which organizational characteristics are most effective in helping associations to attain their goals of influencing public policy? Much of the theoretical perspective developed in this volume is derived from organization literature. Among the issues examined are the "incentive approach," decision participation, legitimate leaders, resource mobilization, goal attainment, and environmental effects.

SOC 559. KOHN, MELVIN L., CARMI SCHOOLER, JOANNE MILLER, KAREN A. MILLER, CARRIE SCHOENBACH, and RONALD SCHOENBERG. Work and Personality: An Inquiry into the Impact of Social Stratification. Norwood, N.J.: Ablex, 1983. 389 pp.
This book studies the effects of jobs on personality; rather than comparing specific occupations, the authors examine such different aspects of jobs as time involved, pressure, and creativity. Other issues considered are women and ethnic groups in the working world. The authors also look at such questions as the effects of job conditions on leisure-time activities, complexity of work and intellectual flexibility, jobs and social stratification, and occupational structure and alienation.

SOC 560. KRIEGER, SUSAN. Hip Capitalism. Beverly Hills, Calif.: Sage, 1979. 304 pp.
Krieger's work presents the history of a radio station that changed its format from foreign language to rock, and became a leader in San Francisco's counter-culture movement. Her book probes the moral implications of "selling out" as the station grew from idealistic origins to commercial success. She traces four periods in the station's development: Beginnings, Legitimacy, Professionalism, and Renewal; Krieger also breaks each period into chapters tracing the chronological growth of the station. Krieger bases her narrative on interviews with station personnel, and includes comments from disc jockeys, salesmen, secretaries, owners, engineers, and listeners as well as from others connected with the station.

SOC 561. LERMAN, PAUL. Deinstitutionalization and the Welfare State. New Brunswick, N.J.: Rutgers University Press, 1982. 246 pp.
Tracing the history of deinstitutionalization, Lerman maintains that the emergence and expansion of the welfare state accompanied changes in "the conception about the dangerousness of mentally ill or retarded persons, shift in treatment modalities and technologies, and the growing preference for proprietary medical and welfare organizations." The author discusses how Federal welfare policy dictates the types of care society provides for the mentally, emotionally and physically disabled and for criminal

offenders. He evaluates specific programs such as the Social Security Act and discusses their effectiveness as methods of social control. Lerman concludes that new forms of institutionalized care, such as short-term therapeutic programs for the emotionally ill and nursing home care for the elderly, offset the decline of traditional institutional care.

SOC 562. LESTER, RICHARD A. Reasoning About Discrimination: The Analysis of Professional and Executive Work in Federal Antibias Programs. Princeton, N.J.: Princeton University Press, 1980. 384 pp.
Lester examines how the process of reasoning or analysis itself influences public policy on discrimination and its enforcement; he argues that misguided enforcement of Federal antibias programs damages the functioning of business enterprises. The author's theoretical framework for analyzing the role played by "reasoning" about discrimination in professional and managerial work is based on three "generating centers of work influence and guidance": the system of work relations that operates within a particular enterprise, the aims and actions of the individual worker, and outside economic forces or market influences.

SOC 563. LEVENTMAN, PAULA GOLDMAN. Professionals Out of Work. New York: Free Press, 1981. 266 pp.
The author focuses on the unemployment of professionals during the 1970s, saying, "Professionals unemployed in the seventies felt a particular sense of betrayal of a society that had allowed them success and esteem as the price of their faith in the system." This book compares the personal effects of the unemployment of the Great Depression and the unemployment of the 1970s. Working from a geographical area of the Route 128 belt loop outside of Boston, Leventman looks at the businesses in the area and the economic, individual, and institutional effects of the unemployment of the decade.

SOC 564. MAJKA, LINDA C. and THEO J. MAJKA. Farm Workers, Agribusiness and the State. Philadelphia: Temple University Press, 1982. 346 pp.
"This book concerns farm workers, their struggle with the large growers of California, and the ways government at all levels has intervened to regulate political and economic conflict." Their analysis informed by their participation in the farm labor movement, the Majkas explore the lengthy history and development of farm worker protest and insurgency (including separate chapters on Chinese immigrant laborers, Japanese farm laborers, the effects of immigration on farm worker insurgency, and the bracero program), the responses and sources of power of agribusiness, and the vicissitudes of state policies in regulating the conflict.

SOC 565. MARIL, ROBERT LEE. Texas Shrimpers: Community, Capitalism, and the Sea. College Station, Tex.: Texas A&M Press, 1983. 222 pp.
This book about Texas shrimpers focuses on "their work, their families, their dreams, and their frustrations. It is also about their place in their communities and about how their communities respond to them. Finally, it is about shrimping as an industry and about how shrimpers are affected by big business, big government, and . . . larger economic forces. . . ." Based primarily on participant observation, interviews, and survey research, Maril examines, first, the personality and social characteristics of shrimpers and the nature and social structure of the work. Second, he analyzes the social history of shrimpers, their families and communities, and their lives on land. Finally, and more broadly, he studies the major external forces—social, political, and economic—that affect shrimpers' lives.

SOC 566. McNALLY, FIONA. Women for Hire: A Study of the Female Office
      Worker. New York: St. Martin's Press, 1979. 214 pp.
The particular focus of this study is women in routine, temporary white-
collar employment. The analysis suggests that women's occupational choices
and responses to work are influenced by a very wide range of variables
which may be divided into three groups: (1) non-work factors; (2) a number
of influences deriving directly from the work situation; (3) the character
of the market for labor. McNally also argues that it is wrong to suppose
that women consistently display a passive orientation to the situation
in which they currently find themselves. Temporary workers exemplify
women's capacity to negotiate actively the limiting structures that confront them.

SOC 567. MEDCALF, LINDA. Law and Identity: Lawyers, Native Americans
      and Legal Practices. Beverly Hills, Calif.: Sage, 1978.
      147 pp.
Medcalf argues that strategies developed by lawyers for increasing the
wealth and power of Native Americans have failed to provide a meaningful
choice for the minority group faced with assimilation into mainstream
American society or maintenance of their separate identity. In examining
the genesis of the Native Bill of Rights, Medcalf shows that legal efforts
on behalf of Native Americans resulted in the imposition of the liberal
political forms of the dominant culture on the indigenous community.
In effect, according to the author, this imposition stymied the emergence
of alternative native forms of political and economic organization.
Medcalf argues against the ethnocentricism of liberal lawyers and in favor
of a greater understanding of cultural diversity in legal processes.
She concludes that, while Native Americans have secured material benefits,
they have at the same time seen the demise of many of their own traditional
cultural practices.

SOC 568. MEISTER, DAVID. Behavioral Research and Government Policy:
      Civilian and Military R&D. New York: Pergamon Press, 1981.
      375 pp.
Meister's subject is the effect of government sponsorship on behavioral
research and development (R&D); he argues that the Federal government
largely determines how such research is conducted and therefore influences
its results. Part one generally discusses the structure and process of
behavioral research; part two analyzes the range and nature of the research
areas that have been funded by government; and the last section addresses
the problems created by the influence of political factors on the methods,
content, and quality of behavioral science.

SOC 569. METZ, DONALD L. Running Hot: Structure and Stress in Ambulance
      Work. Cambridge, Mass.: Abt Books, 1981. 237 pp.
This is a sociological account of the daily life of an emergency medical
technician on the ambulance run. Metz argues that ambulance work offers
variety, challenge, responsibility, and the opportunity to make a contribution to the well-being of the community; it also offers an environment
fraught with stress and difficult conditions of work, and the variety
of activities, occupations, and organizations that together make up an
emergency medical service. He describes the typical ambulance run: the
"crew culture" structured around peculiarities of language and behavior
which in turn reflect the peculiarities of the work; and the recruitment
and training of ambulance workers. Three chapters are devoted to the
relationships between the ambulance personnel and their environment, with
special attention paid to the interaction between the workers and their
employers, the patients, and representatives of other public services
such as fire and police personnel.

SOC 570. MILLER, GALE. Odd Jobs: The World of Deviant Work. Englewood
          Cliffs, N.J.: Prentice-Hall, 1978. 260 pp.
Miller employs two criteria to define deviant work: the existence of
legal norms and law enforcement agencies that place sanctions on certain
types of behavior and the existence of public consensus about the immoral
or threatening nature of some types of behavior. He attempts to analyze
a series of deviant work roles and relationships in terms of the niches
which they occupy within the broader structures of society. Among the
deviant workers examined are the thief, confidence operator, medical
quack, fortune teller, racketeering operator, prostitute, and female imper-
sonator. Miller looks at the work role and rationale behind each deviant
work area. He points to the many similarities between deviant work roles,
the non-deviant work roles of low status, and relative powerlessness, and
those on the fringes of the mainstream economy. He argues that the deviant
worker is not unlike the non-deviant worker in that he engages in those
activities which yield the necessary monetary rewards to sustain a decent
livelihood.

SOC 571. MILLER, S. M. and DONALD TOMASKOVIC-DEVEY. Recapitalizing America:
          Alternatives to the Corporate Distortion of National Policy.
          Boston: Routledge & Kegan Paul, 1983. 215 pp.
The term "recapitalization" refers to increasing the importance of business
and capital in social and economic policy. The authors contend that most
contemporary discussion of American social and economic policy "is mired
within the ideological and political framework of recapitalizing America--
the magical belief that increasing the power and profitability of private
capital will solve the cyclical and structural problems of a faltering
economy." Although the Reagan social and economic programs represent
its most visible and "reactionary" manifestations, the authors maintain
that recapitalization is a general ideology that "precedes and transcends
Reaganism and Reaganomics." Their study is an analysis and critique of
the conventional wisdom of much of contemporary liberalism and conservatism,
and a statement of economic and political alternatives.

SOC 572. MUELLER, ROBERT KIRK. The Incompleat Board: The Unfolding of
          Corporate Governance. Lexington, Mass.: Lexington Books, 1981.
          283 pp.
Mueller's title, inspired by Izaak Walton's The Compleat Angler, implies
that the current corporate boardroom is not yet sublime, although it has
the potential to be. Mueller focuses on the changing nature of the board
from varying perspectives, including the opportunity for innovation in
the boardroom. His approach is pre-normative, avoiding conventional analysis. He concludes that the corporate status quo should not be maintained
in the next decade. Mueller looks ahead to when corporate actions can
be audited by a third party the way their accounts can be examined now,
realizing that a moral and philosophical "top line" is more difficult
to meet than the "bottom line" of profits and loss.

SOC 573. ORNSTEIN, MICHAEL D. Entry into the American Labor Force. New
          York: Academic Press, 1976. 220 pp.
This empirical study treats entry into the labor force as a process of
occupational stratification. It is based on the work histories of approximately 1,600 American males aged thirty to thirty-nine, nearly half of
whom are black. Characterizing the entry job both by wage level and prestige, Ornstein examines the relation between individual characteristics
and entry job, and the relation between the entry job and subsequent mobility. Also discussed are the reasons for a job change and its effects
on wage and prestige, and the effects of military service on occupational
status. Ornstein suggests that entry wage is the most accurate predictor
of subsequent wage level attainment. This fairly technical work represents
a step in bridging the gap between economic stratification studies focusing

on income and wealth and sociological studies which treat stratification
by occupational prestige.

SOC 574. OZAWA, MARTHA N. Income Maintenance and Work Incentives: Toward
           a Synthesis. New York: Praeger, 1982. 279 pp.
This is an attempt to address the question of how this nation can develop
a system of income maintenance that is based on a "coherent incentive
system so as to preserve the work incentive" and yet at the same time
provide adequately for such vulnerable groups of individuals as children,
the elderly, and the disabled.

SOC 575. PARCEL, TOBY L. and CHARLES W. MUELLER. Ascription and Labor
           Markets: Race and Sex Differences in Earnings. New York:
           Academic Press, 1983. 315 pp.
The authors analyze earnings attainment as a function of both personal
and structural characteristics, for workers who vary by race and sex.
The human capital and status attainment variables are generally statistically significant predictors of earnings across status groups; and the
degree of predictive success of these supply factors varies by ascriptive
status. Turning to the structural perspectives, Parcel and Mueller stress
that the structures of local, industrial, and occupational labor market
organization at the respective ecological levels differ from the structures
of these markets as viewed from the perspectives of the several status
groups.

SOC 576. PENNINGS, JOHANNES. Interlocking Directorates. San Francisco:
           Jossey-Bass, 1980. 220 pp.
An "interlock" exists when one individual sits on the boards of two or
more corporations, thus generating a link between these corporations.
This study explores the connections between the boards of directors of
the largest corporate organizations in the U.S. Pennings poses the question of whether or not interlocks afford their organizations an unfair
economic advantage over competitors in the marketplace. He examines the
relationship between the formation of interlocks and economic performance.
The three types of connections—horizontal, vertical, and financial—which
link directorates are examined, together with an analysis of the ties
among 800 large U.S. firms, the links between financial institutions and
their corporate clients, and the impact of interlocking directorates on
organizational effectiveness. The author finds a positive correlation
between the numbers of interlocks and the firms' earnings, return on sales,
return on fixed assets, and sale on assets.

SOC 577. PETERS, THOMAS J. and ROBERT H. WATERMAN, Jr. In Search of Excel-
           lence: Lessons from America's Best-Run Companies. New York:
           Harper & Row, 1982. 360 pp.
Peters and Waterman study sixty-two successful and innovative corporations.
The authors maintain that companies as diverse as Texas Instruments,
McDonald's, and Bechtel share common attributes that combine effective
and vigorous management, novel research and development techniques, and
response to employee skills and customer needs to yield large financial
and productive profits. Peters and Waterman suggest a more flexible "people oriented" organizational style over current management schemes that
draw from derivatives of Frederick Taylor's theory of scientific management.

SOC 578. PRANDY, K., A. STEWART, and R. M. BLACKBURN. White-Collar Union-
           ism. London: MacMillan Press, 1983. 172 pp.
Prandy, Stewart, and Blackburn "demonstrate the limitation of conventional
views of unions as organizations of an industrial proletariat pursuing
sectional interests." They maintain instead that "trade unionism, whether
for blue- or white-collar workers, . . . both contributes to and reflects

a wider social process" to supplant capitalist market criteria with egalitarian concepts and labor union solidarity. The authors treat the public sector separately and chronicle the rise and implications of public provision and administration.

SOC 579. REISS, ALBERT J., Jr., with OTIS DUDLEY DUNCAN, PAUL K. HATT, and CECIL C. NORTH. Occupations and Social Status. New York: Free Press of Glencoe, 1961. 305 pp.
The results of a study in the social status of occupations, the North-Hatt-NORC (National Opinion Research Center) study, are reexamined and reassessed here. The North-Hatt-NORC study produced a prestige-ranking of about eighty occupations; this scale has been used in subsequent studies of stratification as, for example, a skeletal structure by which the rank of other occupations can be inferred, and for cross-cultural comparative studies. This volume evaluates the methodology and results of the NORC study and the usefulness of its results for such sociological investigations. A chapter by Duncan deals with the construction of a socio-economic index of occupations and the relation of that enterprise to the NORC study.

SOC 580. REUSS-IANNI, ELIZABETH. Two Cultures of Policing: Street Cops and Management Cops. New Brunswick, N.J.: Transaction Books, 1983. 145 pp.
This study is based on eighteen months of research conducted in two New York City police precincts, using participant observation, event, and network-analysis techniques. Reuss-Ianni argues that the organization of the police force, popularly viewed as a monolithic community, is best understood in terms of the interaction of two separate and often antagonistic cultures: a street cop culture and a management cop culture. The latter, characterized as middle class, educated, and upwardly mobile, are seen by their former peers (for they have worked their way up from the streets) as professional managers who have lost touch with their roots. Using this dichotomy as the baseline of the study, Reuss-Ianni examines police work, precinct communities, police brutality, suicide on the job, the management by objective plan, and the city-wide blackout from the point of view of both communities of policemen.

SOC 581. RIEMER, JEFFREY W. Hard Hats: The Work World of Construction Workers. Beverly Hills, Calif.: Sage, 1979. 203 pp.
Working with the popular stereotype of "hard hats" in mind, Riemer offers evidence to portray building construction workers as they really are. He finds that the usual indicators of occupational differentiation places construction workers at the highest level among blue collar workers and competitive with some professionals. Riemer, a certified journeyman construction electrician and sociologist, reviews previous "hard hat" research, then characterizes the construction worker's life on the job. He describes how individuals enter the field, the problems women face, and the extent and nature of deviance among workers. Other chapters discuss how contractors and policy makers can improve building quality, and Riemer concludes with a methodological appendix that articulates the problems and techniques of studying construction workers.

SOC 582. RIEMER, JEFFREY W. and NANCY A. BROOKS. Framing the Artist: A Social Portrait of Mid-American Artists. Washington, D.C.: University Press of America, 1982. 89 pp.
This work provides "a social portrait of Kansas artists" in the fine arts, design arts, art education, and art as a hobby. The authors adopt "an occupational sociological perspective" to investigate how artists make occupational choices, receive training and handle the risks, problems, and rewards of art careers. The work employs a comparative approach as well, to clarify the distinctions among the various types of Mid-American artists.

SOC 583. RODGERS, HARRELL R., Jr. The Cost of Human Neglect: America's Welfare Failure. Armonk, N.Y.: Sharpe, 1982. 226 pp.
Rodgers maintains that the American welfare system "provides a select group of America's poorest citizens with benefits that are so modest and so misdirected that most recipients are left in a state of dependent poverty." The author argues for more comprehensive and uniform coverage and rational execution in the Federal social welfare system. Taking as his model European state welfare programs, Rodgers recommends four policies: national health insurance, guaranteed housing, guaranteed minimum income, and a family policy which accommodates changing sex roles. Rodgers also advocates a full-employment economy based on "human priorities" to lower dependence on welfare.

SOC 584. ROGERS, THERESA F. and NATHALIE S. FRIEDMAN. Printers Face Automation: The Impact of Technology on Work and Retirement Among Skilled Workers. Lexington, Mass.: Heath, 1980. 184 pp.
Rogers and Friedman analyze the impact of the technological revolution initiated with the "collective-bargaining agreement signed in 1974 between the Publishers' Association of New York City . . . and Local 6" of the International Typographical Union. The pact granted management full freedom to automate the workplace and to set a moratorium on the hiring of new printers. "In return, printers won job security, a six-month paid productivity leave, periodic cost of living increases, and a dollar incentive to retire." The authors examine the printers' reaction and transition to the new technology, the alternative choice between retirement and continued employment, the union's struggle to retain its strength, and the effect of greatly magnified productivity on various workers. The authors' conclusions place the research in "the context of policy issues now being faced by government, industry, unions, and the individual."

SOC 585. RONCO, WILLIAM and LISA PEATTIE. Making Work: Self-Created Jobs in Participatory Organizations. New York: Plenum, 1983. 212 pp.
This book is an effort to comprehend the nature of job satisfaction by investigating people who "like their work, and work either on their own, with minimal supervision, or in small, participatory organizations." Reflecting their interest in the relation of worker autonomy and control to job satisfaction, they focus on participatory organizations, in which members have a role in determining policies for the organization and in designing their own work settings. They consider these issues in terms of several disparate workplaces: a pottery studio, a fishing cooperative, an architecture firm, a sheltered workshop, a food co-op warehouse, and several managerial jobs (e.g., a high school principal) with a high degree of autonomy and control.

SOC 586. ROSE, ARNOLD M. The Power Structure: Political Process in American Society. New York: Oxford University Press, 1967. 506 pp.
This book analyzes the distribution and nature of political power in modern America. Rose suggests that political power is exerted by a number of groups within the society through different means and in different fashions. He disputes the theory of a power elite. However, he does not accept the popular counter-view that the multiplicity of interest groups working upon the political system in any way results in an even balance of power among them. He examines the political elements of power, the influence of economic elites on politics and government, and the influence of the military and the industrial-corporate complex. He also looks at the power of the American masses as exercised through voluntary associations and local community government and organizations. He concludes that "Political power in the United States, like any other social phenomenon, is changing its locus of concentration, its distribution and its manifestations constantly."

SOC 587. **SACHS, CAROLYN E.** The Invisible Farmers: Women in Agricultural
          Production. Totowa, N.J.: Rowman & Allanheld, 1983. 153 pp.
The primary purpose of this book is to explore the full nature of women's
involvement in agricultural production through the use of historical
research and interviews with contemporary farm women. It is found that
the erroneous assumption that women are not involved in agricultural production in the U.S. has influenced agricultural development throughout
the world. The male bias in the U.S. system of agriculture has been transferred to developing countries, thereby lessening women's power and access
to resources in agriculture. The continual shift to large-scale commercial
agriculture throughout the world has excluded women from decision-making
related to food.

SOC 588. **SCHEVITZ, JEFFREY M.** The Weaponmakers: Personal and Professional
          Crisis During the Vietnam War. Cambridge, Mass.: Schenkman,
          1979. 191 pp.
This study examines the role crisis faced by weapon designers and testers
working during the Vietnam War period. Schevitz introduces the study
with some historical data on the recruitment and retention of weaponmakers
and the large constituency they form within the scientific community.
He constructs a typology of three types of workers and presents in-depth
case studies to substantiate the model: the rationalizers, who rationalize
their work in order to continue in the face of outside criticism; the
drop-outs, who left their weaponmaking or redesigning jobs in order to
eliminate the projects to which they had objections; and the political
organizers, who attempted to organize their colleagues to force changes
in the use of their work. Schevitz analyzes the social determinants of
critical and non-critical orientations toward weaponmaking and the differences between the three basic types which emerged from the study.

SOC 589. **SCOTT, JOHN.** Corporations, Classes and Capitalism. New York:
          St. Martin's Press, 1979. 219 pp.
This study of corporate Capitalism in contemporary Western society raises
the issues of ownership, control, and the relationship to class structure
of the multinational corporation. Scott describes the liberal/pluralist
view of industrial society and the contrary Marxist interpretation of
society as a phenomenon structured around class relations. He argues
that neither theory succeeds in explaining industrial Capitalism satis-
factorily and that a new interpretation, the outlines of which are presented here, is necessary. Among the issues discussed (and substantiated
with empirical data from the U.S. and other countries) are ownership and
strategic control, the corporation and class structure, the mechanisms
of state intervention in the corporate sector, and the internationalization
of capital through the rise of the multi-national company. He argues
that the multi-nationals, in advanced Western societies, increasingly
turn toward each other looking for new investments, and thus create greater
international, economic interdependence.

SOC 590. **SEXTON, PATRICIA CAYO.** The New Nightingales: Hospital Workers,
          Unions and New Women's Issues. New York: Enquiry Press, 1982.
          219 pp.
In chronicling the issues which hospital workers consider crucial to their
job satisfaction, Sexton demonstrates that the voice of a large section
of the female work force has largely gone unheard. Media attention usually
focuses on the demands of the more articulate professional and managerial
women and not on the working-class women who form 80% of the total female
work force. This study is based on data gathered through interviews and
surveys of hospital workers, local union organizers, and top union leaders.
Part One of the study profiles life in the hospital; the workers and their
relationships; the union's history, structure and organization; and the
relation of the hospital workers to the women's movement. Part Two of

the volume details the priority issues raised by the workers themselves--discrimination, institutional segregation, comparable work, wages, benefits, childcare, fairness, work schedules, health, safety at work, stress, supervision, career structure, self-management, and unionism.

SOC 591. SIEGEL, IRVING H. and EDGAR WEINBERG. Labor-Management Cooperation: The American Experience. Kalamazoo, Mich.: W. E. Upjohn Institute for Employment Research, 1982. 316 pp.

Siegel and Weinberg explore the potential for co-operative relations between management and labor in the field of industrial relations, traditionally characterized as a minefield of adversarial confrontation. The advantages and disadvantages of collaboration between management and employees are discussed with reference to sixty-five case studies. The historical introduction includes a review of the American experience and a description of the machinery set up since W.W. I to regulate labor-management relations. The authors analyze the labor-management committees for five industries--steel, construction, retail food, railroads, and men's clothing. Four chapters are devoted to labor-management cooperation within the company with particular regard to communication; consultation arrangements; productivity committees and quality circles; welfare; health and quality of work life programs; flexible scheduling; and incentive programs. Labor-management relations within public agencies are also examined. Comprehensive appendices relating to the many aspects of labor-management cooperation are included.

SOC 592. SIMPSON, CHARLES R. SoHo: The Artist in the City. Chicago: University of Chicago Press, 1981. 276 pp.

Simpson examines the art colony in the SoHo district in New York City to characterize and understand the formation and social structure of a status community, in which participants have defined and constructed an occupational culture. Simpson describes the development of the SoHo community, including the formation of a new housing form, the residential loft, the burden that residential and occupational integration places on the family, and the mobilization of the community into a political pressure group. Simpson believes that the SoHo community reflects and forms a unique part of the American middle class. The SoHo artist retains the middle class value of success and emphasizes the drive for self-achievement as well.

SOC 593. SIMPSON, IDA HARPER, with KURT W. BACK, THELMA INGLES, ALAN C. KERCKHOFF, and JOHN C. McKINNEY. From Student to Nurse: A Longitudinal Study of Socialization. New York: Cambridge University Press, 1979. 266 pp.

The primary objective of From Student to Nurse is to develop a "synthetic" model of socialization. The authors then undertake a longitudinal study of the professional socialization of nurses, a profession that has experienced rapid and substantial changes, as a means of testing their model. The research reported here grew out of a project begun in the 1950s that was designed to measure the acquisition of the nursing subculture as students progressed through their education and into the world. Entering nursing students were studied at regular intervals, from their entrance as beginning students in 1959 to their first year of work in 1965.

SOC 594. SOLMON, LEWIS C., LAURA KENT, NANCY L. OCHSNER, and MARGO-LEA HURWICZ. Underemployed Ph.D's. Lexington, Mass.: Lexington Books, 1981. 350 pp.

This volume is based on five years of research on the job market for doctorate holders in the humanities, the sciences, and engineering. The overview in Chapter One presents information on trends in Ph.D. output, graduate enrollment, undergraduate majors, and in student quality and employment status. Current employment patterns are discussed in a com-

parative context. Part One deals with the humanities Ph.D. in the public
sector, focusing on solutions to the humanities employment crisis. The
emphasis is on finding alternatives to the elusive jobs in academia and
preparing Ph.D.'s for non-academic jobs. Job search methods, changing
career goals and matching the Ph.D. with the job are discussed. The
authors conclude this section with a critical evaluation of humanities
tracking. In Part Two, the focus moves toward science and engineering
Ph.D.'s employed in non-academic jobs. These jobs are evaluated in terms
of job satisfaction, flexibility, and potential mobility. The concluding
chapter turns attention toward a new and different crisis: the prospective
shortage of scientists and engineers in the future.

SOC 595. ST. CLAIR, LEONARD and ALAN B. GOVENAR. Stoney Knows How: Life
as a Tatoo Artist. Lexington: University Press of Kentucky,
1981. 149 pp.
This work evolved from conversations between folklorist Alan Govenar and
tatooist Leonard "Stoney" St. Clair, whose physical handicaps and involvement in the stigmatized craft of tatooing placed him on the outer margins
of society. St. Clair and Govenar chronicle Stoney's career reminiscences
from 1928 until the mid-1970s. Preceded by a short history of tatooing
in America, the work describes Stoney's early years in West Virginia,
his training under famous tatooists, his employment in circuses and carnivals, and his travels as an itinerant tatooist working on transients
throughout America. Stoney's reflection on the artistic significance
of tatooing conclude the book.

SOC 596. STREET, DAVID, GEORGE T. MARTIN, Jr., and LAURA KRAMER GORDON.
The Welfare Industry: Functionaries and Recipients in Public
Aid. Beverly Hills, Calif.: Sage, 1979. 199 pp.
The subject of this book is American poverty and the reform efforts of
the 1960s and early 1970s. The authors focus on urban public assistance
and on efforts to improve the public assistance system. The central finding of this study is that "the rules which aim to govern the relations
of welfare recipients and functionaries are so numerous, complex, contradictory, and vague that they defy routine, rational, and legal interpretation."

SOC 597. SULLIVAN, TERESA A. Marginal Workers, Marginal Jobs: The Underutilization of American Workers. Austin: University of Texas
Press, 1978. 229 pp.
This report on the use of the labor utilization framework is designed
to measure underemployment as well as unemployment. The author attempts
to demonstrate that it is possible to obtain a reasonable and useful measurement of underemployment in the U.S., primarily through an examination
of the "marginally employed" sector of the population. The volume uses
labor force data to enhance sociological as well as economic knowledge.

SOC 598. TERKEL, STUDS. Working: People Talk About What They Do All
Day. New York: Pantheon Books, 1974. 589 pp.
This is a documentary account of America at work. Social critic Studs
Terkel conducted interviews with American workers, from garbage collector
to corporation executive, to provide the reader with an account of their
daily lives. Working provides an in-depth look at the values and attitudes
of farmers, sanitation workers, salespeople, taxi-drivers, waitresses,
brokers, athletes, teachers, doctors, and gravediggers, giving insight
into the broad range of occupations that exist within the American economic
system and revealing the harsh reality of the American work ethic. "This
book," Terkel writes, "is, by its very nature, about violence--to the
spirit as well as to the body. It is about ulcers as well as accidents,
about shouting matches as well as fistfights, about nervous breakdowns
as well as kicking the dog around. It is, above all (or beneath all),

about daily humiliations. To survive a day is triumph enough for the walking wounded among the great many of us."

SOC 599. TORRENS, PAUL R. The American Health Care System: Issues and Problems. St. Louis, Mo.: Mosby, 1978. 120 pp.
This is an overview of the American health care system, how it works, and the problems that affect it. The book is divided into three parts. The first discusses the historical background of the development of health care services in the U.S. Part two identifies some of the salient issues and pressures (e.g., the role of government, technology, and control of the system) confronting health care delivery today and in the future. Part three focuses on the future of health care in America and describes an "ideal" health care system for this country.

SOC 600. WALSH, MARY ROTH. "Doctors Wanted: No Women Need Apply": Sexual Barriers in the Medical Profession, 1835-1975. New Haven, Conn.: Yale University Press, 1977. 303 pp.
This study of medical education for women focuses on the New England Female Medical College and the New England Hospital in Boston in the 19th century. Walsh studies the difficulties women faced in obtaining both medical degrees and employment. She provides portraits of Feminist leaders such as Harriot Hunt and Marie Zakrewska, and negative appraisals of such male doctors as Samuel Gregory and Horatio Storer.

SOC 601. WHYTE, WILLIAM H., Jr. The Organization Man. New York: Simon & Schuster, 1956. 429 pp.
In an analysis of American life in post-W.W. II America, Whyte defines organization men: "They are not the workers, nor are they white collar people in the usual, clerk sense of the word. These people only work for the Organization. They are the ones of our middle class who have left home, spiritually as well as physically, to take vows of organization life, and it is they who are the mind and soul of great self-perpetuating institutions." According to Whyte, the harsh facts of organization life defy the American Dream, the so-called Protestant Ethic. It has been supplanted by the bureaucratic or organizational ethic--the new Social Ethic. The author discusses the ideas that helped to formulate this Social Ethic, such as "scientism," "belongingness," and "togetherness." He then follows the education of the organization man from college through junior executive training, analyzes his neuroses, assesses the impact of the organization life upon him, and examines the new suburbia.

SOC 602. WRIGHT, JAMES D., PETER H. ROSSI, SONIA R. WRIGHT, and ELEANOR WEBER-BURDIN. After the Clean-up: Long Range Effects of Natural Disasters. Beverly Hills, Calif.: Sage, 1979. 230 pp.
This book focuses on the policy question of whether or not U.S. communities require special governmental assistance in the face of natural disasters. The authors reach a number of conclusions concerning (1) the existing data bases that are available to the research community for the study of natural disasters in the U.S.; (2) the nature of the distributions of such disasters for what may be called a typical decade in recent U.S. history; and finally, (3) what sort of relief and rehabilitation natural disasters require and receive in the U.S.

SOC 603. YOUNG, JOHN A. and JAN M. NEWTON. Capitalism and Human Obsoles-cence. New York: University Books, 1980. 253 pp.
This study originated from a five-state regional research project sponsored by the Western Rural Development Center at Oregon State University. The book is organized around a series of case studies of economic underdevelop-ment: wood products in Oregon, mining in Arizona, pineapple production in Hawaii, small farms in California, and entrepreneurs in Lincoln, Washing-

ton. The effects of monopoly Capitalism on each of these economic areas are discussed. The three main questions addressed in this volume are how individuals, families and communities adapt to persistent unemployment and deterioration of their economic position; why people affirm the necessity and propriety of capital development which has made them victims and contributed to the virtual destruction of their communities; and what factors have limited political mobilization and radical change. The researchers argue in conclusion for economic alternatives to corporate Capitalism and the need for more political power for individuals and more control over non-elective state agencies.

SOC 604. ZELIZER, VIVIANA A. ROTMAN. Morals and Markets: The Development of Life Insurance in the United States. New York: Columbia University Press, 1979. 208 pp.
Zelizer's work examines the non-economic aspects of economic behavior. As an example, she studies the major cultural and ideological factors involved in the legitimization of life insurance, and probes the ideological and sociological conditions that changed to make the industry expand dramatically in the 1840s. Her quantitative analysis uses data that included life insurance advertising booklets, insurance journals, widows' and marriage manuals, and government documents. She concludes that changing attitudes about financial evaluations of human life and toward risk and speculation influenced the growth of the life insurance industry.

SOC 605. ZERUBAVEL, EVIATAR. Patterns of Time in Hospital Life. Chicago: University of Chicago Press, 1979. 157 pp.
This volume presents a study in the sociology of time--an analysis of the temporal structuring of social life. Zerubavel locates his theory in practice by observing the temporal structuring of hospital life. He demonstrates the linearity (time) and the cyclical nature (the year, the rotation, the week, the day, the duty period) of hospital life which contribute to a temporal structure of responsibility and a temporal division of labor. He establishes a close relationship between the temporal patterning of work and coverage in the hospital and the general social structure of the organization. Furthermore, the analysis demonstrates that the temporal structure of hospital life also constitutes a significant context within which a large number of cognitive processes relating to temporality are anchored. By constructing a socio-temporal order, Zerubavel locates time in a social rather than personal domain.

IX. SOCIAL PROBLEMS, DEVIANCE, AND SOCIAL CONTROL

SOC 606. ABADINSKY, HOWARD. The Mafia in America: An Oral History. New York: Praeger, 1981. 151 pp.
The primary source in this study of Italian-American organized crime is the life history of a Mafia figure who was contacted and interviewed through the U.S. Marshals Service, which administers the Department of Justice's Witness Program. The author uses this first-person account to examine the structure of organized crime (whether amorphous or bureaucratic), its membership categories, roles, rules, and business operations (legitimate and illegitimate).

SOC 607. AGAR, MICHAEL. Ripping and Running: A Formal Ethnography of
          Urban Heroin Addicts. New York: Seminar Press, 1973.
          173 pp.
Agar has produced a cognitive anthropological study of the heroin addict's
world. He analyzes such key concepts as "hustling" (obtaining money for
drugs), "copping" (buying drugs), and "ripping" (being arrested), and
describing the addict's life in terms of decision-making.

SOC 608. AGETON, SUZANNE S. Sexual Assault Among Adolescents. Lexington,
          Mass.: Lexington Books, 1983. 184 pp.
This is a report emerging from the Sexual Assault Project that focuses
on forced sexual experiences, including so-called "date-rape," among adolescents. The data for the study are derived from a 1976 national sample
of eleven to seventeen year olds, who were then interviewed once a year
for five consecutive years. The authors seek to provide systematic data
on the "incidence, prevalence, and distribution of sexual assault for
adolescent victims and offenders." They also provide a descriptive profile
of adolescent victims and offenders and a description of the sexual assault
experience. Finally, they develop and test a model of adolescent sexual
assault.

SOC 609. ALIX, ERNEST KAHLER. Ransom Kidnapping in America, 1874-1974:
          The Creation of a Capital Crime. Carbondale: Southern Illinois
          University Press, 1978. 222 pp.
Alix examines the evolution of ransom kidnapping legislation in America
in relation to both the consensus and conflict models of law creation.
He begins by differentiating between numerous types of kidnapping and
focuses his analysis on ransom kidnapping—a situation in which the exclusive or primary motivation is the collection of ransom. Alix draws his
data primarily from The New York Times for the period 1851-1974. His
major research questions concern: what has been the American experience
with ransom kidnapping, when were (capital) ransom laws created, what
role did the Lindburgh case play in the creation of ransom kidnapping
laws, and is the sociological literature correct that consensus forces
rather than conflict forces prevailed in the creation of laws against
crimes like ransom kidnapping?

SOC 610. ANDERSON, ROBERT M., ROBERT PERRUCCI, DAN E. SCHENDEL, and
          LEON E. TRACHTMAN. Divided Loyalties: Whistle-Blowing at BART.
          West Lafayette, Ind.: Purdue University Office of Publications,
          1980. 399 pp.
Divided Loyalties is about the three engineers who were fired from the
Bay Area Transit Authority (BART) for insubordination in March of 1972.
The engineers challenged the safety of the train-control system and the
way BART was overseeing its contractors. In the following political struggle, the general director and the Board of Directors were replaced in
a process that involved the engineers, management, the state legislature,
local governments, professional engineering societies, the press, and
private companies. The subject of this book is how such a seemingly insig-
nificant personnel dispute could grow to such proportions, and how these
events relate to the theoretical issues of professionalism and decision
making.

SOC 611. ATHENS, LONNIE H. Violent Criminal Acts and Actors: A Symbolic
          Interactionist Study. Boston: Routledge & Kegan Paul, 1980.
          104 pp.
Athens applies a symbolic interactionist perspective to the problem of
violent criminality. Based on in-depth interviews with fifty-eight
offenders convicted of a variety of serious violent crimes (e.g., criminal
homicide, forcible rape, assault) in which the victim was either physically
injured or sexually violated, the study examines "the interpretations

violent actors make of violent situations, the self images they hold, as well as their violent careers."

SOC 612. BROAD, WILLIAM and NICHOLAS WADE. Betrayers of the Truth: Fraud and Deceit in the Halls of Science. New York: Simon & Schuster, 1982. 256 pp.
"This is a book about how science really works." Well-publicized cases in which scientists have published fictitious results have contradicted the conventional wisdom of scientific objectivity, disinterestedness, and emotional neutrality. Broad and Wade seek to explain how such violations of scientific norms can and do occur. After examining numerous instances of scientific fraud, they reject explanations couched in terms of individual psychology. Instead, their examination of scientific fraud led them to locate its sources within the very dynamics of science itself. This book, therefore, "presents an analysis of what can be seen of science from the perspective of scientific fraud."

SOC 613. BRYANT, CLIFTON D. Khaki-Collar Crime: Deviant Behavior in the Military Context. New York: Free Press, 1979. 388 pp.
Bryant examines crime within the military and demonstrates that crime and deviance in this context represent a much more inclusive set of behaviors than white-collar or blue-collar crime. Bryant's typology arises out of the cross-classification of two dimensions. The first is the type of crime: crimes against property, crimes against persons, and crimes against performance. The second dimension is the context of the crime: intraoccupational (involving other soldiers), extraoccupational (involving civilians), and interoccupational (involving enemy soldiers). Bryant discusses several factors that he argues influence the incidence of military crime: the social composition of the military, the stress of military existence, opportunity structures, military culture, military socialization, official toleration of military deviancy, and the subversion of military training.

SOC 614. CHAMBLISS, WILLIAM J. On the Take: From Petty Crooks to Presidents. Bloomington: Indiana University Press, 1978. 269 pp.
Chambliss began his participant observation study of organized crime in Seattle in 1962. His research took place over the period of a decade, during which he spent hours at cardrooms and taverns talking with patrons and operators, interviewing bagmen and public officials—studying organized crime from the bottom up. From this research he concluded that an economy of vice existed in Seattle, and that it was perpetuated through an alliance of traditional racketeers, legitimate businessmen, corrupt law enforcement officials, and politicians who depended on organized crime contributions to maintain themselves in office. Chambliss contends that the vice industry is an important feature of the political organization and economic structure of modern life.

SOC 615. CLINARD, MARSHALL B. and PETER C. YEAGER. Corporate Crime. New York: Free Press, 1980. 386 pp.
Clinard explores the dynamics of unethical and illegal activities in the corporate world. He focuses on the role of middle managers, who, he maintains, are most responsible in the modern corporation for implementing top management's directives. His study is based on interviews with retired Fortune 500 middle management executives. In these interviews he addresses a wide range of issues concerning why some corporations are more ethical than others. He examines the role of factors internal to the corporation (the behavior of top management and corporate pressures on middle management) and those external to it (the corporate financial situation or unfair competitive practices). Clinard's respondents identify internal factors as the chief causative factors for unethical and illegal corporate behavior.

SOC 616. COHEN, BERNARD. Deviant Street Networks: Prostitution in New
          York City. Lexington, Mass.: Lexington Books, 1980. 200 pp.
This book presents one form of street deviance, namely female heterosexual
prostitution. The author spent hundreds of hours observing thirteen locations of deviant activity in Manhattan, and Deviant Street Networks focuses
primarily on the ecological and social environments in which such deviance
exists. The author contends that visible deviant street conditions exist
when several persons gather on a public street over a substantial period
of time to engage overtly and repeatedly in illegal behavior. This book
deals with spatial distribution of street deviance, stratification of
deviant street networks, and determinants of street locations.

SOC 617. CONRAD, PETER and JOSEPH W. SCHNEIDER. Deviance and Medicali-
          zation: From Badness to Sickness. St. Louis, Mo.: Mosby,
          1980. 311 pp.
The subject of this book is the gradual social transformation of designations of deviance in American society from "badness" to "sickness."
There is a dual focus in this book: it is a historical and sociological
inquiry into the changing definitions of deviance and an analysis of the
transformation from religious and criminal to medical designations and
controls of deviance. The authors develop a conceptual framework grounded
in the labeling-interactionist and conflict approaches to deviance. This
directs their attention to an analysis of the changing conceptions of
deviance and social control rather than to the behavior of deviance or
individual etiology. They pay special attention to the role of the medical
profession and its champions in the creation of designations of deviance.

SOC 618. CURVIN, ROBERT and BRUCE PORTER. Blackout Looting!: New York
          City, July 13, 1977. New York: Gardner Press, 1979. 240 pp.
On July 13, 1977, a power failure in New York City resulted in widespread
looting that led to business and property losses in the hundreds of millions of dollars. This book, commissioned by the Ford Foundation to analyze the looting phenomenon, examines the nature, extent, and style of
the blackout looting in detail. The authors' overriding objective was
to explain the underlying causes of the looting. Accordingly, they
describe the characteristics and motivations of the looters, the role and
response of law enforcement agencies, the relationship of looting to employment and economic and housing conditions, and, in general, how the looting
was related to the sense of the quality of life in the city.

SOC 619. DECKER, SCOTT H. Criminalization, Victimization and Structural
          Correlates of Twenty-six American Cities. Saratoga, Calif.:
          Century Twenty One, 1980. 100 pp.
Decker uses Uniform Crime Reports (UCR) and victimization-survey results
for twenty-six cities to examine the statistical relationships among variables reflecting population characteristics, ethnic composition, economic
circumstances, and crime and victimization rates. He evaluates the statistical potential of victimization data and then relates the victimization
and crime rates to other central-city characteristics. He gives a history
of criminal statistics and of victimization-survey approaches to estimating
criminal activity.

SOC 620. DIETZ, MARY LORENZ. Killing for Profit: The Social Organization
          of Felony Homicide. Chicago: Nelson-Hall, 1983. 230 pp.
Dietz's study focuses exclusively on what she calls "killing for profit."
According to Dietz, killing for profit refers to the cold-blooded, impersonal, and predatory murders that are done for profit or some form of
personal gain. Dietz considers killing for profit to be synonymous with
what is referred to as "felony homicide." Her study is based on her analysis of information contained in police reports. She selected several
hundred cases that met her definition from the files of the Detroit Police

1826

Department. The book is divided into three parts. Part one concerns the nature and structure of three kinds of felony homicides. Part two is her analysis and examination of what she calls the "common interaction patterns" between victims and offenders. In part three Dietz examines the career development of felony murderers.

SOC 621. **ELIAS, ROBERT.** Victims of the System: Crime Victims and Compensation in American Politics and Criminal Justice. New Brunswick, N.J.: Transaction Books, 1983. 352 pp.
The research reported in this book is part of the broader field of "victimology," which focuses on crime victims. Elias's particular concern is with victim compensation programs, which provide "compensation to crime victims as our means of giving assistance, redressing the wrong, and coaxing good will toward government and criminal justice from victims and the general public." Through a systematic research design that included interviews with victims of crimes, Elias evaluates two victim compensation programs in Brooklyn and Newark, respectively, by comparing responses of crime victims who applied for redress under the program with those who made no such claims.

SOC 622. **EVANS, DARYL PAUL.** The Lives of Mentally Retarded People. Boulder, Colo.: Westview Press, 1983. 319 pp.
What is it like to be mentally retarded in a society that places a high premium on competence? This book examines the worlds of mentally retarded people, the increasing role of retarded persons in mainstream society, and the needs and problems that such integration has produced. Evans explores the ways in which professionals, governments, communities, and families attempt to meet these needs and cope with attendant problems. He also probes the special adaptations people made to being mentally handicapped and offers glimpses of their feelings, fears, and frustrations.

SOC 623. **FISSE, BRENT and JOHN BRAITHWAITE.** The Impact of Publicity on Corporate Offenders. Albany: State University of New York Press, 1983. 393 pp.
Is publicity an effective sanction for controlling corporate crime? This is the basic question this study is designed to examine. Utilizing extensive interviews with individuals (including corporate employees and former employees) familiar with the cases, the authors undertake a qualitative analysis of seventeen large corporations involved in publicity crises. A chapter is devoted to each case, which include such infamous moments in American corporate history as the Ford Pinto affair, ITT and covert actions in Chile, bribery at Lockheed, McConnell Douglas, and Exxon, and the electrical equipment price-fixing cases. The authors conclude by suggesting ways in which publicity can be effectively used to control corporate crime.

SOC 624. **GALLIHER, JOHN F. and JOHN R. CROSS.** Morals Legislation Without Morality: The Case of Nevada. New Brunswick, N.J.: Rutgers University Press, 1983. 163 pp.
Galliher and Cross use the anomalies of the Nevada criminal statutes as the focus of their book. Nevada law permits legalized casino gambling, "quickie" marriages and divorces, and prostitution, but simultaneously contains the most stringent penalty in the country for possession of marihuana. They are concerned with determining whether Nevada's public morals laws were based on fundamental moral or religious values. They begin by reviewing previous works that have studied the origins of law, and use the changes in drug legislation in socially and religiously conservative states of Utah and Nebraska as a comparison/contrast to what is happening in Nevada.

SOC 625. **GIBBONS, DON C.** Changing the Lawbreaker: The Treatment of Delinquents and Criminals. Montclair, N.J.: Allanhald, Osmun, 1981. 318 pp.
Gibbons states that his book is intended to be: (1) an inventory and assessment of recent theories and research findings regarding causal processes in crime and delinquency, (2) an overview of social pattrns in correctional organizations, (3) a theoretical venture in "applied sociology," and (4) a contribution to correctional practice theory. The author believes that rehabilitation of offenders depends upon basic knowledge of the causal factors in criminality. He sets forth some central propositions and hypotheses about the causes of crime and delinquency that emerge from the sociological literature.

SOC 626. **GLIEDMAN, JOHN** and **WILLIAM ROTH.** The Unexpected Minority: Handicapped Children in America. New York: Harcourt Brace Jovanovich, 1980. 525 pp.
This book documents the far-reaching and often disastrous consequences for children who must constantly interact with an able-bodied world from which they are excluded. Gliedman and Roth argue that what makes the handicapped "special" are the attitudes and reactions of others who are not handicapped; the greatest harm to the handicapped child or adult stems from this socially engendered impairment of daily life and self-esteem, not from functional impairments themselves.

SOC 627. **HARPER, DOUGLAS A.** Good Company. Chicago: University of Chicago Press, 1982. 172 pp.
This is a descriptive ethnography of homeless men—primarily tramps—presented in the first person narrative by the author, and accompanied by a series of photographs depicting tramp life. Harper seeks to capture—in the words of the men themselves—the tramp world with its cycle of drinking, migrating, and working. In a postscript, Harper briefly describes tramp history and how it has affected tramp culture. He sees the tramp as "organic to the American landscape," a reflection of the fluidity and individualistic nature of American society.

SOC 628. **HASTIE, REID, STEVEN D. PENROD,** and **NANCY PENNINGTON.** Inside the Jury. Cambridge, Mass.: Harvard University Press, 1983. 277 pp.
This study represents an effort to determine empirically how juries behave and to assess the quality of jury performance. The authors accomplish this by a series of simulated jury decisions carried out in actual courthouses with actual court personnel and citizens called to jury duty as experimental subjects. The study focuses especially on the effects of varying the jury decision rule (the quorum required to render a verdict) on jury performance. It also analyzes the jury's behavior during deliberations and the influence of social background differences on juror behavior. Finally, the authors advance a theoretical model of the juror and jury behavior, which, "grounded firmly on systematic empirical research, can," they contend, "reduce the dependence of legal policy makers on the vagaries of intuition and personal experience."

SOC 629. **HEYL, BARBARA SHERMAN.** The Madam as Entrepreneur: Career Management in House Prostitution. New Brunswick, N.J.: Transaction Books, 1979. 276 pp.
This book is an analysis of a single individual's movement from an unconventional childhood through entry into prostitution, and across a twenty-year career as both prostitute and madam, culminating in a return to the "square" world. Its primary goal is to examine the extant theories of prostitution and the development of a new processual model of entry into a deviant career. The book takes an interactionist approach and focuses on the different aspects of prostitution (madaming, pimping, hustling).

Heyl's analysis (1) describes contemporary house prostitution and the training provided, (2) provides life history data on one madam of such a house over a four year period, (3) documents changes in the occupation and how they are dealt with, and (4) illustrates the process of leaving a deviant career to reenter the conventional world. Four major perspectives on entry into prostitution include: psychoanalytic, psychological, structuralist, and sociological.

SOC 630. HIMMELSTEIN, JEROME L. The Strange Career of Marihuana: Politics and Ideology of Drug Control in America. Westport, Conn.: Greenwood Press, 1983. 179 pp.
This book is about the origins of legal policy and public opinion toward marihuana in the U.S. during the 20th century. Himmelstein says the issue of anti-Mexican racism was only indirectly relevant to the Marihuana Tax Act. He says it was the fear of schoolchildren being seduced and corrupted by marihuana, and not an impulse to punish Mexicans, that persuaded legislators and the public about marihuana and the need for its control. During the 1960s, the hegemony of the Federal Bureau of Narcotic's views on marihuana disintegrated. Himmelstein considers two hypotheses, the "embourgeoisement hypothesis" and the "hippie hypothesis."

SOC 631. HOLLINGER, RICHARD C. and JOHN P. CLERK. Theft by Employees. Lexington, Mass.: Heath, 1983. 148 pp.
This book outlines the major sets of variables that have been found to affect the phenomenon of theft by employees in the workplace. According to the authors, sociologists view the phenomenon of employee theft not from a law-enforcement perspective but as a set of behaviors to be explained by way of the various structures and processes operating in the workplace. Hollinger and Clerk believe that a lower level of employee theft may be one valuable consequence of a management team that is responsive to the current perceptions, attitudes, and needs of its work force.

SOC 632. HOLMES, RONALD M. The Sex Offender and the Criminal Justice System. Springfield, Ill.: Thomas, 1983. 236 pp.
Holmes states that his book "is devoted to the discussion of normalcy, deviancy, theories of learning, and a detailed examination of various sex offenders and their offenses." It is divided into twelve chapters, each devoted to cursory descriptions of a wide range of sexual aberrations and crimes, including "nuisance" sex crimes (e.g., voyeurism, exhibitionism); sex crimes against children; child pornography; adult pornography; dangerous sex crimes (e.g., rape, pyromania); incest; and transvestism, transexualism, and homosexuality.

SOC 633. HOLMSTROM, LYNDA L. and ANN W. BURGESS. The Victim of Rape: Institutional Reactions. New York: Wiley, 1978. 320 pp.
This book, which is based on research begun in 1972, "looks at how three major institutions--police, hospital, and court--respond to the rape victim and what impact this response has on victims." Using a combination of participation observation and in-depth interviews, the authors followed a group of rape victims from their appearance at a hospital emergency ward to the end of the legal process involving their assault. The authors demonstrate that few rapists are likely to be convicted and, for the victims "rape does not end with the departure of the assailant," for victims are likely to be afflicted with what they term "rape trauma syndrome." This response is frequently exacerbated by the institutional processing by hospitals, police, and courts that follows the rape, which "can be equally devastating." The 1983 edition, a reprint of the 1978 edition, contains a new introduction that discusses the authors' original findings in terms of more recent research, much of it stimulated by their original study.

SOC 634. JACKSON, PATRICK B. The Paradox of Control: Parole Supervision of Youthful Offenders. New York: Praeger, 1983. 149 pp.
This book studies one aspect of the highly controversial phenomenon of parole--the effects of parole supervision. Because parolees under supervision are constantly threatened with revocation of their parole, the author interprets it as a specific form of social control. The basic question of this study is whether social control as represented by parole supervision results in crime. The author examines this question in a group of 725 parolees in the East San Francisco Bay area of California. The arrest and conviction outcomes of parolees randomly assigned to either retention on or discharge from parole were compared and the findings interpreted in the context of deterrence and labeling theories. The author concludes that parole "may reveal a paradox of control--that it either has no effects on crime or may even exacerbate the problem that it seeks to control."

SOC 635. JACOBS, JAMES B. New Perspectives on Prisons and Imprisonment. Ithaca, N.Y.: Cornell University Press, 1983. 241 pp.
The twelve essays in this volume represent the author's efforts over the past half-dozen years to produce a socio-legal history of the American prison since 1960. The author's goal is to describe and explain contemporary American prisons, and more specifically, to illuminate the dynamics that have been transforming them for the past several decades. Jacobs relies on case studies, survey research, content analysis, multivariate analysis, and reflective social analysis. In addition, as a lawyer, his attention is drawn to prisoners' rights litigation, the controversial role of the Federal courts in institutional litigation, and the impact on prisons of antidiscrimination and collective bargaining laws.

SOC 636. JACOBS, JERRY. The Search for Help: A Study of the Retarded Child in the Community. Washington, D.C.: University Press of America, 1982. 135 pp.
The realities of mental retardation are presented in the words of the parents, siblings or teachers who have most intimately known mentally retarded children. The first section of the book focuses on the parent's approaches to physicians in search of a hopeful diagnosis for the child. The second part is the self-fulfilling character of the diagnosis of mental retardation. Finally, the author returns to the parents of the retarded, and their feelings about the present and the future for their child.

SOC 637. KALINICH, DAVID B. The Inmate Economy. Lexington, Mass.: Lexington Books, 1980. 119 pp.
This monograph is a study of inmate culture in a Michigan maximum-security prison. The author focuses especially on the contraband market, especially drugs, which flow freely through the prison, and the "structural, organizational, and social factors that both create the demand for contraband and facilitate the distribution of contraband goods and services through the sub-rosa marketplace." The author examines both the prison social system, including the informal inmate power structure, and the dilemmas confronting prison administrators attempting to deal with the flow of contraband.

SOC 638. KASINSKY, RENEE GOLDSMITH. Refugees from Militarism: Draft-Age Americans in Canada. New Brunswick, N.J.: Transaction Books, 1976. 301 pp.
Refugees from Militarism is an analysis of the social and personal characteristics of Vietnam War refugees--draft dodgers and deserters--who fled to Canada between 1964 and 1974. It is also an examination of the process whereby these refugees sought exile in Canada and their adaptation to Canadian society. Kasinsky argues that "to comprehend their reasons for going into exile is to understand one of the major socio-political

forces that shaped the lives of all draft-age American males in the Vietnam War period: the continental youth channeling system of North American capitalism, [which] was designed to subordinate these youth to the interests of the American economy, an economy dominated by multinational corporations." Her study is based primarily on six years' experience as a participant observer in the war refugee movement in Canada, primarily in Vancouver, and on data obtained from over 1,200 American war refugees.

SOC 639. KOBIN, SOLOMON and MALCOLM W. KLEIN, written with ELAINE M. CORRY, CARL L. HECK, FRANK R. HELLUM, JOHN PETERSON, and KATHERINE TEILMANN VAN DUSEN. Community Treatment of Juvenile Offenders: The DSO Experience. Beverly Hills, Calif.: Sage, 1983. 341 pp.
This book evaluates the effects of a national, Federally funded program designed to "foster and encourage" the deinstitutionalization of juvenile "status offenders"—youths "whose acts would not be criminal if committed by adults, acts such as incorrigibility, truancy, runaway, and similar strictly juvenile offenses." Introduced by a history of Federal involvement in delinquency control activities, the report describes the objectives of the deinstitutionalization of status offenders (DSO) program, its program structure and design, and its impact.

SOC 640. MARTINEZ, TOMAS M. The Gambling Scene: Why People Gamble. Springfield, Ill.: Thomas, 1983. 231 pp.
This is an assessment of social science and psychiatric knowledge about gambling, based on field observations and participant observation in Nevada casinos, interviews with active gamblers, observations at Gamblers Anonymous meetings, a survey of viewers of television game shows, and studies of a range of gambling activities. Martinez identifies the stages through which compulsive gamblers move. Two important motives that contribute to all kinds of gambling are the need to confirm one's existence and the need to establish one's worth. Martinez discusses the contribution of mass media to popular notions of gambling and the ritualized activities of television game shows. He deals with the occasional poker player, the weekend race-track player, the compulsive gambler, the professional, and the many gradations in between.

SOC 641. McCAGHY, CHARLES H. Crime in American Society. New York: Macmillan, 1980. 368 pp.
Rather than focusing on police, court, and correction policies, McCaghy eschews these traditional categories used in criminology texts. His discussions focus on the results of research conducted on criminal behaviors themselves. In particular, the author divides his attention between those crimes traditionally associated with the lower class, blue-collar crimes, and those generally committed by individuals from the middle and upper classes, white-collar crimes. He argues that the natures of and motivations for these crimes differ widely and that the generalizations made about blue-collar crimes cannot be extended to white-collar crimes.

SOC 642. MILLMAN, MARCIA. Such a Pretty Face: Being Fat in America. New York: Norton, 1980. 252 pp.
Such a Pretty Face combines in-depth interviews and participant observation to obtain autobiographical accounts of the experience of being fat. These are used to demonstrate the symbolic role ascribed to the obese and the way that stigmatization restricts their lives. The first part of this book examines the social worlds of fat people; the second discusses their identity struggles. Three social settings are used to portray their collective adaptations: (1) politically-oriented "fat-rights" organizations in which an aggressive struggle for acceptance is waged by those who have constructed a supportive subculture for themselves and their "fat admirers," (2) weight-loss organizations which ritualize eating to achieve

slimness and use a religious framework to promote weight control, and
(3) weight-loss camps for adolescents, an institution intended solely
to induce weight loss, relying upon powerful social control processes.
A central theme of this book is the relationship between sex roles and
sexuality and obesity in women.

SOC 643. MOORE, JOAN W. Homeboys: Gangs, Drugs, and Prison in the Barrios
of Los Angeles. Philadelphia: Temple University Press, 1979.
239 pp.
This book presents accounts of problems in collaborative research processes
and pre- and post-prison adaptation of tecatos (heroin addicts) and pintos
(convicts). The book's key themes are (1) the persistence and influence
of barrio groups; (2) the growth and spread of drug use and markets; (3)
the continuities of barrio norms during, and after, incarceration; (4)
the wide range of adaptations that co-exist in the barrio; and (5) the
research process itself. The authors focus on three factors that shape
the lives of Chicano East Los Angeles homeboys (individuals from one's
barrio or gang). These factors are the distinctive ethnic context of
Chicanos in Los Angeles; the key institutions of social control and "help,"
and the opportunity structures connecting the barrio to the larger society.

SOC 644. MUEHLBAUER, GENE and LAURA DODDER. The Losers: Gang Delinquency
in an American Suburb. New York: Praeger, 1983. 138 pp.
This study examines hostility and conflict between police and a large
adolescent gang, The Losers, over a six year period in an affluent suburb
of a large Midwestern city. The authors analyze the origins of the gang
and explain how, "in the midst of a community that is modeled after the
original American dream, class conflict and cultural alienation can lead
to the nearly complete disaffection of a large segment of youth from their
peers, parents and established authority." They contend that their study
will "provide insight into the genesis of individual and group deviance
in suburban schools, and describe the toll this process takes on individuals and the community."

SOC 645. PERRUCCI, ROBERT and DENA B. TARG. Mental Patients and Social
Networks. Boston: Auburn House, 1982. 160 pp.
The hypothesis of this study of forty-seven patient networks and the mental
hospital records of these patients is that the properties of social networks help shape the behavior of constituent members and therefore influence the career of the mental patient. The authors examine how changes
in networks influence the decision to hospitalize and how the characteristics of networks influence chances for patient release. Perrucci and
Targ suggest a hypothetical typology of patients based on symptom patterns
and resources, and relate this typology to the medical/psychiatric and
deviance perspective. They advocate a new social network perspective
and offer hypotheses on this perspective.

SOC 646. PROPPER, ALICE M. Prison Homosexuality: Myth and Reality.
Lexington, Mass.: Lexington Books, 1981. 237 pp.
Data for this work were obtained from seven training schools for juveniles;
four housed only females; three, females and males. Two of the four single-
sex institutions were private; the three institutions for females and
males were state supported. The intent of this research was to determine
the extent of homosexuality across institutions and to explain its origin
following the general conceptual orientations provided by the "deprivation"
and "importation" perspectives. The deprivation perspective sees all
anti-social, anti-staff, and anti-institutional behaviors and attitudes
of inmates as adaptive responses to the hostile and depriving nature of
incarceration, i.e., homosexuality. The importation perspective sees
intra-institutional behaviors and attitudes as the result of bringing one's
pre-established social baggage--attitudes, values, beliefs, lifestyles,

and experiences--into the institutional setting. According to the importation perspective, prison homosexuality would likely be engaged in by persons with either prior homosexual experience or a predisposition to engage in homosexual behavior by virtue of background or lifestyle.

SOC 647. PRUS, ROBERT and STYLLIANOSS TRINI. Hookers, Rounders, and Desk Clerks: The Social Organization of the Hotel Community. Beverly Hills, Calif.: Sage, 1980. 279 pp.
This is an ethnographic description of the "hotel" and "bar" community--an arena comprised of hotels and bars that are the haven of prostitutes, strippers, and rounders. The authors used a participant observation approach, as well as interviews, to study the actions and interactions of hookers, desk clerks, bellhops, security personnel, strippers, musicians, comedians, rounders, bartenders, waitresses, and patrons. Hookers, Rounders, and Desk Clerks also contains information about those participants who, although not frequenters of the "hotel" and "bar" premises, have ties with the participants who are frequenters--street hookers, massage parlor girls, call girls, and theatrical agents. Description and analysis of these interaction networks form the basis of this book, as is the analysis of the career patterns and career contingencies of the various participants.

SOC 648. RAFFAELE, JOSEPH A. The Mafia Principle. Washington, D.C.: University Press of America, 1979. 156 pp.
According to the author, in Sicily the term "mafia" originally referred to an informal organization protecting people against oppression by the state. However, in the U.S., the word has come to be used as a synonym for organized crime. Raffaele believes that the "mafia principle" affirms the tendency in Western civilization to encapsulate human activity into ever bigger organizations; to replace individual morality with organizational morality; to subordinate the individual to the demands of organization; and to develop an "equality of mediocrity" that cuts across organizations. Raffaele sees the "mafia principle" as "an exhortation to undertake a critical examination of liberalism."

SOC 649. REUTER, PETER. Disorganized Crime: The Economics of the Visible Hand. Cambridge, Mass.: MIT Press, 1983. 233 pp.
This is an economic analysis of the distribution of power within bookmaking, numbers, and loan-sharking markets in New York City. Reuter disputes allegations of centralized control, domination, and coordination of these illegal activities by the Mafia. He is especially skeptical of the emphasis placed by law enforcement officials on the role of violence in shaping illegal gambling markets, which, he argues, are maintained without violence or intimidation. He concludes that "the Mafia may be a paper tiger, rationally reaping the returns from its reputation [which is reinforced by law enforcement agencies and the popular press] while no longer maintaining the forces that generated the reputation."

SOC 650. RICHARDS, PAMELA, RICHARD A. BERK, and BRENDA FORSTER. Crime as Play: Delinquency in a Middle Class Suburb. Cambridge, Mass.: Ballinger, 1979. 261 pp.
The data for this study were derived from public school pupils from selected Chicago neighborhoods in 1975, with questionnaires directed to three levels between the fifth and twelfth grades. The authors hypothesize that (1) youths who participate heavily in delinquency and those who do not are not very different in their decision-making processes, (2) legal and illegal actions of middle-class adolescents try to maximize returns of their investments of leisure time and money, seeking optimal allocation between legal and illegal activities, (3) some adolescent activities are performed not solely for their return but to get data on likely outcomes from various investments of resources, and (4) experimentation gives the

young persons information and skills that help them handle complex social situations and experience with the tensions of risky situations.

SOC 651. ROEBUCK, JULIAN and STANLEY C. WEEBER. Political Crime in the United States: Analyzing Crime by and Against Government. New York: Praeger, 1978. 244 pp.
Roebuck and Weeber argue that political crime involves either: (1) crimes by the government against the people or (2) crimes by the people against the government. The authors, writing from a critical theoretical perspective that assumes class conflict in an advanced capitalist society, focus primarily on the former. However, they employ a broad definition of political crime that does not separate crimes by government from corporate crime, since they consider government to be "an extension and instrument of the economic system—a system dominated by the corporate structure." The authors develop a typology of political crime, and they focus their analysis on its manifestations in the U.S. from 1960 to 1978.

SOC 652. SANDMAIER, MARIAN. The Invisible Alcoholics: Women and Alcohol Abuse in America. New York: McGraw-Hill, 1980. 298 pp.
Stunned by the inadvertent revelation that one-third of all alcoholics in the U.S. are women, Sandmaier produced this book on the nature and problems of women alcoholics, who, she maintains, have been virtually ignored in the voluminous literature on alcoholism. She rejects the notion that the experience of alcoholic women duplicates that of men. Because there are different social norms surrounding alcoholic consumption, drunkenness, and alcoholism for men and women in our society, the "alcoholic woman lives out a nightmare uniquely shaped by her culture, role, and status." Based on extensive interviews, this book attempts both to raise consciousness concerning the existence of alcoholic women and "to record and interpret women's actual experiences in the grip of alcohol."

SOC 653. SCHARF, PETER and ARNOLD BINDER. The Badge and the Bullet: Police Use of Deadly Force. New York: Praeger, 1983. 254 pp.
It is estimated that about 2,000 people annually are shot by a police officer. In this book Scharf and Binder report results of their investigations of the use of deadly force in the police departments of Birmingham, Miami, Newark, and Oakland. They examine the cultural context and psychological significance of guns in police work, the social factors that influence when police officers will use deadly force, the different kinds of confrontations police encounter, the psychological competencies required for police officers to deal effectively with them, and the impact of police administrative policies and procedures on decisions to use deadly force. It is their overall goal "to describe, as faithfully as we are able, the complex world of the police officer as decision maker."

SOC 654. SHERMAN, MICHAEL and GORDON HAWKINS. Imprisonment in America: Choosing the Future. Chicago: University of Chicago Press, 1981. 146 pp.
This analysis of imprisonment in America and the basic assumptions that underlie it is "explicitly a policy book" that seeks to transcend and, at times, to synthesize liberal and conservative views of the American correctional system. The authors review the essential features of the debates over whether to build prisons and whom to imprison. They contend that "imprisonment is overused because legislatures, prosecutors, and judges do not know what else to do." They propose that the "fusion of punishment with prison" be abandoned and that judicial and correctional officials adopt punishments that do not incarcerate but are still punitive. They conclude with policy proposals concerning prison use and construction.

SOC 655. **SHIBUTANI, TAMOTSU.** The Derelicts of Company K: A Sociological
Study of Demoralization. Berkeley: University of California
Press, 1978. 455 pp.
During W.W. II, Shibutani was a member of Company K, a Nisei military
unit whose poor service record stood in striking contrast to the exemplary
service record of Japanese-Americans. Shibutani's field notes, supplemented by interview data, army records, and material on the history and
culture of Japanese immigrants and their descendants, form the basis of
this study. It begins with a narrative on the historical and cultural
experience of Nisei in Hawaii and on the mainland, and an account of their
reaction to the infamous forced migration and hostile public opinion during
the war. Determination to reverse negative ethnic stereotypes motivated
many Nisei to display patriotism, and those who enlisted in the armed
forces were seen as having a special responsibility to demonstrate the
loyalty of their group. This book is an account of the day-to-day activities of a group of mainland and Hawaiian recruits that was originally
formed as an infantry company at the replacement depot at Fort Meade,
Maryland.

SOC 656. **SIMON, RITA JAMES.** The Jury: Its Role in American Society.
Lexington, Mass.: Heath, 1980. 159 pp.
During the past quarter century, controversy over the effectiveness and
desirability of a jury system has generated considerable research. Such
studies have focused on a wide range of issues and employed a variety
of methods and research designs. Simon provides a brief history of the
American jury and an analysis of how it has been perceived by the American
press, by writers of American fiction, and by legal professionals. However,
her major objective is to "organize, edit, and comment upon much of the
major research that has been done on the American jury from the 1950s
to the present." In the final section, she evaluates the independence
and impartiality of the jury in the three decades following the end of
W.W. II.

SOC 657. **SIMON, RITA JAMES.** Women and Crime. Lexington, Mass.: Lexington
Books, 1975. 126 pp.
Simon's book assesses the impact of the women's movement on female crime
and the effects of social change on deviance. Through a statistical analysis of comparative arrest data for the years 1953-72, as well as data
on convictions and imprisonment, the author presents evidence about the
differentials in crime and punishment between male and female criminals.
She finds that as women have entered the labor market in increasing numbers,
crimes against property committed by women have risen threefold compared
to those of men, while violent offenses have remained steady. Another
finding in Simon's report is that there has been a continued protective
bias toward women in the American penal system. Far fewer women than
men who are arrested are convicted or imprisoned.

SOC 658. **SKOGAN, WESLEY G.** and **MICHAEL G. MAXFIELD.** Coping with Crime:
Individual and Neighborhood Reactions. Beverly Hills, Calif.:
Sage, 1981. 280 pp.
This book on crime and reactions to crime in three large American cities--
Chicago, Philadelphia, and San Francisco--was based on more than 1,300
telephone interviews conducted in 1977, on the content analysis of newspapers, and on field observations that generated almost 10,000 pages of
observer reports. Supplementary data were reported from Census Bureau
victimization surveys conducted in 1973 and 1974 for those same three
cities. Skogan and Maxfield conclude that those most vulnerable to crime
tend to do the least about it, and that those who do react to crime sometimes react in ways that affect adversely the metropolitan areas in which
they live.

SOC 659. SKOLNICK, JEROME H. House of Cards: The Legalization and Control
of Casino Gambling. Boston: Little, Brown, 1978. 382 pp.
Skolnick obtained access to both casinos and the institutions of control
in Nevada and England. This book presents an ethnographic record of the
casino industry and the control system from a variety of perspectives.
There is a guide to casinos and the games of Nevada and a discussion of
varied matters, such as the role of prostitution; class differences in
clientele and their effect upon the organization of gambling; the function
of credit, high rollers, and junkets; the role of casinos in "laundering
dirty money" and in tax evasion; and the myriad opportunities for cheating
the public by casinos and of casinos by their owners and employees.
Skolnick contends that within the casino industry "opportunities for deception abound at every level of the business."

SOC 660. SNODGRASS, JON. The Jack-Roller at Seventy. Lexington, Mass.:
Lexington Books, 1982. 173 pp.
In the 1920s, sociologist Clifford R. Shaw recorded the life story of
a delinquent teenager, Stanley, who was a "jack-roller," or mugger of
drunk or sleeping men. Published in 1930 as The Jack-Roller, the biography
became a classic in the field of juvenile delinquency studies. In 1975,
Snodgrass located Stanley in Los Angeles and established a working relationship with him. This book picks up the narrative of Stanley's life from
the 1930s through to his death in 1982. Stanley's life story is conveyed
in his own words, and this autobiographical account is supplemented by
analyses of his later life by several noted criminologists.

SOC 661. STASTNY, CHARLES and GABRIELLE TYRNAUER. Who Rules the Joint?
The Changing Political Culture of Maximum Security Prisons in
America. Lexington, Mass.: Lexington Books, 1982. 234 pp.
Who Rules the Joint? is a book on the rise and fall of inmate self-
government in the Walla Walla, Washington, state penitentiary. It is told
by Stastny and Tyrnauer through a case study that explores the internal
as well as external political and organizational factors that influenced
the change. This book also includes chapters on American prison history
and the issue of judicial intervention. Walla Walla was the reform that
tried to make prisons bearable by coming to grips with political pressures
building among inmates.

SOC 662. SURREY, DAVID S. Choice of Conscience: Vietnam Era Military
and Draft Resisters in Canada. New York: Praeger, 1982.
224 pp.
Choice of Conscience is a product of the Viet Nam Era Research Project.
It is a study of American draft resisters and military deserters who went
to find refuge in Canada. The two introductory chapters review the history
of American military procurement. Surrey finds class to be the continuing
major factor that determines whether one serves, where one serves, and
one's actual prospect of getting killed or wounded. From the buying of
substitutes, to deferment and exemption for education, occupation, or
conscientious objection, drafts and other military personnel procurement
practices are systematically biased to enable the relatively well born
to avoid service, and especially dangerous service. These class differences are prominent in Surrey's two major "resister" categories: draft
dodgers are more likely to be students and more affluent, while deserters
tend to be less well-educated and less affluent. These differences
affected the assimilation of these two groups into Canadian life.

SOC 663. SUTHERLAND, EDWIN H. White Collar Crime: The Uncut Version.
Edited by Gilbert Geis and Colin Goff. New Haven, Conn.: Yale
University Press, 1983. 291 pp.
Sutherland's study of white collar crime was originally published in 1949.
However, because of pressure from his publishers and his university, the
names of corporations and individuals were deleted. Geis and Goff put
together the uncensored version of Sutherland's study, White Collar Crime;
in addition to the names that were previously deleted, this book contains
three case histories that were not included in the 1949 edition.
Sutherland found that each of the seventy corporations he studied had one
or more decisions against it for criminal activities: restraint of trade;
misrepresentation in advertising; infringement of patent, trademarks,
and copyrights; unfair labor practices; financial fraud and violation
of trust; violations of war regulations; and assorted miscellaneous
offenses. With an average of fourteen criminal decisions per company,
Sutherland concluded that most of the corporations he studied were "habitual
offenders."

SOC 664. TALBOTT, G. DOUGLAS and MARGARET COONEY. Today's Disease: Alcohol and Drug Dependence. Springfield, Ill.: Thomas, 1982.
174 pp.
This study is based on the assumption that the conditions of alcoholism
and drug addiction do not represent "bad habits" or a lack of discipline
or will power. They may be characterized as progressive, genetic, and
fatal diseases; the chemically dependent individual does not have a primary
psychological disorder. Case reports summarize the authors' experiences
in treating hundreds of alcoholics and drug addicts. Talbott and Cooney
argue that alcoholism and drug addiction can be fought effectively only
when they are recognized as diseases.

SOC 665. THORNTON, WILLIAM E., Jr., JENNIFER JAMES, and WILLIAM DOERNER.
Delinquency and Justice. Glenview, Ill.: Scott, Foresman,
1982. 530 pp.
This study is an overview of the extent, causes, nature, and control of
juvenile delinquency in the U.S. Although primarily sociological in orientation, the book views delinquency as a complex and multifaceted phenomenon.
The authors discuss theories about the causes of delinquency from biological and psychological points of view as well as sociological. They also
examine a diverse range of proposed solutions to the problem of delinquency.

SOC 666. TROYER, RONALD J. and GERALD E. MARKLE. Cigarettes: The Battle
over Smoking. New Brunswick, N.J.: Rutgers University Press,
1983. 170 pp.
Cigarettes: The Battle over Smoking defines smoking as a deviant process
that can be understood best from a socio-historical perspective. Troyer
and Markle present documentation of the debate over cigarette use in American society. The authors chronologically review the pre-W.W. I efforts
to prohibit the sale of cigarettes and the eventual repeal of this legislation. After contrasting increasing per capita consumption with medical
science's revelations of the many health hazards of smoking, the authors
conclude with a discussion of the recent government regulatory efforts
to segregate the smoker.

SOC 667. WRIGHT, JAMES D., PETER H. ROSSI, and KATHLEEN DALY. Under the
Gun: Weapons, Crime, and Violence in America. New York: Aldine,
1983. 342 pp.
The purpose of this book is a "sifting and winnowing" of the claims and
counterclaims from both sides of the "Great American Gun Debate"--the
perennial struggle in American political life over what to do about guns,
violence, and crime. One of the authors' major conclusions is that,
despite the large number of studies conducted, many critically important

questions have not been adequately researched, and some of them have not been asked at all. The goal of this book is not to strike out in new research directions, but to compile and assess the research of others.

SOC 668. ZIETZ, DOROTHY. Women Who Embezzle or Defraud: A Study of Convicted Felons. New York: Praeger, 1981. 157 pp.
Zietz uses case studies to delineate three groups of women convicted of violating property rights. The first two groups were women without histories of drug offenses. These women were interviewed and then grouped according to their reasons for accepting positions of trust. The "honest" women had taken their positions without intending to use them to embezzle. The "dishonest" women took their positions or inspired trust in order to defraud. The third group consisted of women who had been convicted of forgery and who had previously been convicted of drug offenses. Zietz notes that men tend to become violators of trust either to cover their errors or to gain status. Many of the women violated trust to contribute to the welfare of their families. Zietz suggests that some of the women knowingly risked punishment, but sacrificed themselves in order to protect valued relationships. The second part of Women Who Embezzle or Defraud identifies three types of women who have worked their way into positions of trust to commit fraud.